Long Distance Voyagers
The Story of the Moody Blues

ALSO BY MARC CUSHMAN

I SPY: A History and Episode Guide of the Groundbreaking Television Series

These Are the Voyages – Star Trek: The Original Series, Season One
These Are the Voyages – Star Trek: The Original Series, Season Two
These Are the Voyages – Star Trek: The Original Series, Season Three

Irwin Allen's Lost in Space: The Authorized Biography of a Classic Sci-Fi Series

Long Distance Voyagers
The Story of the Moody Blues
Volume 1 (1964-1979)

Marc Cushman

Edited by Mark Alfred

Jacobs/Brown Press

San Diego, California

LIBRARY OF CONGRESS CATALOGING-IN-PUBLICATION DATA

Cushman, Marc

Long Distance Voyagers: The Story of the Moody Blues

Volume 1 (1964-1979)

Marc Cushman

Edited by Mark Alfred

Editorial staff: Thomas C. Tucker, Sondra Johnson, and Susan Osborn

Publisher: Matthew Brown

Includes bibliographical reference

Hardcover ISBN 978-0-9988663-9-0

Paperback ISBN 978-0-9995078-0-3

Kindle ISBN 978-0-9995078-1-0

First edition hardcover, December 10, 2017

Library of Congress Control Number: 2017957129

Cover Design: Zack Korn

Front cover image: Promotional photo issued in 1968 by Derek McCormick, manager, Moody Blues. Pictured (L-R): G. Edge, J. Lodge, J. Hayward, M. Pinder, and R. Thomas.

Back cover image: Moody Blues performing in 1965 (author's collection, provenance unknown). Pictured (L-R) M. Pinder, D. Laine, G. Edge, R. Thomas, and C. Warwick.

Inside flap photo of author: Mike Hayward Photography

Hardcover edition manufactured in the United States of America

Jacobs/Brown Press is an imprint of Jacobs/Brown Media Group, LLC

San Diego, California

www.JacobsBrownMediaGroup.com

Acknowledgments

The author thanks Moody Blues co-founders Mike Pinder and Ray Thomas for contributions made to this book, as well as their wives, Tara Pinder and Lee Thomas, for the kindness they have shown.

Requests for interviews were sent to Graeme Edge, Justin Hayward, John Lodge, and Denny Laine, but Jacobs/Brown Press did not receive a response from these members or their representatives, including their various websites, management, Threshold Records, and the Moody Blues' primary record label, Universal Music. We will continue our efforts to make contact and conduct interviews for the second volume of this book. In addition, copies of this book will be sent to all of the Moody Blues. Should they, or you, find inaccuracies, or wish to request that certain quotes, information, or images, be modified or deleted in future printings or e-books, please contact the publisher.

Since we were not able to obtain direct interviews in many cases, and because many of those who worked with the Moody Blues in the 1960s and '70s are either no longer alive or proved unreachable, we relied on over 5,000 vintage newspaper and magazine articles, as well as hundreds of archival interviews, in either print or on the internet, in order to reconstruct the story of this iconic band.

Special acknowledgment and appreciation to Mark Murley, publisher of *Higher & Higher*, for granting permission to use written materials from all 50 issues of the fanzine, published from 1984 through 2006. The conscientious work of Mr. Murley and his co-editor, Randy A. Salas, proved immensely valuable.

My appreciation to Tony Brown for his diligent work in collecting and preserving articles and images pertaining to the Moody Blues for his website, TheMoodyBlues.co.uk. Mr. Brown kindly provided numerous rare documents for my research and images to be used in this book.

My thanks to Taran Berkeley and all the contributors to the website MoodyBluesAttitude, for their industrious collecting and sharing of vintage materials pertaining to the Moody Blues. While I personally gathered hundreds of articles and reviews from various newspaper archives, perhaps half of the vintage material used for research and inclusion in this book came from the site www.tapatalk.com/groups/moodybluesattitude/.

A full list of the newspapers, magazines, websites, CDs, and DVDs from which materials were utilized for research or inclusion in this book can be found in the "Bibliography / Sources" section. But I wish to give special mention here to Mark Powell of Esoteric Records, who has researched and written the liner notes in the excellent reissues of Moody Blues albums on CD, each remastered, with bonus material, as well as doing the same for many of the band member's solo albums. Also, special mention to the website 45cat.com, which has presented high-quality images of 45rpm record labels and picture sleeves. The images of this type presented in this book were gathered from numerous sources, including 45cat.com. Visit that site to see color reproductions of many of the images in this book, and countless others representing the work of nearly every recording artist spanning the 1950s through the end of the vinyl 45rpm single era in the 1990s.

I thank those who have either shared in the past year of work or have given their support and encouragement in other meaningful ways, including Mark Alfred, Sondra Burrows, Andrew Johnson, Steven J. Kates, Susan Osborn, and Thomas C. Tucker.

Finally, my joyful gratitude to all the members the Moody Blues – Justin Hayward, Mike Pinder, John Lodge, Ray Thomas, and Graeme Edge – and, from the band's first incarnation, Denny Laine and Clint Warwick. Their albums, their songs, their messages, they musicianship, and their presence has been a light in my life, as it has in millions of other lives, throughout the decades.

TABLE OF CONTENTS

Preface

One critic described the music of the Moody Blues as "cosmic and sunshiney-style optimism that is solace to some and schmaltz to others."

Until undertaking this book project, and reading through thousands of archival newspaper and magazine articles, as well as deep-diving into internet research, I never knew that there were people who didn't love everything the Moody Blues ever did. In my experiences, particularly when I was young and curious, eager to understand what my peers were thinking and feeling, everybody loved the Moodies. While growing up, I rarely knew anyone who didn't have at least one of the "Classic Seven" albums in their record collections, and sometimes a copy of *Blue Jays* and Justin Hayward's *Songwriter*, to boot. The Moodies were everywhere I went. And they were wonderful. Everyone thought so. Right?

Then I worked on this book. I was surprised to read negative reviews from the 1970s and beyond. Who were these heartless critics who could not hear what I heard; what my older sisters and their friends heard; what my friends all heard – the beautiful, thought-inducing music of the Moody Blues? Some of these reviews from decades past seemed remarkably callous as I read them now – seething with venom, cynicism, and, no surprise, arrogance.

Well, now I do know about these other opinions. It takes all kinds. And some of these kinds are people you or I probably don't want to know – people whose savage breasts cannot be soothed by song, people incapable of being moved by, or even recognizing, a beautiful melody. Thoughtful, poignant lyrics don't intrigue these folks. Disdainful people like this are echoed in today's mean-spirited internet trolls.

What I am grateful for is that I was blessed with the ability – or, perhaps sensitivity – to be deeply moved by a lovely melody, and to be captivated by lyrics which prompt me to think beyond my routine. I am also grateful that I grew up when and where I did, in 1960s and '70s America. I heard pop music from the late 1950s and the early and middle 1960s thanks to my older sisters, and their friends. They introduced me to the Beatles, the Rolling Stones, Elvis Presley, the Supremes, the Beach Boys, the Monkees, Simon & Garfunkel, and so many others. When my sisters went off to college, I inherited many of their records, included newer ones by the Doors, Creedence, Three Dog Night, Elton John, Stevie Wonder, Sly & the Family Stone, and Crosby, Stills, Nash & Young (together or apart). But no Moody Blues! Of course, I had heard the hits the Moodies had in the 1960s and the early '70s on Top 40 radio, and, once I was in high school and also working a part-time job for pocket money, one of the first albums I bought was the five-year-old *Days of Future Passed*. I knew the two hits from it and loved them both, and was curious to hear what other gems might be among the album tracks. I'll be honest: At my age, the orchestration from Peter Knight was a little too old-school and syrupy for me. I have since learned to appreciate it for the masterful work that it is. But I do recall being immediately taken by the songs. This was the most consistently good album I'd ever heard, except for those by the Beatles. For me, there wasn't a bad song among the lot. And, while the Moodies wrote and sounded like the Beatles in some ways, they also had something different – those distinctive vocal harmonies and that hauntingly sad sound of the strings … that weren't quite like strings at all. I found out much later that I wasn't hearing strings at all, but the Mellotron played by Mike Pinder. I was also impressed by how the album had a theme. It was not just a collection of songs.

Later, in 1974, I started visiting my sisters, who were attending college and sharing an apartment with a lovely girl named Nancy. Ah, Nancy. She had very nearly all of the Moody Blues albums. I spent hours devouring that music, and studying the gatefold album jackets. The front covers were like pieces of fine art, each with a story behind it. And the inside of the gatefold allowed me to see what these men who made this sometimes eerie, sometimes beautiful, sometimes exciting music looked like. It was then that I finally was able to hear many of the songs that the older, cooler kids probably already knew by heart. I was surprised to find that I recognized many of the songs that hadn't been issued as singles; they must have received a fair amount of airplay on AM radio. I recognized "Legend of a Mind," "Lovely to See You," "Dear Diary," "Never Comes the Day," and "Melancholy Man." But the other songs, the ones I'd never heard before, were wonderful too. And I loved the spoken-word passages. "Blasting, billowing, bursting forth with the power of ten billion butterfly sneezes." What I liked the most was how all the songs connected together to form a story … or invoke a feeling. The album I remember playing most was *Seventh Sojourn*. I really hadn't heard so many consistently good songs on a single album since, well, the Beatles.

After the school year ended, Nancy moved away, and away went her records too. I had to dig deep into my pockets and start buying the albums for myself.

In the early 1980s, I was dating a delightful girl named Bonnie, who also loved the Moody Blues. She taught me the popular practice of dimming the lights, lighting candles, rolling a joint in the gatefold of *On the Threshold of a Dream* (her favorite of their albums), then sitting back and zoning out to the Moodies. Bonnie had older siblings too, so I expect we were mimicking rituals from a decade earlier. And wasn't it perfect that Mike Pinder's songs were usually near the end of the album … just when our eyes were the most aglow.

It was at this time that *Long Distance Voyager* came out, and Bonnie and I went to see the Moodies when they played the Hollywood Bowl … or was it the Greek Theater? I'll know the answer to that when I've finished researching Volume 2, covering the 1980s and beyond. For now, it's enough to say that I was spellbound the moment I heard the blending of Justin Hayward's and John Lodge's voices, live, on "Gemini Dream." There was *that sound* – that distinctly Moody Blues harmonizing. When Ray Thomas joined in on some songs, it only got richer. The Moodies were exceptional in concert, perhaps as good as any artist I ever saw … and I must have seen all the big names from that era play.

I saw the Moody Blues again a few years later, at the Universal Amphitheater in Los Angeles. But that was the last time. You see, as much as I love the Moodies, I also love dozens of other artists, and there is only so much time and opportunity and money to do the things you love. In fact, I will admit, I hadn't heard some of the individual Moodies' solo albums until working on this book. But, fortunately, my job sometimes allows me to revisit past loves … as well as discover new ones. So, for the last several months I've been on a regular diet of Moody Blues, and solo Blues, helping to keep me focused on my work, and what fun work it has been! I was particularly pleased with the remastered CDs of the band's early albums. Those songs have never sounded better. I've also purchased and watched the many DVDs that are now available, some with performances from the early 1970s. I'm happy to say that the more you know about these talented men, the more you see and hear them, the more you like and respect them. Our world is certainly a better place for having the Moody Blues as part of it.

Marc Cushman

October, 2017.

Author's Note:

I call this book you are holding "a biography of a band ... in its time ... and its place." It's a different type of a biography; a time machine, if you will, designed to take you through each album and each decade, and either remind you, or, if you weren't there at the time, share with you, how it all looked and sounded and felt. You will be reading about it *as it happens* – with many of the words from that time, from the reporters, the critics, the fans, and the Moodies. It's the summer of 1964, and the Moody Blues are forming *now*; it's the fall of 1967, and *Days of Future Passed* is being released *now*; it's the fall of 1972, and "Nights in White Satin" is racing to the top of the American singles charts *now*. In the structure of this book, as the words from the past are woven into the narrative, it is my hope that you will travel to those places ... find yourself in front of the old radios and stereos, or reading the old newspapers and rock magazines ... attending the concerts, and experiencing it all ... as it happens. We're not *looking back*; we're *going back, together*. The story is alive; it's happening now; unfolding in front of our eyes.

It's a big book. Does that mean there is too much information? In this age of instant and abbreviated news – even if you call the stuff on the internet and our chosen channels "news" – some may think so. But the true fans, I expect, will not find this book to be too much. We rarely get bored by the things that are important to us. If you're holding this book, then the Moody Blues are clearly important to you.

On the more than 700 pages to come, you will be reading excerpts from hundreds of album and concert reviews. These are the real deal, not a single retro-review in sight. You'll be reading vintage press releases and excerpts from newspaper and magazine reports, all from "way back when," in the explosive era of the 1960s and '70s. And you will be getting those all-important numbers: record sales, chart performance, concert attendance, and awards received. In all cases, I try to use as much language from the times as "fair usage" guidelines in reporting allow. In some ways, the concept occupies a very gray area. Therefore, should any copyright holders of the decades-old reviews and news articles we have sampled object, then my publisher and I are ready to abbreviate the material. But we think it's vital – and I suspect you prefer it – to hear what the people in the 1960s and '70s had to say, in their own words, be those words positive or negative.

The same applies to the images in this book. Some are 60 years old; the newest is 38 years in age. We licensed many; we received kind permission to print others; and others we believe to be in the public domain. We cite the source for each. If we are in error concerning provenance or subject or our right to use, we will correct or delete.

Still, all of these words, images, and data, are for you – intended to take you back in time to discover – or *rediscover* – the music and the magic of the Moody Blues.

If only you can enjoy this trip as much as I have!

1

Pre-Road Blues

(L-R) Mike Pinder, Denny Laine, Graeme Edge, Ray Thomas, and Clint Warwick: the Moody Blues, circa 1965. (Photo source: Author's collection)

The roots of the Moody Blues were sunk deep in Birmingham, West Midlands, England, which experienced its first boom as a textile manufacturing center. After World War II, the region's economy grew further with the expansion of motor industry plants. The city's population peaked in 1951 at 1.1 million, a majority of whom were factory workers. By the mid-1960s, a couple of thousand belonged to skiffle and rhythm & blues bands. During this period, Birmingham was home of a music scene comparable to that of Liverpool.

Denny Laine said, "The thing about Birmingham – because it was a factory town – is it was a little bit like Detroit. There was a lot of music. Well, you know, after the war, everybody was kind of into doing something to make money, as well, [and] there was a lot of music about. A lot of it was chart stuff or stuff that we heard on Radio Luxembourg, which was the American Forces network in Germany. And so we picked up a lot of music from that. We were more into copying bands rather than playing originals. We weren't like the London scene, which was more traditional jazz and blues-based; we were more sort of R&B/pop type of fans. It was a good scene; there were a lot of bands around. And when I was in school, it seemed like everyone was in a band." (DL-G10)

Birmingham produced no single pop sensation as big as Liverpool did with the Beatles, but was nonetheless described by one journalist as "a seething cauldron of musical activity."

Consider the groups that bubbled forth from the cauldron:

The Moody Blues were the first to achieve worldwide fame, but they were actually predated by one year by the formation of the Spencer Davis Group, which would experience an international breakthrough shortly after the Moodies opened the door. Although named after guitarist Davis, the shooting star in the band was vocalist/organist Steven Winwood. He later joined Dave Mason in 1967 to form Traffic, another band with Birmingham roots, before moving on to Cream, followed by a successful solo career.

The Move got its start in Birmingham shortly after the Moodies, with Roy Wood and, later, Jeff Lynne. This band would evolve into the Electric Light Orchestra.

Birmingham can also claim the birth of heavy metal rock, with the first of many prominent bands in this genre, Black Sabbath and Led Zeppelin, forming in 1968, and Judas Priest, in '69.

Christine McVie came from Birmingham, and would often sit in with the Spencer Davis Group before joining Fleetwood Mac in 1970.

There would be many more. And for each group that found success on a national level, there were hundreds – even thousands – that were popular on the local scene, beginning with the Moody Blues … and, predating their inception in 1964, with the earlier bands in which each of the Moodies cut their teeth.

Ray Thomas said, "I began my musical career playing a one-string bass in a skiffle band called the Saints and Sinners." (RT-MMCD14)

Later, with the Moody Blues, Thomas would write a song called "Nice to Be Here," which included a line about "a guitar with only one string." There really was such a thing.

The Saints and Sinners

Ray Thomas's birthplace, Lickhill Manor, Stourport-on-Severn. (Courtesy Tony Brown)

Ray Thomas was born in Lickhill Manor, Stourport-on-Severn, England, on December 29, 1941. It was the middle of World War II, and nearby Birmingham with its numerous factories was a prime target for frequent, heavy German bombing raids. The Manor had been commandeered by the government for the purpose of taking in expectant mothers, providing a safe haven to deliver their children away from the bombarded cities.

2

Thomas, like fellow Moodies Mike Pinder and Graeme Edge, also born in 1941, and early Moodies member Clint Warwick, born in 1940, spent his first few years of life surrounded by the tensions, heartaches, and sounds of war.

The devastating war in Europe finally came to an end in May 1945. As it often is when following any prolonged period of anxiety and sacrifice, the final years of the 1940s and the new decade ahead brought an excitement of new beginnings, and the much-needed calm of carefree life. Now there was time for joy … and music.

At age nine, Thomas's interest in music was sparked when his father, an amateur harmonica player, began teaching his son to play the instrument. With his powerful baritone voice, Thomas was also encouraged to train as a singer. At 10, he became a member of the Birmingham Youth Choir.

Thomas's family consisted of working-class people, so it is no surprise that he left school at 14 to begin learning a trade – training to be a tool maker – but his interest in music remained.

Interviewed for this book, Thomas said, "I was a big fan of Gene Vincent; really liked his voice and style; also enjoyed Elvis and Johnny Cash. I sang when I was in school; decided I didn't want to spend my life in a factory, and music was taking over everywhere and catching everyone up." (RT-AI17)

By October 1958, at 16, a door to a better life than a factory job opened.

Thomas, along with former Paget Road School chum and future Moody Blues bassist John Lodge, was friends with guitarist/vocalist Mike Brassington, the leader of a local Birmingham skiffle group, the Saints and Sinners. This ragtag band patterned its sound after Lonnie Donegan, the "King of Skiffle." Donegan, who would return later to figure in the story of the Moody Blues, had already scored seven U.K. Top 10 hits, and skiffle was now the rage in Britain.

This homespun genre of music, a combination of jazz, blues, and folk, had originated in the U.S. in the first half of the 20th century. By the 1950s, America was preoccupied with the newer and more exciting genres of rhythm & blues and rock 'n' roll. But skiffle was perfect for the post-war teens of poorer factory towns such as Birmingham and Liverpool. The music was on the radio, thanks to Donegan and other popular U.K. artists, such as the Vipers Skiffle Group. But perhaps the greater appeal was that skiffle was customarily a product of homemade and improvised musical instruments, such as washboards, jugs, "cigar-box fiddle," inexpensive harmonicas, and second-hand acoustic guitars and banjos. With the unappealing future of factory work ahead of them, teens were quick to take to these instruments and hope to become the next Lonnie Donegan. It's not surprising that a city such as Birmingham produced so many young and hopeful skiffle groups. The Saints and Sinners' chances for local fame seemed just as good as anybody else's.

Through his friendship with Mike Brassington, Thomas knew that the five-man Saints and Sinners were losing its tea-chest percussionist. Brassington said, "Ray Thomas – he was a school mate…. And he had always been interested in, you know, in what we had been doing. I think he'd always wanted to be in the group." (MB-CA06)

Thomas asked to be considered as replacement on this "instrument," which anyone with a sense of rhythm might play. He also offered to contribute backing vocals. Brassington enlisted Thomas, but he was asked to also play bass.

The obvious problem was that Thomas had never played the instrument. Another obstacle – the young members of the group came from poorer working-class families and rarely received much pay for their performances. Stand-up bass instruments did not come cheap, and electric bass guitars were even more expensive. Therefore, the members of the group pitched in to improvise their own stand-up bass, something simple enough for a novice like Thomas to handle. Journals kept by the band state that each of the boys chipped in sixpence a week to cover the cost of plywood, glue, varnish, and other needed materials. Then they set about building a one-string, electric, double stand-up bass, which, because of its size and shape, they called "The Coffin." This instrument would become Thomas's primary station in the group. He took to the instrument quickly, recalling that it was "not a problem to master." (RT-AI17)

The Saints and Sinners (circa 1959). Ray Thomas (far left) mans "The Coffin." With him (L-to-R): Ricky Wade (percussion), Mike Brassington (lead vocals and guitar), Dave Jones (drums), and Brian Smith (electric guitar).
(Courtesy Tony Brown)

"The Coffin" is believed to have made its first public appearance on October 17, 1958, when Thomas performed with the Saints and Sinners at Holte Pub in Birmingham.

Accordingly, with the shift in sound, the group was able to distance itself a little from skiffle and move toward the newer, hipper genre of American rhythm & blues. This called for a name change. They were now the Saints and Sinners Vocal & Rhythm Band.

Besides Lonnie Donegan's "Rock Island Line," the new lineup – Brassington on guitar and lead vocals, Brian Smith on second guitar, Dave Jones on drums, Thomas on tea-chest and double bass, and Ricky Wade on washboard and percussion – covered songs such as Buddy Holly's "That'll Be the Day" and "Peggy Sue," and Roy Orbison's "Mean Woman Blues," as well as other formative staples of American rock 'n' roll.

On rare occasions, when Mike Brassington was sick with a cold or flu and not in good voice, Thomas would assume the lead vocals for the group.

On April 18, 1959, the Saints and Sinners, with their nest-egg made up from each member's contribution of sixpence a week, entered Hollick & Taylor Studios in Handsworth to record a demo record. The disc featured a pair of songs written and sung by Brassington: "It's Cold Outside" and "I'll Show My Love Is True." The tunes are catchy and reasonably well recorded for this time, with each demonstrating more than a passing resemblance to the sound of Buddy Holly & the Crickets. Even though Thomas hadn't written or sung lead on the songs, they are nonetheless notable as the first recordings to include a future member of the Moody Blues. (Both are featured on a music bonus disc included with the DVD documentary, *The Moody Blues: Classic Artists.*)

On April 24 and 25, the record was played over the sound system at the Apollo Cinema in Birmingham. Of the five copies of the disc that were reportedly made, only a couple of them were circulated to music "insiders." Due probably to the band's lack of connections with local decision-makers, the recordings fell on deaf ears.

By June 1959, with good-paying gigs few and far between, and members being lured away to more popular area groups, the Saints and Sinners decided to call it a day. Their last known performance was at a talent competition at the Navigation Hotel and Pub on June 29. They won three suitcases, an appropriate prize since the band was packing it in.

Next, Ray Thomas sat in with a rock 'n' roll band known as the Ramblers. This venture was a short one. After the Ramblers disbanded, Thomas decided to start a group of his own, which would team him with a young friend and future Moody Blues member. In time, a third future Moody would come on board.

John Lodge's childhood home, Inland Road, Birmingham. **(Courtesy Tony Brown)**

El Riot and the Rebels

John Lodge, born in Birmingham on July 20, 1945, was typical of many who chose to devote their life to music – he developed a deep and perhaps obsessive interest at a very early age.

Lodge said, "I had violin lessons when I was 11 and played all the hymns in the school orchestra in the morning." (JL-NME70a)

The violin gave Lodge his first musical training and experience at performing, as a member of his school's orchestra. However, Lodge's study of the violin was relatively short. He said, "I was taken out of the music class because I was told music wasn't my interest – because I didn't know the birth date of Beethoven at the time. And I challenged the music teacher to play, I think it was, 'A Whole Lot of Shakin'' or 'Lucille,' on the piano. I said, 'If you can learn that, then I'll find out when Beethoven was born.' He didn't take up the challenge … and I did woodwork after that." (JL-OTR86)

In America, "woodwork" is called "shop class."

Having flunked "music," Lodge was free to follow his own interests. He chose an instrument more in line with a future rocker: "I bought my first guitar when I was 11 years old from a neighbor – it was a Spanish guitar with metal strings – for the equivalent of two pounds, 10 shillings! I didn't know how to play it, so I set about trying to find out how it worked." (JL-BF96)

Anyone who's ever learned to play a musical instrument without receiving proper training knows the trial-by-error method – listening to a song and attempting to find the notes or chords that go along with it. With guitar, if you haven't been trained or seen a book which shows how to form chords, then you have to make up your own – something which may sound close, but not quite right. And for teenagers in England at this time, the BBC's "approved" playlists didn't have much room for teenage fads. Virtually their only exposure to America's rock 'n' roll came from imported records and the occasional movie.

Lodge said, "I was 13, I guess, when the American movies started coming here. I saw every single one – *The Blackboard Jungle*; *Rock Around the Clock*; *Shake, Rattle and Roll* – I couldn't believe this thing called American rock 'n' roll." (JL-H&H88)

The Blackboard Jungle, from 1955, dealt with the dark subject of juvenile delinquency. The film famously featured "Rock Around the Clock" by Bill Haley and his Comets. The movie resulted in the song breaking through to radio in both America and England – so much so, in fact, that it was even given a movie of its own, 1956's *Rock Around the Clock*. This, thought to be the first rock 'n' roll exploitation film, starred Haley and his Comets in a story built around the music business. Also featured in the film were many other songs by Haley destined to become radio hits: "See You Later, Alligator," "Rock-A-Beatin' Boogie," "Razzle Dazzle," "Mambo Rock," and one simply called "R-O-C-K."

The lesser known *Shake, Rattle 'n' Roll*, which Lodge mentioned, was the British title for a 1956 short subject (released as *Around the World Revue* in the U.S.). It featured Haley and his Comets doing the title song, another Top 10 hit.

Besides Bill Haley, Lodge named others who inspired him: "I was a fanatical fan of Gene Vincent, Jerry Lee Lewis, Little Richard, and Eddie Cochran, but there was no one to teach me anything other than classical guitar!" (JL-NME70a)

Lodge's only guide was the on-screen performances of Bill Haley, Gene Vincent, the Jerry Lee Lewis band, the Little Richard band, and Eddie Cochran. But the American rocker who made the greatest impression on Lodge seemed an unlikely type to achieve international stardom. That in itself was part of the appeal. Lodge said, "Then I heard 'That'll Be the Day' by Buddy Holly & the Crickets. That song changed my perception of a lot of things. Up until then, all rock 'n' roll was Elvis, Little Richard, Jerry Lee Lewis, and Gene Vincent. These were really big icons, and in England we had people copying that, [but] there was no way you could elevate yourself to that position as an Englishman. I went to see Buddy Holly at Birmingham Town Hall. He was simply standing on the stage playing guitar, [and yet] he had such a presence. That paved the way for me to become a songwriter." (JL-BF96)

That "presence" showed through, despite Holly's shy ways. He was slight, pale, and sported untrendy eyewear – until *he* made the black horn-rimmed glasses cool.

Lodge was not alone in being struck by Buddy Holly. As we will learn, the singer/songwriter from Texas also made a substantial impression on the Moody Blues' Mike Pinder and, especially, Justin Hayward. It is also worth noting that Holly hit No. 1 with his first single, 1957's "That'll Be the Day." The notable thing was that Holly had several hits which he had co-written, like "Peggy Sue," "It's So Easy," and "Maybe Baby." Few pop artists of the time were writing their own material. Holly died in a plane crash in 1959, but not before serving as an inspiration to countless teens interested in guitar music who, on the surface, seemed unlikely candidates for stardom.

John Lodge, circa late 1950s.
(Courtesy Tony Brown)

Lodge said, "I was fortunate a bit at finding a few people locally who wanted to explore rock 'n' roll itself. And when I was 14, I met Ray [Thomas]… and Ray knew how to sing a few songs and I'd learned to play a few songs on guitar, and so we started playing at youth clubs. We were singing, you know, 'Down the Line,' [and songs by] Jerry Lee Lewis; we were doing rock 'n' roll songs." (JL-CA07)

The group's manager, at the start, was John Lodge's father.

Lodge recalled, "There was a jazz club – I think it was called the Midland Jazz Club – that used to be at that time at 'House in Birmingham.' And my father went along there and said to the [pub owner], 'My son's got a band and would you let him play in the interval, *at no charge?*' And the [owner] eventually said, 'Yes.' … And we went there; we played, and we started to increase the amount of people that were going to this jazz club. It had been, for ages, a hundred people, and then, suddenly, 110 turned up the following week, and then 120 the week after. And I think the pub owner suddenly thought, 'You know, this could be good.' So he asked if we'd like to do our own night, which we said 'yes,' except we only knew eight songs. And he said, 'Well, play them *twice!*'"

Regarding the selection of the group's name, Lodge recalled, "We were looking for a name for the band, and we decided to call ourselves the Rebels. And, at that time, bands were starting to come out of London, like Nero and the Gladiators, and they were dressed as gladiators. And Ray and I thought, 'Well, the Rebels; what are the Rebels? They're Mexicans! Let's get some Mexican outfits!' …

"Ray and I were talking one night and I said, 'We need a name for you.' And we came up with – I don't remember which of us said it – 'El Riot.' So, it became El Riot and the Rebels.

"We thought we'd wear all these Mexican outfits with the great big sombreros. And, as soon as we became El Riot and the Rebels and started wearing these clothes, we suddenly started going further afield, out to Bromsgrove and Leamington and Tunbridge

Above: El Riot and the Rebels, February 1961, at the Coleshill Town Hall. Ray Thomas (El Riot) is on the left, standing, with John Lodge on the right (the only one without coordinating socks). Below: in their Mexican outfits, with Pinder now in the band (far left). Thomas is center, with Lodge immediately to his left.
(Photo source: raythomas.co.uk)

Wells, and places like that, and we started to develop, you know, a huge following. It was fantastic." (JL-CA07)

Ray Thomas said, "I made Alice Cooper look like Mary Poppins in those days. I was a sort of Evel Knievel, dressed in silver skin-tight suits, with silver hair, and I made my entrance springing up a ramp and landing on my knees in the middle of the stage. I've had doctors hammer my knees for hours looking for a reflex action. There's nothing doing. My nerve ends in my knees are all dead!" (H&H85)

John Lodge also took on a new name; he became "Johnny C. Storme," in a nod to Rory Storm & the Hurricanes, a moderately popular English rock 'n' roll band getting their start at this time.

El Riot and the Rebel's lead guitarist Bryan Betteridge took on the name of "Bunny B." Also in the group were Mike Heard on rhythm guitar and Ricky Wade on drums.

At this time, Lodge went electric. He said, "I bought a Rosetti Lucky 7 [electric] guitar and, to try to add more punch, I started playing at the bottom end of the guitar, working out different riffs, all really based on guitar boogie." (JL-BF96)

By playing from the lower strings, Lodge was able to create a bass-like sound, giving the songs a richer "bottom end" register. The only thing better would be an actual bass guitar.

Lodge said, "In Birmingham, there were no bass guitars at the time; I had never seen one. In 1958, I went to see a big American combo from Texas that played in the movie *The Girl Can't Help It*. Right in the middle a guy was playing what I thought was a guitar. I finally realized it was a Telecaster bass. I was mesmerized by this guitar.

"I went back to the music shops in Birmingham where I used to go every Saturday to play every guitar they had. Tuxedo [Guitars] introduced a solid bass similar to the Fender bass. I bought that Tuxedo bass, then I built my own bass enclosure for a 50-watt tube amp. I started to really enjoy playing bass and I listened to record after record to figure out how the bass was played....

"In 1961, I walked into Jack Woodruff's music store. In the window was a Precision bass. That was it... just sitting there saying it was mine! I went home to get my father, saying, 'You'd better come and have a look at this bass with me.' We went to the store and I bought this Precision. It was a total love affair – I still have the bass; it lived with me under my bed, went everywhere I went. Dad and Mum were happy with what I was doing even though I don't come from a musical family. They

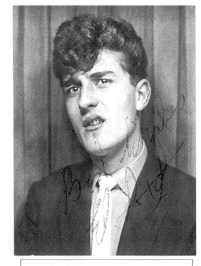

Ray Thomas giving the camera the Elvis Presley curled lip.
(Photo source: raythomas.com)

knew I enjoyed what I was doing, [and] I played all the time; every night." (JL-BF96)

For two years running, El Riot and the Rebels were voted the best R&B band in Birmingham.

It was during the first year when the band picked up a third future Moody.

John Lodge said, "Mike Pinder joined the band as well. Mike was with us for about three years, [or, at least] two years. We worked all around... Birmingham and the Midlands." (JL-SOMB86)

Above: Mike Pinder's childhood home on Chingford Road, Birmingham. (Courtesy Tony Brown)

Mike Pinder was born in Birmingham on December 27, 1941, just two days ahead of Ray Thomas. Pinder was the youngest of four children, with two sisters and a brother.

He said, "Dad was in a dance band and I was weaned on a diet of pop music. I'll always remember coming downstairs one night in 1944. Dad had just come home from the war in France and was having a tremendous 'knees-up' with all his buddies. I came to see what was going on and ended up singing my party piece, [English sing-along] 'Bobbing Up and Down.' For that I got ten bob, a cigarette and a glass of shandy." (MP-DME70)

There was no shortage of musical instruments in the house. Pinder said, "My dad played piano and accordion. My older brother played trumpet. The first instrument I played was ukulele, then banjo. We also had a Steinway upright piano in our home. I can

Young Mike Pinder.
(Photo source: mikepinder.com)

remember as a young boy lying under the piano and reaching up to touch the keys and holding my hand on the strings to feel the vibration that each note produced. The thicker and longer strings were the lower tones. The high strings were short and thin. So even in my early life I was interested in how sound collected."

Pinder remembered his first public performance: "My mom was head barmaid of the Crossway Pub in Birmingham. My dad would play piano for pub patrons. When he took a break I would take over and play. My reward was a lemonade; my dad's reward was a beer. That started me on a lifelong path. My very first performances were in an English pub!" (MP-HDP14)

While Pinder's father made extra money playing in the dance band, he was also an amateur electrician. Pinder said, "We could not have been better suited if I'd chosen him myself." (MP-DME70)

Pinder shared his father's interests in both music and electronics. He fondly recalled, "When I was young I would build radios and amplifiers with my dad in his workshop. I had a natural interest in electronics that stuck with me throughout my life." (MP-HDP14)

By this point in his young life, Pinder cited his musical influences as being the unlikely mix of classical and rhythm & blues, with an added ingredient of rock 'n' roll and jazz. He said, "Besides the music of Mantovani and his orchestra, I grew up listening to Buddy Holly, Nat King Cole, Dave Brubeck, Chuck Berry – we later did a tour with him – Gene Vincent, Everly Brothers, Bill Haley, and the like." (MP-HDP14)

Pinder's interests in spirituality and metaphysics, including out-of-body experiences, were also piqued at an early age. "I grew up thinking everyone had out-of-body experiences," he said, "Every Sunday when I was 8 or 9, I'd lie in my bed and mentally journey into the street to see which kids were playing."

"I would just float out of my body and go through the window and around the corner of the house, and go look in the street…. And then, if it was someone I wanted to play with, I'd get out of bed, dress, go out, grab a sandwich, usually – you know, something to eat – and go out. And the person that I saw *was* there. So I thought everybody could do it.

"And, of course, they *can*. But this relates to the Hopi Indians, as well, who… when they say goodbye to their families, and when they're walking away, they say, 'And don't forget to keep the door on the top of your head open.' … It's an out-of-body experience. And we all do it as children – up until about 12, before the soft spot on the top of our heads… hardens over. But it doesn't stop us from doing it; it's just that you have to work at it more. You know… through meditation." (MP-ET95 and MP-CA07)

Also at 12, Pinder began playing skiffle in clubs around Birmingham. The big step forward came in late 1957/early '58, with Billy Saunders and the Tuxedos. Saunders handled lead vocals and was backed by two guitarists, Tony Carter and John Killigrew.

Alan "Bugsy" Eastwood played drums. With two guitarists in the band, Pinder chose to play piano. Of course, the boys couldn't afford tuxedoes to go along with the group's name, but they did nonetheless try to class up their act a bit. Pinder said, "We wore white jackets and black pants.

"We were playing rhythm & blues, American folk, and pop songs of that time. It was fun but nothing permanent came out of it. Ray [Thomas] and I met and became lifelong friends during these years." (MP-HDP14)

In February 1958, Billy Saunders and the Tuxedos won a band competition at the Birmingham Town Hall, edging out the popular local group, the Tiger Sharks.

By the end of 1961, in order to remain competitive, The Tuxedoes modified its name to the more provocative the Rocking Tuxedoes.

Pinder said, "After a time, I got a bit fed up with playing in the band and joined El Riot and the Rebels for a few shows after Ray asked me to join." (MP-MMCD15)

★ Birmingham's Latest and Greatest
Rock 'n' Roll Group!

El Riot and the

Rebels

M. T. PINDER
158 Chingford Road   ● URGENT CALLS —
Erdington, Birmingham 23 ● Phone—Coleshill 3346

Above: Business card for El Riot and the Rebels, with Mike Pinder listed as contact.
(Courtesy Tony Brown)
Below: El Riot and the Rebels in their final year. Ray Thomas is center stage at microphone; John Lodge, to the right, in dark glasses. Mike Pinder appears to be stage left, on guitar, although picture may be from a period when he was not with band. (Photo source: TheMoodyBlues.co.uk)

Pinder sat in with El Riot & the Rebels during most of 1961 and '62. He was even proactive in trying to find gigs for the band, handing out business cards with his home address and phone number on them.

After a switch in drummers, with Ron Sherwood joining the lineup, the band appeared on the popular TV show *Lunchbox*.

Ray Thomas: "The *Lunchbox* was great – our first telly appearance. John Lodge's Uncle Ray worked on the *Lunchbox* and he convinced some of the people there to come hear us play. That got us two slots on the show." (RT-AI17)

The first of the two appearances came on November 14, 1962, covering the Shadows' hit "Guitar Tango" and with Thomas singing Frank Ifield's chart topper, "I Remember You."

The band also performed on ATV's *The Pop Show*.

Despite local success – which meant the band members could pay for their instruments and have some pocket money left over, while most were still living with their parents – Pinder was not so certain that a "Brumbeat" band, as they

would soon be labeled, was the right path toward a secure future. He explained, "[T]hings got in a bad state in Birmingham for the groups, so I joined the Army. Pretty drastic, right?" (MP-BI66)

Those remaining in the band – including Thomas and Lodge – carried on. But, as 1962 was winding down, Pinder found himself stationed in the icy cold of Germany, as a corporal in the Royal Army Service Corps. It didn't take long before he was questioning the decision to enlist, especially considering the timing. It was during this military exile when the Beatles broke through to popularity.

Pinder said, "When I heard 'Love Me Do,' it was like, 'Okay, that's what I've been waiting for.' I'd been waiting for that signal because the music scene in England up until then was pretty poor; it was a pretty bad scene. That's why I went into the Army, because my brothers, my uncles, my dad, and all my family at one time had been in the military. It was sort of the rites of passage… back then." (MP-CB95)

In early 1963, the Beatles hit again with their second single, "Please Please Me," this time topping the charts. Pinder was about to discover that perhaps music was his true calling. He and a few other younger members in his company with experience at playing musical instruments were struck with an idea. He said, "We persuaded a Colonel to [hand] out £600 to equip a guitar group. It was all Liverpool boom then."

The pleasure of performing music once more had Pinder eager to return to his old life with the bands of Birmingham. He said, "I went to see my CO, and he said, 'Yeah, you can go.' So they let me out, you know; they let me out of my term." (MP-GM09)

It was classified as a medical discharge. Pinder recalled having spent precisely one year and 42 days in the Army. He said, "Anyway, I eventually got out, started working clubs with Ray Thomas. [We did] Shadows stuff. Everyone was copying. But I suddenly came to the conclusion that rhythm guitarists were on the way out, so I switched back to piano. I don't read music, just study the keys, [and] my style developed from Shearing, Brubeck, Oscar Peterson – that sort of stuff. Brubeck is great for his "time" compositions. Anything that is FIRST in a field is great. The Beatles are great. And the Stones, in their style." (MP-BI66)

The Rolling Stones had no record contract at this point, but were playing many of the same clubs in which El Riot and the Rebels appeared.

Thomas, Lodge, and, possibly, Pinder, along with their colleagues in the Rebels, appeared on TV again, returning to *Lunchbox* for the program's April 15, 1963 episode.

Also on April 15, while playing at the Riverside Dancing Club in Tenbury Wells, the group shared the bill with none other than the Beatles, who had just released their first album, *Please Please Me*, and their third single, "From Me to You," both destined to top the charts.

Thomas recalled, "Riverside was the first time we'd met the Beatles. Even though they had just hit in the charts, they still honored the contract they had signed to perform at Riverside. They were great guys." (RT-AI17)

The Beatles were the envy of all the struggling bands, and with this as an incentive, El Riot and the Rebels recorded a 78 rpm acetate with a cover of the Marcels' No. 1 doo-wop hit, "Blue Moon."

Ray Thomas: "Making 'Blue Moon' was rather funny because I couldn't remember the words – no teleprompters in those days! It was never used for anything, but did give us some recording experience." (RT-AI17)

A second song, the Roy Orbison-penned "(Go! Go! Go!) Down the Line," was also recorded, and served as the flip side of the sample disc. (This song, perhaps the only example of Ray Thomas singing rock 'n' roll, can be found on the audio disc from *The Moody Blues: Classic Artists*).

The group was also given an EMI audition. However, despite El Riot and the Rebels' local popularity, they were not offered a recording contract. Lack of further success left the band members looking for better opportunities.

Mike Pinder said, "I stuck around in the band for a while but then got an offer to join another Birmingham group – the Krew Kats. I heard that the band had been offered the chance to play the clubs in Hamburg, and [I] asked Ray to join me." (MP-MMCD15)

The Krew Kats

There were two bands in England during the 1960s called the Krew Kats. The first featured famed English session guitarist Big Jim Sullivan, who had been a member of British rock teen idol Marty Wilde's backing band, the Wildcats. After leaving the Wildcats, Sullivan started his own group, the Krew Kats, and recorded a pair of instrumental singles in 1961, which fused the guitar-rock sound of the Shadows and the surf-guitar music of the Ventures. Neither single hit, and Sullivan and the Krew Kats disbanded. At this time, a group Mike Pinder had played with in 1958, the Rocking Tuxedoes, changed their name to the Krew Kats, thereby capitalizing on the two surf/rock singles which had received some jukebox exposure in both England and Germany. While all the members of this new Krew Kats lineup came from the Rocking Tuxedos, only one – bass guitarist Norman Bradley – was a carryover from the original group from which Pinder had been a member. The new Krew Kats struggled in Birmingham just as the other hundreds of semi-pro bands did, but were able to find work at clubs in the Reeperbahn Red Light District in Hamburg, Germany.

When Bradley was able to arrange for a return booking at Hamburg's notorious Top Ten Club in late 1963, three of his group members – the lead vocalist, the organist, and the rhythm guitarist – were not interested in making the trip. Bradley offered Pinder the gig, for which he would alternate between playing the band's lightweight electronic organ, the clavioline, and rhythm guitar. Bradley knew Ray Thomas from his work as front man in El Riot & the Rebels, and enlisted him to handle lead vocals. Still with the group, along with Bardley on bass, were Ted Tunnicliffe on lead guitar, Ricky Barnes on Tenor Sax, and Eddy Sparrow on drums. Pinder didn't need to have his arm twisted to quit the machinist's job he had found, and he and Thomas left for Germany with the Krew Kats.

The band played four weeks at the Top Ten Club, and, as the Beatles had experienced in 1961 and '62, were subjected to a grueling schedule of performing six days a week for eight or more hours, with few breaks.

Ray Thomas: "It was really hard work playing in those clubs in Hamburg. We played an hour on, then an hour off, at night, from 7 pm until 5 am the next morning." (RT-AI17)

The accommodations in the back of the club were appalling. What happened in the front was worse, with the stage often shared with strippers, performing before drunk and rowdy audiences, sometimes to the accompaniment of gunfire.

Pinder shared, "We were playing the Top Ten Club in Hamburg, and you get a little bit crazy because you're doing a few shows a day, and there's not much you can do [in between sets] but go to the bar, or the coffee-shop kind of thing. They weren't great gigs that we had. But we're on stage one night, and we're just getting ready to open the curtain, and I see this white toilet seat on the left there behind the curtains. And I grabbed it and put it around my head for the opening number.

"And then I found out later, after becoming friends with the Beatles, [when] I was talking to John Lennon about doing that show in Germany and that white toilet seat, and [he said], 'Oh, it's the one I left there!' He'd done exactly the same thing!" (MP-GM09)

Anyone who has read about the Beatles' early days in Hamburg will likely recall the colorful – or off-color – stories of their antics in the wild clubs, including the infamous tale of the toilet seat often worn around Lennon's neck during many performances. Clearly, housekeeping was not a high priority in the Hamburg clubs, and even something as out of place as a toilet seat on the side of a stage could remain there for years. Sadly, this flip-up seat which had adorned the necks of both a Beatle and a Moody was lost to history after this. What a prize it would have made for a pop-music memorabilia collector!

The moments of levity, or good-humored lunacy, eventually gave way to the exhausting workload and the oppressive club owners.

Thomas recalled that the primary owner, Peter Eckhorn, "was a notorious German club owner who had a full blown shooting range in his attic. He [had] Mausers and all kinds of guns up there. He was a bit crazy and used to feed his dog on speed. Him and his cohorts really were gangsters."

Ray Thomas: "The same people who owned the club in Hamburg also owned a club in Hanover, so they sent us up there to play." (RT-AI17)

The Hanover club hadn't been doing well, and the plan was to have the Krew Kats fill in during a month-long interim period before closing the doors.

Interviewed by Mark Powell, Thomas said, "So, we went down to Hannover. We were a pretty good band and, as a result, the business at the club picked up, and so he decided he wasn't going to close it. The problem for us was that he was just feeding us money from the bar sales of this club; we weren't getting our proper wages. Things got quite desperate and we kept on trying to get a hold of him and couldn't. Eventually we went back to Hamburg, basically to get our passports, as he was holding on to them.... When we asked him to pay us the money we were owed, he just told us to 'fuck off.'"

Eckhorn returned Pinder's and Thomas's passports to them – throwing them at the two young men. Thomas said, "When we opened them, we discovered that the bastard had arranged for our work visas to be terminated when we left his club in Hamburg, and so we'd been working for a month illegally.... We couldn't go to the police because our German work permits had expired…. He'd got us over a barrel. We were sorry broke, but at least we got our passports.

"Mike and I decided that we should go straight home, but we had no option other than to walk, trying to hitch rides where we could!" (RT-MMCD15)

Pinder told Ian Dove of *New Musical Express*, "[Ray] and I walked home from Hamburg that time! Yes, *walked*…. [W]e had some contract trouble and ended up with nothing – flat broke. Originally we intended to hitchhike, but it turned into a walking marathon because we only got two lifts – one in an invalid car, a three-wheeled all plastic job driven by a very old Frenchman." (MP-NME65)

Thomas said, "We had some money for a little food but not enough for transportation. At nights we slept in bus stops and nearly froze. We got very few rides from hitching; must have been the long hair! It took us the better part of two weeks to walk through Germany and Belgium." (RT-AI17)

Once in the Belgium coastal city of Ostend, Thomas and Pinder went to the British Consul, seeking help.

Thomas said, "They told us to piss off; they didn't want to know. And so Mike said to me in a loud voice, 'The best thing we can do is to go outside and do what the Liverpool band the Undertakers did!'" (RT-MMCD15)

Thomas told how the Undertakers had a similar problem with their passports after getting stranded in Germany. When denied help from the British Consul, they went out, got drunk, then smashed a plate glass window of a department store. They spent the night in jail, but were warm, safe, and well fed. And then they were deported back to Liverpool, all expenses paid. Thomas picked up on the scam, and shouted, "Well, that's bloody ideal; we'll spend a night in a warm bed, have breakfast and then they will fly us home!"

As Pinder and Thomas had intended, the British Consul official overheard. To forestall this impending crime wave, he took their passports and handed them seven shillings and sixpence each for breakfast. Then they were to go to the dock, where a ferry captain would hold their passports for passage back to England.

Thomas said, "They begrudgingly gave us tickets for the ferry to Dover, England – which we had to repay them back for!" (RT-AI17)

Pinder said, "Anyway, you can see we've knocked about a bit; and the stars knocked out of our eyes." (MP-NME65)

Thomas and Pinder had made it home, but in the explosive 1960s, much could change in the blink of an eye … or after a few months in Germany.

Pinder said, "We found that a lot of the bands had got disillusioned as they weren't really going anywhere. At one point it felt as though 'Brumbeat' would be the next 'Merseyside [Beat]' and become a national phenomenon, but that never happened. Bands were breaking up left, right and center, and, as a result, there were a lot of musicians around in Birmingham looking for something new to do." (MP-MMCD15)

With no immediate prospects on the music front, Pinder answered a "help wanted" ad from Streetly Electronics, looking for someone with both musical and electronic experience. He interviewed with the company and was hired to test a sort of musical "machine" being prepared for marketing.

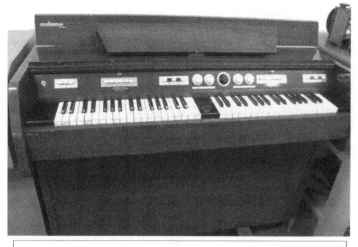

An orchestra in a box – the Mellotron.

Pinder said, "At Streetly Electronics I was introduced to this machine, and the moment I saw it, I thought, 'This is destiny to me.' It was almost like I knew it was there for me to discover and to use."

The machine, as any Moody Blues fan might guess, was a Mellotron.

Pinder explained, "The Mellotron is actually a mechanical device, a playback tape recorder with 70 heads and 70 pieces of tape on a giant pinch roller. When you press down a key, you're literally playing a tape recorder. My job was to play the Mellotron to make sure that each machine worked perfectly and that all the tapes were timed correctly."

"When [each Mellotron] machine was built," he said, "it would be sent to my department and I would put all the tapes in, [then] line them up. They all had to be lined up so that when you hit a [key], it started playing correctly at the beginning of the note. [I was also] tuning, and testing, and all that kind of thing. So, everything that went out of there had my stamp." (MP-EOTS99 and MP-GM09)

Pinder was actually there when the very first Mellotron went out the door.

While the Mellotron was brand new in England, the concept behind it had been born several years earlier in America. In fact, the first keyboard-driven tape instruments were built and sold by Wisconsin-inventor Harry Chamberlin, who had experimented in this field from 1949 through 1956. After relocating to California, he recorded a variety of orchestral notes from the Lawrence Welk Orchestra, with each tape in his "Chamberlin" containing one long note from each instrument.

A travelling salesman for the new and understaffed company, who was supposed to take a demonstration unit across America, sailed to England instead. Once there, he represented himself as having the authority to sell territory rights for the "unnamed" instrument, from which he had removed the Chamberlain label. The Bradley brothers – Frank, Norman, and Les, of engineering company Bradmatic Ltd. – believed they could improve on the design, and acquired the U.K. manufacturing and distribution rights. Bradmatic Ltd. soon joined with Streetly Electronics, and, by 1963, the Bradleys were ready to market their music-and-sound-effects machine.

The machines Pinder was loading with tape, then tuning and testing, were priced at £1,000. (In 2017, this would be the equivalent of £16,000 – or $20,000 – an expensive toy.)

Among the first customers, in the early and mid-1960s, were Princess Margaret, Peter Sellers, King Hussein of Jordan, Scientology founder L. Ron Hubbard, and the BBC Radiophonic Workshop.

While Pinder was becoming an expert with the Mellotron, Ray Thomas had been trying to find a way to stay in the music business as a performer. He said, "There was so much competition [in Birmingham in 1964] that the only way to get gigs was to put together a local super-group, which is what we did over the next few months." (RT-H&H85)

Pinder was intrigued and willing to leave behind his job at Streetly Electronics, provided he and Thomas could find other "stars" to join them.

This brought them to the doorstep of a pair of local musicians named Laine and Edge.

Denny Laine's childhood home, Holcombe Road, Birmingham.
(Courtesy Tony Brown)

Denny Laine and the Diplomats

Denny Laine, born Brian Hines on October 29, 1944, in Birmingham, had just turned 19, and was already a local celebrity of a sort.

Laine told Mark Murley of *Higher & Higher*, "All during my school days, up until I was 16, I was doing everything all over the country, working at night then going to school in the day. I had my own band, eventually called Denny Laine & the Diplomats. We were probably one of the Top 5 bands in Birmingham." (DL-H&H97)

Of course, this status did not come overnight.

At seven, Laine got his first taste of show business when he started performing in an amateur pantomime company. By 11, while attending Yardley Grammar School in Birmingham, he was singing folk songs and playing guitar. Soon after this, he became the guitarist in a local skiffle band called the Deltas, then lead singer for the Hep Cats. After this, in early 1962, he became the leader of the Dominators (named after the Norton motorcycle). He said, "I was probably in about two or three bands at the same time, really. That was what the scene was like in Birmingham. It wasn't a professional thing." (DL-G10)

After leaving school, Laine found a job as a trainee "buyer" in a large department store in Birmingham. He said, "So I went and got a job at a huge store owned by Harrods of London, called Rackhams. I was in the music department as a trainee 'buyer,' so I learned all about pianos and hi-fi equipment. I introduced guitars to that store, because it was a very high-class place, and they didn't have guitars. They had a record section, and people started coming in, like Ella Fitzgerald, Lonnie Donegan, and a lot of people I liked. And I would meet a lot of people from the music business – I would get to talking about records, and playing records, and that kind of thing…. But when I started being late for work, because I was gigging in the evenings with my band, I decided to knock it on the head. I then decided to go professional, because I was making more money at it than at work, and I didn't want to go to the shop." (DL-RM09)

Since he was known as Brian Hines in the music department at the store, Laine adapted the stage name Johnny Dean for this latest band, now with Birmingham pals Tony Elson on rhythm guitar, Dave "Wongy" Wheeland on bass, and Tim Bellamy on drums. During its brief life, the group was known as Johnny Dean and the Dominators.

The band soon established itself in local venues, such as the Mermaid Pub and Hotel, and at Maney Hall, Tamworth. It has been said that the energetic Johnny Dean would amuse audiences by demonstrating his gymnastic skills, doing back flips and cartwheels across the stage.

With so many music groups in the city, and so few paying gigs to compete for, personnel changes were common, and frequent.

Above: Denny Laine and the Diplomats, with (L-to-R) Laine, Phil (Ackrill) "Ralston," Bev (Bevan) "Ralston," and Dave Wheeland. (Photo source: bbc.co.uk)
Platinum bleached: Denny Laine and the Diplomats, circa 1963, with (L-to-R): Bev Bevan, Steve Horton (replacing Wheeland on bass), Laine, and Ackrill.
(Courtesy Tony Brown)

In October 1962, with Laine still on lead guitar and vocals, and Wheeland on bass, Johnny Dean and the Dominators transformed into Denny Laine and the Diplomats (sometimes called the Dynamite Diplomats). The new additions were Phil Ackrill (aka Phil Ralston) on rhythm guitar, and Bev Bevan (aka Bev Ralston) on drums. If the name Bev Bevan sounds familiar, you likely know him from his residency in the Move, starting in 1966, then remaining with the core members as they evolved into the Electric Light Orchestra in 1971. He remained with ELO into the mid-1980s, and then took a turn drumming for Black Sabbath.

Bevan said, "Denny Laine & the Diplomats – we were very successful in Birmingham; we became one of the top groups in the Birmingham area. We all had peroxide blonde hair, and we wore, like, mock-crocodile skin suits, and did anything for a gimmick just to get publicity. But it was a good band and Denny obviously a very talented boy." (BB-CA07)

Two sides to the Diplomats. Above: With Nicky James as the front man.
(Photo source: birminghammail.co.uk)
Below: On their own, with Laine, Horton, Laine, Ackrill, and Bevan.
(Photo source: Fab4Collectable.com)

Laine said, "We were doing, sort of, a lot of our material, you know, as opposed to just doing the hits of the day. And we got kind of known for that." (DL-CA07)

During a trip to the East Coast of England, and while playing a gig at the Baths Hall in Scunthorpe, Lincolnshire (a former indoor swimming house converted into a concert hall), Denny Laine and the Diplomats picked up a fifth member.

Bev Bevan recalled, "There was this rather tough sort of character at the front of the stage, saying, 'Can I sing?'" (BB-CA07)

The character was Nicky James, who was from Birmingham and would later collaborate with Ray Thomas on his two 1970s solo albums. Since the crowd had been somewhat unresponsive up until now, the band invited James onto the stage. And then they witnessed this "tough sort of character" with a heavy Birmingham accent change before their eyes.

Bevan said, "[S]uddenly, he was transformed, and he put on this sort of red satin jacket, and then he says, 'Can you do Elvis? Can you do 'One Night'? 'Okay, yeah.' And we did that [imitating guitar intro to the song], and this guy goes, '*One ... night ... with ... you*!', and in the best Elvis voice you'd ever heard." (BB-CA07)

Nicky James recalls, "And, of course, the next thing you know I've got all the girls at the door screaming their lungs off, because I'm singing like Elvis Presley." (NJ-CA07)

The room immediately started to fill up.

Bevan remembered, "And me and Denny, particularly, we're big Elvis fans, and we just went, 'Wow! What else do you do?' And we ended up doing lots of songs – Elvis songs – and Denny was totally taken with Nicky James. And he said, 'You should join the band permanently.'" (BB-CA07)

James said, "I went back to Birmingham that night, with Denny Laine and Bev Bevan…. And then it became 'Denny Laine and the Diplomats, *featuring* Nicky James,' and that lasted

for a good year – year and a half – and we really did build up in Birmingham at that time, just a fantastic reputation." (NJ-CA07)

So fantastic, that the group starting getting bookings with some of the biggest acts in England. One example came in July, 1963, at Birmingham's Old Hill Plaza:

Laine said, "The most memorable gig prior to the Moody Blues was when the Diplomats played with the Beatles. We opened for the Beatles at the place in Birmingham that has a revolving stage. When we came off, the Beatles came on, and all the leads got pulled out of the speakers because somebody forgot to take them out before the stage moved around. So the Beatles came on to no microphones. The girls are all screaming, but John is pointing at his microphone, saying, 'Where's the f**king microphone?!' …

"I was working at the shop when I first heard 'Love Me Do,' and knew it was gonna be a hit. So, I said [to them], 'The minute I heard "Love Me Do," I knew you guys were gonna be a problem!,' and we all laughed." (DL-RM09)

It was here, and on subsequent meetings, when Laine and Paul McCartney formed a friendship which would one day lead to a musical partnership in Wings.

Also, from this time, the band was invited by record producer Tony Hatch, of Pye Records, to cut a demonstration disc at Marble Arch studio in London. Nicky James recorded two songs, backed by the Diplomats: "My Colour Is Blue" and "Take Me Back." Then, two of Laine's compositions were recorded – "So Wonderful" and "Forever and a Day," with Laine on lead vocal. The Nicky James songs were released by Pye as a single on September 10, 1963 (7N 15560). It failed to chart. (One of the Denny Laine songs – "Forever and a Day" – was later issued on the music CD with *The Moody Blues: Classic Artists*.)

As evidenced by the recording of "Forever and a Day," Laine showed promise as a vocalist and songwriter, and the band certainly had the talent to back him up. Sadly for the Diplomats, Hatch became distracted by all of his other successes, which included writing "Sailor," the No. 1 hit for Petula Clark that year, followed by writing and producing numerous other Pet Clark hits, as well as several for the Searchers and other artists.

The Diplomats give up on being blond, hair now dyed jet black.
(*Birmingham Planet*, January 30, 1964)

The Diplomats were left with a demonstration record, but no record contract, and a long drive home to Birmingham.

In early 1964, Nicky James, with his dark locks, and bad boy good looks, seemed to be getting more attention than the fair-haired boys in the band. So, after two years of being bleached blond, the Diplomats – Denny, Bev, Phil, and Steve – visited the hairdresser's shop.

However, a new look didn't give the locally fashionable Diplomats a new lease on life. By this time, Laine had become disenchanted and was open to the idea of defecting to another band. He explained, "The thing was… Nicky James… was a dead rip-off of Elvis Presley. It was kind of sporty in some ways. He was a good singer, but I didn't want to be in an Elvis copy band. We kind of developed a little bit there, and that started to piss me off. I thought, 'This isn't what I'm all about.' So, the Diplomats were no longer the same band; they sort of became a backing group. I just got fed up with it. I suppose when the Moodies came along with an idea of doing something different, it was just right; it was the right timing for me to do what I wanted to do….

"I know that they [Pinder and Thomas] used to come to Diplomat gigs, and they came up to me one night and asked me if I wanted to put a band together." (DL-H&H97)

Laine recalled another reason he wanted to make a move, saying, "I wanted to move to London and the rest of the Diplomats wouldn't move because of their [day] jobs. It was at that point that I started to rethink my future." (DL-MMCD15)

Regarding his decision to go with Pinder and Thomas, Laine said, "We all wanted to make it. We all wanted to get out of the rut of being a Birmingham band that just played everybody else's hits. So we got together with the idea of being sort of a blues-R&B band. It was only us and Spencer Davis at the time that were doing it….

"I know that Ray was meant to be the lead singer, originally…. He had a really good voice, but Ray's not a blues singer. My quality voice probably isn't as good as his, but I've got more influences in that department, so I ended up being the singer."

"[I]t turned out like a blues band with harmonies, if you can imagine that; a little bit more of a gospel-style thing." (DL-H&H97 and DL-G10)

Laine's final gig with the Diplomats was at Birmingham Town Hall on March 26, 1964, opening for the Rolling Stones.

Days later, the *Birmingham Planet* reported:

> Denny Laine has left one of Birmingham's best-known groups, the Diplomats, to concentrate on R&B. His departure coincides with the break-up of Gerry Levene's Avengers. The result: two of the Avengers, Jim Onslow and Mike Southern, are now Diplomats.

Phil (Ackrill) "Ralston" and Bev (Bevan) "Ralston" would carry on with the two former Avengers and original Diplomat member, Steve Dawson, returning to the lineup.

Payback for a favor brought the new Denny Laine-Ray Thomas-Mike Pinder R&B band its next key member.

Ray Thomas said, "Denny was living at Graeme Edge's at the time because he had some blowup with his mom and dad, and so Graeme's parents put him up for a while. And so, Denny said, 'If I join the band, I want Graeme to join the band.' … [W]e said, 'Fine.' I mean, we knew Graeme from when he was in the Avengers." (RT-DM15)

And Graeme Edge, as they all knew, was one hell of a drummer.

Gerry Levene & the Avengers

Graeme Edge, born in Rochester, Staffordshire on March 30, 1941, was raised in Birmingham.

Graeme Edge's childhood home on Coventry Road in Birmingham, as it appears today. (Courtesy Tony Brown)

Edge had two passions at an early age – drumming and writing poetry, two things that usually don't go hand-in-hand.

Regarding the poetry, he said, "I like to tell the story of when I was about 10 or 11: We had an English test and the master said he wanted us to write an essay about what we'd do with £100 if he gave it to us. Well, I was going to do wonders with it – of course I spent about a thousand – but I did write the essay all in rhyme. It just seemed to come natural to me. When the master saw it, he saw that I didn't know when rhyming you ended a line and started a new one below. I just wrote mine clear across the page. I had no idea that you were supposed to leave the rhyming words at the end of the line. He asked if I'd read poetry and that started him off. He gave me [Alfred] Tennyson and [Lord] Byron, all the Romantics. I still prefer the Romantics; beat poetry and stuff like that doesn't interest me. The thing about poems is you can make them so much denser than essays because you have the tyranny of the meter and rhyming. You're forced into a much more direct and finite universe." (GE-AW12)

As for the drums, they were readily available to Edge when but a boy. His father, who had been a music-hall singer, and his mother, who was a pianist, had the biggest house in the neighborhood. Some of the boys who lived nearby, all older than Graeme, had formed a band and, because their families' homes were smaller, they were allowed to store their equipment in the Edge family home. Of all these instruments, Edge found himself gravitating toward the drums.

Wanting to encourage their son's interest in music, the Edges arranged for him to take lessons. This only lasted a few months, however, since Edge preferred teaching himself, playing along to records, free to develop his own style.

The boy's first opportunity to drum while playing with others his age was certainly not something associated with a future rock 'n' roll drummer. He told an American interviewer, "I had joined the Boys' Brigade. You know, like your Boy Scouts…. I played snare drums in the marching band. It was a lot of fun. From there, I bought a crappy old drum kit, with permission to play it between 5:00 and 7:00 at night, hopefully to keep away the neighbors with their pitchforks." (GE-TWN15)

Edge eventually played with the Blue Rhythms, the group of boys who stored their gear in the family home.

It was a hit-or-miss affair, especially for the new drummer. Edge said, "There was no one around in England to teach us rock 'n' roll drumming, because we were the first. We had to make it up as we went along."

22

Edge would later have to work at undoing some of the habits he had formed while making it up as he went along. He finally accomplished this by reading books on drumming, and said, "Reading was valuable; it taught me that by just copying the sound you can get into trouble. You can play something that sounds similar but, because you're not putting in a double beat on one hand sometimes or starting with the correct hand, you can end up messed up. You can get the fill to sound exactly right, but to get back to a standard pattern, you have to sort of uncross your arms, which makes you speed up. Then you're not in control of the situation." (GE-MD87)

While Edge fussed over the right and wrong way of drumming, his parents had other plans for him and enrolled their son into a proper trade school – Gosta Green College of Advanced Technology. He later said, "I still have dreams about being late for exams. I studied structural engineering – you know, bridges and skyscrapers. I never got past fire escapes." (GE-TWN15)

Maybe not, but Edge did well enough to obtain the Higher National Certificate as a draughtsman, all the while playing with local groups. He said, "I had been playing in various bands on the Birmingham scene. My first band was called the Silhouettes. We liked the Shadows, so we thought we'd call ourselves the Silhouettes! Like all first bands, we were really crap, but we loved it and had fun. And then I moved to the Blue Rhythms, and then Gerry Levene and the Avengers." (GE-MMCD15)

(Courtesy Tony Brown)

In a 1964 Decca records "biography" on the Moody Blues and its members, that band Graeme recalled as the Silhouettes was called the Shades. Another group he played with the Ivor Debman Jazz Quintet. And, during much of this time, he worked as a waiter in a coffee bar in Birmingham.

Regarding the Avengers, Edge said, "I was in the local music store, you know, where everybody used to gather on Saturday mornings and look at all the equipment we couldn't afford to buy. And I was just messing around on the drums and Gerry Levene – his real name was Mike Gibbs – was in there and he saw me playing and sort of said, 'Do you want to come up and play with us?' I think the band was already going, but I think they had just lost their drummer. He'd just quit… he had a nervous breakdown at 18. He couldn't face playing live. It was too tense for him…. He got no joy from it. He enjoyed the rehearsals and all that, but, when he actually got before the public, he couldn't hack it….

"I worked with those guys for about a year and a half…. And we did really well in Birmingham – only on a local level – but we were one of the top five or six local bands." (GR-H&H96)

The other guys, besides Levene on vocals, included Mike "Sprike" Hopkins on guitar; John Watson on second guitar; Peter Cook on keyboards; Jim Onslow on bass, and now, Edge on drums. In time, Watson would leave the group and be replaced on guitar by Roy Wood, who would later gain recognition in three British progressive bands:

the Move, followed by the first incarnation of the Electric Light Orchestra, and then Wizzard.

Edge said, "When we first started out, we were doing things like, basically, the Top 20 – things like Bobby Vee's 'Rubber Ball,' a couple of Everly Brothers tunes, stuff like that. And then we had a week's tour up in Liverpool and saw what they were all playing up there, stuff like 'Some Other Guy,' 'Twist and Shout,' 'P.S. I Love You' – a lot of the stuff that eventually came out on the Beatles' album. All the bands up there were doing [these songs]. And we shot down to the record shops and scurried back to Birmingham with copies of them all, and learned them…. This would be '63, around there. And that was one of the major reasons we became a force to be reckoned with in Birmingham, because we nicked all the songs from Liverpool! ...

"We had a residency Wednesday afternoons and Saturday afternoons at the local ballroom in town. It was the only place to go. Wednesday afternoons you got all the people from the shops [to attend] because the stores used to close Wednesdays. And Saturdays, of course, you got all the kids uptown; there was nowhere else to go all that time. So we did quite well at that time." (GR-H&H96)

In a music competition, "Liverpool v. Birmingham," Gerry Levene & the Avengers represented Birmingham. Their opposition: Liverpool's the Beatles, who

Above: "The Sky's the limit!" Gerry Levene and the Avengers. Levene is pointing the way toward stardom; Edge is second from the left.
(Photo source: gerrylevene.com)
Left: Sheet music for the only "Doctor Feel Good," with Graeme Edge at drums
(Courtesy Tony Brown)

triumphed. As compensation for their loss, Decca Records gave the Avengers a one-off record deal. The result was a single released in January 1964. "Doctor Feelgood" was coupled with "It's Driving Me Wild." (The A-side can be heard on the music CD included with *The Moody Blues: Classic Artists*.)

The band even got on TV, in February of that year, on Rediffusion's *Thank Your Lucky Stars*. They expected to perform the A-side but the producers asked them to play a song called "Hey, All You Women" instead.

Without national exposure, "Doctor Feelgood" never had a chance. Levene said, "It didn't make the chart but it still did pretty well, selling about 6,000 copies."

But 6,000 copies weren't going to get them another record released… nor, for that matter, keep the band together.

Edge told Moody Blues fanzine *Higher & Higher*, "Well, a lot of Birmingham bands broke up around this time [1963-64]. It started after Mersey beat. There was going to be Brumbeat and [the record companies] came down and recorded us all. And we thought we were really going to follow the Liverpool boom, and it didn't happen. By then, I had moved into a position of power in the group, inasmuch as I was getting [the] bookings. It was a thankless task, but it was me who was getting all the bookings and making all of those kinds of arrangements, and [the group] really got sort of [angry] and sort of blamed me [when things started going downhill]. It was almost like I was the manager. So, I got very fed up with that. It became very unsatisfying." (GR-H&H96)

After the demise of the Avengers, Graeme played drums for the short-lived R&B Preachers, a band which featured Denny Laine as vocalist/guitarist (when he was gigging away from the Diplomats) and Clint Warwick on bass.

It was at this time when Ray Thomas and Mike Pinder stepped forward. Thomas said, "We already knew both Denny and Graeme from gigging around Birmingham. At that time everyone was becoming disillusioned because the Brum Beat wasn't taking off like the Mersey Beat had. Lots of bands were breaking up. Mike and I got in touch with Denny and Graeme with the idea of forming a Birmingham Super Group." (RT-AI17)

Concerning the first meeting of the minds with Pinder and Thomas, Edge said, "[Ray Thomas] was with Mike Pinder, and they had John Lodge in their pocket…. They wanted to get me and Denny to join up with those three to form a band, because some of the other players were into rhythm & blues and some weren't. They were quite correct in assessing that it was Denny and I in our band who really wanted to play it!" (GE-MD87)

Edge didn't need to have his arm twisted. Seeing the irony in the situation, he said, "Here I was, the highest qualified man in this small engineering firm I was working for. I was making only half as much as when I played music.

"The music, of course, was much more fun, so I quit my job and that led to forming the Moody Blues. At the time, we never expected to make it big or anything like that. We were just having a good time loonin' around on stage." (GE-CP68)

Despite Edge's lighthearted comment, the members really were taking this new band more seriously. Laine, Thomas, and Pinder were clearly determined that this new Birmingham "super-group," comprised of members from three of the city's most popular groups – El Riot and the Rebels, Denny Laine and the Diplomats, and Gerry Levene & the Avengers – would take them beyond merely being a Birmingham sensation.

2

Early Moods

**The Moody Blues in 1964 (L-R): Denny Laine, Clint Warwick,
Ray Thomas, Mike Pinder, and Graeme Edge.**
(Photo source: Author's collection)

It was April 1964. The lineup for the yet-to-be-named "super-group" was tentatively Denny Laine, Mike Pinder, Ray Thomas, John Lodge, and Graeme Edge. But once it was made clear that the goal was to leave Birmingham, one member immediately dropped out.

Denny Laine said, "When we formed the Moody Blues, we offered John Lodge the gig but he wouldn't come because his girlfriend didn't want him to move out of Birmingham." (DL-H&H97)

There were actually two factors keeping Lodge from throwing in with former bandmates Thomas and Pinder, and new recruits Laine and Edge.

Ray Thomas said, "By trade, I'm a toolmaker, and so is John, but I'd finished my apprenticeship. John's dad said to him exactly what my dad said to me: 'This is a hit or miss sort of business,' he said, 'so finish your apprenticeship, and then you've got something [to fall back on] if it doesn't work out.' I mean, after being in a rock 'n' roll band, the last thing you want to do is go work in a *factory*, in *any* industry! [But] John's dad said the same, word for word, so John had another year to go on his apprenticeship… and so John took his advice, which was good advice." (RT-DM15)

Denny Laine and Graeme Edge had just worked with a good bass guitarist, who Pinder and Thomas knew, as well. They didn't have to look any further.

Clint Warwick, born Albert Eccles in Birmingham on June 25, 1940, become interested in the guitar while recuperating in the hospital from a car accident. Soon, after leaving the hospital and finishing school, he started playing in the Birmingham skiffle group – Danny King and the Dukes. Later, Eccles, as he was still known, formed and led the Rainbows. After no real success there, he joined Denny Laine and Graeme Edge as bass player for the short-lived R&B Preachers.

For the new venture, Eccles decided it was time to adopt a stage name. He chose "Clint" after seeing American TV western star Clint Walker in his *Cheyenne* series, now airing in the U.K.

Mike Pinder: "His real name was Albert, but he liked Clint Walker's rugged image." (MP-EOTS99)

The surname of "Warwick" was taken from American pop singer Dionne Warwick, who had just experienced her first Top 10 hit in Britain, with "Walk On By" (May 1964).

Besides being the oldest member, what set Warwick apart from the others was being the only married member. And a child was on the way.

In the early rehearsals, beginning in late April, 1964, the band nailed down its sound. Ray Thomas: "There were two hundred bands in Birmingham and a hundred thought they were Cliff Richard and the Shadows; the other hundred thought they were the Beatles. We were playing a form of the blues, and the only band playing blues was Spencer Davis." (RT-NME70)

Denny Laine: "[We were] more of a blues-based band, because I didn't want to play all the pop stuff. I was kind of sick of that. So, we had this following as a blues band, really. We had a club there that we played every week and people like Manfred Mann would come there, or the Jeff Beck Group, or people like that. A lot of the blues bands from London used to come up to the various Midlands blues clubs, and that's how I met a few of them." (DL-G10)

According to Mike Pinder, the band's chosen name developed as a ploy to gain sponsorship. He said, "One day, Ray Thomas and I were sitting in a little office of the ballroom where we were working. We were trying to conjure up an idea of how to get some money to fund the band and also to try and get on a circuit. In Birmingham, one of the big breweries there was Mitchells and Butlers. They went by the name of M & B. They owned most of the big dance halls. We thought maybe if we named this new band that Ray and I just put together, using those initials, we might talk them into coming up with some money to fund us, and also to get on their circuit." (MP-CB95)

Clint Warwick: "We had a short residency at the Moat House nightclub and painted 'MB5' on the side of our van. But, almost immediately, the brewery decided they don't like us. I can't imagine why!" (CW-RS02)

Ray Thomas: "They told us to fuck off, to put it mildly!" (RT-MMCD15)

Since the group had already been performing for a few weeks as the MB5 – and, on a few other occasions, as the M&B 5 – they decided to pick another name that utilized the same initials.

Ray Thomas: "Mike apparently [will tell you that he] came up with 'the Moody Blues,' but I always thought that *I* came up with the 'Moody' part of it because I always saw it as a blues band. I think Mike got [the 'Blues' part] from a Miles Davis album, 'Indigo Blue,' or something like that." (RT-MMCD15)

Thomas was almost right concerning "Blues." Pinder said, "When I was very young I heard a piece of music by Duke Ellington called 'Mood Indigo' [a 1930 jazz song]. I really liked the music, but I liked the name of it even better, and it just stuck with me.

"[Also] at that time, I was very interested in the fact that music changed our moods. I had made the realization then [that] it had magical qualities to do things like that. We needed an "M," so that was really easy to come up with the 'Moody.'" (MP-CB95)

Pinder said coming up with the "Blues" part was easy, as well, because that is what the band was playing. But it was he, he said, who thought of it.

Denny Laine's memory differed from both Pinder's and Thomas's. He countered, "This is going to go down on record as the

Above: The Moody Blues 5's first performance, at the Carlton Ballroom, May 2, 1964.
(Photo by Joe Simpson; birminghammail.co.uk)
Below: The Carlton Ballroom occupied the second floor above two retail shops, Dale Forty and Brooks Bros. (Courtesy Tony Brown)

big controversy – *who named the Moody Blues anyway?* I was totally into the Blues then, so I'm sure I put the 'Blues' bit in there. And I was probably the moody one, so who knows? But I'm pretty sure I [suggested the name], so there you go, Michael [Pinder].

"But, anyway, it doesn't matter. The thing was, it was a great name, you know, and that's the way great names come about…. It was just different to anything else that was going on. And it kind of gave us a style, too." (DL-CB07)

For an engagement at the Carlton Ballroom on May 2, 1964, the band, still in a state of transition, was using the moniker "The Moody Blues 5," with the legend, "Rhythm and Blues at its Best." The poster had a picture of the band members wearing matching dark dress suits, much like the Beatles wore at this time, and also wearing distinctive "Beatles boots." The poster also acknowledged that this brand-new band had already secured local management with the claim: "Sole Representation & Management: Midland Top Ten Agency."

The Carlton Ballroom was not as impressive as it sounded. It was a small dancehall above two retail shops – Dale Forty, seller of pianos, and Brooks Bros., men's clothier. The man behind Midland Top Ten Agency was also the owner of the Carlton Ballroom – Phil Myatt.

In the June 12, 1964 edition of the *Birmingham Planet*, Mary McGrane wrote:

... The Moody Blues Five they have called themselves – and all five have one thing in common: they were leaders of well known local beat groups just waiting for the chance to switch over to the music they prefer and make it pay.

El "Kinky" Riot (22) had his own group, the Rebels; Mike "Hands" Pinder (22) led the Daltons; Graham "Plate" Edge (21), the Avengers; Clint "Whiskers" Warwick (22) was leader of Danny King's group, the Dukes, for four years; and 19-year-old Denny "Jingles" Laine was with the Diplomats.

And if you thought they looked as if they were enjoying standing up there banging out Beatles numbers – it was an optical illusion.

Edge, who preferred jazz and rhythm & blues over pop, told McGrane, "When rhythm & blues started to get popular, it was an opportunity we could not afford to miss. If anyone had told me a year ago that we could make a living out of R&B I'd have thought he was mad, but we are playing six nights a week!" (GE-BP64)

Laine told McGrane, "It was very hard work at first. We had to learn R&B from scratch. Playing for two hours is as tiring as working eight hours in a factory. Rock 'n' roll is simple and a good way to start, but we grew out of it." (DL-BP64)

McGrane wrote:

They grew into R&B at a very appropriate moment when places like Manchester' and Coventry are crying out for Blues groups.

What if the Midlands R&B market gets flooded?

Edge answered, "It won't. But if it did, we would just take another step in the direction we are eventually aiming at – modern jazz." (GE-BP64)

At this time, a Birmingham newspaper writer, Janice Nichols, reported:

A new Birmingham beat group who are shortly to wax their first record are going to cause a storm of controversy. For the Moody Blues Five, formed just four weeks ago, have decided to make their disc debut with a pop treatment of the "23rd Psalm." The boys fully expect angry letters from churchgoers and have not ruled out the possibility of the BBC banning their effort. Why then are they still determined to record it?

"We like the tune, and what's so wrong with bringing a hymn up to date?" asks Moody Blueser Denny Laine, their 19-year-old lead guitarist. He points out that the words have not been altered, neither has the melody. "It just happens that we like 'The Lord is My Shepherd' and, as we are beat musicians, we sing it in our usual style."

Teenagers at dances in Erdington's Carlton Club have already heard this version of the psalm. "They really dig it," says bass guitarist "Whiskers" Warwick. "None of them feels it is in any way disrespectful or mocking."

Drummer Graeme Edge points out: "American Negro performers have been doing this sort of thing in their churches for 50 years. There is no reason why a hymn shouldn't swing. And maybe it will make teenagers think about God and religion."

The Moody Blues Five plan to tape another "preaching number," "Thou Shalt Not Steal," for the B-side. The disc may be issued under the heading of "Prayer Meeting."

The Moody Blues manager, Phil Myatt, is convinced he is backing a winner. "Young people will go for this record – it has tremendous appeal. Although I expect opposition from the church authorities, I am prepared to meet any member of the clergy and discuss it."

Three of the combo are ex-leaders – Denny, El Riot, the vocalist, and "Whiskers." El and pianist Mike Pinder have both toured with groups in Germany.

Undoubtedly, they will get the tongues wagging when the "23rd Psalm" is released.

Days after the newspaper piece, the Moody Blues 5 was performing at the Moat House Hotel in Birmingham when they were "discovered" by an aspiring disc jockey named Tim Hudson.

Ray Thomas: "He was from London and later went on to become a DJ in America. But, at that time, he was selling fridges and appliances as a travelling salesman. He really liked us and knew some people in London who were looking for a band to manage and mentioned us to them. These people turned out to have set up a management company called Ridgepride, but they were also the people behind Seltaeb, a company who had the rights on all the Beatles merchandising – the name was actually "Beatles" spelled backwards! They came to see us play and [were pressuring] us to sign a contract with them." (RT-MMCD15)

By this time, Pinder, like Laine and Thomas, was convinced that the thought of any real success while staying in Birmingham was "a bit of a fairy story." He explained, "There were so many groups, really, and all of them undercutting each other like mad. This was, in effect, cutting their own throats, because they were ending up working for expenses – you know, a four-man group doing four hour's work for £1! That's no scene at all!

"We had worked up to getting union rates for the job – only about eight groups are in the Musicians' Union in Birmingham, I think – and we had a fan club, which was unusual. It got to around 300 in the first month or so, and grew from there…. [But] we were working seven nights a week in Birmingham and didn't seem to be getting anywhere. That's the trouble with the beat scene in Birmingham: there's a lot of good musicians there but they don't seem very adventurous – too security conscious. If you want to make it, you have to take a gamble – turn professional.

"And it was a big gamble. Just before we formed the group, we bought new equipment and were about a £1,000 in debt. Then the day before our first booking, Denny Laine, our lead guitarist, had his guitar pinched. So we had to borrow more money….

"But by this time we were determined. We'd been through enough before, had our hopes built up by promoters and so on, and then had them dropped down again. This was *our* risk – if it didn't work, we'd take other jobs; go down the pit, or something like that." (MP-NME65)

The arrangement with Phil Myatt was a loose one, nothing that would prevent the band from signing with Ridgepride. Ray Thomas told this author, "Phil Myatt did represent us but not as a manager. Phil was really more of a promoter and got us some gigs." (RT-AI17)

The men from London appeared to have much more to offer.

Graeme Edge: "They asked us what we wanted, and we told them all the equipment we wanted, *tongue well in cheek*. They came back a week later with a van full of all this stuff! So we signed this piece of paper. And they robbed us blind, of course. But they set things up for us, I suppose." (GE-MD87)

Ridgepride was a partnership of four men – Alex Murray, Jon (aka John) Fenton, Tony Secunda, and Simon Miller-Mundy. The latter was a wealthy young man providing the working capital for the new business. The other three concentrated on handling the talent, of which the Moodies would be the first. And, although two of the Ridgepride partners were connected to Seltaeb, the two businesses were kept separate. Seltaeb, after all, was there to market Beatles merchandise through a licensing agreement with the group's manager, Brian Epstein. Ridgepride, on the other hand, was looking to start a Beatles of its own.

Ridgepride had actually begun with Alex Murray, aka Alex Wharton.

As Alex Wharton, Murray had been part of a singing duo, the Most Brothers (with future famed record producer Mickie Most). They had a residency at the famous 2i's Coffee Bar in Soho, London, often referred to as "the birthplace of English rock." They also toured the U.K. in the late 1950s with early rock 'n' rollers such as Marty Wilde and Cliff Richards. The Most Brothers had three unsuccessful U.K. singles released by Decca Records in 1958 before disbanding.

In 1959, Wharton changed his name to Murray and tried for showbiz success again, this time as an actor. He found work on the stage and was cast a few small film roles. Success again eluded Murray,

Mickie Most and Alex Wharton (aka Alex Murray) as the Most Brothers, 1958.
(Photo source: National Portrait Gallery)

prompting him to try pop music once more, this time as a soloist. Decca issued three singles by Murray in 1960, with him covering songs such as the American hit "Teen Angel." They failed to chart, and Murray took a job with Decca as an A&R man in 1961. He was 21, the youngest man in the country to hold such a position.

Murray's first production for Decca was 1961's "Love Is Like a Violin," by English singer/actor/songwriter Ken Dodd. It went to No. 8 in the U.K. singles chart. Murray followed this with U.K. hits by other Decca artists, such as pop star Mark Wynter, and Rhet Stoller, whose "Chariot" featured the first double-tracked guitar, reaching No. 26. Murray also produced a pioneering stereophonic jazz album, *Sweet Wide and Blue*, as well as albums with Mantovani, before leaving the company, disillusioned over "office politics."

By early 1964, millions of pounds were being made seemingly overnight in the reenergized pop-music business, with beat music now the No. 1 export from Britain to America. Murray, having had success at Decca as an A&R man, decided it was time to do better by himself. He later described Ridgepride as an "off-the shelf company" purchased by himself, Simon Miller-Mundy, Jon Fenton, and Tony Secunda. The initial bankroll for the business came about as payback. Murray had come up with the idea for Seltaeb "over a game of Monopoly," which he gave to Jon Fenton and Simon Miller-Mundy, and which had done extremely well for the two. Now, Fenton and Mundy agreed it was time to cut Murray in by using some of the Seltaeb money to create a partnership between the three, in the booming field of band management. Mundy put up £10,000 to get Ridgepride going. It only occurred to Murray after this that they might benefit from a fourth partner, someone strong in the area of promotion.

Murray had known Tony Secunda from the days of the Most Brothers, when they meet at the 2i's Coffee Bar. Murray was in the Merchant Navy then, but soon found a job working as an office boy for an entertainment manger, thereby enabling him to learn about the business. Now, in the spring of 1964, the two men met again. Murray said, "I called by a shebeen – all night drinking den – and found a dejected Tony Secunda slumped on the floor in a dark corner. He had just finished his night-shift working as a waiter, having recently been released from prison after setting-up a partner with a drug plant and being caught.... I felt sorry for him and took him onboard for his promotions expertise; we'd done a couple of promotional stunts in the past and worked well

Tony Secunda, circa late-1960s.
(Photo source: Discogs.com)

together; and I'd twice forgiven him for stealing from me." (AM-LP06)

Murray and Secunda were provided a couple of desks in the Seltaeb's office – a basement flat at 79A Warwick Square in London. Now with a suitable mailing address, desks, and phones, the two men began the process of searching for a pop sensation of their own, to jointly manage with Fenton and Mundy.

Murray said, "When I was looking for a band to sign... there was a travelling salesman called Tim Hudson – school friend of Fenton. He saw [the Moody Blues] in the Carlton Club and called me to go see, which I did with Secunda, and we made a management offer. Didn't know they had a management contract – still don't know the details of the Myatt connection; thought they'd just been 'booked' to play. They upped sticks and came to London almost immediately to a flat we rented in Kensington, and we took over."

As for the Moodies' Birmingham management, Murray said, "Phil Myatt, owner [of the Carlton Club].... Nice guy, dumped by the boys without recompense when [they] came down to London." (AM-TB09)

Remarks such as this can tarnish the reputations of others. Murray may not have been in the loop regarding all the business arrangements. Simon Miller-Mundy, on behalf of Ridgepride, and listed as "Chairman," signed a contract with Phil Myatt, with the two parties in agreement that Ridgepride would manage the Moody Blues and engage a London agent to handle the group's bookings instead of Midland's Top Ten Agency. In turn, Ridgepride agreed to pay Myatt 10% from its earnings for managing the Moodies. Since Ridgepride was only taking 10% for itself, and Myatt was only entitled to 10% of Ridgepride's 10%, his end represented only 1% of revenue from the Moodies' record sales and appearance fees. It really didn't even amount to 1%, for Ridgepride also stipulated in the contract that they could deduct their business expenses (but not income taxes) before arriving at net earnings, from which Myatt would only then be paid his 10%.

Graeme Edge: "We were picked up by these three guys who told us, 'This is how you comb your hair, these are the trousers to wear,' and the guy who paid for all this was a sweet little feller by the name of Simon Miller-Murphy [sic, Mundy]. He was a millionaire's son, and he got rooked. All his bread was set up in a trust and he couldn't get his hands on it unless he had a job – so these three sharp characters put him on the board of directors of their company, which was supposed to be a showbiz agency." (GE-RS71)

Once in London, the Moodies discovered that their new managers needed more time to arrange for some gigs. In the meanwhile, the accommodations for the band were, to say the least, modest.

Pinder said, "We were all living in this one flat together and never went out those three weeks, except to pictures. There was no question of turning back; we had all agreed that we'd put our return fare away and only go back when the money and the food ran out." (MP-NME65)

Alex Murray said, "We put them on retainers, bought them a VW Kombi, kitted them out, hired a dancehall for them to play in weekly, and started promoting them via the Marquee Club and the National Jazz Federation Agency. At the time they signed the contract – a rip-off percentage-commission deal, which was the norm those days – I told them quietly that, when they made it big and the invested capital had been recovered, we could tear it up and sign a fairer one. I had myself been under such a contract as an artiste and personally considered such deals unfair." (AM-LP06)

While the Moodies were not yet writing their own material, the songs they performed were nonetheless new to the London scene, which started getting the band attention and bookings.

Ray Thomas explained the origins of the Moodies' new songs: "It was a DJ in the States, and he was a friend of one of the guys for our management company. And, [the managers] said, 'If you come across material, can you send it out?' That's how we came across James Brown. We were doing things like 'I Go Crazy' and all that stuff. By then, we'd moved to London and all that stuff hadn't been heard over here." (RT-DM15)

Work picked up and the Moodies began making regular appearances every Friday night at the Richmond Crawdaddy Club, and then received a chance to play London's popular Marquee Club.

The Marquee Club was born in 1958 as the home of the National Jazz Center. In 1961, it broadened its musical tastes and invited in rhythm & blues. By 1963, Manfred Mann (called Mann-Hugg Blues Brothers at first) became a resident band. That opened the floodgates, allowing in the Rolling Stones, the Who, the Yardbirds, the Spencer Davis Group … and now the Moody Blues.

Ray Thomas: "The Marquee was *the* gig to play in London. Manfred Mann had a night of their own; Paul Jones [Manfred Mann vocalist] came down with laryngitis, and we were a working band all the time, and we just happened to have a night off, so, the Marquee people got in touch with our management and said, 'Do you think your band will step in and do these nights at the Marquee to cover for Manfred Mann?' So, we said, 'Yeah!,' because we just wanted to get our foot in the door. We played 'I Go Crazy' and a lot of rhythm and blues… and we went down an absolute storm; they loved us! And so they offered us our own night." (RTDM15)

Now that the band had two steady venues, the next task for Ridgepride was to arrange for a recording contract … for the benefit of the company, not the Moodies.

Murray, with his connections at Decca had little trouble securing a deal to license the Moody Blues' recordings to the record company. It was a unique arrangement. The Moodies weren't signed to Decca, only to Ridgepride. The partners, then, were able to determine when and where they would have the band record, how much would be spent on the sessions, and who would produce.

Ridgepride convinced the Moodies that this was for the band's own good. Record companies took advantage of babes in the woods like the Moody Blues. Ridgepride, the Moodies were told, would make sure Decca didn't. As it turned out, Decca would not. But what of Ridgepride?

Secunda, who would soon become well-known for his gimmicky high concepts in promoting his bands, immediately put one in motion for the Moody Blues – matching blue dress suits.

The Moodies' first recording session for Ridgepride took place on July 24, 1964 at Olympic Studios on Baker Street, in London. With Alex Murray producing, an alleged Denny Laine / Mike Pinder

The Moodies outfitted in matching blue suits (L-R): Thomas, Laine, Edge, Pinder, Warwick, with designer David Skinner. (Photo Source: MoodyBluesAttitude.yuku.com)

composition, "Lose Your Money (But Don't Lose Your Mind)," was committed to tape, along with cover versions of R&B songs recently sent over from America, including "Go Now," "Steal Your Heart Away," "I Go Crazy," "You Better Move On," and "Can't Nobody Love You." Also recorded, the rollicking rendition of the "23rd Psalm." (These recordings would remain unreleased until the new millennium when a two-disc CD set of *The Magnificent Moodies*, with numerous bonus tracks, was issued.)

Above: David Skinner (second from left) with the boys, showing off the finished suits, on a railway platform, November 11, 1964.
(Photo Source: MoodyBluesAttitude.yuku.com)
Below: Decca gets the wrong song title –twice! Note the spelling "Loose" instead of "Lose."

A second session took place at Olympic studios the following day, July 25, resulting in new versions of the two best contenders from the previous day, now recorded with greater care.

U.K. single release:
"Steal Your Heart Away" b/w "Lose Your Money (But Don't Lose Your Mind)"
Decca F.11971; September 4, 1964

An obscure number written by American rhythm & blues guitarist and singer Bobby Parker, "Steal Your Heart Away" had been the B-side of Parker's only U.S. Top 100 hit, "Watch Your Step," from 1961. That single was one of those sent to Ridgepride from America.

Chosen for the flip side was "Lose Your Money (But Don't Lose Your Mind)." The record label identified the song as written by Laine and Pinder, but the copyright taken out on behalf of the two only listed them as having arranged the number. The song actually had a history.

Among the American blues artists the Moodies were exposed to at this time were

36

Sonny Terry and Brownie McGhee. On the duo's 1962 album, *Shouts & Blues* (Fantasy LP 3317), the twelfth and final track was an original called "If You Lose Your Money." The tune to this recording and the one by the Moodies are hardly comparable, except for the choruses, which are slightly similar although using different tempos and arrangements. The Terry and McGhee version is actually fairly slow; more bluesy in styling.

The lyrics are a different story. For instance, Terry and McGhee wrote:

> *If you lose your money, please don't lose your mind.*
> *If you lose your woman, please don't fool with mine.*

Laine and Pinder didn't have access to the original lyric, and they came pretty close. Their version reads:

> *If you lose your money, boy, well please don't lose your mind.*
> *If you lose that woman, boy, well, please don't come for mine.*

In the copyright filing for the Moodies version, it appears that Laine and Pinder, while knowing who sang the song, did not know who wrote it, and may have suspected it was a public-domain title. It would be reasonable to assume that Decca instigated a title search but was unable to find anything concerning the song, which had only been issued in America on the small Fantasy label, from Oakland, California, or felt the two songs had little in common. Decca therefore credited Laine and Pinder with the composition.

Both sides of the single are well recorded, with great clarity and punch – better sounding, actually, than their next three singles, no doubt thanks to being recorded at Olympic while the later songs were not.

"Steal Your Heart Away" had all the qualities needed to be a hit. Considering his young age, 19-year-old Denny Laine gave a surpassingly passionate and soulful reading of the somber song, complimented by the other Moodies' fine harmonizing.

Goldmine rock critic Bruce Eder would later call the recording "one of the most convincingly soulful singles to emerge from the entire British Invasion."

"Lose Your Money (But Don't Lose Your Mind)" is a good companion song for this first single – filled with energy, a driving beat, and an irresistibly catchy title and hook. It also features excellent harmonica playing – both bluesy and soulful – thanks to Ray Thomas.

Despite the quality of the A-side, the flip seemed a better contender for a trip into the British Top 40 during this week in 1964. Consider the competition: "You Really Got Me," by the Kinks, at No. 1, followed by "Do Wah Diddy Diddy," by Manfred Mann; "I'm Into Something Good," by Herman's Hermits; "Rag Doll," by the Four Seasons; "A Hard Day's Night," by the Beatles; "She's Not There," by the Zombies; "I Get Around," by the Beach Boys; "It's All Over Now," by the Rolling Stones, and "Where Did Our Love Go," by the Supremes. Even the slower songs in the British Top 20 at this time were so melodic and catchy that they proved irresistible – such as "As Tears Go By," from Marianne Faithfull. Could the bluesy and slow-paced "Steal Your Heart Away" find a place on the charts among such pop gems? Perhaps "Lose Your Money (But Don't Lose Your Mind)" could.

Either way, breaking a new group is never easy, and co-manager Tony Secunda, demonstrating his brilliance for high-concept promotional stunts, helped the first single take flight. Secunda dispatched homing pigeons to the several music weeklies that crowded newsstands at this time in Britain – *NME* (*New Musical Express*), *Melody Maker, Record Mirror, Disc and Music Echo* (aka *Disc Weekly*), *Pop Weekly,* and *Rave.*

Peter Jones, of *Record Mirror,* was one who responded. He wrote in the magazine's September 11 issue:

> Now when a live, placidly-cooing homing pigeon arrives in the office, I am bound to take notice of it. It arrived in a box, bearing an invitation to meet the Birmingham-based group The Moodybues [sic]. To RSVP, as they say, all I had to do was clip a "yea" or "nay" to the pigeon's left ankle and give it the old heave-ho out of the window.
>
> Meeting the Moodyblues [sic] is well worthwhile. Each of the five were leaders of individual groups until a few months ago when they linked up to become Birmingham's "Boss" R and B group. Incidentally, they already have a fan club of over 2,000.
>
> When they first arrived in London, they worked the Marquee Club and earned themselves an unprecedented reception. Their first disc, "Lose Your Money (But Don't Lose Your Mind)," and "Steal Your Heart Away," produced by Alex Murray, was hailed by dee-jay Alan Freeman [host of BBC-Radio's *Pick of the Pops* series] as "The best first record by any group in this country." ...
>
> I think their debut disc is excellent. I think the group has the ambition, enterprise, and talent to make a very big dent on the group scene. And that homing pigeon clearly agrees with me!

British journalist and pop music critic Don Nicholl gave the single four stars, writing:

> A fine debut disc this, and one which should establish the Moobyblues [sic] group very swiftly. They chant and play their own composition "Lose Your Money" in brisk blues fashion using R and B harmonica in the accompaniment to get current sound. Very difficult for new groups to make an impression at the moment but these lads do it.
>
> For the reverse they offer a slower number, "Steal Your Heart Away," which the lead singer plants solidly.

Based on these two reviews, it was already evident that the B-side was getting the most attention. When the group appeared on the Rediffusion TV series, *Ready Steady Go!,* the producer also picked the up-tempo flip side over the designated A-side.

Regarding the TV taping, Mike Pinder said, "We weren't used to doing television or lip-synching. That was new to us, and it was strange standing there going through the motions of playing, while you sort of heard through a speaker." (MP-GM94)

Bruce Eder later wrote in *Goldmine*:

> The lip-synced performance (available on EMI's *Ready Steady Go! Volume 3*) shows off a remarkably loose band, considering the pressure that it must've been under in what had to be one of its earliest television appearances – Ray Thomas blows on his harmonica with great gusto, while Denny Laine moves lithely around the stage with his guitar, strumming his unamplified instrument and miming to the voice track; Graeme Edge is less effective-looking on the drums, Mike Pinder seems deeply involved at the electric piano, and Clint Warwick looks coolly detached with his bass. On the whole, they look more animated and convincing than many of their rivals, but a good deal less sweaty in their dedication than, say, Van Morrison's group Them, in the same venue.

To further support their first single, the Moody Blues embarked on a tour with Sonny Boy Williamson, an American blues singer, songwriter, and harmonica virtuoso.

Ray Thomas: "We backed practically everybody who came over from America, and Sonny Boy spent a fortnight living with me, which was amazing. He taught me just a huge amount [about playing the blues on harmonica]. We even covered one of his songs, 'Bye Bye Bird.' We learned a great deal from all of them." (RT-GM94)

Despite getting to plug their song on TV, and the positive reviews it garnered, neither side of the single made the British charts.

Graeme Edge later quipped, "[W]e really started with a record called 'Lose Your Money' – *and we did!*" (GE-R68)

Clever line, but not entirely right. The disc sold well in Birmingham, and while the single did not chart nationally, the B-side – that Laine/Pinder "original" with all the bounce and a memorable hook – did become a jukebox hit. The kids couldn't get radio programmers to flip it over, so they did it themselves at teenage haunts where a penny could spin the disc.

This was enough to get Ridgepride to pony up for another recording session and for Decca to be willing to press a follow-up disc. This time the management did a better job in picking from among the demo tapes for an A-side with hit potential.

3

"Go Now!"

Single release:
"Go Now!" b/w "It's Easy Child"
Decca F 12022; November 13, 1964
Peak U.K. position: #1
(Certified silver disc award)

"Go Now!" b/w "Lose Your Money (But Don't Lose Your Mind)"
London 45-LON 9726; January 1965
Canada: #2
U.S. #6 (*Cashbox* and *Record World*)

Alex Murray said, "Tim Hudson had moved to the States and was sending me parcels of single releases for possible covers. 'Go Now!' was one of them." (AM-TB09)

Ray Thomas: "I remember being in the Marquee and this box of singles turned up. We were rehearsing in there during the afternoon of our show, which was great because now we've got somewhere to rehearse, as well. We were going through these singles; there were all sorts, and we came across 'Go Now!' It has Bessie Banks singing on it, which was a lot slower, a lot lighter, but we thought it was the right song." (RT-GM94)

Denny Laine: "It came in one of those suitcases full of records from America. This guy – James Hamilton, his name was; he was a friend of B. Mitchel Reed, who was a [New York] DJ – and he would send this stuff across. So I picked that one out, especially because Mike Pinder was a piano player… Anyway, we did 'Go Now!' because it was a song with a piano in it." (DL-G10)

Mike Pinder: "The song seemed an obvious one for us to cover as it had a descending piano-led chord pattern. We were quite piano-led as a band at the time." (MP-MMCD15)

The original demo of the song, from American rhythm & blues performer and singer Larry Banks, written with Milton Bennett, had been cut by Banks in 1963 with his wife, Bessie, singing the lead. American popular music producers Jerry Leiber and Mike Stoller heard the demo and re-recorded it on November 22 and 23, 1963, with Bessie Banks again taking the lead. She recalled the recording session was interrupted by news of the assassination of President John F. Kennedy. Distraught over the death of the president, they finished the song the following day. It was issued in the United Stated in January 1964. The soulful rendition failed to click; the song only made it into one of America's three national "pop music" charts from this time – *Cashbox* – which listed Banks' version of "Go Now!"for only two weeks, peaking at No. 146 (some internet sources claim No. 40 on *Cashbox*, perhaps referencing a R&B chart). The fact that the song had not been a success in America, and never released in England, made it all the more appealing for the Moodies.

Chosen by Alex Murray for the flip side was an obscure song called "It's Easy Child," which originally was released as a single in America in 1962 by rhythm & blues singer/guitarist Freddie King, with singer Lulu Reed, and which did not make the pop charts – one more of the 45s to be discarded by a New York radio station due to lack of interest, therefore finding its way to Ridgepride management in London and into the hands of the Moodies. For the Moodies' version, Pinder's piano gives the

42

arrangement the feel of Charlie Rich's playful 1965 hit "Mohair Sam." But Pinder wasn't copying – "Mohair Sam" was months away from being released.

Alex Murray said of "Go Now!": "The band had played the song for the first time in London at a Marquee gig and that night they blew the crowd away – took them somewhere else! My spine was electrified when I witnessed it. It was a unique song which matched their unique interpretation, so I knew before we went into the studio that 'Go Now!' was the 'big one' if we could only get it right and recapture the atmosphere they'd created at the Marquee.

"First off we tried recording it at Chappell Studios in Bond Street, but it just wouldn't come together in the three hour session that we'd booked. As the head of the Moodies management company, I had invested a lot of cash into the band for house and flat rentals, transport, clothes, equipment, instruments, etc., so expensive studio time became a real funding issue." (AM-BB09)

In a correspondence to a British music researcher, Murray was more candid: "Equipment and initial promotion cost most of our capital and Ridgepride was broke by the time I needed to make a second single." (AM-LP06)

"I had been talking to Phil Woods," Murray recalled, "who was trying to get a studio together at the back of the Marquee. So, as a cost saving incentive, I decided to go ahead and use the under-construction studio as an experiment. The studio was, in fact, simply a garage with a homemade 12-channel mixer; the only outboard gear being a borrowed echo plate and two Apex recording decks – second hand, one mono and one stereo – from EMI." (AM-BB09)

Murray also remembered there being "an odd collection of old BBC microphones," as well as one "modern condenser mic" for the vocals, a Fairchild compressor for the "vocal sound," and a Broadwood grand piano.

Phil Woods, who Murray described as "an amateur sound engineer and blues buff," had been outfitting the garage to serve as a studio. The National Jazz Federation, owner of the Marquee Club, was footing the bill. With no money to pay for the recording session, Murray agreed to allocate a 2% royalty for record sales to the Federation in exchange for use of the facility.

The session took place in September, 1964, for both "Go Now!" and "It's Easy Child," in the yet unfinished recording studio.

Mike Pinder: "I can remember going into Marquee studios to record the song and realizing that the studio hadn't been fully finished. There were still step ladders and decorators tools in the corner of the studio." (MK-MMCD15)

Ray Thomas: "They literally built the studio around us!" (RT-AI17)

Alex Murray: "The group were tired when they came into the session, but well rehearsed with the song. They had been gigging with it for a few weeks [and] had their individual parts [down] pat, so my only concern with them was a lack of freshness, especially with the backing vocals and lead vocal. A lot of time was spent 'encouraging' urgency in the vocal harmonies and 'identification with character' from Denny. I don't remember how many retakes there were, but they left the studio with sore throats, I'm sure. ...

"The fadeout was so abrupt because poor Denny's voice had been punished during the recording session and, as he was holding the last note, his voice cracked. I was

43

just too exhausted to return to it all again, so I just pulled the fader on the final mix so I could go home and get some sleep!" (AM-BB09)

Graeme Edge: "We had one last little thing to do to finish 'Go Now!,' and it was a drop-in on the piano part. The engineer dropped in the recording but he hit the wrong button and wiped the last 90 seconds of the song. We were left with no choice but to rerecord the whole thing from scratch. Although I wasn't happy, we rerecorded the track from scratch in probably 35 minutes." (GE-MMCD15)

Alex Murray: "Mike Pinder had a lot of 'drop-ins' to do on account of some of the 'sound on sound' bouncing losses. From my point of view, it was a marathon session. The band's recording session itself was about six hours straight. They were recording in between a hectic gig schedule, so they got away lightly because I couldn't keep them there to do more overdubs. …

"The final result sounded like it had been recorded in a public lavatory – dirty but full of ambience, which was what I was after. I was as pleased with it as I was exhausted." (AM-BB09)

In an interview for *New Musical Express* from this time, Pinder said, "Essentially, we want to get the same sound we get on stage, and I think we managed it. Certainly, 'Go Now!' is better technically than our first disc, 'Lose Your Money,' because we ourselves are more used to recording techniques. I think it's the kind of music we play, as well. 'Lose Your Money' was strictly rhythm-and-blues, with the harmonica and maracas and so on, which is only one side of the music we play. …

"Our music evolved over the months quite naturally. For example, there was the time we were in Hamburg when we played until five in the morning. Then, hard drunk, because it was the only way to stand the pace, we'd sit down and play what we called soul music – *our kind of music*. Four of the Moody Blues, myself included, are modern jazz fans. Ray Thomas is the odd man out. He plays harmonica, which is a solo – not a 'chordal' – instrument. He digs country blues and that kind of gear." (MP-NME65)

What influences shaped the Moodies aspirations?

Denny Laine specified the Beatles song "This Boy." The Lennon-McCartney song, in which John sang in three-part harmony with fellow Beatles Paul and George, contained both mellow sections and pained, soulful vocals. Laine said, "Admiring the Beatles as much as I do, I think this really does something for their versatility – a beautiful composition and a knockout harmony vocal sound." (DL-NME65b)

Mike Pinder, the jazz enthusiast and pianist, chose the instrumental "Take Five" by Dave Brubeck: "This really is a terrific disc. It's got just about everything – plenty of soul, a beautiful arrangement and, [jokingly], lovely lyrics." (MP-NME65b)

Ray Thomas went for "Love Me Do," by the Beatles. He explained: "This, the boys' first British disc, has a strong R&B flavor, with nice harmonica work from John Lennon, and a good vocal sound. A very good record." (RT-NME65b)

Graeme Edge liked "Rock Around the Clock," by Bill Haley and his Comets. He said, "It started off all the present music trends, and must be about the most original disc I've ever heard." (GE-NME65b)

Clint Warwick selected "Anyone Who Knows What Love Is (Will Understand)" by Irma Thomas. He proclaimed, "This really is a terrific disc. It's got just about everything – plenty of soul, a beautiful arrangement, and lovely lyrics." (CK-NME65b)

One could say the same of "Go Now!"

"Go Now!" b/w "It's Easy Child" was released on November 13, 1964 in the U.K. The A-side was then, and is still now, immediately accessible and memorable. The lovely melody features another heartfelt lead vocal from Laine, and Mike Pinder's pounding piano accompaniment driving the ballad into the popular mid-tempo pop sound typical of this era. The choir of background singers – Thomas, Pinder, and Warwick – provide excellent support. The frosting on the cake is the instrumental break when Pinder shifts into a melodic refrain with a touch of honky-tonk, just the thing needed for the otherwise somber mood.

For the B-side, Pinder's piano dominates and brings life to "It's Easy Child," with Laine's soulful lead vocal effectively backed by a rich harmony from the other band members. Graeme Edge's unexpected but effective drum breaks add needed accent, making this song worth flipping the record over for. It wasn't going to get on the radio, but with "Go Now!" as the A-side, "It's Easy Child" didn't need to.

Regarding "Go Now!", Alex Murray said, "It was an unlikely chart contender, being in 3/4 time, but they gave it an individual quality that I found inspiring. By this time, we'd released 'Steal Your Heart Away' and it had put them on the map; now we needed to make a real impact." (AM-BB09)

Five days after the single was issued, the music critic for *Record Mirror* said:

> Flip side ["Lose Your Money"] of the group's first one was a big juke-box hit and nearly made the charts. This ["Go Now!"] is another excellent slab of slow, bluesy material – with a load of atmosphere. Lead vocal, pounding piano backdrop, fine percussion work, all ingredients of a single which we think will make the charts in full glory this time! These boys really do have a way-out group talent....

"Go Now!" entered the British singles charts on December 10, 1964. On December 12, Ian Dove, of *New Musical Express*, wrote:

> The Moody Blues play their rhythm-and-blues with a Birmingham accent, but they are still examples of the harder, more aggressive type of new wave British beat groups that are springing up.

45

"Go Now!" is the MB's second record and first one in the *NME* Chart. Says the Moodys' lead vocalist, Denny Laine: "We got the tune from a New York disc jockey, B. Mitchel Reed. We met him when he visited London and got on well together. He's known as 'Mr. Good Guy' in New York and he's certainly been that to us. Originally, 'Go Now!' was arranged for a big band, but we changed brass for voices and got what we wanted."....

[The Moody Blues] were Birmingham's first rhythm-and-blues outfit. Birmingham liked them but they decided that they should come to London to succeed. They stepped straight into an engagement at London's Marquee Club, where, incidentally, "Go Now!" was recorded. "Not live," says Denny. "They have a studio at the back. One of our managers, Alex Murray, recorded us there." ....

On December 22, the Moody Blues appeared on BBC1's *Vision On*, performing the new A-side.

Three days later, on Christmas Day, "Go Now!" jumped into the Top 20 in the British charts – at No. 16. The songs to beat during that week were the Beatles' "I Feel Fine," at No. 1, and, in second spot, "Downtown," by Petula Clark.

That night, the Moodies shared the bill with the Searchers, Hermit's Hermits, and Sandi Shaw, on *Ready Steady Go!* They performed "Go Now!" Suddenly, with a song in the charts, and on England's top-rated music show, the audience reaction to the Moodies changed with the flip of a switch.

Shortly after the appearance, Ray Thomas told Ian Dove of *NME*, "That was strange. We've played for a long time in clubs in the West End, with no protection against the audience – such as an orchestra pit. And we've never been dragged off the stand by fans. In fact, we find the audiences for club work much quieter – they really listen. Still, we were mobbed at the *Ready Steady Go!* Christmas Day party. We closed the show and, just as the cameras switched off us, Graeme disappeared in a sea of girls, with the rest of us following seconds later...." (RT-NME65)

Another TV appearance came days later on STV's *Three Go Round*.

Alex Murray said, "They spent a day at Shepperton Studios – I think – recording a primitive video for one of the TV shows. On the way back to the Kombi van with their roadie, Stephen Christian, I said I could present them 'better than that,' and Stephen – who, prior to this gig, had been Assistant Director on a crew of [the 1962 British film] *A Kind of Loving* – agreed to work with me to make a promo. We formed a company – with no capital – Murray-Christian Films, hired a crew, and shot the film in a day, borrowing the wages for the crew from Lord Ellitor's – another Director of Seltaeb – Trustee." (AM-LP06)

The day of production was Tuesday, December 29. Ray Thomas recalled, "Alex borrowed a Super 8 movie camera and filmed the 'Go Now!' video right there in the Marquee Club." (RT-AI17)

With the borrowed camera, a cheap location, filming against a black background, Murray lived up to his boast that he could do better than the TV studio, succeeding in making one of the first stylistic music promotional films – if not *the* first – of the pop era.

46

The visually striking film seemed to have been inspired by the album cover of the Beatles' second LP, *With the Beatles* (released as *Meet the Beatles!* in the U.S.), in which the Fab Four wear black turtlenecks and stand in darkness, with key lights illuminating their faces. Using this same approach, "Go Now!" appears to be performed by the disembodied heads of Pinder, Thomas, Edge, and Warwick, supporting Denny Laine's lead with a choir of harmony. These shots are intercut with an

December 29, 1964, Alex Murray's stylistic promotional film for "Go Now!"
(Photo source: thestrangebrew.co.uk)

equally stark view of Mike Pinder's illuminated hands pounding on the piano keys to create the dramatic accompaniment. This unusually cinematic and "arty" performance film predated Richard Lester's innovative and stylistic "music video" approach taken in filming the Beatles' 1964 film, *A Hard Day's Night*, by several months.

The "Go Now!" film was offered to TV broadcasters in America and Europe, and even in the U.K. when the Moodies were not available to appear live. (It would be seen on a broadcast of the BBC1's *Top of the Pops* and, in America, on the ABC-TV's *Shindig* series.)

On December 31, the Moodies dropped in on BBC1's *Top of the Pops*, again performing "Go Now!" According to *Melody Maker*, the song had moved up two spots in the Top Singles chart to No. 14.

From January 8 through 31, the Moodies toured the U.K. on a shared bill with Chuck Berry. Ridgepride arranged for Robert Stigwood Associates to book the tour, with the band receiving £275 per week (the 2017 equivalent of nearly $6,000 weekly).

By January 13, "Go Now!" was still on the go, up to No. 6. on *NME*'s chart. Over at *Melody Maker*, it had leapt from No. 12 to the 3, just under Georgie Fame's "Yeh, Yeh" and the Beatles' "I Feel Fine," respectively, prompting the headline: "Moodymania! Brum Boys Shoot Up Nine Places!"

The story in *Melody Maker*:

> It's a Moody scene! The Moody Blues have startled the pop world by leaping to Number Three in the chart with their plaintive beat-ballad, "Go Now!," their first hit....

> One of the exciting new "Sounds of '65," the Moodies are currently touring Britain with the Chuck Berry show and stealing a lot of the thunder....

> Not content with disorganized blues blowing, they arrange their numbers, and use tricky stop timing and breaks to key up the

audience response. Practically a Beatles big band, they charge through numbers like "Bo Diddley" and "Bye Bye Birdie" [sic] and cool down for "Time Is on My Side" and "Go Now!"

From its January 16, 1965 edition, *Record Mirror*'s music critic said of the Moodies' live performance:

> The second half [of the concert] opens with "Time Is on My Side," from the Moody Blues. Highlights for me – and everyone else in the theatre – was a fantastic three minute rendering of "Bo Diddley," the group leaving their instruments to clap only – and building up to a wild frenzy. Four more numbers from the boys just wasn't enough. From the performance, which is as good live as on disc, and audience reaction, the only group to really pull in the screams, the Moody Blues seem set to be one of the really big groups of 1965.

"Time Is on My Side," incidentally, was one more of the songs introduced to the London scene by the Moodies … and, at the same time, introduced to the Rolling Stones, who recorded their own version.

On January 16, the Moodies shared the bill with Manfred Mann, P.J. Proby, and the Rockin' Berries, for that night's broadcast of *Thank Your Lucky Stars*, again promoting "Go Now!" The following day, they were seen doing the song yet again, for the second time on *Ready Steady Go!*

On January 19, the headline at the top of Page 2 in the *Daily Mirror* proclaimed, "It's Go Now! with the Moodies! – They're Tops." Next to that: a picture of Clint, Graeme, Denny, Ray, and Mike looking anything but blue – they were beaming. Patrick Doncaster wrote:

> A new sound has topped the pops – the Birmingham Boom of the Moody Blues. Their disc "Go Now!" has pushed Georgie Fame's "Yeh Yeh" to the Number Two spot – after only a week at the top. And when they heard the news, the sad-eyed soulful lads from Birmingham just could not keep their faces straight.
>
> Before the group's one-night stand in Hull, Yorks, last night, bass guitarist Clint Warwick, 22, said: "We knew the record was moving. We were keeping our fingers crossed…. At first we didn't want this one to be a topper – it's hard to follow an out-of-the-blue hit."

Also on January 19, in the *Birmingham Evening Mail*:

> The Moody Blues, Birmingham's first group to lead the national hit parade, were on their way today to Newcastle-upon-Tyne, where a rousing pop-style welcome was awaiting them. Their "Go Now!" disc yesterday displaced Georgie Fame from the supreme position in two leading national magazine charts….

The Moody Blues group celebrated with a bottle of champagne after their concert with singer Chuck Berry at Hull last night.

Denny Laine told the *Evening Mail*, "We are still knocked out by the news. I don't think it has really sunk in yet that we are now the country's top group." (DL-BEM65)

One day later, *New Musical Express* joined the other British music charts and declared "Go Now!" No. 1 in its chart as well (published January 22). *NME*'s Michael Steel wrote:

> The mood today is far from blue for the five boys from Birmingham who call themselves the Moody Blues. Their disc, "Go Now!," has arrived smartly at Number One in the *New Musical Express* pop charts, thus dethroning Georgie Fame and the Blue Flames....
>
> Success has come just in time for the Birmingham group. Just a few months ago they were so fed up with the pop world that they decided to pack in altogether....

Denny Laine said, "I think the Chuck Berry tour kind of clinched 'Go Now!' reaching the top of the singles chart. It reached Number One whilst we were on that tour and the reaction was fantastic." (DL-MMCD15)

From the January 23 edition of *Disc Weekly*, Ted Scott wrote:

> Denny Laine tore open a telegram, read the message, then excitedly shouted to the other Moody Blues: "Hey, listen to this, fellas. It's from the Lord Mayor of Birmingham... 'Congratulations to all the members of group on award of Silver Disc for recording of "Go Now!" Best wishes for future successes in charts. Am sure this first award to Birmingham group will not be the last."
>
> It was a triumphant return home for the chart topping Moody Blues, whose current tour with Chuck Berry had brought them to Birmingham Hippodrome on Sunday.

Graeme Edge told Scott, "Appearing here at the Hippodrome is very exciting for us. I remember seeing [British comedian, singer, actor] Max Bygraves here once. He was a gas. I never thought one day I'd be performing on the same stage myself!" (GE-DW65)

Clint Warwick said, "We're going to the Moat House Club in Bradford Street after the show tonight. It should bring back memories. We played there every Tuesday night before we moved to London." (CW-DW65)

Laine told Scott, "We all live in a five-bedroom house in Roehampton now. But Birmingham is still home to us because we were all brought up here. We are glad we moved to London because there is more happening there as far as entertainment is concerned. But we miss our local fans, the family, friends, and, of course, home-cooking." (DL-DW65)

Pinder injected, "We managed to pop home for an hour before the show and I had my Dad's Sunday dinner – roast beef and Yorkshire pudding. But I only managed to clear half the plate. I'm not used to such big meals nowadays." (MP-DW65)

Laine said, "I'm the only one not staying at home tonight. I've decided to stay at the Albany Hotel. It's the most modern in Birmingham and it will give me a real kick staying there. You know, I've stood across the road at a hot dog stall [stand] looking up at the hotel late at night more times than I care to remember after a booking with my group. I used to think it would be great to be able to stay there. Well, that's just what I'm going to do tonight. It will be like realizing an ambition." (DL-DW65)

In America, the Moody Blues' single came out in mid-January 1965. London Records passed on using "It's Easy Child" as the B-side and instead opted to pair "Go Now!" with "Lose Your Money (But Don't Lose Your Mind)," previously unissued in the U.S.

On January 23, American trade paper *Billboard* predicted "Go Now!" would be a hit, saying that the song had a "rare beat" and an "interesting gospel-like piano support."

Bessie Banks had seen her version of "Go Now!" come and go in a matter of weeks while barely placing in the charts. A year had gone by, but she was delighted that the song was catching renewed interest. She recalled, "I was happy and excited that maybe this time I'll make it. 'Go Now!' was released and right away it was chosen 'Pick Hit of the Week' on WINS

radio. That means your record is played for seven days….. I was so thrilled [and] when I heard the first line [of the song], I thought it was me. But, all of a sudden, I realized it wasn't. At the end of the song it was announced, 'The Moody Blues singing "Go Now!".' … This was the time of the English Invasion and the end of Bessie Banks' career, so I thought. America's DJs had stopped promoting American artists." (BB-SC04)

Back in England, on January 23,

the five Moodies had the cover of *Disc Weekly*. Across town, *Record Mirror* had a feature story in its issue for that morning. Clint Warwick told staff writer Christine Osbourne: "Anyone can get a record in the Top Ten, but it's up to you whether you live or die on stage. They've all come to see you – to see whether you can stand up to your record's reputation. It's all very well turning out a good record – but if you don't go down well on stage, that's it." (CW-RM65)

Osbourne continued:

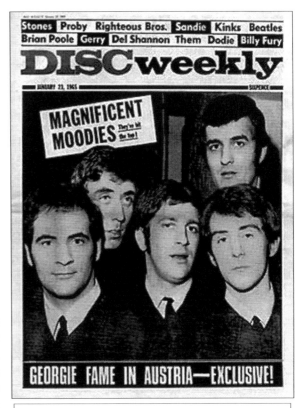

Cover of January 23, 1965 issue of *DISC Weekly.*

> With the Moodies "Go Now!" well up in the charts, here they were on their first tour with everyone watching to see if they could live up to their record's reputation.

I was sitting in their dressing room on the second night of the tour, surrounded by umpteen tins of Coke, packets of cigarettes, and various Moody Blues, with a couple of managers, road managers, and other odd people thrown in for good measure. So how did they feel about playing to such a large, critical audience, I asked. The answers were varied.

Clint "had butterflies," drummer Graeme was plain "frit" – his grammar, not mine! – and pianist Mike felt "'orrible" but "appy" – again, his English, not yours truly's. The other two listened with just a hint of superiority. "I started when I was 11 on a stage the same size as this one," said lead vocalist Denny, "so it wasn't so bad." And Ray wasn't at all nervous. "My first ever show was at the Birmingham Hippodrome when I was 16 – and I was out there all on my own that time!" …

Pinder told Osbourne, "We're planning on changing the routine every week if we have time. Our trouble is we're all perfectionists. We come off stage happy, pleased we've gone down well, but not satisfied. Even while they're still clapping out there, I'm thinking, 'What can we do to better the act?' all the time." (MP-RM65)

Laine said, "We need this tour. We've only been together eight months, so we want to give people the chance to see us and know our record wasn't just a fluke. And working with Chuck [Berry] is a knockout. He's a real showman, which is something I'd like to be." (DL-RM65)

51

"Go Now!" gets Silver Disc! "Thumbs up, boys!"
(Author's collection)

Mike Pinder added, "I was terribly relieved when the first show was over, and terribly, terribly tired. We'd been rehearsing for so long that day." (MP-RM65)

Days later, it was reported that "Go Now!" had been awarded a Silver Disc, acknowledging the sale of 200,000 copies in the UK.

Ray Thomas said, "The Lord Mayor of Birmingham presented our Silver Disc for 'Go Now' – one between five of us! I won the card draw for it; otherwise we'd have needed a silver pizza cutter!" (RT-SM15)

By the final days of January, *Melody Maker* showed the Moody Blues slipping to second place, making room for the Righteous Brothers and "You've Lost That Loving Feeling." Over at *NME*, "Go Now!" was still top song, with the Brothers one notch below.

The performance price for the Moodies went up, accordingly. Prior to the hit, they often worked for as little as £50 a show. After "Go Now!" topped the charts, they commanded £500 or more – and there was no shortage of offers. During January 1965, the Moodies gave 47 concerts in 29 different cities on 30 different days. The band didn't have a single day off throughout the month. The only day they weren't performing – January 7 – they were in London recording TV and radio programs. Additional appearances had to be recorded on some of the days when the band was in London before their nighttime club and music hall shows.

From London's *The Observer*, January 31, 1965:

> Birmingham has been the forgotten town of British beat. Liverpool, Manchester and Newcastle have all produced chart-topping groups. But the Mid-lands made its first major dent in the pop world only in the past month – with the Moody Blues' No. 1 hit, "Go Now!"

> Birmingham isn't behind in sheer beat man-power – about 400 groups, most of them specializing in a hard-driven, bluesy kind of sound. They tend to be short on originality.

> Decca launched a big Brumbeat campaign at the beginning of 1964 when E.M.I. was cornering most of the market with their Mersey Sound [from Liverpool]. Decca signed up more than half a dozen Brum groups, issued a spate of singles and put up a big advertising drive. But it failed to catch on – records sold steadily but refused to develop into hits. And soon the groups (Keith

Powell and the Valets, Dave Lacey and the Corvettes, the Redcaps) were drifting into the background again.

In spite of the Moody Blues, Birmingham is still unlikely to become the centre of a big beat craze. With the group boom undoubtedly on the wane, something extra is now needed to stay at the top.

In *Record Mirror*, February 13, 1965:

The Moody Blues have been spending some time in the recording studios lately cutting tracks for an E.P. [Extended Play record], which is due for release in March. A hectic tour with Chuck Berry didn't give the Moodies any time for recording, but they picked up plenty of material along the way, they told *RM*.

That very night, the Moodies began a short Scottish tour. This was followed by more concerts across England. With their Ridgepride management pushing them to take every paying gig offered – at the rate of one, sometimes two, per day – there was little time to record.

In mid-February, "Go Now!" was holding firm in the British charts. It had relinquished the summit position to "You've Lost That Loving Feeling," and allowed the Kinks to slip into second spot with "Tired of Waiting for You," but was still playing on the hour, firmly set at No. 3.

One day after the publishing of

(Photo source: MoodyBluesAttitude.yuku.com)

that chart, a wire story appeared in newspapers across America, reporting that Brian Epstein, "the famous manager of the Beatles," would be hosting and producing segments in London for the U.S. NBC-TV series *Hullabaloo*. Among the acts to be introduced by Epstein to an American audience were Georgie Fame and the Blue Flames, Billy J. Kramer and the Dakotas [whom Epstein managed], the Searchers, Wayne Fontana and the Mindbenders, and the Moody Blues.

This not only was the first performance of the Moody Blues on American TV, but their first in color. And, while the Moodies were already friendly with the Beatles, this created the possibility for a closer association with Epstein, always on the lookout for another hot band to represent.

In the February 20 chart published in *Pop Weekly*, "Go Now!" was now at No. 5. It would soon be yesterday's news in Britain, but not so in America. The trade paper predicted "Go Now!" would top the U.S. charts. The musical question in the headline of an accompanying feature was "Can the Moody Blues Succeed Again?"

As one consequence of their new success, the Moodies were able to upgrade their digs. They had given up their shared center-of-London "flat" one month earlier and provided with something a bit roomier by their management.

Denny Laine: "We rented a big house. This was just outside of London, in Roehampton, by Richmond Park. We used to throw big parties and everyone in the music business showed up – the Who, Tom Jones, the Rolling Stones, the Animals – just everybody used to come to those parties." (DL-H&H97a)

Mike Pinder: "We had a reputation of being the biggest ravers in the business – and I would never dispute that. 'Go Now' sold two million copies [and] for the first time in our lives we had financial success. Not only that, but the fact that we became so constantly in the public eye, on stage and on TV, naturally our egos were affected.

"We found we each had £40 or £50 a week to spend … so we spent it! It was a natural reaction to stardom and I don't regret those days. It was a phase we had to go through. I'm glad I went through it and learned its lessons." (MP-DME70)

A *Pop Weekly* staffer wrote:

> Tipped in our polls as the "Most Likely to Succeed," the Moody Blues certainly deserve this recognition. Formerly a group called Denny Laine and the Diplomats [sic], the Moody Blues have rapidly established a completely new image for themselves. Once they were just an ordinary rock group. Now they are rated as one of the best R & B teams in the country….
>
> They have just completed a very successful stage debut on the Chuck Berry tour and are now heading for even bigger heights with their record being tipped to hit the charts in no time flat in the United States….
>
> I asked some of the teenagers in the Marquee Club in London who they thought would be the biggest group this year – the biggest *new* group, of course. All of them said the Moody Blues. One can hardly blame them. Apart from their very polished and commercial record, the Moody Blues are one of the few groups to ever have such a stage performance.
>
> I would say without hesitation that if the Moody Blues can continue to make such appealingly commercial platters that their future in the pop world is assured. I doubt whether the Moody Blues could in fact slip out of popularity for any length of time with such a superb stage act….
>
> Everything, of course, depends on their next few records, but knowing that the Moody Blues have such a fantastic range of ideas about discs, I expect to see them high on the schedules at any time for a new release and yet another No. 1.

From the March 1, 1965 issue of England's *Rave* magazine, Lyn Carnell reported:

> The Moody Blues – Denny Laine, Mike Pinder, Graeme Edge, Ray Thomas, and Clint Warwick – live along with Clint's wife, Christine, in a large home in Roehampton, Surrey. There, they make nosh-ups, throw parties, and entertain people to coffee.

Mike Pinder, stretching out in front of the fireplace, told Carnell, "Having a Number One hit makes a difference in life. We've become wanted. It's odd that one record should make such a difference. We had no idea we'd be Number One. We didn't consider it. I suppose it's best that way. Reach for the moon, and you end up in a nut house...."

Pinder turned to Denny Laine, and asked, "Do you reckon we'll end up neurotic and wild-eyed, Denny?" (MP-R65)

Laine responded with a grin, "End up? We're that already." Then, said to Carnell, "Seriously.... We take our music seriously; we study jazz; we enjoy performing live.... We rate our stage act important, because I want us to go on entertaining forever. I think if you can have chart success and back it with a steady, well thought-out act, plus a genuine love of good pop music and jazz, you've got a chance of lasting." (DL-R65)

Clint Warwick put in, "Jazz absorbs us. We like George Shearing, Buddy Rich, Count Basie; we all owe a lot to the jazz musicians. They gave a part of themselves to their music and they kept the flow of beautiful notes going. Some combinations of notes would die if they weren't played by these men. We would forget about them in the gold rush to the top, where only a simple tune is necessary." (CW-G65)

Graeme Edge added, "I would like the chance of proving we are an act and not just a product of a recording studio. Holding a Palladium audience would really do it." (GE-R65)

Decades later, Denny Laine looked back at all the excitement: "Obviously, those early days we had some great fun. We used to shout and scream when things went right. We knew what we wanted. We were a good band. You know what I mean? We got on really well together, as well, even though we had some arguments about the musical side, because it *had* to be right. We also had a very, very strong, demanding manager [Tony Secunda] who wanted it right, as well. It was just the fact that we made it. We all wanted to make it and we all were very professional about the way we went about it. It was just a great thing." (DL-H&H97a)

Graeme Edge reflected, "Naturally, by this time, we were full of ourselves; we really raved it up. Our parties in our house in Roehampton became famous. We got the image of ravers, but it wasn't just talk, we earned it! Everyone used to come to those parties from the Beatles downwards. They were really happenings. People thought we were being flash and extravagant after only one hit record, but it only cost us about £40 pounds each party, and we were wise enough to save half of our earnings!" (GE-R68)

Denny Laine: "We met practically anyone who was anyone in the music business, the fashion business, photographers, everyone. It was just a brilliant period. I would never really compare anything to it. Probably the best period of all." (DL-H&H97a)

Back then, in the spring of 1965, the Moodies were top of the bill – like the night they appeared at Golden Green on March 21. Opening acts including Brian Poole and the Tremeloes, who had made No. 4 in the British charts two years earlier with their cover of a Beatles' cover – "Twist & Shout" – and then made it to No. 1 with a cover of an

American R&B group's song, "Do You Love Me." But, in early 1965, the events of 1963 and '64 were yesterday's news. A current No. 1, like "Go Now!," carried more weight than a six-month-old No. 1 hit, like "Do You Love Me."

Considering what had happened to Brian Poole and the Tremeloes, it's no wonder that the Moodies decided to live it up. After all, success is often fleeting.

The one Moodie with less opportunity for glamour and extravagance was Clint Warwick. Married and with an infant, Warwick hadn't planned on uprooting his family and leaving Birmingham. Now, there was no choice – the band had to use London as its base of operations. Warwick's wife and child came along. Even that, however, didn't ensure a healthy marriage. Warwick said, "Our baby was only three months old and I was having to tell the wife, 'I'm off!'"

Warwick tried to enjoy the band's success and instant – if temporary – fame as best he could. "We ended up in a flat in Chelsea," he said. "I bumped into Ursula Andress coming out of one of the neighboring flats. We quickly befriended all the other bands – the Stones, the Who, the Kinks, the Animals, [Jack] Bruce, [Ginger] Baker and [Eric] Clapton, who were later to form Cream, and, of course, the Beatles, with whom we had a particularly strong friendship. They were just ordinary guys like us and we visited each other regularly. There were no frills, no pretentions. When they played us their demo of 'Paperback Writer' [in the spring of 1966], I said to Paul, 'You bastards, you've done it again,' and he just smiled. But there was no competitiveness – it was very good-natured, no agro [aggression]. We were mates." (CW-RS02)

On the other side of the pond, the Moody Blue's recording of "Go Now!" made the Top 10 on all three U.S. charts. While *Billboard* held the song at No. 10 (on April 17), both *Cashbox* and *Record World* showed it at No. 6 (on April 24).

Regionally, "Go Now!" did better.

The song reached No. 5 in some cities, including New Haven, Connecticut, on radio station WAVZ (in its April 17 survey), and likewise in Milwaukee, Wisconsin, on WRIT (April 18).

It hit No. 4 in various areas, including San Bernardino, California, on station KFXM (in its March 27 survey); in Pittsburgh, Pennsylvania, on KQV (April 6); in Chicago, Illinois, on WLS (April 9); and in Hartford, Connecticut on WDRC (for two weeks, beginning April 12).

"Go Now!" got to No. 3 in numerous cities, including Honolulu, Hawaii, on station KORL (for its March 13 survey); in Hartford, Connecticut, on WPOP (for its April 16 listener survey); in Boise, Idaho, on KIDO (April 18); in Minneapolis-St. Paul region, in Minnesota, on KDWB (April 24); and in Louisville, Kentucky, on WAKY (May 1).

The Moodies made it to No. 2 in many parts of the U.S., including Los Angeles, California, on L.A.'s top-rated pop radio station from the mid-1960s, KRLA (for two weeks, beginning in the station's March 15 countdown survey); in Detroit, Michigan, on WKNR (March 17); in Milwaukee, Wisconsin, on WOKY (April 24); in Springfield, Massachusetts, on WHYN (March 27); in Akron, Ohio, on WAKP (for three weeks, no less, beginning April 9); in Kansas City, Missouri, on WHB (for two weeks, starting on April 9); in Long Beach, California, on KLFM (April 18); in New York City, New York, on WABC (for two weeks, starting on May 1); and, from the same week, in Minneapolis-St. Paul, on WDGY.

It hit No. 1 in some markets, including Port Huron, Michigan, on WTTH (in the radio station's survey on March 21), and in New York City, on WMCA (in its April 15 survey).

On American TV, the Moodies appeared on the March 23, 1965 edition of *Hullabaloo*, with the segment Brian Epstein produced for "Go Now!"

The song was breaking out in other countries, as well. It hit No. 2 in Canada; No. 6 in Hong Kong; No. 10 in the Netherlands; and No. 12 in Australia. It has been reported that, worldwide, "Go Now!" sold in excess of six million copies.

Despite the extremely strong sales, the Moody Blues saw very little of the money that came in. Some sources report that they made as little as £50 each.

Acting under the advice of their managers, the Moody Blues had agreed to allow their recording revenue from Decca to be invested in their future. Laine put it this way: "The big labels sort of supplied their people, but we weren't happy with it.... We kind of built our own companies, you know; we built our own little setup right down to the secretaries." (DL-WS01)

Tony Secunda was trying to be the next Brian Epstein, whose management company NEMS represented not only the Beatles but other Liverpool acts, such as Gerry & the Pacemakers, Billy J. Kramer and the Dakotas, and Cilla Black, all hitmakers. The problem with Secunda's version of NEMS was that, so far, the Moody Blues was its only successful act. Later, Secunda would manage Procol Harum, the Move, Marianne Faithfull, T. Rex, and the Pretenders. But in 1965, it was only the Moodies, and, to keep revenue

Singing for their supper ... and on the road – or tracks – again, Spring 1965.
(Author's collection; also Getty Images)

streams flowing, Ridgepride kept the band on the road, taking nearly everything offered – and then rushing to release a new single ... which, as far as the group was concerned, wasn't even meant to be a single.

Cheers! Six million copies of "Go Now!" had been sold. With the Moody Blues in great demand for concert and TV appearances, and Ridgepride investing the earnings on the band's behalf, the Moodies were assured of a bright future … or so they believed.
(Photo source: Author's collection)

4

The Magnificent Moodies (1965)

In the 1960s, when a pop act in Britain scored a Top 10 single – let alone a No. 1 hit – it was customary for the record company to hurry the artist into the studio to make an album. This was how it worked for the Beatles. Their first single, "Love Me Do," was a Top 20 hit in England (it would go to No. 1 when released a year later in America). Their second single, "Please Please Me," topped the U.K. charts. Before that single lost its forward momentum, producer George Martin wisely brought "the boys" back into Abbey Road Studio to record their first LP, *Please Please Me*, in order to capitalize on the success of the two singles.

The Rolling Stones serve as another example. Their first single, "Come On," failed to make the Top 20, but then John Lennon and Paul McCartney gave them "I Wanna Be Your Man," which went to No. 12. A third single, "Not Fade Away," made the Top 10 and the band was immediately sent into the studio to cut an album, released but two months later.

Typically, things would have gone the same way for the Moody Blues. But at Ridgepride, too much money was going to the management firm, and not enough was set aside to pay for studio time. This kept the Moodies on the road with a new paying gig each night.

Of course, there needed to be a new single, so Ridgepride released a song that had been started in the studio, but not entirely finished. It was also a song which the group had never considered as a potential A-side.

U.K. single release:
"I Don't Want to Go on Without You" b/w "Time Is on My Side"
Decca F.12095; February 26, 1965
Peak U.K. position: #19 (Billboard/Record Retailer)

The top side of the Moodies' third single release in the U.K. was taken from the B-side of an American 45 written and produced by Bert Berns and Jerry Wexler for the Drifters. The hit, from 1964, was "Under the Boardwalk," but the buried treasure on the flip side, "I Don't Want to Go on Without You," seemed just right for the Moodies. It was fairly unknown, and was the sort of American rhythm & blues number the band enjoyed reinterpreting.

Was there a thematic link in the selection of this song to follow "Go Now!"? On the earlier single, Denny Laine sang, "We've already said 'goodbye.' Since you gotta go, oh you'd better go now, go now, before you see me cry." Now, he sang, "It's so bad to be alone, oh baby, come home. I need you, my room is so blue.… Oh my darlin', hear my plea, c'mon back to me."

The problem is that the recording sounds like a demo; a rough run-through. One can't help but wonder if the group was planning to do another take, or at least record some overdubs. One is right to think so.

Alex Murray said, "I managed to get Decca to advance some royalties to Ridgepride… and we made another – not very good – single in the garage [behind the Marquee Club] because, somehow, there was no budget for studios – probably Fenton and Secunda had spent it all in nightclubs; I only ever drew £10 a week." (AM-LP06)

Graeme Edge told *Rave* magazine, "We recorded a beautiful song called 'I Don't Want to Go on Without You,' all done in a bit of a rush and intended really as an LP track. We went off on a ten-day tour of Scotland intending to rerecord it properly when we got back. But we returned to find that the rough track had been released as our new single! We were all angry about that." (GE-R68)

Ray Thomas said, "'I Don't Want to Go on Without You' wasn't finished when it was released. It should've had a flute on it." (RT-H&H86)

"Time Is on My Side," chosen as the flip, was itself originally a B-side to Irma Thompson's 1964's minor American hit, "Anyone Who Knows What Love Is (Will Understand)," a personal favorite of Clint Warwick. It too was yet one more of the dusty

45s discarded by a New York radio station, sent over to Ridgepride and the Moody Blues by their American DJ acquaintance. The Moodies may have considered this for an A-side if the Rolling Stones hadn't beat them to the punch, releasing their version of the song a few months earlier.

Denny Laine: "We were doing 'Time Is on My Side' very early, *before* the Stones were playing it. They were at a lot of our early gigs and saw us doing it." (DL-GM94)

Graeme Edge: "After the success of 'Go Now!' … the next song we recorded was, in fact, 'Time Is on My Side,' which the Rolling Stones promptly stole and made their own. That sort of flattened us." (GE-MD87)

"Flattened" as in knocked down.

The Moody Blues' version of "Time Is on My Side" fares better than their unfinished master of "I Don't Want to Go on Without You," with cleaner and crisper production and more punch, but it wasn't going to make it on radio playlists since the song, with very nearly the same arrangement, had just been a hit for the Stones.

The new Moody Blues single that-shouldn't-have-been was issued on February 26, 1965. This was not the follow-up to "Go Now!" that British pop music journalists and fans of the Moodies had been hoping for. Its main contenders in the charts were the Seekers' "I'll Never Find Another You" at No. 1, followed by, respectively, Tom Jones's "It's Not Unusual," Wayne Fontana & the Mindbenders' "Game of Love," Herman's Hermits' "Silhouettes," and the Animals' "Don't Let Me Be Misunderstood." The pleasant "I Don't Want to Go on Without You" is just not in the same league.

The British music chart cited most frequently on the internet (although not identified by name) shows "I Don't Want to Go on…" with a peak position of only No. 33, contributing to the folklore that the early incarnation of the Moody Blues was a one-hit wonder. Yet, on March 18, for its pop music chart, *New Musical Express* had "I Don't

Want to Go on…" at No. 28. Two weeks later, the song made No. 20. Shortly after this, in the April 17, 1965 issue of *Billboard* magazine, the U.S. trade reported that "I Don't Want to Go…" was at No. 19 in one of the British charts it monitored (although it did not specify which). These two reports document that the single performed far better than some have reported.

London Records in the U.S. passed on issuing "I Don't Want to Go…" as a follow-up to "Go Now!," holding it instead for the first album, as the Moodies had intended.

On April 10, the Moody Blues had the cover of England's trendy *Fabulous* magazine. One day later, the group performed among other *New Musical Express* 1964-65 Poll-Winners at

Cover of *Fabulous* magazine, April 10, 1965.
(Photo source: beatchapter.com)

L-R: Laine, Edge, Clark, Pinder, and Thomas.
(Photo source: garagehangover.com)

the Empire Pool, Wembley, which included the Beatles, the Animals, Wayne Fontana and the Mindbenders, Herman's Hermits, Tom Jones, the Rolling Stones, the Searchers, Dusty Springfield, and Van Morrison & Them. The Moodies were now part of pop music royalty.

One day after this, the band had a recording session for the BBC Light Programme *Saturday Club*. They did a note-perfect rendition of "Go Now!" that actually had a bit more life than the hit single, as well as a James Brown cover – "I'll Go Crazy" – which was both loose, exuberant, and unfamiliar to the ears of Britons. The third song they performed that day for airing on the *Saturday Club* was their new single, "I Don't Want to Go…" It too sounded superior to the studio version, showing what the song might have become with a little more recording time. For the broadcast, Ray Thomas's flute is present, adding greatly to the song. Beyond this, the vocals – both lead and supporting – are more polished and tighter.

In a second TV appearance from this time, Thomas also "plays" the flute – even though the band was really performing a synched version of the record! He recalled, "When we did [it on TV], I just took a flute on and pretended to play it. I got dozens of letters saying how great the flute playing was, *and it wasn't even on it!* That's auto suggestion." (RT-H&H86)

Similarly, Mike Pinder said, "We got letters from fans saying what a raving record it was and the flute was fab gear. We hadn't got a flute on the record. Even TV producers didn't know the difference." (MP-RM65a)

Denny Laine told *Record Mirror*'s Richard Green, "Ray took up the alto flute and, after two weeks' practice, was playing well enough to put it on record." (DL-RM65)

Thomas said, "I was playing more flute by now and less harmonica; I'd changed to a chromatic [harmonica] anyway, which Sonny Boy [Williams] wouldn't have approved of – he could do the same with just a vamper…. But as the new sound lent itself more to flute, I became the first rock 'n' roll flautist." (RT-SM15)

Thomas's flute would be featured on the band's next single.

Despite this, and the disappointment the band felt over Ridgepride's decision, Mike Pinder defended "I Don't Want to Go on Without You." He told Richard Green, "[W]e think our latest disc is a good record. It was a very personal record to the Drifters, but one of them told our manager he was surprised that a white group could sing the number with such feeling." (MP-RM65)

So much feeling, in fact, that the Moody Blues were still very much the rage in England … and across the channel, on the Continent.

For its May 1 issue, *Rave* magazine covered the Moodies' trip to Paris.

L-R: Pinder, Clarke, Edge, Thomas, and Laine.
(Photo source: Past Daily.com)

Denny Laine told *Rave*'s Maureen O'Grady, "It was our first foreign trip as the Moodies. We didn't have a lot of time for sightseeing, but we saw all the most famous places including the Eiffel Tower. We got to our theater, the Olympia, around six-thirty, and from that moment on, it all started happening!" (DL-R65a)

Graeme Edge: "In between our two shows, we went outside for a breath of air, thinking we weren't that well-known. But it wasn't long before we were being mobbed. A gendarme saw us trying to get in the stage door and told us to clear off! In 'French,' of course!" (GE-R65a)

Ray Thomas: "It was quite funny, really. The audiences were fantastic; all these blokes up and shouting '*Vive! Vive!*' as we finished our act. We were quite surprised they even knew us!

"We completed the two shows at about eleven-thirty, and then all the real fun started." (RT-R65a)

Mike Pinder: "At one club we visited, the manager recognized us. He put on all the spotlights, got all these cameras out and took a film of us doing 'the Monkey.'" (MP-R65a)

On May 3, the Moodies recorded two songs for another appearance on *Saturday Club*. This time they played their soon-to-be-released fourth single, "From the Bottom of My Heart (I Love You)," and, as with "I Don't Want to Go on Without You," the BBC series version is superior to the one recorded for single release. (These BBC sessions can be heard on the 50th Anniversary Double-CD release of *The Magnificent Moodies*.)

On Wednesday, May 12, the Moodies were seen again on U.S. TV, this time on the ABC network's prime-time music show *Shindig*, performing "I'll Go Crazy," a preview of their upcoming first album. Sadly, their American record label had yet to follow up on the success of "Go Now!," missing the chance to plug a new record.

Mike Pinder: "We were disenchanted with our original producers. After "Go Now!," they started to release unfinished album cuts in an effort to meet record company deadlines. At the time, we were working hard on the stage and they wanted us to come up

with hit singles in the studio in a couple of hours. That was impossible. So, we just sat there and watched everything crumble around us." (MP-HP69)

U.K. EP release
The Moody Blues
Decca DFE 8622; May 21, 1965

One week before the release of the Moody Blues' fourth single, Ridgepride tried to squeeze some extra money out of the group by having Decca issue a four-track EP which contained *no* new recordings. What *The Moody Blues* EP did feature was both sides of the band's first two singles, in a color picture sleeve. Since anyone in Britain interested in owning a copy of "Go Now!" already had the single, and many others had probably picked up the only other Moody Blues record available – their "Steal Your Heart Away"/"Lose Your Money" single – it should have come as no surprise that the EP failed to make the charts.

U.K. single release:
"From the Bottom of My Heart (I Love You)"
b/w "And My Baby's Gone"
Decca F.12166; May 28, 1965
Peak U.K. position: #16 (*Record Retailer*)

U.S. single release:
London 14-LON 9764; May 28, 1965
Peak U.S. position: #70 (*Cashbox*)

The song the Moodies had wanted to be their third single, a Pinder/Laine original, "From the Bottom of My Heart (I Love You)," was issued as their fourth. With this song, the band competed in the first British Song Festival, May 24 through 26, 1965. On Day 1, for the "First Heat," the Moodies came in third. That advanced them to the next day of the competition and, during the Grand Final category, they were awarded fourth position, out of the ten acts competing.

"And My Baby's Gone," chosen for the B-side, was also written by Pinder/Laine.

Alex Murray wasn't sure that either had what it took to be the A-side of a single and viewed these sessions as being for an LP. He said, "We started laying down rhythm

tracks for an album, but I was so busy with trying to hold the business together that I handed production to Denny Cordell – who I was mentoring as a producer – on the agreement that he would reimburse me with 10% of his production royalties. He never did. He did, however, introduce me to heroin via a mutual friend some weeks later!

"I decided enough was enough and called the boys in, offering to tear up their agreement – as promised – and take on the other directors [of Ridgepride] if they would stand as one with me. They wouldn't. I left the job that night and never went back. Weeks later, I was voted off the board and out of a job with Ridgepride. Tony Secunda abstained in the voting." (AM-LP06)

Secunda, who Murray said he had picked up off the floor of a drinking den and brought into the business, wasn't about to betray his mentor. But, apparently, he wasn't going to stick his neck out for him either. Jon Fenton and Simon Miller-Mundy, who Murray gifted the idea for Seltaeb, closed the door on him.

Denny Cordell was now the Moody Blues producer.

Denny Laine said, "Originally he was just working in the office, sticking press cuttings into a book in the office." (DL-WS01)

Ray Thomas said, "*Everything* was new then. *None* of us were used to recording. Then when Alex Murray left, Denny [Cordell], who'd always been around, just took his chair. He made a name with us – before that, he was the tea boy. We all learnt together, on-the-spot experience." (RT-SM15)

Mike Pinder said of Cordell, "He's a frustrated musician. He can't play, so he gets a good sound from other people in the studio. He can make a piano and the flute sound like 12 violins." (MP-RM65a)

Cordell would go on to have a bright future, with hit records for the Move, Georgie Fame, Procol Harum, Joe Cocker, Leon Russell, and Tom Petty & the Heartbreakers, among others.

Pinder said, "I think 'From the Bottom of My Heart' was the real turning point for the band. That was where we began trying to experiment with sound, writing with ideas that were more sophisticated. We developed a style, using reverb on the vocal, and getting various kinds of sounds and effects out of the piano that we hadn't done before." (MP-GM94)

In addition, "From the Bottom of My Heart" was the first Moodies' record to feature Ray Thomas playing his brand-new alto flute.

Thomas said, "It was no problem switching to the flute [from harmonica]. I'd played the flute as a boy. It was almost a family tradition, because my grandfather played,

and 'From the Bottom of My Heart' was just the first chance I had to use it on a record."
(RT-GM94)

The song is notable for more than being the first known instance of a rhythm & blues (or rock 'n' roll) band featuring a flutist among their members. Graeme Edge said, "'From the Bottom of My Heart' [was the one] which we like to think of as the very first psychedelic record *ever*, with Denny's very high screamy voice at the end." (GE-R68)

Part of that psychedelic feel includes one of the guitars on the track recorded to sound almost like a sitar – a good six months before we would hear the Beatles' first use of the Indian instrument on a pop record, with "Norwegian Wood."

Regarding these innovations, Denny Laine said, "But then that's what it's all about. You've got to keep trying different things, I think; develop all those influences." (DL-H&H97)

In the June 19, 1965 edition of *Record Mirror*, Richard Green wrote that Laine's scream "has been described in many ways, and a lot of older people seem to think he's going through a death agony."

"It's not screaming," Laine countered, "it's a falsetto warble. People like the Ivy League do falsetto, but I get the higher notes." (DL-RM65)

Pinder interjected, "I had a clamp on him when he did it." (MP-RM65)

It should also be noted that the Beatles' similar use of falsetto and head-shaking was driving young girls to screaming frenzies at this time. In the States, Lou Christie, Del Shannon, and the Four Seasons were also renowned for singing in falsetto.

Despite its good standing in the recent British songwriting competition, "From the Bottom of My Heart" seemed yet another questionable choice as an A-side. The song certainly has merit, as a possible B-side or album cut, but it really wasn't suitable for a single release. Its comparatively complex structure makes it somewhat inaccessible, unless heard numerous times. The singing was good – both Laine's lead and the support from the rest of the band – but the confusion of seemingly mismatched elements and time signatures, and the over-the-top falsetto climax, defeated the chances for this one to make the Top 10.

"And My Baby's Gone" perhaps was a better choice for the A-side. It's what they called "a raver" back then – catchy, with a energized beat and rhythmic handclapping, further enhanced by Laine's guitar and Pinder's piano, combining to create a jaunty recurring riff; a second guitar manipulated by a wah-wah pedal (comparable and equally effective as the Beatles' "Yes It Is" from this period); expertly woven lead and backing supporting vocals; and a killer harmonica performance by Thomas. It's one hell of a B-side!

"From the Bottom of My Heart (I Love You)," b/w "And My Baby's Gone," was issued on May 28, 1965. This represented the first time both sides of a Moody Blues' single had been written by members of the group. The obstacles to its success were Sandie Shaw's "Long Live Love," at No. 1 in the U.K. charts, plus other Top 20 contenders such as the Beatles' "Ticket to Ride"; Peter and Gordon's cover of Buddy Holly's "True Love Ways"; Roger Miller's "King of the Road"; Bob Dylan's "Subterranean Homesick Blues"; the Beach Boys' "Help Me, Rhonda"; and Herman and the Hermits' cover of Sam Cooke's "Wonderful World."

While it was the fourth Moody Blues' single issued in the U.K, "From the Bottom of My Heart" was only their second in the U.S. The music critic for *Billboard* magazine gave the song a "spotlight" pick in the trade's May 22 edition:

> To follow up their hit, "Go Now!," the group comes up with another intriguing, off-beat piece of material, much in the vein and rhythm of their current hit.

In the May 29 edition of England's *Record Mirror*, the pop music newspaper's critic wrote:

> Another Festival item. Slightly disjointed opening, but it soon gets into typical "Moody" material – full choral happenings, with some great lead vocalizing.... A ballad-with-blues, jangling guitar, lots of meaningful interpretation... It has originality and commercial impact. Flip is by the same Pinder-Laine team, with high-pitched vocal wildness... [is] rather good, too.

Back in the States, on June 12, music correspondent and critic Sandy Gardner was less sure that this song was right for American radio:

> "From the Bottom of My Heart" is a weird deal from the Moody Blues which builds like crazy and ends with the vocalist going right off his rocker in falsetto fashion. It could snare a bottom rung.

May 29, 1965 issue of Music Business.
(Photo source: MoodyBluesAttitude.com)

"Bottom rung" was chart-watcher's jargon for just outside of the Top 40.

In the May 22 issue of *Record Mirror*, it was reported that the Moodies had several TV appearances on their schedule to support the new single, with *Ready Steady Go!* (May 28), BBC-Light's *Top Gear* (May 29), ABC's *Thank Your Lucky Stars* and BBC-Light's *Saturday Club* (both on June 5), plus radio promotion with Radio Luxembourg's version of *Ready Steady Go!* (June 6) and BBC-2's *Gazooks! It's All Happening!* (date to be determined), along with numerous music hall performances.

Immediately following these commitments, the Moodies were scheduled to go to America on a triple-threat bill with the Dave Clark 5 and the Kinks.

On May 29, the Moodies had the cover of *Music Business*. Much was still expected of them. One day earlier, their fourth single had been released in England by Decca. June Harris wrote about "Go Now" becoming a hit in the U.S., adding:

No one was more delighted than *Music Business*, because we'd flown the record in from England at the beginning of the New Year. We tipped it as a winner, which wasn't really a terribly difficult forecast as it hit the top of the British charts.

We saw the Moody Blues on television too. They had a bit on *Hullabaloo* before it recessed for the summer. They're a very strange looking group in a groovy kind of way. There are five Moodies. They don't always dress alike, but sartorially they always look good. They wear Italian inspired shoes and brush their hair over to the sides of their heads. When they pose for photographs, their faces look like they were cast in stone and their eyes have a passive look.

Musically, they are led by Denny Laine and Mike Pinder, who wrote both sides of their new release on London. Titles are "From the Bottom of My Heart" and "And My Baby's Gone." It doesn't really sound too much like "Go Now," which has a different background altogether. ...

The Moody Blues is a good name for the kind of material they perform, but the quintet doesn't do it tongue in cheek style. They're dead serious about their music. ...

The Moodies arrive here on June 12 for a four-week tour with the Kinks. This will be their second trip out of England – their first was in April, when they headlined at the Paris Olympia. They only stayed 24 hours, but they managed to swing their way through 14 night clubs in addition to playing the date! ...

The Moody Blues are terrifically critical of both themselves and their work. They go for big sounding vocal harmonies, and big sounding instrumental work. After the success of "Go Now" in England, it took five weeks from the release of their next disc, "I Don't Want to Go on Without You," before it hit the charts. They weren't worried, because they said that chart success isn't everything. But the Moodies are coming here in plenty of time to promote "From the Bottom of My Heart."

And, if they had, "From the Bottom of My Heart" may have made the Top 20 in the America as it had done in the U.K. However, due to mishandling by their management, the Moodies had to be drop out at the last minute when the proper work permits could not be secured.

Despite *Billboard*'s confidence in the record, and with the band a no-show on the Kinks/Dave Clark 5 tour, Sandy Gardner's prediction about snaring "a bottom rung" turned out to be right. In America, "From the Bottom of My Heart" barely scraped the bottom of the charts, with *Cashbox* showing it at No. 70 peak. *Record World* stopped the record cold at No. 82, and *Billboard* barely noticed it at No. 92 on June 19.

Local radio listeners in Connecticut were a bit more accepting. For its June 7 survey, radio station WDRC in Hartford put "From the Bottom of My Heart" into the Top 40, at No. 34. Over in New Haven, WAVZ ranked the song at No. 23 (on June 26). In Los Angeles, on top-rated KRLA, "From the Bottom of My Heart" reached No. 38 on June 12. South of L.A., in San Bernardino, KFXM took the song to No. 32 on June 21. Further south still, in San Diego, "From the Bottom…" was played once every two hours on station KCBQ, where it peaked at No. 16 on July 4.

Back in England, "From the Bottom of My Heart" made it as high as No. 22 in *Melody Maker*. Another U.K. chart, as reported in the June 23, 1965 issue of U.S. trade paper *Variety*, placed the song at No. 16.

In May, the Moody Blues are known to have given at least 19 concerts in 18 different venues. The live-performance schedule had been scaled back by nearly a third to allow the band to record its first album, something which hadn't seemed a priority for management, and not even for some in the band.

Ray Thomas told this author, "We weren't that concerned with the time lapse because we were a working band rather than a recording band; we made our living gigging rather than worrying about an album. Secunda had us gigging every night we could, which didn't leave a lot of time to record. You've got to remember that in that time period people were buying singles – 45s. An album in those days was really just a compilation of the singles a band had released, and we *did* release some singles." (RT-AI17)

On the June 1 broadcast of the BBC's *Saturday Night Club*, the Moodies performed a teaser from their upcoming LP with the James Brown cover, "I've Got a Dream," as well as the B-side from their fourth single, "And My Baby's Gone." As with earlier TV performance, the live versions were superior to the vinyl releases. It was a testament to their developing showmanship, but it also demonstrated how hampered the band was in the recording studio under their current management.

U.K. LP release:
The Magnificent Moodies
Decca LK 4711, July 22, 1965
Peak U.K. position: #5 (*NME* chart)

U.S. LP release:
Go Now: The Moody Blues #1
PS 428; July 28, 1965

It had been ten months since their first single release, and nearly six months since they had topped the charts with "Go Now!" But, when Ridgepride finally did deliver the tracks for the LP to Decca, there were only eleven new songs, augmented by the inclusion of "Go Now!" Most U.K. pop albums from this time contained 14 tracks and rarely included a seven-month old single. In the number of songs, it was a skimpy release. Clearly Ridgepride had either not wanted to pay for additional studio time or merely hadn't given the band enough nights off the road for further recording. However, despite the leanness in the number of tracks, when finally issued in the U.K. on July 22, 1965, the long-awaited LP was greeted with both open arms and open ears by the British music press.

Of the 11 new tracks, seven were covers, and four were Mike Pinder-Denny Laine originals.

Denny Laine said, "I wanted to 'make it,' and I wanted to make it doing the kind of music that was more mine, more what I like to do. So, we developed from a straight blues band into a band that wrote its own material. On the first album, you can hear the R&B influence, but then there's a lot of songs that I wrote that Mike Pinder helped me with." (DL-H&H97)

Laine sang lead on most of the songs, with the exception of a James Brown cover, "I Don't Mind," featuring a lead by Mike Pinder, and the George and Ira Gershwin standard, "It Ain't Necessarily So," sung by Ray Thomas.

On Side 1, "I'll Go Crazy" gets things started with a sound trip into a Southern church in the U.S. for a gospel prayer sing-along, before shifting into a fusion of soul and jazz, with hot piano licks, soulful vocals – both lead and backing – richly accented with clear and crisp percussion. The Moodies found the song in a box of 45s sent over from the U.S. It was a somewhat obscure 1960 single by James Brown (who also wrote the number). Brown's version had made the Top 20 on the U.S. R&B chart, but failed to cross over to the pop charts.

Band 2, "Something You Got," was written by Chris Kenner, who had a No. 2 hit in the U.S. in 1961 with his composition of "I Like It Like That." His recording of "Something You Got," however, failed on the pop charts, resulting in this 45 being tossed in the box of discs to be shipped to the Moodies in England. It is possible the group may also have listened to the 1964 cover version by soul singer Alvin Robinson, which had made No. 52 on the *Billboard* Top 100 chart. The Moodies' recording of this song features Ray Thomas on flute, complementing an arrangement filled with amusing shifts in time signatures and playful percussion.

Along with "Go Now!" (the third track), Band 4, "Can't Nobody Love You," provides one of the album's highlights. Written by James D. Mitchell and originally recorded by Solomon Burke in 1963, the song was an R&B hit that crossed over to peak at No. 66 on *Billboard*'s Hot 100 chart. For the Moodies, Laine delivers a moving lead vocal – again, showing surprising blues passion for his age – backed by a choir of doo-wop angelic voices and a "wah-wah" harmonica accompaniment from Thomas. Pinder contributes just the right piano backing and instrumental break, with a tasteful guitar solo by Laine. In the delightful ending – the Moodies croon "Oh, yeah" like the "Amen" at the end of a hymn.

Band 5, "I Don't Mind," was another James Brown song, this one dating back to 1961 when it peaked at No. 47 in the *Billboard* Hot 100. This is the only song on *The Magnificent Moodies* to feature Mike Pinder in the lead vocal spot. He sounds nothing like the Pinder of later Moody releases, as he delivers a gut-wrenching blues reading. The high-ranged vocal accompaniment from the other Moodies makes an effective contrast to Pinder's deeper, soulful voice. As for the backing vocals, you can almost imagine these Birmingham boys as a girl group from 1964 Detroit, Michigan. Pinder's piano again sets just the right tone, somber and poignant, and contributes one of the song's hooks with the descending piano riff which precedes each verse.

"I've Got a Dream" closes out the first side, and Denny Laine delivers a vocal as sweetly as Frankie Lymon and the Teenagers might have. Ray Thomas's flute effectively floats over the top of Laine's singing, combining nicely with a charming piano riff from Pinder and the now-familiar choir of harmonic background voices. The song was an amazing find by the Moodies – the B-side of a release that never even charted, by a group that never made the charts on any other occasion: 1965's "Keep It Up," by the Soul Brothers. But the writers of this obscure song certainly *had* hit the charts, time and time again. Ellie Greenwich and Jeff Barry were one of the most successful writing teams to ever come out of New York City's Brill Building, providing producer Phil Spector with many of his girl-group hits, such as "Da Doo Ron Ron," "Then He Kissed Me," "Be My Baby," and "Baby, I Love You."

Side 2 opens with the first of four Pinder/Laine originals. "Let Me Go" is another of the album tracks enhanced by Thomas's flute playing, combining with Pinder's piano to create an ear-tickling riff at the outset of each verse, smoothly dancing around yet another lovely lead vocal from Laine, with lush backing vocals from the other band members.

"Stop!," again by Pinder and Laine, delivers a tango of strident notes and curious rhythm breaks. With its odd time signatures and sudden stops and starts, it's certainly a distinctive cut. The song even hints at Top 40 possibilities, but the intruding rhythm breaks in the arrangement rendered it a bit too offbeat for mass consumption (as London Records in America would learn when issuing it as a single later in the year).

Graeme Edge: "Denny Laine leaned more toward jazzy drumming. He liked me to be much busier with lots of short, busy little phrases. If you listen to the record called *Go Now: Moody Blues No. 1* there are three or four tracks that are far from mainstream pop. There are some strange time signatures and constant changes in rhythm patterns, which are the kinds of things Denny Laine liked to write…. I liked the technical aspect of playing that material, but it did lack feeling." (GE-MD87)

"Thank You Baby," the third track on Side Two, is another Pinder/Laine original. As with "Stop!," this song seems comprised of parts that are greater than the whole. They fight one another – in the best tradition of jazz, perhaps – but, in doing so, they struggle from verse to chorus to middle eight and back again; it was maybe just a little too busy for popular tastes.

Band Four on side Two, "It Ain't Necessarily So," brings Ray Thomas to the forefront, singing in his best "Old Man River" bluesy, soulful baritone voice, which then climbs into the range of a tenor, sounding a bit like Bobby Darin. Written by George and Ira Gershwin for their 1935 opera *Porgy and Bess*, the song was sung by the character Sportin' Life, a drug dealer, who mocks various Bible stories. The song became an American chart hit for Leo Reisman in 1935 and for Bing Crosby in 1936, but it is likely Thomas knew it from the 1959 album, *That's All*, by Aretha Franklin and Bobby Darin, accounting for his dead-on Darin impression when in the higher register. "It Ain't Necessarily So" is a surprising contrast to the previous cuts, and, after hearing this track, one can only wonder why Thomas didn't sing more leads. He dominates the track, complimented brilliantly by Pinder's ever-present piano, again with the keyboard driving the track, glissando included. And, of course, a choir of voices from the other Moodies that preaches the blues right back at the lead singer. This is another of the album's many highlight.

Regarding the song choice, Ray Thomas said, "I hadn't written any songs and I had always liked 'It Ain't Necessarily So.' I felt like it suited my voice at the time. [Years later] I did have a fan tell me it was the worst song I had ever written!" (RT-AI17)

"True Story," a Pinder/Laine original, makes for a nice shift, with a less heavy, less tricky, and playful blending of Bo Diddley guitar-styling and the Birmingham blues.

With "Bye Bye Bird," the album ends with a punch, courtesy of Laine's frantic vocal and a great harmonica workout from Thomas. The Moodies learned the song from American blues singer Sonny Boy Williamson when they toured with him in late 1964. Williamson taught Thomas to play the harmonica in the sped-up blues style heard here. Denny Laine learned from Williamson too, and often played an added harmonica part for this song when performing live.

Written by Williamson with fellow blues artist Willie Dixon, "Bye Bye Bird" was the B-side of the former's 1963 single, "Help Me," an obscure song itself, which only made it as high as No. 24 on *Billboard*'s R&B chart, missing the pop charts entirely.

Mike Pinder: "'Bye Bye Bird' was one of our most popular numbers onstage, and it not only gave Ray a showcase for harmonica, but [jokingly] gave me a chance to show off my magnificent playing on the maracas. You can see it on the *New Musical Express* poll-winners concert film." (MP-GM94)

In the same way that the Beatles commonly ended concerts and albums with a raver, "Bye Bye Bird" is the Moodies' "Twist and Shout." It combines a savage harmonica with an insanely excited lead vocal, a "crazy, man, crazy" driving rhythm, and maddening energy. Going loony was never so much fun.

The Magnificent Moodies is a mixed bag of blues, overlooked gems, and originals, but, when "Bye Bye Bird" comes to its abrupt conclusion, one can't help but want to start playing the entire record again. It's just too short.

Interviewed for this book, Mike Pinder said, "*The Magnificent Moodies* was really the reflection of our early influences, which – among our styles – was a good measure of rhythm & blues. We were very young and we were learning so much – how to record, how to interpret and arrange songs, how to interact with other musicians, and how to be a band. We were just starting to write in our own voice, too." (MP-AI17)

The albums to beat in the U.K. charts the week *The Magnificent Moodies* was released included the original soundtrack to *The Sound of Music*, at No. 1, followed by Bob Dylan's *Bringing It All Back Home*; Joan Baez's fifth album (titled *#5*); more Julie Andrews, with the soundtrack to *Mary Poppins*; the Seekers' *A World of Our Own*; and a former No. 1 smash, *Beatles For Sale*.

English folk singer/songwriter Donovan was asked to write the sleeve notes for the back cover. He was early in his career, having just scored a pair of U.K. Top 5 hits – "Catch the Wind" and "Colours" – but his unique and offbeat persona was already shining through. Case in point, Donovan's idea of sleeve notes included:

> … *The sounds of blues came mellow*
> *Rolling*

It moved me to somewhere else
The Moody Blues turned me on to their
music that night
Their writing has all the sensitiveness
an' feeling that makes music cool to
listen to
The tracks on this LP will show you the
sort of scene they have got going
You will probably call it contemporary
blues – it could be if you want it to be
It doesn't matter
Just let it pass through you.

After hearing a press preview for the album, Virginia Ironside, music critic for the London *Daily Mail*, wrote such an enthusiastic review that it was printed on the back sleeve as well, crowding Donovan's verse to the side. She said:

> I first heard the Moody Blues on my radio one night, just before going to bed. I caught "Go Now" in its opening bars, and as the record played on, I became more and more hung up, waiting for the D.J. to tell me who it was. And then finally he announced, "… the magnificent Moody Blues." I bought the record at 9:30 the next morning.

> I caught the Moodies live a few weeks later, and their soulful sound knocked me out. Since then, I have been made to wait for almost a year for their first album – and the first chance to get the real feel of the Moodies' own sound.

> Listen to Denny Laine's fantastic timing on "Bye Bye Bird," and his beautiful guitar solo on "Can't Nobody Love You"; the thrust of "Something You Got"; the harmonies and Mike Pinder's piano on "Let Me Go," one of the four stunning Pinder-Laine compositions. All knitted together by Graham [sic] Edge on drums, Clint Warwick on bass, and Ray (flute, maracas, harmonica, tambourine) Thomas. Listen to their solid choral harmonies. Listen to the way they achieve sounds as powerful as a great soulful orchestra without double-tracking a single musician – without any assistance but their own….

And, just for the back sleeve, Ironside added:

> But sleeve note – hell. With the Moody Blues, all you need to write is "MAGNIFICENT" in pink lipstick and leave it at that.

Richard Green of *Record Mirror* found it curious that the album had been recorded in several different London studios. He observed:

It's usual for an LP to be produced in one studio. This way, the group gets the same sound the whole way through and everyone is happy. But not so the Moody Blues.

The reason for using so many different studios likely had more to do with an erratic recording schedule, squeezed between road trips and local gigs.

Denny Laine shrugged it off to Green: "We used four studios in all on our LP. It was a laugh trying out all the studios and seeing which one was best." (DL-RM65a)

One British reviewer wrote:

> The first album from the Moodies [is] a commendable debut in the LP field. What I like particularly about this group is that they never play to the gallery. They don't rouse rabbles in preference to the music they want to play in the way they want to play it. This is mostly rhythm & blues-based material, and it's pretty near to the real coloured thing, vocals and all.
>
> Ray Thomas deserves praise for his lead singing and the mean harmonica he plays for "Bye Bye Bird." Denny Laine's guitaristics are consistently good, too.
>
> Side 1 leans strongly on the James Brown coloured R-and-B scene for material, and the flip spotlights the songwriting gifts of Moodies Denny and Mike Pinder. George Gershwin's "It Ain't Necessarily So" gets an unusual and movingly effective treatment.
>
> A very good set which has a lot for inwardly digesting.

Supporting the album, the Moodies continued to gig across England. On August 6, they were one of the featured bands playing the prestigious 5th National Jazz Festival at London's Marquee Club. Performing with the Moodies that Friday night were the Yardbirds and the Who, each more properly classified as rhythm & blues than jazz. With the tone set, the Saturday night bill carried on with Manfred Mann and Georgie Fame, while Sunday night had the Animals and the Spencer Davis Group. Jazz connoisseurs may have objected, but the Marquee Club made a bundle.

In the July 24 issue of *Record Mirror*, the newspaper's music critic wrote:

> Everybody liked "Go Now!" The other Moodies discs, including this album, have been more and more offbeat. With the accent vaguely on spiritually inclined R & B, this is essentially an LP which you need to listen to several times before receiving the full impact. Once you like it, you'll like it for a long time. Wistful vocal work, interesting backings and everything blending together very well. Four originals on here, the rest are lesser known oldies. A pity, though, that there couldn't have been a few more tracks, especially as everyone already has their "Go Now!," included for some strange reason here.

The Birmingham Planet praised their local boys for the first LP release with a review in the newspaper's August 26, 1965 edition:

> It is my pleasure to rave about two LPs: The Beatles' latest and the Moody Blues first; both of which are, in rather different ways, bordering on the brilliant.
>
> The *Help!* LP contains few surprises; *The Magnificent Moodies*, on the other hand, is full of them. The shadow of Bob Dylan hangs over the former, and that of Steve Winwood over the latter….
>
> From the first few seconds, the Moodies LP demonstrates their assured grasp of musical styles. The beginning of "I'll Go Crazy" sounds like something out of Brubeck. Seconds later, when the vocal starts, it sounds gospely… In fact, the entire record is a model of flair, versatility and well-executed unusual combinations.
>
> As well as the celebrated "Go Now," the new LP includes such tracks as "Something You Got," featuring Denny Laine as vocalist and Ray Thomas on flute, the rather whimsical tune "I've Got a Dream," and a well-balanced treatment of "It Ain't Necessarily So."
>
> I am also unable not to mention Denny's tremendous performance on "Bye Bye Bird," the stabbing piano and guitar backing to "I Don't Mind" (sung by Mike Pinder), but most of all the highly emotive "Can't Nobody Love You," which simply abounds with virtuosic touches – notably Denny's amazingly appropriate guitar solo.
>
> However, the focal points of this album are the four Pinder-Laine numbers, "Let Me Go," "Stop," "Thank You Baby," and "True Story," each of which is a gem.

While *The Magnificent Moodies* failed to make the *Record Retailer/Music Week* chart in the U.K., it did place well on *NME*'s album chart, peaking at No. 5.

The American version of the album, given a different title – *Go Now: The Moody Blues #1* – also had twelve tracks, but with some changes. Dropped were covers of "Something You Got," the Pinder-sung "I Don't Mind," and a pair of Pinder/Laine originals, "Stop!" and "Thank You, Baby," being held in reserve for possible single release. In their place, the U.K.-only single sides "And My Baby's Gone," "It's Easy Child," and "I Don't Want to Go On Without You," as well as the current single in both the U.S. and Britain, "From the Bottom of My Heart."

On August 14, *Billboard* in America gave the U.S. version of the album a "Pop Spotlight," saying:

> Currently riding the British charts with their hot single, "From the Bottom of My Heart," which forms the basis for this LP, the group of five English lads combines a solid blues wail with a driving

dance beat to produce a package aimed right at the teen market. Exceptional cuts are their recent U.S. smash, "Go Now!," "Can't Nobody Love You," and Ira Gershwin's "It Ain't Necessarily So," A rapid chart climber.

Variety (in its September 8 issue) also gave the U.S. long player a positive review:

> The Moody Blues is a suitable moniker for this latest British combo to attempt to crack the U.S. market. The group is deeply immersed in the blues groove and projects the idiom with authenticity and power. Tops in the set are the title song, "From the Bottom of My Heart," "I'll Go Crazy," "And My Baby's Gone," "I Had a Dream," "It Ain't Necessarily So," and "Bye Bye Bird."

In America, despite *Billboard*'s claim that the album was a rapid chart climber, there are no statistics available as to its ranking, suggesting it may not have made the national Top 100 LP chart.

Meanwhile, the Moodies were having trouble with their management.

Alex Murray had left Ridgepride months earlier, and now Tony Secunda appeared to be heading for the door. Birmingham's *Sunday Mercury* reported in May that Secunda had signed another Birmingham band, the Move, and was giving them a £70,000 contract. Mark Gardner, the writer of the article, mentioned that the Move sounded like the Moody Blues. By summer, Sucunda had branched out further, taking on a London Subculture band called the Action. Neither would be managed by Ridgepride, only by Secunda. It is unclear where the money for these new ventures came from, but, Secunda, who was penniless when he joined Ridgepride, had clearly done well for himself. Meanwhile, Ridgepride was unable to pay its creditors.

Not only was Ridgepride deeply in debt, but Seltaeb was collapsing. Regarding the latter, there were too many hands in the kitty – Nicky Byrne and Lord Peregrine Elliot having the largest, with more money being scooped up from secondary partners John Fenton, Simon Miller-Mundy, Mark Warmen, and Malcolm Evans (not to be confused with Beatles' roadie Mal Evans). Worse still, Ridgepride had been biting the hand that fed it – that of Beatles' manager Brian Epstein.

The company, setup in 1963 to handle all Beatles merchandising deals, had taken advantage of Epstein from the outset. He and the Beatles were only getting 10% of the money Seltaeb made from licensing the Beatles' likenesses and good name, minus the company's expenses, of course. By early 1964, with Beatlemania spreading across Europe and now entrenched in America, and merchandising booming as never before imagined, Epstein realized that the partners in Seltaeb had treated him unfairly. He immediately had his lawyer undertake renegotiations, with the threat of taking the dispute into court and a request of early termination. In August of that year, the deal was changed, with Epstein and the Beatles now getting 49%. However, this left far less money for Seltaeb's six partners, and some were killing the goose who had once laid golden eggs with frequent cash withdrawals. Come December, 1964, Byrne was suing

Elliot, and the revenue streams to Fenton and Murphy, as with the other partners, were quickly drying up. Fenton and Mundy were now dependent on Ridgepride to cover the high standard of living each had become accustomed to. That high standard had also been enjoyed by Tony Secunda.

With only one band to support Ridgepride, the debts soon overtook the revenue. Ridgepride was using the Moodies' earnings to cover the rent on the home for the band, and the partner's homes, as well as restaurant bills, liquor bills, party bills, and the many necessities, including office rental, employee wages, attorney fees, accounting fees, and the cost of outfitting the band. From

Above: The Moodies management was bleeding them dry … as this 1965 photo seems to imply. Posing in a graveyard, from left to right, Thomas, Laine, Pinder, Edge, and, looking like Jonathan Frid (as Barnabas Collins) in *Dark Shadows*, Clint Warwick.
(Photo source: prog-rock-70s.blogspot.com)

July alone, this included £45 for a flute and guitar from Jones & Crosslands Ltd.; £281 to Finance Limited of 164 Bristol Street, Birmingham, for a Rickenbacker guitar and case; and £161 to Maple & Company Ltd for a Bentley 6-octave piano. Simon Miller-Mundy signed for the charges, but, by September, many of the charge accounts were delinquent.

On October 21, Murphy wrote to A.I. Lido Park Limited (West-End Flats & Real Estate), stating that Ridgepride was terminating the lease agreement for its office space located at Flat 6, No. 7 Lancaster Gate, with promise to vacate the offices no later than November 21. They actually vacated earlier.

Graeme Edge said, "Ridgepride were making a lot of money from us. They rented us a house in Roehampton and we thought that they were paying the rent for us. It turned out that they *weren't*. We were also told that they would pay all the utility bills, and they *weren't!* They were giving us £20 a week pocket money. … We thought [everything was] getting paid for us by Ridgepride and that they were taking care of our money and investing it wisely for us." (GE-MMCD45)

But they weren't.

Ray Thomas recalled, "We came back off a road trip and headed to Ridgepride, because we needed some money, to find the office closed down and cleaned out. And the guys who ran it had disappeared. They left us high and dry as well as not paying for the hotels and meals while we were on the road." (RT-AI17)

Mike Pinder: "Ridgepride did a 'bonker' and disappeared from sight. The band was left with nothing to show for a No. 1 record." (MP-AI17)

Graeme Edge: "We knew things had to be done at this stage, so we signed with dear Uncle Eppy, who was a wonderful person with wonderful people in his organization." (GE-MD87)

"Uncle Eppy" was none other than Brian Epstein.

5

"Uncle Eppy"

The Moody Blues were rightfully concerned that, thanks to Ridgepride's management, their promising career was on the skids.

At the start of September, Ridgepride had given the group a summer afternoon "off" in order to make themselves available for interviews. One of those talk sessions became the basis for an article in the September 11 edition of *Pop Weekly*.

Top right: The Moodies on the cover of *Pop Weekly*, September 11, 1965.
(Photo source: MoodyBluesAttitude.com)
Above: Brian Epstein, circa 1966.
(Image found at Goldmine.com; BeatlesRadio.com; TheGuardian.com)

Graeme Edge described the condition of the group to *Pop Weekly*'s Gray Powell as, "Getting all twisted up inside, we are." (GE-PW65)

Ray Thomas said, "What's happened is that the things we wanted to do, we haven't been able to do.... We decided that we shall have to make some changes. We are dead scared, and we don't mind admitting it. Things aren't going right. For instance, our last single died, although our LP is doing very well."

Thomas picked up one of the music newspapers. "Look at this! Our LP is No. 4 in the LP charts, but not a word about us in the whole paper, *never*. But look at all of this about the group who are No. 5 in the chart! Somehow we don't seem to be able to hold the fans' interest." (RT-PW65)

Graeme Edge declared, "We look too old on the stage, too somber, yet we are the same age range as the Beatles, but they have this young image while we've got this old man look."

Asked about their management – which had already abandoned the Ridgepride offices – Edge answered frankly, "There were these four blokes who drilled us like we were in the army, so we couldn't say what we wanted. We were the ones that were under the thumb, so that got us together in a way. But we got this somber image. We were pushed from light blue suits to darker blue suits and then into black suits, and we got this dark somber old moody image." (GE-PW65)

The somber Ridgepride image for the Moody Blues, 1964-65.

Thomas concluded, "In [the] future, we are going to restrict ourselves to all our own gear. You might say, making our own records is our last hope. That's why, as we said, we are dead scared and we don't mind admitting it." (RT-PW65)

Gray Powell, who had heard some of the Moodies' latest efforts in the recording studio, wrote:

> It was the end of the Moodies' summer afternoon off. They had 2,000 cards to autograph for their fans in Germany, and were due to leave for their evening show. Somehow I don't think the Moodies have any reason to be scared. Their last single may not have done so well chart-wise, but their LP is doing very well, and if the new tracks they played come out on the final recording as great as they sounded to me, the Moodies will be seeing the right side of the Top 10 pretty soon.

Days after giving the interview, the Moodies followed through on their words and made some drastic changes. Despite being "left high and dry" by Ridgepride, as Ray Thomas put it, Mike Pinder observed, "But we had name recognition now, and we knew that we had an audience. Ray and I were good friends with the Beatles, and… after being abandoned by Ridgepride, Brian Epstein was suggested to us by one of the them; probably Paul." (MP-AI17)

On September 3, 1966, London's *Daily Mirror* reported that Epstein had taken the reins of the Moody Blues. The Beatles' manager's fame was so great that the news didn't just become a blip on the radar screen for the British press, but rippled across the Atlantic to the shores of the U.S. Sandy Gardiner, in his syndicated column, "Platter Patter," reported on September 25:

> Brian Epstein has added another British hit group to his ever-growing musical stable. The Moody Blues are the latest addition

and the Birmingham boys will probably get their biggest push to date.

One of Epstein's first chores would have been to replace the record licensing agreement between Ridgepride and Decca with one directly between the record label and the Moody Blues. However, it's doubtful that he would have been able to better the deal. Ray Thomas said, "Brian didn't negotiate a new contract with Decca. He took us on to manage us and we were on 'free lease' with Decca. If Brian had wanted to negotiate a contract he would have taken us to EMI where the Beatles were – after being famously turned down by Decca." (RT-AI17)

"Free lease" means that neither party is bound to the other for a specified period of time. In the music industry of the 1960s, this type of arrangement was rare and, if it did occur, this would only be after the initial "term" period of the contract had been satisfied. The standard term mandated by record labels in the 1960s was three to five years, during which the artist was exclusively bound to the label and required to produce a certain amount of songs ("sides") per year. But the number of recording sessions or record releases weren't guaranteed to the artist by the label. If the artist's first record performed well, the label would exercise its option to record and release a second, and then continue in that manner. Changes in management, or even losing band members, would not free an artist from their recording contract. There was nothing Brian Epstein could do to change that until the end of the contractual term, which, if for three years, would have the Moodies in a "free lease" arrangement by the summer of 1967. This is likely what Ray Thomas was referring to. Until then, all Epstein could do was help the Moodies with their tour schedules, negotiate higher rates for their appearances, and shoot for higher-profile appearances, such as television. To this end, he made a transatlantic phone call, giving the Moodies their biggest push to date. The man on the other end of the line was Ed Sullivan. Epstein had already put the Beatles on four episodes of Sullivan's top-rated Sunday night series, as well as Gerry and the Pacemakers, Billy J. Kramer and the Dakotas, and Cilla Black. Now it would be the Moodies' turn.

Brian Epstein's formula for success – get his pop bands on *The Ed Sullivan Show* (R-L: Epstein, behind Sullivan, with Lennon, Starr, and McCartney, February 1964). (Photo source: MeTV.com)

Epstein also sent the Moodies back to the BBC. On September 21, for *Saturday Club*, they recorded live-in-the-studio performances of previous B-side "It's Easy Child," the album track "Stop!," and, at Epstein's request, their upcoming A-side – a Laine-Pinder original called "Everyday." The broadcast would take place in the near future as a primer for the single's release in America.

Meanwhile, a letter dated September 28, 1965, from the legal offices of L.M. Doffman & Co., representing Jazz Today Ltd., was sent to Ridgepride Ltd. It stated that Jazz Today had a two-year contract (from January 8, 1965 through the end of 1966), appointing them as sole and exclusive booking agents for the Moody Blues. The attorneys wrote:

> … As a result of information given to us by the solicitors to Ridgepride Limited and to our clients both direct and as a result of press publicity, it appears that your clients [the Moody Blues] no longer recognize Ridgepride Limited as their managers and have entered into fresh arrangements with Nems Enterprises Limited.
>
> It is not, of course, the concern of our clients as to whether Ridgepride Limited or Nems Enterprises Limited are your clients' managers. Our clients have been appointed their booking agents and intend to hold your clients to the Agreement.…

L..M. Doffman & Co., and their client, Jazz Today Ltd., would have to get in line – Ridgepride had many creditors.

It is reasonable to assume that NEMS was also sent a demand letter of this type. Epstein had his own booking agents in house and would not need Jazz Today. He also had good attorneys to handle matters such as these. Jazz Today Ltd. had a contract with Ridgepride. That was who they would need to sue. Be sure, they would.

The Moodies, likely unaware of all the red tape and threats of litigation to be dealt with, didn't know the half of what Epstein was doing for them.

An article in the October 16 edition of *Billboard* reported that Epstein had booked the Moody Blues to appear on the December 19 episode of *The Ed Sullivan Show*, broadcast live out of New York City over the CBS-TV network. He had also booked them and the Fortunes, another of his bands, to be part of the Murray the K's Xmas Show at New York's Brooklyn Fox theater.

Epstein was also making arrangements to have the Moodies tour with the Beatles. The big push was making big news.

Another story from this time (exact provenance unknown) ran the headline, "It's Enough to Make Even the Moodies Smile." The report read:

> The Moody Blues are now being managed by Beatles' boss Brian Epstein, which is one of the reasons why lead singer Denny Laine and pianist Mike Pinder were smiling.
>
> "We used to have to project the moody image," said Denny. "We were always scowling. Now we just act natural and smile if we feel like it."

Mike told me future plans. "We join the Beatles' British tour in early December, then we fly off for a first visit to America. We'll be there for Christmas."

Meantime, they have a cracking new single to set the pace. Title: "Everyday" (Decca).

U.K. single release:

"Everyday" b/w "You Don't (All the Time)"
Decca F.12266; mid-October 1965
Peak U.K. position: #44

U.S. single release:
"Ev'ry Day" b/w "You Don't"
London 9799; mid-October 1965

In mid-October, 1965, Decca released the Moodies' fifth U.K. single. "Everyday" (issued as "Ev'ry Day" in the U.S.) b/w "You Don't (All the Time)," were both Laine-Pinder originals, and, as with their last two singles and album, produced by Denny Cordell. For the U.S. release, the song title on the B-side was shortened to merely read "You Don't."

"Everyday" has curious appeal. Its slight Latin rhythm merges with jazz and British-invasion-era vocal harmonies for an odd combination. It didn't have much of a chance on radio, and "You Don't (All the Time)")" seemed the better choice for an A-side. It's more accessible than "Everyday," although perhaps still too intricate and tricky for mass audience appeal, a common concern with the majority of the Laine/Pinder originals up to this point.

The biggest songs on the radio in the U.K. at the time of release included the Rolling Stones' "Get Off of My Cloud" (at No. 1), Barry McGuire's "Eve of Destruction," the McCoys' "Hang on Sloopy," and Bob Dylan's "Positively 4th Street."

On October 23, *Record Mirror* said:

Written by Mike Pinder and Denny Laine, this is the long-awaited follow-up by the highly-talented group. It's a mid-tempoed beater, with powerfully laid down percussion. Vocal arrangement is a gas! Builds with some complexity, but obvious professional gloss. Good lyrics. Should do well. Same writers for the more straight-forward flip – a bouncy tempo and lots of singing going on.

Another review from this time (provenance unknown) said:

Denny Laine and Mike Pinder wrote this and it reminds me terribly of something else.

It's more tuneful than past records of theirs, for which I am grateful… although it's still typically Moody. I'd like to see them back in the chart, but I don't know whether this will get too high….

Another unidentified reviewer said:

A great record. I love the lead voice. I wish I could tell you more about it. No, I don't know who it is. Ah, the Moody Blues. One of the most talented groups in this country. I feel sad I didn't recognize the group I consider one of the best.

Another picked the B-side as the song worth watching::

One record reviewer said The Moody Blues' last record "contained everything but the kitchen sink." He'd be right on the newie, "You Don't (All the Time)." A very involved record with several changes in arrangement and vocals. An experiment that grows on you and one that should pay off.

On October 30, *Record Mirror* did a follow-up piece. Richard Green met for lunch with Mike Pinder and Denny Laine, finding them as candid with him as Ray Thomas and Graeme Edge had been with Gray Powell of *Pop Weekly* two months earlier.

When asked to describe their new single, Pinder told Green, "We think it's a Mexican number. It's not pretty, as one national journalist said; it's rough." (MP-RM65b)

Laine explained, "We got a backing track and thought it sounded Mexican, so when it came to putting on the voices, we kept in the same vein." (MP-RM65b)

Green added:

This is the first record the Moody Blues have had issued since they joined Brian Epstein's organization a few weeks ago. How much say Mr. Epstein has in the choice of his artists' material I do not know, but he has certainly run up against a bit of opposition with the Moodies.

Pinder complained, "We wanted the B-side as the A-side. But Brian Epstein thought the other side was more typical Moody Blues stuff, so that was that."

Epstein not only designated "Everyday" as the A-side, but, in breaking with Decca tradition, he had a large "A" put on the top side of the single to make sure that DJs knew which song to play.

Besides the disappointment over how the single would be promoted to radio stations, the band members were feeling more and more rundown with their relentless touring. When they weren't on the road, they were booked in London nightclubs, meaning, a seven-day – or seven-night – work week.

Laine told Green, "We're completely shattered. We rush about here and there for dates and [on] our night off we go down to night clubs, and never get to bed early." (DL-RM65b)

Pinder added, "We're off to Cornwall tomorrow and then we've got to go straight up to Manchester for a show. We've just got a new car. We got rid of the old one and we've bought a Chevrolet Impala. It's a great car, but when you have to do two or three hundred miles at a stretch, it gets a bit rough." (MP-RM65b)

The 1964 Chevy Impala, though roomier than most 21st-century autos, was considered medium-sized then. Not only that, it was only a two-door. With four grown men sharing the space (and a fifth Moodie and roadie following in a van), there would hardly be room for comfortable napping.

Pinder talked to *Beat Instrumental* at this time about the rigors of touring: "I just wish I could stick a grand piano in my coat pocket. It's hopeless. Now we have a clause in our contract that the promoter must provide a good piano … yet one bloke the other day offered us a pub-style piano, then said, 'Well, can't you go on without using piano.' Ridiculous. We couldn't … and didn't. We just felt sorry for the fans.

"Another time in Blackpool, we were out in a rainstorm in front of 7,000 people. It was dangerous to use the electrical equipment. So the promoter said: 'Well, do you need to use the amplifiers?' We had spent £600 on our Fender amps and PA system – even Chuck Berry used it when we were together on tour….

"I'm not all that worried about the money, I just want to go as far as I can as a musician. If only people would help more with good equipment; good dressing rooms. We've even changed in a toilet – no hot water – after traveling six hours in a car." (MP-BI66)

To support "Everyday," Epstein sent the Moodies on a short tour from late September into early October, opening for the Rolling Stones. It must have been disparaging for the Moodies to hear the Stones doing their discovery, "Time Is on My Side," to a cheering crowd.

The band also dropped in for yet another BBC recording session to be used in a soon-to-air *Saturday Club*. This time they performed the B-side of their latest single – "You Don't," the side that they preferred Also, a previously unheard R&B cover called "I Want You to Know." The song, and its performance, is a soulful charmer; it's a shame that this number would never be issued on vinyl.

On November 20, *Cashbox* rated the new single, saying:

> The Moody Blues make a strong bid for chart honors with this driving solid funky blues effort. Potent romance lyrics and groovy sound could earn the boys lots of coin.

As for the flip side, the *Cashbox* critic added, "Same bag over here."

That same day, *Billboard* magazine predicted the new single would miss the Top 20, but probably make it into the Top 60 in the American charts. The reviewer said of the A-side, "Easy-go dance beat with good lyric content makes this an exciting entry that should climb the chart rapidly." The same trade showed the song peaking at No. 44 a few weeks later. It missed the charts entirely in Britain.

Meanwhile, the Moodies' status in the U.K. continued to diminish. In late November, they were the opening act on the Walker Brothers tour, a group who had just scored their first No. 1 hit with "Make It Easy on Yourself." Prior to that, the Walkers had only one other Top 20 single in the U.K. – "Love Her" … peaking at No. 20. The Moodies had more hits than that, but the newest No. 1 hit-makers had the clear advantage over a group with a six-month-old No. 1 … just like the Moodies' standing on tour with Brian Poole and the Tremeloes half a year earlier.

Meanwhile, *Shindig*, for its U.S. version, had an episode on November 28 which showcased performances from the nearly three-month old British National Jazz Festival, featuring the Moodies, the Animals, and Georgie Fame.

NEMS did get the Moodies on a short national tour with the Beatles, as reported in the December 1 edition of *Rave* magazine. On that night, they and the Fab Four were putting on a show at the Glasgow Odeon.

Meanwhile, the fourth partner in Ridgepride – the one Graeme Edge described as "a sweet little feller" who "got rooked" – had his day in court.

For an article in the November 30, 1965 edition of London's *Daily Mirror*, Don Short wrote:

> Old Etonian Simon Miller Mundy talked last night of his disastrous venture in the pop world. Twenty-four-year-old Mr. Mundy was co-manager of one of Britain's leading pop groups, the Moody Blues. But the venture ended yesterday with admitted debts of £37,034 – of which Mr. Mundy bears a personal loss of £25,000.
>
> "It's a lot of money, I know. But things went wrong and lack of experience played its part," Mr. Mundy said last night.
>
> Now the Moody Blues are playing on under a manager with plenty of experience … Mr. Brian Epstein, boss of the Beatles.
>
> At the West End hotel yesterday, Mr. Mundy and his co-partner Jon Fenton, 28, attended a meeting of creditors. It was stated that they had put their company into liquidation….

Mundy told Short, "Managing a pop group, however successful the group may seem, is a precarious business. We had internal management troubles and other difficulties. I can't say what I'm going to do now." (SMM-DM66)

Mundy's partner, Jon Fenton, told Short, "I discovered the Moody Blues and invited Simon in as co-manager. He's a bit choked about losing all this money, of course – not with me, but over the way things worked out." (JF-DM66)

Short wrote:

> Next weekend the Moody Blues, with their new record "Everyday" in the charts, are due to start a nationwide tour with the Beatles.
>
> "I would say their prospects are quite fantastic," said Mr. Epstein.

On December 2, 1965, the Moodies returned to British TV with an appearance on BBC1's *Shindig*, performing "I'll Go Crazy," the opening track on their album. It was the same episode that had aired months earlier in America.

In the December 10, 1965 edition of *New Musical Express*, Alan Smith covered the Beatles / Moody Blues concert at the Odeon, in Glasgow. He spoke highly of the Moodies, saying that their stage act, which featured "belters like 'I'll Go Crazy' as well as their slower-paced hits" had given "a performance steeped in professionalism."

The problem was, during much of their set, the audience was shouting, as Smith phrased it: "WE – WANT – THE – BEATLES!! WE – WANT – THE – BEATLES!! WE – WANT – THE – BEATLES!!"

> This was the thunderous, rumbling roar that went up no less than six times immediately before the Beatles came on stage at Glasgow Odeon on Friday.
>
> You could sense the electric, feverish tension hanging over the audience as they waited for the group's momentous first package appearance in 1965.
>
> Suddenly a short instrumental riff was heard from behind the curtains – and it was like flinging open the floodgates of the audience's emotion. Wild, ear-tingling screams bursts over the audience as the curtains parted and the Beatles moved straight into their first number, "I Feel Fine." John sang lead, and was in top vocal – and humorous – form. From time to time he would throw in a funny facial expression that had the crowd roaring with delight.

Smith went on to give a blow-by-blow description of the Beatle's performance, which moved along into "She's A Woman," "If I Needed Someone," "Act Naturally," "Nowhere Man," "Baby's In Black," "Help!," "We Can Work It Out," "Day Tripper," and ended with "I'm Down."

Smith wrote:

> The last raver ["I'm Down"] has become the 1965 "Twist and Shout" for the Beatles – a red-hot finale for their show that leaves the audience begging for more.

By the time the Beatles finished their performance, as the closing act, and Smith finished his report, no one was talking about the Moodies.

Despite this downside, there were plenty of perks to touring with the Beatles, the least of which was playing to sold-out venues every night. Their common management by NEMS also helped to enrich the friendship between the Moodies and the Beatles.

Mike Pinder said, "We were very close to the Beatles, and they liked us; they enjoyed our music. I remember, when they were onstage, we'd be by the stage taking in what they were doing; and when we were playing, there would be the four of them, standing by the side of the stage listening to us." (MP-GM94)

Ray Thomas concurred: "Yeh, we had a lot of fun touring with the Beatles. We used to split up – well, not that way … yet! – and half the Moodies would travel in their car and half the Beatles in ours. So, with four-and-a-half people in each car, it was one hell of a tour, as you can imagine! Yes, they were really good mates, of course. We knew them well before the tour, because, of course, Brian Epstein was also our manager for a while. So we were very close … and, in those days, touring was very different to now. I mean, you played together and you stayed together, and, well, back then, with the fan situation being what it was, we used to have to stay in remote locations – especially when playing around Liverpool." (RT-AC15)

The Moody Blues and the Beatles relax after dinner in their hotel after playing their Sheffield date during their December Tour.

From the December 1965 issue of *Beatles Monthly*. Around table (L-R): Unknown guest, Ray Thomas, George Harrison, Mike Pinder, John Lennon, Ringo Starr, Denny Laine, Clint Walker, Graeme Edge, and Paul McCartney.

On December 4, the Beatles and the Moodies played the City Hall in Newcastle on Tyne. The following night, the two bands took the stage at the Empire Theatre, in Liverpool, then, for December 7, they performed at the ABC Theatre, Ardwick, in Manchester. One day later, they were at the Gaumont, in Sheffield, followed another Odeon, on December 9, this one in the Moodies' home town of Birmingham. December 10, the two bands played yet a third Odeon, this time in Hammersmith. The following night, they performed at the Astoria, Finsbury Park, in London. On December 12, the Beatles and the Moodies shared the stage at the Capitol, in Cardiff.

More help from Epstein came with

The most FANTASTIC game of billiards ever.

Above: John and Paul are ready for the battle. Below: Moody Blues, Clint Warwick on the left and Graeme Edge, sandwich Ringo between them in opposition. Top right: Mike Pinder joins Ringo with John and Paul. But I think they are all going to miss the ball. Bottom right: Ringo and Clint are both determined to hit that shot back if it is the last thing they do.

Above: Yet another perk of having Brian Epstein as manager – a spread in *Beatles Monthly*, December 1965 issue. Top left, Lennon and McCartney; top right: Pinder with Lennon and McCartney; bottom left, Warwick and Edge surrounding Starr; bottom right: Thomas and Warwick with Starr.
(Source: *Beatles Monthly*, December 1965)
Below: On England's *Ready Steady Go!*
(Associated-Rediffusion Television)

a photo spread in the December issue of *Beatles Monthly* featured numerous pictures of the Moodies and the Beatles, including a photo spread of "The most FANTASTIC game of billiards ever." Despite not having a hit record for the holiday season, the Moodies were nonetheless enjoying high visibility.

Under Epstein's direction, the Moodies kept busy with more live gigs and TV appearances. They had already appeared on *Ready Steady Go!* three or more times, as well as multiple stops at *Thank Your Lucky Stars* and *Shindig*, and at least one guest spot each on *Hullabaloo*, *New Musical Express*, and *Top of the Pops*.

Mike Pinder said, "[W]e played a lot on *Ready Steady Go!* We were favorites, because we were based in London, and they had us on the show a lot. I remember we did a Christmas Show where we played James Brown's 'I'll Go Crazy' and we threw a little 'Jingle Bells' into the break." (MP-GM94)

After taping this program, the Moodies were off to America to be part of Murray the K's Xmas Show, where they shared a stage of the Brooklyn Fox Theatre in Brooklyn, New York, with Peter & Gordon, Wilson Pickett, the Fortunes, and the McCoys.

In December alone, the Moodies are known to have performed at least 47 shows in three different countries (England, Scotland, and America).

The Moodies also appeared again on U.S. TV for ABC's *Shindig*, this time for the December 30 episode.

(Source: MurrayTheK.com)

Due to popular demand, the Murray the K Xmas Show had became the Murray the K New Year's Show. The Moodies, the McCoys, the Fortunes, and Wilson Pickett stayed on, and were joined by the Toys, Lenny Welch, and Cannibal and the Headhunters. Each of the acts played four shows a day.

Ray Thomas said, "That first American trip was a complete fuck-up. We were assured that we were going to do the *Ed Sullivan Show*, and to pay for the trip we were booked to play on the bill of Murray the K's Christmas show at the Fox Theatre in Brooklyn. We were supposed to use the fee from those shows to pay for the trip and the idea was that the TV exposure we'd get from the Sullivan show would help us get to a huge American audience. When we arrived in New York they took our visas off us at the airport because the paperwork wasn't correct and the immigration people said we shouldn't have got them. This meant that we couldn't do any television work, but as we were liable to do the live shows with Murray the K, we were able to do those concerts. Basically, we were in the States for a month for *nothing*. All the hotel bills and air fares were paid, but we got bugger all!" (RT-MMCD15)

Denny Laine: "If we'd have done the *Ed Sullivan Show*, I think we would have probably been a lot bigger at that period of time. For me, it was a huge let-down in a way, because everybody else who did the *Ed Sullivan Show* sort of shot to the top, and we'd missed out on that. It left me very disappointed." (DL-MMCD15)

One might wonder if it was possible for a savvy pop manager like Brian Epstein could have dropped the ball so badly. He certainly knew a thing or two about work visas in the U.S., having made the trip numerous times with his other artists. So what happened?

Victor Riesel, a syndicated newspaper columnist based in New York City, was looking into the situation. He wrote:

> Who is "Them"? If you don't know who "Them" is, you definitely don't know what the "Moody Blues" are. So you're not "camp" – which is a junior's way of saying "hep."

> Them and the Moody Blues are rock and roll sensations in England.

They're having difficulties getting into the U.S. on any basis, including, if you will pardon the expression, a cultural exchange.

And who are the cultural arbiters? Who actually rules on who can come and sing and entertain the young (and the old)? Who sets the rules on whether the Blues – and even the Beatles and any other "alien workers" – can enter the U.S.?

The rules should be interpreted by the Justice Dept. or the Labor Dept. But no, this government power, affecting hundreds of millions of dollars worth of business, has literally been taken over by a brace of unions.

These unions are the arbiters. These unions have set up special kangaroo courts in their national headquarters in New York. Into these chambers, day after day, troop the managers and attorneys of the foreign artists, singers, players, rock and rollers, acts of all sorts – be it the Beatles or the Thems....

And any force which has the power to regulate the Beatles is an awesome power indeed, even in the days of Them and the Moody Blues....

Epstein caught a flight to New York to see what he could do to salvage the Moodies' first trip to the States.

The January 8, 1966 issue of *Record Mirror* reported:

Brian Epstein flew to America on Tuesday to visit the Moody Blues and negotiate business deals. The Moodies are having two tracks from their British LP released as a single in the U.S....

Before they return home on January 17, the Moodies will record six TV shows in Los Angeles after their session at the Brooklyn Fox Theatre.

The solution, as indicated in the *Record Mirror* report, was to get the Moodies as far away from New York's musician and labor unions as possible Therefore, Epstein sent them west to tape segments for less-prestigious and less-viewed American series ... such as the

Brian Epstein appeared on camera to introduce the Moody Blues for a 1965 episode of *Hullaballoo*.
(Hullaballoo Enterprises / NBC-TV Network)

afternoon tiny teeny-bopper show, *Where the Action Is*. A step up was an appearance on the January 10 episode of *Hullaballoo*, also beamed from Hollywood across the nation. But neither series could shoot a star into orbit like Ed Sullivan.

U.S. single release:
"Stop!" b/w "Bye Bye Bird"
London 9810, January 1966
U.S. peak position: # 89 (*Record World*)

Based on expectations that the Moody Blues would take the stage of *The Ed Sullivan Show* in late December 1965, London Records greeted the New Year with a new single by the group.

You may recall that London had removed four songs from *The Magnificent Moodies* album before creating its own LP, re-titled *Go Now: The Moody Blues #1*, for American release. Two of these – the Pinder/Laine originals "Stop!" and "Thank You Baby" – were saved for single release later in the year. By then the album track "Bye Bye Bird" had been receiving a fair amount of attention outside of America. It was an audience favorite whenever performed by the Moodies in England and on the European Continent, and was featured on television numerous times to cheers and applause. As a result of all the hoopla across the Atlantic, London decided to drop "Thank You Baby" (preventing the song's release in the U.S. until inclusion on a remastered CD version of *The Magnificent Moodies* decades later) replacing it with "Bye Bye Bird," making for a double A-side. Despite the popularity of the song outside of the U.S., "Bye Bye Bird" was too offbeat and manic for American radio tastes at this time. It was also six months old, having been available in the U.S. on *Go Now: The Moody Blues #1* during all that time. Therefore, U.S. DJs favored "Stop!"

For its January 22, 1966 issue, *Cashbox* picked "Stop!" as the side with the most radio potential, saying:

> The Moody Blues are odds-on favorites to get back in their previous money-making ways with this power-packed newie tabbed "Stop!" The cut is a tender, medium-paced blueser about a romantic triangle with some interestingly off-beat pounding bursts. The coupler, "Bye Bye Bird," is a rollicking, fast-moving, mostly instrumental stanza.

On the same day, *Billboard* deemed the single as a double-A-side, but predicted that the latest Moody Blues disc would *not* make it into its Top 20 chart, despite the quality of the release. It would have to settle for Top 60 honors, said the trade, despite the plug:

One of their strongest entries in some time. Original off-beat material with catchy lyric and rhythm arrangement should spiral *them* rapidly up the chart.

Not rapidly, or far enough. The trade was wrong in its Top 60 prediction for the two tracks. "Bye Bye Bird" missed the charts entirely in the U.S., and "Stop!" barely registered in the Top 100, with *Billboard*, *Cashbox* and *Record World* showing its peak position to be No. 98, 93, and 89, respectively.

One area where "Stop!" did better was in the state of New York, particularly in New York City. The two big Top 40 stations in the Big Apple at this time were WABC and WMCA. When they heard that the Moodies were to perform their new single on the Sullivan show, both jumped on the record. WABC took the song to No. 12 on April 2. WMCA did it one position better, not stopping "Stop!" until it reached No. 11 on March 17. Outside of New York City, in Syracuse, New York, station WOLF made "Stop!" a Top 10 hit, on April 9, with the survey placing it at No. 7. And this was just a small indication of what could have happened if the New York musicians union had allowed the Moodies to keep their date with Ed Sullivan.

The Moodies were on the radio in England, too, but not with a new record. Instead, thanks to a deal arranged by Brian Epstein and Decca, a new group composition was woven into the hook line of the current Coca-Cola jingle. It's a catchy one-minute recording, with the Coca-Cola Company giving the Moodies more radio play than they'd had in several months.

The grind continued. In February 1966, the Moody Blues traveled to France where, two months earlier, Decca had issued "Bye Bye Bird" b/w "I'll Go Crazy" as a single (nearly coinciding with the release of "Bye Bye Bird" b/w "Stop!" in the U.S.). When the Moodies arrived, to everyone's surprise, the band discovered that "Bye Bye Bird" had flown up the charts.

Ray Thomas: "We had an offer through NEMS to go and play in France. However, this French promoter … said, 'Since "Go Now," they haven't had a hit in France.' And the money wasn't that good. He'd pay our expenses but would also get people thinking about the Moody Blues again over there, so we agreed to do it. When we got to Charles de Gaulle Airport, it was packed with photographers and reporters. We had been No. 1 with 'Bye Bye Bird' and didn't know that the French record company had released it! This guy got this No. 1 act for peanuts to play all over France – so he was laughing his socks off!" (RT-RS15)

As in many countries, there was more

than one single music chart ranking record sales and radio play. One online source lists SNEP (Syndicat National de l'Édition Phonographique) as the chart which listed "Bye Bye Bird" at No. 1 in early 1966. Wikipedia reports that the song made it to No. 3 in France, but without a citation to identify which chart listed it at this position.

In England, the Moodies' live shows continued throughout March, April, and May. In May alone, the Moodies are known to have played no less than 28 engagements, which included another trip to France, with a 14-day tour.

Meanwhile, Brian Epstein was stretching himself further. It was reported in the June 18, 1966 issue of *Billboard* that Epstein had taken on an American group – the Cyrkle ("Red Rubber Ball" and "Turndown Day"), adding to his British stable which currently included Gerry & the Pacemakers, Billy J. Kramer, Cilla Black, The Big Three, the Fourmost, the Applejacks, Tommy Quickly, Sounds Incorporated, the Moody Blues, and, of course, the Beatles. And now, by having the Cyrkle open for the Beatles, he was helping to jumpstart the American group's career.

Why them and not the Moodies? Epstein was actually being somewhat crafty in including the Cyrkle in the shows to get around the New York musician's union and other possible labor issues in the States. Since the Cyrkle was an American band, it would be harder for the unions to get an injunction against the concerts, thereby allowing the Beatles to clean up.

Despite missing out on a U.S. tour, the Moody Blues were still working relentlessly on the stage, including more shows planned for Denmark, France, and Belgium in July. But with their recording prospects so dismal, the band began to come apart.

On June 28, the *Daily Mirror* reported that Clint Warwick had quit the group in order to spend more time with his family and search for a proper job.

The July 2, 1966 issue of *Disc and Music Echo* confirmed:

> CLINT WARWICK, Moody Blues bass guitarist, is leaving the group. He decided this week that group work is keeping him apart from his wife and two small children too much.

Warwick told *Record Mirror*, "The travels have kept me away from home too long, and I feel this is unfair to my wife and family." (CW-RM66)

Denny Laine: "[T]he minute he left, of course, the band wasn't as good anyway. He was no fantastic bass player, but he had a style, and he did good harmonies; most of them, in fact. I used to work them out, but he was good at doing what he did." (DL-H&H97)

In the July 14 edition of London's entertainment trade *The Stage*, it was reported that 21-year-old Rod Clarke had been recruited as the Moodies' new bass player. He had previously played with Les Garcons.

Denny Laine: "I know he wasn't around for long. He was a good bass player. He used to be in a really good band in Birmingham…. Like anything else, it would have taken time for him to fit in." (DL-H&H97)

Despite the changes in the band, and their poor showing on the record charts, the Moody Blues continued to work tirelessly through an exhaustive series of live engagements. In August of 1966, they were again one of the opening acts for the touring Walker Brothers.

The August 27 edition of *Record Mirror* narrated the Moodies busy schedule:

> … On August 28, they fly to Paris for the *Music Hall De France* TV shows and, on September 10, play a concert near Amsterdam and do another TV show. The following day (11), they move to Brussels for more TV work.
>
> Their next LP, tentatively titled "Lookout," should be ready for October release and a single, probably self-penned, will follow shortly.
>
> Their British dates include Tenbury Wells Riverside (September 3), Bexley Black Prince (4), Trent Bridge Rowing Club (18), recording *This Must Be the Place* (21) and *Saturday Club* (24).

In other words, just another typical month for the Moodies – trying to squeeze recording sessions in between concerts and TV appearances, but never getting enough time in the studio to really advance their career.

For the October 6 edition of *Record Mirror*, Richard Green wrote:

> Pride is a fine thing to have, but sometimes it can be a great hindrance, as the Moody Blues are beginning to realize. In fact, they blame their pride for their lack of hits lately.

Mike Pinder told Green, "We don't want to record anything just to get in the chart. We've got to the stage where we know exactly what type of music we like and it's what I suppose you can call quality stuff, but that's not the kind of thing you can put on a single. We've done most of it for an LP, which will be out soon."

Green interjected:

> Two numbers the Moodies have recently written and recorded are "This Is My House" and the up-tempo "Really Haven't Got the Time," which sounds like a sure-fire hit. Unfortunately, it looks as though neither will be out on singles.

He asked why the band didn't ask Lennon and McCartney to write a song for them to release as a single, as every other act represented by Brian Epstein had. Billy J. Kramer had made it to No. 1 in the U.K. with "Bad to Me," and to No. 2 with "Do You Want to Know a Secret?" (released before the Beatles included it on one of their albums), No. 4 with "I'll Keep You Satisfied," and No. 10 with "From a Window." The Fourmost had made it into the Top 10 with "Hello Little Girl," then hit again, in the Top 20, with "I'm in Love." Cilla Black made the Top 10 twice thanks to the Beatles' castoffs, with "Love of the Loved" and "It's For You." The Applejacks made the Top 20 with "Like Dreamers Do." And Silkie saw the Top 20 with "You've Got to Hide Your Love Away." These were just the acts handled by Epstein!

Peter & Gordon, not repped by Eppy, but in good company with the Beatles because Paul McCartney was dating Peter Asher's sister, Jane, seemed to make a career from that happenstance. They got into the Top 20 with "I Don't Want to See You Again" and "Woman," then the Top 10 with "Nobody I Know," and hit No. 1 on both sides of the Atlantic with "World Without Love," all Lennon/McCartney songs. At the time, the Rolling Stones too were struggling, unable to make it into the Top 20, so their pals John and Paul helped out, giving them "I Wanna Be Your Man" before Ringo ever sang it. The song took the Stones to No. 12.

Other groups had pilfered Beatles LP cuts which the Fab Four chose not to release as singles. The Overlanders did it, and got to No. 1 with "Michelle" during the same week when David and Jonathan made the Top 20 with the same song. Cliff Bennet made the Top 10 with "Got to Get You into My Life." And the Hollies got into the Top 20 with a George Harrison-penned song, "If I Needed Someone."

The Beatles hadn't forgotten the Moodies. Paul McCartney had tried to interest the Moodies in recording "Those Were the Days," but the group felt the song wasn't right for them. McCartney waited two years, and then produced it as a single for Apple recording artist Mary Hopkins. It went to No. 1 in both the U.K. and the States.

Graeme Edge told Richard Green, "We were offered some songs they wrote, but we turned them down. It was a difficult thing to do. There's always a stigma attached to people who record Beatles songs. I wonder why! People like the Overlanders who have a go at the Beatles are being ridiculous." (GE-RM66)

As Richard Green had said, pride can be a great hindrance. All of Epstein's acts had been successful while under NEMS's management umbrella with one exception – the Moody Blues. And only the Moody Blues had refused the help of Lennon and McCartney. One can only imagine that Epstein was feeling as much frustration as the Moodies … even a fair amount of professional embarrassment. After all, he had a reputation as the pop manager with the Midas touch. Laine/Pinder seemed to want to prove that they could be a Lennon/McCartney in their own right. And this must have irked "Uncle Eppy" even further. Perhaps this was why the group's last single release in Britain – "Everyday" – had been nearly one year earlier.

This was a band that dearly wanted what the Beatles now had – ample time in the studio to make worthwhile recordings for both album and single release, instead of trying to squeeze recording sessions in between seemingly endless live performance dates. Even now, they were planning yet another trip to France.

Graeme Edge told Green, "It's funny, we've never tired of doing 'Bye Bye Bird.' It's still in the charts in France and everyone on the Continent seems to like it. We get more singles out over there than we do here. Our last single here was last October, called 'Everyday.' Can you remember that far back?" (GE-RM66)

Pop music consumers seemed not to.

Richard Green concluded:

> So it looks as though there still might not be a Moody Blues single
> for some time, which is a pity. I'm certain that they'd have a hit
> with "Really Haven't Got the Time." …

For the proposed second album, "Lookout," the Moodies had nearly enough songs in the can – eleven total, including the aforementioned Mike Pinder song, "I Really Haven't Got the Time," a piano rocker with Pinder singing lead. Green was right, it felt like a hit.

Also recorded from April through September 1966 were several Pinder/Laine originals. The electric folk song, "People Gotta Go" would see release in January 1967 on a French EP (*Boulevard de Madeleine*). Future single releases included "Boulevard," "This Is My House (But Nobody Calls)," "Life's Not Life," and "He Can Win." Left in the Decca vault for five decades were the melodic "Sad Song"; the entertaining oddities "Jago & Jilly" and "Red Wine"; and what may have been a commentary on the state of affairs in the band, thinly disguised as a rocking love song, "We're Broken." All were Pinder/Laine compositions. The only cover they recorded during this time sounded like a surefire hit – a rocking version of a Tim Hardin song, "How Can We Hang on to a Dream." It was arranged to fit the groove of "Go Now!," with pounding piano and bass, and a honky-tonk piano instrumental break, all sweetened with the unmistakable Moody Blues choir of background singers. Top 20 was written all over the track, and yet Decca let it and the other songs remain hidden for decades until the reissue of *The Magnificent Moodies* with bonus tracks galore.

Perhaps one track shy of an album, Denny Laine gave notice.

On October 8, 1966, Ray Thomas was quoted in English music trade *Record World*, saying, "Denny left on Saturday and we´re not sure what we're going to do. We´re waiting to see Brian Epstein to talk things over with him." (RT-RW66)

A short while later, Graeme Edge recalled, "At the time, we put the split with Denny down to diverse musical tastes, but in fact it had got to the point where we were gradually hating the sight of one another. Denny decided that the time had come to break with us, go solo and become a star! He gave us four days' notice, but left after three. So there we were with a book full of bookings and left stranded. I think that secretly we were all glad really about the break, because every single day there was a punch up, and always about work. A very delicate period." (GE-R68)

Laine told his side of it in an interview with Moody Blues fanzine *Higher & Higher*: "I was wanting to go into the studio. I wasn't content to just carry on this gig, just to bring money in. Our management thing had all fallen apart. We'd gone with Epstein and that was a disaster. Even though we got a lot of work out of Brian Epstein, as a manager, he didn't have the time to do anything for us. We didn't have that same sort of attention [as the Beatles, Gerry & the Pacemakers, and Billy J. Kramer did]....

"Prior to that, we had our own company that managed us, and various others after us, but we were their solo thing. That was it; that's how come we made it; there was always that going on." (DL-HH97)

Elsewhere, Laine elaborated: "I sort of got tired of it and wanted to go into the studio again and make another album, because we weren't doing too well after the first album. It started to trickle, but it didn't do really well. And all they wanted to do was go to Germany and go to Europe and France – because we were quite big in France – and just work. And I said, 'We've got to go in the studio. We owe them an album.' Otherwise, we were gonna lose this three-album deal. So I said, 'Well, okay, I'm not going to do all of that. I'm going off and do some new recording.' I was still friendly with them; I didn't fall out with them. And I went off and started doing my own thing, and then they were forced to go into the studio to do *Days of Future Passed*." (DL-G10)

It is believed Denny Laine's final day with the Moody Blues was October 1, 1966.

More bad news: the Moodies were about to be without representation.

Graeme Edge, speaking of Epstein's "ever-growing musical stable," said they all fit into one happy category: "The kind of people NEMS never had to push; rather people [such as concert promoters and music reporters] came to them. So they'd never had to sell a group to the public, and they just couldn't get us off the ground." (GE-R68)

Brian Epstein, towering above his three biggest acts (L-R): No. 1 in popularity, the Beatles, followed by Gerry & the Pacemakers, and then Billy J. Kramer & the Dakotas. Was there room for the Moodies?
(Image: rebeatmagzine.com; tumblr.com; forums.stevenhoffman.com; eilatgordinlevitan.com)

The constant low-paying tours had been wearing the band down. And playing for small fees in France after the surprise success there of "Bye Bye Bird" was still sticking in the craw of at least one band member.

Ray Thomas said, "We were pissed off, and so when we got back [from France] we went and saw Brian and told him that he was the head of a crap organization. And he threw us out of his house. He called a meeting for the following day with all his heads of department – publicity, [booking] agency – and we sat there with all the heads of departments, and Brian was there. We always got along with Brian and he was a real gentleman. Brian banged on the table and went around asking all his department heads what they'd done about all this. They all stared at the floor and said nothing. Then he banged on the table again with his fist and said, 'It appears that the boys are right – I'm head of a crap organization!' Then Brian said to us, 'What do you want?' We said, 'Can we have our contract back?' So he said, 'Go and get their contract.' And he ripped it up in front of us, and said, 'There you go. And good luck.' He could have kept us under contract and that would have been crap. So, we said, 'Thank you very much, Brian,' and left." (RT-RS15)

It's been reported that the split between Epstein and the Moodies occurred on October 12, but it was actually later than that. Justin Hayward recalled that Epstein was still managing the band when he joined, and for a brief period afterward. This was likely because the gentlemanly Epstein continued to look after the band, in the interim, as they attempted to reorganize and find new management. He had also already arranged for another single to be released by Decca, and, as he had done with "Everyday," had Decca place a big "A" on the side he felt should be promoted. Once again, Uncle Eppy's ear for a hit proved to be tone deaf.

As happened with the misspelling of "Lose Your Money" on the Decca 45 (as "Loose Your Money"), the record label's proofreaders missed catching "Madeleine" printed as "Madelaine."

U.K. single release:
"Boulevard de la Madeleine" b/w "This Is My House (But Nobody Calls)"
Decca F.12498; October 7, 1966

U.S. single release:
45-LON 1005; October 7, 1966
Peak position: #112 (*Cashbox*)

With the success of "Bye Bye Bird," albeit not on British or U.S. shores, Epstein and Decca decided to issue a single culled from the tracks the Moody Blues had been recording for their second album. It was hoped that "Boulevard de la Madeleine" could capitalize on the French success of "Bye Bye Bird." The B-side, "This Is My House (But Nobody Calls)," was one of the two songs Richard Green of *Record Mirror* had heard and picked as possible hits.

Both songs were Pinder/Laine originals, and featured Laine on lead vocals. "Boulevard," was smooth and melodic, ripe for packaging as a hit – with proper promotion and support from a band that wasn't fracturing.

Ray Thomas said, "Denny wrote 'Boulevard' when we got big in France. We stayed on the Parisian West Bank, and we recorded it there. But the French hated it, because, although we didn't know it, Boulevard De La Madeleine was their red light district! They thought we were singing about picking up hookers." (RT-SM15)

Ironically, the true gem was on the B-side, and might have ensured a return trip to the Top 20 for the Moodies – if any DJs heard it. The rollicking "This Is My House (But Nobody Calls") has the "Go Now!" sound stamped all over it, and was the most accessible and enjoyable recording by the band since that No. 1 hit.

The "Boulevard de la Madeleine"/"This Is My House" single was issued on October 7, 1966.

On October 22, *Record Mirror* said:

Distinct Continental sounds early on here, then it goes into a straight sort of beater. But it's different enough to restore the Moodies to the charts – they still have a substantial following. Well sung, too. Flip is much meatier and more to their usual style. Nice beat.

With a review combined with a news update, Mark Gardner wrote:

> I was unable to track down any of the Moodies for personal interviews. NEMS said: "Frankly, we don't know where Denny Laine is or what his plans are."
>
> "Boulevard de la Madelaine" is a suitably melancholy farewell. It has a typically plaintive vocal from Denny.
>
> Apparently, he and co-composer Mike Pinder penned the song last spring while they were marooned in a Paris hotel gazing dejectedly out of the window at the rain-soaked, wind-battered boulevard.

DJ's copy of the latest Moody Blues single, with the B-side marked by hand as the side to play.
(Image source: 45cat.com)

> The introduction sounds like French café music, complete with accordion. An altogether curious performance.
>
> Another Pinder-Laine song, "This Is My House," is the flipside. Fast and furious, it's a much better number than the "A" and might have stood a chance of making an impression if the coupling had been switched….

Days later, this report came out (provenance unknown):

> Today I am writing the obituary of The Moody Blues, a group that in its day was the most successful to be spawned by the Brumbeat movement.
>
> Guitarist-lead-singer-songwriter Denny Laine has decided to quit the outfit and embark on a solo career.
>
> Denny is virtually irreplaceable and the decision, I fear, will certainly spell the breakup of The Moodies. You can take it that

their just-released single, "Boulevard de la Madeleine" (Decca F.12498), is the last page in the story.

I spoke to Brian Epstein's NEMS Enterprises Ltd., which signed the unit over a year ago. No definite statement was made, the official comment being: "Denny Laine has broken away from the group, who are now taking no engagements in the United Kingdom. The position is fluid at the moment. The Moodies may or may not reform."

Presumably if another Denny Laine could be found they would stay in business, but artists of Laine's talent don't grow on trees.

Why was this excellent group allowed to founder after such a promising start? Why were so many of their later singles sub-standard? Why was their name allowed to vanish from print and mind? These are the questions fans will be asking. Something has clearly gone seriously wrong between January 1965, when the Moody Blues topped the chart with "Go Now," and October, 1966, when the writing is starkly on the wall.

The A-side went nowhere fast. In America, radio programmers preferred the B-side, but too few stations picked it up and the song only bubbled under the Top 100 charts, with *Billboard*, *Cashbox* and *Record World* calling its best show as No. 119, 112, and 114, respectively.

They'd tell you differently in the big state of Texas. At radio station KFJZ, "This Is My House" reached No. 15 on August 14. And they liked the song in the Big Apple. On WMCA, "This Is My House" peaked at No. 37. Things looked better in Syracuse, New York, where WOLF took the song to No. 27 (on July 2), and, in Buffalo, N.Y., where radio station WYSL ranked it at No. 13 on July 24. They loved the record in Cleveland, Ohio. Of the two Top 40 stations there, WIXY charted "This Is My House" at No. 18 on September 12. Two weeks earlier, station WKYL brought the record all the way to No. 6.

We told you it had "hit" written all over it. Critic Mark Gardner did too.

Even with this chart activity, the Moodies nonetheless found themselves minus two members.

Asked why the band, less than two years after a No. 1 hit single, had fallen apart, Ray Thomas answered, "Well, bands are complicated things. It's probably better to ask how they've stayed together, if they have, rather than how they fell apart! On the whole, they're just like 'real people.' So, you're all walking the same road together and then one says, 'It looks really interesting over there; I'm gonna take the next turning.' And another says, 'I really like it here, I think I'll stay put.' And you say, 'I'm happy going in this direction.' That's what happens, isn't it? Anyway, back to the point! So, Denny wanted to pursue a solo career and Clint didn't want to tour at all anymore and went back to running the family business in Birmingham. Well, Mike and I wanted to go on, so it was up to us to find, well, a John and a Justin – which we did, fortunately." (RT- AC15)

101

6

Reformation – The Moody Blues, Mark 2

**The new Moody Blues, circa 1967, performing "Fly Me High" during U.K. TV appearance.
Left to right: Graeme Edge, Justin Hayward, Ray Thomas, John Lodge, and Mike Pinder.**
(Photo source: Alamy Stock Photo)

Denny Laine was out of the band. They were no longer under Brian Epstein's aegis. Under such circumstances, it wasn't surprising that spirits were low. Rod Clark left the disintegrating group for one which seemed to have better prospects – the Rockin' Berries. The remaining Moodies – Pinder, Thomas and Edge – were doubtful if they should continue.

Graeme Edge told Pamela Holman of *New Musical Express*, "Some of our smart London friends dropped us. We became a little bitter but wiser. Denny Laine left; he felt we were holding him back. Finally, the group split up." (GE-NME71)

Pinder found a desk job working for Ember Records. Thomas hadn't yet decided what he was going to do. Meanwhile, Edge was planning on lugging his drums to France where "Bye Bye Bird" had been a hit.

He said, "I got my drums on my back and had a booking on the ferry to France. The others had agreed to let me keep the name – they didn't care. My plan was to go to

Paris, engage four French musicians on low wages and tour the Continent. The name was still fairly big there and I figured I could make a fast buck on one-night stands before word got around that we were selling them short. Then Ray said he'd like to come along with me as he had nothing else to do, and I next heard from Mike who had packed in the £20 a week job he'd got, and who wanted to come too." (GE-NME71)

Pinder had taken a look at his budget: His living expenses, minus food, were 21 pounds, 12 shillings. His pay at Ember Records left him a pound and a half short each week.

Edge said, "This, of course, killed my brilliant plan for a smash-and-grab Continental tour – there wouldn't be much left after a three-way split. However, it did occur to me that here we did have the nucleus of a good band.

"So we got in touch with Johnny, who had finished college and gone professional with a band that was getting nowhere. He agreed to come along." (GE-NME71)

Catching Up with John Lodge:
His Time in Mark Stuart & the Crestas, and the Carpetbaggers

The Carpetbaggers (L-R): Big Al Johnson, Malcolm Bourne, John Lodge, and Rob Sheward. (Courtesy Tony Brown)

Throughout 1964, while Mike Pinder and Ray Thomas were performing with the Krew Kats in Hamburg, Germany, John Lodge remained in Birmingham and attended the Institute of Advanced Technology (now Astor University), where he was working toward an engineering degree. But Lodge hadn't abandoned music entirely: nights and weekends he played with the established Birmingham rhythm & blues band – Mark Stuart & the Crestas.

The band had originally been led by Micky Harris, and was merely called the Crestas. As Harris became less available for the low-paying gigs, rhythm guitarist Brian

Yates (with a name change to what he believed was the more-marquee-friendly Mark Stuart) assumed lead vocals.

At around this time, in February 1964, Dial Records in England put out an album called *Brum Beat*, featuring 14 Birmingham bands, performing one song each. The LP rear crowed that the sampler included "Birmingham's fourteen greatest groups." Mark Stuart and the Crestas were one, with "St. Louis Blues." Another song, the Senators' "She's a Mod," featured a young, pre-Led Zeppelin John Bonham on drums.

But none of the bands that included pre-Moody Blues members appeared. Their acts – El Riot and the Rebels; Gerry Levine and the Avengers; and Denny Laine and the Diplomats, with Nicky James – had either disbanded or were in a state of transition when the album was recorded.

Brum Beat sold fair in Birmingham, but not so well in other parts of Britain, and the anticipated "Brumbeat-mania" never materialized. In disappointment, many of the bands featured on the album fell apart, while others underwent personnel changes. Mark Stuart & the Crestas, for example, were soon minus a bass player. They invited John Lodge from the recently disbanded El Riot and the Rebels. He accepted the offer, but it was a short stay. The Crestas had already lost their momentum and soon fell apart.

In the summer of 1964, at the time the Moody Blues left Birmingham for London (another trip which young John Lodge had declined), the bass guitarist reunited with former El Riot and the Rebels drummer Rob Sheward, as well as organist/pianist Malcolm Bourne and pianist Big Al Johnson, to form a new band. Johnson, who was friendly with American rock 'n' roll singer Gene Vincent ("Be-Bop-A-Lula"), on tour in England at this time, traveled to London to visit with his old friend on the day of a *Thank Your Lucky Stars* appearance. Johnson brought his star-struck bandmates along to meet Vincent. They came upon him reading a book in the studio canteen. After introductions were made, Johnson asked Vincent if he'd like to recommend a name for the new band. Vincent said, "I've got just the name for you. Believe me, it's a good one." He then turned the book over on the table. It was Harold Robbins's *The Carpetbaggers*.

The John Bull Breed (John Lodge, standing, fourth from left). (Photo source: TheMoodyBlues.co.uk)

Lodge remained with the Carpetbaggers for about a year. The group gigged often, including opening for the Animals. They cut a demo disc, pairing a cover of Little Richard's "Tutti Frutti" with a John Lodge original, "Blues Stay Away from Me" (the latter of which can be found on *Classic Artists: The Moody Blues*).

By mid-1965, the Carpetbaggers had run their course. Lodge lost no time, reconnecting with Brian Yates (aka Mark Stuart) to form a new band, the John Bull Breed.

The group caught on fast in the Birmingham area and was soon finding bookings outside of the city. For an article in Birmingham's *Sunday Mercury* (October 1965, exact date not known), Mark Gardner reported that the "J.B.B.'s" Liverpool-based agent was keeping the band "on the move to all points on the compass," including surrounding English towns and cities, plus trips into Scotland, Ireland, and across the channel to the Continent. Yates told Gardner, "We are able to command much larger fees outside Birmingham. Eire [Ireland] is one of our favorite touring spots. We were in Dublin a couple of weeks back and, on the strength of our performance, have been booked for an Irish TV show in December."

The group had also played Hamburg. While most British bands returned from Germany with tales of the low pay, exhausting work, and deplorable accommodations, Stuart remained upbeat: "It was a ball! We enjoyed every minute and, after Christmas, we are going back for another four weeks on the Star Club circuit." (BY-SM65)

By the end of the year, the John Bull Breed was picked as the Midland's most popular band in a newspaper poll. The *Sunday Mercury* reported:

> A sweeping victory for the John Bull Breed in the group category is the shock result of the *Sunday Mercury*'s 1965 Pop Poll. The Breed's fans saw to it that their favorite polled 43 percent of the total votes cast – a sensational win for the Birmingham sextet.

> Their nearest rivals were the Johnny Neal Group (12 percent) and the Spencer Davis Group (11 percent), who just beat the Berries (nine percent) for third place.

> But members of the John Bull Breed also scored heavily in the individual [categories]. Vocalist Mark Stuart was No. 1 male singer, while Michael Heard (lead guitar), John Lodge (bass-guitar), and Graham Hose (drums) all topped their respective categories....

So did Terry Guy, the group's organist/pianist.

More comparisons: Stuart had more than triple the votes of Steve Winwood in the singing category (50 to 13 percent). Guitarist Michael Heard polled 44% of the ballots as lead guitarist, to Winwood's 7%. And Terry Guy trampled Winwood as top organist/pianist 45 to 9%. Yet, in less than a year, the Spencer Davis Group, with Winwood, would be charting hits on both side of the Atlantic.

Winning the Pop Poll ensured the John Bull Breed a recording contract, and Polydor Records was quick to sign the group, now expanded to seven members.

On May 6, 1966, Polydor issued "Can't Chance a Breakup" b/w "I'm a Man" (not the Yardbird's 1965 hit of the same title, or the Spencer Davis Group's 1967 hit, also called "I'm a Man").

Getting an advance copy of the disc, Mark Gardner wrote in the May 1, 1966 edition of Birmingham's *Sunday Mercury*:

> The Breed's single (BM56065) is, I think, the best of the batch [of Birmingham group releases] so far. With a six-man backing,

vocalist Brian Yates gets solid support on the beauty "A" side. Soaring tenor-sax spot keeps the temperature up and the overall sound is crisp and clean.

Despite the plug, the song failed to chart, and the band was soon headed back to Hamburg for nightclub gigs.

Considering the title of the A-side, "Can't Chance a Breakup," it was ironic that the band would dissolve only a few months after the release of the single.

Lodge said, "We went to Germany... but we all got fed up because it wasn't happening. There were seven of us and we couldn't get musical ideas together; there were too many people, so we came home and split up." (JL-NME70a)

Polydor recording artists, briefly, now expanded to seven members (with John Lodge on the left).
(Courtesy Tony Brown)

The timing of the breakup was actually good for Lodge. Only a short while later, an old friend called.

John Lodge: "Ray rang me up and said, 'Denny's leaving the band and Clint's [left] the band.... Have you finished college? Can we get another band together?' And I said, 'Yeah, that's a great idea.' And I don't think we were going to call it the Moody Blues.... We thought of another name, [but I forget], it's gone now." (JL-TS83)

At this time, Eric Burdon was replacing dropouts from his band, the Animals. Ray Thomas said, "I was sitting at a club in London... and I was talking to Eric Burdon of the Animals. Eric had been advertising in one of the trade magazines for a guitarist/singer. He was putting the new Animals together at the same time [as we were reorganizing the Moodies]. He said, 'Since I put an ad in the paper, I found the guy I want.... All I put in my ad was, "Top recording band seeks guitarist/singer." They won't know what band it is, [not] from the ad, anyway. If you want to come around to the office tomorrow you can have all the replies. And that's how we found Justin – a little bit of fate." (RT-RS15)

John Lodge recalled that, although he had talked to Ray Thomas earlier about joining the band, his actual induction happened at around the same time that Justin Hayward came onboard. He said, "I went down to London and we decided to put the band together, and Ray said, 'We found this guy called Justin. Shall we go and meet him?'" (JL-TS83)

Graeme Edge said of Hayward, "We put a guitar in his hand and said, 'Play!' And he did.... He played us three of his songs. We dug him, liked his personality; he was a nice looking cat and we liked his taste in music." (GE-R68)

Justin Hayward

David Justin Hayward
was born on October 14, 1946, in
Swindon, England. His father
taught mathematics at Sanford
Street School; his mother taught
Domestic Science at Drove Road
School. Hayward had an older
brother and a younger sister, and
began taking piano lessons when he
was six.

Hayward said, "I come
from a church-going family, and I
really used to love the music in
church, especially when I was very
young. I took some piano lessons
but I wasn't clever enough to

**Above: Justin Hayward's childhood home, Dean
Street, Swindon.** (Courtesy Tony Brown)
Below: Young Hayward, circa mid-1950s.
(Photo source: *Sur la mer* inner sleeve)

handle the mathematics of it, so my parents bought me a ukulele, which is what I wanted,
and I learned to play that quickly." (JH-H&H94a)

He recalled, "[W]hen I was a small child, I
remember hearing on the radio a guy called Johnnie
Ray who had a kind of cry in his voice, and I think he
did a song called 'Cry,' actually. He had a wonderful
kind of break in the voice, and it always appealed to
me. And then, also, my family had a very strong faith,
so I was familiar with the tunes and the melodies from
the 'New English Hymnal,' which always resonates
with me. But when I heard Buddy Holly, you know,
my whole life was changed, really. Then I was able to
focus on exactly what I wanted to do."

When he was nine, Hayward acquired his first
acoustic guitar. He said, "I did my first gig with a skiffle group in the church hall in
Swindon when I was 10, which was a lot of fun. But we were crap." (JH-HT97)

Hayward was tall for his age. The extra height enabled him to find work on the
stage as a juvenile actor, although he initially joined a repertory theater group to
accompany a performance on guitar. He said, "I went into rep at Lyme Regis when I was
13. At that time I thought I was going to be in the *Guinness Book of Records* because I
was five-foot-eleven, and a real freak.

"We did a different program every week…. It was the first time I'd really seen
show business and what is was like. The next year I went to Jersey with the same
company in a group called the Offbeats; it was a revue and we'd come on and do our bit.
We were really bad; no one came to see us." (JH-NME70)

From an area newspaper at this time (provenance unknown):

A Swindon teenager, Justin Hayward, of 54 The Mall, who saved the show for a repertory company in Lyme Regis last year, has been asked to perform again this summer.

He was on [summer] holiday [last year] when he learnt that a repertory company at the Marine Theatre was in need of an accompanist, and Justin stepped in with his guitar.

This year he has been asked to sing and the company has also invited the [Offbeats group] with whom Justin sings. …

Last year, in addition to accompanying the performers, Justin also had small parts in plays, including Osric in Shakespeare's *Hamlet*. In one plays Justin played a teddy boy and then rushed off stage to change and reappear as a policemen.

Although the group will be given board and lodging, as well as spending money, the manger, Beverly Doughty (17), said, 'They do not play for the money – purely for the fun of it."

Despite a brush with acting, music was still Hayward's first and greatest love. He said about acting, "Because of what I'd seen in those three years, I'd been turned off it. The opportunities of getting anywhere were nil. I suppose I could have stayed on, but it didn't seem to be leading anywhere at the time." (JH-NME70)

Buddy Holly remained Hayward's greatest influence. He explained, "It's the fact that Buddy was all three – he was a writer and a singer and the guitar player. I knew as a small kid, when I got my first guitar, when I was 10 – so that would be about 1956-57 – that I was never going to be like Elvis, to be able to stand out in front of the group and perform like that. But as soon as I saw Buddy Holly, it all made sense to me, because he could be in the group, not be a sort of flamboyant personality, but write the songs and sing, as well, and it

Above: Justin Hayward (far left) with the Offbeats, circa 1959. (Courtesy Tony Brown)

was a revelation. I think it changed a lot of people – the way a lot of people thought about music." (JH-MBT16)

With Holly serving as a role model, and with renewed enthusiasm, Hayward quit the repertory theatre and the Offbeats, then joined a new band

A clipping from a November 15, 1960 Swindon area newspaper reported:

One of the most successful "rock" groups in Swindon, the Rebels' Rock Group, has just recruited a new vocalist. He is tall, 14-year-old Justin Hayward....

(Courtesy Tony Brown)

The group was founded by Ken Emerson and Jeff Bull, pupils at Headlands Grammar School, almost five years ago as a skiffle group. But they changed their style when skiffle died out....

They have over 100 tunes in their repertoire, and have had engagements as far afield as Birmingham.

Justin, although a new member, is anything but inexperienced. He has played the guitar for a repertory company in Lyme Regis.... The company was in need of an accompanist for a musical called *Boy in the Blue Jeans* they were to perform. As Justin was an accomplished guitar player, he volunteered, and remained to the end of school summer holidays....

In the fanzine *Higher & Higher*, childhood friend Lesley Drewett shared:

I knew Justin when he was 14 years old.... I remember that even then he was a wonderful guitarist and singer.

Justin joined a young rock group called the Rebel Rockers [sic] as lead guitarist and singer, and played at local youth clubs, churches and school halls during lunch break sessions. Even in those days he attracted large crowds of enthusiastic fans and supporters, and vowed that one day he would be famous...."

Drewett recalled Hayward as "quiet, shy, reliable, and honest." (LD-H&H94)

Hayward said, "I started to get serious, and I earned enough between the ages of 11 and 15 to buy a Gibson guitar." (JH-HT97)

While Hayward gained experience as a singer and guitarist, he was about to encounter his next great influence. "We had Cliff [Richards] and the Shadows in about 1960. But still we had to wait until the Beatles in '62 before we knew that the whole world was going to be different, musically.... I remember being at home in Swindon; it would have been [late] 1962 or early 1963... and I heard 'Love Me Do' on the radio, and I can distinctly remember going out of the house and walking down the street and thinking, 'My life is going to be totally different now because the Beatles are in it.' I just knew, from one record; I knew they had a lot more to offer, and, of course, they did.

"They weren't particularly welcomed at the time; I remember there was a chap called Steve Race, who seems to do a lot of music stuff on the 'tellie' and on the radio, and he was very insistent, 'Oh no, they'll never last…. No, no, their kind of music will, you know, never catch on.' And I thought then, 'I really don't like you!,' because the Beatles meant so much to me." (JH-MBT16)

Encouraged by the Beatles' success as performers and songwriters, Hayward took a momentous step. In the last months of 1962, as "Love Me Do" was in the pop charts, Hayward left the Rebel's Rock Group and formed his own band, the Whispers, in which he played guitar and sang lead vocals. By the end of 1963, the group had gained a sizable local following. Peter Antony, writing for *The Swindon and District Review*, summed up the year for the group:

> Six months ago, the name of the Whispers was rarely seen on the Swindon beat scene, yet here was a group with enormous potential and greater musical ability than many beat groups. However, in the annual Rock Group Convention of last year [1962] at the Locarno Ballroom, the judges commented that although the group's ability was evident, it was not being fully exploited.
>
> This has proved to be a milestone in the history of the group, for with two changes in personnel and the appointment of a manager, the Whispers have made rapid strides since the competition and are now held in high regard by most local promoters. It seems fairly certain that early in 1964, the group will be generally accepted as Swindon's top group and the 1964 competition should prove the point. Several of the top groups (the Searchers and the Hollies, for instance) have recently commented very favourably on the group, having seen and heard them perform.
>
> Founder member, lead guitarist and principal vocalist of the group is Justin Hayward, only 17 years old, but without a doubt the most talented guitarist on the local pop music scene…..
>
> To be on top of the local scene is not enough and manager Tony Bowd is confident that the group could hold its own in the professional world of pop music. However, with such an enormous number of professional groups in the business today, entry into the business without a hit record can be very risky. So, the Whispers are due to cut their first disc early in [1964] and a short summer tour is planned, on which the group can gain firsthand experience of the hard life which a tour of one night stands entails.
>
> The Whispers are certain to emerge as the town's top group of 1964 and maybe we shall see a hit record by the group in "the charts" sometime during the year. This would certainly be a fine achievement for the group and a chance for the "Swindon Sound" to take a tilt at the "Mersey Beat."

Hayward later changed the name of the band to All Things Bright when he learned that there were other groups using "Whispers" as their moniker.

Mike Greenland, who played rhythm guitar with All Things Bright, had been a fan of the earlier incarnation, the Whispers. He told interviewer Mark Murley of *Higher & Higher*, "I was pleased to be playing with Justin, as he was quite well known at the time. I used to stand outside the clubs, because I was too young to go inside and listen to him playing. When his offer came up, it was like an offer from the Beatles!" (MG-H&H1994)

Dave Miller, the bass guitarist with All Things Bright, said of the band's 17-year-old front man, "He seemed to always know that he would make it, which is a good thing, because, if you're convinced of it, you've got a better chance of success." (DM-H&H94)

Despite Hayward's assuredness concerning his future prospects, he nonetheless emulated his idol Buddy Holly onstage, maintaining a subdued persona when performing.

Greenland, like fellow band mate Dave Miller, and Hayward's childhood friend Lesley Drewett, remembered Hayward as being "a quite shy fellow, really."

It was October, 1964 when Hayward acquired his first "pro" guitar, a Gibson 335 electric. Its unique tone when played with Hayward's distinctive style created the signature Moody Blues guitar sound on such classics as "Ride My See-Saw," "Lovely to See You," "Gypsy (Of a Strange and Distant Time)," "It's Up to You," "The Story in Your Eyes," and countless others.

It has been reported on the internet that Dave Miller left for a better opportunity, resulting in the breakup of the band. This is not true. From late spring 1965, a Swindon newspaper (provenance unknown) reported:

> All Things Bright, one of Swindon's well known groups, go to Germany this week…. The group had a setback earlier this year when Justin Hayward, their lead guitarist, left them to join the Marty Wilde Trio….

According to the article, Michael Greenland advanced from rhythm guitar to lead, taking Hayward's spot. Dave King was brought in from the Strykneens to replace Hayward as lead vocalist. Nigel Norman handed off the bass chores to Dave Miller, switching over to organ. Chris Richardson remained on drums. The new lineup failed to find success.

Regarding the opportunity to play with Marty Wilde, Hayward said, "I was an avid reader of the *Melody Maker*, and I answered an ad… and it said, 'Guitarist wanted for famed singer.' And I went up to the house in East London, and Marty Wilde opened the door!" (JH-MBT16)

Marty Wilde was a star, and a teen idol. He had experienced success in the late 1950s and early '60s by covering popular

Marty Wilde was one of England's biggest rock 'n' roller teen idols from the late 1950s and early '60s.
(Photo source: LongIslandWeekly.com)

American records for the English market, with several U.K. hits in the Top 20 from 1958-1962.

Hayward said, "Marty was one of the great rock stars in the U.K. in the late '50s and early '60s. He was up there with Cliff Richard. So it was a great privilege to work with him. I was working with 'the master,' really. I was 17 when I joined Marty. He would have been 21. So, really, we were *both* just kids.

"I joined first as a member of his group, the Wildcats, but then Marty wanted to do something that just involved his own songs, and I think he thought the best people for that were myself and Joyce, his wife, who was a member of the Vernons Girls, which was a Liverpool group of backing singers." (JH-CB)

Justin Hayward, Marty Wilde and his wife Joyce, as the Wilde Three.
(Photo source: MartyWilde.com)

From the April 9, 1965 edition of the Swindon *Evening Advertiser*:

> An 18-year-old Swindon guitarist appeared on the stage of the London Palladium last night with pop singer Marty Wilde and his wife Joyce Baker.
>
> Justin Hayward, whose parents, Mr. and Mrs. F.A. Hayward, live at 54 The Mall, is a member of the newly-formed Marty Wilde Trio, which has been in circulation for eight weeks.
>
> Justin's mother, Mrs. G.M. Hayward, told an *Evening Advertiser* reporter: "I went up to the show – the Midnight Stars charity show, which was televised. The feeling of seeing my son there on stage with such stars as [Irish pop singer] Val Doonican and [highest paid English pop singer of the day] Alma Cogan was indescribable…."
>
> The trio has been touring clubs in the North of England, and on April 28 leaves Lyneham RAF station for a tour of the New East, entertaining troops in such places as Cyprus, Tripoli and Benghazi….

Hayward said of his time with Marty Wilde, "[T]hat was a wonderful experience for me. It was kind of a baptism of fire, almost going straight from school to that, sometimes three gigs a night doing clubs."

The initiation included traveling outside of England, a first for the young, shy Hayward. He said, "We did the Middle East. That was when I found out the British weren't really popular [there], for all of the occupying of the Middle East countries that they did." (JH-CB)

113

On April 16, 1965, Decca Records issued a record from the trio – "Since You've Gone," b/w "Just as Long." On September 10 of that year, a second single was issued – "I Cried," b/w "Well Who's That." Neither charted and the Wilde Three (aka the Wilde Trio) soon fell into a routine of road trips to cabaret engagements. To appreciate the experience of playing "cabaret" in Britain of this time, one is best reminded of the words to a 1969 Creedence Clearwater Revival song "Lodi": "If I only had a dollar for ev'ry song I've sung, and ev'ry time I've had to play while people sat there drunk. You know, I'd catch the next train back to where I live."

Hayward said, "We did cabaret, but it was a bit of a drag and, emotionally, it was just so bad." (JH-NME70)

In late 1965, Hayward left the Wilde Three to see if he could do better on his own. He recalled some advice from Wilde: "He told me that to survive in this business you must write your own material. So, from that moment on, like, a 16-year-old kid, I thought, 'Yeah, sounds like a good idea; I'll write songs…' So I became really a songwriter…. I think [Marty] was my single biggest influence." (JH-H&H94)

Lonnie Donegan, known as the "King of Skiffle" … and a "mentor" to Justin Hayward.

Thanks in part to his past association with Wilde, Hayward was able to get an audience with skiffle star Lonnie Donegan, who by now had charted a total of 31 U.K. Top 30 singles spanning 1955 to 1962. Two of his British hits also made the Top 10 in the U.S. – 1955's "Rock Island Line," which made it to No. 8 on both sides of the Atlantic, and 1959's "Does Your Chewing Gum Lose Its Flavor (On the Bedpost Over Night)," a novelty record which made No. 3 in the U.K. and No. 5 in the States.

Donegan recalled, "One day, Justin came to me and said, 'I've written some songs, would you like to hear then?' I said, 'They're fabulous; I'll record them next Sunday.' But he said, 'Oh, no, you don't understand; I haven't written them for you; I've written them for me!' I said to myself that this kid had to be out of his mind, because at that time I only had to spit into a microphone and it was a million seller. But he wanted to do them himself. So, I signed him up." (LD-RC87)

The fact was, Donegan would have had trouble selling anything at this point in his career. His last charting record in the U.K. had been in 1962. He had released nine singles since, none making the charts. Donegan's memory differs from that of Hayward, who has stated that he *did* offer Donegan the songs for recording, but that the former skiffle star was more interested in the publishing rights.

Decades later, Hayward said, "I was offered a publishing contract, which I regret signing because it was a terrible contract, and I'm still bound now. It was a mistake. But I didn't know that. I was a very young boy." (JH-HL98)

Toward the end of 1965, Donegan booked Hayward into a studio, where the now 18-year-old singer/songwriter cut his first single – "London Is Behind Me," b/w "Day Must Come." The A-side was an uptempo song with a hint of country-western, telling the story of a man hitchhiking on the motorway, trying to return to his love. (It can be heard on *Classic Artists: The Moody Blues*.) The B-side, slower and less commercial, was more telling of Hayward's future as a songwriter, with the lyrics:

> *Darkness all around me now*
> *Haunting memories of how*
> *you and I have loved*
> *But now it's over.*
> *Alone at night*
> *without you near,*
> *I can see you oh so clear.*
> *Did you have to leave me here*
> *to remember?*
> *Day must come*
> *and I'll forget you*
> *until the night falls again.*

Donegan used his connections to secure Hayward an agent and, in turn, an offer from Pye Records for a one-off record deal to test his appeal.

On December 31, 1965, "London Is Behind Me" b/w "Day Must Come" was released in the U.K. as Pye 7N 17014. The single was also issued in America by Red Bird (RB 10-049). Martin Wyatt (who much later would produce Hayward's 1985 solo album, *Moving Mountains*) first became aware of the singer at this time. Wyatt, who worked for Pye Records, was assigned the job of trying to break Hayward's first single on radio and in record shops. He told Moody Blue's fanzine *Higher & Higher* that "London Is Behind Me" was not considered a major release for the record label, adding, "Justin was completely unknown. Nobody had ever heard of him, and it was really, really hard work

to try and get anything to happen with the record." (MW-H&H94)

Hayward was hopeful, as any 19-year-old wannabe singer/songwriter would be with a record out. One week before the release of the single, he told the *Daily Mirror*, "If they prove popular there is no knowing what the future may hold. I have recorded the songs and hope their success may help me to branch out and write my own musical." (JH-DM65)

Decades later, Hayward, older and wiser, told *Goldmine* magazine, "I had a record on Pye, that they were gracious enough to release, as a formality, and 'London Is Behind Me' was one of [the sides]. I really wrote 'London Is Behind Me' only to fit in with Lonnie Donegan's band, because that was the kind of tempo that they liked. I knew that I'd be working on that particular session with those musicians, so I wrote something that was in character for their tempo." (JH-GM12)

The single didn't chart and, while a follow-up was recorded in the Pye studio, the record label decided not to put the record into release. However, Parlophone, the Beatles' label, did.

On August 26, 1966, "I Can't Face the World Without You," b/w "I'll Be Here Tomorrow," a pair of love songs, were issued in the U.K. on Parlophone (R 5496).

New Musical Express recommended the up-tempo A-side, describing it as "a self-penned rhythmic ballad, dual-tracked, with a sparkling backing of dancing strings, trombones and a pounding beat."

However, the single failed to click with radio programmers and record dealers. Hayward said, "I found that I just didn't have the drive to make it on my own as a singer. It's terribly lonely being on stage with no one to help you, and you don't know if what you're doing is right." (JH-NME70)

Meanwhile, Hayward was running out of money, prompting him to answer the fateful trade-music ad for a band in need of a guitarist – Eric Burdon's group, the Animals.

Hayward differs with this often-told story. He has stated that while it was an ad that led him to Marty Wilde, this new opportunity came about much differently. He recalled, "I thought of myself mainly as a songwriter and put all my energies into trying to promote my songs. That's how I came to the Moodies. I sent my songs to Eric Burdon, to somebody in his office that I knew; that's how it came to Mike Pinder." (JH-CB)

Burdon had by now filled the spot in his own band and passed the material on to Ray Thomas. Neither Burdon nor Thomas understood that the tape had been made to audition the songs, not the singer, songwriter and guitarist. Regardless, Hayward was hurting for income, and was not in a position to turn down an offer for work. He said, "I had already sold all my clothes and record player the day before I got a phone call from Mike Pinder to join the Moodies." (JH-H&H84)

Elsewhere, Hayward recalled, "I knew [of] the Moodies and was most familiar with Mike Pinder's hands [on the piano keys] because of the record, 'Go Now!' The image I had of them [from seeing them perform on television] was that piano riff and Mike playing the song. I knew that the band was a rhythm & blues band. I was really looking for an outlet for my own songs…. My purpose in coming in to the band was that I might get my songs done by a good band. That was my rationale, then, really. I didn't know the Moodies were even looking for somebody, because I had written to Eric Burdon and sent my songs to him. The call from Mike came completely out of the blue. I had to sort of rethink things very quickly. I was happy to go along with it. I'm not sure in truth that any of the five of us was confident that it would last more than a few months; there was no master plan at the beginning, or any plan at all. There was a promoter in Belgium who offered us some gigs, and that was as far as we thought." (JH-GM12)

Denny Laine was happy to hear that his former band had a new lease on life. He said, "All the groundwork was done for Justin and John to just walk in. If they hadn't given it a new lease on life, the Moody Blues would have gone down the pan." (DL-H&H97)

***

Hayward had been a singer/guitarist in two bands. He had served as a guitarist and backing vocalist in a third – the Wilde Three. Now, for the first time, he would serve a group as singer, guitarist and songwriter. And, as he would soon discover, with his voice best suited for covering songs which had originally been sung by Denny Laine, he would also be the front man. It was almost by accident, but for the Moody Blues he would wear the different hats that his early and later idols, Buddy Holly and the Beatles, did.

Hayward said, "Until the Beatles, all these sort of rock artists relied on teams of writers or other writers to provide them with material. That was kind of risky. Then the Beatles changed everything, really, and I was lucky to be in London, in the center of it, when the Beatles happened, and even luckier to get the call from Mike to join him and the other guys. The Moodies knew the Beatles and were mixing in those circles." (JH-CB)

Lonnie Donegan said of Hayward, "We tried to present him then as a star for a year or so, but he really didn't want to be an act. I couldn't make heads or tails of what he wanted to do! Neither could he. Then he met up with the remnants of the Moody Blues, who'd all just broken up. They asked me to go down and hear what they were doing, which was good. So, I fixed them up with a manager and said, 'Right, Justin, go for it!' See what happens? The rest … is history." (LD-RW87)

Hayward said, "None of the boys had any bread; neither did I. I met them on a Sunday and the following week we went off to Belgium." (JH-NME70)

In mid-to-late October, England's *Hit Parader* reported:

> DENNY LAINE quit and he was quickly followed by ROD CLARK, leaving three original MOODIES in their house in Esher sussing out the scene by way of the telephone. After numerous calls they got things together and have now legged off to the Continent where things have been happening for them in a big way.
>
> Their new lead guitarist is JUSTIN HAYWARD from London and, on bass, JOHNNY LODGE – he was, in fact, an original founder member of the group, but when they turned fully pro and

left Birmingham, he stayed to finish studying Mechanical Engineering at college…. Both the "new boys" are tall and blonde, so they fit in and contrast well with dark 6-footers MIKE and RAY!

MIKE has switched to Hammond organ as there were often so many hang-ups involved with out-of-tune pianos on gigs before. When he first got the Hammond he drove everyone out of their heads by experimenting for sounds almost non-stop … but the noise was tremendous. On the vocal front there is no lead singer as such. MIKE, RAY, JOHNNY and JUSTIN will all feature – should be good sounds coming out of the Continent!

DENNY, by the way, is to pursue a solo career, so we should be hearing more of him too.

The Moodies' base of operation on the Continent was the town of Mouscron, in the province of Hainaut, Belgium.

John Lodge: "There were clubs we could play in, to earn enough money to live and, in the meantime, concentrate on writing our own music…. We had been playing Tamla/Motown, some blues songs, James Brown's 'I Don't Mind,' Curtis Mayfield's Impressions – all our influences came from America. We started experimenting with harmony, which was really important – and that has become the mainstay of the Moody Blues. We concentrated on counter harmonies that went against the main melody, and this, I think, came from the Impressions and the Four Tops. But we were really looking for our own direction." (JL-DOTP97)

The group also needed time to bond with Hayward, who said, "Although I'd joined at the same time as John Lodge, everyone else was from Birmingham, and there I was – from a place called Swindon in Wiltshire, that nobody had heard of. I was the country yokel. I had to re-adjust a lot. I'd played with other bands but I'd never worked with people like the Moodies before and I'd never even been to Birmingham….

"I think Ray and I became the closest to start with because I played acoustic and he played flute and we could make sounds together. That helped me settle in."

"It was a gradual thing. Graeme played me his type of records and I played him folk, things like Simon & Garfunkel albums that he had never heard before. In the end, we realized that we dug each other's music, and after that, things were much easier." (JH-DME70 and JH-NME68).

Ray Thomas said, "We were all rock 'n' roll-oriented, but Justin was more folky, so that was the first fusion… a marriage of musical styles, a natural progression. We had some songs we'd intended to record but we couldn't get any studio time to make an album. You needed a hit record for that, so it was Catch-22." (RT-DOFP97)

Since they couldn't convince Decca to provide for further recording sessions, the reformed Moodies set about to stir fresh interest in the band. They soon found steady work, opening for Tom Jones during his "Tom Jones Spectacular" engagement at the Olympia Music Hall, Paris, France. The Moody Blues played the first half of the show, with Jones, backed by the Moodies, closing.

118

Is it hard for you to visualize the Moody Blues backing Tom Jones, as they did during December 1966 and January 1967 for the "Tom Jones Spectacular" at the Olympia Music Hall? Here's what it may have looked like: Jones rocks out to "It's a Hang Up, Baby" with his old friends on the November 6, 1969 episode of *This Is Tom Jones*. (Photo Source: Alamy Stock Photo)

In January 1967, when this engagement ended, Jones' agent, Colin Berlin – who had previously represented Justin Hayward for a short time – came backstage and asked the Moodies to consider letting him book some gigs for them in England. The Moodies, each feeling homesick and understanding their need for greater visibility in Britain, agreed to return to London.

Lodge said, "We met Colin Berlin over there and he brought us back and tried this cabaret thing, which was really dire. We were trying to find ways of getting home from Newcastle every night!" (JL-NME70a)

The business plan wasn't necessarily a good one. Graeme Edge admitted to *Melody Maker*, "The original idea was keeping the Moody Blues name and carry on singing 'Go Now!' and 'Stop!' and all those numbers. I suppose it was a lack of confidence in ourselves but we carried on trading off the *old* Moodies." (GE-MM73)

Hayward added, "I ended up singing ['Go Now!'] because nobody else wanted to do it after Denny had left." (JH-TB13)

Graeme Edge: "But Justin was never ever happy singing Denny Laine's songs…. People wanted us to play 'Go Now!,' but, really, a song like that belongs to the lead singer and not the band that makes it. When a singer leaves, he sort of takes the song with him." (GE-H&H87)

It didn't help that Decca was still releasing material from the previous lineup, reflecting the Moodies earlier style.

U.K. single release:
"Life's Not Life" b/w "He Can Win"
Decca, F.12543; January 13, 1967

This final single with Denny Laine as the lead vocal was issued on January 13, 1967. The Pinder-Laine original, "Life's Not Life," was coupled with "He Can Win," also composed by the two. These songs were left over from the sessions for the unreleased "Lookout" album.

One British music magazine reviewer said of "Life's Not Life":

> A Pinder-Laine composition with a plaintive lyric that belies the happy feel of the disc. Has the usual Moodies' trademark of constantly changing tempos – plus crashing cymbals, tambourine, falsetto harmonies backing the soloist, and an ear-catching flute solo.
>
> FLIP: Like the top side, the most intriguing feature here is the well-conceived lyric. A competently performed medium-pace.

The band had no choice but to tour behind the "new" single. Graeme Edge said, "On the Continent we're 'coining it,' and we always have been. There they think that if you haven't had a hit at home for a time it's because you've been busy playing all the time. In England, we were just a has-been group as far as people were concerned." (GE-NME68a)

Hayward said, "All I know is that the rhythm & blues wasn't working. Quite frankly, we weren't good enough at it. Denny Laine had a great R&B voice, and he was the voice of that previous lineup. When the five of us got together, we were like fish out of water – we were out of character. Mike was writing some lovely stuff, but he was trying to fit it around the piano and a rhythm & blues feel, and it wasn't right, and it wasn't reflecting his own personality." (JH-GM12)

Edge said, "Colin was [still] our manager, but Tom [Jones] had that giant hit, 'Green, Green Grass of Home,' so he hadn't much time to devote to us. Then, when it came to our turn again, Colin got tied up with a new singer, Engelbert Humperdinck, who had a fantastic hit with '[Please] Release Me.' … [Just prior to] the flower power summer of 1967, we were still wearing our neat blue suits, fairly short hair, and still doing 'Go Now!' The two new boys, John and Justin, had been smothered by the old Moodies image, and had never been allowed to express themselves properly." (GE-R68)

Hayward said, "We were just trying to work for petrol – gas for the car. That was about it.… Only three months after I joined I was back with my parents because we had no money." (JH-CB)

7

New Look, New Sound, New Singles

Less moody, more Mod: The Moody Blues, circa late 1967.
(Photo source: Author's collection)

It had been more than six months since the original lineup of the Moody Blues had recorded for Decca. Since then, they had mostly worked on the Continent.

John Lodge said, "[After we] came back to England, we sent some demos of our new songs off to Decca, which led to a couple of singles." (JL-DOFP87)

These demos resulted in a meeting with Decca staff producer Tony Clarke, beginning a long and productive relationship.

Tony Clarke was born in 1941, in Coventry. Like Pinder and Thomas, he grew up to the sounds of his home town being bombed by the Germans during World War II. In his early teens, Clarke became enamored in the skiffle music craze that swept Britain and joined a group. He told interviewer Mark Murley, "I think it was the Strollers. Sounds bad enough, doesn't it? I ended up playing sessions a lot. That's what made me want to be a producer; I kept seeing producers in a suit and [with a] briefcase, and an expense account, and I thought. 'I'm doing all the sessions and getting nowhere, and this guy is what I want to be.'"

Clarke's sessions work engendered many good contacts at the studio. He wrote to Decca and was offered a job in the promotions department. "I was with Decca Promotion for about a year, looking after luminaries like Roy Orbison, Brenda Lee, and Bill Haley and the Comets. Can you imagine? I was about 20 and trying to look after bands like Bill Haley and the Comets, who had seen it all! And I was a young idiot from the record

Tony Clarke, Decca producer.
(Photo source: musicheritageuk.org)

company, buying them drinks, organizing cars, and whatever." (TC-H&H95)

Clarke next worked for Dick Rowe, an executive at Decca.

Clarke recalled, "He was extremely infamous. He said to me, at my interview, 'I guess you will have heard; I'm the guy who turned down the Beatles. But I challenge you to go listen to their audition tape! It's in [our] library; go and listen and tell me what you think…. Yes, I'm the guy who turned the Beatles down, but I signed the Rolling Stones two weeks later, so there!'" (TC-H&H95)

Actually, the Beatles already had two No. 1 singles and a top album by the time Rowe signed the Rolling Stones in the spring of 1963. And, according to Mick Jagger, it was George Harrison whose suggestion brought the Stones to Rowe and Decca, after which Lennon and McCartney provided them with their first Top 20 hit.

Dick Rowe was out of the doghouse after the Stones' version of "I Wanna Be Your Man" made it to No. 12. Other acts Rowe brought to Decca later, in 1964, were the Zombies, Tom Jones, and Them (featuring Van Morrison). 1964 was also the year Rowe signed a record contract with Ridgepride Ltd., bringing the Moody Blues to Decca.

Meanwhile, Tony Clarke was spending as much time in the studio as possible, taking on all types of tasks as a production assistant. Soon he felt, "I can do that; I can do that better than *he* can!" (TC-H&H95)

Among the sessions Clarke was involved with – as an assistant – was "Gloria," by Them. And then he was offered a producing job – for a group called the Pinkerton's Assorted Colours, and their song "Mirror, Mirror." It was a surprise hit, peaking at No. 9 in one British chart. Clarke also produced a single for John Mayall and the Bluesbreakers ("Crocodile Walk" b/w "Blues City Shakedown"), but the record failed, resulting in the band being dropped from Decca. Another assignment for Clarke was producing the Equals' "Baby Come Back," which, while missing the charts in England when first issued in 1966, eventually caught on across Continental Europe, hitting No. 1 in Belgium, No. 2 in France, No. 4 in Norway, and No. 6 in the Netherlands. Due to this success, Decca reissued the song in the U.K. in 1968, when it topped the charts (as well as becoming a Top 30 single in America).

Clarke said, "I remember driving along in my Jaguar – *a second-hand Jaguar* – with the radio turned on, and they said, 'Number One, it's "Baby Come Back."' That's a great feeling. So when I met the Moodies, they had had a Number One [with 'Go Now!'], but so had I!" (TC-H&H95)

This is another great Clarke story, but "Baby Come Back" didn't make No. 1 in the U.K. until its second go-round – in the spring of 1968, a year *after* Clarke first met the Moodies.

As for his introduction to the group, Clarke said, "I was a staff producer at Decca Records in London but had never met them. I'd heard they were moody; that they ate producers, and things like that." (TC-HP71)

Mike Pinder explained, "The record company didn't have much faith in us and we were waiting to show them what we could do. They had the opinion that we were very much untogether because of circumstances and things that had happened in the old days. There were always managerial problems… we never could get along with the manager and we never found a manager that could get along with us…. We always had those hang ups." (MP-C71)

And, now, a bad reputation because of it.

Regarding that first get-together with the Moodies, Clarke remembered, "I met them in a bar right next to Decca. And my boss had said to me, 'See if you can work with them. Here are some [demos] they've done' … and I picked this guitar and voice demo of 'Nights in White Satin' and I said that I thought it had really great potential and that I'd love to do it. So, I met with them a day or two later… in a bar next to Decca…. I was a bit nervous meeting them… but they were great; as easy [to talk with] as anything." (TC-H&H95)

While it stands to reason that Clarke was indeed nervous – after all, he'd only produced one Top 10 hit at this point, and a pair of misses – he couldn't have heard "Nights in White Satin." Justin Hayward hadn't written it yet. What Clarke *had* heard was Hayward's demo of "Fly Me Away" and the Moodies' 1966 recording of Mike Pinder's "I Really Haven't Got the Time."

Hayward said, "I had 'Fly Me High,' and I had quite a lot of things that [were] recorded in a publisher's office in Denmark Street, and some things that I demo'ed up very badly, cheaply and quickly. I didn't really have much else…. 'Fly Me High' was the one that I came with that the other guys in the Moodies really listened to and could see some potential in." (JH-GM12)

Ray Thomas: "Tony was assigned to us by Decca; he was employed by them, and he was the best. We hit it off with him immediately. He wasn't a 'suit,' he was a 'muso' [obsessed with music] himself, so he knew the ropes." (RT-AI17)

Mike Pinder: "Tony, Ray, and I hit it off right away. Tony was a musician – a bass player – as well as a Decca producer, and he had the right sensibilities for us and the music we were composing." (MP-AI17)

From this meeting sprang a longtime relationship that was beneficial to both sides. Clarke said, "It was a meeting of minds, I think. I had wanted a band like that, and I got it!" (TC-H&H95)

U.K. single release:
"Really Haven't Got the Time" b/w "Fly Me High"
Decca F.12607; May 5, 1967

U.S.A. single release:
"I Really Haven't Got the Time"
b/w "Fly Me High"
London 45-20030; June 1967

"I Really Haven't Got the Time"/"Fly Me High" was initially released as a double-A-side, with Mike Pinder's "I Really Haven't Got the Time" listed first. The full catalogue numbering also denotes this detail. "I Really Haven't Got the Time," in the U.K., is identified as Decca F.12067 (DR 4200). "Fly Me High" is F.12067 (DR 4201). It's the same in the U.S., where "I Really Haven't Got the Time" is LON 45-20030 (DR 4200), and "Fly Me High" is LON 45-20030 (DR 4201). It was standard at this time in the record industry that the lower number usually designated the A-side, with the higher number used for the B-side.

"I Really Haven't Got the Time" was also listed first in New Zealand. However, by the time the single was issued in Europe, the sides had been reversed. "Fly Me High" had the lower catalogue number in the Netherlands, Italy, France, and Belgium (the last two being issued with picture sleeves clearly presented "Fly Me High" as the top side).

In the spring of 1967, under the supervision of Tony Clarke, the Moodies entered Decca Studios in West Hampstead to record the Mark 2 lineup's first single.

Clarke recalled the recording session: "It wasn't done in the usual studio; it was done in Decca Number Two, which is a bit of a snake pit. I remember spending hours in the drum booth talking to Graeme. When I think of that session, I think of the drum booth and explaining some aspect of the high-hat [cymbal] to Graeme. It was a pretty good record – it certainly was for them. And I thought at the time, 'Wow, I'm on to something here. This is the direction I want to go in.' I found them so easy to work with, and so funny. Coventry – my home town – isn't far from Birmingham, so I think they accepted me as being from 'the neighborhood.'" (TC-H&H95)

FLY ME HIGH
(really haven't) **GOT THE TIME**

HIT PARADE
79006

DECCA

THE MOODY BLUES

French picture sleeve for single,
designating "Fly Me High" as top side.

Hayward enjoyed the recording too. "It was the first record we did with Tony Clarke, which brought something special; he wanted to contribute. And he really did make it different. And then there was Gus Dudgeon as an engineer, and I think he did a great job, too." (JH-HL99)

Dudgeon would soon become a famous producer in his own right. He first cut his teeth as a Decca engineer on songs such as the Zombies' 1965 hit "She's Not There." Once in the producer's chair, for another label, Dudgeon helmed David Bowie's 1969 hit, "Space Oddity." In 1970, he began a long and rewarding professional relationship with Elton John, with the artist's self-titled album.

"I Really Haven't Got the Time" had been recorded once before by the group, under the supervision of Denny Cordell and while Denny Laine was still in the band. It was intended for the unreleased "Lookout" album. The Moodies of that era, with the Laine-Pinder-Thomas-Clark-Edge lineup, even performed it on television (currently available for viewing on YouTube). Mike Pinder, who wrote the song, sang the lead for the first recording, for the live TV performance, and now for the new version.

Regarding the flip side, Hayward said, "We did one great record called 'Fly Me High' before the Mellotron. We made a few recordings at our own expense, but one that really pricked the ears of Decca's executive producers was 'Fly Me High.' It was the best thing we did pre-Mellotron." (JH-CB)

Lodge said, "'Fly Me High' was the first real progression because that had all the harmonies. It was a turning point." (JL-DOFP87)

On May 5, 1967, "I Really Haven't Got the Time," coupled with "Fly Me High," was issued in the U.K. The biggest competitors on the radio that week in England were Sandie Shaw, at No. 1 with "Puppet on a String," followed by Frank Sinatra and daughter Nancy with "Something Stupid," a song filled with creepy implications. Rounding out the Top 5 were the Mamas and Papas' "Dedicated to the One I Love"; the Tremeloes' "Silence Is Golden"; and the Who's "Pictures of Lily."

When hearing the new single for the first time in May 1967, British DJ Alan Freeman, host of *Top of the Pops* and frequent panelist on *Juke Box Jury*, picked "Fly Me High" as the potential hit, raving, "I love this! They always get such a great feel. Oh, what beautiful harmonies! Fabulous! Notice how they establish it very quietly and build without making a big fuss. The rhythm is very subtle, so cool and so definite. It's a fascinating record altogether. If they don't get right up the charts then there just isn't any justice." (AF-MS67)

Four days after the single was issued, the Moodies had a BBC recording session for the radio show *Saturday Club*. They performed "Fly Me High" and a cover version of the Animals' two-year old hit, "Don't Let Me Be Misunderstood," featuring an impassioned lead vocal by Hayward and atmospheric flute playing by Thomas. (Both songs are featured on the CD *Live at the BBC 1967-1970*).

The American release came a month later. In its "Top Singles of the Week" review column for the June 28, 1967 edition of *Variety*, the trade's music critic picked "I Really Haven't Got the Time" as one of the "Best Bets" of the week's 100-plus single releases:

> The Moody Blues' 'I Really Haven't Got the Time" brings back this British band with a swift-moving pacer touched up by piano and cute vocal roles. "Fly Me High" harmonizes as a strong flip side.

On July 15, *Cashbox* ran its review, also picking "I Really Haven't Got the Time" as the potential hit:

> This one could prove to be a chart-destined vehicle for the Moody Blues. Side is a brisk-moving finger-snapper with a nice beat and strong instrumental backing.

"Fly Me High" was described as an "Infectious swinger."

On July 22 – a Saturday – ABC-TV in America aired a comedy/variety show taped in London, called *Piccadilly Palace*. The Moody Blues performed both sides of their new single.

Another welcome bit of exposure came when the band's promotional contract with Coca-Cola was renewed. The Moodies were photographed in the studio while recording their latest single. Bottles of Coke were strategically positioned in each photo.

New Blues For The Moodies And most welcome ones they are. Johnny Lodge and Justin Hayward, newest members of the "Magnificent" Moody Blues. But new personalities mean new problems. A 10-hour work session, complete with disagreements, discussions, suggestions, brings some answers. But one suggestion needing no discussion is "How about Coke?" The Blues, new and old, drink Coke after Coke after Coke. Only Coca-Cola has the taste they never get tired of. And only Coca-Cola keeps everything going better all through the long exhausting session.

Seventeen—May 1967

This page and next: Cropped image of full-page summer 1967 Coca-Cola print ad featuring the Moody Blues.
(Photo Source: *Seventeen* magazine)

Justin, a bachelor, like his fellow Moodies, feels new group has finally reached its musical peak. "There are no stars. We all contribute to the sound."

Multi-talented Mike Pinder plays guitar, organ, piano. Dislikes "people who try to be something they're not and make a hash of it."

The flute and harmonica man, Ray Thomas, enjoys the reputation of being the only Moody who can sing and tap his foot in different tempos at the same time.

Graeme Edge, his favorite drink nearby, is group's comedian. "Drummers are happy people. They take frustrations out on the drums. Look at Ringo."

The Moody Blues relax with Coke while listening to playback critically as engineer balances sound.

The "Magnificent" Moody Blues recording their final take. With a difficult number nearly wrapped up, both new and old Moodies see repertoire take shape.

As they waited to see if either song might impact the charts, the Moodies had to stay visible – and that meant taking more work in the cabarets. Graeme Edge said, "[In] the summer of 1967, we found ourselves in cabaret in the North of England. It was a fortnight [two weeks] playing to people who didn't know what we had to offer. All they wanted was what we called 'straw hat and red nose' stuff, and it depressed us." (GE-NME71)

Also at the beckoning of the audiences, the band was still performing "Go Now!"

Justin Hayward said, "That song has a lot of bad memories for us…. we played 'Go Now!' and all those numbers into the ground. We were down to £40, £50, still in the blue Moody's suits and doing cabaret in Newcastle." (JH-MM70)

Graeme Edge: "We were living off 'Go Now!,' and we were going the way of all the one-hit-wonders, and the prices were falling down, and the standard of gigs were falling down, and we were gradually becoming more and more disenchanted with the work we were doing. And it got to a period where we went into the 'graveyard of groups' in England, which is 'cabaret,' working in these clubs, and we were a week in Newcastle, and a week in Darlington, which is way up in Northern England, a long way from anywhere I want to be…. And it sort of acted as a catalyst – I mean, something had to come out of that: either the Moody Blues were going to break up, or we were going to *do* something." (GE-OC68)

Justin Hayward: "[I]t really was death. Ray and I had a breakdown and we just got lower and lower, and nothing at all was happening." (JH-NME70)

Graeme Edge: "Justin and John had breakdowns during the cabaret [tours]. There's nothing worse than playing music you don't believe in to Northern audiences who aren't interested." (GE-NME68a)

Justin Hayward: "[T]here was this turning point for us when we were playing at the Fiesta [Night Club] in Stockton [Warwickshire, England]. There was a knock on the dressing room door one night and this guy came in and said, 'I've got to tell you, you're the worst band I've ever seen in my life..... I come here every Thursday with my wife. I pay £2/10 to be entertained and you're bloody rubbish. I just thought I ought to tell you that.' And, on the way back home in the van, it was all silence for the first hour, and then somebody said, 'He's absolutely right, we're bloody awful.' And, literally, the next morning, we threw away the blue suits and, from then on, we worked on our own material." (JH-Q90)

Mike Pinder: "We suddenly realized there were enough people producing cheap temporary pop music and that we were unhappy because we were doing nothing we actually believed in. Gradually, it began to dawn on us that we were looking for the same thing." (MP-R70)

Justin Hayward: "As soon as we started doing our own material – originally I was the only guy writing, with Mike – all of us got behind the material, and everything changed for us. Our audience was suddenly different. People started liking us for the right reasons. There was an honesty about our playing that was completely apparent." (JH-GM12)

Mike Pinder: "We went through a lot of changes before we realized we loved one another like brothers, and if we could only communicate some of our true feelings to others we would find the kind of peace of mind we were looking for. We decided then and there to aim our music at the head and the heart." (MP-R70)

Justin Hayward: "It was in the summer of '67; that beautiful summer which did so much for everyone, that we decided we had to be honest with ourselves and do what we wanted to do. If nobody dug it, then we'd know we had nothing to offer." (JH-MM70)

The Moody Blues performing "Fly Me High" on British TV.
(Photo source: Alamy Stock Photo)

(Photo source: GarageHangover.com)

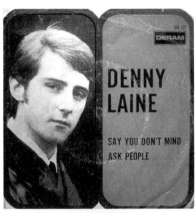

Denny Laine and the Electric String Band

As the Moody Blues underwent changes in both their music and their offstage lives, ex-Moody Denny Laine's life was likewise taking new directions.

He'd left the Moodies at the start of October 1966. Within a couple months, Laine had found his new musical path, and group – the Electric String Band. The group was comprised of Trevor Burton (who had just left the Move) on second guitar; Binky McKenzie (formerly of Free at Last) on bass; Viv Prince (of the Pretty Things) on drums; and, from the Royal Academy of Music, Wilhelm Martin and John Stein on violins, and Clive Gillinson and Chris Van Campen on cellos. Laine and his Electric String Band was doing something that had never been tried before – combining the guitars, electric bass and drums of a pop combo with an amplified string quartet. This was several months *before* the release of *Days of Future Passed*, and four years ahead of the Move's transition to the symphonic rock of the Electric Light Orchestra.

Laine signed with Decca's new specialty label, Deram, and kept Denny Cordell as his producer. Laine also chose to stay with Brian Epstein, even after his fellow Moodies broke with NEMS.

Laine's first solo single, backed by the uncredited Electric String Band, was "Say You Don't Mind" coupled with "Ask the People" (DM 227), issued on April 14, 1967 in the U.K. In

America, the single was cataloged as DEM-7509. Both songs were written by Laine and featured psychedelic rock-era pop tunes enhanced by the strings section. John Paul Jones, later of Led Zeppelin, provided the arrangements.

Laine said, "John Paul Jones was, back in those days, like Jimmy Page, doing all the sessions. So, Denny Cordell was the producer…. [and] my best friend at the time. I went into the studio with those guys and John Paul Jones was playing a little bit of bass, and Danny Thompson [of the band Pentangle] was on double bass…. John Paul Jones was doing a lot of scoring for people, [so] I got him to do the string parts." (DL-G.C10)

A low-budget promotional film, featuring only Laine spinning and tripping out to the beat of the music, was issued. For this film, Laine had patterned his look after John Lennon (as seen on the picture sleeve and promotional video for the "Penny Lane" / "Strawberry Fields Forever" single, issued on February 13, 1967). This included the hairstyle, mustache, and granny glasses. He also wore a Nehru jacket. With his lead vocal, especially apparent on "Ask the People," Laine even sounds like Lennon. Of course, Laine saw Lennon in the flesh, often. As a friend of the Beatles, he routinely visited the group, including during the recording of the soon-to-be-released *Sgt. Pepper's Lonely Hearts Club Band*. Because of this, Laine had the inside track as to what their new music sounded like. "Say You Don't Mind" and "Ask the People" echoed that sound.

Laine's innovative disc, with its pair of pleasant and catchy songs, received good reviews. Influential London disc jockey John Peel, who hosted the popular show *Top Gear*, rated the A-side highly. Despite this, the record failed to chart. (In 1972, its commercial quality was proven when Colin Blunstone, former vocalist of the Zombies, covered the song for a single release, taking it into the U.K. Top 20.)

Laine said, "[T]he single, 'Say You Don't Mind,' had a very good underground following for me. We did a lot of underground clubs and folk clubs and stuff like that. And, on the London scene, it did me a lot of good even though it didn't have any success [in the charts]." (DL-G.C10)

The first known live appearance of Laine and his pop/string band took place on May 19, 1967, at London's Tiles Club (after dropping out of a Saville Theatre show earlier in the month when the band's bass player fell ill). Sharing the bill with Laine and his group was none other than the new lineup of the Moody Blues.

In June 1967, at the Saville Theatre in London, Laine and his innovative band shared the bill with both the Jimi Hendrix Experience and Procol Harum (the latter having just released "A Whiter Shade of Pale").

Laine said, "It was very good for me, because I tried to get recognized for about a year before I got that concert. When I did the concert, Paul [McCartney], John [Lennon] and Peter Asher were in the audience. Everybody liked the show; we had all done very well. And even Jimi Hendrix complimented me on the show, on the fact that I was doing something different, because Jimi was a creative artist and he wanted to move forward with his music." (DL-HC17)

On the morning of August 27, 1967, Laine went to Brian Epstein's house to discuss further bookings. There was no answer when he rang the bell. Epstein *was* home, but had died overnight from an accidental drug overdose. Afterward, Laine went from one former Moody Blues manager to another – the one who predated Epstein, Tony Secunda. Laine said, "He understood me. He backed me in anything I wanted to do." (DL-BB13)

A follow-up single, "Too Much in Love" b/w "Catherine's Wheel" (DM 171) was issued in the U.K. by Deram on January 12, 1968. London Records in America passed on this one.

Again, Laine wrote both sides of the disc, and Denny Cordell produced. The promotion film for the A-side was risqué for its time, as Laine took pictures of a lovely model wearing skimpy, sexy attire, then had her lay on her back, allowing him to straddle her as he pointed his camera downward and snapped more pictures. Both the A-and-B-sides of the single are up-tempo catchy pop, typical of this era, with "Catherine's Wheel" better utilizing the string section. Despite the sexual tease of the promo film, the record missed the charts.

Denny Laine's Electric String Band was winding down, anyway. Asked why he ended the group, Laine said, "Well, the main reason was because I started going on the road with these four musicians from the Royal Academy of Music. They were all soloists and they were all very much busy doing orchestral stuff all around the world, so you couldn't tie them down too much. So, in a way, it was a little bit of a white elephant having the best guys who were the young soloists of the Royal Academy of Music in London; they were so good, there was *nobody else* to replace them.

"It was an exhausting experience. Everyone had to be paid and the bit of money I'd saved up ran out eventually. So there I was again – happy but broke." (DL-G.C10 and DI-BR13)

The Moody Blues were also onto the idea of adding string accompaniment to their music. But they were about to do this without taking on the difficulties of trying to tour with members of a symphony orchestra.

U.K. single release:
"Love and Beauty"
b/w "Leave This Man Alone"
Decca F 12670; September 22, 1967

Another sign of change for the Moody Blues was their first use of the Mellotron.

The musical "machine" which Pinder had spent 18 months in 1963 and early '64 loading with tape, then tuning and testing for Mellotronics of Birmingham (a division of Streetly Electronics), had been very much on his mind lately.

It began one day in early 1967. Pinder was visiting with the Beatles, and was played a tape of a song they were recording that begged for the otherworldly sound only the Mellotron could provide.

He recalled, "One of the biggest things of the whole Mellotron thing was the fact that I actually got to turn the Beatles onto the Mellotron. I told them about it, and they immediately all got one, and I went by a few of the *Sgt. Pepper* sessions and they were starting to use it. And they played 'Strawberry Fields,' and it was, like, 'Wow.'

"Yeah, I did a good thing that day. I did a very good thing [laughs]. I'm probably most proud of the fact that I actually was a factor in their music." (MP-GM09)

Now it was time to factor the Mellotron into the music of the Moody Blues.

John Lodge: "We tried every type of electric organ – Vox organ, Hammond organ – but none of them blended in with the sound we were creating on stage with the flute, and with the vocal harmonies. And we really needed something else that would mask everything; that would fill everything else in; and put [in] the right colors. And then Mike one day said that he'd worked on this thing called a Mellotron, in Birmingham, and he knew where there was a secondhand one – we didn't have enough money to even think about buying a new one!

"At the Dunlop Tire Company, in their social club – which was a club for all the employees – someone had managed to sell them this Mellotron. It had never even been played; *no one knew how it worked!* I don't think it actually had a plug on the cord, and it was just sitting in a corner with chairs on it and beer cans and everything." (JL-MBT90)

Justin Hayward: "[Mike] said, 'I know this instrument and it could really work.' … We found it stuffed up in a corner and paid £25 for it and brought it back down to London." (JH-CB)

Pinder differed on the price. "I remember paying £300 for it…. This one had tapes hanging out the back of the LSO [London Symphony Orchestra] moonlighting, which were triggered by a keyboard." (MP-UN14)

Graeme Edge: "We spent our food money on it. Mike used to work for the company that makes Mellotrons, so he took it all to pieces and did lots of things to it." (GE-NME68a)

As Pinder was putting Humpty Dumpty back together again, Decca invited the Moodies back for another recording session.

Even though "I Really Haven't Got the Time" and "Fly Me High" missed the charts in both the U.K. and the U.S., both songs had garnered favorable reviews and picked up sporadic radio airplay, as well as becoming jukebox hits ("Fly Me High" in particular). There had also been numerous invitations for the band to perform the single on both radio and TV. This attention favored "Fly Me High," which fit so well with the psychedelic trend sparked by *Sgt. Pepper*. Beyond this, the Moodies were getting further exposure from Coca-Cola's omnipresent print ads in numerous music and teen magazines. As a result, the band was given more studio time.

On May 19, with Tony Clarke and Gus Dudgeon again in the control room, Justin Hayward's "Long Summer Days" was recorded. That night, the Moodies shared the bill with Denny Laine and his Electric String Band at the London club, Tiles.

On June 12, they shared the bill with the Who and the Herd at Christ College, Cambridge. On June 22, they appeared at London's "hippie club," the Middle Earth, on a double bill with Pink Floyd.

Another recording session from June 29 resulted in two more new numbers being committed to tape – Hayward's "Leave This Man Alone" and Mike Pinder's "Please Think About It." (The latter song, along with Hayward's "Long Summer Days," remained unreleased until 1977, with the *Caught Live + 5* album.)

On July 9, the Moodies again shared a bill with Pink Floyd, this time at a former London railway "shed" converted into a music hall called the Roundhouse.

The Moodies' new style, featuring the symphonic sounds of the Mellotron, was first captured on tape July 17, 1967, when the band recorded a new Mike Pinder song, "Love and Beauty."

Mike Pinder: "'Love and Beauty' definitely was a precursor to *Days of Future Passed*. Having the Mellotron allowed me to start creating backdrops of lushness and soundscapes." (MP-AI17)

Hayward said of Pinder's skill on the Mellotron: "He was the master. It was a sound effects machine with a few orchestral sounds. Mike took all the sound effects out and replaced it with duplicates of the orchestral sounds, and he managed to play it. You only had eight seconds when you pressed a note down, but Mike managed to do it." (JH-GM12)

Graeme Edge: "There were two major things that caused [the new sound]. One was Justin, because he came from an English folk musical background... more than the straight 12-bar rock we came from; and the other was, of course, Mike Pinder and that magnificent – but dreadfully difficult – machine of his: the Mellotron.... The BBC were the most interested in it, the idea being they had all these tapes with [sounds of] walking on gravel, a dog barking, car door slamming, etc. You could see the potential if you actually recorded instruments [onto those tape loops], because they used a black and white keyboard for access. If someone could read music, you could put C above E and know that was the rocket ship taking off. So you could retrieve the sounds by writing it like a musical form. Mike figured out to add horns, strings, bagpipes and all that sort of stuff behind it and turn it into a more natural musical instrument. That, along with Justin's folk chord-structure background with the tonal variations available from the Mellotron, was what set us on the track that sort of ended up as *Days of Future Passed*." (GE-GM12)

Also recorded on the same day as "Love and Beauty" was Justin Hayward's song, "Cities."

With five songs recorded, Decca selected two for the next single in the U.K. – Pinder's "Love and Beauty" coupled with Hayward's "Leave This Man Alone." London Records in the U.S. passed on issuing the single.

On the charts in the U.K. that month were Engelbert Humperdinck at No. 1 with "The Last Waltz," followed by the Small Faces' psychedelic excursion, "Itchycoo Park"; Scott McKenzie singing the John Phillips song, "San Francisco (Be Sure to Wear Flowers in Your Hair)"; the Bee Gees' "Massachusetts"; the Rolling Stones' "Dandelion"; and the Supremes' "Reflections." And, though no single had been issued, the airwaves were filled with cuts from the Beatles' *Sgt. Pepper*.

TV appearance, circa late 1967. Note that Ray Thomas was the first to sport a moustache. (Photo source: MoodyBluesAttitude.com)

One British reviewer (provenance unknown) said of the new single:

The Moodies' "Fly Me High" met with great success up and down the country from pop fans who caught on to the catchy melody. This new sound is bigger and better but isn't quite as catchy, maybe because of its complexity. Written by Mike Pinder, the sound is deep and echoey, boosted well by strings, a dipping bass, and the big full vocal sound. A pretty, sweeping sound of a record crashing through the rain-clouds and full of surprises. It could be a giant hit providing it gets enough plugs to allow us to become familiar with the sound and lyrics. They're continuing to make good, good sounds.

The reviewer had no way of knowing that the "strings" boosting the song weren't strings at all … it was the Mellotron.

For its September 23 issue, *Record Mirror* also ran a review of the Moodies' new single. Critic Peter Jones gave "Love and Beauty" four stars, writing:

> Very good, commended thusly, just missed a 'tip.' Powerful harmonies, mid-tempo, big arrangement and production – could easily make it with plugs.

The Moodies were willing to do radio and television to plug the new single, should any offers come through. But there was no desire on their part to go on another circuit tour of the northern cabarets.

When issued by Decca on September 22, 1967, the "Love and Beauty" / "Leave This Man Alone" single also failed to chart, but it did establish the Moodies' new sound. Ray Thomas's flute had been in evidence earlier, on *The Magnificent Moodies* and a couple of the group's 1966 singles, but now, and from this time forward, it was featured far more, combining with Pinder's Mellotron for a distinct psychedelic sound.

Justin Hayward: "Mike was thinking of a very different route for the Moodies to go, and it was very brave. I was a huge fan of Mike. He was the one who brought me to the band, and he was a great musician, a lovely guitar player, [and] a beautiful voice, as you know. But what he was doing [as a writer] was very different than what they had done before, and so was my stuff. You certainly couldn't have called it rhythm & blues at all." (JH-CB)

Ray Thomas: "We changed the lineup so there were different influences with 'Just' and John. Mike had been working with Mellotrons, so instead of just going on stage and doing one number after another and taking your bow in between, we thought it would be a nice idea to do, not a medley of songs, but something like a rock symphony." (RT-MSA74)

Graeme Edge: "At that time we used to do two half-hour spots a night. We decided that we were going to do a stage show so that we started and finished the two half-hours without any announcements – straight in and through all the songs."

"With the little money we had left, we decided to lock ourselves away for three weeks of rehearsals – which meant in fact

TV rehearsal, circa late 1967/early 1968. Graeme Edge joins Ray Thomas in adapting the latest Beatles look – the mustached pop star. Can you dig it? (Photo source: MoodyBluesAttitude.com)

The Moodies, circa late 1967, with their new look ... and new sound, thanks in part to Mike Pinder's new instrument – the Mellotron.
(Photo source: MoodyBluesAttitude.com)

that we hadn't any bookings anyway! We were going to start again. We each wrote five or six songs, and worked out eight of the numbers with our new instrument – the Mellotron – and out of this evolved *Days of Future Passed*." (GE-MM73 and GE-R68)

There were no record royalties of consequence coming in from two singles that missed the charts. And, since the Moodies had spurned touring to write an entire show's worth of new material, money quickly grew short. But the group had found a sponsor.

It was the second of the two events which prompted the Moodies' break from touring the cabarets. The first had been the man who came into their dressing room after a show at the Fiesta Club in Stockton, to tell the band that they were "bloody rubbish." This is believed to have happened in the spring of 1967. Now, also in the north, at the Cavendish Club in Newcastle, around the first of August 1967, they encountered someone else, with a completely different opinion of

their music. The band had been running through some numbers in the club before the audience was let in for a show.

Justin Hayward said, "We didn't pay any attention to a man who wandered in and stood listening for a while." (JH-TP67)

Derek McCormick had entered on his own accord, there to see to the installation of air conditioning. He returned to watch the show that night. Mike Pinder

said, "[W]e were playing the Cavendish Club, Newcastle. A gentleman came back stage after the show and introduced himself as Derek McCormick. We found out later he was a millionaire – having made his money in heating and ventilation. He said he had been knocked out by our performance and wanted to help our career. He added, 'Till now, I've been a Sinatra fan. But yours is the most exciting sound I've ever heard." (MP-VT68)

In the first week of November 1967, in Newcastle's *The Journal*, it was reported:

> A young Tyneside millionaire has spent more than £5,000 to put a pop group back on its feet. He is 33-year-old Mr. Derek McCormick, of Fawdon, Newcastle, who owns a heating and ventilation business based in Gateshead factory. The group he has taken under his wing is the Moody Blues, who had a world-wide No. 1 hit in 1964 [sic, early 1965] with "Go Now!" …
>
> Mr. McCormick, reported to be one of Britain's youngest millionaires, discovered them when they were appearing at a Newcastle night club.

McCormick told *The Journal*, "I was there three months ago. I went backstage to have a word with them, and I was very impressed. I could see they had lots of talent, but they were too busy just trying to make ends meet to do any creative work."

The Journal reported that McCormick's first step to put the group back on their feet was to cancel all their bookings, and work out a new policy with their record company. He said, "I'm a business man, and I wouldn't do this unless I thought it was going to be a profitable investment." (DM-TJ67)

The article also reported that the Moodies would have a new single out in one week's time and a new album the week after that.

Days earlier, McCormick told Jack Bentley of London's *Sunday Mirror* (the weekend supplement of the *Daily Mirror*), "I think the Moody Blues are a big business proposition. I have already invested a lot of money in them and am prepared to continue.

"Personally, I don't dig the big beat; I'm a Sinatra fan. But I don't listen to an air conditioning plant for amusement either. I have a good enough ear to recognize that the Moody Blues are producing an exciting new sound and, combining this hunch with advice from experts, I'm convinced I'm on a good proposition." (DM-SM67)

Regarding McCormick, Mike Pinder told Bentley, "He seemed taken with us and, when I told him that we lacked modern equipment, he plunked down a check. This included £1,300 to buy a Mellotron – an electronic instrument which can reproduce something like the sound of a full orchestra.

"Many groups use a large number of 'straight' musicians to back discs now, but can't reproduce the sound on stage. That's where our Mellotron comes in." (MP-SM67)

It is important to note that £1,300 was the price of a brand-new Mellotron in 1967. Also, note McCormick's statement in Newcastle's *The Journal* at the start of November, that he had met the Moodies at the Cavendish Club three months prior, roughly at the start of August. The Moodies had recorded "Love and Beauty" on July 17 with the second-hand Mellotron the band had bought from the Birmingham Dunlop Tire company social center. McCormick wrote them a check to buy a new unit sometime in August. The Moodies now had two Mellotrons, one which they could keep in the studio and one for work on the road. Pinder, of course, customized both.

It also meant the Moodies could continue focusing on writing that 45-minute stage show … which, of course, could also be used as an album.

Celebrating new funding from a new manager ... and the latest rage in Britain – the 1967 film *Bonnie and Clyde*. (Photo source: MoodyBluesAttitude.com)

As a publicity stunt, McCormick rented vintage 1930s American gangster clothing to be worn by the Moodies in a photo shoot. At this time, *Bonnie & Clyde*, the Warren Beatty/Faye Dunaway film, was a major hit in England, prompting this bizarre new look. The gimmick worked and pictures of the Moodies in their new, albeit temporary, attire were picked up by numerous U.K. newspapers. Did this look bode well for the current single release, "Love and Beauty"? Hardly; perhaps more so for the flip side, "Leave This Man Alone."

In the December 1967 edition of *Pop Scene* (on newsstands in late November) Dick Tatham wrote:

> On the comeback trail – our old mates the Moody Blues, with a new sound, Bonnie and Clyde gear, and a backer.
>
> In their line-up, Mike Pinder, Graham [sic] Edge and Ray Thomas are old faithful dating back to the 1964 heyday of "Go Now!" New boys are John Lodge and Justin Hayward. Another addition to the line-up is Derek McCormick, 33, a millionaire in the heating and ventilating business.
>
> McCormick – from Newcastle – tells me, "Last thing I expected was to find myself tied up with a pop scene. But I heard the Moodies and reckoned they were big business."
>
> So, millionaire McCormick has all the cash necessary to bring the Moodies back on the scene in a super-colossal way.
>
> But what has been happening to the group since their last big hit, "From the Bottom of My Heart," back in the summer of 1965?

Mike Pinder caught Tatham up: "There were times when we were right up against it, financially. We made discs which missed the charts. Our stage dates thinned out and the group almost packed up. The turning point came when we were playing the Cavendish Club in Newcastle. Derek McCormick happened to be in the audience. He came back stage and said he was interested in helping our career. So here we are again."
(MP-PS67)

Graeme Edge said, "We told him what we wanted to do and where we wanted to go, and he said 'Okay.' He understood, you see. He digs people who want to have a shot at something. He removed all the financial strain we had on us." (GE-R68)

"Nights in White Satin"

Regarding the origins of "Nights in White Satin," Justin Hayward said, "Graeme and I were sharing two rooms with our girlfriends in Bayswater, and we came back very late at night [from a gig]. They were all asleep, and I sat on the side of the bed with my old 12-string – [which] I was renovating for Lonnie Donegan – and I wrote the basic two verses. One part of it was that I lived out of a suitcase then, I never had any possessions, and a previous girlfriend had bought me some white satin sheets. I was at the end of one big love affair and the beginning of another, and there were a lot of random thoughts by a 19-year-old boy. There's quite a lot of truth in it. I did write letters, never meaning to send. 'Just what you want to be, you will be in the end' is a philosophical thing." (JH-UC14)

Bayswater "bedsitter," home to Justin Hayward and Graeme Edge in 1967, and the location for the writing of "Nights in White Satin." (Courtesy Tony Brown)

Next to Hayward was his sleeping girlfriend, Marie, wrapped in those white satin sheets. He remembered it being between 2 and 4 a.m. In order not wake Marie, he left the room to work out the song on guitar.

Ray Thomas later teased, "Justin won't own up to it now, but he had the idea for 'Nights' sitting on the loo – with the lid down. Nice acoustics, normally." (RT-UC14)

Justin Hayward: "We were living in a tiny bedsitter at the time. In the bathroom, on my 12-string guitar, it sounded great. The only problem was, I did most of my composing on guitar after 1 a.m. It must have driven the neighbors mad." (JH-TS78)

Imagine trying to sleep in the wee hours of the morning, and hearing faintly through the wall from the apartment next door:

> *Nights in white satin, never reaching the end*
> *Letters I've written, never meaning to send*
> *Beauty I'd always missed, with these eyes before*
> *Just what the truth is, I can't say any more....*
>
> *Gazing at people, some hand in hand*
> *Just what I'm going through, they can't understand*
> *Some try to tell me, thoughts they cannot defend*
> *Just what you want to be, you will be in the end*

And I love you, Yes I love you, Oh how I love you...

The lyrics reveal the questions and troubles that afflict us all at some time in our lives, especially in our teens. Salvation seems only possible through love; and that mystical connection to another becomes a lifeline, even when you feel that "Just what the truth is, I can't say anymore."

The subject of that love – Marie Guirron – later told London's *Daily Mail*, "I met Justin through Graeme, the drummer in his band. Graeme knew a friend of mine and we all had been out drinking on a Friday night. Graeme was a little the worse for wear, so my girlfriend and I had taken him to our flat in Bayswater, West London. When I saw the lovely blond man walking up the stairs to my flat the next morning, I thought he was very attractive. I was a part-time model and actress, so I was used to meeting celebrities, but I was still pleased when he asked me for a date." (MH-DM97)

Soon the two were living together, sharing the small two-room "bedsitter" (plus bath) with Edge and his girlfriend. Those nights in white satin led to Justin's and Marie's marriage in 1970, and a daughter. The couple remain husband and wife to this day.

Hayward said, "I did the basic song and I took it in to play to the other guys the next morning, where we kept our equipment. And I played it through a couple of times. And the other guys were, like [yawning], 'Yeah, that's all right.' Mike said, 'Play it again.'"

This time, when Hayward performed the song, Pinder played along on the Mellotron, adding in the haunting string-like arrangement that followed each of Hayward's melodic lines. Hayward said, "I played it again and everybody was interested. So that was the difference [the Mellotron] made to my songs, in one small example." (JH-CB)

At this time, the Moodies recorded a session for the BBC Light Programme show *Saturday Club*, which, as they had done once before, included a cover version of the Animals' two-and-a-half year old hit "Don't Let Me Be Understood." This time, the performance sounded nothing like the Animals and everything like the new Moodies. Also committed to tape at the BBC studio was the new Justin Hayward song, "Nights in White Satin," enhanced by Pinder's Mellotron.

Adrian Day, the engineer on the session, was stunned by what he heard. He later said, "We recorded it on a stereo machine and we had no idea it was so good until then. We had gone out on a limb because it wasn't what was happening on the market at that time – a long, slow record." (AD-MO80)

John Lodge: "None of us had got the full picture of 'Nights' until then. When we went into the control room and listened to it, it was mesmerizing. It was a time when we all felt we were floating on air." (JL-UC14)

Graeme Edge: "[T]he first inclination of something extraordinary was when we recorded the song for a BBC show. There's just a magic when that happens...." (GE-DOFP97)

John Lodge: "[I]t was a fantastic burst to sort of walk into the control room, on a one-track machine, and listen to 'Nights in White Satin' for the first time. And that was one of the greatest moments ever." (LJ-RL86)

The groundwork for *Days of Future Passed* had now been set.

8

Days of Future Passed **(1967)**

U.K. album release:
Deram SML 707 (mono and stereo); November 11, 1967
Peak position in the U.K.: #27
France: #12 (1968); #1 (1972)
Australia: #10 (1973)

U.S. album release:
Deram DES-18012 (stereo); Deram DES-16012 (mono); March 2, 1968
Peak position in U.S.: #2 (1972, *Cashbox*)
(Certified platinum*)
Peak position in Canada: #3
(Certified platinum)
Peak position in Australia: #10

U.K. single release:
"Nights in White Satin" b/w "Cities"
Deram DM 161, November 10, 1967
Peak position in the U.K. (1968): U.K.: #19
France: #1 (in both 1968 and 1972)
Belgium: #1 (1968)
Netherlands: #1 (1968)
Holland: #2 (1968)
Poland: #2 (1968)

Spain: #3 (1968)
Australia: #5 (1968)
Switzerland: #6 (1968)
Argentina: #9 (1968)
Germany: #18 (1968)
Second chart run peak position in the U.K. (1972): U.K. #9
Australia: #8 (1973)

U.S. single release:
"Nights in White Satin" b/w "Cities"
Deram 45-85023; January 1968
Peak position in U.S. (1968): #93 (*Cashbox*)
Canada: #13 (1968)
Second chart run peak position in U.S. (1972): #1 (*Cashbox* and *Record World*)
(Certified gold)
Canada: #1 (1972)

Far East single release:
"Another Morning" / "Tuesday Afternoon (Forever Afternoon)"
April 1968
Peak position in Singapore: #3 (1968) (*Billboard*)
Hong Kong: #7 (1968) (*Billboard*)

U.S. single release:
"Tuesday Afternoon" b/w "Another Morning"
Deram 45-85028; July 1968
"Tuesday Afternoon" peak position in the U.S.: #24 (*Billboard*)
Canada: #12

It began merely as a recording session to make a third single for the reformed Moody Blues. Although "Fly Me High" and its flip side, "I Really Haven't Got the Time," and the follow-up, "Love and Beauty" b/w "Leave This Man Alone," all failed to make the charts, there had been enough positive press, airplay, jukebox action, and TV appearances to warrant giving the new lineup another chance.

"Cities" had been recorded around the time of "Love and Beauty." Hayward said, "'Cities' was another song that had a long time before I joined the Moodies. That was something that I used to do in folk clubs on the big 12-string." (JH-GM12)

The A-side was given to the newest Hayward composition – "Nights in White Satin."

Coupling "Cities" with "Nights" gave Hayward both sides of the new single, meaning he'd receive songwriting royalties, times two, for each single sold. He said, "If we had all known what we know today about B-sides in those days, I certainly wouldn't have had the B-side as well as the A-side." (JH-GM12)

Recording the "Nights in White Satin" single:

The recording date for the single was October 8, 1967. Graeme Edge said, "Till then we had always listened to record company executives who advised us to concentrate on recording three-minute up-tempo numbers with a couple of breaks in the intro, so that a dee-jay could come in with a snappy announcement and then go straight into the record. We had got nowhere on that advice." (GE-NME70)

Decca recording engineer Derek Varnals manning his control booth station, circa late 1960s. (Photo source: MoodyBluesAttitude.com)

Now with Tony Clarke producing, the daring decision was made to record the atypical and lengthy "Nights in White Satin" to be the next A-side.

Hayward said, "Mike and the Mellotron made my songs work. That's the simplest way I can put it. When he was playing piano it was difficult for me to try and find something that would be percussive on piano and that would be interesting. And particularly because Mike had already played, you know, the greatest piano single ever, so that was going to be impossible to follow. But when he found the Mellotron, suddenly my songs worked, you know. The moment we got the Mellotron, everything just kind of opened up a wonderful door to a world of imagination and the landscape of our possibilities." (JH-RC12 and JH-GM12)

Mike Pinder: "I loved the strings, flutes, and orchestra sounds that I could play with my Mellotron. I grew up to the music of Mantovani and the beautiful string orchestral arrangements. I knew the power, depth, and emotional landscape that I could add to our music and musical arrangements using the Mellotron. I could expand the songs we were writing with counter melodies and layers of orchestral sounds." (MP-AI17)

Derek Varnals, the Moody Blues' recording engineer for the next several years, was 22. A friend had gotten Varnals a job at Decca as an apprentice tape operator when he was just out of high school. Varnals told *Higher & Higher*, "[F]or a couple of years, [I was] working with various engineers with various 'histories,' and ages; some of the old-timers had been making records back in the '30s and, to a certain extent, had invented a lot of recording techniques that had become custom and practice. Some of my contemporaries there have gone on to become record producers in their own right. I was a contemporary of Gus Dudgeon, who was a record producer for Elton John [in the 1970s]. He was an engineer and 'tape op' at Decca."

But Dudgeon, who aspired to produce, had been moved up, and now it was young tape operator Derek Varnals' turn. Varnals said, "Basically, it was a very good grounding, because we had to be tape op on all types of recording sessions. Of course, in those days, we recorded real musicians with real microphones; we didn't plug them into anything. We had to learn how to use the room, how to select the type of microphone, how to use the microphones on instruments, how to lay out the studio so that you could record and the musicians could hear each other as well. You could always lay out a room so that you could record it, but if they couldn't hear it, they couldn't play properly. The use of headphones by musicians didn't really [occur at that time]. Drummers used headphones, but you didn't end up with a whole roomful of musicians using headphones. That didn't come until much later." (DV-H&H95)

Elsewhere, Varnals said, "'Nights in White Satin' was recorded as a single before the album was even conceived. The company wanted to get it out because the previous single had failed, and so, with a B-side ['Cities'] already in the can, the session was booked at short notice. The song was recorded in a day, and it didn't even make use of an orchestra or Deramic Sound." (DV-SOS09)

"Decca Panoramic Sound" was called "Deramic" for short. Prior to this, due to technical limitations, stereo recordings of popular music were mixed with certain vocals and instruments to the hard left, center, and right only. Often, the voices would come out of one speaker, with the instrument track emitting from the other. The new concept, however, allowed for more aural "space" between instruments. Decca established the sub-label Deram Records to specialize in recordings with a more natural-sounding stereo spread. Instead of overdubbing and mixing four individual mono tracks from a 4-track recorder, the Decca recording engineers used a pair of 4-track machines to layer multiple 2-channel (stereo) recordings. This new concept permitted the engineer to place instruments more easily in any position within the stereo field.

As with most London recording studios from this time, the control booth was elevated by nearly one story above the recording area. Varnals recalled, "I told the roadie who arrived with the band's equipment where I wanted to set everything up, and he got the bass and the Mellotron the wrong way around. Immediately under the control room window there was a stage area, and then there was a small step, half the height of the stage, down to a mezzanine level that ran the width of the studio.... Since musicians are often creatures of habit or superstition – 'Oh, that's my spot, I go here!' – this setup was cast in stone from then onwards and Mike was playing with his back to the drums, which he was actually happy to do as that's what he did on stage."

The Mellotron required ingenuity in recording. Varnals said, "It was completely new to me, and so I'd just decided to treat it like a keyboard instrument that sounded like strings. The job was to make it sound as sweet and smooth as possible, but of course some of that's down to the player. The Mellotron's 'attack' gives it a percussive quality that strings don't have, but Mike developed the technique of hitting a chord and then using the swell pedal to bring it up a split second later to avoid that attack. Of course, he'd anticipate it by a half a beat, a bit like playing a church organ where the sound doesn't come out straight away...."

"I certainly remember on 'Nights in White Satin' that, while he was putting his usual sound through the Marshall amp, I was getting hold of that amp and trying to find out what I could do to sweeten it up a bit. We needed a certain amount of clarity, but we didn't want shrieking treble, or for it to be too muddy if he was playing low down. You know, if he was playing a gig somewhere, he'd want to fill the hall with sound, but we were only projecting it as far as the microphone. The Marshall had at least three tone controls, so I spent some time trying to get some reasonable ingredients out of it before going into the control room and getting rid of that edgy sound. For that, I kept on using a reverb to blur the edges a bit, and I also gave it 'sustain' that helped Mike and his foot pedal in the chord changes. The Mellotron was *always* a battle....

"By the time we began recording the vocals, the reverb wasn't exactly dominating the track, but it was becoming a feature. The high sound of John's backing vocals was an octave above everything else, so I just pushed up the reverb, attempted to blend it, and the overall effect was quite dramatic." (DV-SOS09)

Tony Clarke in Decca Studio 1 control booth.
(Photo source: Prezi.com)

John Lodge recalled, "Harmonically, the spread is huge.... The scene is set with Justin's singing at the beginning. Every instrument on that record has its own space; nothing gets in the way of anything else, because everything has its own space, everything sounds bigger. I think that's what gives it its lushness, and the dynamics. Your imagination takes over; your brain is filling in the picture. It was like we were recording in Cinemascope. We used to talk about that. 'How wide is the color of the song.'" (JL-UN14)

Ray Thomas said, "John, Justin, Mike, and myself got round the mic. We only had four tracks, so we put four voices on one track, and four on another. When Tony mixed the two together, he said, 'You've got to come and have a listen to this.' When he played it back to us, it freaked us out that we could make such a big sound. We thought, 'Christ, that sounds bloody good.'" (RT-UN14)

Varnals said, "By the time we put the backing vocals on, the record had its own ethos, grand and dramatic, and it encouraged us to blend the voices in with the Mellotron. It starts quietly and builds. It's quite an intense lyric. They'd been playing it onstage, so they knew how to do it. But it needed a lot of reverb to round it out.... It's a very empty, simple arrangement. It's really just the layers of the Mellotron and the backing vocals that give it that drama. And the way the voices sparked off the echo-chamber just right. We tried it on other songs, to give them a similar approach to 'Nights in White Satin,' but the voices never worked like that again.

"Then at the weekly A&R meeting on the 16th, somebody said, 'It's not a single; should we do it on an LP?' That's when one of the A&R people – Michael Dacre-Barclay – grabbed it for a sound series he was already doing, to demonstrate the Deramic Stereo System." (DV-UN14)

Recording the Album

In the late summer of 1964, you'll recall, Ridgepride entered into a recording and licensing agreement with Decca Records concerning the Moody Blues. The standard contract from this period called for the delivery of a minimum of 20 "sides" (songs) per each 12-month period, for at least three years, should the label agree to pay for the sessions needed to record this many songs. This would produce enough new material, annually, for the release of three single and one LPs (with 14 new songs). If the records did not perform well, the label could reduce the amount of songs to be recorded, or cancel the contract.

Between the late summer of 1964 and that of 1965, with four singles and one album (which had 11 new songs), Decca released 19 "sides" by the Moody Blues. In all likelihood there was one more song recorded but not released, bringing the total to 20. All four singles and the album had sold well, and Decca naturally exercised its option for a second year.

For the second term, roughly 20 songs were recorded, which provided the six songs released on three different singles, a seventh song issued on an EP in France, and additional tracks earmarked for a second album, with had a working title of "Lookout." However, record sales were declining, and Decca was no longer making a profit off the Moody Blues. The label chose not to complete and release the LP.

Still, Decca clearly intended to keep the Moodies in its stable. It paid for additional sessions in 1967. Four of those songs had been issued on a pair of singles, with a third 45 now planned. Decca kept the Moodies under contract for a third year. But "Fly Me High," b/w "I Haven't Got the Time," and "Love and Beauty," b/w "Leave This Man Alone," missed the charts. Decca was understandably in no hurry to draw up a new three-year contract. This explains why Ray Thomas remembered the Moodies being in a "lease free" arrangement with the label – a period which would have begun in the fall of 1967. The band didn't owe Decca the remainder of the third year's required 20 sides since the label hadn't called the band in for additional recording sessions during that period. Any new songs recorded in the free lease period would belong to Decca, provided the label paid for the sessions. Decca could then release the songs or not, depending on its whim.

Explaining why the Moody Blues continued to record for the label after the third term of their contract ended, Justin Hayward said, "Although we'd put out a couple of singles for Decca, we owed them quite a bit of money – £5,000 I think – which was a hangover from the early days with Denny Laine. We were lumbered with the debt, and so we couldn't record for anyone else. So, if they asked us to do something, we had to do it.

"We had a phone call from them, asking whether we'd be interested in doing something for a demonstration record series, to show off the Deramic Sound System. The logo was a big ear, *reverberating*! It was really a different way of recording, at full frequency, right across the range. Most rock 'n' roll stuff cuts the top and bottom slices off so you get the maximum level onto the record. This was real high quality recording, classical standard." (JH-TRC96)

Derek Varnals: "At Decca, a guy in marketing [Michael Dacre-Barclay] had developed a stereo series called DSS [Deramic Sound System] which they wanted to promote. [It] was a kind of wide stereo. But not in the traditional early stereo – which we used to call 'ping-pong table-tennis stereo,' [in which] this is on the left, this is on the right; very widely separated kind of stereo. They wanted to have more of a smooth width to it; sort of a Cinemascope stereo." (DV-H&H95b)

The promotional campaign had only been in the works for a few months. Varnals recalled, "Between June and August of '67 Decca Records produced six orchestral albums with the Deramic Sound System. All had 'night' in the title – *Strings in the Night*;

Brass in the Night; *Piano in the Night* – it was a pretty straightforward theme. At some point, Decca decided to liven up the label by having a pop group record with an orchestra…. and for the orchestration they'd be using Peter Knight, who, among other things, had worked on *Voices in the Night*."

"And what [Decca] decided was that this fusion of orchestra and rock group was going to be put on that series. And so they wanted an act that was signed to Decca that would be able to do that sort of stuff. I'd been working as an assistant on a lot of these orchestral sessions – doing some overdubs and mixes – and they felt that the Moody Blues was the act to do it. That was decided, as far as my memory goes, *after* we recorded 'Nights in White Satin.'" (DV-SOS09 and DV-H&H95b)

Justin Hayward: "They wanted a record that would demonstrate that rock 'n' roll could be as interesting in stereo as classical music, because there weren't many rock 'n' roll stereo records. Even *Sgt. Pepper* was hard to find in stereo." (JH-TRC96)

The Beatles had actually only mixed *Sgt. Pepper* in mono, leaving producer George Martin to handle the stereo mix. This was common practice. Singles would be heard on (mono) transistor radios, and few consumers of rock 'n' roll owned stereo systems. Therefore, an album's stereo mix wasn't a high priority in the breakneck pace of pop. For example, only the last two Beatles album, 1969's *Abbey Road* and 1970's *Let it Be*, received their original mix in stereo.

Mike Pinder: "[T]he day came where Decca Records in London wanted to make an album and try to update Dvorak's *New World Symphony*, and someone had the brilliant idea to let a rock group try and do it." (MP-C71)

Czech composer Antonin Dvorak's 1863 "Symphony No. 9 in E Minor" was subtitled "From the New World." Part of its appeal was that the music was in the public domain. No royalties or permissions were involved.

Justin Hayward: "They wanted us to play Dvorak – work out baroque arrangements of the main themes – and then the orchestra conducted by Peter Knight would play real Dvorak in between. That wasn't what we wanted to do, but we agreed because it was our only opportunity to spend more than three hours in the studio." (JH-TRC96)

Graeme Edge: "We were given a copy of Dvorak's *New World Symphony* and told to pick out the melody lines and put a beat to them. Peter Knight was to do the orchestration for the London Festival Orchestra, who were engaged to back us; all very posh and prestigious." (GE-NME71)

John Lodge remembered that lyrics were to be written. He said, "The record company wanted us to take the melodies of Dvorak's *New World Symphony* and put lyrics to it, and make what they called a 'sampler album.' They were exploring stereo, and they were exploring full frequency sound at that time. Decca Records in the U.K. had a hardware department making turntables and amplifiers, but they didn't have the records to go with it to explore stereo full frequency sound. So they asked if we would be interested, and, of course, we said 'yes,' [but] instead of using Dvorak's *New World Symphony*, we started writing this stage show which evolved into *Days of Future Passed*." (JH-GM12)

In other words, Decca wanted something along the lines of the recent Procol Harum single, "A Whiter Shade of Pale," which combined a Bach-derived melody with a contemporary arrangement and lyrics by the song's co-authors Gary Brooker, Keith Reid, and Matthew Fisher.

Ray Thomas's memory differs from the other Moodies; his interpretation of the assignment is certainly the most outrageous. "They wanted us to play tunes like 'Blue Suede Shoes,' 'Rock Around the Clock,' and stuff like that, and wanted Peter Knight and the London Festival Orchestra to play Dvorak's *New World Symphony*. We said that's going to sound bloody awful – one minute they're listening to 'Blue Suede Shoes' and then the next minute to the symphony and us playing something else!" (RT-RS15)

At first blush, this project hardly seemed likely to burnish the Moody Blues' prospects for rock success. But it would at least bring them additional experience in the recording studio, and fulfill their contractual obligations. Then they'd be free to negotiate a new recording contract, with Decca or elsewhere.

Graeme Edge: "Tony Clarke was very instrumental in getting it all together. You must realize that at the time we were stone cold. The Moody Blues were a bubblegum group that had one hit record two years before and we were dead on the scrap heap. People were waiting for us to go home and be butchers and bakers and candlestick makers." (GE-C71)

The group had one other supporter at the label, a bit higher up than Clarke – Decca A&R manager Hugh Mendl, who had been instrumental in the recent establishment of London/Decca's new subsidiary imprint Deram Records. Mendl, as Varnals recalled, was the executive at Decca who would create budgets for various projects and get the go-ahead to proceed.

Justin Hayward: "They put us together with a wonderful man called Hugh Mendl, a walking encyclopedia of Decca.... He was an executive producer, and liaised us and Peter Knight, the orchestral arranger. Hugh just said, 'Do what you want to do,' which [was] the best thing anyone had ever said to us." (JH-TRC96)

What the Moodies wanted to do was the stage show they had been writing. Mike Pinder said, "I had always wanted to create something that was conceptual. I loved the work of Mantovani. I wanted to have our albums on people's shelves – albums that people would want to collect, and play in their entirety." (MP-BCB17)

Graeme Edge: "This will sound either crazy or ruthless, depending on the way you look at it, but no sooner had we heard the idea than we were plotting a major double-cross. The plan consisted of misapplying all Decca's facilities, laid on at great expense, to shelve their idea and record an album of our two weeks' birth pangs, *Days of Future Passed*.

"It first meant talking Peter into becoming an accessory before the fact. Naturally, he was very apprehensive, but he listened to what we had to offer and finally agreed to stick his neck out. I salute his tremendous guts." (GE-NME71)

Justin Hayward: "In actual fact, the idea for turning it around came from Michael Dacre-Barclay, who used to do special projects for Decca – take a quick royalty and bugger off. I have to give him credit for turning it around with Peter....

"So we went to Peter and said, 'We're not that keen on the Dvorak idea, but we have got all these songs that we would like to record.' We played them and he said, 'I think they're great. Why don't we do it the other way round – you do your songs and I'll do the orchestral versions of them.'" (JH-GM12 and JH-TRC96)

Graeme Edge: "Peter was a wonderful guy for taking the project on. He was very well established in the company, so he didn't have to do it. But he was a music man, and when we told him what we had, he said, 'Yeah, I'd much rather do *that* than rehash Dvorak.' So he did it, bless him." (GE-GM12)

Ray Thomas: "We said, 'They'll still get a rock 'n' roll band on there, and they'll still get an orchestra.' But it isn't exactly what they wanted. [Peter Knight] said, 'Well, I'll go along with it.' And Tony Clarke said, 'So will I.' I mean, he could've lost his job over it." (RT-DM15)

Regarding the album's inspiration, Hayward revealed, "At the time there was an album called 'Signs of the Zodiac' out, which impressed us and we thought the idea could be used for a more pop-based form of music. We did it on [*Days of Future Passed*] because we could take the risk – we had nothing to lose." (JH-DME68)

The correct album title was *The Zodiac: Cosmic Sounds*. It was a collaborative concept album focused on the signs of the Zodiac, and was released by Elektra Records in May 1967. The album's twelve tracks were a heady mix of sitar, classical instruments, and an early prototype of the Mood synthesizer, with narration thrown in. It's easy to see echoes of the concept in *Days of Future Passed*.

Of course there was another influence – the Beatles' *Sgt. Pepper's Lonely Hearts Club Band,* released four months earlier.

Graeme Edge: "Like everyone else, we picked up on that album as a magnificent departure from rock music – expanding both a musical and lyrical consciousness.

"The Mellotron had already opened up a whole new era to us but we had found it difficult to use this monster instrument without thinking it would make us sound sugary. When we heard the Beatles and what they did with strings, we realized that there was a way to use this musical flow, this lack of attack, on the Mellotron. Just that record opened the door and allowed us to explore that one scene they highlighted. It was perfect for us at that time and we totally explored the possibilities." (GE-S73)

John Lodge: "When we actually then came to record [the album], we went to Decca and said, 'Can we have lockout time?' – i.e., we wanted the studio 24 hours a day so we could set up all our equipment and just record. In those days, you could only record in strict morning sessions. They agreed and then we [decided] that instead of using the melodies from Dvorak, we would use our own songs." (JL-DAFT97)

Tony Clarke: "We went into the studio under that pretext…. They were doing things like *Brass in the Night* and *Stings in the Night* – all the albums were to come out under the banner of Phase 4… In all the smoke and confusion of that, we got in and got the studio time and made *Days of Future Passed*, which wasn't '*Anything* in the Night'!" (TC-H&H95)

The band members entered the studio on October 18 to begin recording tracks for the newly conceived concept album. Mike Pinder's "Dawn Is a Feeling," the lead-off vocal track on the album, was the first to be committed to tape. Pinder said, "Gradually, it began to dawn on all of us that we were looking for the same thing." (MP-R70)

As this realization came, Pinder worked the word "dawn" into his new song.

> *Dawn is a feeling, a beautiful ceiling*
> *The smell of grass, just makes you pass*

into a dream....

You look around you; Things they astound you
So breathe in deep; You're not asleep
Open your mind.

Justin Hayward sang the verses to "Dawn Is a Feeling." Pinder said, "I felt his voice suited the verses, and I could contrast this with the punch line!" (MP-H&H94)

The punch line was the middle section of the song, which Pinder sang.

Justin Hayward: "Mike's lovely song really turned me on.... 'Nights in White Satin' and 'Dawn Is a Feeling' were the two key songs that gave us the idea of the story of a day in the life of one guy, and that's what our stage show was about before *Days of Future Passed* was mentioned or thought about." (JH-GM12)

Following "Dawn Is a Feeling" and "Nights in White Satin," the third song written for the stage show was Lodge's "Peak Hour."

John Lodge: "I remember it like it was yesterday. I was in the rear of a transit van as we were driving back from a show in the north of England. I could feel this tempo in the van, like a bass drum. I asked Graeme, 'Can you keep this beat going?' He said, 'Yes,' and pounded away while in the back of that van. It is a driving song. In America, you have 'rush hour,' and in England we have 'peak hour.' I wanted to write a rock 'n' roll song with Mike's Hammond B3 organ in the middle, take a choir break, and then back to the tempo, a bit like the Beatles, as we were all growing up [musically] at the same time. With the album, it was a great time to write songs and introduce our different way, experimenting with music." (JL-GM17)

Justin Hayward: "'Peak Hour' is a little gem that I love to this day. It's such a simple little piece of writing." (JH-GM12)

Hayward and Pinder were the two experienced songwriters in the group, and mentored Lodge, Thomas, and Edge. From their guidance, and the jam sessions, came:

... Minds are subject to what should be done
Problem solved, time cannot be won
One hour a day, one hour at night
Sees crowds of people, all meant for flight
Peak hour, peak hour, peak hour
It makes me want to run out and tell them
They've got time
Take a step back out
And look in at their debt
And their time ...

The verses of the song sound are reminiscent of the Beatles' harmonies. This is actually John Lodge and Ray Thomas blending their voices, with a little bit of Mike Pinder in the mix, creating an uncanny John, Paul, and George aural impression.

John Lodge: "We'd developed this vocal sound, and also because Ray Thomas and his flute-playing... we had this orchestral sound within the band.... And the Mellotron was one of those fantastic instruments that blended and gave us exactly what we wanted." (JL-RL86)

In an album infused with lush orchestral interludes, and more orchestration simulated by the Mellotron, "Peak Hour" represents a bold crash of the cymbals. The arrangement, with Hayward's hard rock approach to guitar playing, and driving rhythm section, showcases how the Moody Blues could rock as well as the Who from this period, in startling contrast to Peter Knight's hustle-bustle orchestral section.

Placed on the album between "Dawn Is a Feeling" and "Peak Hour" is "Another Morning," by Ray Thomas. He said, "[E]verybody was writing; everybody was trying it. Some of the stuff got thrown in the bin by everybody – especially when you may have smoked some illicit stuff. You think, 'This is fantastic!', and then you listen to it in the morning and think, 'This is a heap of shit; in the bin!'" (RT-DM15)

The charming "Another Morning" was not destined for the trash bin. But, as with Lodge's "Peak Hour," the experienced songwriters in the band lent a hand to help shape what Thomas had conceived.

Justin Hayward: "For Mike and I, it was almost like school [writing songs]. I had to have everything done before I went into the studio – I had to have *everything* done. For John, Ray, and Graeme, because they hadn't been writers before, [they] came at it from a very different point of view. They would let things happen in the studio and then work on them. That was my experience with the other guys' contributions. I used to love working on Ray's stuff, because I could just make up the chords. I'd say, 'What about this?,' and he'd say, 'That sounds great!' I could have said a completely different chord and he'd say, 'That sounds great!'

"That was the beauty of it. We all came from a different starting point. Mike was a fantastic pub pianist; he could sit there and entertain people for hours and hours. I came from folk clubs and constructing songs for publishing. The others came at it from a completely different point of view, and that's what made the whole thing interesting. Each one of us had different things to bring to the album." (JH-GM12)

Regardless of how many cooks were in the kitchen, Thomas made an impressive debut as a songwriter with his two contributions to *Days of Future Passed*. The first, "Another Morning," offered an infectious melody and lyrics, set to a mid-tempo beat and multiple layers of Thomas's flute, giving the listener a pleasant reminder of the imagination of a child. Thomas sang:

> *Balloons flying, children sighing; what a day to go kite flying!*
> *Breezes cool, away from school; cowboys fighting out a duel.*
> *Time seems to stand quite still; In a child's world, it always will....*

The song's celebration of childhood innocence seemed itself a rebellion against the ever-increasingly complexities of western society.

Graeme Edge: "Ray is a wonderful, natural tenor. He's a Welsh guy. What a surprise! The Welsh are famous for their tenors. He had a very pure, very powerful voice. He also has a very whimsical way of writing. 'Breezes cool, away from school, cowboys fighting a duel.' He brought both a very good voice and a whimsical clown." (GE-GM12)

Hayward chose the afternoon for his next contribution. He said, "So we had those two times of the day ["Dawn Is a Feeling" and "Nights in White Satin"] and the idea [for the album]; then it was just a question of grabbing different times of the day to write

151

about…. I just put my hand up for 'The Afternoon.' So, I ended up with 'Tuesday Afternoon' … I was going back to my parents' house in Wiltshire. I smoked a couple joints, went out into a field with a guitar and sat there and wrote that song." (JH-GM12)

> *Tuesday afternoon; I'm just beginning to see*
> *Now I'm on my way; It doesn't matter to me*
> *Chasing the clouds away.*
>
> *Something calls to me; the trees are drawing me near*
> *I've got to find out why; those gentle voices I hear*
> *Explain it all with a sigh*
>
> *I'm looking at myself, reflections of my mind*
> *It's just the kind of day to leave myself behind …*

Hayward's lyrics are a grand expression of the "Hippie Dream" of 1967, contributing to the mystical labeling the group would soon be given by the press and fans alike. In the decades to follow, the Moodies would often wonder at the way their fans looked upon them as soothsayers. The seeds for that reverence began in songs like these.

Regarding the recording, Derek Varnals said, "The Studio One live area had an old-fashioned sound, and you can hear it on tracks like 'Tuesday Afternoon.' You can hear the drums going around the room and ending up in the acoustic guitar mic. Still, that was accepted back then – it was the old-fashioned way of doing things." (DV-SOS09)

As the recording sessions continued, John Lodge volunteered to write a song about the evening.

> *Evening, has earned its place today; I'm tired of working away….*
> *… Evening time to get away, 'til the next day….*

The theme of escape from the day's responsibilities continues.

Mike Pinder chose "The Sun Set" as the title for his second contribution. As with "Dawn Is a Feeling," Pinder shared the vocal with Hayward. Hayward begins, and then Pinder combines his voice with that of Hayward's for the second verse, then takes the lead on the middle eight.

"The Sun Set" appears to be a very personal song, as the lyrics give indication of Pinder's growing spirituality.

> *When the sun goes down, and the clouds all frown,*
> *Night has begun for the sunset.*
> *See it with your eyes, Earth re-energized*
> *By the sun's rays every day.*
> *Take a look out there; Planets everywhere….*
>
> *I can see it all from this great height.*
> *I can feel the sun slipping out of sight*
> *And the world still goes on through the night.*

Pinder said, "[S]ome people thought we were permanently on drugs and just freaking-out – but this was simply because our change of direction coincided with that period in pop music, which was called psychedelic." (MP-R70)

Ray Thomas's second contribution to the album was "Twilight Time." Over the pounding rock 'n' roll keyboard arrangement from Pinder, Thomas raises his voice an octave, singing a lyric which demonstrates the influence – or collaboration – of poet Graeme "Breathe deep the gathering gloom" Edge:

> *Twilight time to dream awhile, in veils of deepening blue.*
> *As fantasy strides, over colorful skies of form disappearing from view.*
> *In twilight time, dream with me awhile.*

Once again, the Moodies entice the listener to set the cares of the world aside, follow their lead, and "dream with me awhile." It's no wonder that the dreamy music and pseudo-mystical lyrics entranced young listeners. The teenage years are the times when most people search for greater meaning in life.

"Nights in White Satin" followed, and again spoke to yearning young minds, seducing with its eerie otherworldly sounds. Hayward gently told listeners, "Just what I'm going through, they can't understand," but then assured them that "Just what you want to be, you'll be in the end."

Regarding the spoken-word passages he wrote for the album, Edge said, "Unfortunately, being musicians, there was a part of each day that we were not very aware of, which was from dawn to about midday, *because we were usually asleep.* We really didn't have a lot of material for that. I remember, I was sitting with the roadie. We had a Volkswagen van for the equipment, and a four-seated car for the guys – [but] there were five of us! We used to have to take turns to ride with the roadie in the van. It was my turn, and I opened a pack of Players cigarettes, so I'd have something to write on. I was actually trying to write a lyric for a song so that the guys [might] put music to it – to fill in the dawn gap. As part of the writing, it seemed obvious to go to evening as well. I dashed it off during the three-hour drive from London to Carlisle. Then, we were in the studio the next day, because we were doing gigs at night and recording during the day for *Days of Future Passed.* I gave it to everybody and said, 'What do you think?' They all said, 'It's great work – great work, but there's no way we can do music to that. It's just too many words; you can't sing that many words.' Mike [said] that, and he started reading it, and said, 'We'll do it *that* way; we'll just put it in a poem.' From that point on [with the albums to come], it became a tradition, and gave people clues to the theme." (GE-GM12)

> *… Cold hearted orb that rules the night,*
> *removes the colors from our sight.*
> *Red is grey and yellow white,*
> *But we decide which is right,*
> *and which is an illusion.*

The Moodies began recording the album on October 18, and finished nine days later, on the 27th.

Graeme Edge: "It is astonishing what you can sometimes get away with in a big organization. We had one of Decca's main studios for two weeks with a bunch of technicians assisting. Yet no one, but *no one*, questioned what we were doing." (GE-NME71)

For some, the impact of hearing *Days of Future Passed* was immediate. The Moodies' millionaire manager, Derek McCormick, remarked, "I sat in the studio night after night, enthralled as the boys laid down the music for their *Days of Future Passed* album. I was convinced it was revolutionary and I *knew* it was big business." (DM-HT70)

Then it was time to bring in the orchestra.

Peter Knight was 50. He had worked in television – as a composer and musical director – for numerous TV specials, made-for-TV movies, and limited-run series. Among these jobs, Knight wrote the theme music for the British pop music "hit parade" series, *Thank Your Lucky Stars*. Knight was often commissioned to arrange full orchestrations for all types of recording artists, and he soon had his own ensemble – The Peter Knight Orchestra. Just prior to working with the Moody Blues, Knight had experimented with combining pop and orchestral music when he recorded George Harrison's composition, "Within You, Without You" (from *Sgt. Pepper*), and released it as a single on Mercury Records in 1967.

Tony Clarke: "He was affiliated with Decca and he was the logical choice to orchestrate and augment the tracks that we'd done for *Days of Future Passed*. In most cases, the tracks would be done and then the next day we'd race out to Peter Knight's place and play a track to him and say, 'Listen to this,' and he got the gist of what we were saying. The orchestra was put on in one day at the end of it all." (TC-H&H95)

That day was November 3, 1967. Tony Clarke recalled that there were around 45 players in the orchestra, and it was so crowded in Decca Studio 1 that the 'arco bass' player had to be stationed in the doorway. The most difficult section of the score was saved for the end of the day – the orchestral backing track to "Nights in White Satin," beginning at the middle of the song and building to the grand finale.

Derek Varnals: "There was never any plan to have an orchestra on that song. Peter Knight just wrote the little descending woodwind piece before "Nights in White Satin" comes in. And then, he decided it would be hard to pick up the end of the song without an orchestra over the last verse and chords." (DV-SOS09)

Justin Hayward: "I was the only one in the studio when they recorded the London Festival Orchestra. They only did it *once*. They did a rehearsal with Tony Clarke, and prepared the tape [of our recordings]… with blank tape on a 4-track [for the orchestra], with Peter Knight, counting down. It's unbelievable how they did this. They'd already put the songs in the right order with the gaps in between, and then Peter would conduct the orchestra to his own voice counting. They rehearsed it once without [recording] it, no alternative take or anything, then took a break for a cup of tea, then they did a take. And that was it! It was all over." (JH-GC13)

Hayward said Peter Knight's score was "just marvelous," then added, "I'd go through all sorts of traumas if I were trying to write out all the pieces myself. Peter had that gift. The orchestra knew when they turned up for Peter Knight that the writing was going to be great quality." (JH-GM12)

The Moodies were also impressed with the facility, and the two wizards that came with it – Tony Clarke and Derek Varnals. Hayward said, "[T]he quality of the recording was so wonderful. At Decca, we were lucky; we were always recorded beautifully. We were recorded in full stereo. At the time, people weren't even sure that stereo would catch on – 'People won't want to buy two speakers; it's too complicated!' But our songs were done so well, it proved it could be done." (JH-OTH09)

John Lodge clearly remembers the first playback session for the completed album, after the orchestration had been added. He said, "We were so excited about the album. It was recorded in stereo and we had a playback. We put some speakers up in the studio and invited our friends and [some] from Decca down. We turned the lights out and played *Days of Future Passed* from the beginning to the end." (JL-DOFP97)

Ray Thomas: "We sat there and put it through a couple of big speakers. And we freaked out!" (RT-BCB17)

John Lodge: "It was like a concert in the dark. Then it finished, the lights went on and you could see a smile on everyone's face as though something magical had happened. I can still get that feeling now. We knew it was right – I'm not talking about commercial success; I'm talking about what the Moody Blues wanted, a culmination of what we'd done for a year." (JL-DOFP97)

A second playback was then scheduled for the record company heads.

***

As for the different recollections regarding what Decca knew or did not concerning the making of *Days of Future Passed*, we've heard all five members of the Moody Blues and their producer state that the recording sessions were conducted covertly. Hayward said that Decca A&R manager Hugh Mendl advised the band that they should do what they wanted, and then, we may assume, obligingly looked the other way. Hayward also said that Decca special-projects coordinator Michael Dacre-Barclay was in on it. And the entire band credits Tony Clarke and Peter Knight for sticking their necks out and making the entire endeavor possible.

But Derek Varnals never believed it. He felt Decca had to know. Checking his personal journal from that time, Varnals said, "On the 20th [of October], the Friday morning, I went to a meeting when they knocked around the idea of doing a rock band with orchestral bits, in the same way that 'A Day in the Life' [by the Beatles] had. But nobody mentioned Dvorak. I think that's when the concept of an album set over a day was developed, with 'Nights in White Satin' at the end." (DVUC14)

Yet, after referring to his journal, Varnals has also confirmed that the album sessions began on October 18 with Mike Pinder's "Dawn Is a Feeling." If the concept album idea comprised of original Moodies material wasn't discussed until the 20th, then what did those at the meeting think was being recorded on October 18, 19, and 20?

And, for that matter, exactly who was at the meeting? If the picture on the back of the album's cover is any indication – if this was typical of the meetings, or was indeed *the* meeting referred to by Varnals – then those present, along with young Varnals, were the five Moody Blues, Tony Clarke, and one unidentified man. Might that man be Michael Dacre-Barclay, who Hayward acknowledged, along with Clarke and Knight, was responsible for setting the wheels in motion of *Days of Future Passed*?

Regardless, one newspaper article from the time the album was recorded seems to support Varnals' account.

In the October 22, 1967 edition of Manchester's *Sunday Mirror*, staff writer Jack Bentley interviewed Mike Pinder and Moodies' manager Derek McCormick. He reported:

Decca Records seem to share Mr. McCormick's faith in the Moody Blues. They have invested £9,000 on their new LP, *Days of Future Passed*. It will be out November 3, with a single called "Nights in White Satin." I've heard

From the back album cover: A production meeting at Decca between (L-R): Edge, Hayward, Thomas, Lodge, Pinder, Clarke, an unknown person, and Varnals.

[the single] and I wouldn't mind investing a few bob myself.

The single would actually be issued on November 10, followed one day later by the album.

Note the date of this article – October 22. Varnals' logs document that "Nights in White Satin" was recorded on October 8. The album was recorded from October 18 through 27, with the London Festival Orchestra in the studio on November 3. Yet, according to Jack Bentley's article on October 22, Decca already knew the album's title, had a budget of £9,000, and a tentative release date.

This author has heard from a handful of individuals who doubt that the recording of *Days of Future Passed* was a stealth operation, with one citing the October 22, 1967 Jack Bentley article as "proof." Yet, it is difficult to fathom a conspiracy between Hayward, Pinder, Lodge, Thomas, Edge, and producer Tony Clarke to invent a fictional account concerning the making of the album, and to have stuck with that story for decades. And, if fiction, why didn't Hugh Mendl, Peter Knight, Michael Dacre-Barclay, or anyone else at Decca ever dispute it?

All that Bentley's article does prove is that he visited with Mike Pinder and Derek McCormick, and they provided him with the information concerning the project. As they presented it to Bentley:

1) The Moodies were making an album. True.

2) They – and "they" could mean only the Moodies, their manager, and their producer – were planning on calling it *Days of Future Passed*. True again, but this does not mean Decca knew the band's intended title. Nor does this mean that all of the Decca heads were aware of exactly what was going on.

3) That the budget set by Hugh Mendl was £9,000. True. But this could have been for the project as originally planned. Whether recording *Days of Future*

Passed with the Moodies and Peter Knight and his orchestra over ten days in Studio 1, or recording *New World Symphony* with the same people, in the same period of time, the price would have been the same.

4)   That Bentley was under the impression that Decca was supportive of the project. Of course he would be. But did he get this from Decca, or was he basing his assumption merely on his conversation with Pinder and McCormick?

In other words, the Jack Bentley article proves little when questioning the veracity of the account given by the Moody Blues and their producer concerning the making of *Days of Future Passed*. It is certainly possible that the majority of the Decca people did not know what was transpiring in Studio 1.

Ray Thomas: "Every Tuesday, all the producers would bring in what they'd done that week and all these old men would sit around the table, and these guys would play what they'd recorded during the week, and then they'd decide, 'Yes, we will release that and we'll put that amount of money into promoting that,' and all that shit. And so, Tony put it on and they sat through *Days of Future Passed*. They sat through it, and they all said, 'What the hell is it?!'" (RT-DM15)

Graeme Edge: "Picture those pundits sitting in solemn conclave and closing their eyes to listen to what they expected to be a trendy mutilation of Dvorak, and suddenly realizing that they had been horribly tricked. I am told they went 'spare.' Members of the jury were shouting and screaming. They were going to kill it and see that none of us ever worked again, *anywhere*." (GE-NME91)

Tony Clarke: "I remember I couldn't even get them to play 'Nights in White Satin' to certain executives. And when I did, they said, 'Well, it's too long and it's too slow and what's it about?' … The managing director of Decca at that time listened to *Days of Future Passed* and said, 'The Moodies with a symphony orchestra? You can't dance to it – what is this?!'" (TC-H&H95)

John Lodge: "[T]hey had no idea at all what we had recorded. They had no idea what to do with it, and, consequently, they moved away from it; moved away from the whole idea as though it was never going to work." (JL-GM12)

Ray Thomas: "They weren't going to release it." (RT-PROG13)

Graeme Edge: "Then someone pointed out that it had cost them £25,000 [sic] to make *Days of Future Passed*." (GE-NME71)

Ray Thomas: "They were all well pissed off, except one guy called Walt McGuire, who was over – *fortunately* – from the States. He was from London Records, which is Decca-America, and he said, 'If you're not gonna release it here, I'm going to release it in the States; no trouble.' He loved it." (RT-DM15)

Tony Clarke: "[T]he head of the classical division said, 'Well, I think it's extremely good,' so I'm indebted to him because I was in a meeting with all these executives and I was rather junior at the time. He had the foresight to say that he thought it was pretty new and imaginative." (TC-H&H95)

John Lodge: "[W]e had two people there who were really fabulous – a guy who was head of the classical department at Decca Records called Hugh Mendl, and Walt McGuire, the vice president of London Records in New York [who] was actually in London at the time. Both those people knew exactly what we were trying to do, and they became our mentors, really, and they supported it all the way. Beautiful, good music men." (JL-GM12)

Once a decision was reached to put the album out, a sleeve design was quickly conceived. David Anstey, a young Decca artist, was given the assignment. While many consider *Days of Future Passed* a classic album, we've never heard anyone say the same of the album cover.

Justin Hayward: "I find the artwork quite difficult to look at, to be honest, because there's so much going on. It was reduced in scale from David Anstey's original picture. He was just thrown this idea, and we met him in a pub and told him about our songs, and he knocked that out, *and they used it!* It was all very quick and cheap…. We certainly turned that around on the next album. We were lucky enough to have a chance to *make* another album, and from that point on, Phillip Travers, a staff artist in the art department of Decca, did our sleeves." (JH-GM12)

Anstey continued with Decca for another two decades, designing and painting covers for classical music collections devoted to Beethoven and Bach, among others, and, at the other end of the spectrum, British progressive rock bands, including Camel, Caravan, Chicken Shack, Galliard, Savoy Brown, and 10cc.

As for the back cover, Graeme Edge said, "[O]n the first pressing, there was not much of an ego [in the band]. There were no photographs of any of us, except the tops of our heads sitting at a meeting; it was all very low key. The reason for that was we had [been on] a Beatles tour. We were opening for the Beatles. We just saw what a life they led. We said, 'No, no, no, that's not for us!' They couldn't do *anything*. They couldn't get out of their hotel; they couldn't go to a pub or a club; they were trapped in their hotel room every day. It was a bit scary. I'd step out of a hotel, and just because I was short, with long hair – well, long hair then – I'd be chased up the street, and I wasn't even one of 'em! You get four or five of those 14-or 15-year-old girls – *you get four or five of them hangin' on you* – you ain't got a prayer! When they get a bit hysterical, they are strong creatures, so it was very scary. We were so terrified of that." (GE-CA07)

The songwriting credits on the album say "Redwave," where Thomas's and Lodge's names should be – an effort, according to Hayward, by a Decca executive trying to line his pockets.

Therefore, the band requested that their faces not be featured on the record sleeve.

When asked about the curious songwriting credit on the album for "Redwave, Knight," Justin Hayward candidly answered, "Redwave was a Michael Dacre-Barclay way to take a royalty from the publishing. To this day, anybody who was involved in that album walks around shaking his fist in the air. We were on a minute percentage, because we had a debt to

Decca, which we were supposed to be repaying by doing this demonstration album for them. *Days of Future Passed* came out as a demonstration record, and then [Decca] put it up to full price when they realized its potential, and that people were playing it." (JH-GM12)

In time, for future pressings, the credits would be straightened out. Hayward, Pinder, Lodge, Thomas, and Edge would all be acknowledged for the songs they wrote. Tony Clarke would get plenty of acknowledgement, too, as did Peter Knight. The one person who didn't, to Justin Hayward's thinking, was Derek Varnals. He said, "I think that Derek Varnals deserves a great deal of credit, as an engineer. He was classically trained, and he had an ear for the sound that we wanted and how to achieve it, that was extraordinary. He was extremely important to what we did, and he's never been given full credit for it." (JH-GM94)

It is remarkable how fast things were done back in the 1960s in the entertainment world – with television, movies, and music. Budgets were smaller then, time shorter, with far less hindrance or "help" provided by management.

Consider this: Peter Knight and the London Festival Orchestra had but one day to record their contribution to the album – November 3, 1967 – and then the album was mixed and presented to the Decca brass to be judged and discussed. Once a decision was made to release the LP, only a handful of days were left for cover design, sleeve notes, and manufacturing. *Days of Future Passed* was in record shops and the music departments of department stores only eight days later, on November 11.

In such an extraordinary rush to release, Hugh Mendl, the Moodies' staunch supporter from within the Decca management, dashed off the sleeve notes for the back cover.

> In *Days of Future Passed* the Moody Blues have at last done what many others have dreamed of and talked about: they have extended the range of pop music, and found the point where it becomes one with the world of the classics.
>
> Here, where emotion and creativity blend – where poetry, the beat group, and the symphony orchestra feed on each other's inspiration – the Moodys have chosen to paint their picture of everyman's day….
>
> For such a fusion of pop composition and classical writing, it seemed obvious that the Deram Sound System would be the ideal recording technique. And here in the deep, wide spectrum of "all-round sound" it has, we believe, become more possible than in any other way to be totally submerged – and hence totally committed

to such a deeply emotional statement of the human condition today.

Release / Reaction:

U.K. single release:
"Nights in White Satin" b/w "Cities"
Deram DM 161; November 10, 1967

U.K. album release:
Days of Future Passed
Deram SML 707; November 11, 1967

The first positive reaction from outside Decca came from the Beatles. Ray Thomas said, "I recall one particular day when they came over, and played us their new album, *Sgt. Pepper's Lonely Hearts Club Band*. We were so blown away by what they'd done. When we did *Days...* we invited John and George over to hear what we'd recorded. They were really complimentary about the album; it meant a lot." (RT PROG12)

The "Nights in White Satin" / "Cities" single was released in England by Deram on November 10, 1967. One day later, Deram issued *Days of Future Passed* in both stereo and mono.

The songs to beat on the radio in England during this week were "Baby Now That I've Found You," by The Foundations, at No. 1, followed by, respectively: "Massachusetts," by the Bee Gees; "Autumn Almanac," by The Kinks; "Zabadak!" by Dee-Dozy-Beaky-Mitch & Tich; and "The Last Waltz" by Engelbert Humperdinck.

Top 5 albums this week in the U.K.: The soundtrack to *The Sound of Music* (still riding high after two years!); The Beatles' *Sgt. Pepper's Lonely Hearts Club Band*; *The Best of the Beach Boys, Vol. 2*; *Break-Through: An Introduction to Studio 2 Stereo*, by various artists; and another compilation album, *British Motown Chartbusters*.

The single version of "Nights" was different in many ways than that of the album – it was in mono; it was half the length of the LP track, lacking Peter Knight's orchestration and Graeme Edge's spoken-word poem, "Late Lament"; and there was no grand finale leading to a clash of a gong. As issued by Decca in the U.K., the song was 4:26.

One British reviewer (provenance unknown) wrote of the single:

Their first on Deram. It's a somber and somewhat melancholy disc, with the minor-key heightening the doleful effect. The soul-searching lyric is soloed by the leader, whose vocal is framed in a magnificently scored semi-classical arrangement.

As we know, that "magnificently scored semi-classical arrangement" was Mike Pinder's Mellotron.

A review of the album (provenance unknown) read:

Here is a new type group LP, with Peter Knight conducting the London Festival Orchestra behind the Moody Blues, and the whole LP covers a day, from dawn until night, on seven tracks. It's quiet and arresting, with strong, bluesy undertones, and varied vocal and instrumental sound patterns….

On November 26, 1967, London's *Sunday Mirror* called *Days of Future Passed* "Gershwin clad in hippy gear – a great combination."

Disc and Music Echo reviewed the album in its December 2, 1967 issue:

This is a brave and worthwhile venture, blending one of the country's most interesting groups with an orchestra to provide a rich, stimulating album that sets out with an idea. That idea is to paint a picture of a day.

It has moments of rare beauty, with the Moodies in warm, sensitive mood, perfectly complemented by some lush orchestral work…. It is a work of art to blossom into the field of inspired creation. The Moodies have achieved it here, and every pop fan should hear the results.

On December 10, 1967, "HaRo," a music critic for *The Observer* in London, said of *Days of Future Passed*:

An album schemed as an album: a musical picture of a day, using a fusion of pop and classical music with a touch of poetry thrown in. Fascinating enough to keep playing and playing. As worthy of a rave as anything we have heard for months and months.

U.S. Single release:
"Nights in White Satin" b/w "Cities"
Deram 45-85023; January 1968

"Nights in White Satin" b/w "Cities" was issued in the U.S. in January 1968, two months after its U.K. release. London Records used the Deram label, as Decca in England had. The runtime stated on the record is listed as 4:26, the single version's original length in the U.K., but the song had actually been cut down to 3:06. Another error on the initial U.S. release was the songwriting credit, given to "Redwave" instead of Justin Hayward.

Meanwhile, back in England, in the January 13, 1968 edition of *Record Mirror*, Graeme Edge told Derek Boltwood, "Making the album was great…. It was what every group dreams about – being given the run of the studios for three weeks…. [But] we never record a sound that we can't reproduce on stage. We obviously can't take a full-scale orchestra with us everywhere we play… so we use a Mellotron. We use one for recording, and for our live performances few people seem to realize that it is a musical instrument in its own right. Everyone seems to think that anybody can play it, but in fact it's a very difficult instrument. We're lucky because our organist, Mike Pinder, used to work for Mellotron, so he knows just about everything there is to know about the instrument. But it's great – it's not a featured sound or anything, but it fills in the gaps. It makes the effort much more solid." (GE-RM1968)

Above: U.S. single, January 1968. The actual run time for "Nights in White Satin" was much shorter than listed – cut down to 3:06. Also, "Redwave" snatched the writing credit from Justin Hayward.

Derek Boltwood concluded:

> Sound on record – sound on stage. That sound of '68 – that's how the Moodies are being plugged for the new year. And I hope we hear a lot more of them this year, because they have a sound that I like a lot.

From the January 20, 1968 edition of *New Musical Express*:

> … After an appearance on French TV, "Nights in White Satin" was the fastest-selling record in France last weekend – and it is also currently in the Dutch Top Ten. Visits to Scandinavia and America in the near future are being planned for the group. Already set is a German tour in early March.

In addition, the Moodies were booked to perform Cannes, France, on Wednesday, January 24, followed by twelve dates in February which would take the band across England.

Also from January 20, Mike Ledgerwood wrote in *Disc and Music Echo*:

> Worldwide chart smash "Go Now" – circa January 1965 – was the one "bright star" in an otherwise overcast sky for the Moody Blues. It brought them fame and fortune on a grand scale, plus the recognition among record-buyers they so richly deserve. …
>
> Lately people have again been sitting up and taking notice of a delightful new single, "Nights in White Satin," and an incredibly

progressive album made with the "highbrow" London Festival Orchestra, and cleverly-titled *Days of Future Passed*.

So it looks as though the magnificent Moodies are at last winning the long, grueling comeback battle.

Mike Pinder told Ledgerwood, "That crash through with 'Go Now' was straight from obscurity to the ultra big-time. And it almost broke us in many ways. But it did make us internationally known and gave us the opportunity to back up our reputation with a stage show. We wanted desperately to prove that we take care and interest in things; and that we really are deep-rooted musically....

"The group is so completely different now from the original. Now we're five men all on the same wavelength musically. We all talk about the same things; we're all trying to say the same things. The Moody Blues have become a way-of-life to us all. Everything's so much better." (MP-DAME68)

Things became better still when the Moodies arrived on the Continent for concert dates.

Justin Hayward: "We went over to France and played at the MIDEM song festival in Cannes. The Supremes didn't turn up, and they were screaming for someone to play live, because all these other acts had come to mime. So we played 'Nights in White Satin' live and, literally, the next day, the whole of France went bonkers. They released it, straightaway, and within a couple weeks, it was No. 1 – for eleven weeks, would you believe!" (JH-TRC96)

Ray Thomas: "France really put the bacon on the table for us." (RT-UC14)

From *Melody Maker*, February 3, 1968:

> Moody Blues have been swamped with offers to play in numerous Continental countries since their overwhelming success at last week's MIDEM Festival [in Cannes, France]....
>
> Agent Colin Berlin is currently working on a complete concert and TV tour of Portugal, Holland, France, Scandinavia, Germany, and probably other Continental countries as well.
>
> Said a spokesman this week: "This is definitely the re-birth of the Moody Blues in a big way."

John Lodge: "We got a phone call from England and it was No. 19, and selling 20,000 copies a day." (JL-UC14)

No. 19 was the song's peak position in England

Graeme Edge: "We released "Nights in White Satin," which not only got into the charts here, but got to No. 1 all over the Continent. As Justin said at one time, 'I couldn't care less if it's been No. 1 in France for 14 weeks, just to have the record in the Top 30 here for two weeks means everything! It's home; this is where it matters.'

"That really goes for all of us. We seem to have broken back into the British market again now, which makes us all feel pretty wonderful. We made a lot of mistakes that groups are still making now, but we won't make them a second time around. We've learnt our lesson…. You know, I'm glad now that everything has happened the way it did, because had things been different, we might not be doing what we're doing today. And this is, although we never realized it before, what we've always wanted!" (GE-R68)

In both France and the Netherlands, "Nights in White Satin" hit No. 1. In Poland, the song climbed to No. 2; in Spain, No. 3; in Switzerland, No. 6; and in Germany, No. 18. Halfway around the world, in Australia, "Nights" went to No. 5. The song made No. 9 in Argentina, and reached No. 13 in Canada.

Curiously, "Nights" was not issued as a single in the English commonwealth territory of Hong Kong or in Singapore. Instead, Decca issued Ray Thomas's "Another Morning," which peaked at No. 7 and No. 3 in Hong Kong and Singapore, respectively.

Justin Hayward, John Lodge, and Graeme Edge in early 1968.
(Photo source: *teenbeat* magazine)

At the same time the single was peaking at No. 19 in the British charts, the album topped out at No. 27.

Also from February 3, in *New Musical Express*, Keith Altham proclaimed, "Moody Blues Deserve Much Greater Success." Following the headline:

> At a time when the charts do not testify to any great composing originality – except for Lennon/McCartney – there is one disc staggering about the nether regions of the charts which was released last November and deserves greater recognition. It is the Moody Blues opus which combines elements of classical orchestration and poetic narrative – "Nights in White Satin."
>
> It was written by the group and taken from a very listenable album, *Days of Future Passed*, which features their talents coupled with those of the great unknown London Festival Orchestra – a band of highly talented session musicians gathered together by Peter Knight for the purpose of the album….

Despite the Moodies not having many bookings on U.K. TV at this time, the momentum behind the record continued to increase.

Graeme Edge told Keith Altham, "Apart from one TV plug on *Twice A Fortnight* [comedy series, starring Monty Python members] and help from [*Top of the Pops* host] Alan Freeman, we've had hardly any encouragement or promotion on this disc. *Top of the Pops* won't include it because they say it is too long and would slow the program down. The disc lasts for over five [sic; 4:26] minutes, but we refuse to edit it, although they have done so in America [to 3:06]. Frankly, I don't want to hear what they've done – I'm sure we'd hate it….

"Now we're doing things that we really believe in. No musician really wants to cater to the common denominator but very few will take the risk of doing what they want." (GE-NME68)

Altham concluded:

> Personally I approve of both the group's personal integrity and their musical ethics – I think Lennon/McCartney would as well!

For the March 1968 issue of *Beat Instrumental*, a headline proclaimed, "Quality Paid Off for the Moody Blues." "P.G." wrote:

> … [T]he Moodies deserved to hit it big. And they did, via "Go Now," a chart-topper early in 1965. Since then all has been almost silence in their own highly inventive field of pop music. Until, that is, their amazing five-minute-plus [sic] and intricate "Nights in White Satin" single took off … after what seemed an eternity of plug-less weeks following its release. "Too long to play" said some disc-jocks. "Too involved" said others. But quality eventually paid off.

Mike Pinder told "P.G.": "People talk about learning in the University of Life – and that covers us. From the top of the charts to nowhere, and then a slow climb back up. We became known internationally through 'Go Now!,' but everything since has been in the nature of a comeback. What can you do if bookers think of you as a group who *had* a hit but haven't one now? It's a risk for them to book you, even though our name somehow outlived the original hit record.

"Well, these past months have been spent on specialized dates around Britain – colleges and universities, mostly, where you don't have to churn out the pure pop hits and where people are willing to listen to you. And the Continent has been a good spot for us, particularly France where everything is supposed to be years behind the times in popular music – but where they are more aware than most people think….

"We've taken quite a few risks in going out for what *we* want, rather than what we know the mass audiences want, but gradually it's starting to pay off….

"We hope, eventually, to do a concert with the Festival Orchestra at the Royal Albert Hall, which would be quite an experience. Things went well for us at the MIDEM Festival in Cannes and our sales have built marvelously well through Portugal, Spain, Italy, Scandinavia – and France. So the whole of May will be given up to touring there, fitting in as much television exposure as we can. There won't be a new single until the end of March and we can only hope it doesn't take as long to get moving as did 'Nights.'" (MP-BI68)

Actually, there would be no new single at the end of March – not in Britain or the rest of Europe, anyway. But "Tuesday Afternoon" coupled with "Another Morning" would be issued in America.

Pinder said, "But we regard our forthcoming tour of America as being most important. They do know us there and it seems a very good market for the new-style Moodies. Though there are only two comparatively new members, we really are thinking along completely different lines. I said once before that our music has almost become a way of life for us, and that's absolutely true." (MP-BI68)

P.G wrote that *Days of Future Passed* was "another slow starter but still building sales," which led to Decca renewing the Moodies' contract and giving the group "an anything-within-reason blank cheque to produce another album, on similar lines, for the autumn sales rush."

On March 9, 1968, *New Music Express* reported:

> The Moody Blues are to pay a promotional visit to America in late April and early May [it would actually be pushed back]. Their *Days of Future Passed* LP was issued last weekend in the States, where it had a 30,000 advance order. The group's "Nights in White Satin" single, currently No. 1 in France, Portugal and Holland, has just entered the U.S. Hot 100.

A UK publication from this time (provenance unknown) said:

> We somehow suspected that the Moody Blues would return to the charts with "Nights in White Satin," despite their lack of hits during 1967. The single is a track from their *Days of Future Past* [sic] album, which was universally acclaimed by the critics for its conception and originality.
>
> The boys spent 10 days in the studio recording the album, and Decca spent nearly £10,000 on its production. The company's original idea was to produce a specialist album in their new Deramic Sound System and the Moodies decided on the theme. Little did they realize that it would be such a shot in the arm to the group's career.
>
> The boys admitted to us that they had been depressed of late because of their lack of chart success – now they've got rid of the blues! ...

U.S. album release:
Days of Future Passed
Deram DES 18012 (stereo);
Deram DES 16012 (Mono);
March 2, 1968

While "Nights in White Satin" was going around the world, charting high in every English-speaking country, and many in which English was not the primary language, it had yet to have an impact on the

THE MOODY BLUES DERAM

(Courtesy Tony Brown)

national radio charts in America. But the critical reaction had been very positive. *Variety* put "Nights" at the very top of its "Top Singles of the Week" review column for the trade's January 17, 1968 issue. Finding it to be the best of "The 'Best Bets' of This Week's 100-Plus Releases," the music critic said that the song "showcases the British combo on a slow ballad packing big impact." The critic deemed "Cities" to be "a well written piece of material."

In the March 10, 1968 edition of *The Los Angeles Times*, music critic Pete Johnson said of *Days of Future Passed*:

> Blending classical musicians with pop concerts is not particularly new, harking back to records such as the Drifters' "There Goes My Baby," numerous Phil Spector hits and the use of string quartets and orchestras on Beatles and Rolling Stones songs, but a new album offers a particularly grand and pretty hybrid of the two musics.
>
> Some idea of the extent of collusion is revealed by the album's artistic credits: the Moody Blues with the London Festival Orchestra conducted by Peter Night [sic], all in equal type faces. The title is *Days of Future Passed*, the label is Deram.
>
> What emerges is beautiful, massive and thoroughly contemporary, a happy destruction of the artificial borders which cloister taste and experience. …
>
> Unlike some recent experiments with diverse forms of music and the beat genre, this one works all through the album. To quote the for-once-true album notes: "… emotion and creativity blend … poetry, the beat group and the symphony orchestra feed on each other's inspiration."

Three days later, the music critic for *Variety* wrote:

> This is another example of the big-scaled musical enterprises being tried by an increasing number of contemporary groups. The Moody Blues, a standout British combo, has joined with the London Festival Orch, under Peter Knight's baton, in a group of songs pegged to a central theme. The titles tell the story: "Dawn Is a Feeling," "Another Hour" [sic], "Peak Hour," "Forever Afternoon," "The Sunset," and "Nights In White Satin."

On March 16, 1968, Mike Hennessey, the critic for America's *Billboard*, caught a Moody Blues performance in Paris:

> The Moody Blues, who recently returned to the top of several European charts with "Nights in White Satin" after a period in limbo, appeared at the Paris Olympia in "Europe No. 1 Musicorama" concert Feb. 26. With the whole of the show to

themselves, the Moody Blues paced their program well and, aided by the immense versatility of Mike Pinder's Mellotron, achieved a wide variety of musical sounds. Since their reorganization more than a year ago, the Moody Blues have evolved and matured into a highly polished musical group with a fresh approach to composition and a rich range of textures and fine colors.

The first half of the program featured the group's more orthodox material such as "Fly Me High," Sonny Boy Williamson's "Bye Bye Bird," and a superb interpretation of the old Eric Burdon hit "Don't Let Me Be Misunderstood." But the highlight of the first set was a new number by lead guitarist Justin Hayward (who wrote "Nights in White Satin") called "What Am I Doing Here?"

In the second half of the concert the Moodies featured tracks from their album *Days of Future Passed*, and scored heavily with "Nights in White Satin," which has a powerful, oratorio-like quality about it.

It is significant that an audience conditioned to expect temperature-raising stage antics from English and American groups were not in the least dismayed by the Moody Blues' concentration on music and singing. This is a group which has so much powerful and original music in it that the lack of visual stimulus is no handicap to communication.

From the March 19, 1968 edition of England's *Croydon Midweek*, Sandra Grant reported that *Days of Future Passed* had already sold 100,000 copies, a decent number for the U.K. But the Moodies preferred to talk about the music, and not the money.

Mike Pinder told Grant, "The drag is that everybody tends to put everything into a pigeonhole for their own satisfaction, because of their lack of understanding of the mystery of music.... We want to play music with feeling. Music is a form of communication, and we're trying to put something across.

"In the beginning, music was a form of worship and all music was religious. Music wasn't originally intended to make money. Now it's reversed completely and people think that music is only to make money out of. They've forgotten to give pleasure to yourself and other people." (MP-CM68)

Justin Hayward said, "We're trying to elevate pop to a level comparable to classical music. You'll never catch me playing Dvorak's 'New World Symphony.' It's a gas, and I love it, but it's nothing to do with me. I've grown up through rock 'n' roll, and I'm going to carry on with that branch of music, getting more and more involved and better and better.... We're doing exactly what we want to do. And who's to say we can't make – if you want to stick a label on it – pop/classical music?" (JH-CM68)

For its March 23 issue, *Billboard* said:

The Moody Blues who scored with "Go Now" and "Stop Stop" [sic] a few years ago are joined by the London Festival Orchestra in this album as the two excellently bridge symphonic music and pop. The theme is "the day," and the two musically chart the day's routine events such as lunch break and evening. "The Night: Nights in White Satin" is among the British best selling singles and has potential to score.

Meanwhile, despite doing well in some markets, "Nights in White Satin" had failed to take hold in the U.S. national charts. The song's worst showing was in *Record World*, stopped at No. 110. *Billboard* saw things nearly as bad, with the song's No. 103 peak position. Only *Cashbox* called "Nights" a Top 100 contender, where it rose as high as No. 93. The song wouldn't become a national hit in the U.S. until several years after its initial release. But, if you are among those who could swear you remember it being played a great deal on the radio in 1968, you likely were not imagining it. The United States, after all, is a big country. In some regions, "Nights" certainly was a hit right out of the gate.

WINN radio in Canton, Ohio was one of the first in the U.S. to jump on the song, where it peaked at No. 15 on February 9, 1968. WHYN in Springfield, Massachusetts was also an early bird and had the song in its Top 40 list for a couple of weeks in mid-March. KCPX in Salt Lake City, Utah, sent "Nights" to No. 6 on March 29. KFXM in San Bernardino, California, played it too, and the song peaked at that station on April 12 at No. 18. And "Nights" made the Top 20 on WOSH radio in Oshkosh, Wisconsin throughout May of 1968, peaking at No. 6.

Los Angeles was the hip music center of the mid-to-late 1960s thanks to the proactive efforts of the highly competitive local Top 40 AM stations, such as KHJ/Boss Radio, home of top jocks "The Real" Don Steele, Charlie Tuna, Charles Van Dyke, and Robert W. Morgan. KRLA declared themselves "the Beatles station" in L.A. and indeed got many exclusives. The station was home of DJs Jimmy O'Neill, Casey Kasem, Reb Foster, Bob Eubanks, "Emperor" Bob Hudson, Dave "The Hullabooer" Hull, and Johnny Hayes. KFWB, with celebrity jocks such as Wink Martindale and Gary Owens, was the third big pop station in L.A. With these heavy radio hitters, songs that barely broke in other parts of the U.S. often made the Top 10 in L.A. "Nights" was one of those. *The Van Nuys News*, surveying local radio stations and record sellers, charted the single at No. 9 on May 22. The newspaper also charted *Days of Future Passed* as being the No. 3 selling album in L.A.'s San Fernando Valley stores on May 31.

Sales were strong enough in the U.S. for London Records to press a new batch of "Nights in White Satin" singles in the Spring of 1968. The catalogue number was adjusted from 45-85023 to 45-DEM-85023, and Hayward received his rightful credit.

Incidentally, at this time, you could pick up a copy of the LP for only $3.09 at Los Angeles area Broadway department stores.

Days of Future Passed was on the move in other regions of the U.S. as well. On May 17, Loraine Alterman wrote in *Go Magazine*:

The Moody Blues' *Days of Future Passed* album is stirring up quite a bit of excitement because of its artful blend of the pop and symphony form. Although the group faded out of the spotlight for a couple of years, they've now made a solid comeback with the new album.

Not everyone was impressed. *Rolling Stone* magazine had, so far, resisted giving the album a review. But the equally critical *New York Magazine* couldn't resist speaking up. For its May 20 edition, the music critic wrote:

> … Not that we weren't warned 10 years ago when Chuck Berry wailed "Roll over Beethoven and give Tchaikovsky the news," but who could have thought the rock revolution would lead its children to the very gates of High Culture, where they would proceed to peel off the gold paint and sell it as Art? I'm thinking of that mound of thought-Jello called *Days of Future Passed* (Deram) which features the Moody Blues, the London Festival Orchestra, and lots of bad poetry. …

> The Moody Blues are a fine rock band, whose wailing sound dates back to the dawn of Beatlemania. But these days, rock groups change images like a woman discarding nylons. In their new incarnation, the Moodys give us ponderous songs with titles like "Dawn Is a Feeling" and "Forever Afternoon (Tuesday?)." True, there are some stunning string parts on this record, some superb vocalizing, and one haunting ballad called "Nights in White Satin." But even this song is rendered obtuse by the kind of hyper-orchestration that leaves you in the balcony waiting for the movie to begin. …

Few other journalists had their noses in the air when it came to *Days of Future Passed*. In fact, most members of the press seemed genuinely surprised, and impressed, by the Moodies' new album. So impressed, in fact, that many wanted to know what the Moodies themselves listened to. *Hit Parader* asked that question of Justin Hayward and Mike Pinder.

Pinder answered, "My first album is *Sgt. Pepper* by the Beatles; that album is too much. That's the first album to have a real continuity. There's always something new to hear in it." (MP-HT68)

Also on Pinder's short list: *Younger than Yesterday*, by the Byrds; *After Bathing at Baxter's,* by Jefferson Airplane; and Simon & Garfunkel's *Bookends*, which he called "a masterpiece."

Justin Hayward said, "The *Buffalo Springfield Again* is the best American album of last year; it had a lot of depth. *Bookends* by Simon and Garfunkel is absolutely beautiful. Laura Nyro's *Elis Confession* [sic] is also incredible. It's a shame more people haven't gotten on to it. She's a very talented chick; she does everything herself – writes, sings, plays piano and guitar, and does vocal backgrounds. She's got a ton of soul, and she's just beginning." (JH-HT68)

While "Nights in White Satin" failed to make an impact on the national charts in America, Deram decided to pick a second track for single release in hopes of bringing the album to the attention of more record buyers.

U.S. single release:
"Tuesday Afternoon" / "Another Morning"
Deram 45-85028; late May 1968

In late May (many online databases mistakenly list the release date as July 19, 1968), Deram issued Justin Hayward's "Forever Afternoon (Tuesday?)," with the new title of "Tuesday Afternoon (Forever Afternoon)," backed by Ray Thomas's "Another Morning," which had charted high in the Far East a couple of months earlier. Both were savaged by harsh trimming, reducing "Tuesday Afternoon" to 2:13 and "Another Morning" to 2:24. Fortunately, once the A-side started climbing the charts, many radio stations across America opted to play the longer LP version of the song, which, as the first cut of Side Two, was easy to cue up. It was not uncommon, however, that DJs would be caught off-guard and not fade the song down at the end before the segue into "The Sun Set." Some allowed the next song to play in its entirety while others would rush to turn the sound down during the second song's introduction, before the start of the vocal. It was a common occurrence.

The hot five singles in the U.S. at this time were, respectively, "Tighten Up," by Archie Bell & the Drells; "Mrs. Robinson," by Simon & Garfunkel; "Beautiful Morning," by the Rascals; "The Good, the Bad and the Ugly," by Hugo Montenegro and his Orchestra and Chorus; and "Honey," by Bobby Goldsboro.

In the May 29, 1968 issue of *Variety*, the trade paper's music critic picked the pairing of "Tuesday Afternoon" and "Another Morning" as one of the "Best Bets" of the 100-plus single releases from that week, saying that the A-side "provides this British outfit with an offbeat entry with plenty of lyrical and melodic quality." The reviewer described the B-side as "a cute piece."

Billboard magazine gave "Tuesday Afternoon" a "Special Merit Spotlight," recommending the A-side as a "blues mover with clever production and vocal work throughout," and stating that it was "loaded with teen appeal."

On July 25, immediately after reviewing the Band's *Music from Big Pink*, and calling it Capitol Records' most exciting LP since *Sgt. Pepper's Lonely Hearts Club Band*, U.S. syndicated music critic Wayne Harada, in his "On the Record" column, wrote:

> Still another interesting find is *Days of Future Passed* (Deram DES-18012), an example of the fusion of rock and classical forms.... This is a paean to dawn and dusk – and everything in between. One hit already has emerged: "Tuesday Afternoon." For enjoyment at any hour of the day.

"Tuesday Afternoon" entered *Billboard*'s Hot 100 chart for the week ending July 20, 1968, at No. 98. It jumped to No. 71 a week later, then to 48, where it held for two weeks before continuing its upward momentum, to 44, then to 40, then 37. For its seventh week in the charts, "Tuesday" made a big jump, to No. 29, where it held for two weeks. On September 21, the single achieved its peak position, at No. 24.

This time the single that Decca selected had clicked, making the Top 30 in all three of America's major music charts. *Billboard* had it at No. 24, with *Cashbox* and *Record World* close behind, placing the song at No. 26 and 27, respectively.

These numbers may seem a bit low in our collective memories – for those of us who were old enough to be listening to Top 40 radio in 1968. But the national charts can be deceiving. Some songs – such as the latest single at this time from the Beatles ("Hey Jude" b/w "Revolution") or the Rascals ("People Got to Be Free"), or the Doors ("Hello, I Love You") – would break immediately in nearly every city across America because of the immense popularity of the bands. However, for a group such as the Moody Blues, whose last Top 10 hit had been four years earlier, the situation was far different. Some radio programmers heard the hit potential of "Tuesday Afternoon" immediately and added it to their playlists. Others didn't begin playing the song until after it had proven itself in other markets. The result was a longer-than-normal run in the national charts, but a lower peak position.

Sampling radio station playlists from across America during this period, we find that "Tuesday Afternoon" did much better than the national charts indicate, peaking in the Top 20 in very nearly every major city across the United States, and often making the Top 10... just at different times, beginning in June and lasting through October 1968.

It broke in Buffalo, New York early, on WNIA radio, which put the song into the Top 20 in June. But this was rare occurrence on the East Coast. For the most part, "Tuesday" got its start on the west.

In Bakersfield, California, KAFY radio leaped on the song, and the station's listeners approved, flooding the request lines and sending "Tuesday" to No. 1 on July 3.

Also for the week ending July 3, Los Angeles's top-rated station, KHJ/Boss Radio, had "Tuesday" at No. 5. On the other side of the mountain that separates Los

Angeles proper from its suburbs in the San Fernando Valley, Van Nuys' *The News* ran a "Top Hits" list of its own. After surveying local record sellers, *The News* reported "Tuesday" as the top-selling single in the area – a solid No. 1. On the national scene, however, at least in the *Billboard* Top 100 chart, it still wasn't even listed.

On July 14, from his syndicated newspaper column, "The Underground Sound," music critic Scott G. Campbell said "Tuesday Afternoon" was an "easy song with some good piano work," then added, "It's already in the Top 20 on the West Coast and should hit nationwide before too long." Days earlier, on July 12, "Tuesday" was No. 14 on WKLO in Louisville, Kentucky.

On July 26, KFXM, in San Bernardino, California, had "Tuesday" at No. 18.

On August 1, WKNR, serving Detroit, Michigan, ranked the song at No. 15.

On August 3, with KYA, in San Francisco, "Tuesday" was at No. 3.

On August 8, in Newport, Rhode Island, the *Newport Daily News* reported "Tuesday Afternoon" at No. 3.

On August 10, WUBE in Cincinnati, Ohio, had "Tuesday" at No. 4. Incidentally, at this time, *Billboard* showed the song nationally at No. 48 and climbing.

Also on August 10, "Tuesday" was No. 13 in Tucson, Arizona, on KTKT.

On August 13, WJET, in Erie, Pennsylvania, had the song at No. 14.

On August 16, in Newport, Rhode Island, "Tuesday Afternoon" moved up to the No. 2 spot, blocked from top position by the Rascals' "People Got to Be Free."

On August 17, KSDR, in Watertown, South Dakota, listed the song at No. 13.

By August 18, *The Cincinnati Enquirer*'s "Top 10 Tune Consensus" had "Tuesday" at No. 6.

Also on August 18, WING-Radio in Dayton, Ohio, put "Tuesday" at No. 1.

Also from August 18, WNAP, in Indianapolis, Indiana, had it at No. 9.

On August 24, WJBS, in Deland, Florida, placed "Tuesday" at No. 14.

On August 25, KTSA, in San Antonio, Texas, had the song at No. 13.

One day later, "Platter Patter," by Doug Harsh, with a survey of radio stations and record sellers, ranked the song at No. 6, for the first of two weeks. Meanwhile, on the *Billboard* chart, "Tuesday" had just cracked the Top 40.

On August 28, WOR, in New York City, listed it at No. 18.

On August 30, WGEM, in Quincy, Illinois, put "Tuesday" at No. 4.

Also on August 30, KELI, in Tulsa, Oklahoma, ranked it at No. 18.

That same day, KIRL, in Saint Charles, Missouri, took the song up to No. 6.

On September 4, WKYC, in Cleveland, Ohio, had "Tuesday" at No. 15.

On September 7, WBAZ, in Kingston, New York, showed it at No. 3.

On September 9, WLS, in Chicago, Illinois, said No. 12.

On September 10, WIBG, in Philadelphia, PA, had the song at No. 19.

On September 13, KBIL, in St. Louis, Missouri, put "Tuesday" at No. 17.

On September 14, CHUM, in Toronto, Canada, showed it at No. 14.

Also on September 14, WBAZ, in Kingston, New York, took it to No. 2, with only "Harper Valley P.T.A." keeping it from the top position. The situation was the same one week later, for the survey ending September 21. *Billboard* was way behind, with the song at No. 24.

On September 23, WBIZ, in Eau Claire, Wisconsin, had "Tuesday" at No. 13.

On September 25, KILT, in Houston, Texas, ranked it at No. 14.

On September 28, WORL, in Worcester, Massachusetts, took it to No. 9.

To further illustrate how spread out the chart run for "Tuesday Afternoon" was, it wasn't until October 10 when the song finally made the Top 10 list in Belvidere, Illinois – at No. 8.

The Top 20 – and often Top 10 – ranking of "Tuesday Afternoon" in cities all across America prompted *Days of Future Passed* to finally get some momentum on the U.S. LP charts. *Billboard* had listed it for the first time during the week ending May 25, 1968, at No. 150. The highest it reached prior to the release of "Tuesday Afternoon" was No. 138. One week later, it moved up to 132, then No. 98, then 97, 96, 84, 83, 66, 65, 61, 50, and then 48 on the week ending September 14. At this time, the Moodies now had two albums in the U.S. charts. *In Search of the Lost Chord* had just debuted, at No. 122.

Justin Hayward: "I don't think we [thought] there would be a great audience, and initially there wasn't. But it coincided with the birth of FM radio and a lot of the other record companies were making records where you had really bad stereo with the drums on the left and the vocals on alone on the right.... But *Days of Future Passed* was such a beautiful stereo image that when we went to America in that winter [December] of 1968 with the record... FM radio just jumped on it. It was perfect for them." (JH-MBT16)

Helping FM radio to make the jump was a London Records ad campaign targeting a couple of the most influential FM stations on the West Coast.

An article in *Hit Parader* magazine reported:

> ... One of the earliest centers of underground [radio] was the 'far out' city of San Francisco, and this is where the Moody's spanking new LP began to take off first. London, wisely, broadcast FM radio commercials about the LP, and listeners, who were really 'tuned in,' would whisper "Wow!" when they heard those first cuts of the LP on the commercial. After that they were soon hearing the whole album being played, and sales boomed.

But what drew the attention of the vast majority of FM stations – the ones not paid to air the one-minute commercial – was the popularity of "Tuesday Afternoon," now being played every hour or two on AM stations across the country

Hayward said, "'Nights,' of course, will always be the big one for us, but 'Tuesday Afternoon' is the one we think of the most fondly, because that was the one that really broke us in America.." (JH-TB13)

On November 13, 1968, Richard Hull wrote in New Jersey's *Asbury Park Press* to "Classical Rock," writing:

> ... What makes *Days of Future Passed* work, perhaps more than anything else, are the transitions from the Moodys' voices, guitars and drums to the orchestral pieces.
>
> The first of the album's seven bands is exclusively orchestral; the Moodys stay out of it. The orchestra changes "The Day Begins" from a simple overture to a day-in-miniature with chronological

strains from the other six bands, each fighting for domination, almost as in symphonic order.

The second band, "DAWN: Dawn Is a Feeling," begins as slowly and quietly as does consciousness each morning, establishing cosmic implications.

Next, flutes give gaiety to "The Morning." Their happy, light sound implies morning, which, after all, belongs to the very young.

The final song on the first side echoes of typewriters, scurrying feet, and the "busy" sound connected with baroque works, eventually giving way to a driving, singular beat. "LUNCH BREAK: Peak Hour" is a song of self-assertion, made manifest chiefly by the Moodys' guitars.

But what is day without afternoon? "THE AFTERNOON: Forever Afternoon (Tuesday?)" is the album's song of fulfillment: "So gently swaying through the fairyland of love; if you'll just come with me you'll see the beauty of Tuesday afternoon."

Afternoon yields to evening, accompanied by the anxious strains of the closing hours of work. Sounds of tom-toms lend an exotic flavor to "THE SUNSET: Twilight Time" as they beat out a chant to the god of darkness, metamorphosing into a rocking prayer, and culminating in intimations of despair.

The last song deals with the end of the day. "THE NIGHT: Nights in White Satin" is a moaning cry, a realization of defeat.

But the artistry of *Days of Future Passed* doesn't end with the final song. ... "Nights in White Satin" is more than a last reflection of the day; more even than a song that takes Ravel's "Bolero" one step farther. It is the loneliness theme, of remembrance and unfulfilled aspirations which faces man at the closing of life's door: "Gazing at people, some hand in hand; just what I'm going through they can't understand. Some try to tell me thoughts they cannot defend. Just what you want to be, you'll be in the end. And I love you."

At this time in the rock era, the music critics at America's one-year old and arrogantly-cool *Rolling Stone* magazine clearly believed that if an album wasn't unabashed and uncompromising "rock," it wasn't worth listening to. The magazine's writers made an exception for the Beatles, perhaps because, besides leading rock into its new era, the band rarely included singles on their English albums. The magazine was conspicuously silent when *Days of Future Passed* was released, and refused to review the album even after "Tuesday Afternoon" became a hit in America ... or, more likely, *especially* since "Tuesday Afternoon" had become a hit.

By December 1968, *Rolling Stone* could no longer ignore the Moody Blues. *In Search of the Lost Chord* was issued in the U.S., and the band was touring the nation. Bands that *Rolling Stone* admired, such as Ten Years After and the Jeff Beck Group, were opening for the Moodies, no less. "Nights in White Satin," "Tuesday Afternoon," and "Ride My See-Saw" had become popular on FM radio as well as AM. For its December 6, 1968 issue, along with a review for *Lost Chord*, the magazine published a review of *Days of Future Passed*. And, of course, panned it.

Jim Miller wrote:

> … The Moody Blues, on evidence of their most recent recordings, have matured considerably since "Go Now," but their music is constantly marred by one of the most startlingly saccharine conceptions of "beauty" and "mysticism" that any rock group has ever affected. To be specific: *Days of Future Passed* claims to "have extended the range of pop music," finding "the point where it becomes one with the world of the classics." This is pure nonsense.
>
> There are some quite fine rock tracks on *Days of Future Passed* ("Tuesday Afternoon" especially), but all of these songs have next to nothing to do with "the classics." In any case the "classics" for the Moody Blues, apparently, are Rimsky-Korsakov, Brahms, David Rose, and Elmer Bernstein. The London Festival Orchestra is generally used between tracks to play Hollyridge Strings changes on the rock compositions in the album. The whole execution of the album is so perverse that the only real surprise is the discovery that between the movie soundtrack slush there is some quite palatable rock which makes no compromises, even in the direction of orchestral accompaniment…. Then why the Festival Orchestra? Why the hideous spoken introduction and conclusion? If this crap is supposed to be breathtakingly beautiful or the aesthetic *raison d'etre* of the album, god [sic] deliver us back into the hands of prosaic rock, like "Peak Hour, or "Forever Afternoon," or "Nights in White Satin." Or even the triteness of "Twilight Time."
>
> This must remain the real curiosity of *Days of Future Passed* – what is obviously a fine, tight English rock group has chosen to strangle itself in contextual goo. Ironically, almost every one of the rock tracks has something to recommend it – but what might have been a quite capable – even exciting – album is willfully turned into something musically akin to Milo's chocolate cotton … which is too bad. …

Another Day for "Nights"

"Nights in White Satin" and *Day of Future Passed* had staying power, with each having a second run in the charts that would greatly surpass the first. Listener requests to hear "Nights" on the radio both in America and Britain not only stayed strong but built to such a degree that, by 1972, radio programmers were requesting that Decca reissue the single.

Graeme Edge said, "We were about to release another single ['I'm Just a Singer in a Rock and Roll Band' in late 1972] when the American record company got in touch and said, 'Hold off a minute, you've got a "breakout" – a local hit. It was going absolutely crazy in Seattle and had started to spread. Many years later, we discovered the DJ who started it all. He was on 12 till 4 a.m. – the graveyard shift. He told us that he wanted to go smoke his bong, so he went down the authorized playlist and picked the longest record he was allowed to play – 'Nights in White Satin.'" (GE-DOFP97)

Ray Thomas said of this DJ, "The second time he did it, the switchboard lit up like a Christmas tree." (RT-GM14)

It was like dropping a pebble in a pool of water, with ripples spreading out in each direction. More radio stations began getting requests, and, as they played the song, more stations, each further away from Seattle, added it to their playlists. But the original single in the U.S. had a run time of 3:06, and was lacking orchestration and the spoken-word section. The callers wanted to hear the longer version – all the way to the clash of the gong. FM stations didn't mind, but a song of this length didn't fit the programming needs of Top 40 AM stations. The song's original, complete running time of 7:38 was too long for most AM radio stations. For this reason, and due to many requests from radio programmers for a version of the song that would time out somewhere in between the long LP and short 45 released, the U.K. version of the single, with its running time at 4:26, was issued. Accounts vary as to exactly when this took place.

Regardless of its length on the 1972 single pressings, "Nights" became a massive success on both sides of the Atlantic. In England it bested the original chart position by reaching No. 9. In America it hit No. 1 on two of the music charts – *Cashbox* and *Record World* – and No 2 on the third (*Billboard*). For this second life, "Nights" hit the top of the charts in Canada, and had a second Top 10 run in Australia, peaking at No. 8.

Despite becoming a staple of radio playlists to this day, the writer of the song hasn't profited as one might expect. Justin Hayward said, "I get very little financially from it, because when I was 18 I innocently and stupidly signed away my copyrights 'til I was 26 to Lonnie Donegan and his family –

Some sources state that new U.S. pressings of "Nights in White Satin" in 1972 had the same short run time as the Spring 1968 pressing – 3:06 – and it was not increased until either 1974 or '75. But those of us listening to AM radio in 1972 may recall a version shorter than that on the album, but certainly longer than 3:06. As the above image documents, there was a medium-length version issued by London Records (exact date unknown), with a run time of 4:20. The catalogue number was adjusted from 45-DEM-85023 to 5N-85023.

In 1972, "Nights in White Satin" was reissued in Australia with a running time of 5:37. It was also given a different B-side than past releases – Mike Pinder's "Dawn Is a Feeling."

for life! – a deal a judge later described as 'onerous.'" (JH-UN14)

Every song Hayward wrote until he turned 26, in October of 1973, would be subject to Donegan's publishing deal, in perpetuity. And this meant that every song of Hayward's on the "Classic 7" albums, including "Tuesday Afternoon," "Voices in the Sky," "Lovely to See You," "Question," "The Story in Your Eyes," and "New Horizons."

Hayward said of Donegan, "He was a deeply unpleasant man, and he became a parasite on the Moodies. He even sent someone to take the guitar I'd written 'Nights' on while I was out, which was bizarre."

"Bizarre" – but legal. As you may recall, the 12-string guitar on which Hayward composed the song was Donegan's. Hayward shrugged the unpleasant situation off: "But I'm the only person who has the joy to sing it, and for the audience to go, 'That guy did that, and he's singing it for us.'" (JH-UN14)

As for *Days of Future Passed*, it had an impressive 102-week run in the U.S. charts, hitting its peak position of No. 3 in *Billboard* and No. 2 on *Cashbox* in late 1972. It was certified Gold for over a million dollars in sales. Since then, it has gone Platinum, acknowledging the selling of over one million copies.

Justin Hayward said, "[W]e did have the sense that we were creating something really different, and we had the sense that we were creating something that no one was going to listen to. I think we thought that we were making a record – or I certainly did – for a minority audience, for a very small group. I thought that we'd get reviewed in *The Guardian* cultural page…. That's the record I thought we were making, a limited appeal record." (JH-PS95)

Ray Thomas: "It was fantastic because it was all new…. It was a new band playing new material and it was exciting. And especially being this young – *everything* was exciting. We had some breaks, but basically it's like anything else – the harder you work, the luckier you get. I firmly believe that." (RT-DM15)

Graeme Edge: "I'd just have to say that it's orchestral rock… performed by a bunch of guys who were too stupid to know that we *weren't* supposed to be able to do it." (GE-GM12)

Mike Pinder: "We recorded it at a time when music and technology collided. We were young, eager, and ready to be part of the creative London musical landscape. We had the great opportunity during those sessions to reflect the changing times and the inner searchings of young people like ourselves in our songs. And I do feel that *Days of Future Passed* does stand the test of time." (MP-BCB17)

Justin Hayward: "I would say that it's a little work of art that's trying to express things that are not on the surface – and that evolved. It was the meeting of a classical orchestra and a rock group, seamlessly. That's what's lovely about it. It jars when other people do it. I've never heard anybody do it as well as it was done on *Days of Future Passed*. I can't say 'as well as *we* did it,' because *we* didn't do it. It was Peter Knight, Tony Clarke, the whole band, and engineer Derek Varnals recorded it so beautifully for us. We had these simple songs, and the Mellotron made it segue so beautifully. It's a little gem of a record, and it shouldn't be discounted." (JH-GM12)

John Lodge: "Afterward, there was a certain amount of negativity from people who said, 'Well, yeah, it's basically just an orchestra album,' because we had used the London Symphony [sic] Orchestra. So we said, 'Okay, then, what we should do then, just to quell these people on the next album, is to play every instrument ourselves. Even if we can't play it, we'll get a book and learn how to play it.' So that's what we did with *In Search of the Lost Chord*." (JL-GM12)

9

In Search of the Lost Chord (1968)

U.K. album release: Deram SML 711 (mono and stereo); July 26, 1968
U.S. album release: Deram DE 16017 (mono); DE 18017 (stereo): July 26, 1968
Peak U.K. position: #5
U.S. #23 (*Billboard*)
(Certified gold in U.S.)
Germany: #30
Canada: #37
(Certified platinum in Canada)

U.K. single release:
"Voices in the Sky" b/w "Dr. Livingstone, I Presume"
Deram DM 196; June 28, 1968
Peak U.K. position: #27

U.S. single release:
"Ride My See-Saw" b/w "Voices in the Sky"
Deram 5N-85033; Late September 1968
U.S.: #46 (*Record World*)
Canada: #33

U.K. single release:
"Ride My See-Saw" b/w "A Simple Game"
Deram DM 213; October 25, 1968
Peak U.K. position: #42
Netherlands: #12
France: #15
Holland: #16

As reported in the January 20, 1968 edition of *New Music Express*, just when "Nights in White Satin" and *Days of Future Passed* began their chart runs in England, the Moody Blues had already returned to the recording studio.

The sessions were not for the purpose of making a new album. Decca, while waiting for more reviews of *Days of Future Passed* to be published, and for an increase in sales, had no idea what to do with the band next

Tony Clarke said of the songs recorded at this time, "They were done in the gap between *Days of Future Passed* and *In Search of the Lost Chord*... before we got the green light, before *Days of Future Passed* was actually a hit. It was a time when we knew we should be recording but we didn't have an absolute hit in America. They were done without the umbrella of an album concept. There was a need to get into the studio, with the band, when it was available. I remember doing things when they'd be packing the equipment while we were still recording because they'd landed a gig and had to be on the road to somewhere." (TC-H&H95)

The tracks recorded – left unreleased until 1977 and the *Caught Live + 5* album – included John Lodge's "Gimme a Little Somethin'" and two from Hayward – "King and Queen" and "What Am I Doing Here?" There was another one, which would make it on the next album – Ray Thomas's "Legend of a Mind." The session took place on January 16, 1968.

"Legend of a Mind" was the group's most ambitious recording to date, utilizing the Mellotron in ways not attempted on *Days of Future Passed*. It was more "psychedelic" in theme, lyric, and tone than anything on the previous album or single releases.

Mike Pinder said, "The lyrics, 'Timothy Leary's dead, no, no, he's on the outside looking in,' we've taken from the whole idea of the *Tibetan Book of the Dead*, which is about the different bardos, the different states of consciousness, and out-of-the-body experiences that are concerned with that."

Ray Thomas was inspired to write "Legend of a Mind" after Pinder gave the book to him. Pinder said of the song, "It's a metaphysical reference. It's very complimentary in terms of, 'no, no, he's not dead, he's on the outside looking in,' meaning, as far as I was concerned, very much a spiritual connotation." (MP-H&H96)

John Lodge said of Leary, "He represented a part of America. We were always reading about him in England. He was part of everything going on back then – part of Woodstock, flower power and the San Francisco scene. He represented a whole new way of life that was happening then." (JL-BJ96)

San Francisco, and its Haight-Ashbury area, had been ground zero for the launching of the "Hippie Nation" in 1966 and, one year later, its "Summer of Love." (As a reference, the landmark Woodstock concert took place a year after this album's release, in August, 1969.)

Thomas said of Leary, "I'd read about him; I hadn't met him at that point. But 'Legend of a Mind' is very tongue-in-cheek because I saw the 'astral plane' as like a psychedelically painted bi-plane with the hippies hired for a trip around the San Francisco Bay…. I was just taking a piss, really; just having a laugh at all the hippies and what they believed in, and everything in the States." (RT-RS15)

Timothy Leary, 41 at this time, was a psychologist and teacher, and an advocate for exploration of the therapeutic potential of psychedelic drugs … under controlled conditions, of course. In 1963, he was conducting experiments under the Harvard Psilocybin Project, prior to LSD being designated as an illegal substance in the United States. Leary and a colleague were both fired from Harvard that year.

Leary used LSD himself and pronounced its alleged therapeutic benefits, developing a philosophy of mind expansion and personal truth through the use of the drug. All of this brought him a large degree of notoriety, followers, and enemies alike. He was good at seducing some and taunting others with catchphrases such as "Think for yourself and question authority" and, most famously, "Turn on, tune in, drop out."

Leary wrote many books, including the one Mike Pinder and Ray Thomas had been reading – 1964's *The Psychedelic Experience: A Manual Based on the Tibetan Book of the Dead* (written with Ralph Metzner and Richard Alpert) – as well as 1966's *Psychedelic Prayers after the Tao Te Ching*, and 1967's *Start Your Own Religion*.

Timothy Leary had certainly been "searching for someone" … himself, whom he discovered by "dropping acid." Some thought him to be a modern-day prophet. Leary seemed to see himself that way, too.

In "Legend of a Mind," Thomas, tongue firmly planted in cheek, sings about the pusher man who promises spiritual enlightenment:

> *Along the coast you'll hear them boast*
> *About a light they say that shines so dear*
> *So raise your glass, we'll drink a toast*
> *To the little man who sells you thrills along the pier.*
> *He'll take you up, he'll bring you down,*
> *He'll plant your feet back firmly on the ground.*
> *He flies so high, he swoops so low,*
> *He knows exactly which way he's going to go.*

Mystic or pusher? Or madman? Or "Sexy Sadie"? Thomas wasn't saying. What he was willing to say about LSD was, "I got something out of it at the time. You felt nice and 'blah blah blah.' But, after a few times, I wanted to come down and get on with something. It got boring." (RT-PM73)

Hayward had experimented with LSD too, more than Thomas, and taking a bit longer to become bored by it. He said of the drug, of the song, and of Leary, "Some of us in the band – and this was 1966, '67 – were going through our own psychic experiences, as a lot of musicians were at the time, probably being led by the Beatles. We were reading a lot of underground press and reading about Tim Leary, so we put him in.

"[It was] a very cheeky English version – of what we thought things would be like in San Francisco in the 'flower power' days…. but with a background of serious meaning. It did mean something to us. We were using a lot of phrases of the time, extracts from *The Tibetan Book of the Dead*, talking about the astral plane and so forth, and it's a reflection of that." (JH-HC96)

The lyric to "Legend of a Mind" was only half the trip. Equally important, and just as trippy, were the music and instrumentation. Mike Pinder said, "Tony Clarke, Derek Varnals and I were always trying to create new and innovative sounds. A good example of my signature Mellotron swoops are in Ray Thomas' song, 'Legend of a Mind.' I used the speed control on my 'Tron' to create the swoops, and we would take advantage of the stereo effects to make the Mellotron sound, and the movement comes from one side to the other side, i.e., left-right, and right-left. And I would use the reverb to make it come forward and back in the track as well. The listener would get an almost-3D sound that was unique for that time." (MP-SAV14)

Besides Pinder's Mellotron sweeps from speaker to speaker, and Thomas' exquisite flute playing, a third instrument of prominence on the track is the sitar. Justin Hayward had been inspired by the Beatles' use of the Indian instrument on their recent LP, *Rubber Soul*, released in December, 1965. For the song "Norwegian Wood (This Bird Has Flown)," George Harrison played the exotic instrument.

Hayward was intrigued, and was challenged to experiment with the sitar, which is heard on three *Lost*

(Photo source: rockcellarmagazine)

Chord tracks, including "Legend of a Mind." Two other Eastern instruments featured on this track, and elsewhere on the album, are the string instrument, the tambura, which Mike Pinder played, and the percussion instrument, the bongo-like tabla, played by Graeme Edge. Hayward also played three different guitars on the track – both 6-and 12-string acoustics, and an electric guitar. Thomas had the lead vocal, with backing provided by Hayward, Lodge, and Pinder. Lodge's masterful falsetto, used to punctuate sections of the song, offers yet another eerie, "druggy" effect.

In addition to the tabla, Graeme Edge also manned his standard U.K. drum kit, on which he played anything but a standard rock beat. He said, "I like 'Legend of a Mind,' especially where we change into the Indian stanza. I think the tempo change is done in such a way that you don't suddenly notice that we've moved from 4/4 [time] into what it became. I can't remember the time signature, because the Indian music is like a giant riff. Of course, it can be measured out, but you end up doing something daft like 17/8, and it's best not to think of it in those terms. It's best to picture it as the Indians do – as a riff. I was very pleased with the way I crossed over there." (GE-MD87)

As for the melody, Hayward gives full credit to Thomas, even though there had been speculation that some of the music came from other band members. He told Mark Murley of *Higher & Higher*, "[Ray] was very good at melody lines and he would stick to those without changing a note, and that would be it. The job that myself or Mike often had to do… was to listen to the vocal and then put in chords. We even had to choose the key, because sometimes Ray would think two keys were right for it. He could do a line and it would work in C and in G. So you would play around with it and ask him to keep singing this little melody that he had until you got something that you thought was right and original and interesting – which is absolutely wonderful for me, and I loved it because then I could just use little tricks that I learned…. It was fantastic; he was completely open." (JH-H&H04a)

The Moodies recorded "Legend of a Mind" before they had an album commitment because Decca was looking for a single to follow up "Nights in White Satin." "Legend," even if not a traditional "single," was the product.

Recording engineer Derek Varnals said, "The reason we did it was they were performing it on stage, so we thought, 'If they've already got a song they've written and are performing, let's get it down on tape.' It was rare that they would ever perform a song before it was recorded, but that's one of the ones that was, like 'Nights in White Satin.'" (DV-H&H95)

In between sessions, the band was out and about, performing their stage show of *Days of Future Passed*, as well as requested songs and some new ones, like "Legend of a Mind." Among the venues around England that the Moodies visited were the Punchbowl Bar and Restaurant in the picturesque village of Lapworth, on January 19, and, on the 20th, the much bigger California Ballroom, in Dunstable, which could hold 2,000 people.

On January 24, as covered earlier, the Moodies were on the Continent, filling in for the Supremes at Cannes MIDEM '68. Then, right back to London Decca Studio 2, on January 28, with the band recording Justin Hayward's "What Am I Doing Here?," a new song they had been doing live, which fit with the theme of the search for knowledge, faith, and self-acceptance for the upcoming album. Sadly, due to the time constraints of 33&1/3 rpm vinyl albums (roughly 20 minutes per side), the song was left off *Lost Chord*. It remained hidden in the Decca vault until 1977 when finally issued as part of *Caught Live + 5*.

Throughout February, the band played further dates around England, such as the Imperial Ballroom in Nelson on February 3, Liberty Hall in Yeovil, South Somerset (February 8), Portland Building in Nottingham (Feb. 9), and the historic Leas Cliff Hall in Folkestone (Feb. 10).

Additional hurried recording sessions took place in London whenever the band could squeeze into the busy schedule of Decca Studio 2. Like "What Am I Doing Here?," two new songs – Hayward's "King and Queen" (from a session on February 13), and John Lodge's "Gimme a Little Something" (recorded on March 17), would also not be made available until *Caught Live + 5*.

More concerts – including Fitzwilliam College in Cambridge (February 16), Grays Technical College in Grays (17), Civic Hall in Nantwich (24), Country Club in Kirklevington (25), then back to the Olympia in Paris, on February 26 – kept the band out of the studio. The set list at this time included "Fly Me High," "Bye Bye Bird" (from the *The Magnificent Moodies* album), "Don't Let Me Be Misunderstood," "Peak Hour," "Tuesday Afternoon," "Nights in White Satin," and the recently recorded but unreleased "What Am I Doing Here?"

On February 27, the band was back on English soil, playing at Manchester University, then one day later at the Mayfair in Newcastle. On March 1, they were at Headington Tech College in Oxford, then, the following day, at Winter Gardens Pavilion in Weston-Super-Mare. On the 5th, it was Shenley Green Youth Club, Birmingham, then, for the next day, Portsmouth Technical College, then, on March 8, a gig at Sorby Hall in Sheffield. On March 9, they played Sloppy's in Manchester. On the 10th, they were in Germany performing "Nights in White Satin" on German TV's *Beat Club*. On March 13, the band was back in Birmingham, playing the Town Hall. On the 15th: Reading University. On the 22nd: Middle Earth, a club in Covent Garden, London.

Even when their breakneck performance schedule allowed the Moodies additional time for recording, it became a common problem that Decca Studio Number 2 (designated for smaller productions such as rock combos) was often booked. In an effort to get a solid block of recording time to arrange and perform a consistent and coherent album, the group sent a request to Decca head Sir Edward Lewis. They requested the use of the much larger – and frequently vacant – Decca Studio Number 1. This facility was used primarily for orchestral recordings, as it had been for *Days of Future Passed*. By this time, with the positive press in England and the good sales on the Continent for "Nights in White Satin" and *Future Passed*, Lewis agreed.

Hayward later said, "He was the last man I knew in this business with the authority, and with the confidence in an artist, to be able to stand there and say, 'Boys, I don't know exactly what it is you're doing, and I don't understand it, but it's great, and you just do it the best that you can. And we will sell it." (JH-GM94)

In mid-May, the Moodies moved into Decca Studio 1 for a six-week stay, enough time to record the balance of the album.

Regardless of the faith shown toward them by Sir Lewis, sales of *Days of Future Passed* were not as good as hoped for by the band. The same

Sir Edward Lewis, head of England's Decca Records.
(Photo source: jproc.ca)

186

could be said of the situation in the U.S., prior to the release of the "Tuesday Afternoon" single

Graeme Edge said, "In the end, [*Days of Future Passed*] did well, but it certainly didn't come up to our expectations [in that first year]. I remember Justin being very depressed about it when we went in to cut *In Search of the Lost Chord*. I said, 'Don't let it bring you down because that record's too good for something *not* to happen to it.'" (GE-S73)

Morale picked up, once work began in earnest.

The album's theme, the search for life's meaning, came to the Moodies through Transcendental Meditation. Hayward said of TM, "It definitely affected *In Search of the Lost Chord*. There were only four of us who did it – me, Mike, Graeme, and Ray. I'm not sure if Graeme completed the course… but the [other] three of us certainly did. So it was a huge part of our lives, and you never forget that stuff. The initiation and the practice is still with me. When I need serenity, I still go there." (JH-RC17)

Graeme Edge: "We were very hung up on meditation, and this album is a result of that. It was a matter of getting it out of our systems, getting it out of the way so that we can now go on to something else." (GE-RM68)

"*Lost Chord* is our personal feelings," he said, "The tracks are by different [band members] and reflect their thoughts. We wrote it at the time when the Beatles were with the Maharishi. I think they expected too much from him; they were looking for a miracle. At the time, everyone was getting involved in false religions and false philosophies." (GE-NME68a)

Mike Pinder: "I was aware of him [the Maharishi] before he arrived and before the Press got hold of him and the Beatles. I was always reading occult subjects right from childhood days of legends and fairy stories. Meditation showed me it was possible to heighten one's awareness of life. But meditation is only an action, not a method. It will take you there but it won't let you in – that bit's up to you alone." (MP-DME70)

Justin Hayward: "For *Lost Chord*, we sat down and thought how we could string a story together. So we came up with the idea of music around the world – and every musician being in search of the lost chord and unique sounds. It was a good subject to write an album about, and it meant we could include the songs we'd already recorded: 'Legend of a Mind' and 'Voices in the Sky.'" (JH-TRC96)

Recording the Album

Mike Pinder: "When we sat down to do *In Search of the Lost Chord*, we wanted to do a good follow up to *Days of Future Passed*. We wanted every note and word to be written by ourselves, and we also wanted everything to be played by us. We wrote most of the material during the session. While one of us was overdubbing the vocal, somebody else would be in the back room working on another song." (MP-HP69)

Back at the controls were producer Tony Clarke and recording engineer Derek Varnals.

Justin Hayward: "Decca put a lot of faith behind us. They gave us a terrible royalty rate, but a lot of studio time. They encouraged us to make any music we wanted in any way we wanted. That changed our songwriting process." (JH-GP95)

"We were never offered the orchestra again," he said, "although I remained friends with Peter. We all did…. To work with an orchestra, you've got to have someone between you and the orchestra; you've got to have the conductor or the arranger, and that's a difficult job to do. And there's only a certain kind of person who can do that well." (JH-GM12)

Despite lacking an orchestra this time out, Clarke made sure the Moodies had everything they needed to expand and realize their musical ambitions. Hayward explained, "What it did do is it made us realize, if we had the studio time, and you gave us the instruments, with a couple of hours, we could get enough of what we needed out of each orchestral instrument." (JH-GM12)

John Lodge: "We started to write and record in terms of colors. We'd say, here's the type of color we want to achieve.' A lot of instruments just give you one color, but you add a couple of different instruments together on the same part and you get something new. I used to play a cello tuned in fourths against Mike's Mellotron parts, and that was a great sound." (JL-GP95)

Justin Hayward: "We got hold of a chart that had pictures of every instrument in the orchestra. We just kept pointing at things and asking Decca to bring them in for us – 'Yeah, we need that, and that, and that.' We had everything that could be blown into and all sorts of percussion piling up." (JH-GP95)

Tony Clarke: "I brought in more instruments than I ever did on anything. I wanted them to play everything, whereas we had a symphony orchestra on the first album. Everything you hear is played by the band." (TC-H&H04)

Mike Pinder: "We found that we could experiment with different kinds of instruments very successfully. We'd call an instrument rental company, and ask, 'What have you got?', and we'd see if we could work it into whatever songs we were working with. It was that kind of atmosphere – we really felt like there were no limits. Justin and I might pick up sitars, or cellos, or whatever was available." (MP-GM94)

Graeme Edge: "Oh, did we have some bloody nerve! I've seen John Lodge, Mike Pinder, and Justin Hayward sit in the studio for two days trying to get a bloody cello part.

"For some reason we developed this set of morals that we weren't going to have anybody but ourselves on the records. I think one of the reasons was that we were so upset by the fact that everybody thought *Days of Future Passed* was a rock band with a bloody orchestra over everything…. If you listen carefully to that record, the orchestra is never playing when the Moodies are playing. They play the links between the songs, but when the Moodies start playing it's just us and the Mellotron. On the album version of 'Nights,' they come in halfway through the last verse, and it is the orchestra in back of the poem, but, outside of that, it was never at the same time…. So it sort of became an issue. On the next album, we put: 'All instruments played by the Moody Blues.' We listed everything everybody did." (GE-MD87)

Assistant recording engineer Adrian Martins told interviewer Mark Murley, "Tony would always have very definite ideas, and on every track, he was looking for something new – new sounds and everything else. The Moodies were innovative, too…. A lot of friends weren't very good at playing their own instruments, so, basically, the studio would bring in session players to front for them, either their own instruments [bass, guitar, keyboards, etc.] or classical instruments. What the Moodies would do was to go out and buy or rent what they needed and learn it. You'd open up a cupboard and there would be Ray Thomas with an alto flute, actually learning how to play it! If Justin wanted a sitar on something, he'd go out, buy a sitar, and come back and learn how to play it…. Justin's extremely talented. He can pick up any type of guitar and just start singing and playing, and you sit there with your mouth wide open." (AM-H&H97)

"Departure" leads off the album, this time with Graeme Edge reciting his own poem instead of Pinder. Edge builds to a manic frenzy and hysterical laugher, as a single note from the band grows in volume and intensity. The theme for the album is established as Edge tells the listeners that be it from "sight, sound, smell, or touch," we all need to be touched *within*. That connection to life can come from observing a mighty oak tree, or from the "wonder of flowers" which persist in blooming through the cracks of mankind's paved-over world. We can achieve a sense of inner peace, Edge tells us, by listening to the sounds of nature, as we "lie in a meadow and hear the grass sing," or by reaching into the sky ourselves, flying to the sun "without burning a wing." Unless we remain connected to nature, man is on an empty quest, relentlessly driven to find explanation for his existence … and seek out a god … or some substitute for faith. The idea's hopelessness is demonstrated by the wild laugher at the end of the track.

This laughter segues magnificently into John Lodge's rocker, **"Ride My See-Saw."** Here, Lodge combines his voice with those of Hayward, Pinder, and Thomas. The song tells the story of an average young man who left school with a "first class pass" only to be delegated work as a member of the "second class," thus working "like a slave for years." While school taught him "one and one is two," now he knows that answer "just ain't true." In society, "one" is often *not* invited to become part of the club.

The singers offer no answers. They, like us all, are still asking.

Standard Moodies instruments are used on this "rock" track – electric and acoustic guitars from Hayward, Mellotron from Pinder, bass guitar from Lodge, drums and maracas from Edge.

The combined one-two punch of "Departure" and "Ride My See-Saw" gets the album off to an electrifying start. Much credit must go to Tony Clarke, who sequenced the tracks.

Justin Hayward said, "Tony was always able to see the grand picture. He was never a hands-on-the-mixer producer; he was someone who would look at the whole picture and see the album finished when you've only just started." (JH-H&H04a)

Mike Pinder credited Clarke with having a "musical and audio vision." He said, "[Tony] was right up there with [us]. If I mentioned an idea that might be [unusual], he'd be right there with me… and then, 'Derek, how can we do this?' We'd go for it. Anything that would give us more tools, more expression, more vision, we were for it. I think Tony looked at the sound the same way as I did – *visually*. It was a visual conception of the musical landscape. Here we were in stereo… we've got width, we've got placement, we've got left, right, up, down, far away, close up – all of those dimensions for us to use. So that was one of the cool things – experimenting and exploring every possible aspect of stereo." (MP-H&H04b)

"Dr. Livingstone, I Presume" follows. As with Thomas' "Legend of a Mind," it too is tongue in cheek. Thomas has said he did this to offset the heaviness of the overall theme used for this album, and the serious approach of its other tracks.

A bit of backstory concerning the characters in the song:

Dr. David Livingstone was a British medical missionary who gained fame in the Victorian Era for his exploratory missions on the continent of Africa. Livingstone was obsessed with solving an age-old mystery: the source of the Nile River. It was on one such expedition that he came across famed journalist and fellow explorer Henry Morton Stanley, who allegedly said, "Dr. Livingstone, I presume?"

Thomas sings that while Livingstone saw "butterflies galore," and people "big and small," the explorer still hadn't found what he'd been looking for. This was a fair assessment; Livingstone vanished without a trace on one of his expeditions … never heard from again.

Another subject of the song is British Royal Navy Captain Robert Falcon Scott, who led a pair of expeditions into the Antarctic between 1901 and 1913. On the second expedition, Scott and his team perished in the frozen wastelands. Thomas explains that although Scott boldly conquered great distances, seeing polar bears and seals, and great Antarctic eels … but he, too, has not found what he was looking for.

And then there was Christopher Columbus, who stumbled on American in 1492 while trying to find a seaway shortcut from Western Europe to China. He, too, never found what he was looking for. Columbus returned from his final sea expedition ill and then suffered for the remainder of his life, often bedridden. He died at age 54.

Despite being a Ray Thomas song, there is no flute. What we hear: Hayward, playing 6-and 12-string guitars, as well as electric; Lodge on bass; Pinder on Mellotron and piano; Edge on the drums. In addition, Hayward, Lodge, and Pinder provide the backing vocals.

"House of Four Doors" is John Lodge's second composition on the album. He said, "I wanted to write a song that showed how you could live your life. As you're going along, there are doors that you can either open or ignore. My philosophy was always to open the door and see what's inside – it might be something fabulous." (JL-C88)

In two parts, the song is presented in epic proportions, with Hayward on acoustic and electric guitars, Thomas on flute, Edge on drums, and Pinder on piano, harpsichord, and Mellotron. Lodge played cello as well as bass. He said, "I played the cello on that track, and tuned it the same way as a bass guitar. I never realized that a cello wasn't actually tuned that way at all, but we got the desired effect." (JL-ISEOLC08)

And then there was that creaking door. These sounds, as with everything on the album, were created by the Moodies; no sound effects from the Decca library were used. Engineer Derek Varnals said of the creaking door sounds, "That was cello. That was John or Mike dragging a bow across a cello. If you drag a bow across a cello very coarsely without trying to make a note, you can make it really grind and creak. It took several tries but we eventually got one." (DV-H&H95b)

The lyric tells about a group of people wandering through the forest, discovering a lost path leading to the House of Four Doors – a beautiful maze-like structure … and the discovery behind each of the four doors … until they are told at Door Number Four that they will be lost forever. With the opening of each door, we hear music played on instruments representing a specific era. First come an English folk guitar and flute; for the next era, harpsichord; for the third, heavy orchestration courtesy of the Mellotron. When the fourth door opens, we hear psychedelic music representing 1978 … leading into Ray Thomas's "Legend of a Mind." At its conclusion, the door closes and we are back in the "House of Four Doors," for the final revelation of that song, bringing Side 1 to an end.

"Voices in the Sky" opens Side 2. This Justin Hayward-written-and-sung track is another on the album to benefit from Ray Thomas' lovely flute playing. The thematic search continues, with "Bluebird, flying high … tell me what you sing … if you could talk to me … what news would you bring … of the voices in the sky?" And another question: "Just what is happening to me? … I lie awake with the sound of the sea … calling to me."

Hayward plays an acoustic guitar; Thomas is on the flute, supported by Pinder's Mellotron, Lodge's bass, and Edge's drums and tabla.

"The Best Way to Travel," Mike Pinder tells us, is by thinking. He sings: "And you can fly, high as a kite if you want; Faster than light if you want to…. Distance is gone … Will we find how life began … Will we find out? … Speeding through the universe?"

Graeme Edge: "Mike didn't have a very good voice, but he used it so emotionally and so emotively that it came across in his songs so good. He was kind of ethereal and [the] semi-religious aspect of the diamond. They were all facets of the diamond, those four guys – and five, with Tony Clarke." (GE-GM12)

This is the album's most psychedelic song, highlighted by stereo panning, accomplished by use of "pan pots" on the Decca custom-built four-track recording console, which had input jacks for 20 microphones.

Besides singing lead, and working the Mellotron, Pinder also plays the lead acoustic guitar. Hayward contributes electric guitar and sitar, as well as backing vocals. Thomas' flute is utilized, and Lodge and Edge provide the solid rhythm section.

"Visions of Paradise" was a collaborative composition from Hayward and Thomas, and is dominated by Hayward's acoustic guitars (both 6- and 12-string) and Thomas's flute. It is believed Thomas also played the oboe for this track, and Hayward the sitar. Pinder, besides Mellotron, also played the tambura. Edge, besides drums and standard percussion, also played the tabla. Lodge contributed the bass line.

This song's lyrics aren't as obviously concerned with the album's theme of discovery. However, there is a hint of a search of inner awareness, and the idea of sharing and exchanging these thoughts with another: "The sounds in my mind just come to me … Come see, come see … And the call of her eyes makes waterfalls … of me, of me…."

Is the singer in search of love? … Or the touch of flesh? … Or the soothing sound of the beating heart of one's mate? … Or the light in their eyes?

Mike Pinder was content with Moody Blues' lyrics remaining mysterious. He said, "Music is the biggest communication medium of all – it is also the only medium where we can tell the truth without fear of censorship. The real meaning of so much music is disguised and you can't see it until you search for it. But a lot of mysteries of music will come into the open, and in some 20 years time, when our generation becomes the ruling generation." (MP-DME70)

"The Actor," the next track on the album, can be interpreted as a companion piece to "Vision of Paradise," and it is pure Hayward – the only song on the album reminiscent in tone and vocal performance to "Nights in White Satin."

The curtain rises, and, as the play unfolds before the singer's eyes, he realizes that the actor is himself. Love, and the connection with another, is the quest here, as in "Visions of Paradise." The challenge is to see through the masks we all wear – for we all are actors and life is but our stage – with the curtain always ready to drop.

Justin Hayward: "I remember sitting in a little bedsitting-room where I used to live, and I remember me coming back from a gig and writing this song. And it really was about my life at that time, and all the pop businesses [in which we] have been an actor.... I think it's not show business, but it is – it's still the show. So I was working very hard, and sleeping late. It was like a movie screen, with images on a screen. So I just wrote it down." (JH-HL99)

"It was certainly a time for me when I was sort of searching and seeking different religions, psychedelic experiences," Hayward said elsewhere. "I know we've talked about this before, but it was a real time of discovery for me as a young man. So, I was getting stoned a lot and going deeper into music and things. I certainly saw it as a real chance at musical freedom... a way to express the sort of searching, seeking things that we were doing in our lives, or some of us were doing. Some of us were doing this more seriously or more intensely than others. So, the album reflected that....

"My songs form a kind of biography or diary of my life, as they are people I have loved and people I only knew in my heart; places I have seen only for a moment and places I have lived all my life....

"'Tuesday Afternoon' was written on a beautiful day, trees like Tolkien's Ents who take hours just saying 'hello.' 'Nights in White Satin' – about an audience in Glastonbury, a flat in Bayswater, and the ecstasy of an hour of love. 'The Actor' – who is me and you." (JH-H&H04a and JH-RM70)

As in "Visions of Paradise," the prominent instruments here are Hayward's acoustic guitars and Thomas's flutes ("C" and alto flute). Thomas is also the most noticeable of the backing voices.

"The Word," a second poem on the album by Graeme Edge, benefits from a reading by Mike Pinder. "To reach the chord is our life's hope," he tells us, "and to name the chord is important to some ... so they gave it a word ... and the word is 'Om.'"

"Om," written by Pinder, is also heavily influenced with Indian musical instruments and styles.

The word or name "Om," which is chanted in the song, represents "Aum," a sacred mantra in the Hindu, Jain Sikh, and Buddhist religions.

Pinder trades lead vocals with Ray Thomas, with chanting from all five of the Moodies. The song makes use of a variety of instruments – dominated by Pinder's Mellotron, Thomas's flute, Hayward's sitar, and Edge's tabla. Also present: Lodge on cello as well as bass, Hayward on acoustic guitar, and Pinder on tambura.

"Om" concludes the album. But Ray Thomas recalled that there was one last lost chord intended for the very end of the LP. He said, "We were fucking around a lot with sounds, and we discovered that if you took a B-flat down so low you could hardly hear it, then turned it backwards, the pulsation would make you lose control of your bowels. So we thought, wouldn't it be great if we put this on the end of *In Search of the Lost Chord*? Nobody could hear it, and everybody shits themselves! But the Decca powers that be said we couldn't do it; it was highly dangerous. Then, while we were playing [it] in the studio,

Tony walked across the room and all of a sudden it dropped him like a fucking stone; it hit him in the neck! Just after that time, people were starting to experiment with 'sound bombs,' but we were doing it months before." (RT-CRB14)

Regarding *In Search of the Lost Chord*, and all eight albums he produced for the Moody Blues, Tony Clarke said, "One thing I've discovered is that none of the Moodies' music is meant to be listened to in daylight. They were certainly made for in the dark. I find them much easier to listen to at midnight than at midday." (TC-H&H95)

The album was finished, but one more song was recorded at this time – Mike Pinder's **"A Simple Game,"** was put to tape in Decca Studio 2 on October 11 and 12. It was coupled later that month on the U.K. version of the "Ride My See-Saw" single.

Pinder was still in a *Lost Chord* state of mind when he wrote this song, evidenced by the lyric:

> *... When this crazy world is free*
> *When it finds out*
> *Exactly what we're meant to be*
> *Free from doubt*
> *That we are one*
> *We're all the same*
> *And life is just a simple game.*

Derek Varnals said, "It was remarkable how Mike would come up with a good song under pressure. He was one of the last [of the group] to get a song together and he would come up with good ones. Sometimes he would write songs in separate portions, you know – he would have a great middle eight, which, of course, 'A Simple Game' does have – and it's almost as though he had two separate songs and he'd graft them together. A little bit in the way the Beatles did with 'A Day in the Life.' ... He always used to have a better middle eight than the rest of the song. It was one of those things – we always looked forward to his middle-eight pieces; his bridge pieces." (DV-H&H95b)

Regarding the title for *In Search of the Lost Chord*, Pinder shared, "I listened to the radio a lot and when I was about 5 years old, I heard a song by Jimmy Durante called 'The Man Who Found the Lost Chord' [sic]. I remembered that story 23 years later, after the band's hit album *Days of Future Passed*, and I coaxed them into calling the next album *In Search of the Lost Chord*. So you can see that what happened to me as a child had a big effect on my entire life." (MP-EOTS99)

The novelty record by Jimmy Durante was actually called, "I'm the Guy Who Found the Lost Chord," making reference to a poem and song of the same title, called "The Lost Chord."

The more one knows about "The Lost Chord," as opposed to the Durante comedy song, the more one must wonder whether or not Pinder encountered the original poem ... perhaps on a different plane.

"A Lost Chord," written as a poem by English poet and Philanthropist Adelaide Anne Proctor, was published in 1858 by *The English Woman's Journal*.

> *Seated one day at the organ, I was weary and ill at ease.*
> *And my fingers wandered idly over the noisy keys.*

I know not what I was playing, or what I was dreaming then;
But I struck one chord of music like the sound of a great Amen.
It flooded the crimson twilight, like the close of an angel's psalm,
And it lay at my fevered spirit with a touch of infinite calm.
It quieted pain and sorrow, like love overcoming strife;
It seemed the harmonious echo from our discordant life.
It linked all perplexed meanings into one perfect peace,
And trembled away into silence, as if it were loth to cease.

I have sought, but I seek it vainly, that one lost chord divine,
Which came from the soul of the organ, and entered into mine.
It may be that death's bright angel will speak in that chord again
It may be that only in Heaven I shall hear that grand Amen.

One can easily imagine how these words could have made an impression on a young Mike Pinder, just as they did on English operatic composer Arthur Sullivan (of Gilbert and Sullivan). Sullivan was in search of the lost chord to bring comfort to his dying brother. It was while at his brother's bedside that Sullivan resumed an earlier attempt to compose music for the poem. Fred Sullivan died days later, but Arthur Sullivan's composition for Adelaide Anne Proctor's words went on to became popular in its day. So popular, in fact, that Jimmy Durante made a parody record of it. And then, said Pinder, that song gave him the idea for the title to the new album … on which the original poem by Adelaide Anne Proctor might have felt quite at home.

Displeased with the album cover art for *Days of Future Passed*, the Moodies asked manager Derek McCormick to search for a different artist to design the *In Search of the Lost Chord* artwork.

Philip Travers was born in 1945 and studied art design at the Sutton School of Art and the London School of Printing. After five years at Art College, Travers found a job in the art department at Decca Records, designing record sleeves. He left the company after two years to take a position as an illustrator for a design office in Wimbledon.

Travers said, "While there, I was contacted by someone I knew at Decca because, apparently, the then-manager of the Moody Blues had been at Decca to look through their catalogue of sleeve designs and he'd really liked an illustration of mine which I had done shortly before I left. Shortly thereafter, I was invited to an introductory meeting with the Moodies at a pub in London… and, after we'd worked out the details of the commission, I was invited to listen to the soundtrack of *In Search of the Lost Chord* at their recording studio." (PT-TR08)

Travers' reaction was immediate and positive. "I liked it," he said. "And that's the way it always worked with them – I'd get to listen to the record, then discuss the themes and ideas behind it, before any art concepts were developed." (PT-TT15)

The Moodies had an idea of what they wanted – concept-wise – but it would be quite a challenge for Travers to realize those ideas. "The band wanted me primarily to illustrate the concept of meditation," Travers recalled. "This was not something that I had much personal experience of, and so my initial thoughts about such an ethereal subject were, unfortunately, insubstantial. And so, I wasn't producing any cohesive visual ideas,

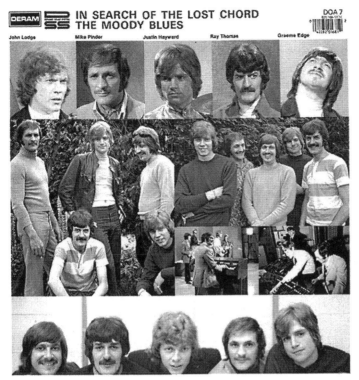

IN SEARCH OF THE LOST CHORD
THE MOODY BLUES

John Lodge   Mike Pinder   Justin Hayward   Ray Thomas   Graeme Edge

with this lack of ideas evident in my first rough designs. In fact, as time was getting short – by the way, *everything was always wanted in a hurry* – I was starting to panic." (PT-TR08)

Travers returned to Decca Studio 1 and asked to have the tape of the album played again. He remembered, "While I was listening to the music, the concept for the cover was actually given to me in some sort of subliminal way. The recording and mixing area of the studio where I was sitting was separated from the area where the band would play by a large glass window and, in the glass, I could see several images of myself – one above the other – almost as if I was ascending up into space…. After that, everything just fell into place….

"It's impossible for me to tell you now how long it took me to produce the illustration, other than to say that, in most cases, I had days rather than weeks to complete them and submit them for approval. As for the way I painted, I used Gouache and some watercolor, and very often I employed an airbrush." (PT-TR08)

There is no question that the stunning, surreal front cover design for *In Search of the Lost Chord* helped to sell the record. Music reviewers praised the bold, innovative design, and displaying the album in record stores certainly translated into sales. With *In Search of the Lost Chord,* you certainly could judge this "book" by its cover. So successful was it that Phil Travers would be called on to design the next several Moody Blues album covers.

The back-sleeve cover was another story. The Moodies had resisted having their faces appear on the cover and sleeve of *Days of Future Passed.* This time there would be a montage of pictures of the band crowding the back cover – four group shots, plus a single image of each band member, plus a picture from the recording studio control room, featuring Tony Clarke, Derek Varnals, and, we believe, tape operator Adrian Martins, working at the recording board. One image crowds out the next. Despite the collision of visual styles, we who missed out seeing the Moodies on TV or in concert from this period, had faces to go with the voices.

On the inside – in the gatefold – Tony Clarke provided the sleeve notes, telling how the Moodies played every instrument and made every sound heard on the album. He described them as "the smallest symphony orchestra in the world."

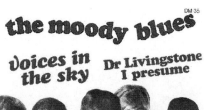

Above: Picture sleeve issued in Belgium.

U.K. single release:
"Voices in the Sky"
b/w *"Dr. Livingstone, I Presume"*
Deram DM 196; June 28, 1968

A full month before the release of *In Search of the Last Chord*, Decca issued an advance tease of the album, coupling Justin Hayward's "Voices in the Sky" and Ray Thomas's "Dr. Livingstone, I Presume."

Why these two songs? Shortly after the album was released, Graeme Edge said that Decca executives "pick what they think is the most commercial track off an album. And they ask, 'Can we release it?' And we've never, up 'till now, said 'no,' because we've got a system – we wipe anything that we don't want released. We never make 'singles' and we never make 'LP tracks'; we just go in and make LPs." (GE-OC68)

At this time, Justin Hayward told Richard Green of *New Musical Express*, "This single will probably help the LP and vice versa. Disc jockeys are more likely to play it than select a track for themselves." (JH-NME68)

There was good reason for wanting to help the DJs along in promoting the album. For *In Search of the Lost Chord*, the Moody Blues used the technique rapidly becoming known as "cross-fading," in which one song would transition (or fade) into another without any space in between. This made it difficult for DJs to play album cuts on the radio, unless the song was first up on either side of the vinyl LP. Having two of the tracks from the album on a single made it possible for the DJs to cue either one. It was simple to set the needle down at the track's beginning and provide a spoken intro, before releasing the record to play.

This was how it worked in the days before "tape carts" (cartridges), or, later, CDs, or, later still, digital playback boards. A DJ, sitting in front of a microphone and between two different turntables, needed not only a nimble tongue, but coordinated hands, an instinctive sense of timing, and, preferably, a pair of 45s, not LPs, on those spinning turntables.

The "Voices in the Sky" single was not issued in America, since "Tuesday Afternoon" was still riding high in the charts. In fact, the very day that "Voices" was

released in the U.K. – June 28, 1968 –
"Tuesday" was in the Top 10 on Los
Angeles, California's popular KHJ/Boss
Radio. More stations across America were
adding it to their playlists each week,
continuing well into October. Deram,
therefore, withheld "Voices in the Sky"
from the U.S. market, allowing American
radio programmers to keep their focus on
"Tuesday Afternoon."

(Photo source: Author's Collection)

The new single missed out being
issued in other countries as well. According
to *Billboard*'s "Hits of the World" charts,
during early August, as "Voices" was
climbing the British charts, "Nights in
White Satin" was still a Top Ten entry in many other countries, such as Argentina, and
Spain, where it was at No. 6 and moving up (it would hit No. 3 one week later).

The songs to beat in the last week of June 1968 in England were, at No. 1, "Baby
Come Back," by the Equals (produced by Tony Clarke), followed by, respectively, "The
Son of Hickory Holler's Tramp," by American soul singer O.C. Smith; "Jumpin' Jack
Flash," by the Rolling Stones; and "Hurdy Gurdy Man," by Donovan. Also high in the
British charts: "Young Girl," by Gary Puckett & the Union Gap; "Mony Mony," by
Tommy James and the Shondells; and "Do You Know the Way to San Jose," by Dionne
Warwick.

The day before "Voices in the Sky" was released, one British music trade said of
the song:

> One of the most publicly ignored groups in the country, the
> Moody Blues, are really good, turning out music of great beauty
> and high standard. This [new single] is no exception. It has a
> lovely controlled jazz opening and then drifts on with a gentle
> voice and soft woodwind. It is totally delightful and should be
> bought and played and appreciated.

The day after the single was issued, *Melody Maker* had its review in print:

> While the group have sunk below the national consciousness since
> their hit days, they have improved vastly and are now producing
> some remarkably beautiful records, including this moody and blue
> ballad.

> Their live performances too are something of a revelation, and if
> the public can be made to forget their "Go Now" image, the
> Moodies should be back in the main stream of pop events soon.

Also on the June 29, *Record Mirror* had its assessment in print:

From the LP *In Search of the Lost Chord* [comes] this rather wondrous production. I'm not saying it is instantly to be labeled "for the charts" because there is a lot happening and it takes time to register. But, if justice still prevaileth, then it will make it. Excellently sung and the backing is quite tremendous, but in a restrained sort of style. Great lyrics. Flip: Let's just say it's a value for [your] money.

That night, the Moody Blues performed a high-profile concert at the London's Queen Elizabeth Hall. The set list included "The Best Way to Travel," "Peak Hour," "Nights in White Satin," and, of course, the two sides to the new single.

On July 5, the Moodies were on David Symonds' BBC 1 radio show, performing the two sides of the single and, from the album, "The Best Way to Travel" and "Ride My See-Saw."

On July 6, David Hughes reviewed the Moodies' Queen Elizabeth Hall concert for *Disc and Music Echo*:

> … For a five-piece group, seemingly of the normal line-up, the Moodies create an incredible sound, or, as the man behind me was heard to remark, "I suppose they're going to reproduce the entire Hall's Orchestra again!"

> Indeed, it is the incredible Mellotron of Mike Pinder that MAKES the Moody Blues. Looking just like yer normal Hammond organ, the machine reproduces any instrument of the orchestra at the flick of a button.

> Thus, "Voices in the Sky," "Knights [sic] in White Satin," and other tracks from their two LPs, roared over the audience like … well, like the Hall Orchestra!

> Lead guitarist and vocalist Justin Hayward is an extraordinary man. Not only can he write poignantly beautiful melodies, but his sad eerie voice sings them like no one else.

> Ray Thomas provided humor, excellent flute, and good vocalizing, and drummer Graeme Edge beamed at everyone, looking like a younger Ringo Starr! …

On July 13, the Moodies were back on the BBC – this time for the *Saturday Club* – with the two single sides and "The Best Way to Travel."

On July 15, it was another trip onto the David Symonds show, and, again, another change to plug the two sides of the single, along with "Best Way to Travel" and "Ride My See-Saw."

From England's *Fabulous 208*'s July 20, 1968 issue, June Southworth wrote:

> The Moody Blues hope you'll be hearing lots of "Voices in the Sky" over the next few weeks. …

"Nights in White Satin" was, for me, THE record of '67. Now they're bringing out an album, *In Search of the Lost Chord*, which has even nicer things in it.

There was a marvelous turnout of Moodies' fans when Mike, Ray, Justin, John, and Graeme played The Queen Elizabeth Hall recently. The Hall is London's latest show-case, and the prestige of playing there is enormous. …

Here is a group that really plays as a group. No one is trying to do a prima donna. The group comes first. Ray's flute is so pretty that you can feel the spring in the air; Mike coaxes a whole orchestra out of the Mellotron; Graeme drums himself into the stage; John's bass is a solid foundation for all the magic of the others; and Justin plays lead guitar and sings with a feel that shakes you sometimes. All the time they play, they watch each other, help each other along, smile to each other when the sound is really happening. Watching them you know that this is what a group sound is all about.

After the concert at The Queen Elizabeth, the Moodies gave a party, and it seemed that anyone who had ever given them a helping hand was there. They had even brought their parents along from their various homes in Birmingham and Swindon, and it was nice, you know, seeing them there.

Justin's mum told me she had never been so proud. Justin was walking around in a little dream, as gentle and genuine as always, despite the fuss. …

Lovely people, the Moody Blues. I hope you'll listen to those "Voices in the Sky" when they come calling you.

More promotion: The band sang the two single sides plus "Travel" and "See-Saw" on the July 21 edition of the BBC radio program, *Top Gear*.

U.K. album release:
In Search of the Lost Chord
Deram SML 711; July 26, 1968

U.S. album release:
U.S. album release: Deram DE 16017 (mono); DE 18017 (stereo): July 26, 1968

In the U.S, at the top of *Billboard* magazine's albums chart the week *In Search of the Lost Chord* was issued, counting down: *Bookends* by Simon & Garfunkel, and filled with hits: "Mrs. Robinson," "Fakin' It," "A Hazy Shade of Winter," and "At the Zoo"; *The Beat of the Brass* by Herb Alpert & the Tijuana Brass, featuring "This Guy's in Love With You"; the soundtrack to *The Graduate*, mostly by Simon & Garfunkel; *A Tramp*

Shining by Richard Harris, featuring "MacArthur Park"; and *Look Around* by Sergio Mendes & Brazil '66, with their U.S. hit, "The Look of Love."

From the July 27 issue of *Record Mirror*, the music trade's critic said of *In Search of the Lost Chord*:

> Powerful and eerie sound from this excellent quintet who have always gone forward with their torrid, sometimes overpowering, music. This is an expedition into the outer atmosphere, specially "Ride My See-Saw," "Voices in the Sky," "The Best Way to Travel," and "Dr. Livingstone, I Presume" (about famous explorers and how they are looking for someone, too). All the numbers are written within the group.... A most impressive album, with arresting Philip Travers painting on the sleeve cover.

From the same day, *Melody Maker* reported:

> The Moodies are currently on a Continental tour which takes them to France, Austria, Switzerland, Holland, Portugal, and Germany. Over 4,000 fans were at their opening in Grenoble last week.

On July 30, the group appeared on a pair of German TV programs, performing "Tuesday Afternoon" and "Legend of a Mind."

The following day – July 31 – they were back in England, where John Lodge wed his true love, Kirsten (and they are still happily together as of this writing – 2017).

On August 3, Derek Boltwood wrote in *Record Mirror*:

> There is somewhere a lost chord. Some people call that chord "God," some people call it "the truth," some people call it "Om." ... The Moody Blues have spent a short period of their lives searching, hoping to find the lost chord through their music. To say that they have found what they were looking for would be ridiculous. But they have, as a result, produced an excellent LP. ...

> When I first heard the album I was struck by the really great sound ... and by its pretentiousness. I was right about the sound and wrong about the album being pretentious. It is held together by the central theme of its title, *In Search of the Lost Chord* – and part of the record's success is that the Moodies have interpreted what could have been a pretentious idea in their own way, proving again, as they did with *Days of Future Passed*, that they are a lot more than just another pop group. They are five very serious musicians, capable of doing great things with pop.

> All the tracks on this LP flow together. The opening "Departure" is a sort of maniac poem that leads into the first song, "Ride My See-Saw." The opening is dramatic, and sets the "big sound" mood that runs all the way through. A big sound produced by the Moody Blues alone, with no assistance from the London Festival Orchestra or from session musicians. Between them they play over 30 different instruments on the album. Breaking into "House of

Four Doors," there's even part of a concerto ("to prove to our critics that we're able to play 'real' music," says Graeme Edge)....

The opening track on Side 2 of the album is "Voices in the Sky," the number which is also on release as their new single.... "Visions of Paradise," I think, is one of the most beautiful tracks on the album – melodic with some very nice harmonies and choruses. The last track on the LP is "Om," a very Eastern sound, very beautiful and strangely haunting – the chanting of a thousand Buddhist monks translated into English....

On the Continent the Moody Blues are massive – in this country they have the respect of all. But they deserve to be "even more massive."

On August 14, across the pond, U.S.A.'s *Variety* said:

Like so many other rock groups, the Moody Blues have been growing artistically. They are now expanding ideological horizons by pursuing some lofty concepts that are indicated by the titles on this new album, such as "Departure," "The Actor," "The Word," "Om," "Legend of a Mind, "Visions of Paradise," and "House of Four Doors." The album, with the new concept of segueing through the "separating" grooves, is excellently produced. It displays topnotch musicianship and a mature approach that should win rewards.

Four days later, American syndicated music columnist Scott G. Campbell devoted a third of his "The Underground Sound" to the Moody Blues:

The single "Tuesday Afternoon (Forever Afternoon)" and the album *Days of Future Passed* were, in part, responsible for the return of the Moody Blues as a top progressive rock group since the success of "Go Now" several years ago. The quintet's newest album, *In Search of the Lost Chord* (Deram DES 18017), should do much to advance that reputation.

All of the songs on the album are well-done, with "Ride My See-Saw," "Om," and "House of Four Doors, Parts I and II" the highlights; each is just a bit harder rock than "Tuesday Afternoon," but each still manages to retain many of the same distinguishing characteristics that mark the songs as "latter-day Moody Blues" (not to be confused with the "early Moody Blues").... These characteristics may stem from the wide variety of musical instruments heard on the album, and the group's members' adeptness in playing them. These range from sitar and tablas to cello and flutes, in addition to the usual guitars and drums.

But, no review of this album is complete without a word or two of praise for Philip Travers' magnificent cover illustration, which has to rate as among the most spectacular we've seen on any album.

To illustrate how much had changed in the nine months since the release of *Days of Future Passed* in England, consider this review from the August 24, 1968 issue of *Disc and Music Echo*:

> Almost overnight and with shattering impact the Moody Blues have suddenly become the elite of the pop world. Only the Beatles LPs are looked forward to with such eager anticipation as a new Moody Blues album. At their rare live concert appearances a sea of avid admirers will always include great chucks of famous pop names who go to worship at the shrine....
>
> Their new album – called *In Search of the Lost Chord* – has been played regularly by top DJs and left the rest of us in some awe.

Justin Hayward said at this time, "It's been a fantastic feeling that our LPs have been so well-received. I'm not being flash, but it's really so nice to have people you respect and friends openly admitting they like your music. And now we're in a position, like the Beatles, where we can take as much studio time as we want to without worrying about money. Most groups have to rush in and do one number then go back next week, and they lose the whole mood. We go in for three weeks, day-and-night without stopping, until it's finished.

"We find our audiences are usually University types and older kids. But the nicest thing is that we're a group in every sense of the word. For a long time I sang on my own and I was useless; I couldn't get anything organized. But with the Moodies it is five people acting like one, and that's great." (JH-DME68)

On August 28, American syndicated music columnist Dave Donnelly ("The Teen Beat") wrote:

> *In Search of the Lost Chord* by the Moody Blues I like very much. Though not really blues in the Mayall sense, the group is musically advanced and does fine material, maintaining a good beat. One song, "Legend of a Mind" (about Timothy Leary), could become a minor classic.

On August 31, Richard Green wrote in *New Musical Express*:

> ... A few weeks ago, the Moody Blues played a concert at the Queen Elizabeth Hall and gave everyone a nice surprise with their musical talent and abilities. Now, their near-perfect album *In Search of the Lost Chord* is climbing the *NME* LP chart and a track from the album, "Voices in the Sky," enters the singles chart this week at No. 27.

That very night the Moodies appeared on a new BBC-1 variety show, *How It Is?* In the following week's *Disc and Music Echo*, Vicki Wickham dismissed the show, but not the Moodies:

> … Supposedly [this show has] it's "something for everyone," but unless you've got the time to sit through an awful lot of what's not for you, and unless you're really a bit square, I don't think [*How It Is?*] is…. The Spinners really aren't "how it is" by any stretch of the imagination. John Williams, "one of the world's greatest classical guitarists," was interesting, but didn't make me want to leap out and see him in concert. But one musical item did – The Moody Blues. They're a 'luvverly'-looking group and come up with gorgeous records and *How It Is?* really did them proud. The presentation on "Voices in the Sky" was an all time best ever. With superb lighting and incredibly beautiful camera shots, nicely superimposed and faded, and the introduction of a light-film over-all at the end, it was terrific. …

While the events of the last week or two were transpiring in England, the Moodies were on the Continent promoting their new album. In fact (although some dispute the exact date in respect to the band's schedule), it is believed that on August 20, 1968 when the Soviet Union struck a blow against freedom, the band was in, of all places, Prague, Czechoslovakia.

John Lodge said, "Of course, it was a time of social change and upheaval, but it was during the era when Alexander Dubček was in power, and everything had become a lot more relaxed. You heard rock 'n' roll music at the airport, and it didn't feel you were in an Iron Curtain country at all." (JL-PROG12)

The people of Czechoslovakia were enjoying renewed freedom under the liberal government of Alexander Dubček, who was daring to open the country up to Western influences. Both Louis Armstrong and American poet Allen Ginsberg had been guests in Prague in 1965, with Armstrong performing at Lucerna Hall. Folklore has it that the Beach Boys performed in Czechoslovakia prior to the Moody Blues, but their appearance there was actually later, in June 1969. Therefore, in the summer of '68, the Moodies made history. They were the first rock act – be it rhythm & blues, rock 'n' roll, English beat music, progressive rock, or whatever else one might call it – to play in the Communist country.

For a television taping, the band set up their instruments on the historic Charles Bridge (constructed in 1357 under the auspices of King Charles IV, and spanning the Vltava River). There, the TV appearance was taped, with Ray Thomas introducing the group, then the Moodies lip-synching to "Nights in White Satin" and "Voices in the Sky." Carefree pedestrians gathered and looked on, then, at the completion of each song, cheerfully applauded.

The Moodies were scheduled to perform a concert that night. Meanwhile, as the sun set, four of the Warsaw Pact Nations (the Soviet Union, Bulgaria, Hungary, and Poland) rolled tanks across the border, followed by 250,000 troops.

John Lodge said, "So we went and did the gig, came back to the hotel, and the manager said he wanted an urgent word with us. He explained that the Russians had invaded the city and had taken over the hotel and we had to move…. We ended up sharing a hotel room somewhere else. That's five members of the band and a roadie, all crammed in!

"Eventually, the only way we could get out of the country was to sneak onto a Pakistan Airlines Red Crescent flight, which is like being on a Red Cross mission. We arrived in the country as rock stars, and left in the back of a Red Crescent emergency aid plane. *That* was a reality check." (JL-PROG12)

Justin Hayward said, "[But] it wasn't until we got back to England that we realized what was going on. It left a big impression on us – and not only because we never got paid! It was kind of like, 'What the f**k's going on?! We thought that was over!'" (JH-OOO)

On September 7, 1968, *New Musical Express* reported:

> The Moody Blues return to London next Wednesday (9) following their current European tour, during which they were the last British group to perform in Czechoslovakia prior to the Russian invasion….

For that matter, they were also the first.

Meanwhile, the French were going wild over not only "Nights in White Satin," but all of *Days of Future Passed*. The Moodies were the rage.

On September 7, *Disc* reported:

> Moody Blues played to one of the largest audiences ever assembled for a pop show when they visited France last weekend. A massive 300,000 fans – THREE TIMES the capacity of Wembley Stadium – watched their open-air concert on the outskirts of Paris. The show was appropriately titled "Festival De Humanite." The festival was held in a series of fields containing a mass of amplifiers and loudspeaker equipment. Moodies have already sold over two million records in France this year.

On September 14, the Moodies appeared on the TV program *Colour Me Pop*, performing a good portion of their new album: "Departure / Ride My See-Saw," "Dr. Livingstone, I Presume," "House of Four Doors," "Voices in the Sky," "The Best Way to Travel," "Visions of Paradise," "The Actor," and "Om" (entire video performance available on *Time Traveler* box set).

Also on September 14, in the new issue of *Top Pops*, Gordon Coxhill glowed:

> After virtually sinking into oblivion for two years, the Moody Blues have emerged as the only group, apart from the Beatles, capable of lifting pop onto a higher plane than it has been.

> Last November, *Days of Future Passed*, an album using a span of 24 hours as its theme, soared high into the LP charts and started everyone talking about the group who had once been top of the charts with "Go Now," an R&B standard.

A single taken from the album, "Nights in White Satin," reached the lower rungs of the best-sellers list in Britain, but topped hit parades all over the rest of Europe. It also chalked up considerable success in America, where "Tuesday Afternoon," another song from *Days*, was issued as the follow-up.

In Search of the Lost Chord is the group's latest collection, and, again, a new single has been taken from it, "Voices in the Sky." It is unlikely it will be a chart topper. There are not yet enough aware pop fans to put the Moody Blues back where they should be. But knowing the group, I know they are not over worried about record sales. They win new fans with every live appearance, especially at their acclaimed concert at the Queen Elizabeth Hall several weeks ago. …

In the September 28 issue of *New Musical Express*, Keith Altham wrote:

The Moody Blues are the sleeping giants of the pop world. They seldom seem to make a dramatic impact upon the charts, but create significant best-selling albums and thoughtful, sensitive singles, like "Voices in the Sky," which meander about the lower regions of the Top 30 for months, being bought by other thoughtful, sensitive people who gradually pick up the good vibrations.

But the giants are walking! When they fly to America in October it is likely they will emerge from their musical cocoon with the kind of status which is now enjoyed by the Cream, Donovan, and Jimi Hendrix.

Mike Pinder told Altham, "Two-and-a-half years ago we shut the factory down and almost broke up when Denny Laine, our vocalist, left. What stopped us was finding two people like John and Justin, who were so much on the same wavelength as us. From that point on we just believe in things that we really enjoyed, like *Days of Future Passed*. It's not completely an accident when you find yourself successfully doing something that you like. If you really enjoy what you are doing, the effort is that much more and the work, therefore, that much better. The mental release is greater.

"*Days of Future Passed* was really a challenge, but it was something that we had always hoped would secretly happen. We shut ourselves away in the studios for 15 days, until it became our domain and what came out was what we thought we could do. What we did was really a diary of our experiences and ideas at that time. I'm sure that's how the Beatles and the Stones work now. It's really all a 'Day in the Life'…." (MP-NME68)

Ray Thomas, joining the interview, interjected, "I don't think that we are musically pretentious. Mike has already said that we do what we have lived through in musical terms…. *In Search of the Lost Chord* is just simply an adventure in mind, really. There are a lot of critics who put the most fantastic interpretations on what we do but it's made worthwhile by just the few who find what we put there.

"One of the most distressing things about the misrepresentation over the album has been that some people have got the impression we are a lot of drug addicts. We go

205

over to Europe and these guys come at us, rolling up their sleeves to show us the needle marks, as if it were some kind of badge! An admission to the club! There are a lot of 'lurky' people who sidle up to you and whisper, 'Wanna drug?,' because you are in a pop group and into things they cannot understand. That's very sad." (RT-NME68)

Concerning the recent Paris concert which attracted 300,000 spectators, Pinder said, "It was really a bit frightening. I'd never seen so many people in my life. There was an exhibition on there as well which included some items from the Vietnam War, including an American pilot's jacket riddled with bullets. That was frightening too, and a bit grisly." (MP-NME68)

By September 21, "Voices in the Sky" had stopped its advance in the charts. At this time, it held for a second week at No. 27 according to both *Record Retailer* and the *NME* chart. Clearly this song was not going to rival the success of "Nights in White Satin." But it was getting enough airplay to make people aware of the new album.

With *In Search of the Lost Chord* now out in the States, and, although "Tuesday Afternoon" was still on the charts, a new single would be needed to alert music buyers of the new LP. The plan had been to issue "Voices in the Sky" there as well. But, since the song failed to crack the British Top 20, it would be relegated to the B-side; a different album track was chosen to represent the top side of the U.S. single.

U.S. single release:
"Ride My See-Saw" b/w "Voices in the Sky"
Deram 45-85033, Late September 1968

The songs to beat in the American singles charts at this time, counting down from the top, were "Hey Jude" by the Beatles; "Harper Valley P.T.A." by Jeannie C. Riley; "People Got to Be Free" by the Rascals; "Hush" by Deep Purple; and "Fire" by the Crazy World of Arthur Brown.

On September 25, 1968, *Variety* chose "Ride My See-Saw" as one of the 15 songs which it ranked as the Best Bets from over 100 single records released that very week. The reviewer wrote:

> The Moody Blues' "Ride My See-Saw" scores for this British combo as a swinging rock slice due for returns. "Voices in the Sky" is slower and pretty by this inventive bunch.

Three days later, *Billboard* put "Ride My See-Saw" into its "Top 20 Pop Spotlight," thereby predicting the song would make the music magazine's Top 20 chart. The reviewer said:

> Just as "Tuesday Afternoon" drops down the Hot 100, this blockbuster rocker comes on strong with all the ingredients to spiral them to the top in short order. A mover from start to finish.

Concerning the album, the trade said:

> This LP has much to appeal to the masses – "Dr. Livingstone, I Presume" is getting wide airplay on progressive rock programs and "Om" and "Visions of Paradise" are strange but appealing tunes. The group's drive is perfection in music and they present here some beautiful works.

It was likely that American DJs imported the U.K. single which featured "Dr. Livingstone, I Presume" on the B-side, thereby avoiding the complications of trying to drop the needle on a song weaved into others by cross-fading.

As the Moodies toured America, from mid-October through mid-December, 1968, sales of "Ride My See-Saw" were strong. *New Musical Express* reported on October 21 that in a period of two weeks, the U.S.-only single had sold in excess of 200,000 copies. As a result of such popularity, it would be issued in England on October 25.

In the U.S., "Ride My See-Saw" entered the *Billboard* Top 100 singles chart on November 2, 1968. You've read the appreciative reviews for this song, which is well-known to Baby Boomers and fans of classic rock. It's surprising that, although it sold 200,000 copies in a mere two weeks, it only peaked at No. 61. *Cashbox* ranked it better, giving the single a two-month chart span with a peak position of No. 41 (also on November 9). *Record World*, a third American national chart, put "See-Saw" at No. 50.

We who were listening to the radio in 1968 probably remember it being a bigger hit. Once again, the national charts are misleading, with the single breaking in different regions at vastly different times. Beginning on October 1, 1968, and lasting all the way through the end of December, "Ride My See-Saw" had a see-saw ride on numerous Top 40 AM radio stations in the U.S. and Canada, usually making the Top 30, but more often placing inside the Top 20, and sometimes the Top 10.

On October 1, CKLU, in Windsor, Ontario, put the new single at No. 12.

October 3: WKNR, in Detroit, Michigan, listed "See-Saw" at No. 20.

October 9: WUBE, in Cincinnati, Ohio, ranked it at No 24.

October 10: CHUM, in Toronto, Canada, had "See-Saw" at No. 16 for three consecutive weeks.

Also on October 10: WHLO, in Akron, Ohio, took the song to No. 15.

October 11: KIRL, in Saint Charles, Missouri, charted it at No. 17.

Also on October 11: WYSL, in Buffalo, New York, had the record at No. 22.

October 12: KYA, in San Francisco, put the song at No. 19.

October 16: KAFY, in Bakersfield, California, had it at No. 11.

October 18: WKLO, in Louisville, Kentucky, sent "See-Saw" to No. 7.

October 21: WCOL, in Columbus, Ohio, took it to No. 16.

Also on the 21: WSAI, in Cincinnati, Ohio, showed the song at No. 24.

October 25: KTRB, in Spokane, Washington, said No. 23.

Also on October 25: WIZE, in Springfield, Ohio, placed it at No. 17.

October 26: WLOF, in Orlando, Florida, listed "See-Saw" at No. 14 for two weeks.

Also on October 26: WNAP, in Indianapolis, Indiana, ranked it at No. 15.

On the same day, WKFR, in Battle Creek, Michigan, had the song riding along at No. 20.

October 30: KHJ-Boss Radio, in Los Angeles, which had taken "Tuesday Afternoon" to No. 5, now charted "See-Saw" at No. 7.

Also on October 30: WKYC, in Cleveland, Ohio, ranked it at No. 12.

Again on October 30: WMCA, in New York City, placed it at No. 24.

November 1: CKRC, in Winnipeg, Manitoba, charted "See-Saw" at No. 18.

Also on November 1: WSGN, in Birmingham, Alabama, said No. 14.

November 4: WVOK, also in Birmingham, put "See-Saw" at No. 11.

November 6: CHLO, in St. Thomas, Ontario, ranked "See-Saw" as No. 22.

November 7: WYBC, in New Haven, Connecticut, called it at No. 11.

November 8: CKOC, in Hamilton, Ontario, put the song at No. 19.

November 11: CKBB, in Barrie, Ontario, took it to No. 16.

November 16: WARM, in Wilkes-Barre, Pennsylvania, sent it up to No. 20.

And, on December 8, the Woolco Department Store in Arlington, Texas, ranking its singles sales, listed "See-Saw" at No. 9.

U.K. single release:
"Ride My See-Saw" b/w "A Simple Game"
Deram DM 213; October 25, 1968

In England, "Ride My See-Saw" had been issued on October 25. Selected for the B-side, a new song – Mike Pinder's excellent "A Simple Game" (not issued in the U.S. until 1974, when included on the compilation album *This Is the Moody Blues*).

For its October 26 edition, *New Musical Express* rated the single:

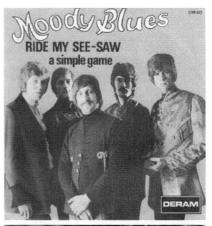

> Progression, experimentation, inventiveness – these are some qualities that we've come to associate with the Moody Blues. Indeed, some of their material has been so far out that it scarcely comes within the bounds of pop music. But their new disc is much less complex and more obviously commercial. It's a fast-moving number, set at gallop pace and featuring a raucous twangy sound – plus underlying and unobtrusive strings. [It] pounds along feverishly, with the boys singing in unison. … Yet, despite their concession to commerciality, the Moodies haven't lost their artistry or class.

Record Mirror said:

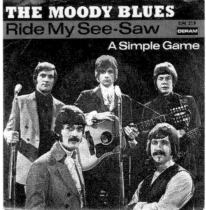

> Already a big hit in the States, this must be equally big here. Starts with a persistent sort of rhythm, then the voices come in, adamantly urgent. It's got style and professionalism, but it's also built on very commercial lines. In an admittedly funny odd week for records, it's a decided stand-out. Never lets up. … CHART CERTAINTY.

The reviewer said of "A Simple Game": "A relaxation of pace and power; a very good number, this."

"Ride My See-Saw" reached No. 42 in the

British charts, not a bad showing for a song available on a three-month old LP, and which had been given airplay by offshore "pirate radio" during that entire period.

It fared better in France, as Moodies' singles often did, peaking at No. 15.

Meanwhile, back in England, as the Moody Blues toured with two albums in the national charts, more critics began to acknowledge the retooled band. This was not always a good thing.

The Los Angeles Times published Pete

Johnson's review on October 27. He panned the Bee Gees' new one, *Idea*, a bad review, accusing the group of not fulfilling the promise of their first album. He added that the brothers Gibb had "slid down to the level of easy listening rock." Then Johnson said that this was "a criticism which can also be leveled at the Moody Blues' *In Search of the Lost Chord*."

> This, too, has some fine songs on it – "Ride My See-Saw" (a single hit) and "Dr. Livingstone, I Presume" stand out – but a lot of the time it leaves you wondering where is the movie to go with their soundtrack.

This was the start of the era of the "serious rock music critic" in America. Following the lead of the one-year-old *Rolling Stone* magazine, these types were only inclined to recommend music so far underground that you would need a flashlight and mining tools to find it. Some even dared criticizing the Beatles. Now can you imagine that?

American syndicated music columnist David F. Wagner also seemed to want inclusion into the small circle of rock-critic elitists. He reviewed *Lost Chord* on November 10. After trashing Steve Miller Band's *Sailor* album – writing "With apologies to *no one* for not liking it, I must say the Steve Miller Band's second album is even more boring than the first…" – Wagner took notice of *In Search of…*.

> In a monetary sense, the Moody Blues' *In Search of the Lost Chord* will be successful; it has "Ride My See-Saw," a catchy single hit which, unfortunately, highlights the album. After the first effort, the album settles down into the patterns of predictability which have made some of this year's allegedly best new groups nothing but tedious experiences on record. Don't misunderstand: the Moody Blues isn't a new group – it just sounds like an extended "Happening '68" new band contest.

> Another point to make clear – the Moody Blues consists of five good musicians who turn out musically tight performances. The material itself is mainly weak. Writing every scrap of music on an album and making it 'Significant' is not easy in these days of rock (nor has it really ever been). …

> Mike Pinder's "Om" has a certain amount of academic interest for students of rock music, as does "Legend of a Mind," but poetry buffs will find nothing to get excited about. Aside from the single, neither will the average rock fan.

On November 16, Hoag Levins of Camden, New Jersey's *Courier-Post*, wrote:

> Their first comeback album, *Days of Future Passed*, was a smash in Europe and did well in the underground [radio] cities here. Their second, *In Search of the Lost Chord* (London Records) has a very unusual sort of classical-mystical-gently rocked but heavy

pulsed kind of sound that is haunting and sticks to the lining of the mind.

Lost Chord had already made it big on the underground stations, and straight AM radio stations are beginning to give it some airtime.

Some of the album's heavy mystical sounds are a direct influence of the group's relation with the Maharishi.

"He wasn't actually a religious experience for us as he was for many other people," Graeme Edge told Levins. "I tried meditation and found it very useful, not religiously, but just as a way to relax and lift one's head up." (GE-CR68)

While the band was motoring to L.A. for more live shows, they turned up in the November 28 edition of New Mexico's *Albuquerque Journal*. Arts Editor Jim Newton gave a positive review for the new Doors' album, *Waiting for the Sun*, then wrote:

The Moody Blues apparently are one more of the proliferation of psychedelic sound groups which have sprung up in the wake of the Beatles mind-bending experimentation.

With *In Search of the Lost Chord* their thing is driving rhythm, shouting harmony, and over-modulated electric guitar, a la Jimi Hendrix.

One really different effect in "Best Way to Travel" is what might be called Doppler-effect progression. An organ chord gains in volume, then slides in pitch (like a train whistle passing) but ends up in a different chord, with the listener not really aware of when the change took place. It's a pleasant experience in an over-populated style.

Who were those other proliferators of psychedelic sounds, springing up in the wake of the Beatles' mind-bending experimentation? A short list would naturally include Jefferson Airplane, the 13th Floor Elevators, Soft Machine, Tangerine Dream, and Pink Floyd. But many were calling the Grateful Dead psychedelic too. And AM hits such as "Incense and Peppermint" by the Strawberry Alarm Clock," "Green Tambourine" by the Lemon Pipers, "Itchychoo Park" by the Small Faces," "Eight Miles High" by the Byrds, "Pictures of Matchstick Men" by Status Quo, "Hurdy Gurdy Man" by Donovan, and "Time Has Come Today" by the Chambers Brothers, were stamped as psychedelic. And that was the problem for the elitist rock critics – the surrealistic sound had crossed over from underground to Top 40 radio.

In the December 6 issue of *Rolling Stone* magazine, the music paper finally decided to review *Days of Future Passed* … together with *In Search of the Lost Chord*. Jay Miller wrote:

… If *Days of Future Passed* is the Moody Blues being self-consciously "beautiful," *In Search of the Lost Chord* is the Moody

Blues being self-consciously "mystical." ... But let us be charitable: we will say nothing further of the seven-minute closer on the album, "Om." Nor the opening "Departure." The rest of the album is very well produced and generally tasteful; John Lodge's "Ride My See-Saw" and Ray Thomas' "Dr. Livingstone, I Presume" are both well done, solid rock tracks. On the other hand we have "House of Four Doors," an overblown piece of literal psychedelic with four (count 'em: *four*) squeaky door sound effects sandwiched in between some rock mood music.

The dilemma of this whole album is illustrated by "Legend of the Mind," featuring a nifty lyric about "Timothy Leary's dead." If you don't listen to the words it sounds like a better than average rock song with interesting flute work by Ray Thomas and appropriately swooping cellos – but then there are those inane lyrics that keep bombarding you with Timothy Leary's name. Mike Pinder's "The Best Way to Travel" sounds indebted to the Pink Floyd [who had two albums out by this time, neither successful in America], while the inevitable sitar pops up painlessly on Justin Hayward's "Visions of Paradise." Whoever does the vocal on "The Actor" [Hayward] and "The Word" [Pinder] (they run together) does one hell of a job; beautiful, unabashedly emotional singing. ...

Hopefully next time around the Moody Blues will leave their London Festival Orchestra and Yantra at home and get together a straight-ahead, no bullshit album of rock. ...

Of course, the London Festival Orchestra *had* been left at home, for *Lost Chord* – everything on that album had been played by members of the Moodies.

The following day, Ramblin' Jim Martin, in an article for Los Angeles-based *Open City* weekly newspaper, began:

The Moody Blues did a Shrine gig recently. I interviewed the group's drummer, Graeme Edge, after the opening. Among the things I wanted to discuss was a bullshit review of *Lost Chord* in *Rolling Stone*. I wanted to give the group their chance to reply if they wanted.

Edge said of the two *Rolling Stone* reviews by Jim Miller, "They were a couple of stinkers, but he can say it if he wants to. He listened to them. We obviously did something to him, because he got steamed up enough to write about us. I don't think he knows what he's talking about; I think he's completely missed the point of it all, of *In Search of the Lost Chord*."

What was the message behind *Lost Chord* that Miller missed? Edge, the atheist in the group, explained to Martin: "We tried to get the big LSD-religious Maharishi Yogi thing into perspective – 'We're all looking for someone' – the need to identify." (GE-CC68)

Speaking for himself, Pinder, Thomas, and Edge, Justin Hayward said, "Hash was the drug really. There's no point saying that it didn't play a part, because it did. But we all had a respect for drugs because we could see what it did to some people. None of us were ever controlled by drugs, whereas the people that were fell by the wayside and died.

"The four of us did it very carefully and took good care of ourselves. Except for the time we left Ray alone in the flat. He was watching the telly. And when we came back, *Crossroads* was on. He was going: 'Man, this is fucking far out!'" (JH-CRM14)

Ray Thomas: "We were very optimistic. We were trying to preach peace, love, and 'outta sight.' And sex, drugs and rock 'n' roll. It was the whole package." (RT-CRM14)

Graeme Edge: "So we just tried to play around with meditation. Everybody – when you mention meditation – everybody immediately thought [and] expected it was some kind of way to nip in and have a quick chat with God. Well, obviously, that's a complete load of cobblers; it's nothing more than … reflection. People say, 'Ah, you're talking about self-hypnosis.' Well, you can call if 'self-hypnosis' if you want to, or 'meditation,' or you can call it 'masturbation' for all I care. I don't care what label you put on it, it calms you down. It lets you take a step back out and look in; it lets you really see what's the point of what you're doing. Is there a point? Is there any need of a point? And, it was very difficult for us, anyway, because the group consists of two very religious guys, two 'Don't Knows,' and one atheist. And so the thing had to be put together in such a form that it didn't upset any of you. …

"[But] that's always a problem when you're making an album. You've got to be so careful when you are trying to do something worthwhile with the album because the line between a good album, a worthwhile album, and a precocious load of shit is so thinly divided; you've got to be so careful you're not putting yourself on a box and dressing yourself up in a white robe and saying, 'Listen, Brothers, I've got it all solved.' And we don't. In fact, when you're into our music, what we try to do is rush around and point out the things we feel are wrong, to try to create a climate so that if some cat does come along who sees these things the way we see them, as being wrong, and is also capable – he'll have to be a genius, capable of giving some solutions. And hope." (GE-CC68)

Just what was in that cup? Spiritualism … Transcendental Meditation with the Maharishi Yogi … drugs … a new religion … or just heady music?
(Photo source: Pinterest.com)

In the January 4, 1969 edition of *Record Mirror*, David Griffiths picked *Lost Chord* as his most-recommended album of 1968. He wrote:

> There are some sumptuous sounds on this LP, all of them made by just the five Moodies. No session musicians, simply the group's instrumental versatility, adroit use of the Mellotron and brilliant sound engineering....
>
> ... [T]he music's often positively beautiful, and the album is based on a good idea – a trippy quest that ends with gods and "Om." It is for that last "Om" track (highly atmospheric) and for the daring and effort that went into *Search* that I have to pick this LP.

In Search of the Lost Chord climbed into *Billboard*'s Top 100 album chart on September 21, 1968, at 95. When the Moodies began touring the U.S., the album moved into the Top 30. It peaked at No. 23 on December 7. It had a 29-week chart run, and was certified Platinum (having sold one million copies) at the beginning of July 1969.

The album made it to No. 5 in the British album charts. With only two albums, the band had achieved a stunning comeback.

The Moody Blues   Management: Derek McCormick   Publicity: Nick Massey
Fan Club: Wendy Kilty, 17 Portland Place, London, W.1, England

1968 Promotional photo listing Derek McCormick as manager and Nick Massey as "publicity."
(Photo source: Author's Collection)

10

Touring America

HEADING FOR THE TOP
THE MOODY BLUES
RIDE MY SEE-SAW

U.S.A. Appearances by the Moody Blues:

Minneapolis	Chicago
New York City	San Francisco
Boston	San Diego
Baltimore	Los Angeles
Philadelphia	Portland
Washington, D.C.	Seattle
Spokane	

85033

DERAM
A PRODUCT OF
LONDON

Producer: Tony Clarke

To many Americans living through the turbulent 1960s, the words of a common Protestant hymn were strangely applicable. Though first published in 1868, the words of John Bode were still relevant to this tormented nation, a century later: "My foes are ever near me / Around me and within."

In many ways, America in 1968 was a nation at war … with itself. In that year alone, Senator Robert F. Kennedy and Rev. Martin Luther King, Jr. had both been assassinated; the U.S. war in Vietnam was escalating and deteriorating, with the Tet Offensive launched by North Vietnam sending U.S. casualties to record heights; and a second war for America loomed due to the Pueblo Incident, when North Korea seized that U.S. intelligence ship. More turmoil came when black athletes Tommie Smith and John Carlos lowered their heads and gave the black power salute while the American National Anthem played at the Summer Olympics in Mexico City. American cities were simmering with racial protests and violence, with hundreds of deaths nationwide, thousands of arrests, and tens of thousands of buildings ablaze. In many places the National Guard was called out to restore order. Anti-war protesters marched on Washington and clashed with police. The Democratic National Convention in Chicago turned to violence, and TV news distributed worldwide the images of Mayor Richard Daley's police beating protesters. Feminists picketed the Miss America Beauty Contest in Atlanta City, and even *Star Trek* fans got into the act, marching on NBC corporate offices in Burbank and New York City, protesting the network's plan to cancel the sci-fi series. Meanwhile, a different person named Spock – renowned baby-authority Dr. Benjamin Spock – was put on trial along with several others, for conspiracy to encourage violation of draft laws. And pop-culture artist Andy Warhol was shot in his New York City apartment. Not surprisingly, a somber President Lyndon B. Johnson, 'with a heavy heart,' informed the nation that he would not seek reelection.

It's no wonder that the teens and young adults, interconnected by media as never before, sought diversions by escaping into TV, underground comix, drugs, or music.

And then the Moody Blues set foot on American soil.

Beginning October 19, and continuing into early December 1968, the Moody Blues supported *In Search of the Lost Chord* with a lengthy and exhausting American tour. This was the second trip to the States for Pinder, Thomas, and Edge (who had only seen New York City and Los Angeles in December 1965/January 1966), and the first for Hayward and Lodge. Making the trip with them: Manager Derek McCormick; press agent Nick Massey; producer Tony Clarke; and roadie Pete Jackson.

Justin Hayward: "We were offered – by a man called Bill Graham – two different gigs. One was at the Fillmore East, here in New York, and the other was at the Fillmore West, in San Francisco. The only thing was, [the gigs] were ten weeks apart. We were earning no money anywhere else. We had no money [for] repayment on our equipment, on our guitars or amplifiers. So we said, 'Listen, let's just go; we've got these two gigs, [and] as long as we're there, we'll pick up the rest of the gigs as we go along.' And that's exactly what we did. We came here [and] we played at the Fillmore. By playing at the Fillmore, we met other people [involved in booking acts]. We just worked our way across the country." (JH-MBS90)

The first concert scheduled was for Minneapolis, Minnesota on October 20, the day after the Moodies arrived in the U.S. The Moodies were there but their equipment was stuck in Boston. The concert had to be canceled. This was only the first in many difficulties the band and their small road crew would have to endure.

The Moodies' press agent, Nick Massey, writing an article for England's *Record Mirror* (December 14, 1968 edition) described their experience in touring America.

> … The first day we got to America, we hit a problem. The Moodies were due to open in Minneapolis the following night – headlining a bill which also included Tiny Tim, the Rascals, Joe Tex, and Tommy Boyce & Bobby Hart. But the cargo plane carrying their equipment over from England lost an engine over the Atlantic and was forced to land in Boston. After endless calls to airports from New York to London, to Senator Edward Kennedy in Washington (the show was part of the John F. Kennedy Foundation charity work), it was clear that the equipment wouldn't show up in time for the show. So, that night the boys were very sad, after having to scrap their first show in America. And the next morning we flew to Chicago after being promised that the equipment would meet up with us there. It did.
>
> The Moodies were appearing at the Kinetic Playground in Chicago (which is the second largest city in America) with another English group who were very popular there – Ten Years After.

The Kinetic Playground is typical of American ballrooms – a vast circular building full of light shows, films, and noise, and capable of holding about 3,000 people. After the two nights there, more than 7,000 people had been to see the Moody Blues.

It was a Saturday night, on October 19 when the Moody Blues took the stage at the Kinetic Playground, followed by a second performance on Sunday, October 20. The other half of the bill went to Decca Records label-mates Ten Years After. The Moodies' set list for these shows, and the entire tour (with occasional modifications) included:

- "Ride My See-Saw" (featuring Lodge, Hayward, and Thomas on vocals);
- "Legend of a Mind" (sung by Thomas);
- "Tuesday Afternoon" (Hayward);
- "Another Morning" (Thomas);
- "Peak Hour" (Lodge and Thomas);
- "Bye Bye Bird" (likely sung by Hayward, and featuring Thomas on harmonica);
- "Don't Let Me Be Misunderstood" (Hayward);
- "Dr. Livingstone, I Presume" (Thomas);
- "The Best Way to Travel" (Pinder);
- "Twilight Time" (Thomas); and
- "Nights in White Satin" (Hayward).

Other sets included "Voices in the Sky."
Covering the show was Robb Baker of the *Chicago Tribune*:

> … England really seems to be where it's happening – all over again – for headliners on Saturday's show were the very good Moody Blues. Though we have found their *Days of Future Passed* album a little uneven, it's clear after seeing them that their work with the London Festival Symphony orchestra on that was excellent training for them. What they've learned about instrumental shading and blend, building climaxes, and making an entire program go together, should make most rock groups sit up and take notice. And this new album is quite good.
>
> The group has not one, but four vocalists it can be proud of, particularly John Lodge, the soft-voiced bassist, and Ray Thomas, who plays a nice flute as well.

It is believed the Moodies picked up a couple of other gigs before leaving the windy city – for October 21 and 22, venues unknown. The next gig was in New York City, at the famed Bill Graham's Fillmore East, on October 25 and 26, where the Moodies would perform two shows each day, on a shared bill with John Mayall and the Bluesbreakers, and a West Coast group called Rhinoceros.

For his *Record Mirror* coverage of the tour, Nick Massey reported:

Transport is a problem in America because of the great distances between cities; to fly everywhere would cost a fortune, so all the groups over there travel by road (for example, Joe Tex has got his own Greyhound bus). So, in Chicago, we hired a transport for ourselves and for the equipment. We kept the two vehicles all the time we were on the East Coast – and after three weeks had clocked over 5,000 miles!

After the Chicago gigs, we had just under two days to get to New York. "Easy," we thought – straight along the Ohio Turnpike… but the journey was over 1,000 miles and it took us 26 hours, driving non-stop, apart from to eat and to change drivers (we all took it in turns to drive). …

The Fillmore, the boys felt, was a big test. Only the hottest acts appear there – Jeff Beck and Tim Buckley the week before and Steppenwolf the week before that – and the word was that the Fillmore audiences were very hard to please.

The Moodies were nervous that night before the show, but at the end of their set – after receiving a standing ovation from the audience – their nerves had been well and truly settled. They were a success.

One of the biggest physical encumbrances while crisscrossing the country was the clumsy Mellotron. John Lodge said, "We were top of the bill at Fillmore East. And they announced us. The curtain opens; we start playing; Mike hits the first chord on the Mellotron, and all of the tapes come out of the back…. It was like spaghetti junction; all this spaghetti; tapes all

Bill Graham on stage at the Fillmore East.
(Photo source: The Woodstock Whisperer)

over the place. And it was like, 'We've come all this way for *this*?' And so, we look at the stage manager, and he says, 'Don't worry, boys,' and they put Bugs Bunny movies on. And so we're at the Fillmore East, and we're playing second bill to Bugs Bunny!" (JL-CA07)

Justin Hayward remembered the frustration of "doing very first gig for Bill Graham at the Fillmore East, and then for the Mellotron to pack up in the first song! And for Mike to spend the first set with his head in the back of the Mellotron was devastating. I just remember the blues guy, John Mayall – who was also on Decca, and extremely pissed off that we were above him on the bill – and seeing him in the wings laughing his head off at Mike." (JH-RC12)

Mike Pinder told this author, "The Mellotron got a bad rap for breaking down, but it was not so much that it broke down but it was often that it was mishandled in moving it. If it was moved improperly, the tapes would get messed up and it was a hassle to put them back into place. It was a problem when you had a show to do! The Fillmore East show being a good example of this." (MP-AI17)

Robert Shelton, reviewing the concert for *The New York Times*, wrote:

> The Moody Blues is a fresh mod quintet that has recorded recently in art-rock and Eastern mysticism veins, with some success. A few numbers gave inkling of fine musicianship, poise and clean vocal work, if not great passion.... [But] mechanical troubles kept the Moody Blues from making any sort of coherent impression at the first Saturday night concert.

Fortunately, there was a second show that night, and this was the one most critics attended … and celebrities.

John Lodge: "David Crosby came to see us. We were standing in this little dressing room and he said to me: 'Where do you get your clothes? Can you put me in touch with somebody? That was the most important thing to him. We were proper English dandies to people like that." (JL-CRM14)

For the second performance, Gene Mallard of *Circus* magazine had a backstage pass. He and the *Circus* photographer, Jeff Mayer, were taken to meet the Moodies. They entered the dressing room with trepidation: journalists aren't always welcome immediately before a performance. Mallard wrote:

David Crosby of the Byrds had his eye on John Lodge … or, at least, on his clothing style.
(Photo source: Pinterest.com)

> To our relief, we were greeted with warm smiles – something we hardly expected! – and they invited us to join the party.

> Jeff immediately started clicking away with his camera, and the Blues were all-too-willing to cooperate. When Jeff felt that he had enough photos, we just stood around and rapped. It was great conversation, and I kept wishing that I had brought a tape recorder. Their heads are really in a beautiful place.

> Time seemed to fly, and soon they were due to play their next set. Before getting up to go on stage, Ray Thomas burst into song, singing "Hey Jude" at the top of his lungs, while everybody present joined in. The song broke up in laughter as their manager,

Derek McCormick, flew into the room, screaming, "You're on next?! Hurry! Hurry!" …

The concert turned out to be quite fantastic. The Moody Blues left people speechless with songs like "Ride My See-Saw" (their opening number), "Tuesday Afternoon" and "Nights in White Satin." The group has the uncanny ability to sound just as good "live" as they do on record. With the help of the Mellotron, an organ-like instrument that can just about reproduce the sound of every instrument in an orchestra, the Moodys left many observers with the impression that they had used [accompaniment] tapes. They hadn't.

Technically, they *had*, since the Mellotron was, in a sense, a giant 80-something-bits-of-tape player … when those tapes weren't erupting from it. Regardless, the Mellotron had passed the test with the second performance.

Happily for the band and their anxious manager, the critics for *Billboard* and *Cashbox* magazines missed the earlier show, arriving for the later (and much better) performance.

Fred Kirby of *Billboard* wrote:

> … Mayall is a tough act to follow, but the Moody Blues rose to the occasion. Relaying mainly on selections from their two most recent Deram albums, *Days of Future Passed* and *In Search of the Lost Chord*, the British quintet displayed tight musicianship and superior material with vital lyrics.
>
> In Justin Hayward, the Moody Blues have an exceptional vocalist whose voice is similar to Barry Gibbs. … [Ray] Thomas's expert flute playing is probably the quintet's most identifiable instrumental sound and Thomas's fluting was excellent. His performance was classical in technique in the group's "Legend of a Mind," but he was in fine form throughout.
>
> Hayward's lead guitar also was topnotch, but it was his singing that stood out, especially in numbers such as "Forever Afternoon (Tuesday)," "White Satin" and "Don't Let Me Be Misunderstood." Lodge on bass guitar and Pinder on organ also were strong instrumentally. …
>
> While there were blues elements in the Moody Blues, the group's sound was sophisticated rather than raw, as was Mayall's. …

The critic for *Cashbox* said:

> Saturday saw Bill Graham's East Coast showplace bulging at the seams with stone blues fanatics there to see their English blues idol John Mayall. It was in this somewhat hostile atmosphere that the Moody Blues scored a phenomenal triumph. As the British quintet opened with their current Deram hit, "Ride My See-Saw,"

sections of the audience began to leave the theater; yet by the end of the second number, a particularly powerful reading of "Twilight Time" from their popular *Days of Future Passed* LP, almost everyone had returned to their seats and began applauding enthusiastically.

The Moodies, radically changed since the days of their "Go Now!" smash, brought with them Mike Pinder's legendary Mellotron on the maiden voyage to America. This strange electronic instrument looked outwardly much like an organ, but there the similarity ended. From its computerized depths came wave upon wave of varying sounds. From the massed string effect in "Nights in White Satin" to the astral sounds of "Thinking is the Best Way to Travel," the Mellotron showed an amazing versatility.

Justin Hayward, interchanging lead vocals with Ray Thomas, proved to the entire Fillmore audience that he has one of the finest voices around. And believe it or not, each song included vocals and harmonies that could actually be heard! A rare group indeed.

…

On October 26, 1968, the second of the two days the Moodies played the Fillmore East, they had the cover of *Cashbox* magazine in the U.S.

Nick Massey's diary of the Moodies' tour of America continued:

Music City's Broad Re-Development Blueprint ••
Top 40 Market Thrust From PlayTape••GRT Into Disks•••
RCA Stereo 8: 8 Millionth Tape Nears••Sippel Mercury Prod. Mgr.••
ABC Re-structuring A&R•••Pocketdisc: More Tests Post-Xmas•••RCA Japan Co.

> … None of us really got a chance to see New York, so the opinion we formed about the city wasn't exactly a good one. All we saw were hotels, restaurants, and the filthy taxi cabs that New York is renowned for. …

> The next town we went to was Boston – 300 miles north of New York. Boston is very much like England – quiet and rather colourful with the college town of Harvard just a few miles away. And in Boston, again, it was the same story – packed houses and another standing ovation at the end.

On November 1 and 2, the Moodies performed at the Psychedelic Supermarket in Boston. On a Moodies internet chat room, one contributor wrote, "I recall seeing the Moody Blues at the Supermarket. Mike Pinder hit the first note on the keyboard and blew every fuse in the place!"

It was a nightmarish echo of the Fillmore East fiasco. Ray Thomas recalled, "The Mellotron was a right pig to travel with. In the States, it broke down more than it worked, but it caused quite a stir over there. It was a great lump! The trouble was, it was fine here [in England] because our electricity supply is so stable, but in the States you could tune everything up in rehearsals and by the time you came to play it, everybody had gone home and put their electrical appliances on and the Mellotron went, like, 'Wooaargh!' – just like having a voltage alternator on the damn thing. It was all over the shop!" (RT-DOFP87)

Nick Massey's travel guide continued:

> We left Boston quite early on a Sunday morning – and the next show was in Baltimore that same night. And Baltimore was 800 miles away to the south, down the Connecticut and New Jersey Turnpikes. We arrived there ten minutes before the show was due to start.

Justin Hayward said, "We played a lot of free concerts and concerts in parks and things like that. We did a lot of psychedelic clubs and underground clubs. And then we got a few dates on the farewell Cream tour, supporting them, which was a great experience. That introduced us to a huge audience; there was us with our little, tiny equipment and the Cream in these huge sort of stadiums." (JH-MBS90)

It was Sunday, November 3. The Moodies opened for Cream for the latter's farewell concert at the Baltimore Civic Center. The cheap seats ran $4. To sit close enough to watch Eric Clapton's fingers dancing across his guitar, you'd have had to cough up ten bucks. According to Nick Massey, there were 13,000 people packed into the Civic Center.

The next morning, the Moodies and their entourage were on their way back to New York City, where they had a four-day layover. The band spent most of that time writing more one-minute songs for Coca-Cola, this time creating melodies with a resemblance to "Nights in White Satin," which would build and climax with the band transitioning into "Things go better with Coke!" They also taped two appearances for *The Merv Griffin Show*.

Next, they traveled to Philadelphia for two nights at the Electric Factory (November 8 and 9), appearing with another very popular "underground" group called Ars Nova, filling in for no-showing Pink Floyd.

On November 10, the Moodies drove the 86 miles from Philadelphia to Cleveland, Ohio, where they played two shows. Some sources say both concerts were at the Cleveland Grande, while others say that the second performance was at the WHK-

Radio Theater. After that, they ping-ponged across the country again, heading back to Chicago – a-346 mile drive – for a return booking at the Kinetic Playground.

Nick Massey wrote:

> Chicago at six in the morning in the middle of November, with an Arctic gale blowing across Lake Erie, is a depressing place, especially when the hotel you were booked into had let your rooms to someone else the previous night!
>
> So, from a phone box on State Street (you know, the one Mr. Sinatra is always singing about), we rang about 30 hotels, and eventually found one that could take us. When we got there, we knew we'd picked a winner – we were in the company of people like B.B. King, Jackie Wilson, Gene Chandler, and countless more "Sock it to Me" artistes!

In other words, after 30 frantic phone calls from Derek McCormick, they landed a hotel that would cater to "colored people" … and long-haired musician-types.

While in Chicago, and before their return engagement at the Kinetic Playground, the Moodies recorded the jingles they had written for Coca-Cola at the famous Chess Records studios, with Tony Clarke producing the sessions (with the help of an American producer, Bill David, who had worked with the Four Tops, among other soul groups).

Mike Pinder said at the time, "Our new producer, Tony Clarke, travels with us now wherever we go. He's very close to us. He knows our music and how we work on stage. We felt it would be very important for him to experience everything with us in America. This two months we'll be spending touring America will largely influence our next album.

"While we're here, I hope to see Simon & Garfunkel and Jefferson Airplane perform. I'd like to talk to some of the guys from Buffalo Springfield too!" (MP-HP69)

Justin Hayward: "My favorite writer is Paul Simon. I'd say he's very English. He must love England and I'd really like to meet him. He writes about America quite often, like on the *Bookends* album, but it's as though he is an outsider. Like, he does that song called 'America' and he's off in search of it." (JH-HP69)

(Notwithstanding Hayward's estimation, Paul Simon is a true-blue American, born in New Jersey; he grew up in Newark and New York City.)

On Friday, November 15 and 16, the Moodies performed at the Playground. Days later, Robb Baker wrote in the *Chicago Tribune*:

> John Lennon maybe was at the Kinetic Playground during the second set by the Moody Blues Friday night. That person in the black peacoat standing unnoticed on the sidelines certainly looked like him…. And of course it's hard to recognize John and Yoko these days with their clothes on anyway. But it would make sense. Although he wasn't really supposed to be here for the world premiere of his and Miss Ono's movies at the film festival, it's hard to believe he'd stay away. And if he were in town, it would make a lot of sense for him to catch the Moodys, who have been around for a long time but suddenly have turned into one of the

best of the British groups. And John's still pretty hip about things like that, even if he did write the lyrics to "Revolution."

The quintet, which boasts four very good vocalists, were every bit as good in this return as they were in their one-nighter at the Playground a month ago. They seem destined to succeed the Beatles in a "Yesterday" lyrical vein (now that the Beatles are interested chiefly in pursuing other directions) – a role most people had assigned the Bee Gees until they fumbled the ball....

From Chicago, the band and entourage motored to Detroit, Michigan (284 miles).

On November 17, in the "motor city," the band performed at the Grande Ballroom, sharing the bill with a fellow Birmingham band, The Move. Martha Kinsella wrote in the *Detroit Free Press*:

> ... From beginning to end, the Moodies put on a tight show which was a delight to the eye and ear. Their sound (producer Tony Clarke refers to them as the "smallest symphony orchestra in the world") is something which even parents could be happy spending an hour listening to.
>
> From the sprightly "Dr. Livingstone, I Presume" to the soft sounds of "Nights in White Satin," and ending with the definitive statement, "Legend of a Mind," on LSD king ("Timothy Leary's dead. No, no, he's on the outside looking in."), the Moodies' sound is characterized by the facile use of such instruments as flute and Mellotron, an organ-like instrument. ...

Producer Tony Clarke was looking forward to visiting Motown recording studios but instead he visited WABX studios. Instead of talking shop with Motown producers, he heard the underground radio station's tapes of The Beatles' new album ["The White Album"]. It was also the first time that the group had heard the new double LP which was first aired by the local station. The English quintet played disk jockey on Dave Dixon's nighttime show for a couple of hours, alternating between the Beatles and the Moody Blues. ...

The "White Album" was in stores on November 22. And the Moodies were back on the road, with four days to make it from Detroit to San Francisco, California (2,400 miles). They'd have to average better than 12 hours a day on the road to make it.

On November 21, the Moodies were seen on *The Merv Griffin Show* (the first of their two appearances taped earlier in New York). Also chatting with Merv were Orson Bean, comedy team Jerry Stiller and Anne Meara (Ben Stiller's mom and dad), and TV critic Cleveland Amory.

That night, and for four days (November 21, 22, 23, and 24, a Thursday, Friday, Saturday, and Sunday), the Moodies were in San Francisco playing at Bill Graham's other big club, the Fillmore West. The Moodies had top billing; Chicago Transit Authority (soon to be known merely as Chicago) and Frumious Bandersnatch opened.

"We were playing the Fillmore West with Chicago Transit Authority and I noticed off to the side of the stage this girl was smoking a joint," Justin Hayward marveled. "There was this policeman standing, watching her and smiling. This was a complete revelation. In England, no one had attitudes that lax!" (JH-GM94)

Assessing America's assessment of the Moodies, Hayward said, "I think that they saw us as a psychedelic band. We were perfect for FM radio; we were deeper than a lot of the other, more R&B/rock-influenced English bands, who didn't fit culturally in America. For some reason, they took to us. Our music was quite different to anything else that was coming out of England, apart from Jethro Tull." (JH-TRC96)

For America, Jethro Tull was still months away. Tull's first album, the very bluesy *This Was*, had only just been issued in England (October 25, 1968), with a U.S. release scheduled for February 1969.

Hayward added, "But the big difference, which set us apart, was that we were prepared to go there and work for next to nothing. We did very long tours of America, and supported a lot of other groups like Canned Heat, who exposed us to a whole new audience. You could hear 'Going Up the Country' and 'Voices in the Sky' on the same stations. We supported the Cream on their farewell tour of America, although they didn't do many dates – about half a dozen. Again, that introduced us to another audience. Even by then, we were starting to get imitators, who were starting to behave like us. We did a tour with Chicago – we toured with them in '68/'69 – and they told us then that the look and the clothes that we wore were unusual in America. People started copying our image.

"There was a whole subculture beginning in America which rejected any hard sell or poppy thing in music. They just didn't see it as hip and they wanted more underground/progressive stuff; and we just fitted the bill." (JH-TRC96)

Indeed, manufactured groups such as the Monkees were losing popularity as quickly as they had obtained it two years earlier. Also slipping down the pop meter: Paul Revere & the Raiders; the Dave Clark Five; Herman's Hermits; the Four Seasons; and even the Beach Boys. Bad boys, such as the Rolling Stones, were maintaining their popularity. And, of course, the Beatles, whose sound continued to evolve one step ahead of the rest in pop music. Gaining strength were underground bands, such as the Jefferson Airplane, Big Brother & the Holding Company, Quicksilver Messenger Service, the Velvet Underground, Frank Zappa & the Mothers of Invention … and the Moody Blues.

Next, the Moodies drove cross-country from California to Idaho for a November 26 concert in the Idaho State University gym, in the town of Pocatello (some sources say the concert took place in a high school auditorium). The distance from Point A to B is 781 miles.

The next show was in San Diego, California – or, at least, near San Diego, in the Grossmont College gym, La Mesa. It was scheduled for the very next day (November 27). This was a 913-mile drive. On today's roadways, that would be 13 hours, without traffic and without stopping. Rest stop breaks, meals, and 1968 road systems, would have made this a much longer trip.

The following day, November 28, the Moodies were driving from San Diego to Los Angeles – a mere 121 miles.

On Friday and Saturday, November 29 and 30, they performed at the Shrine auditorium in Los Angeles. Opening for them were Deram label-mates Ten Years After. The Jeff Beck Group, featuring Rod Stewart as lead vocalist at this time, were the headliners, but took the stage second due to the length of the program. This left the Moodies to close in the wee hours.

Donna Chick was there, writing for the December 3 edition of *The Los Angeles Times*:

… The Moody Blues have dragged themselves back into the money and spotlight with several recent hits starting with "Nights in White Satin" [which had gone Top 10 in Los Angeles, followed by "Tuesday Afternoon" and "Ride My See-Saw," also both Top 10 in L.A.]. Looking like a page out of a men's high fashion magazine, the quintet generally lacked

The "Models from Carnaby Street," as Lodge recalled one critic describing them.
(Photo source: Pinterest.com)

the volume, savage consciousness, and unusual musical ability of the previous groups, but managed to carry the audience a little closer to ecstasy.

Mike Pinder on organ and piano; Ray Thomas (Richard Harris' twin) on flute; Justin Hayward, lead guitar; John Lodge, bass guitar, and lovely Graeme Edge on drums, carried on the tradition of the Moody Blues' simple, Beatle-inspired music without any difficulty.

"Ride My See-Saw" was a rock-out, surging song, which featured Hayward at his best. But after Ten Years After and the Jeff Beck Group, both with honest, soul-bared, unpretentious, unaffected music, the Moody Blues seemed to be afraid to wail, to show emotion to the audience, who sensed this lack of communication and dwindled rapidly.

Of course, the time – past 2 a.m. – might have dampened the crowd's excitement a bit.

John Lodge: "I remember the reviews saying, 'They looked like models from London's Carnaby Street!" (JL-CA07)

Justin Hayward: "People are always asking why we don't go on stage and freak out or ad lib more. I know what they mean. We're not, perhaps, a terribly exciting group visually…. We're not the kind of musicians who can cause a rave-up on stage. I think we'd look pretty silly if we tried. We get more satisfaction if an audience can really sit and enjoy the music, and like it from their hearts rather than liking it from some other part of their anatomy. It's music to listen to and float away on." (JH-DME70)

John Lodge: "At that particularly time, everybody wanted to dance, but we kept to our own guns. We just kept to what we believed. We started spending a lot of money on our P.A. systems, so that the audience could actually hear all the lyrics and all the melodies. And we were trying to get as near perfection as we could, with this new equipment all the time.

"It's true people couldn't dance to it, but suddenly people stopped dancing and started to listen. And, as soon as people started listening to us, we began to really pursue highlighting parts of songs, like flute solos and very high harmonies. And we began putting the melodies and the words of the songs over." (JL-SLPD93)

Cashbox also had their music critic attend one of the concerts given at the Shrine. The trade ran its review on December 14:

> … The Shrine, now cooled by 16 new electric fans, is a mecca for young, hip, teenyboppers, who come to see the talent of the American and English musicians. …
>
> The Moody Blues, a group that has remained quiet for awhile, has suddenly entered the music world once again with "Nights in White Satin." They didn't have the wild appearance and raging, frantic on-stage vitality of the other two groups, but they were accepted by the audience. "Ride My See-Saw" was the highlight by the group…. Their lyrics are moody and often blue (hence, their name?) and other times they dig deep into the hard-rock bag and pull out a few winning songs. More often they are just quiet, assured musicians with expensive clothes and looks of shadowed certainty.

Graeme Edge recalled a groupie that the band befriended in Los Angeles: "She was rather plump and plain, but she was very friendly and she invited us all back to dinner – a knock-out meal of roast beef and roast potatoes, *English style*. She was a divorcee with two lovely kids and she was hung up on English bands.

"We visited her all the time we were in Los Angeles and she was great company. She showed us the beach, and it was just a completely innocent, friendly relationship. But it meant more to us than all the sex-obsessed scrubbers [low-class groupies] in the world. Any British group which has been away from home for a long period and has been repeatedly torpedoed in the stomach by hamburgers, will jump at the offer of a home-cooked English-style meal." (GE-MM69a)

Someone else the Moodies visited while in California was Timothy Leary.

Justin Hayward: "We met him on our first tour when our friends in Jefferson Airplane asked us if we wanted to play what was once called a 'love-in' at Elysian Park in Los Angeles…. So we did it, and Timothy Leary was there. Mike and Ray and I went up to stay at his ranch for the weekend." (JH-GM13)

Ray Thomas: "He loved ['Legend of a Mind'] and knew I was being mischievous with it. The first time I met him, he invited me, Justin and Mike up to his commune just outside of San Francisco. His followers took us inside this longhouse to feed us. But it was all vegetarian, and we were big carnivores. Later, they took us up to Tim's cabin. When he asked if they'd fed us, he went: 'Yeah, it's crap, innit?' And he got out this whacking great steak and banged it on the barbecue." (RT-CRB14)

Justin Hayward: "We were indeed offered some LSD, but I don't think any of us took it at that particular time. I had already done it by then, anyway, [but] it certainly wasn't passed on to me. Those few nights were lovely. We talked on into the night and played music. He wound up becoming a good friend of the band after that, and we would always see him when we were in the U.S." (JH-GM13)

Years later, Thomas said of Leary: "He took me to one side and said: 'I'm gonna tell you something now. And if you tell anybody else, I'm gonna deny it. But that bloody song of yours made me more famous than I did!" (RT-CRB14)

On Friday, December 6, the Moody Blues were again seen (via videotape) on *The Merv Griffin Show*, this time sharing Merv's stage with Rocky Graziano.

That night (and again on Saturday), after travelling the 1,135 miles from Los Angeles to Seattle, Washington, the Moodies performed in Seattle's Eagle Auditorium. Susan Schwartz wrote in the *Seattle Times*:

> … The Moody Blues, five unusually handsome men, drew a lot of "oohs" and "ahs" from the girls. They sang songs they wrote from their two hit albums, *Days of Future Passed* and *In Search of the Lost Chord*. Their style is spiritual lyrics and a melodic, big-band-like accompaniment. …
>
> Their best song was their present hit, "Ride My See-Saw." They played it with the kind of heavy beat that was still exciting even after the sound system filtered much of the music. …

On December 8, the band reportedly crossed the border into Canada and gave a concert in Vancouver, British Columbia's the Garden Auditorium. The opening acts were Mother Tuckers Yellow Duck and the Black Snake Blues Band.

Fusion magazine covered the Moodies' U.S. tour for its end-of-the-year issue. Jeff Maxwell picked the group as one of the primary innovators in the rapidly changing rock scene:

> … Much of the group's impetus stems from the electronic and musical efforts of Mike Pinder, self-appointed tender of the Moody Blues' Mellotron. This fantastically versatile keyboard instrument is not at all like an ordinary organ in that it has no actual pre-set tone controls which can be punched or rotated to give various sounds. … [T]he Mellotron could come very close to

realizing the dream of many artists for an instrument which can augment any melody, accentuate any mood, and achieve any depth required. What is so startling about the custom-built unit is that all of these advantages now can be placed on stage, before an audience. At present, the only serious drawbacks to this new advance are that the Mellotron is incredibly delicate (Pinder spent most of two or three days virtually rebuilding it after a rough trip from England), and that it draws a great deal of electrical power.

The aural impact of the Mellotron is amazing. To hear an entire string section suddenly come to life on the tiny stage filled with mikes and amps is stunning and unexpectedly real. It enables the group to employ the most complex arrangements yet attempted with a band of this size, and frees the members of the Moody Blues to venture into subtleties previously prevented by the need for harmonic support and a full sound. The situation is helped immeasurably by the fact that they sing extremely well; this in itself adds four instruments to the collage.

It is very fitting that the Moody Blues are the first group to have brought a Mellotron into the United States, because their work with the new unit has been the inspiration for others' experiments. The Hollies have used a Mellotron, and the Beatles borrowed Pinder's instrument for the *Sgt. Pepper* album. More will be using it in the future, if the labor problems in the United States don't impede this welcome hint of progress. ...

Mike Pinder: "I think they really liked it because it was so different. All the time we were getting questions – 'What is that box?' ... 'Where is that sound coming from?!' " (MP-GM09)

Next, for December 13, the Moodies were scheduled to share the bill with Vanilla Fudge in Harrisburg, Pennsylvania. They got as far as the U.S./Canadian border, but visa problems prevented them from re-entering the U.S. Exhausted and fed up, the band and their manager decided to end the tour there and return to home.

***

After their return to England, Graeme Edge told *Melody Maker*, "[I]t was just about the saddest experience of my life. We were touring all over the States and we encountered the groupie scene everywhere – but not a single person to whom we could talk intelligently. We really thought – and hoped – that we'd meet people who were on the same wavelength as ourselves. But all we met were groupies claiming to be the best experts on the latest pill, and a lot of middle class bigots who really hate the younger generation." (GE-MM69a)

John Lodge: "If you did a gig, you'd spend hours afterwards meeting people, talking about religion. I grew up through an evangelical church, and the more I talked to people, the more I realized all the things I'd learned at church were relevant – and what everyone was looking for, I was thinking, 'Just a moment, I think I've got that!' That's really when I started to find an inner strength. The '60s was a crazy time in rock 'n' roll, and you could have really gone to extremes in everything. But I found I had inner strength that seemed to see me through a lot of things." (JL-CH00)

Graeme Edge: "I'd always seen America as the place where people went to escape from bigotry and persecution, and to build a new life. But look what they've built! First of all, they have the weirdest class system – starting at the top with the white Anglo-Saxons and then going down through the Poles to the Puerto Ricans and then to the Negroes. ...

"When we went from Chicago to New York via Pennsylvania, we were knocked out by the scenery, the beautiful colors of the leaves and the hills. It was unforgettable. But then we got to the city and passed a shop selling bazookas, shot guns, and hand grenades. And we read advertisements in the magazines which said: 'Protect your children with this machine gun.'" (GE-MM69a)

Justin Hayward: "We didn't realize that, of course, when you're in America, you really should be flying if you want to go somewhere – you know, from one state to another. We even ended up at Greyhound bus stations and things – it was ridiculous!... It was frightening... as if you really *were* in danger." (JH-OFO16)

Graeme Edge: "The middle class Americans are so inflexible that you can understand why the revolutionaries go to such extremes to shock and outrage them. But there are two ways of fighting the establishment – by proclaiming positive, reformist ideas in the face of reactionary complacency, or by making the establishment seethe with anger just for the hell of it. The young Americans seem to have chosen the second way – and it's barren, pointless and pathetic.... As if all you needed to put the world right was to tear your clothes off and sleep around. I can't condemn them on moral grounds, but I'm distressed to think that so many of them confuse free love with free copulation. Everyone expects the younger generation to moan and rebel and to be nonconformist, but it's no good replacing one set of prejudices with another. If you are a girl brought up by parents who say you must never sleep with a man, and you react by sleeping with every man in sight, you are being just as bigoted and fanatical as your parents." (GE-MM69a)

Justin Hayward: "It was a much harder place and life than I thought it would be. I thought it would be a much easier life for most people, but most of the audiences that we saw were leading a sort of a tough, working class life. And, of course, there was the Vietnam War and the threat of the draft hanging over every person of our age when we were playing colleges and things like that." (JH-RC17)

Elsewhere, Hayward said, "In those days, it was very expensive for fans to travel everywhere to see any band. Just about the only people who could do that were the groupies. And we had some who would be at a lot of our shows on tour. Did we ever indulge in activities with them? Well, come on. We were young guys from England, in a successful band and these girls were offering us their services, what do you think happened? Of course we enjoyed ourselves with some of them!" (JH-PROG13)

Ray Thomas remembered the shy Hayward, who had a happy relationship at home, wasn't always that quick to indulge. "In those days, we roomed together. I shacked up with Graeme, while Justin and John shared. Anyway, one morning, John was in the bathroom washing his hair, and there was a knock at the door. Justin opened it to find himself face-to-face with this beautiful, young girl. She had on a fur coat, and that was all. So, she opened her coat and said to Justin, 'Do you wanna have a ball?' You know what Justin said to her? 'Oh, I can't; John's in the bathroom doing his hair'! What a thing to say. He later admitted he wasn't sure why he'd said that, but it was the first thing to come to his head." (RT-PROG12)

Justin Hayward: "There were also the girls you came across in a lot of the cities. You knew they were there for whatever band was in town. But that was the way it worked. It was us one week, and then they'd move on to somebody else, Led Zeppelin or whoever, the next week. But it was a mutually beneficial arrangement. They'd look after you, no strings attached." (JH-PROG13)

Graeme Edge: "The younger generation should be working positively to put things right – but they just don't know what to do. So they settle aimlessly for causing grief to the older generation by smoking pot, using four letter words, and pretending that sex is love. …

"I'm not being prim about sex – I'm just sick of the ludicrous importance which is attached to it and I also feel it's a great pity that most people don't have the opportunity I had to discover the phoniness of the sexual dream as fostered by the communication industry. I've been through it and now, for the first time, I'm finding out what love is; but an awful lot of people will never find it because they've been corrupted by those fantasies. It's the saddest and most devastating confidence trick in the world."

However, Graeme said, "I have to admit that we probably met a non-typical cross section." (GE-MM69a)

Ray Thomas: "It went quite disastrously, actually. We had equipment failures. At that stage, the Mellotron, they don't travel very well, and you have to know how to move them around. And, at that stage, we just didn't. I mean, the thing was put in a box and thrown around in an aircraft, and came out more or less in pieces." (RT-OFO16)

Justin Hayward: "We didn't correctly plan for the number of roadies we would need for an American tour, and that made it very difficult." (JH-GM94)

Ray Thomas: "After our first tour of America, I came home to England after two months a nervous wreck with no money in the bank and asked Jill to marry me before I turned into a vegetable. Those were the days when our so-called manager [Derek McCormick] was booking us in every shed in America and bleeding us white. We were given five dollars a day for food in the cheapest motels. There was no money for calls home and you would really get to know what 'homesick' meant.

"That kind of experience either pulls you together or tears you apart. America does that to you. … You really have no conception of touring and the strain until you have toured America the hard way, driving yourself from New York to Washington [State] and working until you are so tired and ill you are on the verge of collapse.

"On our first tour it was nothing to walk into your room and find 'Jus' [Justin] or someone in tears from sheer exhaustion. You either helped each other or you went under.

"I can remember 'Jus' being so ill with flu that he could hardly move, and he ordered a meal in his room. He got the biggest 'bollocking' I've ever heard from a manager for that because he said we couldn't afford it." (RT-RM72)

Touring was most difficult for Hayward; he was not only the youngest member of the band, but also the shyest. He longed to be home with his live-in girlfriend, Marie.

Marie said, "There were times of great loneliness. The tours were so long. We wrote to each other every day and I still have all Justin's letters in a bundle, tied with a pink ribbon…. But, though the letters were lovely, it was the phone calls that made my life bearable. I have composer Lionel Bart to thank for that; I couldn't afford to call America, so Lionel let me use his phone." (MH-GH97)

Hayward said, "I liked the idea of having Marie to come home to and having a place I could call home. I became very homesick on tour, so the thought of her kept me going. She understood that I was totally involved in my music and wanted it to be the best. I was pretty self-absorbed, I suppose, but she always supported me." (JH-DM97)

Marie said: "If I ever worried about him, [those letters] kept me strong. I knew he was sensible enough not to get involved in drugs or heavy drinking, although everybody dabbled a bit. We knew people who had ruined their lives, but I relied on Justin to know when to stop." (MH-DM97)

Justin Hayward: "Going on tour was difficult; there were all sorts of temptations. Everybody knew what went on. But I never met anybody to match Marie." (JH-DM97)

Marie: "His manager once said to me, 'You must be one hell of a lady, because your husband goes home to his own bed at night.' I was relieved to hear that, but, knowing the life he led and the adoration of the fans, I couldn't help wondering what he got up to when I wasn't there. But I found that if I was to survive, it was better not to entertain those thoughts." (MH-DM97)

Justin Hayward: "You know, a couple of us were ill. But we played a lot of good gigs. We got to see all of the California scene. We played Fillmore West while it was still going in San Francisco. And I'm glad we were there." (JH-OFO16)

However, the strains of the tour, including the head-butting with their young manager, would leave its damage.

As the Moodies saw it, there had been too many miles covered, too little planning, too few roadies, too little food allowance, too few phone calls home, too many "cheap motels," and too much "bollocking" toward ill band members from their millionaire manager. Derek McCormick, who had just put a fair sum of his own money on the line, no doubt had his own side to the story. Regardless, the Moodies would split with their manager. Thereupon, Derek McCormick would sue for breach of contract and unpaid personal loans.

Those things would have to wait. First, the Moodies had another album to make.

11

On The Threshold of a Dream (1969)

U.K. album release:
Deram SML 1035 (stereo), DML-1035 (mono); April 25, 1969
Peak position in U.K.: #1
(Certified Silver in the U.K.)
France: #10
Norway: #12
Germany: #37

U.S. album release:
Deram DES 18025 (stereo); Late April/Early May 1969
U.S.: #20
(Certified platinum in U.S.)
Canada: #26
(Certified platinum in Canada)

U.K. single release: *"Never Comes the Day" b/w "So Deep Within You"*
Deram DM 247; April 2, 1969
Non-charting

U.S. single release: *"Never Comes the Day" b/w "So Deep Within You"*
Deram 45-85044; Late-April 1969
U.S. peak position: #89 (*Record World*)
Canadian peak position: #74

Upon their return to England in mid-December 1968, the Moodies set about choosing a theme and writing the songs for their next album.

The group that had hit No. 1 in 1965 with "Go Now!" no longer carried the stigma of a one-hit wonder. The chart performances of "Nights in White Satin," "Tuesday Afternoon," and "Ride My See-Saw" proved their staying-power. Even more importantly, with the

(Photo source: PastDaily.com)

success of *In Search of the Lost Chord*, Decca knew that *Days of Future Passed* was not a fluke. To the contrary, *In Search of the Lost Chord* had outperformed the earlier album.

Justin Hayward: "When Decca found they could actually sell LPs instead of singles, they went completely overboard on us and just gave the studio time. The chairman famously said to us, 'I don't know what you're doing, boys, just go on doing it, because people love it!' It was fantastic!" (JH-GM12)

The Moodies recorded *In Search of the Last Chord* and *On the Threshold of a Dream* fairly close together in time. They were thinking about the material needed for *Threshold*, and no doubt writing some of it, while touring in support of the former album.

Justin Hayward: "You almost had to. We'd go on the road and be thinking of the next record in the back of our minds. We knew that most groups last about two years, so we were thinking of that. And we had a lot to say.

"There was some pressure, but we had a lot of energy, enthusiasm, and urgency. We were having hits and being successful on the road. It was the days of recording; we put a lot more emphasis on recording than on touring – there wasn't any money in touring in those days. The records were our passport to the world." (JH-OTR09)

Mike Pinder, in early 1969, said, "When we made *Days of Future Passed* we had time to sit back and listen to it. There were let downs in it. Same with *Lost Chord*, but it was much better. We'll apply the experience of these two albums to our next album, which we begin in February. It will be quite a challenge after this American tour...

"I'm quite happy with our studio in England. They've had a chance to improve on it and install 8-track equipment. We use Decca's studio where they record all of their classical music. It's become like home. The climax of the Moody Blues is in the recording studio." (MP-HP69)

John Lodge: "Every album was a journey. There's so much energy in the recording side – the excitement of the finished album; the finished tape – listening to it was pure magic." (JL-OTR09)

Justin Hayward: "What we were saying [on the albums] was sincere; we weren't just picking up bits of information and using them in songs. We were actually living this stuff at the time – I suppose like many other people, but we took it more seriously than most other musicians, and we were able to put it into the music in a more accessible way than some of the other musicians who were really seriously into it, but who were inaccessible in their music....

"But we did have that eagerness of youth that wants to experiment. I was smoking a lot of dope, and it definitely was part of the music. I can't deny that. I wouldn't deny it, because it was wonderful. And, being in a group of people, we had safety in numbers. We could keep cool and be private, and just do our own thing.

"Having said that, there is nothing sloppy or drug-induced about our music; we took that very seriously, and the quality of the musicianship was the most important thing; that never suffered. We never recorded anything if we didn't feel that it moved us – whether we were stoned or straight." (JH-O00)

Assistant recording engineer Adrian Martins said, "A lot of the time it was loose and very friendly. When you work with a band until four in the morning for weeks and months on end, you kind of become family and everyone's input becomes important. We reached a couple of stages where, for example, 'Okay, *In Search of the Lost Chord* is a hit, but now we're doing the next album; which direction do we go in? Do we keep the same direction or do we try something new? And is this the right direction for us?' Those thoughts were in everybody's minds." (AM-H&H97)

Besides the "colors" to the music that widened because of the introduction of a greater variety of instruments, the Moodies had many other experiences coloring the writing of the songs for the new album.

The recording of the album would not go completely uninterrupted. There were many concert dates to contend with.

New Musical Express reported that, according to their "manager," Colin Berlin, the band would play ballroom dates for the remainder of December. Then, during the first two weeks of January, they had reserved the Decca studio to record their next album. Immediately following that, for the rest of January and throughout February and March, they would be touring England.

Colin Berlin had served as the Moodies' booking agent since late 1966/early 1967, but he wasn't their manager. That job, beginning in the fall of 1967, was in the hands of Derek McCormick. However, the tour in America had gone badly. Exactly when the Moodies split with McCormick is not known, but the *New Musical Express* article gives indication that the break may have occurred as early as mid-December 1968, upon their return to England from America.

The trauma of the tour, and the separation from their loved ones for so long, had more than one Moody thinking in terms of marriage. On January 1, Graeme Edge welcomed in the New Year by wedding Carol Mayers, his 22-year-old girlfriend. The writing had been on the wall, anyway – while in America, Edge had told an American journalist that Mayers might be pregnant.

All five Moodies, and Carol Mayers (now Carol Edge), had the cover of *Disc and Music Echo* on January 11, 1969.

Graeme Edge was in *Melody Maker*, too, making a sort of [pre-marriage confessional. "I used to watch the James Bond films and see him pulling beautiful birds right, left and center, and I'd be terribly envious. 'What chance do I have,' I used to think, 'of attracting birds like that?'

"In December 1964 we were in New York for three weeks and, of course, the Beatles had made such an impact that British groups could do no wrong.

"All the girls had to do to get into our room while we were out was to bribe the maids. When we came back we found them in the wardrobes, in the bath, under the bed, behind the curtains. They'd pinch our shirts, cuff-links, ties – anything they could lay their hands on for souvenirs. ...

"Let's own up, it was the biggest mistake of my life, but it was all so new.... They'd come up the fire escape at four in the morning and hammer on the door. They were just as blatant then as they are now [in 1969]. They would walk through the door and grope you, just like that! [with the snap of a finger] ... because they had to make their pinch fast with all the competition around. Well, you can imagine the effect it would have on any normal healthy bloke to be plunged suddenly into that kind of situation. Often, while you made love to them, they'd say, 'Do you know Mick Jagger?' ...

"After a while, when you've been playing James Bond every night for months, you start realizing where it's really at. You stop pulling birds because you know that, after you've satisfied the physical thing, you'll find yourself lumbered, left with a chick who has nothing to say, with whom you have nothing in common. And you think, 'Why the hell did I bother?' I know it sounds blasé, but that's the way it is. That's how animal the whole thing is. I think that anybody in that situation would go through exactly the same sequence of reactions, if they had any feelings at all.

"I've gotten over the James Bond envy bit and I have a much better chance of achieving a lasting relationship with someone – a relationship founded on something more durable than an easy lay." (GE-MM69)

Now he got to sleep with his wife ... a former model.

Recording the Album:

On Thursday, January 9, 1969, the Moodies moved into Decca Studio 1 to begin work for *On the Threshold of a Dream*. The first three days were devoted to setting up the equipment and getting into the vibe. Justin Hayward told *Higher & Higher*'s Mark Murley, "Mostly I remember talking a lot with Mike and being with Mike a lot. I'd already written my songs and was done, but nothing unusual in that. I don't remember much else about the preparation except that this was the first time we were given a free rein with studio time, and we could take two or three weeks. ... So, after *Lost Chord* was out, they said, 'You can block out studio time and take as long as you like.'" (JH-H&H04a)

Producer Tony Clarke: "We were locked in, and that was pioneering stuff. It was like being sealed into a capsule – an experiment where all the guys and instruments are in there. I bolted the doors and that was it.

"I used to lock people in small cupboards [closets] in the studio and tell them to stay in there until they wrote a song. Ray loved it." (TC-H&H04)

Mike Pinder: "I don't actually remember what songs were started before the recordings. Some of it was done in the studio and some of it was done at home. When I wasn't needed, when say, Ray was doing flute overdubs or Justin was doing guitar overdubs, we'd all be scattered in different areas, writing, in one cupboard or another. We had little closets and cupboards and things where we could go and be quite away from the sound, and be able to be creative and write lyrics and songs.

"Usually, Justin would come in with at least a couple of songs and a few things that were started. I would come in with one or two things. … We knew that we could produce it when we went in and got into that creative environment where we were literally locked away with very little interruption. We knew that the juices would flow if we let it happen." (MP-H&H04b)

Beyond this, parts of the studio were made as homelike as possible for the Moodies.

Tony Clarke: "We brought in carpets and lamps and ashtrays, and recorded in the dark. It had to be comfortable and cozy. The sessions tended to go from midday until midnight." (TC-H&H04)

Justin Hayward: "Tony was somebody who stood back and saw the whole picture, but he was a wonderful record producer…. His overall feeling and emotion that he had was wonderful. … It was creating an atmosphere; about creating a sense of importance. 'This recording that you're doing is the most important thing, and the only thing that exists in the world. That's it.'

"I'm so glad that he thought that way, and Derek Varnals was always there to capture that moment. Perfectly recorded." (JH-H&H04a)

Pinder said that he, Clarke, and Varnals were the technical wizards when it came to designing and realizing the way the concept albums were recorded, and how the songs were woven together. "Yeah, we would interface between the three of us, with Derek being the real font of information. Tony is a bass player, and, in fact, he used to play in a couple bands just a few miles from Ray and I. We didn't meet until we met at Decca, which is crazy, but Tony had the background…. It had a lot to do with where he was coming from." (MP-H&H04b)

On the Threshold of a Dream was the first Moody Blues' album to benefit from Decca's newly outfitted 8-track recording console (they had test-driven the new deck with the B-side, "A Simple Game," recorded the previous October).

Travelling through the album:

"In the Beginning," a poem by Graeme Edge set to the eerie "music" of Mike Pinder's Mellotron, opens the program and establishes the theme.

A music journalist in 1970 – Jared Johnson of the syndicated "Teen Times" newspaper service – said it best:

> Several hundred years ago Descartes set out to discover one fact of which he might be absolutely certain, realizing that the senses often deceive. After considerable cogitation, he formulated the famous assertion, "I think, therefore, I am." Of this knowledge, Descartes could be absolutely sure; his own existence devised from introspection and the thought of his own existence. Descartes' "discovery" set the mood for *Threshold* and the eerie, supernatural cover well reflected the music inside.

Graeme Edge launched the musical voyage with "In the Beginning" and a slight modification of Descartes, "I think; I think I am, therefore I am … I think" …

In fact, this first cut was actually one of the last tracks recorded for the album, on Wednesday, January 29. It's also the only Moody Blues spoken-word track to feature multiple members of the band reciting lyrics – performing, if you will, a micro-play.

Derek Varnals: "I don't recall much about doing the vocals, but the casting was obvious. The sort of slightly bemused, lone person, which is Justin, was Voice One. Then Graeme as the maniacal, power-mad, James Bond villain; he was sort of like the Establishment – 'You are all under our control' kind of thing. I recall saying to them, 'Yes, like a bank manager.' That's the way they looked at it; back in those days, about the only thing that was computerized were banks, which was the concept of what Edge was writing about." (DV-H&H04)

According to the written material included with the original album, Justin Hayward's part was described as the "Man," new to life, trying to understand his purpose within the grander scheme of things.

Despite his experience as a juvenile actor on the stage, Justin Hayward felt insecure about his performance on this track: "I felt very self conscious about doing the voice because I'm the first voice that you hear." (JH-H&H04a)

Graeme Edge's role – "Establishment," as identified in the 12-page booklet in the gatefold LP – is the Man's antagonist. After man realizes that, because he thinks, therefore he must be, the "Establishment" tells him, "Of course you are, my bright little star. I've miles and miles of files; pretty files of your forefather's fruit … and now to suit our great computer … you're magnetic ink."

Man protests: "I'm more than that. I know I am … at least, I think I must be."

Mike Pinder provides the voice for the "Inner Man," as identified in the album materials. "There you go, man, keep as cool as you can," he raps. "Face piles and piles of trials with smiles. It riles them to believe that you perceive the web they weave."

Man is told, "Keep on thinking free," as the sounds of the Mellotron build.

These sounds were, as Derek Varnals recalled, intended to convey "the sound of the universe." Varnals said, "I recall Tony trying to describe to me what they wanted. He said, 'We want the sound of everything … but also of nothing.' And I said, 'Oh, sort of like the background radiation in space.' And he said, 'Yes, plus all these little twinkly star things,' which is what we used the Mellotron to create. But we also wanted the steadiness of the high tones and the low tones, and, of course, they are at slightly different frequencies as well, which makes them beat against each other. We created these with oscillators. If you've ever gone on an airplane and the pilot doesn't get the speed of the engines right, you get sort of a throbbing sound when you get two low frequencies close to each other…. When you get frequencies that are not quite the same as each other, they beat against each other. We have them on each side of the stereo. The high and the low frequencies represent everything, from top to bottom. And then there's this sort of third of an octave of pink noise, because white noise is *every* frequency. They used to call it pink noise because it wasn't quite white. And it's a narrow band of noise.

We chose the pitch and put lots of reverb on it to make it sound everywhere and nowhere, if you like. It worked and seemed to be quite atmospheric." (DV-H&H04)

Pinder said, "I used my 'loaner' Moog to create some really high tinkling sounds. We also generated white noise. We used the real Moog bass notes, and then some white noise, or pink noise, and tinkles from the Moog equipment." (MP-H&H04b)

As for the ticking sound, Varnals said, "Well, we got everybody's watch. In those days, we all had battery watches – and they went 'tick-tick.' We put them all together in one heap and put a microphone over them. We had them contained in something; I forget what." (DV-H&H04)

Hayward remembered 'what,' and said, "The 'clocks' were all our watches in an ashtray, as far as I remember." (JH-H&H04a)

Pinder remembered a different "what": "[W]e put all our wristwatches, and a little alarm clock, or something, in a jam jar, and put a microphone in there. And that's how we got [the computer sounds]." (MP-H&H04b)

Varnals said, "And we recorded a couple of layers of those. And for the first time, we recorded the Mellotron without it being played. It has a revolving capstan, which is the rotating spindle that the tapes press against. The motor drives this capstan. On the Mellotron, this is pretty noisy, so we took the back of the cabinet off and put a couple of microphones on the Mellotron clanging away. So, we mixed that in as well…. [W]e were giving the listener the sound as a representation. So, all this 'mad-professor-world' dominated conspiracy is all very mechanical, and that is represented with all this ticking and clanking." (DV-H&H04)

"Lovely to See You" was written by Justin Hayward. Even though it wasn't chosen to be released as a single – with the exception of a 1969 promotional 45, coupled with Ray Thomas's "Lazy Day" (Deram 45-9489) – the song became the album's most-played cut on the radio, and went on to become a staple of classic-rock radio.

Justin Hayward: "'Lovely to See You' was written about a guy I knew from California, who was one of those people who just lit up any room he was in. Whenever he came to stay with my girlfriend and myself it was always a great time, so the song just came naturally." (JH-RS13)

With this song, the theme progresses: The Man has found a friend … "Wonderful day for passing my way / Knock on my door, and even the score … with your eyes."

This new friend has traveled near and far, therefore having acquired wisdom to share ("Tell us what you've seen / In far away forgotten lands / Where empires have turned back to sand…").

This was the second song recorded for the album (following Pinder's "So Deep Within You"), taking only one day, from start to finish on Tuesday, January 14, 1969. Besides being one of the simpler songs, the speed in which it was recorded also had to do with the song being fully written before the session began. Hayward said, "I remember having 'Lovely to See You' and 'Never Comes the Day' already written. I remember working with Mike on 'Have You Heard,' and I remember he had that one already…. I think Mike was often prepared, and I was *always* prepared. It's just the way I am. I just got nervous about it and wouldn't wait. It didn't have anything to do with the studio charges. …

"The basic track for me was always acoustic guitar, bass, drums, sometimes electric guitar, and Mike keeping time either on the tambourine or by some other way. Even if it wasn't used, it was Mike who was in the middle of it." (JH-H&H04a)

Now with the luxury of eight tracks, the band could achieve greater clarity in their recordings. Hayward recalled one track being used for John Lodge's bass, one for his guitar, and then Pinder either on tambourine or with a cowbell, creating, in effect, a time click on a third track, which could later be wiped.

Justin Hayward: "'Lovely to See You' was a guitar riff that was easy to remember. And then I'd just got the [Gibson ES-]335 not long before that, I think, towards the end of *Lost Chord*, and I think 'Lovely to See You' was the first song I recorded with it. I had the luxury of double-tracking myself as well, which I hadn't done before." (JH-H&H04a)

It was that distinctive tone of the electric Gibson ES-335, in combination with Hayward's playing, that gave many Moody Blues songs their signature guitar sound – such as here, and, later, in "The Story in Your Eyes," and so many others.

Derek Varnals said, "Most of the days we worked on these songs were 10-to-16-hour days. We finished this one in a single long session. The song is quite simple – the song itself; the layers. There really isn't a lot to it. There weren't too many overdubs to do, and what was added on was straightforward. The backing vocal lines were quite simple. Not a difficult number to play or get right. That's why it went down so quickly. And I think it's done very well." (DV-H&H04)

In addition to electric guitar, Hayward handles the lead vocals; Lodge the bass; Pinder on acoustic guitar as well as Mellotron; Thomas on tambourine; and Edge contributing drums and percussion. Lodge, Pinder, and Thomas blend their voices for the backing vocals.

"Dear Diary" was both the third track recorded and sequenced on the album. It continues in the tradition established on the previous two albums. Ray Thomas provides charming, dreamy, and almost child-like imagery, with a dash of humor woven in. The song begins: "Dear Diary, what a day it's been / Dear Diary, it's been just like a dream / Woke up late; wasn't where I should have been. For goodness sake, what's happening to me?"

Thomas's inspiration for the lyric is believed to have been the Eastern concept of *Maya*, the belief that the material world is merely an illusion. If life is unreal, it's no wonder that the people passing by don't understand it. The singer tells his secret friend – his "dear diary" – about "So many people by the score / Pushing around so senselessly / They don't notice there's people like me." If only these people "weren't so blind," then "surely they would see … there's a much better way for them to be." The song ends with the narrator remarking that someone has exploded an H Bomb … but, he is pleased to say, not anyone that he knew.

Regarding the H-bomb reference, Derek Vandals said, "Oh, he just made it up as he went along, I think. Then, Bang!, the H-bomb thing. Yeah, we wanted to keep that in because it was witty and quite amusing. And when we did the final mixing of the album, I said to Tony. 'That's the perfect point to cut it dead and bring in the next number.'" (DV-H&H04)

Thomas's voice was filtered through a Leslie speaker to create the eerie, otherworldly effect of a man thinking to himself. The technique had been used first by recording engineer Geoff Emerick for the 1966 John Lennon song "Tomorrow Never Knows," the last track on the Beatles' *Revolver*.

Varnals said, "Ray sang into one of the PA stage mikes, which was fed through a special speaker cabinet that electric Hammond organs use, called a Leslie Tone Cabinet. The bass speaker is in the bottom of the cabinet, and that's got a rotating fan thing, which makes the sound waver slightly." (DV-H&H04)

Regarding the vocal effect, which he supported with an off-beat harmony, Hayward said, "I think that was the way Ray sort of felt it. I thought it was just a great idea for a song. It was an opportunity to do something different that you would never normally have the nerve or courage to do on a recording." (JH-H&H04a)

Thomas' flute accompaniment is a delight, as much a signature for this song as the vocal effects. The band provided their regular support – Hayward's acoustic and electric guitars; Pinder's Mellotron; Edge's drums and percussion. But the bass heard on this track was not Lodge's electric bass; instead, an acoustic string bass was used – provided by Hayward from his growing collection of vintage guitars, and played by Pinder.

Hayward said, "It was one of those where I seem to remember that I always wanted to do a song in that tempo, and I had this double-bass that I bought, and that's my double-bass on it. It's a three-quarter double-bass." (JH-H&H04a)

"Send Me No Wine" and **"To Share Our Love"** are companion songs from John Lodge, and fittingly placed side-by-side. Both are rockers, in the tradition Lodge had started with "Peak Hour" on *Days of Future Passed* and "Ride My See-Saw" on *In Search of the Lost Chord*, providing a bouncy counterbalance to the album's more serious opening tracks.

The dreamlike theme continues with Lodge singing, "… Leave me no time … in your imagination … only to find … words in your mind," and, "For once in my life … I need no conversation … All of my time … I'll spend in fascination." In the next song, the daydream turns to the reality of love: "Now I can see … it takes more than one to give … the life we need … I can't think why … I never thought of this before … Now I know what it means to share … to share my love."

"Send Me No Wine" was the fourth song on the album, and the fourth recorded. It features Lodge on lead vocal, riding along the top of the track while providing the solid bottom with his bass guitar; Hayward plays 6- and 12-string acoustics, and electric slide guitar; Pinder on Mellotron; Thomas on tambourine, Edge on drums. Hayward also provides the harmony vocal.

Derek Varnals: "'Wine' is really a country and western song. When you play it, imagine it slower, with some of the repetition taken out. Listen to the song and note the Mellotron parts are very much like a pedal steel guitar as well." (DV-H&H04)

"To Share Our Love" was first recorded on Sunday, January 26, and then remade on Monday, January 27. While written primarily by Lodge, it is Pinder who sings the lead vocal, with Lodge, Hayward, and Thomas backing. And, here, Thomas contributes flute.

Hayward recalled, "It was a kind of jam session in the studio.… Also, I know at the time we did the original track, I thought, 'I'm playing all over this; I can't imagine how there's ever going to be a vocal on it…' I'd just taken the opportunity to enjoy my [Gibson] 335. I remember it being a solid guitar solo from beginning to end….

"I know there was a vocal line that John put to it that he and I sang…. And then, Mike had some doubts about it and decided to do sort of a little freak out over it. I remember watching him do it after we'd done this vocal. And we thought, 'Oh, that's great!'" (JH-H&H04a)

Pinder explained why he sang the lead: "Because John's version of 'Share' was okay, but it wasn't really happening. We were working on some vocals when all of a sudden it came to me, and I said, 'Hold on there, John, let's see what you think of this…' And I took his lyric and all of a sudden this whole new melody came up out of the harmony I was working on. That's how it happened. John said, 'Yeah, it's better than what I've got. Do it.' And that's how I ended up singing John's song … because I came up with a whole new melody." (MP-H&H04)

"So Deep Within You" was written and sung by Mike Pinder, with accompaniment of his Mellotron. Thomas's jazzy flute is the other dominant instrument on the track. Backing vocals are from Hayward, Lodge, and Thomas, sung over electric and acoustic guitars from Hayward, and the rhythm section of Lodge and Edge. Thomas makes a second contribution via the piccolo, and Edge doubles up on timpani.

Notable here are the romanticism and dreamlike quality of Pinder's lyrics, with lines like, "Talk to me, baby, I want to sleep at night / My heart is heavy, it's weighed down by the night / And now I'm lonely, I want to see the light / So deep within you," and, "Your love's a never ending dream / A castle by a stream … of sweet understanding."

Justin Hayward: "I remember doing that with Mike, sitting together playing the guitars for it. As far as I know he pretty much already had that before we went in, but I seem to remember rehearsing it at his home and then saying how we were going to record it. Lovely, fantastic song." (JH-H&H04a)

"So Deep Within You" was the first song recorded for the album.

Derek Varnals: "I think it is one of Mike's best songs. It's got one of his usual-key-changes-in-the-middle bits, which is the same 'trick' he used in 'A Simple Game,' in the middle eight [bars]." (DV-H&H04)

It took two days to record the song – Sunday and Monday, January 12 and 13.

"Never Comes the Day," written and sung by Justin Hayward, opens Side 2. It's a pure but not simple love song, as the dreams of romance spoken on the earlier tracks now become reality … such as reality is. There is the dark side of the real: "If only you knew what's inside of me now / You wouldn't want to know me somehow," and the brightness of love, awash with hope, and a message to the listening audience: "Give just a little bit more / Take a little bit less / From each other tonight."

Justin Hayward: "'Never Comes the Day' was in an open tuning, actually, and I'm really glad the guys just let me play the open acoustic guitar, as it is. I remember when I first played it to the band, it was just me on the acoustic guitar, with Ray actually accompanying me on harmonica, and I really liked that from Day One." (JH-RS13)

As tricky – and therefore intriguing – as the lyrics were, the guitar work was even more mystifying to any musician who heard and then tried to play the licks. Hayward said, "There are things I do, as a self-taught guitarist, that I would never do if I'd learned to play correctly. ...

"Not long ago, I met a fan who was a guitarist, and he'd been trying to get 'Never Comes the Day' right, and he couldn't, and he asked me about it. He showed me what he was trying to do, and I told him what the problem was – he was trying to play it the way a properly-trained guitarist would, which was wrong. I told him, 'If you do it this way, which is the wrong way, you'll have it right." (JH-GM94)

Part of the magic of the Moody Blues music was that they didn't know *not* to try certain things. Mike Pinder said, "People who don't read music wish they could, and people who do read music wish maybe they didn't because it narrows your creative focus. Taking the course I did forced me to develop a style of my own, which I may not have done had I taken the academic approach. So I'm rather grateful for that. Even though I can't play wonderful scales, I've developed something that was perfect for me. The music that I create is like a landscape painting – it is visual music." (MK-EOTS99)

"Never Comes the Day" was the eighth track recorded for the album, with the session taking place on January 22. Besides electric and acoustic guitars, Hayward also contributes a Mellotron part to the backing track. Ray Thomas plays a harmonica. Lodge and Edge bring forward the rhythm section. Pinder, Lodge, and Thomas blend their voices for the backing track.

Hayward recalled that "Never Comes the Day" was "a song written in the middle of the night all on my own, and then I actually played Mellotron on it, as well. I had a small Mark IV Mellotron that was like a half-size Mellotron, and I had that string line that I wanted to do. I think that was the first time I played Mellotron on a record. I played piano before that, but this was the first time for the Mellotron on a record. I think Mike doubles it; I'm not sure, but I know that I put the line down as part of the original backing track. Then I got to the rhythm bit in the middle, and then Ray said, 'Oh, let me have a look at my bag of stuff,' and he got out his harmonica and did that [bit]....

"And also the [Gibson] 335 was just perfect between the harmonica and the 'Live just a little bit more' [line]. My 335 really sang on that. The 335 in a Vox amplifier in the normal channel – it gave Derek and Tony the kind of sound that they really liked." (JH-H&H04a)

"Lazy Day," this album's second number written and sung by Ray Thomas, describes a carefree Sunday ... the one day of the week designated by society as a period for rest. The dream theme is present ("Soon you'll start to nod off, happy dreams"), but never free of the reality of the other six days of the week ("Today's heaven-sent and you're feeling quite content / You worked all week long / Still, it's quite sad, tomorrow's so bad"). The silver lining of the lazy day has its dark cloud, and Hayward sings the contrasting passage ("It's such a crying shame / Week after week the same / That's how life goes by / Until the day you die").

The song was recorded on Tuesday, January 28. Derek Varnals described it as, "One of Ray's novelty numbers, indeed; another looking-back-at-childhood song; it's a very English, 1950s, rigid family lifestyle sort of situation. Like a lot of Ray's numbers, it's probably autobiographical."

For Varnals, part of the success of the song has to do with contrasting elements – both in the lyric and musically. "Take the contrast between the lead vocal and the backing vocals, and the harmonica solo and the Mellotron setting – this is huge, which makes 'Lazy Day' very tongue-in-cheek. You have this sort of Russian soldier choir singing [on the chorus], and you have this little English novelty number [on the verses]. The whole thing is a humorous little track." (DV-H&H04)

Besides the standard instruments, handled by each band member, Pinder contributes an organ (along with the Mellotron), and Thomas, instead of flute, plays the harmonica … beautifully.

"Are You Sitting Comfortably?" is the second song (as with "Visions of Paradise" on *Lost Chord*) written by Hayward *and* Thomas. Like the earlier song, the prominent instruments are Hayward's guitar and Thomas's lovely flute playing.

The lyric makes dreamy reference to the legend of King Arthur, naming Camelot, Merlin, and Guinevere. The twilight time of reality is ever present, as Hayward sings, "Take another sip, my love, and see what you will see … Let Merlin cast his spell."

Justin Hayward: "'Are You Sitting Comfortably?' was one of those that was written in the broom cupboard at the back of the studio. I already had the guitar riff and the chord sequence, and I had the first line… 'Take another sip, my love, and see what you will see.' I knew I wanted to do a song called, 'Are You Sitting Comfortably?' Lionel Bart [who wrote the liner notes for the album] had suggested the title. It was part of a children's program on the radio. The first words of it would be 'Are you sitting comfortably, children?' Of course, it was just a funny title, but everyone in England knew the phrase. So, I had the title, most of the guitar sequence, and that first line. And then we just took it from there. Ray contributed a lot of lyrics, and we did the fusion guitar run [the descending progression]. We did that together in the room between us. I know the first thing he did was that second line, 'A fleet of golden galleons, on a crystal sea,' which is a very Ray Thomas phrase." (JH-H&H04)

Thomas said, "I used to sit in the broom cupboard at Decca, writing lyrics while Justin was working stuff out on guitar. Then he'd pop into the broom cupboard, we'd smoke a 'j' and just work it out." (RT-CRB14)

The track was recorded on January 30, 1968, the final "song" to be committed to tape (only the recording of a poem was left to complete the album).

Derek Varnals said, "There's a lot of reverb on it. The song is quite mystical, so I had to get it 'floaty.' There are all sorts of things you can do with reverb, but because the song was mystical – the Merlin bit and all that – we wanted to keep it strange and sympathetic." (DV-H&H04)

"The Dream" is Graeme Edge's spoken-word poem, designed to tie all the previous cuts together and set the stage for the album's musical climax. Mike Pinder speaks the words. The theme of love is reinforced: "Just as new life will come from death, love will come at leisure / Love of love, love of life, and giving without measure / Gives in return a wondrous yearn of a promise almost seen."

Early on, Ray Thomas had sung of isolation. Now Edge's words, and Pinder's voice, beckon the isolationists in us all to come out from hiding: "Live hand-in-hand and together we'll stand … on the threshold of a dream."

Recorded in January 31, this was the last track for the album put on tape.

Derek Varnals: "We worked a very, very long day, that day, 'cause it was our last chance to do anything on the record. If anybody was not happy with something, we had to redo it that day."

As for "The Dream," Varnals said, "This one is built up around Mellotrons. There's a descending chord on 'The Dream' as Mike changes the pitch on his Mellotron. This comes in at the end of 'Are You Sitting Comfortably?', where we bring in the eternity sound [which they had recorded earlier as part of 'In the Beginning']. And then at the very end of 'The Dream,' as it goes down to 'Have You Heard' [Part 1], with the line, '… and together we'll stand, on the threshold of a dream,' we took the speed off the track and slowed it down as we move into 'Have You Heard' [Part 2]." (DV-H&H04)

"Have You Heard" and **"The Voyage"** are a pair of gifts from Mike Pinder, featuring a lovely melody and perhaps Pinder's best vocal performance. They are constructed to form a three-part suite – "Have You Heard, Part 1," into the instrumental interlude of "The Voyage," then the reprise of "Have You Heard, Part 2."

The entire suite is rich with a calm dreamlike melody, and the equally melodic instrumentation. Pinder on Mellotron, piano, and cello, trades off with Thomas, on flute and oboe, for "The Voice." "Have You Heard" benefits from Hayward's acoustic guitar, Lodge's bass line, and Edge's rolling drums … rolling and tumbling in the very best tradition of Ringo Starr (*Pepper/Abbey Road* period) – a dead-on imitation.

After the lyrical and musical journey, Pinder gently sings, "Now you know that you are real… Now you know that you are free / Living all your life at ease / Each day has its *always* / A look down life's hallways … doorways to lead you there."

If "Nights in White Satin" is Justin Hayward's signature song, "Have You Heard?" must certainly be the most significant from Pinder.

This three-song sequence made up the fifth, sixth and seventh tracks recorded for the album, over three days (Sunday, Monday, and Tuesday, January 19, 20, and 21).

Derek Varnals recalled, "We recorded the two bits of 'Have You Heard' one right after another, Part One and Part Two, because we knew when this was being done there was going to be a big dramatic musical bit in the middle – which is why the first part of 'Have You Heard' resolves like it does. I'm pretty sure Mike is playing acoustic guitar on the basic track, as well as Justin…. Probably Mike and John were playing the cellos, 'cause there are some real cellos on that." (DV-H&H04)

Pinder, you may recall, played acoustic guitar with several bands before making the move to keyboards when the Moody Blues first formed in 1964. He said, "I never really played electric. I messed around and I had one, but I was nowhere near Justin's ability. I was probably the second best guitar player in the band, with John being third." (MP-H&H04b)

These two sections were recorded in less than a day, on Sunday, January 19. For the remainder of that day and the two that followed, work continued on "The Voyage."

Varnals said, "We spent Sunday, Monday, Tuesday – three long days doing this instrumental. Or, should I say, three days elapsed before we did the next track. Mike had been fooling around for days with the little melody line you hear on the piano coming in on the end – you know, the double-tracked piano [that] comes in after all the pseudo-orchestral stuff – and that was the basis for the whole musical bit at the end of 'The Voyage.' I don't know; he may have been fooling around with it for months before even!

245

... Certainly that little melody line was heard around the studio for days and days and days! But, basically, the intro bit of 'Voyage' was inspired by the classical piece that's used in *2001: A Space Odyssey* – the big chord buildup with the climactic tympani and all that stuff." (DV-H&H04)

Justin Hayward: "The bit in the middle, 'The Voyage,' I think that was where Mike just closed the door to the studio for three or four hours and just did it. I came back and listened to it. I knew what he was going to do but he didn't really like to have other people around when he was really concentrating on that Mellotron stuff....

"The big difference from *Lost Chord* to *Threshold of a Dream* wasn't so much in the guitars, although I could double-track myself much easier because I had the available tracks – it was because they could bounce Mike [and his] Mellotron sound a lot better. And you could really hear the Mellotron sound getting smaller and smaller and sweeter; not quite as [harsh as] on the first couple of albums." (JH-H&H04a)

"The Voyage," in particular, demonstrates Pinder's brilliance on the Mellotron – a true *tour de force*. As the reprise of "Have You Heard?" fades down, we are left with the sound of the Mellotron, humming on its own, bookending the album with that eerie *2001: A Space Odyssey* soundtrack flavor that was so new in 1968 and '69.

Recalling the making of the album, Adrian Martins said, "I remember mainly that we were always cutting new ground. We were breaking barriers. I can't speak for the States, but certainly nobody in this country had reached those heights before."

Of course, there was a price for such innovations. "Derek and myself and a few other guys were the first engineers ever to work the kind of hours that the Moodies worked – until maybe four or five in the morning," Martin said. "[With other artists], sometimes you'd do this kind of work, occasionally, but these were the first albums where you'd run on until really early in the morning, day after day after day. We didn't get paid overtime; we'd just get a meal allowance. So Derek and I would get in at 10 in the morning and work until 4 in the morning, three months [in a row]. We were the people who really negotiated with Decca management and said, 'Okay, we really have to have some overtime, because we're working our butts off and not getting any pay for it!'

"I remember that the Moodies' roadies used to go out late at night and bring back all kinds of Chinese meals, Indian meals and stuff, and we'd eat all that. But one of the other things that would happen was that the Moodies used to raid the biscuit supply that the nine-to-fivers used to eat on their tea breaks. At four in the morning they'd raid a Coca-Cola machine and that would cause great problems with Decca management. Nothing had gone on like that before; nobody was used to bands needing food in the middle of the night. A Tom Jones session would finish at 10 in the evening at the absolute latest!" (AM-H&H97)

***

Mike Pinder credits radio personality Dave Symonds with coming up with the idea for the album's title. He said, "Dave and I were sitting at the coffee table, probably about halfway through making the album. But, basically, when we were kicking some titles around, I remember talking about how here we are, we'd just come through '67 in kaftans, everybody was out in the street, and it was that kind of thing. So, we were

246

thinking, 'Hey, we're on the brink of a new consciousness, a new way of looking at things.' And so we were talking about that, and it was like we were 'on the verge of a human dream; a dream of humanity,' and Dave said, 'threshold,' and I came up with 'of a dream,' and he just gave us the threshold part of it, and it was perfect." (MP-H&H04b)

Regarding the title, Hayward revealed: "I'll tell you the reason the album came to be called *On the Threshold of a Dream* – at least as I recall it. We'd been over to America, touring a lot over there with people like Jefferson Airplane and Canned Heat, who we became very friendly with, and when we came back to do the album we sort of felt that we could be on the verge of something really special. It was like, 'Have we arrived where we dreamed of being, or are we just on the threshold of it,' you know. People always talk about, 'What's your dream?' or 'What do you dream of doing?' But when you're on the 'threshold' of the dream it's a special place, and that led to the idea for the title; it was like a moment in time, if you like." (JH-RS13)

Dave Symonds said, "It was a milestone album… and a band untrammeled by corporate interference. I thought it was a masterpiece. The album really is a great piece of work, but it's the product of the men [who created it]. I was genuinely flattered to see so much of it taking shape as I did, to be involved in the naming of it and to be invited to write the sleeve notes for it. It was a terrific experience." (DS-H&H04)

Tony Clarke: "This album set the standard for how we recorded future concept albums. It's quite important in so many ways. It was the first time we had true freedom in the studio; this was our first chance at being left alone – no men in white coats or people with clipboards. It's still quite lovely. I'm proud of a great deal of it." (TC-H&H04)

Justin Hayward: "For me, it's probably the defining Moody Blues album. It's the time when we critically reached our peak where the media and the press still liked us. I think it talks about a wonderful kind of naiveté, which is so precious. …

"I think *Threshold* is the defining album for the Moody Blues. And it's the one in the '60s that you would find in people's homes when you went; *they would have that album*." (JH-H&H04a)

Besides spending more money on studio time for the Moody Blues, Decca raised the bar concerning the album packaging. As with *In Search of the Lost Chord*, the new album also had a gatefold jacket. This time it also included a 12-page booklet containing song lyrics and liner notes – opening with those from Dave Symonds and closing with the abstract thoughts of Lionel Bart, both of whom had high profiles in the British pop-culture scene from this period.

Among Symonds' thoughts:

> … We never have enough friends and we never have enough learning, but we gain a little more of each every day. It's because we are able to bite off and digest a slightly larger portion of the outside world than we thought we were able to yesterday. And that's a reaction. The problem about reactions is that they tend to need a catalyst to trigger them off, and that's why the Moodies are so important in my life. Their music catalyses. Words, instruments and voices … a controlled power that is all their own.

Among Bart's observations:

... I think ...... I think I love The Moody Blues.
I think ...... I think they turn me on...

... There's no results in art, or life.
Only beginnings.
The Moody Blues and their Producer,
Tony Clarke,
Are six of the World's best beginners.
In my opinion. And yes,
I'm grateful that I live
In the same Universe
At the same time....

Each of the Moodies, and that included Tony Clarke, were provided with a color portrait shot on the inner sleeve. There was also a group portrait, and this time the pictures did not clash with the cover art from Phil Travers, as was the case on *In Search of the Lost Chord*.

At the time of the release of *On the Threshold of a Dream*, Ray Thomas told *NME*'s Richard Green, "Look at that sleeve. Isn't it great? We told Philip Travers our general ideas and he went away and designed it. He brought it along to a session, heard some tracks, scrapped the whole thing and did this one. I think it's beautiful." (RT-NME69)

Mike Pinder, looking over the double-sided album cover, said, "At the top, of course, we've got Merlin's castle – the Camelot-type thing. It looks a little bit like there's a wispy hand, but I don't think it's particularly meant to be that; I think it's just a nebulous thing. Then we've got the galleons of a time gone by – the river or time or whatever. Then we've got the rose, of course, being held by the mechanical establishment vehicle, which is what we've just been talking about, and you can see the rose on the left, in the right hand caliper of the

Photos from the gatefold of the LP, including Tony Clarke as the "sixth Moody," and the group shot taken on a damp winter day in January 1969.

machine. The establishment machine is restricting art. The beauty of the flower is being plucked so that there's no growth; [no] creativity….

"Then, of course, we've got the white eagle of the north over the top there, which has many representations, but I think we generally were looking at it as the new age of information…. That's the way that I see it visually on there. Then you've got the apparent dead branch that has eyes and ears and saw all life, no matter what state it is in, is receptive, cognizant, or something like that. You know, the 'as new life will come from death' line. You flip it over and you see that the cut branch, or dying or dead branch, is actually coming out of the left eyeball of the upside-down skull. Then we've got Merlin there with his little wizard cane. [The art] just sort of fit. It made a statement at the same time; you had these nice *Days of Future Passed* kinds of connotation in a sense of the past, present and possibly the future." (MP-H&H04b)

***

Even before the album was finished, the Moodies were back before a live audience. In late January, they performed at the College of Commerce in Manchester, as well as playing the California Ballroom in Dunstable.

While Clarke and Varnals handled the final mix-down in early February, the Moodies took flight again. On February 1, they played Mothers Club in Birmingham, then, on February 5, the Top Rank in Leicester. One day later, they performed at King's Hall in Aberystwyth.

On February 7, in America, *This Is Tom Jones*, a new weekly one-hour variety series originating from London, premiered. Jones was joined by Mary Hopkins, singing her recent Paul McCartney-produced hit, "Those Were the Days," and the Moody Blues, singing "Ride My See-Saw," among other guests.

Meanwhile, the Moodies continued touring England. On February 8, they were at the University of Southampton, playing in the Old Union Building to a capacity crowd. On February 13, they performed in the Skyline Ballroom in Hull, then, the following day, at Goldsmith's College in London. One day after that, they were at Liverpool University.

On February 18, the band recorded four songs for the BBC radio show *Top Gear* (broadcast on Feb. 23). The numbers included that great single-that-never-was, "Lovely to See You," as well as their current single, also sung by Hayward, "Never Comes the Day," and two up-tempo album tracks, "Send Me No Wine," sung by Lodge, and "To Share Our Love," with Pinder on lead vocal.

On February 21, the Moodies played at Sheffield University. One day later, they appeared at Brunel University, in Uxbridge. On February 25, they were back at Sheffield University, this time sharing the bill with the Hollies. On March 27, they appeared at the London College Student Union. One day later, it was Common Ball, Queen Elizabeth College, Kensington, London, sharing the bill with Pink Floyd and the Settlers.

On March 1, the Moody Blues were in Manchester at that city's Tech College. On March 7, they were in Amsterdam, Holland, sharing a bill with Gladys Knight & the Pips for the Grand Gala du Disque. The Moodies continued to be quite the draw at colleges. In March alone, shows are reported to have taken place at Loughborough

University, Leicester (15); Aston University in Birmingham (22), and Seymour Hall Student's Union, in London (on March 28).

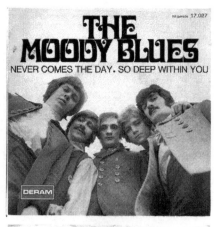

U.K. Single release:
"Never Comes the Day"
b/w "So Deep Within You"
Deram DM 247; April 2, 1969

U.S. single release:
"Never Comes the Day"
b/w ""So Deep Within You"
Deram 45-85044; Late-April 1969

An advanced taste – and tease – of the new album was issued 20 days before the LP's release in the U.K.

The singles to beat in Britain, from No. 1 to 5: "I Heard It Through the Grapevine" by Marvin Gaye; "Boom Bang-A-Band" by Lulu; "Israelites" by Desmond Dekker & the Aces; "Gentle On My Mind" by, no, not Glen Campbell, as Americans would hear it, but Dean Martin; and "Sorry Suzanne" by the Hollies.

"Never Comes the Day" came out three weeks later in the U.S.

The top singles to beat there, from 1 to 5: "Dizzy" by Tommy Roe; "Aquarius/Let the Sunshine In" by the Fifth Dimension; "Time of the Season" by the Zombies; "You've Made Me So Very Happy" by Blood, Sweat and Tears; and "Galveston" by Glen Campbell. Also high in the charts: "Only the Strong Survive" by Jerry Butler; "Traces" by Classic IV; "Proud Mary" by Creedence Clearwater Revival; "Rock Me" by Steppenwolf; "It's Your Thing" by the Isley Brothers; "Build Me Up Buttercup" by the Foundations; and "Hair" by the Cowsills. It was a great time to be listening to Top 40 in the U.S.

On April 30, "Never Comes the Day" made *Variety*'s "Top Singles of the Week" list, one of 15 out of over 100 single releases that week. The plug:

The Moody Blues' "Never Comes

the Day" is a slowly building entry with a husky vocal sound that could command chart status. "So Deep Within You" is a smooth pop ballad with lilting flute and a classical turn via kettle drums.

On May 3, *Billboard* magazine selected the new disc for its "Special Merit Spotlight," meaning the trade was not predicting it to be a radio hit, but nonetheless recommending the top-side song. The reviewer said, "Group offers a compelling rocker from their forthcoming LP with a production that builds to the end."

Also on May 3, rival trade magazine *Cashbox* selected the song as one of a handful of the trade's "Picks of the Week."

Starting in a gentle folk vein, the new Moody Blues' side opens with less than the act's usual impact, but the single grows almost immediately to become a hypnotic outing. This sampling from the upcoming LP continues the evolution that the Moody Blues have undergone in their recent album and singles product. Instant FM success should prompt sizable AM action.

"Never Comes the Day" is a good song, both pretty and, as it builds, invigorating and catchy. It didn't seem a bad choice for a single, although the more obvious one was "Lovely to See You." But "Never Comes the Day" was selected. And then promptly failed to hit as a single. It didn't chart in the U.K. ... and didn't do much better in the U.S., where it barely scraped into the lower rungs of the Top 100. *Billboard* gave "Never Comes the Day" its worst showing, at No. 91 in the first week of April 1969, and kept it on the chart for a mere four weeks. *Cashbox* saw things about the same, with a four-week chart run and a peak position of No. 91. *Record World* was the most generous, but only slightly, raising the single to No. 89.

251

On the day the "Never Comes the Day" single was issued – April 2 – the Moodies recorded "Lovely to See You" and "So Deep Within You" for the BBC radio program, *The Tony Brandon Show* (with one song airing on April 14, the second on April 18).

All of this was in advance to the release of the album, which came on the 18th.

On April 26, the Moodies performed at the Mothers Club in Birmingham. The following day, they were part of a package bill for a one-off concert, "In Aid of Shelter." They played for an hour, starting at 3 p.m., with songs including "Never Comes the Day," "Tuesday Afternoon," "The Sunset," "Dr. Livingstone, I Presume," "Are You Sitting Comfortably?", "Nights in White Satin," "Ride My See-Saw," "The Dream" (and, in all likelihood, it led into "Have You Heard" and "The Voyage").

U.K. album release:
Deram SML 1035, April 25, 1969

U.S. album release:
Deram DES 18025 (stereo); Late April/Early May 1969

At the top of the top of *Billboard*'s album chart the week *On the Threshold of a Dream* was released were, counting down from No 1: the Original Cast album from *Hair*; *Blood Sweat & Tears*, by the band of the same name (containing "Spinnin' Wheel," "You've Made Me So Very Happy," "And When I Die," and "God Bless the Child"); *Galveston* by Glen Campbell; Donovan's *Greatest Hits*; *Cloud Nine* by the Temptations; *Help Yourself* by Tom Jones; *Wichita Lineman* by Glen Campbell, *In-A-Gadda-Da-Vida* by Iron Butterfly; and *Bayou Country* from Creedence Clearwater Revival. Still doing fine, the Fab Four's former chart-toppers *The Beatles* ("the White Album") and the *Yellow Submarine* soundtrack.

Days after the release of *On the Threshold of a Dream*, in the May 3rd edition of *New Musical Express*, Richard Green wrote:

> From conception to completion, *On the Threshold of a Dream* took just three weeks to become reality. From release to entry in the *NME* chart took the same album just three days!

> An amazing success for the Moody Blues, whose singles have become virtually accustomed to withering and dying. As an album group, they stand head and shoulders above most others.

Regarding a recent concert given by the Moodies, Green added:

> The full effectiveness of Mike Pinder's Mellotron was demonstrated at the Moodies' Sadler's Wells Theatre concert on Sunday. A whole range of instruments seemed to be hidden behind a curtain – in fact their sound was being reproduced by the one instrument.

Opening with a beauty, "Ride My See-Saw," the group played 12 numbers in their hour-long set, including "Are You Sitting Comfortably," "The Poem" [sic, "The Dream"] and "Have You Heard," from the new album. The audience's response was, to put it mildly, very appreciative. ...

Numbers like "Dr. Livingstone" (described by Ray as a world-wide "Games People Play"), "Never Comes the Day," with its superb cross harmonies and vocals, their recent American hit "Tuesday Afternoon," and Mike's "Sunset," were exceptional. A first-class show, me boys.

On May 10, in *Melody Maker*, Derek Boltwood wrote:

Always on the threshold, for though the dream is good, the dream that follows is always better. *Days of Future Passed* was a dream of an album. *In Search of the Lost Chord* even better. *On the Threshold of a Dream*, the third volume in the Moody Blues musical autobiography, is so much more. Question: Can you imagine in years to come how good will be that final volume?

From the May 13 edition of American music newspaper *World Countdown:*

The Moody Blues have done it again with their fourth hit in a row, "Never Comes the Day" (the former three being "Nights in White Satin," "Tuesday Afternoon" and "Ride My See-Saw"). Also they have their third album out on the market on the Deram Label, titled, *On the Threshold of a Dream*, and it is equally as fantastic as the two previous ones. ...

"They never come back" is an old show business saying that is generally true. However, there are a handful of artists whose talents and staying power is such that they are not dependent on hit records and sensational news-making stunts. Such a group is the Moody Blues. At the beginning of 1965, they had a world-wide hit with "Go Now!" Suddenly the Moody Blues were the most wanted name in pop. Then, for some unknown reason, their discs became less successful and the group seemed to melt away into oblivion.

The months passed and various fads with them. Then, in the autumn of '67, the Moodies went into the recording studios and emerged with an album called *Days of Future Passed* that has been acclaimed by the experts as a fusion of pop and classical music. A six-and-a-half minute extraction from the LP was issued as a single. It was "Nights in White Satin," and put the Moodies back where they belong, high in the charts. The Moodies have had their share of the doldrums. They are now set to join the Beatles as one of the trendsetting progress chasers of pop. ...

Variety filed its review on May 14:

After a ponderously "significant" intro, this album settles into a more comfortable and conventional groove, for most of the way. This British group delivers some solid ballads with a highly attractive sound. Standout items are "Never Comes the Day," "Lovely to See You," "To Share Our Love," "So Deep Within You," and "Are You Sitting Comfortably?"

On May 17, Richard Green interviewed Justin Hayward for *New Musical Express*. In their discussion, Green brought up how the audiences had changed at Moody Blues concerts. It was true that the screaming young female fans had been replaced with older teenagers, young adults, and college students. As for those in the audience who were still at the pop-star-groupie age, even they appeared more reserved, listening to the music quietly, seemingly in deep contemplation. Green noted that while many top groups preferred to have people pay attention to their music, Hayward had a different reaction to the lack of screaming. He admitted: "Yeah, I miss it, really. We haven't had screams for two years. People do take us too seriously. They try to read meaning into our songs that aren't there.

"We write songs that we like and they don't have to have a message, but people think they do. We often get asked what they mean and we have to try and think of something to please people." (JH-NME69)

Billboard magazine ran its review of *Threshold* on May 24:

> The Moody Blues are off on more of their pop-orchestral excursions through the rock universe with their unique tapestry of sound and suggestion. Scoring heavily on the charts with their previous blends of music and mysticism, the British group should groove again with a more rock-oriented weave that features a new single, "Never Comes the Day," plus FM sure shots like "So Deep Within You," and more.

"Lovely to See You" was becoming a radio favorite, receiving more airplay than the chosen single. This, despite its placement on the LP, required a bit of work for radio programmers to cue up the cut, or to dub it over to a tape cartridge.
Sometimes it was played with the "In the Beginning" introduction, sometimes not, usually depending whether or not the station was AM or FM. Finally, with radio programmers asking for the song without the crossfading deterrent of the LP version, London issued a promotional 45 coupling "Lovely to See You" with Ray Thomas's "Lazy Day." As a result, both songs, but especially "Lovely to See You," gained substantial AM airplay.

From the U.S. syndicated newspaper column, "The Underground Sound," on June 1, Scott G. Campbell wrote:

> A listing of the few truly consistently creative record acts in the field today would have to include Britain's Moody Blues in the prominent spot. They are one of an even more exclusive class whose music, in addition to being constantly changing and

exploring new dimensions, also possesses a certain indefinable quality all its own.

The Moodies, as you may remember, launched their recording career four or five years ago with a nice Top 40 song called "Go Now," which still keeps popping up on the radio with some regularity as a favorite requested golden oldie. But it was not until the somewhat belated success of the *Days of Future Passed* album, however, that the quintet came to be especially well-known and loved by progressive rock enthusiasts. The LP, which contained such favorites as "Tuesday Afternoon" and the great "Nights in White Satin," also featured the talents of the London Festival Orchestra, and added what amounted to a new dimension to pop music. …

Now the group has presented us with a third package, entitled *On the Threshold of a Dream*. … While this venture is more closely related musically to *In Search of the Lost Chord* than *Days of Future Passed*, it is still quite a bit different from anything the group has done before.

What the Moody Blues does on this album, as in the past, is to combine music and mysticism. An example of this is the opening cut, "In the Beginning," which is a confrontation between man and computer (the latter is labeled "Establishment"). "Dear Diary" is another song which follows the same theme of individuals vs. the Establishment.

The group's new single, "Never Comes the Day," is a highlight of the album, which incidentally was produced by Tony Clarke. While nearly all 13 original cuts on this LP are solid and smooth, and meaningful as far as lyric content is concerned (a 12-page booklet is included for lyrics), two more highlights are "So Deep Within You" and "Have You Heard (Parts One and Two)."

On June 5, another syndicated newspaper music columnist, Wayne Harada, was equally enthusiastic:

The Moody Blues, a British quintet, continues to show rare form with each album release. The latest, *On the Threshold of a Dream* (Deram DES 18025), advances the group into the sea of artistic success.

With inventive care and a brooding, sensitive feel for the currents of today's scene, the group delves into a subtle series of mind-blowing experiences, minus hard rock. Their moving blues form is epitomized in "Never Comes the Day," the cream of this crop. There are several other rock ballads grooved in the blues vein – earthly, rich, sensuous. Witness "Lazy Day," "Have You Heard," "Lovely to See You," [and] "So Deep Within You." …

On June 7, and perhaps dreading the thought of another American tour, Ray Thomas married 21-year-old Gillian Jary. He was the second Moody, following Graeme Edge, to tie the knot.

A nice present to the newlyweds was the *Billboard* LP chart for the week ending June 7, 1969. *On the Threshold of a Dream* jumped into the Top 100 from its debut position of 132 a week earlier, now all the way up to No. 38, "with a bullet." In the U.K., *Threshold* topped the album chart, becoming the Moodies' first No. 1 album.

Justin Hayward: "I think that album overall was the one where Decca finally believed, and we believed as well, that we were a band who could really have some longevity. The album made No. 1 in the U.K., which was a huge moment for us; really important." (JH-RS13)

Pete Johnson, who worked hard searching for faults when reviewing *In Search of the Lost Chord* for *The Los Angeles Times* a few months earlier, was singing the

Disc and Music Echo—June 14, 1969

Above: From *Disc and Music Echo*, June 14, 1969: "… Moody Blue Ray Thomas took the great step over the threshold on Saturday when he married delightful 21-year-old Gillian Jary at London's Caxton Hall. Funny, though, the only Moody missing is drummer Graeme Edge – who's also the only other married member! …"
(Lower imagephoto source: Pinterest.com)

same tune – acknowledging the band's quality, and talent for melody, but nonetheless hell-bent on finding a flaw. His review of the new album in the June 8 edition of the newspaper read in part:

> … Like its predecessors, it contains a number of strongly melodic compositions, beautifully arranged and performed. Also like its predecessors, it is a bit pretentious, but it is worth putting up with some overblown nonsense to hear songs such as "Never Comes the Day," "Lovely to See You," "Dear Diary," and "Have You Heard?"
>
> Their sound could be described as a symphonic variety of rock, though they are no longer working with a full symphony orchestra.

For its third week in the U.S. *Billboard* chart, *Threshold* moved up one position, to No. 37.

From June 15, Robb Baker of the *Chicago Tribune*, a great supporter of the Moodies Mark 2, up to now, reviewed the new album:

> *On the Threshold of a Dream* is a disappointment mainly because it measures up so poorly to the group's recent *In Search of the Lost Chord*, which toyed with greatness.
>
> There's only one really good song this time – Justin Hayward's "Never Comes the Day," which is strong both musically and lyrically (featuring an unusual interplay between strings and harmonica at one point). But most of the lyrics are somewhere between pedestrian and pedantic, and the melodic (at times almost symphonic) quality that marked the group's previous two albums is almost wholly lacking (except in Mike Pinder's "The Voyage," which is over too soon).

But if there was only one good song – Hayward's "Never Comes the Day" – then why was Pinder's "The Voyage" over too soon?

Baker's opinions couldn't stop the forward momentum of the album in the charts. On June 21, *Threshold* jumped from No. 37 to 28 in *Billboard*, where it would stay for two weeks, before continuing its climb. On July 5, it rose to No. 22, then up to 21, then, on July 26, peaked at No. 20. Not as high as one might think, especially since it topped the charts in Britain, but this was merely the ninth week … out of a stunning 135-week chart run in the States. The album would be certified Gold in America in October.

Meanwhile, the Moodies were supposed to appear at the Woodstock Music & Art Fair spanning August 15-18, and their name was used to sell tickets. The contract between Zell Enterprises, International, Inc./Woodstock Ventures and Umbrella Management Ltd, the latter representing the Moodies, had been signed by the promoters on June 25, with the Moodies given a $2,500 retainer (half their performance fee) to deliver "One show approximately 45 minutes between the hours of 9:00 PM and 11:00 PM" on August 17. The contract was signed and sent to Umbrella Management with the retainer check. The Moodies were to appear on the third and final day of the festival. They never made it, accepted an offer to perform in Paris instead.

The Moodies did take part in England's version of Woodstock – the 1969 Isle of Wight Festival. The biggest name associated with the program was Bob Dylan, followed by the Moodies and the Who. Also there: the Band, Joe Cocker, Free, Richie Havens, and the Nice, among others. Attendance was estimated at around 170,000. This

257

event was but a warm-up for the 1970 Isle of Wight Festival, at which the Moodies would be one of the headliners, and which would exceed the attendance of Woodstock.

John Lodge wrote in the September 20, 1969 edition of *New Musical Express*:

> We enjoy 'live' shows because audiences now are 'giving' so much, almost marking the end of the "doer" and "receiver." This was so noticeable at the Isle of Wright festival. People are identifying themselves so much with the music they have become part of. …

> We are at the moment preparing for a new coast-to-coast U.S. tour in November and a British tour in December. (JL-NME69)

Shortly after missing Woodstock, the Moodies were seen in America by an audience even bigger than the 400,000 people who attended the historic festival. On September 5, they appeared on U.S. TV with an audience of several million, performing on the ABC-TV summer replacement series *The John Davidson Show*. The band played "Send Me No Wine" and "Never Comes the Day."

From the fall of 1969, Chris Hodenfield wrote in *Go* magazine:

> … Nobody in the world uses a Mellotron like the Moody Blues, probably because no one can handle it. When you hear these long sweeping notes coming from the band, sounding something like Spector-shattered orchestra, from a seemingly empty stage, it's the Mellotron. It works on the principle of, say, a bank of tape recorders. Pinder has recorded all kinds of sounds on the tapes, such as an orchestra hitting a C-note, and when he presses the key on the keyboard, he gets roughly the same sound, pumped out through his amplifiers. And the sounds he has recorded get pretty far out.

> As can be expected, this machine runs on hair-line tolerances and it breaks down frequently. (Another reason nobody uses one on the road.) At the Fillmore concert last year, the audience got a free 45-minute concert on how to fix the Mellotron. … Pinder, however, used to work for the factory, and is perfecting it.

New reviews were still coming in through the end of the year. From November 1969, "P.R." of *Stereo Review* wrote:

> Hey, are you ready for this? A rock group that sounds sophisticated? Not commercial, *sophisticated*. By that I mean they combine intelligence, poise, and an electric ease. That may not mean sophisticated to you but it does to me. … The Moody Blues members wrote all the songs heard here, and the winner by an arm's length is Mike Pinder, who contributes three excellent songs: "So Deep Within You," "The Voyage" and "Have You Heard?" They are beautifully performed by this group and seem to suit its style (a rock, gentle-blues, faintly jazz-inflected one) much more than some of the other efforts.

The album is lavishly packaged, with an insert that gives all the lyrics, unfortunately in an almost unreadable type face. The album is superbly produced by Tony Clarke. Not for hardcore rocknicks, but, for those who enjoy something a little different, this is an album worth listening to.

On November 8, syndicated music columnist John Sunier took a look at both *In Search of the Lost Chord* and *On the Threshold of a Dream*:

> While the current fashion in rock demands a return to the simple, often sparse instrumental sound with little amplification and orchestral backing, the Moody Blues buck the trend with two excellent albums abounding in very artistic employment of the "big sound." Their producer refers to them as "the smallest symphony orchestra in the world."
>
> The British quintet has to have a great deal of versatility to bring off their enveloping sound-poems; for example Justin Hayward is heard on guitars (12-string, acoustic, electric, and bass), sitar, tablas, piano, harpsichord, Mellotron, and percussion, besides his vocal work.
>
> The *Threshold of a Dream* album is the masterpiece of the two – a complete and beautifully-paced journey into inner thought. The truly fine poetry of the lyrics is printed on the record sleeve. It's very difficult to mention specific tracks since both albums are such totalities in themselves. Bravo producer Tony Clarke and the Moody Blues for some rock creations in the best of taste and full of sensitivity!

To promote *On the Threshold of a Dream* in America, the Moodies undertook a 30-day tour of the U.S. throughout November 1969. This also gave an advanced plug for *To Our Children's Children's Children*, already recorded and schedule for release at the end of the month. Their first planned concert was at the Los Angeles Forum, on a double bill with Jefferson Airplane.

For a syndicated article, Kathy Orloff, of the *Chicago Sun-Times*, wrote:

> At a time when rock was boasting of its new direction and intelligent motivations, and all we had for proof was *Sgt. Pepper* and [Chad & Jeremy's 1967 album] *Of Cabbages and Kings*, along came the Moody Blues and *Days of Future Passed*.
>
> The album, which nestled quietly among the private delights of those with enough sense and sensitivity to listen, became popular with the chart rise of two tracks: "Nights in White Satin" and "Forever Afternoon (Tuesday?)." Even with the incredible beautiful melodies and thoughtful lyrics, the songs were and are only part of the odyssey, a journey through time and the times,

presented by one of England's most underrated and super-talented groups. …

The second album, *In Search of the Lost Chord*, took them further along, as did the third, *On the Threshold of a Dream*. The dream will be fulfilled with *For My Children's Children's Children* [sic], which will be the last in the four-part series and will be the first released on the group's own label, Threshold Records. Like four-part harmony, the albums are at once successive and simultaneous in their expression. In the future, their music will evolve, new directions will be explored, and possibly they will go back a little to those enigmatic "roots" musicians search for today.

Orloff interviewed Mike Pinder and Graeme Edge, who were in America making arrangements for the upcoming tour. She shared:

[T]heir remarks were some of the most positive, thought provoking and sensitive of any I have heard from musicians this year.

Acutely aware of the proliferating absurdity of the "super-hip" subculture, which is rapidly becoming more absurd than the establishment it so vehemently battles, they reflected on a new positivism that will hopefully infuse some objectivity and joy into music and life in general. Pinder and Edge rejected the negativism and destructive themes of much of the music of the '60s, saying that people are slowly coming to realize that there has been a strong overreaction against traditional values and as feelings and standards are brought more into focus there will be a huge coming together of groups which have never before understood each other.

The thought in itself is a positive one, much better than predicting universal doom through dry rot as so many musical "prophets" have done; better and most likely more musically pleasing and creative.

Ironically, the Moodies will appear in concert in Los Angeles sharing the bill with Jefferson Airplane, a group that has had the reputation of being rather disruptive. …

The concert, scheduled for October 31 at "the fabulous" Forum, had to go on without the Moody Blues, who were detained getting into the country due to "immigration difficulties."

Reportedly, the band gave their first U.S. show for 1969 in San Diego, California, on

THE MOODY BLUES

(Photo source: 1969 tour booklet)

November 1, in the Golden Gym at California Western College. After this, they hightailed it up to Los Angeles (about a three-hour drive back then) for a show on November 2 in Elysian Park with the band they had stood up days earlier. The event was called "Love In," and the Moodies shared the bill with Jefferson Airplane, Hot Tuna, and Wolf Gang.

Hayward, recalling the event, told Mary Campbell of the Associated Press, "Before we became concerned with managers and agents, we would take everything that came our way…. [Grace Slick] said, 'We've got this truck where you can let the side down and you can put your equipment on it, and you can turn up in a field and play. We announce at a concert [that] in three days time we're going to turn up in a park and play. Why don't you come with us and do it?'" (JH-LPT91)

John Lodge added, "We were with them at Elysian Park in Los Angeles, with 20,000 people." (JL-IPT91)

This was 5,000 more than would have seen them a few days earlier at the Forum.

The set list for these engagements was: ""Gypsy," "Dr. Livingstone, I Presume," "Never Comes the Day," "Tuesday Afternoon," "The Sunset," "Are you Sitting Comfortably?", "The Dream," blended into "Have You Heard, Part 1," "The Voyage," and then "Have You Heard, Part 2," followed by "Legend of a Mind," "Nights in White Satin," and "Ride My See-Saw."

On November 6, the Moodies were seen coast to coast for the second of three appearances with their old friend Tom Jones, on *This Is Tom Jones*, over the ABC-TV network. They performed "Are You Sitting Comfortably?" from their soon-to-be-released new album. Also on the show were actress/singer Connie Stevens, singer Matt Monro, and comedian Shecky Greene.

From L.A., they travelled north to Washington State, giving a concert on Thursday, November 7, at Gonzaga University, in Spokane. On Friday, Nov. 8, they appeared at the PNE Agrodome in Vancouver, British Columbia, Canada, sharing the bill with Canned Heat. On Saturday, November 10, the band was back in Washington State performing in Seattle's Center Arena. Janine Gressel attended, and wrote in the *Seattle Times*:

> The Moody Blues overwhelmed a capacity crowd at the Arena Saturday night. The British quintet overcame some sound equipment problems and presented a concert that was brilliant and satisfying.

The band often came closer to classical than rock in its musical form. The Moody Blues songs were carefully constructed compositions that seldom followed a simple verse-chorus-verse style. The music was complex and explored a wide range of instrumental sounds.

Moody Blues albums have been formed like suites, where all songs, poems and instrumental works contributed to a single theme. For this reason, there was speculation on how the group would come across in a "rock-show" situation. The performance was great. The band lifted songs from their albums, but managed to do so without losing the atmosphere of each work. This was mainly due to the quintet's exceptional instrumental ability. Even songs from the album, *Days of Future Passed*, which the Moody Blues recorded with the London Festival Orchestra, sounded nearly as good live with five musicians as they had on the album with the entire orchestra.

A huge slice of dynamic instrumental work was due to Mike Pinder. The organ Pinder played ranged in sound from church organ to violins to a trumpet. The artificial "instruments" were not used in a gimmicky way, but were simply in the background to give the subtle aural illusion of a fuller, more varied sound.

The Moody Blues also were excellent vocally, although at times the balance between vocals and instruments was not too good. They used four-part harmonies on most songs (apparently only Graeme Edge, drummer, doesn't sing) and Pinder, Ray Thomas and Justin Hayward all took turns as lead singer.

Pinder and Hayward were particularly outstanding vocalists. Pinder's singing was deep and rich. He also recited Graeme Edge's poetry, both on the albums and at the concert. His speaking voice sounded much like Richard Burton's.

Hayward's voice is in a slightly higher range and has an extremely emotional quality to it that makes his vocal interpretations highly dramatic.

With Johnny Ray, and the singer's "Cry," as his earliest vocal influence, how could Hayward miss?

From there, it is believed the Moodies gave concerts in Utah and Kansas (unconfirmed) before playing the Houston Music Theatre, Texas, on November 13, with opening act Bodine. Then, back to California to take the stage in the Swing Auditorium, San Bernardino, on November 14. Continuing north, they appeared in Sacramento on Nov. 15, for Cal Expo, sharing the bill with Country Joe & the Fish.

Having learned from the last tour of America not to drive across country, the group took to the air for Detroit, Michigan, where they gave concerts at the Grande-Riviera Theatre on November 18 and 19. Opening for the Moodies was Humble Pie, featuring a young Peter Frampton. On the 21st, the Moodies played at Maritime College in the Bronx, New York, then, for the next day, they performed two shows at Stony Brook University, N.Y.

On November 27, they teamed again with Humble Pie for two separate shows at the Fountain Street Church in Grand Rapids, Michigan. On November 28, they were back in New York State, again with Humble Pie, at the Kleinhans Music Hall, in Buffalo. Turning north again, both the Moodies and Humble Pie crossed into Canada to play the Massey Hall in Toronto, on November 29. The two groups then returned to America and the state of Illinois, for a concert in the Chicago Auditorium.

Covering this final show of the tour, Linda Winer wrote in the *Chicago Tribune*:

> More vibrations from Britain. First the reverberation of bare feet crossing Abbey Road, then the sounds of the Stones rolling across the country, and last night the music of the Moody Blues, who returned to Chicago for a concert at the Auditorium before heading home.
>
> Similarities stop after accent. The Moody Blues, five musicians known best for their single, "Tuesday Afternoon," written by lead guitarist Justin Hayward, suggest none of the suggestiveness of the Stones, nor do the M.B.'s songs require Beatlian analysis. Mostly the Blues play straightforward, strongly rhythmic rock, and sing optimistic lyric pastoralism. …
>
> Most of their songs came from the three past albums, plus a new one not yet released here. Messages are positive: "love of love and love of life," "we're all looking for someone…," "take a little bit less from everyone today," and voices, sweet and harmonious, if not loud enough to stand up to the electronics. The words go to your mind, while the beat works on your gut; sometimes unfortunately they cancel each other out. …

From December 13, George Knemeyer wrote in *Billboard* magazine:

> Going to a concert by the Moody Blues can be a deceiving experience. If one just listens to the music, and doesn't watch it being played, he would claim that the five-man British rock group was being backed by a symphony orchestra. Actually the embellished sound of strings is produced by Mike Pinder playing an instrument known as the Mellotron.

Pinder told Knemeyer, "The music we recorded in early 1968 [sic] on our *Days of Future Passed* London Records' album had the backing of the London Symphony Orchestra. In order for us to recreate or even come close to the original sound, we have to use an instrument such as the Mellotron. In our past two albums and our upcoming one we have used many different instruments. The Mellotron helps recreate those sounds since some of the instruments are too bulky to carry around on a tour." (MP-BB69)

Knemeyer continued:

Ray Thomas is the only other member of the Moody Blues that uses an instrument strange to rock music in live performances. He uses a flute, but not in the way the instrument has been used in the past.

Thomas said, "On most rock records made, a flute is used only as background. I try to bring the flute to an 'up front' position in the group. It's more than a 'fill in' instrument; it's part of the total sound we try to create." (RT-BB69)

It was while touring the States that they noticed a profound change in the way their fans were reacting to the group.

Mike Pinder told Keith Altham of Britain's *Rave* magazine, "In America we were amazed to find that some people hailed us as gurus and the acid freaks were convinced *Days of Future Passed* was some kind of gigantic trip!" (MP-R70)

Justin Hayward told Royston Eldridge of England's *Melody Maker* magazine, "One of the problems we found in the States, not here, was that people were leaving everything to follow us. They thought we were spirits on some sort of different plane. They were reading too much into the music. They're looking for a leader.

"There's no real problem here [in England] with the Establishment, but over there the generation gap is so wide. They have been forced to think a lot more through the music, but they are taking it to an extreme." (JH-MM70)

Ray Thomas, recalling one of the concerts in America from this time, told interviewer Rob Hughes, "This guy turns up, built like a brick shit-house. He gets down on his knees in front of me. We'd just finished a gig, so I've got a Scotch and Coke in one hand and a cigarette in the other. He says: 'I want you to do the laying on of hands.' Someone had told him that after one of us had done this he was going to Nirvana and Krishna would take over his body. That's why he'd been preparing himself as he had done. It must've taken years to get into that shape. This guy had clearly been crazy for a long time!"

Thomas told Hughes about an even more disturbing fan encounter, which happened soon after the Moodies' return to England at the beginning of December, 1969. *To Our Children's Children's Children* had just been released. Thomas was coming home to his new wife, but somebody else was there. "One woman from St. Louis broke into my house and lived in my garden for about three weeks, covered in shit and crazy as a box of bloody frogs. She came in and lay with the sign of a cross on her face, in floods of tears, like a nun. She expected me to screw her and said the offspring was going to be the Second Coming. In the end we had to have her deported. Then she'd write reams of letters to me, saying things like, 'The Easter eggs are under the sea! The Easter eggs are under the sea!' I had a death threat from her – she even told me what type of bullet she was going to use. She was going to shoot me, then I'd resurrect myself, just so she could prove who the hell I was. It really frightened the shit out of me." (RT-CRB14)

12

Establishing Threshold Records

Kings of their own castle.
(Photo source: 1968 Coca-Cola print ad)

Mike Pinder: "I can remember talking to Mo Ostin [President of Warner Bros. Records] sometime in the 1960s, and thinking, 'God, if we could go to Warner, what they would give us.' By that I mean that the support and creative control. We might have left Decca, except that the contracts that we'd signed left us at their mercy. We couldn't get out... so we formed Threshold instead, to give us some measure of control." (MP-GM94)

Of course, the Moodies already had *carte blanche* in the studio when recording, but they were equally concerned about escalating resistance from Decca concerning other production aspects such as the extravagant artwork for the album covers and sleeves. Those gatefold jackets were significantly more time-consuming and expensive to design and print than standard LPs. Further, the band chafed under the realization that company executives exerted veto power on what was released, including what songs would be promoted as singles.

Justin Hayward: "We wanted control over the way that our albums were released, and, basically, Threshold gave us that – we could design the jackets and anything that went with them, and devote a certain budget around [them] which we could work. If we wanted something printed a certain way, it could be done. Of course, all of this cost us, and we were paying for Threshold and anything extra that was done with our records, but we had the control." (JH-GM94)

Threshold was not the first name considered, nor was it known at first if Decca, in the U.K., and London Records, in America, would release albums by other groups on the Moodies' new label.

From the May 3, 1969 issue of *Billboard*:

> Decca group the Moody Blues is seeking an American record company to handle their new record label, Circle, which will feature artists produced by the group in association with their producer Tony Clark [sic]. This follows failure to reach agreement on terms with British Decca with whom the Moody Blues have a contract for their own recordings until January 1972.
>
> Graeme Edge, drummer with the group, told *Billboard*: "We had hoped to place the label with a British company, but now it looks as though we shall have to accept an American offer."
>
> So far the Moody Blues have signed no talent to the new label but a British group, King Crimson, is expected to be the first to be released on Circle....

And King Crimson, as we would soon learn, often emulated the sound of the Moody Blues.

`On May 10, in *Melody Maker*, Derek Boltwood wrote:

> In the first week of release of [*On the Threshold of a*] *Dream*, while it sold 35,000 copies, already the Moodies have started work on their next album. Progression always – musical; personal.

Regarding *Dream*, Justin Hayward told Boltwood, "This album was finished months ago, but it took a long time to arrange getting the cover we wanted, and so it's only just been released.... We've found a theme for our next album now, and so we'll be starting work on that shortly.

"In [the] future we'll be releasing two sorts of albums – 'A' stream and 'B' stream. 'A' stream will be the group albums, like our last three – featuring the group as a whole with a different musical theme for each release. 'B' stream records will be a completely different sort of thing – the albums will feature what we would like to record, but in a different direction to 'A' stream; the sort of things that we couldn't put on the general Moody Blues albums. For example, Ray and I would like to do a complete album of his poetry. They'll still be Moody Blues' albums, but not the sort of thing that's expected from the group.... So I think it's sensible to separate our releases into two distinctly different sorts.

"At the moment, though, we're involved in the business of setting up our own management and production company – and we'll have our own record label as well. Obviously we won't be on our own record label as we have a world-wide recording contract with Decca – but I think we've learnt enough to pass on some of our experiences to the new company. For example, it's been important to us to have a lot of studio time – and so we won't try to limit the groups who record for us.

"The thing is that we've done a lot of talking about the incredible things we intend to do with our new company, and so now it's important that we get down and do them. But the fact that we haven't kept our intentions quiet is good, because it more or less forces us into doing everything we said we would. We're running around a lot, seeing solicitors and that sort of thing – some of it is quite enjoyable. But we have board meetings sometimes, and I tend to fall asleep halfway through them. I'm looking forward to the time when we get everything going through.

"I think a lot of our success is due to the fact that we work well together as a group of people…. The group works because there's a harmony between us – a unity, and we tend to progress because we stimulate one another by developing our ideas together." (JH-MM69)

Shortly after the formation of Threshold Records, Graeme Edge told *Hit Parader*: "The main reason we wanted to have a label was to get rid of the bloodsuckers in the business, you see. I'm not sure what the scene is [in America], but in London if you want to get any kind of recognition, you need to get yourself a manager who wants something like 20%, 25%, and then an agent, who wants 10%, 15%, and then a press man/promotion man who wants 2.7% of all the records. And you end up doing free concerts everywhere [because the money goes to the manager, the agent, and the press man]…. We want to use the success of the Moody Blues to get the label off the ground. And we have a high standard of quality of acts, so the label comes to stand for something, so that eventually the situation comes to be that, if we find an act that we think [has] something to say, people need to listen to them. We can release them on the label, and they won't have all these commercial hang-ups – they won't need these people, because the label would be sufficiently known for them to be able to sell enough to make a living, by virtue just of the fact that it's on a particular label that it is on. So we can wipe out all these horrible people who corrupt the industry that keeps bringing up the dreadful commercial junk and push artists sometimes down the wrong road, and trap them in the commercial aspects of the business. [It] does terrible numbers on your mind." (GE-HPY70)

If there was any question that the Moodies had broken with their manager, Derek McCormick, the latest remarks from Edge settled it.

Mike Pinder said, "The music business shouldn't be made purely for commercial end. It should be for art's sake. And we're hoping to preserve a little bit of artistic integrity, for most of it's gone down the drain." (MP-HPY70)

The Moodies were also clearly following in the footsteps of the Beatles, who had started their own record label – Apple – one year earlier, for art's sake. With Apple, the Beatles would no longer be at the mercy of Capitol Records in the States, where the label shuffled Beatles songs to create "new" albums and released album tracks as singles at their whim. But the Beatles were not businessmen. In time, Apple would become an unsupervised money pit, and the strain of running such a venture would contribute to the breakup of the band. If the Moodies had known this, they might have thought twice about starting Threshold.

The Beatles in 1968, setting up their Apple Corps. Left to right: John Lennon, Peter Brown, Paul McCartney, Derek Taylor (facing away), and Neil Aspinall ... and the headless suits. (Photo source: Newsweek)

In the spring and early summer of 1969, however, and without the advice of a business manager, they were as recklessly ambitious and blissfully ignorant as their friends and role models, the Beatles.

Pinder said, "We have played the music we liked to the successful tune of ten million dollars' worth of records sold. We want to extend that same musical freedom to other artists and groups that we enjoy. If a group or a solo artist is given complete freedom within the framework of a record company, it follows that they will put more enthusiasm and intent into their work so that the public get the best." (MP-R70)

Justin Hayward told *Melody Maker* magazine at this time: "Now that we've got our own freedom, we can do all the things that we want to do. Graeme wants to do a total concept epic type of album, and Ray and I are doing an album together, which will be mainly acoustic material. It's getting away from the Mellotron sound and we've been working on it for about 18 months.

"Mike's working on his own thing; he's into electronic sound, particularly sound and vision. He's got a few revolutionary ideas which even I don't really understand." (JH-MM70)

With these concepts, the Moodies were again following the Beatles' lead. George Harrison had issued a pair of side projects, the soundtrack LP *Wonderwall Music* and the experimental (some said annoying) *Electronic Sounds* album; John and Yoko were in the process of issuing a trilogy of *avant-garde* records, such as *Two Virgins* and the *Wedding Album*; Paul McCartney had written and produced songs for his discoveries, Mary Hopkins and Badfinger; and Ringo Starr was making an album of pop standards, called *Sentimental Journey*, featuring renditions of the title track and other songs of a bygone era, such as "Bye Bye Blackbird."

As talented and ambitious as the Moodies were, and as popular as they were becoming, they were not the Beatles. But, with Derek McCormick suddenly out of the picture, who was going to remind them of this fact?

Rationalizing the side projects, Graeme Edge told *Melody Maker*, "A lot of the things I write don't fit in with the Moody Blues; sometimes I get a little too bitter and cynical, which doesn't suit the group. Mike gets a little occult and he wouldn't want to do that with the group, either. So, we're doing an electronic album together, while Justin and Ray are working on what we call 'the acoustic album.'

(Photo source: MoodyBluesAttitude.com)

"As the Moody Blues, it's hard to change too quickly; people expect a certain something from you, so you have to ease them to what you're doing. It's a gradual weaning. People will know that these two albums are not the Moody Blues as a group.

"Mike and I have a lot of experimenting to do; we've already got miles of tape, so we might have something already, but there are an incredible number of things involved. We've got a Moog which gives us complete control of any sound frequency that the human ear can hear, and we plan to use the Moog to make the tapes for the Mellotron. We'll use the two combined, and the Mellotron will eventually be a play-back machine for the Moog."
(GE-MM70)

After three successful albums, the band was no longer on the threshold of the dream of success; they had passed through the doorway. Wishing to placate their top act, and keep them under contract longer, Decca was soon dealing. With the contract that was renegotiated in early 1968 between Decca and Derek McCormick, the label had the Moodies under through early 1972. Their new arrangement let the Moodies record for their own label, along with whatever acts they wished to sign up. In turn, Decca would get a longer contract – through the end of 1976, tying the Moodies to Threshold, and Threshold to Decca.

From the fall of 1969, *Go* magazine's Chris Hodenfield wrote:

> … For "artistic leverage," the Moodys are starting their own record label, called Threshold. Reasons given are standard for any band that does this. Freedom, chance to break in other worthy groups, kick out the monopolies of the fat old men, replace their capitalism over the existing one. It will still be distributed by the old folks, though. Decca in England, Deram/London in America. Their first album will be called "For Our Children's Children's Children." (Suitable title, say, for a time capsule). They comment that their album will be that far advanced. I was given an advance listening, and while it sounded like a terrific album, it didn't sound like the same contribution and advancing like in the first album.

> What the Moody Blues do have, that not many others do, is a way with the melodies and song structures. Like the Beatles, who have cycles of song flowing from their fingertips, the Moodys have a natural way with their dulcet silvery harmonies. That they are still mucking around with *Sgt. Pepper* ideas while the movements

seem to be returning to that natural gut feeling in music ("Get Back"?), is another matter. There is still a place for the mind, their own euphonious karma.

In the October 2 edition of London's *Daily Mirror*, Don Short reported:

> ... Today, Decca will announce an entirely new project in the recording industry field. It is to sponsor – to the tune of £400,000, I understand – an independent company to be run by one of its star recording groups, the Moody Blues.
>
> With the capital, the Moody Blues will set up their own organization... with offices in London's Soho [district]. They will be able to call on all Decca offices and know-how, but essentially they will be self-sufficient.
>
> They will make all their own records, engage and promote other artists, arrange concert tours, and launch their own music publishing company. The name of the company will be "Threshold," a term which, it is hoped, will signal a new era.
>
> Decca officials, although reluctant to talk of the threat of artists leaving their label, agree that "something had to happen."

Decca artists' manager Hugh Mendl told Short, "There is a great change in our business and Decca sees it as a very healthy one, and we are ready to meet it. Over the years, we've had pressure from numerous groups to run their own operation. But we've never been keen on the idea because it has usually meant that all they wanted to do was satisfy their own egos. But with the Moody Blues, we felt that here was a team of people who were serious, responsive and creative, and who were going places. We have no control over their operation. There is a contract, of course, but really it's all down to mutual trust." (HM-DM69)

Graeme Edge said, "It's taken us a long time to convince Decca that this was the best thing to do. We could have stayed with Decca as the Moody Blues and kept on recording, but where was the challenge? Most of all, we wanted our artistic freedom. It was great to find that Decca finally believed in us." (GE-DM69)

From *Variety*'s London office, October 14:

> The Beatles started the trend with their own business empire in Britain, other top acts have threatened to follow. Some have made feeble attempts and now the Moody Blues pop group is having a corporate fling. Part of their setup includes an independent disk label. ...
>
> Over the past two years they have sold nearly $10,000,000 worth of product for Decca.... They were one of the first to realize the potential of albums that followed one theme rather than just containing a collection of tracks. Their new label, Threshold, will

follow this trend and all singles issued will comprise tracks from albums.

Talks between Decca, the group, and their producer, Tony Clarke (an equal partner in Threshold) began nearly a year ago. Decca had rejected similar proposals from other groups but eventually decided to back the venture with a five-year contract, reported to be worth $960,000. …

Though Decca has been making polite and contented noises over the arrangement, it really had little choice. At the moment Decca is in a precarious position with its three hottest properties – Tom Jones, Engelbert Humperdinck, and the Rolling Stones – all indicating a desire to operate more independently when their present contracts run out. Obviously if the Moody Blues pact works out okay for both sides, then other artists may be persuaded to retain the same sort of ties with Decca.

The Moody Blues say that they are more interested in satisfying the musical ego than in money by waxing what they want and not what a "commercially based" company thinks is best for the market. Nevertheless they will be appreciably better off. Instead of receiving a cut of 18¢ per album, they will now pick up nearly 30¢. …

But the Moodies would now be responsible for the costs previously absorbed by Decca, such as art and layout.

In November 1969, for an article called "New Blood on Moody's Label," Justin Hayward told Richard Williams, "After we'd completed each of our albums we found that we had so many ideas left over and we had nothing that we could do with them. As well as that, we felt that we weren't able to exercise sufficient control over the material. The rules of the game were getting too strong, so we decided that the best way out would be to make our own [rules].

"We're going to make nine albums a year – but they won't all be Moody Blues albums, of course. Three of them will be by the group, and the other six will be other artists produced by us. …

"We're able to use the full facilities of Decca for Threshold, and they're really behind us in the project, and they're looking after us because, after all, it's in their interest too that we should succeed." (JH-MM69)

The band was aiming high. They would never realize three group-effort albums a year, nor would they manage six albums a year by other artists. The reality would be less than half of those numbers.

Hayward said the change in business structure would not change the music. "It will still be Moody Blues music," he said, "and Tony Clarke will still be producing us. What we're after is artistic satisfaction. Every artist has a problem when other people control his output. You make a tape, it's whisked away, and that's the last you see of it until the record comes out. Now we have full control over things like sleeve design and promotion, which are really important."

Williams pointed out that while the Moodies albums had been a "spectacular success," their singles, at least in Britain, had been "something less than earth-shattering in impact." He asked if, now that they owned their own record company, would they "try harder to crack the singles market?" Hayward answered, "No. Our singles have always been taken off the albums, because we think they make good 'trailers' for them, and they're good for plugging." (JH-MM69)

The fact was, making hit singles and hit albums usually required two different mindsets. There were groups who had a long string of hits, but had never made a standout album, such as the Supremes, the Four Seasons, Herman's Hermits, the Dave Clark Five, Tommy James & the Shondells, the Turtles, and the Monkees, to name but a few. For the most part, their albums were a collection of singles and missed attempts at singles. On the other hand, there was an entire genre of album artists – it was called AOR, "album-oriented rock." It was championed by the new FM music scene and in music magazines such as *Rolling Stone*. Many of these bands remained "hitless" according to the singles charts, but had a deep, long-lasting fan base. These included groups like the Velvet Underground, the Band, Moby Grape, Traffic, Ten Years After, and Frank Zappa and the Mothers of Invention. Of course, there were those who could do both – make respected albums and, without appearing to sell out in the eyes of rock elitists, have hit singles too. The Rolling Stones managed, as did Creedence Clearwater Revival, the Doors, the Who, Simon & Garfunkel, and, of course, at the top of the list, the Beatles.

Ray Thomas explained one of the goals of their new imprint: "Threshold is our freedom and we hope to lend that same liberty to those artistes who join our label. We have established our success on the basis of composing and interpreting the kind of music we like ourselves. It should be quite obvious that the happier you are in your work, the greater the mental release and, consequently, the better the product. People who buy a Threshold recording can therefore be certain they are getting the best that the artist can produce.

"As musicians ourselves, we know the frustrations and limitations of working for a huge impersonal concern, but as a smaller company we can relate to our artistes with some personal and sympathetic attention." (RT-TCP69)

Tony Clarke said, "We are concentrating upon producing and encouraging the kind of talent and records which have some lasting quality. There is an ever increasing market for good progressive music with durable qualities as opposed to discs which are hits today and forgotten tomorrow." (TC-TCP69)

Here is the business plan which was developed:

Each Moody was given an office. John Lodge would handle sales; Ray Thomas and Justin Hayward would take care of advertising, press relations, and promoting the company's records; Mike Pinder would be the sound studio chief; Graeme Edge would serve as general manager, handling commitments and contracts; and Tony Clarke would be recording manager. And Clarke, the man with actual business experience, had big plans. In the October 10, 1970 edition of *Melody Maker*, he wrote:

> It is well known that we don't hear entirely with our ears, and
> bone conduction – the rib cage, for example, picks up and registers
> bass levels – is something which is bound to be considered by the

record producer. We know that certain sound levels can produce physical reactions in people, and this need not be reduced to 1984 terms. You should be able to induce in people the feeling of relaxation, peace, ecstasy, and contentment, as opposed to any unpleasant side-effects.

Stereo has done for music what Cinema did for the small screen, but it is only the beginning; the end is an absolute and total involvement which may not be so far in the future as some anticipate. …

Mike Pinder said, "The Moodies have moved both with the lyrical content and ideas of our times and the electronic development of pop music. Our producer, Tony Clarke, is one of the foremost exponents of stereophonic effects in recording.

"People always tend to discover the bad things about scientific development first. They found the atom bomb before they harnessed its power for the use of more peaceful and constructive purposes.

"Electronic sounds can be produced to do good things and I believe this is a development that we will go into during the '70s to produce a feeling of peace, relaxation and confidence in the listener. It's really only a logical extension of the maxim that music has the power to soothe the savage breasts!

"Music is now a tremendous communicator throughout the world and we are very conscious of its influence. We want our music to be a source of inspiration for happiness and peace. The only thing which dispels fear is knowledge, and you can help to spread that through your music. There are a million places your senses can go and music can take you to almost all of them.

"Pop music is no longer the shallow and temporary thing it was in years gone by. We know and have proof that our albums recorded three years ago are still selling. People are still getting the same sense of validity from 'Nights in White Satin' now as when we recorded it so long ago. We are delighted to learn that people collect our albums rather like volumes of an encyclopedia – go back and still enjoy them." (MP-R70)

Ray Thomas, while discussing the Moodies' experiments with sound with *Record Mirror*'s Keith Altham, was still fascinated with the idea of using certain frequencies and chords to stimulate the human body as well as the mind. He reiterated, "[I]t is a scientific fact that if you take a certain note, record it and slow it right down until it is oscillating, then reverse it, the sound produced will hit the stomach muscles and subsequently make the listener's bowels work. Imagine that as an encore at the Albert Hall!" (RT-RM70)

Now, with the freedom of having their own record label, one might no longer be limited to merely imagining it.

13

To Our Children's Children's Children (1969)

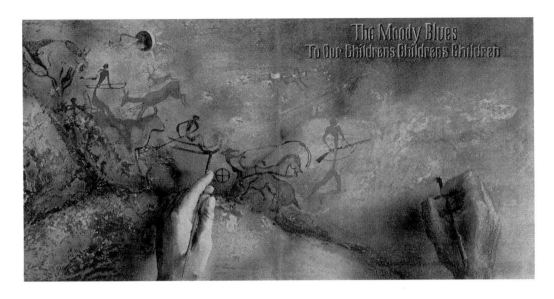

Album release:
U.K. and U.S. Threshold THS 1; November 21, 1969
Peak position in the U.K.: 2
(Certified silver in the U.K.)
U.S.: 14
(Certified platinum in the U.S.)
Canada: #11
(Certified platinum in Canada)

U.K. single release: *"Watching and Waiting" b/w "Out and In"*
Threshold TH 21; October 31, 1969
Non-charting

Recording of the magnificent *To Our Children's Children's Children* began May 10, 1968, continuing through the 24th. Two more sessions spanned a period in July.

On that first day in the studio, in early May, it had been a mere eleven weeks since the completion, mixing, and overdubbing of *On the Threshold of a Dream* … and only a month since that album's release. This was a remarkably short amount of time from the completion of one album to the start of the next – but the Moodies were eager to get a project ready for the launch of their new Threshold label. Decca was just as eager for there to be a new album for the Christmas buying season of 1969.

Part of the milieu prompting the album's theme of space travel was Stanley Kubrick's epic *2001: A Space Odyssey* , released in May of 1968 – and, now, the United States was preparing to put a man on the moon. The Apollo 10 mission was scheduled to launch on May 18. This was the fourth manned space mission from the U.S. Apollo program and the second (following Apollo 8) to orbit the moon. It was considered a "dress rehearsal" for the first moon landing, planned for three months later. Apollo 10 would also set the record for the highest speed attained by a manned vehicle – 24,791 miles per hour – during its return trip from the moon.

Apollo 11 would launch on July 16, 1969, with Mission Commander Neil Armstrong and pilot "Buzz" Aldrin landing the lunar module "Eagle" on the moon on July 20. Armstrong became the first man to step foot on the moon's surface six hours later, on July 21.

There was another "space" event in England at this time. On July 12, 1969, *Star Trek* premiered on the BBC (with the episode "Where No Man Has Gone Before") and was an immediate hit. Chances are, Graeme Edge – later to declare himself a Trekkie – was watching.

With the continuing focus on space in the cinema, on TV, and the real world, producer Tony Clarke was determined that "space … the final frontier" would be the theme of the Moodie's new album.

Tony Clarke: "I must say, *To Our Children's Children's Children* is the most self-indulgent of the albums that I did. I remember paying for everybody to go to the cinema, and I think we all went and saw *2001*. I very much wanted us to make a space album, and, at the time, I was very immersed in that sort of thing. Now that was my frame of mind, and I rather pushed it in that direction, so everybody capitulated." (TC-H&H95a)

Justin Hayward: "[T]he main mover with that album was our old producer, Tony Clarke, who was very, very hung up on astronomy and would always whiz down to NASA, and they were all showing him 'round things there." (JH-RL88)

Ray Thomas: "We were talking with Tony 24 hours a day, not just music but philosophy and astronomy too. He had a huge telescope on the roof of his house and we'd go up there, look at the moon and stars, and talk about *everything*." (RT-CRB14)

John Lodge: "When we knew that they were going to try the landing on the moon, we decided to write an album first, before it took place, to say, 'What would it be like? How would we feel as ordinary people about flying to the moon?' And we wrote *Children's Children* as about being this sort of astronaut; this traveler." (JL-SP93)

Justin Hayward: "Tony Clarke was a 'boffin' producer who could see the whole thing cinematically. He'd describe it in this Stanley Kubrick way – 'And then we fade across the setting sun, and sparks come out!' He was straight! Four of us were pretty stoned – [but] not John." (JH-UC14)

Graeme Edge: "Landing on the moon. That was in that period of time which was very exciting; it was a feeling of being in history. We used to think of it – God, the conceit of it! – as the record to put under the foundation stone of some building, because that's what it says on the top: 'To our children's children's children.'" (GE-MD87)

Talking with *Melody Maker* shortly after the release of the album, Hayward said, "We found that it's easier to write when we all have something specific to write about. It keeps the feeling going. It meant that when people bought the album they were listening to the whole of it instead of just one or two tracks. Maybe that's a bit selfish but we realized that we were an album group and just couldn't make singles." (JH-MM70)

Indeed, no single from the album would be released in the U.S.

Recording the Album:

The songs were put to tape in the following order, with the corresponding dates:

1. "Gypsy" (Hayward) on May 10, 1969;
2. "Eyes of a Child, Part 1" (Lodge) on May 11;
3. "Eyes of a Child, Part 2" (Lodge) on May 12;
4. "Sun Is Still Shining" (Pinder) on May 15;
5. "Watching and Waiting" (Hayward/Thomas) on May 17;
6. "Floating" (Thomas) on May 19;
7. "Beyond" (Pinder/Edge) on May 22;
8. "Candle of Life" (Lodge) on June 25;
9. "Out and In" (Pinder) on July 11 and 12;
10. "Eternity Road" (Thomas) on July 29;
11. "Higher and Higher" (Edge) on July 30;
12. "I Never Thought I'd Live to Be a Hundred" (Hayward) on July 31;
13. "I Never Thought I'd Live to Be a Million" (Hayward) on July 31.

Moving through the album, in track order:

"Higher and Higher," with verse written by Graeme Edge, music by the band, and studio wizardry by producer Tony Clarke and engineer Derek Varnals, was the launch on the album, both thematically and audio-wise.

The track was recorded on July 30, 1969, nine days after man first walked on the moon, which Graeme Edge has said was his inspiration for writing the words ... and clearly inspired the recording of the music and effects.

John Lodge: "We got in touch with NASA and said we'd like the sound of one of their rockets taking off so we could put it on the front of our album, which we were doing. And they sent us some sound over, but, actually, it wasn't very good. So, we got in the studio and we spent a couple of days and made our own space sound of a rocket taking off and sent it back to NASA and said, 'Perhaps you'd like to use this on your future missions.'" (JL-ST93)

Derek Varnals: "The rumbling sound of a rocket blasting off was several layers of instruments. We had guitar amplifiers turned up really loud with no instrument playing. You can get the sound of a general 'white noise' roaring away on an amp. We had a Hammond organ and Mellotron motors going with microphones right by the motors. We had muffled drums being rolled and maybe a couple of electronic things in there. It begins with a cymbal crash ... [and] I think we had the Hammond and Mellotron gradually working their way up to give you the idea of a crescendo. The idea is to give you the impression that you are going up into orbit, leaving the [booster rocket] behind, as we've all seen film of the third stage separating and falling back to Earth." (DV-H&H95)

Mike Pinder: "It was armfuls of keyboards being played. It was crossed arms on the keys, starting at their instruments, letting loose. I liked what we did, sound-wise, behind [the vocal] – the fact that we actually conjured up the sound of a rocket taking off with nothing more than musical instruments. I definitely felt a sense of achievement with that." (MP-H&H95)

For the track, Pinder spoke Graeme Edge's verses, with Hayward, Thomas, and Lodge joining in for the dramatically building chorus of "Higher … and … higher!"

Mike Pinder's plucking of a harp, augmented by Ray Thomas's bass flute, creates a transition from "Higher and Higher" into "Eyes of a Child, Part 1."

Tony Clarke told *Melody Maker*, "The Moodies must be the best band to record in the world, because they can play practically any instrument under the sun. If you want any woodwinds, or even a harp, one of them will be able to play it. That's why I call them the world's smallest symphony orchestra." (TC-MM70)

"Eyes of a Child, Part 1," written by John Lodge, was recorded on May 11 (the second session for the new album, following "Gypsy," laid to tape the day before).

John Lodge: "I really thought, if you were out there, 'What would you expect; what would you see if you were on the spaceship going out?' And I suddenly realized, if you went up there with all preconceived ideas and preprogrammed ideas in your mind, you'd probably miss everything. And I realized then, that's how a child works. When a baby is growing up, everything is wonderment. He'll find a piece of paper and spend hours with it, or he'll find some cloth, or a flower, or a tree; whatever it is. And he'll spend ages looking and learning. And I thought that's really how we'd have to see; you'd have to see everything through the eyes of a child." (JL-20CG00)

The harp that transitioned "Higher and Higher" into "Eyes of a Child, Part 1," continues into the song, joined by a glockenspiel. Mike Pinder said, "I think Justin played the glockenspiel on that. I definitely played a beautiful, seven-foot golden harp on that…. I particularly like that song; I like the sentiment that John came up with." (MP-H&H95)

Sentiments, such as: "Listen, hear the sound / The child awakes / Wonder all around …. Earth falls away / New life awaits / Time, it has no day / New life awaits."

"Floating," the next track on the album, was actually the sixth to be recorded (on May 19). Like many of Ray Thomas's contributions, such as "Another Morning" on *Days of Future Passed*, "Floating" is another of the writer's signature "child's world" songs, this time describing the awe of leaping about on the moon.

> *Floating free as a bird / Sixty foot leaps, it's so absurd*
> *From up here you should see the view*
> *Such a lot of space for me and you….*
>
> *Now I know how it feels / To have wings on my heels….*

Graeme Edge: "My favorite track on *To Our Children's Children's Children* is 'Floating.' As always, you can count on Ray to poke a bit of irreverent fun just when we are all strutting around a little too pompously!" (GE-H&H95)

The song utilizes all the band members in their most familiar roles – Thomas's flute, Pinder's Mellotron, Hayward's guitars, Lodge's electric bass, and Edge's drums and percussion. But, with the Moody Blues, nothing was ever as simple as it might sound.

Mike Pinder: "There's a lot going on keyboard-wise in that one. I think I used a Mellotron vibraphone setting; some of the guitar [setting] off the Mellotron in there, too. I seem to remember that there were at least three or four different Mellotron parts." (MP-H&H95)

Pinder's Mellotron does some floating of its own, from one stereo channel to another. Tony Clarke explained that this effect was accomplished by means of "a very early use of the old pan-pot" – sometimes requiring several people to manually turn dials and slide fader controls up and down on the mixing board.

Tony Clarke: "The round-and-round panning effect was a step easier to accomplish than on 'Thinking Is the Best Way to Travel' [from *In Search of the Lost Chord*]. By then, we had built a panning device that went left to right, then forwards and backwards…. It took three or four people to operate. Derek tells me that he had two faders, I had two faders, and Graeme had a fader or two." (TC-H&H95)

This effect was accomplished while mixing, not at the actual time of recording. As far as the recording was concerned, Derek Varnals was out sick for a few days. He missed the session for "Floating" (as well as "Sun Is Still Shining" and "Watching and Waiting"). His assistant Adrian Martins manned the controls for most of those recordings.

"Eyes of a Child, Part 2" was recorded on May 12, the day after "Part 1" had been put to tape. Other than some of the lyrics, it is actually a different melody and arrangement from what was heard in the recording from one day earlier. And far more dramatic.

John Lodge: "[T]he first part, I thought, was a very particular and personal part of the song. [For Part 2], I thought it'd be a great idea to do it in a choral version where everyone's singing like the finale in a stage play…." (JL-20CG00)

> *I'm gonna sit and watch the web / That you will build this day*
> *Will it be a thread of love you weave….*
>
> *In the eyes of the child / You must come out and see*
> *That your world's spinning 'round / And through life you will be*
> *A small part / Of a hope / Of a love*
> *That exists*
> *In the eyes of a child you will see.*

"I Never Thought I'd Live to Be a Hundred" was a solo spot for Justin Hayward – as writer, vocalist, and guitarist. It is the simplest arrangement and execution ever applied to a Moody Blues track. This snippet of a song, and its companion piece, "I Never Thought I'd Live to Be a Million," were the final two tracks recorded for the album – both on July 31, 1969.

"Beyond" is Mike Pinder's solo spot – with the Mellotron carrying the track, via its abilities to mimic organ, guitar, flute, and bass. The only other Moody present on the track is Graeme Edge, on drums.

Interviewed for *New Music Express* in 1969, Pinder described the track as being "like a mini 'Planets' suite; it has three parts. One bit is like Saturn with this big thing in the middle going 'ooom,' and these thing spinning round it."

Perhaps because Pinder didn't consider "Beyond" to be a song – merely an experiment with sounds and Mellotron riffs in the studio, set to the theme of other worlds, and the beat of Graeme Edge's drums, he chose to give authorship to Edge. This translated to money in the pocket for the drummer, for this credit included the publishing rights, too.

The track was made on May 22, the final recording completed before the band took a month-long break.

"Out and In" was another of Mike Pinder's contributions to the album, and, again, an example of his generosity – this time, he shared the writing credit with John Lodge for the original vinyl pressings (although, by the time the records were reissued on CD, the song writing credit would cite Pinder alone).

Pinder told Mark Murley of *Higher & Higher*, "I wrote 'Out and In.' John Lodge threw in a couple of ideas. I shared the boon, as I did also with 'Beyond.'" (MP-H&H94)

This was the only song for that album that took more than a single day to record. The recording spanned two days – July 11 and 12.

Mike Pinder: "It is still one of my favorite songs. This was written 'within me,' and draws from the experiences I had as a kid, looking up into the night sky." (MP-H&H95)

Tony Clarke: "It's lovely. I like that 'push beat' in it. The feel rather comes from Mike's rhythm acoustic-guitar playing. There was a time when he did wear a guitar a lot." (TC-H&H95)

"Gypsy," by Justin Hayward, was called "Gypsy Comet" when recorded. It tells the story of a space venture ... with no hope of finding a way home:

> *A gypsy of a strange and distant time*
> *Travelling in panic all direction blind*
> *Aching for the warmth of a burning sun*
> *Freezing in the emptiness of where he'd come from...*
>
> *Speeding through a shadow of a million years*
> *Darkness is the only sound to reach his ears*
> *Frightening him with the visions of eternity*
> *Screaming for the future that can never be*
> *... Left without a hope of coming home.*

Hayward said, "I can't say that I was really influenced by *Doctor Who* [as some may think], although it sounds a bit like that. It's just an idea of a lost spaceship, and gypsies in space, really." (JH-OM00)

It's a straightforward back-to-roots recording – the only one that the Moodies felt able to perform live at the time of the album's release. Hayward sings the lead, and plays both acoustic and electric guitars; Pinder mans his Mellotron; Thomas on the bass flute; Lodge on bass guitar, and all three provide backing vocals. Edge, of course, pounds out the beat.

This was the first song recorded for the album, on May 10, 1969.

Mike Pinder: "I love it. It was one of those good songs; it has a really good rhythm and it was something that enabled me to use the Mellotron in a nice way.

Musically, it was one of those songs that would definitely lift you up and away; in the same way that 'Out and In' did." (MP-H&H95)

Tony Clarke: "I like 'Gypsy' very much; I like the tempo and I like the urgency in the vocal. It really does encompass a lot of things and colors." (TC-H&H95)

"Eternity Road" is one of the best songs contributed by Ray Thomas to date. It flows out of "Gypsy" with thoughtful execution … continuing along the theme of a traveler … in search of himself … with no course home.

> *You'll see us all around, turning, spinning, catherine wheeling*
> *For ever changing*
> *There's no beginning; you're so very far from home....*
>
> *And so very much alone, travelling eternity road*
> *What will you find there?*
> *Carrying your heavy load, searching to find a piece of mind.*

The song was the tenth to be recorded for the album, after the band returned to Decca Studio 1 on July 29, following a two-and-a-half week break from recording.

Mike Pinder: "I would say that with 'Eternity Road,' it was Ray's lyric and melody, but it was a real cooperative effort between Justin and myself. I think that 'Eternity Road' is one of the better examples of songs that were not written by myself or Justin that shows how well he and I co-arranged together." (MP-H&H95)

Tony Clarke said of Hayward's guitar playing on this track: "The guitar is three-part harmony, from the electronics. I was always begging him to go for another [harmony part], exactly the same, just a third up or a third down. He's very good at that." (TC-H&H95)

"Cradle of Life" was the only song for the album recorded in the month of June. Decca Studio 1 was unavailable, so the Moodies attempted to make the track on June 24 at Lansdowne Studios in London. Graeme Edge recalled, "We found the Lansdowne Studio to be too small and communication with the control room was difficult. Wessex Studio was better for us." (GE-H&H95)

The Lansdowne session was aborted and the band reconvened the following day at Wessex Studio. Derek Varnals was not available, so the recording engineer for this song was Robin Thompson.

Although written by John Lodge, the lead vocals are handled by Justin Hayward, with backing from Lodge.

If not for following "Gypsy" and "Eternity Road," Lodge's "Candle of Life" might not appear to represent the theme of the album. But consider the previous two tracks depiction of a lonely space traveler lamenting the vastness of space, and longing to return to his love. Lodge's song certainly echoes their sentiments, with lines such as, "Something there outside, says we're only in the hands of time, falling slowly… burning slowly, the candle of life."

The time-capsule concept is represented well in the chorus, with a look at the youth movement of the Sixties: "So love everybody … and make them your friend."

On the instrumental front, Pinder shines with a piano arrangement that is at the same time commanding and beautiful.

"Sun Is Still Shining," Pinder's second composition for the album (excluding the instrumental "Beyond"), is supported by an Indian musical flavor, as Pinder had done in the past with both "Sunset" (from *Days of Future Passed*) and "Om" (from *Lost Chord*). This direction gave Justin Hayward another opportunity to play sitar. Pinder, besides the Mellotron, also played the tamboura on this track – an Indian instrument that is similar to the sitar but fretless.

Mike Pinder: "As with 'Out and In,' 'Sun' was a nice little vehicle for me to do the 'Mickey the Moonboy' thing." (MP-H&H95)

"Mickey the Moonboy" was a nickname given to Pinder when a child, due to his fondness of lying on his back in the yard at night and staring into the starry sky.

The song also speaks of Pinder's belief in out-of-body experiences:

Everything's turning, turning around
See with your mind, leave your body behind
Now that we're out here, open your heart
To the universe, of which we're a part.

But if you want to play
Stay right back on earth
Waiting for rebirth.

Pinder continued, "The middle-eight – 'So if you want to play, stay right back on Earth, waiting for rebirth' – was sort of a wake-up call…. But it's come to represent the drudgery or the mediocrity in life in our civilization. All of this [technological] greatness has only resulted in the sense of the mundane that prevails." (MP-H&H95)

"I Never Thought I'd Live to Be a Million" was an extension of Hayward's "I'd Never Thought I'd Live to Be a Hundred" on Side 1, committed to tape on the same day as the former, the last two tracks to be recorded for the album.

Why one million? Graeme Edge explained: "Tony Clarke had the idea to make an album that would serve as a time capsule – to be buried and discovered millions of years later." (JH-BBC81)

Gerry Hoff, label manager of Threshold at this time, explained further: "It's like you see a star explode in the sky and you catch the light, it may have exploded two hundred thousand million light years ago; it hasn't existed for an incredible length of time, but you're just seeing it right now, and time is really not relevant at all." (GH-HP71)

By this light, the singer might be dead, but, in a sense, he lives on a hundred – or million – years hence, through his voice, his words, his song … when the time capsule is discovered.

"Watching and Waiting," a collaborative work between Hayward and Thomas, was recorded on May 17, halfway through the sessions for the album. The song echoes the concept of "I Never Thought I'd Live to Be a Million." The writer/singer has been waiting a million years to be unearthed and discovered … and heard. "Watching and waiting / for a friend to play with / Why have I been alone so long? / Mole, he is burrowing his way to the sunlight / He knows there's some there so strong. … Soon you will see me / 'cause I'll be all around you / But where I come from I can't tell / But don't be alarmed by my fields and my forests / They're here only for you to share. … Watching and waiting / for someone to understand me / I hope it won't be very long."

Justin Hayward: "I was just talking about the inside of myself, I would think. I have always written what seems wondrous to me. Songs are about invoking a feeling; there doesn't have to be a real plan of saying some certain thing in particular. If it makes you feel good or better, then that's great….

"To tie it in with the theme [of the album], I changed it to make it, you know, a 'being' from a lost world – a beautiful, lonely world. I altered it from being just a straight love song, to give it that dimension for the sake of the album. Probably I made it much more obscure than it needed to be, but it still moves me, and I'm not sure that I can explain why. I feel every single word of it; it invokes images within me that I find particularly moving. It does have a spiritual dimension to it, a religious-almost dimension to it." (JH-RN92 and JH-MWE00)

No matter how disguised the lyric – which, in many ways, only made the song more intriguing – the melancholy mood resonates with great poignancy. Hayward said, "I think that it was a sad time for me…. My father had just died, and it was a very painful thing for me." (JH-MWE00)

The track is rich in a haunting Mellotron arrangement from Pinder, and a fragile and even ghostly vocal by Hayward, his voice seeming distant, as if softly calling from "the other side." The combined effect is both eerie and hypnotically seductive.

Tony Clarke: "It's a great song. It worked beautifully and the sounds are lovely." (TC-H&H95)

Mike Pinder: "A favorite of mine; a very, very special song, in my opinion. Again, this is one on which Justin and I worked together intensely [in devising the arrangement]. The vast majority of the song – 90% – is Justin and myself, because it's the Mellotron and his voice. Justin's voice and my 'wrapping around' Mellotron arrangement give it that magic feel. Justin was able to come up with things like 'Watching and Waiting' that I could really go to work on." (MP-H&H95)

Pinder also played a stand-up acoustic bass for this track

The final sessions for the album took place on August 8, 9, 11, 18, and 19. These five days were used for additional instrument overdubs and backing vocal work on the various tracks.

The Moodies, with Clarke and Varnals, had made what many would consider yet another masterpiece. The downside – very little of it could be reproduced on stage.

Tony Clarke: "A few of them, upon playback and mix, would say, 'How are we going to do *that* on stage?' and I would say, 'That's *your* problem.' That didn't matter to me – maybe it should have. The point was that we had to be as far reaching as we could and then a little time later we could worry about how to bring it about on stage. And I think they did quite a good job of that [starting in the 1980s], meeting the challenge by adding another bank of keyboards or whatever to bring the effect." (TC-H&H95)

Justin Hayward: "The only problem with that album was that we'd gone so far down the studio recording route that when we went back on the road and tried to play stuff from it, it was just impossible. In fact, the next album, *A Question of Balance*, was very much a conscious effort to step back from that, and make it much more suitable to play live. It was very difficult to promote the *Children's Children* material live, because there was so much that we simply couldn't perform live." (JH-RS13)

Mix-down sessions took place on August 22, as well as September 4 and 5. On the latter day, there was also a playback session for over a dozen people. Derek Varnals said, "The band generally weren't there to hear the mixing. Then, for playback [day], wives, girlfriends, managers, and executive producers – about 12 to 16 people – would arrive…. *To Our Children's Children's Children* was a very effective playback because the whole album was put together very nicely and it ends with 'Watching and Waiting.' Of course, we'd play it back in the dark, in low lighting…. It was always good to hear the Moodies albums in the dark." (DV-H&H95)

In the September 20, 1969 issue of *New Musical Express*, Justin Hayward said, "I'm looking forward to the release of the album we've just finished. There are several more varied styles of music than we've ever tried before. That's the beautiful thing about being in a group where all five members write material. You get so many different ideas and opinions verbally as well as musically, there's never a dull moment." (JH-NME69a)

For the same article, Graeme Edge said, "Music – along with the other arts – is an expression of the soul. It is the only thing that man has that no other animal has, and to present it in its best form, the musicians playing it must have a deeper understanding of each other and the music than merely what chord comes next." (GE-NME69)

Ray Thomas told *NME*, "To me, the Moodies are a family. I remember my parents saying, 'You can't pick your family, but you can always pick your friends.' … This is obviously true to a point, but after a time I found myself in the beautiful position of having four brothers of my own choosing all on exactly the same scene, and that's really too much." (RT-NME69a)

Graeme Edge: "Suddenly, all the things you wished for were there. You had your own studio, you could make your own music, people were coming to see you play; all your dreams were right there in your hand. The world really was ours for a song." (GE-CRM-14)

After the completion of *To Our Children's Children's Children*, Mike Pinder told *Record Mirror*, "Our current album really sums up all we have been saying in our first three albums and puts a nice little ribbon around them. We hope people will regard them almost as a set because we have closed that particular chapter of our musical lives.

"People have been trying to categorize what we have been doing ever since *Days of Future Passed* and we're talked about in terms of "underground," "psychedelic," and "mind-music." On our first trip to America a few acid freaks thought we were gurus and read all kinds of misinterpretations into our work!

"Our albums have really been nothing more or less than the changes we have been going through – sort of musical diaries and the message… 'Be yourself,' because that's what we are trying to do and not 'This is where it's at!' …

"I've always felt that a lot of today's music is under the balls! It's aimed directly at the genitals and is just about as lasting as a cheap thrill – very temporary music. We think that there are a large number of people interested in more aesthetic and subtler human emotions. We made up our minds three years ago to aim our music at the heart and the heads!

"Music to me is not a shallow thing and its influence and effects are limitless. If they are used in the pursuit of peace and love then there can only be good effects. Many years ago the Tibetans, for example, discovered that certain music affected the metabolism and certain changes in the body chemistry took place. People became more relaxed and peaceful listening to certain sounds – they became more aware of their own entity." (MP-RW69)

With reflections like these, it really was no wondered why the "acid freaks" in America thought of him and his fellow Moodies as gurus.

Pinder was not just looking inward, but toward a different dimension altogether. At this time, he told *Disc and Music Echo*'s David Hughes of an incident that occurred while the Moodies were touring England: "We were driving home down the M1 about 3:24 a.m. after a gig in Manchester. I was lying in the back in the back seat looking at the stars, which had always fascinated me, when I saw a red light which I thought was a radio tower.

"We were doing about 80 mph and after four miles we had still not passed the light; it was still in the same place. We drove through a wood and out the other side and there was this light, 'sitting' in a ploughed field just like a big red moon.

"We stopped the car, got out and watched. The color became intense and turned to amber with all reds and greens. It seemed to be pulsating and was very psychedelic. We were only 200 yards away from it and I estimate it must have been 60 feet in diameter and 20 feet off the ground. All the time it was getting nearer and nearer, and then suddenly changed direction and I could see there were two of these objects side by side, not just one as we had thought.

"Then one of the lads got scared and we drove away, but looking back down the motorway I can remember it crossing almost the point where we had stopped.

"I have always come to the conclusion that these and other UFOs are not metal spaceships…. They are *beings* from another dimension… but are not here for an evil purpose….

"Skeptics say, 'Why haven't these beings contacted us?' The answer is simple: If you went by rocket to another planet where the inhabitants were all ape-men, how would you make contact with them? To these superior beings we are like ape-men. As the famous Yogi Paramahansa Yogananda says, 'It is easier for a man to contact an angel than for an angel to contact a man.'

"UFOs are nothing new, of course; they have been seen for thousands of years and are always described in the same way –'like a ball of light or a ball of fire.' I believe the UFOs we see today are the same beings who, for example, guided the Israelites in their flight from the Egyptians. In the Book of Exodus it says they were guided by a pillar of light.

"Jesus says in Revelations, 'I will come to you on clouds on the day of judgment.' And, of course, the most famous UFO of all was the Star of Bethlehem." (MP-DME70)

***

RELEASE DATE: NOVEMBER 1969
ORIGINAL U.K. CATALOGUE NUMBER: THRESHOLD THS 1
HIGHEST U.K. CHART POSITION: 2
HIGHEST U.S. CHART POSITION: 14
U.K. SINGLES: WATCHING AND WAITING

BAND LINE-UP:
JUSTIN HAYWARD
MIKE PINDER
JOHN LODGE
RAY THOMAS
GRAEME EDGE
PRODUCER: TONY CLARKE

Top image: David Wedgbury's print of the group in the
photo studio. Above: Phil Travers's composite image,
including his illustration of the interior of the cave.

As he had done before creating the artwork for *In Search of the Lost Chord* and *On the Threshold of a Dream*, Phil Travers met with the band and discussed the theme of their latest album, then listened to the finished tracks.

John Lodge: "In the '60s, we wanted to record a point of view, not just make a record. The sleeve was part of what we thought was the music of our albums. We would sit with a designer and exchange ideas and build up the image we wanted to convey to the listener, *visually*." (JL-RGJ95)

Phil Travers: "This was one occasion when the band had a pretty good idea of what they wanted illustrated." (PT-H&H95a)

Mike Pinder: "The front part – with the handwriting and cave paintings – were in a sense the legacy that had been left for us from a long, long time ago, and had been written onto cave walls. In a sense, the album itself was *our* cave-wall drawings that we were doing." (MP-H&H95a)

Phil Travers: "The wall texture was initially created by a layer of paint, and allowed to dry and then scraped and manipulated until I had a surface interesting enough to build on." (PT-H&H95a)

Earth tones are prominent, a study in browns, oranges, and various subtle colors. The series of simple figures depicted in Travers's painting is based on authentic – and well-known – European cave drawings. It also shows two human hands – representing the artists of these drawings – one hairy, one hairless.

The photograph used for the interior of the gatefold was taken by David Wedgbury, and depicts the five Moodies inside a cave, gathered around campfire. Wedgbury took the picture with the group members sitting in front of a black backdrop, allowing Travers to determine what the interior of the cave would look like. Travers drew in the campfire, as well as modern comforts, such as books stacked in a small bookcase, a lamp on a small table, a computer, a TV screen, what seems to be a combination turntable/reel-to-reel recorder … and a dog.

Graeme Edge: "I thought the album sleeve design was the best of all our many sleeves." (GE-H&H95a)

Even with the creation of Threshold, there was still pushback from Decca regarding the cost of the packaging.

Justin Hayward: "We had to establish a new price…. We had to also find another printer that could do just that booklet for slightly cheaper, because the printers weren't set up for doing that. Originally the booklet – the insert – was actually stapled into the album. That was a mess, really. That was so expensive. In the end, they put it inside…. But I know it cost a shilling for every album. There was a massive debate about that [among the Decca] people. Nobody was willing to give up any [profit, so] I think we ended up paying [it ourselves]." (JH-H&H04a)

Despite the Moodies making it a habit not to put their faces on the front cover of their albums, and to generally not seek recognition, the British pop press was not about to let that happen. Rock bands, even progressive rock bands, still fell under the category of "Pop Stars." In England, pop stars made for good press, and were quickly exploited.

Before long the members of the band were pigeonholed into character templates.

Of the five Moodies, Mike Pinder became the "deep" one, Graeme Edge the outrageous one, John Lodge the quiet, polite one, Ray Thomas the earthy one, and Justin Hayward the shy, pretty one. The two who got the most press were, not surprisingly, Edge and Hayward – one for his attention-grabbing quotable remarks, and the other for his good looks and introverted (therefore mysterious) demeanor.

Hayward later commented, "In this business there is an element of vanity involved, which is probably essential. At least that's my excuse. That vanity has been there right from the day when I got my first guitar and started posing in front of a mirror to see how I looked. I enjoyed every minute of being described as 'the prettiest man in pop.' I had my 15 minutes of being famous in teenage girls' magazines in the late Sixties, and loved it." (JH-DM94)

Release / Reaction:

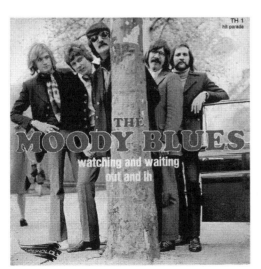

U.K. single release
"Watching and Waiting" / "Out and In"
Threshold TH 1, October 31, 1969

"Watching and Waiting" is exquisite, but wasn't a suitable candidate for Top 40 radio in America. "Out and In," another lovely and distinctively Moody Blues song, may have had a better chance to get into the charts, but it too would have been a long shot for the AM radio market. Therefore, London Records chose not to issue the single. This was unfortunate, if only

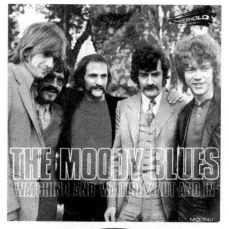

WATCHING AND WAITING
(Hayward/Thomas)
THE MOODY BLUES
Producer: Tony Clarke
(from: the Threshold album "To our children's children's children)

OUT AND IN
(M. Pinder/Lodge)
THE MOODY BLUES
Producer: Tony Clarke
(from: the Threshold album "To our children's children's children)

for the reason that the two songs were ripe for FM radio in the U.S., but, because they were positioned as the last tracks on the two sides of the LP, subject to crossfading, they were difficult to isolate and play as separate tracks. DJs working for radio stations not equipped with tape-cartridge playback – still the majority at this time – would have appreciated the "clean" introduction to these two excellent songs which a single release would provide. As it turned out, the song to get the most radio action – on AM as well as FM – was "Gypsy," the first track on Side Two of the LP. It could be cued up for radio play, and then faded down at the end to avoid the crossfading into "Eternity Road." It also sounded more like a single than any of the other album tracks.

In the U.K., it was also unlikely that "Watching and Waiting" was going to ascend the charts, but the Moodies nonetheless felt that it was the song to best represent their new album on the radio. To better appreciate what radio was looking for at this time in the U.K., the Top 5 singles were: "Sugar, Sugar" by the Archies, at No. 1, followed by, respectively: "Oh Well" by Fleetwood Mac; "I'm Gonna Make You Mine" by Lou Christie; "He Ain't Heavy … He's My Brother" by the Hollies; and, something America never heard, an oddity called "Return of Django / Dollar in the Teeth," by the Upsetters.

From the November 1, 1969 issue of *Disc and Music Echo*:

From their eagerly awaited – as usually – album, *Our Children's Children's Children*, comes this single track with all the identifiable Moody sounds.

It opens vaguely like "Space Oddity" and then goes into the vocal of drifting echoey unearthliness that has become their trademark.

This group are in a class of their own, and it's hard to judge them on the usual commercial level. I don't think they should have bothered to release this as a single. I don't see it doing much because everyone will clamber over each other for the album – where it belongs.

From the same day, in *Record Mirror*:

> Predictably high standards here on this track from the group's new album. A lovely big sensitive slow-building atmosphere and lyric given a haunting promotion. Not entirely sure about its single chances, but it is a magnificent preview of the LP. Organ, voice, simplicity.

Ray Thomas told *NME*'s Richard Green, "We all chose this to be the single. We all fancied it. We decided to release the single as a trailer to the album, but I don't think it'll do well if the album's going to. But it may get people interested in the album." (RT-NME69b)

Justin Hayward: "We'd put out that single, which was called 'Watching and Waiting,' which we all thought would … finally be a big follow-up to 'Nights in White Satin.' We put that out and we all totally believed in it. It sold about 10 copies." (JH-BBC81)

Mike Pinder: "We hoped that a wide audience would be ready for a song like that. Of course, it didn't do too well as a single and that was our disappointment. Yet it was one of our most progressive and intricate songs. It embodied so much of what is good about being a human being and living on this planet, in this solar system, in this universe. How can I put it? It was just too much quality. It was like a Rolls-Royce that was affordable to everyone, but everyone was programmed into thinking that they could never own a Rolls-Royce." (MP-H&H95)

London Records wasn't about to try to attempt to ship a Rolls-Royce to the airwaves of American Top 40 radio. The company declined to issue the 45 in the States.

Also in the *Record Mirror*'s November 1 issue, David Griffiths, having gotten an advance copy of the album, described to his readers what they could expect in a few weeks when the LP was issued. Signaling a turn against the band from some in the British music press, Griffiths's high expectations for the melodically lovely, lyrically poignant album were unfulfilled. His review:

> A portentously voyagistic *2001*-style opening, with whooshing sound effects, leads into a "Heavenly choir," then solid beat music and a bit of narrative with strong poetic and philosophical ambitions – that's the opening attempt to get "Higher and Higher" and it nearly sets the album's tone. The next track, "Eyes of a Child," is pleasantly pretty. "Floating" is relaxed and space-minded. On the "Eyes of a Child, Part 2" – much more rugged eyes this time. Tender guitar work introduced "I Never Thought I'd Live to Be a Hundred," a very short bit of bemused wonderment. "Beyond" is a slightly corny instrumental, reminiscent of [U.K. instrument group] the Tornadoes. That leads into the last track on Side One, "Out and In," some trippy musing on the meaning of life and that.
>
> Side Two and "Gypsy," with a big, cunningly produced sound, giving an air of profundity, but the lyrics could do with more than references to visions of eternity to give the song any genuine significance. A smooth slide into the plaintive "Eternity Road," a

typically Moody Blues quest for peace of mind, excellently played and sung, at considerable length. Abrupt switch to "Candle of Life," but maintaining the flourishes on this one which most progressive listeners will consider a bit pathetic. "Sun Is Still Shining" invites us to open our hearts to the universe – a delightful performance but an embarrassingly naïve song. "I Never Thought I'd Get to Be a Million" is just a few seconds long and is no more than a mathematical increase of the sentiment expressed on Side One. "Watching and Waiting" wraps up the show with soothing strings and sincere-style singing about the pursuit of love. …

From the November 8 edition of *New Musical Express*, Richard Green was still on the Moodies' side:

Being a gambling man I don't really like odds-on bets, so I won't be putting any money on the chances of the Moody Blues new album, *To Our Children's Children's Children*, getting to No. 1 as the last one did!

It's a cert to make the top of the chart and even though the group will be on a four-week tour of America when it's released on their new label Threshold on November 14, hordes of fans and believers will buy it. It has, I'm told, an advance order of 50,000.

U.K and U.S. LP release
November 21, 1969

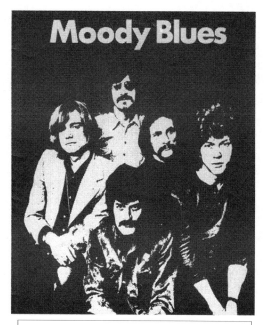

1969 tour book (this page and next).

The albums to beat during the week that *To Our Children's Children's Children* was released in England were: the Beatles' *Abbey Road*; a various artists' collection called *Motown Chartbusters Vol. 3*; a live album recorded behind prison bars, *Johnny Cash at San Quentin*; Led Zeppelin's second LP, *Led Zeppelin II*; and *Tom Jones in Las Vegas*.

In America, the top five contenders, counting down from No. 1, were: the Beatles' *Abbey Road*; Led Zeppelin's *Led Zeppelin II*; Creedence Clearwater Revival's *Green River*; Santana's self-titled debut LP; and Janis Joplin's *I've Got Dem Ol' Kozmic Blues Again, Mama!*

In support of the new album in their home country, the Moodies spent the first two weeks of December touring, with stopovers in Manchester, Newcastle upon Tyne, Edinburgh, Bristol, London,

Southampton, and then finishing in Birmingham. This time they toured with the Threshold Records fellow artists Trapeze and Timon.

For their engagement at Usher Hall in Edinburgh, *New Musical Express* reported on December 13:

> It was the first-ever Sunday night pop concert Edinburgh Corporation had allowed in their beloved hall. Not even in the Beatles and Stones era would they permit the doors to be opened on the Sabbath. If the Moodies and the crowd kept the thing nice and orderly, other Sunday concerts would follow. Well, we can look forward to more Sunday sessions. The Moodies behaved themselves (what else do the City Fathers expect?) and the 2,420 fans who packed the house offered not the slightest hint of trouble.

On December 20, from *Record Mirror*:

> … The magnificent Moodies, who certainly live up to their "dubbed" name, had their sound perfectly attuned to the vast, completely filled surrounding. They opened with a superb rendition of "Dr. Livingston, I Presume," and "Are You Sitting Comfortably?," which was followed by a poem from Graham [sic] Edge.

When the Moodies take the stage, even a tambourine is employed as a fluent musical instrument and they make good use of Mellotron, with each member coming to the fore in the breaks. After featuring additional tracks from their albums *Days of Future Passed* and *In Search of the Lost Chord*, including "Nights in White Satin," and a number dedicated to Timothy Leary, "Legend of a Mind," the group were called back by a standing ovation to round off a brilliant set.

Disc and Music Echo had its music

critic at the concert too. From the December 20 issue of the music paper:

> ... It's a treat we don't get the chance to see very often, but when it comes ... well, if you've seen them live you'll know what we're talking about. Moodies have just finished their British concert tour... and this Sunday guest on the first of three *This Is Tom Jones* shows to go out during Christmas week. The group's *To Our Children's Children's Children* is at Number 4 in the LP charts.

Richard Green of *New Musical Express* wrote:

> I was fortunate enough to see the Moodies' concert at the Royal Albert Hall and what impressed me was the absolute professionalism of the three acts – the others being Trapeze and Timon, who are both signed to the Moodies' own label, Threshold. The whole show was recorded and there is a chance of it being released as a double album....

It would be, in 1977, as *Caught Live + 5*. The reason the Moodies only performed enough material to fill three sides was that the first side of the double LP was planned for Trapeze or Timon, or a combination of both.

Richard Green of *New Musical Express* had questions whether or not *To Our Children's Children's Children* would go to No. 1. In fact, it would have to settle for No. 2 honors. The top spot for that month and then some belonged to the Beatles' *Abbey Road*.

Children's Children was out in the States by Christmas 1969. In the January 3, 1970 issue of *Billboard* magazine, the trade's critic wrote:

> The Moody Blues inaugurate their London-distributed Threshold label with a highly original LP that displays their superb vocal and instrumental talents and should extend their long string of album hits. Among the songs combining realistic commentary on the present with bright optimism for the future are "Higher and Higher," "Floating" and "Watching and Waiting."

On January 17, 1970, American syndicated entertainment writer Jared Johnson reported:

> The new Threshold label was officially born with the release of the Moody Blues new album, *To Our Children's Children's Children*. As usual, the sleeve artwork is fantastic, this time a prophetic look into mankind's future, portrayed in cave-man drawings on the wall of a cave; not just cave-men with rocks and spears, but "cave-men" with guns and modern weapons. ...
>
> In keeping with past albums, *To Our Children's Children's Children* is the epitome of the total concept album. The performances are skillfully and smoothly blended together to form

a unified whole, a reflection of the images invoked by the cover mural, the future of the human race, mankind's aspirations and his destiny or fate, depending on whether you adopt an optimistic or pessimistic attitude.

The Moody Blues are one of today's most talented progressive rock groups and presently occupy a position in this country similar to that of the Who for so many years. While extremely popular in Britain (their last album, *On the Threshold of a Dream*, went straight to Number One in England) they haven't yet achieved that well-deserved degree of popularity in this country. …

Also, the Moody Blues are probably the only group today that can create the sound of full orchestral accompaniment while playing all the instruments themselves, further testimony to their ever-widening talents. …

They handle everything from soft-orchestrated rock to hard progressive rock, with touches of folk, while generating a magnificent majestic quality throughout this epic work.

To Our Children's Children's Children is a truly beautiful album, no better way to start off the New Year. As long as albums like this fail to reach Top Ten, the Moody Blues remain one of the most underrated groups in this country.

But just wait. One of these days they're really going to catch on big.

Also on January 17, Richard Green wrote in *New Musical Express*:

If you've ever wondered how the Moody Blues manage to turn out consistently good albums while their rivals disappoint now and then, the answer is to be found in one word – TEAMWORK. This, explained John Lodge, is the open secret of the group's ability to get things done and done well.

Almost every track of every album stands up on its own and at the same time fits neatly into the general theme of the LP. This is all the more surprising when all five members write.

Lodge explained: "One of us writes the song and, as the concept of how the finished album should sound approaches, the six of us, including Tony Clarke, say, 'Let's put a flute part in there,' and then we discuss what it should be.

"We leave it to the individual writer, who'll do six or seven songs, but from those there'll only be two he'll put forward as his own particular favorites. Nobody tells anybody else what to write. It's only at the final stages that we discuss the final formations of each song. …

"The reason we wait until just before the album to write is because then we're all writing at the same time with roughly the same ideas. You can hear emotions and thoughts of a certain period in each album. All our albums are musical diaries.

"We're as tight as a community can be without living in the same house. All our wives are friends and all our best friends are in the band.

"We've never had a violent row; there are opinions, but this is good because then you can explore things. This is what a discussion group is all about." (JL-NME70)

On January 31, 1970, Mike Jahn, a music columnist for Pop Scene Service, syndicated to newspapers across the United States, wrote:

> The Moody Blues have released their newest album, *To Our Children's Children's Children*, another significant step in their musical-philosophical journey. ...
>
> Their reputation is based on one excellent LP, *In Search of the Lost Chord*, which established the Moody Blues as the only popular rock group which can sing of cosmic beauty and universal truth without seeming stupid and pretentious. ...
>
> The new album isn't as pointed and specific as *In Search of the Lost Chord*. And it has a certain sameness of melody and feel. But the Moody Blues' music is so unique and effective one doesn't mind hearing it again. ...

One day later, another syndicated columnist in America, Scott Campbell, with his "Sounds – From the Underground," wrote:

> The Moody Blues' two greatest assets are originality and versatility, married to an almost unlimited amount of talent. Originally one of the forces of the famous British Invasion launched by the Beatles in the mid-Sixties, the group emerged from a later popularity slump to combine rock music and classical arrangements in the *Days of Future Passed* album. From there, as one observer commented, the Moodies ceased utilizing an orchestra and instead became one. ...
>
> The Moody Blues' fifth album, *To Our Children's Children's Children* (Threshold THS1) is out now on the group's own new record label. As expected, it fulfills every promise made by previous LPs. It is very much a continuation of the last album, *On the Threshold of a Dream*, with the new set reaching a higher level of musical advancement and complexity.
>
> I have found practically everything the group has ever done a source of fascinating listening, and the 13 cuts on the LP are no exception.

For a United Press International wire story, in newspapers in February 1970, John J. Meehan asked the musical question, "Is Message of Rock Music Only for

Young?" Among the artists Meehan took an objective look at were the Beatles, Bob Dylan, the Rolling Stones, the Jefferson Airplane, the Lovin' Spoonful, Jimi Hendrix, Frank Zappa and the Mothers of Invention, and the Moody Blues. Each artist, or one member from each group, was interviewed, and a topic of discussion was the generation gap ... the void that seemed to exist between the music listened to by the over-30 crowd and that of the young. Hendrix told Meehan, "I'm going to write an album which will simplify it all and bridge the gap between parents and kids."

Meehan wrote:

> ... The Moody Blues feel they have begun a bridge. This British group's album *In Search of the Lost Chord* traces what they see as their contemporaries' quest for truth. The record trips through educations and personal experiences and, frankly, into drugs. Explorers Livingstone and Scott fail to find full answers in Africa and the Antarctic; neither does the answer lie, according to the Moodies, in the LSD of Dr. Timothy Leary, who will "take you up ... let you down ... plant your feet back firmly on the ground." The Moodies leave Leary's hallucinogens about where accepted psychiatrists place them, possible keys for further understanding of the mind, but dangerous for indiscriminate use. "Timothy Leary's dead," the group sings. "No, no, he's on the outside, looking in" to where the answer lies.

Graeme Edge told Meehan, "We were saying, 'Acid is too dangerous to run around using by yourself.' The album describes a search. It's meant to kind of show that the answer is not in the physical. It's in the metaphysical. You've got to try to change people's hearts and minds. That's what you've got to do." (GE-MEP70)

Meehan continued:

> The Moody Blues recent album, *To Our Children's Children's Children*, begins with the electron roar of a rocket thrusting into space where the Moodies discover, not a momentous mechanical achievement, no Soviet or American first, but a child's uncluttered outlook on the world and universe. Space flight they see as a "climb to tranquility ... finding its real worth, conceiving the heavens flourishing on Earth. ...

> "With the eyes of a child ... you must learn how to see ... your world spinning 'round ... and for life you will be ... a small part of the hope ... that exists in the eyes of a child."

Edge said, "A child doesn't have any of the preconceived ideas of truth and beauty that we build up as we get older. The child has the truly open mind. That's what we should try to keep, an open mind all our lives. So many people are hung up on how different they are to everybody. They ought to start concentrating on how they're the same." (GE-MEP70)

Also on February 14, Justin Hayward had the cover of *Fabulous 208* magazine. Inside, Georgina Mells wrote:

Justin Hayward is the original beautiful dreamer. Very tall and unbelievably skinny with shaggy fair hair and intense dark eyes, he looks like an eighteenth-century poet. He smiles rarely but insists he is a happy person.

Hayward told Mells, "I daydream all the time; that's why people sometimes think I look sad. I find illusion makes me happy. For me songs are daydreams – like cartoons where anything is possible, where you can extend reality. When I write, it's always about me and always starts from something that happened to me; important things like my first love affair."

But Hayward did admit that four years with the Moodies, of which three had been wildly successful, had changed him. "I think I've changed a lot in that time, mostly in the things I want. Once it was very important to be in the charts, to appear on *Top of the Pops*, but now we realize that if you concentrate on singles you are only as good as your last one, and recording under pressure sometimes gives results you're not happy with. With albums, there is time to care, time to get involved. I'm much happier now, more relaxed and less ambitious. My tastes are simple and I have everything I could want materially with an opportunity to explore the business of giving pleasures."

Hayward acknowledged that he shied away from publicity. "It scares me a bit – I'm not sure I'm someone who should be noticed. It's a strange responsibility when your opinions start to count. The only other thing that scares me is being alone; losing people I love. Friends and family are very important to me. In fact, I just like being with people, at the fish-and-chip shop or in a crowd. One of the saddest things is that the shy fans, the ones you'd like to meet, aren't the ones with the determination to get backstage." (JH-F70)

Days later, Richard Green of *New Musical Express*, did a profile on Hayward as well, as part of his ongoing "Doing a Moody" series. His observation:

> Justin Hayward is intense and serious. … When he talks about things other than his music, he seems to have a pre-occupation with setting the world right without having the complete knowledge of how to do it.

Hayward told Green, "I have certain religious beliefs; I believe in Jesus Christ. I wouldn't try to put my views over to others, though. All I know is, things have got to change. There is no real need in this country to break away from the Establishment, there is no real problem. In America, you can see the extremes and you have to choose which side you're on – there's the plastic America and the young America, which, in its own way, is just as mixed up.…

"There have been people who have tried to alter things and they've all been crucified in the same way – Kennedy and Martin Luther King, and people like that.…

"It's difficult to just sit here and say what I feel, but when I write a song I can put down what I feel. The songs are really what I feel and things that I can't just say in a pub at lunchtime." (JH-NME70)

February 21, 1970: Another review from America. Dave Donnelly, syndicated music columnist – he wrote "The Pop Beat" – turned his attention to the Moodies:

> Quietly, and without a great deal of fanfare, an English group has been busy creating a number of unified albums – unified in the sense that *Sgt. Pepper* or Side Two of *Abbey Road* is unified – and the time has come to recognize them for it.
>
> The group is the Moody Blues, and their latest LP, *To Our Children's Children's Children*, begs our attention for a number of reasons.
>
> It is the group's fourth consecutive release which attempts to be more than a collection of short, snappy tunes – that aims, in fact, as high as pop albums dare to aim at this stage in rock's development. …
>
> In their latest album, the Moody Blues have chosen nothing less than the course of history as their theme, and while any dealing with such a vast subject needs be superficial, the melodies are pleasing, the voices harmonious, and the lyrics thought-provoking enough to make a successful album. It's not background music, to be sure – *To Our Children's Children's Children* must be listened to attentively, without interruption. And the Moody Blues and their producer, Tony Clarke, must be watched carefully, to see what they'll come up with next.
>
> Also, dig the album's art work (by Phil Travers) – it says it all!

Not everybody embraced the Moody Blues. From March 15, music critic David F. Wagner wrote in his syndicated newspaper column:

> A great deal of inter-industry trade paper talk has gone down about [the] Moody Blues' new album. I forget the actual wording, but something to the effect that it's the top accomplishment of the last decade – at least in rock, which is silly. …
>
> Although I've enjoyed them in the past, the latest work struggles through an entire side before it gets untracked, if that term is apropos for recordings. … "Gypsy," on Side Two, offers some of Moody Blues' better works, but compositely the album is not significant. The best that can be said of it is that it's often pleasing.

The vocal on "Gypsy" is tight and the number is as close to traditional rock as M.B. gets. "Eternity Road" is typically over-arranged, as most Moody Blues ballads are.

On Side One, the reliance on electronic effects is tedious. The lessening of this procedure on Side Two goes a long way toward bringing the group back down to earth and, when it relies on guitars, Moody Blues is far more bearable.

In America, where the band's popularity was still growing but far from peaking, *TOCCC* peaked at No. 14 in *Billboard*. Despite this, by mid-1970, it had sold in excess of 500,000 units and became the Moody's second Gold Record there.

As Justin Hayward later said in "Top Rank Suite," on the Moodies 1978' *Octave* album: "We were on our way to the big time, babe; to the great gold record in the sky."

***

On Saturday and Sunday, March 20 and 21, 1970, the Moodies kicked off yet another tour of America with two performances per day, at the Fillmore East in New York City. Opening for the Moodies were soloist Lee Michaels and English band Argent. The Fillmore sold out for all four appearances, at $5.50 admission fee, generating $62,000, a hefty purse for 1970. So popular was the engagement that two more performances had to be added on for Monday, March 22.

Even though *To Our Children's Children's Children* was new in the record stores, the Moodies' live set list only featured one song from the album – "Gypsy."

Because no single was taken from *TOCCC* for the American market (even though "Gypsy," an FM staple, would have sufficed), London Records wanted to release a new song for a 45. Although not a "singles" band, the Moodies went into the studio and produced a song they felt might get radio play – "Question." It was included in their set list.

"Jeff," a critic for *Variety*, covering one of the Fillmore East concerts, wrote in the trade:

> … The Moody Blues worked their way through a variety of songs from their albums, displaying their instrumental versatility and fine vocal harmonies. Mike Pinder's keyboard work, Justin Hayward's vocals and guitar, and Graeme Edge's driving percussion provide simulation of classical themes with a rock format. The group's new single, "Question," proved a potent hard rock number. …

From its March 22 edition, *Rolling Stone* magazine, and music Mike Jahn, assessed one of the Moodies' Fillmore East ventures … and, surprisingly, liked it.

> … The Moody Blues, a British group that played Friday and last night, and will appear again Monday evening at the Fillmore East, is a fine example of creative pretension. It is virtually the only rock group that sings very straight-faced of cosmic truth and eternal beauty and emerge with credibility intact.
>
> The British musicians' credibility always seems to be *In Search of the Lost Chord*, or music about *Days of Future Passed*, to mention the titles of two of their albums. Their music is lush, romantic, melodic and slightly Wagnerian. It is centered on the flute and the Mellotron, a keyboard instrument that manages a reasonable facsimile of an orchestra's string section. With these instruments, the players provide themselves with a sweet, harmonious and extremely dramatic backing. Consequently, no matter how many lost chords they search for in their lyrics, musically they can back up their dreams with drama.
>
> They also have written many beautiful songs. They are talented musicians, and their ensemble singing is quite good. Even in such an inventive field as rock, their sound is unique. In the concert this weekend, they offered a good selection of their songs, all played perfectly. To hear such an involved, powerful music played by five people was quite an experience. …

Billboard magazine's music critic was there, too, but appeared on the fence in his reporting. For the trades April 4, 1970 edition, Ed Ochs wrote:

> … When the British rock Brahman weren't confusing matters with erratic reproductions of their masterfully produced disks, the burden of carrying the group fell to Justin Hayward, whose straining voice changed the Moodys into an extraordinary folk-rock group. "Never Comes the Day" showed that the group could adapt their beautiful compositions from the master plan. Also outstanding was Ray Thomas' "Dr. Livingstone, I Presume."

Circus had this to say:

> The five rather dapper looking musicians on the Fillmore East stage began a song, and some members of the audience craned their heads to look for the orchestra that evidently backed the group. The Moody Blues, champions of symphonic rock, do it all themselves, with their beloved Mellotron. Mike Pinder, who operates the machine, "knows more about it than the people who built it in the first place," according to flautist Ray Thomas. The orchestral sound that Pinder produces on his Mellotron is more reminiscent of Kostelanetz and Mantovani – i.e., contemporary

symphonic pop – than any distinctly classical tone, but it sounds real pretty just the same.

"We like gentle, smooth music," Mike explained, and bassist John Lodge backed him, saying, "We don't like anything that grates the ear." This preference puts the group closer to the pop tradition than to the "art rock" label that the rock press had conferred upon them, along with Procol Harum, Deep Purple, and the now defunct Nice.

"The Mellotron turns our five pieces into about twelve pieces," Lodge continued. "The range of tone color you can get out of that machine is fantastic." …

Their music may be subject to criticism at times, but these five musicians, all things considered, are currently enjoying the fruits of a hard-earned, and justly deserved, success.

From New York, the band moved on to Boston, Massachusetts, to play the Boston Gardens on March 24 (unconfirmed), with the Steve Miller Band opening, then followed by the John Mayall Band, before the Moodies took the stage. One day later, they were in Hartford, Connecticut, this time with only the John Mayall Band as warm-up.

In the March 26 edition of Connecticut's *Hartford Courant*, J. Greg Robertson wrote:

The young audience showed their credentials – a ticket, long hair, bell-bottoms, and facial hair and an Army field jacket, if possible – and heard examples of the best and worst in rock music Wednesday night.

His audience was ready but John Mayall was late, his sidemen were disorganized, and product, bluesrockjazz, was unpolished to the point of being insulting. The Mayall group jammed with limited success for 40 minutes until John, buckskinned and hair swept tightly back into a ponytail, arrived to pull them somewhat close together. Mayall can do better. Mayall has done better. Mayall should do better.

In contract, the Moody Blues, 'heased' (since when has 'rehearsal' become a dirty word?), and [were] well-received by the audience.

The group brings to its sensitive, image-filled songs a feeling of tremendous, but restrained, power. … Their vocal and musical blending is nothing less than beautiful. …

Robertson also talked about the Mellotron, as nearly all who reviewed Moody Blues concerts in the 1960s and very early 1970s did. Its versatility made it something like the musical eighth wonder of the world.

JAM PRODUCTIONS & KTSA PRESENT

MOODY BLUES

SAN ANTONIO HEMISPHERE ARENA
MARCH 31 AT 7 P.M.

TICKETS — $3, $4, $5

On March 26, the Moodies took the stage of the Allen Theatre in Cleveland, Ohio, following an audience warm-up from the John Mayall Band, and Argent.

On March 31, the Moodies were in San Antonio, Texas, performing in the Hemisfair Arena. Poet and musician Turley Richards opened. Seat prices ran $3, $4, and $5.

On April 1, the Moody Blues reportedly played the Terrace Ballroom in Salt Lake City, Utah, with Cold Blood as their opening act (unconfirmed).

On April 2, the Moodies were in the Berkeley Community Theater in Berkeley, California, with Tom Rush doing warm-up.

For April 3, the Moodies were at Cal Poly University in San Luis Obispo, California. Cold Blood opened the show.

On Saturday, April 4, now down into Southern California, the Moodies were in the Long Beach Arena. They had the Steve Miller Band as their opening act. Tickets ranged from $3.50 to $5.50. Robert Hilburn of *The Los Angeles Times* got in for free. Mr. Hilburn acquired a reputation over the next few decades as the hard-as-nails music critic in L.A. He evidenced a fondness for radical rock acts, and a disdain for anything that might please the masses. It's surprising he decided to show up at all. His opinion:

> For those who judge rock concerts by their length, the Moody Blues-Steve Miller Band affair Saturday at the Long Beach Arena was a bonanza. Too bad most of it was such a bore.
>
> In many ways, the failure of the evening (which stretched from 8 p.m. to 1 a.m.) was caused by an audience that was as noisy, restless and generally unattentive [sic] as any I've seen. …
>
> The Moody Blues, an English group that has attracted a degree of respect and popularity in rock circles by its occasional use of classical music, was a general disappointment. But again, the audience may have contributed to the downfall.
>
> Lead singer-guitarist Justin Hayward deserves special praise for not missing a line or note despite the dozen semi-clad 15-year-old girls who gyrated at his feet all evening. …
>
> Rather than stick to its excellent, melodic rock (as shown in such songs as "Ride My See-Saw," "Lovely to See You," "Never Comes the Day," and "Send Me No Wine"), the Moody Blues have a tendency to engage in some pretentious classical and poetic side trips. …

Though the group finished with a rousing rendition of "Ride My See-Saw," most of what went before it was so weighted down with the lesser elements of the group's abilities that the whole appearance seemed like a long disaster. Audience response was favorable, however, for the group.

Obviously Hilburn felt he knew better than the audience.

The day after the Long Beach show, the group was seen on the TV show *Get It Together*, hosted by Mama Cass. They performed "Candle of Life" and "Floating." Meanwhile, that same evening, they were at the Santa Clara County Fairgrounds in San Jose, California, that evening. Norman Greenbaum ("Spirit in the Sky") was their opening act. This show concluded the short U.S. tour.

In the April 15 edition of *Variety*, it was reported that the Moodies, all totaled, gave 17 consecutive one-nighters, and grossed $200,000. They were now safely back in Mother England.

Ray Thomas told Tony Norman at England's *Music Now!*, "We are still picking up [sales] in the States – it's so big. The last album, *To Our Children's Children's Children* sold as many in Los Angeles as it did in the whole of Britain. That's what the groups are aiming for when they go over there. You get over half the world's record-buying population in one land mass. ...

"We are not going to do any more stadiums over there. We want to stick to concert halls. We played to 15,000 people in one stadium [Long Beach Arena]. That's just ridiculous; there's just no contact with the audience at something like that. The Isle of Wight show was even bigger, but that was just an experience; the thing I liked was that it was just down to good vibes. Nobody wanted to hassle you. In a big concert in the States, you get at least 40 or 50 police. ...

"But, really, I don't like the States too much. It's too violent and too hectic."
(RT-MN70)

Justin Hayward had a different opinion regarding America. On the same day that Ray Thomas's interview appeared, so did one with the focus on Hayward, in the May 9 edition of *Disc and Music Echo*. Hayward told Penny Valentine, "America is really the hope of the modern world, which may be a frightening thought, but it's true. England is the only country to live in and I love it here, but we never really get involved with much. You couldn't exactly say the future of the world revolved round this island.

"Our attitude to America's changed – I think because our fear of it has gone. The first time I went there I was positively petrified. There was this terrible undercurrent of physical damage and violence. The second time that undercurrent was there but suddenly it was exciting. Now there's so much happening there, so much to become involved in that the fear has completely gone.

"The American attitude to music is so different to anywhere else in the world. There's so much musical freedom – if you switch a radio on there you don't find a series of DJs on ego-trips but people who are interested in the tracks they're playing. Even the musicians have a different attitude.

"Like any group, the Moodies are influenced by the music we hear and how much music we're exposed to. In America you're exposed to the maximum, and naturally that affects you." (JH-DME70)

Regardless of the overwhelming job of doing a cross-country tour of the U.S., the band enjoyed performing live and had especially enjoyed their tour of England prior to embarking to America.

Ray Thomas said, in an interview with David Hughes for *Disc and Music Echo*'s May 30, 1970 issue: "We don't ever intend giving up live work, partly because when you're on tour you're in the company of the people who buy your records and you can get a better idea of the direction you're heading, and partly because it's good for our egos to be on stage! We love to play to people, and if we go down well it knocks us out – like our last British tour. That was the first time the Moody Blues had ever toured Britain as a top of the bill act. It was fabulous!" (RT-DME70)

***

To Our Children's Children's Children was nominated for a Grammy in America as Best Engineered Album. Because it was released so late in the year in 1969, it did not qualify for that year's awards (given out in early 1970) but, instead, was put into the competition for albums released in 1970, with the awards handed out in early 1971.

Derek Varnals said, "It was a tough year. *Bridge Over Troubled Waters* won it, and that won about eight categories that year." (DV-H&H95b)

14

A Question of Balance (1970)

U.K. and U.S. album release:
Threshold THS 3; August 7, 1970
U.K. peak position: #1
U.S.: #3
(Certified platinum in the U.S.)
Australia: #2
Canada: #3
(Certified platinum in Canada)
Norway: #5
Netherlands: #8

Single release: *"Question" b/w "Gypsy"*
U.K.: Threshold TH 4; U.S.: Threshold THS-67004; April 24, 1970
U.K. peak position: #1 (*New Musical Express* and *Disc & Music Echo*))
U.S.: 19 (*Cashbox* and *Record World*)
Holland: #1
Netherlands: #1
Belgium: #3
France: #7
Canada: #8
Germany: #10

Single release: *"Melancholy Man" b/w "Candle of Life"*
TH 30005 (French release); November 1970
Peak position in France: #1

At the time that the Moody Blues were recording *A Question of Balance*, Mike Pinder told Keith Altham of *Rave* magazine, "There was a very real danger at one time that we would become so involved in our recording techniques that we would no longer bother with personal appearances, but we discovered in time that nothing takes the place of a live audience. You lose that communication with a live audience and you lose so much – you can feed off the enthusiasm of an audience and give them back interest in return." (MP-R70)

Hayward said, "For us, we had a delicate balance. We weren't ever able to get it right on stage. We had a power and energy on stage, but we never got the balance right, until the '80s actually, when technology finally caught up with us. Before that, it was sheer power; great big stacks of Marshalls' [amplifiers].... At one show, I remember looking at Ray, and he was standing in front of Mike's speakers, and his trousers were literally flapping with the movement of the air!" (JH-OTR09)

To ensure that the use of studio techniques wouldn't prevent them from touring, as it had with the Beatles after the making of *Sgt. Pepper*, the Moody Blues decided to simplify the instrumentation on this new album.

Justin Hayward: "From the beginning of our recording sessions we were all convinced that we had to record an album of songs that could easily translate into effective live performances. In a way, we almost reverted to perforating live in the studio, without venturing too much into the world of overdubs." (JH-QOBCD08)

In another interview, he elaborated, "[T]here's actually very little double-tracking on that album – even on the track 'Question,' which has some nice echo, but not much beyond that. Mike may have double-tracked some Mellotron here and there, but apart from that it was all single voice, single guitar kind of stuff." (JH-RS13)

As for a theme for the album: Rock bands work and live in a world that has no conventions, nothing normal, especially in respect to the times they are touring. The hours are upside down, the schedules are exhausting, and the group must remain isolated from its public. This is simply because of the fans who live out the term "fanatic" – and the Moodies certainly had their share. All of these factors impacted the Moodies' choice of theme for their next album.

Justin Hayward: "What I remember most about that period was struggling a little bit to get the balance right in our own lives between the touring side of things, and being physically out on the road in America, or what have you, for long periods, and then going back into the studio. It's such a different physical environment that it can be very hard to get out of the 'road fever' mentality, which comes from being on tour for long periods away from home. After a few years, something has to give in a way." (JH-RS13)

After their first American tour, and before recording *On the Threshold of a Dream*, many of the Moodies had remarked to press that their next album would reflect what they had seen while crisscrossing the U.S. This idea was jettisoned in favor of something more subtle – an examination between the differences between reality and dreams, and how the two can resonate, enforcing each other, or clash horribly … and what it is to be on the threshold of the latter.

This intended examination and commentary on modern culture, with primary focus on America, was again postponed when Tony Clarke lobbied for the follow-up to *Threshold*, also to be recorded and released in 1969, to be an album with a theme of life in the space age, presented as a time capsule to be unearthed one million years hence.

Now came the dawning of a new decade. With *A Question of Balance*, the band could finally express their reflections and feelings about modern-day life in America, as well as the rest of the modern world, and even touch upon the extreme fan worship they had witnessed while touring the U.S.

Question probed many aspects of humanity out of balance – with religion, science, militarization, ecology, and inner perception and peace … or lack of it. America, as the Moodies had witnessed on their treks across the nation, was perhaps the most ambitious and powerful country on Earth, and, frighteningly, in some ways the most imbalanced. The generational divide, and the opposition between Hawks and Doves, between the races, between the sexes, between the churches, between the class systems, between industrialists and environmentalists, were tearing the country apart.

When the touring Moodies arrived at a particular place in this patchwork nation of conflicts, some praised them, some dismissed them, some loved them, some hated them, and some worshiped them. Amidst all of this, the Moodies were seeking balance in their own lives.

Mike Pinder in particular seemed to be in deep contemplative search of something. At the time *A Question of Balance* was being recorded, David Hughes of *Disc and Music Echo* visited Pinder's home, for a March 28, 1970 article called "Moody Mode of Travelling – On the Planet." Hughes observed:

> Mike Pinder – moody blue and an adult 28-years-old. Dark brown hair receding at the front but well compensated by a distinguished full mustache. Immaculately, yet colorfully dressed. Cool, calm and very calculating. Brimming with ideas and beliefs – astronomical, astrological, philosophical, and religious. Businessman and musician, animal and garden lover. Above all – infinitely likeable human being!
>
> To Mike, music and the Moody Blues are means to a far greater end – his small part in trying to bring peace and understanding to a troubled world; a world he says will end during his lifetime. If that sounds pompous and unnatural, it's simply the result of reading it in cold print. Mike Pinder is sincere without being a bore.

Pinder was living in a "delightful" £15,000 60-year-old house in Cobham, Surrey, which, he told Hughes, "belonged to a schoolmaster, has an acre of ground, and looks very like something out of Stratford-on-Avon [a "market-town" near Birmingham]."

There, Hughes noted, Pinder lived with his goldfish and dozens of wild birds and grey squirrels. Part of his daily ritual was surveying his garden of 4,000 daffodils, looking for any sign of spring. In his house was shelf after shelf containing 300 books on theology and theosophy. High on his list of plans: to build a recording studio in the summerhouse and garage.

Pinder told Hughes, "The best way to explain how I feel now is that I have no fear of death. I have a certain realization now and I know I will have complete realization when I die. I want to die conscientiously; I want to die awake.

"I believe in life after death, and I think we will see the end of the world as it is now, in our lifetime." (MP-DME70)

Pinder came to believe this from reading ancient philosophies, both Christian and the occult, which, by his interpretations, had the same forecast for the world's end. He said, "Throughout the Bible it says the world will end by fire. I don't believe that will be by pressing a button and starting a nuclear war. This planet is destined to go through a change, not because we are on it, but because of where it is, on the very edge of the galaxy. In our galaxy, the moon goes round the Earth, which goes round the sun, which goes round the galaxy. And our galaxy, the Milky Way, is in a constellation moving in a spiromatic way. Our galaxy vibrates a certain rate – everything vibrates; the very reason we live is because of our vibrations. But not everything vibrates at the same frequency – spiritual bodies exit, but they vibrate at a much faster rate. This is why a Buddhist monk, for example, can set fire to himself and not feel or register pain.

"I believe our Earth is moving into a galaxy which is vibrating at a far faster rate – the dawning of the Age of Aquarius. And this is what the Book of Revelations and Jesus Christ are talking about. The magnetic field of this planet will be upset and there will be fire, volcanoes and earthquakes as a direct result of the new vibration. The vibration can be compared with the human voice, which can shatter a wine glass with its vibrations. This new vibration will shatter the Earth. In every single work of wisdom ever written they prophesy this in much the same way.

"The Children of God will be saved, the non-believers will perish, says the Bible, and the Children of God will be recognized by the eye of God – the third eye, on their foreheads.

"In modern terms, I believe the people who will be saved from destruction are those who are spiritually aware and can understand our relationship with the universe – for the higher you get, spiritually, the higher you vibrate, and if your vibrations are high enough, you will be able to adapt yourself to the new world.

"And I want this catalytic upheaval to come, because I believe this planet is now in the grip of evil forces. Make a list of all the evil things happening in the world; then of all the good things – the evil will far outweigh the good.

"I hope I shall survive." (MP-DME70)

A question of balance? Or a question of destiny?

With these events, influences, and distractions under consideration, the Moodies embarked on a journey to ask questions and perhaps offer solutions for the essential balance that all sensible people seek in their lives.

Recording the Album:

A Question of Balance was made in three periods, the first spanning 14 days, from Saturday, January 17, 1970, through Saturday, January 31. These sessions produced, respectively, "It's Up to You" (Hayward); "Tortoise and the Hare" (Lodge); "And the Tide Rushes In" (Thomas); followed by a track that didn't make the original album, with the working title, "Mike's Number One"; then on to "Don't You Feel Small" (Edge, with uncredited collaboration by Hayward); and "Question" (Hayward).

The group returned to the studio for the second batch of songs, recorded from March 10 through 13. These four days produced one new track, John Lodge's "Minstrel's Song."

The final session of recordings took place from June 1 through 6. From these dates came two songs from Mike Pinder – "Melancholy Man," followed by "How Is It (We Are Here)?" – and, the last track to be recorded, the Edge/Thomas collaboration, "The Balance."

Graeme Edge: "That [album] was the start of where we were almost treated as semi-deities, and we very much wanted to reflect what the title says: that maintaining yourself is a question of balance. It's very hard to maintain your equilibrium under those pressures." (GE-MD87)

Hayward told Tony Norman in August 1970: "On the first side, we were asking ourselves the questions, and, on the second side, we are starting to answer it. Looking for the answers will keep us going for a long time." (JH-MS70)

"Question" is actually two-songs-in-one by Justin Hayward. It was recorded on January 24, 1970. (It is believed additional work on the song took place on January 30 and 31.)

Justin Hayward: "There were a lot of things happening in the world, and in my life, and I was getting a bit upset. I'd also lost someone that was very dear to me, which was part of it as well, and there was a kind of anger about that loss. And it turned out not so much a personal song, but more, I suppose… to do with war in the world and problems of the world in general." (JH-WNEW87)

Elsewhere, Hayward said, "The song was about the anti-war movement, which we somehow seemed to be involved in around the world, particularly in America, and in France, as well, in '68, with the student uprising. It was a protest song that was also about a world that we were beginning to believe was lost." (JH-TRC96)

> *Why do we never get an answer*
> *When we're knocking at the door,*
> *With a thousand million questions*
> *About hate and death and war?*
> *'Cause when we stop and look around us,*
> *There is nothing that we need,*
> *In a world of persecution*
> *That is burning in its greed.*

In another interview, Hayward said, "'Question' was two songs that I'd written separately – one frantic; one very slow. And then I was sitting at home one day and I thought, 'Hang on a minute; one of them is half the tempo of the other one. So, maybe, let's go from one into the other, and see what happens, and then come back out of it.' [The recording session] was very quick. We'd just gone through this period of not doing too many overdubs and trying to pull back to a live feel. We recorded it on Saturday; Tony Clarke mixed it on Sunday, and Decca had it for their Monday meeting." (JH-CC88)

Graeme Edge: "Do you play football? Have you ever had that experience, that feeling, when you play a move, make a shot that normally would have been impossible? That surge of elation, seeing the light? Well, that happened two or three times to me on our albums. It happened on a *Question of Balance* session. The first time we did ['Question'], we were all miked up, ready to go. We sat down and everybody played what they wanted to play, and all the way through I was shitting myself because I didn't know it that well. Normally, we play over and over again until we have it right. But we always have the tape running. And 'Question' just happened, right there and then. It was like playing darts and getting 'treble twenties' the whole time." (GE-RS71)

Another song committed to tape during this session, which did not make the cut for the album, was by Mike Pinder. (Known simply as "Mike's Number One," the January 24 recording is a bonus track on the 2008 remastered *Question of Balance* CD.)

After these two songs were recorded, the Moodies took a break from further work in the studio to undertake another American tour (March 1970, covered in the previous chapter). Work on the album resumed in June 1970 at the Threshold studio in the Decca West Hampstead recording center. "How Is It" was the first Moodies recording to utilize Mike Pinder's newly acquired Moog synthesizer.

"How Is It (We Are Here)" was written and sung by Mike Pinder – a song filled with questions: "How is it we are here / On this path we walk / In this world of pointless fear / Filled with empty talk..."

Mike Pinder: "The song is based on the simplicity of asking the questions that have always been asked; using the song as an excuse to say other things, which is usually the way I've always written. You start off with something so you can actually say something else." (MP-H&H96)

Pinder found it curious that man would unearth precious things, only to hide them again in an underground vault. He commented on this with the lyrics: "Man's mighty mine-machines digging in the ground / Stealing rare minerals where they can be found / Concrete caves with iron doors, bury it again / While a starving, frightened world fills the sea with grain."

"And the Tide Rushes In" was written by Ray Thomas after a fight with his wife, symbolizes how a tide rushes in and washes away sandcastles, symbolizing a relationship. Thomas sings:

> *I've been searching for my dreams*
> *A hundred time today*
> *I build them up, you knock them down*
> *Like they were made of clay*
> *And the tide rushes in*
> *And washes my castles away*
> *Then I'm really not so sure*
> *Which side of the bed I should lay...*

With this song, the question of balance has to do with love and communication between two people.

Thomas recalled that producer Tony Clarke was especially pleased with the song and recording. Thomas said, "I remember Tony Clarke saying to [my wife] that she ought to have more rows with me because he considered it such a great song." (GE-QOBCD08)

While making *A Question of Balance*, Thomas told *Hit Parader*, "We have had people break down and cry hearing our records. And that really is a kick because it means they are feeling emotions we put into the song. We've had tears on the album we are working on now. Someone heard it and said it was how they were feeling but were unable to express it to anyone." (RT-HP71)

The song was recorded January 22. In addition to acoustic guitar, Justin Hayward played a mandolin.

"Don't You Feel Small," credited solely to Graeme Edge, was actually a collaboration. Edge said, "I presented [the song] with a guitar and played a sort of skeleton-ish chord sequence, and Justin... took over on guitar and just virtually wrote the music, although he never asked me for any piece of the publishing or anything." (GE-ITS89)

At the time of the album's release, Edge told an interviewer, "[That song] started, basically, as a bit of a go about ecology, and then I [added] a lot of things [about] the way people seem to be allowing themselves to be made to feel very insignificant.... [T]he point of the song is, 'Don't *you* feel small; [don't you *allow*] yourself to feel small – not that you *are* small." (GE-H&H96)

> *Ask the mirror on the wall*
> *Who's the biggest fool of them all,*
> *Bet you feel small*
> *It happens to us all....*
>
> *Look at progress,*
> *Then count the cost*
> *We'll spoil the seas*
> *With the rivers we've lost....*

The original intent was to have Edge sing the song.

Derek Varnals: "This was the first time we had Graeme attempting to sing, as it were, other than doing a speaking part." (DV-H&H96)

Tony Clarke: "We wanted to have him sing this originally, but Graeme can't sing, and I think he'd be the first to admit this." (TC-H&H96)

So he was asked to whisper it instead, with Mike Pinder and John Lodge whispering along. This made for a unique track, not only for the album but for all of pop music. Can you think of another song that was whispered? To everyone's delight, it works, and works well.

"Tortoise and the Hare" is John Lodge's song based on one of Aesop's fables, making comment on the wastefulness of the rat race – aka the human race – always racing through life, with few of us ever crossing the finish line which marks the goals we set for ourselves.

The recording session took place on January 19.

"It's Up to You" was the first song recorded for the album, started on January 17, 1970, and completed the following day. Justin Hayward had gained a reputation as the group member who would usually start the new albums off, since he always came prepared with one, two, or more completed songs.

The song started off with a guitar hook. Hayward said, "That's probably my guitar favorite, because I love the way my Gibson 335 sounds on this track." (JH-GW93)

Elsewhere, he added, "I just know that I love that type of song. I'd done a couple of them before and I'd enjoyed them so much. I think another one was 'Lovely to See You.' The same kind of thing; same key – I think it was in E; it was just a natural for the 335 as well; for the D28 and the 335 to make that kind of sound…" (JH-20CG00)

Another song of this type, with that melodic lead guitar sound, would be "You and Me" from *Seventh Sojourn*. The same parallel could be drawn with a track from *Every Good Boy Deserves Favour*, "The Story in Your Eyes."

For very nearly any other band, this recording would have been issued as a single with certain Top 20 possibilities. But the Moodies were not trying to dominate the singles market … or be trapped by it. "Question" had been such a great success as a single prior to the release of the album, they didn't feel a need to follow it with a second single release.

Mike Pinder: "Another great song of Justin's…. 'It's Up to You' is very much a starker reality that people still need to realize, that it's up to the individual to make anything better, whether it be a political vote in conserving water or in not polluting the planet." (MP-H&H96)

"Minstrel's Song," written and with lead vocal by John Lodge, delivers another Moody Blues positive message: "Hear the nations sing / Our minstrel's song / As he walks by in their lives / Soon the spring will come / And everyone will all be singing, bringing / Love – Love. Everywhere love is all around."

"Minstrel's Song" took longer to record than any other track on the album. The taping spanned four days, starting on March 10 and wrapping on the 13th.

Tony Clarke: "[I]t was around this time that we got into the thing of Mike and Justin playing acoustic guitar at the same time. That saves a tape generation, meaning, less tape hiss …. [and] the acoustic guitars sound great…" (TC-H&H96)

"Dawning Is the Day" is Justin Hayward's third composition and lead vocal on the album. Ray Thomas had only contributed one song this time out, making room for this number. The gentle and lovely song is surprisingly punctuated by louder-than-expected drum rolls from Graeme Edge.

Edge said, "What I enjoy about Jus's work is the depth of the emotion, the soul, and the obvious effort that has been put into writing the song. With regard to the drums, his songs really don't want hitting-every-drum-in-sight Keith Moon fills. The word 'delicate' comes to mind. There's great satisfaction in holding a simple beat right to the edge of monotony and then giving the song a release in the right place, kicking it on." (GE-MD87)

Hayward sings:

Rise, let us see you, dawning is the day.

Miss, misty meadow, you will find your way.
Wake up in the morning to yourself and
leave this crazy life behind you.
Listen, we're trying to find you....

"Melancholy Man," features a captivating sing-along melody and a curious lyric by Mike Pinder. Pinder, followed by the band during the second chorus, sings:

... When all the stars are falling down
Into the sea and on the ground,
And angry voices carry on the wind,
A beam of light will fill your head
And you'll remember what's been said
By all the good men this world's ever known....

Meanwhile, Pinder, in the lead, sings the verse:

I'm a melancholy man, that's what I am,
All the world surrounds me,
And my feet are on the ground,
I'm a very lonely man, doing what I can,
All the world astounds me
and I think I understand
that we're going to keep growing, wait and see.

A quarter of a century after writing the song, Mike Pinder said: "The single most incorrect interpretation of 'Melancholy Man' has been that maybe it was a song about *me* being melancholy. I used that as a way of saying that there are different levels of melancholy, and that this was a melancholy for the whole world, because of the impending breakdown of the structure in all things that we have seen happen since the song came out, 26 years ago. What we're seeing now is just more results of what was being done then, and what continues to be done by the industrial giants and governments of the world, and the greedy little cigar-smoking guys, like [the one depicted] on the album cover." (MP-H&H96)

Derek Varnals said, "It was a curious thing. As soon as they started playing the first run-through – and Mike was playing acoustic guitar with Justin on it – the key they were playing it in and just the general feel of it made me say to Tony: 'This sounds like the soundtrack to a French film.' And I said to Mike: 'I hope you don't mind, but I'm going to very much try and make it sound like a French film,' which is why I made the song a little bit echoey. I usually employed echo to make things sweet and smooth, but I thought this one should sound a little bit more brittle, a bit stark, a bit sort of black and white. That was the flavor that it gave me, and that's what we did to the basic guitars. Interestingly enough, it was a very big success in France. I'm not sure if it was a case of 'selling ice to the Eskimos,' but it had that sort of feel about it." (DV-H&H96)

The song is constructed around the twin acoustic guitars of Pinder and Hayward – each overdubbed twice, bringing forth the blending sound of four guitars, with Pinder strumming chords and Hayward doing, as Pinder described it, "the picking; the little movements."

Pinder also plays the Moog synthesizer on this track.

Graeme Edge: "You knew straightaway that you didn't need to do a lot to [it]. All you needed … was to reinforce the harmonies that were coming off the piano … without changing the chord sequences, the two different melody lines, and then the way the two melody lines intertwined. If you would have over orchestrated it, it would have actually spoiled [the effect]." (GE-H&H96)

"The Balance," by Graeme Edge and Ray Thomas, combines a poem by Edge (with collaboration from Thomas), set to music by Thomas and an uncredited Mike Pinder.

Regarding the lyric, which sounds biblical, Edge told Keith Altham of *Record Mirror*, "I had the idea for that piece in my head and written [it] out several times, but although I knew the sentiments were right, it laid itself open to the kind of criticism we have experienced before. I rewrote the piece in Biblical terms because it took it right over the top. It was so open; so vulnerable, that we couldn't have dared to do it unless we meant it!" (GE-RM70)

This is what Edge, with Thomas, dared to do:

> *… And he thought of those he angered,*
> *for he was not a violent man.*
> *And he thought of those he hurt,*
> *for he was not a cruel man.*
> *And he thought of those he frightened,*
> *for he was not an evil man.*
> *And he understood;*
> *he understood himself.*
> *Upon this he saw that when he was of anger*
> *or knew hurt or felt fear,*
> *it was because he was not understanding,*
> *and he learned … compassion.*
> *He saw his enemies like unto himself,*
> *and he learned love.*
> *Then, he was answered.*

The group then sings:

> *Just open your eyes*
> *and realize, the way it's always been.*
> *Just open your mind, and you will find*
> *the way it's always been.*
> *Just open your heart,*
> *and that's a start.*

Mike Pinder: "It was really quite amazing, because [religion] was not something that Graeme paid a lot of attention to. He still is a self-professed atheist, and religion was not something that he would be spending a lot of time on. He would be spending a lot of time on astronomy, science, and math, and those kinds of things. So when that kind of imagery came through, it was obvious that he had opened himself up to some wonderful outpourings." (MP-H&H96)

While promoting the release of the album, Edge told *Disc and Music Echo*, "Poetry is a way of transmitting human emotion. Because of the relationship between the Moodies, we were able to relearn and rediscover the basic truths of the old writers. Those cats, Confucius and Jesus Christ, they were right – they told us to love one another. And that's what we're doing.

"We are rewriting it just with different techniques. You get back what you reflect. If you give out good vibes, you'll meet nice people. If you are an aggressive person, you'll meet with the same treatment....

"Society forces people into a narrow way of life. I believe that people are essentially good; it's the society which is bad." (GE-DME70)

"The Balance" was recorded on June 6 and 7, 1970, bringing the sessions for the album to a close.

Justin Hayward: "It was quite refreshing, actually, doing the *Question of Balance* album after the concept stuff and all the studio trickery of the *Children's Children* album; getting back to that place where we could just get a bunch of songs together with a bit less instrumentation going on, that we could just sit around in a room and play." (JH-RS13)

Assistant recording engineer Adrian Martins said, "We used to book the album playbacks at Trident Studios, where there would be a bit of a reception. I remember it was a bit like the Gilbert and Sullivan things where Tony Clarke would sit outside with his head in his hands and moan, 'What's the reaction going to be from the press? Are they going to blast it?' It was always a success, but Tony was always worried that the new album would be the one where they'd say, 'Ah, you've overstepped the mark with this one; you're finished!'

"But Tony was a brilliant producer; he always put his heart and soul into the Moodies, and really knew how to get the best from them." (AM-H&H97)

Between the formation of Threshold one year earlier, and now, with the completion of the band's second album for their own label, Hayward's emotions were high. He told David Hughes, for the May 30, 1970 issue of *Disc and Music Echo*, "The last seven months have been like a dream to me. Now anything is possible and… the group, as a whole, works even better together now than before. We understand each other better. Whatever we do, it's we six who stand to gain or lose – it's a marvelous feeling of independence." (JH-DME70a)

***

As the album was being mixed and prepared for release, a cover design was needed. As usual, it was needed quickly.

Phil Travers: "The cover concept was pretty much down to me. I think the band did mention Einstein. We may have had some preliminary discussions about how it should feel, but it was pretty much down to me.

"I think we had three days to complete it, from start to finish, and so I can tell you categorically now that I had absolutely no sleep for three nights and two days; I just worked solidly on it. I had meals, obviously, but I didn't have any sleep at all…. The last day, I had the printer breathing over my shoulder to take it away, while I was trying to finish off these clouds on the bottom." (PT-H&H96a)

One of the reference images Travers used in prepping the art for *A Question of Balance* was a photograph of Colonel John Nicholas Blashford-Snell, OBE, a well-known British explorer, which had appeared in a copy of *National Geographic* magazine.

Colonel Blashford-Snell was a former British officer turned explorer and author. Among other accomplishments, he founded Operation Raleigh (a sustainable development charity which works primarily in Africa and South and Central America aiding poverty victims) and the Scientific Exploration Society. His books chronicled his many expeditions.

Travers told Mark Murley of *Higher & Higher* that he closely reproduced the image, as part of his cover, which was painted once again in Expressionist style. In his drawing, Travers took liberty with the likeness of Snell, in pith helmet, and had him brandishing a pistol, seeming to be aimed at the head of an elephant. The depiction came to Snell's attention after the album was released, and he brought legal action against Decca Records and the Moody Blues.

Above: Colonel John Nicholas Blashford-Snell, OBE, pith helmet included.
(Photo Source: Daily Telegraph)
Below: Original LP cover drawing and replacement image.

Travers told Murley, "Snell said he was embarrassed being on this cover. 'A source of constant embarrassment being on the cover,' I believe was the expression that he used." (PT-H&H96a)

Tony Clarke recalled, "Snell saw this artwork and sent us a letter of complaint. He was very agitated about it, and we had to come to some settlement with him. I personally was annoyed and said to the lawyers, 'Why are we doing this? This is just a painting of a man holding a gun.' But [Snell] was objecting to the fact that he was being portrayed as a white hunter." (TC-H&H96a)

Travers changed the illustration, altering the likeness of the man depicted and losing the pith helmet. Decca used this as the new cover in England.

Travers said, "The only trouble was that Decca, in its infinite wisdom, printed up new covers in this country [England] but they didn't think to do it abroad, apparently. So then there was another action against Decca, this time involving a lot of money, I heard." (PT-H&H96a)

Anyone who has a copy of the album which shows a man wearing a pith hermit has a collectable item.

Also depicted on the cover, from top left and working clockwise:

- A missile representing nuclear threat;
- A cigar-smoking man with his hand outstretched (Travers said it was "your average sort of tycoon; it was no one at Decca," but Tony Clarke laughingly referred to it as "the guy at our record company, his hand outstretched, saying 'Where's the new album? Where's the new album?'");
- Smoke surrounding Earth (Travers said, "Well, we were all heavily into pollution in those days, plus the lyric mentioned it somewhere");
- A Raven (Travers noted, "Oil slick; again, the pollution theme);
- A pistol-brandishing man with gun aimed at elephant's head;
- Foliage (Travers said, "Other than the obvious environment tie-in, this was primarily done to provide some color");
- An orange (in reference to the fruit in 'The Balance');
- Approaching storm clouds looming over idle beachgoers (Travers explained, "The people on the sleeve are actually just sitting there, on holiday, basking in the sunshine with presumably not a care in the world; they just don't notice what's coming up at them and probably won't until it's too late");
- The Threshold logo on a flag on the beach tent;
- Falling people, a TV, a car, a motorcycle (Travers explained, "They're trying to get up the ladder of success, wanting things like TV sets and to get more than the person next door, keeping up with the Joneses, you might say.");

- Albert Einstein (Travers: "Because, if you like, he was feeling partially responsible for the weaponry developments and is looking a bit perplexed and sort of awkward about it. He's thinking: 'Oh, my God, what did I start?!'").

U.K. and U.S. single release:
"Question" b/w "Candle of Life"
Threshold TH 4; April 24, 1970

Since the last two Moody Blues singles – "Never Comes the Day" from *On the Threshold of a Dream*, and "Watching and Waiting" from *For Our Children's Children's Children* – had failed to impact the charts, a decision was made. The Moody Blues would do something they had not done since 1967 – release a single well ahead of the album.

A song that the band had put to tape a couple of months earlier was chosen, coupled with "Candle of Life," a track from the previous album that radio programmers would be happy to have without any crossfading at the start or the end.

Of course, the Moody Blues, being the Moody Blues, put out a single that did not fit the mode of most singles aimed toward AM radio. It had dramatic time signature shifts, and ran nearly five minutes in length.

For its April 18, 1970 issue, *Cashbox* magazine selected "Question" as one of its 16 "Picks of the Week," in the company of other sure winners such as "Up Around the Bend" by Creedence Clearwater Revival; "Reach Out and Touch Me" by Diana Ross; "Daughter of Darkness" by Tom Jones; "Westbound #9" by the Flaming Embers; "Soolaimón (African Trilogy II)" by Neil Diamond; and "Spill the Wine" by Eric Burdon & War, all destined to become U.S. hits.

The trade said of "Question":

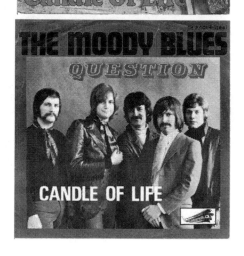

> Working into this side with a guitar intro in the Who manner, the Moody Blues churn up instant listener interest from the start for a contemporary question song bound to capture tremendous programming on both FM and AM outlets. Side alters midway to

become a brilliantly presented ballad in the M.B.'s own tradition….

In the April 25 issue of *New Musical Express*:

> The Moodies are essentially an LP group, but now they've come up with a track designed specially for the singles market – and they may well make a profound impression with it even though, because of its violently contrasting tempos, it's hardly danceable!

> Opens at a frantic gallop pace, with the blistering rhythm strummed out by acoustic guitars and string bass. Then midway through, it changes to a slow and rather wistful ballad with a clinging melody – before reverting to the breathless up-beat, this time with full orchestra support.

> …. The lyric is deep-thinking and absorbing. Altogether a remarkable piece of work.

Steve Zinz, reviewing the single for his "Sounds Good" column in the May 3 edition of Maryland's *The Baltimore Sun*, said:

> This British group has not made the [singles] disc scene for a long time, but with this sound they should once again set up camp on the charts. "Question" begins as a slow sound but builds tempo only to reverse again. The Moody Blues have a great deal of talent, but they get hung upon variations of speeds and sounds too often.

Apparently Zinz was confused. He reported that "Question" begins slow, then speeds up, then slows down again. But the tempo changes were exactly the opposite! One can only wonder what Mr. Zinz was smoking.

The following day, *The Baltimore Sun* was on the subject of "Question," with an article from Bob Lardine. After interviewing Graeme Edge, Lardine wrote:

> The Moody Blues have a brand new single out on Threshold Records called "The Question," but Edge is pessimistic regarding its chances to become a hit.

Edge told Lardine, "The disk is almost five minutes long and most radio stations won't play it because it interferes with their commercial breaks. But the record should get plenty of air time on FM radio." (GE-BS70)

Lardine told how the group also had a new album in the works, tentatively titled, "Stand Off and Be Counted."

Edge said, "Our new album will be a little more militant. It definitely will be antiwar, but not specifically the Vietnam War. We have to talk in generalities because, as Englishmen, we're foreigners concerning America and its involvement. Many people in England are frightened as to what's happening in your country. We look to the United States for leadership, but then comes the mockery of the Chicago Seven trials, and we just sit back, astonished." (GE-BS70)

In the May 9 edition of England's *Music Now!*, Tony Norman wrote:

> The Moody Blues' albums have given me great pleasure. Their concert at the Royal Albert Hall was one of the finest I have seen in "Home of the Instant Encore." I like all their songs, but Justin Hayward's [songs] rise above the splendor of the rest for me. They contain that rare quality of romance and beauty.
>
> Perhaps I had come to expect too much from one of my favorite bands, but when I heard their new single, "Question," I was bitterly disappointed. Justin wrote it but, to be honest, it left me cold. Happily, you, the record-buying public, have found interest where I found nothing. I am glad so many people are getting more out of it than I am.
>
> It could be a chart record – not that that matters, except it will mean it is in a lot of homes, which is always a nice thought. I am content to wait for their next album.

Despite being left cold by the Moodies' new single – or perhaps because of it – Ray Thomas gave Norman an interview … and defended the song. "We all like 'Question' from the start. Justin played it to us on guitar – that's the way we usually work it. Really, we released it just for kicks. We don't usually bother with singles because they are too expensive. Eight bob for one record is a lot, isn't it. Still, this one is four minutes, fifty seconds, which makes it better. This is the first time nobody has told us to cut down on the time. That happened on 'Nights in White Satin.' We resisted it there, but they just chopped a lump of it out in the States. It was so obvious – it sounded terrible. It's quite something to be able to play a single that long on *Top of the Pops*, as well. They wouldn't play 'Nights' because it was too long." (RT-MN70)

But *Top of the Pops* was willing to make an exception this time. "Question" was ascending the charts too quickly to be ignored.

Regarding their next album, Thomas said, "We've done seven tracks. I don't know really what the finished article will be like…. The songs are basically about things we have experienced since the last album. They will link together, but I don't think it will be the same basic format as the other albums. That's really up to our producer, Tony; he pieces it all together, but we all agree we are about due for a change…."

"One new thing will be a song written by Graeme. He's tone deaf, so a lot of effort went into that one!

"Basically, we all love melodies. We get what we want to say without just shouting out a protest song. It's more subtle than that and I think it's more effective." (RT-MN70)

With the release of "Question," the media attention given to Justin Hayward above the other Moodies continued to escalate. On May 9, Penny Valentine wrote in *Disc and Music Echo*:

> Justin Hayward is the tall, slim, delicate, sensitive-looking lead singer with the Moody Blues, who is still considered by many outside the group as the "newcomer." In fact, Hayward has been with them for nearly four years, and has had a tremendous impact and influence on their music – music which has put them very high on a pinnacle of success, alone and unrivalled.
>
> He has now established himself with the Moodies beyond question. It was he, in fact, who was almost totally responsible for their re-emergence from being just a pretty good group with a lot of internal hang-ups, to a highly praised and exalted musical force.
>
> He did it by writing "Nights in White Satin" – the track that did more for the Moodies than any of the "Go Now" and "Fly Me High" numbers. ...
>
> The fact that their new single – the first for four years NOT to have come off an album – was also written by Hayward should not go unnoticed.

Nor should the contributions from the other Moodies go unnoticed, as they were in Valentine's article. For instance, Mike Pinder's orchestration in both "Nights in White Satin" and "Question" – vital contributions.

According to Valentine, *Days of Future Passed* was selling up to 15,000 copies a month in America ... more than two years after its release.

In its May 9 issue, *Melody Maker* reported that the "Question" single had sold 15,000 copies in its first three days in record shops, and had, so far, sold 70,000 copies in America.

A surprised Ray Thomas told Richard Green of *New Musical Express* (May 16 issue), "Yeah, we've sold out. We've definitely sold out!"

Green wrote:

> The Moody Blues are about the last group in the world that needs a hit single. The group's phenomenal album sales – all its LPs are still in the American chart somewhere or other – more than compensates for an absence from the Top 30. ...

Thomas told Green that it was unlikely another "trailer" would be released before the issuing of their next album. He said, "There's not much point, really. They never sell a great deal; people always waited and bought the albums. …

"We're still not sure whether to put 'Question' on the album. I don't think it's really a good idea. Americans seem to like it, but I don't think people do here.

"We've got seven tracks done and the rest'll be finished over the next few weeks. I don't know when the album'll be out yet. It always takes time to sort out things like the art work for the cover and the reductions and editing." (RT-NME70a)

On May 18, in only its third week on the *NME* singles chart, "Question" leapt to No. 2 under the novelty record, "Back Home," by England World Cup Squad.

In the May 23 issue of *Record Mirror*, Keith Altham asked:

> When is a single not a single? Apparently when it is the Moody Blues. The Moodies have broken into the Seventies with every indication of making it a record shattering year for their newly baptized label, Threshold, on which they soared to the highest position ever in the U.S. charts with *To Our Children's Children's Children* and followed that with their first single, as such, in five years, which is currently gracing an otherwise ungracious Top 20.

Not entirely "ungracious." Other songs in the U.K. Top Ten this week included Norman Greenbaum's "Sprit in the Sky," Christie's "Yellow River," and Creedence Clearwater Revival's "Travelin' Band." Declining, but still in the Top 20 were the Beatles with "Let It Be," and Simon & Garfunkel's "Bridge Over Troubled Water."

Regarding "Question," John Lodge told Altham, "In a sense this is an 'anti-single.' We've made absolutely no concessions to the popular conception of what a hit single should be – in fact, almost the opposite. By generally accepted standards, 'Question' is too long, un-danceable, not easy to remember, and has a long instrumental introduction which usually displeases DJs.

"In spite of all that it is being played in its entirety, and *Top of the Pops* agreed to let us present it without any edits. If there was any compromising to be done, it has really been the media who have met us rather than we it.

"It was never conceived as a deliberate assault upon the Top 20, but was simply a track we were recording for an album by Justin, and suddenly we got the feeling about the song like we did for 'Nights in White Satin.' The only criterion we had for releasing it was that we all liked it so much we hoped others would as well. It got mixed reviews but as soon as [BBC Radio DJ] Tony Blackburn said it was not a chart record, we knew we had a chance!" (JL-RM70)

On May 23, *Record Mirror* reported that – even without the benefit of a hit single – *To Our Children's Children's Children* had just been awarded a Gold Record. Meanwhile, "Question" was in the U.K. Top 20. And the Moodies had just committed to a "mini-tour" of selected colleges during the month of June … having finished their next album beforehand. Stops would include Sheffield University, York University, Hull University, and Leeds University.

On May 25, "Question" kicked the England World Cup Squad all the way "Back Home" and became the new No. 1 single in *New Musical Express*. The other top U.K.

chart – *Melody Maker* – had "Question" at No. 2, its peak there, and still trailing the World Cup gang. Over at *Disc and Music Echo* (for its May 30 issue), "Question" was No. 2, kept from the top spot by Christie's "Yellow River." The following week "Question" made No. 1 there too.

Justin Hayward said, "It was No. 1 at the time but we've since been demoted to No. 2 because everybody has gone over to the BBC chart. But in *NME* and *Disc and Music Echo* it was No. 1. But at No. 1 in the BBC chart was a BBC record, "Back Home" by the England World Cup Squad. They fixed it!" (JH-TRC96)

"Question" hit No. 1 in Poland and Holland, and made the Top 10 in Canada, as well as South Africa.

"Question" peaked on the *Billboard* chart in America on June 13, where it held at No. 21 for four weeks. It peaked on *Cashbox* two weeks later, and held at No. 19 for two weeks. The third big national chart in the U.S., *Record World*, also placed "Question" at No. 19.

For you original Moodies fans, if this sounds too low, then you may suspect – after reading about "Tuesday Afternoon" and "Ride My See-Saw" – that the national charts are again deceptive. Correct! Once again, a Moody Blues record was slow to gain support from broadcasters because of its length. With stations coming on board at different periods over the course of several months, the single made Top 10 in most markets, but only Top 20 in the nationals.

In the interest of pacing, we'll skip the stations that put "Question" into the Top 20 and only list those stations known to have taken the song into the Top 10.

May 8: KCBQ in San Diego, California, was one of the first stations to jump on the record, and brought it up to No. 8;

May 10: KFRC, in San Francisco, California, ranked "Question" at No. 8;

May 13: KAFY, in Bakersfield, California, sent it to No. 4;

May 16: WSAI, in Cincinnati, Ohio, showed "Question" at No. 8.

May 20: CKOC, in Hamilton, Ontario, took it to No. 7;

May 29: KOL, in Seattle, Washington, brought it to No. 6;

May 30: CHUM, in Toronto, Ontario, for two weeks, had the song at No. 7;

June 3: KYND, in Fresno, California, ranked it at No. 8;

June 3: KADI, in St. Louis, Missouri, ranked it better, at No. 5;

June 5: WHYN, in Springfield, Massachusetts, sent it to No. 10;

June 6: KYA, in San Francisco, California, called it at No. 8;

June 8: WCOL, in Columbus, Ohio, took "Question" to No. 7;

June 10: KGB, in San Diego, California, brought "Question" to No. 10;

June 10: KAKC, in Tulsa, Oklahoma, said No. 6;

June 11: WZMF, in Milwaukee, Wisconsin, had it at No. 4;

June 11: KVDL, in Kansas City, Missouri, it was at No. 4;

June 13: KIRL, in Saint Charles, Missouri, went for No. 6;

June 16: WJET, in Erie, Pennsylvania, raised it to No. 5;

June 19: WKOS in West Muncie, Indiana, ranked the song at No. 8;

June 20: CFRA, in Ottawa, Ontario, showed it at No. 9;

June 20: WKBW, in Buffalo, N.Y., saw its peak as No. 4;

June 20: KXOK, in St. Louis, Missouri, listed it at No. 6;

June 20: KSEE, in Santa Maria, California, said No. 7;

June 22: WYSL, in Buffalo, New York, for two weeks, held it at No. 6;

June 22: WCFL, in Chicago, Illinois, put "Question" at No. 10;

June 25: WHFM, in Rochester, N.Y., got it all the way to No. 2

June 25: Rival Rochester station WSAY also had it at No. 2;

June 25: The third Rochester Top 40 station, WBBF, ranked it at No. 3;

June 27: WHB, in Kansas City, Missouri, for two weeks, ranked it at No. 7;

July 1: WOLF, in Syracuse, N.Y., called it at No. 6;

July 5: WPTR, in Albany, N.Y., sent the song to No. 10;

July 10: CKVN, in Vancouver, British Columbia, took "Question" to No. 2;

July 12: KAST, in Astoria, Oregon, put "Question" at No. 6;

July 13: KDWB, in Minneapolis-St. Paul, Minnesota, for two weeks, had it at No. 3;

July 15: WNHC, in New Haven, Connecticut, said No. 9;

July 17: WDRC, in Hartford, Connecticut, had "Question" at No. 5;

In addition:

The San Bernardino County Sun polled its local record sellers and, on June 9, ranked "Question" as No. 6 in area singles sales.

Freemont, California's *The Argus* did likewise, and, on June 11, ranked "Question" at No. 7.

Los Angeles's *The Van Nuys News* polled local record sellers and found "Question" to be No. 3 in top-sellers for the week ending June 12.

This list, of course, is not definitive. But you get the point.

Album release:
Threshold THS 3; August 8, 1970

Interior gatefold LP design.

In the August 1 issue of *New Musical Express*, Richard Green gave his readers a preview of the new Moody Blues album. He had been treated to a garden party and playing of the album for the press by the Moodies and Tony Clarke. Clarke commented to Green, "I wish I could have heard it like you – for the first time." Although very proud of the work, Clarke was too close to the album for an objective appraisal. He could no longer hear it through fresh ears.

But we have Richard Green's first impression:

> … This latest album struck me, on first hearing, as being far better than anything they have done before. It must be a massive hit.

The highlights for Green included Lodge's "Tortoise and the Hare," of which he wrote:

> Up-tempo but at the same time basically light. Lines like "your friend was heavy, but he was ready" underline the theme. As the track progresses, things liven up and the Mellotron forces its way in, counter-balanced by the lead guitar. Vocal harmonies in the background lend weight to the lead vocals. One of the best tracks on the album without a doubt.

Of "Melancholy Man." Green said:

> Great song, perhaps my favorite on the album. A couple of acoustic guitars open it up before Mike Pinder's distinctive voice takes over at a slow pace with a chorus behind and a plodding drum beat comes in. I've rarely heard instruments used so well to relay the theme of a song; they're quite faultless. Pathos and woe spreads all over the place and I don't recommend listening to it after you've had a row with your loved one.

Regarding "The Balance":

> Graeme speaks the introduction; then there's a brief piece of action when vocals take over and some heavy playing. Back to Graeme for a longer spoken passage, then a return to the other side. Both parts are played off against one another very well and make a nice balance. It could have turned out pretty corny if it hadn't been treated just right – a lot of groups wouldn't have had the expertise to carry it off. Another standout number.

Andrew Means from *Melody Maker* was at the premiere playback as well. He wrote in his paper's August 8 issue:

> Moody Blues releases have become much-awaited and almost religious moments, and last week saw the launching of their new album, *A Question of Balance*. Since the success of *To Our Children's Children's Children*, which topped the British LP chart, their records seem to attract the respect usually reserved for vintage wines – it doesn't matter whether you dig the taste, just as long as you can pronounce the names.
>
> It is almost a status symbol to possess one of the early albums – *Days of Future Passed* and *In Search of the Lost Chord*,

325

especially, if you claim to have bought them at the time of issue. All the albums, apart from *In Search of the Lost Chord*, have now sold a million in the U.S. ...

On the Threshold of a Dream and *To Our Children's Children's Children* were the latest to go Gold, joining *Days of Future Passed*, which had never charted high, but sold steadily since the spring of 1967

Regarding the latest album, Means said:

> ... There is both an internal theme – briefly summarized as Man's relationship with his Earthly and unearthly environment – and a distinct link with previous LPs. ... The first side begins with a version of "Question," and remains on this familiar note of questioning and searching with one composition from each member of the group. ... Suggestions, rather than answers, color the second side. One of the attractions of the group's music is that they refuse to be trapped into a doctorial "telling it like it is," as if we were all sitting on the same side of the pitch. The balance between the group members is an improvement on previous albums, and Graeme Edge and Mike Pinder produce very good work at the end of the new release. ...

Also from August 8, the reviewer for *Disc and Music Echo*, having attended the premiere, told his readers:

> Even before you play this latest masterpiece you know what it's about – thanks to another poignantly descriptive cover from artist Phil Travers. The British holiday-maker sits blissfully on the beach, totally unperturbed by the terrible things that go on in the world around him.
>
> Side One is the questions, Side Two puts forward solutions. Moodies have come down from their ethereal cloud to tackle the root problems on Earth.
>
> Musically, this does not on first hearing have as many instantly memorable tunes. "Question" is enlarged musically so that it punches over with double the impact, and, typically, two other Justin Hayward compositions are the most immediate – "It's Up to You" (bearing some resemblance to "Lovely to See You"), and "Dawning Is the Day," made even more impressive by "padding" drum work from Graeme Edge. ...
>
> Key, emotionally, to the whole album, is Graeme's poem, "The Balance" – "With his eye of compassion he saw his enemies like unto himself, and he learned love. Then, he was answered."
>
> Like any Moody Blues album, singling out tracks is unfair. Listen to the questions – try to find the answers. They may be different but the musical enjoyment meanwhile is ease itself.

By August 22, *A Question of Balance* was No. 2 in the *NME* chart.

More Moodies news, as reported that day by *New Musical Express*: In America, the band had just been presented with a Gold album, for *In Search of the Lost Chord*. Now, all four of the Moody Blues Mark 2's previous albums had turned to gold.

On September 2, *Variety* reviewed the album:

> Chalk up another sales success for England's Moody Blues. Utilizing a myriad of instruments, the Moodies again achieve their distinctive orchestrated rock sound. The disk includes their hit, "Question," which rates as top effort. Other highlights of this disk, whose balance leans toward similarity, are "It's Up to You," "Dawning Is the Day" and "And the Tide Rushes In."

One of those highlights, "It's Up to You," was getting substantial radio action. The song could have clicked as a single on its own merits, if released. Easily accessible as the first track on Side 2, it made it onto radio nonetheless.

From September 9, the *Milwaukee Journal* opined:

> The Moody Blues' new album, *A Question of Balance*, on Threshold, is the fifth volume in a musical and conceptual history that began with *Days of Future Passed*, went on to the magnificent *In Search of the Lost Chord*, with "Om" number, that is perhaps the finest single pop composition of the last five years; and continued with *On the Threshold of a Dream* and *To Our Children's Children's Children*.
>
> There is probably no other word in the language capable of describing the sound of the Moody Blues than "beautiful." Their music is symphonic, filled with great swelling strains of Gregorian chant, hymns of hallelujah, and mournful processionals about the passing scene. But always there is the gently preaching teaching: a belief that the human spirit will transcend its current condition. As the Moodies have said before: "Thinking is the only way to travel." …

Interviewed for the September 11 edition of the *Detroit Free Press*, Tony Clarke told Mike Gormley, "We have always tried to keep a good balance on the albums. The Moodys have never gone in for the hard, freaky music. Also, when you see them live you'll find out they aren't all that soft. They are loud and much of what you hear on record is increased in volume on stage." (TC-DFP70)

Gormley commented:

> Soft could also describe a form of music rather than volume. The Moody Blues are soft in that there is a trace of classical and folk in their music. You hear violins and "other fancy stuff" on their albums. "The strange thing about that," and nobody believes Tony when he says it, is, "we didn't use any violins or any other

instruments on any Moody album [sic; since *Days of Future Passed*]. All that is done with the group." ...

In the September 12 edition of *Billboard*, the trade's reviewer wrote:

> The Moody Blues have once again turned in an album of thinking man's music with some intelligent lyrics and some arrangements that just soar away. It stays firmly on the right side without venturing into the realm of pretention. The album contains a longer version of their single, "Question," and the whole thing moves smoothly between the acoustic and the heavy sounds.

From the Morningside Heights, New York *Columbia Daily Spectator*, on September 29, Vernon Gibbs wrote:

> ... If you are looking for music that is neither pretentious nor limited, then the Moody Blues are the kind of change you need. Their latest album is not their best (*Children's Children* was more complete), but it is among the best of the last month's releases, and it contains some extremely powerful moments on it. My favorite is "Melancholy Man," but only because it reminds me of "Nights in White Satin" or *On the Threshold of a Dream*, both of which, to the accompaniment of some dynamite Panama Red, had me falling away in pieces and drifting into eternal sunrise, and so on. It is, of course, not necessary to have this kind of accompaniment, but if by accident it should offer itself, take it. Many of the songs on this album have that same ethereal quality, the strangely hypnotic force that makes the Moody Blues the unique group that they are.

You could own *A Question of Balance* for only $3.98 ... plus tax ... at the Record Bar in Chapel Hill, North Carolina. And, while there, you could pick up *Days of Future Passed* and *In Search of the Lost Chord* for $2.99 each! Panama Red (a strain of cannabis) was extra.

On October 10, *A Question of Balance* peaked on the *Billboard* album charts at No. 3, early in an impressive 74-week stay on the chart

In mid-October, Robert Hilburn, the resident music critic for *The Los Angeles Times*, had come to the conclusion that he no longer liked popular music. He complained:

> It is often well to pause to remember there is slight, if any, correlation between sales and quality in pop music albums. Four new albums, all instant best-sellers, reinforce that point.
>
> The Moody Blues' *A Question of Balance* ... Santana's *Abraxas* ... the Jackson 5's *Third Album* ... and the Carpenters' *Close to You* ... are all soaring up the sales charts and reflect a wide range of musical styles, but are rather undistinguished.

Then he directed his jaundiced eye at the Moodies:

… Only portions of the Moody Blues' album contain any real measure of musical inventiveness or excitement. In *A Question of Balance*, the Moody Blues demonstrates once again that it can be both (a) one of the world's best rock bands, and (b) one of the most pretension-prone groups in pop music.

At its best, the Moody Blues features a splendid combination of orchestral glitter and rock rhythm. It is difficult, however, to determine whether the group's weaker moments are caused by pure pretentiousness or just an inability to carry out some occasional lofty themes – themes that often wander into all sorts of musical metaphysics.

It is chiefly on songs by Justin Hayward ("Lovely to See You" and "Never Comes the Day") and John Lodge ("Ride My See-Saw" and "Send Me No Wine") that the English quintet does its best work. Perhaps then, it is only natural that the best selections on the new album are on Hayward ("Question" and "Dawning Is the Day") and Lodge ("Minstrel Boy") [sic] songs. The best effort, by far, is on Hayward's "Question," a multitude of themes and rhythms compressed into a single song. The only other noteworthy song on the album is "The Balance," an interesting, if not totally successful, blend of music and narrative.

A Question of Balance remains short of the perfect Moody Blues album, short by quite a distance. But the group, it seems clear, is capable of extraordinary things.

Another heavily referenced syndicated rock critic, David F. Wagner, turned his thumbs decisively down over *A Question of Balance*. Writing in his mid-October column, he opined:

When I suggest this one fails, perhaps I should amend it by saying that while it is good at what it attempts, I don't feel it interesting. Analyzing the success of Moody Blues, I conjectured the group seems to appeal to those who don't dig the blues or jazz and are nearly totally Caucasian in their musical orientation. That isn't me. Personally, Moody Blues seemed to peak with "Ride My See-Saw."

In the October 16 edition of *Thunder Word*, the newspaper of Highline College in Midway, Washington, Mike Heavener seemed to have read reviewers like Hilburn and Wagner:

Most groups are taken fairly seriously by reviewers when they release an album. One group, however, seems either to be ignored or some sort of a joke to these same persons. The group is the Moody Blues. …

Now the Moody Blues have released another album, their fifth.... An album called *A Question of Balance*. This performance is possibly the best effort of the group and certainly is not to be ignored or taken lightly. The themes are rather complex, some of them shared by several of the cuts. The leading track, an effort called "Question" by Justin Hayward, was released as a single early in the spring; its inclusion in this album is necessary, as it states the mood of the record.

The record is timely in that these fellows, in more polished poetry than most performers, point out exactly what they think is wrong with the world today, and they don't waste words doing it. Hayward tells everyone that "... the truth is hard to swallow.... in a world of persecution that is burning in its greed."

Looking at the gap between many of the people, Ray Thomas explains "You keep looking for someone / To tell your troubles to / I sit down and lend an ear / Yet I hear nothing new." ...

Mike Pinder asks, almost immediately, in "How Is It (We Are Here)," what scientists are doing to help save the natural ecology of the world ... "will they save us in the end, we're trembling on the brink." As far as he is concerned, nature "... sends us her glory, it's always been there ...," but it is up to us to solve the problems.

In "Don't You Feel Small," Graeme Edge admonishes everyone to "Look at progress / Then count the cost / We'll spoil the seas / With the rivers we've lost." ...

Most of the record is in the same serious vein, especially when Hayward, in another cut, tells us that we have "No reason to hide from what's true."

John Lodge seems to be the man who gives the album its lighter touches. He gives us a musical rendition of Aesop's "Tortoise and the Hare." Again, in "Minstrel's Song," he wants us to "Hear the morning call of waking birds / When they are singing... / Everywhere love is all around."

Typical of all Moody Blues albums is the interpretive reading, here performed by Graeme Edge, who can be commended upon his excellent diction as well as his thought in the last band of the record, which also makes up the end of the album's title.

A note on the liner tells us that all instruments are played by the Moody Blues, making them a most talented group. Arrangements are also by these fellows; everything they touch is golden.

Those people interested in rock music are advised to listen to the group before you condemn; you won't be disappointed. If social comment is your bag, analyze the cover while you listen to the words. Music fans won't find their ears assaulted by the Moody Blues; changes are delicate and chords are well thought out. In addition, this group has discovered, as in past records, that loudness and sheer volume are not an end; the sounds here are not overwhelmed but enhanced. …

Also from mid-October, syndicated "Teen Times" contributor Jared Johnson asked, "Who are the Number One progressive rock group in the world today?" Then answered: "The Moody Blues."

Johnson rationalized his claim:

Now the Beatles are gone and pop music must search out new leaders. The Stones went to the top automatically. For superstar and supergroup status, Mick Jagger and the Stones have been second only to the Beatles for years. However, not speaking strictly in terms of sales or popularity, only one group can claim the title of Number One progressive rock group in the world today, the Moody Blues. …

Their probing lyrics magnificently complement their vibrant and highly cerebral music: "Vast vision must improve our sight."

"Gazing past the planets, looking for total view."

"Searching with this life of ours, you've got to make the journey out and in."

"Traveling eternity road, what will you find there, carrying your load, searching to find peace of mind."

"Blasting, billowing, bursting forth with the power of 10 billion butterfly sneezes."

Classic Moodian metaphors.

Call it majestic rock, mystical rock, religious rock, philosophical rock. Whatever, the sound swells to break and transcend the mundane limits of the earth-chained human mind, as well as conventional musical boundaries. Their music catalyses. It is controlled power with unequalled breadth, depth, and feeling. …

The Moody Blues' new album, *A Question of Balance*, is a further development in the total concept album, this time dealing with ecology in a far broader sense than we've been exposed to from environmental biologists over the past year. For the Moody Blues this means spiritual ecology or ecology of the mind – the relationship between man and the world and how they perceive this world – there has to be a balance!

"How is it we are here, on this path we walk, in this world of pointless fear, filled with empty talk...."

Just how wasteful is man? And how full of misunderstanding? "Look at progress, Then count the cost. We'll spoil the seas, with the rivers we've lost. See the writing on the wall, hear the mirror's warning call. That's why you feel small, it happens to us all."

In relationship to the entire universe, man may feel small. Some things, of course, are beyond his control. There are certain facts he must accept. "No one tells the wind which way to blow."

The Moody Blues express their views on these problems with lyrics of extraordinary sensitivity, aiming toward universal vision and wisdom. Their songs are a mystic quest, leading the soul's ascent up the scale of reality to the heights of mystic vision – to full understanding, wherein the problems facing us may be solved.

For the Moody Blues, the universe has a purpose that is constantly unfolding. And we are part of it. It is up to us to make an effort to understand. "Just open your eyes, and realize, the way it's always been. Just open your mind, and you will find, the way it's always been.... Just open your heart. And that's a start!"

The Moody Blues have always been in the vanguard of progressive rock. Now they are destined to lead it.

Also from October 1970, in Australia's *Ram* magazine, the music critic wrote:

If you've never bought a Moody Blues album, then *A Question of Balance* is possibly not the best one to start with. Of course, it's a great record; the Moodies are never less than great. But other albums give a better introduction to their brilliance, for example *Days of Future Passed* or *On the Threshold of a Dream*.

If you have bought Moodies albums before, let me assure you this one maintains the tradition – grand soaring echoing melodies, played on a multitude of instruments by the five Moodies alone.

There's just a shade of receptiveness in this one, which suggests that they should aim for some new styles on their next album, but they still top most modern groups. ...

Also from this time, again from Australia, *Go Set* magazine published its review:

... There was a very distinct danger that [the Moodies] would become very artificial and very much a studio concoction after the last album, but this album has convinced me firmly once more of the group's brilliance. They've come back towards a group sound with guitar solos and things, and beautiful songs.

The other thing they've avoided falling into is the trap of their albums' themes. The last one was strongest in that it was unmistakably the story of a trip into space and a better future. The theme here (if there is one) is much less tangible and thus the songs are much more enjoyable. I'd say that with this album, they've really made it, and at last have avoided the pretentious tag which for so long has been their millstone. Their best album to date.

Mike Jahn, rock music critic for *The New York Times*, with many of his stories syndicated to newspapers across America, wrote in his November 1 "Sounds of the 70s" column:

> ... If rock has periods like classical music, the Moody Blues clearly represent the Romantic. They mix lyrical grandiose, semi-religious conceptions of the way life is ordered, with very round, melodic, almost pretty melodies that are amplified with incredible force, like a Wagnerian opera. This theoretically should earn them a chorus of laughter from an American rock audience today, but they have a large fanatical following. This is probably not because of belief in their romantic theories, but because they do it so well. Their singing is perfect. Their songs are all well constructed and exciting, and could stand with or without words.
>
> *In Search of the Lost Chord* is a masterpiece, their best recording to date. *To Our Children's Children's Children* is good also. Its opening track, "Higher and Higher," is guaranteed to blow your neighbors right through their dinette sets.
>
> *A Question of Balance*, the new album, is better than *To Our Children's....* It has solid form and represents a total concept album like the group's others. (A total concept album is a kind of symphony, more than just a bunch of songs stuck together on a long-playing record.) It flows well, with fine mood and tempo shifts, particularly in the opening track, "Question." It's so fine to hear an acoustic guitar strummed double-speed, with the precise choral effect swaying under it and the Mellotron blasting up from underneath like a roomful of cellos.
>
> The Moody Blues are making a very special place for themselves. Chances are they are unlike anything you have heard, imaginative and audacious.

On November 11, way down under in Sydney, New South Wales, Australia, Gil Wahlquist savaged the new Blood, Sweat and Tears album (the one with "Hi-De-Ho" on it) in *The Sydney Morning Herald*. Then he turned his critical eye toward the new Moodies LP:

> Moody Blues have a stirring introduction to their new album *A Question of Balance*... "Question" is the title of the track and the

hot acoustic guitar choruses dispel any idea that the Moodies are about to try another over-written symphonic experience.

The tunes are good. After being suspicious of the Moody Blues when first hearing them, I'm warming to them with this album.

Should one wish to seek out the November 12 edition of *Rolling Stone*, one may be amused by John Mendelsohn's attempt to write comedy. His review of *A Question of Balance* is a couple of columns of sarcasm. Pointed tongue in cheek, Mendelsohn describes that a thing of beauty recently came to him, a thing which warmed his soul and opened his mind. This treasure: the new Moody Blues album, not something to be stored among other records, but to be placed within a cardboard shrine, "that houses your *Nam myoho renge kyo* scroll."

After the comedy bit, Mendelsohn added an aside:

(Really, friends, doncha think [its] sad that this group – who, were they to quit regarding themselves as seers, hock their Mellotrons, and let Justin Hayward do all the writing and singing, might make some damn fine straightforward rock and roll – think themselves above making fine straightforward rock and roll?)

Incidentally, Mendelsohn, notorious for using his sarcastic "wit" to pan the first two Led Zeppelin albums, among many other classics, attempted and failed at launching a music career of his own. Perhaps his own rock 'n 'roll was not "straightforward" enough.

From the December 3, 1970 *The Honolulu Advertiser*, entertainment correspondent and critic Wayne Harada said of the Moodies and *A Question of Balance*:

The Moody Blues long has been an underrated British import. Each LP is a montage of marvelous composition and performance. This is no exception. From "Don't You Feel Small" to "It's Up to You," from "How Is It?" to "Dawning Is the Day," the Blues are supreme.

 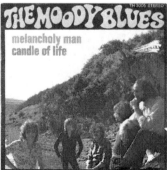 

Single release:
"Melancholy Man" b/w "It's Up to You"
Japan TH-4, 1970

"Melancholy Man" / "Candle of Life"
France TH 3005, November 1970
Germany TH 5, 1971
Netherlands 6101 600, 1971

"Melancholy Man" / "Don't You Feel Small"
Italy TH 101, 1971

On January 31, *Billboard* magazine reported that "Melancholy Man" was No. 1 in numerous European charts and, in four weeks, had sold close to 150,000 copies there.

Despite this, the single would not be issued in Britain or the United States. Nonetheless, the song was no stranger to FM. Broadcasters would often import overseas singles such as these to have better access to the songs without cross fading … and all the easier to cue up.

Syndicated music journalist and critic Jared Johnson had been predicting that it was only a matter of time before the world agreed with him that the Moody Blues were one of the most important bands around. And he continued to lobby for this cause when selecting his choices for the 14 "top albums of '70." In the company of the Beatles' *Let It Be*, the Bee Gees' *Cucumber Castle*, Crosby, Stills, Nash and Young's *Déjà vu*, George Harrison's *All Things Must Pass*, Jefferson Starship's *Blows Against the Empire*, Joni Mitchell's *Ladies of the Canyon*, Simon and Garfunkel's *Bridge Over Troubled Water*, Neil Young's first solo album, *Neil Young* (even though it was released in 1969), and his third, *After the Gold Rush*, and the self-titled debut albums for a pair of English bands – Fotheringay and Renaissance – Johnson picked *To Our Children's Children's Children* (a carry-over from late 1969) and *A Question of Balance*. Of the latter, he said:

> This was the album that really broke through for the Moody Blues. It had taken them a while, so they slowed down just a bit to let listeners catch up. As Justin Hayward sang on "Dawning Is the Day," "Listen, we're trying to find you." *A Question of Balance* made No. 3 [in the U.S.] on the album charts, so now it's "Listen, we think we have found you." But, the Moody Blues' musical evolution will not stop here. Their progress will continue. "We're going to keep growing, wait and see." - "Melancholy Man" (Mike Pinder).

Scene magazine finally got around to reviewing the "new" album on January 7, 1971. Sam Milicia wrote:

> A smash new LP from one of the best groups around. The Moody Blues have composed music which both talks about and reflects the more important questions of the day – questions involving love, hate, war, and the world around us. "Melancholy Man" and "Minstrel's Song" are some of the heavier cuts. This LP may create a musical explosion, destining it to become one of the musical and popular successes of all time.

On January 30, 1971, *New Musical Express* published the results of a readers' poll, which placed the Moodies' *A Question of Balance* as the fourth best British album of 1970, following, respectively, The Beatle's *Let It Be*, George Harrison's *All Things Must Pass*, and *Led Zeppelin III*. "Question" was ranked as the fifth best British single of the year, behind Mungo Jerry's "In the Summertime," Free's "Alright Now," the Beatles' "Let It Be," and Dave Edmunds' "I Hear You Knocking."

15

Isle of Wight, 1970 … and Back to America

To support *A Question of Balance*, tours were arranged for England, Continental Europe, and America. The first scheduled appearance was destined to become an event on par with Woodstock.

Isle of Wight, August 26-30, 1970

In *Melody Maker* on August 22, 1970, the big news was about the Moodies pulling out of the 1970 Isle of Wight Festival.

I.O.W. Publicity Officer Pete Harrigan commented, "We're all very disappointed about the whole business. We think the Moodies are the best of the British groups, musically speaking, and we were going to pay them £2,500 – five times what they got last year." (MM70)

A statement issued by the Moodies regarding the reason for withdrawing:

> In our opinion the Isle of Wight Festival will promote enormous financial gain for persons connected with the festival and is not being conducted in the best interest of music for the fans. (MM70)

John Lodge told Richard Green of *New Musical Express*, "I think everybody was keen on the idea of doing the festival thing because of what it was. We were going to do Bath but that was rained off for us and when we did the Isle of Wight [last year] … well, you saw the scenes. Festivals are, or rather, *were*, a good idea, but so many things happen in between your agreeing to do them and actually appearing that you begin to wonder." (JL-NME70)

Graeme Edge added, "They've become a dinosaur – the body's too big for the brain." (GE-NME70)

Despite all the talk to the contrary, just a few days later the Moodies did appear at Isle of Wight, as one of the prime headliners of the fifth and final day of the festival.

It was England's answer to Woodstock. That event, in New York State, spanning four days from August 15-18, 1969, had attracted an estimated 400,000 people. The first Isle of Wight music festival in 1968 had an estimated attendance of 10,000. In 1969, just eleven days after Woodstock, the second Isle of Wight Festival brought in around 150,000 spectators. Now, for the third consecutive festival, it is believed attendance was around 600,000, making this the largest rock event to date.

(Photo Source: UK Rock Festivals)

There had been four days of performances by over a dozen legendary acts, and many aspiring ones, before the Moodies took the stage on Sunday, August 30. Highlights had included Kris Kristofferson; Supertramp (their debut album had been released one month earlier); Chicago; Procol Harum; John Sebastian; Joni Mitchell (whose performance included her song "Woodstock"); Tiny Tim (and, yes, he sang "Tiptoe Through the Tulips"); Miles Davis; Ten Years After; Emerson, Lake and Palmer; the Doors; the Who; Sly & the Family Stone; Melanie; Donavon; and then the Moodies.

Justin Hayward said, "We played all three, in '68, '69 and '70… and I remember not getting paid for any of them! We also got a bit stoned, then *very* stoned, and we wondered how we were gonna pay for the petrol to get back home. Although we'd had hits, we still didn't have any money then – it took years, as we were on lousy publishing and recording deals.

"There was terrible trauma and fights backstage at the Festivals, with people trying to get their money. The guys from Free went in to beat up [festival producer and master of ceremonies] Rikki Farr and there was a lot of 'effing' and 'blinding.' I thought, 'That's how you do it – all go in and kick his head in!' And it worked.

"I wouldn't have missed it, although I don't think we were very good. But it was of its time and the last of an era." (JH-RC03)

Graeme Edge: "… I remember – and if you've seen the video, you'll know this – just by pure fluke, 'cause the whole thing was totally unorganized, but we actually played the song 'Sunset' when it was actually sunset, and I remember staring at the sun dropping down the horizon while we're singing, 'As the sun goes down and the clouds all frown.' It was cool. I enjoyed that." (GE-GM14)

The Moodies played a 14-song set, including three songs from *Days of Future Passed* ("Tuesday Afternoon," "The Sunset," and "Nights in White Satin"), two from *In Search of the Lost Chord* ("Ride My See-Saw" and "Legend of a Mind"), four from *On*

338

the Threshold of a Dream ("Never Comes the Day," "Are You Sitting Comfortably?," "The Dream," and "Have You Heard?"), one from *To Our Children's Children's Children* ("Gypsy"), and four from their new album, with "Question," "Tortoise and the Hare," "Minstrel Song," and "Melancholy Man."

Ray Thomas: "Oh, that was one of the biggest audiences I have played, probably the biggest audience we *ever* played. It was colossal. Viewing the audience from the stage was phenomenal. When they announced us, the warmth of the people was unbelievable. Six hundred thousand people sent their loving like a jumbo jet taking off. A long uproar, you know." (RT-DM15)

Justin Hayward: "[I]n the immediate lead-up to the 1970 one, we'd just had that huge success with 'Question,' which helped us enormously in getting the crowd on our side. A lot of the acts got a pretty rough ride at that festival; there were some quite unpleasant crowd reactions. But, when we came on, we were definitely helped by being on that wave of chart success, and we went down really well." (JH-RS13)

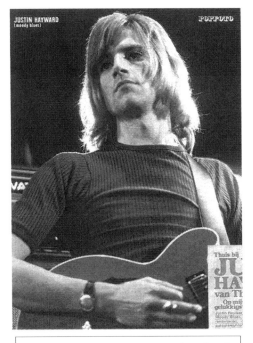

Justin Hayward on stage at the Isle of Wight Rock Festival.
(Photo source: 1970 issue of Dutch music magazine, POPFOTO)

(Photo source: Cameron Life Photo Library)

Mike Pinder: "Having that many people – 600,000 people – gosh, that hasn't happened in England, other than maybe something the Beatles or the Stones did." (MP-GM09)

Pinder underestimated the magnitude of this latest rock concert event. Neither the Beatles nor the Stones had seen a crowd this size. Nor had anyone else, except for those sharing the stage at Isle of Wight, 1970.

Justin Hayward: "I recall that Ray may have had a few drinks that day and was lively to the point of kicking over a chair or two. However, his playing was very solid that day, and he may very well have held the whole thing together." (MP-GM09)

One of the things that needed help keeping it together was the Mellotron, which was adversely affected by humidity and unstable electrical current, both of which were in abundance at the Festival. Hayward said, "Mike was having a challenging time, as the Mellotron kept going out of tune." (JH-RC03)

Mike Pinder: "[I remember thinking] 'Can I keep this Mellotron on the tracks?' … [B]ecause, in the middle of nowhere, anything can happen with the power. I mean… if we were doing a fairly early show, say 6 or 7 o'clock… we'd be on stage, but then, all of a sudden, all of the moms at home would put their electric cookers on, and things like that, and the power would go down. The

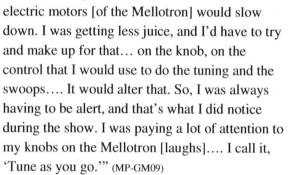

electric motors [of the Mellotron] would slow down. I was getting less juice, and I'd have to try and make up for that… on the knob, on the control that I would use to do the tuning and the swoops…. It would alter that. So, I was always having to be alert, and that's what I did notice during the show. I was paying a lot of attention to my knobs on the Mellotron [laughs]…. I call it, 'Tune as you go.'" (MP-GM09)

Pinder is seen on the DVD documentary, *The Moody Blues: Live at the Isle of Wight Festival*, working those knobs. And Hayward is heard and seen playing electric guitar on "Tuesday Afternoon" instead of acoustic guitar. He explained, "In 1970, it would be hard to use an acoustic guitar when you've got a full drum kit behind you, and be able to be heard" (JH-GM08)

After the Moodies, performances on this last day continued with Jethro Tull; Jimi Hendrix; Joan Baez; Leonard Cohen; and Richie Havens.

Whether the Moodies were paid or not, the appearance certainly gave a good plug to *A Question of Balance*, the main purpose for gigging at this time.

Following the festival, on August 7, the Moodies performed at Belfry Hotel in Sutton Coldfield. Dennis Detheridge of *Melody Maker* reported:

> There was no Isle of Wright style encore from the Moody Blues at the Belfry at Sutton Coldfield on Monday. But no one in the capacity crowd really expected one after the Moodies had played their hearts out for 90 minutes on their final British date before starting another American tour.
>
> With relatives and old friends out front – the Moodies used to live in nearby Birmingham – it was a hero's return for the local boys

who have made good. We had heard the music before, of course, but the atmosphere of the occasion seemed to inject something extra into their performance. …

A new group called Kiss opened for the Moodies.

Richard Green was there, and wrote in the September 13 edition of *New Musical Express*:

> … It was a bit like being at a Kenwood concert, except that the music wasn't classical, in the true sense at least, though it was in the Moodies' way. They played "Minstrel Song" from the new album for the first time on stage, and the beautiful "Melancholy Man," and a lot more besides. …

Green had heard the rumblings of the self-proclaimed ultra-cool in the music world, that the Moodies music was pretentious. He added:

> The Moody Blues are about as pretentious as a Yorkshire pudding and anyone who thinks otherwise obviously misunderstands them or hasn't bothered to listen to their music properly. It's now something of a monkey on their collective back to have the accusations leveled at them week in, week out. …

A tide was turning for the Moody Blues, a critical backlash resulting from their being the darlings of the press for three consecutive years. Now, some of those who had praised the Moodies now felt a need to overcompensate by over-criticizing them, to clear the way for the latest pop flavor of the week.

(Photo source: MetroLyrics.com)

Back into America:

A Question of Balance had indeed been a breakthrough album for the Moody Blues in America. They had been gaining positive attention, their fan base steadily growing, and record sales steadily improving for three years. Now, as if overnight, their popularity soared. The band had no idea how much had changed for them since they last toured the U.S. earlier in the year, but they would soon find out.

The set list for this plunge into America – which always allowed for some changes at the discretion of the band – was "Gypsy" (Hayward), "The Sunset" (Pinder), "Minstrel's Song" (Lodge), "Tortoise and the Hare" (Lodge), "Question" (Hayward), "Tuesday Afternoon" (Hayward), "Are You Sitting Comfortably?" (Hayward), "The Dream" / "Have You Heard, Part 1" / "The

Voyage" / "Have You Heard, Part 2" (Pinder), "Tuesday Afternoon" (Hayward), "Melancholy Man" (Pinder), "Never Comes the Day" (Hayward), "Nights in White Satin" (Hayward), and encore numbers: "Legend of a Mind" (Thomas) and "Ride My See-Saw" (Lodge).

Tuesday, Wednesday, and Thursday (September 15, 16 and 17) are believed to have been the first three U.S. concert dates, but no details are known.

Friday, September 18, 1970: Cobo Arena, Detroit, Michigan, with Van Morrison opening. Tickets: $3.50, $4, $5, and $6.

Following the concert, Mike Gormley reported in the *Detroit Free Press*:

> The Moody Blues deserved every one of the seven or so standing ovations they received during their performance at Cobo Hall Friday. Despite some off key music and a touch of poor singing, the group came through to prove itself one of the most brilliant groups to come along for years.
>
> The last time the Moodies came to Detroit, about two years ago, they were so mistreated by the promoter they hated the thought of returning to this city. This time, though, over 12,000 people blessed the Moody Blues with screams for more and a standing ovation after almost every song. The crowd cheered when the man on the Mellotron talked about Timothy Leary, and then released remorseful moans when the lead guitarist mentioned he was losing his voice. …
>
> Unity seems to be the reason for the fine music…. All the five musicians in the group work together rather than fight for solo spots, something found in most bands. …
>
> A relatively new instrument to the world of music is the Mellotron, an instrument the Moody Blues use with style. In short, it serves as an orchestra complete with brass and strings. It's the sound that sets this group apart. The instrument gives a full sound to the group, something most bands find extremely difficult to present to a live audience. With the Mellotron's help, the Moody Blues gave a highly enjoyable show, for the most part.
>
> "Tuesday Afternoon" was beautiful with its floating and distant beginning sliding into a solid beat. It would have been better if the lead singer's microphone hadn't been in the process of dying, however. "Sunset" sounded like a sunset, and songs from the group's album *Days of Future Passed* put you in that twilight zone with its driving and space-like sound. It boggles the mind to think what it would be like if the Moody Blues had ironed out the mistakes. …

This time out, the Moodies found a "name" opening act that wasn't about to steal away their thunder. Gormley described Van Morrison as looking "like a little lost boy who was too frightened to get off the stage," and:

… He just stood there, and ran through his songs with nary an introduction. As opposed to the unity of the Moody Blues, the Van Morrison Orchestra was a group of men fighting to play solos. If Morrison hates performing so much it would be better if he just wouldn't.

Saturday, September 19, 1970: Milwaukee Arena, Milwaukee, Wisconsin. The opening act was the James Gang, with front man Joe Walsh.

Sunday, September 20: Buffalo Festival, War Memorial Auditorium, Buffalo, New York, with the James Gang, and Dion.

Monday, September 21: Burlington's Memorial Auditorium, University of Vermont, with the Moodies opening a series of fall concerts in the venue. Concert promoter Jack Trevithick told *The Burlington Free Press*, "Rarely has a concert attracted so much enthusiasm. Series tickets were sold out quickly and campus bulletin boards are posted with notes offering scalpers' prices for tickets for the opening concert."

Brady Street PRODUCTIONS Presents …

MOODY BLUES

with the
james gang and bob reitman

MILWAUKEE ARENA
September 19th. 8:00 P.M.
ALL SEATS RESERVED
$4.50 Advance/$5.50 Door

Tickets available at Arena Box Office,
Gimbels — Milwaukee & Madison stores,

also at 1812 Overture

Following the concert, John D. Donoghue wrote in *The Burlington Free Press*:

The University of Vermont's White Lane Series concerts opened Monday night with one of the biggest putdowns of the young people who came to Memorial Auditorium. With consummate arrogance, the Moody Blues, scheduled to begin at 8:30, never started to play until 10. It wasn't a waste of time since Dion made an unscheduled appearance with his winning smile and his guitar and his fine songs.

The young are forgiving. They greeted the Englishmen as though they were old friends, and by the time the over-30 set had left for quieter realms, the Moody Blues had the high decibel set applauding rapturously. They did their own stand-up for the finale at 11:15.

Justin Hayward, Mike Pinder, Ray Thomas, John Lodge, and Graeme Edge are good musicians when they let themselves be heard. Distrustful of a New England sound system, they brought their own and it couldn't have happened to a nicer bunch. The King's English, which used to be one of the Empire's better exports, got lost somewhere between the marbled mouths and the most intimidating collection of loudspeakers that set our ears to ringing. One had to be carted away – a loud speaker, that is. …

The Moody Blues – what a Spoonerism that would make – also had trouble with their instruments. The lead guitar had a D that kept going out of pitch regularly and the insides of the organ had a minor ulcer.

However, their tunes – many of them their own work – are well enough known so that an opening chord drew the applause of recognition. They offered such tunes as "Sunset," "Never Comes the Day," "The Tortoise and the Hare," "Melancholy Man," "Are You Sitting Comfortably?" "The Dream," and "The Legend of a Mind." There were lots more to drown us in sound. ...

John Lodge said, "We tried to build our own P.A. systems to get that right, but it was impossible. Every venue was different." (JL-OTR09)

The hardest part of touring continued to be lugging Pinder's Mellotron. John Lodge told interviewer Joe Benson, "Actually, the size was the big problem – getting it on airplanes, we had to find out the size of the door on every plane; it had to fit in. In the end, we found the best thing was to have three or four Mellotrons and leave them in different places. I remember we had one show in Los Angeles, and the Mellotron was happily winging its way to Hawaii!" (JL-OTR09)

Despite the Moodies themselves knowing that there was a problem in amplification in certain venues, Donoghue's review struck a negative chord with many of the college students who populated the audience that night in the Burlington's Memorial Auditorium. The newspaper shared the indignation:

Is it too much to ask, when a musical event is to be reviewed, that a qualified person be utilized for the task? I am, of course, referring to the rather poor excuse for a review which was conjured up by John Donoghue for the Moody Blues concert at Memorial Auditorium, Monday evening.

Taking things in order: Anyone who frequents concerts by "name" bands such as the Moody Blues realizes that there is almost always, without exception, a back-up group or performer who starts the show. Therefore, one does not go to a rock concert expecting the top-billed group to appear first. As for Dion's "unscheduled" appearance.... Fact: Dion was contracted for the concert and was not merely added to the show at the last minute as an afterthought.

I wonder if Mr. Donoghue could clarify what is inherently excellent about "New England sound systems," and why he apparently feels offended that the Moody Blues chose to use their own equipment. Fact: Almost universally, rock bands use exclusively their own equipment, not because of inane geographical prejudices as Mr. Donoghue seems to imply we should believe, but simply because sound systems normally found in auditoriums and such places are seldom equal, never superior and practically always inferior, to the equipment which the band has purchased for the express purpose of musical instrument and vocal amplification.

Finally, on the purely subjective side, I wonder what is Mr. Donoghue's basis, if any, for comparison of performance quality. I have seen, in person, somewhat over 30 major nationally and internationally known groups ranging from the Airplane to Zappa and have yet to see some members of each group not have some technical problems – yes, even an out-of-tune D string if you like nit-picking. Comparatively speaking, relative to other live performances, the Moody Blues put on an excellent performance as was evidenced by the more favorable audience reaction.

Mr. Donoghue would have been wiser to simply declare that he did not like the Moody Blues' music. Since appreciation of music is a subjective and aesthetic process, no one would then be able to argue with Mr. Donoghue's opinions except with his own equally valid or invalid opinions. However, when the reviewer ventures beyond his scope as a music critic, I strongly suggest that he first make an effort to know what he is talking about.... – Gary Thayer, Student, University of Vermont.

Tuesday, September 22: Music Hall, Boston, Massachusetts (two separate shows). Poco opened.

Wednesday, September 23: Felt Forum, New York City, N.Y., again with Poco (two performances).

"Jeff," a reviewer for *Variety*, wrote:

> The distant rock sounds of the Moody Blues and the spirited country-rock of Poco drew an enthusiastic, sellout audience to the Felt Forum, N.Y. last Wednesday evening (23). With tickets scaled to $6, the Ron Delsener production grossed $47,000. The two shows were marked by professionalism and high caliber talent in both groups.

> Although much of their set had an air of familiarity and predictability to it, the Moody Blues continue to amaze with the large orchestrated sound they achieve in person. Much of the latter is due to the Mellotron, a synthesizer that allows the Moodies to produce a myriad of instrumental shadings. The quintet stuck to its past hits, with "Question" demonstrating their ability to fuse tranquil elements with driving rock. ...

Ed Ochs covered the concert for *Billboard*:

… As always, the Moodys were energetic and beautiful to hear. Unfortunately, they are a pop act who take themselves too seriously, mistaking sound effects for musical literature, and coming out from behind their elite disk image they appear obsessed as pompous aristocracy with their "statement." Packed into Mike Pinder's Mellotron all the pop-mystical bursts, rushes and echoes exquisitely recorded into their colorful Deram and Threshold albums, as Justin Hayward's brave, probing vocals illustrated the high sentimentality of "Question," "Never Comes the Day," "Nights in White Satin," and others. No mistake about it, though, the know-it-all Moodys have a schmaltzy gimmick – a sound – and they devotedly crank out beautiful cosmic rock, symphonically splendorous, rock's classiest light-heavyweight and easiest listening. …

Thursday, September 24: Cleveland Public Auditorium, Cleveland, Ohio. Poco continued as opening act.

Friday, September 25: Cincinnati Gardens, Cincinnati, Ohio, with Van Morrison opening. Prices: $4.50 in advance; $5.50 at the door.

Jim Knippenberg attended for *The Cincinnati Enquirer*:

> Van Morrison and the Moody Blues put on a two hour rock concert at the Cincinnati Gardens Friday night. Between the two of them, they pulled in more people than I can remember being assembled there in a long time. Remarkable enough, almost everyone went home happy. No thanks to Van Morrison. He opened up the show and was pretty much of a disappointment. … For one thing he has absolutely no stage presence. He stands there and sings, nothing more. There's no dialogue with the audience, no movement, very little personality; he just stands there looking semi bored and now and then utters a curt "thank you" after a song. …

> But the Moody Blues made up for it and took away all semblance of disappointment. They came on the stage accompanied by a deafening roar from the nearly full house, performed their first number and completely cleaned up the bomb Van Morrison left. The group came on all revved up and got the audience into the same state in a matter of seconds. And it's small wonder – they were devastating.

They brought with them a big, almost symphonic, sound which managed to switch from "good ole rock" to what might be called classical rock, at the drop of a drumstick. They gave away lots of good, gentle vibes that did beautiful things to your head.

One of the good things they did to the mind was to keep it jumping. By playing a lot more than everyday rock, mixing in numerous motifs, they kept everybody active and thinking. The contact highs were free, yours for the asking. All you had to do was listen. The Moody Blues generated enough excitement to prompt one ardent fan to take off his clothes. He was escorted to the exit.

But it was that kind of a show. They made you feel like you could do anything or go anywhere just with their music. Music for the spirit, music for the mind, music for the body – put it anywhere, it's dynamite.

The audience showed their appreciation with a couple historic ovations, forcing the group to stay on stage a bit longer than anticipated. And that was great too.

Whatever harm Van Morrison did with his ultra cool approach, the Moody Blues made better with their talent, versatility, sophistication, and incredible energy. However unpromising the evening started, it ended eight miles high – and that's good news.

Saturday, September 26: Duke University, Durham, North Carolina. Dion was the opening act.

Sunday, September 27: The Spectrum, Philadelphia, Pennsylvania, with Van Morrison and Dion as opening acts.

Jack Lloyd wrote in *The Philadelphia Inquirer*:

… The Moody Blues was the big powerhouse attraction, of course. Aside from the fact that flutist Ray Thomas fell through a "hole" in the backstage area as the group maneuvered in for their set, everything was fine.

"Flute Broken." That's what a member of the group announced, at any rate. Thomas – who might have been inspecting the Spectrum's ceiling at the time – reportedly did not break anything but his flute and no further explanation of the "hole" was given.

Fortunately rock crowds are invariably prepared for any emergency and someone in the audience just happened to have a spare flute tucked under his poncho.

And so Moodies finally came on to give a first-rate demonstration of the brand of music that inspired many fascinated observers to talk about the group as revolutionary back in the days when hard rock was king.

Such devices as cello, flute, harpsichord, and a Mellotron – an electronic instrument that produces a kind of organ sound – mixed with the more familiar rock tools were the basis for this "revolutionary" talk. But whatever you call it, the Moody Blues' approach to modern music is impressive. ...

About that hole Ray Thomas fell through, Justin Hayward recalled, "At this one place – the Spectrum in Philadelphia – they left a little triangle, because the wall was curved where it went around as you walked on to the stage. But the scaffolding was square, so there was a little bit of a triangle of empty space. And we'd always go on in the same order – superstitious thing, or it just worked – and I always followed Ray on stage. So, I'm blindly following Ray on stage with my guitar, and all of a sudden, he's not there... 'schwoop,' he's completely disappeared. And I just looked down and I could just see the top of his head sticking out, and he says, 'I'm fucking stuck!' ...

"And, poor Ray, he'd fallen down this hole and twisted his ankle, and he was just suspended in the scaffolding underneath it.... And some people had to go underneath and push him back up. Dear Ray. But the worst thing was he'd broken his flute. That wasn't so funny. In fact, he didn't think it was funny at all, any aspect of it....

"[W]e got Ray onto the stage, but he had no flute.... And one of us made an announcement to say, 'Ray Thomas has broken his flute. Just by any chance, there's nobody here with a spare... is there?' And, 'Yeah! I've got a flute!' And this guy came up with a complete C flute. The things people bring to concerts, it's amazing!

"Yeah, Ray played this guy's flute for the whole concert. Sounded lovely."
(JH-CAMB06)

And, according to a report in *Record Mirror*, he did so with a bruised back, sprained ankle, and two broken toes. Fortunately for Thomas, the Spectrum engagement was the last scheduled stop on the tour. This proved fortunate for Pinder too. The *Record Mirror* article stated that, while the Moodies had returned home "from their highly successful American tour last week," they were minus Mike Pinder, who was resting in a Los Angeles hospital following an operation for the removal of a cyst from his larynx. He was expected to be discharged from the hospital in two weeks. Some concerts that had been set for Italy had to be cancelled, but Pinder was able to rejoin his colleagues in time for further European engagements (Amsterdam on October 23, and continuing in Germany on October 24 to 26). Uriah Heep was the opening act.

On October 10, Keith Altham commented in *Record Mirror*:

> The Moody Blues – trick or treat? Their talent and ability to produce their unique sounds on live appearances is undeniable but a hard core minority both in the Press and out of it seem to suspect their motives.
>
> There are very few people indifferent to the Moodies and more often than not it is a case of canonization or crucifixion. Very few seem to have realized that simple truth of perspective which the Moodies have adequately pointed out on their Number One album that it is indeed *A Question of Balance*. ...

The Moodies themselves are less incensed by the injustice of some of the accusations leveled at them of "pretentiousness" than their fans. ...

Edge told Altham, "In a sense I think it is something of a compliment to be called 'pretentious.' We leave ourselves open to that kind of criticism by the opinionated material that we produce. We have very definite opinions on certain subjects and we feel they are important enough to be said in public, which is bound to cause a reaction – we'd be disappointed if it did not." (GE-RM70)

On November 6, 1970, having returned to England, Mike Pinder was at the Epson Registry Office where he married a 19-year-old secretary from California named Donna Arkoff, the daughter of American International Pictures co-head Samuel Z. Arkoff. All four fellow Moodies were with Pinder and his bride.

One British newspaper reported:

> The couple will live at Mike's house in Cobham, but there is no time for a honeymoon just yet as the Moodies are now back in the studios again! The group has now moved its headquarters of its Threshold Records company out of London, and has opened offices in Cobham – where they all live.

It was also reported that the Moodies would begin their latest American tour on December 3, playing mainly West Coast dates, before traveling east for the final date in the schedule, at New York City's Carnegie Hall on December 14 – the group's first appearance at the celebrated venue.

For the November 14, 1970 issue of *Sounds*, Penny Valentine wrote:

> Mention the Moody Blues to a lot of people and they curl up their mouths and snort derisive things like "pretentious," "rubbish" and other gentle phrases. Mention the name to others and they'll gawp and say: "Oh, the Saviors" – and really both are just as bad. It's the kind of reaction the Moodies don't need, but seem to have laid themselves open to in the past couple of years.
>
> Through their work on albums like *Days of Future Past* [sic] and *Children's Children's Children*, they have established a very individual and unassailable niche for themselves in the music field. But its kickback has been an unfair amount of criticism simply because the Moodies' work, to some minds, has come to mean something above and beyond their actual music.

Lodge told Valentine, "I don't mind any criticism as long as it's justified.... I think criticism is good because if you don't get it you really are too close to your work to be able to judge properly. It does you good for someone to point something out....

"Of course, criticism of any kind can throw you a bit – just as all that crap about being 'The Saviors' can. Just before our last British tour we were really paranoid.... We

349

were really cap in hand until we heard it was sold out before we started. Even then, I thought maybe they were coming along to boo us.

"But when it all comes down to this 'pretentious' label – well, it was us who initially made *Days of Future Passed* and it was us who stood up and played it."

As for why the band returned to America so frequently, Lodge explained, "Most of our U.S. tours are only in two-week stretches. The last one covered the East Coast and Mid-West. It's a much easier way of working – even though it still means travelling at least 500 miles to each concert across country in 12 days.

"I think we have acclimated ourselves to America now. When you first go it's such a different attitude and way of life from everything you've known that you really have to get your head in a different place….

"I suppose, really, American audiences do take preference – simply because of their sheer volume and force. When 15,000 or 20,000 people actually bother to come out and see you, then, naturally, it's a tremendous boost even before you set foot on stage."
(JL-S70)

The second leg of the *Question of Balance* tour of America began on Wednesday, December 3, 1970, at the Maples Pavilion, Stanford University, Palo Alto, California. Threshold band Trapeze was the opening act for the entire tour.

Thursday, December 4, 1970: San Diego International Sports Arena, San Diego, California. A writer for the San Diego area *Chula Vista Star-News*, using only his last name, the eye-catching – for this era – "Lennon," described the event:

> … Houselights flashing a warning of the show's beginning focused many-colored eyes on the stage. …
>
> Trapeze is the three-man warm-up group. They are very talented and promising. So the crowd reacts well to them as joints light up and house-lights dim down. …
>
> [After the warm-up act], a local disk-jockey addresses the non-listening audience. He doesn't say anything very important and everyone knows it. … The lights go out as the DJ continues to talk and no one listens. The Moody Blues sneak onto the dark stage.
>
> Mike Pinder, their leader, interrupts and demands that the lights go on so his group can tune their instruments. The crowd laughs and joins Mike Pinder in heckling [the DJ], as he smiles shamefully and hurriedly finishes his announcement. He then tucks his tail between his legs and leaves the stage to the Moody Blues.
>
> Joints light up again, the crowd applauds and the Moody Blues continue their tuning. Their amplification system is one of their finest in the world. They finish their tuning and make a good start with Justin Hayward's "Gypsy." The crowd cheers Hayward's guitar and voice in the song. He is really a gifted musician and songwriter. Long applause follows. …
>
> "Tuesday Afternoon," another Justin Hayward song, follows. One begins to feel that Hayward could make it on his own if he had to,

though it seems he enjoys sharing the leadership of the Moody Blues with Mike Pinder.

Pinder remarks about our smog-filled sky, and introduces a trio of songs from their recent *Question of Balance* album. John Lodge's "Tortoise and the Hare" explains that we are moving much too fast and that progress will kill us. The crowd agrees, with applause.

The crowd goes wild over Hayward's excellent guitar and voice in "Question." ...

The Moody Blues have been dropping LSD for several years and some think they now have strong and powerful minds. Many of their songs give quite accurate descriptions of LSD trips and of how the drug magnifies the senses.

In "Departure," the first song on the *In Search of the Lost Chord* album, Graeme Edge tells of their reason for dropping: "... Or to fly to the sun without burning a wing ... to lie in the meadow and hear the grass sing ... To have all these things in our memory hoard ... And to use them to help us to find ..."

What exactly the Moody Blues are trying to find is the true meaning of life and the achievement of perfection. They have done well in perfecting their talent: for they each play a score of instruments on their albums and have recorded five within two years [sic; three years].

The five members of the group sound, on record and in concert, like a huge symphony orchestra. What makes them so exciting to watch in concert is their precision timing. Listening to the group one imagines that they all possess the powers of mind-reading, seeing to the ends of the universe and forecasting the future. ...

Now comes the Moody Blues finale. "Legend of a Mind" by Ray Thomas tells the story of Timothy Leary and was the first of the group's acid songs. We are held breathless, filled with emotion, at the end. The Moody Blues leave us at a standing ovation. They do not care for America and Americans, and so they make us beg for many long minutes before they finally come back.

John Lodge's best creation, "Ride My See-Saw," ends the show as the crowd surges to the front of the stage. The Moody Blues disappear again and leave everybody jumping up and down, cheering and waving their arms in adoration of the five gods of music. But the Moody Blues are too proud to come back, and leave us shouting for more in hopeless dismay.

We left and began the endless search for our cars. It's fun to watch all the stoned people try to figure out where they parked. It's even hard when you're straight. ...

Friday, December 5, 1970: Municipal Auditorium, Kansas City, Missouri.

Saturday, December 6, 1970: Dallas Memorial Auditorium, Dallas, Texas. The Moodies continued to marvel over the effect their songs had on some people in America – the biggest state in the Union included.

From this time, Ray Thomas told Keith Altham of *Record Mirror*, "In Dallas, there is a radio station devoted almost exclusively to readings from the Bible and the background music is often taken from our albums. I suppose it is justified by turning people on to good books like the Bible, but when they take very innocent lines like 'The rain is on the roof' and infer it has some direct reference to a Biblical prophecy, it's laying an unnecessarily heavy number on someone's head. ... One guy turned up in Texas outside our dressing room dressed as the Pope in full ceremonial gear – the MITRE, cloak, jeweled gauntlets, rings, staff, and a goblet from which he invited we 'brothers' to drink. He even had a girl dressed as a nun with him! I suggested he try and kick the habit!" (RT-RM71)

"The Whistler," music reviewer for Texas's *The Waxahachie Daily Light*, wrote:

> Blasting, billowing, bursting forth with the power of ten billion butterfly sneezes, the Moody Blues gave the most dynamic performance concert of the year 1970 (as far as I am concerned, all years) on Sunday afternoon of December 6, 1970, at Memorial Auditorium in Dallas. The Moody Blues always come on strong and engulf their audiences with a sea of profound thought and astound them with their unbelievable musical ability, but this Sunday's concert was like a wave of Merlin's wand. The Moody Blues don't stop with music in their concerts, they create a mood – a state of mind that no other group before them has ever been able to create.
>
> The Moodies bounded into the stage and struck into "Gypsy" and immediately had the throngs of listeners (a capacity crowd at Memorial) entranced in their solid sound. The group worked with the strong guitar of Justin Hayward, the throbbing band and backup vocal of John Lodge, and symphonic harmonies of Mike Pinder's organ, the mystic flute and voice of Ray Thomas, and the unmatchable percussion of Graeme Edge. Working like smooth and fine machinery, they took the minds of the listeners and produced visual images of what they wanted to say through music. As the red, blue, orange, and yellow spotlights caught the musicians in their mystical beams, the masses sat silently spellbound as the Moodies played. ...
>
> They sing of hope of life for the better. They sing of the beauties of nature and the majesty of creation. In their praise of majesty, they can't help but praise the creator at some time. ...
>
> The Moodies played their famous sequence from their *Threshold of a Dream* masterpiece and then they hit "Legend of a Mind." The concert ended and the [audience] went wild. Cheers virtually

352

shook the roof. The group went off but they were brought back for an encore. They played "Ride My See Saw" as the thronging multitude clapped time to the music. The lights came on and the spotlight swept the floor. Everyone was together. …

The people just wouldn't leave. For about 20 minutes, the multitude stood in their seats chanting "More & more!" The very structure was pulsating with [the] intensity of the noise. Several times the road manager came out on the stage and gazed in disbelief into the throng. … The audience responded with an ecstatic 'Yes!' Finally the lights went out again and the crowd cheered. The Moody Blues struck up "Never Comes the Day" and the people shouted their approval. It was truly a magnificent experience for us and for the group, I'm sure. Two encores that would not stop – they were overwhelmed. As they finished they stood in gratification, giving peace signs and smiling gratefully. "Goodnight. We're coming back as soon as we can. Thank you. Good night and God bless you."

Isn't that the answer?

Monday, December 7: Municipal Auditorium, Austin, Texas.
Tuesday, December 8: University of Oklahoma, Norman, Oklahoma.
Wednesday, December 9: Sam Houston Coliseum, Houston, Texas.
Thursday, December 10, 1970: St. Louis Arena, St. Louis, Missouri. Thomas B. Newman wrote in the *St. Louis Post-Dispatch*:

> The Moody Blues, one of the youth culture's personifications of Pan, took rock back to the Renaissance last night as they shook the walls and rafters of the Arena with sound. But the Blues didn't stop with electrifying sixteenth century chamber music sounds. They ranged through much of today's rock sounds while more than 16,000 rock music fans shrieked and applauded. At the end, the audience was standing, wringing hands and writhing in pleasure. In fact, the adulation for the Moody Blues surpassed, perhaps, the yells attended at any game of the St. Louis Blues, not a rock band but a hockey team, that most often plays in the Arena.

> Blues, oranges and violet lights bathed the Blues as they ripped it out. Some members of the audience, no doubt, saw more colors than the ones mentioned above.

> One must note that the Moody Blues are heavily into electronic gadgetry in their music. This accounts in large measure, perhaps, for the fact that the five British lads have scored four gold albums in the last three months. …

> The Mellotron, an instrument that produces an organ-like sound, is a key claim to fame of the Moody Blues. In with this electric instrument are guitars, drums, and the flute of Ray Thomas, one of the Blues, who last night managed some fine obbligato. … The

acoustics of the Arena seemed more gracious to the instruments than to the voices. …

Friday, December 11: Denver Coliseum, Denver, Colorado.

Saturday, December 12: Los Angeles Forum, Inglewood, California, with Trapeze opening; then, for this night only, followed by Spirit, before bringing out the Moodies.

Ray Thomas told *Record Mirror* at this time, "In Los Angeles, we had one guy who got backstage, walked into the dressing room and dropped onto his knees in front of Mike. Poor old Mike was there until one o'clock in the morning trying to straighten him out. These people are exceptions, of course, but there is a hard core minority who persist in reading everything we write as apostolic. Now, I understand how McCartney felt when they went through that period when everything the Beatles wrote was analyzed and all kinds of misconceptions placed upon the simplest song." (RT-RM71)

John Lodge: "It was a different world. They were freaky times. It was a huge time of looking for things. We used to spend night after night sitting in hotel rooms with people we'd never met before discussing everything – flights to the moon which hadn't even happened yet, looking for all the different religions and the mystical things, the astrology and Christianity, everything. Everything was there, you know, and you were looking all the while, and this had to reflect in the songs you were writing." (JL-Q90)

Justin Hayward: "We only had ourselves to blame for all that, really. We were just expressing things that we'd read, and experiences that we'd had, and spiritual things that we'd had, and we were just expressing them in a very open and honest way without trying to be clever about it.

"It was a generation in America where they had the Vietnam war going on and there was a great need for some sort of philosophical sort of guidance, and they saw that in a lot of the groups, and particularly in the Moodies, because we were English. We weren't involved in their war, we came from a quaint little country, and that made us even more meaningful somehow. We had all these people at our feet, saying, 'What is the word? What is the answer?' And we could only say, 'Well, you know, try and make the world a better place.' At gigs every night there were people saying, 'You've got to come with us; you've got to go up the mountain; the end of the world is coming and you are the great leaders and you're the only ones that have the secret.' They treated us as gurus, and it was scary." (JH-Q90)

John Lodge: "It happened here in England, too. You'd come home from a tour in America and there would be all these people sitting in your drive and they'd look at you and say, 'We're waiting for you to take us away.' And you'd go, 'Oh, yes? Well, er, I'm going shopping, actually.'" (JL-Q90)

Ray Thomas: "America is a fascinating collection of loose ends and mixed-up people. But it is a totally materialistic society which is constantly being confused – 'Drink this cough mixture and you'll live to a thousand!' … 'Buy this car and be the envy of your friends!' … 'Take this pill and be happy!'" (RT-RM71)

Speaking of mixed-up people, the Forum concert was covered for *The Los Angeles Times* by John Mendelsohn. You may recall Mr. Mendelsohn as the fellow who was trying so hard to be funny while writing his album review of *A Question of Balance* for *Rolling Stone*.

At the time Mr. Mendelsohn reviewed *A Question of Balance*, he admitted that while the Moodies had talent, and were popular, he didn't take them seriously because the only worthwhile pop music was "straight-out rock and roll." For Mendelsohn, the problem with the Moody Blues were: 1) they didn't just play straight-out rock and roll; 2) they took themselves too seriously and used pop music to make statements; 3) Justin Hayward was the only Moodie who should be allowed to write and sing.

Mendelsohn ditched the sarcasm for his review in the *Times*, but his tune was otherwise the same:

(Photo source: Author's collection)

Were the Moody Blues both less democratic and less dedicated to the proposition that rock is indeed art, they would most likely be one smashing rock 'n' roll band. Although smashing as they are or not, it must be noted that they're popular enough to sell out the Forum, as they did Saturday evening. …

As for their rock-as-art excesses, they'd be worlds easier to take seriously were Pinder's classics-derived Mellotron (orchestra-in-a-box) embellishments not constantly reminding us what weighty stuff their music is.

Finally, if the Moodys were to stop regarding themselves as Junior sages they might be less inclined to writing such distressingly pedantic, pompous and stilted lyrics as, "Why do we never get an answer … to our thousand million questions about hate and death and war?"

For all their faults, the Moodys are always at least listenable, occasionally forget themselves and rock 'n' roll splendidly, and are infinitely preferable to the vast majority of their neighbors in the Top Ten. …

Daily Variety reported that the Forum concert, with a "standing room only" attendance of 18,732, grossed $103,000. Mr. Mendelsohn clearly felt that 18,731 of those in the audience had no idea what good music was about.

Sunday, December 13 was a travel day from West to East Coast.

Monday, December 14: Carnegie Hall, New York City, New York.

Mike Jahn reported for *The New York Times* and *Rolling Stone* magazine:

The Moody Blues played a set Monday, at Carnegie Hall, before a packed house. The concert, advertised as "special, two-hour performance," turned out to be a little over an hour by the Moody Blues. The rest was taken up by a half-hour show by Trapeze, a loud Grand Funk Railroad style group that the Moody Blues produce, and a long intermission. The fact that the group abbreviated its concert caused only minor grumblings from the rather festive audience, who amused themselves during the intermission by sailing hundreds of paper airplanes from the balconies and applauding particularly long flights.

The Moody Blues played some of their familiar songs, such as "Timothy Leary's Dead" [sic] (refrain: "… no, he's outside looking in"), an old song that has assumed new significance lately; "A Question of Balance," which provoked the greatest audience response, and "Ride My See-Saw."

Because of the volume of the group's instruments, the lyrics were largely unintelligible, but that is not exactly a new problem in rock. Mike Pinder gave the Moody Blues' finest performance yet on the Mellotron, the amazing keyboard instrument that makes reasonable imitation of an orchestral string section.

In all, it was a fine concert; one could have better appreciated it were one's ears not benumbed by Trapeze earlier in the evening, but still it was very worthwhile.

Fred Kirby covered the concert for *Billboard* magazine:

The Moody Blues, one of the most imaginative, original groups around, gave a high-caliber concert in the first of two Carnegie Hall concerts Dec. 14, a concert of the caliber that has become their trademark. … At all times, the group injected subtle refinements not usually associated with rock acts. …

"Have You Heard" was a fine example of the melodic and rhythmic variety used by the Moody Blues within almost every number. "Question" and "Melancholy Man" were among the gems from their latest Threshold album, *A Question of Balance*, while "Forever Afternoon (Tuesday)" was a winner from *Days of Future Passed*, the Deram album, also distributed by London, which established this former rock group in its more modern course. "Legend of a Mind" again was the solid closing number. Throughout instrumental work and vocal work both shone.

Trapeze, in its first U.S. tour, were perhaps too heavy for the hall, especially the overpowering lead guitar. …

On Wednesday, December 16, still in New York, at a reception at the Friars Club hosted by London Records, the Moodies were presented three Gold Record Albums by

Sir Edward Lewis, chairman of Decca Record Company of England. The awards were for *In Search of the Lost Chord,* on Deram, and *To Our Children's Children's Children* on Threshold, and also for their latest album, *A Question of Balance*, also on Threshold. Earlier in the year, the Moodies had gained Gold Albums for *On the Threshold of a Dream* and *Days of Future Passed*, meaning that they were now five-for-five.

Three days later, on December 19, 1970, Justin Hayward married his long-time girlfriend, Marie Guirron.

Marie said, "I'm from Birkenhead [near Liverpool] and I used to go to the Cavern Club in Liverpool to see all the groups, so by the time I married Justin, when I was 26, I knew what the pop business was all about. I took the attitude that what my eye didn't see, my heart couldn't grieve over. I tried not to let my fears get to me, but I also realized Justin was different. He was deep, and still is – that's what attracted me in the first place. There's a side to him I still don't know after all these years." (MH-GH97)

Justin Hayward and Marie Guirron, wedding day, December 19, 1970.
(Photo source: MoodyBluesAttitude.com)

The marriage would endure ... through "all these years," but the wedding and honeymoon were something groom and bride would rather forget.

Hayward later spoke candidly of the spontaneous affair: "Marie and I had known each other for three years and been living together for two. We bought the house that we still live in [in 1994] before the wedding. We'd thought about getting married – we knew we would but we never nailed it down. Then I came back from a tour with the Moody Blues and just decided to do it.

"We got married in the church just around the corner and the service was taken by a young priest who was a friend of my family.

"The other guys in the band were away in various parts of the world. It was December and we couldn't rustle up that many people. Basically, the guests were my family, and Marie's family, plus a few friends, including our record producer, Tony Clarke, and the local doctor who lived down the road. My brother was the best man. ...

"Everyone came back and joined us at home for the reception and we cut the cake that my mother had made for us. It was 19 December and so close to Christmas that we had decided to book the bridal suite at the Dorchester for the weekend and stay in England. ...

"Looking back, we were well out of our depth because it was all so posh; we really didn't know what we were doing. We simply hadn't thought the thing through. Sunday morning came and the weather was miserable, [so] we hung around in the room and managed a brief walk in the park.

"That evening was to be the centerpiece of the occasion. I had booked a table at the Dorchester Grill and we both got all dressed up. This was the big treat for the weekend. I'd brought along the suit I'd worn for the wedding, the first proper one I'd ever owned, bought specially in the Beatles' Apple boutique, and I put it on again because I knew you had to wear a suit and tie to get in.

"It's probably true to say that the hotel wasn't particularly thrilled with my type. I had long hair and there was still a lot of prejudice around against that in those days. We went downstairs to the restaurant and I went up to the maître d' and explained that I'd booked a table. He said: 'I'm sorry, sir, but I can't possibly let you in.'

"I told him that I had put on a suit and tie specially for the occasion because I knew the rules. He said, 'It's not you, sir, it's madam. She is wearing a trouser suit when she should be wearing a dress.' I was flabbergasted.

"As we'd only brought proper clothes for that one evening, there was nothing Marie could change into. We were completely deflated and embarrassed.

"We went back upstairs, took all the posh gear off, put on ordinary clothes, and headed out into Park Lane. We found this hamburger bar just before you got to the Hilton on the left, and that was where we had our big honeymoon meal. Then we went to the cinema, saw *Women in Love*, with Alan Bates and Oliver Reed, and, on Monday morning, packed our bags and went home." (JH-DM94)

Such was the life of a pop star in England, 1970. Justin and Marie Hayward would return to the Dorchester restaurant 25 years later, celebrating their silver anniversary. This time they got a table with no trouble at all.

16

Their Own Realm

John Lodge and Ray Thomas in front of the Threshold Record shop in Cobham, England. The top two floors above the shop comprised the Threshold Records offices. (Courtesy Tony Brown)

Charles Alverson wrote in the April 30, 1970 edition of *Rolling Stone*:

> … The Moodies began thinking about their own label 18 months ago when they got rid of their managers and started managing themselves. Decca wasn't happy about the idea, and it took a lot of persuading and three years tacked onto the distribution contract for the Moodies to break away. But so far the relationship has been amicable.

Tony Clarke told Alverson, "We've got complete freedom. All we had to promise Decca was no tits and toilet seats on the album covers, and that's not our scene anyway." (TC-RS70)

Regardless, according to Alverson, there had been conflict between Decca and Threshold. The Moodies spent 25% more making *To Our Children's Children's Children* than *Days of Future Passed* had cost. One fight was over the cost of the LP sleeves. In the end, Threshold took over the contracting of the sleeves' printing, for delivery to Decca.

Mike Pinder: "We've found out that no matter how hard we work in the studio, our records can turn up in the shops totally destroyed. Through Threshold we're able to follow our records clear to the shops and know the buyer is getting good value for money. When we were just artists, we were told to shut up and sing. But, as a record company, we can influence the distribution in the way we think they ought to be." (MP-RS70)

Tony Clarke: "You'd be surprised at the impact on sales of a small thing like record sleeve orders. Some prick decides to play it safe and under-orders sleeves, so one of our records stands still or slips in the charts. I'd rather burn a few thousand sleeves to make sure they are there when we need them." (TC-RS70)

The Moodies were, they said, not copying the Beatles lead with their Apple Corps. Unlike the Beatles, the Moodies wanted to keep Threshold a small company run by the band and their producer. Pinder said, "In a way, we're very lucky to have Apple as an example to us. Everybody here at Threshold has to be totally involved. We're too small to carry any deadwood. But we're not looking for an Allen Klein. We don't need any heads chopped off." (MP-RS70)

For some Beatles fans, the reference to lawyer Allen Klein were fighting words. Klein was a New York music manager for the Rolling Stones, who achieved some influence with the Beatles after Brian Epstein died. Lennon, Harrison, and Starr were in favor of Klein. They realized that their company Apple had become overloaded with staff and acquisitions. Paul McCartney didn't trust Klein and refused to be managed by him. But the other three felt that a "shark" like Klein could rid Apple of the leeches and hangers-on who had turned a promising company into a money pit. In April 1970, the conflict over Klein, perhaps more than anything else, torpedoed the Beatles.

***

In 1970, Tony Clarke bought a home in Cobham, Surrey, about an hour's commute from London. Also at this time, Mike Pinder, John Lodge, Ray Thomas, and Graeme Edge bought homes in Cobham. Justin Hayward had moved to nearby Teddington.

At the end of the year, Threshold relocated their offices from London to Cobham, to a three-story brick building. The top two floors were used for office space and the bottom floor turned into a record shop.

John Lodge explained to Tony Norman of *Music Scene*: "We were spending two hours on the train every day going up to town, then seven hours sitting in our office. At night we'd feel really shattered and in no mood to do anything creative. It was like two hours for the music and nine for the business, whereas it should have been the other way round.

"All this really hit us one night when we were sitting in our First Class compartment of the commuter special back to Cobham. I think I was sitting next to Ray at the time, and we were surrounded by all the bowler hat brigade with their smart suits, umbrellas, and brief cases. We looked at each other and it just clicked that we were getting to be exactly like the rest of the guys in the carriage. We had our brief cases up on the rack above our heads. All we needed was a bowler hat each and we would have been away!

"It was a frightening thought, I can tell you. So we decided to get an office in Cobham and it has worked out really well. I think we avoid a lot of the pressures that you get up in town and that helps us to get more done in a shorter amount of time." (JL-MS72)

Also interviewed in 1970, Tony Clarke said, "The band and I all recently moved to a small village outside London where we'll work from. Other than removing the need to commute, we also get to control our business hours. A few hours each week takes care of our work. We can then spend the rest of the time doing what we really like to do. If you allow yourself to get deeply involved in the business side of a record

Above: Decca Records, London, England – the business world's idea of the music business. Below: Threshold Records, Cobham, England – the Moody Blues' idea of the music business.
(Photo source: MoodyBluesAttitude.com)

company you lose sight of the creative side. That's hurt groups before and we don't want it to break up the Moody Blues." (TC-DFP70)

Another reason for the move, according to Mike Pinder, was to escape the cynics, as well as the evil that infested many people and places on Earth. The Moody Blues' success enabled them the freedom to create their own Nirvana – or try to, anyway.

In June 1971, a regional newspaper covered the event of the Moodies' attempts to assimilate into the village of Cobham:

> The Moody Blues, one of the top recording and concert groups, have put down their roots in Cobham and fitted into local life.
>
> In the past 18 months, all the Moody Blues have bought houses in or near Cobham, and, after much soul searching, the group then decided to base its Threshold Records Company in Cobham.
>
> Since moving into Threshold House in Cobham High Street about six months ago, they have centralized their business in Cobham, and

expanded the Moody Blues "family" with the addition of their American friend, Gerry Hoff, who arrived in Cobham at the beginning of this year, fresh from Los Angeles, to be General Manager of Threshold Records.

At the time, Ray Thomas told *Disc and Music Echo*, "We found we couldn't be creative and be businessmen at the same time, so we've had to let someone take control of the business side. But our objectives remain the same – no one who signs to Threshold will get a poor deal in the way that we used to. Do you know how much I received for 'Go Now!,' which sold three million copies? £50!" (RT-DME71)

"Pete," a writer for *Jackie* magazine, shared an insider's look at the place we'll call "Moodyland" for the magazine's September 25, 1971 issue. He wrote in part:

> Once a year, the Moody Blues hold court and throw their homes or their office open to the press. It's a well-planned ritual, timed to coincide with the release of each Moodies album. [It's] that precise business sense which has made the Moody Blues one of Britain's most successful and exclusive groups. …
>
> In the main street, they've recently bought a modern, red-brick three-storeyed office block, and have since opened their own record shop – Threshold Records – on the ground floor. It was there at their headquarters that this year's Court was held.
>
> First, the Moody Blues trooped down the banks of the River Thames nearby to pose for a select group of invited photographers; then a champagne buffet was served and the press… were invited to the board-room premiere of their latest LP. …

The Moodies in 1971, on the banks of the River Thames, Cobham, Surrey, in promotional image circulated after a day with the press.
(Photo source: teamrock.com)

The organization was impressive. But then it always is. Stories of the Moody Blues and their wheeling and dealing are becoming almost legendary. They were the first to secure a £250,000 advance on royalties from Decca. Then they offered to take over the packaging of their LPs, and did it at a profit. Then they costed the running of their London office, and found it was cheaper on time and money to operate from the country – and promptly opened in Cobham. Having done so, they've opened that record shop – and imported an American recording executive to manage their record company. …

When the Moodies go on the road it means a concert tour of the United States, or the Far East, playing to audiences of 15,000 or more each night. But when the work is over, it is back home for the Moodies. Ray Thomas summed up the group's feelings: "We've done so much traveling that we really value the time we are able to spend at home in sunny downtown Cobham."

Pete described some of the Moodies' indulgence. Tony Clarke, a "keen astronomer," had a 12-inch diameter Cassegrain telescope – "one of the most powerful telescopes in Britain!" – installed in a "roof studio" at his nearby home. Graeme Edge was also "dabbling in space exploration," as well as writing his sci-fi stories and poetry, and working to develop an electronic drum set. As for the others, Pete wrote:

Mike Pinder has just finished a six-month building program, completing his own five-roomed recording studio. It's been built in the grounds of his house, complete with eight-track recording equipment, and three acoustic chambers.

Ray Thomas has joined nearly every angling club along the banks of the River Mole. One afternoon recently he caught 15 perch – another day he landed a 4 ½ pound chub. …

Justin Hayward is settling down with his newly-wed wife in the house they bought from [pop star and actor] Tommy Steele.

Edge boasted, "Justin spends most of his time songwriting. And so does John Lodge – he's really taken to songwriting now. John's also moved to a new house about half a mile away from the old one he had. And Justin's become quite a guitar freak – he's got 22 guitars now!" (GE-J71)

Pete noted:

And so this quiet, well-ordered, happily domestic life that the Moody Blues lead rolls on. They're always popping in and out of each other's homes for dinner, their children play together, and their wives are close friends. …

Ray Thomas told David Hughes of *Disc and Music Echo*, for the paper's August 21, 1971 issue: "This is the first year since the Moody Blues made it that I've felt free. It's also the first year that we've been able to sit back and take stock of ourselves.

"I get uptight just driving to London. I get to Hammersmith Bridge and I'm immediately aware of all the hustle and bustle. And it's just the opposite the other way round – people who come down to Cobham to see us always remark how quiet and peaceful it is. London is a very lonely place – you have 'friends' when you have money, but they're friends not worth having. In Cobham, my friends are real people… My best friend down there drives a van for the local fruit shop and is the secretary of one of the fishing societies.

"It's now a whole ritual with me, this fishing. Apart from the fish there are huge hares bobbing about, and water rats, and wild geese. It's so much better for me both mentally and physically than raving around Piccadilly until four in the morning."
(RT-DME71)

Thomas talked about the new record shop: "It was an accident, really. We bought a two-story block in Cobham to house our Threshold offices and our own offices and it happened to have a shop on the ground floor, which had previously been a bookshop, selling Bibles and things for the Christian Aid Society. We thought it might be a good idea to continue using it as a shop, but, when we asked for advice, [our solicitors] came up with a launderette. We didn't think the idea of a little old lady and a lot of washing machines was quite Moody Blues, and the obvious solution was a record shop

Launch of Threshold Record shop in Cobham, with (L-R): Lodge, Hayward, shop manager Don Mackenzie, Thomas, Edge, an unidentified person.
(Photo source: Pinterest.com)

"There was no record shop in the village, although the electrician sold a few, and it's this which really seems to have brought us into the village community. What is such a gas, too, is that we're selling records right across the board, from reggae to classical. And doing well, too. We had a fear that people might just regard the shop associated with us as for progressive music only. But we're selling everything."
(RT-DME71)

Penny Valentine, of *Disc and Music Echo*, talked to Mike Pinder about the band's prog-rock image. She said, "I wondered if this was one of the reasons the Moodies have often been labeled as a pretentious group, because many journalists, especially, were very aware of how you lived and couldn't equate that with your music."

Pinder responded, "[T]here are people who question our ethics, but who questions *theirs*? Who watches the watcher?... I think the media all over the world – TV, press, radio – is misused. Ninety-seven percent of the material they use is trivial, and even the newscasts are biased. It's rubbish – the system is filling the minds of the people with rubbish so that people don't get time to think about anything else. ...

"I read a report in the paper today – from Switzerland, that was given out to the press – that all the seas on this planet are going to be dead of life in 25 years. And it was on Page 3 in a two-inch column, and on the front was a picture of Kosygin in a head-dress! And, for me, the fact that the seas are going to be dead should have been a headline. That was the real, biggest piece of news to date!" (MP-DAME71)

The Moodies' success, Pinder pointed out, didn't automatically make the group's observations insincere. He had devoted much of his time to reading, exploring various beliefs, concepts, cultures, and religions. He had been on a spiritual search ever since 1967, just prior to *In Search of the Lost Chord*. The statements in his songs from that album forward were his own questions, concerns, discoveries, and answers. They were the truth as he understood it. And, if sincere, then how could they be pretentious?

For the December 1972 issue of the American music magazine, *Circus*, Ward Beaverman told his readers about "a point of contention which has been driving the Moodies up the walls for years now – specifically, the criticism that they are aloof, pretentious pseudo-philosophers."

Beaverman noted that after a Chicago newspaper ran a concert review with the mocking headline, "Rock Gods Descend from on High," Ray Thomas took the stage in Chicago and, "obviously, ... not amused," remarked, "You know I took a stroll across the lake before coming here." When an English journalist had pushed for a reaction to being called "pretentious," Graeme Edge fired back, "Pretension to me means pretending, and I don't pretend, so I'm not pretentious as far as I can see!"

For the article, Beaverman went to Cobham himself. His report:

> When you get down to the basic facts of the Moodies' lives, you begin to understand that Graeme and Ray and the others have a perfect right to be annoyed by these critical suggestions. Really pretentious things – like half a dozen sports cars and several castles – have no place in their lives. All they really want to do is play music and hang around the British countryside with their wives and kids.
>
> Were it not for an overabundance of British architecture, the town of Cobham could very well be any hamlet in New England. Except for the accents, the people seem the same – tight-lipped little old men and tweedy little old women, people who still do double-takes at the sight of a long-haired male. Browsing through the scenery you find lots of trees and grass, a little brook with a watermill, gobs of flowers, maybe some gold-fish.

Before the Moody Blues moved there… the biggest thing going in Cobham was the local football team. Even now, when a Moody wanders into the local pub, conversation stops dead and pints of bitter halt in mid-air. Out on the street, English mums in sensible shoes turn to their friends and whisper, "There goes one of them," every time a patchwork boot passes by. Hardly what you'd call Mount Olympus, or wherever it is that a "rock god" would reside. …

The Moodies enjoyed living in plain sight. No one bothered them in Cobham. Some didn't even dare talk to them. John Lodge amusedly told *The Popular Voice* in 1973 that many residents weren't even sure who lived in his house. He said, "This electrician I met told me about a man in the local [union] who was telling his mates: 'A lot of people would like that house, but one of them bloody Rolling Stones has got it.' I've lived in that house five years. That's how much impact we've made in Cobham." (JL-PV73)

Graeme Edge told *Sounds* magazine, "We don't believe we're these gigantic worldwide superstars. Maybe on the plain level of how many actual records we've sold – well okay. Not on an ordinary level; we haven't got these gigantic extrovert personalities.

"We're not stars – we're your plain musicians. If you level it out by the dirty dollar, then we may be thought of as stars, in that bracket. But as household names, we're not. As names or faces, only a few people recognize us. We are proper musicians in the old fashioned use of the term. " (GE-S73)

Now these latter-day minstrels were living in an old-fashioned hamlet.

***

The plan in forming Threshold had been for the Moodies to be able to branch out – to do two or three group albums a year, or for individual members to produce albums by other Threshold artists. And they also had planned to do solo albums.

But, as the Moodies gained popularity in America and Canada as well as Britain and Continental Europe, the demands for them to tour increased. Each tour became longer and more exhausting than the previous one. It soon became apparent that the band would not be able to release two to three albums each year. One every 12 months was more likely. And any time that members might have used on individual projects was also curtailed, delaying or canceling those ideas. Still, the Moodies remained determined to use Threshold to launch new careers.

The first act that Threshold had wanted to sign was King Crimson (as reported in the May 3, 1969 issue of *Billboard*). The group, with Greg Lake on guitar and lead vocals, and Ian McDonald on flute and Mellotron, had released their first album, *In the Court of the Crimson King*, in October 1969. It has long been rumored that Tony Clarke produced the album. Folklore has it that when the band signed with Island Records instead of Threshold, Clarke's name was withheld. True or not, the group took the credit for producing themselves.

There had also been talk of signing a new band called Genesis (with front man Peter Gabriel), but they too went with a different and more established label.

Above: Gatefold of first Trapeze album. Original lineup: Glenn Hughes, Mel Galley, Dave Holland, Terry Rowley, and John Jones.

The first act actually signed to Threshold was Trapeze.

Formed in 1969 by vocalist John Jones and guitarist/keyboardist Terry Rowley (both former members of the Montanas), Trapeze also included guitarist Mel Galley, singer/bassist Glenn Hughes, and drummer Dave Holland, all from a previous group called Finders Keepers.

Glenn Hughes said, "We were greatly influenced by the great American soul records of the 1960s, but we were essentially hard rock musicians. The fusion of the two styles of music only seemed natural to us at the time." (GH-SCT94)

The band had built a reputation performing concerts around England and caught the ear of more than one record company. Hughes said, "We had five labels that wanted us. We had the Beatles' Apple label, we had John Lodge and their new label, Threshold, we had EMI, we had CBS, and Warner Brothers. And, for some reason or another, we went with the Moodys, [probably] because they were touring America a lot. We really wanted to go to America, so, I think, we did it for that reason alone." (GH-GM94)

Terry Rowley remembered another reason. "[We had] several offers, but the Moodies' was the best simply because the deal was so personal. It's so great to be working with businessmen who are really artists. They don't smoke long cigars and go on about how much money you must earn; they are sympathetic and, in that way, I'm sure they're getting the very best out of us." (TR-DME70)

John Lodge said, "I found Trapeze through various people and, as everything we do has to be unanimous, I asked the others' opinion. Everyone was unanimous that they were talented. I ended up producing them and it was a great experience.

"I'd never done it before and I had fears about it, but just in case I goofed; I wasn't scared of going in and doing it. I had an idea for the single, but we produced the other songs first to get to know each other." (JL-NME70a)

Threshold had launched in November 1969 with the Moody Blues' album *To Our Children's Children's Children* (THS-1), and their single "Watching and Waiting" b/w "Out and In" (TH 1). Trapeze came next, on November 21, with the John Lodge-

367

produced single "Send Me No More Letters" b/w "Another Day" (TH 2). It missed the charts, but Lodge told the British press that sales were nonetheless good; he was encouraged by the band's prospects.

To support the release of *To Our Children's Children's Children*, the Moodies spent the first two weeks of December touring, with stopovers in Manchester, Newcastle upon Tyne, Edinburgh, Bristol, London, Southampton, and finishing in Birmingham. The opening "warm up" acts were Trapeze, and another artist signed to Threshold, Timon.

Above: First Threshold single release by Trapeze, produced by John Lodge. Below: Single released on Threshold by Timon, produced by Justin Hayward.

On December 20, 1969, from *Record Mirror*:

> Preceding the Moody Blues at a live concert is a hard task for anyone, but Trapeze, John Lodge's new discovery, battled hard against the bad acoustics of the Albert Hall.
>
> They emerged with some nice easy vocals, but were a little too loud for their own good. The following act, featuring the lone figure Timon, with only guitar for company, proved to me a little embarrassing, though the audience gave him the necessary support.

Shortly after Trapeze was launched on Threshold, Justin Hayward oversaw the production of a single for Timon.

Hayward told *Melody Maker*'s Richard Williams, "John Lodge is recording a group from Wolverhampton called Trapeze, and I'm producing a singer called Timon, who was with Apple but didn't do anything there. He just wandered into our office and started playing these beautiful songs. He writes, plays good guitar, and sings, and he just needs some backing." (JH-MM69)

Tymon Dogg (as he would later spell his first name) was born Stephen John Murray. As a singer-songwriter and multi-instrumentalist, he began his career at the Cavern Club and the Peppermint Lounge in Liverpool when only 15. Moving to London at age 17, and using the name Timon, he signed to Pye Records, where he recorded a single that featured studio musicians Jimmy Page and John Paul Jones, pre-Led Zeppelin. It didn't chart and Pye chose not to renew its option. Timon moved to Apple Records next and recorded some tracks for producer Peter Asher, featuring Paul McCartney on piano and James Taylor (also

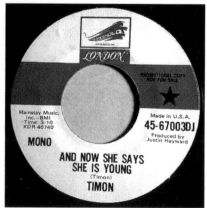

signed to Apple) on guitar. These songs were not released, and Timon left Apple to join Threshold.

Timon's first and only single on Threshold, catalog number TH 3 (issued as 45-67003 in the U.S.), was released in early April. For its April 8, 1970 edition, *Variety* picked the record as one of its "Top Singles of the Week."

> Timon's "And Now She Says She Is Young" gives the Moody Blues' recently formed Threshold label a strong entry via a smooth vocal and instrumental performances set in a subdued rock groove. Flipside "I'm Just a Travelling Man" is an okay folk flavored slice.

In the May 30 issue of *Disc and Music Echo*, Hayward said of Timon, "He hasn't really found himself yet. After all, he's only 18 now. He's trying to get a group together and find the place he should occupy. But at the same time he is playing music that desperately needs to be heard. Basically, he's just a tramp-like person, wandering from place to place, occasionally playing with Fairfield Parlour and other groups." (JH-DME70a)

Timon was soon back to the life of a "wand'ring minstrel." Living on squatter property in Westgrove, London, Timon made a living playing folk clubs. His first album, *Tymon Dogg*, was released in 1976 by Outlaw No 1, a record label so far underground it doesn't even register on the internet. He would release more albums, for other small or underground record labels, in the 1980s and beyond.

Threshold next released the Moody Blues' single "Question" b/w "Candle of Life" (TH 4) in April 1970. One month later, the label issued the self-titled Trapeze album (THS-2), produced by John Lodge.

Terry Rowley told *Disc and Music Echo*, "Freedom is the whole thing – with Threshold you can do what you like … within reason. John, who produced our single and LP, never brought his influence too much to bear on our music. He let us get on with the writing, and then adapted some of the songs in arrangement." (TR-DME70)

Despite his elation, shortly after the release of the album, Rowley, as well as John Jones, returned to Montanas, leaving Galley, Hughes, and Holland to carry on as a trio.

The Moodies' *A Question of Balance* came out next (THS 3), as well as the European single release of "Melancholy Man" (TH5). In November, *Medusa* (THS 5), a second album from Trapeze, was released, and again produced by John Lodge.

During the first two weeks of December 1970, the Moodies toured America, with Trapeze serving as their warm-up act.

Mike Jahn, covering a performance at New York's Carnegie Hall for *The New York Times* on December 16, 1979, called Trapeze "a loud, Grand Funk Railroad style group," who performed a 30-minute set. After stating that the Moodies gave "a fine concert," Jahn added that, "one could have better appreciated if one's ears were not benumbed by Trapeze."

Covering the same concert, Fred Kirby said in the December 26 issue of *Billboard* that Trapeze was "perhaps too heavy for the hall, especially the overpowering lead guitar."

Away from Threshold, Tony Clarke, Mike Pinder, and Justin Hayward took on a side project – writing and producing and performing on a single for the Four Tops.

Pinder told Mark Murley of *Higher & Higher*, "Tony had been asked to produce the Four Tops by Motown and also to supply material. Tony said immediately, 'I know a bloke who has a couple of songs that would be great for them.'" (MP-H&H04)

The "bloke" was Mike Pinder, and one of the songs Clarke had in mind was "A Simple Game," recorded by the Moody Blues but released only in the U.K. as a B-side in 1968 (to "Ride My See-Saw").

"You Stole My Love," the song chosen for the single's flip side, was not by Pinder, but written by Clarke and, under a pseudonym, Justin Hayward.

Pinder said of the recording session for the two songs, "Actually, Justin and I ended up singing backgrounds on those two songs with the Tops. It was great fun." (MP-H&H94)

The song barely showed up in *Billboard*'s Hot 100 Singles chart in early 1972, at No. 90. It fared better on the trade's Hot Black singles chart, reaching No. 34. But in England, the single flew up the chart to No. 3.

Pinder was especially gratified by one consequence of the song's release. Years later, he told this author, "Awards don't mean much to me, but 'Simple Game' did get the Ivor Novello Award for social comment and it was an honor that the Four Tops recorded the song." (MP-AI17)

In March 1972, Threshold launched a third artist with a single by Sue Vickers, the wife of Manfred Mann's Mike Vickers. "Loving You the Way I Do" b/w "Will You Take Me With You" (TH 8), produced by Michael Aldred made no impact. Nothing further was heard from the singer-songwriter, on Threshold or any other label.

Above: Sue Vickers
(Photo source: indiemusicpeople.com)
Below: Asgard, circa 1972.
(Courtesy Tony Brown)

Threshold almost tried again with a fourth artist, the band Hollywood Freeway. A single was recorded – "I've Been Moved" b/w "Cool Calamares" – again produced by Michael Aldred. The single, however, was cancelled without even promo copies getting out, and the catalogue number, TH 10, was reassigned to the semi-progressive rock group Asgard, for their single "Children of a New Born Age" b/w "Friends (Where Are Your Friends)," issued on April 28,

1972. The group's name, taken from ancient North European mythology, means "castle of the gods." The A-side was produced by Tony Clarke, with Gerry Hoff producing the flip side. An album, *In the Realm of Asgard*, was released later in the year. Both single and album failed to chart, and Asgard never returned.

Trapeze's third Threshold album, *You Are the Music … We're Just the Band* (THS 8), produced by Neil Slaven, was issued in late 1972.

With Gerry Hoff still managing the company, Threshold tried to launch a few more careers in 1972, including Sally Pickard, who recorded some tracks which were never released, singer/songwriter Nicky James, and the six-piece American rock band Providence.

Providence, blending rock combo instruments with violin, cello, and viola (played by Jim Cockey, and brothers Tim and Tom Tompkins, respectively), would also record and tour with Justin Hayward and John Lodge during their 1975 *Blue Jays* period. An album, *Ever Sense the Dawn* (THS 9) and single, "Fantasy Fugue" b/w "Island of Light" (TH 14), all produced by Tony Clarke, went nowhere.

SALLY PICKARD

Above: Threshold artists Sally Pickard never had any of her recordings released by the label. (Courtesy Tony Brown) **Below: Jacket to first of two Nicky James albums issued by Threshold.**

Nicky James had known the Moodies in the early 1960s in Birmingham, and often performed with Denny Laine and the Diplomats. Threshold tried him out with a single, "Why" b/w "Foreign Shore" (TH 12, December 1, 1972), which was produced by Gerry Hoff. An album was released at the end of the year, *Every Home Should Have One* (THS 10), also produced by Hoff. Neither clicked.

Over the years, the Moodies reflected on their attempts to launch other artists through Threshold.

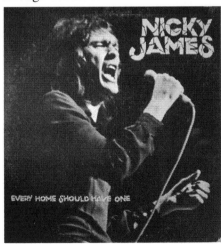

John Lodge said, "[I]nitially we fell into the trap that other record companies have, and still are falling into – if you give an artist money 'up-front,' you're really giving him the illusion that he's made it before he's had a chance." (JL-DME73)

Ray Thomas said, "We just let Timon go, and it was the same old scene. He wrote a load of songs, and we were impressed by them, but we just got into a lot of [business] complications there.

"I thought Sally Pickard was a gas. I'd still like to see those songs released. Trapeze are

371

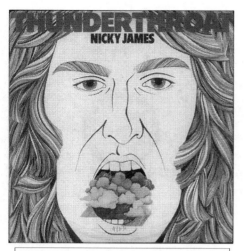

playing in the States. I think they're a great band. But I think the organization around them is poor, and I've told them so....

"We've financed Trapeze on about four separate occasions. But the only bread-winners in Threshold are the Moodies.

"There are too many little agents and promotion men around all groups. They've their own little this, and their own little that. I want to speak to the people – to the artists. I don't want to speak to a bloke in a charcoal grey mohair suit....

"All the people want is bread. They rave around, saying, 'Peace' and 'out-of-sight,' and all this, and it's all a load of baloney. When it comes down to it, they're on a bread trip.... We even had discussions with the Stones. And all they were talking about was bread. They weren't talking about ideals or anything.

"We tried to step out of that and get the scene together, so that people could be artistic and creative. But people have done nothing at all but say, 'If you want to sign us, it's going to cost you five grand.' At first we started to do that, but ... I've lost more money on Threshold than I've made. Without a doubt, Threshold is costing us a fortune to try and achieve the aims we set out to achieve. It'd be far cheaper for us to close the office down." (RT-DAME71)

A second single from Nicky James, "Black Dream" b/w "She Came to Me" (TH16), again with Hoff producing, was issued in March 1973. A third, "I Guess I've Always Loved You" b/w "My Style," with Hoff still at the controls, came out in July of that year. As with everything Threshold put out other than Moody Blues records, they went nowhere.

A fourth Trapeze album, *Final Swing*, was released in 1974, but this was a compilation LP featuring cuts from the first three albums plus two new tracks produced by Threshold's Gerry Hoff. Glenn Hughes left the band after this, and a reformed unit continued on with two unsuccessful albums for Warner Brothers in the late 1970s.

A second album from Nicky James, *Thunderthroat* (THS 19) and final single, "I Guess I've Always Loved You" b/w "My Style" (TH25), with A-side produced by Hoff and B-side by John Lodge, were issued in 1976. At this time, James was also writing songs with Ray Thomas for the latter's two solo albums, released in 1975 and '76. Despite both talent and a good effort on the part of Threshold, James never found consequential success.

Meanwhile, the Moody Blues popularity continued to increase.

17

Every Good Boy Deserves Favour (1971)

Album release:
Threshold THS-5; July 23, 1971
U.K. peak position: #1
U.S.: #2
(Certified gold in the U.S.)
Canada: #2
(Certified platinum in Canada)
Australia: #5
Norway: #5
Netherlands: #6

U.S. single release: *"The Story in Your Eyes" b/w "Melancholy Man"*
Threshold/London THS 67006; July 23, 1971
U.S. peak position: #14 (*Cashbox*)
Canada: #7

European single release: *"The Story in Your Eyes" b/w "My Song"*
Various dates, including August 27, 1971
Netherlands/Holland (6106 601): #11
Belgium (3.0064): #22

Towards the end of 1970, the Moodies had completed a fall tour of the United States. The trip had ended badly, with Ray Thomas falling through a hole in the stage in Philadelphia, and Mike Pinder having a cyst removed from his larynx in Los Angeles. Following these difficulties, the Moodies regrouped in November 1970 to begin work on their next album – the sixth by the classic lineup. Tony Clarke was again producing, with Derek Varnals as engineer. New to the team was assistant recording engineer Dave Baker, taking over for Adrian Martins.

Baker told *Higher & Higher*, "I had gone to the last big Isle of Wight Festival to see Jimi Hendrix, who was performing on a Sunday night. The Moodies were playing on a Saturday night [sic; Sunday]. I became a fan of theirs, more or less, that moment." (DB-H&H96)

A short while later, Baker was hired by Decca to work as a "tape-op" (tape operator). After an apprentice period of a few months, working sessions by artists such as ballad singer Donald Peers and the more energetic Tom Jones, Baker – a fan of rock music – finally was assigned to a band he took a personal interest in. The call came from Derek Varnals, inviting Baker to work the board for the Moodies' sixth album, which Baker recalled being described to him as a "new direction" album.

Dave Baker: "I was pleased that Derek had asked me to do the sessions, because I knew I had a lot to live up to with Adrian Martins.… I was in awe of the situation to start with. Being about five years younger than Derek, these guys had already been at it for five albums and it was a really successful team; so I was conscious of the fact that I had to do well to make any grade that needed to be made." (DB-H&H96)

At this time, Tony Clarke told Nick Logan of *Hit Parader*, "Usually we arrive at the studio, sit around a coffee table armed with acoustic guitars, and everybody is most reluctant to start. While we are in there, there is no Threshold business… or phone calls. We do a lot of talking first, everything from the state of the world to the price of fish, and then we will goad somebody into being the first victim. One of them will say, 'I have this verse and first chorus but no middle eight,' and then we're away." (TC-HP71)

Also from this period, Justin Hayward told Nancy Erlich of *Hit Parader*, "When we do an album, we're spending a lot of time together, the five of us – the six of us, with Tony Clarke, our recording manager. He's the sixth Moody Blue, really; he just doesn't come on the road, doesn't appear on stage. But we talk a lot and we've found we're often thinking about the same things at the same time, because we are so close as a band. It just works out that way; it just falls together that way. Usually it isn't until afterwards that we say, 'There is a pattern after all,' and Tony juggles them around and puts them together, and all the pieces fit in a jigsaw." (JH-HP71)

This new album was recorded in a series of sessions, interrupted by more concert commitments. In fact, in December, 1970, just weeks after beginning work on the project, the band was back in America for more concerts. In January, 1971, additional recording sessions were scheduled, this time at Wessex studios in London.

As he had begun to do on *A Question of Balance*, Mike Pinder was transitioning from the clumsy Mellotron to the easier to program and play Moog synthesizer, featured on many of the tracks in both that album and this. But the Mellotron was still very much in use.

Dave Baker: "I think we spent the first week of the recording session recording Mellotron tapes. I thought: 'These guys are recording their own instruments even before we start making the record!'" (DB-H&H96)

Moving through the album, in chronological order:

"Procession," the only track on a Moody Blues album to share writing credit among all five members of the classic lineup, was designed to describe the evolution of music, with sounds and a chant of three words: "desolation," "creation," and "communication," then the introduction of various musical instruments and styles.

Graeme Edge told interviewer Mark Powell, "We had nerve in those days! We decided that we could create a piece that would show the history of musical evolution. We began by making grunting sounds and hitting hollow logs. This evolved into both Eastern music and, eventually, Western music." (GE-EGBDFCD08)

The track opens with a scenario like the "Dawn of Man" sequence which began the 1968 film *2001: A Space Odyssey*. Mike Pinder, either on Mellotron or Moog, conveys the idea of a spaceship descending to Earth, kicking up winds, and then bringing forth a storm. Primitive man reacts, and huddles together, grunting in fear. Then the vocalizations take on the form of a chant. As mankind develops, the chanting voices begin to harmonize, and the beating of the log transitions into a rhythm, which then emulates drums accompanying a march. Thus the origin of music, which evolves from primitive instruments to ones more advanced and intricate. Snippets transition from Eastern sitar and flute to the English Elizabethan era, represented by the harpsichord. A pipe organ segues to orchestral music. Last, the electric guitar of the rock era takes us up to the sound of Moody Blues, circa 1971, and the start of the following song, "The Story in Your Eyes."

While the album was recorded, Graeme Edge and Mike Pinder were interviewed by David Erlich of *Circus* magazine. Edge said, "We believe in art, and music is basically the only art form that lots of people can make their living at and devote themselves to; it is essentially the human thing, because there is nothing else that human beings have that animals haven't got. We're trying to find what it is about music, that it is in some strange kind of way the expression of the essence of humanity. Art." (GE-C71)

(Of course, music isn't the only "art" which distinguishes mankind from animal. In addition, what about cooking, or the alphabet?)

Amplifying Edge's point, Pinder told Erlich, "Music is an obvious, fantastic power source. It's something that you don't understand; it's a mystery, and seems to have a level of communication that is much subtler than anything we've got. The big high on art was in the 17th, 18th, 19th centuries.… Although the expression in painting is quite fantastic, they can't quite get it across to so many, because they've basically got only one painting to start with… it's difficult to make that speak with a loud voice to a lot of people. And we've got to the stage [in music] where we've got all this technology with 8, 12, 16, 24 track machines. And can you imagine Stravinsky or Wagner or Bach, or any of those guys, in a 24 track studio?" (MP-C71)

It turned out that "Procession" was the final track recorded for the album. By that time, the album's theme and title were known. So, Pinder added one final element to the track. The title – *Every Good Boy Deserves Favour* – was taken from the student mnemonic for the lines of the treble clef: E-G-B-D-F. This procession of notes is played by Mike Pinder on piano in "Procession." And, you'll see, this mnemonic makes a space-saving abbreviation for the album's name.

"The Story in Your Eyes," a melodic rocker by Justin Hayward, manages to combine urgency, angst, lyrical imagery, and a poignant theme, in only three minutes.

At first listen, perhaps hearing the song on a car radio, one might think this is a direct man-to-woman song. But it's something more than merely that. When examined and interpreted, the song seems to be more about the state of the Moody Blues … and, beyond that, a relationship between man and God.

Hayward's religious upbringing, and fondness for church hymns when he was a boy, makes a religious interpretation valid, even probable. One thing is certain: This song, like many from the Moodies, is at least partly autobiographical.

Consider the opening lines: "I've been thinking about our fortune, and I've decided that we're really not to blame, for the love that is deep inside of us is still the same."

Mike Pinder later revealed that Hayward was speaking directly about the "fortunes" of the Moodies. Along with hard work, a good bit of happenstance or luck had been part of their success. Meanwhile, this prosperity had severed them in many ways from their much less glamorous origins, for better or worse. And now many in that outside world were attacking them, calling them "pretentious." These critics believed the Moody Blues were hypocrites. They sang of spiritual quests, yet were rich enough to indulge any whim or heart's desire. Some resentful folk felt that the group's musical indulgences were an expression of too much money, too much license, and a sort of musical snobbery.

In "Story," Hayward responds to these feelings of resentment, saying that they – the Moody Blues – were really not to blame for their level of success; that their music was sincere; their lyrics honest; their quest for spiritual enlightenment true; and the love that was deep inside of them was still the same.

The song continues with: "And the sound we make together is the music to the story in your eyes. It's been shining down upon me now, I realize." Whose eyes does the singer refer to? The audience, perhaps? Or do those eyes belong to someone or something on a higher plane, able to "look down upon" him?

Perhaps referring to the history of mankind, he sings: "Listen to the tide slowly turning, wash all our heartaches away. We're part of the fire that is burning, and from the ashes we can build another day." Even more telling are the lines, "But I'm frightened for your children, and the life that we are living is in vain, and the sunshine we've been waiting for will turn to rain." The reference to "*your* children" could certainly apply to mankind – all children of God – and reference to "the sunshine we've been waiting for" might represent the second coming of Christ, or merely the answer the band members had been seeking since they wrote – and experienced – the songs that made up *In Search of the Lost Chord*.

Lastly, Hayward sings, "When the final line is over and it's certain that the curtain's going to fall, I can hide inside your sweet, sweet love for evermore."

He could be referring to the group's lineup, as well as the final line of the song. The falling curtain could represent the end of a concert, a career, or life itself. We can only hope that an earlier line, "And the life we've been living is in vain," doesn't come true.

And the final passage – when the singer hopes to hide in someone's "sweet, sweet love forevermore" – could be a romantic exaggeration, but it might also stand for eternity – in a place called Heaven.

Regarding the recording of the song, and, in fact, the entire album, Hayward said, "[W]e deserted Decca [recording studio] at that point, which to this day I can't recall exactly why – probably a few of us were a bit too stoned or whatever, and decided the grass was greener [elsewhere]. There were some decisions going on – for example, when we did 'The Story in Your Eyes,' we ended up recording it in Mike's garage! God only knows what possessed us to end up there instead of a nice comfy studio with Derek Varnals! In hindsight, it was probably the beginning of the end of that sort of era – I mean, I quite like the album, I think there's some good stuff on there, but we'd maybe gone about as far as we could in that particular style before something had to give." (JH-RS13)

"Our Guessing Game," by Ray Thomas, could have been inspired by his divorce. The melancholy mood certainly supports this. But the lyrics also imply that this is another song hinting at a man's faith, and his nature to question his own place in the greater scheme of things. Thomas sings, "There are times when I think I've found the truth / There are times when I know that I'm wrong / And the day when I try to hide my fears / Bless the day when I'm feeling strong. Wonder why we try so hard / Wonder why we try at all / You wonder why the world is turning around / When in the end it won't matter at all…. And with tomorrow / What will they make of me / It leaves me so much to explain / That's the start of our guessing game."

The verses are lovely, but a blemish on the track is the cluttered chorus, in which too many voices, too many instruments, and a rushed tempo detract from the quality of the composition.

There would be some criticism leveled against this album over certain aspects of its production, with statements from reviewers which echoed a line in Thomas's lyric: "Wonder why we try so hard?"

"Emily's Song" was written and sung by John Lodge to his infant daughter, Emily. Lodge sings: "Lovely to know the warmth your smile can bring to me / I want to tell you but the words you do not know … Rivers of endless tides have passed beneath my feet / And all soon they had me standing on my own / Then when my eyes were closed you opened them for me / And now we journey through our lives to what we will be…. And in the morning of my life / And in the evening of my day / I will try to understand in what you say…"

The production tries to convey the feeling of a new life, and the simplicity and love of a child. The arrangement may seem too "sweet" for some, but its sentimentality is intentional.

"After You Came" was credited solely to Graeme Edge. The other Moodies helped with the melody and arrangement.

Graeme Edge: "I'd say that when one of us writes a song, he really writes only 50 percent of what ends up on the album. The other 50 percent comes in contributions from the other members – except for Justin. He writes about 75 percent of what comes out." (GE-T73)

Mike Pinder: "If Ray or Graeme needed help finishing a song, we were always there. One of my functions at that time in the band was to move among the others and provide the orchestration that might make a song work better…. 'After You Came' was one song that started out as a poem by Graeme, with no melody. Graeme would be the first to tell you that he has no singing voice, and the rest of us just grabbed it – the chords and the tempo." (MP-GM94)

The song is a chronicle of a lost love. According to the singer, "For some short time / For a while you and I were joined to eternity / Then we split in two, back to me and you / Like the rain rising from the sea…. We all can see what we shall be / But knowing's really not controlling. With time perhaps I will pass the traps / and find some peace / and understanding. After you'd come and while you're gone / You leave me guessing – It's depressing / Never to know the way to go / to find some time…. So you just have to laugh / When it hurts so much / You're so far away and so hard to touch. I have reached the top of my wall / And all I've found is another way to fall."

"Our Guessing Game" is a well-presented song, though of course its subject is sad, even depressing. Perhaps this is why the Moodies treated it with an upbeat melody and arrangement. This makes for a curious combination, not entirely unsuccessful.

"One More Time to Live," John Lodge's second offering, is an epic production, and one of the album's stronger tracks. The words chanted in "Procession," such as "desolation," "creation," and "communication," return here, helping maintain the album's thematic framework. In fact, the idea began here, with this song written and recorded before "Procession."

Lodge sings: "One more time to live / and I have made it mine / Leave the wise to write / for they write wordly rhymes / And he who wants to fight / Begins the end of time…"

"Nice to Be Here" is Ray Thomas's second song on the album, and a bit of a trip through the looking glass – with Thomas, like Alice, entering into a wonderland of surreal lights, sounds, and concepts. "All the leaves start swaying / To the breeze that's playing / On a thousand violins / And the bees are humming / to a frog sat strumming / on a guitar with only one string … I can see them / they can't see me / I feel out of sight / Much to my delight. And it seems worth noting / Water rats were boating / As a lark began to sing / The sounds kept coming / With Jack Rabbit loudly drumming / On the side of a biscuit tin."

Thomas said, "That song was great fun to record. Particularly trying to get Justin to play a guitar solo using only one string, like the frog in the lyric. He actually managed to get it down to *two* strings!" (RT-EGBDFCD)

The playful song is the album's only instance of levity, yet an important addition to the collective work.

"You Can Never Go Home," one of the album's stronger tracks, is by Justin Hayward. With a beautiful melody, and a cry in his voice, Hayward laments: "I don't know what I'm searching for / I never have opened that door / Tomorrow may find me at last / Turning my back on the past / But time will tell / of stars that fell / a million years ago. Memories can never take you back / Home, sweet home / You can never go home anymore."

Kudos to Mike Pinder for the descending piano chords that begin the song, nicely setting the mood, and the Mellotron string arrangement, as effective here as on other melancholy Hayward compositions such as "Nights in White Satin" and "Watching and Waiting."

378

The song has an intricate design, comprised of six parts in its structure instead of the standard three in pop songs (verse, chorus, and middle eight).

Also noteworthy is Hayward's lead guitar work during the second of the two chorus sections, reminiscent of the style used in "Lovely to See You," then, during the middle eight, a shift, with the same Gibson 335 guitar, to a mood foreshadowing much of what was heard on 1975's *Blue Jays*.

"My Song" is Mike Pinder's only composition on the album (other than his contribution to the opening cut, "Procession"), and the track that is the most "cosmic." Pinder sings: "How can I tell you all the things inside my head / The change in these past years / Has made me see our world / In many different ways…"

Pinder's Mellotron gets a workout on this number, to excellent results. The middle section of the song, as was the case with "The Voyage" between "Have You Heard" parts 1 and 2, from *On the Threshold of a Dream*, showcases Pinder's talent on the instrument. He reimagines some of the sounds heard in *2001: A Space Odyssey* – conveying the "sound" of space, and the breathing of an astronaut, amplified within his space helmet. Ray Thomas also shines during this interlude, with a haunting flute melody, complemented by Pinder's Mellotron.

Talking to Tony Stewart of *New Musical Express* at the time, Thomas said of Pinder's work on the Mellotron, "Mike is the best at it. And that's not just another Moody shooting the shit. He's the best at it; you can ask Mellotronics. They've stripped his machine down every time he's made a modification, and had a look at it. It's not a Mellotron anymore, and it hasn't been for the last three years. It's a 'Pindertron' – that's what we call it." (RT-NME72)

As for the sound of breathing, Tony Clarke disclosed, "I got Mike to wear a cardboard box over his head, which had me in stitches. And it worked beautifully. The Neumann microphone was inside the cardboard box as well. It was a 3M Scotch brand recording tape box and it actually worked. It gave us the sound of being inside a claustrophobic space helmet. But it had me crying with laughter at the time." (TC-H&H95)

The only flaw in this track is Pinder's vocal, which sounds more like a "scratch track" (a temporary vocal intended to be replaced later after all the instruments had been recorded). A more polished vocal from Pinder, like those heard on "Out and In" and "Have You Heard," would have greatly benefited this intricate and lush track.

During the mixing and sequencing of the songs for the album, Tony Clarke talked to Nick Logan of *Hit Parader*. Describing the amount of separate recordings used to construct the final album, Clarke held his hand high, likely over his head, saying, "It's a pile of tape that high. The boys go away at that stage; they are never there to mix. Although they have some idea, they never know what the final running order will be. They hand it over and say, more or less, 'Do your worst.'" (TC-HP71)

This time it seemed that Clarke did. He excused "the boys" too early, before they had recorded enough standout tracks to create an album that could stand as tall as their previous works. While there are certainly no bad songs on *EGBDF*, the percentage of great ones may have tapered off.

Did the Moodies know that they weren't rising to the level set by their previous albums? At the time of the making of *EGBDF*, Graeme Edge told popular music correspondent Jared Johnson, "It's getting to be a bit difficult after six albums … to keep fresh…."

Johnson said, "I can see where a group like the Who was really faced with a problem after *Tommy*, but I see you faced with that same problem after *every* album."

Edge candidly admitted, "It seems to be that way, yes." (GE-TMN71)

Hayward said, "[W]e were trying to come to terms with the fact that our music wasn't underground anymore, with a small audience; we were having to [present] ourselves to stadiums in America. We were changing as people, and that's very much reflected in *Every Good Boy*. It's almost apologetic, I find." (JH-TRC96)

In another interview, conducted at the time the Moodies were recording *Good Boy*, Hayward told Nancy Erlich of *Hit Parader*, "We can never really honestly hear our own music. We can never hear it like you hear it, because we know every single note and every moment in the recording session, and remember it all. One day I'd like to be hypnotized and be somebody else and just listen to it, just to see what it sounds like. A time period of maybe two or three years has to go by before you can really forget the circumstances surrounding the recording of the album – the making of it and the writing – and you can begin to step outside it. It takes that long. It really does." (JH-HP71)

Life was speeding by quickly for the Moodies. They had enjoyed a steady four-year rise in popularity, the making of six albums, and the formation of their own record label. There had been seemingly non-stop touring and TV and radio appearances. When had there been time to assess their lives, let alone their latest album?

At this time, Hayward, trying to make sense of his life, the world around him, and the message of his own music, told *Hit Parader*, "There is no final judgment; for me certainly not yet. I'm not prepared to say, 'This is the way and the light,' and that kind of thing, because I can only relate what I'm feeling at that particular time. I believe we really have a long way to go into finding a real faith and happiness. I knew someone, though, someone very close to me, who had a very strong faith. He's gone now. It just gave me faith as well. I don't know what in, but he just had such tremendous faith, it did him such a lot of favors. You know, there's a time for us to catch up on that kind of thing in years to come. The kind of life we are leading just at the moment, on the road, in the studios, doing gigs, in airplanes, that kind of thing… there will come a time pretty soon when we will be able to sit and reflect." (JH-HP71)

Many years in the future, Hayward did indeed reflect on this album and the state of affairs surrounding its making. He said, "I think that *Every Good Boy Deserves Favour* is a kind of searching, seeking record. It was made at a time of tremendous success for us, and that brought on all of the feelings of guilt, inadequacy, and self-doubt that accompany that kind of success. It's a bittersweet record that pointed the direction of the next album, which was a full stop." (JH-EGBDFCD08)

Shortly after the album release, Mike Pinder told *Sounds*, "*Every Good Boy Deserves Favour*, we just about got through that by the skin of our teeth. Probably by listening to it you can detect circles within circles within the band. To a certain extent complacency crept in, the greenery of Cobham has seeped into our lives somewhat. I've always been frightened of that, and I've been rebelling against even living here for the past year.

"I think what's really happening is that the music's caught up with us. In other words, all our ideas and things expressed in our albums were true; I mean, we really felt these things… we've always tried to put a lot of hope in our music…. But what I think happened was that the music caught up with us because it got to the stage where all the money and stuff started rolling in, and we started the record company, and even that's been questioned of late – whether we should even bother with that, because just the mere fact of having a company, it makes a part of you another person. So, consequently, I think the time has come, especially now, for us to make a stand in the same respect as [for] our music, and start living what our music says." (MP-S71)

Looking back at the sessions, from the safe distance of the 1990s, Hayward said, "I think *Every Good Boy* was a start of us trying to struggle to find good songs and [new] ways to recording, and already there was some uncomfortable feelings beginning to create [tension] then, which manifested [in] *Seventh Sojourn*…. So I just remember it as a struggle." (JH-HL99)

These words from the Moodies show in a variety of ways that *EGBDF* was a difficult album to make, and may not have represented them at their best. In spite of these feelings, and despite some of the hostile reviews on the following pages, it is only fair to point out that some Moody Blues fans love this album and even rate it as among their favorites. In hearing from these fans, it is interesting to find that nearly all were introduced to the group with *EGBDF*. When "Procession" started playing for the first time on their record or CD players, they did not have the high expectations of others who had already experienced the opening of, say, *In Search of the Lost Chord*, *On the Threshold of a Dream*, and *To Our Children's Children's Children*. But they listened with an open mind, perhaps with no expectations at all. And they liked all of what they heard. You can find their comments on Moody Blues chat rooms online. Read a few, then ask, is it possible that there is really nothing wrong with *EGBDF*? Can it be that those of us who don't rate it as favorably simply listened with unrealistic expectations? After all, how could the Moodies (or anybody) continue to outperform themselves with each new album?

***

Also recorded at the time of the album was **"The Dreamer,"** a collaboration between Hayward and Thomas. The song didn't make the cut for the album, even though it would have easily fit in with the other songs. Thomas sings: "I am the Dreamer / With such a life to tell / I got no answers / But a lot of dreams to sell."

The simple uptempo track – *simple* melody, *simple* lyric, *simple* production – is appealing for this very reason – its simplicity – and might have made a nice addition to the album. It could have served as an intermission of a sort between the album's big production numbers on Side 1 and 2, and, if placed at the halfway mark, would have continued the pace of "After You Came," before returning to the slower songs that dominated the album. Side One is roughly 19 minutes long; Side Two is a little more than 20 minutes, so there was certainly room for the song's four minutes at the end of the first side.

Thanks to the 2007 remastered CD with bonus tracks, you can try sequencing the CD to add in "The Dreamer" as the sixth song to be played. You may also find that allowing the CD to continue playing after "My Song," into the other bonus track, an alternate version of "The Story in Your Eyes," with a more prominent vocal from Hayward, an extended ending, and the unexpected snippet of studio banter and laughing, will add further to your enjoyment. With 11 tracks instead of nine, and with "The Story in Your Eyes" nearly serving as bookends, and, because of the slightly rough edges of that alternate version, you will experience the Moodies letting their hair down a little. Experience *EGBDF* in this way, then perhaps you will agree that the album rises to the level of some of those which preceded it.

***

After Tony Clarke sequenced the album, Phil Travers was brought in to create the sleeve art. This one is especially alluring – in both concept and execution – and can be interpreted in numerous ways. We'd like to suggest one:

The front cover depicts an old man – soothsayer, mystic, prophet? – enchanting, even seducing, a young, impressionable boy, with a glowing jewel on a (swinging?) chain. Turn over the album jacket and see the rest of the story – with two other youths, their faces blank, very nearly featureless, as if their personalities have been wiped away. One holds a rose, symbolizing the heart; the other holds out a teddy bear, a symbol of the innocence of youth – two things at risk if the boy doesn't look away from the hypnotic charm on the chain, breaking the spell.

We could also suggest the opposite: Maybe the two figures on the left are proffering false sentimentality (the rose) and a retreat to the false security of uninformed childhood (teddy bear). That could be why they have no faces, because they represent falsehoods. By contrast, the wonderful, wise old man is offering the only good thing, the light of knowledge and wisdom.

Either way, someone is trying to manipulate the boy and lure him into false beliefs.

Consider Mike Pinder's line of thinking for an interview given shortly before the release of the album. He told Penny Valentine, of *Disc and Music Echo*: "I've been on a search for a few years now and I've been into every occult subject, without ever joining a club or anything, which I believe [to join would be] wrong. But I've been into all the occult subjects you could name and at some stages I really thought I had found the truth. And, suddenly, until very recently, I found I was nowhere at all. I'd only actually been a part of the confusion. ...

"And the whole essence of doing this interview is that I think that what we're really all trying to communicate is the sum total of our experiences, which we can all learn from. And what I have learnt over a period of years has been that it's no use wasting our time on occult subjects and magic of one kind or another, because that is all part of the confusion which is being put on this planet by man, as it says in the Bible. And I've been 'into' all these people that came along and said, 'This is the way to God; sit here for half an hour looking at your navel ... all of those who are actually leading millions and millions of people astray – because while people are heavily into that they're not being open to the simple truth, which is the word of God. All that other stuff is just a spiritual ego trip, and I'll own up to myself about that." (MP-MM72)

The cover for *EGBDF*, another beautiful work of art by Travers, seems to illustrate these concepts … and messages.

The inner gatefold depicts music, as a conductor – Tony Clarke, perhaps – giving direction, and musicians playing, and the dancers spinning, caught up in the swirl of sound. Among the faces drawn into the painting are those of the five Moody Blues.

***

As to why the Moodies had let nearly a year lapse between the release of *A Question of Balance* and *Every Good Boy Deserves Favour*, in an era when pop artists usually released two albums a year, Graeme Edge told "Pete" of *Jackie* magazine, "We're very careful not to saturate people with our music. That's why we wait before releasing another one. People save up to buy albums, and it's a mistake to release a new album before fans have been able to save up and buy your last one." (GE-J71)

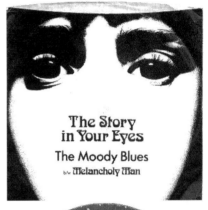

The Moodies were becoming astute businessmen, and all without the benefit of a personal manager. Other groups were taking notice and, starting at about this time, the norm would be to release a new album annually instead of bi-annually. By the 1980s, most recording artists would take an average of two years between releases.

Album release:
Threshold THS 5, July 23, 1971

U.S. single release: *"The Story in Your Eyes"* b/w
"Melancholy Man"
Threshold THS 67006; July 23, 1971

The Top 5 albums to beat the week *EGBDF* was released in the U.K. were, from No. 1 to 5, respectively: *Bridge Over Troubled Water*, by Simon & Garfunkel; *Sticky Fingers*, from the Rolling Stones; *Blue*, by Joni Mitchell; *Ram*, which was Paul McCartney's second solo outing; and *Every Picture Tells a Story*, by Rod Stewart.

For the A-side of the single, "The Story in Your Eyes" was the obvious choice. With no other track on the album having the "feel" of a radio hit, London Records opted to utilize "Melancholy Man"

383

from the previous album as the flip side. The song had scored well in Europe when issued there as a single earlier in the year, and had picked up a great deal of airplay on FM radio in the States. By issuing it on a 45, free of the cross fading technique used on the album, AM radio stations could now access the song with ease. As a standalone track, it would also be more accessible to FM, creating the possibility of additional play on those stations. The prime competitors in the U.S. single charts at this time were Carole King's *Tapestry*, at No. 1, followed by Paul McCartney's *Ram*; James Taylor's *Mud Slide Slim*; *Jesus Christ Superstar*, featuring a variety of artists; and the Carpenters' self-titled second album.

The press received the album about a week before it was available for sale.

Rolling Stone in the U.S. had never been warm toward the Moody Blues, but, with the band's popularity soaring, the music magazine was changing its tune. From the June 19, 1971 issue, Stu Werbin said that "Each album has been a worthy product. The latest offering is no exception." He continued:

> We cannot point to outside influences on this album for all the stylistic inspirations seem to come from the individual composer and his relationship to other members of the group. Neither is any dynamic new direction taken with this album. Just more good Moody's music, played perhaps a bit mellower.
>
> Lead guitarist Justin Hayward had traditionally been responsible for providing the strongest love ballads on previous albums. ... His "You Can Never Go Home" is the prettiest song on Side Two, but is outclassed by bassist John Lodge's "Emily's Song" on Side One. ... [Lodge] rises as more of a force on this album. "Emily" contains not only the most classically beautiful melody on the album but also the most pleasant lyric: "Sing me a lullaby / And I will listen, for there's beauty where there's love."
>
> Lodge's second contribution, "One More Time to Live," is the most powerful and most intricate number on the album, and it is from it that the "Desolation ... Creation ... Communication" theme from the opening "Procession" is drawn.
>
> Hayward's second song, "The Story in Your Eyes," is closer to the bouncy move-along-and-through-to-the-next kind of thing that Lodge did on the other albums.
>
> Flautist Ray Thomas also has two offerings: "Our Guessing Game" is his strongest composition since "Legend of a Mind." It moves swiftly through a lyric in which he tries to appraise his own mind and its continuous flights of fantasy. ...
>
> Percussionist Graeme Edge gives us the closest thing to a rock song on the album with "After You Came," which closes the first side. The Moodys are not known for their rocking, but this is a pretty good attempt.

I feel Mike Pinder should have stayed in the studio a little while longer with "My Song." It's a fine vehicle for his modified Mellotron, but he has performed it better live.

In short, if you're still listening to your old Moody Blues albums, there's not a reason in the world that you won't like this one. They're still the Sistine Chapel of popular music.

From July 24, 1971 issue of England's *Disc and Music Echo*:

Moody Blues' *Every Good Boy Deserves Favour* (Threshold THS 5, £2.19) will be hailed by their fans as great, while their critics will immediately dive into dictionaries for a new word meaning "pretentious." There are nine tracks, mainly running into each other, and it's quite heavy going listening to at volume. Opening track is "Procession" which seems to be a time travelogue. Something lands from outer space on a desolated planet (presumably this one), then the rains come, bringing the jungle before some Neolithic chants. Then it goes all Asian. Pictures in sound! What you can't do with a Mellotron and recording studio? …

"One More Time to Live" starts Side Two and reverts to the history of mankind idea hinted at in "Procession." This contains lengthy chanting of relevant words like "Desolation, Creation, Evolution, Pollution," in fact all the "tions" you can think of! It merely becomes a list of words, and you are very tempted to add "alliteration" and "constipation." …

On this LP some of the melodies are good, the production is superb, the arrangements are all incredibly over-dramatic, and their lyrics are generally trite and naïve. But we can't all be Dylan Thomas or Bob Dylan, so if the Moodies write with sincerity, which they probably do, they can't be pretentious. Can they?

Also on July 24, Andrew Means of the U.K.'s *Melody Maker* gave his verdict:

… Perhaps it is inevitable that arid slopes should border the fertile plain, that crests should be matched by hollows.

A question of balance. It is obvious on this new album that the Moody Blues have not been motivated by the same degree of imagination that has peppered their creative past. There are lines that strike home and the LP has its attractions, but albums are not made by lines, they are made by songs, and it is solid compositions with a validity of their own and in the general context that are lacking. …

One infers from the title (the treble lines on musical score sheets are *EGBDF*) that any theme will be fragmentary. But before this is confirmed by the lyrics there is an intense, partly electronic introduction, "Procession," which virtually demands more emotional response than the rest of the record.

To some extent, *Every Good Boy Deserves Favour* is a parody of previous albums. It sounds as if the Moodies are following their own formula for success, with a consequent degree of predictability that is not the necessary result of group style. Idiosyncrasies are carried to excess. ...

The songs that have most to offer are Mike Pinder's "My Song" and Graeme Edge's "After You Came," for both indicates a mood of development and changes that are reticent elsewhere. As "My Song" fades and the needle lifts off, there is lingering disappointment and a conviction that the Moody Blues can do better than this, if they really are going to deserve favour.

Not all were critical of the album. Only about half. Representing the 50% that liked it was the critic for *New Musical Express*. From July 1971:

The album begins with "Procession," which all the group wrote. There are *Star Trek* sounds at the start, then the bass moog, shouted voices *a la* Arthur Brown ("Fire"), the sound of rain falling, jungle noises, [American bass singer] Paul Robeson chants, black magic atmospherics, a sitar, Eastern music, a flute, harpsichord, the sound of a symphony orchestra, and a rock passage. ...

Ray's "Our Guessing Game" is the sort of thing you expect to hear on a juke box in Italy while you're laying on the back with your lady. Except that it's a million times better in terms of musicianship and production. It's romantic, though not really in the love sense, beautiful and simple and, at the same time, occasionally involved.

Regarding "Emily's Song," the *NME* critic found it to be a "song that is peaceful and lovely," in which "Childlike passages of utter simplicity are strung together by a father's understanding.... Among my favorite tracks."

Concerning Thomas's "Nice to Be Here," the critic described it as a "nice open-air song" with a "feel of a sunny day in the country away from the fume-emitting lorries, ringing phones, and bus queries – very suited to the occasion, in fact. Lyrically and musically it's the type of adult's song that children will love."

As for Hayward's "You Can Never Go Home," it was "gloom-laden," but "with rays of hope in the lyrics as the tale progresses. A very good number about someone's search for something, they know not what, and definitely my favorite track."

Over at London, England's *Record Mirror*, the word was also encouraging:

If this really is the last huge Moodies album – incorporating that very total cosmic sound they've become almost infamous for in the past five years – then it's a good one to go out on. Although

Every Good Boy Deserves Favour holds fast to Clarke's production of great sweeping magnitude – the sudden swelling of tracks to take off pitch, the flourishing awe inspiring moments where tracks sound like the opening for a religious epic – it also innovates a much more melodic feel.

I think a lot of this has to do with the fact that each song is a very personal statement from each member of the band and stands alone. The progression from past albums like *Children's Children* and *Threshold* is an obvious one and should stand them in good stead for moving away from such huge back-up pieces in the future. ...

The overall feel of this album stays cathedral like and vast, needing a long time of living with it to judge it absolutely as an overall work, but on the first few plays there are tracks that jump out with some nice direct lyrical simplicity and some very strong melodies – particularly "Emily's Song," "You Can Never Go Home," and Ray's quirky little nursery-rhyme, "Nice to Be Here."

On July 28, *Variety* magazine in the U.S. placed "The Story in Your Eyes" at the top of its "Top Singles of the Week" picks, calling it "another fine driving rocker from this vet British combo."

Billboard said:

The Moody Blues' long awaited single is a typically fine and complex musical theme with a contemporary love lyric culled from their soon to be released LP; it should at least match the Hot 100 success of last year's hit, "Question."

The songs to beat at this time in the American charts were, from No. 1 to 5, respectively: James Taylor with the Carole King-written "You've Got a Friend"; the Raiders (with Mark Lindsey), singing "Indian Reservation"; Carole King with the double A-side, "It's Too Late" and "I Feel the Earth Move"; Jean Knight with "Mr. Big Stuff"; and Tommy James with "Draggin' the Line."

On July 31, back in England, and back on the negative side, Bill McAllister of *Record Mirror* said of the new album:

What the Moody Blues have to offer contemporary music seems extremely in doubt after this album. *Every Good Boy...* doesn't stretch beyond what they have done in the past (and theirs has been a continuous development from *Days of Future Past* [sic], right through to *On the Threshold of a Dream*), but then neither does it consolidate their past work. Instead it merely marks a stopping point in their development ... and a very negative one at that.

The pretty melodies are still there, and the use of rich, heavily textured instrumentation, and the use of heavenly voiced choral work, but all it adds up to is a very poor rehash of the past.

The opening track, "Procession," for instance, is a drab, uninteresting instrumental. It lacks the bite and fire, a demand for attention that has nearly always been a hallmark of the Moody Blues' work in days gone by. As always, the lyrics are passable, acceptable … and ultimately that must be the downer on them. No, Moodies, this isn't quite good enough to favour with money being as tight as it is.

Was John Lodge making excuses for *EGBDF* when talking to Robert Green for the July 31 edition of *New Musical Express*? He said, "The thing is, with this album in particular, we started recording it about last November and it's the album that's stayed with us the longest because we did two American tours in the meantime. We've played it and played it and played it, listened to it and dissected it. All you can rely on is someone else's judgment; you can only do so much. When it's out it's too late to change anything…."

Pinder, Hayward, Lodge, Thomas, and Edge during photo shoot in Cobham, England, 1971.
(Photo source: Grammy.com)

As for the theme of the new work, Lodge explained: "The basic thoughts behind it are as basic as *Days of Future Passed* – that was a theoretical point of view on, 'This is what life is.' *In Search of the Lost Chord* was philosophical, sort of, 'Wouldn't it be nice if things could be like this?' *Threshold* sort of linked the two things together and said the theory was all right but the practicability wasn't. *Children's Children* was about now and the future. And *Question of Balance* was what is happening in the world today, and, if we're not all cheerful, we'll blow it all up. This one is: 'We couldn't even keep the question of balance together; let's start again at the beginning." (JL-NME71)

In America, "The Story in Your Eyes" entered both the *Billboard* and *Cashbox* singles charts on August 7 at No. 88 and 73, respectively.

Days earlier, on August 4, *Variety* rated the new album, saying:

Vet English combo the Moody Blues continue their love affair with the concept LP. This disk, as others, deals with the search for truth and sanity in a chaotic world. While no solution to the problems, except love, are really offered, the set is none the less musically impressive. Strings and horns on ballads provide a fine balance to the trippy, high voltage electronics on the rockers. Best tracks are "Procession," "Emily's Song," "You Can Never Go Home," "My Song," and "The Story in Your Eyes."

On August 14, *Billboard* reviewed *EGBDF*:

> The Moody Blues have always had some righteous things to say in rock's religious renaissance, and again they beautify the picture with more of their space-age blends of studio technology and timeless wisdom. Justin Hayward's "Story in Your Eyes" is the new single, while "My Song" and "You Can Never Go Home" rise in relief from the moving whole, bound to turn into more gold.

On August 21, *Every Good Boy Deserves Favour* entered the *Billboard* album chart at No. 30.

On August 22, Tony Palmer of London, England's *The Observer*, wrote:

> One of the strangest success stories in pop has been that of the Moody Blues. From being a second-rate combo from Birmingham, washed up in the wake of Beatlemania, this five-man group has developed into a clever, articulate and musically accomplished ensemble, whose records may not be to everyone's taste but which can certainly be admired for their skill.
>
> Over the last four years, the group has produced six albums whose sound is a curious blend of orchestral and rock 'n' roll and whose style is the most polished example of symphonic pop music – if that's not too preposterous a description – to be heard today. Starting with an LP called *Days of Future Passed*, they have progressed to their latest album – *Every Good Boy Deserves Favour*, which is as near to a contemporary song cycle as you are likely to get. …
>
> But somehow, within its modest limits, the music has a consistent directness and unity which outstrips, for example, the more strident patchwork of the Who's *Tommy*. Whereas the Who's rock opera relied heavily on the repetitive use of *leitmotiv* to hold the whole thing together, the Moody Blues have constructed a 40-minute piece whose design, although diffuse, seems to have a natural and spontaneous development.
>
> The subject matter, as in their previous records, is largely autobiographical, charting their rustic origins and their consequently contented view of life. For theirs is music which lacks the urgency of self-conscious suffering or overt propaganda – it is music of happiness – the most difficult to write and certainly the most difficult to make sound convincing.
>
> They are lucky in that they are now protected by having their own record label – Threshold – on which they and they alone record all their material, and in their choice of recording manager, Tony Clarke. His use of stereo and other electronic effects marks out the Moody Blues records as technically the most sophisticated products this side of the Atlantic. Particularly, his involvement of

389

the Mellotron (an electronic keyboard instrument) has provided many of the sounds that one might otherwise be forgiven for thinking were orchestral. ...

Not taking any glory away from Tony Clarke, we all know – even if Tony Palmer did not – that the credit for the Mellotron, and all those other "electronic effects," goes to Mike Pinder.

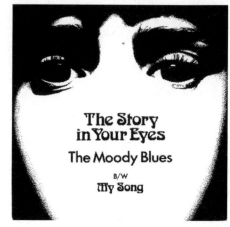

European single release:
"The Story in Your Eyes" / "My Song"
Threshold TH 6; August 27, 1971

"The Story in Your Eyes" was issued in Europe over a month *after* the album came out, with varied release dates in different countries, beginning on August 27, 1971 in a few nations, then continuing through the year and even into early 1972 for the remainder of the Continent. Because "Melancholy Man" had already been issued as a single in early 1971 in Europe, a different B-side had to be chosen. The honor went to Mike Pinder's "My Song." However, when the single was issued in Japan on October 1, 1971, the B-side was given to John Lodge's "Emily's Song."

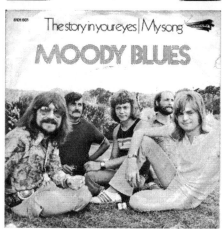

"Story" was not released in the U.K. was not issued in the U.K. Justin Hayward explained, "That was us being really pedantic and arty, thinking we could control all our releases. We just decided that we didn't want any singles out then. London Records snuck it out in the U.S., and I'm damn glad they did, as it gave us a No. 1 [sic] there." (JH-RC03)

For the September issue of *Phonograph Record*, Jon Tiven, joining the anti-Moodies critical movement, wrote:

> Clad in lush blue and scarlet robes, a monk descends from the sky. Raising his brow, and pointing his forearm at the heavens, he cries out: "Let there be Moody Blues!" And there was Moody Blues. And there were albums, with atrocious covers and two or three good tunes packaged between mounds of dung.
>
> And then there was a new album. With a tolerable cover. And a very pretentious beginning, sounding like something a tired minister would program in his movie about the rise and fall of mankind.

The hit "The Story in Your Eyes" is a dynamite song right out of the back pocket of the Beatles or Ian Matthews, but that's OK, if the rest of the album was like this. But it isn't. The next cut is a eunuch procession march; all their songs sound either castrated of forcefully asserted.

Have they changed? No, not at all. The same type of tunes as always, pretty melodies that go virtually nowhere. They don't write pretty songs as well as Paul [McCartney]. And Paul rocks well, at least when he wants to. Not that Paul is supermusicman or anything, but he sounds like the Stones next to the Moodies. Ho-hum.

Mike Pinder was scheduled to be interviewed for *Melody Maker*'s August 28 issue. But, one week earlier, *MM* ran the tease for its upcoming issue: "Moodies – Do They Try Too Hard?" Pinder saw that "trailer," and felt the interview he had been asked to give was a set up for a put-down. So, he had Keith Altham, the Moodies' publicist, call *Melody Maker*'s Roger Hollingworth to say that the interview was off. However, the interview's space had already been reserved for the next issue. Instead, those pages were filled with a picture of Pinder and the catty article, "Doing a Moody: Presenting the Bizarre Tale of Roy Hollingworth's Non-Interview with the Moody Blues' Mike Pinder."
Hollingworth wrote:

> We'd just got it into our heads that the Moodies' music might be suffering because the Moodies were perhaps beginning to believe their own propaganda. And that they might be trying too hard to find that lost chord. It was a question of balance, if you like – but it stumbled, and fell. Pinder cancelled the interview because of that trailer. ...

Hollingworth told how Keith Altham called to say that *Melody Maker* "blew it." According to Hollingworth, Altham said, "I had in mind you interviewing them; Mike Pinder, in fact, because I feel it's he who should be interviewed. But Mike's a sensitive person, and would need to speak to someone who's sympathetically inclined towards the band."
Hollingworth wrote:

> The *MM* conference was about an hour away. ... I was finding it strange that a Birmingham beat group had blossomed into some sort of God-like establishment, far removed from the tittle and tattle life of such mortals as us. They had one of those auras, this whole *To Our Children's Children's Children* thing. ...

> Comments like this could be put to Pinder – one hoped he'd brush them aside with a "bah, rubbish," and then talk in very basic terms. Or maybe we'd get some interesting chat. ...

> It was funny, but Moodies were brought up at the conference [editorial meeting]. There were several remarks made, several

regarding the band believing their own propaganda – some of the remarks were, I felt, a little harsh. "They really blew it not doing the score for *2001*," was one. The word "boring" was frequently mentioned. In fact, every other word was "boring." The point that had to be accepted was that Moodies were No. 1 in the album charts. They had released *Every Good Boy Deserves Favour*, and it had just sold straight to the top. You can't ignore things like that, you just cannot ignore them. ...

If it was preconceived that we were going out to put the Moodies down, well, as far as I was concerned, that was wrong. If it was preconceived that we were going to ask questions that weren't sometimes sympathetic towards the band, then that was right. Dead right. We were aiming for a critical appraisal of the Moody Blues from Mike Pinder. We wanted to ask if he thought they were trying too hard. It seems silly, sickening, and extremely sad that a band of the Moodies' stature can't bring themselves to answer more than one question. It's childish, actually. ...

Who were really being childish – Pinder for dodging a hostile interview, or the *Melody Maker* people, by calling Pinder "childish," "sad," and "sick," because he had spoiled their fun?

Graeme Edge, the warrior, agreed to field Roy Hollingworth's tough questions for the September 4 issue. Predictably, Hollingworth asked, "Are the Moodies trying too hard?" Edge replied, "Trying too hard. Mmmm.... If you asked me if I thought the last album was overproduced, then I'll say, 'Certainly, there were items which were overproduced.' Nobody's ever perfect, and I feel on certain items we did tend to take the production too far. There was a lot of material written for that album, and a hell of a lot was thrown away." (GE-MM71)

Like the good "straight-forward" rock 'n' roll track "The Dreamer."

But Edge probably knew what Hollingworth really wanted to say, and, sure enough, the *Melody Maker* man used the dreaded "P" word. Edge stayed cool. He replied, "Pretention. Well ... you'd have to tell me what songs you thought were pretentious, and I'd tell you what they were about. 'Pretention' means to 'pretend' – and we don't pretend."

Edge wasn't through having fun. He impishly told the writer, "I have been tempted, many times, to be pictured sitting on the toilet on an album sleeve, or picking one's nose. Yeh, picking one's nose – that would be better. But it would just be misunderstood. We are just five guys, who get on, and we work well together, and we make music.... We write songs, and we have freedom within those songs to do what we wish. We try to deliver freedom, peace, and love. And how corny it sounds to say that? Just how corny?" (GE-MM71)

On September 4, in the U.S., *EGBDF* leapt from No. 8 to No. 2 on the *Billboard* album chart, replacing McCartney's *Ram* and now sitting under the seemingly unbudgeable *Tapestry* album from Carole King. This was only the third week in the chart for *EGBDF*. It would hold at No. 2 for three weeks, under *Tapestry*, before slipping down one position for a two-week stay at No. 3, behind *Tapestry* and Rod Stewart's *Every*

Justin Hayward John Lodge Graeme Edge Michael Pinder
Ray Thomas

The Moody Blues

Picture Tells a Story. By the end of that second week in third place, the album was certified Gold by the Record Industry Association of America (RIAA). It stayed on the chart for 43 weeks.

In this examination of the press reaction to *EGBDF* in the year it was released, we have passed over many regional newspaper reviews of the album, not because they were negative (and some were), and not because they were positive (and many were), but because they were indistinctive, merely saying what had been said before in much the same way. But one regional review, from Henry Mendoza in the September 14 edition of *The San Bernardino County Sun*, warrants inclusion.

Mr. Mendoza said, in part:

… The album is not full of a lot of musical tracks, but does employ a wide variation of sounds making the ultimate product. And the sounds are quite a way from the old electronic twang and noisy drum. Since *Days of Future Past* [sic] the Moody Blues has been recognized as a musically tight rock group. This album should enhance their reputation.

"The Story in Your Eyes," which as a single is getting a lot of attention, opens the album. As a cut, it probably best epitomizes Moody Blues. The group is built around rich acoustic guitar leads with a strong supporting electric bass line. The combination has always been part of the Moody Blues, but only recently has gained popularity with other groups. On "The Story," the acoustic guitar opens the cut with a pronounced rhythm section. An electric guitar joins the acoustic lead, introducing the lead vocal. The transitions are smooth and the sound is made tasteful throughout, building nicely. It's a fine song done by some obviously fine musicians. …

Ray Thomas does a fine vocal job on "Our Guessing Game," a cut which includes some of the most exciting sounds on the album. "Emily's Song" is a beautiful folk song with enchanting lyrics.

"One More Time to Love" opens Side Two, with a fantastic thing called the "Middle 8" on the cut. The lead vocal sings a word, or two, which is answered by a background chorus, again demonstrating the group's vocal blend as well as musical imagination.

It's an album you hear differently each time you listen to it. It's full of fine musicianship and good sounds. A dubious critic might again say the album is above the rock audience's head, but sales figures would squelch that argument. Along with McCartney's *Ram*, and Rod Stewart's new album, the Moody Blues finally helped dislodge *Jesus Christ Superstar* from one of the longest stays in *Billboard*'s Top 5 sales list in recent memory.

In the September 16 issue of *Rolling Stone*, Andrew Bailey was now jumping on the negativity bandwagon and hitting the Moodies with the hard questions … and the same description.

One word keeps cropping up in connection with the Moodies – pretentious. None of the Moodies writes music down conventionally. In the studios, they use comic strips, pictures, and maps to get across the song to each other. They were going to include some of the relevant maps with the new album. "But," said John [Lodge], "people would have called it pretentious."

Instead, the album has a painting on it, which was described by one critic as … pretentious.

John Lodge responded to Bailey, "Our biggest headache is knowing what to call an album. We don't start off saying, 'Right, this is going to be called 'The Answer to the Mystery of Life,' like some people think we do. Usually somebody comes up with a title and we all agree it's right.

"Tony Clarke said this album is like a grand symphony. 'The Seven Ages of Man.' We couldn't use that as a title; that really would be pretentious. So, instead of being called a symphony, it's called *Every Good Boy Deserves Favour*, one of the first things you learn about music.

"I'm not sure all of this gets across to the listener. All you can hope is that the people who buy our stuff think like that anyway. We're not your sex pot idols; we're not gurus; and we're not good looking; and we don't say 'Power to the People.' But we do stand up and play in front of 20,000 people, so we must have something." (JL-RS71)

Mike Jahn, rock music critic for *The New York Times*, who once sang the praises of the Moody Blues, had now defected to the other side. On September 19, the word was "disappointment." Jahn wrote:

A disappointment, in which the Moodies let their previously effective cosmic kitsch ("everything is everything" and all that) become formalized and trite.

No songs stand out, just the fact that perhaps too many years of searching the cosmos for *the* Answer had led them to believe they may really be the ones ordained to find it.

"The Story in Your Eyes," a song we contend definitely *did* "stand out," peaked in the *Cashbox* chart at No. 14 on September 25 for the first of two weeks. Over at *Billboard*, the single peaked at No. 23 on October 2, for the first of two weeks. *Record World*, the third big U.S. national chart, showed the song's peak position as No. 16.

Meanwhile, with a great "trailer" out to promote the album, rock critics continued to dissect the Moodies' latest offering, including Thomas Popson in the October 10 edition of the *Chicago Tribune*:

> The Moody Blues always seem to be teetering on the brink of musical excess, just one misstep away from too-lavish arrangements, too-grand lyrics, and too-sweet harmony. Yet on each of their albums, the Moodies have usually managed to avoid going over the edge. They keep performing those lush, soaring songs with lofty lyrics, but for the most part they stop just short of becoming pretentious or cloying.
>
> The latest release from the Moodies – *Every Good Boy Deserves Favour* (Threshold) – finds them doing it once again. Like other Moody Blues albums, it has that luxuriant sound, and, like the other albums, it is always highly listenable.
>
> Part of the reason their songs remain palatable is that the band never really abandons straightforward rock 'n' roll. They do a marvelous job of covering it up with Mellotrons, harpsichords, flutes, and the like, but if you dip into their material and push aside the embellishments, you find some crisp, exciting rock at the core.
>
> Occasionally, tho, they do trip and fall. "One More Time to Live" on the *Favour* album comes on strong with near-majestic instrumentation and simultaneous vocals, one of which seems to promise in its obscure working a solution to mankind's problems. Even the Moodies can't touch that without sounding a bit too self-important.

From the *Detroit Free Press*, October 24, 1971, John Weisman wrote:

> Despite the current backlash, the Moody Blues are still, when they're in form, one of rock and roll's better ensembles. Their latest album, *Every Good Boy Deserves Favour*, is an excellent example of the kind of continuing kinetic growth that the group enjoys. Engineered well, and beautifully produced, the album is really first rate. "Our Guessing Game" by Ray Thomas and John Lodge's "One More Time to Live" are but two examples of the individual sound that the Moodies produce. Whereas sometimes in concerts the vocals tend to be covered by heavily amped instruments, *Every Good Boy Deserves Favour* has the clean sound and good tones of a fine LP.

In the November 1971 issue of *Circus*, the magazine's record critic wrote:

> The Moodies have done it again. Done what? If you have to ask, you may not enjoy the latest effort by this British quintet. But if you've let yourself be drawn into the dreamlike web of their unique music over the years, you should find *EGBDF* right up to snuff. "The Story in Your Eyes," which has done quite nicely for the boys as a single, is included, but the longer cuts, those which enable the group to really step out, give the album its strength. Mood plays a large part in the proceedings, most notably in "My Song," a composition by Mellotron master Mike Pinder, which swirls and flows like a river. "Nice to Be Here" is the kind of song which quickly slips into your consciousness and takes up residence there like an old friend. "Procession" and "One More Time to Live," with their dramatic intonations, are a bit too weighty for comfort, but the gentle excellence of the remainder of the set more than makes up for these excesses.

In November, Judy Hugg of Copley News Service (syndicated to newspapers across North America), wrote:

> The never-ending battle for the top spot among English and American rock groups just doesn't seem to let up. However, you can bet your knickers that the Moody Blues are here to stay.
>
> Attesting to the fact is their latest album on their own Threshold label entitled *Every Good Boy Deserves Favour*. The platter, which struck gold only eight days after its release, is their fifth [sic; sixth] straight – a sure sign of success for an English group on the American pop scene. ...
>
> Of course, everyone remembers the Moody Blues' old greats like "Have You Heard," "Timothy Leary" [sic], and "Nights in White Satin," which made them what they are today. But one must listen to this new album to appreciate the real down-to-earth factor which keeps the group on top, consistently earning new fans. ...

The point-counterpoint continued. From the December 1971 issue of *Hi Fidelity* magazine:

> The LP opens with a windstorm, followed by the spoken word "desolation"; similarly, "creation" is intoned after a thunderstorm effect, and "communication" follows native drums. This kind of echo-chamber emotion is a familiar tactic with the Moody Blues, one of the few groups still concerned with the cosmic questions raised during the Haight-Ashbury period of youth culture. Musically the group is the Wagner of its day – romantic, lush, and a bit pretentious.... [D]espite the complexity of their music and the brilliance with which it is assembled, the pretention does get to be tiring after a while. ...

Pretention is valuable – where would art and politics be without it. But it's tricky business, and must be done well. The Moody Blues, on this LP, aren't doing it as well as they once did.

The opening line from one song is, "I don't know what I'm searching for," and though the group searches for it with great clamor, the goal is not approached.

From a syndicated "Teen Times" review in December 1971, in various newspapers across North America, Jared Johnson wrote:

> … If you're planning on buying only one new album this year, this is it! Listening to the Moody Blues is an exhilarating experience. Not everyone likes them, but it's interesting to note the comments from those who don't, seeming to indicate that somewhere deep down they are vaguely embarrassed because they aren't able to appreciate the Moody Blues.
>
> "The Moody Blues? They're too much for me. Their music escapes me." "I just don't understand them. I don't understand what they're trying to do. I guess I just can't get into that kind of music." "They're too elaborate. I like something loud, but not too deep." A few observations for what they're worth.
>
> Once again, a prophetic look into the future, the album is a continuation of some of the lyrical themes initiated on *To Our Children's Children's Children*. "And I'm frightened for your children, and the life that we are living is in vain, and the sunshine we've been waiting for will turn to rain." "The Story in Your Eyes" (Justin Hayward)….
>
> For a reviewer who has been writing on their music for years, even back when the usual response to bringing their name up was, "Moody who?", it has been a very satisfying experience to watch them grow. The Moody Blues have always been in the vanguard of progressive rock. Now they are destined to lead it!

Even after 1971 gave way to 1972, rock journalists were still talking about *EGBDF*. In the New Year, Rick Gould, of *The Gold Bug* music magazine, wrote:

> … *Every Good Boy Deserves Favour*, as released last summer, is a musical reaffirmation and consolidation of the Moodies' patented musical expression. "Story in Your Eyes," "After You Came," "You Can Never Go Home," and "My Song" all betray two concurrent themes: evolution and mankind's spirituality. Christian shadows are again lurking in this puzzling and at times enigmatic work…. I am reassured that the music of the Moody Blues is "music to listen to and float away on."

18

U.S. Tour 1971: Enter Jerry Weintraub and Tom Hulett

Jerry Weintraub of Concerts West, circa early 1970s. (Photo source: Variety.com)

The Moody Blues had taken their longest break in touring – nearly nine months. Now they were going back on the road to support the release of *Every Good Boy Deserves Favour*.

John Lodge told Hal Speck of *Record Mirror*, "If it wasn't for Pete [Jackson] we might never have gone back on the road. He was with us right from the early days when he was our road manager and he was the best. He hurt his back and we told him it didn't matter because we wanted him to handle the paperwork and administrate on the tours. [But] Pete thought we were offering him a free ride and his pride wouldn't let him take the job. He got married and left us for a year." (JL-RM72)

Recalling the injury and his time away from the Moodies, Peter Jackson said, "We continued to tour up until 1970, when I got a busted vertebrae from picking up a microphone onstage. I had guys helping me then, but I used to set the mics and run the soundboard. Basically, I felt my days were done after that; 'I'm finished.' I got an offer to become an agent in the States, so I left the band. I thought I couldn't help them anymore.

"I moved to America with my wife in November of '70, but the job never materialized. The guy who offered me the job was fired, so it never panned out. [Meanwhile, the Moodies] missed dates and the crew they had replaced me with just didn't work." (PJ-PS00)

Lodge said, "We did a tour with some other roadies and it was chaos – that was particularly the reason we didn't work for a year [mid-December 1970 to late September 1971]. Finally, we were able to persuade Pete to come back and convince him that 'tour manager' was no picnic." (JL-RM72)

Jackson said, "The band asked me to come back to England. They had set up Threshold Records and asked if I would run the management for the band. I would hire a new crew and put the touring division together, basically. So I returned to England and ran the touring division of Threshold Records.

"When they were finishing [the *EGBDF*] album, our [U.K. booking] agent called me and said, 'This American company wants to sit down and ask the band to become their new agent/promoter.' … Concerts West was a national tour promoter, which in those days was absolutely unheard of. So, I jumped on a plane to L.A. and met with Tom Hulett and Jerry Weintraub." (PJ-PS00)

This began a new phase in Moody Blues tours, which eventually led to a new management deal for the band. For the remainder of the 1970s, Tom Hulett, a partner in Concerts West, and Weintraub, of his own Weintraub Entertainment, would become factors in the career of the Moody Blues.

This part of the story begins with Pat O'Day and Dick Curtis, a pair of DJ's at Seattle, Washington's top radio station, KJR, which played Top 40. O'Day, in fact, was one of the city's highest-profile DJs and dance promoters, who organized and sponsored local "sock hops." By 1963, O'Day not only had KJR's top-rated show during the afternoon drive-time, but had become the station's program director. Curtis held down the evening shift at the station. This position brought about their first encounter with Jerry Weintraub, New York-based manager of the Four Seasons and, later, The Young Rascals.

Curtis recalled, "Weintraub was brilliant. He telephoned program directors at the leading rock stations all over the country asking them if they wanted to be partners in presenting the Four Seasons. The group had exploded a year earlier with their No. 1 hit, 'Sherry.' 'Big Girls Don't Cry' was the follow up, another No. 1 smash. Jerry was asking program directors to come up with $5,000 and then take 50% of the profits. Of course, there was the cost of promoting the show; hall rental, advertising, etc.

"O'Day had gone to all the KJR DJs and asked them if they'd like to participate. Two thousand a piece, he told them. I borrowed the two grand from my brother and his wife and before long I was thrust into a business I knew nothing about. None of the others at KJR chose to participate.

"A concert producing company was quickly formed called 'Pat O'Day and Dick Curtis Presents.' We rented a small apartment on the west side of town and sparing no expense, equipped it with a typewriter and an answering machine. That was basically it. In order to satisfy KJR management, we needed to keep our concert business outside of the radio station.

"The show would be held at the Seattle Center Opera House, which seats about 3,000…. It was all so new. Ticketing, [and] this included ticket agencies; ticket printing and scaling of the facility (deciding how much each seat would cost) [was my job].

Responsibilities of the Seattle Center personnel, including off-duty police, stagehands, ushers, was shared by the two of us. …

"The concert was a huge success! So big, we sold out two shows the same day! O'Day and I each pocketed a few thousand and we were on our way." (DC-BW11)

Soon O'Day and Curtis were partners. The business had a new name: Pat O'Day and Dick Curtis Presents. Beside local dances, they continued to book area concerts, including shows with national headliners such as Little Stevie Wonder (as he was billed then), April Stevens & Nino Tempo, the Exciters, Del Shannon, the Beach Boys, Jan & Dean, the Righteous Brothers, Bobby Vinton, Jackie DeShannon, the Shangri-Las, and Roy Orbison.

Curtis continued, "Everything we touched was turning to gold. If it hadn't been for Jerry Weintraub odds are I would have never delved into show business other than being a radio deejay." (DC-BW11)

As O'Day and Curtis became busier with larger concerts, as well as their ongoing "day job" on radio station KJR, they needed someone to take over the sock hops and other smaller programs. In 1965, Terry Bassett joined the company, with the business name now changed to Pat O'Day & Associates.

Meanwhile, the concerts became bigger, with such groups as the Mamas and Papas, the Lovin' Spoonful, and English Invasion-era the Rolling Stones. Their biggest booking and largest venue became the Beatles in the Seattle Coliseum.

With the company's success came the need for more helping hands.

Tom Hulett, who would go on to become the Moody Blues manager throughout the 1980s and first half of the '90s, had been a football quarterback for the University of Washington in the late 1950s, then the Seattle Ramblers (which became the Rangers of the Continental Football League) in the early 1960s. In the middle of the decade, after laying down the football, Hulett worked in sales, mostly automotive. In 1965 he went to work for Pat O'Day & Associates, brought on-board by Curtis. The two were good friends and golf buddies.

Curtis said, "I knew Tom when he was a $12,000 a year guy impounding cars when owners failed to pay his employer, Universal CIT Credit Corporation. I'd lied to my partner, Pat O'Day, and told him Tom was making $16,000 so we could pay him $20,000 as an inducement to leave a solvent business, give up a medical plan, and join Pat O'Day & Associates. Tom knew nothing about the concert business when Pat and I first hired him in 1965 to sell our teen fair booth space.

"Say what you want, Hulett was a hell of a salesman. He and O'Day together made a combination that was hard to top when it came to sales. My gut instincts were right. He went on to sell out all the booth space at our Teen Fair in 60 days." (DC-BWB11)

By 1967, Pat O'Day was dominating Puget Sound Radio, as program director and top DJ on KJR, as Pat O'Day & Associates ruled the local live music scene with concerts and dance-hall events. Their influence was such that a Federal anti-trust lawsuit was filed against him and his partners.

As a result of the suit, Curtis chose to leave the company at this time. He also left KJR, moving to rival Seattle Top 40 station KOL. O'Day, Bassett, and Hulett remained; they reorganized and changed the company name to Concerts West. Because O'Day was still employed with KJR, new regulations were put into place, to make the company distinct from his work at the radio station. Hulett, with no radio ties, was named the new president.

Concerts West soon picked up Vanilla Fudge, Led Zeppelin, and Jimi Hendrix for local concert appearances. In fact, Tom Hulett personally took charge of arranging all of Jimi Hendrix's concert bookings and arrangements, both in Seattle and throughout the United States. He also shepherded Frank Sinatra

Soon Jerry Weintraub joined O'Day, Hulett, and Bassett, bringing John Denver, Neil Diamond, and Dolly Parton.

When Elvis Presley decided to begin touring again at the start of the 1970s, Pat O'Day was determined to add the King to the Concerts West roster. With the support of his partners and the added financial muscle of Weintraub's involvement, he was able to secure a loan of $1,000,000 in order to present Colonel Tom Parker with a cashier's check in that amount – Parker's asking price for exclusive representation of the King on the road.

Concerts West was off and running, now operating on a national level. Besides the Seattle office, more offices were opened in Los Angeles, Dallas, New York, and Miami.

By 1971, Concerts West had lost Hendrix to a drug overdose, but, along with Presley and Sinatra, the company was now handling the U.S. tours for other major early 1970s acts, such as Creedence Clearwater Revival, Three Dog Night, Chicago, Bread, Led Zeppelin, the Beach Boys, Eric Clapton, the Rolling Stones, and Elton John.

Now they were making a play for the Moody Blues, who would very soon be selling out arenas faster and more consistently than these other artists.

Because Pat O'Day was still one of the top DJs in the state of Washington, Concerts West received another perk. Dick Curtis said, "More than any other person, Pat was responsible for the place that Seattle had in the nation as an area that broke records. He simply was a phenomenon." (DC-SPI02)

Among the records O'Day would have a hand in "breaking" in the Seattle area, in the fall of 1972, was "Nights in White Satin," provoking the domino effect across America which sent the five-year-old single to the top of the national charts. O'Day was not the first to play the record in that region, but his influence helped to move the song into bigger markets.

This is why, after receiving a call from Concerts West, Peter Jackson hopped on a plane and flew from London to the U.S. West Coast to meet with Tom Hulett and Jerry Weintraub.

Peter Jackson: "When I met with them, they said, 'Hey, we got this idea. We'd like to do a national tour with the Moody Blues and we'll do an 85-15 deal.' Up until then, the deals that used to be done were, well, put it this way – if you sold out, the promoter made nearly as much money as the band made. So this was quite a new idea.

"When these people offered the deal, I said, 'Well, we've had so many problems with people and contracts, we don't sign contracts. I'll shake your hand and you got a deal. We'll do a tour. Yeah, 85-15, fine.' And that's what we did. This was right about the same time Led Zeppelin did the same thing with Concerts West.

"So that was it for the next three or four years. The Moody Blues would come over here for usually three-week runs at a time, and they would put the shows on sale and just sell out immediately. It was unbelievable." (PJ-PS00)

The management of Weintraub and Hulett put the Moody Blues into much larger venues, setting the stage for something that would take the U.S. music press by surprise … and impress the Moody Blues, too.

Above: Promotional picture used for the fall 1971 U.S. tour.
Below: Back to America.
(Photo source: quickywiki.com)

The set list for the Moodies' 1971 tour of America was "Gypsy" (Hayward), "Tuesday Afternoon" (Hayward), "Tortoise and the Hare" (Lodge), "Our Guessing  Game" (Thomas), "Melancholy Man" (Pinder), "One More Time to Live" (Lodge), "The Story in Your Eyes" (Hayward), "Are You Sitting Comfortably?" (Hayward), "The Dream" (Edge; with Pinder reciting), "Have You Heard, Part 1"/"The Voyage"/"Have You Heard, Part 2" (Pinder), "Nights in White Satin" (Hayward), "Legend of a Mind" (Thomas), "Question" (Hayward), and "Ride My See-Saw" (Lodge). Some concerts

403

included "My Song" (Pinder). Country-rock singer/guitarist Charlie Starr was engaged to be the warm-up act for the entire tour (except for one hastily added show in Los Angeles).

For the October 1971 issue of *Circus*, Penelope Ross wrote about the upcoming tour, and another milestone for the Moodies.

> … Trevor Taylor, a member of the English table tennis team that was invited to play in China, had bought a copy of *To Our Children's Children's Children* in Singapore and took it with him over the border. Once there, he convinced the interpreter to play it for a large group of people. Taylor says they weren't sure about it at first, since Western music is totally unknown there. But eventually the audience began to appreciate what they considered its revolutionary content.

Newspaper photo (provenance unknown), with caption:
"On his historic return from China, table tennis player Trevor Taylor was presented with a complete autographed set of the Moody Blues' LPs. Trevor is a Moodies fan and took their *To Our Children's Children's Children* LP to China to play the Chinese. He reports: 'They seemed to like it.' In the picture are (L to R) Justin Hayward, Trevor, Jerry Moss (Threshold Records business manager), Graeme Edge, and Moodies' producer Tony Clarke."
(Photo source: MoodyBluesAttitude.com; posted by Ros)

Ross added:

> Maybe the content is revolutionary. Certainly, it radically departs from what is normally considered rock. And it's not jazz and it's not pop. Love or loathe it, the Moody Blues create unique music.

> Finally it seems that this music is going to get the recognition it deserves. Until last year the group's success was steady. … All of [their albums from 1967, '68, and '69] sold well enough at the time of release, but it wasn't until 1970 that the band really broke through [with the release of "Question" and *A Question of Balance*]. Then in a remarkable spurt that may be a record of some

sort, all five of the albums were certified gold by the R.I.A.A. in a two month period. And their current LP, *Every Good Boy Deserves Favour* (distributed by London), began to get heavy airplay on the FM stations at least a month before it came out. ...

Saturday, September 25, 1971: The tour opened at the Seattle Center Coliseum, in Seattle, Washington, with singer/guitarist Charlie Starr as the opening act. Janine Gressel attended for *The Seattle Times*:

> "We've not been on stage for nine months," Mike Pinder told the crowd, "and we're bloody terrified." ...
>
> The British band, which has five Gold albums to its credit, had nothing to fear. The Coliseum – Gargantua of Seattle rock halls – was filled nearly to capacity. ...
>
> The Moody Blues have done with rock-and-roll what Duke Ellington has done with jazz – made it bigger, more dramatic, more symphonic. With the use of an electronic instrument called a Mellotron (Pinder plays it – it looks like an organ), the Moody's music, both on record and on stage, sounds as if it were performed by a full orchestra and chorus.
>
> Their music is complex; a cut above most good rock, and immeasurably better than the abundant bubble-gum music. ...
>
> The Moodys played for almost an hour and a half, offering music from all six of their albums. As each member composes, the concert showcased all five members individually as creators as well as performers. The only member who wasn't heard vocally was Graeme Edge, the percussionist. His talents were much in evidence, however, through his outstanding drum work and through his poem, "The Dream," recited by Pinder. ...
>
> If the Moody Blues began their show with some trepidation, they must have ended it with new confidence. They were a smashing success in Seattle.

Sunday, September 26: For the next concert on the tour, the Moody Blues and Charlie Starr appeared at Memorial Coliseum, in Portland, Oregon.

Tuesday, September 28: they played the Los Angeles Forum, Inglewood, California.

While in Los Angeles, the Moodies were presented with their sixth gold album award. Reporting the event back in England, *New Musical Express* told its readers:

> When it was decided that the Moody Blues would receive their sixth gold record (representing $1,000,000 worth of sales) for *Every Good Boy Deserves Favour* during their Hollywood press conference, their press representative, Connie DeNave, cabled

them in London asking whom they would like to present them with the award.

A one-word cable came back with the response: "TONTO." Connie sent a second cable: "REPEAT MESSAGE." Again the response" "TONTO. TONTO. HI-HO SILVER, TONTO."

And so it was actor Jay Silverheels, veteran "Tonto" of decades of both radio and television broadcasts as the Lone Ranger's trusted Indian companion who made the presentation. Silverheels seemed honestly impressed and honored with his mission, and the Moody's stood around him very much like small children who were meeting their idol for the first time. ...

An unidentified writer from *Rock* magazine was there to cover the event. He reported:

> ... The day the group played in Los Angeles, and before my interview, a press conference was held at a flowery, luxuriant West L.A. hotel. *Teen Magazine* was there, so were these middle-aged reporters from CBS, but I guess that's who these press conferences are for.
>
> Before the actual conference commenced, an aging Jay Silverheels was chosen to present the group a gold platter for their latest LP, *Every Good Boy Deserves Favour*.... (Edge explained later that the group

Above: Jay Silverheels and Clayton Moore in *The Lone Ranger*, 1949-1957.
(Apex Film Corp./ABC-TV Network)
(Below image: *Billboard*, Dec. 25, 1971 issue)

chose Tonto because he was one of the first symbols that the group identified with America, or something like that.)

John Lodge explained, "Believe it or not, I grew up watching *The Lone Ranger*. Though it was aimed at a young market, *The Lone Ranger*, to this

The Moody Blues receive a gold LP for their latest effort from actor Jay Silverheels.

day, has remained a popular television series in England, even among adults; and Jay Silverheels is well-known in England because of his role as Tonto. …

"What Jay Silverheels did with Tonto, he showed us that the red man contains the same capacity as the white man to possess integrity, exhibit loyalty, and perform good works. It's not a matter of liking Tonto better than the

(Photo source: MoodyBluesAttitude.com)

Lone Ranger. I like both of them, but being an Englishman and not having many common reference points with America's past, I've always been fascinated with the American Indians. … When he played the part of Tonto, that part was the piece that became real – Tonto became a reality for me.

"So it was an honor for myself, and the band, to meet Jay Silverheels. … He was larger than life. … We were at the Bel Air Hotel in Los Angeles. It's a fabulous hotel, and we had terrific photograph sessions there. Jay made the presentation to us, and afterwards, we started talking, and he told us all about how he had become an actor in Hollywood, and about his family. He explained how thrilled and proud his family was that he had become a movie star, and a television star; from that our friendship really grew." (JL-WWM98)

The unidentified writer for *Rock* magazine was still on hand, but unimpressed. His report continued:

> … Mike Pinder is quite clearly the most pretentious and verbose of the group; he likes to babble in long streams about anything, especially mysticism. … At one point toward the end of the conference, Mike candidly admitted, "We alone can't save the world." Whirling around on stage, blowing peace signs to *everybody*, Mike is as he'll always be. …
>
> It's harder to make each LP, Mike says, and he's right. The Moodies are ever looking for new techniques and new ideas. *Days [of Future Passed]* was written and recorded in a little more than a week, but their last LP required over fifty days in the studio. …
>
> The band played the Forum that night. I wish I could accurately tell you how thrilling the Moody Blues were – and they were – but I can't as the seats the PR people gave me were located behind the stage on the very highest row – the worst seats I've ever had. And but for satisfying you, *Rock* readers, I wouldn't have bothered

doing this article, such indifferrence I received by all those involved. …

With Concerts West organizing the tour, the Moodies crisscrossed America by skyway rather than highway.
(Photo source: MoodyBluesAttitude.com)

Back to the tour:

Wednesday, September 29: The tour continued, now in Vancouver, British Columbia, Canada.

Thursday, September 30: Due to the sellout just days earlier at the Forum in the Los Angeles area, a return trip was arranged to L.A., this time with the Moodies appearing at the Hollywood Bowl. Charlie Starr wasn't available, so Concerts West arranged for Poco to open.

Friday, October 1: Oakland-Alameda Coliseum, Oakland, California. Charlie Starr was back with the tour.

Saturday, October 2: Arizona Coliseum, Phoenix, Arizona.

Sunday, October 3: Memorial Coliseum, Dallas, Texas.

Monday, October 4: The Coliseum, Houston, Texas.

Tuesday, October 5: Mid-South Coliseum, Memphis, Tennessee.

Wednesday, October 6: Municipal Auditorium, New Orleans, Louisiana.

Thursday, October 7: St Louis Arena, St. Louis, Missouri. After the concert, Thomas B. Newsom wrote in the *St. Louis Post-Dispatch*:

> … The British lads traveled from New Orleans to St. Louis yesterday and set the Arena on fire again last night before about 18,000 screaming rock music freaks.

It does not appear that the Moody Blues have made any marked musical progress since their autumn 1970 appearance at the Arena. Yet their electronic gadgetry and their musical style has a certain appeal. …

The Moody Blues performance was quite solid and heavily laced with selections from their latest album, *Every Good Boy Deserves Favour*. One cannot deny the success of this quartet in the rock idiom. Their five gold albums [sic; now six] are testament to acceptance. …

[T]he group displayed a professional touch with the vocal chords as well as with their throbbing instruments. To cite but one, Mike Pinder's offering of "Melancholy Man."

Pinder is the genius on the Mellotron, a vital instrument in the Moody Blues' show. This is a keyboard instrument that looks rather like an organ. Its sound is produced by pick-up heads and pinch rollers gripping tape, rather than plucking of strings or air rushing through pipes. The instrument has a limited range of about three octaves, but the combination of sounds available from its track selections range from whispers to gigantic boom-roar.

In addition to the Mellotron, the personnel of Moody Blues play a range of instruments from sitar to an ear-shattering flute. …

Their work last evening was quite professional and faithful to the expectations of the Moody Blues fanatics in the St. Louis area.

Friday, October 8: Cobo Hall, Detroit, Michigan. John Weisman covered the event for the *Detroit Free Press*:

…. Their sold-out concert Friday night at the Cobo Auditorium was an excellent chance for Detroiters to hear a replete example of the Moody Blues' talents. The quintet, Mellotronist Mike Pinder, flautist Ray Thomas, bass guitarist John Lodge, [drummer Graeme Edge] and lead guitarist Justin Hayward, played a baker's dozen tunes – 12 in the regular set and one encore, when the cheering crowd wouldn't let up, stomping, applauding and whistling for perhaps three or four minutes until the group came back onstage.

The musical range of the Moody Blues is stupendous. There's the often-whimsical "Legend of a Mind," by Ray Thomas, a song which chronicles the story of Timothy Leary. It's a mixture of English music-hall comedy, a "Daphnis and Chloe"-like flute solo by Thomas, and a folksy riff behind everything.

Then, conversely, there's the almost-epic "One More Time to Live," by John Lodge. In that, the "middle eight," as the Moody's call it, is a contrapuntal arrangement of a narrative line with the choral "Tell me, someone, why there's only confusion? Tell me, someone, that this is all an illusion? Tell me someone ... changes in my life, changes in my life." It's a bit flat on paper, but live it is beautiful.

The instrumental voicing of the Moody Blues have a kind of Middle Ages virility in them. Mike Pinder's souped-up Mellotron bends tones with the grace and ease that a Sherwood Forrest archer lent to aiming his longbow, the tapes inside his instrument making it sound one moment like a string orchestra, the next like a hunting horn.

Graeme Edge's drumming is always on top of things. He's not fancy, but he's thorough and inventive – a palpitating heartbeat to the group. Justin and John have seemed to find the right balance between them, combining a variety of styles into a euphonics totality that is pleasing and finely executed. ...

Saturday, October 9: Two shows at the Minneapolis Auditorium, Minneapolis, Minnesota, both sell-outs. Charles Quimby wrote in *The Minneapolis Star*:

... The Moody Blues are much more mood than blues – a group dangerously close to being buried by their own classical roots. Saturday's concert demonstrated a welcome retreat to a more subtle, but still highly orchestral style.

The old lyrical progressions of ascending and descending flute still are evident, floating above the distinctive melophone [sic], with layers of heavier sound shifting and swelling in massive waves. A single song may range from circus to opera to piano bar. ...

"Melancholy Man," sung by Mike Pinder at his haunting best, typifies both the reach and the limit of the band. The song is almost pastoral, a multi-colored dance of slow falling leaves at hurricane volume. And somehow very, very, melancholy.

Even their faster, more urgent, more commercial efforts exert a strangely quieting effect. "The Story in Your Eyes" brought a burst of cheering from the crowd. But the burst was unsustained above the sadness in the depths of the song. ...

The Moody Blues are very much a group. They avoid both showy extroversion and sullen me-and-my-music ego trips. Superficial crowd pleasing, such as the obligatory drum solo, is left alone. ...

October 23: The Moodies' final U.S. appearance for 1971 was had Madison Square Garden in New York City for two sold-out shows.

Before departing America, Mike Pinder and Ray Thomas chatted with Dick Kleiner, a columnist for Newspaper Enterprise Association, for a syndicated article. Kleiner wrote:

… The group is one of the most distinctive of the current rock crop. In an era when rock groups come and go like new washday wonders, the Moody Blues seem to show shocking signs of sticking around. One reason, perhaps, is that these are five serious gentlemen, who won't just wander in off the streets, joints at the ready, and record whatever comes to mind. These five spend a lot of time and effort on each of their albums, and it shows.

They also have some pretensions, but maybe that's not bad.

Mike Pinder told Kleiner, "We're trying to break down national barriers. We want to show that we're all Earthmen." (MP-NP71)

Kleiner continued:

They're making huge sums of money now, but claim that money doesn't particularly interest them. Drummer Edge pours it back into his art – he recently spent more than $15,000 in trying to develop an electric drum kit. (Consider your ear drums warned.)

Pinder plays the Mellotron, a keyboard instrument which uses tapes of pre-recorded sound. He says he's spent upwards of $75,000 on his equipment.

Pinder added, "And I spend most of my time underneath the Mellotron – I've got two bloody great burns on my fingers now from the soldering iron." (MP-NP71)

On October 30, the Moodies, in an onstage photo, had the cover of *Cashbox* magazine.

Surviving the "backlash" that music critic John Weisman had mentioned in his review of *EGBDF* (*Detroit Free Press*, October 24, 1971) was an important damage control operation for the Moodies. The album was already out – nothing could be done about that now. People would like it or not, and based on the sales and chart positions on both sides of the Atlantic, the album was earning strong support. After an initial blast of hostile reviews, the mood shifted, and notices became more complimentary. Then the U.S. tour became a triumph, as sold-out stadiums, happy audiences, and mostly positive reviews prevailed. Now they returned to England to turn a tide of negative press that had suddenly erupted.

The primary criticisms had been that the band were becoming "pretentious" and, as

October 20, 1971 issue of *Cashbox*.
(Photo source: MoodyBluesAttitude.com)

one critic sniffed, "boring." Others had chastised them for not delivering "straightforward rock and roll." The Moodies first chance to prove the home critics wrong was an October 30, 1971 concert date at Royal Festival Hall in London. They came, they played, and, by all accounts, they conquered.

On November 6, Andrew Means, wrote in *Melody Maker*:

> An electric charge swept through the audience. It was almost as if London's Festival Hall had taken an almighty breath and couldn't hold it in any longer.
>
> Eighteen months of pent-up emotion exploded from both sides of the speakers as the Moody Blues terminated a long absence from British stages. The sheer volume, intensity and expanse of the music, were physically overwhelming. One actually felt their opening number, "Gypsy," smash against the anticipant shoreline like an Atlantic breaker.
>
> Everyone from musician to listener was so obviously excited by the concert that nothing was allowed to interfere with its success. It hardly mattered that Graeme Edge's "moog"-type drum kit couldn't make its debut; he spent most of the concert clowning around the stage and the audience loved it. ... Their set appeared well-rehearsed, for it is only with such a basis that spontaneity and Edge's looning could have been allowed to develop without detracting from the music.
>
> The tension remained until the end, which built up to a voluminal finale with "Nights in White Satin," "Legend of a Mind," "Question," and "My Song" as an encore.

From this time, when asked if the band ever grew tired of performing, say, "Tuesday Afternoon" or "Nights in White Satin," Justin Hayward replied, "[Y]ou never get bored with it. Because there is always scope for changing them, every night. If you've got a solo to do in 12 bars, or 8 bars, you can ad lib in that 8 bars. Tastefully. And every place sounds different. You never get bored of playing. That's one thing we'll never do, is come off the road. I don't believe so." (JH-HP71)

Melody Maker's Means was not alone in forgiving any past transgressions. Richard Green was there, as well, for *New Musical Express*. In that paper's November 6 issue, he wrote in part:

> ... Any resemblance between the Moody Blues of their last tour here or even the Isle of Wight fiasco last year is purely physical. There is now so much more gusto in the music that they can be counted among the world's greatest rock bands.
>
> Opening with "Gypsy" and its rock, they followed with "Tuesday Afternoon," which has its moments of thrills as well. ...

More rock followed with "Tortoise and the Hare," one of John's songs, Ray blasting away on harmonica, Justin Hayward playing some brilliant lead guitar, and Graeme punishing his drum kit. It was the sort of music that hits you right in the guts, something which the Moodies have always believed.

But it wasn't all rock. Mike Pinder's beautiful and moving "Melancholy Man" had the audience absolutely silent and attentive as he sang and used the Mellotron with its string effect as a supreme asset. The combined chorals of Ray, Justin and John added to the pathos of the number which is without a doubt one of the classic songs of all time – in any field.

"Guessing Game" from the new album proceeded "After You Came" with more rock and Mike on the guitar for a change, the powerful "One More Time to Live" and then the final sequence from the *Threshold of a Dream* album which consists of "Are You Sitting Comfortably?", Graeme's poem, "The Dream," which Mike recited, and "Have You Heard?" The audience response to that trilogy was one of utter and complete acceptance.

"Knights [sic] in White Satin" and then the beloved "Question," which was packed with enthusiasm, extended to over five minutes and presented as the perfect closing number. There then came the sort of standard ovation that is reserved for superstars only. No screams and hysterics, just insistent and prolonged applause that rose in volume as it continued. …

Despite the worst criticism having come from their homeland earlier in the year, the Moodies had wisely refined their act in America and returned ready to dazzle the music press.

After crisscrossing England a few times, with Hot Legs as their warm-up attraction, the Moodies returned to America. In the States, their opening act was the husband-and-wife folk attraction, Fat City.

Most sources state that the set list was identical to the fall 1971 tour of America: "Gypsy"; "Tuesday Afternoon"; "Tortoise and the Hare"; "Our Guessing Game"; "Melancholy Man"; "One More Time to Live"; "The Story in Your Eyes"; "Are You Sitting Comfortably?"; "The Dream"; "Have You Heard, Part 1"/"The Voyage"/"Have You Heard, Part 2"; "Nights in White Satin"; "Legend of a Mind"; "Question"; and "Ride My See-Saw." But at least one reviewer mentioned that the Moodies performed a few unfamiliar songs from a yet-to-be-released album, and it does seem unlikely that they would not be plugging their new single "Isn't Life Strange?"

Regardless of the set list, things kicked off on March 22, 1972 at the International Amphitheatre, Chicago, Illinois.

It was here that a girl rushed the stage and grabbed Ray Thomas. He told *Record Mirror*'s Hal Speck, "It scared the life out of me. It hasn't happened for years. I rang my wife later and told her I'd been 'mobbed' by a girl. There was a pause at the other end of the line and she said quietly, 'Of course. What do you expect, darling, you're my little superstar.'" (RT-RM72)

Speck said Thomas's face "underwent the look of a lemon that had been trod on."

March 23, 1972: University of Illinois, Assembly Hall, Champaign, Illinois.

March 25, 1972: Cobo Hall, Detroit, Michigan.

Hal Speck, who accompanied the Moody Blues on their tour, reported back to *Record Mirror*:

> The Moodies still draw a few freaks of course, like the gent in Detroit who got backstage and wanted to take them out that night in his rocket for a trip to Mars.
>
> "You can't do that," explained Threshold manager Gerry Hoff patiently. "We have to be in Syracuse tomorrow."
>
> "Oh I know that – I can have 'em back before then," scoffed the man.

March 26: Onondaga Memorial Auditorium, Syracuse, New York.

March 27, 1972: Baltimore Civic Center, Biltmore, Maryland. James D. Dilts wrote in *The Baltimore Sun*:

> The Moody Blues – contemporaries of the Beatles, the Stones, the Who – is one of the oldest surviving British rock bands. And they have written some passable songs, for example, guitarist Justin Hayward's "Knights [sic] in White Satin." But if they have anything else to recommend them, it was not evident at their concert Monday night at the Civic Center. The quality of their material was pedestrian, its musical execution mediocre and the stage presentation boring to the point of being soporific. Schlock rock. …
>
> The Moodies' singing was uneven and the words were inaudible, due in part to the fearsome amplification. Not that it made that much difference to the sellout audience at the Civic Center, which applauded enthusiastically after each song and gave the band a standing ovation at the end.

How dare the audience be so enthusiastic!

March 28, 1972: Maple Leaf Gardens, Toronto, Ontario.

March 30, 1972: Boston Gardens, Boston, Massachusetts.

Critic Peter Herbst, of a Boston-area newspaper (provenance unknown) caught the Moodies at the Garden, and wrote:

> In Boston, the measure of a rock group's importance is the ability to fill Boston Garden. Jethro Tull, Leon Russell and of course the Rolling Stones were able in the last several months to reach that milestone. When tickets for last night's Moody Blues concert at

the Gardens were put on the market, they were sold out immediately. Quietly, without the aid of press hoopla and without gimmicks, the Moody Blues have become a supergroup.

They are certainly a strange and surprising supergroup, because their stage act is devoid of almost any motion, relying instead on the highly theatrical, melodramatic music they play. The key to the sweeping, orchestral sound this five-man group produces is Mike Pinder's Mellotron, an electronic keyboard instrument about the size of an organ with a range of three and one half octaves, capable of producing a sound not unlike a full orchestra.

The combination of Pinder's Mellotron, Justin Hayward's full-sounding guitar work, John Lodge's moving bass guitar and Graeme Edge's booming, grandiloquent drums filled the Garden on Wednesday night with the clearest, most undistorted sound the Garden has witnessed in some time.

The band came charging out with their recent hit, "Story in Your Eyes," followed with "The Tortoise and the Hare," from the excellent *A Question of Balance* album, and polished off the segment with "Tuesday Afternoon." …

In order for the fans to get an encore from the band, they had to applaud for five minutes, during which time about ten thousand matches were lit in the dark, creating a matchless spectacle which stunned the Moodies when they returned to the stage. …

Nonetheless, they have demonstrated their importance to Boston by filling Boston Gardens with highly appreciative Moody Blues fans who seemed to enjoy the concert's weaker moments.

March 31, 1972: Memorial Auditorium, Buffalo, New York.
April 2, 1972: Convention Center Arena, San Antonio, Texas.

According to *Record Mirror*'s Hal Speck, who was present, the owner of the auditorium came backstage after the performance, saying, "I just wanted to tell you guys that was one of the most successful concerts we have ever had here and one of the most pleasant to witness. That was a packed, standing ovation, and when I look down in my auditorium afterwards there was not a chair out of place."

Speck wrote:

The only bad apple in San Antonio was a character called "The Queen" who had suffered a traumatic experience following the last Moody Blues concert when Ray looked at him in the front row of the audience and [the Queen's] tooth fell out.

The freak decided this was a sign, a portent of the end of the world, no less, and sat out by the freeway for 50 days until their current visit predicting the end of the world on their next appearance.

He came screaming at them from the other side of the road when we got in the cars to go to the auditorium, but was headed off by the hotel security. To some it might seem funny and it has that side to it, but the Moodies were visibly upset and Pete [Jackson] went to great lengths to see that the freak did not reappear.

Ward Beaverman, of *Circus* magazine, soon afterwards described the strange occurrence this way:

> … [A]n hour or two before the Moody Blues were to go onstage for a concert in Texas, into their dressing room floated none other than the Queen of Norman, a previously unknown doomsday prophet. The Queen, who happens to be a guy, must be given credit for the novelty of his approach – this time, *he* was the guru and *they* were supposed to be the disciples. (Right?) Singling out Justin Hayward, the Moodies mild-mannered and unbelievably shy lead guitarist, the Queen ranted into a revival pitch with lots of words and little success. When Justin remained unconvinced by the rhetoric, his royal holiness began to get a little too physical. At this point Peter Jacks [sic; Jackson] entered the picture and caught sight of some long, tall lunatic shoving Justin across the room.

Jackson told Beaverman, "I'm really a very easy-going sort of guy, you know. But this guy was really getting scary. So I just pushed him out the door and slammed it behind him. And I slammed it so hard that the doorknob came off in my hand." (PJ-C72)

After this story was reported in *Circus*, the Queen sent the magazine a letter.

> If people so desire, they can change their heads with time, and it is with this premise in mind that I would like to publicly apologize to the Moody Blues for the unfortunate incident that occurred outside the San Antonio Hilton Hotel on Easter Sunday of last year…. Earlier in the day, I had intruded on Justin Hayward's privacy at the Hilton and had been a little too "pushy" in trying to convey some religious ideas on him. I was ushered out of the room and reacted like an obnoxious little boy by screaming at them as they came out of the hotel and entered the limousine: "You cowards! I've come to save the world on Easter Sunday!" This was a very screwed up thing to do, and I have often regretted it. I hope that you will print this letter, for when a person changes, he wants to make amends to the people he hurt before he changed.
>
> Sincerely,
> J.P.B. [name withheld for this book]
> The Ex-Queen of Norman
> Norman, Oklahoma.

April 3, 1972: Tarrant County Convention Center, Fort Worth, Texas.

April 5, 1972: Sam Houston Coliseum, Houston, Texas. In this month's *Sounds*, Penny Valentine wrote:

A notice outside the theatre box office in San Antonio over Easter had a hastily scrawled message on it: "Moody Blues sold out," it read. Then underneath it added, "Elvis Presley tickets still on sale."

"Well," said Ray Thomas, laughing, "He does charge a bit more than we do. We try to keep ticket prices down." ...

Success in America is no stranger to the Moodies. Thomas reckons that the last three tours have been comparable in sizes of audiences and halls and that really over that period they've reached the top and haven't much space to climb any higher.

But this tour certainly has been notable for a few things of its own making. Their publicist, for instance, who was dragged out into the fray last week, witnessed the Houston concert only to remark that he'd seen it all – he's seen the opening of the Stones and the closing night of the Beatles, but he'd never witnessed anything like Houston....

American promoters have also informed the band that they've broken all the American box-office records for consistent audience attendance. And to cap it all a gentleman of the press got in such a froth during one review that his biblical bent got the better of him – culminating in a historic quote that: "And the rock gods came from on high." ...

April 7, 1972: Orlando Sports Stadium, Orlando, Florida.
April 8, 1972: Hollywood Sportatorium, Hollywood, Florida. In that morning's *Fort Lauderdale News*, entertainment editor Jack Zink warned his readers:

The Moody Blues, who four years ago began searching for "the lost chord" and are the rock musicians who seem to have found it, appear at the Hollywood Sportatorium tonight at 8. The concert is expected to be a sellout by this morning, with record-setting attendance figures in the offing. Absolutely no tickets will be sold at the gate, no one will be allowed onto the grounds without a ticket. ... Security is being beefed up for this occasion.

Doors open at 3 p.m. today, with a major traffic tie-up expected by 6 p.m. on West Hollywood Boulevard. The Sportatorium holds 15,000 people and is serviced by that single, two-lane highway. If you've got tickets, pack a lunchbox and leave early.

The group is one which has always seemed a step ahead of current trends in rock music. Part of the impression is due to the fact that the Moody Blues were taking their music seriously long before the charts had heard of people like Emerson, Lake and Palmer.

Although they have roots in acid rock along with many of today's acts, their approach has been less toward acoustical gymnastics than their contemporaries.... The liner notes of the *Lost Chord* album describe them as "the smallest symphony orchestra in the world." Nothing could be closer to the truth. ...

The notorious Sportatorium, outside Hollywood, Florida.
(Photo source: SouthFlorida.com)

Hal Speck of *Record Mirror*, still traveling with the Moodies, covered the event:

In many ways the last gig was the most memorable, although our first sight of the vast Miami Sportatorium situated 30 miles outside the city in the middle of the everglades where even the alligators are leaving home, was something of a shock.

The venue itself looked like an abandoned aircraft hangar – Mike perhaps summed it up better by referring to it as "that oversized air-raid shelter" – surrounded by barbed wire entanglements like some grotesque concentration camp.

This was to be the site of the largest rock concert gathering ever seen in Miami and its isolated position in some reflection of how paranoid the local populace are of such large gatherings. ...

That was the night they packed the auditorium that Zeppelin's manager Peter Grant was alleged to have said could never be packed after his group only managed to three quarters fill it last year. The Moodies collected a capacity 15,000 crowd with a further estimated 10,000 outside who could not get tickets! ...

After the concert, Jack Zink wrote for the *Fort Lauderdale News*:

The Moody Blues have succeeded in rock during the past few years with a musical style that borders on the mystic. The group has used the electronic capabilities of its instruments to set a mood of wonderment both in the concert hall and the recording studio. They repeated that formula Saturday night to more than 15,000 persons, many of whom had waited five hours for the show to start.

It took the group some time to catch the fire of the occasion, as several of the early numbers rang flatly against the cavernous walls of the Sportatorium. They had opened in a strong blues vein, a more up-tempo style which the group hasn't exploited much and in which they don't seem to be fully at home. They began to simmer with "Tuesday Afternoon," followed by an interlude punctuated with several sharp numbers. *Threshold of a Dream* thickened the atmosphere about halfway through the evening. From that point on, the audience simmered nicely.

Much of the acoustical handiwork comes by way of the Mellotron, played by Justin Hayward and Mike Pinder on alternate occasions. That, plus some unusual work on the acoustic guitar helps the group move into dimensions not regularly explored in rock music – or in any forms of music, for that matter. Add to these some of the deepest sounds ever to come from the bass guitar and you have what the Moody Blues are all about.

The crowd was estimated beforehand to be the largest ever to pack into the Sportatorium. …

A wire-story concerning the aftermath of this concert got as far as California's *The Van Nuys News*:

At the Moody Blues' final concert on its U.S. tour in Miami's Hollywood Sportatorium, 15,000 people crowded into a packed arena while the same number of people wandered around outside trying to get in.

Those on the outside reportedly created a 25-mile long traffic jam. …

Hal Speck capped the story, for his article in the April 22 edition of *Record Mirror*:

"GI-NORMOUS" is the only word to describe the Moody Blues' present status in America. … It is really only possible to ascertain just how big the Moodies now are in America by seeing them in concert on the road. That was the experience I shared on their recent U.S. tour which was, significantly enough, promoted by Jerry Weintraub (Presley's current coordinator). …

The Moodies have shattered every attendance and percentage record by a British group in America, having sold out every auditorium on a three week tour from Chicago [International Amphitheater] to Miami Sportatorium, which was the largest rock concert ever seen there. ...

That last night was topped off by a police escort from the gig with sirens going like *Hawaii Five-0* gone mad and an end of tour party at which the Moodies presented their thanks to their American on-the-road team in the shape of cameras, travelling cases and a computerized world clock to promoter Jerry Weintraub. ...

Perhaps the amiable young stage manager I talked to back stage at Miami put the verbal seal on the Moodies success when he said to me: "You know, some of the English groups who come over here can be real shits and their music just leaves you partially deaf, but these guys are different. What I like most about them is that their music may be high in the sky but their feet are on the ground."

How long I wonder before England realizes just how big a group the Moodies are and gives them the recognition they really deserve. Maybe the Empire Wembley Pool will serve to open a few more eyes on April 22 and their new single, "Isn't Life Strange," will establish things in a clearer perspective.

On April 19, *Variety* reported:

The Moody Blues grossed $920,000 in their 14-city U.S. tour, which wound up April 8 with a turnaway 15,000 crowd in the Hollywood (Fla.) Sportatorium. Promoter Jerry Weintraub of Management Three is booking another tour for the British group, which will begin in October.

Was Britain ready to acknowledge just how big a group the Moodies had become, as Hal Speck wondered?

In the April 29 issue of *Melody Maker*, Andrew Means reported:

From the biggest British group in America to the Empire Pool, Wembley. A gig that probably came as close to their American triumphs as the Moody Blues are likely to experience in this country. A giant venue and a group whose gigantic influence is frequently underestimated. ...

The show might have been lifted to new heights by the injection of fresh material. As it was, not even the group's new single, "Isn't Life Strange," got a plug.... If their material broke no new ground, the sound quality probably did. Almost alone in the world of electric music, the Moody Blues can make use of vast waves of volume without becoming painful to listen to. One could feel these currents rolling out and then dying away, each chord superseded by the next.

Penny Valentine was there, too, covering the return of the Moodies for *Sounds*. On the newsstands the same day as the Means' review, Valentine told her readers:

> They were back! And the Moody Blues entered like a team from the first division up the ramp onto the stage. Brought the packed crowd at Wembley's Empire Pool to their feet last Saturday night. …

> Like most bands, the Moody Blues respond musically much more powerfully when an audience is totally responsive, and you could feel this playback from the stage to auditorium on Saturday as they went through some of their most rewarding numbers. …

> Nearly two hours later the 10,000 strong audience were on their feet again – giving the Moodies an ear-shattering five minute ovation until they came back on for their final encore. …

> The audience reacted as only the Moodies audiences can – rising at the end as one huge entity to reward their heroes with a total heartfelt enthusiasm.

To learn all about the single and its album, read on.

19

Seventh Sojourn

U.K. album release: Threshold THS 7; October 23, 1972
U.S. album release: Threshold THS 7; November 17, 1972
U.S. peak position: #1
(Certified gold in the U.S.)
Canada: #1
(Certified platinum in Canada)
Australia: #2
U.K.: #5
Netherlands: #7
Norway: #10

Single release: *"Isn't Life Strange" b/w "After You Came"*
U.K.: Threshold TH 9; U.S: Threshold 45-THS-67009; April 21, 1972
France: #4
Canada: #9
U.K.: #13
U.S.: #20 (*Cashbox*)

Single release: *"I'm Just a Singer (In a Rock and Roll Band)" b/w "For My Lady"*
UK: Threshold TH 13; U.S.: Threshold 45-67012; January 19, 1973
France: #1
Holland: #4
U.S.: #8 (*Cashbox*)
Belgium: #13
U.K. #36

Any observer of the Moody Blues' personal and professional lives could sympathize with the title of "Isn't Life Strange," the preview track from their upcoming *Seventh Sojourn* album.

Many of their experiences while touring, especially in America, had become increasingly surreal. Attendance continued to swell, and each new album broke the sales record of the previous one. Yet, the bigger the Moodies became, the harsher their reception from some of those in the rock press. The over-the-top level of hostility from this very vocal minority was itself surreal. Some of these writers and reviewers were savaging any and all things that weren't "the next big thing" ... even when the critics' targets were the very artists they had championed a mere year or two earlier.

It had started with the near-brilliant *A Question of Balance*. After singing the praises of the Moodies for two and a half years, even comparing some of the Moody Blues' work with the Beatles, some of the critics acted as if the band had overstayed its welcome. Complaints included: the band's musical styles weren't evolving fast enough; they were too democratic in their song selections; and that only Justin Hayward should be allowed to write and sing. With *Every Good Boy Deserves Favour*, some of these critics were even attacking Hayward. One such reviewer said that one of Hayward's two contributions to the album – the moving "You Can Never Go Home" – was "the sort of song that people happy-doing-nothing-because-they-don't-need-to-do-anything write." While reviews of this type were in the minority, they would nonetheless be painful for any moderately sensitive artist.

It had to have been worse for the other Moodies, though, to hear from more than one reviewer that they were inferior to Hayward. The cruelest barbs had been directed at Mike Pinder, the biggest advocate among the band for concept albums and orchestral arrangements, and the most determined of the five Moodies to write and sing songs filled with hope, peace and love – the very topics some critics now mocked.

Even with the Moodies' soaring record sales and dramatically increased concert attendance – and with the majority of the press still in their court – the sheer nastiness of the naysayers had left some in the band shaken.

It was with these feelings of confusion and hurt that the Moodies came together in January 1972 to begin work on their latest album. The sessions took place in a home studio built by Mike Pinder inside a converted garage on his property, outside Cobham.

Justin Hayward: "It was a ludicrous situation; we could afford to record anywhere in the world, and there we were in our keyboard player's garage. We were so frightened of failure that we just tried to make ourselves smaller and smaller." (JH-SSCD08)

Three songs were attempted. Hayward had one song that he had written with the help of Graeme Edge, appropriately called "You and Me." Mike Pinder brought in a song about the darkness he had seen in some people, called "Lost in a Lost World." And John Lodge had a song that seemed to sum up everything everyone in the band must have been feeling: "Isn't Life Strange." As indicated by the absence of a question mark, this title was not asking a question but making a statement.

Instrumental tracks were laid down for Hayward's and Pinder's songs during these sessions. The only one of the three songs to be completed was Lodge's observations on the vagaries of existence.

Regarding the writing of the song, John Lodge told interviewer Mark Powell, "I was having dinner one night with some friends and heard the song in my head whilst I was eating. I went straight to the piano and, within 15 minutes, I'd got the outline of the song finished." (JL-SSCD08)

Talking with a writer for *Sounds* magazine in 1972, Lodge said, "We'd built the studio and went in to cut stuff for the new album. It was during the power cuts [as a result of a British coal miners' strike]. It was really a busy time – we'd had five days of the British tour, then the U.S. tour, then the Continent, and then Wembley Pool to do. So all we got done was this track." (JL-S72)

The original recording of "Isn't Life Strange" is actually in excess of eight minutes, and includes a two-minute instrumental passage, prominently featuring Ray Thomas's flute, Hayward's acoustic guitar work, and a masterful orchestral interlude composed and performed by Pinder on a Chamberlin (an instrument similar to the Mellotron).

Regarding the song, and pressure on the group to finish the track before departing for the States, Lodge recalled: "Justin and I went into the studio on Friday night to finish the vocals; we left the next morning for our U.S. tour and took the tape with us. We dropped it off in New York on Saturday, and it was released the following week while we were on tour. That was the speed of things in those days." (JL-OTR09)

To make the song suitable for single release, the two-minute instrumental portion was edited out.

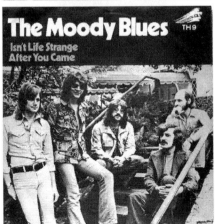

U.S. single release:
"Isn't Life Strange" b/w "After You Came"
Threshold/London 45-67009; April 21, 1972

U.K. single release:
"Isn't Life Strange" b/w "After You Came"
Threshold/Decca TH 9; April 21, 1972

With only one new song available for a single, "Strange" was coupled with "After You Came," from *Every Good Boy Deserves Favour*. Credited to Graeme Edge as writer and featuring Hayward, Lodge, Thomas, and Pinder on vocals, it had been one of the more heavily sampled songs by radio from the previous LP, prompting the decision to free it from the crossfading inherent on the album.

At the time of the record's release, Ray Thomas told *New Musical Express*, "I think it's a good single. It's value for [your] money." (RT-NME72)

The public agreed and the single quickly ascended the charts on both sides of the Atlantic,

THE MOODY BLUES
ISN'T LIFE STRANGE
AFTER YOU CAME

despite the 6:03 running time of the A-side.

John Lodge told *Sounds* magazine, "We weren't going to put anything out until September – when the album's due to be released – but we thought it would be a good idea to have a track that bridged that space in time. The singles' market is still an unknown entity to us, really, and I'm surprised we've broken it with a single that's over six minutes long." (JL-S72)

Well, not entirely an unknown entity, and not the first time they had broken the singles market with a longer-than-normal song. They had made the British Top 20 in early 1968 with a four-and-a-half-minute version of "Nights in White Satin," then again, in 1970, topped the charts with the five-minute-long "Question." Regardless, the six-minute "Isn't Life Strange" was their longest, perhaps strangest, single yet.

At the top of the *Billboard* singles chart during the week "Isn't Life Strange" was released was Roberta Flack's "The First Time I Ever Saw Your Face." Michael Jackson's "Rockin' Robin" was at No. 2, followed by Joe Tex's "I Gotcha," America's "A Horse with No Name," and the Dramatics' "In the Rain."

In Britain, "Amazing Grace," by the Royal Scots Dragoon Guards, was the chart leader, followed by Ringo Starr's "Back Off Boogaloo," Nilsson's "Without You," the Chiffon's "Sweet Talkin' Guy," and Vicky Leandros's "Come What May," respectively.

On April 19, 1972, *Variety* ranked "Isn't Life Strange" at No. 4 on its "Top Singles of the Week" picks, saying that the song "gives the British combo a pretty contemporary ballad which builds into potent impact."

Come April 22, the reviewer for *Sounds* wrote:

I have a bet on with the office that this will reach Number One in very few weeks. Against are two – both betting 10s if you're interested – plus one erstwhile staff member who thought it was the Bee Gees, so I don't count him. On a more serious note … this is one of those rare Moody tracks cut solely for the singles market. Written and sung by John Lodge, it opens with some rather disturbing "dying swan" violin work, and I must admit at the beginning the vocal does sound rather Bee Gees' oriented. It's

426

extremely gentle, rather mournful, and builds up with flute, guitar and Mellotron…. Very fine.

The single – objectionably long for American AM radio stations – had a good chart run, nonetheless. It peaked on *Billboard* on June 10, 1972, at No. 29. The other U.S. charts ranked it better, with *Cashbox* taking the A-side to No. 20, and *Record World* placing it at No. 23.

"Isn't Life Strange" peaked on the British radio charts at No. 19 on May 21, 1972. However, it continued selling steadily in shops and hit its peak in sales on June 10, at No. 13 (according to *Record & Tape Retailers*, reporting to U.S.-based *Billboard* magazine).

Recording the Album:

From the very beginning, events seemed to be working against *Seventh Sojourn* coming to be.

The first try, from those sessions in Pinder's garage during January 1972, hampered by the frequent power cuts, resulted in only one completed song, and one backing track to be utilized for a second song.

In February, the group stopped recording to embark on a European and British tour, which was cut short when John Lodge came down with the flu. After time taken for Lodge to recover, the Moodies were off to America for a spring tour (covered in the previous chapter). This spanned parts of March and April. Then the band returned to England to make up the dates which had been cancelled as a result of Lodge's earlier illness. It was June before work resumed on the album, this time in a proper facility – Decca studios in London – with a push to have it completed before the next tour commitment in the U.S., in the fall.

Ray Thomas: "By the time we began the sessions, I think we needed a break from each other. Up to that time, everywhere one of us went the others would be there too. All my experiences were *their* experiences. It was a strained and awkward period for us. Mike Pinder, particularly, found it difficult. We were all exhausted and had become prisoners of our own success." (RT-SSCD08)

Rolling Stone magazine hoped to get one of their writers into the sanctuary of the Moodies' recording studio, to witness the making of the group's seventh sojourn into the realms of album making. James Horwitz expressed his difficulty in getting behind the recording scenes:

> … [A]nyone who knows anything at all about the Moody Blues knows that they hate to come out from behind their record albums to do interviews and things like that, and the chances of getting all five of them together for anything public except playing their music is, well, practically impossible.

Talking to a different magazine (*Tambourine*), Edge said, "We never allow anyone else in the studio except for the band and our producer, Tony Clarke. We don't even allow an extra engineer there – it's such a close thing that it would be like allowing a guy in bed with you and your wife." (GE-T73)

Regardless, Horwitz did make it into the studio for a time. John Lodge told the *Rolling Stone* writer, "We decide we're going in on a particular day and then we just start talking about what we're going to do, like a discussion group." (JL-RS72)

Ray Thomas injected, "Group therapy. We write independently but we arrange the whole thing collectively." (RT-RS72)

Tony Clarke added, "It's like a confessional in the studio, with nobody there to upset, or whatever. It's almost an agony…. When any song is being recorded there are just six chairs in a darkened studio and a few guitars lying around, and whoever's turn it is bares his soul and looks 'round for help, and everyone helps, and we're off recording a song." (TC-RS72)

Graeme Edge told Horwitz: "We always start with one of Justin's songs; that's a superstition." (GE-RS72)

John Lodge said, "But we start by sitting around together, talking, trying to paint a picture of what the song's about. And after we've talked it through so everyone knows, we just get up and do it. But it's only from the discussions we find the direction. Nobody says the direction; it's just that our minds work together. …

"Most of the albums we've done have, like, a beginning and an end, but this one is like a discussion where we just sit down. There's no beginning or end; it's just a discussion that goes from subject to subject. That's why we called it *Seventh Sojourn*, because it's like a group of people just sitting down and talking together." (JL-RS72)

This was the second Moody Blues album to involve assistant engineer Dave Baker. He remained impressed with the professionalism of both the band and their producer, the "sixth Moody."

Dave Baker: "Tony Clarke was, I think, an exceptional producer. He got a lot from the band, and I would think they would have to be fairly grateful to him for extracting some of the performances. He's certainly one of the most patient and hard-working producers I've come across. Most of the ones I've seen were like roadies – very laid-back individuals. Tony was very much: 'We're going to get on with this and it's going to be a really good album.'" (DB-H&H96)

Going through the album in chronological order:

"Lost in a Lost Land" was written by and featured Mike Pinder on lead vocal. Pinder begins on a pessimistic note:

> *I woke up today, I was crying,*
> *Lost in a lost world,*
> *'Cos so many people are dying,*
> *Lost in a lost world.*
> *Some of them are living an illusion,*
> *bounded by the darkness of their minds.*
> *In their eyes it's nation against nation against nation.*
> *With racial pride, sad hearts they hide,*
> *Thinking only of themselves,*
> *They shun the light; They think they're right,*
> *living in their empty shells.*

Setting *Seventh Sojourn* apart from the previous six albums is Pinder's keyboard orchestration, sounding lighter, cleaner, gently bathing most of the tracks in a gentle string arrangement. This is actually not Pinder's familiar Mellotron, but a new instrument he acquired and mastered by this time.

Justin Hayward explained, "We'd found a great replacement for the Mellotron, an American instrument called the Chamberlin. It worked on the same principle as the Mellotron, but had much better quality sounds – great brass, strings, and cello, and so on. With a Mellotron you had to overdub and overlay it, adding echo to get it to sound nice. The Chamberlin was a louder instrument and had a much better sound quality." (JH-SSCD08)

The Chamberlin, as discussed in Chapter 1 of this book, was actually the father of the Mellotron. Streetly Electronics of Birmingham, England (aka Mellotronics) had taken the early prototype of the Chamberlin, imported from America in 1963, and made alterations. Mike Pinder, working for Streetly at that time, made further changes.

Meanwhile, Harry Chamberlin continued to tinker with his invention in the U.S., making improvements throughout the 1960s until coming up with the version Mike Pinder purchased, and promptly customized, which is so impressively displayed on *Seventh Sojourn*.

"New Horizons," as melancholy as it may sound, was actually a love letter from Hayward to his new wife, Marie, and the child they were expecting. "I've had dreams enough for one, and I've got love enough for three," he sings, referring to himself, wife Marie, and child on the way.

Their daughter, and, as it would turn out, only child, was born on December 3, 1972, less than a month after the release of *Seventh Sojourn*. Justin and Marie Hayward named their baby girl Doremi. The solfège music education system, popularized in *The Sound of Music*, uses "do, re, mi, fa, sol, la, ti" as a teaching tool.

While the lyrics to the song seem upbeat on paper, the blue mood of the melody and the song's arrangement continue as Hayward sings, "But I'm never gonna lose your precious gift, it will always be that way. And I know I'm gonna find my own peace of mind, someday, some way."

It's even more touching to reflect that Justin and Marie Hayward remain husband and wife as of this writing … in 2017. But the haunting, sad "feel" of the song prevails. Hayward later explained, "I have to write about things that move me, and 'New Horizons' really moved me. It was a very, very traumatic time in my life; very troubled. I'd lost someone; it was a very strong emotion and it went onto the record. Something must mean an awful lot to me before I write about it."

Hayward seemed to relive these feelings any time he performed the song. He said, "That meaning is contained in every performance that I give. Everyone can identify with it; that's a simple way of putting it." (JH-TRKS96)

There is a lovely musical signature in the song each time Hayward finishes singing "someday, some way," with Mike Pinder's Chamberlin proving especially effective. That lilting keyboard "riff" is one of the song's most enduring hooks. This remains one of Hayward's most beautiful songs.

"For My Lady" follows. In some ways, this is Ray Thomas's "New Horizons" – in theme as well as mood. In what may be his most beautiful and enduring song, Thomas sings: "My boat sails stormy seas / Battles oceans filled with tears / At last my port's in view / Now that I've discovered you / Oh I'd give my life so lightly / For my gentle lady / Give it freely and completely / To my lady."

As with "New Horizons," the melody and heartfelt vocal performance convey a sadness despite the positive nature of the lyrics.

"Isn't Life Strange" has been discussed. Unfortunately, time limitations on the vinyl LP prevented the presentation of the full eight-minute, 10-second version; the edited single was used instead. Seek out the remastered CD from 2008, which includes the longer version. You'll likely be moved by the two minutes of added beauty, Ray Thomas's lovely flute melody, and a truly inspired Chamberlin sequence by Mike Pinder.

"You and Me," a collaboration between Justin Hayward and Graeme Edge, is another one of those Moody Blues hit singles that never were. However, the song did find its way onto many radio station playlists in late 1972 and early '73 thanks to being easily accessible, as the first track on Side 2.

The multi-layered and highly melodic guitar passages by Hayward, opening the song and taking it into an extended play-out at the end, are as hook-laden as they are fluid, weaving in and out of the framework of the song.

Justin Hayward: "'You and Me' was one of three tracks recorded at Mike Pinder's studio in Cobham. It started off as a guitar riff that I wrote, which turned out to be a complete song. At both ends of the tune we used acoustic guitar, bass, drums, and a little Mellotron. I played two electric guitars on top of that, and played the riff in harmony." (JH-MM74)

This song marked the only contribution Graeme Edge made to *Seventh Sojourn* as a writer. Shortly after completing the album, he told *Sound*'s Penny Valentine, "I could have done more but … by the time it came to the recording session, all the writing I'd done didn't really stand up. Eighteen months ago I split from my wife and wrote some very bitter poems. For a year I was on my own and during that time I went back to the life I led before I was married. It was empty and juvenile and it left what might be called the intellect of my soul very lacking. Then I got a new lady who has given me a good calm base to operate from. When the album was being made I'd mellowed right out – and those earlier words would have just seemed so much bullshit." (GE-S72)

But these words, written in collaboration with Hayward, work fine. The lyric fits with the message that opened the album, in Pinder's "Lost in a Lost World," and which closes the LP, Lodge's "I'm Just a Singer (In a Rock and Roll Band)." Taking the lead from Pinder, with his plea to all the lost people to find solace in love, (Pinder also sang, "Come on my friends, we've got to bend / On our knees and say a prayer"), Hayward now sings, "We look around in wonder / At the work that has been done / By the vision of our father / Touched by his loving son."

These words were likely written by Hayward, the devoted Christian. Hayward and Edge come together as the singer tells the "so many people" of Pinder's "lost world": "What will be our last thought / Do you think it's coming soon / Will it be of comfort / Or the pain of a burning world?"

More poetry from Edge, shaped and put to music by Hayward, seems directed toward the Moody Blues' fans, as seen from the band's vantage point on the concert stage. "You're an ocean full of faces / And you know that we believe / We're just a wave that drifts around you / Singing all our hopes and dreams."

Even with this uptempo number, the melancholy that permeates *Seventh Sojourn* remains, although less apparent here than elsewhere. Hayward said, "I still find that album quite painful to listen to, to be honest with you – not because the material isn't good, but because it has so many uncomfortable memories for me of tension in the studio. In fact, I think the song 'You and Me' was about the only song which didn't have that tension with it, probably because that song was a collaborative effort between myself and Graeme, so it didn't 'belong' to anyone in the way of being my song, or John's song, or Ray's song, or what have you. There was a lot of 'alpha male' behavior coming into the picture at that time, and it was difficult…. [But] it was a strong album on its own merits – it's beautifully recorded, back with Derek Varnals again, and there are some really good songs on there. Unfortunately, for me, it's just a little too painful with the associated memories that it conjures up." (JH-RS13)

"The Land of Make Believe" was written by Justin Hayward. From a musical standpoint, it has much in common with "Are You Sitting Comfortably?" Lyrically, it hints at the earlier song as well. Still, these words are very much at home on *Seventh Sojourn* and this strange time in the Moodies' lives. Hayward sings, "We're living in a land of make-believe / and trying not to let it show / Maybe in the land of make-believe / Heartaches can turn to joy. We're breathing in the smoke of high and low / We're taking up a lot of room / Somewhere in the dark and silent night / Our prayer will be heard, make it soon."

"When You're a Free Man" seems in some ways Mike Pinder's sequel to Ray Thomas's "Legend of a Mind." More so, it's a love letter to a friend.

Timothy Leary had been arrested on drug charges more than once and, at this time, facing a lengthy prison sentence in the U.S., he fled the country. Whenever Leary came out of hiding in some foreign land, Richard Nixon's White House stepped up efforts to have him extricated to the United States.

Pinder wrote: "Time quickly passes by / If only we could talk again / Someday I hope I'll see you smiling / When you're a free man again. High on a mountainside / We laughed and talked of things to come / Someday I know I'll see you shining / When we're all free men again. / You left your country / For peace of mind / And something tells me / You're doing alright. …"

Pinder even sent a hello to Leary's wife, Rosemary in his lyric.

It wouldn't work out so well for Leary and Rosemary. Various times in jail, and life on the run, had taken a toll on the marriage. The couple divorced before the end of 1972. The long arm of Richard Nixon also caught up with Leary, and he was returned to the United States, incarcerated in California's Folsom Prison. California Governor Jerry Brown – the yin to Nixon's yang – had Leary's sentence reduced, and the famed drug guru was released from prison in 1976.

While the lyric is not one of Pinder's more subtle, the tune, vocal performances, and overall production are lush and appropriately calming – the melancholy of *Seventh Sojourn* is present even here.

"I'm Just a Singer (In a Rock and Roll Band)" was no more shrouded in lyrical mystery than "When You're a Free Man." All of the Moodies had made comments to the press about their discomfort when people misinterpreted their lyrics and elevated them to the position of rock soothsayers. (We hope this book isn't a modern example.)

John Lodge wrote the song. Despite a fast tempo, and the locomotive beat of Graeme Edge's drums, "I'm Just a Singer" also has a profound sadness to it.

John Lodge: "It really was part of *Seventh Sojourn*; part of us starting out as just five people. People were giving us attributes we didn't have – 'You *do* have all the answers to the world' – and we were in our mid-20s! We had to say, 'We're just singers in a rock and roll band…. Just look at the questions for yourself and try to figure it out." (JL-OTR09)

"I'm Just a Singer" combined with "Lost in a Lost World" bookends the album's central theme, with "Isn't Life Strange" and "You and Me" anchoring the middle. Here, Lodge and his fellow Moodies sing, "How can we understand / Riots by the people, for the people, who are trying to destroy themselves / And when you see a frightened person / who is frightened by the people / who are scorching this earth."

Ray Thomas contributes saxophone to the recording. He said, "For my money, you can't beat natural sounds. I've been using baritone sax. I played it on 'Rock and Roll Band.' It was an old silver thing that had obviously been on stage with Eddie Cochran!" (RT-NMA74)

"I'm Just a Singer" brings the album to a close, as Graeme Edge's drumming slows, then comes to a stop amid the dubbed-in applause and whistles of the band members.

John Lodge: "I really like the album, actually; it's one of my favorites to this day. What I particularly liked about it was its honesty, because we'd had so much stuff getting out of control from people who were asking us things, almost expecting us to have the meaning of life or whatever, and that's where my song 'I'm Just a Singer (In a Rock and Roll Band)' came from, because at the end of the day that's what I was. I don't have the answers; I'm not going to fly you away in some spaceship to escape the cares of the world. At the end of the day, I'm just the guy who likes playing rock and roll." (JL-RS13)

***

The Moodies worked on *Seventh Sojourn* right into September, when they had to prepare for their next tour of the U.S.

John Lodge told Tony Newman of *Music Scene* magazine, for its November 1972 issue, "It took us seven weeks. I'd usually leave [Cobham] around two in the afternoon and get back around five the following morning. So, what's that, about 15 hours a day? Of course, we weren't working all that time. One of the problems with living here in this neck of the woods is that it takes a while to get to the recording studio in London.

"I hate driving up to town. You get caught in all the traffic jams and I think it's fair to say that by the time you arrive a bit of your creative spirit has been worked away! So, we just sit around and chat and relax for a while. Then, when we're in the right sort of mood, we get down to work." (JL-MS72)

The accumulation of work was also taking a toll.

Ray Thomas: "If you want to tot up how many songs we've recorded with this lineup and include albums and singles, it comes to about a hundred songs. It's got to get more difficult because you don't want to repeat yourselves.

"*Seventh Sojourn* took two months, but then *Sgt. Pepper* took nine months and the Beach Boys spent two years on *Heroes and Villains* and still had to scrap it. The longer you go on, the more difficult it's got to become." (RT-MSA74)

Justin Hayward: "The album took a long time to make and I found it a painful experience. It became obvious to me that the five of us wouldn't make another album. We didn't argue, it was just an unhappy time." (JH-SSCD08)

Despite the struggle, and the remarkably unwarranted hostility soon to be heard from some critics, *Seventh Sojourn* is among many Moody Blues fans' favorite albums. This author's, as well. Both of Pinder's contributions are sublime (even though a bad mix buried the vocal – and therefore many of the words – in "Lost in a Lost World"). All three of Hayward's songs are a joy – albeit one is a sad joy. To these ears, "For My Lady" is the most lovely song Ray Thomas has written, and among his finest vocal deliveries. And John Lodge hit a pair of home runs with his two entries. Beyond the eight well-crafted and inspired songs, the performances and production are impeccable. All the instrumentation is inspired, but Pinder's work on the Chamberlin gives *Seventh Sojourn* a unique sound and casts a spell over many a listener. From the haunting strings of "New Horizons" to the gypsy violin touch added to "I'm Just a Singer," to a bonus of the instrumental passage in the long-version of "Isn't Life Strange" (finally made available on the 2008 CD reissue), this album brings us one treasure after another, all the more glistening with their digital remastering.

Decades after the original release, Edge told Mark Powell, "At the time of recording *Seventh Sojourn* it was my least favorite album. But years later, after coming to it with fresh ears and away from all the pressures of that time, I realized that it was really rather good!" (GE-SSCD08)

While the album represented a difficult time for the band, none of the Moodies had lost affection for one another. Shortly after the completion of the album, and, as they were beginning their fall 1972 American tour, Ray Thomas told Tony Stewart of *New Musical Express*: "I love them. I think they're the greatest.... They're the nearest thing to me that I'll ever come across.... I understand them. And they understand me, which *is* very important." (RT-NME72)

Also interviewed by Norman, this time for *Music Scene*, John Lodge said, "It really is just a nice circle of friendship. Like on Sunday, it was my son's christening, so everyone was round here. This week Ray's moving house, so a couple of the boys are round there helping him out. I'll probably drive his car over to the new place for him this afternoon. And, really, it's all down to that sort of thing.

"We don't think it's anything fantastic; it's just the way we are. But I'm glad we don't have the personality clashes that some groups have to put up with. We just help each other out when we can and it's nice to know you've got people around who you can really rely on." (JL-MS72)

Surprise hit:
"Nights in White Satin" / "Cities"
May through December 1972

There is a reason why *Seventh Sojourn* was released a month later in the U.S. than in Britain and Europe. It had to do with the unexpected return of "Night's in White Satin" and *Days of Future Passed* to the American charts. With a five-year-old song on the radio, and hundreds of thousands of customers across the nation purchasing its equally old album, the decision was made by London Records to delay *Sojourn* in America.

In England, the music press was attempting to make sense of his resurgence in America. Doug Jones explained in the November 4, 1972 issue of *New Musical Express*:

> … This particular musical snowball was initially rolled last May by an influential DJ called Robin Mitchell in Seattle, who resurrected the album on his station KOL and started a chain reaction through the United States, resulting in sales of 1 ½ million for the album, and over a million on the single.

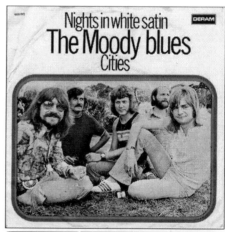

Mitchell's action on KOL in Seattle – the same station where Pat O'Day of Concerts West worked – was taken up by neighboring radio markets. By June, it was the album version that most of these stations were playing, all six-and-a-half minutes of it. The 45, last pressed in April 1968, wasn't easy to come across, therefore, in late July, a new pressing of the single was ordered by London Records and rushed into record stores coast to coast.

The demand had been there for a few months prior to July. Justin Hayward told Mary Campbell of the Associated Press, "We didn't rerelease it; it had never been taken off release. But we had just put out a single, 'Isn't Life Strange,' and we were afraid it would jeopardize that. So we didn't ship 'Nights in White Satin' to shops until after that went off the charts."
(JH-CGD72)

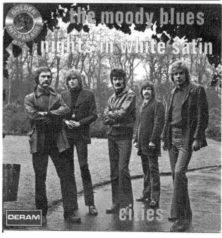

The Top Five songs in the *Billboard* singles' chart for the first week of August, 1972 were Gilbert O'Sullivan's "Alone Again (Naturally)," at No. 1, followed by, respectively, "Brandy (You're A Fine Girl)," from Looking Glass; "If Loving You Is Wrong, I Don't Want to Be Right," by Luther Ingram; "Daddy, Don't You Walk So Fast," by Wayne Newton; and "Too Late to Turn Back Now," by the Cornelius Brothers & Sister Rose.

In the August 4, 1972 issue of *Variety*, the trade listed "Nights" as its second pick for the top release of the week, following "Black & White" by Three Dog Night" (which, incidentally, would go to No. 1).

One of the first Top 40 stations to add "Nights" to its rotation playlist was WDRC in Hartford, Connecticut, making the station's Top 30 survey (at No. 29) for the week ending August 4, 1972. One week later, the song had moved up to No. 22.

On August 19, *Billboard* picked "Nights" as one of the four "breaking" songs showing the most "Hot Chart Action." This placed the Moody Blues' five-year-old single in the company of "Hold Your Head Up," by Argent; "Play Me," by Neil Diamond; and "Honky Cat," from Elton John. The trade said:

> … Formerly on their *Days of Future Passed* LP, cut has made a giant chart move in two weeks with additions in Top 40 radio showing in Kansas City, Syracuse (WNDR) joining Indianapolis, Hartford, and Minneapolis who started it three weeks ago. Dealer sales activity reflected in 13 of the 21 markets checked.

The station in Hartford, Connecticut, was WDRC, "The Big 'D' in Sound Survey." On August 21, it put "Nights" in its Top 20 at No. 12.

On August 26, over at WMBG, in Newport News, Virginia, "Nights" jumped from No. 40 to 29.

Two days later, "The Big 'D'" in Hartford advanced the song to No. 8.

On September 7, KHJ Boss-Radio, in Los Angeles, responded to listeners' requests despite the song's long running time, giving the disc Top 10 status, at No. 8.

Four days later, in West Palm Beach, Florida, WIRK, which operated both a stereo FM channel and an AM station, had "Nights" at No. 11.

On September 16, radio station WAMS, in Wilmington, Delaware, took "Nights" from No. 7 to 2 on its "Super Hit Survey." On this day, the song had just gotten into *Billboard* magazine's national chart, at No. 20.

One day later, KISD, in Sioux Falls, South Dakota, showed "Nights" jumping up its "More Music Survey" from No. 11 to 4.

That same day, WIRK, in West Palm Beach, Florida, raised "Nights" from No. 11 to the top, becoming the new No. 1 hit in town on both its AM and FM outlets.

Back in L.A., the listeners of KHJ Boss-Radio pushed the song from No. 8 to 3.

One day later, back at WAMS, in Wilmington, Delaware, the song made the final move from second place to No. 1.

Two days later, KISD, in Sioux Falls, South Dakota, jumped the song from No. 4 to second spot, bested only by Three Dog Night's "Black and White."

That same day, in Rochester, New York, "Nights" made the Top 10 survey on WSAY, at No. 9.

In Buffalo, New York, on radio station WKBW, "Nights" moved up to No. 4. And it was holding at No. 1 for a second week at WAMS, in Wilmington, Delaware.

By the start of October, the song was Top 10 at WPIX-FM, in New York City.

Meanwhile, the surprise success of the "Nights" single rekindled interest in *Days of Future Passed*. Although rarely absent from *Billboard*'s album chart since 1968, the album was shooting upwards, making the Top 20 on October 7 (at No. 14).

By October 11, with "Nights" just outside the Top 10 in *Billboard* (at No. 12) and one notch higher on *Cashbox*, it topped the charts in Philadelphia (on WFIL), Buffalo (on WKBW), and in Peoria, Illinois (on WIRL).

By the 14th of October, *Days of Future Passed* was No. 7 on *Billboard* and No. 13 on *Cashbox*.

This situation was so unprecedented that news had rippled across the Atlantic. In the October 21 issue of *New Musical Express*, following the headline "Moodie Mania in U.S. Over 1967 Recordings":

> The Moody Blues have suddenly and unexpectedly been swept to a new peak of acclaim in the United States, on the strength of their first album, *Days of Future Passed*, and their single, "Nights in White Satin," initially released five years ago. Both are now in the Top Ten of the respective U.S. album and singles charts, and are challenging strongly the No. 1 positions. And there has been unprecedented reaction to the news of their latest American tour, beginning this weekend and running until November 4.
>
> Their opening venue on Saturday at Hampton Roads Coliseum is a complete sell-out, as is their double concert next Monday at New York's vast Madison Square Garden – which sold out two 35,000 capacity houses within five hours of the box office opening. The 18,000-seater Los Angeles Forum (November 1) cleared tickets in 3 ½ hours, but the fastest sale was at Boston Gardens (for next Wednesday) where 19,000 tickets were sold in 90 minutes. ...

At this time, Ray Thomas told a writer from *Rolling Stone*, "[T]he success of *Future* and 'Nights in White Satin' now, I don't know why that's happened. In a million years I couldn't explain that. I thought it was good at the time and I was disappointed it didn't do so well [in America]... but, I mean, why has that happened now? It's rocketing up there. It's Number Four and the album is Number Five!" (RT-RS72)

A writer for the *North Country Catholic* newspaper commented, "It's a sign of the times that the Moody Blues' 1967 hit song, 'Nights in White Satin,' has returned to the Top Ten charts." To this critic, the "good old days" of pop music were a mere five years ago:

> "Nights in White Satin" is a song from an album that deserves to be on everyone's record shelf. It's a record of firsts. It was one of the first records in the rock field ever to combine rock music with classical music. It was one of the first records to use a symphony orchestra along with rock instruments. In other words, it was the forerunner of an important trend in rock music that culminated in

albums such as *Jesus Christ – Superstar. Days of Future Passed* was also one of the first theme albums. …

The song comes at the very end of a very important album. The album's theme can be considered a story in the life of a man. "Nights in White Satin" is the description of night time. The night of the soul, if you like.

Combined with the music, the song's lyrics raised vivid images – the cold hearted moon, casting only colorless shadows; the loneliness and isolation of man; the difficulty in understanding other's feelings, emotions, thoughts; the uncertainly about right and wrong; the frustrations brought about by dreams unrealized, things left undone; the joy of being young, and the fear of growing old.

And through it all, somehow coloring everything even in this colorless world, the love that man admits to, the love for another person.

There is much sadness here, tempered by the realization that man is not completely alone, that he needs not be always alone. If he loves, he shares. If he shares, he can in the end be what he wants to be. …

On October 21, *Billboard* advanced "Nights in White Satin" to No. 5 on its "Hot 100" singles' chart. At *Cashbox*, it was No. 7. *Days of Future Passed* was No. 9 on *Cashbox*, and had jumped to No. 3 on *Billboard*.

October 21 was also the day the Moody Blues began their latest U.S. tour.

The set list for this outing was, in most performances: "The Story in Your Eyes" (Hayward on lead vocal); "Tortoise and the Hare" (Lodge, leading the others); "How Is It (We Are Here)" (Pinder); "Tuesday Afternoon" (Hayward on lead); "Our Guessing Game" (Thomas on lead); "When You're a Free Man" (Pinder on lead); "Land of Make-Believe" (Hayward); "I'm Just a Singer (In a Rock and Roll Band)" (Lodge with Hayward and Thomas); "After You Came" (group effort on vocals); "One More Time to Live" (Lodge); "Melancholy Man" (Pinder); "Are You Sitting Comfortably?" (Hayward); "The Dream" / "Have You Heard, Part 1" / "The Voice" / "Have You Heard, Part 2" (Pinder); "Nights in White Satin" (Hayward); "Legend of a Mind" (Thomas); "Question" (Hayward); and "Ride My See-Saw" (Lodge and the others). Note that the set list included several songs from the *Seventh Sojourn* album, even though it had not yet been issued in the States … but not the one song from the album which was currently in release, as a single: "Isn't Life Strange."

The opening acts were Albert Hammond, who had a fast-rising hit with "It Never Rains in Southern California"; and Dianne Davidson, described by one newspaper as a purveyor of "cosmic country" music. Davidson's current single, "Delta Dawn," became a No. 1 hit for Helen Reddy a year later.

For a fall 1972 issue of *Circus* magazine, Ward Beaverman wrote of the events that preceded the start of the tour.

... It's late September and [Peter Jackson] has just arrived in the States to finalize arrangements for the Moodies' historic October and November U.S. tour. As he leans back and tries to pull his thoughts together, the phone on the large wooden desk in front of him rings constantly – newspaper editors are requesting tickets for concerts which had sold out weeks in advance. One editor of a large daily newspaper, after hearing about the ticket situation, mumbled, "I see …," and then asked, "But tell me, who *are* the Moody Blues?"

Despite twenty million LP's, a new album that turned platinum [with advance orders] a month before it came out, an L.A. Forum concert that sold out in less than an hour, and a record that miraculously zoomed into the Top 20 a full five years after it first came out, the Moodies' traditional lack of interest in publicity has left them an unknown name outside the rock scene. As the song says, "Isn't life stray-yay-yange…" …

As many a frustrated writer can tell you, the Moody Blues are just plain weird when it comes down to doing interviews. Having found in the past that they were expected to answer questions they would prefer to avoid (on subjects like politics and religion, for example), now, except in cases of dire emergency, they shy away from the press altogether. As Gerry Hoff puts it, "Everything they have to say, they've said in their music. It's all there in the albums." …

Saturday, October 21, 1972: Hampton Roads Coliseum, Hampton Roads, Virginia. Attendance was at capacity – more than 11,000. Linda Cooley covered the concert for Newport Beach's the *Daily Press*:

> … Despite the poor sound balance for those in some parts of the coliseum, the Moodies came across to the vast expanse of fans without the usual rock and roll strutting and fluttering. It was as if the crowd had the words memorized anyway, so it was only the group's penetrating presence that mattered.
>
> Composed of five highly-talented British musicians who have been together for more than six years, the Moodies come on like a group that's got it made and knows it – A group that doesn't have to depend on adolescent amplifier feedback to get wooly heads moving.
>
> Only a couple of numbers performed, including "Just a Singer (In a Rock and Roll Band)," were regular rock and roll type instruments, something the group is not known for. Perhaps what makes the Moodies so unique is the use of the "Mellotron," an electronic instrument that produces swelling lush tones that make you think the Boston Symphony is playing back-up. Mike Pinder

is undisputed master of the Mellotron. He was the first to use it, and, for many years, the only one.

For those who paid to get in, plus about 30 who crashed the front doors, according to Hampton police, the numbers that drew a good share of applause were those who have gotten Top 40 radio air play, including "Tuesday Afternoon" and "Nights in White Satin." Also included in their two-hour long performance were two numbers from their new and seventh album to be released this week, *Seventh Sojourn*.

If there were any doubts as to the enduring quality of the Moody Blues material, they would have been dispelled by audience reaction. …

It had been a long way from their adolescent "Go Now" phase. They had made it in America again, this time grown-up.

Seventh Sojourn would not make it out "this week," as Cooley had reported … unless one were willing to travel to England to pick up a copy.

Sunday, October 22: Civic Center, Baltimore, Maryland. Ray Thomas told a writer for *New Musical Express*, "In Baltimore we had a bomb scare back stage and the cops made us all stand perfectly still for a couple of minutes while a guy with earphones clamped to his head ripped a black briefcase to shreds only to find a set of maintenance tools. Shows how sick it's getting over here. Someone finds a heavy bag backstage that shouldn't be there and immediately leaps to the conclusion it's a bomb." (RT-NME72)

Monday, October 23: Madison Square Garden, New York. *New Musical Express* had Doug Jones tagging along with the band. As an Earthman landing on an alien world might make curious observations about the strange sights and creatures about, it seemed that Jones was trying to explain to the readers back in England just who and what these American fans of the Moody Blues were.

… Their audience varies between [age] six and 60 with the majority in their late teens and early twenties, and seems to appeal to all races, creeds and color. Even the normally taciturn Madison Square Gardens' security squads were attentive, and refrained from stuffing their ears with the conventional cotton wool reserved for most rock groups. …

"Melodic Rock" sounds like a contradiction in terms until you hear that contemporary paradox, the Moody Blues. I watched them last week prove their point to shattering effect before 50,000 people during two houses at New York's massive Madison Square Garden, where the Moodies won standing ovations on both shows.

Be-stetsoned promoter Gerry [sic] Weintraub was ecstatic over their reception and the fact that the group sold out their two shows in less than five hours. In fact, there had been sufficient response for them to have filled the Gardens yet again that day if they had had the time.

Jerry Weintraub told Jones, "Presley can do it on the strength of his sex appeal and Jagger with his showmanship, but the Moody Blues are the only group in the world who can do it purely on the basis of their music – the kind of music you will probably still be buying in 50 years' time. Within two years we should be able to equal anything the Beatles ever did on tour." (JW-NME72)

"Kirb" covered the Madison Square Garden concert for *Variety*:

> … The British super group, who sold out the skedded evening performance so quickly promoter Jerry Weintraub added an afternoon Veterans Day show, which also went clean. The double bill grossed $264,000 at a $7.50 top.
>
> An excellent sound system proved invaluable as the many musical subtleties of this quintet came over. … The vocals of lead guitarist Justin Hayward were among the big plusses as his "Nights in White Satin," revived as a current click, gained one of the longest of ovations. But its predecessor, a medley from *On the Threshold of a Dream*, beginning with a recitation by Mike Pinder over his Mellotron, [demonstrated] a key to the Moody's sound. The instrumental work was a beauty as Pinder was joined by flutist Ray Thomas, Hayward, bass guitarist John Lodge, and drummer Graeme Edge. …

Don Heckman was also there, covering the event for *The New York Times*. He opined:

> What happens when the Moody Blues, the ultimate apostles of sound as substance, of medium rather than message, appear at Madison Square Garden? For the jam-packed audiences at Monday's two concerts, the answer was instant Nirvana. …
>
> Because that, in effect, is what the Moodys are all about: they are virtually identity-less as individuals, sacrificing all for the group music consciousness to create a music whose lyrics and sounds tell us that the everyday hassles are meaningless, that what really matters is the Karma of some sort of vaguely mystical togetherness.
>
> Out-of-date acid-head music? In some ways, perhaps, except that the Moody Blues have always followed a slightly separate, if parallel, path from that of the usual hard rock, acid groups. The wash of sound they produced, strongly influenced by the sound of the Mellotron, is downer music – music intended not for physicality but for inner psyche inspection. …

Also at the Garden party was Nancy Erlich, for *Billboard*:

440

Reports have it that the Moody Blues' afternoon concert at Madison Square Garden was as engrossing and dynamic a show as we're used to seeing from this established, professional group. By the evening, however, it seemed that the Moodies have sojourned one too many sojourns. It was a bored, tired and uncharacteristically sloppy group that churned out their act for the cheering throngs.

Sure, it's a grueling tour schedule and stadiums are hard places to play and it's rather a drag to play the same material for five years; but didn't the Moodies create all those conditions yesterday for themselves.

Yes, the group can have a bad night, but nobody seemed to put much energy into trying to make it work.

Regarding this type of criticism, Graeme Edge said, "Unfortunately, we have a problem, we have nobody with stage presence. We perform like old time artists, we play a number, and say, 'Thank you.' We haven't got anyone who can lay all kinds of rubbish on an audience. I'd often like to speak, but it's hard to reach the mike [from behind the drums]. I think we're basically shy." (GE-MM71)

Elsewhere, Edge said, "We're a bunch of corpses on stage. We stand and fall by the notes we play. I think that's the problem a lot of people have with us. We haven't got a leader, no sex symbol, we're *not* that revolutionary, *not* that established, *not* that pop, *not* that far out. Which leaves us slap bang in the middle of the road – and yet we're not a middle of the road group. So, really, we don't belong anywhere." (GE-S73)

Associated Press correspondent Mary Campbell visited with the Moodies after the concert. For a widely syndicated AP wire-story, she wrote:

The Moody Blues gave two concerts in one day in New York's 20,000-seat Madison Square Garden. We went back to the dressing room after the first one and found a few friends with the group, but no groupies, and a very relaxed, friendly atmosphere.

How, we asked Justin Hayward, can you be so relaxed? Isn't there a lot of tension at the top – the last six albums have been gold and *Seventh Sojourn* has an early November release on Threshold Records. ... Also, the single "Nights in White Satin" hit No. 1 on the best-selling chart on Oct. 28. ...

Hayward told Campbell, "It isn't tense for us. There hasn't been any hype to get us where we are. People just play our records. There hasn't been much in the way of advertisements or promotions or interviews. We're pretty quiet as people. We just like to lead our own lives, and go perform. We're our only real close friends – each other and our wives and girlfriends and mums and dads. It is a big family." (JH-CGD72)

Tuesday, October 24: The Spectrum, Philadelphia, Pennsylvania. Jack Lloyd, covering the concert for *The Philadelphia Inquirer*, reported that 2,000 additional seats had been added to the Spectrum, making it possible for the Moodies to break the attendance records from their previous visit.

> The Moodys lured 19,000 fans – and the seats were sold out in one and a half days six weeks ago. … The figure is not only a new Spectrum record, but a new indoor record for the entire state. …

> Unfortunately, though, the concert did not warrant such a prestigious greeting. Without first-rate sound, the Moodys are in serious trouble. The sound – built around an incredible arsenal of instrumental depth and a device known as the Mellotron – is everything, the element that makes the Moody Blues unique. And on Tuesday night, the sound was simply off, deadening much of the luster that one expects from this durable group from Birmingham, England.

Although lamenting bad acoustics in the Spectrum, Lloyd was nonetheless aware of the scope of the presentation, and how, for good or bad, "the Moodies are capable of unloading just about any instrument ever created."

> … More remarkable than the music itself is the fact that the Moody Blues began performing this brand of rock five years ago when every other British group worth its weight in long hair was tearing things up with straight hard rock.

> There's hardly any doubt that the Moody Blues take their music seriously. Heck, back in 1967 the group even recorded with a symphony orchestra. And it was this experience which obviously set the tone for the Moody's future direction.

> This approach has withstood the test of time. Records turned out back then, such as "Nights in White Satin," are becoming hits for the second time.

Hugh Cutler, covering the same concert for Wilmington, Delaware's *The Morning News*, didn't seem to have any issues with the sound. Perhaps he had better seats. Here's what he heard … and saw:

> The Moody Blues' annual extravaganza in the City of Brotherly Love is a fitting forum for these five limey lads who boast a "universal conforming spirit" behind each of their album tracks, though individually written, because "we are so close that we have always thought alike on most subjects."

> "Alike" is an understatement. The work of the present band – three members go back to 1965, the days of their single, "Go Now," among the best in the first post-Beatles British rock invasion; guitarist Hayward and bassist John Lodge joined in 1967 – is overwhelming in its unity of tone and purpose. …

442

After "Melancholy Man" from the *Question* album, flutist Ray Thomas introduces "three movements or bits" from the *Threshold* LP: "Are You Sitting Comfortably?," which he co-wrote with Hayward; "The Dream," a recitation written by Edge but narrated by Pinder (which gets an ovation); and Pinder's own trilogy: "Have You Heard? (parts 1 and 2)" with "The Voyage" (instrumental) sandwiched between. The totally sold-out Spectrum house goes into rapture at the close. …

Pinder intones, dirge-like yet underlain with optimism, that he's a "melancholy man … all the world astounds me and I think I understand that we're going to keep growing; wait and see." His Mellotron, vaguely akin to an organ but substituting electronic recording tapes for pipes, builds a wave behind him like a heavy tuba section in a slow processional. Justin Hayward's careful, lyrical acoustic-like lines on an electric guitar are swallowed in the crescendo. …

Then the 11th song of the eve, "Nights in White Satin" from the *Days* LP, draws a sustained applause at its first few notes as Hayward, looking like a blond angelic groupie-gatherer, reels back on each chorus for an extended echo-wail aimed at the rafters: "Ohh, how I lovvvveeee youuuuu!" … Pinder may be the wizard of the Mellotron's orchestration, but Hayward steals higher honors as lyricist, as flash guitarist who still knows impeccable taste, and as one of rock's two or three finest vocalists. …

Doug Jones, of *New Musical Express*, continued his behind-the-scenes report:

The concert that night at the Spectrum was not a good one by the group's own standards. There were too many niggling problems with the P.A. and sound system in an auditorium. … The sound was messy, despite which the Moodies gave a professional performance and were again recipients of a standing ovation which lasted some ten minutes.

It was a different scene backstage…. "That was enough to drive you to drink," said Graeme Edge, suiting action to words and reaching for the brandy bottle.

[Live audio sound supervisor] Gene Clair comes into the room shaking his head apologetically. "You know what happened in 'Nights in White Satin' when the whole thing went dead," he says angrily. "The cop tripped over the lead and pulled it out of my mixer – the sonofabitch was supposed to be guarding it so no one would get near it. I almost strangled him!"

Like a football team who have won only by the odd goal, they go over their program and iron out the technical hitches. Mike Pinder points out his microphone is falling to bits and a new one is ordered. Gene discovers what was going wrong for them on stage and goes away determined to see it will not happen again. None of this was really as serious as it sounds, but the Moodies, like any good group, are only happy with perfection.

Michael Pinder   Graeme Edge   Ray Thomas   Justin Hayward   John Lodge

The Moody Blues

LONDON
RECORDS & TAPES

With "I'm Just a Singer (In a Rock and Roll Band)" in the set list, Ray Thomas added saxophone to the instruments he played during the tour.

Wednesday, October 25: Boston Garden, Boston, Massachusetts. Doug Jones continued his report, telling how the Moodies were an anomaly when it came to the behavior expected from most rock bands on tour. From his observations, the group seldom if ever went out "clubbing," or, for that matter, even ventured out of the hotel rooms at night. Ray Thomas's idea of a high time was to watch an old Humphrey Bogart movie on TV when he could find one. John Lodge's favorite pastime appeared to be playing ping pong with tour manager Pete Jackson … when a table-tennis setup was offered by the hotel. There were no "groupie scenes," no fights over the best rooms, and, most surprisingly, no damage to the rooms.

The group's American tour coordinator, Danny Fiala, told Jones he was accustomed to having to pick up the pieces when babysitting rock bands on tour. He said, "I couldn't believe it when I first worked for [the Moodies]. I went down to the hotel desk after the first day… to pay off the usual damages and breakages, plus extra charges. When [the desk clerk] told me there were none, I almost fell through the lobby. In fact, they told me there was a rebate on some rooms because [the Moodies] had doubled up. Then I went to wake them up and there they were in the coffee shop, packed and ready to go – they'd been up for two hours, fishing!" (DF-NME72)

Friday, October 27: Missouri Arena, St. Louis, Missouri. Dick Richmond of the *St. Louis Post-Dispatch* was there. He relayed the experience in the newspaper the following day:

> Almost 20,000 persons jammed into 'The Arena' Friday night to see the Moody Blues compete with the acoustics. The Moody Blues won.
>
> Often one rock group will sound pretty much like another. What sets the Moody Blues apart from the others is the flute of Ray Thomas.

Thomas isn't the only standout in this British band. Drummer Graeme Edge could have been an actor. He's dramatic; he'll hold his arms high to crash the sticks down on the cymbals at just the right moment or pound across the drums so fast that the listener gets the impression that someone is helping him. He has to have two of the heaviest feet in the business; they're constantly pounding the two bass drums.

Others in the group are Justin Hayward on guitar, John Lodge on bass, and Mike Pinder on Mellotron, a keyboard instrument that resembles an organ but sounds like a lot of other things. They're good, but it's the flute that makes the group outstanding because the other instruments work around it....

When Richmond's review appeared in the next morning's newspaper, the Moodies had yet to leave town. Ray Thomas was the first to read it.

Ray Thomas was the star of this latest review, and you can be sure he read it. Doug Jones, still traveling with the band, revealed in *New Musical Express*:

... The last I saw of Thomas, his bags packed and ready for the next gig, he was swaggering about the hotel like a dog with two tails, brandishing the review under the amused noses of Messrs. Edge, Hayward and Lodge, who were just finishing breakfast.

"Come on you lot," he rumbled straight-faced. "I've known for years I've been carrying you and this review confirms it. If you're not out in five minutes I'm just going to find myself another backing group – you musicians are ten a penny, yer know." ...

Thomas told *New Musical Express*, "One of the funniest quotes I read was in a review in the States. It said our album was from 'The Five Veteran Cosmic Rockers.' We just fell about." (RT-NME72)

For the week ending October 28, 1971, *Days of Future Passed* spent its second week at No. 3 on *Billboard*, trailing only *Superfly*, by Curtis Mayfield, and *Carney*, by Leon Russell. *Cashbox* called it better for *Days*, raising the album to No. 2 on its chart, under *Superfly*. On the singles charts, "Nights in White Satin" had moved up to No. 3 on *Billboard*, under Chuck Berry's "My Ding-A-Ling" (No. 1) and Elvis Presley's "Burning Love" (No. 2). *Cashbox* believed that only "Ding-A-Ling" was ahead of "Nights," and ranked the Moodies at No. 2.

Saturday, October 28: The Arena, Milwaukee, Wisconsin.

Sunday, October 29: Metropolitan Sports Center, Minneapolis, Minnesota. John Carman of *The Minneapolis Star* reported that a capacity audience of 15,000 was in attendance. His observations:

In these days of slumping quality in rock music, performing artists have turned increasingly toward stunts to gain notoriety. Notoriety, in turn, sells records and fills concert halls, which of course pads bank accounts. Alice Cooper does about everything on stage but stand on his head and spit nickels. Ian Anderson of Jethro Tull kicks over chairs and does the splits. Dr. John and Night Tripper comes on looking like an aborigine. This is a long way of saying how good it was to see and hear the Moody Blues last night at the Metropolitan Sports Center. ...

Alternating from high pitch to delicate lyricism, [the band] never lost their grip. They played mostly what the audience came to hear ("Tuesday Afternoon," "Question," "Nights in White Satin," "Melancholy Man," "Timothy Lear" [sic], "Have You Heard"), as well as some less familiar cuts from their half-dozen albums.

Appropriately, because the Moody Blues helped pioneer the concept of rock albums as integrated musical packages rather than nonrelated pieces, one of the best portions of the concert was a medley from Side Two of the *On the Threshold of a Dream* album.

Seeing the Moody Blues perform in a sports arena might seem as incongruous as watching ballet on the floor of the Roman Coliseum. Yet, the Britons never veered from what could be expected from a reputation for solid professionalism, and the sound was true. With recording-studio precision, they brought off their distinctive changes in tempo – from even-flowing rock beat to flute or electric keyboard solo and back again – gracefully and intelligently.

So, unlike other groups that draw crowds to see stage acrobatics of a superstar figure, the Moody Blues has found its niche in faultlessly giving audiences an emotional experience of the most exquisite kind.

Tuesday, October 31: Salt Palace, Salt Lake City, Utah. Brent Mower, writing in the *Deseret News*, brought a bit of the concert to Utah residents who couldn't get tickets before the event sold out:

This Halloween was not only a night of ghosts and goblins, but an evening of a superb concert performed by Moody Blues before a sellout audience at the Salt Palace.

The major objective of the Moody Blues is communication and their ability to realize this end can be measured by their shatteringly successful concerts throughout the world. Their only dictum is "be yourself and be kind." .... Each of the six Moody Blues albums has sold well past the million mark; such figures indicate that their communiqués are being received and understood. ...

Electronics help any rock concert but without talent they can be wasted. The Moody Blues joined together these two virtues into one great show. ...

446

Wednesday, November 1: Los Angeles Forum, Inglewood, California. Following the show, Robert Hilburn had his say in *The Los Angeles Times*. It was the same broken record -- Hilburn still felt the Moodies weren't living up to their artistic possibilities.

> The Moody Blues is one of the best rock 'n' roll bands in the world, a fact the group seems only occasionally interested in documenting on stage or on record. Part of the problem is the democratic nature of the English quintet. As desirable and fulfilling as it may be in the course of human affairs, democracy doesn't always best serve a rock group or its audience. In most cases, the strength of a group comes from a single person's vision. There are cases (i.e., the Beatles and Rolling Stones) where two people shared control of the group's material, but normally it is up to a Pete Townsend or Ray Davies or Robbie Robertson to guide a group's destiny. Remember what happened to Creedence Clearwater after leader John Fogerty began sharing writing-vocal-arranging chores with the other members of the group?
>
> The Moodies have two fine writers in Justin Hayward and John Lodge, but the group, unfortunately to my mind, believes it has five fine writers. Thus, it devotes much of its time to the works of Mike Pinder, Graeme Edge and Ray Thomas rather than concentrating on the works of Hayward and Lodge. ...

Hilburn said that the low spot for him was whenever the group would go though "some metaphysical meanderings, complete with poetry that seems so totally overblown," and how he couldn't understand why "the audience doesn't hoot Pinder off stage when he begins telling us, in measured tones, about the '... white eagle of the north ... flying overhead.'" Hilburn didn't seem to understand that the fans *wanted* each Moody to take the limelight from time to time. The audience's appreciation was for the individuals, as well as the group.

Ray Thomas said, "I understand the Press has got a lot of power. But I think, basically, the critics are a load of comics.... I'm not trying to be flash, but one thing that annoys me is when somebody who's passed a few English examinations – so he's quite a good reporter – can have so much power. If you write for *The Times* you've got a vast audience, yet you might not even be able to sing in tune let alone know anything about music." (RT-NME72)

Lambaste as he might, Hilburn had to concede one point:

> Despite my reservations, the band's democracy and/or dual musical personality has certainly not hurt its popularity. Tickets for its appearance Wednesday night at the Inglewood Forum and tonight at the Long Beach Arena were gobbled up as fast as promoter Jerry Weintraub could put them on sale. And the group's "Nights in White Satin" single (recorded in 1967, but recently re-released) is the nation's best-selling record, while the album from which it was taken, *Days of Future Passed*, is streaking its way back up the sales charts. ...

In the same city, at a different paper (*The Valley News*, in Van Nuys, a suburb of Los Angeles) Paul Scott had this to say about the very same concert:

> A balloon floated softly through the air over the Forum crowd on Wednesday, Nov. 1, as the lights dimmed and the mood of anticipation reached its peak among the 17,000 fans. Then there came a roar from the audience as the Moody Blues entered and went into the first number, "The Story in Your Eyes." For the next two hours the English rock group enchanted the sellout crowd with its rich and full sounding music. ...
>
> The Moodies as a group have been together since the mid-60s and their music has been consistently fine. ...

Friday, November 3: Sports Arena, San Diego, California.

For the week ending November 4, 1972, "Nights in White Satin" peaked on *Billboard* at No. 2, under Johnny Nash's "I Can See Clearly Now." *Cashbox* did "Nights" one better, raising the song to No. 1. *Record World*, the third big national record surveyor in the U.S., agreed with *Cashbox*, giving "Nights" top honors.

Saturday, November 4: Auditorium, Long Beach, California. Covering the last concert of the short tour was Denise Kusel, of the Long Beach *Independent*. She reported:

> ... The last stop on a 12-city tour that began in Hampton Roads, Virginia, ended Saturday night at the Long Beach Arena with a sell-out house. It's not fair to call the Moody Blues' performance a concert. It was a statement. A statement of electronic power, mingled with a reflective journey through orange and gold autumn.
>
> The last city on a tour can mean one of two things to a rock group: a worn out, tired performance, or a burst of energy to the finish line. The Moody Blues sprinted across with style in an explosive crescendo. The energy kept building, gaining momentum, beginning with "How Is It (We Are Here)" and "Tuesday Afternoon," and winding with a tight rendition of "Question."
>
> Justin Hayward's lyric-poetry was a feast of imagination.... Hayward's dreams mesmerized the audience; lulled them into respectfulness, almost docile, they were carried along on a Ferris wheel of time. I had the feeling of being out in space on an electronic wave – awake and sensitive – and then lured back to earth by middle-register flute sounds.
>
> There's something about the Moody Blues' sound that makes you feel the whole world is up there on the stage, turning electronic dials, listening and building for some terrific finale – and always the question "Why?" drifting from their lips. ...

It was predictable that the "Question" would close the show. To use the old cliché, it's a hard act to follow. …

The sprint left the audience hungry for more. It left the Moody Blues on a mountain, shouting down echoes and shattering them against time.

The purpose of the tour had been to support *Seventh Sojourn*. It is ironic then that due to the success of "Nights in White Satin" and *Days of Future Passed*, the album the band had come to America to promote was withheld until after the tour ended. *Seventh Sojourn* wouldn't make it out in America until 13 days *after* the end of the tour.

For the week ending November 11, 1972, *Billboard* held "Nights in White Satin" at No. 2, still blocked from the top by "I Can See Clearly Now." *Record World* still listed the Moodies' single at No. 1. At *Cashbox*, it slipped from top spot to No. 5. On the album charts, *Days of Future Passed* slipped down one on *Cashbox*, from second place to No. 3, under new chart leader, *Catch Bull at Four*, by Cat Stevens, and runner-up, *Superfly*, by Curtis Mayfield. *Billboard* also listed *Days* at No. 3.

Two and a half weeks earlier, Seventh Sojourn had been released in Britain.

U.K. album release: *Seventh Sojourn*
Threshold THS 7; October 23, 1972

On November 11, *Melody Maker* published Andrew Mean's review of *Seventh Sojourn*. You may recall that Means, an advocate for constant change in rock music, hadn't been very kind to the Moodies in his previous album and concert reviews. Means now wrote:

> The continual pursuance of one mode of expression almost inevitably results in staleness. For too long the Moody Blues have hammered out repetitions of the International Brotherly Love theme without adding anything. The message is creditable – we all want peace, don't we?

> But musically it can become intolerable to have the same words remixed, to have to listen to variants on the same melodic master pattern. The same old story with a different title. Their lyrics have become bankrupt, and their music has now been swamped in the delusion that the grander the scale, the greater will be the impact. The only way in which *Seventh Sojourn* can be said to be a progression is in studio technique. In terms of musical and poetic inspiration there's no change. The ideas behind this album found expression in *On the Threshold of a Dream* and *A Question of Balance*, and were all but exhausted on *Every Good Boy Deserves Favour*.

> Sure, there are some attractive tunes and some impressive studio sounds, but it's over a year since their last LP release, and three hundred and sixty five days usually produces changes in people.

The same might be said of Means and his opinions; they remained the same. He could not see that Mike Pinder had *not* written a song quite like "Lost in a Lost World" before. The theme may have been somewhat reminiscent of some of the band's previous works, such as portions of Justin Hayward's "Question," but this new track was a much different commentary on life than we had heard from Pinder before. Means evidently could not see that Hayward had never written a song about the specific subject of "New Horizons" – with his family now three. Or that Ray Thomas's "For My Lady" – a beautiful song – was unique in that Thomas had never done a straight-out love song before. He was better known for writing quirky, tongue-in-cheek pieces. And "Isn't Life Strange" wasn't like anything John Lodge had written before. This too was new territory for the Moodies, including the first time they had sounded a bit, well, Bee-Gee-ish … which they pulled off, beautifully. "I'm Just a Singer (In a Rock and Roll Band)" is also unique. The Moodies had never done a song that sounded like this before – with those locomotive drums picking up speed in the beginning and slowing to a stop at the end. Never before had the fans been so clearly reminded the Moodies were seekers, not saviors. If only Means had been able to get that message, too.

Perhaps, when Mike Pinder wrote about the "so many people" lost in a lost world, he had a particular "mean" fellow in mind.

Justin Hayward said, "Probably the last good review we had was for *Threshold of a Dream*. After that, we lost the British press. British music is thrilling and exciting, because it changes very quickly. You have to be thick-skinned and realize that if you're hip, you're going to be unhip pretty quickly, which happens to this day. We just weren't their cup of tea anymore." (JH-TRC96)

With the exception of critics such as Robert Hilburn, the Moodies' reception remained warmer in America.

From November 11, 1972, Gregor Vaule, music director for radio station KYSN, in Colorado Springs, Colorado, had brought in a copy of *Seventh Sojourn* from England. He gave a sneak peek:

> The Moody Blues is one of the few mid-sixties British rock groups to survive with any kind of following in the 70s … and what a following they have!! Since the personnel overhaul in 1967, the Moodies have been responsible for an almost mystical brand of music found nowhere else in rock. The latest Moody Blues' release, *Seventh Sojourn*, is better than *Every Good Boy* … if that's possible. The cuts have a flowing quality that makes favorites hard to choose. Aside from a song that was a big hit on KYSN a couple of months ago, "Isn't Life Strange"; "You and Me," "New Horizons" and "Lost in a [Lost] World" are sure winners.

These songs were indeed getting a great deal of airplay on radio stations, even though none would be released as single.

On November 13, radio station WSAN, from Allentown, Pennsylvania, which billed itself as "Progressive AM," said of *Seventh Sojourn*:

This review is probably not necessary. *Seventh Sojourn*, one of the most awaited albums of the year, has finally arrived. The Moody's new album was well worth the wait. Although there is no real change in the Moody Blues' style from previous albums, the abundance of timely lyrics accented by very listenable and moody music makes it another fine album. All cuts are excellent.

And this meant that "all cuts" would be featured on the radio station, with broadcasters already leaning heavily toward "I'm Just a Singer (In a Rock and Roll Band)," "New Horizons," "You and Me," "Lost in a Lost World," and "For My Lady," usually in that order.

**U.S. album release: *Seventh Sojourn*
Threshold THS 7; November 17, 1972**

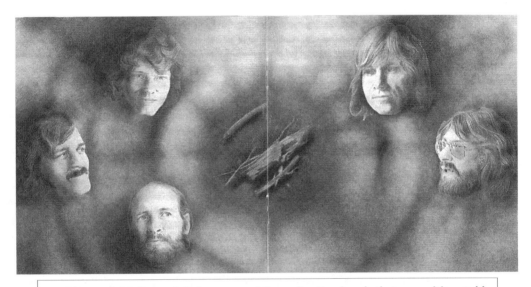

Inside gatefold, *Seventh Sojourn* ... and those floating heads that one critic would reference.

One day after the release of *Seventh Sojourn* in America, for the week ending November 18, 1972, "Nights in White Satin" was on its way down the charts, at No. 5 on *Billboard* and No. 11 on *Cashbox*. *Days of Future Passed* was hanging in there, though, at No. 3 on both charts, still under Curtis Mayfield and Cat Stevens.

Back to England, Tony Stewart's review of *Seventh Sojourn* was published in the November 18 edition of *New Musical Express*. His review seemed a rebuttal to the viewpoint of critics like Andrew Means. Stewart acknowledged that anything the Moody Blues put out was going to be "musically good, with an incomparable production." *Seventh Sojourn* continued in that vein. But ...

... After previous works, the Moodies have a lot to live up to, regarding material and melodies. Once again they have taken their usual theme of social conscience, implying that we could make this world a lot better if we tried, and that there could be an atmosphere of universal love.

But the explanation of their themes through eight songs is different to their previous sets. So surely we can't discard their efforts as repetitive – after all, a relevant argument may be presented in many different ways.

Again, the musical presentation is interesting, sometimes crossing from ballads such as Ray Thomas's "For My Lady" and Mike Pinder's "When You're a Free Man," into good old rock and roll on "You and Me" and "I'm Just a Singer (In a Rock and Roll Band)."

Perhaps I'm looking a little too deeply into the meaning of this album, but I cannot help feeling that the "sojourn" mentioned in the album title comes with "New Horizons" and maybe "Isn't Life Strange" – the latter a blissful love song with just a tinge of melancholy.

The starting point for the group's questioning does come from the philosophical Mike Pinder with "Lost in a Lost World," which states that the cruelty and injustices of the world are not moral as we all belong to the same family. ...

As I was saying before, one has to decide whether it is good to listen to or not. I'll dawdle no longer – it is a remarkable album which will be seldom off my deck.

Back in America, disc jockey and newspaper music columnist/reviewer David F. Wagner in the Appleton/Green Bay area of Wisconsin.

... The M.B. must have hit on something universal, or at least basic, because despite all the intellectual reasons in the world for not liking what they do, I find it easy to get in the mood for digging them. I tell myself they are pretentious, that their lyrics are tritely sentimental, and the music itself over-orchestrated and lacking substance. Yet, they sound pretty good.

The key may be their simple melodies underlying all the super-production effects. Once one of those melodies gets caught in my mind, I hum it for days. "Isn't Life Strange" is an example. I played it on my radio program nearly a week before I wrote this and still the melody lingers on. ...

By November 25, *Seventh Sojourn* leapt onto the *Billboard* Top 20 album chart, at No. 12, with *Days* close behind at No. 14. *Cashbox* had *Seventh Sojourn* in the Top 20 a week earlier (at No. 13) and now said it was the ninth best-selling album in the U.S., with *Days* still at No. 3. *Billboard* was still charting "Nights in White Satin," now at No. 9.

Tony Palermo, of *The Pittsburgh Press*, for the newspaper's November 26 edition, commented:

> There was a time, I guess, when the gospels according to St. Moody Blues bowled people over with profundity – no problem of mankind was too great to be solved with a little love. But the often-repeated head-in-the-cloud philosophies the Moodies offer on *Seventh Sojourn*, their latest LP, are wearing thin, in my book.
>
> What's still interesting is the thick, somber guitars, keyboard and vocal work, scooped around some pleasant melodies like, "Lost in a Lost World," "For My Lady" and "The Land of Make Believe."
>
> A first-rate Moody Blues package, this isn't. But let's face it, they'd have a tough time topping some of their earlier Sojourns.

Seventh Sojourn was doing all right by itself. It didn't appear to need the Moodies on tour to sail up the album charts. On December 2, it was at No. 5 in *Billboard* and No. 6 on *Cashbox*. *Days* was at No. 15 and 10, respectively. *Billboard* still showed "Nights" in the national Top 20, at No. 17.

On December 9, *Billboard* reported that *Seventh Sojourn* had been certified by the RIAA as the Moodies' seventh consecutive gold record (having earned in excess of a million dollars in America). According to *Rolling Stone* magazine, in its December 21 issue, the album actually had an advance order in the U.S. of 1.5 million copies, which meant that it shipped platinum. This was also the week that *Seventh Sojourn* hit the top of *Billboard*'s album chart, displacing Cat Stevens's *Catch Bull at Four*. *Cashbox* showed the new Moodies album at No. 4 and climbing.

One week later, the week ending December 16, *Cashbox* was in agreement with *Billboard* and had *Seventh Sojourn* at No. 1. *Days* had its final week in the Top 20, with *Cashbox* listing it at No. 14. "Nights" had dropped out of the Top 40 on both trades' singles charts.

For the week ending December 23, 1972, *Seventh Sojourn* remained at No. 1, according to both *Billboard* and *Cashbox*. One week later, on December 30, the Moodies held at No. 1 on *Billboard*, but *Cashbox* let *Seventh Sojourn* drop by one, and called Carly Simon's *No Secrets* – the album containing "You're So Vain" – the new No. 1.

For its year-end issue, *Stereo Review* rated *Seventh Sojourn* as "Excellent":

> This is one of the best Moody Blues albums so far. As usual, the instrumental work is lithe and responsive, and, also as usual, the performances have clarity and true musicianship. What makes this album stand out is the quality of the songs; almost without exception they are poetic without straining and convey a directness of communication that I haven't heard from the group before. The opening song, "Lost in a Lost World," immediately sets the quietly reflective tone of what's going on here. Perhaps the best track is "Isn't Life Strange," which conveys what seems to be deep personal feelings through an ironic and wistful lyric. The album ends with "I'm Just a Singer (In a Rock and Roll Band),"

which is saved from bleakness by the hopeful streak of optimism that runs all through this group's work. Tony Clarke's production is splendid, perfectly capturing the intimate atmosphere of a rap session between people of sense and sensitivity. This is a recording worthy of your full attention.

On January 2, 1973, and clearly looking ahead, it was reported that both *Cashbox* and *Record World* magazines had chosen the Moody Blues as the Number One album sellers of 1973. The year had just started, but *Seventh Sojourn* was No. 1 in two of the three national charts, as well as *Billboard*, and *Days of Future Passed* was still flying high.

On January 6, 1973, *Melody Maker* reported that "I'm Just a Singer (In a Rock and Roll Band)," coupled with "For My Lady," would be issued as a single on January 19 "because of the response both tracks have received over the past few weeks." And that meant that radio was already favoring these two songs over any of the other *Seventh Sojourn* tracks.

For the week ending January 6, 1973, *Billboard* still showed *Seventh Sojourn* as the top-selling album in the U.S. *Cashbox* said it was Carly Simon's *No Secrets*, one place above the Moodies.

One week later – January 13, 1973 – both *Billboard* and *Cashbox* showed *Seventh Sojourn* at No. 2, under *No Secrets*.

Rolling Stone magazine filed its review of the new album in the New Year, on January 18, with Steve Ditlea at the typewriter.

> … The Moody Blues' seventh visitation on vinyl weaves some new strands into the consistent fabric of their work. The five members of the group seem to share the awareness of worldly problems once only articulated by Mellotron wizard Mike Pinder. … Musically, they use rhythmical accents more than before, and even sing sometimes close to out-and-out rock.

> Despite these changes, it's still the same old Moodies; the five-year-old "Nights in White Satin" could easily fit on this album. The recent success of that song testifies to the group's ability to transcend the vagaries of pop styles, even if their approach may be occasionally cloying with its cotton-candy cosmicness.

> … There's a follow-up song here about Doctor Tim (remember "Legend of a Mind" with Ray Thomas' haunting refrain, "He's on the outside looking in"?), this time a dirge by Mike Pinder looking forward to "When You're a Free Man." Lead guitarist Justin Hayward, composer of "Nights in White Satin" and the most melodic of the Moodies, continues the group's preoccupation with dreams and fantasy in "The Land of Make Believe" and "New Horizons," the most memorable and sinuous song on the album. Ray Thomas contributes a charming chanty about search for love on life's sea, "For My Lady." And John Lodge turns in the by-now-familiar "Isn't Life Strange," as well as the Moodies' answer to those who would make sages of them, "I'm Just a Singer (In a

Rock and Roll Band)." Gone are the days of "Minstrel's Song" and its optimistic celebration of music's power….

Their lyrics could be analyzed for their mundane imagery or their representation of a prevailing ethos, but I'd rather leave that to the poets and the clowns. On this album, as well as their earlier ones, their most satisfying music is also their most tactile, with a variety of rich and flowing textures. Give your intellect a break. *Seventh Sojourn* is music to bask in and feel with your pores as well as your ears.

Single release:
"I'm Just a Singer (In a Rock and Roll Band)"
b/w "For My Lady"
UK: Threshold TH 13; U.S.: Threshold 45-67012; January 19, 1973

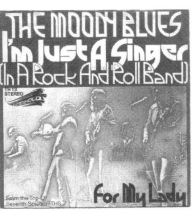

The day after the release of the "I'm Just a Singer," issued simultaneously in the United Stated and the United Kingdom, Tony Stewart of *New Musical Express* reported:

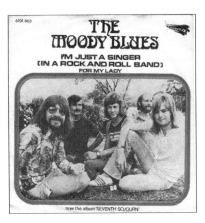

> The release of the single track, "I'm Just a Singer (In a Rock and Roll Band)," comes about now because anybody who was going to buy the album has done so, and they are attempting to pick up sales to a few more intelligent souls. It comes as something as a shock to Lodge to realize he's a commercial writer.

Lodge said, "I think you're surprised when anything seems to have a commercial value – when you do something and people say it's right. Perhaps that's what success is."
(JL-NME73)

Tony Stewart followed up:

> Whether you approve of the fact or not, being in a successful band today means high money stakes and wealth. Touring, albums, royalties, and, once again, singles, all ensure the artist of a position as impressive as that of a movie idol. There are country mansions, Jags, Rolls Royces, and the other trappings. Now the Moody Blues are way out front, and

… Graeme Edge has talked of his problem of being classless while pouring out champagne and handing round the catalogue shots of a yacht he's bought himself. His roots are working class – and [yet the upper class] reject him. Or perhaps the subtlety is rather that they don't accept him. But his mental attitude and upbringing estrange him from any other class. Hence, he is, in his words, classless.

From the same day, Chris Welch of *Melody Maker* wrote:

Graeme Edge's drums take care of the introduction, accelerating into a dramatic performance, rich in vocal harmonies in which the boys insist they are merely singers in a rock and roll band, thus I suspect, denying any ascendency to the gods that over enthusiastic fans may conceivably conclude has taken place. A fairly commercial recording from the boys. …

Billboard in America rated the single in its January 27 issue:

A slight change of pace for the group, as they move to an upbeat rock sound as opposed to their usual more mellow material. Top musicianship and harmony should still give them another winner.

From the March 1973 issue of *Let It Rock*, Simon Frith admitted that the he got a scare when he looked at the inner gatefold of *Seventh Sojourn*, with the drawing of Mike Pinder's "disembodied head floating across the inside of the sleeve, a look of maniac inspiration in his eyes." Frith wrote:

I don't know which one he is but I bet he plays the Moog and inspires the words:

Oh can you feel the world pining
Pining for someone who really cares
Enough to share his love
With all of us, so we can be
An ever loving family….

After laying this on us, the Moodies have got the cheek to claim just to be singers in a rock and roll band. …

The Moodies' art is to build a portentous superstructure on a meagre structure – they always sound important and it's difficult to say why. Shitty lyrics, poor voices, uninspired instrumentalists, boring tunes, and all arranged, synthesized and produced with the utmost loving care.

The Moodies' charm is the gap between the use value of their products and their exchange value. If they weren't so successful and didn't have moustaches they'd almost be punks. "Isn't life stra-a-a-ange" – by the time they finish with it, this mundane cliché has been invested with a mystical fervor. Life just isn't strange, it's blessedly strange.

456

The touching thing is the earnestness. The Moodies believe in their lyrics, they believe that their music is beautiful and their convictions gives the bland sermonizing whatever rock force it has. …

Despite his efforts to sneer the Moodies away, Simon Frith admitted:

The Moodies (or at least their producer) have a feeling for sound qualities which can't be sneered away. Every track has stirring moments (especially in the use of the guitar as a genuinely electronic instrument) and both "Isn't Life Strange" and "I'm Just a Singer" made good radio singles. The Moodies are still the best group of their genre….

***

Since "Nights in White Satin" had performed so well in the U.S., Decca finally decided to issue the song in a longer version in various other countries, such as in portions of South America. Threshold followed suit, doing the same in Australia. This version ran 5:37.

20

The Last Tour of the Moody Blues, Mark 2 (1973-74)

World tour, 1973-74.
(Photo source: derekmo.net/moodyblues, courtesy Derek Morris)

The years 1973-74 brought about the Moody Blues' most ambitious tour to date, and the put them at the pinnacle of their popularity. But no new album.

Each of the Moodies approached songwriting in a very deliberate manner. When they had an album to record, preferably with a concept in mind, the group members demonstrated an ability to be quite prolific. In between albums, however, each member seemed hesitant to finish the songs they had begun on their own.

When asked in 1972 by Penny Valentine of *Sounds* if the band did more songwriting than was apparent on their albums, John Lodge answered, "There's a private collection upstairs on bits of paper that will never get recorded – they're very private, personal songs that I couldn't record to make bread. I don't know why, that's just the way I feel about them. I think the whole band has this kind of collection – things that will never get recorded, things very specifically for ourselves." (JL-S72)

Justin Hayward said, "The stuff I actually record at home isn't stuff the band would do... It's mostly instrumental stuff I do at home and I call it 'fill music,' because that's what it is. I find that if I finish something, I don't listen to it anymore. But if I leave something undone, I'll listen to it quite often and maybe play along with it to work something out.... If I sit down for a day and play around with a chord and it works well, and I think it might be good for the band, I don't record it; I want to go in a proper studio and record it. I would rather not take any chances with it." (JH-S93)

Of the five Moodies, Hayward was the most disciplined songwriter, but, in the year between the making of *Seventh Sojourn* and the attempts to record an album in the spring and summer of 1973, it appeared he had few songs ready for recording. For the most part, only bits and pieces, like "letters I've written, never meaning to send."

In 1972, John Lodge explained the songwriting process that he, Hayward, and, very likely, the other Moodies often took. "There are three buzzes as a songwriter – one is actually getting an idea, which is a ridiculous buzz and takes you over completely. The next is when you've written it and you play it again – I mean, maybe you finish it at 5 a.m. and think it sounds great, but if it still sounds that way the next day, when your mind's at its worst receptive level, *that's* when you get the buzz. The other is going into the studios with the boys and cutting it, because that's what the Moodies are all about – there's no 'all your own work' business. The great thing is to see what other people see in your songs and work on them with them." (JL-S72)

Threshold Records had given the individual members of the Moody Blues opportunities to make solo albums. Projects had been announced, but none were realized. It seemed that time was always the primary problem, due to the Moodies' busy touring schedule. Another hindrance seemed lack of motivation. Without the pressing drive to communicate, the artist falls mute. Each of the Moodies seemed content to be involved in just one album per year – containing, on average, two songs from each member.

For the September 1, 1972 issue of *Record Mirror*, Justin Hayward told Rick Sanders, "At odd times I've tried to do solo recordings for an album, but when it comes down to making it, if I want a bass player, who do I ring but Johnny. For a piano, it's Mike, and so on. In fact, some of my proposed solo stuff has ended up on Moody albums." (JH-RM73)

During the making of *Seventh Sojourn*, Ray Thomas told Tony Stewart of *New Musical Express*, "Mike was going to do an electronics thing, and Graeme was [also] inclined. Justin and I had a few dry runs as far as an album was concerned. We wrote together on two tracks – that was "Are You Sitting Comfortably?" and "Visions of Paradise." With "Visions," Jus wrote the lyrics and I wrote the music, and on "Sitting Comfortably," I wrote the lyric and he wrote the music. It came out well. [But] that's about it at the moment." (RT-NME72)

The songwriting within the Moody Blues was usually motivated by the need or desire to record an album. But, following the harsh reception for *Every Good Boy Deserves Favour* and *Seventh Sojourn* from a vocal minority in the music press, the band was understandably hesitant to create an eighth album. This didn't mean an attempt wasn't made.

From the March 11, 1973 issue of *Melody Maker*, a reader asked if the Moodies would be releasing a single soon … and would they be making any more cosmic-sounding albums? Peter Jackson of Threshold Records wrote the reply:

> Moody Blues will be releasing a new single in March and an LP in
> May. Both will feature their usual sound, which is a combination
> of their individual talent and the skill of their record producer,

Tony Clarke. The Moodies don't make cosmic-sounding records; they make Moody Blues sounding records. It is perhaps the blending of sounds and the use of Mellotron that gives rise to such descriptions as cosmic, space rock, spiritual rock, God rock, etc....

The Moodies, with Tony Clarke producing, had begun that album in January and February 1973. One track, Justin Hayward's "Island," featuring a lovely accompaniment by Mike Pinder on Chamberlin, was recorded on February 14. (This song was released 35 years later on the remastered *Seventh Sojourn* CD.)

Whatever else may have been recorded has yet to be made available. Knowing the Moodies' policy for "wiping" tracks that didn't meet their standard, it is possible that no other recordings survived the session.

According to Graeme Edge, a second stab at working on the next album was attempted in March. For the September 22, 1973, issue of *Melody Maker*, he told Geoff Brown, "We've written a few numbers. And we went in [to the studio] in January and tried to record them, and then went in [during] March and tried to record them, but we was churning out standard, safe Moody Blues crap. We kinda went 'waaaah.'" (Brown said the sound Edge made was an impression of a balloon gently deflating.) "We'd made it through seven albums and worked a lot, and needed a rest. We took the last seven months off." (GE-MM73)

Those several months off took them into the fall of 1973. Explaining the long layoff , Hayward told Ray Hammond of *Sounds*, "Well, we were planning to do a world tour in the early part of the year but, for a reason I don't think any of the boys have talked about before outside of the group, we had to suspend all our activities. In the first part of this year we were involved in a big court case and that knocked everything out. It came up all of a sudden, although it concerned something which happened several years ago." (JH-S73)

The Moodies had been plagued by management difficulties throughout their career. This commenced with Ridgepride, who worked the band relentlessly but paid them very little. Troubles continued under Brian Epstein, who the band discovered was too busy with the Beatles and his other Liverpool acts to be of any real help. Colin Berlin came next, and while no one in the band said anything bad about Berlin, some felt he got too busy with Tom Jones and Engelbert Humperdinck, and didn't find enough time for the Moodies (although he did continue to serve as their booking agent for a couple of years). And then there was Derek McCormick, the alleged "millionaire" from Manchester, who had no experience in entertainment or in band management, but knew a money-making prospect when he saw one. In interviews from late 1967 and early '68, that was how the manager described the Moodies – as a business venture bound to see a good return on his investment.

Hayward explained, "We signed a management contract with a Newcastle heating and ventilation engineer who we thought had some bread and might be able to help us. Later we discovered that it wasn't really working out.... and we broke away from him after about 18 months. That was in 1968 during the *Days of Future Passed* period, and we've been sort of hoping that problem of that contract would go away." (JH-S73)

461

It didn't. And now that the Moodies were one of the biggest rock bands in the world, Derek McCormick, that "heating and ventilation engineer" from Newcastle, filed a lawsuit against the group.

Hayward said the Moodies lost about six weeks of their lives over the legal action, before settling out of court with their former manager. This unpleasantness forced the group to abandon their commencement of an eighth album. Hayward seemed skeptical it might even be made, after the difficulties in completing *Seventh Sojourn*.

It had now been more than a year since the Moodies last recorded. Was the delay caused by a lack of good material … concern for certain critics' opinions ... or simple inertia?

Graeme Edge rationalized to Keith Altham of *New Musical Express*, "We consider the way we work gives our audience the best. We would rather write ten songs a year [each] and let the public hear the best two. It's full frontal nudity when you let a song go, and we like to be heard at our best." (GE-NME73)

But a year had now passed, with no evidence of any new songs – much less ten apiece. Ray Thomas told Al Rudis of the *Chicago Daily News* Service, "Decca Records, our parent company, are screaming blue murder at the moment for an album, and we went in and tried to comply. We worked for three weeks in the studio, eighteen hours a bloody day, sweating our guts out, and came up with nothing. Okay, you know, it sounded all right, but it just wasn't good enough. And so we said, 'Swallow it!' …

"It's just getting more and more difficult all the time. There about 75 songs all in all [on our previous albums and singles], and so it's very hard not to repeat yourself . You could get away with it if you were trading more on the image of the group, like the Rolling Stones and Mick Jagger, but we are trading on one thing only – that's music." (RT-PM73)

With the album abandoned for now, Tony Clarke had turned his attention to a different project.

In the May 5, 1973 issue of *New Musical Express*, Tony Tyler reported that Clarke's "new self-imposed project while the eighth sojourn matures in the minds of the procrastinating Moody Blues" was to transform all of the previous albums into quadraphonic remixes – the much-ballyhooed "next step" in the advancement of stereo.

Clarke told Tyler, "I'm pretty exhausted. Remixing seven albums into quad, one after another, is quite a strain. In fact, I haven't got round to remixing *Lost Chord* yet because it was recorded on four-track originally and that requires a little, er, trickery to get what is, in effect, a simulated quadraphonic sound." (TC-NME73)

The same went for *Days of Future Passed*, also recorded on four tracks.

Meanwhile, as far as that eighth album was concerned, the Moodies did what Tyler suggested they were doing – they procrastinated further … by preparing for a tour instead.

Graeme Edge told *Sounds* magazine that being on the road was a form of escape … and an "addiction." Talking with Penny Valentine, he said, "Financially, obviously, we don't need it, but the Moodies started playing because they wanted to get on stage, and we've always kept that.

"When you get a little success – *oh, who am I kidding?* – when you're as successful as we are, you get entwined by the establishment, which forces you into dealings with money, with the tax man, and so on."

And a lawsuit with a former manager. "So, for a period of your life, you're something you never wanted to be. Out on the road I can say, 'I am the drummer of the Moody Blues, and do not bother me!' Even after all this time it's such an incredible emotional thing to get on stage – it's a much more addictive trap than heroin. We couldn't stop doing it; it's become too much of a turn on for us." (GE-S72)

With the recording sessions cancelled, a blueprint for the tour was put to paper. A press release from early August 1973 announced the touring schedule, which would begin in Stockholm, then, cross Continental Europe, followed by numerous dates in England. After this, a tour across America, then off to Japan, then, lastly, additional U.S. dates before returning to England. It was the most ambitious tour schedule the band had ever attempted, spanning four months. The encouragement to get back to work and go where the money was came from Jerry Weintraub, Tom Hulett, and Concerts West, explaining one reason for the sudden wanderlust. Perhaps conveniently, a tour would necessitate putting off an eighth album.

For the August 18, 1973 issue of *Sounds*, Ray Hammond wrote:

> It was November [1972] when the Moody Blues last played together. That was an American tour, the highlight of which was a superb set at the Madison Square Garden. Until last month the boys did nothing (nothing as a group, that is) when they announced that they were undertaking a world tour bigger than anything they had done before. Since the announcement, the group have been having rehearsals and slowly bringing the mighty Moody machine back into running order.

"Yeah, it's stupid," Hayward said to Hammond. "Well, certainly, by far the biggest."

Hayward seemed aware of the internal problems that had recently splintered many of their contemporaries, such as the Beatles, Creedence Clearwater Revival, Simon & Garfunkel, Bread, and Crosby, Stills, Nash and Young. He said, "The current atmosphere of group splits and departures naturally prompted the question whether this giant tour wasn't some sort of planned farewell trip…. No, I don't think so. There's just no need for the band to split. Anything we want to do we can." (JH-S73)

Hayward was referring to Threshold Records' intended capacity to release solo albums from the Moodies. But this had never happened. Another sign that the Moodies felt more comfortable as a unit was their efforts to build their own recording studio. Hayward said, "I think we've found the site for it now. It's out of town in West London, but we've yet to finalize the deal that will get us the premises. We've got all the equipment organized and we're looking forward to having our own studio. Ideally, we'd like to record our next album in our own studios, but, as they won't be open until around Christmas, we may record somewhere else.

"The problem with using other people's studios is that you can't get in them immediately. If I've got an idea, I want to be able to go to the studio tonight, rather than have to book up two months ahead." (JH-S73)

When asked if he was concerned about attempting such an ambitious touring schedule after such a lengthy layoff, Hayward answered, "No, I don't get nervous, really. Somehow all the preparation is going on and I'm talking about going and playing a gig in L.A., or Japan, or somewhere, and it's not me that I'm talking about. It's a bit unreal. It's not me until the day of the gig, and I think, "Christ, it's tonight!' [And then] I don't feel anything for the first ten minutes of the set…. It's so unreal, it's like someone else is Justin Hayward. But it's me that's going to [get] the shits in Germany and cholera in L.A. There is a very definite sense of unreality about my whole life, rather like it's happening to someone else. It's ridiculous, really…." (JH-S73)

Isn't life strange? It certainly was for the Moody Blues, on their tightrope between snapping critics and adoring fans.

with The Nicky James Band

The set list for the 1973 tour was "Higher and Higher" (with Pinder reciting Edge's poem); "Question" (with Hayward on lead vocal); "Out and In" (Pinder); "The Story in Your Eyes" (Hayward); "One More Time to Live" (Lodge); "Tuesday Afternoon" (Hayward); "Legend of a Mind" (Thomas); "Watching and Waiting" (Hayward); "Eternity Road" (Thomas); "Melancholy Man" (Pinder); "Are You Sitting Comfortably?" (Hayward); "The Dream" (Pinder reciting Edge's poem); "Have You Heard, Part 1" / "The Voyage" / "Have You Heard, Part 2" (Pinder); "Nights in White Satin" (Hayward); "I'm Just a Singer (In a Rock and Roll Band)" (Lodge leading Hayward, Thomas, and Pinder); "Question" (Hayward); and "Ride My See-Saw" (Lodge).

The tour kicked off in Copenhagen, Denmark, on September 4. On September 5, they were performing in Stockholm, Sweden. One day later, in Göteborg, Sweden. Then, another show in Copenhagen, on September 7. They played in Frankfurt, Germany, on September 8. On the 9th, they were in Bern, Switzerland. For this concert, at Fest-Halle, the Moodies set a new attendance record for this venue – 8,200. One day later, the band performed in Munich, West Germany. They had a day off on the 11th, before playing in Brussels, Belgium, on September 12. The concert in Paris, France took place on the 13th. On the 15th, they performed in Rotterdam, Holland. Then, one day later, back into West Germany, to perform in Hamburg.

After returning home, and a week of rest, the band kicked off the British phase of the tour – at the Apollo in Glasgow on September 27, then the New Guild Hall in Preston, on September 28, then to the Gaumont Theatre in Hanley on the 29th, and the Empire in Liverpool, on the 30th. On October 2, they played at the Gaumont in

Southampton; then into the Rainbow Theatre in Finsbury Park, London, on October 3 and 4. On October 5, there was a concert in the New Theatre, in Oxford. For October 6, it was the University of Leeds; then Usher Hall, Edinburgh, on the 7th; and Free Trade Hall, Manchester, on the 8th.

Barry Coleman covered the final English concert, in Manchester, for London's *The Guardian*:

> … The majority of the Moodies' music contributed to an unusual atmosphere at the Free Trade Hall in Manchester last night. There was all the excitement and the air of privilege of the big occasion, but surprisingly none of the usual slightly desperate hysteria. It was worth being there for that alone. The Moodies, as might be expected at this stage, have a masterly grasp of stage presence, and from the start they gave the impression that what they were doing was important as well as entertaining.

> This impact of their work derives to a very large extent from the closeness of its meshing, which sometimes means that it lacks edge. Mike Pinder's astonishing Mellotron playing sweeps the band into grand, even majestic reaches. The effect can be both moving and dramatic but can also have the feel of an epic film score (albeit a good one), or even 'easy listening' on a sort of cosmic scale.

> The Moody Blues have earned their place in the world's top half dozen bands. …

In the October 20 issue of *New Musical Express*, Keith Altham said:

> So the Moody Blues have just finished their cathedral-rock tour of Europe and Britain – their first British dates for over a year. As usual there were full houses, and also, as usual, numerous critics descending from great heights to declare them suitable cases for canonization … or crucifixion.

> In the event, it is well to remember that for the vast majority of Moody Blues followers – it is only a tiny minority of fanatics who misguidedly regard them as Rock Gods From On High – the group's appeal lies simply in the strength of their songs and their ability to contain melody within a rock and roll framework.

> And in all fairness to the band themselves, they are seldom as presumptuous as their analytical assassins, and usually a great deal more objective. …

> They are the only rock group in the world who can fill vast auditoriums like the 22,000-seat Madison Square Garden twice in the same day purely on music – without the theatrical additives of sex appeal or showmanship.

Graeme Edge told Altham, "Our problem is that we don't get into any trouble. We got through all that screwing and silliness over five or six years ago. We don't cause any scandals or sensations, and we lead nice calm, happy lives, which is what we are trying to get everyone else to do. It's not good for the press but it is good for audiences.

"I know we are not exciting enough for some journalists. I mean, what can you write about five guys who are making what I believe to be professional, competent music, doing a straight stage show, and singing piously about a few things they believe in? It's not 'copy,' is it? The press want full frontal rape and seduction.

"Our ideas are not considered revolutionary because we don't want to blow anyone up to get our way....

"We leave ourselves open to that kind of criticism by the very nature of the material we write. We write opinionated songs about things which we consider important, and that is bound to create a reaction – we'd be disappointed if it didn't." (GE-NME73)

By the third week of October, 1973, the Moody Blues were flying to North America. This was the first time Hayward had been out of England for an extended period of time since the birth of his daughter, Doremi, on December 3, 1972. The separation would be particularly hard on his wife, Marie.

She said, "The worst period was after our daughter, Doremi… was born. Justin was away a lot, and, although having a baby was wonderful, she took over my life completely. I remember phoning my doctor and asking, 'What's wrong with me?' Luckily, he was very understanding and realized I had post-natal depression." (MH-GH97)

While families at home anguished, the tour across America was less of a strain for the Moodies – although just as surrealistic, perhaps more so, then ever before. This time, "hitting the road" was merely a figurative phrase. Concerts West provided the Moodies with a chartered 707 – nicknamed Starship One – big enough for band, crew, and equipment.

Wednesday, October 24, 1973, the Moody Blues performed at the Montreal Forum in Montreal, Canada. Threshold artist Nicky James was the warm-up act.

Bill Mann, writing for Montreal's *The Gazette*, said:

> … The show started with a Pink-Floydish explosion of smoke and colored lights, before the music eased in and took over. And rarely has the Forum been stiller for a show: the kids usually found wandering around aimlessly were few and far between. Nearly everyone was watching with rapt attention.

466

It's the Mellotron that does it, no doubt about it. The Moody's stuff on record is lushly produced, with vocal tracks all doubled and often tripled. But in person, you hear what musicians call "naked vocals," and Justin Hayward's vocals sound rather weak out there in front, all alone. But Pinder and that Mellotron just keep creepin' across your brain, and he soars and dips and rises majestically again with his electronic simulated strings. "Tuesday Afternoon" and "Solitary [sic, "Melancholy"] Man" are songs of unmatched contemporary beauty, and "Nights in White Satin" might just end up as the classic album cut of the '60s when music historians go back a few years from now.

Most of the time the Moodys can't honestly be called a rock band in the true sense of the word, even though drummer Graeme Edge (an original Moody) is always in there, blasting away.

The Moodys are odd in another way, too. Only the most devoted fan could tell you all five members of the band. None stand out especially; the group is an unparalleled contemporary exercise in group consciousness.

The show, their first on a North American tour, closed off with "A Question of Balance" [sic, "Question"], a richly-textured composition with a message as old as humanity but still ahead of its time in realization. No one can ever accuse the Moodys of being followers and not leaders.

The group has been called pretentious from time to time by some critics (myself included), and I suspect they are. But they have the impact to make you forget about it.

Any group that can get the high-energy Forum freaks calmed down must have something going for it. Parents: your children behaved themselves last night and listened, for a change. ...

Thursday, October 25: Civic Center, Pittsburgh, PA. Pete Bishop attended on behalf of *The Pittsburg Press*. It was a festive, packed house – a new record attendance, with 14,534. Sadly, the Moodies were late to the party. Their equipment had been delayed at the Canadian/American border – "new customs procedures" – and a show that was supposed to start at 8 didn't get underway until 11:15.

Word was the truck drivers didn't have the proper forms to get across the border, so it was necessary for someone to return to Montreal to fetch the all-important papers.

Despite the wait, Bishop remained open-minded. The vocals could have been better, he felt, but otherwise, well … we'll let him tell you.

The Moodys are masterful musicians, as they've proven album after album, and they have a large repertoire from which to draw. …

Flautist Ray Thomas is the most outstanding individual musician, as he proved on "Legend of a Mind," but Mellotron man Mike Pinder isn't far behind. Every song was well done, instrumentally well blended. …

(Photo source: Pinterest.co.uk)

Their concerts have been described as dull and boring; their show last night was not. Their music is not instant turn-on; they left the "sweaty blues band" era, as Thomas termed it, years ago for a softer, mellower act.

The music itself is often disparaged as pretentious; it is not. It's tuneful, serious and entertaining, all in one. You just have to listen; you can't expect to boogie your brains out and catch the quintessential Moodys. …

Mike Kalina covered the concert for rival newspaper *Pittsburgh Post-Gazette*. He was less forgiving of the Moodies' very late start, saying that "the wait really wasn't worth it." However, Kalina had to admit that the Moodies were "accomplished musicians and they all proved their proficiency and versatility at the concert," and that "Thomas's flute playing was outstanding, as was the Mellotron work of Pinder." All in all, he admitted, "the group presented a well-rounded repertoire which included all of their single hits and a good cross section of album cuts." Oh yes, and "The crowd reaction to the group was strong throughout."

So why was the performance not worth the wait? Perhaps because "the Moodies opened their show in a cloud of smoke – the latest rock cliché. It seems every show I go to, the group enters in a cloud of smoke." Besides this, and despite finding the Moodies' voices to be "captivating," Kalina did note that more often than not the "harmonizing was pretty bad," and there was "some unevenness in their instrumental work." One more thing – the sound system was "mediocre."

Moody Blues, circa 1973.
(Photo source: MoodyBluesAttitude.com)

Friday, October 26: Madison Square Garden, New York, N.Y. Joseph Tripodi was in the house, and wrote in the *Albany State Student Press*:

... "Higher and Higher" begins the evening, as the effect of dry ice billows and blends with the electric excitement of an elated mass. The men who for so long have verbalized and orchestrated the thoughts and wishes of millions, are here to rock us on and mellow us down.

On the rock side, the Moody Blues musically kick the Garden's ass. "Story in Your Eyes" and "I'm Just a Singer" are about as driving and soulful as rock and roll can get. What's fascinating, though, is that the Moody Blues can rock you and comfort you at the same time, with the same song. Ray Thomas' "Eternity Road" is done well, with more feeling than the otherwise sterile studio version.

The mellow side of the Moody Blues speaks for itself tonight. Michael Pinder's "Melancholy Man" pleases the crowd, and perhaps represents why everyone is here. Twenty thousand are assembled to listen to five mutual friends: "All the world astounds me and I think I understand that we're going to keep growing, wait and see." ...

... [T]he high point for me is the big favorite, "Nights in White Satin." Slowly, almost hesitantly, guitar, bass and Mellotron paint the musical background for Justin Hayward's solo. Softly, he sings the feelings of his mind. (At the risk of sounding terribly trite, I think Justin Hayward has the most beautiful voice of any living male singer).

John Lodge's perfect falsetto during the chorus effectively off-set Hayward's lead. The break is crisp, and Ray Thomas' lilting flute solo is excellent, as expected. Back again to close the song, Justin Hayward delivers a devastating variation from the studio vocal and proves "Nights in White Satin" to be one of the greatest musical expressions of love ever written. ...

The big-time critics were there too. "Professional" critics are rarely as easily impressed as those reporting for student newspapers. Phil Gelormine gave his opinion in the pages of *Billboard* magazine:

Sports arenas have never been the ideal venues to fully enjoy a live concert in. More often than not, lighting is shoddy, viewing is poor and sound dismal. Forget intimacy, these places are made for hockey players, not musicians. ... The Moody Blues, so meticulously recorded on records, were ravaged by a sound system designed for the ears of the deaf. Credit the group with valiantly trying to override the problem, at least acknowledging it. Distortion plagued the entire set, especially the vocals when Justin Hayward would reach for notes like those written for "Nights in White Satin." And it's very annoying listening to sound cut in and out while a group is playing, more so when it's a group as professional as the Moodies. ...

In all fairness to the band, the music they selected to play was a thoughtful representation from past London/Deram/Threshold albums and would have been delightful had the Sound Gods been kind. The audience deserves kudos for being both respectful and responsive in light of the situation, which at best was tolerable. …

Saturday, October 27: The Spectrum, Philadelphia, Pennsylvania. Hugh Cutler was there, and wrote in Wilmington, Delaware's *The News Journal*:

Superficial study shows no single sign suggesting why the Moody Blues sound is so superbly satisfying. But, damn, is it ever! …

They trotted out at the Spectrum, its sell-out 19,500 seating stuffed to its ceiling rafters. The day after its ticket office had opened for Moody concert sales, all those tickets were gone. …

Hayward's lungs are the single most amazing instrumental asset in the group, as anyone who's ever heard him sing "Nights in White Satin" may likely attest. Cherub-faced Hayward's song-writing is perhaps the most poetically lyrical of the five and his Gibson guitar-picking the most fluid and delicate music they make. That may be why many a Moody fan seems drawn to study Hayward's mood immediately, to despair if he seems not all there.

But the ensemble sound – the enchantment woven as sweetly as celestial chamber music mixing with a snake charmer's sinuous melodies – soon ensnared the choirboy guitarist as surely as the crowd, easily the most respectful bunch of real listeners to fill the arena in months.

The Moody Blues open on mad-monk Mellotronist Mike Pinder's "Om," the prayer-chant which ends their second album, *In Search of the Lost Chord*. And smoke bombs shoot out underfoot. Immediately they slide to the ensemble ascending-chord crescendos signaling "Higher and Higher" from the fourth album, *To Our Children's Children's Children*. Pinder, again, in his Richard Harris-narrative baritone, intones those exquisite opening lines penned by drummer Graeme Edge. "Blasting, billowing, bursting forth with the power of 10 billion butterfly sneezes… Man with his flaming pyre has conquered the wayward breezes … Higher and higher, now we've learned to play with fire…"

Just as easily, the bass-plucks of John Lodge, obviously tonight's most high-spirited dude on the dais, melt into Pinder's Mellotron magic on "Out and In," an intergalactic travel tune they co-wrote for the same *Children* album. …

Amidst the ritual flickering, I stand and clap till my hands turn raw.

Sunday, October 28: The Nassau Coliseum, Long Island, N. Y.

Tuesday and Wednesday, October 30 and 31: Chicago Stadium, Chicago, Illinois. Lynn Van Matre of the *Chicago Tribune* was at the first show. She was not a fan.

… Last night's repertoire ran heavily to older Moody material, the lyrics either cloaked in ambiguity or so obvious as to be downright banal. The gist of "One More Time to Live," for example, is "pollution, population, degradation, annihilation," while "Nights in White Satin" deals more in mood than concrete meaning. And, as usual, the five Moodys shared the stage equally. …

It was a pleasantly peaceful evening, tho the sameness of the Moody's material tends to become boring long before they run out of repertoire, and their static stage presence doesn't help matters much. The layers of sound segue into each other and roll on full of cosmic slush and more than a little dreaminess – the sort of thing, in fact, that has made the Moody Blues' music a staple in the musical therapy programs at Maryland Psychiatric Institute. Think about that one for awhile.

Thursday, November 1: Freedom Hall, Louisville, Kentucky. Present for the waves of sound was Jeff Harrell of *The Indianapolis Star*.

Freedom Hall at Louisville, Ky. was the scene of two special events recently. For the first time since the mid-1960s, the hall was filled to capacity. The first event was a good performance by the Nicky James Band, but the 20,000 people had come to see the final and main attraction, the Moody Blues.

Since the Moody Blues are one of the world's most popular groups, fans from Indiana, Ohio, as well as Kentucky and other states, were on hand for the performance. The group gave the audience more than their money's worth along with a few surprises, one of which was an excellent performance in solo work by the Moody's lead guitarist, Justin Hayward. …

… Their equipment was fantastic. Amplifiers were stacked on top of each other and the organ was a sight in itself. Along with the drums, the Moody's organ was their music's chief background sound. Since it sounds like a symphony orchestra, their music has a classical mood. Pinder plays the sound superbly in concert, but the other four musicians, Thomas, Hayward, drummer Graeme Edge, and bass guitarist John Lodge, do their part to make their concert sound as clear and harmonies as [they are on] their recorded sound. … When the five musicians broke into "Tuesday Afternoon," one could almost feel the crowd vibrate. …

The Moody's then broke into "Nights in White Satin," played superbly to the accompaniment of Mike Pinder's symphonic-sound organ. The acoustics were excellent and it seems like the capacity audience now was hearing what they came to hear. …

471

Friday, November 2: Louisiana State University, Baton Rouge, Louisiana.

Saturday, November 3: Tarrant County Convention Center, Fort Worth, Texas.

Covering the concert for *The Dallas Times Herald* was Susan Barton.

> The Moody Blues' sound is somehow more than just sound. It is a thing, an object, hanging there in the air of a theater. You feel as if you can touch and taste, as well as hear the Mellotron-wrapped music of the mystical five-man group.
>
> The Moodies have created a new thing in music with their smooth orchestra rock. It is a large, enveloping sound, more than a loud, intense one – and it is as homogenized and creamy as a milkshake, despite the definite rock beat that pulses continually in the vortex of the Mellotron whirlpool. It is the kind of sound that makes you want to simply sit back and let it wash over you. And that is what some 14,000 listeners did in the band's sold out concert at Tarrant County Convention Center Saturday night. It was the most quiet, relaxed crowd in many a concert, rising en masse only at the end of the show to bring back the Moodies for wave after wave of applause. …
>
> Images of the sea and sky tend to crop up frequently in describing the Moodies' music and a mental picture of the band members as gurus, deliverers of their own cosmic words is prevalent. All that is highly appropriate. The Moodies are in the midst of a tour of the world in their own chartered jet with a cosmic name. They touch down in city after city, dispensing a dose of their particular sound and mystique to the masses, then fly off into the night to return some other year. …

Sunday, November 4: Houston Coliseum, Houston, Texas.

Tuesday, November 6: Omni, Atlanta, Georgia.

Wednesday, November 7: Convention Center, Cleveland, Ohio.

Thursday, November 8: Crisler Arena at University of Michigan, Ann Arbor, Michigan. On hand was Tom Kippert of *The Michigan Daily*.

> Mellowly soaring, the Moody Blues enchanted a most receptive following at Crisler Arena last night. The five English musicians took charge completely from the first tune of the set and remained exciting even until the final one, "Ride My See-Saw."
>
> The moodiness that this band creates on their LPs was definitely paralleled in this live performance. The extra dimension in the Moodies' music results from the use of the particularly British Mellotron. Playing this delicate instrument machine, Mike Pinder subtly adds new energy to the rock being played. …
>
> The group puts down a base of rock rhythm intertwined with the beautiful coloring that Pinder and Justin Hayward (on lead guitar)

evoke. Hayward's [guitar] lines on "I'm Just a Singer" and "Story in Your Eyes" are particularly interesting as he instinctively took the emotions higher with his biting guitar.

Looking at the material the Moodies covered is quite inspiring. Most bands could not hope to match the variety of music that the Moody Blues play. Rocking, they attack the scene with a sneaky drive. Even mellowing out, they put the audience in a trance that can't easily be forgotten.

Rounding out the quintet, Graeme Edge's drumming puts a spark into the band's total effect. He is quite powerful, even though not as fast as other others.

John Lodge takes his role in the band seriously as bassist. He joins with Mike Pinder and Ray Thomas to render some of the finest live vocal harmonies heard in rock today.

Ray Thomas, playing flute, sax, and percussion, furthers the already chilling melodies on some of the more melancholy pieces.

As writers, all five Moodies have a good sense of how to translate a wide range of emotions into words. Their ability to describe both happiness and despair so realistically has made their lyrics such a success. ...

Like comedy, appreciation for certain types of music is a subjective thing. One man's treasure is destined for another man's junkyard. Bruce Meyer, of United Press International, saw the Moodies music as belonging in the yard with the junk. His UPI wire story following the Moodies' hop across the United States gives insight into the thinking, and frustration, of a person who was not able to feel what was in the music. Meyer wrote in part:

I had never seen the Moody Blues in concert before their recent quick tour of the U.S., but the concert I attended was an enlightening experience. It was terrible – I mean, really awful. ... Yet the Moody Blues are one of the most phenomenally successful rock bands in history.

- Their seven gold albums have sold well over 20 million copies throughout the world;
- They have sold more than 50,000 albums in India!;
- They have been invited to appear at the Bolshoi Theater in Moscow, but turned down the offer because of anticipated difficulties getting their equipment in and out of Russia;
- Their records sell an average of 10,000 copies a week in Los Angeles alone;
- During their recent tour they sold out the L.A. Forum (18,000 seats plus) in less than an hour.

How could they be so bad and so popular at the same time? I'm forced to consider three possible conclusions.

First, they might have just been "off" the night I saw them.

Second, perhaps they simply can't do on stage what they can do with long hours of work in the studio.

Finally, it may be that whether they play well or not has nothing to do with their popularity. ...

But Meyer was never able to put his finger on what that attraction might be, which brings up a fourth possible conclusion: Different strokes for different folks.

In the November 24 issue of *Sounds*, it was reported that the Moodies might be the first Western band to break through the Bamboo Curtain to play concerts in the People's Republic of China. It truly looked as though it might happen, and you can be sure this was big news at the time. Also big news in the article was that the group's eighth album would be recorded in late winter – during a break from touring – for release in the spring of 1974.

If you are keeping count, this would be the third try at putting together an album in the recording studio. The first came in January/February, a second in March, and now this, in November/December ... not that it would ever happen.

Two days after the announcement in *Sounds*, a different rock music magazine, *Tambourine*, had a contradictory report, saying that the Moodies wouldn't head back into the studio until after the world tour was finished, in March of 1974. Justin Hayward, interviewed by the magazine, admitted that they didn't yet know what the theme of the album would be. The best he could do was to say, "We've written some songs that could be on it, but we might write something the night before we go into the studio and record it. It's what we're into at the time." (JH-T73)

Moody Blues

マリーヴ・ブルーイオのイベル、ニダル、最新するのオルバムの発見を防止する
（ムーディー・ブルース）

Japan, 1974.
(Photo source: MoodyBluesAttitude.com)

The Final Leg of the Tour:

January 18, 1974: Budokan Dai-Hall, Tokyo, Japan.

January 19: Nagoya-shi Koukaido, Nagoya, Japan.

January 21: Kyoto Kaikan Daiichi Hall, Kyoto, Japan.

January 22 and 24: Kouseinenkin Kaikan Dai-Hall, Osaka, Japan.

Sunday and Monday, January 27 and 28: Honolulu International Center Arena, Honolulu, Hawaii. Present, and spellbound, was Beverly Creamer, covering the concert for the *Honolulu Star-Bulletin*.

> … The Moody Blues first concert in Hawaii last night at the Honolulu International Center Arena changed me. I couldn't hear for three hours.
>
> It was an inauspicious beginning. Up the stairs by flashlight, onto the stage single file in darkness with catcalls from us out there. They turned up in the dark arena, five young men from Great Britain with their electric hair silhouetted in blue lights. …
>
> The blue lights turned red, the stage filled with smoke and the Moody Blues burst into view, singing "Higher and Higher," with Mike Pinder oozing his fingers from key to key on the Mellotron. The English band plays something which has come to be called "symphonic rock" and it's the Mellotron that creates their sound. Something like an organ, it produces a complete orchestral sound. …
>
> "The Mellotron – that's what the Moody Blues are," says one of their promoters, a New Yorker named Jerry Weintraub. The instrument was created primarily by Pinder and has been perfected by him over the past six years. He's the only one who can play it, according to Weintraub.
>
> Though they are one of the foremost bands on the contemporary rock music scene, the Moody Blues have not created the personality cult which surrounds musicians like Mick Jagger or Elton John. Their performance is tight and well-orchestrated but it lacks that certain flash of showmanship. That's the way they want it, according to Weintraub.

Justin Hayward would later say that Jerry Weintraub was the closest thing the Moodies had to a manager at this point in their career. Weintraub handled their bookings, and was now speaking on their behalf. He told Beverly Creamer, "Most rock bands have to resort to theatrics. We don't. We play music, beautiful music. Without a doubt these guys are the crème de la crème. There is no star. Everybody writes. Everybody contributes." (JW-HSB74)

But this was a year of sensationalism. The flamboyant David Bowie was breaking big in the United States, already having achieved notoriety in Britain. Outlandish Elton John was on his way to becoming the top pop star on the planet. The flashy Gary Glitter and cadaverous T. Rex (Mark Bolan) were hot in Britain. Flashy and bizarre were suddenly in vogue. The comparatively tame Moodies were becoming harder to fathom for some in the press.

Ms. Creamer attempted to give the members of the band some individual identification:

Lead guitarist Justin Hayward, a slim longhaired blond, is featured on "Nights in White Satin," and it is his guitar work that cuts through in the enchanting "Dream."

Graeme Edge, on drums, the only bachelor, plays as if his life depends on it. His mouth works like a blowfish and half the time he appears to have just had a coronary.

John Lodge, the fuzzy-headed bass player, and Ray Thomas, on flute, saxophone and tambourine, round out the group.

Still, Pinder's my favorite, bringing a gentleness to the group's live performance, which is far more evident on their records. Looking like a Sunday-school picture of Jesus, he is smooth, calm and solemn. Only when he left the stage did he flash a lingering smile, his fingers held in peace signs.

January 30: Los Angeles Forum, Inglewood, California. Singer/guitarist Shawn Phillips was with the tour now, as opening act. Dennis Hunt was the critic sent out by *The Los Angeles Times*. He wrote:

Mike Pinder, "peace and love," 1973. (Photo source: Wikipedia)

The members of the Moody Blues are masterful musicians who play complex, unusual music that would seem to appeal only to a small group of fans. But this English group is very popular and, judging from the hordes of teenagers at the Inglewood Forum on Wednesday night, has many young fans. The show, which also featured rock singer Shawn Phillips, was sold out. Those who berate young people for having deplorable musical taste should have seen that young, enraptured audience. ...

The Moody Blues' songs, which are all composed by members of the group, are enigmatic, highly rhythmic rhapsodies. It is eerie spacey music that creates an atmosphere of edginess and desolation. What is unique about them is their reverence for melody. Their songs are among the most melodic in all of rock music. No matter how oblique a Moody Blues number becomes, the melody is never buried or hopelessly fragmented.

Their songs were full of surprises, partly because they used a variety of rhythms and shifted tempos suddenly. For example, segments of their finest song, "Tuesday Afternoon," were slow and moody, while other segments were fast and clamorous. ...

Even the critic from *Rolling Stone* appeared caught up in the mood of the evening. David Rensin wrote:

> Great music has a timelessness of appeal to varied and progressive musical generations. All artists endeavor to attain this quality in their work, but the gift belongs only to a select few. At a recent sold-out LA Forum date, in an atmosphere of togetherness reminiscent of 1969-70 Crosby, Stills, Nash and Young concerts, the Moody Blues proved they are among the select few.
>
> It was incredible – the band playing essentially spaced-out, late/Sixties music, falling somewhere between the innovations of the Yardbirds and the surrealism of Pink Floyd, and making it work. …

February 1: San Diego Sports Arena, San Diego, California. Robert V. Weinstein of *Modern Hi-Fi & Stereo Guide* asked Justin Hayward about the difference between audiences back in England and in the United States. Hayward answered, "I think English audiences have always been far more reserved than American audiences, particularly for a band like ours. American audiences always seem to go out to have a good time. They seem to be freer when they are at a concert. But you have to remember that it also has a great deal to do with the type of theatres we are playing. For instance, in England we often have to play cinemas and modest-sized theatres because they are the biggest places around. Whereas the States has huge places, stadiums, and large halls like Madison Square Garden and the Nassau Coliseum. In such larger places an audience will quite naturally feel freerer." (JH-MHF74)

The down side, of course, was that most of these coliseums, such as the San Diego Sports Arena, had been designed for sporting events, not music programs. Weinstein continued:

> … All the nuances, fragile lines, finely wrought melodies were gobbled up in an auditorium that is only equipped to recreate massive sound and insensitive to just transporting "music." … It's unfortunate that one cannot experience the Moodies in concert without being assaulted by an overbearing sound. Their all too infrequent trips to the United States necessitate playing stadiums and gigantic auditoriums. A less extensive and more concentrated tour, playing moderate sized theatres, would present the group in a more accurate light.

February 2: Cow Palace, Daly City (San Francisco), California. Attending the concert was Philip Elwood, of the *San Francisco Examiner*:

> Electronic music is the most exciting innovation in the performing arts during the past decade and no group, whether "classical" or rock-blues-jazz oriented, has managed to get their artistic attitudes and electronic conceptions more together than the Moody Blues.

The five man British group gave a perfect concert last night before a sold-out Oakland Coliseum crowd.... It is seldom that an arena show can be turned as well as this one. The sound was excellent, the lighting imaginatively handled, and the concert's pace sensible. ...

The Moody Blues have their own sound system, a huge multi-speaker affair mounted on two towers; and they have their own music, like the gorgeous "Tuesday Afternoon" with its shifting rhythms, or the exciting "Just a Singer (In a Rock and Roll Band)."

The three-part *On the Threshold of a Dream*, an intense rock suite: "The Dream" / "Have You Heard?" / "The Voice" / "Have You Heard, Part 2"; "Question," "Nights in White Satin" ... or "Watching and Waiting," each, and all, have the mark of the perfect electronic rock synthesis.

"Story in Your Eyes," also, is first rate – as is "One More Time to Live." Ray Thomas' flute and sax are fine solo leads and he, as well as principal guitarist-composer-singer Justin Hayward (an immensely attractive artist) project, along with Pinder, a professional competence usually lacking in concert rock groups. Bassist John Lodge and drummer Graeme Edge also play out their roles to perfection. Without ever soloing, Edge demonstrates better rhythmic concepts than his more demonstrative counterparts in other super rock groups. ...

The audience, of rather broad range for a rock show, was enthusiastic without ever becoming rowdy. They dug the music and showed it, their attitude and attention was an acknowledgement of the class and quality of the Moody Blues' and Phillips' artistry.

No one knew that this was the last time Mike Pinder would perform in concert with the Moody Blues.

Justin Hayward: "For about two years in the Seventies we demanded the Starship One 707 plane to fly us from gig to gig on our American tours. And we even had an organ player who used to sit at the end of the bar, playing away. The most ridiculous thing about it was that the plane would be full of people I didn't even know. I would go up to them and introduce myself and they'd say: 'What do you do?'" (JH-CR12)

Graeme Edge: "I tell you how decadent it was. We had the world's longest running blackjack game happening on that plane. We played it all over the world, with all sorts of currencies on the table. Who won in the end? It was our manager, Jerry Weintraub. I wouldn't say he cheated, but he was the only sober one at the table!" (GE-PROG13)

21

1974: A Hiatus … a Compilation … and Edge Goes Solo

Album Release: *This Is the Moody Blues*
Threshold/Decca MB 1/2 (U.K.); Threshold/London THS 12/13 (U.S.); October 8, 1974
Peak position in Canada: #2
(Certified platinum in Canada)
U.S.: #11
(Certified gold in the U.S.)
U.K.: #14
(Certified gold in the U.K.)

Single release from the Graeme Edge Band: *"We Like to Do It"* b/w *"Shotgun"*
Threshold/Decca TH-18 (U.K.); Threshold/London 5N-67018 (U.S.); July 19, 1974
Non-charting

Recalling the surrealism of the year before, John Lodge told Tom Hibbert of *Q* magazine, "We'd made the *Seventh Sojourn* album and we went on this huge world tour and we chartered this huge 707 called Starship One – we had that name painted huge all down the sides of the plane. It was the biggest plane in the world at the time and we even hired an organist to play on a little dance floor in this plane. This is how bizarre things had become. And one night we were flying from wherever we were and there was just the five of us on the plane, and I was walking down the plane and I went past a bedroom which was empty, and I went past the state room with a fireplace, which was empty. This huge, enormous plane was *empty* – it was flying nothing, except for us five huddled in the front, realizing we'd totally run out of conversation. Something went 'Ding!' in my head. We'd got it all wrong. People had bestowed so much on us and things had just got out of hand." (JL-Q90)

In 1974, Graeme Edge chatted with a freelance newspaper writer Barbara Rowes about the band's plans for a Threshold recording studio. Decca had gifted their London Studio Two to the Moodies, which Tony Clarke was having upgraded and modernized. Edge enthusiastically told Rowes, "In our new studio, we will use the same tape mechanism that NASA developed to shoot for the moon, an instrument that automatically set off a 24-track relay of instructions for the astronauts to follow aboard the Apollo. This is the most perfect equipment today according to the sound experts who recommended that we purchase it directly from the Houston Mission Control Center. …

"It will be the first studio in the world designed as a complete, enormous instrument. The room itself is constructed in an oval shape to absorb every sound frequency. In other words, there are no false echoes from sound waves hitting the walls and bouncing back. …

"We all realize now if we just stay together, we have it made. Not one of us is an outstanding musician, but each of us is good and work solid. We do our homework, know our music, know what we are doing, and know how to do it. After ten years of working together, we understand each other when we're on that stage. We instinctively respond to one another's timing now. That is when music has a chance of becoming really original, when sets really take off. We are now free to explore the great and unknown dimension of rock music. Like Beethoven, we are free to reach beyond. Most groups split up before they achieve the musicianship to realize rock's potential as a serious musical form. But with our new recording studio, we have the best facilities in which to create. It is within our grasps." (GE-NYT74)

In the March/April issue of *Modern Hi-Fi & Stereo Guide*, Justin Hayward said, "As a group we have never been concerned or worried about disbanding. Expanding is our goal. We know we have to grow and there has never been any question of going any other way. As far as each one of us wanting to do something different, well, we have managed to do that simply by realizing that we all play a part in each other's lives.

"The five of us have been together for a long time. But the important thing is that we are all equals. Each of us always has the opportunity to do things that are important to him. On any given album containing ten or twelve tracks there is room enough for all of us to express ourselves. Some do more than others, but everybody gets his share. …

"Every album is completely different. Sometimes we have material before we go into the studio, and on other occasions we have very little. There are some people who like to prepare their material beforehand and there are bands who prefer to actually write in the studio. We usually prepare by just talking and being together. Even while we are on tour, we will prepare material. And we find that when we actually go into the studio we think in terms of the whole, not separate particles of sound.

"We are always experimenting with new ideas. This is almost inevitable. One doesn't do this consciously. Many people have asked us if we are consciously experimental. That question is almost impossible to answer. We do what we feel we have to do at any given moment, whether it be an experimental voyage or a return to something in our past. We don't necessarily try to strike a balance between experimental, and previously tried and tested material. We're working on a new album now but don't know when it'll be released." (JH-MHF74)

A letter to an American syndicated newspaper columnist in early April 1974 echoed a question being sent in to journalists on both sides of the Atlantic. Stan Morszewski of Corning, New York, asked:

> The Moody Blues have not released an album since *Seventh Sojourn*, and did not even have a new one during their latest tour, which is quite unusual. Do they intend to rest on their laurels or do you know if they have any plans to record a new album?

Columnist Barbara Lewis answered on April 21:

> Unlike most groups which coincidentally release albums in conjunction with tours, the Moody Blues elected to wait until their 44-city tour was completed before going into the studio. Their manager Gerry Hoff [sic; he was the directing manager of Threshold Records] said, in explaining the delayed action, "We consider it dishonest and a disservice to the fans to put out an album with which we were not satisfied just for the sake of having an album on the shelves during a tour."

> Hoff said that the group would cut their eighth album in London during May and June.

As for the recording sessions, assistant engineer Dave Baker recalled, "I don't recall those sessions as a great deal of serious recording. We may have run tape while they basically jammed in the studio, but, as far as I'm concerned, that material, if it existed, was fairly incomplete." (DB-H&H96)

Hayward wasn't talking to the press at the time, but later went on record with Bruce Eder for an article in *Goldmine* magazine. "I had gone into the studio to begin work with Tony Clarke on a new album early in 1974, and we met with the others, and they were supposed to be working with us. And suddenly nobody wanted to do the next album. This was very frustrating because I was all set to do the record. Tony and I had done some work on it already, and we finally had Threshold Studios up and running, and this would be our first album there, and nobody wanted to go on. The group was breaking up." (JH-GM94)

Elsewhere, Hayward said, "I'd just laid down a couple of untitled songs that were really good, with Tony Clarke, when there was a call from the canteen downstairs. We went down and the others were sitting there and said, 'We've decided we're gonna pull out and not continue recording.' That was it." (JH-RC03)

Mike Pinder told Mark Murley of *Higher & Higher*, "My recollection is of sitting there in the studio thinking, 'What are we doing here? We should all be home doing something much more important.' There was no creativity; the juices had stopped flowing. I don't actually remember us recording anything; we attempted a couple of things, but I don't particularly remember anything going on tape. There aren't any lost masters or anything. It was just the situation I think where everybody was sitting there staring into each other's eyes. It just had to be said that we were wasting our time there. We'd come in from an academic point of view instead of a creative point of view." (MP-H&H94)

Ray Thomas's memories were similar, but didn't agree the band had "run out of juice." They just had not been able to top themselves. He told *Beat Instrumental*: "It wasn't a fact of running out of ideas; it was trying not repeat what you'd already done. We've all got our own individual style of playing, which, when you put it together, is 'the Moody Blues sound.' It gets more and more difficult to maintain that, but we utilize new sounds to make it sound different. That was our biggest problem. It wasn't a drying up of material or anything; it was just trying to make 'em sound newer." (RT-BI75)

Other than Justin Hayward, who was left at the altar of the new Threshold studio, each Moody had his own reason for wanting to take a break. Edge, perhaps more than any of the others, wanted time to get settled after the craziness of a major tour, playing to tens of thousands of people in each city. He was tired of feeling the worship of fans who seemed ready to bestow godhood on them. Conversely, members were also conscious of iconoclastic critics– some of them rock "purists" – who seemed eager to tear down the Moodies after each achievement. It also staggered John Lodge, and Justin Hayward, to see just how big their company had become. There were so many employees whose names they didn't even know … and some employees who didn't even know the names of those in the band. For four lads from the working-class ranks of Birmingham, and one from Surrey, the reality of being part of the Moody Blues organization was becoming overwhelming.

There was another motivating factor for applying the brakes, shared by Edge and Thomas. Interviewed in the early 1970s, Ray Thomas told one journalist, "We've reached a stage now where there's very little incentive to work, simply because the taxman takes so much away. At least 90 percent of my earnings goes to the Government. So at the moment I'm living solely on my share of the royalties from our British record sales. All our foreign earnings stay abroad – our money in America both from records and from live appearances stays in America, simply because it's not worth our while bringing it back to Britain.

"Why do you think the Stones and Donovan are living abroad? Simply because they're fed up with the taxman taking all their earnings." (RT-DME71)

Graeme Edge shared different feelings with Richard Green of *Music Scene*: "A penalty of success is you can't work; it gets hard to get five of you together in the right state of mind. There hasn't been a Moody Blues album for two years, but what we were recording [during that time] hasn't been thrilling and exciting stuff. We'd have got away with it if we'd released it, and [we would have gotten] the usual mixed Moodies reviews, but there's a lot more to it than just one more album. I hope to be making music for the next thirty years. …

"We've done seven albums and another Moody Blues album has got to say a lot of new things. Because of the gap, people assume we're breaking up, but we won't put out an album until it's what we feel is right, and that's the only reason for the delay. …

"You've got to let the pot fill up again. In the past, it's been acceptable for very successful artists to take three or four years off before they come up with anything new, but in this immediate, disposable age, you're expected to churn albums out like a sausage machine." (GE-MS74)

Actually, no rock act had taken three or four years off between albums while maintaining their star status. In fact, the longest break any band had taken so far in the rock era between album releases was Simon & Garfunkel. Twenty-one months passed between the April 3, 1968 release of *Bookends* and *Bridge Over Troubled Water*, on January 26, 1971. But they did at least bridge this gap with the release of "The Boxer" single in the late summer of 1969.

Bob Dylan took a break of 19 months between *Blonde on Blonde* (May 16, 1966) and *John Wesley Harding* (December 27, 1967). The Rolling Stones took 16 and a-half months between *Let it Bleed* (December 5, 1969) and *Sticky Fingers* (April 23, 1971). The Moodies had almost matched that time, with nearly 16 months passing between *Every Good Boy Deserves Favour* (July 23, 1971) and *Seventh Sojourn* (November 17, 1972). But no one had gone two whole years … until now.

Edge told Barbara Rowes, for an article that would appear in *The New York Times*: "We were all very aware – becoming *more* aware – that after ten years, it wasn't working. We were hoping we could make it through. But the pressures finally got to all of us. …

"It's the thing that the public does to you about having to be what you are. The public locks you into being a Moody Blues. And that means, no matter what, you have to play the group's hits. It is a static repertoire for which audiences pay $7.00 or $7.50 per concert, and, sure, they are entitled to hear what they pay to hear. But I can't express to you what that does inside the head of the individual musician, if he is a serious musician. Because if you don't play the Moody Blues things, members of the audience are outraged. They come up to you, very irate, and scream, 'Why didn't you play so and so tonight?' In other words, 'Why aren't you being a Moody Blues?'

"And, for a while, it's very safe and staid – a kind of infallible insurance, and the bread rolls in. But, at the same time, almost without realizing it, you almost cease to be a functioning active musician. You start becoming a sort of robot churning out the same songs in the same styles." (GE-NYT74)

Reflecting on this time in 1987, Edge told interviewer Robyn Flans, "None of us ever had any doubts that we would perform and record together again. I think it grew from that attitude of playing all the instruments ourselves. Also, we had become very, very popular, and we had become totally isolated from the world and totally incestuously lumped all together. We went in to make an album, we had about four tracks, and it was junk. You could hear that one song we previously recorded was the father of those four songs. So we wiped the lot, and we realized we couldn't work together and make stuff that came up to the standard that we wanted. So we went out to get some other experience, working with other people, and also to let the major stardom thing die down.

"Those were strange times. Now the rock stars are [thought of as] people. Admittedly, they're sex objects and all that, but they're people. But in '72, people thought of us almost as semi-deities. People used to ask us to bless them. They thought we were in touch with some cosmic thing, and that's horrifying. Mike Pinder never recovered from it." (GE-MD87)

Pinder countered, in 1994: "I never had a problem with people seeking the answer to those questions, because I've looked for those answers myself. I can show you pictures taken backstage, with me and some fans who've met us, arms around each other, and you don't see any problems. I do wonder if some of what was said about my supposed problem with the fans didn't really have more to do with how some of the others felt." (MP-GM94)

To fully appreciate the magnitude of a Moody Blues split in mid-1974, one must understand the band's popularity at this time:

Throughout the 1960s and into the early '70s, the crown of rock royalty had remained with the Beatles, and continued to be held by them even after their last group release, *Let It Be*, in mid-1970. The individual Beatles had been so successful, even when competing with one another, that they – as the Beatles – remained at the top of popularity polls in both the U.K. and America through the end of 1971. Close behind were acts such as Creedence Clearwater Revival, Simon & Garfunkel, and Crosby, Stills, Nash and Young. Other groups may have had more singles on AM radio, such as the Jackson Five, the Osmond Brothers, Three Dog Night, and the Carpenters. And there were certainly groups whose albums were selling well, with strong concert attendance, such as the Rolling Stones and Led Zeppelin. But to the world in general, no one had achieved the influence that had been enjoyed (or endured) by the Beatles. By the end of 1972, the Moodies seemed poised to occupy a similar place. They bridged AM, FM, and concert performances with great success. Another rising star from this period was Elton John, but he didn't achieve superstar status for a few more years. As a result, for more than a year (late 1972 through the end of 1973), the Moody Blues were (to borrow the words of a later song by Queen) "the champions of the world" of rock music.

Now, in mid-1974, the Moodies announced a hiatus from recording. This opened the door for other performers. Elton John was primed to take the lead and become the next big thing, with Paul McCartney and Wings hot on his heels.

The July 13, 1974 issue of *Sounds* reported:

> All the members of the Moody Blues are currently engaged on solo projects, but the group WILL be staying together, despite rumors to the contrary, and will record and tour as a group as soon as the individual efforts are completed.

> The first solo Moodies record to be release will be a single, "We Like to Do It," which is by the Graeme Edge Band – drummer Graeme Edge plus brothers Adrian and Paul Gurvitz, from Three Man Army. Guitarist Adrian was previously with Gun, and Paul was with Parrish & Gurvitz and Badger. The single is produced by Tony Clarke, [and] will be followed by an album in early autumn.

> John Lodge and Justin Hayward are currently recording an album together in the group's own Threshold quadraphonic studio, being used for the first time this week. A number of prominent American musicians will be flying in to help.

Ray Thomas is writing material for a solo album, and Mike Pinder, whose wife is American, is recording his in Los Angeles.

The group's RM man, Nick Massey, described the sudden flood of solo records as "a logical development. They have only waited this long because they have been waiting for the studio to be completed!"

One week later, in the next edition of *Sounds*, Bill Henderson interviewed the most talkative Moodie. Graeme Edge explained his reason for branching out with a band of his own. "It was a combination of being bored and being trapped – because the Moody Blues is a heavy philosophical band. Now I can be heavy and philosophical in me moments but I can also be a right 'ligger' [freewheeler]. And I was always getting trapped with work that I've done years ago when I was a slightly different person to what I am now. And although the Moody Blues is going to stay alive, it's going to change; it's got to change.

"It's not going to be five insular guys as we were known for being. We didn't like – or didn't get involved with – the normal trappings of stardom; never got caught peeing up lamp posts or stuff like that. We just got shut down and narrowed down and 'blinkered off' as the Moody Blues; blinkered off and pushed down a line that maybe half the time we didn't want to get involved in anyway. And the only way to break out is to become separate musical performers. Like, I separated from the Moody Blues and formed a partnership with Adrian, and I'm making another kind of music." (GE-S94)

The Graeme Edge Band would be a trio. Adrian Gurvitz told Bill Henderson, "It was me and Graeme who decided to do it originally. But we needed a bass player. So, rather than go out and hire a musician or something, my brother, Paul – of Parrish and Gurvitz and latterly Badger – just happens to play bass. We could have used Graeme's bass player [John Lodge] or my bass player; it was just the one who was available, the easiest whenever we wanted him." (AG-S74)

Since Edge was a member of what had recently been the No. 1 band in the world, he felt it only natural for the new group to be called the Graeme Edge Band. Threshold and Decca agreed. Adrian Gurvitz went along with the idea, but candidly told Bill Henderson, "It really stinks; this business stinks! But… music's my life. If I can't make music, I can't do anything." (AG-S74)

There was no plan to tour any time soon. Edge said, "There's a whole lifetime ahead of us and if 'Abe' and me keep making music together, of course we're going to play live one day. We'd both love to, anyway. It's just that I've just done a lot of traveling and living in and out of a suitcase. We just finished a world tour in March, which has kind of satiated my on-the-road feeling. Now I wanna put me arse somewhere and let some roots grow down. I've got tomatoes growing in me greenhouse, got some lovely sugar beets coming up; lovely stuff. Me peas are just fattening out; never touched by mankind spray of any kind." (GE-S74)

Although Hayward was disappointed that his fellow Moodies hadn't rallied around him and Tony Clarke earlier in the year to make an eighth album, he nonetheless was in no hurry to resume touring. His daughter Doremi was a year and a half old; Hayward seemed happy to stay home.

One positive signal that the Moodies were not disbanding was a report in the July 24, 1974 issue of *Variety*, saying that Jerry Weintraub would now takeover the management of the band, as well as Threshold Records. The Moodies had resisted having a manager since 1968. But now, with Mike Pinder moving to California with his American wife, the five members of the group would not be able to have their customary group board meetings. Each had made the decision to pursue solo projects, so the joint affairs of the band and its holdings would need a superintendant. Weintraub had done well for them as a promoter, and he was trusted.

It was further reported in *Variety*, on August 14, that Gerry Hoff would remain with the organization, as European manager of Threshold. Peter Jackson, not needed at the moment as a tour manager, was reassigned as liaison manager between Weintraub and the four Moodies in London.

Single release: The Graeme Edge Band
"We Like to Do It" b/w "Shotgun"
Threshold/Decca TH-18 (U.K.);
Threshold/London 5N-67018 (U.S.);
July 19, 1974

Graeme Edge told *Music Scene*, "I really want to make people laugh and there's no way you can do that under the banner of the Moodies. I want to lighten things up again. This single is my way of doing that. So, I'm getting it out of my system, and the others are doing their albums without the Moodies splitting up." (GE-MS74)

Billboard called the single "a rollicking novelty, as double-entendre as its title would indicate, somewhat in the vein of the Beatles' 'Why Don't We Do It In the Road?'"

Edge's efforts to promote his first solo single, however, also fanned the flames of the rumor mills, which had begun months earlier when a new Moody Blues album had failed to materialize as promised.

On September 14, 1974, *Billboard* magazine in America reported:

> London Records' high-energy push for the debut Graeme Edge Band single, "We Like to Do It," revealed an entirely different major story which had not been previously reported. The Moody Blues have apparently packed it in after five [sic; six]

years of consistent gold albums and SRO auditorium concerts.

Edge, the Moodies drummer, was refreshingly frank during his whirlwind one-week U.S. promotion tour for the single. "We just can't create new music together anymore," he says. "It's not a matter of temper conflicts or anything like that. We'd get into the studio and everything that came out was a carbon copy of our earlier things."

According to Edge, the Moody Blues are holding back 90 minutes of studio tapes which they do not want released.

"This last world tour we finished in February – 85 shows in 15 countries – was an attempt to break our creative slump," says Edge. "But the group has decided we don't want to keep going on for now if we can't honestly give audiences our very best." ...

Edge made similar statements about his group disbanding on several taped radio interviews. Whether the Moody Blues are in a temporary hiatus or permanent dissolution – and many major groups that disbanded "permanently" got back together after a few years away from the grueling pressures of rock star touring – they are clearly at a key decision point in their career. ...

The "90 minutes of tapes" likely included all the group's unused songs, dating back to 1968.

Music columnist Robert Scott looked into the rumors about the Moody Blues breaking up. One day after the *Billboard* article, Scott reported:

Hearts of rock music fans around the world had a stop-and-go rhythm this past week when *Billboard* magazine announced that the famed Moody Blues had broken up.

According to the Moody's business manager, Jerry Weintraub, the lads aren't breaking up. He described the report as "erroneous."

Various solo projects have given rise to rumors, but fans must presume the Moodys are just stretching their musical muscles like their countrymen, the Who.

Weintraub said there will be a new Moody Blues album after the first of the year and a major tour around the corner.

Sure hope there's no fire at the bottom of the smoke.

Rolling Stone jumped on the story, assigning Andrew Bailey to get the facts, and then syndicating his report to newspapers across America. On September 24, Florida's *The Pensacola News Journal* quoted Graeme as saying, "I suppose that we've created something of a Frankenstein. This thing has grown bigger than all of us." (GE-PNJ74)

Bailey continued:

The monster he's talking about is the Moody Blues, which its five creators are now giving an enforced rest.

After seven albums, all of which sailed past the million mark, the Moodys have found that their creative juices are not flowing so freely. But, they insist, it's only a temporary state. It's been two years since the group cut an LP, and two recent attempts in the studio ended in frustration.

Edge told Bailey, "After recording 80 songs over an eight-year period, adding up to 12 hours of music, it got to the point where we'd be halfway through a new number and then, wallop, we'd suddenly realize that it was beginning to sound like something we'd done before. Obviously it was time for a break." (GE-PNJ74)

From California's *The San Bernardino County Sun*, on September 26:

… The Moodys are not splitting up, that is clear. But this band, which has always worked out decisions by committee, has decided to clear the blockage by working on solo projects.

Mike Pinder, keyboard player and technical whiz, now lives in Los Angeles, where he is working on an album. There, he can escape Britain's punitive tax rates, which are hitting rock musicians hard – sending into exile, among others, the Who's Keith Moon. But Pinder can visit England only 60 days a year, under the law, and the Moodys are aware of the logistical problem that creates for them.

John Lodge and Justin Hayward are cooperating on a joint album and calculate that the results should be in the shops by Christmas. Edge is also partway through an album, with Adrian Ben Gurvitz, and is hoping for a release in December. Flautist Ray Thomas is the late starter, so far only at the writing stage.

In another article printed this day, in New Jersey's *Asbury Park Press*, Edge said, "The group was always to be the star, not the members." (GE-APP74)

This strategy had afforded the five members a measure of individual anonymity. But, as a result, they weren't individually familiar – weren't easily recognizable, easily marketable faces. They had put the group first; subduing their separate personalities; never featuring their faces on the front of an album jacket, and rarely appearing on U.S. TV. The comparatively low public awareness for single members had protected their privacy, but could now be seen as a detriment. John, Paul, George, and Ringo were known worldwide. They each had a step up in launching solo careers. But what of Mike, Justin, John, Ray, and Graeme?

Edge said, "Our followers expect a particular thing from the Moodys. I don't think that people look at us as individuals. I mean, we're thought of as a heavy band; strange ethereal creatures who deliver pearls of wisdom."

Brandishing his solo single, he continued, "If we put this out, the reaction would vary from suicide to threats of assassination, because it's really nothing more than a piece of good-time summery nonsense." (GE-APP74)

Radio agreed that it was nonsense and didn't spin the record. Its failure to chart made Edge – the first Moody out of the gate – the first to fall down. Regardless, the band members remained determined to chart their own courses, and each continued to work on their side projects.

In the September 28 edition of North Carolina's *The Gastonia Gazette*:

> ... Ray Thomas, after a quick reconnoiter of the others' studio sessions, described Edge's sound as being "more towards the heavy rock thing," and Hayward-Lodge's as being "more Moody's in feel; softer." And his own? "I can't tell you because I don't know. I'll be doing some sax playing, though, which up to now has only been on a joke level."

In the September 29 edition of Florida's *The Palm Beach Post*:

> ... The low in the Moodys' career, said Thomas, has come after a heavy year during which he estimated that they took in 76 concerts in 15 countries. "The group has come to a crossroad, just like it did before *Days of Future Passed* in 1967." ... [That] LP to date has sold around 2 million copies.

Thomas said, "That's how it started for us. It was hit or bust. That's where we are now, and it's stimulating. We were pioneers in those early days, and that's what we want to become again. When you think that *Days of Future Passed* was done on a four-track, imagine what we can do with our new 24-track [studio]." (RT-PBP74)

Edge commented in the October 10 issue of *Zoo World*, "This happened to the Beatles. We've done seven albums, had seven Number One singles [sic] and seven platinum albums. We've sold out shows around the world and we reached the point where we thought, 'What else can we do?' We were at a stage where nothing turned us on." (GE-ZW74)

To keep the record straight, the Moodies hadn't achieved seven No. 1 singles. They did have four to their credit: "Go Now!" (in England, in 1965), "Bye Bye Bird" (in France, in 1966), "Nights in White Satin" (in France, in 1968, and the U.S., in 1972, among other countries, including Canada and the Netherlands), and "Question" (in some English charts, in 1970, and also in the Netherlands that same year). There would be more to come. And, since Edge referenced the Beatles ... For the record, that group had 20 platinum albums by this time (in the U.S. and the U.K., with more to come), and 36 different No. 1 singles (around the world) ... plus many more to come as solo artists.

Edge continued, "People think there's been a big argument; a fight. There's been none. It was decided for us. We weren't making worthwhile music anymore. Actually, 'break-up' is a bad term for this.... Ours might be forever, but then we could regroup any day. It got to the point where we had a choice: whack out another three albums [to fulfill their contracts], rip-off the fans' money and destroy all we set out to do, or call it quits." (GE-ZW74)

According to this *Zoo World* interview with Edge, "two whole albums" had been recorded by the Moody Blues during 1973 and into '74, which were then "destroyed." (The other Moodies and their producer dispute that the amount of material recorded had been this high.)

Edge's promotion for his new single kept the rumors of a Moody Blues breakup in the public's ears. In *Concert* magazine, with an interview for its November 1974 issue, John David Kalodner asked how the mutual enthusiasm in the Moody Blues got lost. Edge said, "It is very simple – through constant repetition. I mean, take 'Nights in White Satin'; I must have played it probably two thousand times. And you can't put it down; they [the audience] won't let you. And they have a right... they have paid their $7.50 and they want to see the Moody Blues they know, and they've got a right to expect 'Nights in White Satin' and all the others. I'm proud of that music, but now instead of getting to the point that we are forced to hate it, we have to put it all down. ...

"To tell you the truth, I thought a few months ago that I had lost music. I got to the point that I never played the drum kit outside of a working situation. Unless it was something I had to do, like practice to be able to build the stamina to do an hour and a half on stage every night for weeks on end. But I never played them any more for the joy of it. I thought for a while it was because I was changing as a person, but I have now discovered that with my new music I haven't changed, and the joy of playing drums has returned."

Regarding the Moodies' various attempts to make a worthwhile eighth album, Edge divulged, "We went in the studio a couple of times, and just sat looking at each other and did a bit of this, a bit of that, and played it back, and it was horrible, and that was it. The last time we were actually in the studio as the Moody Blues was last fall (1973). And when that failed, and it without a doubt did, we thought we would go on the road – on the worldwide tour... and see if we could get all the excitement and energy back. But it didn't come back, and, in fact, the touring just made it worse. And so, with reluctance, regret, sadness, and a great deal of nostalgia, we put the work of the Moody Blues down for a while. ...

"The final tour was a real endurance contest for the band. And it was a make or break proposition – seven months, 15 countries, 80 gigs. And, in the end, it broke. ...

"[W]hat I did learn was how much the Moody Blues meant to me. I mean, if the concept didn't mean so much to me, I would have just gone right on 'milking' it for all it was worth. We would have released that album we made a year ago; people would have bought it, but it just wasn't inspirational to us."

Kalodner asked for clarification – was there really a complete album? Edge answered, "Oh yes, we have well over one full album 'in the can' that we have 'thrown away' – about 70 minutes of music."

How did the decision to disband, even if only temporarily, come about? Edge said, "Well, it was complicated. The feeling spread, sort of, in order. It took a period of three or four months from the time [of the] first one making that decision to the last.... Mike Pinder decided first. And I was probably the last one to really come to realize that it was time to put our work down. I really didn't want to for quite a while.

"There will be solo albums by Mike, Ray, and, of course, myself, and a duo effort by John and Justin. I am dying to hear Justin and John's work. I have enormous respect for Justin as an artist and a performer, and it will be so nice to hear an album of his songs that I have not been involved in the 'blood, sweat and tears' of. I'll just be able to hear the works of my fellow Moodys by putting them on my turntable and listening to them front to back, completely fresh and unburdened from all the gory details of their creation."

Other than talk to the press, Edge wasn't intending to do anything to help promote the single or the upcoming album. He said, "I don't really have the spirit to go back on the road for a while. Originally I thought it would be the 'right thing to do,' you know, tour while your new album is out. But then I thought to myself, 'Hey, what are you doing? This is what was wrong with the Moody Blues, you were doing what you thought you had to do instead of doing things when you felt right and you were all full of enthusiasm.' So I went to nurture and develop this new enthusiasm and joy, and then do it when it feels right." (GE-C74)

Decca had been pushing for a new album. Now that it was clear one was not coming, the label requested permission from the Moodies to release a compilation LP – a two-disc "best of" album. The Moodies granted the request and gave their input on song lineup and artwork.

Album release:
This Is the Moody Blues
Threshold/Decca MB 1/2 (U.K.); Threshold/London THS 12/13 (U.S.);
October 8, 1974

No tracks pre-dating *Days of Future Passed* were included, meaning that the material from the original lineup of the band, including the No. 1 hit, "Go Now!," was skipped over, as well as the 1967 singles by the Moody Blues. Nor were any of the band's unreleased tracks included, such as "Long Summer Days," "Please Think About It," "King and Queen," "Gimme a Little Something," "What Am I Doing Here?" and "Island." The album would, however, include one rarity – Mike Pinder's "A Simple Game." The little-known song had been released in England as a B-side, but this was the first time it was made available in the U.S.

Also on the album:

From *Days of Future Passed*: "Tuesday Afternoon" (Hayward), "Nights in White Satin" (Hayward), and "Late Lament" (Edge/Knight);

From *In Search of the Lost Chord*: "Ride My See-Saw" (Lodge), "Legend of a Mind" (Thomas), "The Actor" (Hayward), and "The Word" (Edge; recited by Pinder);

From *On the Threshold of a Dream*: "In the Beginning" (Edge), "Lovely to See You" (Hayward), "Dear Diary" (Thomas), "Never Comes the Day" (Hayward), "The Dream" (Edge; recited by Pinder), "Have You Heard, Part 1" (Pinder), "The Voyage (Pinder), and "Have You Heard, Part 2" (Pinder);

From *To Our Children's Children's Children*: "Eyes of a Child" (Lodge) and "Watching and Waiting" (Hayward/Thomas);

From *A Question of Balance*: "Question" (Hayward), "And the Tide Rushes In" (Thomas), and "Melancholy Man" (Pinder);

From *Every Good Boy Deserves Favour*: "The Story in Your Eyes" (Hayward);

From *Seventh Sojourn*: "New Horizons" (Hayward), "For My Lady" (Thomas), "Isn't Life Strange" (the 5:32 U.S. single edit; Lodge), and "I'm Just a Singer (In a Rock and Roll Band)" (Lodge).

Omitted, due to space/time constraints, were popular songs. Also, the version of "Question" on the album is a different mix than the one released on *A Question of Balance*.

In its November 16, 1974 issue, *Billboard* said to record dealers:

> Superb double set of some of the best of this amazing supergroup who enjoyed but a few "hit" records yet became one of the biggest disk sellers and concert draws in history. Reportedly the band has broken up, and if this is true the set becomes all the more important. As the first major band to make the Mellotron an integral part of its sound and as one of the first to employ intricate vocal harmonies and a number of lead singers, the Moodies set several styles that have been copied by a number of others. This set, which amounts to a virtual history of the group following their "comeback" in 1968 [when *Days of Future Passed* was issued in the U.S.] is a must for collectors and new fans alike who want a more complete introduction to the group than what's been on the radio. Contents lets one know just how much good music the Moodies did make together. ...

> Dealers: You know the Moodies sales record. Just display this one.

From the same day, *Melody Maker* said:

> ... They deserve much of the credit for broadening the spectrum of rock, one of the first bands to demonstrate how strings could be used without diminishing the credibility of the music. *Days of Future Passed* was quite a momentous album in its day and opened the way for the introduction of much deeper and more serious elements in contemporary music... Sweetness and melody are in abundance, and even after listening to a double album of the Moodies, there's no denying their worth. It's unfortunate they have to make such a big drama of everything, when the lyrics aren't always the most scintillating. ...

On November 23, Tony Stewart wrote in *New Musical Express*:

> ... As each of the Moodies' albums have been profoundly thematic, one of the basic problems, which has never fully resolved here, is to compile an album of various tracks which makes some sense as a whole. ...

> Producer Tony Clarke, who compiled and re-mixed the cuts, was obviously aware of the possibility that he could undermine the Moodies work, and has, I feel, attempted to add new dimension to the music, and perhaps illustrate that many of the songs can individually exist on their own merits. ...

Naturally, the other most obvious aim of the collection is to show that all five members are capable of writing reasonable songs. Although Justin Hayward contributes seven numbers, Ray Thomas, John Lodge, Mike Pinder, and Graeme Edge all have a fair crack at the whip by putting in four each (though the latter's are all poems). …

Clarke, though, has insisted upon mixing one track over another on what appears to be an effort to give the album unnatural fluidity and momentum. This practice does not always work. … Depending on how you view the Moodies this is either an abortion of their material or an excellent impression of their better moments. …

It was unfortunate that Clarke chose to use that cross-fading technique to link the various songs on the compilation. One thing that had kept many Moody Blues songs off the radio in the past was that disc jockeys did *not* have clean individual tracks to play, except for those songs released as singles. The problem continued with this release.

Freelance writer Barbara Rowes had an article in *The New York Times* (November 24, 1974 edition):

"We'd like to mean as much in the history of music as Beethoven," announced Graeme Edge, drummer and spokesman of the celebrated five-man rock group the Moody Blues. "We believe we're on the threshold of the greatest revolution in sound."

A pop pipe dream? Evidently so. For that was Edge speaking last January when the Moody Blues, having enjoyed their 12th anniversary together, were supervising the construction of a million-and-a-half-dollar recording studio near London, possibly the most sophisticated studio of its kind in the world. And Edge spoke for a group of musicians then confident that their elaborate equipment would provide them with the means to make their eighth album a Beethovenian masterpiece. But that album was never made. And today, the super-studio is empty [sic; Hayward and Lodge were recording the "Blue Jays" album there at this time], the Moody Blues have split up, and instead of the eighth album we have the recently released two-record requiem of the greatest of their hits of the past, entitled *This Is the Moody Blues*. This album at least deserves praise for being a thoughtful and well-integrated *in memoriam*. The sole original song in the collection, "Simple Game," may be the group's eulogy to its own career. Already it has won an English award for songwriting. A straight-forward declaration of independence composed by group member Mike Pinder, "Simple Game" emphasizes the word "free": "As time goes by, you will see that we are going to be free." …

The official word from London is that each musician is going to be making his own album. Edge already took the first step last August with a bouncy single entitled "We Like to Do It," which barely made the charts. His solo album, scheduled for release in October, still is being recorded; ditto Justin Hayward and John Lodge, who are reportedly collaborating on an album. Mike Pinder has moved to Los Angeles where he is living on a commune and allegedly composing. Ray Thomas still has not decided in which direction to turn.

So instead of the magical eighth album which the group mutually heralded as the masterpiece of its career, a two-record requiem of 26 of the group's greatest hits has just been released. Edge still insists that the musicians are busy scheduling recording sessions, but no new sounds have been launched with the NASA equipment. Instead, the multimillion-dollar recording studio is still only a monument to the promise of the music of tomorrow.

Jim Knippenberg, for his "Young Music" column in the December 14 edition of *The Cincinnati Enquirer*, said:

One of the major joys of the album is that it demonstrates, more than any one of the group's others, exactly how versatile the MB can be. There is absolutely no way to classify the music, but the influences you can hear range from the very strong classical lines through straight on rock and roll. …

In the December 16 edition of West Palm Beach, Florida's *The Palm Beach Post*, Tony Clarke was interviewed by Thom Smith. After Smith asked Clarke if the Moodies had in fact broken up, and destroyed two albums' worth of material because they were not good enough to be released, Clarke snapped, "Rubbish! Yes, I've heard that about the Moody Blues breaking up. We've got a lot of letters about it. We had fans literally on the doorstep of our offices from America, asking if the Moodies had broken up. Somebody's drawn the conclusion that since we haven't got a record out in two years, and since we aren't touring, that they've split up. But a band that's been together for 14 years [sic], that's achieved all what they have, doesn't break up."

Clarke was clearly counting the time that Thomas, Pinder, and Lodge had worked together, in El Riot & the Rebels.

Regarding the "destroyed" tapes, Clarke did some spin-doctoring: "There are *no* tapes. The people from Decca would ask, 'What tapes? Why did you destroy them?' It's hard to explain that we didn't have any."

So, had Edge imagined those 70 or so minutes of recorded music which, he claimed, he had taken part in making? And what about "Island," a Justin Hayward song recorded in January 1973, which has since been added to the 2008 remastered version of *Seventh Sojourn*?

Regarding the 1973-74 tour, Clarke admitted, "It was too long. But it was sort of expected of them. Everybody was making world tours, but it took too much of them; it's a big strain. I've seen them come back from a concert ashened. They won't do a thing like that again."

Clarke was in favor of the group not releasing what they may or may not have recorded. He told Smith, "I tell them, two or three years, it doesn't matter. We can't put out rubbish. The people will come back as long as it's good music. To put out a quick version would be suicide." (TC-PBP74)

Mike Daly and Paul Speelman, for their column, "New Notes," in Melbourne, Victoria, Australia's *The Age*, wrote:

> It's been a long time – too long – between releases for England's master musicians, the Moody Blues. But now they're back for the first time since their *Seventh Sojourn* – and with a double-album surprise package. It's a surprise particularly to the many devoted Moodies fans.
>
> *This Is the Moody Blues* is intended to be a compendium of their seven highly successful and much-imitated albums. Instead it's more a reprise with the Moodies indulging themselves in a little re-arranging of numbers that were perfect in the first place. Take the driving orchestral introduction from "Question" off the *A Question of Balance* album – it's been replaced with a longer guitars-only intro. Nowhere near as effective.
>
> But we're quibbling. The majestic Moodies are still the same superb poets and musicians. And, anyway, really devoted Moody Blues fans, like us, have the whole seven albums anyway.

In the December 21 issue of *Billboard*, it was reported that *This Is the Moody Blues,* only two months after its release, had become the band's eighth consecutive gold record in America. It would go gold in the U.K., as well, and platinum in Canada.

On the charts in America, *This Is the Moody Blues* did best on *Cashbox*, where it peaked on January 4, 1975 at No. 4, for the first of two weeks. *Billboard* ranked it just outside of the Top Ten, at No. 11. The peak in the United Kingdom was No. 14. In Canada: No. 2.

In the meantime, Justin Hayward, John Lodge, and Tony Clarke had been at work in the Threshold Studio. Joined for the first time since 1967 by Peter Knight, they began to make music for what might become the next Moody Blues album.

22

Catching Up with Denny Laine

(Photo source: UltimateClassicRock.com)

When we last looked in on Denny Laine, he had maintained his relationship with Brian Epstein and Decca Records, and released two singles on Deram – "Say You Don't Mind" b/w "Ask the People," in April 1967, and "Too Much in Love" b/w "Catherine's Wheel," in January 1968. For a touring band, he had hired guitarist Trevor Burton, formerly of the Move; drummer Viv Prince, formerly of Pretty Things; and a procession of orchestral musicians. However, after a year and a half of struggling, Laine came to the conclusion that the cost of trying to travel with members of an orchestra was cumbersome and hardly cost-effective. Discouraged, he pulled the plug on his Electric Sting Band.

In February 1969, Trevor Burton formed a group called Balls, with Steve Gibbons, who had fronted the long-established Birmingham group, the Uglys. Also onboard were the Uglys' rhythm section of Keith Smart and Dave Morgan, and keyboardist Richard Tandy (who later played with the Move and its offshoot, the Electric Light Orchestra). Balls was managed by Tony Secunda, who had left Ridgepride and the Moody Blues, but remained active in the music business, managing Procol Harum and the Move. In the Summer of 1969, Morgan left Balls and was replaced by Denny Laine. But this lineup was short-lived. The group split up by the end of the year, but reformed in 1971).

Meanwhile, in 1970, both Laine and Burton played in Ginger Baker's Air Force. Laine knew Baker from back in 1964, when the Moody Blues toured with Chuck Berry. Baker, and future Cream bandmate Jack Bruce, were also on the tour as part of a group

known as the Graham Bond Organization. Laine and Baker had remained friendly, which created the opportunity for them to work together, with another mate from Birmingham, Steve Winwood.

The first album, *Ginger Baker's Air Force*, was issued in April 1970, and featured Laine on guitar and backing vocals. He stepped up to share the lead vocals with Baker on one track, "Early in the Morning," and sang lead on a second song, "Man of Constant Sorrow," a traditional number which he also arranged. When *Ginger Baker's Air Force 2* came out in December, Laine contributed guitar, piano, and backing vocals, and also co-wrote one song with Baker for the album. The tune, "You Wouldn't Believe It," appeared on German, French, Australian, and New Zealand versions of the LP, but not on the U.K. or United States release.

Above: Ginger Baker, drummer for Cream, Blind Faith, and Ginger Baker's Air Force.
(Photo source: Pinterest)
Below: Balls with Denny Laine (second from right).
(Photo source: DennyLaine.WordPress.com)

Laine said, "I was in the band until it broke up. But that was really because of Ginger's situation, you know, with – I hate to say it, but – his addiction situation." (DL-RM09)

By this time – late 1970 – Laine, Burton, and Steve Gibbons had reteamed for a new lineup of Balls, with ex-Spooky Tooth drummer Mike Kellie. The group stayed together during the Spring of '71, releasing a single – "Fight for My Country" b/w "Janie, Slow Down" – in September of that year. The

A-side was an anti-war anthem written and sung by Burton, with backing vocals from Laine. Burton and Laine shared the vocals on the B-side. But even before the single's release, Laine had left the group to form Wings with Paul McCartney.

Laine said, "It was because I was in the Moody Blues and we were friendly with the Beatles. Paul and I were pretty good friends, or, shall I say, acquaintances, before. I was doing something of my own after I left the Moody Blues [the Electric String Band].... I think [seeing me performing with them was] what gave Paul the idea of doing something with me, because he knew me, and he wanted to do something original, and he couldn't go on following the Beatles. So, he had to put a band together and do his own thing." (DL-HT17)

McCartney had experienced great success as a solo artist in the past year and a half since leaving the Beatles, but at a price. He was commonly blamed for the breakup, and many in the rock press were resentful, rooting against him. While it was not true – Lennon had actually been the first to exit – McCartney had been the first to announce that he was leaving. Further, he did so in a most dramatic way, timing the release of his *McCartney* album to go head-to-head against the last Beatles LP, *Let it Be*. Despite its pinnacle atop the LP charts – and at least one undeniable classic, "Maybe I'm Amazed" – many critics savaged *McCartney*, finding the one-man band album both underwhelming and, they said, insignificant. Time has proven but viewpoints wrong.

In the Spring of 1971, after filing a lawsuit against John Lennon, George Harrison, Ringo Starr, and manager Allen Klein to dissolve the Beatles, McCartney came back with a Top 5 hit single, "Another Day" b/w "Oh Woman Oh Why." In the Summer of '71 came a chart-topping second solo album, *Ram*, plus a U.S. No 1 single – "Uncle Albert/Admiral Halsey." Again, reviews were mixed; many critics savagely attacked *Ram* as overblown and trivial. Years later, the album would be reassessed as a classic, but 1971 was a year in which McCartney could do no right with the music press. Perhaps in reaction to this, McCartney set out to assemble a group for his next album. For the project, he recruited a pair of Dennys – his old friend, Denny Laine, and session drummer Denny Seiwell, who had played on *Ram*.

Introducing first lineup of Wings, while rehearsing their first album on McCartney's Scotland farm, late summer 1971. L-R: Denny Laine, Denny Seiwell, with Linda and Paul McCartney. (Photo source: Pinterest)

Wild Life was recorded in July and August 1971, when *Ram* and "Uncle Albert/Admiral Halsey" were riding high in the album and singles charts.

Many of the songs were recorded live in the studio, in single takes. In fact, on "Mumbo," the opening track, you hear McCartney call out to his recording engineer, "Tape it, Tony!"

This Tony Clark, not to be confused with Moody Blues producer Tony Clarke, said, "We did the initial tracks in one week and it took two weeks in all…. The whole essence of the feeling that was going on was to get it as 'live' as we possibly could in the studio." (TC-NME71)

Regarding his decision to record an album in such a freewheeling manner, McCartney told *New Musical Express*, "The thing is, having a new group, and it being a new set-up, it came very naturally. Denny [Laine] got about three days rehearsal on some stuff, but that's the way I wanted it. I'm sure a lot of the music I like was put together that way – it's the immediacy." (PM-NME71)

"Immediacy" seemed to also mean announcing the next album (and group) before McCartney's current album or hit single had even vacated the top slots in the respective American LP and singles charts. On September 2, 1971, *Rolling Stone* reported:

> Paul McCartney has formed a band behind him, with both records and live performances in mind. The group includes wife Linda on piano and vocals, Denny Laine on guitar, and Denny Seiwell on drums. ...
>
> Laine has played with the Moody Blues and Air Force, and made an album with a group called Balls that was never released, presumably because there would never have been airplay on the BBC. ...

Wild Life was issued in December, and, just as the two previous albums from McCartney, it received mixed reviews.

Denny Laine: "You can't expect to be as good as the Moody Blues or the Beatles when you just get together, no matter who you are. It just takes time, and, of course, in our case, we just recorded whatever we did, as we did it, and put it out." (DL-G10)

In the December 18 issue of *Billboard*, the trade's music critic was one of the kind reviewers, writing:

> The McCartneys (Paul and Linda) have solicited the talents of the Dennys (drummer Seiwell and guitarist Laine) to become the first supergroup of 1972. The LP is more acoustic and less gimmicky than McCartney's last two and, among the eight songs, four are triumphs: "Bip Bop," "Tomorrow," "Wild Life," and [a cover of] Mickey and Sylvia's "Love Is Strange."

Allen Evans of *New Musical Express* was also charitable:

> Paul McCartney's third album since the days of the Beatles is a bit odd, though not in any derogatory sense. Depending on which side you play first you will find yourself either bouncing up and down

500

to good old-fashioned rock 'n' reggae, or closing your eyes, enjoying soft, dreamy romantic songs. ... But it is, nevertheless, a good, solid album and one that should draw forth favourable criticism from even the most biased quarters. ...

Some of the most "biased quarters" could be found at *Rolling Stone*, where John Mendelsohn said that the LP was "largely high on sentiment," and then quipped, "but rather flaccid musically and impotent lyrically...."

Robert Hilburn of the *Los Angeles Times* didn't much like it either, but at least he resisted using sexual metaphors to make his point. The headline over his review said it all: "McCartney's Third Disappointment."

Denny Laine: "The reason the critics knocked it was because they were expecting a big production. But, you know, you have to understand that, when a band is just starting, you're not in the mood to go in and do that. We were not trying to follow the Beatles or the Moody Blues; we were just trying to do our own thing. ... So that album really was a result of that band [and] where we were at that time." (DL-TH17)

Like the Moody Blues before him, McCartney was deeply affected by rock elitists' attacks on a heartfelt project. Years later, in recalling the period, Linda McCartney revealed that her husband had fallen into a serious depression. Laine saw this too, and was very aware of how much McCartney depended on his wife, the reason why he had wanted her onstage with him.

Denny Laine: "I liked Linda a lot. She was a great influence on [Paul], so that made it easy on me. I didn't know Linda until I was in Wings, [but I could see how] she was very good for him at that time, because he was going through a lot of Beatles' legal problems – the whole Allen Klein situation. It all made him literally retreat to the hills of Scotland. She was his support system. I liked her for that alone, but I also liked her because she was very honest about things. She was not trying to be some big star; she got pushed into that more than she wanted to be. She was not a musician and she was the first one to own up [about that]. She didn't want to be in the band, but he got her into it. ... She was misjudged by people a lot, I think. Really deep down, she was a good lass. She had his back, which was great." (DL-TH17)

Wounded by the plethora of negative reviews, McCartney turned his back on *Wild Life*. The band made no radio or TV appearances to support the LP; there were no promotional videos filmed; and no singles were released, even though the album contained a pair of promotable tunes – "Some People Never Know," which, according to the *Los Angeles Times*, was the most-sampled song on radio at the time of the LP's release; and "Tomorrow," which Robert Hilburn called "probably the best selection on the album." It's not widely known, in fact, that a single had been planned: the quirky, reggae-styled remake of "Love Is Strange." The idea was scrapped when McCartney saw the beating the album was taking. As a result, *Wild Life* only managed No. 6 in the U.S. (*Cashbox*) and No. 11 in the U.K. a lackluster showing for a former Beatle.

Things were better for Denny Laine, who by now was familiar with the diminishing returns of a career after being part of an immensely popular group. In January 1972, former Zombies front man Colin Blunstone covered Laine's 1967 song, "Say You Don't Mind," and took it to No. 15 in the U.K. singles charts. This, in combination with Laine's alliance with an ex-Beatle, served as a shot in the arm for his career.

Meanwhile, McCartney was eager to take his security blanket – wife Linda and the two Dennys – on the road, and added a fifth member to Wings. Since he would be playing bass guitar on stage, with his caring wife on keyboards at his side, McCartney asked Laine to suggest a second guitarist to play lead to Laine's rhythm guitar. Laine arranged for his boss to meet Henry McCullough, formerly of Joe Cocker's touring group, the Grease Band. After jamming with the band, McCullough had the job.

To coincide with the low-profile warm-up tour, Wings issued its first single, the highly controversial "Give Ireland Back to the Irish." Many in the music press felt that McCartney was trying to imitate the political songwriting style of his former partner, John Lennon, the darling of the music press. In response, McCartney

And then there were five. L-R: Seiwell, Linda and Paul McCartney, Laine, and new member Henry McCullough.
(Photo source: Pinterest)

insisted that making a political statement in a song was his right as much as anyone else's. He said, "I figure I'm a [tax] payer, so that entitled me to an opinion. I'm living in the West, so we're allowed to talk over here, right? So, when the English paratroopers – *my* army who I'm paying for – go into Ireland and shoot down some innocent bystanders … I'm moved to make some kind of protest.'" (PM-BOTR03)

Laine was reportedly against issuing the song as a single. The other band members were equally concerned.

Henry McCullough told author Garry McGee, "I joined the band and then we came out with 'Give Ireland Back to the Irish,' and I thought, 'God, I have to be careful where I stand here.' In saying that, I had a brother who was in an Irish pub in London, and he was asked if he was my brother, and he said he was. And he was asked again, 'Did he play on that record, "Give Ireland Back to the Irish?", and he said he did. And he ended up with a bottle in his face over it." (HM-BOTR03)

To little surprise, the song was banned from radio play in England. Nevertheless, the single sold well, making No. 16 in the U.K. charts and going to No. 1 in Ireland. In the U.S., "Give Ireland Back to the Irish" only managed No. 21 on *Billboard*.

In early February 1971, Wings took to the road, albeit a seldom-travelled one. McCartney said, "In the beginning we had to swallow our pride and do some small, anonymous concerts. It was necessary to get the group used to the idea of being a band." (PM-LAT73)

Wings takes flight, with families, dogs, and two vans, in February 1972.
Pictured, L-R: Two roadies, Paul & Linda McCartney, their daughters Mary and
Heather, Denny Seiwell (and significant other), Henry McCullough, and Denny Laine.
(Photo source: exchange.nottingham.ac.uk)

Wings' first concert was at Nottingham University in the Portland Ballroom, on February 9, 1972. McCartney told the Nottingham *Campus News*: "We decided we'd just go on the road with no plans, no hotels booked, no gigs booked; a complete blank canvas. So we set off with the band, the family, the dogs, the babies – up the motorway. We headed north and saw a sign that said Ashby de la Zouch, so we got off the motorway there and asked where the nearest 'uni' [university] was. This became the idea that the only place we could maybe find a captive audience would be somewhere like a 'uni.' So, we were directed to Nottingham Uni and that's how we found it. It was the first time we had tried that idea. I'm really glad we did. It's a completely off-the-wall idea for someone who had been in the Beatles, to go and completely start from scratch again and, you know, looking back at it, I was like, 'Why did we do it?'" (PM-NCN)

Reuter News Service reported:

> Former Beatle Paul McCartney and his newly formed group, Wings, gave their first public performance Wednesday after a spur-of-the-moment decision. And 1,000 surprised and delighted students at Nottingham University got the pop music treat of the year. …

Denny Laine: "The fact that we went out and started turning up at Universities just to play meant that we needed to play live to an audience to get the feel of the band;

get into the confidence, and the rest of it. … So, we decided to jump in a van just like the old days and pretend we were just a band from wherever, starting up. Our roadie would go and say, 'We've got Paul McCartney in the van.' They'd say, 'No, you haven't!'" (DL-TH17 and DL-MNT17)

Henry McCullough: "On several occasions, they didn't believe that Paul McCartney was sitting in this van with dogs and a couple of kids… and they had to come out to double check, so to speak. But once they realized it was Paul McCartney with his new band Wings, then it was no problem. And after the gig… there'd be a bag of money, and it'd be, 'Two for you; two for me.' It was great. It was like pocket money. It was a great way to work." (HM-BOTR03)

Denny Laine: "It was a good way of getting the band in shape, basically, and to get used to playing live. And we had some fun staying in cheap hotels, under the radar." (DL-MNT17)

After getting banned from the BBC with the first Wings single, McCartney chose a safer song for the group's second 45 release – a retooled version of the nursery rhyme, "Mary Had a Little Lamb," a song his infant daughter Mary loved to hear her father sing. To make this gentle tune a little easier for rock-music fans to accept, McCartney put the catchy piano rocker "Little Woman Love" on the B-side. Denny Laine advised against releasing "Mary Had a Little Lamb" as a single. The other band members questioned the decision too.

When asked his impression of the song, Henry McCullough said, "'Mary Had a Little Lamb' was a little strange. … [Paul] was the leader, so to speak, and the way it worked, at that particular time, [was] he was strictly the boss." (HM-BOTR03)

McCartney told *Melody Maker*, "I was the only one who thought it should have been a single.… But on tour the audience really picked up on that one and sang the la lahs. … 'Mary' sold as many copies as 'Tumbling Dice,' in England, y'know. So there!" (PM-MM72)

"Mary Had a Little Lamb" reached No. 6 in the U.K. charts. America wasn't as amused. Despite the group appearing on the *Flip Wilson Show* to perform the song, its best showing in the U.S. was No. 28 on *Billboard*. In fact, many American radio stations chose to play the flip side, "Little Woman Love," instead.

Next, McCartney wanted to tour Europe in an open-air bus. As with the university jaunt earlier in the year, the chosen venues were intentionally small, averaging at about 1,000 people per show. The first concert took place at the Centre Culturel at Chateau Villon in South France.

Denny Laine: "The way things were going in the early days, it was too chaotic, because we were starting again but we were very aware that we were being looked at; stared at. And we were nervous." (DL-BOTR03)

Wings travelling Europe by open-air bus, Summer 1972.
(Photo source: Pinterest)

Among the tour stops was the Olympia in Paris. Laine was no stranger to the venue, having performed there with the Moody Blues.

In its July 29, 1972 issue, *Billboard* reported:

> Paul McCartney made a triumphant return at the Olympia with his band, Wings, for a two-concert stint eight years after appearing with the Beatles. …
>
> Throughout most of the set, Paul played bass and was accompanied by two fine guitarists, Denny Laine and Henry McCullough, with strong drumming from Denny Seiwell. The band shows every sign of becoming a tight, coordinated group, although the inexperience of Linda McCartney, both as a singer and keyboard player, is still disconcertingly apparent. The band gains from the solo talents of Laine, who sang well on his own "Say You Don't Mind" ….

In December, Wings' third single, "Hi, Hi, Hi" b/w ""C Moon" was well received by fans and critics alike. The A-side shot into the Top 10 on all three U.S. national singles charts, with its peak position on *Cashbox* at No. 6. In Britain, the BBC again banned the record, this time claiming references to both sex and drugs.

Fortunately, DJs in England flipped the disc over and "C Moon" became the hit, peaking at No. 5 in the U.K.

In the Summer of 1973, Wings released its second album, *Red Rose Speedway*. This time, McCartney's name came before the group's – and an attention-grabbing picture of their front man occupied the cover. To sway the critics back to his side, McCartney and Wings delivered an album far more polished than *Wild Life*.

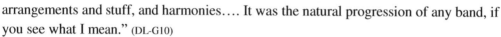

Laine said, "[O]f course, the next album was a little bit more intricate. We went for a lot more arrangements and stuff, and harmonies.... It was the natural progression of any band, if you see what I mean." (DL-G10)

Perhaps predictably, Robert Hilburn of *The Los Angeles Times* panned the record:

> ... Paul McCartney, my instincts told me, was due for a worthwhile album. He's simply too proven a talent to continue producing material so far below expectations. ... But *Red Rose Speedway* reflects little improvement over McCartney's other post-Beatle projects. Because his vocal skills and feel for melody remain, McCartney never really makes an unlistenable record, but he simply hasn't produced anything in *Red Rose Speedway* that touches you in either an entertaining or emotional way. It's merely a competent album. It doesn't even contain "Hi, Hi, Hi." So much for instincts.

Billboard was kinder, calling the album "a rockin' good new set." Jim Conley, in his syndicated newspaper column, called it "very pleasant listening," adding, "What seem at first just to be catchy little tunes turn out to grow within your head."

For *Rolling Stone*'s review (July 5, 1973), Lenny Kaye noted that "as the best of *Red Rose Speedway* indicates, Paul McCartney's music tends to crumble under prolonged examination." He concluded:

> Still, despite expected hits and misses, I find *Red Rose Speedway* to be the most overall heartening McCartney product given us since the demise of the Beatles. After

much experimentation with how best to present himself, Paul has apparently begun a process of settling down, of working within a band framework that looks to remain stable....

Despite mixed reviews, *Red Rose Speedway* topped the U.S. album charts. It also did well in Britain, hitting No. 5. "My Love," released as a single, also topped the U.S. charts, and made the Top 10 in the U.K.

At this time, McCartney and Wings had a national TV hookup in America with *James Paul McCartney*, a 60-minute primetime television special on ABC-TV.

Robert Hilburn called it "traditional" and "middle of the road," with McCartney and his group "involved in several stylized, beautifully photographed 'segments,' most of which could be lifted and inserted as nice, but certainly forgettable, guest spots on a Flip Wilson or Dean Martin variety show."

Picture used in *TV Guide* Close-Up listing for *James Paul McCartney* (ABC-TV, 1973).
(Photo source: stltoday.com)

McCartney said, "The feedback had been 50-50. Part of the problem was the sponsor, Chevrolet. Some of our ideas were a bit mind-blowing for them. We wanted to have a drag scene, like Diana Ross in drag. All the band would be dressed as ladies and Linda would be a fellow. ... but Chevrolet heard about it and said 'no.' They wouldn't let us do 'Hi Hi Hi' either, which was funny because that segment was run in England where the song had been banned from the radio, but not in the States." (PM-LAT73)

Only two months after topping the U.S. charts with "My Love," Wings did it again with "Live and Let Die" (No. 1 on both *Cashbox* and *Record World*; No. 2 on *Billboard*). The title song to the latest James Bond movie went Top 10 in the U.K. *Rolling Stone* magazine called it "the best record Paul McCartney has made since 'Let It Be'." For the B-side, Laine was given the spotlight, taking the lead vocal on the McCartney-written "I Lie Around."

Laine released his first solo album, *Ahh...Laine!*, in November 1973 on the U.K.'s Wizard Records label. It comprised 12 original songs. Warners/Reprise handled the release in

the U.S., and issued a single from the album – "Find a Way Somehow" b/w "Move Me to Another Place" – but both LP and single failed to chart.

For the next Wings album, McCartney chose an EMI recording facility in Lagos, Nigeria. Explaining the curious decision, he told Chris Welch of *Melody Maker*, "We got a list from EMI of all the studios [they own] around the world; it's a big company. We checked on the availability of Lagos and it turned out it would be free for the three weeks we wanted to record. So, we thought, 'Great – lying on the beach all day, doing nothing; [then] breeze into the studio and record." (PM-MM73)

Shortly before Wings was due to fly to Lagos, guitarist Henry McCullough and drummer Denny Seiwell dropped out.

McCartney said, "Henry left over what we call 'musical differences.' … We were rehearsing and I asked him to play a certain bit. He was loath to play it, and kinda made an excuse about it couldn't be played. I, being a bit of a guitarist myself, knew it could be played, and rather than let it pass I decided to

First Wings, late summer 1973, about to be grounded. L-R: Seiwell, Laine, McCartney, McCullough, and McCartney. (Photo source: tumblr.com)

confront him with it, and we had a confrontation. He left rehearsals a bit chocked, then rang up to say he was leaving. I thought 'fair enough,' so it was exactly the stereotyped 'musical differences.'" (PM-MM73)

According to McCullough, it was anything but "fair enough." The tensions had been building for a while, and were not limited to musical differences. He said, "We didn't get paid for tours; we didn't get paid accordingly; we didn't make money with Wings. You were with one of the most famous bands in the world at that point, but we were still on a smallish retainer. … We were promised different things initially – in the beginning – about when things got up and rolling as Wings, then we would be sort of treated a little bit better, financially. But it never came about. I think that was one of the problems that occurred; it was also part of Denny Seiwell's reason for getting out of it as well. We'd been up to Scotland rehearsing *Band on the Run* for like two weeks prior to going to Lagos to do it, and three days before – no, four days before – we were due to go, I couldn't take it anymore." (HM-BOTR03)

As for drummer Seiwell, McCartney said, "Denny didn't want to come to Africa. … [He] rang up an hour before we left from Gatwick [Airport] to say he couldn't make the album. So, that was panic time." (PM-MM73)

Although two-fifths of the band had jumped ship, the two McCartneys and Laine flew to Africa and made the album on their own.

Denny Laine: "So me, Paul and Linda go out there and the studio wasn't that great. It was all kind of old equipment, you know, hand-me-down EMI equipment. And nobody really knew what they were doing out there. But we had Geoff Emerick, who was the Beatles' engineer, with us." (DL-G10)

Laine played numerous guitar parts, and contributed percussion sounds and backing vocals. McCartney sang lead vocals, played bass, guitar, keyboards, and drums. Linda McCartney sang harmonies, combining her voice with her husband and Laine to create the distinctive three-part Wings' vocal sound. All the songs were written by McCartney except for "No Words," a collaboration with Denny Laine. Laine said, "'No Words' was two [of my] songs that were put together. It was Paul's idea to [make them] one song, and then he added a few lines in the last verse, and helped me put it together. So it came to be, you know, a dual composition. But, basically, it was my song and all the rest of the songs [on the album] were his." (DL-G10)

The recording sessions were problematic. The McCartneys were robbed at gunpoint on the streets of Lagos, and there were unfounded accusations from the locals that the band was "stealing their music."

Following these difficulties, the band fled Lagos for the comforts of a London recording studio, where the album was completed with the help of former Beatles producer George Martin. It was then aptly named *Band on the Run*.

The McCartneys and Laine in Lagos, Nigeria, 1973. (Photo source: Inner sleeve, *Band on the Run*)

A preview, or "trailer," came in the Fall with the single release of "Helen Wheels," released in October, 1973. It went Top 10 in the U.S., and hit No. 12 in the U.K. Upon its release in November, *Band on the Run* jumped to the top of the charts in both the U.S. and the U.K.

Laine said he was "very proud" of *Band on the Run*. "I think it has a special feel because it's just me and Paul playing the instruments, and it had a different feel to any of the other albums." (DL-HT17)

Chris Welch of *Melody Maker* said, [W]ith this album, Wings prove they are not just a flutter, or playthings, but a highly valued addition to the ranks of music makers."

Even *Rolling Stone* liked it. Critic Jon Landau called *Band on the Run* "the finest record yet released by any of the four musicians who were once called the Beatles … with the possible exception of John Lennon's *Plastic Ono Band*."

Charles Shaar Murray, reviewing the LP for *New Musical Express*, called it "a great album," adding, "If anybody ever puts down McCartney in your presence, bust him in the snoot, and play him this."

Remarkably, even McCartney's most heralded album couldn't get a thumbs up from Robert Hilburn, who clearly was begging for somebody to bust *him* in the snoot. The hypercritical critic said:

> … I can predict rather easily that *Band on the Run* won't be remembered as anything more than a slight upturn in a what has been a steadily declining artistic barometer for McCartney.

Another miss for Hilburn the soothsayer.

Band on the Run spawned two additional hit singles. "Jet" came out in January 1974, making the Top 10 on all three U.S. charts, and going to No. 7 in the U.K. The LP's title track followed in April, shooting to No. 1 in the U.S. charts, and No. 3 in Britain.

To satisfy McCartney's desire to take to the road again, Wings was augmented with two additional musicians – former Thunderclap

Newman guitarist Jimmy McCulloch and, formerly of American bands Jam Factory and Tall Dogs Orchestra, drummer Joe English. The first fruits of their labors was a double-side hit single, "Junior's Farm" b/w "Sally G," released in the Fall of 1974. "Junior's Farm" made the Top 5 on all three U.S. charts, and "Sally G" went to No. 17. The single scored a No. 16 slot in Britain.

Wings, 1975 (L-R): new members Jimmy McCulloch and Joe English, with Paul, Denny, and Linda.
(Photo source: SomethingElseReviews.com)

This brings us back to the stopping point of our story of the Moody Blues. As 1974 wound down, the Moodies were on hiatus. Elton John had becoming the new "world's most popular rock artist," followed closely by Wings.

Peaking ahead into Denny Laine's not-too-distant future, McCartney and his new Wings lineup released *Venus and Mars* in 1975. For this album, Laine was featured as lead vocalist on the McCartney-written song "Spirits of Ancient Egypt."

Denny Laine: "That was mainly at Paul's instigation; he wanted it to be that way. He didn't want the spotlight to be on him all the time; he was kind of sick of that. You've got to remember that Paul – and he won't mind me saying this – was a great bass player and harmony singer. That was his role in the Beatles and, also, obviously, he wrote a lot of his own stuff and did his own thing. But his forte was as a great bass player and great harmony singer, and John Lennon was kind of the more [dominant] guy of the Beatles' co-written stuff…. Well, I mean, the main hits; let's put it that way. And then Paul went on to be his own man, as far as writing, [with] his songs – 'Yesterday,' and all that stuff, [like] 'Fool on the Hill.' But in Wings, he became the lead singer…. and that was a lot on his shoulders, you know. So he wanted to bring us in to balance it out a little more. … He tried to get us all to do stuff, to the point that he would write a song for me to do, like 'Spirits of ancient Egypt' and 'The Note You Never Wrote.'" (DL-G10)

The reviews were mostly good.

Greg Shaw of *Phonograph Record* called *Venus and Mars* McCartney's "most advanced, refined, diverse effort yet," adding that the album "should allay the fears of those who suspected that, after one good album he might go back to nursery rhymes or one of the other forms of mediocrity of which he's proven more than capable in the past."

The music critic for *Billboard* wrote:

> Mr. & Mrs. McCartney & Wings have a strong candidate already for album of the year in this one. The former Beatle's talents become more and more obvious with each new venture. As with *Abbey Road*, it's an interconnecting work which makes striking sense the more one listens to each song, alone and in sequence.

Even Robert Hilburn had learned to appreciate Paul McCartney and his Wings. In *The Los Angeles Times*, he covered the new album and evidenced a reappraisal of *Band on the Run*:

> Paul McCartney, after finally regaining his artistic balance in *Band on the Run*, has come back in his new *Venus and Mars* with what is not only the most appealing album by an ex-Beatle since John Lennon's *Imagine* but the first genuine Beatle sounding album of the 1970s. … The album, in fact, is so much like a Beatles package that you can spot one tune that Ringo Starr would surely have sung and a couple that reflect the intensity that John Lennon would probably have brought to the project. … By all rights, *Venus and Mars* should be enough to formally put McCartney back on top of the pop music hill, but someone else – Elton John – is already there and he shows no sign of stepping aside. …

Paul Nelson of *Rolling Stone*, however, wasn't buying it. He called *Venus and Mars* a "disaster" which "comes with more extraneous junk (not all of it in the grooves) than it can sustain." Nelson felt that the entire package – record, gatefold cover, two posters, and stickers – "seems more an inadvertent definition of artistic emptiness."

Did you think that *Rolling Stone* only went after the Moody Blues?

The naysayers in the music press couldn't keep *Venus and Mars* from shooting to the top of the charts in both the U.S. and the U.K. Its first single, "Listen to What the Man Said," was also a chart-topper.

Laine's travels with McCartney and Wings continued through the rest of the 1970s, and the former Moody Blue became more visible with each new Wings album and tour.

With 1976's *Wings at the Speed of Sound*, which topped the U.S. album charts and hit No. 2 in Britain, Laine took the lead vocal spot on two songs – one which he composed, called "Time to Hide," and the afore-mentioned McCartney-written "The Note You Never

Back cover, *Wings at the Speed of Sound*.

Wrote." Also in '76, Wings took flight for a sell-out world tour, for which Laine performed "Go Now!" The set list also included him taking the spotlight for "Sprits of Ancient Egypt" and "Time to Hide."

"Wings Over America" tour, 1976, with (L-R) McCulloch, Laine, McCartney, and McCartney.
(Photo source: onstagemagazine.com)

"Wings Over the World" and "Wings Over America," as the two legs of the tour were called, was an eye-opening experience for Laine. He had never played venues as large as those that Wings easily filled to capacity during 1976. The Moody Blues always played "very close-up to audiences," as Laine put it. "In other words, playing small places – bars, clubs, etc. We went on to doing theaters – that's as big as we ever got, with the Beatles, and on the Chuck Berry tours. But we never did a big arena gig. I think the only arena gig I ever did [with the Moodies] was the Wembley Arena, because it was the *New Musical Express* Poll Winners Concert. …

"So, we went on to those big stages. … It took five hours to set up our stage and lights and all that stuff. And everywhere we went was the same set, same crew, same show, and it gets to become really smooth and easy. … Of course, we didn't even know what the lights looked like from the audience's point of view, until we saw the *Wings Over America* [movie] footage. And then it was like, 'Wow, that's great! I would have liked to be in the audience for this one!'" (DL-RM09)

In May 1977, Laine released his second solo album, *Holly Days*, covering songs

Buddy Holly had first recorded. McCartney sat in as producer and arranged for the album to be released by EMI.

Denny Laine: "Originally, I was going to do it with session musicians in Nashville, but the producer, Ray Stevens, wasn't available at the time… so Paul started to make the backing tracks in Scotland. When I went up there, we finished up the album. … It turned out pretty good, because it was more fun to do that with a friend." (DL-HC17)

Despite being "pretty good," the album missed the charts.

In November 1977, Wings scored their biggest hit ever in England – which was also the all-time top-selling single in that country. With 2.5 million copies sold, it topped the 2 million sold by the previous title holder, the Beatles' "She Loves You." The new champ was the McCartney/Laine collaboration, "Mull of Kintyre."

WINGS DOUBLE A

MULL OF KINTYRE

Denny Laine: "[Paul] had the idea for a song. I went up to have breakfast with [him and Linda] up in Scotland. ... I heard the chorus and I said, 'That's a potential hit song.' So, the next day, we went and finished it off; we sat down and wrote the lyrics and put it together. Then we brought in the Campbeltown Pipe Band, and they were all excited. It was the first time they'd ever been in a studio...." (DL-TH17)

Later in the year, the sixth Wings studio album, *London Town*, was released, making No. 2 in the U.S. and No. 4 in the U.K. Laine co-wrote the title song with McCartney, as well as "Don't Let It Bring You Down," "Morse Moose and the Grey Goose," and two other songs which featured Laine on lead vocals – "Children, Children" and "Deliver Your Children."

Another Wings album, *Back to the Egg*, followed in 1979 with Laine singing lead on the McCartney-written "Again and Again and Again." One year later, he released a third solo album, *Japanese Tears*.

But we're getting ahead of ourselves. Now, we return to 1975, with Wings' *Venus and Mars* at the top of the album charts, and Robert Hilburn declaring the band the second most popular recording act in rock music, bettered only by Elton John. Moody Blues fans had been wondering what happened to their favorite band, and why the Moodies had relinquished the pop crown without a fight. It had been nearly three years since their last studio album, *Seventh Sojourn*, and over a year since the group last performed in concert. But now, three of the six Moodies (including Tony Clarke, as the other five band members did), were about to return, with the classic Moody Blues sound.

23

Blue Jays
Justin Hayward and John Lodge, 1975

Album release
Threshold/Decca THS 12 (U.K.); Threshold/London THS 14 (U.S.); March 10, 1975
U.K peak position: #4
U.S.: #7 (*Cashbox*)

Single release: *"I Dreamed Last Night" b/w "Remember Me"*
Threshold/Decca TH 19 (U.K.); Threshold/London 5N-67019 (U.S.); April 18, 1975
U.S. peak position: #29 (*Billboard* Adult Contemporary)
U.S. Top 100 singles chart: #45 (*Cashbox*)

Single release: *"Blue Guitar" b/w "When You Wake Up"*
Threshold TH 21 (U.K.); Threshold 5N-67021 (U.S.); June 27, 1975
U.K. peak position: #8
U.S.: #82 (*Cashbox*)

John Lodge said, "As the Moody Blues, we never made a decision *not* to do anything. We made a decision not to do anything about *doing anything*. So, Justin and I just carried on." (JL-CR75)

Hayward and Lodge told Peter Crescenti of *Circus* magazine that they had hoped to recruit Mike Pinder, Ray Thomas, and Graeme Edge for the sessions, but all three were unavailable.

Justin Hayward: "I was under a lot of pressure from Decca to come up with something to release, so I actually went to America to do something with Mike, between the two of us. Then Tony Clarke and John turned up at Mike's house as well. Mike took me in the other room and said, 'I don't want to work with anybody else; I'm out of this project.' So then it became me and John and Tony Clarke." (JH-SSI13)

Pinder remembers it differently, telling *Higher & Higher*, "While I was in America, [Justin] decided to do it with John Lodge instead.... I *was* available. But they seem to have the mindset that anyone who isn't living within five miles of them isn't available. I thought of it as being only eight hours away by plane." (MP-H&H94)

Twelve hours, actually, not counting getting to and from the airports, with layovers between flights.

The backing band: Kirk Duncan and Graham Deakin (standing between Hayward and Lodge), and Jim Cockey, with Tim and Tom Tompkins.
(Photo source: Pinterest.com)

The sessions were moved to London and the Threshold Studios, with John Lodge taking Pinder's place, and other musicians recruited to take the place of the other absent Moodies. They were Kirk Duncan, on keyboards, and Graham Deakin on drums.

John Lodge: "We met Kirk and Graham at some session they were doing in the past, while the string players come from a band called Providence." (JL-RI75)

Tony Clarke had suggested having the string section from Providence come aboard. They were Jim Cockey on violin and French horn, and brothers Tim Tompkins, on cello, and Tom Tompkins, on viola. Hayward said of Clarke, "Musically he had a big influence on us with this album because he knew Providence, the group we worked with. He discovered them and recorded them in the first place...." (JH-ZZ76)

Assistant recording engineer Dave Baker said, "We had the Providence guys and they were really nice people; very genuine, very concerned, no kind of rock star-ishness about them. If the Gurvitz brothers [of the Graeme Edge Band] were some of the [most difficult] people I've ever met, these guys were among the nicest. They never put their instruments down. Once they stopped working at the microphone, they just went somewhere else in the building and started writing. So you'd walk around the corner and suddenly stumble on three hairy guys playing strings!" (DB-H&H96)

Recording the Album:

The sessions for *Blue Jays* took place at the new Threshold Westlake Audio Studios (formerly a Decca studio) in West Hampstead, London. The recording phase was broken into two extended sessions. Hayward told Andy Childs of *ZigZag*, "We started in June '74 – and don't forget this was a brand new studio which had never been tried out, and, although nothing went wrong with it, we spent a lot of time working out things that happened in the studio, like, getting the 2-track to work took about two days. But it never broke down. Fantastic place. We went in June, took August and September off, [returned in October] and finished it in December, in time for Christmas." (JH-ZZ76)

The reason for the two-month layoff, according to John Lodge, was to help assemble and then oversee the making of the *This Is the Moody Blues* compilation album.

Moving through the album one track at a time, in chronological order:

"This Morning" has the sound of classic Moody Blues, from the first notes, into Hayward's vocal, the beautiful melody, and the words that so perfectly begin the journey:

> *As the dawn is breaking on your future, my child,*
> *Is there none of your love alive?*
> *If every door you open closes on me,*
> *I don't know if I can survive.*

Hayward told interviewer Andy Childs, "There were only three of us on it originally. Kirk did the backing track… then it changes tempo at the end and turns into a big instrumental. It's got very close harmonies – we worked out the harmonies all the way through in thirds between John and I and, I think, it was the first vocal session we did." (JH-ZZ76)

While the album credits do not list that a Mellotron was used, some of the tracks certainly bear the touch of a synthesizer of some kind. Many commenters, in print and online, have the same impression.

"Remember Me, My Friend" represented a couple of firsts. It was the first songwriting collaboration between Hayward and Lodge. It was also the first backing track made for the album, therefore the first recording made in the new Threshold Studio.

John Lodge: "During the Spring of '74, Tony put together our studio in London, and Justin and myself came in, and the first song that we made together – wrote together, played together on – was 'Remember Me, My Friend,' and it seemed to state the road that we were going to take." (JL-MOBJ75)

Hayward told *Circus* magazine, "It was easy for us in so many ways, because we'd always shared the same side of the stage, and we are both guitar players, which made a lot of difference. It meant that we could just sit in our room and play together. That's how the first song we wrote for the album came together – 'Remember Me' – because we sat down and just went through a few pieces, and it fell together." (JH-CR75)

One friend sings to another: "You don't need to ask me if I'll be your friend / I am / I am / You don't need to ask me if I'm sure, my friend / I am / I am."

John Lodge: "With 'Remember Me, My Friend,' there is a joining of the minds.... When you find somebody, who is a friend, it is one of the greatest things in the world. It can be a spiritual thing." (JL-GM17)

Hayward said, "It was also the first time we met the other guys. We rehearsed it up in the afternoon and put it straight down.... We rehearsed it with everybody and it went down first take all the way through....

"[T]hat track was really the beginning because it had a lot of energy going for it, and also it was a very spontaneous thing that actually went on for 9 ½ minutes. But we cut it back to 4 ½ just to get it on the record. It was an exciting start and we knew we were on to something; the band had taken on an identity, and it was something [John and I] had written together." (JH-ZZ76)

As of this writing, in 2017, the longer version has not been released. However, on the cassette tape and reel-to-reel versions of the album, sold in 1975 and for several years after, the version heard is about one minute longer than that on the vinyl (and now CD) releases.

In a different interview given at the time of the album's release, Hayward said, "For everybody it was like a little happening doing our first number in the studio. And when we'd done the take, we knew it was *the* one. Everybody looked around and said, 'Okay by me; great.'" (JH-CR75)

Elsewhere, Hayward said, "And then about a week later, Providence turned up. We played them the track; they added their bit, and there it was; [we] couldn't believe it. It was at that point that we realized that it wasn't just a collection of songs we were knocking out; it was going to be a proper album, and it sort of snowballed from there." (JH-ZZ76)

"My Brother" was a song many felt Hayward had written to Mike Pinder, across the sea, in America.

Hayward sings: "My brother, if you could cast a little light on someone, it's not too soon. You took me half way round the world / I'm running out of time and reasons. My true friend, if you could tell me what it is that keeps you from coming down / You left me way up in the clouds / The higher you fly, the less I see you. So far cross a wild and windy sea / So far that our voices are divided by an ocean."

Hayward said of the sessions, "'My Brother' was the third one we recorded. It was a time when everyone was feeling relaxed, everyone was friends, there was nobody that was not going to be there at the end of the album. We realized that, and that relaxed feeling comes through on the track." (JH-ZZ76)

"You" was written and sung by John Lodge, reminiscent of his "Isn't Life Strange" in that the melody is both rich and memorable.

He said, "I've got a favorite guitar at home – it's an old Harmony Sovereign which I bought in the States on my first trip across – and I thought it was about time it wrote me another song. And out came 'You.'" (JL-MOBJ75)

Regarding the recording of this track, Hayward said, "It was the first time we'd both played lead guitar.... We did a lot of the electric guitar right into the box. We were able to do that in the control room itself – some of it – and we just sat facing each other in the control room. It was really 'too much' with a Fender plugged in and a Gibson 335 straight up the desk. Knockout – with it coming back at you in Quad. Great feeling."

Lodge added, "All the lights out, no one in the studio; no one at all." (JL-MOBJ75)

What they accomplished sounds quite Beatles-ish at times.

"Nights, Winters, Years," written and sung by Hayward, is a song for the dead of night where loneliness lives. Hayward sings, "Pain, sorrow, tears / Long, lonely years / With love having passed me by. I could live a lie for you, but truth is the road I choose / knowing all I need to do … is give to you. Down, down, down where your dreams are found / They're sleeping inside us all."

This song brought about a reunion of the two Moodies and their producer with Peter Knight and his orchestra, the first since *Days of Future Passed* in fall 1967.

Hayward said, "It was the first of three songs on the album we did with Peter Knight. It was purely coincidence, really; we had to speak to him to see if he got his gold record for *Days of Future Passed*. He hadn't, as it turned out, and we told him we were in the studio and asked him to come along. He came along and we played him a few things, and we mutually agreed that we'd like to work together again, like, eight years later! So we did a little demo of each of the songs and he took them away. 'Nights, Winters, Years' was the first we did with an orchestra on. It was really a simple song which I played to people at home. And Peter carted the orchestra in and made it into *this*. Incredible, fantastic feeling! He's a wonderful guy, he really is. I think he's the best musical director in the country." (JH-ZZ76)

Knight's excellent orchestral score highlights the track, accompanying what many consider among Justin Hayward's finest vocal performances.

Tony Clarke: "I just want to say that it's an unbelievable experience being able to sit there and watch a performance sung… but to hear it the first time, and watch it grow – performances like 'Nights, Winters, Years'!" (TC-MOBJ75)

"Saved by the Music" was the closest thing to an up-tempo number on the album, even though it shifts between fast and slow. John Lodge said, "'Saved by the Music' was a lot of fun to do. I suppose it shoots back to 'Just a Singer (In a Rock and Roll Band.' [The song] means that everybody else's music is important to me as well. Certainly I sit at home and listen to records… and sometimes people think you don't do that, for some strange reason." (JL-ZZ76)

Aware of what other's music had done for him, Lodge sings, "When you're following all life's lies … and find its meaning and truth still hides / Don't cover your face / Let the warmth come flowing through / Welcome dawn new morning dew. This time I'm saved by the music, saved by the song we can sing / This time I'm saved by the music, saved by the song that you bring."

Justin Hayward: "John had written this song called 'Saved by the Music,' and we knew, from when we started the song, it was a kind of 'anything goes,' and it was a kind of experimental thing, as much for us in that it was one of those numbers where everybody tried out what they could do on different instruments. And, in the end, we got a whole little orchestra of our own going…. French horns, you know, and stuff, and guitars all over the place, and little piccolos and the high flutes. Knockout." (JH-MOBJ75)

John Lodge: "We had great fun making that track. Providence are in there, and we worked a French horn part in there, [but] nobody could play a French horn! Jim

Cockey, the violinist, got a book called *How to Play the French Horn*, with diagrams and everything! He learnt from that." (JL-ZZ76)

This is yet another track that recreates the feel of the Moody Blues, with use of piano, flute, and what sounds like a synthesizer in the mix.

"I Dreamed Last Night," by Hayward, is the best-known track from the album due to its release as a single.

Justin Hayward: "'I Dreamed Last Night' was one of those songs that turned out to be really easy to write. I remember it was done in just an hour or so, the whole thing! And you consider yourself lucky when those come along. And, in the end, it turned out to be an easy song to record, too, because it was one take. It was one [of the three songs we did] with the orchestra with Peter, and we had one run through; one take, that was it. And it turned out a knockout." (JH-MOBJ75)

"Who Are You Now," a melodically simple yet lovely song, is also by Hayward. He said, "I remember coming to the studio, and it was just one verse long at the beginning – it must have been the shortest song I'd ever written; about a minute. And everybody said, 'It's got to be longer; got to go round again.' So, I did another quick verse, and that was it – I put it down. " (JH-MOBJ75)

He sings: "Somewhere on this crazy island, a familiar stranger sleeps so far away / But wonder in the eyes of children, and the smile of fortune, helps the memory fade / 'Cause they are all there is to know … about me. Who are you now?"

Justin Hayward: "It's a very personal type song – memories of a few years ago – and I think we all must wonder when we look back, and we'd love to see people again. And I'd just like to know, 'Who were you, and who are you now?'" (JH-MOBJ75)

John Lodge called this "the only real acoustic number on the album – no double-tracking anywhere, it was done straight off." He added, "There are a number of songs that are to do with definite statement in as much as it must have happened to everybody – they'd like to know who somebody was, or they'd like to see somebody they knew ten years ago; first love, etc." (JL-ZZ76)

"Maybe" is by John Lodge – another one of those "You"-like songs, with a simple yet strikingly pretty melodies … an area of songwriting shared with "Isn't Life Strange."

Regarding the instrument he'd used while composing the song, Lodge said, "At home I've got this harmonium which I think is about 150 years old, and it seems to play itself."

A harmonium is a pump organ that generates sound as air flows past a vibrating reed. In a drafty house, the instrument will indeed "play itself," starting with a single musical tone, which can them change with the force of the draft.

Lodge continued, "I was sitting in the kitchen one day and I suddenly could hear this harmonium playing. I went into the dining room, started to play it, and I wrote a song called 'Maybe,' and it just seemed to write itself all the way through from start to finish." (JL-MOBJ75)

He told *ZigZag* that the harmonium had belonged to Mike Pinder, adding, "It's got a great tone. Unfortunately, the air leaks out of it, so I couldn't use it on the album – I use a pipe organ instead." (JL-ZZ76)

"When You Wake Up," written by Hayward and Lodge, is the last track on the album, and also was the last song recorded for *Blue Jays*.

Justin Hayward: "I can remember, actually, we just had it written on a piece of paper, and it was, 'When you wake up, you will find that you're not where you left yourself.' And I remember I kept passing that piece of paper around and looking at it. And John and I had been working on another thing… and one day we said they were made for each other. It was probably the most written-in-the-studio number that we'd done." (JH-MOBJ75)

John Lodge: "As a matter of fact, we were just going to venture onto something else, and it was, literally, 'Hey, do you remember that piece of paper on the piano?' [This was] at 12 o'clock, in the control room. And, by 4 o'clock, we knew what we were trying to do, as it were. It was also done on a note of optimism. We'd just about finished the album and everybody was in on that session – roadies, everybody. It was like the final statement of the album, and we wanted everybody to take part in it." (JL-ZZ75)

You would swear Ray Thomas's voice was included on the chanting of the chorus … and Pinder's piano styling.

Throughout the album, and very prominent with this last track, is Hayward's use of the electric guitar to create melodic lead solos. Scan through the radio … or internet radio … and land on a station playing Jimi Hendrix. Before you hear his voice, you recognize his guitar. The same can be said of George Harrison, or Keith Richards, or David Gilmour. There are many great rock guitarists, but only a handful have such a distinctive style, and sound, that you can recognize them after only several seconds of a guitar solo. Justin Hayward, sadly underrated, grossly overlooked, is one such classic rock guitarist, in our opinion. This song demonstrates his style, his sound, and his talent, beautifully.

***

Tony Clarke: "*Blue Jays* is probably, in reality, a year's work, putting it together in the studio and then recording the album, and seeing the album through, because there's an awful lot of things that have to be right before an album gets to you. And I think it's the most harmonic and melodic [of the records we made] – and it's an honest album. I'm very proud of *Blue Jays*." (TC-MOBJ75)

Assistant recording engineer Dave Baker, reassigned from the *Blue Jays* project to work on the Graeme Edge Band's debut LP, *Kick Off Your Muddy Boots*, left the sessions before the last song was recorded. He was so put off by the experience of dealing with the Gurvitz brothers that he was seriously considering finding a new profession. However, working on *Blue Jays*, he recalled, was a pleasure. He said, "That was a good album. The atmosphere was very creative and there were some good songs on that album. It's one I still listen to. You could see things taking off in a different direction and it had a good feel to it, especially after *Seventh Sojourn*, which had been quite hard work. The atmosphere on that album was superb." (DB-H&H96)

Shortly after completing *Blue Jays*, John Lodge enthused, "There was a difference working with other people, but there was no difficulty because everyone really wanted to give everything they had. Everybody who worked on the album wanted to give a one hundred and one percent effort. It was just fantastic." (JL-CR75)

Justin Hayward, always cautious regarding his music, told *Beat Instrumental*, in 1975, "Even though we are pleased with it, it's not 100 percent perfect. Whatever is? On reflection, you often think that an album could be a little better, but it must be that way. You must have an impetus for future recordings." (JH-RI75)

When the mixing sessions were complete, Tony Clarke went on holiday with his wife and children to Disney World in Florida. While there, he gave an interview to Thom Smith for the December 16, 1974 edition of *The Palm Beach Post*. Clarke said of the not-yet-released *Blue Jays*, "It's the biggest album of my life. It's bigger, wider, and more musical.... We've worked harder on this album than any we've ever done. That's why I took this holiday; we were worn out [from] 14 and 15 hours a day in the studio." (TC-PBP74)

As for the new Threshold Studio, Clarke called it "the best in Europe; it's like *Star Trek*."

First Reactions (pre-release):

Reported in the March 1, 1975 issue of *Record Mirror*:

> A world premiere at New York's Carnegie Hall will launch the debut album from Moody Blues hit writers Justin Hayward and John Lodge. Called *Blue Jays*, the album will be played back in quadraphonic sound to an audience invited from all over the world. *Record Mirror* will be there.
>
> The event is already being billed as "the musical occasion of the year" and strict security surrounds the release of the album. No-one will hear it before the March 10 premiere, when it is also released in the States. British release follows on March 14. ...

From that same day, in *Melody Maker*, it was reported that the album would premiere in front of 2,800 people, a combination of members of the music press, DJs, and fans.

> ... The campaign is one of the most expensive in Decca Records history and is certain to renew speculation about the future of the Moody Blues. ...
>
> Edge is now recording an album with Ginger Baker and Adrian Gurvitz, to be released in early summer. Mike Pinder, the band's keyboard player, has been living in Los Angeles for the past 10 months and is also recording a solo album.

A spokesman for the band told *MM*: "It's not true the Moodies are defunct. The band will be back together again after the various solo projects have been completed. Mike Pinder is living in the States because he has an American wife. And, besides, he has two homes – one in the U.S. and one in Britain. But he'll be back with the band when they start work again. It's more than likely that'll be before the end of this year. There will always be a Moody Blues."

MM also reported that "Remember Me, My Friend" was to be the first single issued from the album.

From *Melody Maker*, March 22, Ray Coleman reported:

> It was the most expensive promotional undertaking by Decca, who release the Moodies' Threshold label. The launch cost 100,000 dollars (about £45,000). A total of 2,800 people heard the Carnegie Hall playback – 300 disc-jockeys and writers, 2,500 winners of a New York radio station contest.

Rolling Stone magazine had Ed McCormack there. He reported:

> … As responses to a ticket contest sponsored by radio station WNEW snowballed toward an unmanageable 35,000 requests, Weintraub asked the city for permission to broadcast the proceedings to the luckless throngs who would surely be grieving outside the hall. Fearing trouble, the police refused, but on the big day, orderly lines of fans waited peacefully in the cold even as the privileged cynics of the press partied with the two Moodies amid the wilted canapés of the Carnegie Tavern.

McCormick described Jerry Weintraub as a "robust, sun-tanned man who proudly admits that his patron saints are P.T. Barnum and Mike Todd."

> … But then the hall lights dimmed and the faithful fluttered into place, focusing their attention on a giant album cover which featured a schlock surrealist landscape in which the tiny figures of Hayward and Lodge stood at the edge of a cliff.

> Incredibly, the fans greeted the cover with a standing ovation.…

The U.K. magazine *Sounds* sent Pete Thomas to cover the event:

> Uncanny! The florid splendor of Carnegie Hall must have known many strange occasions but this little episode surely takes the cookie. Picture yourself if you will a grander version of your average town hall. The stage is bare save for large banks of speakers, very tastefully arranged, of course, and a screen suspended centre. As the lights go down there's that air of hushed expectancy found at most concerts, then the album sleeve design is projected onto the screen and the music begins – a reverent silence lasts for just a few seconds. Magic is afoot here. A few bars into this opening track and the crowd are applauding wildly. …

Justin Hayward: "It was the most incredible thing I've ever seen in my life. There's John and me in the dressing room at Carnegie Hall, and the house is full, and all there is on stage is a record player with a couple spotlights on it. And they say, 'Ladies and gentlemen, the very first performance of *Blue Jays*!' And then someone plonks the record on. It was ridiculous." (JH-Q90)

Record Mirror was also on hand for the "ridiculous" record premiere, reporting on March 15:

> ... A minute into the quad playback there was no mistaking the sound. The invited audience of 2,800 broke into a spontaneous roar of approval.

New Musical Express, also there, added:

> ... The sound system was magnificent as it projected the first acoustic bar of "This Morning," and then, just as the song went into a tempo change on the last word of the first verse, there was a standing ovation. By including 1,000 [sic] fans, the atmosphere was guaranteed. Going into a publicist's office to hear a new album will never be the same. ...

Record Mirror:

> ... In a more refined way, the complete Moodies tradition of dreamy songs overlaid with synthesizer, Mellotron or orchestra, is maintained. It is perfectly relaxed – jangly acoustics prefacing most songs and, of course, a stunning display of studio technique.

Rolling Stone:

> ... As the playback washed through the impressive quadraphonic sound system installed by *Blue Jays* engineer Tony Clark [sic] it became increasingly clear that Hayward and Lodge had transplanted the patented, ponderous arrangements and poignant Oliver Twist vocals of the mother band. In effect, they had made a Moody Blues album. ...

Sounds magazine:

> ... The album cannot be accepted as anything less than another Moody Blues product, and by presenting it to the world with such flash and style Jerry Weintraub – MB manager – has made sure this fact does not go unnoticed. Even so, the spectacle of an audience applauding passionately after each track and giving the completed playback a standing ovation was very odd.
>
> That the two of them didn't at least walk on stage to acknowledge the crowd was even odder still. In the event, they remained back stage wondering what to do with the adrenalin buildup. ...

Melody Maker:

... John and Justin sat backstage while [the album] was played in the darkened theatre, too nervous to join the audience. It was, they said, like being present at one's own gig but not being on stage. As weird scenes go, this was one of the weirdest. ...

John Lodge said, "And, at the end of it, everyone stood up and shouted for more. It was quite bizarre. And we never even went out on stage. We wanted to go out and say 'thank you,' but they said, 'No, you shouldn't do that; it'll spoil the atmosphere.' Strange." (JL-Q90)

Rolling Stone:

> ... Most of the faithful remained in their seats until the end, even after it was clear that the principals who'd warranted such respect would not favor them with appearances. Then they rose and left, nearly all wearing their complimentary Jerry Weintraub buttons which bore the message of the day: "I heard the *Blue Jays* album at Carnegie Hall."

(Photo source: MoodyBluesAttitude.com)

Melody Maker:

> On the face of it, the costly operation was a lunatic's flight of fancy by music biz operators who ought to know better ways of investing money during an economic recession, but the man behind the stunt appeared to be no ordinary mortal. ...

Far from "ordinary," he was Jerry Weintraub, manager of John Denver, the Moody Blues, and tour promoter for Led Zeppelin, Frank Sinatra, and Elvis Presley, and rapidly becoming a legend in his own time ... and mind.

Weintraub, surveying the crowd at the Carnegie Hall, boasted to *Melody Maker*'s Ray Coleman, "The record would be a smash without any of this, but it's a 'first' of its kind, this event, and what the hell are we all doing in the music business if we can't have a bit of fun?! And Carnegie Hall is the best place in the world in which to hear music. This event ensures that disc-jockeys and writers can listen to *Blue Jays* without their wife shouting at them, or the baby crying, or the doorbell ringing while the record is playing." (JW-MM75)

From *New Musical Express*, reactions from the floor: An American DJ identified as "Billy the Beard" was saying, "Well, it's the first time anything like this has been done, and there was a lot of criticism about it, a lot of speculation, a lot of people were thrown back by the whole thing, and a lot of people were even thinking about the pomposity of it all But no matter what they thought, it came off!"

Billy the Beard had an opinion about why Weintraub made the premiere so, well, over-the-top. He speculated: "He's always had a great, great desire to own a circus. And deep down in his head and his heart he's a circus owner. He wants that excitement; that constant activity; that constant three ringer of what's going on, of something new happening, and of something fresh."

Hayward and Lodge were finally allowed to speak … to the press, at least, but at a different location.

Pete Thomas wrote:

> … Back at their hotel suite overlooking Central Park, Jus and John look more than a little relieved. "Yeah, it was strange," says John. "I just wished we'd played a gig. I suppose this sort of thing has never been done before."

> He explains that Jerry Weintraub thought of the idea after visiting England to hear a private playback of the album on New Year's Eve. He travelled from Los Angeles, heard the album, then returned to L.A. …

Lodge told Thomas, "On the way home, he thought, 'That's silly, I've just travelled 12,000 miles to hear an album.' But he dug it and thought the whole idea was great and decided we should do this in New York. He rang us up four days later and said, 'I've booked Carnegie Hall for the playback.' And we said, 'You what?!'" (JL-S75)

Hayward told Thomas, "What could we say? We're proud of it anyway, and, if it can't stand up on its own, there's something wrong with our judgment. We made a record we like." (JH-S75)

Did the release of *Blue Jays* give credence to the rumors of a Moodies breakup? Hayward told entertainment correspondent Kim Garfield, "The breakup was news to us, and we should have been the first to know." (JH-SJ75)

Lodge added, "I don't even know how the rumor got started; we just wanted to keep on working after we finished our world tour." (JL-SJ75)

Garfield asked Hayward and Lodge why, after such an ambitious tour, spanning the autumn of 1973 into early winter of '74, the two of them had chosen to commit to making such an extravagant LP – without Pinder, Thomas, and Edge. Hayward answered, "Recording was our relief. We had a lot of songs we wanted to record and we had a brand new studio of our own to work in. This was our way of relieving all the strain that had been built up from the tour. …

"We began writing the songs after the world tour, although the bits and pieces of them were developing for some time. Actually, if you know you're not going to record right away, you're better off leaving the bits and pieces in the drawer instead of trying to finish them."

Regarding the name *Blue Jays*, Hayward said, "So many albums use surnames, but we felt that 'Hayward and Lodge' was just a bit too impersonal. We wanted a one-word title and we finally discovered it after the artist came up with our cover drawing. We noticed the birds, and since both our names begin with the letter 'J,' we came up with 'BlueJays.' Also, many of the songs are love songs and mention birds here and there. The artist did the drawing after he heard the music." (JH-SJ75)

That artist was Phil Travers. For his design, Travers changed the one-word title, "BlueJays," to *Blue Jays*.

According to Garfield's article, Pinder, Thomas, and Edge each sent Hayward and Lodge telegrams wishing them well with *Blue Jays*.

Of course, the now-familiar "Moodies Backlash" was striking hot again. Many in the press lashed out at the hype of the Carnegie Hall premiere, and the money spent. John L. Wasserman wrote for the *San Francisco Chronicle*, in its May 17 edition:

> … How can I communicate to you the cosmic nothingness of the occasion? How to express the transcendent irrelevance of it all? What can one say about the non-event of the 20th century?

And, from the May 24 issue of *Melody Maker*:

> How could anyone justify hiring Carnegie Hall, flying dozens of mass media men across the Atlantic, wheeling in hundreds of their American counterparts, just to listen to a new album being played?

Justin Hayward: "None of us really anticipated fully that there would be such a reaction. The whole thing just turned into a story that got exaggerated. Somehow the point that was missed was that this was a good way of releasing an album. In the States, if one FM station gets an album first and plays it first, then the others aren't too interested. The Carnegie Hall launch was the best way of alleviating this problem. I mean, you can work in devious ways or do something straight. As soon as you do something straight, people think you're being devious." (JH-MM75)

Album release: Threshold THS 12 (U.K.) and THS 14 (U.S.), March 10, 1975

Justin Hayward told Tony Stewart of *New Musical Express*, "It's exactly what we wanted to do, and you can only trust your own judgment in what you make and what you like. And if it doesn't sell a copy, it will destroy my faith in what I think is good, because I think it's good. And I think it's good for *everybody*. I'm proud of it, for everybody [involved]. I'm proud of it for everybody in the Moodies as

From the Moody Blues comes Justin Hayward and John Lodge comes "Blue Jays."

The album of 1975

well – because the music's being played and the fans have got stuff to listen to, and I think it's what they want. They've desperately wanted some albums out of us." (JH-NME74)

In the March 22, 1975 issue of *New Musical Express*, Tony Stewart had a full-page review of the album, saying in part:

> … They sing as they do with the Moodies, they play as they do with the Moodies, they write as they do with the Moodies. … Ironically they have made an album of ten tracks which betters several of the MB's albums, even though they're three short on what are theoretically *integral members* of the band. …

> Melodically the material is invariably stronger, particularly exemplified by Lodge's "You," Hayward's "I Dreamed Last Night," and their two co-operative compositions, "Remember Me, My Friend" and "When You Wake Up." The latter includes some excellent examples of their quite extraordinary harmony work. …

> But what makes this set even more like a MB album (in particular *Days of Future Passed*) is that they've enrolled the services of conductor Peter Knight, whose head is still apparently in a 1967 cloud. Certainly the track "Nights, Winters, Years" would slide very neatly into *Days of Future Passed*, as regards both concept and total sound. …

> Generally, though, the main advantage this work has over, say, *Seventh Sojourn*, is its consistency of style and instrumentation (even if this is a mixed blessing), which does in itself create one drawback for some MB fans, in that, if they prefer Mike Pinder's or Ray Thomas's work to Hayward's and Lodge's, they won't like this album. However, considering the success of the band's singles, most of which were written by one or other of the "Blue Jays" combo, that's unlikely. …

Also from March 22, Ray Coleman of *Melody Maker* wrote:

> … Within a few days of its announced release, *Blue Jays* had shipped gold, as they say in America, and the word is that it will be a massive British seller too. This week, the two artists are doing the rounds of a British commercial radio tour for promotional interviews. … What about the music though? …

Certainly the album carries a lot of Moody Blues hallmarks, with heavy string sections featured on most of the tracks; with Tony Clarke, as ever, producing; with swirling violins; with the vocals commanding each song with great strength, and with lyrical clarity a major characteristic.

Justin and John trade song for song throughout the record, although they co-wrote two, and, for me, the most immediately attractive tracks are "Who Are You Now?" by Justin – always the band's finest writer – and "Maybe" by John Lodge. …

All told, it strikes as a trifle bland, but on the whole – a Very Nice Album. …

Pete Thomas of *Sounds* said:

… The album is everything an avid Moody Blues freak would wish to fill the gap left by that band's retirement. More important though, it establishes these two as "keepers of the keys" during the self imposed solo period all of the old group are going through. Jus and John have unashamedly adopted the Moodies sweeping lyrical stance and so continued a great tradition. It begins with the sleeve – designed by the Moodies regular artist – and continues through each of the ten songs. …

With this new album, Justin and John have proved that they can make as good, if not better, albums than the old group as a whole. …

Record Mirror:

From now on, for Moody Blues, read Blue Jays. Two songwriters – Justin Hayward and John Lodge – who premiered their debut solo album here today, have taken up where the old band left off.

The two members of the Moody Blues are fully aware that it is a Moodies album. "We feel as though we are carrying the flag for the fans," said Justin Hayward, admitting this new phase could last a long time. …

From the March 22 issue of *Billboard*:

The Moody Blues have officially disbanded, but you won't be able to convince anyone who listens to this set put together by two of the driving forces behind the group. Cut with a symphony orchestra, the album brings back memories of the "Nights in White Satin" days, with smooth, flowing cuts, powerfully soothing production and solo and harmony vocals that are reminiscent of the best of the Moodies. To be honest, there is not a great difference here between the overall sound of the duo and that of the Moodies – and the Moodies were one of the biggest groups in pop history. Expect immediate FM play (response is already strong). Best cuts: "The Morning," "My Brother," "Nights, Winters, Years," "I Dreamed Last Night," "Maybe," "Who Are You Known [sic]."

Dealers: Let the customers know who this duo is and you've got a super seller on your hand.

Mike Diana, writing in his U.S. newspaper column, "Hear Say," on March 30, admitted that he was *not* a fan of the Moody Blues:

> … They have that certain something that makes them one of the most listened to groups in the world and that makes me want to go screaming from the room. …

> *Blue Jays* opens with an impressive tune called "This Morning." The song, written by Hayward, is complex and rather interesting. It blends orchestration, guitars, drums, etc., with a strong melody line and moody lyrics (no pun intended). Hayward does the lead vocal work and Lodge fills in the back-up. The song has enough substance to be embellished by a 2,000 piece [sic] symphony orchestration and not submerged and drowned out ala Moody Blues.

> "Remember Me, My Friend," cut Number Two, is so stuffed with garbage that the basic song is jumbled and lost. The tune straightens itself out (and really gets going) in the fadeout, of all places. The symph drops out and we are suddenly confronted with piano, bass, drums, acoustic guitar, and congas.

> "My Brother" is not orchestrated. That is a point in its favor, believe me. Lodge is supposed to be a bassist and Hayward a guitarist – this is the first opportunity to hear them out from under the landslide of various and sundry overkill. …

And so it went.

Single release:
"I Dreamed Last Night" b/w "Remember Me, My Friend"
UK: Threshold/Decca TH 19; U.S.: Threshold/London 5N-67019; *April 18, 1974*

Interviewed for *ZigZag* magazine shortly after the single's release, Hayward said, "Well, the single is really a double A-side. There's 'Remember Me,' which the band wanted – *we* wanted as a single – and 'I Dreamed Last Night,' which, like you, everybody said has got to be the single. Fortunately, it's a hit in America." (JH-ZZ76)

A spokesman for Threshold Records told *Record Mirror*, "After meeting people in America and in this country, these are the two tracks to be picked up by both AM and FM operators. The double A-side leaves programming up to the station's discretion."

This single – at least as issued in the U.K. – was not without a unique aspect. The version of "Remember Me, My Friend," was a newly recorded version of the song with subtle changes from the version on the album.

In America, the album version of the song was put on the single, but the DJ-only "promotional" single featured an edited version of "I Dreamed Last Night," slimmed down to a running time of 2:49.

The album had been out for five weeks. Radio had been playing both of these songs, as well as others from the album, so issuing the two tracks now on a 45 did not make them "new" to the listeners. And leaving it to the discretion of each radio station to pick which song to add to their playlists created the old "divide and conquer" scenario. In a nation as spread-out as the United States, a song needed uniform play among Top 40 stations to go high in the national charts. Having some stations playing one song, and others playing the flipside, wouldn't help either to chart very high. The days of the double A-side had ended a few years earlier, with the breakup of the Beatles and Creedence Clearwater Revival, a pair of bands

that often released singles on which both songs were strong enough for radio play.

Meanwhile, the album reviews for *Blue Jays* continued to flow in.

Bob Bonn, for his column in Pennsylvania's *Beaver County Times*, wrote:

> There is something about the Moody Blues' sound that is somehow unique, something that makes the listener think of winter days, something that makes the music sound as if it's coming from far away, something that makes it different and somehow a bit more classy than a lot of what's going down today.

Before you even get to the first note, you can tell this album is simply oozing with class. You can tell just by looking at the cover. It's a surrealistic, enchanting painting of a sunrise and moonrise over a foggy, mysterious valley as the album's two heroes, Justin Hayward and John Lodge, look out from the ruins of a crumbling archway....

Hayward and Lodge are guitarist and bassist for the Moody Blues, and the duo album, *Blue Jays*, is done with all the class that the whole group would have insisted on had they all been there. But the whole group isn't there. Three Moodies are missing, yet Hayward and Lodge put together an album that is, for all practical purposes, the Moodies eighth sojourn. ...

William E. Sarmento, the drama critic for Massachusetts' *The Lowell Sun*, had attended the Carnegie Hall event. On April 18, wrote:

One of the best groups to come upon the contemporary rock scene in recent years was the Moody Blues. The group represented an answer in pop rock circles to those fans who wanted something less acid than the sounds distributed by such other popular figures as the Rolling Stones and Led Zeppelin. ...

It is no secret that London Records thinks it has another Simon and Garfunkel in Hayward and Lodge. They both sing; they both compose; and they both work well with each other. ... The album contains 10 songs all by Hayward and Lodge and their music is decidedly rock and not in the folk idiom which was very much Simon and Garfunkel. However, don't let the word "rock" throw you. This is anything but "hard rock." It has the beat and the drive, [but] the ballads have a softness to them. The overall result is an album that looks like a big one for the newly formed partnership. ...

On April 19, *Record Mirror* had this to say of the single:

This is scarcely a worthy ambassador for the fine *Blue Jays* album, from which it's taken. The tune isn't that strong, the arrangement is unnecessarily muddy and the way they make three syllables out of the word "you" in the lyrics sounds just plain ugly. The other side, "I Dreamed Last Night," is a much better choice.

This critic's opinion wasn't singular. It transpired that Hayward's "I Dreamed Last Night" was the side most U.S. radio stations chose to program.

On April 22, *The Los Angeles Times* published Robert Hilburn's review. You may recall that Hilburn had been hard on the last few Moody Blues albums, along with one concert he attended. He'd been an advocate for the band to become less "democratic," meaning, less from Pinder, Thomas, and Edge. He felt if the Moodies would only feature songs written and sung by Hayward and Lodge, the group would have greater success as artists. Now he reminded his readers of this, and then wrote:

532

... It isn't surprising, then, that this collection of 10 Hayward and Lodge songs (only two were written jointly) captures the best elements of the Moodies' work (the lovely melodies and majestic arrangements) without the tedious, overblown metaphysical exercises that some of the members of the band seemed to bring to the group's music. But the album does have a flaw.

While some of the songs in *Blue Jays* (e.g., Hayward's "Where Are You Now" and Lodge's "Maybe") rank with the writers' best, there's a mellowness and lack of ultimate boldness that keeps the album from being a wholly satisfying work. It's all too easy, for instance, to put the needle down at any two points and find an all-too-similar tone. The range is simply too narrow.

The irony of the album, then, is that the five or six best songs here would have been standouts on a new Moody Blues album, but the three or four other songs provided by Hayward and Lodge aren't really all that much more interesting – though certainly less pretentious – than the tunes that probably would have been contributed by the other Moodies. ...

It seems ironic that a Moody Blues album featuring all five members was too musically diverse for Hilburn. But now that he heard a release from but two of the Moodies, he complained that the music didn't have enough variation!

Rolling Stone reviewed the album for its May 8 issue. Stephen Holden said in part:

At least in terms of sound, Justin Hayward and John Lodge, guitarist and bass player, respectively, with the currently inactive Moody Blues, have created in *Blue Jays* the ultimate Moody Blues album. It is the same sound that established the Moodys' mass popularity in 1968 with *Days of Future Passed*: basic rock instrumentation heavily overlaid with Mellotron or strings orchestra, and vocals treated as instruments in the Wagnerian manner. In strictly musical terms, however, the Moody Blues are far from Wagnerian. Simple melodic themes are elongated to accommodate a dramatic sense, but about as sophisticated as a mediocre Fifties soundtrack, their emotional import exaggerated by such devices as rapidly swelling orchestration and gargantuan crescendo. ... As a result, *Blue Jays* leaps off the turntable, a tidal wave of romantic bombast that would have reduced Cecil B. DeMille to jelly. ...

Blue Jays is a tonal bath, all sound and nothing but sound, the perfect background music for the kind of person who whispers "I love you" to a one-night stand.

For an article in the *Denver Post*, Jared Johnson talked to John Lodge about the *Rolling Stone* review. Johnson said, "I thought it was one of the best albums of 1975, but they said the album was about as sophisticated as a mediocre Fifties soundtrack and went on with the usual – too lush, too pretentious, 'I don't like the flowery lyrics,' blah, blah, blah, blah. I'm not really sure what direction the reviewer was coming from other than he was probably listening to Aerosmith while writing his review."

Lodge responded, "Well, you can't stop that, but there are a lot of people out there who are going to be happy if I or the Moodies do something we really believe in. And that's what counts. I mean, I can't help it if some people don't like it, but I know there are people out there who *will* like it. I think a lot of reviewers are frustrated musicians anyway. They expect to be part of the rock music scene." (JL-DP77a)

John Wisniewski, writing for May 10 edition of *The Youth Post*, wasn't whispering "I love you" either.

> … *Blue Jays*, like almost every Moody Blues album, comes across as a pretentious attempt at the apocalyptic. Overuse of full-blown orchestration and crescendo (a la the Beatles' "A Day in the Life") is the fatal flaw of most Moody Blues albums and *Blue Jays*. The strings do little but add syrup to this collection of stale musical pancakes. Any sense of the dramatic attempted here never materializes.

Was Wisniewski saying that the Beatles' "A Day in the Life" was flawed? Or just songs that patterned themselves after "A Day in the Life"?

(Photo source: Pinterest.com)

The May 12 issue of *Broadcasting* had this to say of the single:

> Most industry-watchers sympathized with London Records' corporate wince when the Moody Blues broke up two years ago [sic, one year] at the height of their commercial success, but a best-selling greatest-hits package and this single from a hit album by two group members should help the label – London distributes

the group's Threshold product – make up for lost time. "I Dreamed Last Night," like most of the *Blue Jays* album from which it is taken, is instantly recognizable to any Moody Blues fan, and its smooth, medium-tempo flavor and lush orchestration should make it popular among Top 40 and Adult Contemporary audiences. ...

The *Blue Jays* album enjoyed an impressive 23-week chart run on *Billboard*, reaching its peak position for the week ending May 17, 1975, at No. 16. *Cashbox* showed it peaking one week later, at No. 7, and staying at that position for two weeks. A third national chart in America, *Radio and Records*, took it up to No. 8.

In the U.K., *Blue Jays* went as high as No. 4.

Talking with Andy Childs of *ZigZag* magazine, Justin Hayward was asked if he felt "bemused or bitter" over the treatment the Moodies had received from the press in the last few years. The normally soft-spoken Hayward candidly answered, "Actually, it's sort of split down the middle, because the press either fuckin' hate us or we're okay.... Years ago they said we were good, 'progressive' and 'underground,' and all that, and we were certainly never an overnight success. *Blue Jays* is coming up to being the biggest thing we've had in England, which is insane. [It's] great, but strange. It hasn't been knocked very much in the press because it's a good album. We're proud of it." (JH-ZZ76)

Even so, many members of the press who'd had such a good time hating the Moody Blues kept up the job for *Blue Jays*.

Crawdaddy magazine unloaded at *Blue Jays* in its June, 1975 issue. The unidentified reviewer pronounced:

> Hayward & Lodge were in the *original* Moody Blues, and I'll tell ya – when these two split the modern Moodies to go solo-duet, I had high hopes of resurrection of the original Moodies sound, "Go Now," that period back when blood and guts were attached to their vision. How naïve can I get – *Bluejays* smells even more like musk oil than anything the Moodies ever did. More sympho-melodrama.

Perhaps the naïveté belonged to the reviewer. First, Hayward and Lodge were *not* in the "original" Moodies. Second, they did not "split" the group. Third, the album's title comprised two words, not "Bluejays."

The unattributed commentary continued:

> ... Not really surprising [that the album] is "sympho-melodrama" after this many years behind the Great Spector [Phil] of Pseudoclassical Orchestration. The sound, like musical propaganda, has insidiously blemished its way into Hayward & Lodge's collective brain. As the politically wary warn us to kick out the Mellotrons, this writer suggests consuming large quantities of meat as a spiritual antidote. Urp.

Despite the derisive reviews, "I Dreamed Last Night" peaked in America on *Billboard* for the week ending June 21, 1975 at No. 47. *Cashbox* showed the single at its peak position one week later, at No. 45. On *Billboard*'s Top Adult Contemporary Chart, it made it to No. 29.

For its July 1975 issue, *Stereo Review* said:

> The Moody Blues were just about the best at what they did, which was a little schlocky but awfully nice sometimes, and it isn't surprising that ex-Moodies Justin Hayward and John Lodge, backed by some non-Moodies, still have that sound, that gentility suggesting old wood and leather and a time when melodies, by Gadfrey, were melodies. And, er, when words tended to be either pompous or frightfully banal, depending on whether they were Making a Statement or passing the time. Well, we can't have everything. "You," in any case, is, with all its fancy orchestration, a nice tune, catchy the way a good Moodies tune was catchy, while "Remember Me, My Friend" is catchy the way a bad one was, the kind that gets on the radio and hangs on like a toothache. "Saved by the Music" indicates some of the bad ones *aren't* catchy and that however you strip down the Moody Blues they were always a bit awkward at rocking. But the rest of the album is only a *little* schlocky, and awfully nice in spots.

Also in July, *Gramophone* gave its verdict:

> *Blue Jays* (Threshold THS12) is the long-awaited dual effort from two of the Moody Blues, Justin Hayward and John Lodge. It is already high in the pop album charts so there is not much that is new that I can add except that I found it totally absorbing and thoroughly brilliant. Although they have gone it alone, or together as this is the case, there is still more than a hint of the Moody Blues in the arrangements.

Associate Features editor George Bacso reviewed *Blue Jays* in a syndicated newspaper column from August 1975:

> The Moody Blues have not released an album of new material since 1972, and have at least temporarily broken-up. But Moodies mourners will take heart in this natural collaboration between Moodies' guitarists Hayward and Lodge (bass). Hayward and Lodge recruited Moodies producer Tony Clarke and also used the Peter Knight Orchestra, who appeared on the group's *Days of Future Passed* album. The result is that this is a Moodies LP, lacking only the five-part harmonies [sic; four-part] distinctive of the group as a whole. Hayward and Lodge contributed equally in the song writing area, and have combined their talents for the first time to co-author two tunes. One, "Remember Me," is especially memorable, along with "I Dreamed Last Night." Soft, lush, Mellotron-dominated and orchestrated. *Blue Jays* will please most Moody Blues fans and perhaps make several new ones.

Fred De Van gave the album an "A+" rating for his review in the November 1975 issue of *Audio*.

> … The music is magnificent, by any standard. The lyrics are universal in feeling and meaningful in content. As usual with any Moody Blues/Tony Clarke production… the voice is used totally as a musical instrument that also happens to possess the capability of speaking English. The result is stunning. *Blue Jays* is difficult to listen to casually, although it will be welcomed as it becomes more familiar. It is an awesome experience to just sit down and listen to the whole thing at anywhere near its proper level (LOUD!).
>
> The dynamics are indeed awesome because the music is so rich and full. The sound of the record is part of the music. The performance is a construction of seemingly limitless dimension and subtlety, and it's difficult to deal with one without mention of the other. The words are eloquent in concept, meaning, and delivery, yet, as songs would, take on different character and impact without the specifically-ornate music that they dwell within. This independence of elements is what makes the music what it is. …
>
> Despite its epic proportions, producer Clarke makes the myriad pieces mold themselves into magnificence. … It all works. It all fits. This is fine contemporary music. …

So many of the songs from *Blue Jays* became familiar on radio, that, rather than take a second single from the album, a new song was recorded … and one from the album was rerecorded for the B-side.

Single release:
"Blue Guitar" b/w "When You Wake Up"
Threshold TH 21 (U.K.); Threshold
5N-67021 (U.S.); September 26, 1975

On October 4, 1975, Ray Fox-Cumming reviewed "Blue Guitar" in *Record Mirror*:

> Not, as you might imagine from the title, purely instrumental, but very much the kind of single you'd expect from these two gentlemen – melodic, dreamy and sumptuously arranged (production by 10cc and Tony Clarke). Maybe not quite epic enough to be a big hit, but it could easily make a minor impression.

Also on the 4th, C. Charlesworth wrote in *Melody Maker*:

After an introduction that sounds vaguely reminiscent of Hank Marvin and the Shadows with added orchestra, the two Moodies wade into a very slow, slushy and sentimental song that puts me in the mind of Mantovani. Very like the Moodies during their dreamy moments, but it comes in a nice printed sleeve and they're going on round the road, so the chances are it'll be a hit.

In the October 11 issue of *Record Mirror*, Hayward and Lodge posed with their framed silver disc awards for *Blue Jays*.

Peter Harvey wrote:

> According to the yanks, Blue Jays are this year's Number One new duo – which is nice for Justin Hayward and John Lodge.
>
> Originally they had meant "Blue Jays" to be just the title of their debut solo album as members of the Moody Blues.
> "But the name stuck," says John Lodge, "So now we are Blue Jays."

Regarding the new "Blue Guitar" single, Hayward told Harvey, "We've known 10cc for a long time, right from their Hot Legs days. Their first gigs on the road were with us.

"So we were at Strawberry in Manchester around Easter time and the studio was free when Eric [Stewart, of 10cc] asked if anyone had a song."

Hayward did, so Stewart brought his electric guitar and recruited Graham Gouldman (acoustic guitar), Kevin Godley (drums) and Lol Crème (gizmo). Hayward recruited Tony Clarke to produce (or, as the record label credit says, co-produce).

Hayward added, "We're putting out this single because everybody said we should. It's my song so I was least sure about it, but 'Blue Guitar' is a grower. There's a feeling about it." (JH-RM75)

C. Charlesworth of *Melody Maker* was right when he predicted that "Blue Guitar" would "probably be a hit." The song peaked at No. 8 in the British singles chart on November 9, 1975.

"Blue Guitar" didn't fare as well in the U.S. – it didn't have the "feel" of an American AM radio hit – and, on December 27, 1975, only reached No. 96 in *Billboard* One week later, *Cashbox* ranked it at No. 82.

Touring with the Album:

From the September 27, 1975 issue of *Melody Maker*:

Justin Hayward and John Lodge take another giant step away from the Moody Blues this autumn when they embark on their first British tour.

The concerts have been prompted by the huge success of the duo's debut album, *Blue Jays*, which has notched up over a million sales throughout the world. And because of the album's hit status, the group will be billed on the tour as "Justin Hayward and John Lodge – Blue Jays."

Backing the two Blue Jays were Trapeze alumni Mel Galley (guitar) and Dave Holland (drums), and (as featured on the album) Providence members Jim Cockey (violin), Tim Tompkins (cello), and Tom Tompkins (viola).

The dates were Birmingham Hippodrome (November 16); Glasgow Apollo (17); Edinburgh Usher Hall (18); Manchester ABC (19); Lancaster University (21); Stoke Trentham Gardens (23); Hammersmith Odeon, London (25); Bournemouth Winter Gardens (26); Bristol University (27); Southport Theatre (28); Leeds University (29); and Hull ABC (30). Before the tour even commenced, *Melody Maker* (November 15) reported that popular demand had prompted additional shows to be added. Royal Albert Hall, London, now scheduled for December 10, would conclude the tour.

Peter Harvey, of *Record Mirror*, was at the second concert, at Glasgow Apollo.

… There's a nervous expectant tension that boils to the surface once the new band walk on stage at the sold-out Apollo. …

Then, right from the first strains of "Saved by the Music," it's evident that here is an exciting natural band. The three string players from Boise, Idaho, positively glow, and the three guys who normally make up Trapeze know how to rock very hard. Then there's Justin and John, vocally not yet strong enough but growing all the time.

By the fourth number, "This Morning" (from *Blue Jays*) it's really tightening up and the band begin to relax. "You," "You and Me," "My Brother," and, finally, with great excitement, "Isn't Life Strange," wind up the first set.

… The harmonies and characteristic Mellotron sound of the Moodies is missing, but in its place is a harder, funkier sound which shows guitarist Jus, and bass player John, to be more than just the faces behind some very strong songs. True, the Moodies numbers were best received, but they were played in a way that gave them new life. The mixture of strings (viola, violin, and cello), two guitars, bass, keys, and drums is very different.

(Photo source: MoodyBluesAttitude.com)

The acoustic set which follows proves even further the versatility of the lineup. "Who Are You Now" and "New Horizons" spotlight Justin's compelling vocals, while John's "Emily's Song" has the audience singing along. The set closes with "I Dreamed Last Night," one of Blue Jays' best, to pave the way for an incredible finale. It starts with an orchestral version of "Knights [sic] in White Satin" while the stage is re-set, and erupts with the reappearance of the full band playing that very song. From then on, the show is just one climax after another as a now infinitely more controlled outfit hit with "Just a Singer (In a Rock and Roll Band)," "When You Wake Up," and, to encore, "Question" ("You're beautiful," someone yells).

By then everyone was standing and Justin Hayward and John Lodge looked about twice as large as they did at the start of the show. They had to come back again to deliver "Ride My See-Saw," and that was it.

Back stage, Lodge admitted to Harvey that he was "scared to death" before he went on, but, "I'm on top of the world. I haven't slept for four nights, I'm so excited. It's been a hell of a year; a hell of a gamble." (JL-RM75)

Robin Denselow, of *The Guardian*, caught the Blue Jays at the Hammersmith Odeon in London. He had an opposed reaction to Peter Harvey's enthusiasm.

The Blue Jays are yet another example of the worst kind of instant success: bands who are famous simply because they are built around members or ex-members of a genuinely successful, established group. …

The trouble was that while Hayward and Lodge were (mostly) pleasant and tuneful, they failed to produce the sophisticated sound or the professional show that the Moodies could guarantee. The sound balance was very poor, and Lodge in particular showed that his voice is too weak to sustain so many solos.

Harry Doherty covered the London concert for *Melody Maker*:

> I'm still trying to figure out what John Lodge and, in particular, Justin Hayward, were scared of when they presented their Blue Jays act at London's Hammersmith Odeon on Tuesday of last week. It was strange to witness the timidity of two such accomplished songwriters and experienced performers. …
>
> Lodge appeared extremely diffident about what he was doing. Hayward's performance, though, was even more disconcerting. He had the air of a little boy singing at a family party for the first time, reduced to almost whispering lyrics as if he was too shy to let his audience hear what he had to sing, and glancing occasionally at fellow band members for reassurance. It was a pity, for it marred what could have been an excellent performance. …

Doherty had other bones to pick. The sound system was "pathetic" and the soundman was "equally poor," missing cues and too slow to compensate for balance issues. And, with the exception of their contribution to a handful of numbers, the three-man string section "did nothing to enhance the grace of other songs" and should have been replaced with a Moog.

Doherty closed:

> Despite the endless list of faults, 3,000 fans got off on what the Blue Jays did. But Hayward and Lodge have to iron out the many bumps, get a better grip on things and, for God's sake, have a bit more confidence in themselves. …

Reviews such as this certainly weren't going to boost anybody's self-esteem.

Incidentally, at this time it was announced that Hayward and Lodge would go back into the studio after the Christmas break and finish recording a second album, started while they were still recording the first LP. This was to be followed by a tour of America. Neither would happen.

Justin Hayward told interviewer Mark Powell, "We toured the UK and Europe with the album with some success, but never toured the United States. There was more resistance to us touring over there because a lot of people had vested interest in the Moody Blues and didn't want to back our solo projects."

The primary reason, however, was Hayward's reluctance to once more be part of a big, involved group. He worried that it might require the same levels of coordination and bother as the Moody Blues' success had brought. He said, "[I]t was a happy time, because we had a good success, but, after the one album, I didn't want to continue anymore, because it started like this: 'Oh, this is the new Moody Blues!' I didn't want that to happen. I wanted to preserve the Moody Blues in their own right, not have a New Moody Blues. So, after the one album, it was enough for me. I just wanted to do things of my own." (JH-SWCD04)

Asked if John Lodge agreed with the decision to retire the Blue Jays, Hayward answered, "No. Not at the time." (JH-HL98a)

24

From Mighty Oaks
Ray Thomas, 1975

Album release:
Threshold/Decca THS 16 (U.K.); Threshold/London THS 16 (U.S.); July 11, 1975
U.S. #68 (*Billboard* Top 200 Albums chart)
U.K. #23

Single release: *"High Above My Head" b/w "Love Is the Key"*
Threshold/Decca TH 20 (U.K.); Threshold/London 5N-67020 (U.S.); June 27, 1975
U.S. #117 (*Cashbox* singles chart)

From Mighty Oaks was a stunning solo debut from Ray Thomas. In 1975, it came as a surprise. Thomas, always good for a song or two per album with the Moody Blues, was now able to shine, and with greater impact than many had thought possible.

Thomas's powerful voice and passionate singing often sent the melodically rich songs from this collection soaring. With the support of a strong rock combo – guitar, keyboard, bass, and drums – and support from Richard Hewson's sweeping orchestral arrangement, *From Mighty Oaks* makes an exhilarating listening experience.

Preparing the Material … and Finding a Band

As a flutist and harmonica player, both primarily lead instruments, Ray Thomas was not versed on guitar or piano. For his songs with the Moody
Blues, he had Justin Hayward, Mike Pinder, and John Lodge to help fit his melodies to

specific chords on either guitar or piano. In preparing his latest songs for recording, he chose a new collaborator – fellow Midlander Nicky James, who had performed with Denny Laine and Graeme Edge before the Moody Blues were formed. Lately, he had been a Threshold Records solo artist, and served as the opening act on a Moody Blues tour.

Thomas said, "Nicky was from the midlands and I first met him when he signed to Threshold and went on tour as a support act to the Moody Blues on a Threshold tour. … Nicky was a frequent visitor to my house, and would play me new material that he had written…. We began writing together to see if something worthwhile might emerge. I realized quickly that we collaborated well together, and the music on *From Mighty Oaks* was the result…. Some of the melodies were mine, others were his, and it was the same when it came to lyrics." (RT-FMO11 and RT-FMOCD95)

Recording at Threshold Studio was a matter of first come, first serve. Justin Hayward and John Lodge were quick to reserve the facility for their *Blue Jays* album, with sessions commencing in June 1974, immediately following the redesign and refitting of the old Decca studio. As Hayward later revealed, the studio was in fact tested in action with the recording of *Blue Jays*; some bugs still needed working out, such as a temperamental 2-track machine.

Graeme Edge had been the second to reserve the studio. In July 1974, he announced his plans to make an album, with hopes of releasing it in October of that year.

Ray Thomas was the third to get into line, with plans to begin recording following the completion of the Graeme Edge Band's album.

Partly because of some problems which arose in the first use of the studio for Hayward and Lodge, *Blue Jays* had taken longer to record than expected. Another reason for the delay was that *Blue Jays* was such an ambitious album. The project didn't wrap until December, pushing the start of the making of the Graeme Edge Band album back considerably.

Edge was left with very little time to record his album, so Thomas volunteered to delay the start of his, allowing Edge and his colleagues a wider window of time for their sessions. This was actually helpful to Thomas, as well, allowing him more time to prepare.

Ray Thomas: "For me, the fact that I had written everything for my first solo album prior to entering the studio was a real plus. It meant that I wouldn't have to worry about using studio time to write new material, and rushing things. I could concentrate instead on perfecting recordings of songs that I had already finished." (RT-FMOCD11)

Now that he had a writing partner, and an album's worth of songs, Thomas needed a band. He told Chris Charlesworth of *Melody Maker*, "I didn't know where to look for musicians; I've worked with the Moodies and no one else for so long. All the guys I used to know in Birmingham are either dead or they're back on the buses." (RT-MM75)

The fact that the Threshold Studio was unavailable as Thomas and James were perfecting their material actually created the opportunity for them to find their band mates.

Thomas told Jack MaDonough, a newspaper man from New York, "Nicky and I went down to a country studio in Kent to lay down some tracks. The Jones brothers,

Trevor and John, and Dave Potts, were there because they were affiliated with the studio. So I asked them if they wanted to do some session work. Then Mike Moran was recommended to us. It all fell together nicely. I didn't have to go searching or hold auditions, which is not really my style." (RT-RD75)

John Jones played acoustic guitar, electric guitar, and provided backing vocals; Trevor Jones contributed bass guitar and backing vocals; Mike Moran played the keyboards; Dave Potts, the drums. Nicky James also sang backing vocals, and played percussion. Ray Thomas sang lead vocals, plus playing flute, bass flute, and

From the interior gatefold, *From Mighty Oaks*. Clockwise: Nicky James, Trevor Jones, Mike Moran, John Jones, and Dave Potts.

harmonica. Also hired for the sessions were B.J. Cole, on pedal steel guitar, and Mike Silver, on acoustic guitar and backing vocals.

Recording the Album

After rehearsing with the band at the country studio in Kent, Thomas and James, along with their session players, hit the pavement running when they entered Threshold Studios in the spring.

Thomas recalled, "The process of completing the album was very quick. From start to finish it took just over a month to record and mix. As a band, we were well prepared before we entered the studio. We had run through all the material in a series of rehearsals and everybody knew what was wanted of them." (RT-FMOCD11)

It is unknown why Tony Clarke did not produce *From Mighty Oaks*. He had produced the *Blue Jays* album for Hayward and Lodge, and the debut single for the Graeme Edge Band.

Assistant recording engineer Dave Baker revealed who the intended producer was. "We started off with a different producer on *From Mighty Oaks*, a guy called Del Newman, who worked with Cat Stevens. He didn't get a credit on the album. Del and Ray couldn't get on at all, and that changed fairly quickly. Del left, and Derek and Ray produced the album between them." (DB-H&H96)

Thomas recalled, "Although I was initially a little daunted by having to assume the role of producing the music for the album, I soon felt comfortable taking charge and really got into the sessions. My role as producer was made much easier by the presence of Derek Varnals as co-producer."

As for the decision to engage an orchestra, Thomas revealed, "I had really enjoyed working with an orchestra on *Days of Future Passed* and thought it would be a great idea to use an orchestra on *From Mighty Oaks*. We assembled a 38-piece orchestra for the recording sessions. I found it quite stressful to suddenly be responsible for all of these talented musicians and to be the person who ultimately had the responsibility of judging whether a 'take' was good enough. …

"As an engineer, no one could come close to Derek when it came to tasks such as recording an orchestra. He had worked on many famous Decca classical recordings, and would often have to come to the studio the day before an orchestra arrived to arrange the microphones and seating arrangements of the musicians to achieve the very best sound quality. I left all the technical side of things to Derek and I knew I was in safe hands." (RT-FMOCD11)

The album's introductory track, **"From Mighty Oaks"** was an overture based on the various melodies heard on the album, with an arrangement written by Richard Hewson, played by the full 38-piece orchestra. In his liner notes for the remastered CD release of the album, Ray Thomas revealed, "I paid Richard to write all the arrangements for the songs, and when I explained to him that I wanted to open the album with an overture, he went away and wrote a fabulous arrangement. … When I heard the orchestral arrangements of 'From Mighty Oaks,' I was blown away. It began quietly and suddenly built to a crescendo that made the hairs on the back of my neck stand on end!"

When the album had been completed, Thomas asked Hewson how much he wanted for writing the arrangement to the "From Mighty Oaks." Track. The answer: "Nothing. That's on me." (RT-FMOCD11)

"Hey Mama Life," like all but two of the songs on the album, was written by both Ray Thomas and Nicky James.

Thomas had struggled in his early years as a musician. Before his success as a Moody, he was often down to his last dollar, and no stranger to cheap booze. Thomas sings: "Hey, hey, mama, life is a lonely time for a man who drinks his whiskey by the jar. Now I do believe the life I lead won't get me very far. I was once told the streets were paved in gold. Now I know them for what they are."

Now successful, he replies to himself: "Hey, hey, mama, life has a sweeter sound for a man who lives his life for his dream, yet he must be aware there are those who care, and of those who would bring him down. Separate trust from your cut and thrust; the truth can still be found."

And then he sings of lessons learned: "Take the pride from a man, you're left without a meaning. Take the wings from a bird, how can it fly. Give him hope, give him trust and a little understanding; give him back his pride, you'll be satisfied."

In a promotional record sent to disk jockeys and newspapers by London Records in the U.S., Thomas explained, "It's really about a few illusions – people damned for various reasons or built up for various reasons. All this track is really about is, 'See it as it is.'" (RT-SGM75)

It's a beautiful marriage of music and lyric, with an impassioned delivery by Thomas. His core band of acoustic guitar, piano, bass, and drums, jells wonderfully on this track. The added bonus of a double-tracked electric guitar solo (sounding very much like Justin Hayward), with Thomas's flute, creates a recording in the style of the Moody Blues, with strong musical and lyrical hooks throughout. The restrained orchestration, and choir of background singers – all from the core band – slowly build in the latter part of the track, heightening the climax. It made for an impressive start to the album, and could have, and perhaps *should* have been, the single from the LP. The song is catchy on first listening, a hit by any other name.

"Play It Again," another Thomas/James collaboration, plays with the theme and metaphor of "Love's a simple melody, two souls in harmony." Thomas sings: "Let's play our song again, make me remember when we both chased our rainbows through the rain. Our lives belong within this song, that's something we cannot change, so whatever you do and wherever you go, the memories will always remain. Play it again, oh play it again for me."

At the time of the album's release, Thomas said, "You might say it's a pure love song. It's basically about the end of a love affair. I use musical terms in the lyrics because I think, you know, love is like a melody." (RT-SGM75)

It was not only a pure love song, but, some might say, a pure Bee-Gees-type love song. Although Thomas was a baritone, and the Brothers Gibb were tenors, the distinctive voice warble so identified with the Bee Gee's is very prominent here, which, depending on one's taste, is not necessarily a bad thing. Once again, the core band of acoustic guitar, piano, bass, and drums create a supple backing, augmented by a Justin Hayward-like double-tracked melodic guitar solo, and a hint of orchestration, with strings and choir in the ever-building musical refrain.

"Rock-A-Bye-Baby Blues" was the only song on the album not written or co-written by Thomas. This one came from Nicky James.

A dash of Lovin' Spoonful's "Daydream," and Thomas's own Moody Blues' track, "Lazy Day," along with a breath of pop country, mix to make for an easy-going and pleasingly flowing charmer. It's catchy and good-humored … with background singers giving playful support with a series of "ooby-dooby-doo" vocals which might remind you of Roy Orbison. Try singing along without breaking into a smile..

"High Above My Head" may not offer one of the album's better lyrics, but it was chosen to occupy one side of the single. The song's arrangement, and Thomas's lead vocal, would have fit nicely on Ringo Starr's *Ringo* or *Goodnight Vienna* albums ("Oh My My," anyone?). Perhaps it was this in mind that "High Above My Head" was put out as a single. If Ringo could have hits with three-and-a-half minute of pop, why not Ray Thomas?

One of the pluses of *From Mighty Oaks* is that it isn't locked into one style; one sound; one rhythm. It's far more eclectic than *Blue Jays* was, and makes for a fine potpourri of pop.

Despite making a good album cut – with an energized harmonica performance by Thomas – "High Above My Head" proved a poor choice for a single.

"Love Is the Key," selected for the other side of the single (distributed as a Double A-side), is another dose of easy-to-swallow pop. Thomas pleads: "Come on, let's fill our world with laughter; let's put the sunshine into everybody's heart / Then peace will last forever after; oh, what a lovely start."

Thomas, the hippie-dreamer and idealist, said of this song: "There's plenty of room and plenty of food as far as the whole world's concerned. I don't know why we don't distribute food [and] wealth a little bit to everybody rather than knocking everybody's head together." (RT-SGM75)

As an album cut, "Love Is the Key" does fine. But whoever chose this song and "High Above My Head" for this album's only single didn't display an ear for picking hits.

"You Make Me Feel Alright." Thomas sings: "And if I was to say you are my everything, could you believe it? Would you believe you're my life? I found out what true love's about; you came into my life; you make me feel alright … feel alright."

Yet another example of a well-crafted pop song – pleasant melody, catchy hook, polished performance – "You Make Me Feel Alright" may not stand out individually, but it should have you "feeling alright."

"Adam and I" is a love song to Thomas's young son. He sings: "I waited so long for you to come along; hoping and praying my love would bear a son / Now I see that love, it shines within your eyes; we're going to take a journey, Adam and I."

At the time, Thomas said of Adam, "He's two years old. I'm just wild about him, and the song is a message to him. What do you tell a kid? Basically, it's how I live my life – you reap what you sow and don't harm anyone intentionally." (RT-SGM75)

This song would have been another good choice as a single. It is very much in the style of "White Bird" by It's a Beautiful Day, which, while not a Top 100 hit, was a staple on American radio throughout the 1970s. The appeal of "Adam and I" is immediate, especially to anyone who loves the "Classic Seven" period of the Moody Blues. The acoustic guitar-picking intro, combined with Thomas's flute, weave together and remind us of Hayward/Thomas collaborations like "Are You Sitting Comfortably?" The acoustic guitar lick, which serves as a signature to this song (and was incorporated into the overture), also provides one of the song's hooks. Another plus is the subject itself. This is a passionate and honest expression of love towards a son from a father. Who wouldn't mind hearing a sentiment like this on the radio from time to time?

"I Wish We Could Fly" was written by Ray Thomas on his own. Besides being the most dramatic and soaring track on the album, it might have made for a good single. Thomas's elevated voice proclaims, "I wish we could fly; oh how I wish we could fly / Then we'd see far more clearly / Maybe then we'd know the best way we should go / Man just has to grow… and grow…"

Ray Thomas: "It's just another way of saying, 'If we could [step] back out of our environment and just stand there or just circle around and … see what kind of a mess it is … you'd be able to see the wood through the trees.'" (RT-ID75)

Lyric, melody, arrangement, and performance combine to create the album's most striking track. When we reach the inspiring climax, with a spirit-lifting choir backing Thomas's soaring lead, we can imagine his face tilted up, singing to the sky, "I wish we could fly … oh, how I wish we could fly!"

The orchestration during these passages is invigorating; the small choir of multi-tracked voices is stirring. The hook is penetrating … swelling with the power of Thomas's voice.

Recording engineer Dave Baker referred to Thomas as "such a professional…. His voice dubbing is very much the material from the Welsh valley. He doesn't do many takes; he likes to do performances, and that comes across really well. He's a good singer and not difficult to record." (DB-H&H96)

Thomas was equally impressed with the support he was given. He said, "It was a shot in the arm to work with other guys; I really dug it. It was fresh blood, fresh ideas and it worked well."

Regarding the absence of the flute on much of the album, he said, "You can't sing and play the flute at the same time, so I wanted to leave myself open so I could perform the material live." (RT-MM75)

As for the orchestration, Thomas said, "That was the only part of making it that gave me the jitters. I produced this myself and it was the first time I'd done that too. I did all the orchestration in one day and it's bleedin' expensive using 40 musicians!

"They really know their game and technically they're much better than I am because I don't have a clue when it comes down to actual dots. I only had to stop them twice, but you have to make sure that what you're saying is correct when you press that button.

"I think Mike pushed the Mellotron as far as you can push it in its present form. I think you have a lot more scope if you use the real thing, but it's a damn sight more expensive though. It costs £1,500 in the studio from half-past ten in the morning until six, and if you run into overtime you can end up paying another thousand quid extra. I tell you, we finished, 'bang,' on the dot. It was beautiful. It was the only time I've ever watched the clock in my own studio!" (RT-MM75)

As a result of the material being ready by the time the band went into Threshold studio, the recording of *From Mighty Oaks* moved fairly quickly. It was released in mid-July 1975, with an advance single in the shops two weeks earlier (only three-and-a-half months after the release of *Blue Jays*, and even before the release of the first album from the Graeme Edge Band, which had been recorded first).

Regarding choosing a name for the album, which also became the name of the opening track, Thomas admitted that the old English adage, attributed to "stout-hearted Englishmen" ("Mighty oaks from little acorns grow"), was only part of the inspiration. He said, "I have a lot of oaks on my property and I got into the question, 'Which came first, the chicken or the egg; the oak or the acorn.' I thought about calling it 'From Little Acorns,' and I thought, 'Well, let's reverse it' and called it *From Mighty Oaks*." (RT-SGM75)

After listening to the album, Phil Travers gave *From Mighty Oaks* the full Moody Blues treatment, incorporating the various themes from the album's songs into a lovely front and back cover drawing, with Thomas fishing, and reading a book, on what one may imagine to be his Cobham property. His son, Adam, plays nearby, sailing a toy boat on the pond. A dog, a family of swans, a rainbow, and a fairytale castle in the distance are also pictured. This cover perfectly reflects the music within – wholesome, comforting, with themes of peace and love, father and son, God and Man, accented by flights of fantasy.

Chris Charlesworth, of *Melody Maker*, asked Thomas why he was making a solo album – a curious question, and one that gives the impression that the expectations of the British press were low – just as they had been for Ringo Starr when the Beatles broke up.

Thomas politely responded, "Well, we have this really fine studio that we've built and no one was using it. That seemed stupid to me, so I thought I'd go and make use of it for myself. Mike has gone off to live in California, Graeme has buggered off around the world on his boat, and John and Justin have made *Blue Jays*, so it seemed stupid to have a really fine 24-track studio just sitting there and no one using it…

"There's nothing else for me to do. We'd just done a world tour and that took up lots of time and energy, and, when it was finished, there were no plans for us to do anything as a group. We've got all the machinery to make and release records, so why not?

"Plus, [there's] the fact that you've got to work to live in this country now. You can't just sit on your backside any more. The bloody taxes are ridiculous."

Thomas said nothing about having a passion to create. Yet the album is certainly an inspired work of love.

Returning to our "Ringo" comparison, the reaction from the music press in 1975 was very much what one might have expected in 1971 if Ringo Starr had released an album which stood tall next to John Lennon's *Imagine*, Paul McCartney's *Ram*, and George Harrison's *All Things Must Pass. From Mighty Oaks* was of the caliber of *Blue Jays*. These songs were as good or even better than anything we had heard from Thomas before.

Thomas agreed with Chris Charlesworth that the material and overall sound of the album was very much in the Moody Blues vein. "It's gotta be, really, hasn't it?" he said. "I didn't sit down and try to make it very different, but, then again, I didn't sit down to make it exactly the same. It's just what it is.

"The same thing happened with John and Justin and *Blue Jays*, because as soon as they open their mouths to sing or play their instruments, it's got to be the same style. I think if you played my album at the same time as theirs, and then added Mike's, when he's finished his, you'd end up with a Moody Blues album."

Regarding the current state of the Moody Blues, Thomas said, "I think, musically, it's a breath of fresh air for us. The Moody Blues have always been constantly putting out things, and you can't go on churning out things forever without a rest. You just get stale, and we were starting to get that way.

"I mean, we had millions of ideas when we came to do the first album, but, when you get to the eighth, it's different. We're our own worst critics, too, and when we came to laying down tracks we'd think, 'Oh, we can't use that because we did it on such and such an album.' I think we could have got away with a lot if we'd wanted, but we didn't want to try."

Regarding a Moodies reunion, Thomas said, "Well … it's been going on a bloody long time. And you can't really operate a band when one of the members lives 6,000 miles away." (RT-MM75)

Single release:
"High Above My Head" b/w "Love Is the Key."
**Threshold TH 20 (U.K.); Threshold 5N-67020
(U.S.); June 27, 1975**

Billboard reviewed the "High Above My Head" single in its July 5, 1975 issue:

Another ex-Moody Blues takes the solo route with a rocker that sounds a bit like Ringo in spots. Note the strong similarity to the group heard in the Hayward/Lodge product, though the influence is there.

Cashbox was a few weeks behind *Billboard*, when it picked "Love Is the Key," the flip side, as more suitable for contemporary radio.

Out of Thomas' *From Mighty Oaks* LP, this is already getting FM airplay. His association as a Moody Blue is obvious: the classical trappings behind the vocals identify in a good way. Proud and honest … and that's a lovely start.

The music critic for *North Country Catholic* (A New York State-based, nationally circulated Catholic magazine) wrote:

Every once in a while you hear a song that really makes you feel good. For this reviewer it happened with Ray Thomas's single "Love Is the Key." Poetic lyrics accompanied by a Moody Blues-like melody combine to create an easy listening song with a sunshine personality. The refrains are perfect for a bright spring day. …

But the most important ingredient to happiness, according to Thomas, is love. That is the "Key to open any door" that has closed in the past. If one has love, he has the power to conquer all kinds of obstacles. These obstacles may include lack of self-confidence or too much self-centeredness. Either way, love can make things a little easier.

When we love someone, we are forced outside of ourselves so that we can give to another person. By the same token, love makes it easier for one to come out of "hiding."…

An important characteristic of love is that it spreads from the two people who share it to all the people with whom they are in contact. If the love is alive it is impossible to keep it hidden. Thomas finds that the love he shares with this woman encourages him to try to spread peace and sunshine to everyone and everything. He wants peace on the physical earth – he questions how anyone could pollute the beautiful seas, land and skies. And he also wants peace to be in the hearts of human beings. He hopes to try his own "wings" of love and spread joy to the brotherhood (and sisterhood) of all people. With this accomplishment the world will have a "lovely start" of a brand new day.

**Album release: *From Mighty Oaks*
Threshold/Decca THS 16 (U.K.);
Threshold/London THS 16 (U.S.);
July 11, 1975**

NOW...from The Moody Blues
Ray Thomas

In an interview with Tony Stewart published in *New Musical Express* on August 2, Thomas admitted, "I've done the best I can at this time, both production and performing-wise. But if I wasn't pleased with it, I wouldn't release it. And, if I wasn't proud of it, I wouldn't release it. At the same time, I know full well it isn't perfect. If it was, then I wouldn't bother with another one, because as sure as shit I'm not going to do it a second time. Am I? ...

"Now I'm going to make sure it gets a fair hearing by doing promotion here and in the States. And then I want to go out and do some gigs. If all the Moodies aren't available, then I'll go out on my own.

"And then, in February, I'll go in the studios and have another crack at making another album." (RT-NME75)

On August 2, 1975, *Billboard* said to industry insiders:

> Thomas, Moody Blues' flautist and composer, has got himself a very respectable first solo LP. The blend of classical and rock with several other musical elements is close to perfect. All the pressings are in quad sound and this adds another beautiful dimension to Thomas' compositions. Not relying strictly on his group's past merits, Thomas instead throws in bits and pieces of the Moody's intermixed with creative pen of this man. Sharing the composing chores on the album is Nicky James, a British performer who is finally coming into his own.
>
> Best cuts: "From Mighty Oaks," "Play It Again," "High Above My Head," "Love Is the Key," "I Wish We Could Fly."
>
> Dealers: Stick this in the Moody's section, but most importantly let the buyers know where this man came from. The cover art is beautiful.

From August 7, *PTP* magazine in Europe said (English translation):

From Mighty Oaks is the title of the album of Ray Thomas with a beautiful sleeve, again a design by Phil Travers. ... [T]he album is a real pleasure for your turntable. ...

It's temporary that the Moody Blues are apart, and, in fact, it is a pleasure, for this is already the second solo album to be released and they are really much better than the Moody Blues albums. Masterpieces of high quality!

Bruce Westbrook, in the August 17 edition of the Texas newspaper, *Waco Tribune-Herald*, said:

For all practical purposes, this year has marked a revival of the Moody Blues' distinctive brand of music. Oh yes, the group disbanded after their last album, *Seventh Sojourn*, was released almost two years ago. And Graeme Edge and Mike Pinder are not to be heard from. But the group's other three members have released two "solo" LPs, both of which incorporate the soaring, symphonic sound of the Moodies, maintain their excellent vocal styles, are lyrically similar to the Moodies' idealistic work, are recorded on the same Moodies-created label, and even employ the same type of colorful cover art. ...

The latter [*From Mighty Oaks*] is an admirable effort, in some ways superior to the successful Hayward-Lodge collaboration. It is definitely a "concept" album, embodying a recurrent, simple, life-loving philosophy in songs such as "Love Is the Key," "I Wish We Could Fly," and "Adam and I," a tribute to Thomas's son.

Like Hayward and Lodge, Thomas (who plays flute) assembled a group of backing musicians, and he sings all leads himself, with a wonderfully insistent, joyful resonance. But unlike his former partners, Thomas has combined his talents with another musician – drummer Nicky James – on the compositional work. Unfortunately, some of the Thomas-James lyrics lack the dignity necessary for singing the glories of such high-flung ideals as uniting the world in a brotherhood of love, peace and understanding. ... But that's picking nits. The album has some marvelous music, with the best cut the aforementioned "Love Is the Key." There's also a lovely orchestral medley leading off the disk and alluding to its forthcoming highlights. ...

From Tom Von Malder, in Arlington Heights, Illinois's *The Des Plaines Herald*, on August 22:

... This often stunningly beautiful album is a worthy follow-up to Justin Hayward's and John Lodge's *Blue Jays* album (also Threshold), which has been the only other album from the Moodies in the past two years. ...

553

A superb blend of classical and rock elements, the instrumental title song opens the album. The crisp, excellent production found throughout the album is immediately noticed.

Thomas' familiar voice fares equally well on love ballads as "You Make Me Feel Alright" and the good change-of-pace, country-style "Rock-A-Bye Baby Blues." The album's two highlights, though, are the soaring sounds of "I Wish We Could Fly" (which is the closest to the Moodies' sound) and the classy rocker "High Above My Head," which seems a sure bet for a hit single. ...

The cover, as usual, features an excellent illustration by Phil Travers.

From Chris Carson, in the August 23 edition of Binghamton, New York's *Press and Sun-Bulletin*:

This album takes a lot more getting to like than the first solo project by a fraction of the Moody Blues. *Blue Jays* swept you right away, from the opening notes into Hayward and Lodge's dreamy world. Sticking to a style they knew best, Hayward and Lodge came up with an exceptional album. ...

Most of *From Mighty Oaks* is like pages out of "Dear Diary," one of Thomas's more memorable contributions with the Moody Blues. Two exceptions, however, interrupt the surrealistic and moving mood of the album. "Rock-A-Bye-Baby Blues," the only non-original done here by Thomas, is too much like a Ringo take-off, while the following "High Above My Head" is muddled by too many horns and is a far shot from the rest of the album.

As for the other material, Thomas's vocals are crisp and open, while the album flows with a mild mellow bounce added to the Moody mythical mood. The overall production is superb, as are all the products of Threshold studios.

For a syndicated newspaper wire story at this time, Stephen Ford wrote:

... *From Mighty Oaks* frequently contains the familiar mournfulness that soaks the Moodys' works – the ennui, the metaphysical awe for Yahweh and His creations. On the other hand, it also oozes like Crème de Menthe with an obsequiousness that straddles naiveté and an overdose of bliss – just like the Moodys' sometimes musical marzipan.

Thomas's pleasing baritone inexplicably reminds one of Robin Gibbs' eerie vocals even though the Bee Gees singer is a tenor – maybe because they share that quivering, hypnotizing delivery.

Ray Thomas told Ford, "I have no track record of my own. I'll be very glad if the public accepts my album the way they do the Moodys. But this solo business is all very exciting. It's my album, my chance, and I've really put my heart into it. …

"I want to see how the album does before I tour. Hiring an orchestra is a very expensive item. I'll probably make a few TV appearances before then, though."

Asked if the Moodys would reunite, Thomas answered, "I certainly think so. We hope to reunite next year. After all, we still own our own studio and the Threshold Record label. That's when Chapter Two begins." (RT-DS75)

From August 31, in the *Detroit Free Press*, Bob Talbert wrote:

> Now that the Moody Blues have disbanded, each of those brilliant English musicians has launched a separate solo career, but the sound of the Moody Blues lingers over all efforts to date. Ray Thomas, the Moody Blues' flute genius and sometime lead singer, doesn't discard his Moody Blues background, but he does make an effort to open himself up for new directions. Best songs for my ear are "I Wish We Could Fly" and "Love Is the Key." A nice effort, but listening to some cuts makes you realize how much the Moody Blues will be missed.

In Wisconsin, on September 14, Warren Gerds wrote in the *Green Bay Press-Gazette*:

> From a mighty oak (the Moody Blues) a little acorn (Ray Thomas) has fallen. …
>
> *From Mighty Oaks* is the second album to come out of the now dead but still famed and fantastic Moody Blues. John Lodge and Justin Hayward combined for *Blue Jays*, and their effort is okay, but terribly melancholy. Those two also sound like the Moody Blues all over again. Flautist-singer Thomas gets more away from miming the eerie choral and massive synthesizer formula, but his conception of scope is a carryover – and his voice is easily recognizable as coming straight from the midst of the Moody Blues crowd.
>
> The packaging for *From Mighty Oaks* is dandy. The cover art by Phil Travers is a foldout painting in soft hues and delicate details of a country scene. A man fishes and reads at a meandering stream while a boy plays with a boat nearby. In the distance is a fantasy-like castle. It's one of those album covers you could look at for hours – well, a couple of minutes.
>
> Some of the cover's mood and quality carry onto the disc. There is the grand scale – in the title cut, an orchestrated piece that does have the feel of might to it. There is the healthy-hearty man-boy relationship – in "Adam and I," which is a personal favorite. Thomas has sensitivity to put all the warmth and love and hope he feels for his son, Adam, into this touching song.

Other songs have various troubles. Sometimes it's a choral effect gone flat. But most often the paper thin lyrics undermine things. They're either stilted or present themes we've heard ad infinitum in pop lyrics. "Love Is the Key," for one. ...

For the September 20 edition of *Ram*, an Australian music magazine, Tony Stewart wrote:

> Unlike his (former?) colleagues Justin Hayward and John Lodge, who earlier this year released what was virtually an attempt to create a Moody Blues' album on their own (*Blue Jays*), Ray Thomas (star of flute, vocals on such ditties as "Legend of a Mind" and "Dr. Livingstone, I Presume") has taken an entirely different direction. The album seems to be marked with Thomas's personal style, which incidentally given another album or two could see him emerge as a significant solo performer. The strength (and occasionally failure) in the music of his first offering lies with the arrangements and the instrumentation provided by a full orchestra (which opens and closes the set very grandly with first the title track and "I Wish We Could Fly"). ...

> Lyrically the songs are sometimes a 'leetle' bland, although "Hey Mama Life" has words which illustrate Thomas's insight into the problems of the down and out, and, "You Make Me Feel Alright" and "Adam and I," although profoundly sentimental, are poetically worded and perceptive.

From October 3, 1975, Al Rudis' *Chicago Sun-Times* review was syndicated to other newspapers, including Florida's *The Miami News*.

> ... Thomas has always had an excellent ear for catchy melodies and unusual lyrics. He wrote "Legend of a Mind" and "Dr. Livingstone, I Presume" among other Moodies standouts.

> On this album, he collaborated with Nicky James, a talented musician who has remained on the fringes of success for many years, and the two turn out to be a strong songwriting team. The songs are pure pop, and the lyrics aren't very deep, even though heartfelt. The Moody Blues were both worshipped and denigrated for their pseudo-profound musical philosophizing, but Ray and Nicky don't go much further than an occasional line like, "The earth is good, why do we abuse it," or "Take the pride from a man, you're left without a meaning." Most of the time, the two writers stick to the senses, and they're on firmer ground with songs about love and joy in life.

> The arrangements are often a bit inflated, but never so lush that they disturb the [listener]. The playing is excellent, with a country tinge provided by B.J. Cole on pedal steel guitar. Ray's vocals show that he's also been listening to country music. He saves many a line that could be too saccharine with his fine vocals.

From Mighty Oaks is an album that most Moody Blues fans will enjoy.

Steven Holden gave his verdict on October 23 in *Rolling Stone*. You may recall that Holden was one of those Blue Meanie-types who seemed determined to hate "all things beautiful," limiting his choices to "straightforward rock 'n' roll." He didn't much care for *Blue Jays*, and now took glee in stomping on Thomas's musical dream. He considered it to be "as silly as its title and fake English Romantic cover art might indicate." Holden found the nine tuneful songs to have a "melodic thinness" which he felt could not "sustain the weight of [the] heavily orchestrated arrangements." He also thought Thomas's "semi-operatic vocals" suffered from "a harsh vibrato and a bad sense of pitch." The lyrics, he said, were "preachy," "self-aggrandizing," and the work of a "comic-strip romantic." And he compared *From Mighty Oaks* to *Blue Jays*, saying that the latter "maintained the grandiose spaciousness of sound that was the Moodys' most marketable asset," but Thomas's album "doesn't even make it as wrap-around mush."

Also on the negative side was the review in the November issue of *High Fidelity Magazine*:

> ... The recording opens with the title theme, "From Mighty Oaks," as stirring an orchestral work as could be obtained from one of the great Hollywood film-score composers. Cornball? Yes! Effective? Yes!
>
> From then on, Thomas peppers this set with a number of ballads, all expertly crafted, played, sung, and recorded, all dripping with the kind of sentimentality one can't bear to hear any more. ...
>
> Commercial and performed with care, *From Mighty Oaks* and its show tunes, with their goody-goody themes done up as middle-of-the-road rock, can't miss with the Moody Blues horde of fans. It'll probably also corral a bunch of those who are addicted to Paul McCartney's twirpings.

McCartney, as covered in the chapter devoted to Denny Laine, had already released *McCartney* ("Maybe I'm Amazed"), *Ram* ("Uncle Albert/Admiral Halsey," "Too Many People, "Smile Away," "Heart of the Country," and "Eat at Home," all on the radio), *Wild Life* (remember the lovely "Some People Never Know" and "Tomorrow"?), *Red Rose Speedway* ("My Love"), and *Band on the Run* ("Helen Wheels," "Jet," the title track, and "Let Me Roll It to You" were on the airwaves). He'd also released several additional singles, including "Another Day," "Hi, Hi, Hi," "Live and Let Die," and "Junior's Farm," respectively. But, according to this critic, McCartney's output was "twirping."

On the subject of the Moody Blues and his solo record, Ray Thomas told *ZigZag* magazine, "It's a successful format, obviously. The Moody Blues, as we call it, has its own sound, a distinct sound, and I wouldn't knock it. I'm proud of being a member of the Moody Blues because there are a lot of bands who I think have been a lot luckier with only half as much talent. I won't name anybody, but there are a few bands about that have got away with murder, and I don't think the Moody Blues would do any kind of rip-off. I think everybody got value for money and we did the best that we could all the time; and the only reason we're taking a rest now is so that we don't fall into that trap – and it's the hardest thing to do at the moment. I think everybody really wants me to say how much I hate everyone else, and I don't. I love 'em." (RT-ZZ75)

The majority of music critics praised *From Mighty Oaks*, but "High Above My Head" and "Love Is the Key" did not make a strong single release. "High Above My Head" only made one of the American charts, *Cashbox*, where it bubbled under at No. 117 on July 26, 1975. "Love Is the Key" did not chart.

Imagine if the single had been "Hey Mama Life" b/w either "Adam and I" or "I Wish We Could Fly," in all likelihood a Top 40 contender.

Despite the failure of the single, *Oaks* had a not-so-mighty but respectable eleven-week run in the *Billboard* album chart, peaking at No. 68 on September 27, 1975. On the U.K. album chart, it did better, reaching No. 23.

Considering that *Blue Jays* made the Top 10 on most charts, both in England and America, Thomas's album may have been considered a commercial disappointment by comparison. But a placement at No. 23 on one British chart certainly warranted a second album.

Regardless of whether Thomas and his record label(s) viewed *From Mighty Oaks* as a success, Thomas was able to end the year on a happy note. "Adam and I" gave clear indication as to how Thomas cherished being a father. On December 18, his wife, Julie, gave birth to their second child, a daughter this time, named Nancy.

25

Kick Off Your Muddy Boots
The Graeme Edge Band, 1975

Album release:
Threshold THS 15; September 1975
U.S. peak position: #107 (*Billboard* Top 200 Albums chart)

Single release: *"The Tunnel" b/w "Bareback Rider"*
Threshold/Decca TH 22 (U.K.); Threshold/London 5N-67022 (U.S.);
November 11, 1975
Non-charting

Graeme Edge and Adrian Gurvitz returned to the Threshold Studio in December 1974, after the *Blue Jays* duet album was finalized, making *Kick Off Your Muddy Boots* the second Moodies side project recorded, even though Thomas's *From Mighty Oaks* was released before.

Returning from the sessions which produced the "We Like to Do It" single earlier in the year were the lineup of Edge on drums, Adrian Gurvitz on guitar and lead vocals, Paul Gurvitz on bass, and Mick Gallagher on keyboards.

Adrian and Paul Gurvitz had been members in the 1960s English rock trio, the Gun, and scored a U.K. Top 10 single in 1968 with "Race with the Devil." Currently, they both played with the Baker Gurvitz Army, with a name inspired by Ginger Baker's previous band, Ginger Baker's Air Force.

Mick Gallagher had played with the 1960s psychedelic rock band, Skip Bifferty, and would later go on to be a member of Ian Dury and the Blockheads.

Graeme Edge and Adrian Gurvitz, circa 1975.
(Photo source: GettyImages.com)

Former Cream drummer and vocalist Ginger Baker, still active currently in the Baker Gurvitz Army with the Gurvitz brothers, made a guest appearance, co-drumming with Edge on "Gew Janna Woman."

Brian Parrish, who had an earlier band with the Gurvitz brothers called Parrish & Gurvitz, made a guest appearance and sang the lead on "My Life's Not Wasted."

Ray Thomas, and his collaborator, Nicky James, appear on *Kick Off Your Muddy Boots* as backup singers, along with singer/songwriter Lesley Duncan (she wrote "Love Song" for Elton John's *Tumbleweed Connection* album); Barry St. John (aka Elizabeth Thompson), who had a minor U.K. hit in 1965 with "Come Away Melinda"; Sunny Leslie, who was part of Brotherhood of Man, which had a 1970 hit with "United We Stand"; and backup singers Joanne Williams and Ruby James.

The last time a Graeme Edge song or poem had been issued on a record was in 1972 with the Hayward-Edge collaboration, "You and Me." That year, when asked why he hadn't contributed more to the writing on the Moodies' *Seventh Sojourn*, Edge told a journalist that his poetry of late had been fairly dark, due to the failure of his marriage. Remember this when you consider the moods found on *Kick Off Your Muddy Boots*, in 1975. While some songs on the album only credit Adrian Gurvitz as writer, Graeme Edge has said that all the tracks were collaborations.

From the first track, **"Bareback Rider,"** the lyrics contain the lines: "I am the clown in the show / She is the star, don't you know / She is the knife in my life…"

In the second song, **"In Dreams,"** Gurvitz sings: "In dreams sometimes I'm aching / Hoping for someone to wake me / Running for my life… all night."

And in the third song, **"Lost in Space,"** Edge writes: "I find myself suspended in a vacuum / A vacuum that goes either way / But there must be something else to it / 'Cause the sun comes to me every day."

From the fourth track, **"Have You Ever Wondered"**: "Tell me the fruit is yours, grown off a tree / Tell me you grew it and don't you see / You didn't grow it, you're not the sun or the rain… / I lie awake wondering what went wrong / The world was ours for a song."

The sixth song is **"My Life's Not Wasted."** The lyric includes: "Try not to hurt me with problems / 'Cause problems ain't what I want / They'll just distance me from trying to love you…. I've got to try before I die to make these dreams come true / All those years and all those tears / I have to come thru."

From the eighth track**, "Shotgun"**: "Far off in a distant land / A man lying dead in the sand / Lying by his side was a song / Written down on a parchment fair / Overgrown with aging hair / You could see this man died alone."

From the final track, **"Somethin' We'd Like to Say"**: "Last night I nearly died / I nearly cried / My heart inside me, aches me / Takes me / Breaks me / Fakes me so / No sign of love, no hope of anything."

Clearly there is a lyrical pattern.

While the lyrics are mostly dark, expressing states of confusion and the loss of love, the tunes sound mainly upbeat, often featuring heavy – for their time – rock arrangements. This point-counterpoint is not always successful.

Kick Off Your Muddy Boots may not appeal to many Moody Blues fans. For the most part, it doesn't *sound* like the Moody Blues. Guitarist Adrian Gurvitz often coaxes a shrilling sound from his instrument, more in line with some hard rock bands. There is a piercing quality to his voice, as well. He can certainly sing – he hits the necessary notes – but he often sounds strained, at the top of his range. In time, it gets to be a bit grating. Each song benefits greatly when the background singers, including Ray Thomas and Nicky James, add their voices, helping to soften and enrich Gurvitz's singing.

Of course, taste in music is subjective, and some will find the overall sound of this album appealing. But, based on the lack of chart success of *Kick Off Your Muddy Boots* and its accompanying single release of "The Tunnel" b/w "Bareback Rider," fans who found this LP a worthy addition to their record collection were clearly in the minority.

It also seems odd that a band named after its drummer did not feature Edge's drumming to a greater degree. The beat is always there, steady and reliable, with expertly executed fills and rolls, but the spotlight is always on the singer, Gurvitz. In comparison, consider that Ringo Starr's 1971 single "It Don't Come Easy" begins with a cymbal, and Starr provides the vocal. Likewise, Ringo's 1972 single, "Back Off Boogaloo," also prominently featured the drums at its very outset. One might expect that on *Kick Off Your Muddy Boots*, but the musical presentation seems all about Adrian Gurvitz.

Graeme Edge: "I don't have musical expertise to work on my own, and I sound like a bullfrog with somebody stepping on its toe when I sing, so you can't really call it a solo album. It was really a collaboration with Adrian. We co-wrote the material, but for marketing purposes, it was called the Graeme Edge Band.

"It was great working with Adrian, because even though I love the Moody Blues music, like any drummer, sometimes I want to really give it some stick. It was also very much removed from Moody Blues music. I wanted to get completely away, which is why the name of the first album is *Kick Off Your Muddy Boots* – 'muddy boots' being 'Moody Blues.'" (GE-MD87)

Edge had a ball recording an album with his new band. Not everyone in the studio held the same sentiment.

Recording engineer Dave Baker said, "That album was the day I decided I didn't want to do this [job] anymore. I liked Graeme very much, but Adrian Gurvitz – he was one of the most unpleasant people I've met in the whole of my life. His brother wasn't as difficult, but he had his moods, too. I'm a very laid back individual and this guy really got to me. That was the day I said, 'I can't do this anymore.' I didn't get any credit on it because I bowed out; I worked on the album for only a couple of days. If you look at the number of credits on that album, you'll see that every engineer in the studio worked on that, because nobody really wanted to be there." (DB-H&H96)

Tony Clarke may have had enough too, after producing the Graeme Edge Band's 1974 single, "We Like To Do It." He didn't return to work on this album, and the album's production credits go to Gurvitz and Edge.

Joe Petagno provided the gatefold cover art. He gained attention through his black light posters in the early 1970s, which led to assignments creating covers for science fiction books, as well as progressive rock albums. At this time, he had already designed the covers for 1973's *High on the Hog*, for Black Oak Arkansas, and, from 1974, *Rampant,* for Nazareth; *Turn of the Cards*, for Renaissance; and the self-titled debut album for Baker Gurvitz Army. From 1975, Petagno created the cover art for the second Baker Gurvitz Army album, *Elysian Encounter,* and *Soap Opera*, by the Kinks. The cover for *Kick Off Your Muddy Boots*, perhaps more than any of those that came before, signaled the direction Petagno's rock art would take in the future, as he moved into the heavy metal genre, including many album covers for Motörhead.

Album release:
Threshold THS 15; September 1975

In the September 6, 1975 issue of *Melody Maker*, Chris Charlesworth said:

> … *Kick Off Your Muddy Boots* by the Graeme Edge Band featuring Adrian Gurvitz is a lot more listenable than the recent schmaltzy Ray Thomas record, *From Mighty Oaks*.
>
> From the credits it appears that Adrian Gurvitz had more to do with the album than Edge himself. He wrote five of the nine tracks himself, and co-wrote another (a disco-type funk instrumental) with brother Paul and Edge. He sang lead on all the tracks and plays lead guitar throughout, and his influence on Edge is seen in every track but two, both of which are straight from the Moody Blues songbook.

The most interesting track, "Shotgun," almost parodies the shrill slide guitar of George Harrison's *All Thing Must Pass*, but it does contain a beautifully constructed, if rather short, acoustic guitar solo. It's too long for a single, but the opening track, "Bareback Rider," would be ideal. It's short, sharp, riffy, and suitably catchy.
...

Edge told Charlesworth, "It seemed an exciting thing to do, to get involved with Adrian. He's a massive personality, a challenging man to work with, and a big guy at that. Fortunately we never came to blows.

"It was an exciting change because over ten years the Moodies have made nine albums, including two that we didn't release, and we'd got so stylized in the studio and so set in our ways that we were almost like an old married couple. It was so great to be in a studio and have someone challenging what I was saying, and playing with somebody different.

"The Moodies had their arguments five or six years ago, and it was known who was expert at this and who was expert at that, and we had it down pat. The problem was that we had a pattern which wasn't changing. There were no sparks and no rubs, and for me, anyway, it was getting a bit stale. ...

"The funny thing about the Moodies is that none of us have really ever emerged from the blanket name, the Moody Blues. As a group we were well known, but the individuals were a bit anonymous. People didn't know us and so they didn't know that we might have a variety of things to say outside of the Moodies. Now we're coming out and making our various statements, but, hopefully, I expect that one day the Moodies will come back together and we'll all be better for it.

"In fact, we have decided that around next spring we'll record together again.

"I think mine is a harder album than the Moody Blues albums, but you'll still find my Moodies roots somewhere in it. Personally, I found the soft, melodic aspect of the Moody Blues very restricting. I do like a nice flowing song and a flowing melody and a vague lyric... but I also like a good, raunchy bit of slap, and somehow the Moodies weren't capable of doing it. So when I was let loose on my own, it was great to have a heavy electric guitar and really let loose. Actually, the sleeve notes are not strictly correct because we wrote everything together, but various credits went to either of us for publishing reasons." (GE-MM75)

In the September 20, 1975 issue of *Billboard*, the trade said of the Edge/Gurvitz album:

> Man who is best known as the drummer of the Moody Blues teams up with guitarist/vocalist Adrian Gurvitz for a mix of Moodies' sounding strings arrangements and segues and a touch of good old rock courtesy of Gurvitz, who is one of rock's more tasteful guitarists. Far superior to the single Edge released about a year back, with the blend of vocals and instrumentals (particularly those that combine an electronic and rock feel) quite successful. Good backup vocals from Nicky James and Lesley Duncan as well as former ex-Moody Ray Thomas. ... Dealers: Let customers know Edge's origins.

Al Rudis, of the *Chicago Sun-Times*, had his review syndicated to numerous other newspapers across America during the first week of October. Of the three Moody Blues offshoot albums released to date, he was least impressed by *Blue Jays* and most partial to *From Mighty Oaks*. *Kick Off Your Muddy Boots* fell somewhere between. Rudis commented:

> … Edge, the Moody Blues drummer, found in Gurvitz the equivalent of Thomas's [Nicky] James – someone to aid in writing and developing new approaches.
>
> Gurvitz, a member of Baker Gurvitz Army, also dominates the album's instrumental music, playing some inspired lead guitar.
>
> The numbers – five by Gurvitz, two by Edge, and one collaboration – are harder edged than Ray Thomas's, but most of them didn't have much to recommend them. … [T]he instrumental work manages to cover up a lot of the shortcomings.
>
> The one standout on the album is a thing called "Gew Janna Woman," which is strong in all departments, and, with a powerful rhythm and hot sparks from the guitar of Gurvitz, seems to boil over with excitement. …

Robert Scott wrote in the October 31 edition of Lafayette, Indiana's *Journal and Courier*:

> … It's painfully obvious from the start that drummers should drum and forget about "poetic" lyrics. Adrian Gurvitz is a competent guitarist but mediocre with his vocals.
>
> Ginger Baker lends his drumming on "Gew Janna Woman." It doesn't help.
>
> The Moody Blues should give up their respite and get back together.

Mike Diana, writing in the November 2 edition of Newport News, Virginia's *Daily Press*, took an original approach, in the form of a letter from a despairing fan … that, as you will see, was not a fan at all.

> Dear Moody Blues: Why did you have to break up (so to speak)? Don't you see what you have done? You are out to destroy your good name and reputation…. Why did you leave the multi-million dollar Moodies and go off on your own? I weathered the other two releases [*Blue Jays* and *From Mighty Oaks*] but the Graeme Edge Band is the last straw.
>
> The group should be called the Adrian Gurvitz Band with Graeme Edge. After all, he wrote all but three of the nine cuts, arranged,

co-produced, did all the guitar work, and sang lead on all but one cut. Aside from that, Paul, Adrian's brother, did all the bass playing, co-wrote a tune and sang back-up. Ginger Baker even does the drums on one cut. What gall, Mr. Edge! The only thing left is for Gurvitz to have a third brother who plays drums and you would be out of a job.

All I can say is that Moody fans (those many misguided souls) who don't like the sound of the Baker Gurvitz Army will be buying the Edge album under false pretenses. Edge's background drum flailing does not a group make.

Gosh Moodies, don't you see? There's safety in numbers. ... So please, please get back together. Then maybe only once a year will I have to put up with a Graeme Edge, Ray Thomas and the rest. I'm asking you nice. ...

Meanwhile, Edge was making the rounds in the U.S. – but promoting, not performing the music. He told "Pop Scene Service" writer Kim Garfield for a syndicated wire story, in newspapers during November, that it would likely be another 18 months before the Moodies came together to record their long-delayed eighth album. Edge said, "Four of the boys met recently in England but the feel just isn't there for an album now. We're in more or less permanent contact with each other because our business lives are so entwined, so we've no problems in that respect. But it's so nice to have put that monster down. It was gobbling us up." (GE-MEP75)

Edge had referred to the Moodies' accompanying media crises as a "monster" before, when he was promoting his "We Like to Do It" single in the late summer and early fall of 1974. The situation had become that traumatic for him. He explained now, "For some people, we were 'pretentious snobs,' for others we were 'stale, old musicians,' and for still others we were semi-deities. Actually, we were just like anybody else singing about love, peace, and happiness, and wondering how we could achieve these things.

"Myself and everybody else [in the Moodies] will be delighted if and when the day comes when there's an album to be done by the Moodies. But from the plans we're making, it's not ready to jell. Maybe when we've each made our individual statements, we can get together again. And nobody will be happier about it than me." (GE-MEP75)

Edge was asked about projects the other Moodies might be planning. He told Garfield, "I've heard a couple of Mike's tracks and he's moving into a sort of jazzy rock. He's also getting back into playing piano again. Ray's album is symphonic and also an intensely personal statement, and John and Justin's *Bluejays* sort of carries on the Moody Blues banner."

He described the music he had been making with Adrian Gurvitz as "melodic rock." (GE-MEP75)

Garfield commented:

… And while the rock is melodic and the lyrics poetically sensitive, the album cover is a real puzzler. A masked warrior is perched atop a purple, break-nosed horse, galloping past a dead cowboy whose severed arm holds a piece of sheet music.

Edge, a history buff and sci-fi buff, explained, "The dead cowboy represents old America. The modernistic freaky figure on the horse is a projection of future America – with all of its lovely gimmickry and high-speed technological and biological advances. It's marrying of animal and mechanical into a future being … who's still a cowboy….

"America is a warrior country – full of fight and vigor. With all of its problems of Watergate and ghettos, it's still the best anybody has ever put together and Americans should never lose sight of that. You're still alive here, there's still things to do and ambitions to fulfill." (GE-MEP75)

Single release:
"The Tunnel" b/w "Bareback Rider"
Threshold/Decca TH 22 (U.K.);
Threshold/London 5N-67022 (U.S.);
November 11, 1975

It seemed a strange marketing move to issue the first – and only – single from the album two months *after* the LP had been released. "The Tunnel," for the most part an instrumental (what little singing there is, if you can call it singing, is fairly inaudible), was trying to be another "Shaft." Except Isaac Hayes's "The Theme from Shaft" had much more meat to it, and was tied to a hit movie. "The Tunnel" has a "Shaft"-like guitar framework, but that's about all it has going for it.

One music critic had suggested "Bareback Rider" might have hit potential, so it was stuck onto the B-side. Radio was uninterested.

Threshold/Decca of France had better judgment, releasing "Have You Ever Heard," one of the albums's better cuts, as an A-side, with the unmemorable "The Tunnel" as the flip.

From the December 7 issue of the *Green Bay Press-Gazette*, Warren Gerds wrote in his "Records in Review" column:

> … Just as with the other ex-Moody members, drummer Graeme Edge has come up with a product that's decent, but nothing spectacular. Actually, it's not so much his album but Adrian Gurvitz's. Gurvitz, who plays a strong, clear guitar, wrote all but three of the nine songs on album (Edge's are the others) – and he has the bulk of the lead vocals.

566

The Edge-Gurvitz team is a good one. They crank up and let 'er rip in controlled, semi-sophisticated rock (not on the Moody Blues level), and have obvious enjoyment doing it. A good mood emanates from *Kick Off Your Muddy Boots.*

With Edge not willing to go on the road to promote the album, or even perform on television for that matter, *Kick Off Your Muddy Boot* had a short life span in the charts. In America, on *Billboard*, it only charted for nine weeks, peaking for two weeks at a dismal No. 107 in mid-to-late November 1975.

The single released from the album, "Bareback Rider" b/w "The Tunnel," missed the charts entirely.

In the January 21, 1976 edition of Florida's *The Orlando Sentinel*, Richard Santoro picked *Kick Off Your Muddy Boots* for his list of the ten best albums of 1975, alongside top-sellers such as *Procol's Ninth*, by Procol Harum; *Gorilla*, by James Taylor; *Frampton*, by Peter Frampton; and *Face the Music*, by Electric Light Orchestra. Santoro said of *Muddy Boots*:

> Graeme Edge was the first to quit [sic] the Moody Blues. He got tired of playing the same thing album after album, so he got together with one of England's top guitarists, Adrian Gurvitz, and put out an album that astounds on several levels. Edge wanted an album that was totally different from anything the Moodies had ever done; in that respect he has failed. There are Moodies influences here – they were inevitable. But, what he has recorded so totally surpasses anything they ever did, that it is a forgivable error. The resulting hybrid sounds something like a cross between Steely Dan, the Baker Gurvitz Army, and the Moody Blues. It's an interesting and unusually compatible mixture of sounds, with Gurvitz' searing guitar, a mellow string section, and some jazz-flavored keyboards.

A counterpoint view, in the February 1976 issue of *Stereo Review*:

> Graeme Edge of the Moody Blues and Adrian Gurvitz have teamed up to write, produce, and perform in this album, and they've come up with an amiably gaudy time waster. Edge's talent on drums remains, and he can work up a kind of vitality and energy that the material certainly lacks, but Gurvitz's work on the lead vocals is so undistinguished in every respect that the tracks blur into a pleasant sort of background noise. Lots of good, tricky production work and excellent recorded sound make it listenable in a vapid way.

The Graeme Edge Band featuring Adrian Gurvitz would try again the following year. Before then, it was Mike Pinder's turn to try as a solo performer.

26

The Promise
Mike Pinder, 1976

Album release:
THS 18; April 1976
U.S. #133 (*Billboard* Top 200 Albums chart)

U.K. single release: *"Carry On" b/w "I Only Want to Be With You"*
TH 23; June 11, 1976
Non-charting

In late 1974, Mike Pinder left England for California. He told Ernie Rideout of *Keyboard* magazine, "When I came to the States in 1974, it wasn't intended to be a split with the band. America was the place to be, and people were inventing incredible things in their garages. In England, the Labour Party had just got in, and I hadn't seen the sun in about six months. We had just finished a world tour and, for me, what was left to do? I could've kept on doing that, or I could've fulfilled other things in my life." (MP-KB94)

The Promise was recorded at Indigo Ranch Studios in Malibu, which was founded and built by Pinder and partner Richard Kaplan, one of those people who had been inventing incredible things in his garage. The studio would become famous, and see the likes of Bob Dylan, Neil Diamond, Neil Young, Van Morrison, Olivia Newton-John, Canned Heat, The Go-Go's, Sting, and the Moody Blues.

Richard Kaplan was from Southern California, having attended USC and Cal State Northridge before becoming an innovator of light-show technology with a company he co-founded in the early 1970s, Nova Lighting

He told Larry Crane for an article in *Tape Op* magazine, "I was living in a basement in Woodland Hills, California, having just returned from the Midwest where a partner and I had run the Nova Lights show. Nova Lights was the first on-stage laser show in the world, written up in *TIME* magazine in the '60s. We were doing polarized lights and laser techniques. ..."

Mike Pinder moved to California with his first wife, Donna Roth, and son Daniel, in 1974.
(Photo source: Alamy.com)

"Mike had married the daughter of Samuel Z. Arkoff, of American International Pictures – he produced all those B-horror movies in the '50s. Her cousin was one of my best friends, and Mike happened to be talking to him about stage lighting. He said, 'You should talk to this guy Richard.' So, Mike came over and visited me. I showed him some of the lighting stuff I was doing, and he said, 'I've never seen anything like that! I want you to fly to England. I want you to be the special effects guy for the Moody Blues.' A month later, I was on my way to England. They went on tour, and I ended up going with them all over America and England, as well as being their photographer."

Kaplan worked with the Moody Blues during their 1972, and 1973-74 tours. He said, "They were the biggest band in the world for two years. Mike and I got to be best friends. I was his sort of right-hand man, lackey, gopher, photographer, and special effects lighting guy. He was building a little studio in his house, and he was going to have this Aengus console shipped to England. England's economy was approaching the bottom in '73, and he said, 'This is crazy to finish this studio up here. I want to live in the United States. Let's go find a place in America and build the studio there.'" (RK-TO14)

Pinder told interviewer John Baccigaluppi, "My ex-wife was from Los Angeles. She wanted to move back with our young son. As I had always loved my tours and visits to California, I was happy to move across the ocean. I was tired of the English rain and was ready for some California sunshine." (MP-TO14)

Kaplan said, "We started looking at properties, all the way from Santa Barbara to Costa Mesa, and nothing seemed to be right.... Then I got a call from Mike, and he said, 'I'm in Malibu.' We drive up to this place, it's like a mile of dirt road, and we finally get to the end and there's a one-story ranch house with a big parking area in front of it." (RK-TO14)

The 60-acre bowl-shaped property included a large rock formation on the ranch's northwest boundary. There was also a seasonal stream which created an 80-foot-tall waterfall. The property had a striking view of the Pacific Ocean, and contained pine trees, citrus and avocado orchards, and a wide variety of fragrant plants. It was an idyllic setting that had once been used by the Chumash Indians for their yearly drum festivals.

Pinder, who had bought the property, said, "I wanted some place where I could have a house, as well as a recording studio; and I loved the privacy and view of the ocean from the Malibu property." (MP-TO14)

The history of the land was as rich as the surroundings were scenic and lush. The original owner, dating back to the early 1900s, was the head of the Stetson Hat Company. He used the Malibu property as a hunting lodge, since the area featured a wide variety of game, including deer, wild boar, and bear. One frequent visitor was famed actor John Barrymore, Sr.

Kaplan said, "John Barrymore, Sr. was [the owner's] best friend, and the Stetson guy lived back East. John was a horrible alcoholic, so when they had to dry him out for a play or a production they would send him up to this place where he couldn't get out." (RK-TO14)

It was hoped that the property's isolation – and the winding, narrow mountain road (later named Barrymore Drive) leading to it – would cut off Barrymore's access to spirits. But ...

Kaplan said, "As we were building the studio there were a lot of boards that were loose, and behind every one of them was a 50 year-old bottle of something!" (RK-TO14)

Designing the Indigo Studio

Richard Kaplan: "We built the studio largely on Mike Pinder's acoustic intuition. The control room was the best-sounding control room I've been in before, during, or after. I took every penny I earned and put that into gear. It was a phenomenal collection." (RK-TO14)

Contributing to its special atmosphere was a tree growing through the front roof overhang. Also, the studio was but a few steps from The Chalet, a bunkhouse where musicians could "crash" after marathon recording sessions.

Kaplan said, "Mike and I basically built it for our own in-house projects; it was never intended to be a commercial studio. We were originally going to get a Neve or an API console, but we ran into these guys from Aengus [Enterprises]. This was the best console we'd ever heard." (RK-TO14)

Aengus Enterprises was a recording studio in London, as well as an equipment manufacturer and distributor, established in 1968.

Kaplan said, "On the day of delivery of the console in 1974, we're waiting for the truck, and this guy comes strutting down the driveway. He says, 'Hi, I'm here to supervise the installation of the console.' We said, 'No, that's okay; we flew David Hawkins in from England.'

"[Dave Hawkins] had done probably half of the big installations in Europe; very, very sharp guy. We said, 'Thank you anyway. What was your name?' He says, 'Deane Jensen.' ... We didn't even know who Deane Jensen was. We had just come back from Europe, and Deane didn't have the fame there that he had here." (RK-TO14)

Jensen was the son of Dr. Arthur S. Jensen, who was an electronic-imaging expert, awarded 25 patents, taught physics at the U.S. Naval Academy, and later worked for RCA Laboratories and the Westinghouse Defense and Electronics Center. Son Deane recalled visits by Albert Einstein to the family home.

In the late 1960s, Deane Jensen worked for Quad-Eight Sound as a systems engineer, advancing to VP of engineering in 1971. While working for Quad-Eight sound, Jensen installed soundboards which were used by Jefferson Airplane, Van Morrison, the Doobie Brothers, and Crosby, Stills, Nash and Young, as well as utilized for the recording of Bob Dylan's 1974 live album, *Before the Flood*.

Jensen believed that the problem of bad-sounding mixing boards and audio systems were caused by the bad interaction between transformers and active circuits. To solve this, he needed more computing power, and thus created the Comtran Circuit Modeling software for the Hewlett Packard computing calculators. This revolutionized sound recording.

Kaplan said, "David Hawkins knew who [Deane Jensen] was, and said, 'Don't send him away!' So they start putting the console in. About an hour later Mike and I were sitting out on the bench in front of the studio, looking at the ocean while having a cup of tea, and David comes out. We said, 'What do you think of this Deane guy? Should we just send him home?' He said, 'After an hour of working with this guy, I feel like he should be doing the console, and I should be soldering AC cords!' ...

"Deane Jensen – he was *the* guy. Deane looked at a studio as not simply being a bunch of components stacked together; he looked at it as one integral unit. He was very much into level and impedance matching. That studio was so full of transformers. Good transformers are like the difference between a Cadillac and a Volkswagen." (RK-TO14)

Pinder chose the name for the studio, which was taken from the same song that had served as the inspiration for the Moody Blues' name. He later said, "I always loved 'Mood Indigo' [by Duke Ellington]. 'Moody' was used, and 'Indigo' was left." (MP0TO14)

Recording the Album

Richard Kaplan: "The first album I did with Mike Pinder, after we opened the studio for personal use, was called *The Promise*, and the cover is a photograph of one of my polarized light crystals."

The credit in the gatefold of the album read: "Organic crystal formation developed by Richard Kaplan at Indigo Ranch Laboratory." Kaplan also took the pictures of the musicians for the album cover. (RK-TO14)

Pinder chose to produce himself, and brought in recording engineer Robert Margouleff to man the board. Margouleff was, in fact, an electronic-music pioneer, who, among many other credits, had been the recording engineer for the Alexander Courage sessions that produced the music for the two original *Star Trek* pilots – 1964's "The

Cage" and 1965's "Where No Man Has Gone Before." Later, he worked for Stevie Wonder on the electronic music synthesizer programming which gave an innovative sound to Wonder's 1970s albums, including 1972's *Talking Book*, 1973's *Innervisions*, and 1974's *Fulfillingness' First Finale*. Margouleff shared a Grammy award for the latter.

John Baccigaluppi was hired to work as tape op. He later said, "One of the earliest sessions I did in my early twenties at my first 'real' studio job, was with Mike Pinder....

Above: Mike Pinder and Kaplan, Indigo Studios, circa 1976. (Photo source: MikePinder.com)
Below: Inner gatefold from *The Promise*, picturing (clockwise) Bill Berg with Flynn J. Johnson, Jim Dillon, Susann McDonald with Pinder, and the view from the Indigo Ranch.

I remember that Mike knew his way around a studio and was a nice guy, which was good, since I was a bit nervous about working with one of the founding members of the Moody Blues." (JB-TP14)

During the recoding of the album, Pinder, as well as writing, producing and providing all the lead vocals, played both 6-string and 12-string acoustic guitars, as well as piano and Mellotron.

Jim Dillon played acoustic and electric guitar. Throughout his career, he has backed up the likes of John Lee Hooker, B.B. King,

Bonnie Raitt, Carlos Santana, Bruce Springsteen, Sting, and Bob Weir.

Steve Beckmeier also contributed electric guitar. In the future, he would perform with Greg Allman, Billy Preston, Jackie Lomax, and Tom Jones.

Flynn J. Johnson and Fred Beckmeier played electric bass guitars. Beckmeier had performed on occasion with the Paul Butterfield Blues Band and Gregg Allman.

Bill Berg played drums. A noted jazz and fusion drummer, Berg had already played on Bob Dylan's 1975 album, *Blood on the Tracks*, and was forming the future Emmy-nominated band Flim & the BBs, which released their first album in 1978. He also worked with Cat Stevens and Leo Kottke.

Other musical contributions were made by Tom Peterson, Steve Madaio, Susann McDonald, Michael Azevedo, and backing singers Maxine Willard, Jeannie King, Julia Tillman.

The opening track on *The Promise* is **"Free as a Dove."** Pinder sings: "One day… amidst the dark confusion, I asked, 'Where could be found the answer to our problems.' And then out of the dark, a voice was saying, 'Listen … listen to your heart … we are all wise within' … and … Only you, only you can change the way you are, and only you can find your morning star."

The song ends with a pronouncement: "All light and sound is perpetual motion … If you understand then one day you'll be free … Free as a dove."

Such cosmic musings are what we might expect from Mike Pinder. The more cynical among us may scoff, although the more sentimental and spiritual will likely be warmed by the message. The choices made recording of the song are also interesting, and work (or not) depending on the mindset and tastes of the listener. More than any other song on the album, "Free as a Dove" has a very informal, spontaneous feel to it, almost like a jam session, recorded live in the studio. This makes for an unexpected start to the first album by someone such as Pinder, always a careful craftsman when in the studio. Perhaps he was being equally careful here. Consider the title of the song, and its theme. "Free as a Dove" takes flight, with no constraints or concerns. The band and backing singers join the flight, with the mood of a joyous gathering, not a meticulously planned performance. It is very much as though Pinder, right out of the gate, was trying to debunk the "pretentious" tag the press had pinned him with.

For the recording, Pinder contributes an acoustic guitar. Jim Dillon is all over the place on the electric, as if experimenting during the jam, or rehearsal, trying out different guitar parts to see what may fit the best. This helps to create the jam-session feel to the track. Again, this is good or bad, depending on your taste.

In **"You'll Make it Through,"** Pinder sings: "If you're caught in darkness, holding on for dear life, remember where you started and how you knew what was right. And now if you're lonely, and the feeling ain't right … Hold on, don't give in! … You'll make it through the night. Hold on, you'll make it through this life!"

For this second track, the arrangement is more in line with what the listener was likely expecting – an ethereal lyric, a relaxed melody, Pinder's smooth vocal, the majesty of his Mellotron sound (although this time courtesy of an ARP synthesizer), and additional accompaniment from piano, also from Pinder. This recording would have sounded very Moody Blues-ish if not for the choir of background singers during the choruses, including female voices, and a very loose approach to harmonizing. This was also very likely a deliberate choice from Pinder, to stake out his own musical territory as a solo artist.

For **"I Only Want to Love You,"** the recently divorced Pinder sang, "Past lives that I've lived, only lead up to a Gift, of speaking out my thoughts in my songs … I only want to love you, I only want to care, I'd like a friend to talk to / My feelings are to share … my life with someone … I hope it's you and that you'll care."

Besides the lead vocal, Pinder plays 12-string guitar in a style that may remind one of Peter Frampton from this period. He also mans the Mellotron.

There are no female backing singers for this one, and the song is kept in the Mike Pinder/Moody Blues vein. As-is, the song could easily have been included on any of the group's albums. This may have been the reason it was chosen as one half of a double A-side single. "I Only Want to Love You" was not really "hit" material, but if given even a small amount of exposure on the radio, it could have served as an effective "trailer" for the album.

With the next song, **"Someone to Believe In,"** the lyric reads: "I've travelled this illusion… Light show extraordinaire… Been searchin' for a reason… A 'why' we all can share…. A man needs someone to believe in, or else he's gonna blow his mind. There's something more to life than TV; you know it's gonna make you blind."

Of course, Pinder was probably suggesting moral, not physical, blindness from too much exposure to television's "vast wasteland." The sentiment was married to a light jazzy track, driven by tenor flute and saxophone (both played by Tom Peterson), and complemented by an upright acoustic bass (Joe DiBartolo, long-time bass player for Doc Severinsen on *The Johnny Carson Show*, as well as nearly 100 film and TV scores). Pinder played acoustic guitar.

While "Someone to Believe In" would have made for an offbeat track on a Moody Blues album, it nonetheless could have fit in among other group efforts. Pinder had done this type of jazzy music before, featuring Ray Thomas on flute. Songs like "So Deep Within You," from *On the Threshold of a Dream*, and "When You're a Free Man," from *Seventh Sojourn*, had established Pinder's fondness for light jazz arrangements of this type.

In **"Carry On,"** Pinder rejoices his salvation from a dark time: "Carry on, the past has gone and paid for, Solo on, through the door you're made for; Love flows on through the Gates of Heaven; We are one, by the light of seven."

Did "solo on" refer to a solo career after the Moody Blues, or life after the end of his marriage … or both?

Pinder played acoustic guitar on this track. The loose-harmony backing singers have returned, making this one of three tracks on the album – along with "Free as a Dove" and "You'll Make It Through" – which is anything but "Moody" in arrangement.

From this point on, though, the sound of *The Promise* becomes very much a Moodies affair.

"Air" is an instrumental that one critic said reminded him of "Never Comes the Day." You can imagine singing the chorus to that Moody Blues song over the instruments in two different sections of this track. But there is much more to enjoy in this "airy" rock track. Pinder's instrument of choice here was 12-string guitar.

With **"Message,"** for Moody Blues fans – but certainly not most rock critics – *The Promise* shifts into its most satisfying phase – the start of a suite which includes "Message," "The Seed," and into *The Promise*'s title song. This is pure "Classic Seven" Moody Blues, and would have fit in beautifully with the songs of *On the Threshold of a Dream* and *To Our Children's Children's Children*. The journey begins here, with Pinder playing piano, RMI, and ARP (synthesizer), and Jim Dillon playing sitar.

Pinder sings: "I'm writing this message today / I'm thinking that you'll have a way / Of hearing the notes in my tune. Where are you going? / Where have you been? / I can imagine other worlds you have seen / Beautiful faces and music so serene."

"The Seed" has Susann McDonald on harp, Dean Olch on shakuhachi, and Pinder on the ARP synthesizer; he also contributes a breathy spoken-word verse: "The secret of the seed is in the fragrance of the flower, as the petals open up and bow their heads toward the power. …"

"The Promise" is the real prize of this album. This sounds more like the Moody Blues than anything on *Blue Jays*. With a lovely melody line, and smooth vocal delivery, much in the style of "Have You Heard," Pinder sings: "Oh sweet loving music, I hear your tender call. To me, you are a river / Pure love, your waterfall / A tide forever bathing a rough and rocky shore... Please take us on a journey so we can learn some more."

The dreamy journey is propelled by Flynn J. Johnson's bass; Bill Berg's drums; Susann McDonald's harp; Jim Dillon's electric guitar; and Pinder playing 12-string guitar, Mellotron, ARP, and providing the tender lead vocal.

Interviewed for this book, Mike Pinder reflected on the making of *The Promise*, its inspiration, and some of its results. "*The Promise* was an opportunity to delve deeper into music and the cosmos. That really is where my interest has always been. Since a child, I have loved to tinker and use my imagination. I used to build radios with my dad in the garden shed; I would lie under the piano and touch the keys and touch the vibration of the strings to hear what sounds they would make; I would lie in a box in the garden and watch the stars and the planets; I would lie on my bed as a child and astral travel to see who was playing in the streets; I would ride my bike to Sutton Park in Birmingham and look for birds' nests (I have had a lifelong love of birds). So my childhood pursuits and interests led me to love music, to build my own recording studio as an adult, build my own computers, write songs for the Moodies, delight in nature, and nurture a family.

"I think I have always had my feet firmly planted on the ground, but my head has been above the clouds, endeavoring to learn and imagine why is it we are here on this planet." (MP-AI17)

Few musicians in our time have experienced things as Michael Pinder has...his years with the Moody Blues...his retreat in the California hills and privacy. Those years that now bring us Michael Pinder's solo LP... "The Promise" Michael Pinder.

"It's been my goal for nine long years to write this song... so I can say...exactly what I believe is coming down..."*
MICHAEL PINDER

MICHAEL PINDER
The Promise

LONDON

***

The Promise is historic for reasons other than being Mike Pinder's first solo album; it was the first album recorded at the famed Indigo Ranch Studios – where *Octave*, Pinder's last album with the Moody Blues, was recorded 1977-78.

Pinder said, "When I lived at the Ranch, I only recorded for personal use, although I did do a couple of projects for friends, and friends of friends." (MP-TO14)

Richard Kaplan said, "Around 1978 or 1980, [Mike] wanted to move on; he'd gotten married [to Taralee, his second wife] and wanted to put his equity into a house and various other things. We worked out a buyout for the equipment and the property that took years to pay off, but we did it. We continued our good friendship and relationship through all of that. It was an amicable parting." (RK-TO14)

Pinder said, "I moved to Hawaii with my new wife, Taralee. Richard Kaplan and Michael Hoffman bought the property and the studio from me. They opened the studio commercially at that time.

"Living and working at Indigo Ranch was a wonderful experience. I was surrounded by friends and talented people. It was really a loving, supportive, and creative environment. Richard is a very warm and intelligent guy, and learning engineering was second nature to him. Richard and I were very dear friends, and became close, like brothers, during those days. It was a special time for me, and I think the magic of Indigo remained for the musicians that followed." (MP-TO14)

Kaplan said, "In 1975 or '76, Canned Heat was our first customer; they came in and recorded half a side of an album, and then the world literally beat the door down. We had hundreds of great albums that came out of there."

Above: Indigo studio stage, as seen from the control booth, for the cover of Neil Young + Crazy Horse's _Ragged Glory_.

Besides the draw of the relaxing and picturesque setting, Kaplan believed the sound, or "feel," of the studio, was a factor in its popularity among recording artists. He said, "It was the sound. People were hearing little demo bits that were coming out of there, and it was like, 'God, I've never heard anything like that.' Back in the '70s and '80s, when Indigo first started, you'd hear an Indigo record on the radio, and it would just obliterate whatever was played in front of it or after it. The sound was just dazzling."
(RK-TO14)

Some albums recorded at Indigo Ranch Studio were 1978's _Too Hot_ by Olivia Newton-John; Neil Diamond's _I'm Glad You're Here With Me Tonight_ and _You Don't_

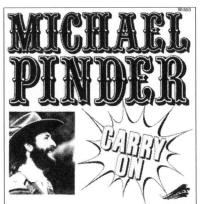

Bring Me Flowers (both from 1978), and _September Morn_ (from 1979); _Vacation_ (1982) the Go-Go's; Neil Young's _Hawks & Doves_ (1980) and _Ragged Glory_ (1990); and numerous albums by Korn.

Album release:
Threshold THS 8; April 1976

U.K. single release:
"Carry On" b/w "I Only Want to Be With You"
Threshold TH 23; May 14, 1976

From the April 4, 1976 issue of *Melody Maker*, the bold headline read, "Pinder's Broken Promise." To explain the headline, the reviewer wrote:

> … Not that this isn't a pleasant, even enjoyable, album. Parts of it, notably the openers on both sides, which groove along quite happily, are even mildly stimulating. But as I write, while the second side of the album runs out at the end of what is the fourth or fifth time of playing, there is hardly anything good that catches in my memory. There are some things that stick for the wrong reasons, however, because they are so predictable, unbearably kitsch, like the breathy spoken "verse" on "The Seed" on Side Two, in which portentous sentiments are intoned while a woodwind doodles around a number of phrases seemingly lifted from Debussy's "Clair de Lune." …

Judging by both the sleeve design, which combines various religious symbols, mandalas and such, with what looks like microphotographs of crystals, and the words of the title song, there is a deep significance about the album which somehow doesn't get out of the grooves. Pinder seems to have been reading Von Daniken, but if he believes he has finally achieved his goal of saying "exactly what I believe is coming down," then so far as I am concerned he has failed. …

According to *Cashbox* on April 17:

> In this tasty solo effort, Michael Pinder establishes himself a viable solo artist. Pinder, late of the Moody Blues, displays his many talents filling the roles of writer, producer, arranger, engineer, and multi-talented musician. The songs bear a light jazz feel with pleasing vocal lines which should make it a popular play in the MOR market. Some progressive airplay can also be expected, though the tunes really do not lend themselves to pop play, where many of Pinder's Moody Blues followers are.

On the same day, *Billboard* told industry insiders:

> Ex-Moody Blues member Pinder does a pleasant set of easy to listen to rock with a few tinges of jazz and symphonic rock tossed

in from time to time. Mellow, flowing vocals are reminiscent of the Moodies, as are the smooth, full instrumental arrangements. Synthesizers and harp also add fullness to the set.... Expect heavy FM play, as well as some MOR. Pinder is at his best when combining the Moody styled instrumentals (minus the booming crescendos) and his own distinctive vocals.

Best cuts: "You'll Make It Through," "Someone to Believe In," "Message," "The Seed." Dealers: Pinder's name is a major selling point.

Also on the 17th, but across the pond, England's *New Musical Express* had an exclusive – the first Michael Pinder interview in four and a half years. He met with *NME*'s Steve Turner in New York at the Hilton Hotel, accompanied by Threshold's Gerry Hoff ... and hundreds, perhaps thousands, of Trekkies. A *Star Trek* convention was taking place at the hotel, turning the surroundings into a surreal fantasy.

First things first. The *New Musical Express* man wanted to know on behalf of his readership what the status on the Moody Blues was. Pinder explained, "After *Seventh Sojourn* I thought there might be another album. But we went in and – nothing. The Moodies were always a band of principles, and that's why we broke up, because of our principles." (MP-NME76)

At last, one of the Moodies had spoken those two words that the members of the press had bantered around since fall of 1974 – "broke up." Graeme Edge had almost said it, but then quickly backpedaled to the "we're just taking a rest" line. Pinder, who Edge had told the press was the first to leave the band for that much needed rest, was now the first to dare to say they had indeed broken up.

But this breakup was not meant to be permanent. Pinder explained, "Someday everybody is going to be in the same place at the same time and *they're* going into the studio to make the wipe-out album of the year. But nobody's saying Wednesday at 3:30 on April the 15th. ...

"My statement in terms of the Moody Blues is this: the getting back together of the Moody Blues, the reformation of the Moody Blues, should be left entirely up to the Moody Blues, and not the public, not the agents, not the record company, not the press; not anybody. It should be left to the individuals. And when *they* feel like doing it, then it's going to happen."

It was curious to hear Pinder refer to the Moody Blues as "they," not "us." Read the statement again. It's plain that "they" referred not to his friends in the band, but to the corollary encumbrances and commitments which had grown around the group.

Pinder continued, "And when it happens for *them* is when it'll happen for the fans, because, if we went in there and did something that our hearts weren't in, you might as well burn every Moody Blues album that has ever been bought. That's what I really honestly feel about it, and that's my statement about it. That's all there is to say, really." (MP-NME76)

Regarding his solo album, his statements, and this rare interview, Pinder told Turner, "What we should have done is sent the album out as an interview, because that's basically what it is. I conducted my own interview with myself, plus all of my inspirations, my dreams, my hopes, my experiences. All we can do now is elucidate upon the album … um … unless you have some other kinds of questions." (MP-NME76)

Turner had heard the album, and told his readers:

> Fortunately for Pinder, *The Promise*, like the two other solo albums released [sic, three] by M. Blues members largely avoids the leaner aspects of the Moody Blues – the tendency toward lushness, lack of cojones, etc. A couple of the tracks may even do well in discos. Consequently, I wondered, had Pinder harbored a latent distaste for his lack of guts?

Remarkably, Pinder didn't take offense from the inference that he had lacked guts, or "cojones," in the past. Perhaps he had accepted that many in the music press were – let's be frank here – remarkably tactless assholes. He seemed to accept that rude behavior had become the norm among the elitist ranks of the press. But it *is* surprising that he went along with the sentiment. "Definitely." He said. "That's very much what I'm trying to do with my stuff now. ...

"What I'm offering you is to share in something that I have found for myself, and, if an individual is in trouble, then I can help give them some clarity. I am a man of convictions, and a man of convictions can usually help people who don't have convictions." (MP-NME76)

Pinder felt he was getting his message across. Others didn't. Bob Bonn, writing for Pennsylvania's *Beaver County Times,* was quite certain that …

> … The disappointing thing about Pinder's album is the quality of songs he's included in it. It's been three years since the last Moody Blues album, and you'd think in that time he could have written a collection of songs capable of knocking us all right out, especially since he composed some of the better tunes [songs] in the Moody's repertoire (including "Melancholy Man," "Lost in a Lost World" and "Simple Game," among others).
>
> There are some genuine goodies in *The Promise*, especially the opening and closing tracks of the album. But mostly, the songs are average, something the Moodies as a group would never have tolerated.
>
> Pinder was to a large degree responsible for the lushness of the group's sound, working his Mellotron to full advantage and making the five-man band sound like an airy rock symphony. Naturally, he continues this sound here. Also, the album is beautifully recorded, as were the others – all of the Moodies are real pros in the studio.
>
> One problem with the Pinder album is his lack of variety in subjects. He keeps harping on what seems to be his only theme – peace and love. Not that there's anything wrong with these concepts, but one can only write sweeping generalities about loving thy neighbor for so long before every set of lyrics begins to

sound alike. Pinder, especially with the release of this album, has gone past the limit. I've had it up to the ears with brotherhood.

Pinder's solo album is not a bomb, yet it is not a totally satisfying album either. It is important for Moody Blues fanatics, and marks a significant point in the un-group's development. For folks who don't share the fanaticism for the Moodies, however, this LP is sadly dispensable. There are too many average albums on the market now anyway.

On May 15, Dennis Hill wrote in New Jersey's *The Daily Journal*:

Michael Pinder's *The Promise* offers very little change from his easy style he was so noted for with the Moody Blues. The music is basically middle of the road and the words play heavy into mind and religion.

Side One is a bit boring and nothing on the side really stands out musically. Side Two is more of a concept piece in the true line of what the Moodys are so famous for. The song "Air" is a mix of the old song "Never Comes the Day" and it at least held my interest to an extent. Pinder does his recital act on "The Seed." It's nice and the point is well made.

In total the album has few high points but the low points far outweigh them. In truth, I can't wait till the Moody Blues get back together and do something constructive

Another regional review came on June 20, from Pete Bishop in *The Pittsburg Press*. His felt that Pinder's *The Promise* was "filled with tasteful arrangements of strong melodies."

… It's a mixed bag: ballads ("I Only Want to Love You"), funky rock, [like] "You'll Make It Through" (check out the Jim Dillon slide guitar work); and fast folk-rock that gets downright rowdy ("Free as a Dove"). Everything is okay or better, except perhaps, "The Seed."

Lyrically, mysticism is rampant (in keeping with the gorgeous cover), usually less than meaty and often too ethereal ("Message," "The Seed").

Pinder has an adequate voice and enhances, rather than dominates, the total sound with his keyboards. *The Prom*ise is uncluttered, pleasant listening.

This seemed to be the general consensus.

In the July 1976 issue of *Gramophone*, *The Promise* was described as "not startling," but "pleasant and undemanding."

Alex Ward wrote in the July 20 issue of Australia's *Ram*:

So. The fifth member of the Moody Blues has chanced his charm. It must be said that his solo debut is not particularly impressive. In fact, it just demonstrates what many have thought all along – the particular lovable/hate-able magic (depending on your view of the Moodies) of the group's albums was a combination of talents. They egged each other into producing one or two good songs. Each member seemed to have a beneficial effect on the other members' music, and the competition amongst the five for song space on each Moody's album also seemed beneficial in terms of quality of songs and pace.

Taking the five solo albums [sic; four] the various Moodies have produced over the past year and a half, you'd have a little over one usual quality Moody Blues album. ...

Pinder sings of romance, universal love and God. The songs are melodic, though mostly mundane. Despite a wonderfully clear production quality, the arrangements are invariably stilted and cluttered with excessive, easy-going instrumentation. "Free as a Dove" and the title track seem to be the closest Pinder gets to those magic moments you all loved/hated on full Moody Blues productions. ...

From the August 27 edition of Chicago, Illinois's *The Daily Herald*, Tom Von Malder wrote:

> ... Pinder's album is a statement of his beliefs and the viewpoint is very optimistic throughout. Both the title piece and "The Seed" contain bits of mysticism, the latter also using the Indian instrument shakuhachi for an Asian sound.
>
> Some listeners may find Pinder's approach to life a bit too corny. Still, the album's music is of a very pleasing quality – soft over-all with traces of jazz, such as the tenor sax and flute on "Someone to Believe In." There are several love songs, including "I Only Want to Love You" ....
>
> It is a collection of songs with no underlying theme. The music is brighter and more up-tempo, and there are nice classical touches throughout, such as the string bass on "Friends." ...

In the September, 1976 issue of *Stereo Review*:

> Michael Pinder, of the Moody Blues, has written and arranged all of the songs here and come up with a competent, likable solo album debut. His voice isn't exactly anything to write home about, no matter where he lives, but his guitar playing is absolutely front-rank. The songs are the regulation high-class mush that passes for sentiment these days. "The Seed," for example, has lyrics that sound as if they were lifted from a TM primer, and they are

delivered as if Pinder were carefully reading a prescription over the phone to a non-English-speaking pharmacist. The arrangements, however, on this and most of the other bands [tracks], are really beautifully done – transparent but lush, imaginative, and unstrained. It's something of a put-down, I guess, to rave about Pinder's arranging talent when he tries so hard in other creative directions, but that is about the only really striking area of the album. Better luck next time.

The album only managed to place at No. 133 on the *Billboard* album chart, while not registering in the U.K. The single, released in England, received a bit of radio sampling, but did not chart. In the U.S., no single was issued.

Considering that it was an album from the eight-times-gold Moody Blues, *The Promise* deserved a bigger push from London Records in the U.S., Jerry Weintraub, and from Mike Pinder. Other than for *New Musical Express* in England, Pinder gave few interviews, no concerts, and no television performances. The flare of the extravagant launch Jerry Weintraub gave to *Blue Jays* was missing for the Ray Thomas and Graeme Edge albums, and for *The Promise*. As for London Records, and the America-based Threshold Records branch, they passed on issuing the "Carry On" / "I Only Want to Love You" single. If the feeling was that these songs wouldn't appeal to American radio programmers, then London and Threshold were likely right. This album had not been made as a showcase for singles. Still, Threshold/London should have at least issued a promotional single, coupling two of the most engaging tracks for radio sampling. The album's title song would certainly come as music to the ears to Moody Blues fans, something radio programmers could have understood. It is surprising London didn't issue it at least as a DJ promo single.

Case in point: After the release of Pink Floyd's *Dark Side of the Moon* in March 1973, and "Money" becoming a hit single, Harvest Records sent out a promotional EP to radio stations containing four songs from the album – two per side, with no crossfading. Two of the songs began getting airplay, so, a few months later, Harvest issued "Us and Them" b/w "Time" as a 45. It didn't chart well, with "Us and Them" only bubbling under at 101 on *Billboard*, but both songs gained substantial airplay on FM and progressive rock AM stations across the nation. This helped send *Dark Side of the Moon* higher in the charts. It doesn't require rocket science to send an album up the charts – just a little effort.

It certainly seems that Pinder had been greatly let down, by his record label, his manager, and himself. After all, why make a record if you're not willing to help it sell?

By this time, Justin Hayward and John Lodge were each preparing solo albums. One step ahead of them, however, and continuing to surprise both the music press and Moody Blues fans, was Ray Thomas. The laidback Thomas had suddenly become quite prolific. For the second time in less than 12 months, he had a new album ready for release. Next up: *Hopes, Wishes and Dreams*.

27

Hopes, Wishes and Dreams
Ray Thomas, 1976

Album release:
Threshold/Decca THS 16 (U.K.); Threshold/London THS 16 (U.S.); June 1976
U.S. #147 (*Billboard* Top 200 Albums chart)

Single release: *"One Night Stand"* b/w *"Carousel"*
Threshold/Decca TH 24 (U.K.); Threshold/London 5N-67023 (U.S.); June 11, 1976
Non-charting

For his second solo album, Ray Thomas co-wrote eight of the ten songs with Nicky James, plus one credited to only himself. One song on the album was credited only to James. Thomas played flute, bass flute, and harmonica.

Most of the core band from *From Mighty Oaks* returned, with John Jones on acoustic and electric guitar, his brother, Trevor, on bass, and Mike Moran on keyboards. Missing was drummer Mike Potts, replaced by *Blue Jays* drummer, Graham Deakin.

Barry St. John returned, again joining Thomas and Nicky James on backing vocals. Additional singers joined the project. They included Liza Strike, who had sung lead for Liza & the Jet Set in 1965 and was heard on hundreds of other records as a background singer, for star performers such as Elton John, Pink Floyd, the Who (on *Tommy*), Gary Wright, Carly Simon, Peter Frampton, Rick Wakeman, Nazareth, Small Faces, Steven Stills, and many others. Also singing backup was Helen Chappelle, who had taken the lead when she recorded a couple of solo singles and with the group Hawk

& Co. As a frequently employed background singer, she supported artists such as the Firm, Albert Hammond, Bryan Ferry, and Allan Clarke.

Thomas again produced, with assistance from Derek Varnals.

Thomas was feeling confident after the experience of recording *From Mighty Oaks*. It had garnered mostly positive notices, as well as a respectable chart ranking. Talking to John Dearing of *The Michigan Daily*, Thomas once more addressed why the Moodies had stopped working together and why making his own records was such a pleasure: "We had said the same thing to each other for ten years. We had nothing left to talk to each other about. Besides, it really felt good entering the recording studio to do the things I wanted without wondering if the others liked it. The great thing about solo albums is that if the effort isn't successful, it doesn't hurt anyone else's reputation." (RT-MD78)

Thomas's second album is less classical in approach than *From Mighty Oaks*. An attempt was clearly made to make a record that was more contemporary pop. But what might work for Elton John or the Bee Gees wasn't necessarily going to click for Ray Thomas, a baritone, who was nearing middle age by the standards of rock music.

"In Your Song" opens the album, and is the only song not credited to Ray Thomas as either writer or co-writer. Nicky James takes the honors, and, from a songwriting perspective, it's not bad. The arrangement, however, clearly tries to be "current," but fails. John Jones's musical choices on the electric guitar are questionable as well, not only here but on several other tracks on the album. The guitar sound may work for some, but others – this author included – found it grating. Had Jones been taking tips from the hard-rocking Adrian Gurvitz?

Beyond this blemish, "In Your Song" comes off like a mediocre Bee Gees song from 1975's *Main Course*, or 1976's *Children of the World* – not quite disco, but leaning in that direction.

"Friends" reaches back to the familiar and fertile soil which nurtured Thomas's *Mighty Oaks*, but somehow comes off like a leftover from the earlier sessions. And the piercing electric guitar is present here, as well, and just as unhelpful. Everything in this song was stated better in Elton John's "Friends," or Carol King's classic, "You've Got a Friend" – both from 1971. The sentiments are the same, just not as well-phrased.

"We Need Love," like the opening track, is trying for a more contemporary feel, and this time nearly pulls it off. The opening piano riff is reminiscent off Charlie Rich wannabe – "(Hey, Did You Happen to See) the Most Beautiful Girl in the World" – while John Jones's acoustic strumming recreates the mood of the opening of Justin Hayward's "I Dreamed Last Night."

"We Need Love," like the opening track, is trying for a more contemporary feel, and this time nearly pulls it off. The piano riff near the beginning is reminiscent of Charlie Rich's 1973 "The Most Beautiful Girl" – while John Jones's acoustic strumming recreates the mood of the opening of Justin Hayward's "I Dreamed Last Night." Together, the opening of "We Need Love" sounds eerily prescient of Bob Seger's 1980 "Against the Wind." Thomas sings: "My love song is a sad song / I sing it to say 'I'm sorry' / Then maybe, just maybe / You'll learn how to love again.…"

The album comes alive with this track … despite John Jones's guitar remaining in the same groove as on the first two tracks. Wasn't it time to change things up?

Despite these observations, "We Need Love" is a stirring song, much like the best heard on *From Mighty Oaks*.

"Within Your Eyes" is a lovely song. Thomas sings: "Within your eyes, so many good hellos and sad goodbyes / Your future shines, the past reclines / Yet still you seek to find / A place to run…."

The track starts out with Thomas on harmonica. Visions of Huckleberry Finn may appear in your mind as you listen. His use of the flute, to the accompaniment of an acoustic guitar, conjures up memories of the beautiful harmonic partnership of Justin Hayward's guitar and Thomas's flute on many Moody Blues tracks. You could imagine this recording as part of a future album from the Moodies.

Thomas also displays his vocal range, singing the verses in a baritone, then switching to a tenor vocal delivery for the choruses, both relaxed and impassioned.

"One Night Stand" closes out the first side of the original LP. It was also picked as the top side of the album's only single. Sadly, the piercing electric guitar is back. Almost as distracting, or perhaps aggravating, is the background singing from Barry St. John, Liza Strike, and Helen Chappelle – these English white girls are trying too hard to sound like three soulful black girls. It's all laid on a bit thick and loud, taking charge of the song instead of providing support to Thomas.

Otherwise, the core band jells nicely. John Jones cleverly arranged the brass, creating a signature hook for the track … and almost making up for his indulgent and intrusive electric guitar fills.

Side Two, and **"Keep On Searching,"** begins with promise. Thomas sings, "Well, I've always been a dreamer, and I sometimes play the fool / But when the lights go down and I hear the crowd, then I'm cool / Then I sing my songs of freedom, and I sing my songs of love / But there's nothing changed / 'Cause I'm still the same as I was."

This might have made a good track for Ringo Starr, on his solo albums from this period. It has a lot of the boogie-woogie hustle of "Oh My My," from Starr's 1973 *Ringo*. But just when everything seems to be clicking, there's that annoying electric guitar sound from John Jones – tuned and amplified to sound like it did on four of the previous tracks. In a word, grating – and this is coming from a listener who rarely had issue with Jimi Hendrix, and was weaned on Steppenwolf. Pair the axe's howls with those southern gospel singers (from England), and a honking *Saturday Night Live* theme-sounding sax part. When unrestrained, the life of the party can kill the mood.

"Didn't I" is a song with elements that may seem not to belong together, but which somehow blend smoothly. Consider Randy Bachman's work on the Guess Who hit, "These Eyes," combined with the haunting cry of a Mexican trumpet (ala "The Lonely Bull"), along with understated but effective orchestration, rock-ballad drum fills, and a delicate vocal from Thomas. The choir here is more reminiscent of the male voices on *From Mighty Oaks*, and just as pleasing.

Thomas laments: "They say that love should last forever / Forever's such a long, long time / And my darling I still love you / Is that a crime? … Didn't our love burn like the sun / Didn't our passion run so very high / Didn't we aim for the moon / But our love died too soon / And that's no lie."

You'll want to play this one again.

"**Migration**" continues to raise the bar. It could have been a hit for the soundtrack of the 1973 film *Jonathan Livingston Seagull*. It's a tasteful number, and almost classical in its presentation, with Thomas's lovely flute leading the way.

He sings: "Trees are bare, snowflakes are falling / You can hear their leader calling / 'Follow me, fly strong my brother / Be strong of heart and help each other home' / And here I am, I'm just a man / And there you are among the stars, flying high / Searching for a new tomorrow / I wish I could follow."

The music and instrumentation is in the style of the standout *From Mighty Oaks*' track, "Adam and I," with a theme reminiscent of that album's "I Wish We Could Fly." It's a wonderful marriage, and one of the best tracks on *Hopes, Wishes and Dreams*.

"**Carousel**" must certainly have been a favorite of both Thomas and James, for it was chosen as the flip side of the single. It's no "Being for the Benefit of Mr. Kite," and won't please all (in fact, one critic singled this out as one of the album's worst two moments), but it is nonetheless an impressive recording. It sounds like a show tune, and, in that context, a good one. "Carousel" is a little stage play or movie within a song, and goes down nicely, for the less cynical among us.

The last song is appropriately titled "**The Last Dream.**" Thomas's vocal is reminiscent of Roger Whittaker. It may be no coincidence that the title is "The Last Dream" when you recall that Whittaker's biggest song from this period is 1974's "The Last Farewell." It shot to No. 2 in the U.K. charts and made Top 20 in the U.S.

"The Last Dream" also plays a bit like a show tune, in the tradition of songs like "The Impossible Dream." It has all the dramatics, and a strong, confident vocal projected towards the back row of a theater, perhaps.

It's a tale of a man's life coming to a close. Thomas tells us: "A simple man had the strangest dream / He stood in a garden of flowers / That overlooked the sea / And there sailing by / Were his truths and his lies going home ... At last he knew his act was through / with no applause and no encores / Though the house was full / So bring the curtain down / Lay him on the ground / For he's gone home ... Memories of youth had passed before / He and he alone could count the score / Now he is free, he is free / This was his last dream / Now he is free."

Tasteful and effective piano and orchestration sweep around Thomas ... as he takes this one home.

Assistant recording engineer Dave Baker said, "Both [of Ray's] albums were a lot of fun. ... Ray's albums were the ones where we did a lot of verbal sparring and we had some good fun. The people in the band had a sort of acid wit, and there were barbs flying all the time. ...

"Of all of them [in the Moody Blues], I got closest to Ray. We like the same things: fishing, and other things. We used to go to restaurants together occasionally. He's a great guy." (DB-H&H96)

Phil Travers, another fellow who shared a long past with Thomas, designed the gatefold album cover.

Album release:
Threshold/Decca THS 16 (U.K.); Threshold/London THS 16 (U.S.); June 1976

RAY THOMAS

"HOPES WISHES & DREAMS" TH 17

Single release:
"One Night Stand" b/w "Carousel"
**Threshold/Decca TH 24 (U.K.);
Threshold/London 5N-67023 (U.S.); June
11, 1976**

Thomas abandoned his second solo album and single at birth. He didn't promote it to the degree that he did with his first outing, nor did he tour. With each suffering diminishing returns; with the last Moody Blues album of new material three-and-a-half years in the past; and in a continuingly changing pop music market, *Hopes, Wishes and Dreams* just didn't interest radio programmers and consumers. Thomas's hopes, wishes and dreams weren't supported by record sales. Without a tour to support the album, or TV appearances to stimulate interest, there would be far less reviews, far less articles, far less coverage of any kind than in the past – as a result, far less sales.

One of the few critics to take notice was Alan Forray, who wrote in the August 15, 1976 edition of Kingston, New York's *The Kingston Daily Freeman*:

> The second solo album by this longtime member of the Moody Blues is a beautiful work fulfilling the promise and upholding the tradition of the Moody Blues music. My personal favorite this week.

The other albums Forray reviewed that week were *Whistling Down the Wire*, by David Crosby and Graham Nash; *Music, Music*, by Helen Reddy; and *Frampton*, by Peter Frampton.

Gus Walker, writing for the *Arizona Republic* of August 20, 1976, said:

> Flautist Ray Thomas, who with keyboard player Mike Pinder, formed the Moody Blues, promised his new album would contain no heavy concepts to bog down listener's minds, and has

proven true to his word. In fact, he's produced the best solo effort of any of the ex-Moodys.

Hopes, Wishes & Dreams features Thomas's distinctive voice backed by the flowing guitar leads of John Jones and the bubbly bass of Trevor Jones. This musically interesting album proves that at least one of the group can break out of the Moody Blues mold.

For the August 27 edition of Chicago, Illinois's *The Daily Herald*, Tom Von Malder wrote:

> … Thomas and guitarist Nicky James each wrote one song alone and collaborated on the rest. The album's title, which comes from a line in "In Your Song," written by James, is one of the highlights.
>
> There is a mix of soft and rock styles, with "One Night Stand" best of the rockers.
>
> With the many production touches and use of full string arrangements, Thomas comes close to the Moody Blues' sound several times. But it is a sound he is entitled to copy as he, with Pinder, cofounded the Moodies.

The headline over Sandy Poiarkoff's review in the September 22 edition of Pennsylvania's *Beaver County Times* was "Ray Thomas Hopes, Wishes, Dreams, Fails." Poiarkoff's beef with this second Thomas solo effort was that it sounded too much like one. She liked *From Mighty Oaks* better, which she felt sounded more like the Moodies *en masse*:

> Ray Thomas is like Eve in the old movie, *The Two Faces of Eve*. On one side, he sounds almost like the Moody Blues; flip the coin and he's a gospel revival singer and a honky-tonk piano player [even though someone else played the piano].
>
> His second album, *Hopes, Wishes and Dreams*, many times lacks the sound of the Moody Blues – music that makes a listener believe it is coming from another planet. The LP doesn't have the power of the Moody Blues. It is like a boxer who is punching with hands made of Silly Putty – forceless.
>
> Thomas tries to capture the Moody Blues effect in all but two of his songs – "Carousel" and "One Night Stand" – [and they] totally ruin the attempt at recreating his days with the Moody Blues. The first song sounds like a revised "Palisades Park." The only good thing about it is the listener is able to visualize what he is singing about. He even feels like he is riding a merry-go-round, up and down on a wooden horse. The other song is like a finale that would be in a soap opera. It's a fast, catchy tune, with words slightly reminiscent of "I'm Just a Singer (In a Rock 'n Roll

Band)," but the choir singing the refrain sounds like a bunch of drunks.

While these songs spoil the album, three others definitely hint of a taste of good Moody Blues music. "We Need Love," "The Last Dream" and "Migration" were written with strong instrumentals and a sound typical of the Moody Blues – a feeling of cold yet comforting times.

… The extra singers add strength to Thomas's already deep, sexy tones. His sound, eerie yet pleasing, is reminiscent of the Moody Blues, like his first solo venture was.

It would be nice if Thomas and the other Moody Blues members reunited. With the songs that Thomas, John Lodge and Justin Hayward have been writing, the group could definitely start fresh and come out with another welcomed, successful album for their diehard fans.

Poiarkoff's comments – she'd like Thomas more if he parroted his past achievements – are reminiscent of G. K. Chesterton when he wrote, "and these critics may be said to praise with faint damns."

From the December 1976 issue of *Stereo Review*:

Ray Thomas, whose fan club is in Surrey (England, that is), writes his own songs and sings them in a self-pitying treble which should keep the letters comings as long as there is an England. Several times I was tempted to write him a comforting little note myself, as he chanted his ballads of sleepless nights, thwarted dreams, disappointments in love, and fading memories. The performer's songs are so insipid and his way with them so depressing – the album ends with "The Last Dream," in which he has a vision of his own death (in the middle of a performance, if I got it right) – that I had to wait almost five minutes after listening to him before I was able to go on with my life. …

Hopes, Wishes and Dreams failed to make the U.K. album charts. In America, on *Billboard*, it peaked at a dismal No. 147.

This was the last album released on Threshold by a member of the Moody Blues. At the end of the year, Threshold Records would cease operations. The Moody Blues remained on Decca (Deram in the U.K. and London in the U.S.); as a group they still owed the company two more albums on their current contract.

Following the failure of *Hopes, Wishes and Dreams,* Thomas career as a solo recording artist abruptly ended.

28

Natural Avenue
John Lodge, 1977

Album release:
Decca THX 120 (U.K.); London PS 683 (U.S.); January 28, 1977
(U.S. release from April 1977)
U.K. peak position: #38
U.S.: #121 (*Billboard*)

U.K. single release:
"Say You Love Me" b/w "Natural Avenue"
Decca F13682; January 28, 1977
Non-charting

U.K. single release:
"Children of Rock 'N' Roll" b/w "Piece of My Heart"
Decca F 13695; March 18, 1977
Non-charting

U.S. single release:
"Natural Avenue" b/w "Say You Love Me"
London 5N-1069; May 1977
Non-charting

U.S. disco 12-inch single release:
"Natural Avenue" b/w "Children of Rock 'N' Roll"
London Disco 3005; June 1977
Non-charting

U.K. single release:
"Summer Breeze" b/w "Rainbow"
Decca F 13717; July 8, 1977
Non-charting

U.S. single release:
"Summer Breeze" b/w "Children of Rock 'N' Roll"
London 5N-1072; July/August 1977
Non-charting

John Lodge told an American writer in early 1977, "It was incredibly exciting when Justin and I followed through with the Blue Jays." (JL-TT77)

After that album's release came a tour of England in autumn 1975. It was announced at that time that Hayward and Lodge had recorded about half of an album's worth of additional material during the 1974 *Blue Jays* sessions, and would return to the studio following the tour to record more songs, completing a second album. However, after reconsidering, Hayward felt that he and Lodge had produced a project that sounded too much like the Moody Blues, and he pulled out. According to Hayward, Lodge wasn't in agreement with the choice of terminating the Blue Jays ... at first. After another year had passed and Lodge recorded a solo album, he echoed Hayward's line of thinking.

Interviewed by Harry Doherty for the January 29, 1977 issue of *Melody Maker*, Lodge said, "The Blue Jays were becoming safe. On tour, there were nights when we could have gone on stage and played anything and got off with it as long as it sounded remotely like the Moody Blues. I didn't like that; it was too safe. ...

"The band was never called 'Blue Jays,' but people decided for themselves that it was, and then suddenly I felt myself getting immersed in another band and I didn't want that at all. ...

"You know that sometimes you can never be as big as the event. That's the way it was for us. We could do a Moody Blues-type tour of America with the Blue Jays but the biggest you could do would be Madison Square Garden, and the Moodies played there twice in one day. ...

"There was another thing that got a bit silly about the Blue Jays. A lot of the letters we got from people were asking when the rest of the boys were going to join the band; bring the Moodies back together. I wasn't going to develop another band to detract from the Moody Blues.

"When I was in America, that attitude qualified itself. I thought, 'Well, if I haven't got the Moody Blues, then I would like to work with as many people as I can. I don't want to stand in one place.'" (JL-MM76)

Talking to American music correspondent Lisa Hemby during a visit to Los Angeles, Lodge said, "It all began when I came over to the U.S. in February of '76. I was really excited about the music business here – there was Fleetwood Mac, recording right next door to the Tower of Power – it just went on and on; all incredibly exciting. So I decided to go back to England with this excitement." (JL-TT77)

When he returned to England, Lodge recruited several session musicians whose work he appreciated, meeting some for the first time. They entered the Threshold One Studio in the summer of 1976.

For the album, Lodge played an assortment of instruments, including 12-string acoustic guitar, bass, and harmonica.

Kenney Jones (drums and percussion) had played with the Small Faces (1976's "Itchycoo Park") and the band's early-1970s incarnation, Faces (with Rod Steward). Shortly after working on *Natural Avenue*, and following Keith Moon's death in 1978, Jones would drum for the Who.

Mick Weaver was on keyboards (piano, organ, electric organ, and celeste). He had been a member of the British band, Wynder K. Frog, who released albums in 1967, '68, and '70. As a session musician, he played on 1970's *Jesus Christ Superstar*, and performed with Joe Cocker, among many other artists.

Steven Simpson, a session guitarist, had previously been a member of several groups and released two solo albums over his career. He played Spanish guitar, 6-string acoustic, and electric guitars, and contributed background vocals.

Chris Spedding also played electric guitar. He had been a member of a late 1960s English band, Frank Ricotti Quartet, which released an album in 1969. As a solo artist, Spedding had a Top 20 U.K. hit in 1975 with "Motor Bikin'." As a session player, he contributed to many popular albums, including Harry Nilsson's *Nilsson Schmilsson* (1971) and *Son of Schmilsson* (1972).

Lodge said of his session players, "I had never met any of these people before but admired them all. I think there's a natural balance when you like musicians. Kenny plays rhythmically and musically as well, and then I wanted a strong rhythm behind the melody with a reaching guitar – thus, Chris Spedding." (JL-TT77)

Assistant recording engineer Dave Baker said, "I think John was incredibly impressed with Spedding, and just sort of let him go [play]. I remember the case of putting the red light on and John saying, 'Chris, just go out there and play something fantastic,' and we'd record it. There's some very good guitar playing on that album." (DB-H&H96)

Also heard on the album's title cut: Mel Collins, on soprano saxophone. He had been a member of King Crimson (1970-72) and also contributed to Justin Hayward's *Songwriter* album (released immediately following *Natural Avenue*). He had also played on songs by Bad Company, Camel, Eric Clapton, Humble Pie, the Rolling Stones, and Uriah Heep.

Brian Rogers provided the orchestral arrangements, performed by his Brian Rogers Orchestra. Lodge told Mark Murley of *Higher & Higher*, "I played all of the songs live for Brian. … I remember sitting 'round with a guitar, playing them, and sitting 'round the piano at home with Brian, working out the arrangements together.

"We had quite a few pre-recording meetings gathered around the guitar where we discussed where the songs should go and how they should develop." (JL-H&H86)

Rounding out the team was producer Tony Clarke, with Derek Varnals as recording engineer.

Regarding his decision to make a solo album, Lodge told Susan Ahrens of *Crawdaddy*, "The Moodies, to me, were sort of the perfect band. All the things that I wanted to do could come out of the Moodies. But as you get more and more successful, the touring becomes longer and it becomes longer between albums, so it means that I would only be writing and recording maybe two songs every two years or so, which doesn't help anybody creatively. If the Moodies could have made an album every four weeks or maybe even two a year, it could have been different.

"When I came to record *Natural Avenue*, I was in the throes of 'Who am I?' and 'What am I doing?' On *Seventh Sojourn*, I stated that I was just a singer in a rock and roll band, and suddenly I'm not in a band anymore." (JL-C77)

If nothing else, an identity crisis can spark creativity, and spur a great deal of songwriting. Lodge said, "None of the songs was sitting 'round at all; they were all written for the album." (JL-H&H96)

He told *Record Mirror*, "Everything seemed to fit together so well. The songs flowed very naturally. In the first number I tried to reflect the Moodies, then I launched my own style. I've always retained my love for a big melodic sound." (JL-RM77)

But big melodic sounds were not what was expected of John Lodge.

Dave Baker: "The biggest surprise was that it wasn't a rock 'n' roll album. I thought, once he had the discipline of the other [Moodies] removed and he could do whatever he liked, that he would do a rock album…. Also, I had followed him from on *Blue Jays*, where John seemed to be straining at the leash a bit to do some sort of driving rock 'n' roll…. So I was quite surprised when I listened to the tracks, that it was a very sensitive and reflective album in many ways, and that he was very much relying on his talents as a songwriter." (DB-H&H96)

Tony Clarke: "Well, we did call John [by the nickname of] 'Rocker' …. It was based on the songs that he wrote. [However, the *Natural Avenue* songs] were the kinds of song ideas John had, and that really charted the way he had to go. Except for the title cut, there weren't really any hard rockers on the album.'" (TC-H&H96)

The album was recorded in two long sessions. The first began in mid-June 1976 and lasting until the middle of July. The second session ran from early October to mid November.

Here is what they recorded (as sequenced on the album):

"Intro to Children of Rock 'n' Roll." John Lodge begins the album, singing, "You have to know where you're going / Before you can say 'goodbye' / You have to know what you're asking / Before you ask 'why' …"

Where he was going soon became apparent. John, the rocker, had become John, the balladeer.

The brief opening track featured Lodge and Steve Simpson on acoustic guitars. This curtain-raiser led into…

"Natural Avenue." Lodge sings: "All my life I've tried / Oh how I've tried / Suddenly I'm there / There's a feeling in the air / Here on Natural Avenue…"

This showed the excitement Lodge had brought back from America. If there had been more tracks like this on *Natural Avenue*, the reaction from the critics would have been much better, spurring sales. "Natural Avenue," the song, is infectious rockabilly-to-rock 'n' roll. The saxophones are the frosting on the cake, but the cake itself is the core band instruments of guitar, piano, bass, and drums, with playful vocals. The energy is high, exactly what one might have hoped from the writer of "Peak Hour," "Ride My See-Saw," and "I'm Just a Singer (In a Rock and Roll Band)."

On the recording, Lodge played four different instruments: 6-string and 12-string acoustic guitars, electric bass, and harmonica. Session men Mel Collins and Martin Dobson played the saxophones.

For **"Summer Breeze,"** Lodge sings sweetly: "Summer Breeze / Whisper softly through the trees / Make my cares slip away / My thoughts drift away from view / Summer Song / Make my day / Make it long / Help this world walk on by / On its Natural Avenue."

Although the polar opposite of "Natural Avenue," "Summer Breeze" is just as appealing in its own relaxed way. It is hard to imagine anyone – any Moody Blues fan, anyway – hearing the first two full songs on this album and not thinking they were in for a wonderful listening experience. "Summer Breeze," not to be confused by the Seals and Croft hit from five years earlier, is reminiscent of some of the gentler work of Ray Davies and the Kinks ("Waterloo Sunset," "Celluloid Heroes"), as the song drifts along, swaying, lazing, floating down a stream into a surreal place and time. The saxophone solo by Jimmy Jewel is candy for the ears, and the backup vocals bring their own pleasing touch.

Assistant recording engineer Dave Baker said, "I remember the sessions being very much like the Moodies' vocal sessions, especially the backing vocals. It was John, downstairs with the guys, working out the vocal overdubs and parts as they went along. Again, I think it was a case of, 'Let's run through and get some ideas,' and then he took command of how he wanted the overall backing vocals to sound. And obviously Tony Clarke had his say in how things came together." (DB-H&H96)

Those backup singers were Gary Osborne (who co-wrote Justin Hayward's hit "Forever Autumn"), John Richardson, Alan Williams, Billy Lawrie, guitarist Steve Simpson, and, of course, John Lodge.

At this point, *Natural Avenue* was setting a high standard for any other Moodies' solo efforts.

"Carry Me" was written by Lodge for his son, Kristian. As with "Emily's Song," written for his daughter in 1970, Lodge crafts a song for the innocent world of a child. He intones: "Drift on the warm wind of your secret world / Hang on to your star stream / Make the sun reappear / Make the dark disappear / From my night sky / Fly away...."

The dreamy orchestration invites you in from the very start of the song, and "Carry Me" makes for a lovely companion to "Summer Breeze," a double-dose of tranquil lullabies. The production is exquisite, the recording quality from the Threshold Studio One impressive.

"Who Could Change" presents another lush vocal, as Lodge coos: "Somewhere in this crazy dream / That we call life / Someone who can give / You time and rest from strife / Take it away … From me.…"

By this point on the album, the listener had been given three solid tracks in a row, but after the easy and breezy back-to-back mood of "Summer Breeze" and "Carry Me," we were in need of another "Natural Avenue." "Who Could Change" is not a bad song – far from it. But it doesn't stand up to the two ballads that came before. Also, the building drama introduced by the orchestration and repetition of the chorus threatens to turn this delicate, simple song saccharine. It's like putting a homemade Valentine into a gold-plated envelope.

The shot in the arm – or, if you prefer, the kick in the butt – that most listeners longed for was missing, as the first side of the original vinyl LP came to a soporific end.

"Broken Dreams, Hard Road" opens Side Two. Lodge sings: "Wish I could write of the love I have known in my lifetime / Wish I could find just one word, one small line, when I'm down / The world has gone and changed its face / The world has gone and changed its place / While we were dreaming for the Human Race / I know I've been down this road many times, many ways, in my lifetime….."

While the pace begins quicker here, the tempo soon slows, right where we left off at the conclusion of Side One. Somehow, after a fine start, the songs have begun stepping down in quality *and* emotional affect. The album's excitement is leaking away like a weary balloon.

"Pieces of My Heart" doesn't come to the rescue. It's another slow-tempo song, as Lodge sings: "High on our hillside we both shared the view / Talking of people we thought we knew / How could that dream fade away and fall on the ground where we lay / 'Cause you're the one that went and stole a piece of my heart / Oh well, you must be twenty-three by now / Married and kids of your own / And the little boy is three / Does he look like me.…"

The song is reminiscent of Justin Hayward's "Who Are You Now," from *Blue Jays*, but the concept has less success here.

By now, the listener wanted a pick-me-up, not a dirge. *Natural Avenue* was continuing to lose the promise established in the first few tracks on Side One.

"Rainbow" continues in much the same sentimental mood. Lodge sings: "If I have to lose you for a while / If I have to lose your loving smile / If I have to lose your loving ways / If I have, make my life worthwhile / Make my life a rainbow / Paint it every day / Make my heart forever sing / Do it right away."

"Rainbow" is a lovely song … but it's too much of the same. Despite the lyric, alternating between romanticism and emotional desperation, the overall effect threatens the listener with a sugar overdose.

If the tune isn't familiar, the presentation certainly is. We'd heard it before on "Carry Me" … and "Who Could Change" … and we'll be hearing it again on this album.

With **"Say You Love Me,"** we are again presented with a lullaby-like vocal. Lodge gently sings: "If I could read you like a book / If I could read your second look / If I could be the one you love / The one you're thinking of / I wouldn't need these eyes / I wouldn't need to see / I wouldn't need to hear your voice / Say you love me.…"

"Say You Love Me" is lovely, but a little variety would be nice – not another lush ballad.

Finally – on the last song! – the pace picks up, with **"Children of Rock 'n' Roll."** With a bit more energy, Lodge reflects, "I remember all the words of love that we sang out of tune / Waving goodbye to a generation as we danced by the light of the moon / I remember oh so clear how the world looked from Blueberry Hill / When you sang all the songs on a six-string guitar / And made you a rock 'n' roll star…."

Lodge said this about the song: "It refers back to being a teenager, being in cars, if you were in America…. It's a statement… of what we all are, and what John Lodge is in relation to everyone else – John Lodge in the audience, as well as John Lodge in the Moody Blues." (JL-TT77)

If only there'd been another rock 'n' roll number like this, somewhere at the halfway point of the album! Such a stronger number might have brought a much different (and better) reaction for *Natural Avenue*, and John Lodge's career.

The question is, why didn't his producer tell him that?

Tony Clarke: "I should have pushed him in that direction a bit more, but that was the way it was panning out at the time. John was into the smooth ballad then and the high harmony, as I recall. But perhaps we should have stuck in a couple of [additional] hard-rocking things.'" (TC-H&H96)

Indeed.

Considering the ethereal sweetness captured on tape, it's surprising to know that England was experiencing a heat wave when *Natural Avenue* was recorded. And, in this era's London, air conditioning was not yet prevalent – especially in recording studios, where the sound of forced air could be picked up by the microphones.

John Lodge said, "[I]t was a fantastic summer in England the year that we recorded the album. I remember some mornings – it was like, four o'clock in the morning – we'd be sitting outside on the steps of Threshold, looking over Broadhurst Gardens. It was so hot. It was so unusual, at that time." (JL-H&H96)

Derek Varnals said, "It was very, very hot and very, very hectic. It was so hot that we turned off lights, equipment, anything in the control room to reduce the temperature." (DV-H&H96)

Hot, yes, hectic, maybe, but, according to Dave Baker, pleasant. He said, "The sessions were held in a good atmosphere and it was a nice album to work on." (DB-H&H96)

If you take into account the overall sameness of the ballads on the album, *Natural Avenue* can be every bit the "nice album" that Dave Baker recalled making. It may not be music for a road trip, but it's fine for a lazy Sunday afternoon, or right before bed. If you're not expecting Lodge to rock your world, *Natural Avenue* is actually quite a charmer.

Roger Dean, along with brother Martyn, created the gatefold album cover. Roger Dean designed many of the album covers for Yes and Asia. At this time, to his credit, were: *One Fine Morning* by Lighthouse (1970); *Demons and Wizards* (1972) and *The Magician's Birthday* (1971) by Uriah Heep; and *Octopus* by Gentle Giant (1972). He also designed numerous album covers for Yes, such as *Fragile* (1971), *Close to the Edge* (1972), *Yessongs* (1973), *Tales from Topographic Oceans* (1973), and *Yesterdays* (1974).

John Lodge said, "I always liked Roger Dean's work, but Roger was always a bit further out on the sci-fi spectrum part of artwork. I'd thought it'd be fantastic if we could combine what I was trying to get to and what he was fantastic at doing. I had a meeting with him, and it just felt really right. We discussed how we'd like [the art] to be, and he came up with the artwork, which I was really pleased with. I could have gone in exactly the same way as a Moody Blues piece of artwork, but I really didn't want to do that. It had to reflect what I was doing." (JH-H&H96)

***

As 1976 turned into 1977, both Justin Hayward and John Lodge were finalizing their solo albums. The question was, what label would release them?

Threshold Records ceased to exist as a label at the end of 1976 when its distribution deal with Decca Records in England and London Records in America came to an end. The Moody Blues, however, were still bound to Decca, with two group albums still due on the previous contract.

In early 1977, when asked by American music correspondent Jared Johnson as to why the plug was pulled on Threshold Records, Justin Hayward replied, "That's the way the record company and the management wanted it. The end of Threshold, which is sad, but it wasn't really fulfilling its original promise." (JH-DP77)

John Lodge told Tom Hibbert of *Q*, "It got so out of hand. We had a Christmas dinner and we hired a restaurant and we had rooms filled with people who were working for us and I didn't recognize *anybody*. I didn't know who any of these people were. And we had an office in Soho with secretaries and desks. It was the desks that got to me because [I was told] they all had antique desks. I could never ever find the place. I never went there. Did you go there?"

Hayward, with Lodge during the interview, answered with a question: "What? Rathbone Place?"

Lodge said, "No, the office in Soho Square."

Hayward answered, "No. I went to our office in Rathbone Place but I can't even remember having an office in Soho Square. Did we?"

Lodge said, "Yes, yes. It had whole teams of people there and the only reason I realized it was because I saw this requisition once for this antique desk."

Hayward said, "Bloody hell. I never knew we had an office there. You live and learn." (JH-Q90)

Lodge commented, "It *was* just like Apple; probably worse. It was just totally out of hand. Financially, it was a total disaster." (JL-Q90)

Lodge, also referencing the Beatles' rotten Apple, told Jared Johnson, "It's a strange phenomenon. Threshold Records began as a workshop, hopefully a workshop for other artists to come and use. But over the years it evolved into a conglomerate empire – you know, lawyers, etc. – and it became a business situation.... If anybody got together to do anything – to do anything musically – it became business. It got totally away from what we wanted initially; what our aspirations were. We found we couldn't get rid of all the business. We wanted to keep Threshold but we couldn't get rid of the business. So we just dumped the whole thing." (JL-DP77)

Hayward said, "We tried desperately to cut down the business activities. The business complications were a very big part of the group's breakup. As a recording band, the personality balance in the group was perfect, but at the business conference table the power structure drastically changed." (JH-DP77)

Besides the Moody Blues, the only act Threshold had under contract that was successful – and only marginally successful, at that – was Trapeze.

Glen Hughes of Trapeze said, "We did three great albums and three tours of the US, along with the Moody Blues. I learnt a lot off them, though they kept to themselves and they were very cosmic – especially the keyboard player – though not as cosmic as you may imagine." (GH-RC99)

Suddenly, there was no Threshold Records to release John Lodge's solo album, or Justin Hayward's first solo effort, also completed at this time. This didn't concern them, for how hard could it be to find a company willing to release a project by a member of the Moody Blues?

Lodge quickly arranged a deal with Decca and London to distribute his solo venture. Hayward was doing the same, but with a surprising stipulation (covered in the next chapter).

U.K. album release:
Decca THS 120; January 28, 1977

U.K. single release:
"Say You Love Me" b/w "Natural Avenue"
Decca F13682; January 28, 1977
Non-charting

Natural Avenue was issued in the U.K. three months before London Records' release in America. The English label's idea of a radio hit was, surprisingly, "Say You Love Me," with the more obvious contender, "Natural Avenue," delegated to the B-side. They were wrong, of course, and British radio showed little interest. The album reception was a different story.

In the January 29, 1977 issue of *Record Mirror*, Robin Smith said:

> As you sit among your Habit furniture sipping tequila and watching the sun go down over Neasden, this is the album to listen to. Full of rich themes and strong harmonies, Lodge has produced a superb album, maybe a bit too rich in places and over sentimental, but otherwise flawless. Compared with the other tracks, "Natural Avenue" seems a strange inclusion. It's a rocker sounding like a spot of boogie from the Forties. "Summer Breeze" reminds you of those balmy days last year, while "Carry Me" continues the theme with a Spanish flavor and strings that develop into a mini-symphony. Everything's thrown in on "Broken

Dreams Hard Road," starting with some basic rock and then joined by the orchestra, including booming kettledrums. An album for the late night antics.

U.K. single release:
"Children of Rock and Roll"
b/w "Piece of My Heart"
Decca F 13695; March 18, 1977
Non-charting

Two months after using "Say You Love Me" as the trailer for the album, Decca Records scrambled to do better and issued the uptempo "Children of Rock 'N' Roll" as the next A-side, coupled with "Piece of My Heart."

Record Mirror said of the A-side:

> After an unpromising start this develops into a well rounded rocker which sounds slightly American. There's a nice controlled guitar section which lifts the song out of the ordinary and into a comfortable plane of its own.

Whatever existed on this plane, British radio wasn't interested.

U.S. album release:
London PS 683; April 1977

At the start of April, 1977, London Records in the States finally released *Natural Avenue*, but hesitated on issuing a single. The record men were waiting to see which songs radio picked up on before making a choice.

From *Billboard*, April 2, 1977:

> Guitarist and writer-singer Lodge is the latest of the disbanded Moody Blues to arrive with his solo album. His hallmark is a softly dreamy music something in the genre of Bread. His light, sensitive voice works well with his feathery orchestrations and folk-like rhythm sections to create a relaxed, open mood. Best cuts: "Children of Rock 'N' Roll," "Who Could Change," "Summer Breeze."

In its April 14 issue, *Circus* said of *Natural Avenue*:

… A strong album, capturing the Moody Blues spaciousness of sound on rock and orchestrated ballads; there are also a few harder rock numbers, notably the title track, befitting the man who wrote "Ride My See-Saw" and "Just A Singer." …

U.S. single release:
"Natural Avenue" b/w "Say You Love Me"
London 5N-1069; May 1977
Non-charting

The title song was one of the album's most-sampled songs on the radio. One month after the release of *Natural Avenue*, the album, along came "Natural Avenue," the single. Learning from Decca's mistake of two months earlier, London made sure the album's title song, and not "Say You Love Me," was the favored side. Promotional copies of the single didn't even include "Say You Love Me." Instead, DJs were given "Natural Avenue" on both sides, one in stereo, the other in mono.

However, it seemed in the spring of 1977 that very few Americans knew who John Lodge was. If the average music consumer were asked to name an individual Moody Blues member, many could only come up with the name of Justin Hayward. The others were just, well, the other Moody Blues. "Natural Avenue," the single, didn't sound like the Moody Blues, so it was ignored. *Natural Avenue*, the album, didn't sound very Moody either. It charted in America, but not much higher than the recent albums from Graeme Edge, Mike Pinder, and Ray Thomas.

From the May 20 issue of Australia's *Ram* music magazine, Simon Richardson reviewed both *Natural Avenue* and Justin Hayward's *Songwriter* (which also had been released by this time). He considered the two albums, combined, as "one-and-a-half strong reasons why the Moody Blues should never have stopped making records." Richardson said:

> I mean some people are going to buy these sets (just as they've bought the previous five solo sets from ex-Moodies) to put next to their Moody Blues volumes, hoping to find the same rich mixture of cosmic overflow, beautifully balanced harmonies and musical textures.

For the record, Richardson only considered *Songwriter* as half a reason why the Moody Blues should have continued recording as a group. This meant he found the album to be *half*-good. It was Lodge's album he credited as being a reason in its own right for the end of Moody Blues' solo albums. He continued:

> In the case of John Lodge they should get their money back. Songs full of maudlin self pity in the "I tried so hard but no one listened" variety, and limp, lachrymose arrangements. Some semblance of

life can be found in the title track, mainly due to the combined saxes of Mel Collins and Martin Dobson.

Surprisingly, Robert Hilburn, of *The Los Angeles Times*, didn't come down too terribly hard on *Natural Avenue*. He liked two of the songs, maybe three. In the May 29 edition of the *L.A. Times*, Hilburn wrote:

> Justin Hayward was the most engaging writer in the Moody Blues, but Lodge – whose "Ride My See-Saw," "Send Me No Wine" and "Isn't Life Strange" added substantially to the band's catalogue – has come up with the most appealing of the many post-Moody solo efforts. The title tune has a punchy boogie-woogie base, while "Summer Breeze" recalls much of his old band's melodic grace. Most of the LP, however, is ordinary and shows why Lodge only contributed one or two songs per Moody album. "Broken Dream, Hard Road" tends toward the group's philosophical sludge. Ditto for the belabored "Children of Rock 'N' Roll."

U.S. disco 12-inch single release:
"Natural Avenue"
b/w "Children of Rock 'N' Roll"
London Disco 3005; June 1977
Non-charting

Disco was the latest craze in America, and hit singles were being born on the dance floor, with extended 12-inch versions. When the May release of the "Natural Avenue" / "Say You Love Me" single failed to get on the radio, London reissued the top side in a 12-inch dance mix. For the B-side, the only other danceable song on the album, "Children of Rock 'N' Roll," was chosen. However, this release couldn't shake a hip like Donna Summer's "Love to Love You Baby" or K.C. & the Sunshine Band's "(Shake, Shake, Shake) Your Booty," two recent hits.

Rolling Stone magazine, of course, was not about to soften the blow, which arrived in the magazine's June 16 edition, courtesy of Charley Walters:

> *Natural Avenue* is weak, overly precious music, an unsuccessful stab at gentle, slightly ethereal ease. The Moody Blues' bassist's melodies and vocals are sweet but forgettably airy. Lyrically, Lodge's childlike simplicity betrays naiveté. Aiming for grandeur, the orchestration is plain and unimaginative; it sometimes seems to be present for its own sake. The percussion, which could have

added conviction to the scoring, is instead obscured by flat engineering, and the lazy backbeat only emphasizes the dragging effect. Even the capable backup Lodge employs – Chris Spedding on guitar, Mel Collins on saxophone, Kenney Jones on drums – succumbs to the frailty of the whole affair.

In the June 22 issue of *Variety*, Lodge was asked why he wasn't touring in support of his album. He answered, "With the Moody Blues, when an album came out we could do a quick tour around the world and get a great deal of promotion, especially on radio. I can't do it as a solo artist because I'd have to do so many more. I did 26 dates in the U.K. with Bluejays. But in Europe and the U.K., radio airplay is not as heavy. There's a concentration on TV. I've done 20 TV shows all over Europe and I'm going back to do more. It releases the adrenalin."

Lodge had come to accept that solo recordings would not rival the releases from the full band. He said, "First, the Moody Blues sold millions, so if a solo album does one-fifth or one-sixth as well, I'll be happy." (JL-V77)

U.K. single release:
"Summer Breeze" b/w "Rainbow"
Decca F 13717; July 8, 1977
Non-charting

After failing to interest British radio with the "Say You Love Me" or the second A-side release, "Children of Rock 'N' Roll," Decca tried a third single: the lovely, Kinks-like "Summer Breeze." The ballad "Rainbow" was chosen for the B-side.

If this had come out as the first single from the album, it might have gone places.

Meanwhile, back in the States, from the July 9 edition of Bridgewater, New Jersey's *The Courier-News*, Karen Herman Steffaro wrote:

> John Lodge joined the Moody Blues in 1966 and composed "Isn't Life Strange" and "I'm Just a Singer," but unfortunately his new album, *Natural Avenue*, doesn't have the same quality, even though the ten songs are his own words and music.
>
> It almost seems it would have been better titled "For Lovers and Others" – Side One for lovers, as he sings of lofty ideals, [like] "would you believe when I tell you all the dreams you have found are mine" … and Side Two for others who are more familiar with unrequited love.

U.S. single release:
"Summer Breeze"
b/w "Children of Rock 'n Roll"
London 5N-1072; July/August 1977

Having failed with "Natural Avenue" as a single, London Records combined the A-sides from the next two U.K. singles onto one release. "Summer Breeze" was given the top side of the disc. Surprisingly, this exceptionally pleasant and catchy song failed to get into the charts on either side of the Atlantic.

From the October 27 issue of *Circus*, Michael Bloom was blunt:

> … *Natural Avenue* is something in the nature of a sellout. Not quite MOR, not quite funky, only somewhat overproduced, it ends up such a horrid compromise of half-measures that there hardly seems room for ex-Moody John Lodge's personality at all…

From the *Scottsdale Community College Free Press* in Arizona (those college kids always loved the Moodies), Patti Bruno said *Natural Avenue* was "a pleasant surprise." She continued:

> … It features delicate orchestral passages, vocals, and songs similar to *Blue Jays* as well as some rock and roll pieces.
>
> This album is set apart from Lodge's past work in that he rarely, if ever, sang without back-up vocal harmonies. Though a very good songwriter, he never seemed to be an exceptional singer (and was overshadowed by Justin Hayward). On "Carry Me," "Say You Love Me," and "Who Could Change," he dares to let his voice carry the songs alone. His voice is airy, light, and quite strong. In the chorus of "Say You Love Me" he sounds almost like Roger Daltrey. These are probably the best Lodge vocals ever recorded.
>
> Lodge's style seems to be leaning toward romantic ballads, and his typically "understated" lyrics are less vague.
>
> For those of you who like a visual treat to accompany your audio-enjoyment, the Roger Dean cover art is nice and should challenge your imagination beyond a few earthy limits.
>
> Maybe this will hold you until a new Moodies album is released.

Natural Avenue had respectable sales in England, peaking at No. 38. It barely registered in America, with *Billboard* listing it at No. 121. None of the singles charted.

29

Songwriter
Justin Hayward, 1977

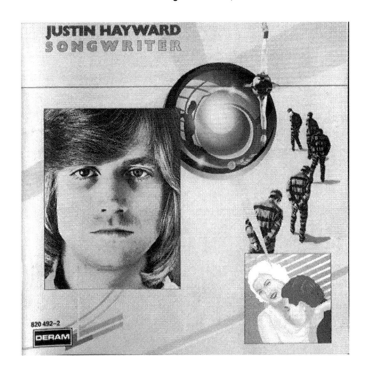

Album release:
Deram SDL 15 (U.K.); Deram DES 18073 (U.S.); February 11, 1977
U.K.: #28
U.S.: #37 (*Billboard*)

U.K. Single release:
"One Lonely Room" b/w "Songwriter (Part 2)"
Deram DM 428; February 4, 1977
Non-charting

U.S. single release:
"Lay It On Me" b/w "Songwriter (Part 2)"
Deram 5N-7541; March 1977
Non-charting

U.K. single release:
"Country Girl" b/w "Doin' Time"
Deram DM 429; April 22, 1977
Non-charting

U.S. single release:
"Country Girl" b/w "Songwriter (Part 2)"
Deram 5N-7542; June 1977
Non-charting

U.K. single release:
"Stage Door" b/w "Lay It on Me"
Deram DM 430; July 29, 1977
Non-charting

Blue Jays was the most successful Moodies side project, outselling all the other solo albums by the various band members. The only one that came close in sales and positive critical reaction was Justin Hayward's *Songwriter*. But as this album's recording progressed, some felt that its mere existence would not only derail a follow-up "Blue Jays" LP, but postpone a Moody Blues reunion.

From the July 20, 1976, edition of *JUKE* magazine:

> A projected get-together by the Moody Blues for an album and English tour has fallen through. Four members of the band – whose management always emphasizes that there has been no "split-up," just a temporary stop of group activities – were believed to have been keen to reform but it is understood that lead guitarist Justin Hayward did not want to rejoin the group at the moment. Hayward told *JUKE*'s Jillian Hughes that he didn't think the time was quite right for the MBs to get back together again. Justin, who with John Lodge, recorded the most successful of the Moodies' solo projects with *Blue Jays*, has also split from Lodge and is recording a solo album at the moment and intends to tour America in October.

A few months later, Hayward told *Melody Maker*, "People were calling us the 'New Moodies,' and I never wanted to wipe out the Moodies' memory. The Moody Blues were very, very big, and it's stupid to take on that mantle. John and I had some fun, enjoyed it, and now it's time to go it alone. After all, this phase of my career is ultimately the most important. I'm on my own for the rest of my life." (JH-MM77)

Hayward told Tom Stock of *Beat Instrumental*, "I never felt restricted [in the Moody Blues] – the only thing that I did think was that I felt that we didn't record enough and there wasn't sufficient product; for me to have only three songs to show for a year's work. I was writing a lot more than that, and I found that I was only able to record the material that I had written immediately prior to a Moodies recording session. I found that if I didn't have a project in mind it became difficult to continue writing, because the way wasn't left open to develop and complete material that was already written – if you see what I mean." (JH-BI77)

Hayward had said before that he wasn't the type of songwriter to prepare songs if there were no immediate plans to record them. He discovered that if finished songs were set aside for months or years, they became stale in his mind, and no longer interested him. He felt he needed the pressure of a looming recording date to stay creative. It seemed much the same with the other Moodies. John Lodge too said that he was usually inclined to leave "bits and pieces" of songs scribbled on pieces of paper, waiting for a pending recording session to prompt their completion. The lack of output from Edge, Thomas, and Pinder gives indication that they were much the same way. Case in point: Thomas had averaged only two to three songs a year while recording with the Moodies (1967-72). Then it took him nearly three years to put out his first solo album, with most of the songs written with Nicky James shortly before recording. Pinder had taken three and a half years between *Seventh Sojourn* and his solo album *The Promise*, which only contained nine songs – meaning his average of two to three songs a year had continued even after the Moodies took a hiatus from recording.

In the interview with Stock, "Of course, I'll always be grateful for being a member of the Moodies, but now I would like to have a real constructive outlet for the work that I do, which is write songs. The album is called *Songwriter* and that's exactly what I am – and I can't help myself from doing that. I also feel a certain responsibility to myself and my family, because I know somehow it comes through me, and I'm able to do it. I've got to put it down in some way, so whatever happens I'll never stop recording, whether it's with the Moodies or on my own." (JH-BI76)

That continued to be true. Hayward has been the only Moody who has put out a consistent stream of product, both as a soloist and as a member of the group. He seemed the only songwriting Moody prolific enough to make solo albums and still be available for group projects, as long as the recording or touring dates did not overlap.

There had been another obstacle to bringing back the Moody Blues, which neither Hayward nor any of the other Moodies had felt inclined to discus from the middle of 1974 until the start of 1977. In an interview with Ray Coleman of *Melody Maker*, Hayward admitted that the separation had been more than merely needing a rest. Just as running their own record company had contributed to the breakup of the Beatles, Threshold had provoked contention among the Moodies. Hayward told Coleman, "When we were together recording, everything was exactly right. Our personalities were right for each other. But when we got round that board table, the power-balance shifted drastically. We were all playing a game but we hardly knew the rules, let alone how to deal with the in-fighting that goes on. We launched this label, Threshold, and it's plain to me now that we hardly knew what to do with it.

"We started to fall out – five guys who had previously grown up together, learned all their adolescences together! I mean – I joined the band when I was 19. We came though a lot, considered ourselves grown-ups, but we fought like children! Ridiculous.

"All we should have been doing was making more records, but business took over. I hated it all so much that I decided to quit several times.

"Mike Pinder was the first to crumble, though. He realized it was crazy, so he skipped to the States. Mike loathed all the business things we ever did. Now I'm determined not to get involved again. But I do want to surround myself with people who feel close to music. Lawyers and accountants worry me. …

"I look back on America and all the hotel rooms and Starship One – we were the first rock band to use that plane – and the world tour taking in Japan and Hawaii, and I think we were wrong to chuck it up. But we've done it all. That's the problem that affected our heads in 1974 – sold-out concerts everywhere, millions of record sales, nothing to achieve. The routine of success together with the business hassles – that's what killed the Moodies. ...

"I'd like to think we could get together again, one day; continue it in some way as the same people. You can't put the clock back, but – well, sometimes I feel the Moody Blues will never go away from our lives, so we may as well play some things together and make a few thousand people happy. Put it this way, we're better mates now than we've ever been. ...

"Maybe one day, though ... we'll have to see what's in the air. ...

"Not one of us will never be as big, solo, as the Moodies were as a band. We have to face that. ... [But] the only important thing to me now is to establish my own career. I need that for survival. The Moody Blues as people had become far too dependent on each other. It's time to step out now." (JH-MM76)

Hayward told Patrick MacDonald of *The Seattle Times*, "*Blue Jays* sounded more like the Moody Blues because we were still growing out of that experience at the time. Now that's in the past and writing on my own comes easier. I'm happier with *Songwriter* than anything I've done in years." (JH-ST77)

Returning to work with Hayward were many of the players from *Blue Jays*, including, from the Threshold band Providence, Jim Cockey on violins, Tom Tompkins on viola, and brother Tim Tompkins on cello. From Threshold's Trapeze: Mel Galley on bass, Terry Rowley on guitars, and Dave Holland on drums. Hayward said of Galley, Rowley, and Holland that they "were the backbone and strongest supporters of *Songwriter*." (JH-RYM09)

Ken Freeman was recruited to play keyboards, including synthesizer. He had worked with David Essex and would reunite with Hayward for the soundtrack of *Jeff Wayne's Musical Version of The War of the Worlds* in the near future. Hayward said, "I had heard of the wonderful Ken Freeman, the supreme master of the synthesizer, and when I met him I was instantly taken aback by his gentle spirit, his true emotion in everything he played and his capacity to give himself to every track."

Hayward played acoustic and electric guitars, as well as taking turns on keyboards, bass, drums, violin, cello, flute, and tambourine. And, of course, all the lead vocals. In many ways, he seemed as musically fluent as Paul McCartney, who'd played all the instruments on his first solo album, 1970's *McCartney*. Hayward said, "I got to play a lot of instruments myself – piano, keyboards, guitars, and even drums, and the album became my life for several months."

Peter Knight arranged and conducted the string section on two of the tracks. Hayward said, "Peter Knight likes to use his own rhythm section on the tracks he arranged, but always had me play acoustic guitar live in the middle of it all – a bit daunting." (JH-RYM09)

Tony Clarke produced.

Hayward said, "[A]lthough Tony is the producer, in many ways you could say we coproduced it. If he tells me something that he believes I should do, I believe him because we're both working towards the same thing; and, equally, if I believe something is right, then we'll do that. But the great advantage with Tony is that he's an engineer as well, which is something that I'd never be able to do." (JH-BI76)

The album, in chronological order:

Regarding **"Tightrope,"** Hayward told *Record Mirror*, "'Tightrope' is about being a performer and the short-lived experience it can be." (JH-RM76)

It also seems very autobiographical. He sings: "I used to walk the tightrope every night / But it got too tight / I walked the straight and narrow line / My head was spinning round / I walked without a safety net / But it was such a long way down / Oh you might have seen us / If we came to your town / The game's made for heroes / And clowns."

As for the recording, Hayward told Jared Johnson, for a May 29, 1977 article in the *Denver Post*, "'Tightrope' is almost a live session. There's hardly any overdubbing at all. The vocals are the original vocals that were put down with the first drums and guitar and bass." (JH-DP77a)

The concept for the song was a good one, coming from a former member of the Moody Blues – the story of a tightrope walker … or rock star … looking back at the surreal days of "not thinking about tomorrow" and only "living for today." The sound of a calliope closes the track, a perfect comment on the circuslike world of the Moodies.

Unfortunately, the production is too busy; the tempo forced. Worse is the opening fanfare – the synthesizer which provides a cheesy and even grating imitation of trumpets. It is believed Ken Freeman was the culprit, but Hayward too played synthesizer on the album. The song's message suffers under the weight of the clutter and gaudiness … until the song ends with Hayward's distinctive blue guitar sound drifting above the calliope.

"Songwriter" has a lilting melody, a pleasant production, and candid lyrics. Hayward sings, "This ain't the best number that I ever wrote," and that the song is constructed on "worn out chords." While not the best, Hayward adds, "But I wrote it for you."

"Songwriter, Part 2" turns the song in an unexpected direction. As the rhythmic piano chords are overtaken by wailing synths and howling guitars, another side of Hayward escapes. It's up to you whether it grates, or if it's a welcome release, as the group kicks out the stops for far too short a time. (You can tell what we think.)

"Country Girl" features synths again, including banjolike licks. It's one of the album's gems. As with most of Hayward's songs, it seems autobiographical. He had been raised in a small town, in the country, and had never been to a city until age 16. That city – London – had him longing to move out, back to a quiet rural life. Lyrically, this is a simple story. Musically, it's rich in melody, with catchy hooks ("No deposit, no return, 'cos I knew I had to return") throughout. This one had "single" written all over it … but perhaps in an earlier era of pop music.

"One Lonely Room" is instantly recognizable as having "the Moody Blues sound." It could have easily fit onto a group album, although one might expect Graeme Edge or one of the other boys would have helped to refine the lyrics. As it stands, or falls, lines such as "You took the wind out of my sails / You took my train right off the rails / You left a car that had no wheels / You left some shoes that had no heels" seem like placeholders for solid lyrics to express the same thoughts.

611

Musically, it has a rich melody with that tender, crying voice of Hayward's, reminiscent of his vocal on "Nights in White Satin," and a lush but not overwhelming strings arrangement by Peter Knight. Our hearts are captured as Hayward begins, "One lonely room / No footsteps on the floor / Nobody needs to answer the door," but it all falls apart when the "sails/rails/wheels/heels" rhyming begins. Some listeners have commented that this ruined the song for them. Others, like me, are able to let the inanities pass while enjoying the song as a whole.

In **"Lay It on Me,"** Hayward sings: "I get a yearning when the sun goes down / To hold your body close to mine / I get a feeling to come round your house / And light the fire and drink some wine / I'll keep you safe and warm and free from harm / It's understood / Oh darling, take your worries and lay them on me."

"Lay It on Me" would have complemented any Moody Blues album. The melody, guitar work, and production are in the same vein of Hayward/Moody songs such as "It's Up to You," "You and Me," and "The Story in Your Eyes." Hayward's signature electric guitar is on magnificent display.

"Stage Door," another look at the spectacle of showbiz, was the second track on the album to feature orchestration from Peter Knight. Hayward has said the song was based on a letter written to him by his parents, when he was a boy spending his school break as part of a summer stock troupe. In the song, the letter develops into a drama of its own, rich in melody. "Stage Door" is not everyone's cup of tea, but this listener finds it enchanting.

Hayward liked it, too. Liz Derringer of *Circus* (August 19, 1977) said that he said Tony Clarke's work on "Stage Door" was "a masterpiece," with Hayward adding, "Tony should get an award for that one."

"Raised on Love" is one of two songs in this collection for which Hayward reportedly played all the instruments. But he didn't provide all the voices. His four-year old daughter, Doremi, is also heard on this song. It's a nice touch – a simple and charming melody and lyric, with a little girl's angelic voice in the mix. It doesn't sound like the Moody Blues, and that's all to the good.

"Doin' Time" is a creditable rock song, featuring excellent lead guitar work from Hayward, who, we have heard, also did all the vocal harmonies. It's a driving track, and an asset to the album, changing up the musical styles, alternating a ratio of one rocker for every two ballads.

The final track, **"Nostradamus,"** was another song on the album which has a reputation as one in which Hayward served as a one-man band, playing all the instruments. Perhaps this is true of the basic track, but Hayward did have help. He later said, "If I needed a sound that we couldn't play, as on 'Nostradamus,' we would just call a famous classical musician – often more adaptable than pop session musicians – and they never failed to get into the spirit." (JH-RYM09)

Hayward called "Nostradamus" "a gloomy song about the guy who prophesies disaster for the world, and he was certainly right." (JH-HL98a)

He sings: "Do you ever get the feeling / What was prophesized was true / And it's all being witnessed now by you / The faces of the children / In the artist's loving hands / Are all returning into sand. / The waters of the oceans / Like the rivers running dry / It brings a tear to your eye."

Did Hayward believe in all that? He told one journalist, "It was not my point of view then. It's just, I think everyone always assumes that when someone writes a song it's always about them, or it's about how they feel. But that's the same [as] saying when someone writes a book it's always about them. It's like saying Agatha Christie always wrote about herself. Well, she didn't; it's just a story. I was interested then in Nostradamus because I just read the book of those prophecies. But that's all. I didn't believe all of this; it was just an interesting subject for a song. Just that." (JH-HL98a)

"Nostradamus" boasts a pulsing, tom-tom driven arrangement, highlighted with strings and wailing flute sounds which recall Native American melodies. It could have graced one of the late 1960s Moody Blues album, with its topic and choir of Moody-like voices. Peter Knight is not given credit on the album for the string arrangement, and Hayward has stated that he brought in some well known classical musicians to realize the effect. It is magnificent, bringing the song to its stunning conclusion.

Upon the release of *Songwriter*, Justin Hayward told American journalist Jared Johnson, "I'm very happy with [my album], both myself and Tony Clarke, who's my producer. We both believe it's the best thing we've ever done. I think it differs in many ways [from the Moody Blues]. But, you know, I can't get away from the sound of my own voice, which I don't want to escape from, [nor] the style which I suppose is identifiable with a lot of the things the Moodies did. But this time I wanted to make an album that would entertain and also be different in subject material. I'd felt that sometimes, with the Moodies, we'd taken ourselves a little too seriously, and I don't think this album does." (JH-DP77)

***

John Lodge's *Natural Avenue* was the first album from a Moody Blues member to be issued after the closing of Threshold, even though it was completed after *Songwriter*.

Hayward told Jon Tiven of *Rock*, "It's a very personal record; it took me about a month to write, and the only reason it took so long [after *Blue Jays*] to record and release was that I had to book the time in the studio and then we had to wait for the other Moodies to release their records. We try to coordinate things as best as possible so that we don't all come out with records as the same time. The album was complete in August [a month before Lodge started recording *Natural Avenue*], but it got held up in release." (JH-R77)

Lodge's album was issued by Decca in England, and London Records in the U.S. Hayward's *Songwriter* would also be distributed by Decca and London, but on the specialty label, Deram, making Hayward the only Moody still associated with the label. In fact, he was the only current artist on Deram. He said, "At least, I'm the only *living* artist recording for it. ... Procol Harum used to be on it, and no one else was using it. So I called up Sir Edward Lewis, the head of Decca, and asked him if I could be on Deram. So here I am." (JH-R77)

U.K. single release:
"One Lonely Room"
b/w "Songwriter (Part 2)"
Deram DM 428; February 4, 1977

One week before the release of
Songwriter, Deram issued a "coming attraction" in
the form of "One Lonely Room." Despite the
simplicity of the lyrics – this was the one with the
"sails/rails" and "wheels/heels" rhyming –
Decca/Deram thought "One Lonely Room" was a
track that would excite radio programmers and pop
music fans in England. Their instincts weren't
completely out of whack, but perhaps a little
disconnected in time. Several years earlier, "One
Lonely Room" surely would have done well. After
all, the Turtles got into the Top 10 in 1968 signing,
"Eleanor, gee, I think you're swell / And you really
do me well" and "I really think you're groovy /
Let's go to a movie." Of course, they were singing
tongue-in-cheek, making fun of the simplicity and
silliness of much of the music on the radio at that time. But the times were a'changin'.

In the February 19, 1977 issue of *Rock Star*:

> Depressing moaner/groaner from "Suicide Justin." After listening
> to this, I felt so down I wanted to disappear. I yawned instead;
> much more healthy, you know. Thank God for rock.

Radio programmers, however, were quick to add "One Lonely Room" to
playlists. The last time a single had been released by Justin Hayward in Britain (1975's
"Blue Guitar") it shot into the Top 10. The expectations of "One Lonely Room" were
high, and, even if not a "hit" by 1977 standards, it did make for a good "trailer" to the
album, out seven days later.

Album release: *Songwriter*
Deram SDL 15 (U.K.); Deram DES 18073 (U.S.); February 11, 1977

After the success of *Blue Jays*, the release of *Songwriter* was highly anticipated.
Chas De Whalley wrote for *Sounds* in February:

> … Moodies and Blue Jays fans will not be disappointed with the
> new album. I found it lighter and less pretentious than what I
> remembered of Justin Hayward's earlier work. What can't be
> debated though [is] the strength of Hayward's writing and an
> added stylistic variety that you wouldn't perhaps expect of him.…

In the February 12, 1977 issue of *Record Mirror*, Robin Smith wrote:

> Sentimental, yes; over-rich in parts, agreed – but I like it. I like it because I'm fed up with hearing so many weak lyrics and everybody leaping aboard the punk and funk bandwagons. If you want to relax, this is your album. The man who brought you "Nights in White Satin" and "Question" has come up with 10 more evocative songs.
>
> "Tightrope" is a strong opener, reflecting on the perils of being a performer. Pity about the cheers and whistles at the end though.
>
> The record mellows with "Songwriter," a soft piano intro and Hayward's close-to-tears voice before the orchestra takes over. "One Lonely Room" has a similar feel to "Nights in White Satin" – a lonely sax providing a mournful background for Hayward's voice. Strings follow, merging with guitar.
>
> Lighter touches are provided by "Raised on Love" and "Country Girl."
>
> Over the years, Justin Hayward's talents as a songwriter haven't diminished one bit.

From the February 26 issue of *Billboard*:

> The latest solo effort from a former member of the Moody Blues shows guitarist-singer-writer Hayward as an impressive talent in his own right. Though not as cosmic as the entire Moodies in full swing, Hayward is well into the synthesizer-orchestra sweeping sound with massed sweet tenor vocal harmonies that characterized the group at its most successful. The main departure is that he prefers to write lyrics about personal, intimate situations rather than the determined poeticizing of the Moodies. Best cuts: "Tightrope," "Raised on Love," "Songwriter."

Also on February 26, Richard Green reviewed the album for *Melody Maker*:

> I recently heard a deejay describe this album as a continuation of the Moody Blues. He was only partly right. There are some places in this, Hayward's first solo album, where the Moody Blues' influence comes through, and that was bound to happen, because Hayward contributed so much to the band's sound. ... Really, it's Hayward's own sound as perfected with the Moody Blues, rather than the Moody Blues' sound influencing Hayward.
>
> It's an entertaining album – the all-important first track on the first side, "Tightrope," has the necessary impact of an album intro (there's a beautiful fairground instrumental passage at the end) – and the album never sags. In fact, it gets better. The title track, or

should I say 'tracks,' because it's in two parts, seems to float into the ears rather than assail them. Midway there's a fast and slow instrumental passage leading to Part Two, a more raunchy and punctuated piece.

An up-tempo "Country Girl" follows, and then it's into the track that's been culled as a single, "One Lonely Room." I can't really see this as a single hit; to me it's more of an outstanding album track. It's certainly one of the best cuts and has a soft, rippling intro before the strings come in at full flow, with Hayward adding some fine vocals and guitar touches.

"Lay It on Me" has Hayward dual-tracking and did remind me of some numbers he did with the Moodies. It's got fine lyrics, a catchy rhythm, and could've been the single release.

For me, the knock-out track on the album is "Stage Door." It starts with shimmering strings and a fanfare, then drifts into a ballad with a slight Latin feel. A dreamy sax weaves its way in and out, but it's the lyrics that grab – all about a boy's Ma and Pa coming to see his band perform and leaving a note saying they're with him tonight, and that there's always clean sheets on his bed at home. Sounds corny and insipid but it isn't, not the way Hayward puts it over on the record.

Green felt the next track, "Raised on Love," was the album's only "dud." He likened it to Ray Stevens's "Everything Is Beautiful," which begins with children's voices, and said that "Raised on Love" was "the kind of track that would get played a lot down the Bible Belt in the States." He called "Doin' Time" Hayward's "prison song," which boasted a "very slight blues feeling with, as always, perceptive lyrics." "Nostradamus," he said, was "something the Moodies might have recorded."

Green concluded:

It's a satisfying first album with Hayward's lyrics like paintings depicting landscapes of the human mind rather than nature. The music has a soft, ethereal quality and it's a soft, moody (sorry about that), late-night listening kind of album. Hayward almost buries the Moody Blues and Blue Jays with this album, but I can't help wondering whether he will win any new converts. But it's a beautiful, artistic record that stands a lot of plays.

Jackie Finch, of *National Rock Star*, wrote:

… There is a distinctly relaxed, uncomplicated and simply good-to-listen-to feel to it. … Justin Hayward is essentially a very sensitive and entertaining writer.

From the March issue of *International Musician and Recording World*:

I like this album despite myself. …

Knowing how incredibly important this solo step is must make the decision about the type of thing to do very hard. Sensibly, Jus has just pulled together the best of his new songs and recorded them with no other comment, concept or continuity link. ... I liked several of the songs without reaching that rare state of reviewer's orgasm, I was indifferent to several and I couldn't make my mind up about a couple.

The album has been produced with considerable care by Tony Clarke, and it's a tribute to his skill that the producer's role cannot be heard on the vinyl. Finally, the album left me with less satisfaction rather than more because of my patchy likes and because I didn't find any one track good enough to hang the whole project on. But even as I write this, there's a warning bell ringing. "Nights in White Satin" was, to say the least, a sleeper, and I've got a suspicion that something in that category could be lurking here. ...

From March 12, Patrick MacDonald wrote in *The Seattle Times*:

... *Songwriter* has the lush instrumental arrangement and dreamy, spacey lyrics that were trademarks of the Moody Blues, and includes some outstanding single cuts that show Hayward's special gifts as a songwriter, singer and musician.

It shouldn't be surprising that Hayward would be the one to finally turn out something worthy of a former Moodie – he wrote almost all the Moody Blues' finest songs, including "Nights in White Satin," "Tuesday Afternoon" and "The Actor."

Hayward called the other day as part of a series of promotional interviews for the album. He was calling from a studio in New York.

"I'm here trying to pick out a single from the album," he said over the phone in a smooth British accent. "As usual, I can't make up my mind so I'm giving them three – let them decide. 'One Lonely Room,' which is already a hit back home in England, but they say it's too slow for American radio, so we may go with 'Songwriter' or 'Country Girl.'"

"One Lonely Room" did receive a fair amount of initial airplay in the U.K. prior to Hayward departing for the States, but Richard Green was right when he wrote that it didn't sound like a hit single to him, but more a standout album cut. It quickly petered out and missed the charts.

One of the songs Hayward offered London Records as a candidate as a single was "Lay It on Me."

U.S. single release:
"Lay It on Me" b/w "Songwriter (Part 2)"
Deram 5N-7541; March 1977

This had hit written all over it – catchy, melodic, energetic, finely produced, and with that familiar voice that immediately evoked memories of "Tuesday Afternoon," "The Story in Your Eyes, "Question," and "Nights in White Satin." It couldn't miss … could it?

From the March 23 edition of the *Beaver County Times* in Pennsylvania, Bob Uhrinak reviewed *Songwriter*:

> This is the best Moody Blues' album recorded since the group stopped recording and performing together over two years ago. …
>
> *Songwriter* is a first-rate album that will complement any record collection. It is full of good – if not outstanding – songs that are performed and arranged with taste. All the elements of a good

Moody Blues album are there – the strings and synthesizer, Justin Hayward's quivering voice, the flawless production.

> The songs rate with the best Hayward has ever written. There is not a bad song on the album (although he does come close to losing a few with his "flower power love is the answer" lyrics). … The theme of universal love that was so over-worked by the Moody Blues only raises its head a few times on the album, most noticeably on "Raised on Love." …
>
> The melodies are interesting and have good hooks. All in all, a very good album. …

Patti Bruno wrote in *Scottsdale* [Arizona] *Community College Free Press*:

> Moody Blues fans may recognize this name. He is the Voice and songwriter behind such hits as "Tuesday Afternoon" and "Nights in White Satin," and one half of the Hayward and Lodge team which released *Blue Jays* in early 1975. Now Justin Hayward has finally gone solo.
>
> Don't expect this album to lead you on an ethereal mind trip like *Seventh Sojourn*. "The songs are more direct than those in the past. There are no hidden meanings," he told *Rolling Stone*.

618

Also gone is the Phil Travers' painting which decorated each album cover. In addition, Hayward's wife Marie and 4-year-old daughter Doremi sing on several cuts – a hint taken from Ray Thomas, Michael Pinder, and Graeme Edge, all of whom included the female vocals in their solo efforts that never occurred on a Moodies album.

Justin Hayward still is, nevertheless, a Moody. The songs are still unmistakingly melodic in the old tradition. He plays nearly every instrument on the album (with guests Peter Knight and the London Festival Orchestra, who also appeared on *Days of Future Passed* and *Blue Jays*).

On "Songwriter, Part 2" he plays piano and synthesizer reminiscent of Michael Pinder (and Rick Wakeman). The guitar and vocals are undeniably Hayward. "Part 2" is a daring piece of music that will surprise hard core Moodies fans.

"One Lonely Room" is the one song on the album that is close to earlier Hayward, containing melancholy lyrics and a heavy, depressing melody.

"Lay It on Me" is a faster song, a possible single, and certainly rock and roll at its best. …

[I]t will be an easy album to get into. There's a bit of music on it for everyone.

From the April 10 edition of *The Pittsburgh Press*, Pete Bishop wrote:

Of all the solo albums by ex-Moody Blues members, Justin Hayward's *Songwriter* (Deram DES 18073) sounds the most like the old parent group. Unfortunately, the material is nowhere near as strong. Granted, *Songwriter* teems with good melodies, but the lyrics rarely are on the same plane, just like Ray Thomas's and Michael Pinder's LPs.

Where the words show some bite and maturity are the high spots: "Tightrope" (fast rock with fanfare opening), "Lay It on Me" and "Doin' Time" (rock out a little harder) and "Stage Door" (ballad from a loving family to a star).

Moodys' fans will recognize Hayward's clean, rather delicate voice immediately – when they can hear it, that is. Basically a guitarist, Hayward also is credited with a hand on piano, drums, percussion, and keyboard, plus he's got some helpers, too, and he and producer Tony Clarke seldom spare music. The result often is an overdone jumble which even sturdier material couldn't support.

Songwriter is basically acceptable, although continuing proof that the Moody Blues apart are far from what they were together.

In its April 18 issue, *People* magazine said:

> The creamily buoyant voice of the moribund Moody Blues is alive and still lushly homogenized. Hayward has even dubbed in wife and daughter on "Raised on Love" – move over Paul and Linda. *Songwriter* should appease Moodies' fans in their fourth year of waiting for a reunion.

U.K. single release:
"Country Girl" b/w "Doin' Time"
Deram DM 429; April 22, 1977

Hayward credited his friend Eric Stuart from 10cc for picking "Country Girl" to be a single. It's a lovely pop song with an infectious chorus. As with "One Lonely Room," if this single missed the charts in Britain, chalk it up to changing times and fickle musical tastes, not the caliber of the material.

Rolling Stone magazine wasn't interested in singles, only albums. The rock magazine finally got around to *Songwriter* with its May 5 issue. Alan Niester wrote:

> *Songwriter* is the first ex-Moody Blues solo album to approximate the vitality and appeal of the group albums that sold so well to long-haired kids with latent MOR tendencies in the late Sixties. And well it should, since Hayward has exerted a lot of effort to recycle the hooks, riffs and vocal inflections of those albums. Since Hayward's voice was always an integral component of the Moody Blues, *Songwriter* amounts to a follow-up to *Every Good Boy Deserves Favour*, six years later. All the features of the Moody Blues are here – the upbeat "Ride My See-Saw" number with the drawn-out guitar notes ("Tightrope"), the introspective questioning of the fates ("Doin' Time," "Nostradamus"), the angel choir vocal tracks (everywhere). Material that doesn't draw directly from the past is the least appealing; witness attempts at making Hayward a singer/songwriter a' la Neil Sedaka on "Country Girl" or "Raised on Love."

Hayward has lost little over the past few years (granted, he's gained equally little), and although this album seems unlikely to draw any new converts it will at least do well in the instant-nostalgia market.

From the May 13 edition of Van Nuys, California's *Valley News*, Richard S. Ginell said:

> There's a rumor going 'round that the Moody Blues are planning to reunite. If so, then this LP stands as filler in the interim between now and the next Moodies album because … let's face it … Hayward needs the group more than they needed him. The songs are decent enough but the extra spark of something or other which the group was able to supply to his songs is missing.
>
> The album, like all Tony Clarke products, shows craftsmanship and care, and the sonics, while not spectacular, are helpful to the cause.

On May 20, Simon Richardson reviewed both *Songwriter* and John Lodge's *Natural Avenue* in the Australian music magazine, *Ram*. He detested *Natural Avenue*, finding the rocking title song to be one of the few listenable tracks. Richardson was kinder to *Songwriter*, calling it a "creditable solo album." He said of Hayward:

> … He was always the least wimpy of the Moodies anyway; at least the one with the strongest rhythm and best lead vocals. He revives bits and pieces of his Moody work (as does Lodge) but they work well in their new, more straightforward setting. "Tightrope" is a neato medium-paced rocker summing up his attitudes to the music bizz. "Raised on Love" has some simple and beautiful choral work. "Nostradamus" builds to an eerie coda.
>
> Justin Hayward and John Lodge's first effort after the Moody Blues disintegrated into Cosmic Dust was as a duo, *Blue Jays*. Their album was just so-so. Justin Hayward's solo is about twice as good as that, and Lodge's twice as insubstantial. …

Robert Hilburn of *The Los Angeles Times* spoke up on May 27. You may recall that Hilburn had lost his love for the Moody Blues back around 1971. But he seemed to like Hayward and Lodge and had hoped they would either take over the band or go solo. When presented with *Blue Jays*, Hilburn tried to like it, but felt something was missing. It didn't occur to him that what *was* missing might have been Pinder, Thomas, and Edge. Now he wrote:

> … Hayward's stirring melodies were the strongest element in the Moody's sound, but the music in his solo debut is too plain. The interchange with the other members of the band gave a majesty and splendor to such Hayward tunes as "Lovely to See You," "Tuesday Afternoon" and "Nights in White Satin" that are absent here. Thin.

In other words, maybe Pinder, Thomas, and Edge, with Lodge, served a purpose after all.

U.S. single release:
"Country Girl" b/w "Songwriter (Part 2)"
Deram 5N-7542; June 1977

Surprisingly, the catchy and uptempo "Lay It on Me" failed to find a home on American radio. London Records came back with a second offering, the same A-side that Decca/Deram in England had recently issued.

The week "Country Girl" was sent to DJs across America, K.C. & the Sunshine Band's "I'm Your Boogie Man" was No. 1 on *Billboard*'s Hot 100 singles chart. Also in the Top 5: Fleetwood Mac's "Dreams"; Marvin Gaye's "Got to Give It Up"; Bill Conti's "Gonna Fly Now (Theme from 'Rocky')"; and Foreigner's "Feels Like the First Time." "Country Girl" was just as catchy … but, perhaps, just out of its time.

Regardless, the album was selling steadily and moving up the charts.

His high confidence in the new album was setting Hayward up for a disappointment. He told American journalist Jared Johnson, "A lot of writers said great things about us in the early days, and I think they probably ran out of good things to say. But I don't see how they can knock this album." (JH-DP77)

Well, they could.

From the July 7, 1977 issue of *Circus*:

> … [W]hatever the Moodies may have lacked philosophically, it must be admitted that, having assumed the responsibility of leading their fans to glory, they always delivered. Their last album is as convincing and comforting as their first.

> … Where the Moodys seemed to do it all for you, Hayward on *Songwriter* shows the stamp of selfishness as self-indulgence. In "Tightrope," the thinly disguised message is that playing with the Moody Blues was too much of a strain: "I worked without a safety net / But it was such a long way down." The singer's conclusion appears to be that he wasn't saintly enough for the job, but his delivery is so smug that the song comes off as a sneer at his former fans. Hayward often places himself in a world of no more than two people – a man and a woman – shutting himself off from the listener as the Moodys would never have done.

> … Producer Tony Clarke used to exercise impeccable judgment in his deployment of instrumental colors; here, he just flexes his mixing-board muscles as the star throws in everything but the

proverbial kitchen sink. If the liner notes are to be believed, Hayward plays all of the instruments, except for a few violin lines. His synthesizer work is too perky to be tolerated, and he simply is not a drummer.

Although Justin Hayward wrote the lion's share of the Moody Blues' most memorable work, he wasn't the prime mover of their success. This album proves that. *Songwriter* doesn't live up to any of its promises.

From the July 9 edition of Bridgewater, New Jersey's *The Courier-News*, Karen Herman Steffaro wrote:

> *Songwriter* by Justin Hayward is just as its name suggests, a collection of songs ... a songwriter's thoughts.

> There are calliope sounds in the backgrounds and echoey tones reminiscent of the early Moody Blues. It's a soft dinnertime album with nothing really memorable except perhaps a line of lyric, "Where is the Eden we dreamed of" ... [That Eden is] back with the Moody Blues as a group....

U.K. single release:
"Stage Door" b/w "Lay It on Me"
Deram DM 430; July 29, 1977

Decca in England tried one more time to find a hit on this album filled with pop confections. "Stage Door" struck the label as enough of a novelty to have a chance in the British charts, where novelty records had often performed well. But this came many months after the release of the album; the chance for striking gold on the radio had come and past.

While *Songwriter*'s chart positions on both side of the Atlantic were respectable, it nonetheless underperformed when considering the success two years earlier for *Blue Jays*, and the expectations from the music industry.

In England, *Songwriter* peaked at No. 28. In America, a bit lower, at No. 37, but it stayed there for 16 weeks, and sales remained steady for a year following its initial Stateside release.

On July 23, 1978, Bart Mills reported in the *San Francisco Examiner & Chronicle* that *Songwriter* had sold 500,000 copies, had already been presented with a gold record award, and was well on its way to being certified platinum.

Justin Hayward told Mills, "I can make more money working solo than working as a Moody Blues." (JH-SFE&C78)

But money had never been the top priority of any of the Moodies. They had demonstrated that time and again. And, just as "Stage Door" was issued as the third single in England, rumors were making the rounds in the press that the Moody Blues were preparing to come back together.

To whet the fans' appetites, Decca Records in England and London Records in the U.S. had already planned an album release for 1977, bringing out previously unreleased Moody Blues material from the Decca vaults.

30

Paradise Ballroom
The Graeme Edge Band, 1977

Album release:
Decca TXS 121 (U.K.); London PS 686 (U.S.); April 1977
U.S. peak position: #164 (*Billboard*)

Single release:
"*Everybody Needs Somebody*" b/w "*Be My Eyes*"
Decca F 13698 (U.K.); London 5N 1071 (U.S.); June 1977
Non-charting

If you felt we were a bit hard on the Graeme Edge Band's first album release, *Kick Off Your Muddy Boots*, our criticism was no harsher than what came from Edge.

Graeme Edge told Susan Ahrens of *Crawdaddy*, for the magazine's August 1977 issue, "After listening to *Kick Off Your Muddy Boots* really hard and getting over the shock that it didn't go straight to Number One – because your ego is still geared that way – when it looked like it was about to stiff, that really brought me back to earth and I started listening to what I had done. It was made in haste, and it lacked certain subtleties. I was determined that this time it wasn't going to happen again." (GE-C77)

For a London Records press release, Edge told how he sailed around the world on his 75-foot yacht to prepare for making the album. He said, "The influences for this new album, *Paradise Ballroom*, came from the music I heard on my trip. I was fascinated by some of the other writing methods I discovered, especially the use of alternative chord structures. I also uncovered a wealth of new drumming styles, ranging from the controlled but exhilarating excitement of the Greeks to the seemingly disjointed rhythm of the Basques to rhythms of the Caribbean, where each island has its own beat, be it calypso, reggae, samba, or any of the other whose names aren't yet household words in our music." (GE-LR76)

Elsewhere, Edge said, "I felt I had to prove myself. The band was sort of hovering on coming back together, and I felt I needed to say, 'This is what I've been doing; this is where I've been, and this is where I am now.' A year on the boat really built my confidence in myself, and I went back and really took charge of the second album, so much so that Adrian and I never worked afterwards because he's a very powerful ego of a man, and I asserted myself a couple of times and said, 'That's my way. Stuff it.' It was a little bit unfair to him, because he put a lot of work into the album, but I never had the slightest intention of going on the road with it because I always knew the Moodies would be back. I suppose in a way I used him. But I suppose in a way he used me, too." (GE-MD87)

This time, Edge made sure to get a co-writing credit on all the songs, and promoted Adrian Gurvitz's brother, bass-player Paul, to handle many of the lead vocals. His singing voice was fuller, perhaps less strident than brother Adrian. But Adrian is still the dominant voice on this second album, though his voice is sometimes cushioned by harmony vocals from Paul. And when Adrian does step out in front, it is on songs more within his range. We seldom get the sense that he is straining or singing in a register that was unnatural for him.

The album kicks into high gear right out of the gate, with the extravagant **"Paradise Ballroom."** The guest roster is impressive, with Strawbs keyboardist Blue Weaver on organ, Traffic's Rebop Kwaku Baah on percussion, and the Memphis Strings and Horns giving the track added life. Adrian and Paul Gurvitz share the vocals, and Adrian's lead guitar is less abrasive on the ears than most of *Kick Off Your Muddy Boots*, yet just as lively.

The second track, **"Human,"** is something Moody Blues fans should like. It's a lovely ballad, with pleasant production. The Gurvitz brothers blend their voices this time around into smooth harmonies. Nothing on the first Graeme Edge Band was this heartfelt, or soothing. The melodic, jazzy piano interlude is especially welcome, and the lead guitar elevates this otherwise gentle song without being intrusive. Edge's drumming is perfect, giving the track punch without taking away from its beauty.

"Everybody Needs Somebody" is both eccentric and fun. It samples the first few notes from the 1964 Dean Martin hit, "Everybody Loves Somebody" – but then turns the listener's expectations upside-down. The most curious element – right up front, throughout – is the playful, soulful organ. There were four different keyboardist featured on this album, but credits were not provided for individual tracks. The hands on the keys could have belonged to Ann Odell, Tony Hymas, Blue Weaver, or Adrian Gurvitz. Whoever it was, take a bow!

So infectious is this recording that it was selected as the single to promote the album. It should have been a hit. When comparing this to the last Moody Blues solo venture, Justin Hayward's *Songwriter*, and its three singles, "Everybody Needs Somebody" succeeds where the Hayward singles did not – it didn't sound dated when released in 1977. Its sound was fresh; it really doesn't sound dated, even today. It defies musical trendiness. It's unique.

"All Is Fair in Love" is energized funk, with electrifying (but not harsh) lead guitar work, matched with an equally invigorating performance from the Memphis Horns, and, again, led by first-rate vocals – the two Gurvitz brothers complementing one another rather than competing.

"Down, Down, Down" is the next surprise in this album filled with surprises – it's a sweet country-western uptempo ballad, with an exquisite, sweeping steel guitar throughout. The melody is enchanting, with a smooth flow, augmented by Graeme Edge's tasteful and punchy drum fills. Adrian Gurvitz continues to play his electric lead guitar in the higher register, but shows appropriate restraint, blending with the steel guitar. "Down, Down, Down," from start to finish, goes down nice.

"In the Night of the Light" has the sinuous string backing of many a disco hit from this era. It's a bit of disco, a bit of funk, set to a pleasant tune, a soulful vocal (which sound more like Adrian than Paul, but fits the mood and lush backing). The Memphis Horns, sounding reminiscent of Earth, Wind & Fire, add the punch, elevating this track above the run-of-the-mill disco and funk that prevailed on radio in 1977. It's catchy and playful.

"Caroline" closes the album on an introspective note. But, like the other quasi-ballads on the album, this too has bite. The inventive background singing, the bouncing guitar licks and fills, along with the thump-and-roll perfect drumming by Edge, and the cushion provided by the Memphis Horns (sax up front), all blend to make for a delicious finale.

If Adrian Gurvitz was indeed the controlling force behind *Kick Off Your Muddy Boots*, and Edge was making the choices for *Paradise Ballroom*, then Gurvitz should be grateful. Gurvitz comes across better in every possible way on the album, as a co-writer, singer, guitarist, and pianist. Sometimes talent just needs a little coaxing – or reigning in.

Paradise Ballroom is an album that all involved should be proud of, and is worth hearing, time and again.

Joe Petagno, who designed the album jacked for *Kick Off Your Muddy Boots*, returned to provide the artwork for this latest album. The results are stunning, and hint at the musical choices for the album. A dancing disco queen never looked so good.

Album release:
Decca TXS 121 (U.K.); London PS 686;
April 1977

Decca Records in England graciously held back the release of the next Moody Blues album, the compilation *Caught Live + 5*, in order to not crowd the release of

Paradise Ballroom. Did they know that they had something special in this second LP release from the Graeme Edge Band? In America, however, London Records rush-released *Caught Live + 5*, in stores on April 30, just weeks after the release of the new Graeme Edge Band LP.

Robin Smith wrote in the May 7, 1977 issue of *Record Mirror*:

> Don't like Justin Hayward or John Lodge? Then give Graeme Edge a listen. The Moody Blues drummer turns out stuff 10 times heavier. For openers there's "Paradise Ballroom," a beefy thigh slapper with his crisp drumming surging along and showing the number forward. "Human" is back to the Moodies style, a tender ballad spoilt somewhat by the well-worn cliché of introducing a string section at the end. Back to the stompers again with "I Need Love," throbbing drums and bass topped off by a curious Sixties electric organ feel – fascinating in a strange way. An album that's more rough and ready than other efforts by ex-Moodies, but still very enjoyable.

From the May 21 edition of *Sounds*, Phil Sutcliffe said:

> Adrian Gurvitz is again Edge's collaborator in this "solo" enterprise. An unlikely partner for a former Moody Blue I'd have thought. Gurvitz isn't exactly svelte in either playing or personality – built like a second-row forward, and bristling with ginger hair and beard, he can make you feel as if you are a china shop and he's the bull. But somehow the blend works and the bull puts in exactly what you'd expect – balls.

> … Edge takes credit for co-writing some appealing songs, co-producing a big sound which still manages to put the emphasis in the right place, and for letting the whole thing happen. …

> The new spheres explored are the non-heavenly worlds of funk, soul and country. Surprisingly the former cosmonaut and the old raunch 'n' roller of the Gun and Baker-Gurvitz Army don't foul up once. …

> The first tracks on each side, "Paradise Ballroom" and "All Is Fair," feature a hot big band sound with the Gurvitz guitar riding on top of the mix, neat and punchy, no heavy metal extravagances, and the odd quick fire variation taking him into Dimeola territory. His voice ranges from raw shouting to convincing handling of the steel guitar ballad, "Down, Down, Down" (not an idiom I enjoy but he gives it the personal touch that the more accepted practitioners always seem to miss out on). And single-handed he makes the one rather dull item, "In the Night of the Light," jump to the funk despite a tediously routine tune and arrangement.

> It ain't the millennium but it is an enjoyable album. …

Single release:
"Everybody Needs Somebody"
b/w "Be My Eyes"
Decca F 13698 (U.K.);
London 5N 1071 (U.S.); June 1977

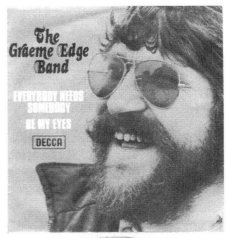

"Everybody Needs Somebody" was chosen as the "trailer" for the album. With the novelty approach of the song, it was hoped it might score on its own as a single. It should have even without the nod to old Dino, especially at a time when the Captain & Tennille's "Muskrat Love" was in the national Top 10.

The B-side, "Be My Eyes," was not included on the original album, but did show up on a later reissuing of the album on CD. It opens as a song by a band named after its drummer should, with the drums, the first time Edge had done this since "I'm Just a Singer (In a Rock and Roll Band)." We had mentioned earlier how Ringo Starr used this approach on his hits "It Don't Come Easy" and "Back Off Boogaloo."

Edge now joins the "star drummer" club, and rises to the occasion. In addition to the signature opening, the drum breaks at various points in the song remind the listener that the spotlight isn't only on the lead singer and guitarist.

In the June 11 edition of *New Musical Express*, Chris Salewicz opined:

> The Graeme Edge Band features shameful Adrian Gurvitz on guitar and keyboards and his brother Paul on bass. It is, therefore, the Baker-Gurvitz Army with a different, stellar drummer.

> It features seven expertly recorded and astonishingly ponderous tracks of cocktail lounge white blues. I suspect it's probably not a vital recording.

On June 18, *Billboard* told industry insiders:

> Jazz flavored instruments coupled with rock vocals makes for an interesting blend. The jazz guitar is the outstanding instrument

here. Strong vocals by lead singer are good. Much of this LP is mellow and as much instrumental as vocal. Best cuts: "Paradise Ballroom," "Human," "Caroline," "All Is Fair."

From the July 9 edition of Bridgewater, New Jersey's *The Courier-News*, Karen Herman Steffaro reviewed *Paradise Ballroom*, as well as *Natural Avenue*, and *Songwriter*, all released at about the same time:

> Edge's *Paradise Ballroom* makes the boldest statement of all three newly released solo albums.
>
> Edge, master drummer of the Moody Blues for ten years, shares the writing credits on his second solo album with Adrian Gurvitz, who comes through on the lead vocals and guitars.
>
> He assembled a new band for the album which features arrangements of Willie Mitchell who had produced Al Green, Ann Peebles and Syl Johnson.
>
> Using new musicians, in 1975, Edge returned to his yacht in the Mediterranean and sailed across the Atlantic for the Bahamas, all the time working on the album. It was a trip that provided the motivating influences in the music: alternative chord structures, drumming styles and snatches from Greek excitement of the rhythms of the Basques and those of the Caribbean. It features the most diversified orchestration of any of the solo albums with the musical interludes between lyrics featuring drum solos and horns.

Adrian Gurvitz's reputation among the music press had, generally speaking, been on the decline for a couple of years. In the October 27, 1977 issue of *Circus*, Michael Bloom said:

> *Paradise Ballroom* is the latest documentation of an ongoing con game by guitarist Adrian Gurvitz, who may be the stupidest man in rock but who always manages to rope some drummer into taking him in for a few albums. When Ginger Baker, his last employer, wised up, Gurvitz made a beeline for ex-Moody Graeme Edge, who is himself much dumber than Baker. Don't touch this turkey with a 10-foot pole.

Paradise Ballroom only stayed in the *Billboard* album chart for four weeks. Two of those weeks were spent at its peak position, a dismal No. 164. It was a shame, in the opinions of those of us who liked the record.

In any event, there was a new sail on Edge's horizon. The Moody Blues were returning.

31

Caught Live + 5 (1977)

U.S. album release: London 2 PS 690/691; April 30, 1977
U.K. album release: Decca MB 3/4; June 1, 1977
U.S. peak position: #26

Threshold Records had turned into a headache for the Moody Blues, even contributing to the band's long hiatus. As a result, the Moodies chose to drop their own label at the end of 1977 when the Threshold Distribution deal with Decca expired.

In the June 4, 1977 issue of *Billboard*, the New York office reported:

> With the resignation of Gerry Hoff as president, Threshold Records becomes a label in name only.
>
> London will continue to distribute the Moody Blues-owned label, which includes several platinum LPs, but no replacement is planned for Hoff, who returns to the West Coast to operate his own company.
>
> Decca will "administer" Threshold affairs in the U.K., a spokesman for the Moody Blues says. …
>
> "There will be no new product issued on the Threshold label," the spokesman said. …

Within months of giving up their label, the Moodies had cause to regret the decision, which also released the band's control over their catalog. Decca (along with its

U.S. partner, London) was now free to release further compilations of both previously released and unreleased material. The first of these releases was *Caught Live + 5.*

Justin Hayward told *Highland* magazine, "They didn't need our agreement. There was a contract with Threshold that said we could control what was released… [but] that contract expired. Because we didn't make records, we were obligated by [the Decca] contract, so they said, 'You haven't come to us with a new Moody Blues album since *Seventh Sojourn,* so we are releasing this material that we already have.'" (JH-HL98a)

The material Decca chose was a 1969 concert which had been recorded at Royal Albert Hall for possible release, but tucked away when the Moodies felt it was not up to their standard. The performance was only about an hour long, enough for three sides of a vinyl album. For the fourth side, Decca dusted off five master tapes from the vault, songs which had been recorded in 1967 and '68. One, "Gimme a Little Somethin'," had been written by John Lodge. It featured his voice most prominently on the choruses, while Justin Hayward sang the verses. Mike Pinder's "Please Think About It" was also resurrected, with Pinder on lead vocal. The three remaining tracks were written and sung by Hayward – "Long Summer Days," "King and Queen," and "What Am I Doing Here?" All three were good songs; the last had received positive notices in 1968 whenever the Moody Blues performed it in concert. It could have been a hit if released as a single that year. But since the song didn't fit the theme of the albums the group was making that year or the next, into the vault it went. Nine years later, the Moodies were not in favor of these older tracks being released on a "new" album

Hayward told Ray Coleman of *Melody Maker,* "Threshold gave us control of our own product, and control on sales and promotion, and it was the right move for us at that time. [But] look at what's happened to us since we don't have Threshold as a label anymore! Decca puts out this compilation, *Live + 5,* and it's no credit to the Moodies. We said, 'Please let us mix it,' and asked for some say in how it appeared. But we couldn't insist, because the tape didn't belong to us. That's the sort of thing you leave yourself open to when you're controlled by others. Look, if we thought that album was any good, we'd put it out in 1969, when it was made." (JH-MM78)

Regarding the recording of the songs that made up the "+ 5," Hayward later said, "At the time, we were under a lot of pressure from the record company to have a follow-up to 'Nights in White Satin.' Those songs were attempts to satisfy the record company."

The appearance of these "songs from the vaults" on *Caught Live + 5* reinforced the Moodies' belief that they should never preserve abandoned songs. Hayward referred to this when he said, "We learned long ago not to leave finished tracks 'in the can.' Once, we came to the end of a record contract and had several songs lying around [that] we didn't think were good enough to put out. The record company released them anyway." (JH-PD86)

Regarding "Please Think About It," one of the "+5" songs, Mike Pinder told Mark Murley of *Higher & Higher,* "That was a sort of connect-the-dots kind of song. I considered it feeble songwriting, really; one of those tracks that didn't really happen."

As for Decca's choice to include it on *Caught Live + 5,* Pinder said, "Record companies do amazing things, don't they?" (MP-H&H04)

Hayward and John Lodge, each having recently released his own initial solo album, and Graeme Edge, with the second album from the Graeme Edge Band issued at nearly the same time in America as *Caught Live + 5*, had further reason to be bothered by the record company's decision.

In the June 22 issue of *Variety*, when asked about the release of his first solo album, John Lodge said, "I was on the wrong foot to start with, because I was John Lodge of the Moody Blues. Now the Moody Blues latest album [*Caught Live + 5*] is out, so I'm competing with *myself*. Listening to some of the tracks on the 'new' Moodies album, they're so old I can't remember them!" (JL-V77)

In Britain, Decca delayed the release of *Caught Live + 5* until June, giving the Graeme Edge Band's *Paradise Ballroom* a six-week lead.

**U.S. album release:
London 5 PS 690/691;
April 30, 1977**

The Wherehouse record stores – and there were 44 of them just in the Los Angeles area in 1977 – had the two-record set on sale for $7.19, down from the list price of $10.98.

From *Billboard*, May 28:

> ... The concert sound is solid, doing justice to the lavish synthesizer production concepts so familiar in Moodies standards like "Nights in White Satin" and "Tuesday Afternoon." There are also several interesting and commercially viable songs among the five new titles. This is the first-ever Moody Blues, as a group, [and they] still retain a vast armada of loyal fans despite several years of only solo activity, and this set provides a new angle of vision on the soft vocals-lush synthesizer style that made the Moodies a top worldwide attraction. ...

> Dealers: This release should re-focus attention on the entire Moody Blues catalog and its various solo spinoffs, which are all still selling steadily.

From June 3, 1977, in Ontario, Canada's *The Ottawa Journal*, Ian Haysom called this release a "Moody Blues Must."

> This double-LP set is possibly the definitive early Moody Blues album. It contains, as the title suggests, three sides of live concert (the band's Albert Hall classic in 1969) and one side of five previously unreleased offerings. These five were recorded between May 1967 and November 1968, so there's no attempt at

pretending it's a new album, and obviously no hint of the later solo leanings of Hayward, Pinder, Thomas, Lodge, and Edge. But it's a must for Moody Blues fans and destined to become a collectors' item. The concert features most of the group's early biggies – "Never Comes the Day," "Nights in White Satin," "Ride My See-Saw," "Tuesday Afternoon," and "The Sunset" – and also shows how remarkably inventive they were as composers and stage performers. Some of the songs have interesting concert arrangements and the Albert Hall atmosphere has been captured perfectly. You can even hear the fret-moves on Hayward's guitar.

The other five offerings are all interesting, particularly Hayward's "King and Queen." ... The concert is a valid experience which deserves to be preserved and Side Four also deserves to see the light of day. In all, an exceptional classic. The Moody Blues' older music can still outpace most of today's loftier offerings.

U.K. album release:
Decca MB 3/4; June 1, 1977

By June 1, 1977, Decca of England felt both John Lodge's *Natural Avenue* (released in late January), Justin Hayward's *Songwriter* (from mid-February), and the Graeme Edge Band's *Paradise Ballroom* (issued in April) had been given a wide enough berth to leave their mark. *Caught Live + 5* was issued on June 1.

From the June 11 edition of *New Musical Express*, Chris Salewicz wrote:

> ... Although [releasing seven-year old material] does seem just a little redundant, it does serve to emphasize that the Moody Blues were the progenitors of the European School of Techno-flash Rock. They were already gargantuan – especially in the States where they were worshipped with an almost religious fervor – when E£P [Emerson, Lake and Palmer] was not even a twinkle in Greg £ake's eye.

We presume that Salewicz's use of the British pound symbol was an intentional implication that, in his opinion, ELP were just in it for the money.

Mr. Salewicz continued:

> … Now, not only did the Moody Blues get that symphorock number together and underpin it with their vocal and instrumental harmonies, but they had another very powerful string to their commercial bow – they wrote Meaningful Lyrics. They wrote about Life. Does not Ray Thomas state on "Dr. Livingstone, I Presume" that "We're all looking for someone?" And if you're into Rod McKuen that can seem like pretty heavy stuff. …

> Actually, what listening to Moody Blues *Caught Live + 5* really drives home is that they were the Eagles of their day. Beneath every histrionic arrangement or piece of bubblegum psychedelia (hints of Dave Mason-written Traffic numbers can be heard in several places on the three live sides) lies a string, well-arranged, late '60s pop song – having five writers in a band is always an advantage. And, as is also the case with the Eagles, the Moody Blues almost never rock out but stick to quasi-ballads.

> This is all reinforced by the five – as of in the album title – "new" (recorded in '67 and '68 actually) numbers. … [A]ll of them could probably have been hits for someone if they'd had cover jobs done on them. "Gimme a Little Somethin'," for example, has a vocal chorus line that could be the Tremeloes if one didn't know otherwise.

Melody Maker (date unknown) said:

> … They deserve much of the credit for broadening the spectrum of rock, one of the first bands to demonstrate how strings could be used without diminishing the credibility of the music … and opened the way for the introduction of much deeper and more serious elements in contemporary music … there's no denying their worth. …

Steve Rosen reviewed the album for *The Los Angeles Times*' June 17 edition:

> This two-record set culled from a 1969 concert exposes the frailties and shortcomings the English quintet all too often experienced on stage. The vocal harmonies are correct but possess none of the elegance nor gracefulness which characterized their recorded voices; the Mellotron (the instrument responsible for the string and horn sounds) is rarely in tune here and captures little of the orchestral majesty present on in-studio recordings. The five never-before-released studio tracks were recorded in 1967 and 1968, and except for Justin Hayward's "King and Queen" – a delightful cut a la "Tuesday Afternoon" – are a little more than novelty interest.

For the June 19 edition of *The Pittsburgh Press*, Pete Bishop wrote:

> The polite applause between songs on the Moody Blues *Caught Live +5* is so British it hurts. But, then, the Moodies, one of the best "listen-to" bands ever, never did lure the rowdies, and if you feel like just listening, you could do lots worse than this two-record set of their Royal Albert Hall concert Dec. 12, 1969.
>
> It has two of their infrequent hit singles, "Nights in White Satin" and "Tuesday Afternoon," and good jobs on lesser-known numbers like "Dr. Livingstone, I Presume," "Legend of a Mind" and "Peak Hour." It also includes the closing 12 minutes from *On the Threshold of a Dream*, and this was wise of them because to detach Moodies' songs is a bit unfair. Their albums should be heard uninterrupted to preserve the carefully crafted ambience.
>
> The "+5" refers to Side 4, five previously unreleased studio tracks. Only "Please Think About It," a ballad, doesn't measure up to other Moodies' work; the others, especially "Gimme a Little Somethin'," (easy rock, flows nicely) certainly do.

Texas's Doug Pullen, of the *Lubbock Avalanche-Journal*, opined on July 31:

> … As expected, the live segment is the most interesting. Recorded when *To Our Children's Children's Children* was the group's latest album, *Caught Live* opens with "Gypsy" and concludes with a fast moving version of the already harried "Ride My See-Saw."
> …
>
> The musicianship of keyboardist Mike Pinder, a virtual pioneer of the Mellotron, and guitarist Justin Hayward, makes itself apparent on *Caught Live*. Pinder's work is graceful and surrealistic, and his Mellotron fills on "Gypsy" are some of his best. Hayward is equally good, commanding his axe to bounce in minstrel-like fashion for some pieces and burn for the rock 'n' rollers.
>
> The "Plus Five" portion of the album is just that, five songs tacked on to warrant the release of a two-album set. The five songs included on Side Four are embarrassing, much like most of the Rolling Stones' *Metamorphosis* album which was released under similar circumstances.

From the October 27 issue of *Circus*, Michael Bloom wrote:

> … Listening to *Caught Live + 5*, I now know the story. It should have been obvious all along; The Moody Blues were the first of the ultra-produced pop legends, with a zillion guitar overdubs and all sorts of orchestral noises on every one of their favorite tracks. For them to reproduce all of that in concert would have taken a platoon of guitarists and pianists. Needless to say, since they

brought none of the above onstage with them, their live sound was as full of holes as any garage band's.

They did possess one quality that no garage band had, though: their ultimately serene and mellifluous aahs. This was the heart of the Moody Blues' appeal: their aahs and oohs transmitted more pure sybaritic delight than a school of whales lolling at low tide or harem right in any Arabian court. Even when they did it onstage, that sound bypassed the brain's intellectual circuitry and nestled up the pleasure center like a kitten in one's lap.

Only two of the dead dogs tacked onto *Caught Live + 5* are worth a second listen, and, predictably, they're both by Justin Hayward. Hayward has always been the master of the joyous moan because his voice is the warmest and his compositions the least preachy. This double set is for hardcore fans only.

Such critical disparagements aside, there were plenty of fans who handed over their money at the record stores. *Caught Live +5* was the ninth Moody Blues album – following the "Classic Seven" studio albums and the *This Is the Moody Blues* compilation – to go gold in America. In fact, it shipped gold. And, according to London Records, sales of all Moody Blues albums combined had now passed the 25 million mark.

Caught Live + 5 peaked in *Billboard* on July 22 at No. 26 (for two weeks of its 15 week chart run).

In England, where the trendiness of pop music was far worse than in America – "when you're hot, you're hot; when you're not, you're not" – the album failed to excite. It was the first Moody Blues LP to miss the charts.

A second compilation was being prepared for the English market at this time – *The Great Moody Blues* – and, for this, the great Moody Blues regrouped, to be sure that *this time* they were okay with the repacking of their songs. This, in turn, stimulated the rumor mills concerning a reunion.

Sometimes, after all, rumors turn out to be true.

32

Octave, 1978

Album release:
Decca THS 129 (U.K.); London PS 708 (U.S.); June 9, 1978
U.K. peak position: #6
(Certified gold in the U.K.)
Netherlands: #7
Canada: #9
(Certified platinum in Canada)
Norway: #9
Sweden: #12
U.S.: #13 (*Billboard* and *Cashbox*)
(Certified platinum in the U.S.)
New Zealand: #14
Germany: #15

Single release:
Justin Hayward: *"Forever Autumn"* b/w *"The Fighting Machine"*
CBS 6368 (U.K.); Columbia 3-10799 (U.S.); June 2, 1978
U.K. peak position: #5
U.S.: #20 (*Billboard* Adult Contemporary)
U.S. Hot 100: #34 (*Cashbox*)

Single release:
"Steppin' in a Slide Zone" b/w "I'll Be Level with You"
Decca F 13790 (U.K.); London 5N270 (U.S.); July 14, 1978
U.S.: #39 (*Billboard* Hot 100)
Canada: #41
Australia: #78

Single release:
"Driftwood" b/w "I'm Your Man"
Decca F 13809 (U.K.); London 5N273; October 6, 1978
U.S.: #38 (*Billboard* Adult Contemporary Chart)
U.S. #59 (*Billboard* Hot 100)
Canada: #60

Single releases:
"Had to Fall in Love" b/w "I'm Your Man"
Decca Y-11833 (Australia); 1978
"Had to Fall in Love" b/w "Steppin' in a Slide Zone"
Decca 6103 116 (Netherlands); 1978
Decca 26.566-Y (Belgium); 1978
Chart positions unknown

Single releases:
Justin Hayward: *"Marie" b/w "Heart of Steel"*
Decca F 13834; April 13, 1979
Non charting

In late June, 1977, rumors began circulating – the Moodies were reuniting to make a new album … and this time it seemed for real.

The rumors arose after a series of meetings between Hayward, Lodge, Thomas, and Edge over Decca's decision to release a "new" Moody Blues compilation album. The press was late in finding out about this – the meetings had actually occurred the previous year.

Hayward told interviewer John Reed, "Mike Pinder was in America and we were in England, so we weren't seeing much of him, but the other four of us were meeting up and just laughing and joking and having a good time. So we thought, 'Why don't we just get together for old times' sake?' So we decided to set a date in the future, about 18 months ahead… to reconvene on that day and record." (JH-TRC99)

On July 9, 1977, Karen Herman Steffaro reported in Bridgewater, New Jersey's *The Courier-News* that Hayward, Lodge, Pinder, Thomas, and Edge were "officially back together again" with plans to enter the recording studio in September.

Weeks later, on July 30, in a wire story out of New York (home base of London Records), Sue Byrom reported:

The Moody Blues, who haven't worked together since the beginning of 1974, are now re-forming.

The British band was one of the most successful in the world at the height of its career. The members have been working as solo artists since they disbanded three years ago and have had considerable success as individuals, but nothing quite like the success they had together with songs like "Question" and "Knights [sic] In White Satin."

A couple of months ago, London Records released a group album called *Caught Live Plus Five*, which was their first live release and included five previously unreleased tracks. The album is a big hit and has gone gold.

Now the five Moodies: Graeme Edge, Justin Hayward, John Lodge, Michael Pinder, and Ray Thomas are going to re-group and record a new album. The group has booked studio time from September through November in Los Angeles, so the new album should be out sometime in the New Year. It will be the eighth album they've recorded together.

Talking with Ray Coleman of *Melody Maker*, Hayward said, "We never closed the door. Through all the solo albums and the success of *Blue Jays*, we all said to each other from time to time that we might get together again when it felt right.

"Around the middle of last year, we were all round at Ray Thomas's house and we said to each other that the solo pieces seem to have run their time, how about getting the band back together again? So we put it in the book for September 1977....

"Sure, there's been friction in the band, but it's not likely to break up again over ego. We realize now that we're a band full of producers, and as long as the guy who writes the song gets the last say on the approach and the sound, there shouldn't be any real trouble.

"Sometimes the writer of the song can't see the end of the tunnel, and for that reason we need a strong producer sometimes, to put his stamp on it. But I think we're older and wiser now. We know the ropes and how far we can push each other. The future looks good." (JH-MM78)

Recording the Album:

Even though the Moodies had their own studio in London, the decision was made to record the new album in Los Angeles. In exile from the punitive British tax man, Mike Pinder was living on a ranch in Malibu, in Los Angeles County. There were other reasons Pinder had made the decision to leave England, but taxes were certainly at the forefront. The same had been the case when Graeme Edge took to his yacht for the better part of a year.

The Beatles had sung about it on their 1966 album, *Revolver*, with George Harrison's bitter "Taxman." In Britain a multimillionaire could be taxed as much as 95%

of their earnings in the 1960s, '70s, and '80s. It was called the "Supertax." Under this structure, each time a person's annual income went up, they were bumped into a higher tax bracket. The result was that many rock stars actually took home less money than when their records sold half as many copies. That's why Harrison name-checked Conservative Party leader Harold Wilson and Labour Party leader Edward Heath, echoing the government's tax demands: "There's one for you, nineteen for me."

One break in the tax law came into effect if an individual, or group, spent a year outside of England. This prompted many bands to go on extensive tours abroad, or record albums in other countries. The Rolling Stones fled England because of the crushing tax laws. When they recorded 1971's *Exile on Main Street* in France, it was corporate taxes which drove the Stones from their homeland. John Lennon had left England by this time, for New York City. Others to travel outside of the country to live, or record albums: Cat Stevens, Jethro Tull, Tom Jones, Bad Company, Ringo Starr, Rod Stewart, David Bowie, and Marc Bolen (T. Rex). So, it wasn't completely unexpected when, in 1977, the rest of the Moody Blues and their producer Tony Clarke flew to L.A. to join Pinder.

Record Plant West, at 8456 West 3rd Street, Hollywood, was chosen for recording a "reunion album" for a group which had never officially dissolved. The studio had a rich history, beginning at the outset of the 1970s when it first opened for business. Among some classics recorded there prior to *Octave*: *James Gang Rides Again*; America's *Homecoming* and *Hat Trick*; Billy Joel's *Piano Man*; the Eagles' *On the Border*; Lynyrd Skynyrd's *Second Helping*; Joe Walsh's *So What?*; John Lennon's *Rock and Roll*; the Allman Brothers Band's *Win, Lose or Draw*; Boston's self-titled debut; Fleetwood Mac's *Rumours*; and Supertramp's *Even in the Quietest Moments*.

Not all the Moodies were keen on leaving England for an extended period, especially when they had their state-of-the-art Threshold Studio One available. Justin Hayward told *Sounds* magazine, "As long as I've got what I need I'm fine. I wouldn't get up and shift out of England just for money. Things would have to get pretty desperate, and I don't think that would happen. I always have 'Nights in White Satin,' and I'm getting cover versions of it every week!" (JH-S78)

But Hayward felt he had little choice in the matter. He told interviewer Mark Powell, "Mike had moved to California and didn't want to come back to England to record, so for the first time we left Britain and made an album in America. I think we all felt like fish out of water." (JH-O08)

The sessions began with the last song heard on the LP. Hayward told Jon Bream of *The Minneapolis Star*, "On our first day of recording – September 1, 1977 – we went into the studio in Los Angeles and somebody said, 'Anybody got any songs?' I played 'The Day We Meet Again,' and then everybody said, 'Let's do it!' We got something down the first day. It kind of broke the ice." (JH-MS78)

Come the New Year, the Moodies were still recording songs for what would become *Octave*. But then the first major mishap in the making of *Octave* occurred. On January 10, Studio C at Record Plant West was destroyed in an electrical fire. At the time, rocker Marshall Chapman was working in Studio B. While the fire department was en route, Chapman, along with other musicians and engineers, carried master recordings to safety outside the building, including many of the *Octave* tapes. She said, "We might as well have been rescuing Rembrandts from the Louvre. ... I remember seeing "Hotel

California" [written] on one, and "John Lennon" on another. I nearly fainted when I saw I was holding a box containing the master tape from Stevie Wonder's *Songs in the Key of Life*." (MC-GLRAR04)

Despite the efforts of many to save the valuable recordings, much of the material the Moodies had recorded was lost. Only a handful of songs were salvaged.

With the studio closed for months, Mike Pinder offered his home studio at Indigo Ranch, in Malibu. The band began the process of rerecording the material destroyed in the fire.

THE MOODY BLUES

Justin Hayward: "The songs we did in the funky studio sounded better in the laidback studio, and we were able to see the musical return of the Moody Blues in a different light, just from that experience which resulted from the fire. ..." (JH-MM78)

As for the approach to the album, the Moodies were dead set against following trends, just as they had always been. Hayward told Linda Barber of the *Detroit Free Press*, "We established ourselves a long time ago, and we're not at all influenced by the trends. I don't think our fans would want us to be. New Wave and Punk have been good for the business. The musical energy in England over the last five years has been tremendous – so many things have come out of it – but it doesn't affect the Moodies or the Moodies' audience." (JH-DFP78)

While Hayward may have liked the sound they were getting better in Pinder's studio compared to "the funky studio," Record Plant West, problems continued to plague the band. Tony Clarke said that recording at Indigo was difficult because it was "15 hundred feet up in the hills of Malibu," and much of that drive was on a windy dirt road. This became even more treacherous because January is the height of the rainy season in Los Angeles. In 1978, the torrential rains had been particularly bad, resulting in massive mudslides.

Tony Clarke: "They never had rain like it in living history. The roads were washed out; people's swimming pools would be hanging out over the Pacific Coast Highway with no soil underneath. It was so dreadful. And Justin and I were in a car crash, because the mud was so deep. I mean, we're talking nine or ten inches of mud, with the whole thing trying to head toward the Pacific. ... We were in a hired car, and Justin was driving, and I was in the passenger seat. And I saw a car about a mile away, heading toward us. It was night, and this car got nearer and nearer, and we actually collided at the light. There was no way [to avoid it]; no traction; you couldn't stop. And... the police came and arrested Justin, *for about three minutes* – [and held him] in the back of a black and white, being interviewed, as an *alien*! ...

"I remember one night it was so washed out I had led a torch light procession – we couldn't take the car any further; we had to go on foot. So, with torch in hand, we made it the rest of the way up there to Indigo Ranch, to do *nothing*." (TC-CA:TMB06)

Justin Hayward remained more upbeat … for a while. He told *Sounds* magazine, "We just had a lot of bad luck…. Still, once we had that studio door closed, everything was fine. We actually spent about three months in the studio out of the six." (JH-S78)

The album, in order:

"Steppin' in a Slide Zone" might be John Lodge's chronicle of being whisked away from home, with someone else in the driver's seat, to make the Moody Blues' new album. Once in California, "I took a ride in a limousine / I took a road I've never been / I met a stranger by the way / His coat was torn but his eyes were clear / Standing in a slide zone / I could be steppin' in a time zone."

With all that was going wrong, it's no wonder that Lodge began to wonder whether carrying on with *Octave* was the right decision. He explained, "I started to question – in my heart, and philosophy, and karma – I questioned the whole thing about, 'Should we be making this album.' … And so, I wrote a song called 'Steppin' in a Slide Zone.'" (JL-CA:TMB06)

Further metaphors in the lyrics: "He went to find a shooting star / Around the bend, that's where they are / I went along just for the ride / Suddenly I began to glide / Standing in a slide zone / I could be steppin' in a time zone."

The song opens the album with the building sounds of a synthesizer. It's the perfect accompanying soundtrack for a journey through time … from 1972 … to 1977, the distance between the recording sessions for *Seventh Sojourn* and *Octave*. Justin Hayward plays slow, bluesy guitar licks over the synthesizer, leading into the vocal portion of the song.

What we hear from this point out is certainly faithful to the Moody Blues sound, as all the voices join in three-or four-part harmony. But the layers of voices, instruments, and synthesizers combine to create a muddled wall of sound. The melody of the song is limited, even redundant, as if Lodge was trying for his own "Tomorrow Never Knows" (from the Beatles' *Revolver*). But it never really hooks the listener enough to succeed.

It is interesting to compare it to the live version of this song, recorded in 1978, included on the 2008 remastered *Octave* CD. The opening "journey through time" sequence has a great deal more clarity and punch, and the vocals throughout are cleaner, the words more audible. It is superior in very nearly all ways to the studio version, even though this was captured with primitive 1978 audio equipment at the Summit, Houston, Texas, before an audience of thousands.

"Under Moonshine" was the first of Ray Thomas's requisite two tracks per album, both with orchestration arranged and conducted by Dr. Terry James, who worked with Thomas on his solo ventures.

Justin Hayward: "The group's always gotten along well; we've never had any ego problems, and everybody wants the same thing – for it to be good, for it to be the best. What makes that possible is that each of the members contributes, and makes the band what it is – five completely different personalities. That's what makes it right." (JH-DFP78)

Or, sometimes, five Moodies can make it wrong.

"Under Moonshine" has a lyric that is hard to comprehend. The lines are interesting: "Creator of dreams that melt with the sun / I'll tell you the things this man has done / He was a saint and a sinner rolled in one / But I'll miss him now that he's gone." Who was Thomas singing about? Himself, or a long-lost acquaintance from his days in the Saints and Sinners? And what does the rest of the lyric have to do with this individual? Lines such as, "Under moonshine, that's where I've been / Under moonshine, I'm clearly seen," only add to the confusion. They seem to be mere fragments that don't fit together.

The same can be said of the tune. Just as the words were challenging, it is equally difficult to grasp the structure of the melody. All the different sections – verse, chorus, middle eight, alternate verse (as it seems to be), and alternate chorus (as it seems to be), seem to relate to each other, but also seem strangely incompatible.

There are other voices on the song – the other Moodies. Sometimes they sing in harmony with Thomas, such as on that first chorus; other times they come close to singing a countermelody. What they mostly seem to do is step on one another.

At one point in the song, Thomas sings, "Or maybe I'm crazy / Also they say I'm lazy / But I'll have my days / When I do as I please / You won't see the woods / While you're a tree...."

The song does seem a little crazy. Its ambiguous structure does seem a little lazy. Thomas was indeed doing as he pleased. And it certainly is difficult to see the forest through the trees with this song.

The good news is that the song benefits greatly on the 2008 CD remaster. When played on a good sound system, all the intricacies of "Under Moonshine" can be recognized, even if they still seem somewhat ill-suited for one another.

Coming on the heels of "Steppin' in a Slide Zone," which challenged the listener in its own ways, the album was now two for two with songs that didn't quite live up to the listeners' expectations of the Moody Blues, especially after more than a five-year wait. A pair of missteps right out of the gate – even if only on first and second listening – can taint an album for a reviewer. All the good that follows may fall on deaf ears.

Fortunately, the charming **"Had to Fall in Love"** helps the album reconnect to the listener. Unlike the previous two cuts, this relaxed and pleasant Justin Hayward song, enhanced by a lovely down-home harmonica accompaniment from Ray Thomas, is immediately accessible.

Hayward sings: "The places I've seen / And the roads in between / Make me wonder why / I'm searching for my dreams up in the sky / I heard the call / And in the mirror I saw / The writing on the wall / And I had to fall ... in love with you."

One reviewer compared this track to the sound of Neil Young, no doubt because of the soulful, mournful, melodic harmonica. Whether one agrees with this comparison or not, "Had to Fall in Love" is lovely.

Mike Pinder liked this song, but found the guitar part to be very monotonous, and he couldn't find anything to add to the track. Keyboards didn't work, nor did the strings of a Mellotron or Chamberlin. Fortunately Ray Thomas was able to find the perfect addition.

Regarding **"I'll Be Level with You,"** Graeme Edge told Bob Edmands of *New Musical Express*, "My song is about my new son, who's 18 months old, and what I hope for him in life. That's all we can write about; what's going on around us." (GE-NME78)

As with many of the songs credited to Graeme Edge, the other Moodies lent a hand in the creation of the tune and the arrangement, and then shared the vocals. In four-part harmony, the band sings, "Little guy, little hands, little eyes and lots of time / What you gonna be, what you gonna see / When your eyes are level with mine? / I'll be level with you / I don't know what I would do / If I had to face the things that you've got coming down the line."

In the 1970s, there was a great deal coming down the line. People were talking about overpopulation (Dr. Paul Ehrlich's 1968 book *The Population Bomb*). A change in world climate was feared, with scientists pointing out evidence of a coming cooldown – in 1974 and 1975 both *Time* and *Newsweek* printed articles about an impending "Cooling World." Political terrorism, the threat of nuclear war, and increased drug use were other controversial topics for news *and* the arts. The ever-changing music scene was pushing into disco, then punk, and away from the seemingly harmlessness of our rock and roll roots.

Wanting to protect your child from the outside world's turbulence is admirable. But the way this sentiment is turned into a pop song is not entirely successful. The song feels rushed, and too busy. Once the singing stops and the instruments are allowed off the leash, so to speak, potential begins to show. But, by then, the track is too soon fading down.

From this point forward, every song on *Octave* is a winner. But, of the first four tracks, three came across awkwardly, and the one that worked felt more like a solo recording than a group effort. This would be reflected in many of the reviews.

Now on, to calmer seas.

Like "Had to Fall in Love," **"Driftwood"** compares extremes, from ambition and stardom to personal relationships and the elation of finding love, and the fear of losing it.

Hayward sings: "Just like the driftwood of a dream / Left on the seashore of sleep / Just like the words that wouldn't rhyme / Lost in the desert of time / Time waits for no one at all / No, not even you / You thought you'd seen it all before / You really thought you knew … I've shattered the illusion / Of fortune and fame / But, darling, now I know you / Life can never be the same / Oh no, don't leave me driftwood on the shore."

The melody is beautiful, much in the style of "New Sensations" from *Seventh Sojourn*. R.A. Martin contributed the lovely and bluesy saxophone accompaniment. The string sounds that you hear aren't strings at all, but either a Mellotron or Chamberlin, no doubt courtesy of Mike Pinder.

"Top Rank Suite" might have fit Justin Hayward's *Songwriter* album more than a Moody Blues LP. But it is an enjoyable track and one of *Octave*'s highlights.

As for the mystifying lyrics, Hayward seemed to be writing his own "American Pie," using metaphors to trace the evolution of rock 'n' roll. "Top Rank Suite" uses the same approach in retracing the story of the Moody Blues.

When Hayward sings, "They made a good bowl of chili at the jazz club," he is likely alluding to the early Moodies' reputation and local fame at London's Marquee Club, known for presenting jazz music. The Moodies weren't a jazz band, but rhythm and blues, which may explain the reference to them making chili – a dish considered too hot for the venue, but which went down fine nonetheless.

When he sings, "They played a good game of football in Mucron," the line likely refers to the reformed Moodies in late 1966 making the decision to perform their own stage show, and trying that show out in Mucron (also spelled Mouscron), Belgium.

The lyrics "They got everyone off at the Top Rank, babe / If you could ever get into their suite / Avenue Tombola and social / We just drove right on by" is a gabfest of odd images, and likely refers to the time when the Moodies returned to London, recorded *Days of Future Passed*, and then went on the road to introduce their new image and music to England. There is a series of music halls in England called "Top Rank Suite." "Tombola" was the name of the "social" club where Justin Hayward and Mike Pinder purchased the band's first Mellotron, the instrument that brought about the greatest change in the Moodies' recorded music and stage shows.

Easier to interpret are the lines, "We're on our way to the big time, baby / To the great gold record in the sky / But can you tell me why?" The Beatles were the only English band to have been presented with more gold and platinum record awards than the Moody Blues had been by this time – those great gold records in the sky. But the immense success had taken its toll on both the Beatles and the Moodies, prompting the question, "But can you tell me why?"

R.A. Martin, who played the saxophone on "Driftwood," returns, arranging and playing the saxophones heard on this track.

"I'm Your Man" is deeply personal. Ray Thomas's marriage had hit a difficult period prior to the making of *Octave*. The subject of "For My Lady" now appeared to be the recipient of "I'm Your Man."

Thomas sings: "Here I go again / Finding it so hard to explain / The way I feel when I hold you near / Still, it hurts when you cry / Maybe you think love has passed you by / Don't you know I need you so / But I guess you'll need to know / I'm just a man, that's all I am / I'm just a man that's yours."

The jazzy arrangement fits the broader picture of the Moody Blues sound. Mike Pinder and Graeme Edge, like Thomas, were fond of jazz music; you may recall that the early Moodies thought of themselves as a combination rock & soul, jazz, and rhythm & blues combo. It made an interesting combination, and "I'm Your Man" is a very pleasant track. This was also the second of two songs – both by Thomas – to benefit from a string arrangement from Dr. Terry James.

"Survival," written by John Lodge, has a simplistic structure built around a rich and distinctive melody. The Moodies, like the Beatles, had a gift for creating tunes that were instantly accessible and moving, filled with catchy hooks, and recorded with lush beauty, usually augmented with exquisite vocal harmonies. This is all present in "Survival."

Shortly after the release of *Octave*, John Lodge told a reporter, "Although I think the Moodies' music has been [described] as being grand, pretentious, or ethereal, or lush, or whatever adjective it is, the important thing is that it takes time making it still sound simple, if that makes sense. It's very easy to put 50 notes into a bar of music. It's very difficult to just put two notes in but give it the same effect." (JL-OWH79)

The structure of a typical hit single – since the origins of sound recording in the 1900s – was simplicity: Verse, chorus, verse, chorus, middle eight (bars), verse, chorus. "Survival" excels with this formula – a hit by any other name. It's too bad that it was not issued as a single (except in Italy).

The orchestration on this track was arranged and conducted by Jimmie Haskell, the composer of numerous film scores, and three-time Grammy winner, for orchestrating Bobbie Gentry's "Ode to Billie Joe," Chicago's "If You Leave Me Now," and Simon and Garfunkel's "Bridge Over Troubled Waters."

"One Step into the Light" is Mike Pinder's only contribution to the album as both writer and lead singer. Graeme Edge said, "Mike's song is very introspective. Typical of Mike." (GE-NME78)

Pinder sings: "One step into the light / One step away from night / It's the hardest step you're gonna take / The ship to take you there / Is waiting at the head of the stairs / That leads up through your opened mind."

Mike Pinder often received criticism for writing "cosmic" lyrics like this, but others appreciated his beliefs, convictions, and boldness. Pinder was never pretentious because he truly believed in what he wrote. And the messages were always positive. On the other hand, the current trend was musical questions such as "Do you think I'm sexy?" Few critics seemed bothered over this. Strange days, indeed.

Many responded to the spiritual, and even the religious, aspects of those songs. Justin Hayward said at the time, "I can understand the religious aspect. We were born in the psychedelic era and we had a lot of religious ideas ourselves. Songwriting is a spiritual kind of feeling. One minute your mind's empty, the next minute you've got something. You've created something out of thin air. It's a very spiritual feeling. ...

"The Moodies are based on that original premise – expressing the problems of ordinary people and the hopes of a generation in a sincere and honest way." (JH-MS78)

I ask you – what on earth could be wrong with that?

Beyond its lyric, the song is tastefully symphonic, with Pinder performing his magic on Mellotron and Chamberlin. His vocal is gentle and soothing, making "One Step into the Light" one of the album's finest tracks.

"The Day We Meet Again," by Justin Hayward, was the first song recorded for *Octave*. Hayward said, "We started the recording with a song that I had written called 'The Day We Meet Again,' which is quite appropriate. And, as I put the cans [headphones] on and ran it down, I thought, 'Yeah. That's that band again.'" (JH-SP78)

Graeme Edge said, "Justin's written a beautiful song called 'The Day We Meet Again,' which could be about a boy and a girl, or about us 'lot' meeting in the studio. Depends on how you want to look at it." (GE-NME78)

Shortly after the completion of the album, Hayward said, "The music reflected the things we were going through in our own lives. We had settled down. We didn't develop a theme, though half way through [making the album] we had five tracks that fit a concept. It was the story of a guy we call 'The Moody Blues.' If you put each of us together to make one guy, it would be his story." (JH-MS78)

When you read the lyric, and consider the song's circumstances, it is hard to imagine it not being about the reunion of the Moody Blues.

Hayward sings, "The day we meet again / I'll be waiting there / I'll be waiting there for you / 'Cause the years have been so lonely / Like a dog without a home / It's dangerous when you find out / You've been drinking on your own … But just in case you're wondering / What was really on my mind / It wasn't what you took, my love / It's what you left behind / And just in case you're wondering / Will it really be the same / You know we're only living for / The day we meet again."

The melody and arrangement, driven by keyboards and augmented by Hayward's twelve-string, is remarkably uncomplicated, yet the pure and simple beauty carries it through for all of its more than six minutes.

***

There was more going wrong for the Moodies while trying to make *Octave* than mere fire and rain, mudslides and car wrecks. John Lodge said, "Absolutely *everything* that could go wrong making an album went wrong. … Tony Clarke, who's producing it – his marriage went wrong. So… his mind was elsewhere." (JL-CM:TMB06)

Graeme Edge: "Tony Clarke was going through severe domestic problems – deeply broken-hearted kind of 'severe.' In fact, I don't think he ever recovered." (GE-CB:TMB06)

Tony Clarke: "I was going through a personal crisis, and we were far from home – which was unusual – for a long time. … I don't think anybody was particularly happy with *Octave*. It was done under great duress." (TC-CB:TMB06)

Something was also going wrong between Mike Pinder and the four other Moodies. He said, "We'd had four years apart because we'd done the world tour which ended in 1974… we were then apart 'til 1978 [sic; September 1977 through early 1978]. The band was totally inactive, on a sabbatical. New people came into our lives; people got married; people got divorced; all those kinds of things. When we got back together… it wasn't the same thing." (MP-CB95)

Justin Hayward: "The album was a little painful to make. … It was quite obvious after a few weeks [at Indigo] that Mike's heart really wasn't into it anymore…" (JH-O08)

Pinder doesn't concur with this. He believes other complications were at play, giving one example: "I was working out a song with Justin, and [Graeme] kept interrupting me. And I was being creative – in terms of it was the idea of the moment, with the song, which is the way that I always worked with Justin. … You know, the juices were flowing – and it was like, 'Can you hold off?' And he wasn't, so I just said something wrong. … 'Can you shut up; you're just the drummer,' or something like that. And of course I hurt him. And of course I realized it. And I really didn't mean it."

Pinder believes that Graeme Edge has not yet forgotten the outburst or forgiven the remark. He added, "And I've tried various ways to sort of let him know – through other people – that, you know, I'm sorry that *that* happened. So, that's unfortunate." (MP-CA:TMB06)

One can certainly understand Edge's feelings. He was not "just the drummer," but also a lyricist for the band. His poems, and Pinder's recital of those verses, had made for a wonderful collaboration; all the more reason for the sadness associated with an unfortunate incident.

To better understand Pinder's state of mind, consider his description of another incident. "Justin had already got a song that was written, and already got a guitar part – that was a very monotonous part. It was a good song, but the guitar part was very monotonous, and it went all the way through. And I tried putting some Mellotron on there, and piano, and said, 'I'm sorry, just nothing fits with this. It just isn't happening, you know.' So, I just didn't know where to go with it. Things just sort of went downhill. I think maybe they thought I wasn't able to do it anymore, or something. … But you can't put strings to everything… and it just wasn't working out, and I was just getting frustrated. And I remember Graeme coming up to me one day while we were there and he sort of let me have it – his opinion of what was going on. And he couldn't have been more wrong." (MP-CB:TMB06)

Edge, as well as Justin Hayward, felt that Pinder didn't care anymore, or care as deeply. To that opinion, Pinder said that Edge couldn't have been more wrong. There were other things Pinder felt Edge was wrong about. Consider the following statement by Edge, concerning Pinder: "He was a very talented man before he believed his own press. A great, great guy – a great asset. … I don't want to say too much about Mike because I don't want to put anybody down, but he got religion bad. One week he was a Hopi and the next week he was worshipping the sun. He hardly worked at all on the album. Most of the keyboard parts were done by John and Justin, who, given enough takes, are very competent keyboardists." (GE-MD86)

Hayward talked about Pinder's level of commitment: "I think there was a feeling [from Mike] that it was over. It was like *Octave* was, 'Okay, it's a comeback album, but then it's finished.' Well, the rest of us didn't feel like that – *the other four guys didn't feel like that*." (JH-CB:TMB06)

Graeme Edge: "Well, it was a very difficult time for us because, as it turned out, two men weren't really 'on.' So the other four of us had a real struggle to get through that one. And Mike Pinder, in my opinion, just seemed to run out of feeling for it." (GE-H&H87)

Justin Hayward: "I saw the split coming. Towards the end of making *Octave*, I could see it all falling apart. I was frightened we were going to lose Tony and Mike…. I could see the same danger signs I saw when we broke up in 1973 [sic; 1974]. With all this going on, the sessions were a bit difficult." (JH-LAT81)

Before long, the prediction came true. But were the others right that Pinder wanted out, or did he feel he had to leave because of the vibe he was picking up from the them? It's an unknowable "chicken-or-egg" situation.

Mike Pinder: "At the point with *Octave* where things got bad, it was like, 'I don't want to be a part of this anymore. If it's not all fun and love and happiness, and [us] getting along with each other, then I don't want to be a part of it. And so I ended up not going to the sessions anymore, because it was, like, 'Why do I want to go somewhere where I'm going to be unhappy?' So I just stepped away." (MP-CA:TMB06)

Justin Hayward: "I was really annoyed that Mike didn't want to go on, and that he wasn't writing enough great songs, so I could play on them, and show off my guitar techniques on. But that's life, and you mustn't expect people to be what you want them to be. … I respected the courage [Mike and Tony] had, to take the position and say, 'That's it for me.' It's very brave." (JH-CA:TMB06)

This too is a telling statement, Hayward's judgment that Pinder "wasn't writing enough great songs." Pinder may have sensed this reaction to his material. In numerous interviews, nearly all the Moodies admitted shyness about presenting their latest songs when the time came to record a new album. The band members, as well as Tony Clarke and recording engineer Derek Varnals, have said how, at the start of each album, the band would sit around a table, with guitars, and each would present their latest songs. It was difficult to get someone to go first. It's easy to understand this, since the songs the Moodies wrote were often intensely personal.

Justin Hayward: "I was never in competition with Mike, whereas a lot of the other guys have always thought they were in competition with me. Mike never thought he was in competition with me and I was never in competition with him, and our egos never clashed. But he knew I loved the stuff he did and, in truth, I don't think we did justice to a lot of his things, maybe because it was so many big egos; five big egos in a group." (JH-RC12)

Mike Pinder knew that Hayward loved his songs … during the making of the first seven albums. But this appeared to have changed, and it's human nature to want to be around the people who appreciate us the most.

Mike Pinder: "I left the group to lead a normal life. I realized that if I put so much energy into writing a song, why not put that same amount of energy into raising a family and holding a marriage together, which is exactly the reason why I decided to give it up. Plus, the time was right. I felt that we'd done our best work." (MP-CB95)

Immediately after the completion of *Octave*, Pinder married Tara Grant, whom he had met one year earlier, and the two moved to Hawaii where they had two sons – Michael (born in 1979) and Matthew (born in 1980).

Pinder told *Echoes of the Sixties* authors Marti Smiley Childs and Jeff March, "I experienced and had all of the things I could possibly want and all of the experiences money could buy, and I came back to what really is what I consider to be the most valuable thing in life – raising a family. Having children is the greatest test that any human being can take, without a doubt." (MP-EOTS99)

Justin Hayward: "Mike, for me, was one of the greatest musicians and talents that ever played in a rock group. … I knew he was leaving; it was coming on and I could see it coming. So, it wasn't something sudden. It was a big empty space in my life. And I still miss him to this day. … I looked up to him, and to have him there in the early years was my one big inspiration. I have to put it like that. … But he's always been sadly missed. But he didn't want to do it, and that's it." (JH-RC12)

Tony Clarke was the next to go. Marital problems caused Clarke's return to England, away from the sessions for a while. Hayward said, "With Mike and Tony now gone, it concentrated our resolve as it was down to the four of us to finish the album. I think it was that experience that brought us together and we resolved that we would carry on." (JH-O08)

Graeme Edge said of *Octave*, "That's just full of pain. Poor Tony Clarke was going through such agonies, and losing Mike Pinder was hard. … Poor Tony Clarke was just going through a divorce, and it took Justin half an hour to talk him off the edge of a cliff…. That's just what you need when you're making your comeback album. It was a bit of a mess, but the four of us came out of it solid." (GE-MD86)

Pip Williams, who would replace Clarke as the Moodies' producer for the next couple of albums, also confirmed that Clarke didn't make it to through to the end: "He had bowed out halfway through *Octave*, which was finished by John and Justin." (PW-MW83)

But when asked if he walked out before the completion of the album, Clarke contradicted statements made by Hayward, Edge, Williams, and others, saying, "No, indeed. I went the distance. *We all did*."

According to Clarke, he continued working on the album long after the recording sessions had ended. Again, responding to any statements that he left the project prematurely, Clarke said, flatly, "I dispute that. If that was the case, how come I was cutting [*Octave*] in New York months later? I saw the album right through to the end and out the other side. I was responsible for that album, don't forget, and I had to deliver it, which I did. I've never walked out on a production." (TC-H&H85)

Part of Clarke's statement is confirmed by a news story from spring 1979 – that he was at least involved in the post-production phase of *Octave*. The April 21, 1978 issue of *Back Stage* reported that Clarke was mixing the sessions from both the Record Plant and Indigo Ranch at Little Mountain Sound in Vancouver, Canada. The article reported:

> Producer Tony Clarke, used to European studios, has been searching for a North American facility with the same super-sensitive monitoring capabilities. He said he found it at Little Mountain Sound.
>
> Engineer on the mix, Little Mountain's Roger Monk, described his equipment: "It scares some producers away," he said. "They're not ready to hear what they've really got on tape."

Clarke obviously wanted to hear what he and the Moodies had really gotten on tape.

***

The music industry of 1978 seemed light years away from that of 1974, when the Moody Blues had last worked together, a time when they were able to maintain control over their releases. And it was felt that new times called for new approaches in record cover/sleeve designs. At first, the Moodies were all right with the idea.

Justin Hayward told Linda Barber of the *Detroit Free Press*, "We just wanted a change in covers, and we don't have the amount of control as we did. And we've changed, as well. The music is a little bit harder, a bit more gutsy than anything we've done before." (JH-DFP78)

Although the band posed for the album cover, they weren't entirely sure of this new direction, which included their photo on the cover rather than a work of art, depicting the theme of the record.

Hayward said, "I'm not sure if we actually all agreed on that sleeve – it was a record company design, and it just got taken away from us and slipped through our hands

652

a little bit. In fact, the next time we got involved with the sleeve design was with the following album, *Long Distance Voyager*, when I was determined to use that painting. …

"The thing around *Octave* was partly due to the fact that, as record company staff increased, they started creating jobs for themselves. Suddenly, someone would say, 'Oh, I'm the sleeve guy now; we don't let the artists do that anymore,' which was ridiculous. These things go in cycles, though." (JH-RS13)

John Kosh, recent Grammy winner for his work on Linda Ronstadt's *Simple Dreams* LP, got the assignment. He was the creative director for the Beatles' Apple Records in the late 1960s and oversaw the design of the *Abbey Road* and *Let It Be* album covers. Kosh came to the project with outstanding credentials.

Regarding the album cover, Mark Mehler wrote in *Circus* magazine:

> On the cover of the Moody Blues' new album, *Octave*, the five band members are pictured walking through a doorway into a blinding white light. Drummer Graeme Edge, like Lot's wife in the Bible, is looking over his shoulder, as if to say goodbye forever.
>
> Opening up the gatefold, however, the Moodies are depicted walking confidently back through the same door. With purposeful strides, they seem to challenge the browser to buy the album.

John Lodge told Mehler, "What we wanted to say on the cover, is that the Moodies are a continuous thing – it's like getting on an elevator at one floor and getting up to the next floor. You're not in the same place, exactly, but you're still in the same building." (JL-C78)

***

For the May 1978 issue of the Australian music magazine *Union Recorder*, Mark Robinson wrote:

> They said it would never happen. Now it has! The Moody Blues are on the verge of return….
>
> The Moody Blues have been out of the music scene since 1973 [sic; 1974]. During the five [sic] years of their absence, they have been the focal point of much speculation concerning their

comeback. November '77 saw the production of *Octave*, their eighth album. ... Can it possibly achieve the acclaim they received for their last work? *Seventh Sojourn* earned a place in the Top 10 Australian albums of 1973. In the same year the Moody Blues were hailed as the "World's No. 1 Rock Band" by several English and American music papers. ...

The Moodies were often criticized for introducing on a large scale electronic music. It was said it took the "feeling" out of creativity, but instead it opened up new horizons in music potential. ...

Melodies that would stay in the mind, music that at times would leave you gasping and lyrics with something to say were the Moody Blues. ... The Moody Blues are still one of a kind. How many five-man bands are there that have four lead singers, five songwriters, and are capable of playing over 33 instruments? And well!

Here they stand, poised on the threshold of return. Can it ever be the same? ...

It was reported in May, before the release of *Octave*, that the worldwide sales of Moody Blues records now topped 26 million.

On May 6, Adam White reported in *Billboard* magazine:

First new record in 5 ½ years by the Moody Blues will ship next month, when London releases the band's *Octave* album. The label is preparing a simultaneous launch of the disk via 500 radio stations throughout the U.S. and plans a major sales and in-store merchandising program in support. ...

Octave is also the Moody Blues' first album of new material to appear on London since the quintet quietly dissolved its own Threshold label last year.

There is no single from the LP presently planned. London says a decision on this will depend on radio reaction, and consultations with the group.

The label adds that *Octave* was cut between September 1977 and this March, though it will not disclose the recording location (one newspaper report pinpoints Los Angeles). ...

The speculations about studio locations are an indication of the secrecy that surrounded the recording of the album. The Moodies were equally secretive as to their relationship with London Records. The article stated that the band's contractual commitment to the label was unknown, "though some sources say that they re-signed for five years upon the rundown of Threshold."

Billboard also reported that tight security would surround London Records' plan to premiere the album on hundreds of AM and FM radio stations with a pre-taped, one-hour "Octave" program. Stations would receive the tape on airdate, or the day before. In major markets, it would be hand-delivered.

Octave actually premiered one week ahead of schedule, on Saturday, June 10, 1978, on approximately 500 radio stations. It was estimated that an audience as high as 60 million may have been listening.

Right before the release of *Octave*, Tony Clarke told *Music Week*, "We spent some nine or ten months in the U.S., and when you are that closely involved with an album project, then obviously you arrive at a stage where it becomes difficult to be constructive about the end result. However, I did listen to the album the other day, and I must say that I was delighted with the way it turned out." (TC-MW78)

Years later, when interviewed for the Moody Blues fanzine, *Higher & Higher*, Clarke had a change of heart. Talking with interviewer Randy A. Salas, Clarke said that his history with the group was "too long, maybe. Maybe that was wrong – ten years with the same band. It's very difficult. You find yourself trying not to copy yourself, let alone [anybody] else. I think that for a long time I was one of the band; if the ideas and viewpoints change, well, things have to charge. … I didn't like the direction it was going on *Octave*. That spirit was missing, I thought." (TC-H&H85)

Justin Hayward was more upbeat. He told James Simon of the Associated Press, "There's a Moody Blues sound and we weren't about to move too far away from it, because it's *our* sound, *our* music. It's a good Moodies album, I think our best, and our old fans will be pleased … I think." (JH-TT78)

John Lodge told Mikal Gilmore of *Rolling Stone* that *Octave* was "1978 Moody Blues, with some healthy contrasts in style, including some straightforward rock 'n' roll tracks. … [O]bviously, we have a concern whether our audience is still there, but we're not going to know that until *Octave* comes out. All I know is that when I was in America last month, the amount of Moody Blues songs I heard over the airwaves was phenomenal. And the amount of mail we received saying it was unfair that we didn't make any new records, when people had followed us for such a long time, was touching. There's a responsibility there, whether you uphold it or not. We don't see this album as a one-shot thing." (JL-RS78)

Justin Hayward wasn't worried about changes in pop music; he believed there was room for Moody Blues music too. "People make the mistake of thinking that all young people are automatically going to be new wave fans. Not so. Millions of young people don't care about that sort of thing and want good songs done by anyone, nothing to do with how old the musician is. We know we can write songs well and we're going to get on with it for a second season, so to speak." (JH-MM78)

Single release:
Justin Hayward: *"Forever Autumn"*
b/w "The Fighting Machine"
CBS 6368 (U.K.); Columbia 3-10799 (U.S.);
June 2, 1978

Days before *Octave* was released, Justin Hayward had a new single out. He told Jon Beam of *The Minneapolis Star*, "If there's one thing I learned during the hiatus, it's that I realized there is room for both my solo career and the Moodies if I pace it right." (JH-MS78)

A big part of that solo career was Hayward's collaboration with Jeff Wayne (on this and future projects).

American-born actor, singer, and producer Jeff Wayne was the son of another American actor, singer, and producer – Jerry Wayne.

Jeff Wayne was the keyboardist for the Sandpipers, a group he left in 1966 to travel with his father to England, where the elder Wayne was appearing in a stage production of *Guys and Dolls*. No sooner had young Wayne left the Sandpipers, when the group struck with the 1966 U.S. Top 10 single, "Guantanamera."

While in England, Jeff Wayne composed the score for his father's 1966 West End musical based on Charles Dickens' *A Tale of Two Cities*, which caught on and spent two years at London's Palace Theatre. Following this, Wayne began writing commercial jingles. By the end of 1973, he estimated that he had written close to 1,200 of the ditties.

This prolific activity gave Jeff Wayne many inroads into other areas of the music world, allowing him to branch out into production. After seeing singer/actor David Essex in the role of Jesus in the London production of Godspell, Wayne produced *Rock On*, the first of several hit albums he made with Essex, which included the No. 1 single of the same title.

Jeff Wayne: "Back in the 1970s when I was working with David Essex… my father reminded me that one of my aspirations as a composer at the beginning of my career was to find and interpret two or three stories that I felt passionate about, and to conceive my take on them. It was in the second year of touring with David that someone passed me a copy of the book of H.G. Wells' *The War of the Worlds* to read, and what I discovered was this fantastic Victorian tale that had great vision, and I just fell in love with it." (JW-DOG09)

David Essex: "Jeff and I had done about five albums together. Then one day he said, 'I'm thinking about doing this concept album, *War of the Worlds*.' I told him it was a great idea, because it had been very controversial when Orson Welles did it as a radio play [on Halloween's Eve, 1938] in America." (DE-TG14)

Jeff Wayne: "I envisioned my version of *War of the Worlds* as an opera – story, leitmotifs, musical phrases, sounds and compositions that relate to the whole." (JW-TG14)

Much as Mike Pinder had done, Wayne had been experimenting on various electronic keyboards, such as the various early versions of the Moog synthesizer. He recalled, "[B]y the time the mid-1970s came around, when *The War of the Worlds* was my challenge, I was by then familiar with not only the Moog 3C, but all the synths that were growing out of those first generation of synthesizers, and *The War of the Worlds*

FOREVER AUTUMN

Recorded by JUSTIN HAYWARD on Columbia Records

Lyrics by PAUL VIGRASS & GARY OSBORNE   Music by JEFF WAYNE

DUCHESS MUSIC CORPORATION & JEFF WAYNE MUSIC LIMITED
Administered by MCA MUSIC PUBLISHING, A Division of MCA., Inc.
1755 Broadway, New York, NY 10019

Higher & Higher Sheet Music Insert #03

was the right story to blend both worlds – meaning, that when the story is being seen from the human characters' eyes the music was all orchestra and organic, whereas when it is seen from Martian eyes, with all their weaponry and machinery, it was all about the synths and the guitars. That was what was going on in my head!" (JW-DOG09)

The music tracks for most of Wayne's *War of the Worlds* were recorded in June 1976, utilizing the backing band Wayne had assembled for David Essex. Essex was cast for the spoken-word role of the Artilleryman, with third billing.

Wayne said, "During the composing period, I realized the Journalist character was the key – the thread that ran through the whole thing. I wanted someone with a voice that would take the listener right inside this world. In my view, Richard Burton's voice was like a musical instrument, so I wrote him a letter – no emails in those days – addressed to the theatre in New York where he was doing *Equus*. A few days later, his manager called to say Richard loved the idea. 'Count him in, dear boy!' he said. I'll never forget those words. I was in shock. Richard was about to go to California to do *The Exorcist* follow-up, so I took David out there to record with him." (JW-TG14)

Richard Burton's role as the protagonist was recorded on June 22, for narration only. When "the Journalist" character takes to song, the voice was Justin Hayward's.

Wayne told *Higher & Higher*, "I obviously knew of him and the Moody Blues, and of his work with John Lodge [*Blue Jays*]. The reason I thought of Justin for what he wound up doing was because, in my writing, I was thinking of somebody whose vocals were very spacious and had a particular sound about them. Justin was the first name I put on a list. That turned out to be a long list in case Justin didn't want to do it. But he was, in my point of view, first and foremost in my mind. ...

"As a matter of fact, it was seeing Justin and John as the *Blue Jays* singing 'Blue Guitar' on TV that reminded me of the loveliness of their voices. It was from that point that I started to contact Justin, because I didn't know him then. ... It sort of refocused my mind that they were possibly in England. That's how we started on the trail. ... If he was working outside the Moodies [as he had with *Blue Jays*], maybe he would consider a project like *War of the Worlds*.

"Justin had just about finished *Songwriter*. I think he had finished the recording and was working on the artwork. I know that John was working on his solo album that was still being recorded. They were both going on at the same time. ... I was just exceedingly fortunate to work with Jus as it evolved." (JW-H&H84)

Justin Hayward: "With Jeff, I just got a call completely out of the blue. He phoned the office, and they called me, and said, 'There's this guy trying to get in touch with you...' I called him... and he said, 'I'm doing this project called *War of the*

Worlds…' The first thing he asked me was, 'Are you the guy who sang "Nights in White Satin"?,' because he wasn't sure which one of us sang it. I told him I was. 'Then I've got this song for you.'

"So, I went down to this little studio called AdVision, on Oxford Street, and Jeff had [created] all the atmosphere [in the studio]; he was an atmosphere kind of person. You know, lights [set just] right, scarf over the lamp, and all that sort of stuff; he had to have the mood right. He'd done everything [on the track], except the vocals. Then he explained everything to me about the project. The next few weeks, I got more involved with the project; played the guitar, and did some other songs on it; generally sort of hanging around. I took a fee… I'd done a lot of these things before and nothing had ever happened, so I got used to saying, 'I'll have the money up front.' I knew the music was great, but I thought, 'Who the hell's going to buy it?'" (JH-O00)

Hayward performed on two songs – "Forever Autumn" and "The Eve of War."

Jeff Wayne: "The 'Forever Autumn' part – with its hook, 'Because you're not here' – actually started out as a jingle for a Lego commercial, sung by Gary Osborne and Paul Vigrass. The advert got a great reaction, so we added lyrics and turned it into a single. The result was a big hit in Japan. Later, as I was writing *War of the Worlds*, I reached the bit where the Journalist discovers his fiancée is missing, and it reminded me of 'Forever Autumn.' It was all about loss. Although I was trying to write an original work, I kept thinking the song was a perfect fit. I had my own little battle with myself, but I went for it. It's the only piece on the album that pre-existed." (JW-TG14)

"Forever Autumn" had been recorded prior to *Octave*, but was not issued until the same week as the Moody Blues album came out. The song became a minor hit in America, reaching No. 34 in *Cashbox*. *Record World* agreed on the Top 40 status, placing the single at No. 38, while *Billboard* held it back at No. 47. It fared better on *Billboard*'s Top Adult Contemporary chart, peaking at No. 20.

But "Forever Autumn" did exceptionally well in many markets around the world, especially in the United Kingdom, where it went to No. 5 in the British singles charts.

The songs that placed higher in England during the week of August 20, were, respectively, "Three Times a Lady," by the Commodores, "You're the One That I Want," by John Travolta and Olivia Newton-John, and a pair of songs that America took a pass on – "It's Raining," by Darts, and "Rivers of Babylon," by Boney M.

Neither of the Moody Blues singles released shortly after – "Steppin' in a Slide Zone" and "Driftwood" – did as well in the U.K. charts, although the former did make the U.S. Top 40, very nearly matching the popularity of "Forever Autumn" in the States.

"Forever Autumn," however, took the cake. It was Hayward's biggest hit of 1970s, in the U.S. as well as the U.K. He said, "It was bought by a lot of young kids, then, suddenly, it appeared in the charts. The record company called and said, 'Would you go on *Top of the Pops*? Your song is the hit.' So, it was wonderful. I went all over the world with it; it was a hit all over the world." (JH-O00)

Album Release:
Decca THS 129 (U.K.);
London PS 708 (U.S.);
June 9, 1978

Mick McDonagh, publicist for Decca Records in 1978, was assigned the job of creating a newsworthy launch for *Octave* in London – at a time when the British music scene was consumed with New Wave and Punk. Interviewed for the documentary *Classic Artists: The Moody Blues*, he said, "Really, London was the last place you wanted to have to be launching – or re-launching – the Moody Blues at that particular time." (MM-CA:TMB06)

While millions of Moody Blues and classic-rock enthusiasts were happily anticipating the return of the group, the British music

Photo op from the Decca garden party to relaunch the Moody Blues.
(Photo source: MoodyBluesAttitude.com)

press, having become increasingly caustic since the dawn of the 1970s, was less likely to hail the return of "the messiahs of cosmic rock."

McDonagh was given only ten days to plan the event. Since he saw the Moody Blues as "rock royalty," he decided the best affair would be a classic spring garden party, such as the Queen of England used to throw, with smoked salmon and champagne. Adding to the surreal scene, McDonagh arranged to parade out the Moodies' platinum-record awards with a uniformed and helmeted security team, surrounding an armored truck, adorned with the disks.

Following this, 20 carriers on motorbikes would enter, each picking up a copy of the new album, and then dispatching them to the various newspapers and radio stations across England. Next, the Moody Blues would be presented with platinum-record plaques from Decca head, Sir Edward Lewis.

It was a lavish, gaudy, and somewhat risky affair.

Mick McDonagh: "I knew the Moody Blues as legend, but I'd never actually met them.... And of course I never met Mike Pinder, because he never did show up on the day, which was another huge problem for us, because [we] set up this enormous launch to say the Moody Blues are back and reunited, and he didn't show on the morning of the gig; he stayed in America. So... I thought, 'Well, because they're not exactly fashionable at the moment, a number of the press might not notice. So... we brought out Tony Clarke, the producer, as another member, and I did the introduction *quickly*, [hoping] nobody would notice that there was one missing." (MM-CA:TMB06)

As McDonagh made the introductions, the Moodies exited the back of Sir Edward's mansion in close order, to the scattered applause from the members of the press who were present. Over a PA system, McDonagh told the guests, "Ladies and gentlemen, welcome back Justin Hayward, Graeme Edge, John Lodge, Ray Thomas – the Moody Blues."

Special Occasion: In one of his rare public appearances of recent times, Sir Edward Lewis is pictured here with members of the Moody Blues in London during June, 1978. At that ceremony, which also saw the launch of the group's "Octave" album, the late Decca chairman awarded the Moodies a slew of platinum disks for worldwide sales topping 26 million.

Tony Clarke, mustached and with thinning hair on top, a reasonable stand-in for Pinder, followed the others and took one of the five seats set out for the band. The ruse seemed to be working.

McDonagh announced, "And please welcome the chairman of the Decca group of companies, Sir Edward Lewis."

Lewis took the microphone, appearing uncomfortable in the spotlight, quite aged and not entirely well. He began, "Moody Blues, I'm afraid, will be written on my gravestone, probably."

It was a morbid joke, considering how Sir Edward appeared, and now knowing that he was in the last two years of his life.

After a chuckle from the guests, Sir Edward continued, "In the last eight years I've spent so many days and hours and weeks, from the day I gave them four discs, I think, in the Friars Club in New York...."

Sir Edward didn't finish his thought, but, instead, looked over at the "five" Moodies, as if directing his next line to them. "That must be six, seven years ago, and I think that was four discs at half a million each ... or something like that."

Back to the press, he spoke: "That was a very exciting occasion. But, since then, of course, we've had traumatic experiences, also...."

Then, stronger, "But here we are again, everybody's together, and we're looking forward to another great future. The seven platinum discs will be to each of the five gentlemen here, which makes 35, and there'll be the discs for Mike Pinder, who, unfortunately, couldn't be here; he's in Hollywood."

Mick McDonagh later said of his dodge to give the illusion of a completely united Moody Blues: "But then Sir Edward came on and let the cat out of the bag." (MM-CA:TMB06)

The bag, and the cat, and the whole affair was filmed, and you can find it online. Be warned, it's awkward.

On June 17, 1977, *Music Week* reported:

> After long hours of agreeing over how to launch the new Moody Blues' album *Octave*, Decca and the Moodies' management finally settled on an elegant garden party at Surrey with transport down the A3....

[Sir Edward] handed over 42 platinum – seven to each member of the band present for sales of their seven albums since *Days of Future Past* [sic]. (Mike Pinder could not be there.) Decca claim it was the greatest number of platinum discs awarded to any artist anywhere in the world. …

In another part of the same issue, a mini-review … more of a sneak preview:

It has been five and a half years since the last official Moody Blues album – since then of course there have been compilations, the *Blue Jays* album, and various solo albums. So the arrival of a new Moody Blues album must be awaited with bated breath, [and] many fans are going to ask – was the wait worth it?

The answer – emphatically, yes. *Octave* proves that the Moody Blues have lost none of their collective magic over the years, and they still rank as one of the world's top rock groups. …

Bob Edmonds was at the garden party, covering the event for *New Musical Express*. To little surprise, *NME* chose to send someone who proudly admitted in his article, from June 17, that he had never bought a Moody Blues album.

Edmonds reported:

… The Moodies were presented with what was described as "the greatest number of platinum discs awarded at any one time."

Draping yourself, as the Moodies did, around all this platinum, is the nearest anyone can get in public to rolling about in money. But then all big rock stars do that.

What was particularly offensive was the way the discs were delivered. They were trundled in aboard an armored car belonging to the Security Express private police force. And as the Moodies posed for the cameras, guards in civilian battledress hovered nearby.

As a piece of radical theatre, it could hardly have been bettered. The rich have always used violence to hang onto their money. Rock superstars tend to be very rich indeed. And The Moody Blues are a prime example.

(Photo source: Alamy.com)

It's a massive irony, of course, that they got that way through an avowed concern for humanity's cosmic destiny. They found their lost chord all right. You can hear it ringing out from cash registers all over the world.

Edmands made his way to Graeme Edge, who was used to hearing condescension from the press. The journalist asked Edge if it didn't worry him that he'd "made so much money out of things spiritual."

Edge said, "No. Not in the slightest."

Edmands edged closer. "No?"

Edge said, "No. Because I pass it all over to the Government anyway."

Edmands then wrote:

> Graeme Edge, who is not one of the blonde hairdressers [Edmond's derogatory description of Hayward and Lodge], has a nifty way of dealing with aggressive questions. He gives replies that consist of one short sentence each, says them in a sweetly reasonable voice, and smiles.

Edmands asked Edge if the Moodies "got back together for business reasons"?

Edge said: "No. No, not at all."

So why regroup?

Edge said, sweetly, succinctly, "To play with the guys." Then he smiled.

Edmands inquired who had prompted the reunion.

Edge answered frankly, "Our manager. But then, he's had a try, regular as clockwork, every six months. This last time we felt it seemed like a good idea. Enough time had passed for things to get a bit more normal. In 1972, they were a bit abnormal and a bit frightening for us."

Edmands then demanded, wasn't it the case that the Moodies had gotten back together because their solo projects "floundered"?

(For the record, *Blue Jays* hardly floundered. And Ray Thomas' first album had done respectable business, and, for that matter, so had Justin Hayward's.)

Edge didn't blink. He said, "Oh, no, I'm ever so proud of my solo albums. I play them and enjoy them."

But they weren't a commercial success, were they?

Edge said, "Well, I'm lucky. I'm in a position where I don't really need that side of it." (GE-NME78)

On that note, Edge thanked Edmands for his kind interest, and went on his way.

Edmands had the last word, in print. The title of his article was "Hairdressers and Brummie Businessmen Quit Day Jobs to Form Mystical Alliance (& Make Bucks)."

Justin Hayward later said, "We split up for three or four years in the Seventies and after we got back together, the *New Musical Express* had a field day with us. They loved us when we were progressive and underground, but when we started selling zillions of records in America, they sent us up something rotten." (JH-DM94)

On June 10, as reported, 500 U.S. radio stations premiered *Octave* in a one-hour special. Canada took part in the simultaneous broadcasts as well. *Billboard* reported:

... Close to 50 Canadian radio stations accepted the Moody Blues one-hour radio special, which was broadcast internationally on June 10. Response to the program, which debuted *Octave*, was so strong at Vancouver station CKLG-FM that the special was rebroadcast in its entirety the following night.

TV appearance for the Decca launch. (Photo source: Pinterest.com)

As part of the U.S. promotional campaign, blue vinyl copies of the record were sent to radio stations. The Canadian arm of London Records went one step further by making 40,000 albums pressed on blue vinyl available to the public. The *Billboard* report continued:

> ... It is believed that the Canadian operation is the only one to have made color vinyl pressings commercially available on the album, which shipped gold, according to a company official. Reorders have it hovering close to the platinum mark, five days after the initial shipment, reports the spokesman. ...

Release / Reaction:

In the June 1978 edition of Sydney, Australia's *Union Recorder*, Mark Robinson wrote:

> The eighth album by the Moody Blues is a dramatic change in style for the band, in that they have now made it apparent that they do not intend to revert to their old formula for making big-selling records. ... During the five [sic; four] years the Moodies have not been together, styles have developed that never sold well on record [sic, *Blue Jays* and "Blue Guitar" were substantial hits, as were, to a lesser degree, *From Mighty Oaks* and *Songwriter*].

Octave seems more of a compilation album of these different styles, and is perhaps intended to shed some light on the Moodies' solo careers. A haunting introduction opens on the album from which a mild "rock" song emerges, courtesy of John Lodge. Lodge's other song on Side Two is the most instantly likable, called "Survival." Justin Hayward's songs have always been magical, and his four contributions to *Octave* are no exception. The first two are semi-acoustic love ballads minus the grandeur of "Nights in White Satin." His third song is a very fast-moving sax based piece. A Hayward track closes the album impressively. Titled "The Day We Meet Again," it could be a monster single if only it wasn't six minutes long. ...

Octave itself is an important album from one of the most significant and influential groups in the world. What better recommendation?

Melody Maker was one of the first to get a review out in Britain, in its June 17 issue. "C.W." wrote:

> ... They start proceedings in typically mysterious style with "Steppin' in a Slide Zone" and the question all Moodies fans will be asking is: "Does it have all that old Moodies SOUND?" I can only answer, yes. There's your flute! And, by George, listen to those vocal harmonies! Are there pretty melodies and haunting vocal refrains; do the keyboards wail long block chords? All this and more, my children of Raan. Look – there's a spiritual song by Mike Pinder all about the Savior, called "One Step into the Light."

> And just to show the Moodies are not all mysticism and can rock, earthily, there's a fine Justin Hayward tune, "Top Rank Suite," complete with wailing saxophone and Graeme Edge goading his drums, just as he did in even earlier days when the Moodies played rhythm and blues at the Marquee.

> Sweeping strings are added to such John Lodge compositions as "Survival" and Ray Thomas's "Under Moonshine," the latter opening in dramatic style: "The dawn crept into my room and stole my dream," chortles Ray. Rather a nifty line, matching for poetic imagery his further observation that, "While you're a tree, no, you'll never see the words. While you're a tree." I shall ponder the significance of that for several weeks.

> Thus everybody gets a whack at writing, including Graeme, who contributes "I'll Be Level With You." But I suppose the prettiest songs of all come from the pens of Messrs Hayward and Lodge, like Justin's "Had to Fall in Love," complete with wailing harmonica and acoustic guitars. ...

My tips for hit singles? "Steppin' In a Slide Zone" and "One Step into the Light" should receive major airplay. Dealers should stock with as many units as feasible. …

On June 18, Aaron Gold reported for the *Chicago Tribune*:

The Moody Blues may not have performed in concert or cut a record for four [sic; five] years, but their fans haven't forgotten them. The group's new album, *Octave*, was released this week and it already sold more than 700,000 copies.

Robert Hilburn was quick to review *Octave* for *The Los Angeles Times*, with his predictable verdict making print on June 20. He even used "predictable" right off the bat.

… [T]he group is in the position in *Octave* of a once-champion prizefighter stepping back in the ring only to find what was once natural and commanding is now a bit sluggish and uncertain.

While there is more than enough of the Moodys' convincing melodic splendor to keep the album from being the embarrassment of so many reunion packages, there's little in it to regain for the band its old classical/pop-rock crown. That title seems safely in the hands now of the more versatile, vigorous Electric Light Orchestra. …

In *Octave*, the group has wisely turned to the two writers for six of the album's 10 songs, but the results are uneven. While Lodge's energetic, slightly mystical "Steppin' in a Slide Zone" would have been rather attractive a few years ago, it now seems little more than a filler track from an ELO album. Similarly, Hayward's plaintive "Driftwood" has some instrumental verve but ultimately succumbs to such dreadfully tired imagery as "Oh no … don't leave me driftwood on the shore."

Hayward fares better on the graceful romanticism of "Had to Fall in Love" and the spicy, saxophone-assisted playfulness of "Top Rank Suite." Lodge's "Survival" is in the classic Moodys tradition of a lushly arranged search for emotional balance and understanding.

But the search bogs down in Michael Pinder's "One Step Into the Light" where we are asked to pick our way through such cosmic cobwebs as "The river of living breaks / Is flowing through the sun." Things get even worse in Ray Thomas' "Under Moonshine": "The dawn crept into my room / And stole my dream / Now, I'll never know / Just what that means." Beats me, too.

Supported by Tony Clarke's usual immaculate production work, *Octave* has enough superficial dazzle to return the Moodys to the Top 10, but it lacks the adventure and purpose to regain the band's original momentum and glow. …

In the June 21 issue of *Semper Fi* magazine, Gus Strachan commented:

… The first track, "Steppin' in a Slide Zone," is instantly recognizable as it carries the Moody Blues trademark of pulsating rhythms richly infused with background vocals and the inevitable Mellotron. It is a pleasant rocky number that certainly doesn't disturb the listener.

"Had to Fall in Love" has some laid back acoustic guitar which is highlighted by emotive blues harp and vocal harmony passages. The interesting combinations of instruments are typical of the album as a whole. Acoustic guitar, brass, organ, Mellotron, bass, vocals, and strings are all employed in a variety of arrangements which are very tastefully chosen. …

Each track is distinctive for at least some facet of its structure. The solos are never over indulgent and blend well within the texture of the song. The use of sax on such tracks as "Top Rank Suite" and "Driftwood" is very good and the various lead breaks maintain a subtle complexity due to their melodic depth. …

The Moody Blues are very proficient musicians and definitely have a unique brand of music. Perhaps the most memorable characteristic of this album is the manner in which the group arranges their musical competency. The songs are manifest with interesting melodic structure and musical intensity is reached and maintained by the use of fine solos and superb harmony vocals. For some, this album might be disappointing because it lacks the spark that earlier Moody Blues had when they were in earnest search of the answer, not to mention "the meaning of life." Perhaps they haven't been consuming enough LSD which seemed to be a staple diet for many of the successful bands early in the decade. …

From June 23, in the *Philadelphia Daily News*, Rich Aregood said "the songs wash over you without sticking. It's kind of like bathing in 10W-40 motor oil."

The new record is OK. You just start to come up with a theory about time passage. How could it be that a group from the mid-60s can sound more dated than John Philip Sousa? …

They're still pretty much where they were, despite the world's having moved far away from that reference point. It doesn't matter all that much that the music still sounds about the same. It does matter that the insipidity of the thought behind the songs is also the same. ….

For its June 24 issue, *Billboard* magazine picked *Octave* as its "Spotlight" album:

… It seems so easy to reacquaint oneself with the Moody's music as the familiar vocal harmonics and melodically structured songs come at you in alarming force and precision. … As in previous efforts, emphasis is on the orchestral backdrop and easily identifiable, yet nonetheless irresistible vocals. Tony Clarke also returns as producer, so whether or not this is a teaser or the first of more to come is unknown, and its forthcoming tour might just decide that.

Best cuts: "Steppin' in a Slide Zone," "Driftwood," "One Step into the Light," "Had to Fall in Love," "The Day We Meet Again."

Dealers: Like the CS&N reunion, the fans are waiting for it.

Also on the 24th, *Cashbox*, the other big American music trade magazine, told industry insiders:

After a six-year [sic] hiatus, the Moodys are back, and as strong as ever. The group's unique ability to forge classical and rock influences into its own distinct musical style remains intact. Each member of the quintet penned at least one of the ten stellar tracks. Standout tunes include "Steppin in a Slide Zone" and "The Day We Meet Again," although AOR and pop programmers have plenty of great cuts to choose from. Should be a retail giant.

Concerning the confusion from the music press as to exactly when the Moody Blues had last worked together:

The last album of new music from the Moodies, *Seventh Sojourn*, had been released in November 1972. It was now June 1978. That was a gap of five and a half years. *However*, the last Moodies hit, "I'm Just a Singer (in a Rock and Roll Band)," peaked in March 1973. If you date the hiatus starting then, then the gap is five years. *However*, the Moodies toured through the end of January 1974. If using that date, then the hiatus comes to less than four-and-a-half years. *However*, the band was still together and even trying to record an album in early summer of '74. At year's end, *This Is the Moody Blues* was released. Using that as the starting date for the hiatus, it lasted less than four years.

From June 25, Lynn Van Matre wrote in the *Chicago Tribune*:

After five years apart and various solo projects, the Moody Blues – creators of some of the most lushly orchestrated sounds on the late '60s and early '70s rock scene – are back together on record with *Octave*… and a couple of lines from John Lodge's "Steppin' in a Slide Zone" sums up the whole affair pretty well: "Standing in a slide zone, I could be steppin' through a time zone…" With this album, the Moodys, too, seem to have stepped into a time warp, turning out the same songs and sounds of creamy dreaminess they did for years, with little musical progression. Despite this disappointingly warmed-over aura, fans of the band probably will find *Octave* pleasurable enough listening, though the Moodys have produced better.

From the June 28 edition of Binghamton, New York's *Press and Sun-Bulletin*, Chris Carson was doing his version of the arithmetic:

... Although they never have officially broken up, there hasn't been a new Moody Blues studio album since *Sojourn*. ... Each member of the group, however, has released at least one solo project since 1972 [sic; 1974], with Hayward and Lodge's *Blue Jays* the most successful commercially. When combined, these solo outings could easily fill the void left by the absence of a Moody Blues album. But, the solo albums naturally lack the lyrical unity of the group's previous albums, although the studio professionalism equated with the Moody Blues is still apparent. ...

Not surprisingly, the Hayward and Lodge compositions are the most accessible here. John Lodge's "Steppin' in a Slide Zone" could easily be coupled with *Seventh Sojourn*'s closing charger, "I'm Just a Singer (In a Rock and Roll Band)." Lodge's other entry, "Survival," gradually builds to a rousing finish like Justin Hayward's songs generally do, and it is one of the album's peaks, alongside Hayward's "Top Rank Suite." The latter is easily one of the freshest songs on this album, while Hayward's three other songs probably influence the overall dreamy scenery of *Octave* the most.

The band's members showed some ambitiousness mixed with that typical Moody Blues' flavor on their solo projects. You would think some of that ambition would show up on their new group effort, but *Octave* comes across as a 1978 successor to their 1973 sound. And while *Octave* is still good by today's standards, what it really demonstrates is how progressive the Moody Blues *were* in the late '60s and early '70s.

Let's hope their next group album will be more ambitious. This time the six-year wait has definitely helped *Octave*, by increasing its impact on listeners. But if they release another album with a similar sound in a year or two, the Moody Blues may sound too familiar to sell well.

On June 28, Sandy Poiarkoff wrote in the Pennsylvania's *Beaver County Times*:

Four years of separation dealt a blow to the Moody Blues. I never thought I'd say that. Isn't life strange!

I ran out the first day their eighth album went on sale, brought it home, settled back with a glass of Moody Blue wine and was ready to hear the Moody Blues again and get the same feeling I got when I was first introduced to them. What a letdown *Octave* is. The wine couldn't even lift my spirits. ...

Octave isn't a Moody Blues album – it's an album of five separate musicians, not the unique sound they had together for seven years. …

Hayward's "Top Rank Suite" says, "We're on our way to the big time, baby, to the great gold record in the sky." There's no doubt *Octave* will achieve that status but it'll be only because fans are dying to hear the Moody Blues together again. …

Fans no doubt will be watching and waiting for an album like *Threshold of a Dream* but it may be just that, a dream.

From the June 30 edition of *The Seattle Times*, in a page full of reviews, Patrick MacDonald gave high marks to Bob Dylan's *Street Legal*, Quincy Jones's *Sounds and Stuff Like That!!*, and Bruce Springsteen's *Darkness at the Edge of Town*. *Octave* also did well.

The Moody Blues are back! And it's as if they'd never left. Listening to this album is like going back to the late 60s and early 70s. It's way better than any of the efforts by the five individual Moodies over the past six [sic] years, but not as much of a "grabber" as previous Moody Blues albums. Ray Thomas is still writing silly singsong poetry, John Lodge is as spacey as ever, and Justin Hayward still writes a nice tune. The production is rich and full of textures and the vocals are strong, especially the harmonies. On a couple of songs it all comes together: "Had to Fall in Love," "Survival" and "One Step into the Light." Should be quite a comeback for the boys.

From *Gallery* magazine at this time:

… *Octave* is the Moodies' first album back together again, and it makes you hope that this reunion will be permanent.

The Moodies are to rock of inner space what the Pink Floyd are to rock of outer space. The mind, consciousness, the universal life force – these are the Moody Blues' principal preoccupations. This concentration on the inner life rather than outward appearances and realities, shapes their music into majestic panoramas of sound. You do not just listen to the Moody Blues, you are enveloped by their music, surrounded by the tonal textures that produce an almost trance-like effect. …

Octave's opening cut, "Steppin' in a Slide Zone," immediately plunges into a warp in the space-time continuum. Literally. A stately synthesized orchestral prelude is gradually enriched by slivers of electric guitar and astral whooshes. The lyrics are vintage Moodies, devoted to otherworldly concerns as the narrator meets an enigmatic stranger who leads him into another time-space dimension.

"Under Moonshine" glows with an opening synthesized pastoral, before a deliciously fruity light-baritone intones, "The dawn crept into my room / And stole my dreams." They are counterpoint to open up new mental dimensions in the listener, nudging him toward a fuller awareness of the infinite.

Still, ever since their breakthrough [with] "Nights in White Satin," this basically other-worldly group has conjured up a string of ballads that approach romance from an oblique angle. These tender ballads are represented amply on *Octave* with "Had to Fall in Love," "Driftwood," and the enthralling "I'm Your Man."

From the July 1 edition of Allentown, Pennsylvania's *The Morning Call*, Paul Willistein Jr. wrote that the Moodies' long-awaited eighth album "sounds as stunning as their first."

The album opens with a familiar Moodies' phasing flourish on John Lodge's "Steppin' in a Slide Zone," a trip into the realm of creativity....

Ray Thomas contributes two songs. "Under Moonshine" (apparently the lunar kind) and "I'm Your Man." Both show the more serious side of rock's own Lewis Carroll. In content they are more similar to Thomas's thoughtful "And the Tide Rushes In" than the whimsical "Nice to Be Here." Thomas establishes the tone of the album – one of reflection, of stepping back from the brink of heightened awareness: "You've got to stand tall / With your feet on the ground."

Graeme Edge contributes the LP's best-crafted song, "I'll Be Level with You." As though he were bouncing his son on his knee like a nervous father, he asks: "Little guy, little hands, little eyes and lots of time / What you gonna be, what you gonna see / When your eyes are level with mine?" With a perfect lyric and melody, Edge reassures: "But you have to have a world you can live in / Not a world where all the hope is gone."

Justin Hayward, with four songs, is the most prolific songwriter here. He's hopeful too, if a little more cynical. On "Top Rank Suite," an Elvis Presley rockabilly satire of the promoters and victims of fame, his frustration finds no answers: "We were on our way to the big time, baby / To the great gold record in the sky / But can you tell me why?" ...

The Moodies' music has survived beautifully. As the album art symbolizes, though the group is no longer perched on the threshold, they have passed through the door, gaining a creative and personal maturity that only comes with the passage of time. ...

670

... Welcome back, Moody Blues. Lovely to hear from you again.

Also from July 1, Ron Hawkins's review appeared in the *Muncie Evening Press*. He raved over the Rolling Stones' new *Some Girls*, but was unable to muster enthusiasm that Paul Willistein Jr. showed for *Octave*. Hawkins lamented:

> The reunion of the Moody Blues on *Octave* is not as joyful an occasion as one would hope. The group members' solo efforts since the Moodies' seventh album seem to have been harmful as individual members seem more concerned with their own compositions. Each song on *Octave* has but one composer, lacking the fluidity of the group's prior communal efforts. ...

> John Lodge's "Steppin' in a Slide Zone" opens the album impressively with a mysterious tale of a "stranger" who leads the narrator to a place of heavenly delight. However, it is followed by "Under Moonshine," "Had to Fall in Love" and "I'm Your Man," the most clichéd songs the band has ever recorded. Even if the band was still able to harmonize as effectively as in days of old, these songs would fall flat.

> Graeme Edge's "I'll Be Level with You" is clichéd in its "you can't be me" approach, but is gripping nonetheless. "Survival" is another song rich in mood and image by Lodge. "The Day We Meet Again" features excellent keyboard work and a pleasant "see you again" farewell.

> But, the Moody Blues do not really exist here. *Octave* is more like an album of solo efforts by ex-Moody Blues members. ...

On July 2, Gary Mullinax wrote in Wilmington, Delaware's *The Morning News*:

> ... This album will probably be a monster seller, as most of their records have been. Their secret? Lush harmonies and orchestral textures. In the past the group's most bombastic music was often its most popular, while it seemed that the more pretentious the lyrics the better. ...

> The Moodies' lyrics are the usual sort of thing for this kind of arty rock: lots of stuff about "creators of dreams that melt in the sun," "time waits for no one at all" and (yecchhh) "... slowly breathing in / feel the life force streaming in." But despite these inevitable Moody excesses, this is a pleasant album that warrants playing when you want to sit back and relax.

Also on July 2, Henry McNulty gave his view on *Octave* for Connecticut's *Hartford Courant*.

... So now there is *Octave*, the eighth album (get it?) by the group, and things are back to normal again. "Normal" means that Hayward is playing guitar, Lodge is on bass, Mike Pinder is at the keyboards, Graeme Edge is behind the drums, Ray Thomas is playing flute, the whole ensemble is singing, and strings are everywhere. ...

We are catapulted back in time. Disco influences? Forget it. Remakes of oldies? Not a one. Punk rock? Not a chance. The Moodies are untainted by the events of the last half-decade. If you liked *Sojourn*, or any other Moody Blues album from *Days of Future Passed* on, *Octave* is for you.

Admittedly, for devotees of the group, there are a few discernible changes. The group seems less inclined to preach Eastern philosophy these days – or to search for lost chords, to teeter on the threshold of a dream or otherwise to pursue some mystical path. The lyrics are mostly straightforward, if hackneyed at times ("Time waits for no one, my love," writes Hayward; "The world keeps turning," says Thomas). Pinder, however, continues to write about "cosmic circles ever turning" and "the life force streaming in."

"Top Rank Suite," despite the name, is one of the shortest songs on the record, and uncharacteristically funky. This Hayward composition with honking saxes and a thumping beat, is almost unrecognizable as a Moody Blues tune – except for the rich, textured harmonies.

Most of *Octave*, however, is so typical of the Moodies' orchestral rock that listening to it is almost nostalgic. "Survival," a superb song by Lodge, uses his old trick of cutting through the gumbo with a slightly-fuzzed, high-pitched guitar solo. "Steppin' in a Slide Zone," the record's other Lodge composition, overdubs the Moodies' usual five-part [sic] harmony so thickly that the group sounds like a rock choir. It is the LP's best rocker. ("Slide Zone," which leads off the album, begins with a couple of minutes of outerspace noodling on synthesizers coupled with *Star Trek* wails. The Moodies' records and those by the Electric Light Orchestra apparently originate in the same corner of the galaxy.) ...

Octave is summed up well by two lines from the LP's closing songs. "The years have been so lonely," says Justin Hayward. And Michael Pinder assures us: "There's one thing I can do / Play my Mellotron for you."

From July 2, Pete Bishop, writing in *The Pittsburgh Press*, said:

... Time seems to have passed the "thinking man's rock band" by. Had they done "Survival" over a hustle beat, they might have had a hit. And the ethereal philosophy of "One Step into the Light" is dated as all get-out; the Age of Aquarius dawned and set awfully quickly from a musical standpoint.

The easy-rocking, lyrically accessible "Driftwood" is good; "Had to Fall in Love" (more easy rock) and "I'm Your Man" (slightly soulful ballad) are OK. The rest? Ordinary, very ordinary. *Octave* is extremely disappointing.

From the July 14 edition of Ontario, Canada's *The Ottawa Journal*, Chris Cobb wrote:

Together again after four years with an aptly titled eighth album, the Moody Blues look set for a new lease of life. Unfortunately, if the band gets one, it will be 70 percent on past reputation and 30 percent on the basis of *Octave*. Essentially, the album is a series of individual efforts totally void of any feeling of togetherness. Some of the songs, particularly Ray Thomas's "Under Moonshine" and "I'm Your Man," make the band sound like Las Vegas hopefuls and shouldn't even have been included. Justin Hayward wrote most of the tunes, the best being "Had to Fall in Love."

There are flashes of the old, solid, tight Moody Blues style, but one gets the feeling the quintet had lost an opportunity because they wanted to please one another. Admittedly, all five have been getting individual musical experiences since the 1974 split but, for *Octave*, a greater fusion was called for. ...

Another Canadian newspaper, Ottawa's *The Citizen*, had Bill Provick's review on July 15:

... *Octave* is not a totally triumphant return but starved Moody Blues fans should welcome this new release with open ears. ...

The album's biggest asset is also its biggest drawback. The basic sound is fairly close to that established in the past. It means Moody Blues fans won't be confused by an alien musical outlook and style but it also means there's little to set this album apart from past successes and classic albums like *On the Threshold of a Dream, To Our Children's, Children's Children* and *A Question of Balance* that will never be matched.

Fortunately, the album doesn't appear to even attempt to compete with such old favorites and thus even the most traditional-sounding tunes bear a warm, non-combative comfortability that becomes more and more pleasurable with each listen. Better yet, there are a couple of surprisingly strong cuts that are worth the price of the album alone – songs like "Driftwood," "Top Rank Suite" and my personal favorite, "Steppin' in a Slide Zone." ...

Single Release:
"Steppin' in a Slide Zone"
b/w "I'll Be Level with You"
Decca F 13790 (U.K.); London 5N270 (U.S.);
July 14, 1978

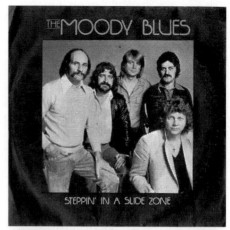

For the Moody Blues' first album of new material in over five years, a hit single was not really needed to get fans to rush to the record stores. So Decca, in England, and its U.S. arm, London Records, waited five weeks from the release of the album before issuing a single. By then, they had seen which tracks were getting the most attention from reviewers and spins on the radio.

John Lodge's "Steppin' in a Slide Zone" had been the favorite of both reviewers and radio programmers, thus was picked to be the A-side. "I'll Be Level with You," credited to Graeme Edge, but the result of a communal effort – the most group-oriented cut – was chosen as the flip.

On July 22, *Billboard* said of the top side:

> The first single from the new *Octave* album is a fast paced rocker featuring the textured vocals and sound layers that have trademarked the best of the Moody Blues' material. Tight instrumentation and strong lead vocal highlight.

Hit Parader magazine interviewed Justin Hayward about the "shortcomings" of the album, and the underwhelming chart performance of the "Steppin' in a Slide Zone" single.

Hayward made it clear that "Slide Zone" was far from an unanimous choice as a single release. He told *Hit Parader*'s J.C. Costa, "If you'll remember, we used to have our own record label [Threshold] and more control over what we released. Now that's over and we're back with Decca [London in the U.S.] where we don't really have a say over what gets released.... I don't think I would have chosen that particular song." (JH-HP78)

Costa agreed:

> "Steppin' in a Slide Zone," the turgid John Lodge drone that opens Side One had a brief life on the U.S. single charts before plummeting into oblivion. ...

> Because of its extraordinary verve, humor and specificity of images – for a Moody Blues song – Hayward's "Top Rank Suite" might have been a better choice. A relatively hot rhythm track

674

propels this light-hearted vamp about the rush to the top peppered with nostalgic asides like, "They made a good bowl of chili at the jazz club / They played a good game of football in Mucron" and "Avenue Tombola and Social / We just drove right on by." ….

Other songs from *Octave* were released as singles for specific markets. "Had to Fall in Love" was issued as an A-side in Australia, Belgium, and Holland; "Survival" saw release in Italy. "Driftwood" would have its moment soon.

In the August 7 issue of *People* magazine, the writer mused:

> The Moodys haven't recorded together in over five years, but their sound has hardly changed. The English quintet's lush vocals, string arrangements and listenable pop melodies are all still intact, although this album offers little beyond that reassurance. With the exception of two cuts, the material is far from memorable despite the extravagant production. The two happy exceptions are "Had to Fall in Love," a charming folkish tune with an acoustic guitar backing, and "Top Rank Suite," the only cut that has any rocking life to it. Unfortunately, for all but starved Moody-maniacs, the rest of the album is bound to create a longing for more fulfilling and captivating oldies like "Nights in White Satin."

Crawdaddy reviewed *Octave* in the magazine's September 1978 issue (out in mid-August). The headline said it all – "Breathe Deep the Gathering Gloom." Benson Worthington Laing wrote:

> … Clearly, the Moody Blues have transcended the odious realm of rock 'n' roll. They now dwell in the heavens, far above the likes of Black Oak Arkansas and Debby Boone. However, trauma has accompanied godhood and it is this trauma, like alienation, that the listener encounters throughout *Octave*. In short, the Moodies have a bad case of the cosmic blues; a condition experienced only by the very saintly, the very boring or key members of Jackson Browne's backup band. …
>
> *Octave* opens with "Steppin' in a Slide Zone," an enigmatic up-tempo tune which, I believe, deals with finding salvation through farming in the state of California before the entire land mass falls into the ocean. After a very cosmic blues-riff-shuffle, this karmatic caper builds in intensity via a musical bridge of Hermann Hesse-inspired handclapping.

Wikipedia break. Hermann Karl Hesse, who had been dead for 16 years at the time of Laing's review, was a German-born Swiss poet, novelist, and painter, who was a 1946 Nobel Prize in Literature, and had written *Demian*, *Steppenwolf*, *Siddhartha*, and *The Glass Bead Game*, each of which explored an individual's search for authenticity, self-knowledge and spirituality. Not sure what the hand-clapping thing is referencing.

Back to the funny critic from 1978:

... The other songs explore the pits of fourth dimensional heartbreak. "Deep inside I pour like rain" offer the band, evoking images of ruptured meteorologists in "Under Moonshine." In "Had to Fall in Love," a moving acoustic dirge, we hear the voice of a wounded romance croon "In the mirror, I saw the writing on the wall." The hidden meaning here is obvious. Everything in life is backwards, except for certain sections of the Beatles' White Album. ...

There's more. But we'll skip it, and ponder what handclapping has to do with the author of *Siddhartha* and *Steppenwolf*.

Stephen Holden hadn't cared all that much for *Blue Jays*. He cared even less for *Octave*. Holden is a continuing example of the acerbic critics who wrote for major rock music magazines of the time.

He told us that the new album faithfully recreated a signature sound that was "almost certain to be regarded as tomorrow's camp: simple rock and folk tunes blown up into a pseudo-classical, quasi-religious choral music, driven by plodding, militaristic rhythm tracks and mixed into a turgid murk that blurs the distinction between rock and orchestral instrumentation."

Holden found only two songs to his liking, both by Hayward – "Had to Fall in Love" and "Driftwood." Still, he felt that neither was as good as "Nights in White Satin" or "Question." Those two songs were times when the Moodies "created tunes to match the grandiosity of their aural style."

Holden ended his review with a clever line. He wrote: "*Octave* is another cathedral of twigs built on a mud slide."

The irony here is that among other challenges the Moodies encountered while making *Octave* were mudslides.

In the October 3 edition of Alexandria, Louisiana's *The Town Talk*, the unidentified music critic wrote:

> If you could buy a single with "Steppin' in a Slide Zone" on one side and "Had to Fall in Love" on the other, there would really be no pressing reason to get *Octave*, the Moody Blues' latest album. You'd miss two lyrical Justin Hayward ballads and a funky sax-punctuated rhythm-and-blues number he also wrote, but that would be about it.

"Steppin'" and "Love" both feature the Blues' typically lush sound but in a very different way. The former, written by John Lodge, is the kind of hard-driving rocker that stays in your head hours after you've heard it, while Hayward's "Love" is as wistful as the harmonica in the background. They're both cuts above the rest of the album.

Single release:
"Driftwood" b/w "I'm Your Man"
Decca F 13809 (U.K.); London 5N273;
October 6, 1978

On October 21, 1978, *Billboard* reported:

... The Moody Blues tour, the band's first in five years, starts Nov. 3 in St. Paul, Minn., and wraps up Dec. 12 in Los Angeles.

London is releasing a new single from *Octave*, entitled "Driftwood." Ironically, this goes into competition with group member Justin Hayward's "Forever Autumn" 45 on Columbia, taken from *Jeff Wayne's War of the Worlds* concept package on which Hayward guests as a solo artist.

It is not clear whether he will perform "Forever Autumn" on the group's tour. ...

London Records would have frowned on Hayward performing "Forever Autumn" while touring America, so that single would have to stand or fall on its own. He would, however, be performing "Driftwood" as part of the concert's set lists.

"Driftwood" entered the U.S. *Billboard* chart on November 4, 1968, for seven-week run, peaking at No. 59 on December 9. The single spent seven weeks on the *Cashbox* chart, as well, and also peaked on December 9, but only managed to make it to No. 68. *Record World* had the song in its singles chart for five weeks, only managing to get as high as No. 85. On *Billboard*'s Adult Contemporary chart, the song peaked at No. 38.

Considering that "Driftwood" was one of the most appealing tracks on the *Octave* album, this was indeed a poor showing. But the album had already sold well over half a million copies, and "Driftwood" had gained airplay even before it had been released as a single. By early December, the track was too familiar now to be pushed as something new.

Single releases:
"Had to Fall in Love" b/w "I'm Your Man"
Decca Y-11833 (Australia); 1978
"Had to Fall in Love"
b/w "Steppin' in a Slide Zone"
Decca 6103 116 (Netherlands); 1978
Decca 26.566-Y (Belgium); 1978

The Decca Records regional offices in three countries – Australia, the Netherlands, and Belgium – opted for Justin Hayward's lovely "Had to Fall in Love" as a single release over "Driftwood." In Australia, it was coupled with the B-side which had served "Driftwood," Ray Thomas's "I'm Your Man." In the two European nations, it was paired with "Steppin' In a Slide Zone" as a double A-side.

Meanwhile, in the November 19, 1978 edition of *Asbury Park Press*, as the Moodies were touring the U.S. (the reunion tour to be covered in the next chapter), Pete Settles wrote of *Octave*:

> … Their new album has already been labeled "gold" by the Recording Industry Artists Association. …

> … The single cut off the album, "Steppin' in a Slide Zone," is reminiscent of Pink Floyd's *Dark Side of the Moon*, with the electronic background. But the Moody Blues just don't seem to be playing together as closely as they once did.

> … Many of the songs on the new album start out with great potential but the buildup never really peaks. "I'll Be Level With You" is another rock 'n' roll song that starts out with a nice beat and has good guitar and piano work but tends to get a little too complex with the use of electronics.

> "Had to Fall in Love" has a taste of Neil Young, complete with harmonica, and could classify as easy listening music.

> "Top Rank Suite," which is the first cut [on] the flip side shows better than most of the other songs and doesn't seem to change beats until the ending. With saxophone and guitar, the song has a fast tempo and with a little bit of imagination, the listener might think the Grateful Dead is somewhere in the background.

> But, unfortunately, the new Moody Blues haven't really been successful at putting together a top rated album, even though the "gold" label was applied just ten days after its release. …

By this time, the Moody Blues were touring the U.S. That is, most of them.

33

The *Octave* Tour: A Change in the Band –
The Road Ahead, 1978-79

The Moody Blues American Tour 1978

John Lodge, Justin Hayward, Patrick Moraz
Graeme Edge, Ray Thomas

A wire story making the rounds to American newspapers in late September 1978 brought news with both encouraging and disheartening aspects. Soon there would be an official announcement: the Moody Blues would tour North America, for the first time since early 1974. The bad news: Mike Pinder wouldn't be on the tour. The report continued:

> When discussions first began about a tour, Pinder was less than enthusiastic, and has now definitely dropped out of the plans, although it is still uncertain whether this decision is permanent as far as future recording is concerned.

> Replacing Pinder will be Patrick Moraz, who seems to be making a career of replacing departing group members.... Moraz is currently with the remaining members of the Moody Blues (Justin

Hayward, Ray Thomas, John Lodge, and Graeme Edge) in England's Threshold Studios rehearsing....

When asked about a Moody Blues *Octave* tour, Mike Pinder told Bruce Eder of *Goldmine* magazine, "Suddenly, there was this urgency to go out on tour, and it didn't make sense to me. I don't think the record was very good, or that we should go out on tour behind it. I questioned why we should tour at that particular moment, and I just couldn't see any reason to do it behind that album." (MP-GM94)

One reason, of course, would be to help the record company which had paid for the album, whether or not the Moodies felt it was as good as it should be. It had been over four years since the Moodies had toured – all the more reason to kick up their public profile. There was a third reason: It's what the fans wanted, and they had certainly waited a long time for it.

Years after the fact, talking to Betty Webb of Arizona's *Tempe Daily Tribune*, Pinder explained his other reasons for passing on the tour. "Basically, my split with the Moody Blues came about because I didn't have my Green Card yet. In 1978, my marriage had fallen apart and I wanted to stay in California to maintain close contact with my young son, Danny, who was living there with his mother. If I'd left the U.S. on the *Octave* tour like the band wanted me to, it would have jeopardized my residency.

"Looking back on it, I'm afraid they found my stance arrogant – and I don't blame them. But I was so concerned about my son I just wasn't thinking of how I was coming across.

"Human relationships are the most important part of my life. Leaving the band was the right thing to do, even though my income dropped sharply. But I always said that if you take care of the music, the music will take care of you, and that turned out to be right. The music [royalties] gave me enough to have a normal life in a normal neighborhood among normal people." (MP-TDNT95)

You may remember that ex-Beatle John Lennon, another Britisher-turned-American resident, also feared to leave the U.S. for fear he wouldn't be allowed back in. Lennon's troubles were also spurred by his political activism, stirring resentment from President Richard Nixon's administration.

No matter how delicate his legal status, Pinder was not about to risk it by leaving America. Therefore, when the Moody tour was set, it would be without him.

The *Octave* tour would begin in October and cover 30 cities.

Chris Welch of *Melody Maker* was allowed to visit Threshold Studios while the new lineup rehearsed for the upcoming tour. His account appeared in the September 30 issue. From the West Hampstead tube station, Welch made a sharp left and continued down to the old Decca studios. "For it was here," he wrote, "that the Moody Blues have been beavering away these past weeks in a state of terror and excitement, preparing for their return to the world's stage for the first time in five years."

Welch spent time chatting with the Moodies' replacement keyboardist, Patrick Moraz.

Moraz, 34 at this time, was a Swiss musician who had recently spent two years playing keyboard for Yes, a progressive rock group that owed more than a small nod to the Moody Blues.

Patrick Moraz.
(Photo source: Classic Rock Here and Now)

As a child, Moraz was first trained on violin, but then branched out to piano, harpsichord, church organ, synthesizers, and Mellotron, as well as other instruments. His first band was a jazz trio. When Moraz was 16, he won first-place honors at a Zurich jazz music festival, the youngest soloist to win this award.

Moraz's first rock band was the British group Mainhorse, who recorded one album, their self-titled 1971 debut. The album was not a success, but Moraz found work as a film composer with 1971's *The Salamander*, 1973's *The Invitation*, and 1974's *The Middle of the World*.

Next, Moraz was invited to join the Nice after Keith Emerson left the group. The new configuration took a new name – Refugee – and released a self-titled album in 1974.

Patrick Moraz: "The Nice had been split-up for more than three years when we formed Refugee. Also, in Refugee, we were playing all original music, which I composed for the group, so I did not have to copy or replicate parts which had been recorded before me. The only reference to the Nice was the fact that I was playing with the same rhythm section, Lee Jackson and Brian Davison, both excellent players and showmen, as well as contributors to the group." (PM-LIR00)

At this time, keyboardist Rick Wakeman departed from Yes during the recording of *Relayer*, the group's seventh album. Moraz was invited to audition as Wakeman's replacement. He told *Keyboard* magazine, "When Yes called me, they knew I was not exclusively signed to anything. I was still involved with Refugee, but it wasn't happening; it wasn't essential music. It was interesting, but we had management problems, we had a record company pushing us for more commercial things, and I felt that I was ready to leave. …

"I had seen [Yes] play before and didn't think their music was very alive; it sounded dead. But seeing them rehearse 'Sound Chaser' [from *Relayer*], I thought they were incredible. Plus I had never seen anything like them before. There were armies of roadies, and they were rehearsing into a 24-track recorder. It took a lot of courage for me to get up and play along with them." (PM-K81)

The audition went well; Moraz was offered the job. He played on *Relayer* in a limited capacity, since much of the material was already developed, then toured with the band in support of the album. A short time later, Moraz played on Yes member Steve Howe's 1975 solo album, *Beginnings*, and on Chris Squire's *Fish Out of Water*, from the same year. He also made his first solo album during this time, 1976's *The Story of I*.

Late in 1976, Moraz regrouped with Yes for a tour, followed by recording sessions for 1977's *Going for the One*. Halfway through the making of the album, however, Moraz was asked to leave to make room for the returning Rick Wakeman.

Moraz didn't see this change coming. He candidly admitted, "Unfortunately, I was forced to leave. And, even though, at the time, the split 'was supposed to appear acrimonious,' I suffered extremely and extensively. To be 'asked to leave' so suddenly put me in a lot of turmoil and disturbance. The fact is, I was never compensated for anything. I never ever got paid for any of my tour participation in the extremely successful and extensive Yes tour of 1976, which comprised about 65 concerts, many of them in front of sold-out audiences of more than 100,000 people. After all, as a member of the band, I was entitled to a 20% cut from what the band was getting. ...

"In addition, it was an extremely complicated and difficult situation for me to be stranded on the street, with my baby daughter who was only one-month old, and her mother, without any transport or money, in the cold winter of Switzerland. Then the fight for survival to stay alive; it all became surreal." (PM-LIR00)

Moraz continued with his solo career, recording his second album, 1977's *Out in the Sun*, then a third, 1978's *Patrick Moraz*. Having experienced the thrill of giving concerts in front of thousands of cheering fans with Yes, Moraz hoped to get back onto a major tour of that proportion. He told *Melody Maker*, "I sort of unofficially let it be known to people that I was mentally and physically ready to go on the road once again...." (PM-MM78)

The timing meshed well with the Moodies' need for a keyboardist. During this period, John Lodge told a reporter, "Mike's slightly disenchanted with the business. So Graeme Edge got the idea to call up Patrick Moraz and ask him to join the band as our keyboardist...." (JL-PDN78)

Moraz said, "I knew the Moody Blues' material and how influential they had been – especially in rock symphonic work. ... After the Beatles' *Sgt. Pepper*, it was really the Moodies' *Days of Future Passed* that saw the breakthrough of symphonic rock. That first album was very influential. ...

"I had to go back to Europe for a solo concert and I suggested we meet and play together. I really couldn't join a band without playing with them first!" (PM-MM78)

This audition took place in July 1978, one month after the release of *Octave*.

A short time later, Moraz told Jon Bream of *The Minneapolis Star*, "They were nervous because they hadn't played together in so long and they didn't know what we should do. They hadn't seen so many keyboards; I think I brought 10 along!" (PM-MS78)

Hayward recalled, "We all sat at our studio in West Hampstead in London and messed around, not knowing quite what to do." (JH-CE78)

Moraz said that this awkwardness lasted "two or three *hours*," adding, "Finally, I said, 'Let's play "Tuesday Afternoon,"'" which was one of the three numbers I had learned before I went there." (PM-MS78)

The other two songs were "Nights in White Satin" and "Legend of a Mind."

Engineer Norman Goodman told Mark Murley, "I was lucky enough to be present when they brought Patrick in, although it wasn't exactly an audition. That was an interesting time, because it was very clear that he was the right guy for the job. I think it was quite unanimous straight away, as soon as he started playing. They all played together in the studio. … Patrick [had] obviously learned the songs and he was a Mellotron player. … [H]is orchestral approach was obviously just right for them; it sounded like the Moodies straight away." (NG-H&H96)

Moraz was hired immediately. He said, "I was happily surprised. It happened at the right moment because I was thinking about putting a band together myself. Then I began thinking about who they were. The Moody Blues were the main influence on Yes, King Crimson, Genesis, and even Kansas. That they thought of doing a rock album with an orchestra in 1967 was incredible." (PM-MS78)

Moraz told *Melody Maker*, "I'm committed to the music, and I'll contribute as much to the Moodies as I did to Yes. My role is to be the orchestra for the band. When the Moodies play it touches the hearts of the people everywhere. When Justin plays a guitar solo, it flies; it's rock 'n' roll.

"We'll be playing two or three cuts off each album, from *Days of Future Passed* to *Octave*, and I've had to learn all their material very quickly. We've been rehearsing for weeks, up to eight hours a day. The tour starts on October 19 in Germany, then we go to America in November. The band has not been on the road for five years and they are pretty scared. But they are in very good shape and they are playing with more power than you hear on the record.

"I've got great respect for Mike Pinder – his early work with the Moodies was incredible. He was the first guy to bend a note on a Mellotron!

"We'll just go on stage and play the songs. The songs are great – they don't need expensive artifices. We'll play tunes like 'Driftwood,' and 'Slide Zone,' and, sure, we'll play 'Nights in White Satin.' It's funny, in ten years I'll know all the British bands' material. I've done the ex-Nice trip, the Yes-trip, and now the Moody Blues-trip! All I need now is to join Led Zeppelin." (PM-MM78)

It took about a week for the word of Pinder's replacement to get back to America. In its October 7 issue, *Billboard* reported:

> … Moraz was approached after founder-member Mike Pinder had declined to tour with the Moodies. Pinder is currently living the life of a recluse, devoting himself to study of the Hopi culture, and his future with the band must be uncertain.
>
> In Britain there has been speculation that Pinder means to take legal action, but as drummer Graeme Edge points out, "We are not closing the door on Mike, it is rather a case that by his refusal to tour, he has walked out through it." …
>
> The band will go into the studio in the new year, but it is not yet known whether or not Moraz will record with them.

Justin Hayward: "We were nervous, but when we struck up the first note at the first gig in Germany, we knew it would be okay. It was exactly the right time for us to come back." (JH-MM79)

At the start of November, after road-testing their act for four or five shows (accounts differ) in Germany, the Moodies undertook a five-week tour of 32 performances in 30 cities spanning North America. The 18-song set list included:

"Steppin' in a Slide Zone" (Lodge); "Tuesday Afternoon" (Hayward); "Twilight Time" (Thomas); "The Day We Meet Again" (Hayward); "The Story in Your Eyes" (Hayward); "I'm Your Man" (Thomas); "Top Rank Suite" (Hayward); "Isn't Life Strange?" (Lodge); "Driftwood" (Hayward); "I'll Be Level with You" (Hayward, Lodge, and Thomas singing); "Gypsy" (Hayward); "Survival" (Lodge); "The Balance" (Edge); "I'm Just a Singer (In a Rock and Roll Band)" (Lodge); "Nights in White Satin" (Hayward); "Legend of a Mind" (Thomas); "Question" (Hayward); and "Ride My See-Saw" (Lodge).

Rockers on the rocks (l to r): Justin Hayward, John Lodge, Ray Thomas, Patrick Moraz and Graeme Edge.

Caption (top right image): "Drugs are out, Gatorade is in, and these veterans are back in the rock cosmos. Caption (bottom right image): "Rockers on the rocks (l to r): Justin Hayward, John Lodge, Ray Thomas, Patrick Moraz and Graeme Edge."
(Provenance unknown)

The North American tour opened on Friday, November 3, 1978, at the Civic Center, in St. Paul, Minnesota. The next day, the *St. Paul Pioneer Press* reported:

> … Like the Bob Dylan reunion four days earlier, Friday night's group drew some 17,000 fans who proved to be more interested in listening than hassling. Sure, there was an abundance of beer drinkers, marijuana smokers (the aroma was unusually strong on the floor), and others who smuggled in wineskins filled with their

favorite spirits. But, for the most part, those who shelled out up to $10 a seat avoided confrontation with the law and concentrated instead on the entertainment provided by the group during its first stop on a 30-day tour. ...

The good news... the crowd helped set a record. The show apparently marked the first time in Civic Center history that two concerts – Dylan was the other – in one week have been sellouts.

Inside the auditorium, James M. Tarbox was covering the concert for the *St. Paul Pioneer Press*. The headline for his report set the tone: "Moody Blues Still Magical."

> ... After a five year hiatus from public performing... the Moody Blues returned to St. Paul Friday night to open the biggest tour they've ever undertaken. If the tumultuous reception they garnered here is any indication, there was no love lost in the interim.
>
> At 8:45, a pair of tremendously bright flood lights played across the floor of the arena as a cacophony of sound welled from the PA system. And in a flash the Moodies were into the opening number of the current album *Octave*. Next came "Tuesday Afternoon" ... and they had the crowd in the palms of their collective hands. ...
>
> The concert was comprised of a healthy selection of songs from the new record, and a smattering of things from the legendary seven – which in effect turned out to be a "greatest hits" format. There probably were few among the nearly 18,000 in attendance who would have complained about the way things were presented. ...

But Tarbox had a few complaints. He felt the Moodies stuck too close to the recorded versions of songs, saying "It was not until the last two songs ("Legend of a Mind" and "Question") that they allowed themselves any room for improvising."

He felt that Patrick Moraz ("sitting in for Michael Pinder, who is not making the tour") was kept too much in the background, limited to "playing chords and glissando." He added, "Finally, he and guitarist Justin Hayward got a little 'dialogue' going, but by then the show was drawing to a close."

Tarbox, clearly well-versed in music (he used "glissando," didn't he?) noticed that Ray Thomas's tambourine got out of tempo with Graeme Edge's drumming occasionally, resulting in a couple of songs getting off on the wrong foot, "but they always were back on track within seconds, an indication of the unyielding professionalism of the group."

The review continued:

> All of this can be laid to the fact that, outside of a few rehearsal appearances in Germany to try the show out, this is the Moodies first live appearance in five years (they last played in San Francisco in 1973) [sic, January 1974]. That's also why the tour opens in the relative wilderness of the Midwest. ... The critics

here may not be as influential as those in New York or Los Angeles. ...

And, finally, Edge, whose immaculate narrative voice and delivery is an object lesson in oral interpretation, was relegated to a sole reading to introduce "The Balance." He could turn the phone book into a love poem.

While the band was in town, Jon Bream of *The Minneapolis Star* interviewed Patrick Moraz. Moraz gave Bream an exclusive: "They have asked me to join whether or not Mike wants to still record with them."

One wonders if anyone had let Mike Pinder know that!

Bream continued:

... Moraz adds a new dimension to the band's classical-rock sound. While Pinder specialized on the Mellotron, Moraz travels with about a dozen different keyboard instruments. "I play the same chord," he said, "but I try to enhance the music."

Moraz's style is more energetic and more rock-oriented than Pinder's. In fact, the Moodies whole sound, especially Justin Hayward's guitar work, sounds harder than before.

If the Moodies' albums are immaculately lush in sound and production, then Friday's 90-minute concert was strikingly stark and spare by contrast. It was definitely more rock-and-roll than orchestral. Furthermore, it was a very straightforward presentation with simple lighting and staging (save some stage fog on one number). ...

Bream observed that "the sold-out crowd of 17,500 people seemed to be cheering as much for the songs and what they have meant as for the band's performance, which was uneven, at best."

Michael Anthony, also writing for the Minneapolis *Star Tribune*, noted that the Moody Blues had chosen the Twin Cities to begin their very first tour of America ten years earlier. They now began their first tour in five years from the same starting point. He observed:

... Apparently, the fans hadn't forgotten. The concert at the St. Paul Civic Center sold out in a couple days, and the same thing is happening elsewhere on the 30-city tour. (All 20,000 tickets for the Nov. 27 concert at Madison Square Garden went in less than a day.) Not surprisingly, the response given to the five musicians as they took the stage Friday night (Patrick Moraz replacing Michael Pinder on keyboards for this tour), and as they continued through the 85-minute set, was tantamount to hysteria.

Understandably, there were some technical problems the opening night of the tour. ("This is our first gig in America, so if we forget a few lyrics bear with us," lead singer-guitarist Justin Hayward told the audience after the first two numbers.) Actually, the lyrics were all more or less in place, but Graeme Edge's drums were under-amplified in the first number... and once or twice in up-tempo numbers Hayward lost pace with the band.

Also, "the ensemble vocals – so rich a part of the Moodies' recorded sound – were often out of sync and pitch, as though they were having trouble hearing one another." But none of this mattered in the end. Anthony explained:

> The Moodies, after all, are credited with starting the classical-rock vogue of the late '60s (Electric Light Orchestra has taken up the calling in the last few years): intricate arrangements, opulent orchestrations and, in the lyrics, a sometimes turgid quest for emotional balance and understanding. Their strength has always been in the melodic appeal of their material, especially the songs of Hayward and John Lodge, and the power of that material made for an impressive set Friday, despite the noted imperfections. ...

Saturday, November 4: University of Iowa, in Ames. Jonathan Engel attended, and wrote for *The Des Moines Register*:

> It was worth the wait. After warming up with some new material, the Moody Blues brought a homecoming crowd of nearly 11,000 to its feet in Hilton Coliseum here Saturday night with a series of soaring renditions of the songs that helped them sell some 29 million records before they split up five years ago. ...

> Justin Hayward was both delicate and dynamic in his guitar work, but many times his vocals could not be heard clearly. Yet he belted out "Nights in White Satin," and the crowd stood and kept standing from then on. Ray Thomas's flutes spoke with hollow eloquence, especially on "Legend of a Mind" (about LSD-tripper Timothy Leary), in which he also sang lead vocals. Graeme Edge on drums and John Lodge on bass provided more than a beat – they thundered to the fore when quiet intricacy moved to intensity, and then fell back again, as in "Question," where Hayward again showed his voice can reach the heights trade-marking the group's harmonies.

> The result was a whooping, pounding call for an encore, which continued for minutes and roared to the loudest sound of the night when the band reappeared for "Ride My See-Saw," a big hit from their third album. ...

> Their musical importance is undenied. The characteristic woodwinds of Jethro Tull, the keyboard wizardry of Yes, and the echoing vocals of Pink Floyd owe more than a little to the Moody Blues.

Sunday, November 5: Dane County Coliseum, Madison, Wisconsin. Reserved seats ranged from $7.50 to $9.50. Joshua Leibner was there, covering the concert for *The Daily Cardinal*.

> … They were warmly greeted here as they opened with a disco-like tune from *Octave*, "Steppin' in a Slide Zone." Fortunately, this wrong was righted with a stunning "Tuesday Afternoon." That alone was enough to bring back faded memories of the start of the psychedelic era ten years ago.
>
> Throughout the evening, the Moodies interspersed their new material between acknowledged classics such as "The Story in Your Eyes," "Isn't Life Strange" and "A Balance" [sic], until all but one new song had been included in the line-up [sic; six of the ten were from *Octave*]. The group didn't feel comfortable playing its *Octave* material, but were put up to it by the record companies to force interest in the album so they could recoup their losses.

Time out. The album had already sold well in excess of 500,000 copies. There were no "losses" to recoup!

Leibner continued:

> … For all the time that was needlessly used up for the newer songs, the audience could have been treated to such spurred elegant classics as "Eyes of a Child," "The Voyage," "Dear Diary," "Never Comes the Day" and "Lovely to See You," just to name a few. …
>
> It's amazing, but after all these years the group is still note-for-note brilliant. … Patrick Moraz, the multi-talented keyboardist who was recently jilted by Yes, took the place of reluctant regular Michael Pinder. Moraz filled Pinder's shoes superbly, and seemed happy to be playing somewhere.
>
> The evening concluded with five knock-out punches, as the group took the audience on a stroll down memory lane with the powerhouse "I'm Just a Singer (In a Rock and Roll Band)" and then encoring with "Ride My See-Saw." Sandwiched in between were celestial remembrances of "Nights in White Satin" and "Question."
>
> The Moody Blues gratefully threw in an extended 10-minute version of "Legend of a Mind" complete with special lighting effects and some added fluting by Thomas to the Madison audience, which is only the third stop in the current tour. "The Timothy Leary anthem" was the unquestionable highlight of the night's 17-song repertoire and still walks hand-in-hand with "White Rabbit" as the king of the hill of the drug ballads. …

Monday, November 6: Market Street Arena, Indianapolis, Indiana.

Tuesday, November 7: Riverfront Coliseum, Cincinnati, Ohio. On the day of the concert, Justin Hayward explained the absence of Mike Pinder to Cliff Radel of *The Cincinnati Enquirer*: "For the last couple of years he didn't enjoy touring very much. We all have enough respect for each other that if somebody doesn't want to do it, that's fine by us."

Hayward confirmed that Moraz would remain with the Moodies and participate in the recording of their next album, sessions for which were already tentatively scheduled. "We all live in England, except for Mike; he lives in California. We'll be recording in London after Christmas and Patrick will still be with us."

Hayward said he felt no animosity toward Pinder, and missed him: "His work with the Moody Blues was always my favorite." (JH-CE78)

After watching the concert, Cliff Radel remembered Hayward's pre-concert statement about missing Mike Pinder:

> I'll second that. Tuesday night, everyone missed Michael Pinder. Hayward, John Lodge, Graeme Edge, Ray Thomas, and the 14,000 spectators that showed up to see the Moody Blues in concert....

> So, while Pinder stayed home, Patrick Moraz, late of Yes, took his place. Well, he did not actually take his place. Moraz is Pinder's inferior when it comes to playing keyboards.

> Moraz's performance went from weak, [as] he groped his way through the organ part to "I'm Just a Singer (In a Rock and Roll Band)," to draggy, for "Legend of a Mind," flutist Ray Thomas's ode to Timothy Leary. Moraz lagged too far behind the beat.

Radel also felt Moraz was sprinkling in too many electronic sound effects, intruding on songs which didn't need them, such as "Question" and "Ride My See-Saw." Radel continued:

> Since keyboards constitute a principal voice on the Moody Blues' records, it is imperative the player maintain their status in concert. Moraz could not. The best he could do was drown out Thomas's vocal on "I'm Your Man." True, Moraz's keyboards were dominant, but this was not the dominance the Moodies sought when they settled upon their style. ...

And then there was the balance between old and new songs. Radel said:

> Granted, the Moodies, like all artists, want to be recognized as viable performers. To be creative they must move on, not look back. This attitude cannot be questioned. And it is not. What *is* is the band's overcompensating for not releasing an album for five years.

> *Octave* songs like "Top Rank Suite," where Hayward used his rich baritone to give deep expression to his lyrics, deserves a hearing. Nevertheless, so do the earlier additions to the Moody Blues'

oeuvre. There are many works of art in that repertoire. To deny them their place on the program shortchanges the Moody Blues' legacy. ...

Of all the Moodies, Hayward has shown the most artistic growth since the band's layoff. His "Nights in White Satin" singing was more impassioned than the recorded version. And his guitar playing, which he discounts, has moved, in Pinder's absence, to the forefront of the band's instrumental array.

Regarding his guitar work, Hayward told Radel, "I've never pretended to be the world's greatest guitar player. That's the last thing I'd want – everyone to turn up every night to see what my left hand's doing. I can't imagine that to be too much fun." (JH-CE78)

Thursday, November 9: Olympia Stadium, Detroit, Michigan. John Dearing covered the concert for *The Michigan Daily*, but what he most wanted to share with his readers was the aftermath.

... Backstage, the Moody Blues are relaxing after their Olympia show. Thomas is leaning against a railing, watching the road crew take down the equipment they will bring to Chicago for a show the following night. Thomas is drained from performing, but is personable and responsive to questions. ...

Justin Hayward, a master at making his guitar weep, converses with an older man holding a baby. Hayward looks considerably older than he did in the group's heyday, but is as dapper as ever. One of the original Moody Blues is not present.

"Mike Pinder, our keyboardist, didn't want to tour," explains Thomas. "It's not for religious reasons or anything; he said he'd simply had enough of the whole scene. Since we really couldn't blame him, [and] we got Patrick Moraz to take his place."

Listening in on a conversation between Lodge and Hayward, Dearing noted, "Some of the band members don't seem overly pleased with the Olympia performance." Thomas felt the same, and explained, "Justin and I really didn't perform up to our own expectations. Near the end of some of the songs we were kind of sloppy. But then, again, this is the first tour we've done together in, what, four or five years?" (RT-MD68)

For any reviewers who thought the band didn't care – they did.

Friday, November 10: Chicago Stadium, Chicago, Illinois. Covering the concert for the *Chicago Tribune* was Lynn Van Matre:

... Though the lineup featured Patrick Moraz (one-time Yes man) on keyboards rather than the non-touring Moody Michael Pinder, the sound retained essentially the same familiar lushness, whether threading through more contemporary Moody material or reprising the vintage "Nights in White Satin," surely one of the group's most appealing songs. And for all of the references to time that pepper the Moodies' lyrics (along the lines of how it waits for no one, and so forth), the music itself has a certain timeless quality.

It remains, at its best, a sound to be swept away by; a sound to plug into when overtaken by a craving for the strains of full-blown romanticism. …

If there was a "best," then there was also a "worst." Van Matre had a problem with the acoustics of the stadium which, like most stadiums of this time, were not built for music but sporting events. Another problem, said the *Tribune* writer, was the Moodies' "lack of live performance panache."

They are amiable and pleasant, yes – but exciting or even engrossing, no. Like some other groups – the Band, for example – who score far more points in the recording studio than they do on stage, the Moodies are musicians, not entertainers. Like the Band, they simply stand there and take care of business, and the occasional helping of mist from a fog machine isn't going to change things. …

A critic from a rival newspaper – Rick Kogan of the *Chicago Sun-Times* – felt the same.

Until Friday night, the Moody Blues had not played in Chicago for five years, and one can only wonder why 20,000 people packed the Stadium for 90 minutes of their music.

The Moody Blues' attraction stems mainly from their albums – full-production anthems dedicated to vague philosophical notions and crushing symphonic punctuation. On record they are somewhat hypnotic and slightly annoying. Ah, but in concert they are mush. …

With a stage presence vaguely reminiscent of grazing sheep, the Moody Blues performed more than 15 songs. Like any group that has been around for more than a decade, they played some songs from their latest album (the million-selling *Octave*) and some hits from the past. But everything sounded the same; songs became indistinguishable from one another in a tangle of cosmic Muzak. …

Granted, there's a "Moody Blues sound." But indistinguishable "cosmic Muzak"? Really, Rick? Maybe it's your musical taste that's been homogenized …

Saturday, November 11: Lexington Center, Lexington, Kentucky.

Sunday, November 12: Middle Tennessee State University, Murfreesboro, Tennessee.

Tuesday, November 14: The Omni Arena, Atlanta, Georgia. Russ DeVault reported in the *Atlanta Journal*:

... They came together at the Omni Tuesday night for a crowd of about 10,000. It was obvious that regular keyboard player Mike Pinder was missing, but the crowd had Justin Hayward, John Lodge, Ray Thomas, Graeme Edge, and Pinder-substitute Patrick Moraz to perform 18 songs, so all was forgiven.

Their best effort was "Nights in White Satin," their 15th of the night. It brought the crowd to its feet for the first time, but was unfortunately followed by a version of "Legend of a Mind" interrupted by a fan's fall down the steeply slanted steps of a stage-right section.

"Oh (expletive)," said Thomas, the band's flautist, in mid-song.

Everything was not downhill after that, however. The band churned on through the remainder of its program without losing the beat and the crowd's response indicated Hayward's vocals deserve the extra emphasis given them in recent concerts. ...

Wednesday, November 15: Coliseum, Greensboro, North Carolina.
Thursday, November 16: Capital Centre, Landover, Maryland. Present was Elaine Dickinson, on behalf of *The Washington* [D.C.] *Star*.

It's hard to believe that a musical group that has not performed in over five years can sell out the Capital Centre. But the Moody Blues did that last night. Unfortunately for their admirers, the group sounded as though it hadn't practiced in five years. ...

Signs of life returned with "Gypsy," but a low point was reached when the Moodys performed "The Balance," including the poem which was recited by Graeme Edge, who possesses a terrible speaking voice. This inclusion sounded trite and dated, especially out of the *Question of Balance* album context.

The Moody Blues were warmly received by the audience, especially when they played it safe with "Nights in White Satin" and "Timothy Leary" [sic]. At the very end of the show, they revived their flair for real rock and roll with "The Question" and "Ride My See-Saw," which brought standing ovations. ...

The group's stage presence was non-existent, and one felt no rapport between audience and musician. Singer Ray Thomas, paunchy and moving with marked clumsiness on-stage, looked as if his clothes were picked out of a laundry basket. Somehow, an old Moody Blues fan expected a little more class and a lot more musicianship.

A second Washington, D.C. newspaper – the *Washington Post* – likewise had a reviewer at the concert. Jennefer Hirshberg wrote:

... With much that is both moody and blue, their material featured strong melody lines colored with broad strokes of the melancholy and high-lighted by Ray Thomas's haunting flute.

They began with "Steppin' in a Slide Zone" from their latest album (seven of the 18-song set were from *Octave*), and, ironically, the title provided an uncomfortable commentary on the first half of their set. ... Their new material seems to borrow much from Bread, in both melodies and harmonies. Their lyrics are less obsessively arty. But whether changes bode well for the band's comeback is open to question.

Friday, November 17: Springfield Civic Center, Springfield, Massachusetts.
Saturday, November 18: Memorial Auditorium, Buffalo, New York.
Monday, November 20: Boston Gardens, Boston, Massachusetts. It transpired that the band's trip out of Boston was a perilous one.
United Press International reported:

Snow and freezing rain turned expressways into bobsled runs from the Midwest to New England Tuesday. At least two traffic deaths were blamed on the storm, which brought the first snow of the season to portions of Boston, New York and Chicago. ...

Snow delayed the rock band Moody Blues, which was leaving Boston after a concert Monday night. The group's double-decker bus skidded a few feet and became stuck beneath the Boston University Bridge.

"It took about a half hour to back the thing out," police said. ...

Tuesday, November 21: Veterans Memorial Coliseum, New Haven, Connecticut. Folk singer Jimmie Spheeris was the warm-up act. Randall Beach reported for the *New Haven Register*:

"A bloody lousy day," ended with a splendid night Tuesday as the Moody Blues made a late arrival to the New Haven Coliseum, but enthralled a sell-out audience until nearly midnight.

With their plane broken down in Boston, the band was forced to drive to New Haven in the sleet and snow. By the time the show finally began, the crowd was getting edgy, the boos intensifying. Fortunately the Moody Blues draw a more mellow clientele than most rock groups. ...

Flutist Ray Thomas, who stunned the audience with his solos, may be the only rock performer who says, "God Bless You" to his fans. But he also sounded off about Tuesday's travel hassles: "We've had a bloody lousy day. The engine fell out of the plane." ...

Guitarists Justin Hayward and John Lodge, dressed as country gentlemen in white sport coats, alternated vocals with Thomas in a beautifully balanced program. Keyboardist Patrick Moraz (filling in for regular Michael Pinder) delivered booming cathedral music and percussionist Graeme Edge recited poems when not flogging his drums.

Some of the band's material is so carefully crafted in the studio that it would seem impossible to perform faithful live versions. But they rendered "Isn't Life Strange" as delicately as on the record. …

Ted Drozdowski, writing for a different Connecticut newspaper – Meriden's *The Morning Record-Journal* – had a grumpier tone. He complained:

> … Most of the evening's program was from their latest and blandest album, *Octave* (an effort that would have been fine if it were recorded by a group like the Bee Gees).
>
> "Steppin' in a Slide Zone," the album's only successful single to date, was the opener suffice to note. A ray of hope drifted into the eyes of the old timers (and there were many in the auditorium) when "Tuesday Afternoon" and "Sunset" from *Days of Future Passed* followed. But, from the pinnacle of their art the Moodies plunged to onstage mediocrity by playing more songs from *Octave* for almost a half-hour. Another glimmer of astral light crept from behind the speaker banks when "Driftwood" floated through the arena. The best cut from their last album, it typifies Hayward's new songwriting bent toward soft-throated, slightly depressing love ballads. His current single from the Richard Burton narrated *War of the Worlds*, "Forever Autumn," a truly fine song, is another example. …
>
> Mike Pinder is, probably for the better, abstaining from the current tour. Mr. Mellotron has supposedly refused to hit the road because he has become so enamored with the home life. Judging by the caliber of his live replacement, it might be healthy for the Moodies if Pinder stayed out of the studio as well. The man who's standing in, Patrick Moraz, played many of the trademark overdone Mellotron passages with his sparkling-sounded synthesizer. Moraz's technique seems to flow like a fountain through one ear and out the other, bubbling over the brain. …
>
> The most commanding aspect of the Moodies' performance was, is, and forever shall be the vocals. Thomas, Hayward and Lodge come together in a perfect, uplifting, inspirational harmony. The raw spiritualism in their voices was the grace that carried, smoothed, and saved what might have been an uninteresting concert (as a whole) or an unchallenged musical drill for Edge and Moraz.

Wednesday, November 22: The Spectrum, Philadelphia, Pennsylvania. Jack Lloyd of *The Philadelphia Inquirer* was on hand, later saying:

> When the Moody Blues released a debut album titled *Days of Future Passed* shortly after the group's formation in 1965 [sic: they formed in 1964, *Days* was released in 1967], the world of pop music snapped to attention with its first taste of something called "classical pop." …
>
> Now they are back, and a capacity crowd of 18,000 that showed up at the Spectrum Wednesday night made it clear that an absence of five years had not dimmed the loyalty of the Moodies' fans.
>
> The only member missing was keyboardist Michael Pinder, a vital cog in the machine since the group's "classical" sound was so dependent on the array of synthesizers manned by Pinder. Pinder performed on the group's reunion album, *Octave*, released in August, but decided shortly before the start of this 30-city [sic] tour that he would pass. …
>
> Utilizing an uncluttered staging motif – devoid of the usual exotic trappings so common at rock concerts these days – the Moodies presented their music with crisp execution for the most part. The sound mix was a trifle off-balance, though.
>
> Not too much has changed, it would seem. Just as a reminder of those old accusations of pretentiousness, "I'm Just a Singer (In a Rock 'n' Roll Band)" was introduced with the notation, "Just so certain people don't think we're pretentious." …
>
> The charge of being pretentious is quite unfair. Credit must be given for what the Moodies have attempted and what they have achieved. …

Thursday, November 23: Civic Center, Providence, Rhode Island.
Friday, November 24: Hershey Park Arena, Hershey, Pennsylvania.
Sunday, November 26: Scope Arena, Norfolk, Virginia. Mike Diana was in the audience, assessing the performance for the Newport News, Virginia's *Daily Press*. Diana, not always inclined to compliment the Moodies in the past, stayed true to course:

> … For a group that has been rated superb since their inception in the late 60s, through their breakup in the mid-70s, and list of records that sold in the millions (and probably still does), the Moody Blues showed to be shadows of their former selves.
>
> They played all their hits and most popular pieces too fast, and could not keep in time with each other.
>
> The main culprit was Ray Thomas. He constantly over blew his flute which gave it the tonal quality of a police whistle. When he

didn't have the flute to play he mercilessly beat on a tambourine. Half the time he didn't pay attention to the beat or the dynamics of the particular piece.

Drummer Graeme Edge could have been beating garbage cans. His playing was suspect if not just plain bad. When a drummer gets out of shape he has trouble sustaining meter through an entire number. Edge drove "I'm Just a Singer (In a Rock and Roll Band)" past Warp 10.

Patrick Moraz, who replaced Mike Pinder on keyboards for the tour, kept stomping his foot and searching for eye contact in a vain effort to keep everyone playing at the same speed. ...

The group did a poor rendition of "Twilight Time" and a lousy rendition of "Story in Your Eyes." For best number in the show my vote goes to "Nights in White Satin" (which really deserved the standing ovation it received) and "Timothy Leary" [sic]. ...

A more appreciative attendee, Nancy N. Lloyd, fired a letter back to the newspaper, and Diana:

... Are you for real? Obviously Mike, you don't know the Moody Blues music or you don't know how to appreciate it. I was very pleased with their performance and so were many others. Why do you think there was a standing ovation? ...

Ray Thomas is not a culprit, and I've never heard a flute sound like a police whistle. In fact, I thought he performed very well.

Are you a musician or just a small time critic? I mean, really, "garbage cans"? Why don't you look up the meaning of some of your adjectives. Garbage cans are used for garbage (i.e., empty beer cans, egg shells, your review), not for music. ...

The Moody Blues have been around for a long time and with the reputation of their music, they will probably be around a lot longer than you will with your degrading interpretations of famous musicians!

Monday, November 27: Madison Square Garden, New York, N.Y. The Nicky James Band served as the opening act. Phil Gelormine was in the building, for *Billboard*. His take:

... Sports arenas have never been the ideal venues to fully enjoy a live concert in. ... The Moody Blues, so meticulously recorded on records, were ravaged by a sound system designed for the ears of the deaf. Credit the group with valiantly trying to override the problem, at least acknowledging it. Distortion plagued the entire set, especially the vocals when Justin Hayward would reach for notes like those written for "Nights in White Satin." ... In all fairness to the band, the music they selected to play was a thoughtful representation from past London/Deram/Threshold albums and would have been delightful had the Sound Gods been kind. The audience deserves kudos for being both respectful and responsive in light of the situation, which at best was tolerable. ...

Robert Palmer covered the concert for *The New York Times*:

> ... Even though the quintet's live sound fell far short of the orchestral richness of its recordings – *Days of Future Past* [sic], which the group recorded in 1969 [sic: 1967] with the London Symphony [sic: the London Festival Orchestra], was a landmark album in the development of symphonic rock – its fans were entranced.
>
> The band did sound good, and in a much more basic and satisfying way than its records. For although it has written some memorable melodies and come up with some pretty, ethereal music, the Moody Blues have also, and often, been cosmic bores. ...
>
> The evening obviously meant a great deal more to the group's longtime fans than it did to this writer, who found it pleasant but not earthshaking. It did seem worth noting that the Moody Blues, who are often dismissed by younger rock musicians as "dinosaurs," still seem capable of playing that is energetic and even gripping.

Wednesday, November 29: The Forum, Montreal, Quebec. Interviewed by the Canadian Press wire service, Justin Hayward was asked if the Moodies were nervous about audience reception for their first tour in five years. Hayward admitted, "I think we probably were, which is why we did a few warm-up gigs in Europe first. The reception there was so tremendous that we came over here with a lot of confidence, and it seems to be going very well. The crowds everywhere are fantastic – really better than before. The people who grew up with us, they're still with us. And there's a tremendous amount of younger people as well, which really knocks me out. A lot of them couldn't have been more than five years old when *Days of Future Passed* came out." (JH-SP78)

Hayward's good feelings weren't echoed by the critic sent by *The Gazette*, the only English-language daily newspaper in Montreal, Quebec. Juan Rodriguez reported:

> Performing locally for the first time in nearly six years, the Moody Blues were greeted with nostalgia last night at the Forum. There was thunderous applause for long-awaited versions of the quintet's revered songs, most of which are nearly a decade old, while the new ones were greeted politely. The fact that the Moodies were at long last back on stage was enough for the 10,000 fans, yet the group did virtually nothing to warrant the reception. ... Indeed, with the exception of keyboardist Patrick Moraz, they had the spirit of sleep-walkers. Never particularly exciting live musicians

– they have the stage presence of bank tellers – they let their equipment do the talking for them. …

Thursday, November 30: Maple Leaf Gardens, Toronto, Ontario.

Friday, December 1: Richfield Coliseum, Richfield (Cleveland), Ohio. In attendance was Mark Faris of *The Akron Beacon Journal*. Other reporters described dull presentations; Faris seemed to have witnessed a different group.

> … The Moody Blues, the legendary, 13-year-old British band of mind-expanding melodies, was back. After five years, they had returned to the concert stage and, based on their performance Friday, their genius for producing supersonic symphonies of color and vision has not diminished. …
>
> The delicate amalgamation of their individual contributions produces an overwhelming, magnificent tidal wave of complex, orchestrated sound that fills the head with images of beauty, contentment, almost unearthly perception and sometimes just plain roaring rock and roll.
>
> They tell of veins in leaves, the balance of the universe, and singing in a rock-and-roll band.
>
> Hayward, Thomas and Lodge blend their voices into a single soaring strain of harmony while Edge's superb, creative percussion simultaneously leads and follows them through every note.
>
> The overall sound of the Moodys is so strong that individual talents are often overlooked. But each man, especially Edge, is more than a capable virtuoso. …
>
> The new music, particularly the beautiful "Driftwood," are classic Moody Blues melodies. But the frantic crowd was really devastated by early hits like "Tuesday Afternoon," "The Story in Your Eyes," "Ride My See-Saw," and "Question."
>
> Other old Moody hits such as "Isn't Life Strange," "I'm Just a Singer (In a Rock 'N Roll Band)" and "The Balance," had the people on their feet and almost breathless. And "Gypsy," "Nights in White Satin" and "Legend of a Mind" stopped the show.
>
> A lot of young faces in the crowd may never have seen the Moody Blues before. After Friday's introduction, they'll never forget them.

Also present for the same show was Bill Camarata of *Scene* magazine. His opinion:

For the first Moody Blues tour since 1973, it was damn good. Since their coming has always been an experience of style, bringing in a different crowd than most of your average events around here, the crowd was also damn good, probably the best I've seen around here in a long time – responsive, polite, and open. The television projection screens in the Coliseum were used for this occasion, bringing to every crack and crevice of the auditorium a decent view of a rare treat. …

The music was modified in its live setting by the conveniences of a loud but very clean sound system, good harmonies (finally), Graeme Edge's syndrums, and, most importantly of all, the keyboards of Patrick Moraz. … His synthesizer stylings and Mellotron playing, along with occasional piano, pulled the whole collage of notes together into one cohesive unit. His piano during Ray Thomas's flute solo was particularly complementary.

Of course, there were highlights to the set, those being the obvious ones. "Nights in White Satin" was amazingly smooth…. "Question" drove the audience nuts, due to all of the pauses in the song. After each pause, the Moodies drew another reaction, and then another, and another, bringing the song to a dramatic explosion at the end. "I'm Just a Singer (In a Rock and Roll Band)" gave us a bit of fun, as did the encore, "Ride My See-Saw." Done faster (as I wish it were always done), it topped off a pleasurable evening. Now let's hope they don't make us wait another five years.

Also at the concert was Bruno Bornino, for the *Cleveland Press*. Said he:

No one in the Coliseum crowd of 20,000 last night knew what to expect. The members of the Moody Blues – at one time the classiest rock band in the world – were on their first concert tour in five years. Longtime fans were hoping – perhaps even praying – that the Moodies would be as good as they remembered them. Other spectators, of course, were there to see and hear whether the band members lived up to their reputations as masters of symphonic rock. …

All doubts vanished during the opening number when the group members dazzled the crowd with perfect vocal and instrumental harmonies on "Steppin' in a Slide Zone." It was clearly evident that the Moodies were still in a class by themselves.

Then came their million-selling "Tuesday Afternoon," and all the fans sat back in their seats and relaxed. They knew this was going to be a special night. And was it ever!

The four veteran Moody Blues – Justin Hayward on guitar; John Lodge, bass; Ray Thomas, flute; and Graeme Edge, drums – couldn't have been better. And the same goes for keyboard wizard

Patrick Moraz, a fine solo performer who used to fill in for Rick Wakeman with Yes, made the fans forget Pinder, who elected to stay home on this tour. ...

Bornino had talked to Ron Hrovat, vice president of marketing at the Coliseum. The official felt that this was the first rock audience that actually came to hear the music. "At other rock shows," said Hrovat, "the fans wander through the halls while the band is performing. The spectators stayed in their seats for this one."

Bornino continued:

> And no wonder. The Moodies are true professionals who obviously would do anything possible to enhance their show. For example, they were the first major act this year to allow the coliseum to use the closed-circuit television system so that every fan could see as well as hear the show.

> Hayward – the Robert Redford of rock – was totally believable when he told his fans, "It's lovely to see you, and great to be back." ....

Did the Moodies' performances really ride a see-saw of quality, alternating between excellent performances and terrible ones? Or could it be that some critics simply have better hearing ... dispositions ... or predispositions?

Saturday, December 2: The Moodies were seen on TV, appearing on the late-night program *Don Kirshner's Rock Concert.* Also on the show: Thin Lizzy, Evelyn "Champagne" King, and Disco Dance Dimensions.

Sunday, December 3: Checker Dome (also called Checkerdome), St. Louis, Missouri. Kim Plummer of *The St. Louis Times* was on the scene, talking to concertgoers.

> ... The Moody Blues' concert Sunday night was the group's first here in more than five years. It drew more than 17,000 to the Checkerdome, including many people who said they had not been to a rock concert in years. ...

> Although most of the audience was under 25 and in denim, there was a sizable segment over 30 – some in sports coats and ties. ... Several couples said that they had thought their rock concert days were over – until they heard that the group was coming to town.

Among the latter, a 35-year-old St. Louis woman told Plummer: "I first listened to them when I was in college and messing around with dope. I still like to listen to them, but now I'm messing around with two kids."

Paul Hale, 32, of University City, said, "It used to be that only hippies and teenyboppers would dare come to something like this. But now we're beginning to see rock music fans who also are parents."

A young woman said, while swaying to "Nights in White Satin," "I smoked my first joint listening to that song. That was the big thing to do when I was in college – get stoned listening to the Moody Blues."

Moodys' St. Louis Blues

Pickwick International's St. Louis promotion director, Greg Hagglund, took time to present the Moody Blues with official St. Louis Blues hockey jerseys during their recent sold-out U.S. tour. The occasion was greeted with enthusiasm by the band, since they all happen to be hockey enthusiasts. Pictured from left: Greg Hagglund, Pickwick St. Louis; group members Ray Thomas, Patrick Moraz, Graeme Edge; George Hornfeck, London Records; and John Lodge, Justin Hayward of the Moodys.

RECORD WORLD DECEMBER 30, 1978

Jan Korschgen, 35, of South St. Louis County, said, "Unless you count Neil Diamond, I can't remember the last time I went to one [concert]. But I couldn't miss the chance to see a group that has been important to me for nearly 10 years. I thought it was important for my daughter to see them, too."

Dan Goddard, 29, a South St. Louis man wearing tweed pants and a navy turtleneck, said, "Age has nothing to do with how much a person enjoys a rock concert, especially when it's by a group like the Moody Blues. The idea that rock concerts are just for teenagers is old-fashioned. … That is an idea that is as dead as the hippies and flower children."

Monday, December 4: Kemper Arena, Kansas City, Missouri. Jimmie Spheeris was the opening act. In one of the better seats was Nancy Bill, Arts and Entertainment Writer for the *Kansas City Star*. From her vantage point, she observed:

> … Concentrating mainly on material from their new LP, *Octave*, with a few well-chosen oldies thrown in for flavor, the group played for nearly two hours with Hayward, Thomas and Lodge dominating. The most significant change is the absence of Mike Pinder, whose masterful playing of the Mellotron and other keyboard instruments filled out the Moodies' sound since the beginning. Though he is included on the new album, Pinder chose not to make the tour and was replaced by Patrick Moraz, who similarly filled in for Rick Wakeman of Yes a few years back. …
>
> It was impossible to fill Mike Pinder's shoes, but Moraz did a good job in his own. Though his approach to the Mellotron was

701

different than the powerful punch that Pinder used to crank up, Moraz filled in with some other inventive work on some small Moog synthesizers. ...

The Moody Blues wrote some of the most beautiful music of the 60s and they still have the wisdom to know that melodic tunes and skillful scoring are just as powerful as dissonance and thousands of decibels of volume. Like the Beatles, they were responsible for a profound change in the emphasis and direction of rock music, and with plans for a new LP and solo projects underway, the Blues look like they plan to be around to stay.

Tuesday, December 5: Myriad Convention Center, Oklahoma City, Oklahoma.
Wednesday, December 6: Tarrant County Coliseum, Fort Worth, Texas. Pete Oppel of the *Dallas Morning News* was on hand. His report started:

The Moody Blues carefully built what began as a good but mechanical concert into one of almost breathtaking proportions Wednesday night before 14,000 persons at the Tarrant County Convention Center. ...

Thomas's vocals and flute playing were impeccable throughout, as were the guitars and vocals by Hayward. John Lodge did not score quite as well on vocals, but he maintained a solid bass rhythm throughout the evening. Edge was simply incredible on drums without ever becoming even slightly overbearing. Moraz tried a few too many tricks on keyboards, including a *Star Wars* sound that lost its novelty after the first 600 times. ...

Thursday, December 7: The Summit, Houston, Texas. John Atkinson, of the *Houston Post,* attended. He wrote:

... The high points of a Moody Blues' concert were all present ("Question," "Story in Your Eyes" and "Nights in White Satin") but a little rain must fall in every concert-goer's life – tunes like Ray Thomas's "I'm Your Man" and Edge's "I'll Be Level with You" were as dull live as on their reunion album, *Octave*. ...

Whether or not the band enjoys continued recording success is up in the air (*Octave* was far from the smash of albums like *A Question of Balance* or *In Search of the Lost Chord*), but it looks as though they will retain a pretty interesting concert following. The songs that made the band's fortune still sound much the same as they did on past tours, or on the records for that matter, but a good deal of continued excitement about the Moody Blues seems to stem from an almost morbid preoccupation among rock fans yearning for the days of yore, when the Moodies embodied some sort of mystical power. ...

"The Day We Meet Again" was recorded at this concert. It's featured on the 2008 remastered CD version of *Octave*. Also on the CD are live performances of three other *Octave* songs from a later performance. The song that Patrick Moraz allegedly defaced with *Star Wars* effects was "Top Rank Suite," performed at an even faster tempo than on the album. "Driftwood," performed without a saxophone, relies more on the simulated strings of an electronic keyboard and is more faithful to the sound of the Moodies. The sound is pristine, the performances very nearly flawless, instrumentations and vocal harmonies uniformly excellent. So good, in fact, that they match or may even surpass the versions from the recording studio. If the Moodies didn't sound good at some of their concerts during this tour, blame the venue, not the band. The proof, as they say, is in the pudding ... or in the listening.

Before leaving Texas, Patrick Moraz talked with Pete Oppel, who had given the Moodies a good review for their Dallas concert a few days before. Oppel told his readers:

> Patrick Moraz, contrary to published reports, is not officially a member of the Moody Blues, but he probably will be before long.
>
> Moraz, who was asked to replace long-time Moody keyboard player Michael Pinder when Pinder decided not to tour with the band, told *The News* this week he has been asked to join the band on a permanent basis, but that nothing has been signed to make it official.

Moraz said, "I'm very happy with the Moody Blues. I think this tour has been happening tremendously well. I feel very good with them because they're like a bunch of good old friends, although I didn't know them before. I'm probably going to record with them for the next album and subsequent albums and I'm probably going to tour with them more. They've asked me to join on a permanent basis. ..." (PM-DMN78)

Sunday, December 10: The Coliseum, Oakland, California.

Monday and Tuesday, December 11 and 12: The Forum, Inglewood, California. Terry Atkinson was there taking notes for *The Los Angeles Times*.

> England's Moody Blues ended its first tour in five years with appearances Monday and Tuesday night at the Inglewood Forum, sounding much like it did during its early '70s heyday. The quintet seemed less insistently grandiose, but this may have been due as much to an observer's changed perspective as to the group's diminished use of sumptuous orchestral effects.
>
> One reason for the Moodies' long hiatus could have been its subjection to the slings and arrows of outraged critics, who by and large found the group's lush, classical-influenced albums too rich to digest. It's easier to appreciate the band's accomplishments now that the ensuing years have brought far less pleasant popular outfits with similar ambitions, i.e., Styx and Kansas.

This is a rare and important statement from a member of the press elite (the *L.A. Times* was one of the biggest newspapers in the world, and centered right at the heart of the entertainment capital). Terry Atkinson was speculating that the press's hyper-criticism of the Moodies in the early to mid-1970s may have prompted the band's reluctance to issue an eighth album.

Equally notably, Atkinson tried to construct a historical model for the Moodies' influence on lesser, later groups (in his opinion). To the list of acts whose sound was foreshadowed by the Moody Blues, Atkinson could have added King Crimson, Genesis, Yes, Pink Floyd, Jethro Tull, Queen, Supertramp, Electric Light Orchestra, and the Alan Parsons Project.

Atkinson continued:

> The group in its present form, as Monday's show demonstrated, is also worthy of more applause than brickbats. Though a bit rough in spots, and shallow in others, the 90-minute set before a full house was well paced and tightly performed. The quintet – with ex-Yes keyboardist Patrick Moraz substituting for Mike Pinder, who doesn't like to tour – alternated between familiar oldies and several selections from the recent *Octave* album. …

> The tunes from *Octave* also benefited from vigorous renditions. Most displayed a new feeling of economy and crispness, but perhaps the most alluring one ("Driftwood") seemed close to the group's old romantic style. …

It's interesting to note that three days earlier, a different music critic in the same newspaper had slammed the Moodies for the very thing Atkinson was praising – modifying their sound slightly.

In that commentary, Dennis Hunt had sniffed:

> Pop goes the Moodies. A lot of people can't believe this has happened. It seems incredible that the Moody Blues, the same band whose complex, grandiose music helped popularize classical-rock in the late '60s, is now playing the kind of simplistic pop performed by the likes of Foreigner, Boston and Peter Frampton. …

Hayward, no doubt tired of such opinions, told Hunt, "When we were making the album, we weren't trying to do songs that would fit the current pop scene. You drive yourself crazy when you set out to be commercial. Who really knows what's commercial anyway? All you can do is trust your judgment and believe in what you're doing. We've never been affected by any trend that's come along. We have our own sound and we can't escape it. Our music comes from us, not from any trends." (JH-LAT78)

Speaking of "us," would Michael Pinder be returning to the flock?

Hayward answered, "We don't know if Mike will do the next album. Patrick may do it. We haven't gotten that far in our plans yet." (JH-LAT78)

Ed Harrison was at the final Forum concert, and wrote in *Billboard*:

… Judging by its live performance Dec. 12 before a sold-out audience, it is hard to find fault with the Moody Blues. The band firmly re-established its magnetism and musical muscle. …

Still intact are those marvelous three-part harmonies by Justin Hayward, John Lodge and Ray Thomas. Cohesive were the pulsating instrumental passages, aided immensely by the madcap keyboard wizardry of Patrick Moraz who replaced original keyboardist Mike Pinder on this tour….

After 13 years as a unit, the Moody Blues still came off sounding as fresh and energetic as it did on its early albums. Hayward handled the majority of lead vocals, while Thomas and Lodge shared the spotlight on the remainder of tunes. Yet it's the multi-dimensional textured harmonies that came across best, as those high notes were still hit with immaculate precision. …

The Moody Blues, unlike many of the new rock acts of today, don't need fancy lights and gadgets to hide its music behind. Sure, the group can be criticized for not being visually exciting, but it lets its music speak for itself. …

Even though much of the material is nearly 10 years old, the intricate melodies and song textures still hold up and are far superior to much of the paltry stuff of today. Hopefully, the Moody Blues won't fade away again.

Justin Hayward told James Simon of the Associated Press, "We were somewhat apprehensive about what kind of reception we'd get, but the offers we've gotten for our concerts now are larger than they were when we were at the height of our popularity." (JH-TT78)

***

There had been talk of a new Moody Blues album to be recorded in the spring of 1979. What was put to tape instead was a new Justin Hayward single issued in England. For the A-side, a highly personal song written for his wife of nearly a decade – "Marie." On the flip side, another Hayward original – "Heart of Steel." The sentiment to the top-side was lovely, the song pleasant, but it was hardly hit material, and London Records passed on giving the single a U.S. release. Hayward didn't seem bothered. This one was for Marie.

The band returned the following May for a 25-day tour of U.S. cities with arenas that were skipped the previous fall. This included a return to the ghastly Hollywood

Sportatorium, Hollywood, Florida, on Thursday, May 3. Jon Marlowe of *Grooves* magazine was there. His report:

> If there is a hell on earth, it is the Hollywood Sportatorium. This 18,000-capacity rock concert venue is actually a lopsided concrete airplane hangar erected in the middle of a swampy, boggy no man's land. A one-lane road is the only entrance and exit, resulting in endless fender-bender traffic jams before and after concerts. And once inside, things only get worse!
>
> No matter what particularly highly specialized, finely tuned, electronic machinery is in use, amplified sound is turned immediately to flying mud. It bounces off the decaying concrete walls like a ricocheting musical rubber ball, destroying any carefully constructed harmonies and/or musical passages that might be coming from the stage. …

Chris Welch of *Melody Maker* was visiting the band for a feature article to appear in the U.K. The Moodies had yet to tour England since they had reformed in the fall of 1977, and for two good reasons: The lack of large venues, and the hostility of the British music press. The band wanted to be sure they were fully broken in before placing themselves at the mercy of the English music critics. But they trusted Welch to give them a fair shake, and he was willing to wing it all the way to Florida to see them perform before an enthusiastic American audience. With 10,000 cheering U.S. fans, the Moodies were bound to look good in front of the *Melody Maker* man, even at the horrid Sportatorium.

As the Moodies prepared to kick off the second leg of their U.S. *Octave* tour, Welch told *Melody Maker*'s readers:

> … Some hours after I arrived in Miami, the Moodies checked-in and we met up in the bar. There was Patrick Moraz with an exploding hair style, clutching an expensive camera; Justin Hayward, blond and reserved; John Lodge, a smile surrounded by ringlets; Ray, a moustache and a swagger; and Graeme Edge, short, sharp and cheerful. …
>
> They're not hung up, angry, confused, pissed-off or frustrated. They are content, happy, carefree and extremely rich. …

Remember, in these days of Punk Rock, all these adjectives – "hung up," "angry," "confused," "pissed-off," and "frustrated" were part of the acceptable persona of a "star." Examples: punk bands like Big Balls and the Great White Idiot or The Nipple Erectors, and front men with names like Sid Vicious or Johnny Rotten.

Thomas spoke to Welch about Moraz: "He's fitted in really well, and I can play a lot better with Patrick around because he's a sympathetic player. It's very difficult playing the flute unless you can hear it, and with Mike there was always a lot of volume. The sound is clear now, and, more sophisticated." (RT-MM79)

Graeme Edge interjected, "And the band is much funkier. More exciting. Patrick has a very percussive side to him. The band has a lot more energy and drive. We really want to play England, but all the big halls are booked up so far in advance. We don't mind losing a bit of money by touring England, but we don't want to lose a lot by playing very small places. The total cost of running a band like ours is frightening. On a tour of America, playing to big audiences, we can just about cover all the costs in three weeks, and then we have to sell out every night." (GE-MM79)

Welch turned his attention to the venue.

> ... The following day the concert was to be held in the Sportatorium, several miles out of town, where the wilderness nudges up against the usual American landscape of gas stations and freeways. Here snakes, 'gators and bugs infest the low-lying swamp lands. "How do you catch an alligator?" I wondered.

Ray Thomas, the one with a passion for fishing, had the answer: "Carefully. You're supposed to put a loop over their mouth, but then you've got to watch their tail lashing about. What a terrible position to get into." (RT-MM79)

Graeme Edge had a thought: "Sounds like my first wife. I bet she could open and close her mouth under water. She could certainly open my wallet." (GE-MM79)

Welch was grateful as they "left the creek and its pesky mosquitoes and went into the Sportatorium, mercifully air-conditioned and bug-free." The crew was setting up the stage, "tastefully carpeted for the occasion in blue." He was informed that "some 15,000 fans" were expected to crowd into the Sportatorium for the show that evening.

Edge recalled the last time the Moodies played there, in 1973. "We got mobbed. We had a police escort from the hotel to the gig, and the show was sold out in a day. It's not quite like that anymore. The kids have been spoilt – saturated with rock shows." (GE-MM79)

Welch talked to Patrick Moraz about the album that had been discussed at the end of 1978, when the Moodies toured last. Word was that it would be recorded in early 1979. But those sessions never came about and, as Welch put it, "Patrick seemed pretty gloomy about the contract problems which prevent him from recording with the Moody Blues."

Those "contract problems" had to do with Mike Pinder's first right of refusal on the keyboardist job.

Moraz told Welch, "Sometimes I feel like I'm right back at the beginning of my career again. I've got so many interests in different kinds of music, from electronics to disco. I'd like to do an acoustic piano tour of Europe, or record with Chick Corea, or form my own band...."

But he was sticking with the Moodies for now, enjoying the relationship and the live music they made together. He hoped that when the next album did get recorded, that he would be part of it. He added, "I like to think it'll be long-term. I like the band, and we have a good relationship. This is a very seasoned band, you know. No problems!"

No problems ... except for Mike Pinder? Since he had declined to tour with the band, he could hardly object to their taking along a replacement ... could he? But then there was the question regarding the recording of future Moody Blues albums.

Furthermore, on the first leg of the U.S. tour in the Fall of 1978, Moraz told the press he had been invited to record with the Moodies on their next studio album. Others in the band had said this to the press too. They didn't know if Pinder would return, but they wanted Moraz to be part of the sessions. And those sessions were tentatively scheduled for early 1979. It was now May, and nothing had been recorded. The only word was that "contract problems" were preventing Moraz from recording with the band at this time … and that the ninth studio album which had been hinted at several months earlier had now been postponed.

Jon Marlowe of *Grooves* magazine was also visiting with the band in Miami. Justin Hayward told him, "Mike really doesn't enjoy touring at all anymore. He's had his fill of it and just doesn't want to know about it. He just doesn't have it in him anymore to go back out there, and the rest of us can respect that. But still, the other four of us wanted to tour, so now Patrick has been on the road with us in his place.

"His position with the band … well, let me see what I can say.… It takes a long time to become a Moody. He isn't a full-fledged member of the band – but he isn't just someone along for the ride, either. It's basically a wait and see attitude on his part – and on ours." (JH-G79)

After attending the concert at the notorious Sportatorium, Chris Welch reported:

> … The audience left no doubts about the venerable group's drawing power as the Seventies come to a close. … But it was no good asking for more. The band, including myself, were already packed into a convoy of limos lined up to escape the Everglades rush-hour. And ah – shades of the Sixties – we did have a police escort.

Friday, May 4: Lakeland Civic Center in Lakeland, Florida. It was sold out, as all Moody Blues concerts in America seemed to be. Bob Ross was there for the *St. Petersburg Times*.

> The loyal were enthralled, the dubious were pleasantly surprised. And the Moody Blues – making their first Suncoast visit after 15 years atop the symphonic album-rock pile – proved to be neither moody nor blue as they astonished 10,000-plus fans Friday night in a jam-packed Lakeland Civic Center arena.
>
> To probably everyone's surprise, the five "Moodies" – four originals and a tour-hardened substitute – turned out to be a dynamic, crowd-pleasing bunch of rockers – a band far more interesting than the mushy orchestral jive that has sustained its commercial life for the last decade.
>
> Despite a five-or-six-year layoff between *Seventh Sojourn* and *Octave*, their seventh and eighth major studio albums, the Moodies remained a durable influence on American album-oriented and progressive rock radio. … Listening to their 1 ½-hour concert Friday, one was sharply reminded how popular the Moody Blues' finest album cuts have remained through the years. Just as FM disc

708

jockeys have been doing for 10 years, the Moody Blues played one or two numbers from each of their best-loved albums. It was surprising to hear so many familiar songs bunched into one show – one tends to forget that the Moodies' music is considered "classical" to many members of the acid-rock generation. But such songs as "Tuesday Afternoon" and "Nights in White Satin," both from the 1968 groundbreaker *Days of Future Passed*, sounded fresher than they have in years of radio repetition. ...

Clean, crisp audio disproved a widely held prejudice against the Lakeland arena's acoustic quality. Fact is, the room's acoustics are only as good as the rented sound system being used at any given time, and Friday night's set-up provided excellent frequency response, audible way up front, far in the rear and at most spots in between. By suspending banks of loudspeakers over the stage instead of stacking them to the side, sound crews gave listeners a rare chance to hear live rock music – in a monstrous room – with range and balance of nearly studio quality.

Purity of expression – with little stage patter and even less visual folderol – made the Moody Blues concert something far more inspiring than the reunion of ageing comebackers that one could have expected. Plainly, the five-year hiatus did the gentlemen some good. ...

Also in attendance was Susan Marshall of *The Orlando Sentinel*. You may find this refreshing, but two different critics, from two different newspapers, in two different cities, were in agreement. Marhsall observed:

The nature of Moody Blues music is so spiritual, so soaringly mystical, that many followers never venture to picture the Moody Blues as a group of talented mere mortals. ...

What we get from the Moody Blues is a sense of their having been somewhere and seen something the rest of us haven't. So despite the fact that one of their themes is the plight of the common man, we aren't sure they should be, simply, another one of us.

But there they are, five human-type guys running onstage like other stars Friday night at the Lakeland Civic Center. The nimbus one might expect to see encircling the heads which created albums called *To Our Children's Children's Children* and *On the Threshold of a Dream* is not there. Nor has there been any divine oracle forbidding screeching mikes, or the pushing, pulsing mass of humanity that reeks of rock concert. So you shut your eyes, forget that people are standing up in front of you – it doesn't have to matter – and let "Legend of a Mind" carry you up river toward euphoric oblivion.

The band is notably low-key; they strike no theatrical poses, shun gimmicks. They can afford to. The music stands on itself and provides as much stimulation as receptive sensibilities can absorb.

What you see is, for instance, an almost retiring Justin Hayward singing "Driftwood" ... from inside out, movingly introspective. And you see "our new brother," as Ray Thomas introduces Mike Pinder's replacement, Patrick Moraz, as he gets totally caught up in the performance, hands flying across the keyboards. As "Isn't Life Strange?" ends, Thomas and Moraz unobtrusively reach out to shake the other's hand. Not for show, I think, but for fraternity.

To fans, each concert number was a hit. ... Then again, something in some of the concert numbers drove it home even harder than do the albums: The clarity of Hayward's and Lodge's voices, heard live, stuns; "Survival" where all forces blended to send you reeling; and "Balance," in which Graeme Edge's oratory, to flute and organ accompaniment, was even more legitimately dramatic, sending us unto some far-removed plane of existence.

There are critics who look down their noses with sanctimonious snickers as they rate this group's haunting songs of disillusionment, and the pleas for what could be as naïve, pretentious. Naturally, a rock group which records with the London Symphony Orchestra and sings of "... the love that you see in the eyes of a child..." is not for everybody. But then neither is caviar.

Days later, Marshall filed another report, taking her readers backstage with the Moodies:

In case you haven't heard: There is a new Moody Blue. ... Former Yes member [Patrick] Moraz is Swiss, but now lives in Brazil – when he can get home, which isn't often. He has a dark mane of hair, a bit of the good-life gut and is so nice, so unassuming, it's hard to believe he's who he is. ... An acquaintance of and strong believer in Moraz mentions that he is restraining himself, subduing his style to play with the Moody Blues but that he loves doing it – it's yet another channel for the talents of a versatile, multi-faceted musician. ...

But what of charter Moody Mike Pinder? Somebody comes out of the dressing room at the Lakeland Civic Center (where the Blues appeared last Friday) and remarks that "Pinder's off climbing a mountain." Literally.

The other band members are as cordial and down-to-earth as Moraz. ... They were quiet, chatted easily with whomever was around, signed autographs for friends of friends and security guards.

710

John Lodge smiles a lot, as he does on stage; and he seems amused, but a little self-conscious about a camera eyeing him in conversation. So, he clowns around and the camera finally goes away to leave him in peace. While Lodge lets more come to the surface, Justin Hayward appears slightly withdrawn – not unpleasantly so, but as one whose time is spent in deep thought. He, more than the others, might fit a preconceived notion that the Moody Blues are philosophically or spiritually removed.

Somehow, though they've just driven a stadium of fans wild (some of whom staggered away teary-eyed), and in spite of the powerful, presumably tumultuous, workings in those minds, the level of calm is consistent.

An amazed security guard revels in the present lack of hassles which often accompany these events. Sure, there were the usual sisters of Graeme Edge, students of Hayward, and neighbors of Lodge's cousins pleading to get backstage. But everything's gone smoothly.

The guys get in their limousines, waving as they leave. Those pedestals that so often crumble when an idolized dancer, actor, writer or singer turns out to be a creep face-to-face, remain intact in the case of the Moody Blues. The demeanor matches the product.

Saturday, May 5: Jacksonville Memorial Coliseum, Jacksonville, Florida.

Monday, May 7: Birmingham-Jefferson Civic Center, in Birmingham, Alabama.

Tuesday, May 8, Hirsch Memorial Coliseum, Shreveport, Louisiana. The concert was supposed to take place at the Mississippi Coliseum in Jackson, Mississippi. But bad weather and flooding caused a rescheduling that unexpectedly brought the group to Shreveport. The largest venue available in the small city was the Hirsch Coliseum, which only held 4,500, whereas the coliseum in Jackson held 6,500. However, it was at Hirsch that, in 1956, the storied words "Elvis has left the building!" were first heard.

Local radio station KMBQ lobbied to bring the Moodies to Shreveport, promising a Moody Blues weekend on the station. The city government also offered to support the effort. The Moodies agreed and changed course, from Jackson, Mississippi to Shreveport, Louisiana. There would be a concert … maybe.

John Andrew Prime reported for Shreveport's *The Times*:

> … Without an opportunity to properly market the show in this area, cancellation was considered, according to Anne Adams of London Records, the group's label. And the band members experienced ill luck with their tour transportation. The performing group traveled by private jet. Their sound and light equipment, complete with operators, traveled by other means. The Moody Blues arrived in Shreveport. The rest of the crew was not able to be found. In the scheduling change, the crew got lost.

"But the Moody Blues wanted to go through with the concert," Adams explained. "They thought of all the people who had bought tickets, and they didn't want to cancel."

So, in spite of bad advance sales and the better-than-even chance that the experienced, seasoned sound men and lighting people might have to be replaced, the show went on. ...

London Records distributed 300 free tickets, many allotted to radio station KMBQ as a "thank you" for helping promote the last-minute concert. The Mayor's office distributed another 800 to charities, the disadvantaged, and the handicapped. That left close to 3,500 to be sold. However, every one of those went by the time the concert was ready to begin.

John Andrew Prime got one of those free tickets, and covered the concert for his newspaper. Prime, however, didn't feel the Moodies were at their prime. The headline over his review proclaimed, "Moody Blues Out of Balance." The copy read in part:

... What should have happened didn't. Any legendary band should have rocked the roof off of the old building during 100 minutes, even on a slow night.

The building wasn't entirely at fault, though the cement walls and terrible acoustics wreaked some havoc with John Lodge's bass lines. The mixing work could have been at fault. ...Bad mix or bad acoustics, the fact remains: for the first few songs of their first appearance in Shreveport, the Moody Blues didn't have their act together. The vocals were weak and the drummer, bassist and guitarist weren't always playing in time. They seemed to be resting on their laurels. ...

The first six songs were slow and a bit lifeless, even though [the capacity crowd] of some 4,500 fans were vocal in appreciation of the music. Until "Top Rank Suite," there were no standout performances. Then, during that seventh song, guitarist Justin Hayward stepped out and performed an interesting, pure rock 'n' roll passage that harkened back to the better rock of the '60s.

"Driftwood," the ninth number, contained much-improved vocal harmonies, and "Gypsy" contained clean, interesting bass work. ...

It wasn't all bad. In fact, Prime's review had a certain balance of its own. He conceded that Ray Thomas was "tasteful and original" with his flute playing, and Graeme Edge took "a well-deserved bow" at the end of the show. But that "out of balance" line created some heat for the critic in the days to come. His newspaper shared several letters from readers, including:

... Four thousand and five hundred people loved the concert and 4,500 people cannot be wrong. Stick that in your hat, John Andrew Prime.

And:

The critic who wrote his opinion for the Moody Blues concert does not seem to be very well balanced himself....

And, just sharing the love:

Thank you, KMBQ, for your Moody Blues weekend, and thank you, Moody Blues, for your Shreveport concert. Loved them both.

Wednesday, May 9: Mississippi Coast Coliseum, Biloxi, Mississippi. Allison Simpson of Jackson, Mississippi's *Clarion-Ledger* reported:

At first the show was not that good because of faulty speakers that couldn't hold all the sound the Moody Blues were pushing out. However, their material was great, especially songs like "Time Zone" [sic; "Steppin' in a Slide Zone"] ... a cut from their new album. Another song that thrilled the crowd of 10,000 was "Time Waits for No One" [sic; "Driftwood"], one of the group's more popular songs. ...

Friday, May 11: Kansas Coliseum, Valley Center, Kansas.

Saturday, May 12: Omaha Civic Auditorium, Omaha, Nebraska. Before flying to Nebraska, John Lodge spoke by phone to Steve Millburg of the *Omaha World-Herald*, stating that there had been not a change but a shift in the sound of the Moodies. Touring Patrick Moraz's high-energy approach to keyboard playing clearly did have an effect on the band. Lodge said, "I don't think the actual sound of the Moodies has really changed. I think the one thing that is different is that the band is more – I don't know – more up tempo. Even the slow numbers have got a backbeat.... It's more rock 'n' roll, if the Moody Blues could ever get rock 'n' roll." (JL-OWH79)

Monday, May 14: Dallas Convention Center, Dallas, Texas. Pete Oppel gave his opinion of the concert in the *Dallas Morning News*:

Midway through the show Monday night at the Dallas Convention Center Arena John Lodge announced the next song on the Moody Blues program would be "Octave" from the album *Driftwood*, when he meant to say "Driftwood" from the album *Octave*. It was that kind of night for the Moody Blues. For some reason, they just didn't seem to have their minds on their work.

Compared to other concerts available, the Moody Blues concert was no slouch. But the Moody Blues are unique; it's impossible to compare them to just any band on the circuit. The final measurement stick has to be how this concert stacked up against other Moody Blues performances. Using this criteria, then, Monday's show was, to put it kindly, less than inspired. ...

Tuesday, May 15: University of Texas Special Events Center, Austin, Texas. Tickets ranged from $7.50 to $9.50. Prior to the concert, *The Waco Citizen* stated:

> Legendary is an adjective which has most often been applied to the Moody Blues. One of rock and roll's most enduring bands, the Moody Blues has set innumerable precedents in their 13 years together. They've sold over 29 million records, performed in nearly every major city in the world, and touched a whole generation of music listeners. More importantly, they pioneered the merger of classical orchestration with rock instrumentation to forge a new musical style, classical rock. The Moody Blues are a main chapter in rock and roll history. ...

Gary Parsons wrote in Sequin, Texas's *The Sequin Gazette-Enterprise*:

> The Moody Blues came to Austin on May 15 and graced the Special Events Center and a crowd of over 10,000 fans with their own flowing style of rock and roll. ... The legendary band played near faultless music for almost two hours.
>
> For most people in the audience, the Moody Blues were a symbol of the past. The band took people back to the days of the late 60s, when Timothy Leary was a household word among the young, and a higher state of consciousness was a common goal. ...
>
> Flutist and vocalist Ray Thomas hypnotized the audience with his "Legend of the Mind" [sic] solo. Using reverb during the solo, Thomas seemed to have two or three equally talented flutists hidden somewhere in the wings, but the sound was all his own.
>
> The angelic voices of bassist John Lodge, guitarist Justin Hayward, and Ray Thomas remain as the distinct symbol of the aesthetic rock band.
>
> Keyboardist Patrick Moraz, subbing for original Moody Michael Pinder performed as though he had played with the Blues since the 60s.
>
> While setting the poetry of drummer Graeme Edge to their own flowing classical-rock style, the Moody Blues realized that people had come to hear the old tunes. "Legend of the Mind," "The Question" and "Ride My See-Saw" brought the audience to their feet. ...

Thursday, May 17, University of Texas, El Paso, Texas.

Friday, May 18: Tucson Community Center, Tucson, Arizona. In the house, Jose Galvez of the *Arizona Daily Star*. He reported:

... Playing to a sell-out crowd of 9,000 at the Community Center last night – the first concert there since Linda Ronstadt's performance last December – the Moodys showcased most of their new album, *Octave*. Sandwiched in between were all the hits which have carried them through the years.

Most of *Octave* [when played live] is rock 'n' roll. Not that the group hasn't been playing that all along.

Even though the Moody Blues were one of the first groups to come out with "concept" albums, *Octave* is not a "concept" record. It is rock 'n' roll with a dash of the old Moodys thrown in here and there for good measure. For instance, "Steppin' in a Slide Zone' is reminiscent of "Melancholy Man." It's not the mellow, stoned-out sound that got us through the '60s and early '70s, but then, most of the crowd last night were teenagers who were not raised on that sound. ...

Thomas's "I'm Your Man" was the softest of the night. Good, old love songs have a habit of being that way. It is a catchy little number that has Thomas pausing for a second to be answered by Patrick Moraz – substituting on keyboards for [Mike] Pinder. Moraz is followed by Hayward's guitar. Very effective syncopation.

And the hits continued to pour out – "Gypsy," "Balance," "Singer In a Rock 'n' Roll Band," "Nights in White Satin." ("We'll do the whole lot," Thomas told a heckler.) There are so many that the whole night could have been spent playing them. ...

Saturday, May 19: ASU Activity Center, Phoenix, Arizona. Before the concert, Justin Hayward chatted with Gary Houy of the *Scottsdale Daily Progress*. "We do things from just about every album. There are a lot of songs we just couldn't leave the stage without playing. I think people would feel cheated if we didn't play 'Nights in White Satin' or 'Tuesday Afternoon' and the old stuff, you know, like 'See Saw.' We love it, anyway. Every night it gets better for us. I never get tired of playing the old stuff....

"Our audiences seem to have grown up with us. I think it's because the band has never been hyped. It's never been thrust down anybody's throat. There's never been any sort of 'Moody mania.' People have just taken to the band. It's sort of a personal experience." (JH-SDP79)

Gene C. Siegel, writing for area newspaper, *Suntracks*, said:

... A sold-out audience greeted the Moodies with a resounding ovation. Unfortunately, the hazards of cavernous concert halls immediately became apparent. Without warning, Ray Thomas clutched his flute tightly after it was struck by an errant Frisbee toss. There was obvious damage and Thomas seemed to suffer throughout the show as a result. This unfortunate event points to the serious drawbacks incurred when holding concerts in large arenas.

The band began with "Tuesday Afternoon" (from *Days of Future Past* [sic]) and the volume was too high. Full appreciation of the Moody Blues requires optimum sound and it was quickly apparent that the Activity Center might not oblige. "Twilight Time" seemed to vanish somewhere in the rafters (the Activity Center's open ceiling defies acoustic control).

Despite such problems, the group was somehow able to adjust their sound effectively. "The Day We Meet Again" had a beautiful synthesizer opening, and I could actually understand Justin Hayward's vocals. Graham [sic] Edge laid down some intense rolls, interspersing clever paradiddles as the sound improved. ...

"The Question," "The Balance," and "Nights in White Satin" were treated beautifully. The group's emphasis carried the audience on a lyrical and melodic journey. ...

Overall, the concert was a special event. Not many groups can reach the emotions stirred by the Moody Blues. ...

Monday, May 21: McNichols Sports Arena, Denver, Colorado.
Wednesday, May 23: Portland Memorial Coliseum, Portland, Oregon. Present was John Wendeborn of Portland's *Oregonian*. His impressions:

Nostalgia in the form of celestial and sensitive mid-to-late-'60s rock music pleased a sellout crowd of some 10,000 Wednesday night at Memorial Coliseum and the subject of it was the Moody Blues. The band, which last appeared in Portland seven years ago, was in excellent form, even though the music was mostly "down memory lane," as one of the five members of the band said midway in the two-hour set.

The Moodies were at the beginning of art-rock a decade ago and while the form has gone off in a variety of directions, their sound was still vibrant. ...

Vocally, the group handled harmonies and solos with ease, and the harmonies, in the mostly low range, were interesting. Instrumental solos were at times beautiful, especially some of the work of flutist Ray Thomas, whose late-in-the-show solo on electronic flute was a highlight. ...

The crowd loved most of the work but saved its longest ovations for early Moody Blues music. There was also a wide range of ages attending the concert, from about 13 to mid-50s, a tribute to the band's staying power and also its history. ...

Thursday, May 24: Pacific Coliseum, Vancouver, British Columbia, Canada.

Friday, May 25: Seattle Convention Center, Seattle, Washington. Patrick MacDonald of *The Seattle Times* had a V.I.P. seat. From there, he heard and saw:

> The Moody Blues ended its 1979 American tour Friday night before a packed house of adoring fans in the Coliseum. The Supergroup That Wouldn't Die gave the crowd what it wanted – note-by-note recitations of songs made famous a decade ago.
>
> The Moodies wrote much of the soundtrack for the psychedelic '60s. From 1968 through '72 the British quintet was the reigning king of classical-rock, i.e., the use of a symphony orchestra with a rock band. …
>
> The crowd seemed to love everything the band did in concert, but I found it a bloodless exercise with the only sparks of excitement coming from, of all people, Patrick Moraz on keyboards. He was the only non-original, replacing Michael Pinder "for the purposes of the tour," according to the press kit.
>
> Moraz, whose playing was so heavy-handed and trendy when he was here with Yes a few years back, added imaginative touches to many of the tunes, even daring to stray from the rigid formula of such established classics as "Tuesday Afternoon" and "Twilight Time." Because he was the only one who wasn't tied to the past, he could fool around with the songs a little and give them some new life. They needed it badly.
>
> Don't get me wrong, I like and respect the Moody Blues immensely. It's one of those bands – like the Beatles and the Jimi Hendrix Experience – that made such an impression that I remember the moment I first heard *Days of Future Passed*, the first [sic] album. The group's first concert here at Eagles Auditorium is a vivid memory; it was transcendental, man. And I played Moody Blues records hundreds of times as a disc jockey from 1969 to '72, when the band *was* current. But that was then. The songs were part of that era. Now they sound dated. … The Moody Blues' songs are nostalgic….

Not all felt that the Moodies were mere nostalgia, or that popular music didn't have room for them among the disco groups and punk bands. Interviewed by Jon Marlowe of *Groove* magazine while on this tour, Justin Hayward said that he had recently attended a party thrown by the British new wave/punk band The Stranglers, who had burst onto the music scene in 1977 with the first of more than a dozen U.K. Top 10 albums. Hayward was approached by the group's drummer, Jett Black. Hayward told Marlow, "[Strangler's drummer] Jett Black called me over and said, 'Hey, listen, it's nice to see you guys are back together again. Really, I mean it; I've always loved your music. Everybody in the band is happy you're making music again.'

"See? That whole punk thing – them saying the Moodies are too old or boring or pretentious or whatever they're calling us this week – that makes for great press…. It makes for great quotes that people put in large type and get all excited about…. But you soon find out that on the road, or backstage, there's none of that going on. All musicians belong to a special brotherhood…. They all understand that in the end the music is what it's all about." (JH-G79)

After reading Patrick MacDonald's critical review of the Moodies' Seattle concert, area resident Al Kiest wrote in to *The Seattle Times*.

> Patrick MacDonald: A response to your unfair and inaccurate review of the Moody Blues…
>
> … You recognize that the band is a classical-rock group but then criticize them because the arrangements closely resembled the recorded versions. It isn't fair to apply the standards of a jazz or pop-rock group to the Moodies. … They aren't concerned with transient pop trends and it would be superfluous to add unneeded jazz riffs to the live performances. …
>
> I don't think your review will have much impact on the 15,000 who attended the concert. Their enthusiasm showed continuity throughout the show. Those Moodies fans who couldn't make it can make their own judgment when the recording of the concert is broadcast on nationwide radio July 28.

The concert had indeed been recorded, airing on a national radio hookup on Saturday, July 28th. Since then, the recording taken from the soundboard at the Seattle Convention Center all those years ago has been widely bootlegged, and is not only available through certain sellers as a CD, but can be heard on various online websites. You can listen for yourself and, as Mr. Kiest suggested, arrive at your own conclusions. To our ears, the Moodies sound spectacular.

Incidentally, at the time the radio special aired, it was reported that *Octave* had sold in excess of one million copies, crossing over from gold to platinum.

In a "Teen, Inc." syndicated newspaper wire story from August 1979, entitled "Moody Blues Is Still on Top":

> … With the tour and *Octave*'s continued success, the Moody Blues continue to assert their preeminence as the world's premiere rock and roll band. The Moody Blues are back to stay.

From the October 27, 1979 edition of the *Glasgow Herald*, Andrew Collier wrote:

> … Sound crews working for the world's top rock bands are not an unusual sight at Prestwick Airport. But when about 30 of this phenomenally popular group's roadies step on to Scottish soil today after a flight from America, their appearance will be a little bit special.

Over the next two days, the band's highly-qualified team of workers and technicians will be preparing for one of the most important shows the Moody Blues have ever played. On Monday, at the Apollo, the group will play to a home British audience for the first time in six years.

After more than 10 years at the very summit of the music business mountain, the Moodies have little left to achieve. Their mellow, melodic brand of contemporary pop may be the very antithesis of new wave's raw-edged aggression, but the fans still remain in their legions. Their British tour is sold out before it starts....

It was a short tour of the United Kingdom, starting at the Glasgow Apollo Theatre in Scotland on October 29, then on to Bingley Hall, Stafford, on October 31 and November 1, Wembley Arena in London on November 3 and 4, and finishing at Brighton Centre, in Brighton, on November 6. On the 9th of November, the Moodies performed at the Ahoy in Rotterdam, Netherlands.

THE MOODY BLUES  PolyGram Records

As a new decade approached, the Moody Blues were about to embark on yet another chapter in their musical career. They'd started as a "Brummie" Birmingham rhythm & blues band, with the spotlight on Denny Laine. After Laine's departure and the arrival of Justin Hayward and John Lodge, they became symphonic rock innovators. They became one of the most influential groups on Earth in the early 1970s. In their new incarnation, they remained true to their "classic" sound.

Some of their all-time greatest hits were yet to come, in the 1980s. There would be ups and downs along the way. They'd face lawsuits, the deaths of mentors and trusted colleagues, and various personal crises. But they would also experience levels of success beyond their wildest dreams. And their music would even travel into outer space.

The story of the Moody Blue's career and musical legacy is too big for one book. *Long Distance Voyagers: The Story of the Moody Blues* will conclude with Volume 2, as the Moody Blues arrive at the threshold of their next, and perhaps greatest, dream.

Appendix

MOODY BLUES DISCOGRAPHY (1964-1979):

Boldface used for LP and EP titles; Single A-sides and Double A-sides titles; and chart positions.

Song titles are listed as they appeared on records (note occasional differences in titles between U.S. and U.K. releases, plus rare spelling errors, as printed on record label).

U.S. chart position listed is best showing in either *Billboard, Cashbox, Record World.,* or *Record & Radio.*
BB = *Billboard* Hot 100;
CB = *Cashbox* Top 100;
RW = *Record World,* 100 Top Pops;
R&R = *Radio & Records;*
AC = *Billboard* Adult Contemporary;
MR = *Billboard* Mainstream Rock.
TCD = *Billboard* Top Compact Discs.

U.K. chart position listed is best showing in either *Melody Maker, New Musical Express, Record Retailer,* or OSC (Official Singles Chart, combining various U.K. charts).
MM = *Melody Maker;*
NME = *New Musical Express;*
RR = *Record Retailer* (as reported in the U.S. by *Billboard*)
OCC = U.K. Official Charts Company, referenced by Wikipedia.

AUS = Australia; CAN = Canada; FRA = France; GER = Germany; NETH = Netherlands; NOR: Norway; SIN: Singapore.

Australian chart sources: *Go-Set* magazine (1964-74); The Kent Report (1974-88); ARIA (1989-2017).
Canadian chart source: *RPM Weekly* (Records, Promotions, Music).
French chart source: SNEP (Syndicate National de l'Edition Phonographique).
German chart source: *Der Musikmarkt*/Media Control.
Netherlands chart sources: Hilversum 3 Top 30 (1969-74); Nationale Hitparade (1974-93; Mega Top 50/100 (1993-2017).
Norway chart source: VG-lista.
Singapore chart source: *Billboard* "Hits of the World."

Date:	Title:	US:	UK:	Other:
Sept. 4, 1964	**Steal Your Heart Away** (UK; Decca F.11971)		-	
	/ Lose Your Money (But Don't Lose Your Mind)		-	
Nov. 13, 1964	**Go Now!** (UK; Decca F.12022)		**1** (NME)	
	/ It's Easy Child		-	
Jan. 1965	**Go Now!** (US; London 5N-9726)	**6** (CB/RW)		
	/ Lose Your Money (But Don't Lose Your Mind)	-		
Jan. 1965	**Go Now!** (Canada; London L 9726)			**2** (CAN)
	/ Lose Your Money			-
Feb. 26, 1965	**I Don't Want to Go On Without You**		**19** (RR)	
	/ Time Is On My Side (UK; Decca F.12095)		-	

721

Date:	Title:	US:	UK:	Other:
May 28, 1965	**From the Bottom of My Heart (I Love You)**		**16** (RR)	
	/ And My Baby's Gone (UK; Decca F.12166)		-	
May 28, 1965	**From the Bottom of My Heart (I Love You)**	**70** (CB)		
	/ And My Baby's Gone (US; London 45-LON 9764)	-		
May 28, 1965	**From the Bottom of My Heart (I Love You)**			**23** (CAN)
	/ And My Baby's Gone (US; London 45-LON 9764)			-
May 21, 1965	**THE MOODY BLUES** (UK EP; Decca DFE 8622)		-	
	Side 1: Go Now / Lose Your Money			
	Side 2: I Don't Want to Go On Without You			
	/ Steal Your Heart Away			
July 22, 1965	**THE MAGNIFICENT MOODIES** (UK; Decca LK 4711)			**5** (NME)
July 28, 1965	**GO NOW: THE MOODY BLUES #1** (US; London PS 428)	-		
Oct. 1965	**Everyday** (UK; Decca F.12266)			**44** (OSC)
	/ You Don't (All the Time)			-
Oct. 1965	**Ev'ry Day** (US; London 45 LON 9799)	-		
	/ You Don't	-		
Dec. 1965	**Bye Bye Bird** (Decca 72.056)			**1** (FRA)
	/ I'll Go Crazy			-
Jan. 1966	**Stop!** (US; 45 LON 9810)	**89** (RW)		
	/ Bye Bye Bird	-		
Jan. 1966	**London Is Behind Me** (Hayward)		-	
	/ Day Must Come (UK; Pye 7N 17014)		-	
Feb. 1966	**London Is Behind Me** (Hayward)	-		
	/ Day Must Come (US; Red Bird RB-10-049)	-		
Aug. 26, 1966	**I Can't Face the World Without You** (Hayward)		-	
	/ I'll Be Here Tomorrow (UK; Parlophone R 5496)		-	
Oct. 7, 1966	**Boulevard de la Madeleine** (UK Decca F.12498)		-	
	/ This Is My House (But Nobody Calls)		-	
Oct. 7, 1966	**Boulevard de la Madeleine** (US London 45-LON 1005)	-		
	/ This Is My House (But Nobody Calls)	**112** (CB)		
Jan. 13, 1967	**Life's Not Life** (UK Decca F.12543)		-	
	/ He Can Win		-	
May 5, 1967	**Really Haven't Got the Time**		-	
	/ Fly Me High (UK; Decca F 12067)		-	
June 1967	**I Really Haven't Got the Time**	-		
	/ Fly Me High (US; London 45-20030)	-		
June 12, 1967	**Fly Me High** (Netherlands; Decca AT 15 072)			-
	/ Really Haven't Got the Time			-
Sept. 22, 1967	**Love and Beauty** (UK; Decca F 12670)		-	
	/ Leave This Man Alone		-	

Date:	Title:	US:	UK:	Other:
Nov. 10, 1967	**Nights in White Satin** (UK; Deram DM 161) / Cities *(Single charted #1 in France and Netherlands)*		**19** (OCC) -	
Nov. 11, 1967	**DAYS OF FUTURE PASSED** (UK; SML 707)		**27** (OCC)	
Jan. 1968	**Nights in White Satin** (US; Deram 45-85023) / Cities *(Single charted #13 in Canada in 1968)*	**93** (CB) -		
March 2, 1968	**DAYS OF FUTURE PASSED** (US; Deram DES-1812) *(LP charted #1 in France; #3 in Canada)*	**2**		
April 1968	**Another Morning** / Tuesday Afternoon (Forever Afternoon) *("Another Morning" reached #7 in Hong Kong)*			**3** (SIN) -
July 19, 1968	**Tuesday Afternoon (Forever Afternoon)** / Another Morning (U.S.; Deram 45-85028)	**24** (BB) -		
June 28, 1968	**Voices in the Sky** (UK; Deram DM 196) / Dr. Livingstone, I Presume		**27** (NME/RR) -	
July 26, 1968	**IN SEARCH OF THE LOST CHORD** (UK; Deram SML 711)		**5** (NME/RR)	
July 26, 1968	**IN SEARCH OF THE LOST CHORD** (US; Deram DE 16017)	**23** (BB)		
Sept. 1968	**Ride My See-Saw** (US; Deram 45-85033) / Voices in the Sky	**46** (RW) -		
Oct. 25, 1968	**Ride My See-Saw** (UK) / A Simple Game		**42** (OCC) -	
April 25, 1969	**ON THE THRESHOLD OF A DREAM** (UK; Deram SML 1035)		**1** (OCC)	
April 25, 1969	**ON THE THRESHOLD OF A DREAM** (US; Deram DES 18025)	**20** (BB)		
April 2, 1969	**Never Comes the Day** / So Deep Within You (UK; Deram DM 427)		- -	
April 2, 1969	**Never Comes the Day** / So Deep Within You (US; Deram 45-85044)	**89** (RW) -		
Oct. 31, 1969	**Watching and Waiting** (UK; Threshold TH 21) / Out and In		- -	
Nov. 21, 1969	**TO OUR CHILDREN'S CHILDREN'S CHILDREN** (UK/US: Threshold THS 1)	**14** (BB)	**2** (OCC)	**11** (CAN)
April 24, 1970	**Question** (UK: Threshold TH 4; US: THS-67004) / Gipsy	**19** (CB)	**1** (NME)	**1** (NL)

Date:	Title:	US:	UK:	Other:
Aug. 7, 1970	**A QUESTION OF BALANCE** (UK/US: Threshold THS 3)	**3** (BB)	**1**(OCC)	**3** (CAN)
Nov. 1970	**Melancholy Man** (France: Threshold TH 30005) / Candle of Life			**1** (FRA) -
July 23, 1971	**EVERY GOOD BOY DESERVES FAVOUR** (UK/US: Threshold THS-5)	**2 (BB)**	**1** (OCC)	**3** (CAN)
July 23, 1971	**The Story in Your Eyes** (US: THS 67006) / My Song *(Single charted at #11 in Netherlands)*	**14** (CB) -		**7** (CAN) -
April 21, 1972	**Isn't Life Strange** (UK: TH 9; US: THS 60079) / After You Came *(Single charted at #9 in Canada)*	**20** (CB) -	**13** (OCC) -	**4** (FRA) -
July 1972	**Nights in White Satin** (US; Deram 45-85023) / Cities	**1** (CB/RW) -		**1** (CAN) -
July 1972	**Nights in White Satin** (US; Deram DM 161) / Cities *(Single re-charted at No. 1 in Netherlands)*	**9** (OSC) -		
Oct. 23, 1972	**SEVENTH SOJOURN (UK: Threshold THS 7)**		**1** (OCC)	
Nov. 17, 1972	**SEVENTH SOJOURN (US: Threshold THS 7)**	**1** (BB/CB/RR)		**1** (CAN)
Jan. 19, 1973	**I'm Just a Singer (In a Rock And Roll Band)** / For My Lady (UK: TH 13; US: TH 45-67012)	**8** (CB)	**36** (OCC)	**4** (NL)
1973	**You and Me** (Japan TH8) / Lost in a Lost World			
July 19, 1974	**We Like to Do It** (Graham Edge Band) / Shotgun (UK: TH 18; US: 5N-67018)	- -	- -	- -
Oct. 8, 1974	**THIS IS THE MOODY BLUES (COMP)** (UK: Threshold MB 1/2; THS 12/13)	**11**(BB)	**14** (OCC)	**2** (CAN)
March 10, 1975	**BLUE JAYS** (HAYWARD & LODGE) (UK: Threshold THS 12; US: THS14)	**16** (BB)	**4** (OCC)	**19** (CAN)
April 18, 1975	**I Dreamed Last Night** (Hayward & Lodge) / **Remember Me** (UK TH 19; US: 5N-67019)	**29** (AC) -	- -	- -
Sept. 26, 1975	**Blue Guitar** (Hayward & 10cc) (UK: TH 21) / When You Wake Up (Hayward & Lodge)	**82** (CB) -	**8** (OCC) -	
June 27, 1975	**High Above My Head** (Thomas) / **Love Is the Key** (UK: TH 20; US: 5N-67020)	**117**(CB) -	- -	
July 11, 1975	**FROM MIGHTY OAKS** (Thomas) (UK/US: THS 16)	**68** (BB)	**23** (OCC)	
Sept. 1975	**KICK OFF YOUR MUDDY BOOTS** (Graeme Edge Band) (UK/US: THS 15)	**107** (BB)	-	

Date:	Title:	US:	UK:	Other:
Nov. 11, 1975	**Bareback Rider** (Graeme Edge Band)	-	-	
	/ The Tunnel (UK: TH 22; U.S.: 5N-67022)	-	-	
April 1976	**THE PROMISE** (Pinder) (UK/US: Threshold THS 18)	**133**(BB)	-	
June 11, 1976	**Carry On** (Pinder) (UK: Threshold TH23)	-	-	
	/ I Only Want to Be With You	-	-	
June 1976	**HOPES, WISHES AND DREAMS** (Thomas) (UK/US: Threshold THS 16)	**147** (BB)	-	
June 11, 1976	**One Night Stand** (Thomas)	-	-	
	/ Carousel (UK: Threshold TH 24; US: 5N-67023)	-	-	
Jan. 28, 1977	**NATURAL AVENUE** (Lodge) (UK: THX 120)			**38** (OCC)
Jan. 28, 1977	**Say You Love Me** (Lodge) (UK: Decca F13682)		-	
	/ Natural Avenue		-	
March 18, 1977	**Children of Rock 'N' Roll** (Lodge)	-		
	/ Piece of My Heart (UK: Decca F 13695) (UK)	-		
April 1977	**NATURAL AVENUE** (Lodge) (US: London PS 683)	**121**(BB)		
May 1977	**Natural Avenue** (Lodge) US: London 5N-1069)	-		
	/ Say You Love Me	-		
April 1977	**Natural Avenue** (Lodge) (US: London Disco 3005)	-		
	/ Children of Rock 'N' Roll	-		
Feb. 11, 1977	**SONGWRITER** (Hayward) (UK: Deram SDL 15; US: Deram DES 18073)	**37** (BB)	**28** (OCC)	
Feb. 4, 1977	**One Lonely Room** (Hayward) (UK: Deram DM 428)		-	
	/ Songwriter (Part 2)		-	
March 1977	**Lay It on Me** (Hayward) (US: Deram 5N-7541)	-		
	/ Songwriter (Part 2)	-		
April 1977	**PARADISE BALLROOM** (Graeme Edge Band) (UK : TXS 121; UK: London PS 686)	**164** (BB)	-	
April 8, 1977	**Everybody Needs Somebody** (Graeme Edge Band)	-	-	
	/ Be My Eyes (UK: Decca F 13698; US: London 5N 1071)		-	
April 22, 1977	**Country Girl** (Hayward) (UK: Deram DM 429)		-	
	/ Doin' Time		-	
April 30, 1977	**CAUGHT LIVE + 5** (US: London 2 PS 690/691)	**26**		
June 1, 1977	**CAUGHT LIVE + 5** (UK: Decca MB 3/4)		-	
June 1977	**Country Girl** (Hayward) (US: Deram 5N-7542)		-	
	/ Songwriter (Part 2)		-	

Date:	Title:	US:	UK:	Other:
July 8, 1977	**Summer Breeze** (Lodge) (UK: Decca F 13717) / Rainbow		-	
July 29, 1977	**Stage Door** (Hayward) (UK: Deram DM 430) / Lay It on Me		- -	
Aug. 1977	**Summer Breeze** (Lodge) (US: London 5N-1072) / Children of Rock 'N' Roll	- -		
1978	**THE GREAT MOODY BLUES (COMP) (UK)**	-	-	
June 2, 1978	Forever Autumn (Hayward) / The Fighting Machine (UK: CBS 6368; US: Columbia 3-10799)	**20** (AC)	**5** (OCC)	**73** (CAN)
June 9, 1978	**OCTAVE** (UK: Decca THS 129; US: London PS 708) *(Album chart at #8 in Canada and Norway)*	**13** (BB)	**6** (OCC)	**7** (NL)
July 14, 1978	**Steppin' in a Slide Zone** (US/UK) / I'll Be Level With You (UK: Decca F 13790; US: London 5N270)	**39** (BB)	-	**41** (CAN)
Oct. 6, 1978	**Driftwood** (UK: Decca F 13809; US: London 5N273) / I'm Your Man	**38** (AC)	-	**60** (CAN)
1979	**Had to Fall in Love** / I'll Be Level with You (Australia: Decca Y-11833)			
April 13, 1979	**Marie** (Hayward) (UK: Decca F 13834) / Heart of Steel		- -	
Oct. 22, 1979	**OUT OF THIS WORLD (COMP) (K-Tel) (UK)**		15	

MOODY BLUES DISCOGRAPHY (1980-2017):

A more detailed listing, with catalogue numbering, will be included in Vol ume 2.

Again, the highest known chart positions are listed for both the U.S. and U.K. All rankings will be listed in Vol. 2 in various chapters for the albums and singles. Using the 1986 single "Your Wildest Dreams" as an example, for this quick reference list, we list only *Billboard*'s Hot Adult Contemporary Singles chart ranking of No. 1. The single also reached No. 2 on *Billboard*'s Hot Mainstream Rock Tracks chart; No. 9 on *Billboard*'s Hot 100 Singles chart; and No. 10 on *Cashbox*'s Top 100 Weekly Singles chart.

Date:	Title:	US:	UK:	Other:
May 1980	**Night Flight** / Suitcase (Hayward) (US/UK)	122	-	
June 13, 1980	**NIGHT FLIGHT** (HAYWARD) (US/UK)	166	41	
Sept. 12, 1980	**Nearer to You** / It's Not You (Hayward) (US)	-		
Sept. 1980	**A Face in the Crowd** / A Face in the Crowd (Hayward) (US)	-		
Oct. 3, 1980	**Street Café** / Threw It All Away (Lodge) (UK)		-	
March 3, 1981	**Unexpected Song** (Marti Webb & Justin Hayward) (UK) / Angry and Sore (Marti Webb)		-	
May 15, 1981	**LONG DISTANCE VOYAGER** (US/UK)	1 (BB)	7 (OCC)	1 (CAN)
May 19, 1981	**Gemini Dream** / Painted Smile (US/UK)	12 (BB)	-	1 (CAN)
July 23, 1981	**The Voice** / 22,000 Days (US/UK)	1 (MR)	-	9 (CAN)
Nov. 10, 1981	**Talking Out of Turn** / Veteran Cosmic Rocker (US/UK)	60 (CB)	-	27 (CAN)
Aug. 28, 1993	**THE PRESENT (US/UK)**	26 (BB)	15 (OCC)	11 (CAN)
Aug. 1983	Sittin' at the Wheel / Going Nowhere (US)	3 (MR)	-	18 (CAN)
Nov. 12, 1983	**Blue World** / Sorry (US/UK)	32 (MR)	35 (OCC)	40 (CAN)
Dec. 1983	**Running Water** / Under My Feet (US)	-		
Nov. 21, 1984	**VOICES IN THE SKY** (COMP) (US/UK)	132 (BB)	-	91 (CAN)
Aug. 1985	Silverbird / Take Your Chances (Hayward) (UK)		-	
Sept. 16, 1985	**MOVING MOUNTAINS** (HAYWARD) (UK)		78 (OCC)	
Nov. 1985	**The Best Is Yet to Come** / Marie (Hayward) (UK)		-	
April 4, 1986	**THE OTHER SIDE OF LIFE** (US/UK)	9 (BB)	24 (OCC)	46 (CAN)
April 9, 1986	**Your Wildest Dreams** / Talkin' Talkin' (US/UK)	1 (AC)	-	20 (AUS)

Date:	Title:	US:	UK:	Other:
Aug. 8, 2000	**HALL OF FAME – LIVE AT THE ROYAL HALL** (CD + DVD)	**185**	-	
Feb. 6, 2001	**THE SINGLES** (COMP)	-	-	
April 24, 2001	**JOURNEY INTO CAVES**	-	-	
Jan 14, 2003	**SAY IT WITH LOVE** (COMP)	-	-	
Oct. 28, 2003	**DECEMBER** (US/UK)	-	-	
Dec. 28, 2003	December	-	-	
Feb 24, 2004	**20TH CENTURY MASTERS: THE DVD COLLECTION**	-	-	
June 29, 2004	**THE LOST PERFORMANCE: LIVE IN PARIS 1970** (DVD)	-	-	
March 1, 2005	**GOLD** (COMP)	-	-	
May 31, 2005	**LIVE AT MONTREUX 1991** (DVD)	-	-	
Nov. 15, 2005	**LOVELY TO SEE YOU (LIVE AT THE GEEK THEATER)**	-	-	
Feb. 27, 2007	**COLLECTED** (COMP)	-	-	
March 26, 2007	**LIVE AT THE BBC (1967-70)**	-	-	
April 24, 2007	**CLASSIC ARTISTS: THE MOODY BLUES** (DVD)	-	-	
April 29, 2008	**PLAYLIST PLUS** (COMP)	-	-	
July 6, 2009	**LIVE AT THE ISLE OF WIGHT FESTIVAL 1970** (DVD)	-	-	
Aug. 11, 2011	**ICON** (COMP)	-	-	
Feb. 12, 2013	**SPIRITS OF THE WESTERN SKY** (HAYWARD)	-	-	
June 3, 2013	**TIMELESS FLIGHT** (COMP)	-	-	
Aug 19, 2014	**SPIRITS: LIVE AT THE BULKHEAD THEATER** (HAYWARD) (DVD)	-		-
May 5, 2015	**10,000 LIGHT YEARS AGO** (LODGE)	-	-	
2016	Isn't Life Strange (unplugged) / Simply Magic (unplugged) (Lodge)	-	-	
Dec. 14, 2016	**ALL THE WAY** (COMP) (HAYWARD)	-	-	

Bibliography / Sources:

Books:

Band on the Run: A History of Paul McCartney and Wings, by Garry McGee (Taylor Trade
   Publishing, 2003)
Echoes of the Sixties, by Marti Smiley Childs and Jeff March (Billboard Books, 1999)
Goodbye, Little Rock and Roller, by Marshall Chapman (St. Martin's Press. 2003)
It Was All Just Rock 'n' Roll: A Journey to the Center of the Radio & Concert Universe, by Pat
   O'Day (St. Joseph's Print Group, 2002)
Joel Whitburn Presents The Comparison Book: Billboard/Cash Box/Record World 1954-1982, by
   Joel Whitburn (Record Research Inc./Sheridan Books, Inc., 2015)
Joel Whitburn's Top Pop Singles, 12th Edition (Record Research Inc., 2009)
Moody Blues Companion, The, by Edward Wincentsen (Wynn Publishing, 2001)
Timeless Troubadours: The Moody Blues Music and Message, by Charles L. Whitfield, MD, and
   Barbara H. Whitfield, CMT, RT (Muse House Press, 2013)

Websites:

AcousticMusic.com
AllMusic.com
AnneCarlin.com
AntiMusic.com
BackStageAuctions.blogspot.com
BestClassicBands.com
BigMovieZone.com
Blatherwatch.blogs.com
BlindedBySound.com
BluegrassMusic.com
Brumbeat.net/dlaine
ClassicRockDaily.com
ClassicRockRevisited.com
DailyClassicRock.com
DailyTribune.com
Demme.net (Let It Rock)
DenOfGeek.com
DiscussionsMagazine.com
DVDTalk.com
EagleRockEnt.com
Examiner.com
Exchange.Nottingham.ac.uk.
FemaleFirst.co.uk
FolkAlley.com
ForGuitarPlayersOnly.com
45cat.com
GetReadyToRock.com
Gibson.com
GlideMagazine.com
Grammy.com
Heraldtribune.com
HighDefDigest.com
Hit-Channel.com
HitsOfAllDecades.com
HybridMusic.com
LiverpoolSoundAndVision.co.uk

Marmalade-skies.co.uk
MiamaNewTimes.com
MoodyBluesAttitude.yuku.com
MusicStreetJournal.com
MusicTap.com
NewsReview.com
NoDepression.com
Otten.freeshell.org/moodyblues
PopDose.com
RaySasho.com
Review-mag.com
RockDaily.com
ScreenReviews.com
SeaOfTranquility.org
SomethingElseReviews.com
SongFacts.com
SongWriterUniverse.com
SoundAndVision.com
Starling.rinet.ru
Tallahassee.com
TapaTalk.com
TeamRock.com
TechnologyTell.com
TheBlog.com
TheMoodyBlues.co.uk (Tony Brown's The MoodyBlues.co.uk)
TheMoodyBluesToday.com
TheMusicBox.com
ThisWeekNews.com
VintageRock.com
VivaScene.com
Wingspan.ru
WriteOnMusic.com
ZoiksOnline.com

Videos:

The Source, November 1983, NBC, interview with John Lodge.
Entertainment Tonight, July 2, 1991, interview with Justin Hayward and John Lodge.
Rock Family Tree, "The Birmingham Beat" segment, July 1, 1995, with Pete Frame interviewing
The Moody Blues.
Classic Artists: The Moody Blues, April 24, 2007 (Image Entertainment).
Sammy Sultan Interview with Justin Hayward, February 9, 2013, YouTube (Hotseat
Entertainment).

Radio:

Off the Record, Westwood One, December 1981, interview with Justin Hayward.
BBC radio, 1981, Anne Nightingale's interview with Justin Hayward.
Rockline, June 30, 1986, interview with John Lodge.
Off the Record, Westwood One, July 6, 1986, interview with John Lodge.
Off the Record, Westwood One, May 10, 1986, interview with Justin Hayward & John Lodge;
host Joe Benson.
WNEW, 1987, interview with Justin Hayward.
In the Studio, 1989, interview with Graeme Edge.

The Moody Blues Story, Unistar, February 17, 1990, hosted by Ray Sciaky, with Hayward and
    Lodge.
Strauss' Place, KTAR, Phoenix, Arizona, September 27, 1993, interview with John Lodge.
WPCH (Atlanta), 1997, Hayward interviewed by Steve Gross.
Rockline, August 1, 1998, interview with Justin Hayward.
Rockline, August 4, 1999, with Bob Coburn, interviewing Hayward and Lodge.

Records:

The Making of Blue Jays, March 1975, U.S. Radio Promo, Threshold Records.
*New ... From The Moody Blues, Ray Thomas Discusses the Preparation and Production of His
    First Solo LP, From Mighty Oaks* (International Distribution vinyl album Threshold
    THSX-102, 1975).

CDs:

A Question of Balance, issued 2008, remastered edition, with booklet by Mark Powell.
Days of Future Passed, issued 1997, sleeve notes and interviews by John Reed.
Every Good Boy Deserves Favour, issued 2008, remastered edition, with booklet by Mark Powell.
From Mighty Oaks, issued 2011, liner notes by Ray Thomas.
In Search of the Lost Chord, issued 2008, remastered edition, with booklet by Mark Powell.
The Magnificent Moodies, issued 2014, remastered edition, with booklet by Mark Powell.
Moody Blues Live at the BBC 1967-1970, The, issued 2007, with booklet by David Wells.
Moving Mountains, CD issued 1989, liner notes by Justin Hayward.
Seventh Sojourn, issued 2008, remastered edition, with booklet by Mark Powell.
Songwriter, issued in 2004, remastered edition, with booklet by Mark Powell.

Correspondences/contracts:

Ridgepride Ltd. agreement with Phil Myatt/Midlands Top Ten Agency to take over management
    of the Moody Blues, Summer 1964; exact date obscured on document (Courtesy of Tony
    Brown).
Marquee Artists/Jazzassociates Ltd. contract Robert Stigwood Associates for Moody Blues tour
    with Chuck Berry, dated December 2, 1964 (Courtesy of Tony Brown).
Jones & Crossland Ltd. bill to Ridgepride Ltd. (Courtesy of Tony Brown).
Finance Limited of 164 Bristol Street, Birmingham Hire-Purchase Agreement with P.P.
    Ridgepride Ltd., dated June 30, 1965 (Courtesy of Tony Brown).
Demand letter from L.M. Doffman & Co. to Ridgepride Ltd., September 28, 1968 (Courtesy Tony
    Brown).
Maple & Company Ltd. invoice, to Ridgepride Ltd., October 1965 (Courtesy of Tony Brown).
A.I. Park Ltd. acknowledgment letter, October 23, 1965, for termination of office space rental
    agreement with Ridgepride (Courtesy of Tony Brown).
Maples & Co. Ltd. letter to Ridgepride, acknowledging satisfaction of debt for piano purchase,
    October 28, 1965 (Courtesy of Tony Brown).
Woodstock contract, between Zell Enterprises, International, Inc/Woodstock Ventures and
    Umbrella Management Ltd., June 25, 1969 (courtesy of Tony Brown).
Alex Murray to Lucy Purdon, May 6, 2006 (courtesy of Tony Brown).
Alex Murray to Tony Brown, January 27, 2009 (courtesy of Tony Brown).

Magazines and newspapers:

Clipping (Swindon area newspaper; title unknown), November 15, 1959, newspaper clipping:
    "Saved a Show at Thirteen."
Clipping (unknown Swindon, England newspaper), late 1959, "Justin Plays an Encore."
The Swindon and District Review, late 1963, "With the Whispers," by Peter Antony.
Birmingham Planet, January 30, 1964, "A New Look for the Diplomats."

Birmingham Planet, early May 1964, "Two Avengers Join Diplomats."

Newspaper clipping, Summer 1964, "Now – A Blues Recording of 23rd Psalm," by Janice Nicholls.

The Birmingham Planet, June 11, 1964, "The Moody Blues Five," by Mary McGrane.

The Moody Blues: The Magnificent Moodies CD box set, with press clipping from unknown British newspaper, on or around September 11, 1964, review by Don Nicholl of "Lose Your Money" / "Steal Your Heart Away."

Record Mirror, September 11, 1964, "Five Leaders in One Group," by Peter Jones.

Record Mirror, November 28, 1964, review of "Go Now!" / "It's Easy Child."

New Musical Express, December 18, 1964, "Brum Accented Moody Blues," by "I.D."

New Musical Express, January 1, 1965, "Moodys Film Their Current Hit," and "Moody Blues Almost Gave Up!," by Ian Dove.

Chuck Berry Tour Book, January 8, 1965, with biographical info on the Moodies band members.

Melody Maker, January 14 or 15, 1965, "Moodymania! Brum Boys Shoot Up Nine Places."

New Musical Express, January 15, 1965, "Moody Blues Are Really Quite Happy," by Ian Dove.

Billboard, January 23, 1965, "Singles Reviews," with "spotlight" on "Go Now" and "Right Out of the Blue," by Michael Steel.

New Musical Express, February 12, 1965, "Top Ten by the Moody Blues."

Rave, March 1, 1965, "The m'm'moody blues boys," by Lyn Carnell.

Golden Green show poster, March 21, 1965, with the Moodies topping the bill, above Brian Poole and the Tremeloes.

New Musical Express, April 11, 1965, listing Moody Blues among 1964-65 Poll winners.

Clipping (unknown Swindon, England newspaper), Spring 1965, "Pop Group Bound for Germany.

Daily Express, December 24, 1965, showing "Go Now" at No. 16 in British pop music chart.

New Musical Express, January 15, 1965, "Moody Blues Film for *Tops of the Pops*."

Record Mirror, January 16, 1965, "Chuck Berry, Moody Blues, Graham Bond Organization: Lewisham Odeon, London."

Daily Mirror, January 19, 1965, "It's Go Now with the Moody Blues – They're Tops," by Patrick Doncaster.

Birmingham Evening Mail, January 19, 1965, "Moody Group Anything But Blue Today."

New Musical Express, January 23, 1965, "*NME* Top Twenty," with "Go Now" at No. 1.

Record Mirror, January 23, 1965, "Anyone Can Make the Top Ten," by Christine Osbourne.

Disc Weekly, January 23, 1965, "'Brum Is Still Home!' Say the Chart-Topping Moody Blues," by Ted Scott.

The Observer (London, England), January 31, 1965, "Brumbeat."

Record Mirror, February 13, 1965, "Moodies E.P."

Hartford Courant (Connecticut), February 14, 1965, "Brian Epstein Taping Pop Acts in London."

Pop Weekly, February 20, 1965, "Can The Moody Blues Succeed Again?"

The Times (Port Huron, Michigan), March 21, 1965, "Top 20 Hit Tunes," by Tom Kane – WTTH," with "Go Now" at No. 1.

Record Mirror, March 27, 1965, "Moodies to Use Flute."

Daily Express, April 1, 1965, with Top 30 chart from *NME*, with "I Don't Want to Go On Without You" at No. 20.

Evening Advertiser (Swindon, England), April 9, 1965, "Palladium Debut for Swindon Boy."

Record Mirror, April 10, 1965, "'How the Beatles Helped Us,' Say the Moody Blues," by Richard Green.

Billboard, April 17, 1965, with "I Don't Want to Go On Without You" at No. 19 in British charts.

Rave, May 1, 1965, "Getting the Blues in Paris," by Maureen O'Grady.

KRLA BEAT, May 12, 1965, "Derek Taylor Reports."

Billboard, May 22, 1965, "Singles Reviews," with "spotlight" on "From the Bottom of My Heart."

Record Mirror, May 22, 1965, "Moody Blues Dates."

British Song Festival ad, May 24 & 26, 1965, with the Moody Blues capturing fourth place for "From the Bottom of My Heart."

Record Mirror, May 29, 1965, review of "From the Bottom of My Heart" single.

Music Business, May 29, 1965, "London's Moody Blues Set a Brum (Birmingham) Blues Beat," by June Harris.

The Ottawa Journal (Ontario, Canada), June 12, 1965, "Platter Patter," by Sandy Gardiner, with review of "From the Bottom of My Heart."

Record Mirror, June 19, 1965, "Story Behind That Scream," by Richard Green.

The Ottawa Journal (Ontario, Canada), July 10, 1965, "Britain's Airwave Rulers."

Record Mirror, July 24, 1965, "Moodies – Off-Beat New LP," record review of *The Magnificent Moodies.*

The Moody Blues: The Magnificent Moodies CD box set, with press clipping from unknown British newspaper from late July or early September 1964, reviewing The Magnificent Moodies (Decca LK 4711).

Billboard, August 14, 1965, "Album Reviews," with review of *The Moody Blues #1.*

The Birmingham Planet, August 26, 1965, "Reviews of Two Brilliant L.P.'s: Moodies Debut." (Courtesy of Tony Brown.)

Daily Mirror (London, England), September 3, 1965, "Epstein Signs Moody Blues."

Variety, September 8, 1965, "Record Reviews," with The Moody Blues first album.

Pop Weekly, September 11, 1965, cover story: "The Moody Blues on a Summer Day," by Gray Perell.

Record Mirror, October 23, 1965, "review of "Everyday" single.

Sunday Mercury (Birmingham, England), October 1965, "John Bill – from Germany," by Mark Gardner.

Record Mirror, October 30, 1965, "Moodies Lose Out to Brian Epstein!"

Cashbox, November 20, 1965, review of "Everyday" single.

Billboard, November 20, 1965, "Spotlight Singles," featuring the Moodies' "Every Day."

The Walker Bros tour program, November 21, 1965, with the Moodies as opening act.

Daily Mirror, November 30, 1965, "The Moody Blues Cost Him £25,000," by Don Short.

Rave, December 1, 1965, "Dodo's Pop Diary," reporting Moodies touring with Beatles.

New Musical Express, December 10, 1965, "The Beatles, The Moody Blues: Odeon, Glasgow," by Alan Smith.

The Sydney Morning Herald (New South Wales, Australia), December 11, 1965, "Christmas Discs," by Craig McGregor.

Billboard, December 16, 1965, "Music Capitals of the World."

Newspaper clipping, likely the *Daily Mirror* (London, England), mid-to-late December 1965. (Courtesy of Tony Brown.)

Sunday Mercury (Birmingham, England), January 1966, "A Sweeping Win for John Bull's Breed."

Record Mirror, January 8, 1966, "Moodies U.S. Disc."

Cashbox, January 22, 1966, "Record Reviews," with critique of "Stop!" / "Bye Bye Bird."

Billboard, January 22, 1966, "Spotlight Singles," with review of the Moodies' "Stop!"

Sunday Mercury (Birmingham, England), May 1, 1966, "The Move Sign a $70,000 Contract."

Record Mirror, May 7, 1966, "Early U.S. issue for Moodies."

Billboard, June 18, 1966, "Epstein Goes American – Forms Firm with Lawyer."

Daily Mirror, June 28, 1966, "A Moody Blue Quits."

Beat Instrumental, approx. Summer 1966, "Profile: Mike Pinder," by Pete Goodman.

Disc and Music Echo, July 2, 1966, "Bassist Clint Leaves Moody Blues," plus, "Not Only … But Also," with tour dates for Denmark, France and Belgium.

Record Mirror, July 9, 1966, "Moody Quits."

The Stage and Television Today (London, England), July 14, 1966, reporting that Rod Clarke is new Moodies bass player.

Deseret News, July 22, 1966, "U.S. Unions Bottle Up Beatles," by Victor Riesel.

New Musical Express, August 26, 1966, "Recommended," with review of Justin Hayward's single, "I Can't Face the World Without You."

Record World, August 27, 1966, "Moody Blues for Europe."

The Ottawa Journal (Ontario, Canada), September 25, 1965, "Platter Patter," by Sandy Gardiner, reporting Brian Epstein now managing the Moody Blues.

Rolling Stones Tour Programme, October 2, 1965, with Moody Blues opening for the Stones.

Record Mirror, October 8, 1966, "Single Truth," by Richard Green.

Hit Parader, October 1966, "Moody Blues Changes."

Record Mirror, October 22, 1966, single review, "Boulevard De La Madeleine" and "This Is My House."

New Musical Express or *Melody Maker*, January 1967, review of "Life's Not Life" single from newspaper clippings collection, exact publication and date unknown.

Seventeen, May 1967, Coca-Cola full-page ad: "New Blues for the Moodies."

Variety, May 3, 1967, "On the Upbeat: London," reporting Dru Harvey as the Moodies' new agent.

The Post-Crescent (Appleton, Wisconsin), June 25, 1967, David F. Wagner's review of *The Zodiac: Cosmic Sounds*.

Variety, June 28, 1967, "Top Singles of the Week," with the Moodies "I Really Haven't Got the Time" selected as a "Best Bets" contender.

Cashbox, July 15, 1967, "Record Reviews," with "Best Bet" pick of "I Really Haven't Got the Time."

Record Mirror, September 23, 1967, review of "Love and Beauty" single, by Peter Jones.

Sunday Mirror, October 22, 1967, "Gear Change: Moodies Return with Millionaire Backer and Thirties Wardrobe," by Jack Bentley. (Article courtesy Tony Brown).

The Journal (Newcastle, England), early November, 1967, "Making a Sound Investment." (Article courtesy Tony Brown).

Variety, November 15, 1967, "On the Upbeat: London," reporting Tony McCormick now managing the Moody Blues.

Top Pops, November 25, 1967, "Gordon Coxhill Meets the Moody Blues," by Gordon Coxhill.

Sunday Mirror, November 26, 1967, review of *Days of Future Passed*.

Pop Scene, December 1967, "Moodies Meet a Millionaire!" by Dick Tatham.

Disc and Music Echo, December 2, 1967, "Moodies Move On," album review of *Days of Future Passed*.

Disc and Music Echo, December 2, 1967, blurb on Moodies.

The Observer (London, England), December 10, 1967, review of *Days of Future Passed*, by "Habo."

New Musical Express, January 6, 1968, "Moodies Classical Again."

Disc and Music Echo, January 13, 1968, "Moodies Dislike Charts," by Derek Boltwood.

Variety, January 17, 1968, "Top Singles of the Week," with review of "Nights in White Satin."

New Musical Express, January 20, 1967, "London Concert, Europe Trips for Moody Blues."

Disc and Music Echo, January 20, 1968, "Now the Moodies Ain't Got the Blues," by Mike Ledgerwood.

Melody Maker, February 3, 1968, "Moodies 'Reborn.'"

New Musical Express, February 3, 1968, "Moody Blues Deserve Much Greater Success," by Keith Altham.

Beat Instrumental, March 1968, "Quality Paid off for The Moody Blues," by "P.G."

New Musical Express, March 9, 1968, "Blues Spring to U.S."

The Los Angeles Times, March 10, 1968, "Grand Hybrid by Moody Blues," review by Pete Johnson.

Variety, March 13, 1968, "Record Reviews," with *Days of Future Passed*.

Billboard, March 16, 1968, "Moody Blues Stages Well-Paced Concert," stage review by Mike Hennessey.

Croydon Midweek (London, England), March 19, 1968, "Making Money Is A Gas, But It's Secondary," by Sandra Grant. (Courtesy Tony Brown.)

Valentine magazine, March 22, 1968, "The Moodies Ride Again!" by Dick Tatham. (Courtesy Tony Brown.)

Billboard, March 23, 1968, "Album Reviews," with *Days of Future Passed*, and "Hits of the World," with "Nights in White Satin" at No. 1 in France.

Billboard, March 30, 1968, "Hits of the World," with "Nights in White Satin" at No. 1 for second week in France and first week in Belgium.

Billboard, April 13, 1968, "Hits of the World," with "Nights in White Satin" at No. 2 in Poland, while "Another Morning" peaks at No. 3 in Singapore.

Go Magazine, May 17, 1968, "Scene" by Loraine Alterman.

New York Magazine, May 20, 1968, "Separating Artistic from Arty," by Richard Goldstein.

Billboard, May 25, 1968, "The Marquee Club: Talent showcase."

Variety, May 29, 1968, "Top Singles of the Week," with review of "Tuesday Afternoon."

Hit Parader, June 1968, "My Favorite Records," by Mike Pinder and Justin Hayward.

New Musical Express, June 1, 1968, "Moodies Single, LP."

Billboard, June 1, 1968, "Specialty Merit Spotlight," with review of "Tuesday Afternoon."

Newspaper clipping (unknown British Music trade), June 27, 1968, review of "Voices in the Sky."

The Los Angeles Times, June 28, 1968, with KHJ Radio showing "Tuesday Afternoon" at No. 10.

Melody Maker, June 29, 1968, review of "Voices in the Sky."

Record Mirror, June 29, 1968, review of "Voices in the Sky."

The Los Angeles Times, July 4, 1968, "Tops in Pops," with KHJ Radio showing "Tuesday Afternoon" at No. 5.

Disc and Music Echo, July 7, 1968, "Moody Blues," with review of concert at Queen Elizabeth Hall, by David Hughes.

Valley News (Van Nuys, CA), July 12, 1968, "Top Hits," with "Tuesday Afternoon" at No. 1.

Arizona Republic, July 14, 1968, "The Underground Sound," with review of "Tuesday Afternoon" by Scott G. Campbell.

Fab 208, July 20, 1968, "Faces," by June Southworth.

The Honolulu Advertiser, July 25, 1968, "On the Record," by Walter Harada, with review of *Days of Future Passed*.

Record Mirror, July 27, 1968, "Moodies Move On," with review of *In Search of the Lost Chord*.

Melody Maker, July 27, 1968, report of the Moodies touring the Continent.

Battle Creek Enquirer, August 3, 1968, "BC's Top 20," with "Tuesday Afternoon" at No. 19.

Record Mirror, August 3, 1968, Derek Boltwood's review of *In Search of the Lost Chord*.

Newport Daily News (Rhode Island), August 8, 1968, "Top 20 Records," with "Tuesday Afternoon" at No. 3.

The Cincinnati Enquirer (Ohio), August 10, 1968, "*Enquirer* Top 10 Tune Consensus," with "Tuesday Afternoon" at No. 9.

Melody Maker, August 10, 1968, Chris Welch review of *In Search of the Lost Chord*.

Variety, August 14, 1968, review of *In Search of the Lost Chord*.

Newport Daily News (Rhode Island), August 16, 1968, "Top 20 Records," with "Tuesday Afternoon" at No. 2.

The Cincinnati Enquirer (Ohio), August 17, 1968, "*Enquirer* Top 10 Tune Consensus," with "Tuesday Afternoon" at No. 6.

Arizona Republic, August 18, 1968, "The Underground Sound," with Scott G. Campbell's review of *In Search of the Lost Chord*.

Billboard, August 24, 1968, "Hits of the World," with "Nights in White Satin" at No. 9 in Argentina, and No. 3 in Spain, as "Voices in the Sky" moves up to No. 36 in Britain.

San Antonio Express (Texas), August 25, 1968, "KTSA Top 30," with "Tuesday" at No. 13.

The Times Recorder (Zanesville, Ohio), August 26, 1968, "Platter Patter," with "Tuesday Afternoon" at No. 6.

Honolulu Star-Bulletin (Hawaii), August 28, 1968, "The Teen Beat," with Dave Donnelly's review of *In Search of the Last Chord*.

Disc and Music Echo, August 24, 1968, "Moodies Haven't Got the Blues Any More."

Billboard, August 31, 1968, "Hits of the World," with "Voices in the Sky" up to No. 29 in Britain.

New Musical Express, August 31, 1968, "Moody Blues Full of Surprises," by Richard Green.

Rave magazine, September 1, 1968, "The Day The Moody Blues Should Have Been Called The Broody Moos!"

The Times Recorder (Zanesville, Ohio), September 3, 1968, "Platter Patter," with "Tuesday Afternoon" at No. 6.

Billboard, September 7, 1968, "Hits of the World," with "Voices in the Sky" up to No. 28 according to Britain's *Record Retailer*.

The Kingston Daily Freeman (New York), September 7, 1968, "WBAZ Jet Set Survey," with "Tuesday Afternoon" at No. 3.

New Musical Express, September 7, 1968, "Moodies Czech Trip Over."

Star Tribune (Minneapolis, Minnesota), September 8, 1968, "Top-Selling Records," with "Tuesday Afternoon" at No. 8.

The Kingston Daily Freeman (New York), September 14, 1968, "WBAZ Jet Set Survey," with "Tuesday Afternoon" at No. 2.

Top Pops, September 14, 1968, "Moodies ... No Message ... Just Meaning!," by Gordon Coxhill.

The Kingston Daily Freeman (New York), September 21, 1968, "WBAZ Jet Set Survey," with "Tuesday Afternoon" at No. 2.

Disc and Music Echo, September 14, 1968, "Tele-scope," by Vicki Wickham.

Disc magazine, September 14, 1968, report from "Festival de Humanite" in Paris.

Variety, September 25, 1968, "Top Singles of the Week," with review of "Ride My See-Saw."

The Kingston Daily Freeman (New York), September 28, 1968, "WBAZ Jet Set Survey," with "Tuesday Afternoon" at No. 4.

Billboard, September 28, 1968, "Spotlight Single," with review of "Ride My See-Saw."

New Musical Express, September 28, 1968, "Moodies Sleeping Giants," by Keith Altham.

Belvidere Daily Republican (Illinois), October 10, 1968, "Survey," with "Tuesday" at No. 8.

New Musical Express, October 21, 1968, "Moodies Next."

Chicago Tribune, October 23, 1968, "The Sound," by Robb Baker, with review of Moodies concert in Chicago on Saturday, October 18th.

New Musical Express, October 26, 1968, "Less Complex, More Commercial Moodies," with review of "Ride My See-Saw."

The Los Angeles Times, October 27, 1968, Pete Johnson's review of *In Search of the Lost Chord*.

The New York Times, October 28, 1968, "Three Groups Rock at Fillmore East," with Robert Shelton's review of concert.

The Los Angeles Times, November 1, 1968, "Tops in Pops," with "Ride My See-Saw" at No. 7 on KHJ Boss Radio.

Record Mirror, November 2, 1968, review of "Ride My See-Saw" / "A Simple Game."

Billboard, November 9, 1968, "Mayall, 'Blues' Paint Blues Red," with review of concert at Fillmore East by John Mayall and the Moody Blues.

Cashbox, November 9, 1968, "Moody Blues – John Mayall" concert review from the Fillmore East.

Green Bay Press-Gazette (Wisconsin), November 10, 1968, David F. Wagner's review of *In Search of the Lost Chord*.

Asbury Park Press (New Jersey), November 13, 1968, "Classical Rock" column, with Richard Holl's review of *Days of Future Passed*.

Courier-Press (Camden, New Jersey), November 16, 1968, interview with Graeme Edge, by Hoag Levins.

Chicago Tribune, November 19, 1968, "The Sound," by Robb Baker.

Detroit Free Press, November 22, 1968, "Soft Sounds of Moody Blues," with concert review by Martha Kinsella.

Albuquerque Journal (New Mexico), November 26, 1968, Jim Newton's review of *In Search of the Lost Chord*.

The Los Angeles Times, December 3, 1968, "Three Rock Groups Perform at Shrine," with review by Donna Chick.

Rolling Stone, December 6, 1968, Jim Miller's reviews of *Days of Future Passed* and *In Search of the Lost Chord*.

Open City, December 7, 1968, "Moody Blues," by Ramblin' Jim Martin.

Seattle Times, December 7, 1968, "British Rock Groups Play a Bit of Melody at Eagles," with concert review by Susan Schwartz.

New Musical Express, December 7, 1968, "Moodies Return."

Cashbox, December 14, 1968, concert review from the Shrine Auditorium.

Record Mirror, January 4, 1969, David Griffith's review of *In Search of the Last Chord*.

Fusion magazine, January 6, 1969, "Rock: Change Had Better Be Now," by Jeff Maxwell.

Variety, April 30, 1969, "Top Singles of the Week" with review of "Never Comes the Day."

Hit Parader, May 1969, "The Moody Blues Visit America."

Billboard, May 3, 1969, Special Merit Spotlight review of "Never Comes the Day."

Cashbox, May 3, 1969, "Picks of the Week" review of "Never Comes the Day."

New Musical Express, May 3, 1969, "Moody Ray Talks About *Threshold*."

Melody Maker, May 3, 1969, "Sex, Love and Pop."

Billboard, May 3, 1969, "Moody Blues Seeks U.S. Co. for New Label."

Record Mirror, May 10, 1969, "Getting Better All the Time," by Derek Boltwood.

Melody Maker, May 10, 1969, ""Sex, Love and Pop" (Part 2), by Jean Elliott.

World Countdown Music Newspaper, May 13, 1969, "The Moody Blues Have Done It Again."

Variety, May 14, 1969, review of *On the Threshold of a Dream*.

New Musical Express, May 17, 1969, "Surprisingly, Moodies Miss Screams," by Richard Green.

Billboard, May 24, 1969, review of *On the Threshold of a Dream*.

Arizona Republic, June 1, 1969, "Moody Blues Music Has Quality All Its Own," by Scott G. Campbell.

The Honolulu Advertiser, June 5, 1969, "On the Record," by Wayne Harada, with review of *On the Threshold of a Dream*.

The Los Angeles Times, June 8, 1969, Pete Johnson's review of *On the Threshold of a Dream*.

The Times (San Mateo, California), June 14, 1969, Pay Less ad for *On the Threshold of a Dream*, priced at $2.97.

Chicago Tribune, June 15, 1969, Robb Baker's review of *On the Threshold of a Dream*.

New Musical Express, September 20, 1969, "Moodies Write for You."

Go magazine, approximately Fall 1969, "… Thinking With Your Mind," by Chris Hodenfield.

Daily Mirror, October 2, 1969, "Why the Moody Blues Want a Bigger Bite at the Apple," by Don Short.

Variety, October 15, 1969, "Moody Blues Join That Corporate Trend & Form Own Label, Pub. Co."

The Corpus Christi Caller-Times (Texas), November 1, 1969, *Chicago Sun-Times* syndicated article, "Now Sounds of the Moody Blues," by Kathy Orloff.

Record Mirror, December 20, 1969, "Forget Pop! What About the More Aesthetic and Human Emotions?"

Stereo Review, November 1969, with review of *On the Threshold of a Dream*.

Melody Maker, November 1969, "New Blood on Moody's Label," by Richard Williams.

Disc and Music Echo, November 1, 1969, review of "Watching and Waiting" single.

Record Mirror, November 1, 1969, review of "Watching and Waiting" single, and David Griffiths review of *For Our Children's Children's Children*.

Daily Independent Journal (San Rafael, California), November 8, 1969, "Around the Stereo Scene with Sunier," with John Sunier's reviews of *In Search of the Lost Chord* and *On the Threshold of a Dream*.

New Musical Express, November 8, 1969, "Ray Thomas, New Moody Blues," by Richard Green.

Seattle Times, November 10, 1969, "Moody Blues Thrill Full House at Arena," by Janine Gressel.

Chicago Tribune, December 1, 1969, "Electric Rock Pastoralism," by Linda Winer.

Threshold Concert Program, December 5, 1969, "An Anatomy of Threshold."

Billboard, December 13, 1969, "Mellotron Embellishes Moody Blues' Sound," by George Knemeyer.

New Musical Express, December 13, 1969, report on the Moodies' December 7th performance at the Usher Hall in Edinburgh.

Record Mirror, December 20, 1969, review of Moodies concert at Albert Hall.

Disc and Music Echo, December 20, 1969, "Moodies Join Tom Jones."

Hit Parader Yearbook, Winter 1970, "The Moody Blues Speak Out."

Melody Maker, January 3, 1970, interview with Justin Hayward, by Royston Eldridge.

The Morning News (Wilmington, Delaware), January 17, 1970, "Artists' Own Companies Increase Their Freedom," by Jared Johnson.

New Musical Express, January 17, 1970, "Moodies Success Secret Is Teamwork," by Richard Green.

The Journal News (White Plains, New York), January 31, 1970, "Moody Blues Cut Album," by Mike Jahn.

Arizona Republic, February 1, 1970, "Sounds – From the Underground," with Scott Campbell's review of *To Our Children's Children's Children*.

Muncie Evening Press (Indiana), February 14, 1970, UPI syndicated wire story: "Is Message of Rock Music Only for Young?" by John J. Meehan.

New Musical Express, February 14, 1970, "Doing a Moody: Ray Thomas," by Richard Green.

Fabulous 208, February 14, 1970, "Justin The Moody Blue," by Georgina Mells.

New Musical Express, February 21, 1970, "Doing a Moody: Justin Hayward," by Richard Green.

Honolulu Star-Bulletin, February 21, 1970, "English Group Stirs Interest," with Dave Donnelly's review of *To Our Children's Children's Children*.

New Musical Express, February 28, 1970, "Doing A Moodie: John Lodge," by Richard Green.

Green Bay Press-Gazette (Wisconsin), March 15, 1970, David Wagner's review of *To Our*

Children's Children's Children.

Rolling Stone, March 22, 1970, "Moody Blues Bring A British Version of Rock to Fillmore," by Mike Jahn.

Variety, March 25, 1970, "Concert Reviews: Moody Blues, Lee Michaels, Argent," by "Jeff."

Hartford Courant (Connecticut), March 26, 1970, "Outasight: Moody Blues," by J. Greg Robertson.

Disc and Music Echo, March 28, 1970, "Moody Mode of Travelling – On the Astral Plane," by David Hughes.

Rave magazine, April 1, 1970, "Moody Blues Sound Effects," by Keith Altham.

Rolling Stone, April 3, 1970, "The Moody Blues, Chumps No More," by Charles Alverson.

Billboard, April 4, 1970, "Talent In Action: Moody Blues, Lee Michaels," by Ed Ochs.

The Los Angeles Times, April 7, 1970, "Moody Blues at Long Beach," by Robert Hilburn.

Variety, April 8, 1970, "Top Singles of the Week," with review of Timon's "And Now She Says She Is Young."

Variety, April 15, 1970, "Moody Blues' 200G Take."

Cashbox, April 18, 1970, "Picks of the Week," with review of "Question."

Melody Maker, April 25, 1970, "New Pop Singles" with Chris Welch's reviews of "Candle of Life" and "Question."

New Musical Express, April 25, 1970, "Five-Minute Bargain from Moodies," with review of "Question."

The Baltimore Sun (Maryland), May 3, 1970, "Sounds Good," with Steve Zinz's review of "Question."

The Baltimore Sun, May 4, 1970, "The Moody Blues – Name No Reflection on Style," by Bob Lardine.

Music Now!, May 9, 1970, "The Moody Blues Have Grown Up," by Tony Norman.

Disc and Music Echo, May 9, 1970, "How Justin Beat the Yokel Image," by Penny Valentine.

Melody Maker, May 9, 1970, "Moodies Aim for the Head and Heart," by Royston Eldridge.

Billboard, May 9, 1970, review of Trapeze self-titled debut album on Threshold.

New Musical Express, May 16, 1970, "A Hit Single? We're Just Getting Our Kicks, Says Moody Ray Thomas," by Richard Green.

Melody Maker , May 16, 1970, "Tony – the Sixth Moody," by Richard Williams.

Record Mirror, May 23, 1970, "The Moody Blues: When Is a Single Not a Single?" by Keith Altham.

New Musical Express, May 25, 1970, "NME Top 30," with "Question" at No. 1.

Disc and Music Echo, May 30, 1970, "Top 30 Singles," with "Question" at No. 2; plus "The Business of Being Moody," by David Hughes; "The New LPs," with review of Trapeze debut album on Threshold.

Circus, August 1970, "The Moody Blues: Gentle, Smooth and Nice."

New Musical Express, August 1, 1970, Richard Green's track-by-track preview and review of *A Question of Balance.*

Disc and Music Echo, August 8, 1970, "Moodies Leave Their Cloud," with review of *A Question of Balance.*

Melody Maker, August 8, 1970, "Moody Commune – In the Stockbroker Belt," by Andrew Means, plus review of *A Question of Balance.*

Disc and Music Echo, August 15, 1970, "Graeme – the Drummer with a Head Full of Words."

New Musical Express, August 22, 1970, "Moodies Tour" and other news.

Melody Maker, August 22, 1970, "Moodies Pull Out of IOW."

Variety, September 2, 1970, review of *A Question of Balance.*

The Milwaukee Journal Green Sheet, September 9, 1970, "Sounds of Times," with review of *A Question of Balance.*

Detroit Free Press, September 11, 1970, "A Moody Producer Sees Detroit," by Mike Gormley.

Billboard, September 12, 1970, review of *A Question of Balance.*

Melody Maker, "Caught in the Act," by Dennis Detheridge.

New Musical Express, September 13, 1970, "Moodies Act As Music Guides," by Richard Green.

The Burlington Free Press (Vermont), September 19, 1970, "Moody Blues to Open Lane Series."

Detroit Free Press, September 21, 1970, "The Moody Blues at Cobo – Hampered by Problems," by Mike Gormley.

The Burlington Free Press, September 22, 1970, "Moody Blues Sound Drowns Rapturous Young Audience," by John D. Donoghue.

The Burlington Free Press, September 25, 1970, "Music Review Criticized."

The Philadelphia Inquirer (Pennsylvania), September 28, 1970, "Moody Blues Begins New Rock Season," by Jack Lloyd.

The Cincinnati Enquirer, September 28, 1970, "Van Morrison Disappointing," by Jim Knippenberg.

Columbia Daily Spectator (Morningside Heights, New York), September 29, 1970, "The Moody Blues' A Question of Balance," by Vernon Gibbs.

Variety, September 30, 1970, "Moody Blues / Poco, Felton Forum, N.Y."

Hit Parader, October 1970, "More Moody Blues News."

Ram, circa October 1970, review of *A Question of Balance*.

Go-Set magazine, circa October 1971, review of *A Question of Balance*.

Billboard, October 10, 1970, "Moody Blues / Poco."

Record Mirror, October 10, 1970, "Two Moodies Injured – Gigs Off," and "Why Do People Get Moody About the Moodies?" by Keith Altham.

Melody Maker, October 10, 1970, "Giving Birth to Quads," by Tony Clarke.

Thunder World, October 16, 1970, "Moody Blues *Question* the World," album review by Mike Heavener.

The Morning Call (Allentown, Pennsylvania), October 17, 1970, Teen Times syndicated story, "Jared: Moody Blues Number One in Quality," with Jared Johnson's review of *A Question of Balance*.

The Des Moines Register (Iowa), October 23, 1970, *The Los Angeles Times* syndicated wire story: "Best Selling Pop Albums Not Necessarily Quality," with Robert Hilburn's review of *A Question of Balance*.

The Post-Crescent (Appleton, Wisconsin), October 25, 1970, David F. Wagner's review of *A Question of Balance*.

Billboard, October 31, 1970, reporting *Days of Future Passed* and *On the Threshold of a Dream* having now sold enough copies in the U.S. to qualify for Gold Record awards.

Star Tribune (Minneapolis, Minnesota), November 1, 1970, "Moody Blues: Is the Answer in the *Rock?*" by Mike Jahn.

The Sydney Morning Herald (New South Wales, Australia), Gil Wahlquist's review of *A Question of Balance*.

Variety, November 11, 1970, "Marriages," Mike Pinder to Donna Arkoff on November 6th.

Rolling Stone, November 12, 1970, John Mendelsohn's review of *A Question of Balance*.

Newspaper clipping, November 14, 1970, "Moodies Play Carnegie Hall," plus Mike Pinder wedding to Donna Arkoff.

Sounds, November 14, 1970, "Why US Audiences Take Preference," by Penny Valentine.

The Honolulu Advertiser (Hawaii), December 3, 1970, Wayne Harada's review of *A Question of Balance*.

St. Louis Post-Dispatch (Missouri), December 11, 1970, "Other Blues Get Cheers at Arena," by Thomas B. Newman.

The Los Angeles Times (California), December 14, 1970, "Moody Blues Evening Sellout at the Forum," by John Mendelsohn.

Daily Variety, December 14, 1970, "3 Rissmiller-Wolf Bashes SRO Here."

The New York Times, December 16, 1970, "Moody Blues Offer Loud Rock Concert," by Mike Jahn.

The Waxahachie Daily Light (Texas), December 18, 1970, "Moody Blues Enchant Dallas," by "The Whistler."

Billboard, December 26, 1970, "Talent in Action: Moody Blues / Trapeze," by Fred Kirby, and "3 Gold Albums to Moody Blues."

Hit Parader, January 1971, "The Electronic Moodies: Mellotron and Moog."

The Morning Star News (Wilmington, Delaware), January 2, 1971, "Top Albums of '70," by Jared Johnson.

Scene, January 7, 1971, Sam Milicia's review of *A Question of Balance*.

Chula Vista Star-News (California), January 7, 1971, "The Woodstock Feel," by Lennon.

New Musical Express, January 9, 1971, "The Day We Had to Con Our Label," by Graeme Edge, as told to Pamela Holman.

Record Mirror, January 16, 1971, "The Moody Blues: Now I Know How McCartney Felt," by Keith Altham.

New Musical Express, January 30, 1971, "Poll Supplement."

Billboard, January 30, 1971, "From the Music Capitals of the World: Paris."

Billboard, February 20, 1971, "Special Merit Picks," with review of *Medusa* by Trapeze.

Daily Press (Newport News, Virginia), February 28, 1971, "Rock Revived by Trapeze," by Mike Diana.

Variety, March 10, 1971, "Top Singles of the Week," with review of Threshold's group, Trapeze, and its "Black Cloud" single.

Circus, April 1971, "The Moody Blues Flow Methodically Onward," by David Erlich.

Hit Parader, April 1971, "A Producer's View: Moody Blues," by Nick Logan.

Billboard, April 10, 1971, Fred Kirby's review of Kinks / Trapeze concert.

Billboard, May 15, 1971, "Trapeze, Southwind concert, reviewed by George Knemeyer.

Hit Parader, June 1971, "Moody Blues … From the Beginning," by Nancy Erlich.

Rolling Stone, June 19, 1971, Stu Werbin's review of *Every Good Boy Deserves Favour*.

Disc and Music Echo, July 24, 1971, "The Moodies Give Pretentiousness a New Dimension," the Disc Panel's review of *Every Good Boy Deserves Favour*.

Melody Maker, July 24, 1971, "Moodies: Can Do Better," with Andrew Means's review of *Every Good Boy Deserves Favour*.

New Musical Express, July 1971, review of *Every Good Boy Deserves Favour*.

Record Mirror, July 1971, review of *Every Good Boy Deserves Favour*.

Variety, July 28, 1971, "Top Singles of the Week, with review of "The Story in Your Eyes."

Billboard, July 31, 1971, "Top 60 Pop Spotlight," with review of "The Story in Your Eyes."

Record Mirror, July 31, 1971, "Sounds of Moodies Past," with Bill McAllister's review of *Every Good Boy Deserves Favour*.

New Musical Express, July 31, 1971, "Moodies Musical Advance," by Richard Green.

Variety, August 4, 1971, review of *Every Good Boy Deserves Favour*.

Billboard, August 14, 1971, brief review of *EGBDF*.

Disc and Music Echo, August 21, 1971, "Lord of the Manor," by David Hughes.

The Observer (London, England), August 22, 1971, "Happiness Blues," with Tony Palmer's review of *EGBDF* … and the Moody Blues.

Melody Maker, August 28, 1971, "Doing a Moody," by Roy Hollingworth.

Phonograph Record, September 1971, Jon Tiven's review of *EGBDF*.

Rolling Stone, September 2, 1971, "Paul McCartney Forms Band."

Melody Maker, September 4, 1971, "Blunt Edge," by Roy Hollingworth.

The San Bernardino County Sun (California), September 14, 1971, "New Sound Far from Noisy!" with Henry Mendoza's review of *Every Good Boy Deserves Favour*.

Rolling Stone, September 16, 1971, "The Moody Blues," "What's Trite?" by Andrew Bailey.

The Baltimore Sun (Maryland), September 19, 1971, *New York Times* News Service piece with Mike Jahn's review of *Every Good Boy Deserves Favour*.

The Morning News (Wilmington, Delaware), September 25, 1971, "Teen Times" syndicated article, "Moody Blues Produce 'Total Concept Albums,'" by Jared Johnson.

Sounds, September 25, 1971, "Percussion: Graeme's Got a Shocker, " by Penny Valentine.

Jackie, September 25, 1971, "Pete Meets the Moody Blues."

The Seattle Times, September 27, 1971, "Triumphant Return for Moody Blues," by Janine Gressel.

New Musical Express, circa September 1971, report of gold record ceremony in Hollywood for Moodies with Jay Silverheels as presenter.

Circus, October 1971, "The Elusive Moody Blues," by Penelope Ross.

Billboard, October 2, 1971, "Gold Awards," with *EGBDF* certified gold.

St. Louis Post-Dispatch (Missouri), October 8, 1971, "Moody Blues Appear at Arena After Trip From New Orleans," by Thomas B. Newsom.

Chicago Tribune, October 10, 1971, "Moody Blues Keep Rock at the Core," with Thomas Popson's review of *Every Good Boy Deserves Favour*.

Detroit Free Press, October 11, 1971, "Rock's 15th Century Moody Blues – Stupendous Range."

The Minneapolis Star (Minnesota), October 11, 1971, "Twice-Packed Concert Evidence Moody

Blues Didn't Blow Mood," by Charles Quimby.

Detroit Free Press, October 24, 1971, John Weisman's review of *EGBDF*.

Melody Maker, November 6, 1971, "Moody Blues" concert review by Andrew Means.

New Musical Express, November 6, 1971, "Moodies: One the World's Top Rock Bands?" by Richard Green.

News-Press (Fort Myers, Florida), November 7, 1971, NEA wire story: "The Moody Blues Forever," by Dick Kleiner.

Sounds, November 8, 1971, "The *Sounds* Talk-In: Mike Pinder," interviewed by Penny Valentine.

Rock, November 8, 1971, "The Moody Blues."

Kingston Post, November 11, 1971, "Moody Blues Are Noted for Simple Honesty, with Judy Hugg's review of *Every Good Boy Deserves Favour*.

New Musical Express, November 20, 1971, Paul McCartney Is Like a Man Who Has Dodged the Death Sentence," by Richard Green, plus review of Wings' album *Wild Life*.

Hi Fidelity, December 1971, M.J.'s review of *Every Good Boy Deserves Favour*.

Boston, Massachusetts newspaper clipping (exact publication unknown), 1971, "Moody Blues Brings Clear Sound to Garden," by Peter Herbsy.

The Los Angeles Times, December 8, 1971, "McCartney's Third Disappointment," by Robert Hilburn.

Billboard, December 18, 1971, review of Wings' *Wild Life*.

The Morning News (Wilmington, Delaware), January 1, 1972, "New Moody Blues Album Deserves Favor," by Jared Johnson.

Melody Maker, March 18, 1972, Moody Views," by Andrew Means.

Rolling Stone, January 20, 1971, Wings' *Wild Life* album review by John Mendelson.

The Ottawa Journal (Ontario, Canada), March 24, 1972, Reuter wire story: "Paul's Wings Fly in Debut Outing."

The Baltimore Sun, March 29, 1972, "Moody Blues Material Pedestrian and Execution Mediocre," by James D. Dilts.

Fort Lauderdale News (Florida), "Security Up for Blues' Appearance," by Jack Zink.

Fort Lauderdale News (Florida), April 10, 1972, "Moody Blues' Musical Style Borders on Mystic," by Jack Zink.

Sounds, April 15, 1972, "And The Rock Gods Came From On High," by Penny Valentine.

Variety, April 19, 1972, "14-City U.S. Tour Hits 920G Payoff for Moody Blues," and "Top Singles of the Week," with review of "Isn't Life Strange."

Record Mirror, April 22, 1972, "The Moody Blues," by Hal Speck.

Sounds, April 22, 1972, review of "Isn't Life Strange."

Melody Maker, April 29, 1972, "Moodies Big Search," by Andrew Means.

Sounds, April 29, 1972, "Moodies: Heroes at the Pool," by Penny Valentine.

The Times Recorder (Zanesville, Ohio), May 25, 1972, "Platter Patter," with "Isn't Life Strange" at No. 8.

The Times Recorder (Zanesville, Ohio), June 3, 1972, "Platter Patter," with "Isn't Life Strange" still at No. 8.

Sounds, June 3, 1972, "Moodies: Isn't Life Strange?" by Penny Valentine.

New Musical Express, June 3, 1972, "Moody Music: The Place of Electronics," by Tony Stewart.

Billboard, June 19, 1972, "Hits of the World" with "Isn't Life Strange" at No. 13 in Britain.

The Van Nuys News, June 23, 1972, wire story: "Traffic Jammed as Moody Blues Ends U.S. Tour."

Billboard, July 29, 1972, "Wings – Olympia, Paris," concert review.

Variety, August 2, 1972, "Top Singles of the Week," with "Nights in White Satin" review.

Billboard, August 19, 1972, "Hot Chart Action: Breaking," with "Nights in White Satin."

The Gold Bug, September 26, 1972, "Records: Sound from Surrey," with Rich Gould's review of *Every Good Boy Deserves Favour*.

Sounds, September 30, 1972, "Graeme Edge Talking to Penny Valentine."

New Musical Express, October 6, 1972, "Moody Music."

The Journal News, October 21, 1972, "Pop Scene Answer Man," by Adam Di Petto.

New Musical Express, October 21, 1972, "Moodies Mania in U.S. Over 1967 Recordings."

Daily Press (Newport News, Virginia), October 23, 1972, "Police Arrest 17 on Drug Charges at Rock Concert," and "Moody Blues Please Crowd," by Linda Cooley.

The Philadelphia Inquirer (Pennsylvania), October 25, 1972, "19,000 Jam Spectrum to Hear Moody Blues; Set Crowd Record," by Jack Lloyd.

The New York Times, October 25, 1972, "Moody Blues Lifts Its Audience to Instant Nirvana at Garden," by Don Heckman.

The Morning News, October 28, 1972, "Moody Blues' Sound Drifts Disembodied at Spectrum," by Hugh Cutler.

St. Louis Post-Dispatch (Missouri), October 29, 1972, "The Moody Blues Perform at Arena," by Dick Richmond.

The Minneapolis Star (Minnesota), October 30, 1972, "Good Sound, Not Gimmicks, Makes Moody Blues Go," by John Carmon.

Music Scene, November 1972, "A Family of Moodies," by Tony Norman.

Variety, November 1, 1972, concert review of Moody Blues at Madison Square Garden.

Deseret News, November 3, 1972, "Moody Blues Shade Halloween," by Brent Mower.

Billboard, November 4, 1972, "Talent in Action: Moody Blues," reviewed by Nancy Erlich.

The Los Angeles Times, November 4, 1972, "Can the Moodies Survive Democracy?" by Robert Hilburn.

New Musical Express, November 4, 1972, "Doug Jones on the Road with the Moody Blues," by Doug Jones.

Independent (Long Beach, California), November 6, 1972, "Moody Blues Not Really a Concert, But a Statement," by Denise Kusel.

Casa Grande Dispatch (Arizona), November 8, 1972, AP wire story: "Tension Is Absent in Moody Blues," by Mary Campbell.

Valley News (Van Nuys, California), November 10, 1972, "Moody Blues Forum Date Attracts Crowd of 17,000," by Scott Paul.

Colorado Springs Gazette-Telegraph, November 11, 1972, "Record Rap," by Gregor Vaule.

Melody Maker, November 11, 1972, "Isn't Life Strange?," with Andrew Means's review of *Seventh Sojourn.*

WSAN Review newsletter (Allentown, Pennsylvania), November 13, 1972, with review of *Seventh Sojourn.*

New Musical Express, November 18, 1972, "Albums," with Tony Stewart's review of *Seventh Sojourn.*

The Post-Crescent (Appleton, Wisconsin), November 19, 1972, David F. Wagner's review of *Seventh Sojourn.*

North Country Catholic (Ogdensburg, New York), November 22, 1972, "Mission: Music."

The Pittsburgh Press (Pennsylvania), November 26, 1972," with Tony Palermo's review of *Seventh Sojourn.*

Circus, December 1972, "Inside the Moody Blues' American Miracle," by Ward Beaverman.

Melody Maker, December 2, 1972, "Mary Had a Little Lamb ... Those Lyrics Are a Heavy Trip."

Billboard, December 9, 1972, "Gold Awards," with *Seventh Sojourn* both certified gold and on top of the *Billboard* album chart.

Variety, December 20, 1972, review of Threshold album, *You Are the Music ... We're Just the Band,* by Trapeze.

Rolling Stone, December 21, 1972, "In Search of the Moody Blues," by James Horwitz.

Democrat and Chronicle (Rochester, New York), November 26, 1972, "Moody Blues: Ponderous Sojourn," with review by Mark Starr.

Stereo Review, circa Fall 1972, "Recordings of Special Merit: *Seventh Sojourn.*"

The Lowell Sun (Massachusetts), January 2, 1973, "The Moody Blues Carry On."

Melody Maker, January 6, 1973, "Moody's Next."

Rolling Stone, January 18, 1973, Steve Ditlea's review of *Seventh Sojourn.*

Melody Maker, January 20, 1973, Chris Welch's review of "I'm Only a Singer (In a Rock and Roll Band)."

New Musical Express, January 20, 1973, "Moody Blues: Motive Force Behind the Money," by Tony Stewart.

Billboard, January 27, 1973, review of "I'm Just a Singer (In a Rock and Roll Band."

Sounds, February 3, 1973, "*Days of Future Passed*," by Penny Valentine.

Let It Rock, March 1973, Simon Frith's review of *Seventh Sojourn.*

Circus, March 1973, "Letters," and review of Trapeze's *You Are the Music ... We're Just the*

Band.

Melody Maker, March 11, 1973, "Letters."

New Musical Express, May 5, 1973, "The Tape Wizard of the Moodies," by Tony Tyler.

The Los Angeles Times, May 13, 1973, "Hunch Cracks Up on McCartney's *Speedway*," by Robert Hilburn.

Billboard, May 16, 1973, review of Wings' LP *Red Rose Speedway*.

Abilene Reporter-News (Texas), "Platter Chatter" with Jim Conley's review of Wings' LP *Red Rose Speedway*.

Milwaukee Sentinel, August 18, 1973, "Moody Blues Start Tour on Sept. 5."

Sounds, August 18, 1973, "The Moody Machine Returns," by Ray Hammond.

Disc and Music Echo, August 25, 1973, "Coming Up the Hard Way: A Moody's View on the Struggle for Survival."

The Los Angeles Times, August 31, 1973, "Paul Reliving the Beatles' Struggle with Wings Group," by Barbara Charone.

Record Mirror, September 1, 1973, "Justin and Four Brum Teds," by Rick Sanders.

Senior Scholastic, September 27, 1973, "On the Road with Paul McCartney," by Ed Sparn.

The Popular Voice, September 30, 1973, "Moody Blues, Happy Family."

The Guardian (London, England), October 9, 1973, "Moody Blues in Manchester," by Barry Coleman.

New Musical Express, October 20, 1973, "Moody Blues: Saints or Sinners?," by Keith Altham.

The Gazette (Montreal, Canada), October 25, 1973, "Moody Blues Transform Forum," by Bill Mann.

The Pittsburgh Press (Pennsylvania), October 26, 1973, "Delay Leaves Area Crowd Moody, Blue," by Pete Bishop.

Pittsburgh Post-Gazette, October 27, 1973, "Moodies' Concert Just Another Show," by Mike Kalina.

Pottstown Mercury, October 30, 1973, *Chicago Daily News* Service wire story: "Moody Blues Keep Searching for Creativity," by Al Rudis.

Chicago Tribune (Illinois), October 31, 1973, "The Moody Blues: Music, Not Madness," by Lynn Van Matre.

Albany State Student Press, November 1973, "Five Friends at the Garden," by Joseph Tripodi.

The New Journal (Wilmington, Delaware), November 2, 1973, "Moody Blues Superbly Satisfying," by Hugh Cutler.

The Dallas Times Herald, November 5, 1973, "Moody Blues: 'Smooth – like a Milkshake,' 'One Giant Tranquilizer,'" by Susan Barton.

The Michigan Daily, November 9, 1973, "Moody Blues Enchant Crisler," by Tom Kippert.

The Indianapolis Star (Indiana), November 10, 1973, "Moody Blues Packs 'Em In At Louisville's Freedom Hall," by Jeff Harrell.

Billboard, November 17, 1973, "The Moody Blues: Madison Square Garden, New York," by Phil Gelormine.

Sounds, November 24, 1973, "Moodies to Open Up the Curtain."

Tambourine magazine, November 26, 1973, "Moody Blues: Universal Experiences – Universal Sounds," by Daniel Goldberg.

Melody Maker, December 1, 1973, "Paul McCartney," by Chris Welch.

The Los Angeles Times, December 16, 1973, Robert Hilburn's review of *Band on the Run.*

Courier-Post (Camden, New Jersey), December 26, 1973, UPI wire story: "Moody Blues Really Awful, But Popular," by Bruce Meyer.

Honolulu Star-Bulletin (Hawaii), January 28, 1974, "Moody Blues, a Tight Show," by Beverly Creamer.

The Los Angeles Times, February 1, 1974, "SRO at Moody Blues Concert," by Dennis Hunt.

San Francisco Examiner, February 1, 1974, "A Perfect Concert from a Very Together Group," by Philip Elwood.

Modern Hi-Fi & Stereo Guide, March/April 1974, "What's Happening with the Moody Blues?" by Robert V. Weinstein.

Rolling Stone, March 14, 1974, "Performance: Moody Blues, L.A. Forum, January 30th, 1974," by David Rensin.

Hattiesburg American (Mississippi), April 21, 1974, "Here's the Answer," by Barbara Lewis.

Evening Herald, April 30, 1974, "Rock Talk," by Tom Malafarina.

Hattiesburg American (Mississippi), June 9, 1974, "Here's the Answer," by Barbara Lewis.

Sounds, July, 13, 1974, "Moodies Solo albums; Single from Edge Band."

Sounds, July 20, 1974, "Edging His Bets," by Bill Henderson.

Variety, July 24, 1974, "Weintraub to Rein The Moody Blues."

Melody Maker, August 10, 1974, "You, Me – and Justin."

Variety, August 14, 1974, "Reshuffle Moody Blues, Threshold Label Setup Following London Meet."

Music Scene, September 1974, "The Mixed Up Mood of the Moodies," by Richard Green.

Journal and Courier, September 12, 1974, "Moody Blues Still Tight Despite Breakup Rumors," by Robert Scott.

Billboard, September 14, 1974, "'We Couldn't Create New Music' Says Disappointed Drummer Edge," by Nat Freedland.

Pensacola News Journal (Florida), September 24, 1974, Gannett-Rolling Stone wire story: "Moodys Pass Million Mark, Find Monster Needs Rest," by Andrew Bailey.

The San Bernardino County Sun (California), September 26, 1974, "Moody Blues Take Enforced Rest After 8 Years Together," by Andrew Bailey.

Asbury Park Press (New Jersey), September 26, 1974, "Moody Blues Taking Rest," by Andrew Bailey.

The Ottawa Journal (Ontario, Canada), "Rock's Frankenstein Moody Blues Retire," by Andrew Bailey.

The Gastonia Gazette (North Carolina), September 28, 1974, "Rolling Stone," by Andrew Bailey.

The Palm Beach Post (West Palm Beach, Florida), September 29, 1974, "The Moody Blues: The Monster Takes a Rest," by Andrew Bailey.

Zoo World, October 10, 1974, "The Moody Blues."

Concert magazine, November 1974, "Graeme Edge: On the Threshold of a Dream," by John David Kalodner.

Billboard, November 16, 1974, review of *This Is the Moody Blues*.

Melody Maker, November 16, 1974, review of *This Is the Moody Blues*.

New Musical Express, November 23, 1974, "Platters," with Tony Stewart's review of *This Is the Moody Blues*.

The New York Times, November 24, 1974, "A Requiem for the Moody Blues and the *Days of Future Passed*," by Barbara Rowes.

The Cincinnati Enquirer, December 14, 1974, "Moody Blues Music With All the Filler Junk Thrown Out," with Jim Knippenberg's review of *This Is the Moody Blues*.

The Palm Beach Post (West Palm Beach, Florida), December 16, 1974, "Moody Blues Alive and Well," by Thom Smith.

Billboard, December 21, 1974, RIAA Gold Record Winners," including *This Is the Moody Blues*.

Music Scene Annual, 1974, "Under The Moodies Influence," by Richard Green.

The Age (Melbourne, Victoria, Australia), February 1, 1975, "New Notes," with Mike Daily's and Paul Speelman's review of *This Is the Moody Blues*.

Beat Instrumental, March 1975, "Ray Thomas."

Record Mirror, March 1, 1975, "Solo Time in New York City: Moody's Branch Out in Quad."

Melody Maker, March 1, 1975, "Moodies: On the Threshold of a Break."

Record Mirror, March 15, 1975, "The Blue Jay Way," covering premiere of Blue Jays album.

San Francisco Chronicle, March 17, 1975, "People Came from Miles Away," by John L. Wasserman.

Sounds, March 22, 1975, "Blue Jays & Happy Days," by Pete Thomas.

Melody Maker, March 22, 1975, "I'm Justin, Fly Me...," by Ray Coleman.

New Musical Express, March 22, 1975, "A Moody By Any Other Name ... Still sounds Pretty Much the Same," by Tony Stewart, and "The Importance of Being Ernest," by Tony Stewart.

Billboard, March 22, 1975, review of *Blue Jays*.

Daily Press (Newport News, Virginia), March 30, 1975, "Hear Say," with Mike Diana's review of *Blue Jays*.

Record Mirror, April 12, 1975, "Moody Two Remember: First Single, TV and UK Dates Soon."

Beaver County Times (Pennsylvania), April 16, 1975, "Two Former Moody Blues Still Oozing

With Class," with Bob Bonn's review of *Blue Jays*.

The Lowell Sun (Massachusetts), April 18, 1975, "*Blue Jays* Hayward and Lodge Continue Moody Blues Tradition," by William E. Sarmento.

Record Mirror, April 19, 1975, review of "Remember Me, My Friend" single.

The Los Angeles Times, April 22, 1975, Robert Hilburn's review of *Blue Jays*.

Rolling Stone, April 24, 1975, "Moody Vets Non-Live Onstage," by Ed McCormack.

The Salina Journal (Kansas), May 5, 1975, "Moody Blues Not Breaking Up: Blue Jays Just a Side Project," by Kim Garfield.

Rolling Stone, May 8, 1975, Stephen Holden's review of *Blue Jays*.

The Youth Report, May 10, 1975, "Stale Offerings in *Blue Jays*," by John Wisniewski.

Broadcasting, May 12, 1975, "Breaking In," with review of "I Dreamed Last Night" single.

Melody Maker, May 24, 1975, "We're the Biggest Underground Band."

Crawdaddy, June 1975, review of *Blue Jays*.

Beat Instrumental, June 1975, "Blue Jays: Moodies Going Solo!" by Chris Simmons.

The Los Angeles Times, June 8, 1975, "Paul Never Better; Elton Still Best," by Robert Hilburn.

Billboard, June 18, 1975, review of Wings' LP *Venus and Mars*.

Stereo Review, July 1975, review of *Blue Jays*.

Gramophone, July 1975, review of *Blue Jays*.

Billboard, July 5, 1975, review of Thomas' "High Above My Head" single.

Melody Maker, July 12, 1975, "In the Moody," by Chris Charlesworth.

Cashbox, circa August 1975, review of "Love Is the Key."

Circus, August 1975, "Moody Blues – How Hayward & Lodge's BLUEJAYS Keep the Astral Band Aloft," by Peter Crescenti.

New Musical Express, August 2, 1975, "Mighty Acorn," by Tony Stewart.

Billboard, August 2, 1975, review of *From Mighty Oaks*.

PTP, August 7, 1975, "Ray Thomas: 'What Else Can I Do?'"

Waco Tribune-Herald (Waco, Texas), August 17, 1975, "Moody Blues Cut Solo Albums," with Bruce Westbrook's review of *From Mighty Oaks*.

The Des Plaines Herald (Arlington Heights, Illinois), August 22, 1975, "Playback: Moody Blues' Composer Records His Own Album," by Tom Von Malder.

Press and Sun-Bulletin (Binghamton, New York), August 23, 1975, Chris Carson's review of *From Mighty Oaks*.

The Daily Tar Heel (Chapel Hill, North Carolina), August 25, 1975, Associate Features wire-story: George Bacso's review of *Blue Jays*.

The Desert Sun, August 28, 1975, NEA wire story: "Rock Millionaire Club's Elite, by Steven Ford.

Detroit Free Press, August 31, 1975, "A Moody Blue Solos Nicely," with Bob Talbert's review of *From Mighty Oaks*.

Melody Maker, September 6, 1975, "Edge of a Dream," by Chris Charlesworth.

Music Week, September 6, 1975, "Taking the Edge Off Exile, " by Terri Anderson.

Green Bay Press-Gazette (Wisconsin), September 14, 1975, "Records in Review," with Warren Gerds' review of *From Mighty Oaks*.

Reporter Dispatch, September 17, 1975, "Ray Thomas Emerges from Blues," by Jack McDonough.

Ram, September 20, 1975, Tony Stewart's review of *From Mighty Oaks*.

Billboard, September 20, 1975, review of *Kick Off Your Muddy Boots*.

Melody Maker, September 27, 1975, "Blue Jays Hit the Road."

The Miami News (Florida), October 3, 1975, *Chicago Sun-Times* syndicated story: "The Moody Blues Pick Up the Pieces," by Al Rudis.

Record Mirror, October 4, 1975, Ray Fox-Cumming's review of "Blue Guitar" single.

Variety, October 8, 1975, review of *Kick Off Your Muddy Boots*.

Record Mirror, October 11, 1975, "The Blue Jays Say: 'We've Always Been Years Ahead or Years Behind," by Peter Harvey.

Sunday Gazette-Mail (Charleston, West Virginia), October 12, 1975, "*Mighty Oaks*, Rock with Class," by Jim Carnes.

Rolling Stone, October 23, 1975, Stephen Holder's review of *From Mighty Oaks*.

Journal and Courier (Lafayette, Indiana), October 31, 1975, Robert Scott's review of *Kick Off*

Your Muddy Boots.

Audio, November 1975, Fred De Van's review of *Blue Jays*.

High Fidelity Magazine, November 1975, review of *From Mighty Oaks*.

Daily Press (Newport News, Virginia), November 2, 1975, Mike Diana's commentary concerning *Kick Off Your Muddy Boots.*

Muncie Evening Press (New Jersey), November 15, 1975, "Pop Scene Service" interview with Graeme Edge by Kim Garfield.

Record Mirror, November 22, 1975, "Blue, But Not Moody," by Peter Harvey.

Circus, November 25, 1975, "Moodies Planning to Record Again."

The Guardian (London, England), November 26, 1975, Robin Denselow's review of Blue Jays Hammersmith concert.

Melody Maker, December 6, 1975, "Caught in the Act," concert review of Blue Jays by Harry Doherty.

Green Bay Press-Gazette (Wisconsin), December 7, 1975, "Records in Review" with Warren Gerds's review of Kick Off Your Muddy Boots.

Zigzag, January 1976, "The Moody Blues," by Andy Childs.

The Orlando Sentinel (Florida), January 21, 1976, "The 'Best' Albums of '75," by Richard Santoro, including *Kick Off Your Muddy Boots.*

Stereo Review, February 1976, review of *Kick Off Your Muddy Boots.*

Melody Maker, April 10, 1976, "Pinder's Broken Promise," with review of *The Promise.*

Cashbox, April 17, 1976, review of *The Promise.*

New Musical Express, April 17, 1976, Michael Pinder interview by Steve Turner.

Billboard, April 17, 1976, review of *The Promise.*

Beaver County Times (Pennsylvania), May 5, 1976, "Pinder's Promise Completes Solo Cycle," by Bob Bonn.

The Daily Journal (Vineland, New Jersey), May 15, 1976, Dennis Hill's review of *The Promise.*

The Pittsburgh Press (Pennsylvania), June 20, 1976, "Moody Blues Player Promising On Own," by Pete Bishop.

Gramophone, July 1976, review of *The Promise.*

Ram, July 20, 1976, Alex Ward's review of *The Promise.*

JUKE, July 20, 1976, "No Moodies Revival."

The Kingston Daily Freeman (New York), August 15, 1976, with Alan Forray's review of *Hopes, Wishes and Dreams.*

Arizona Republic (Phoenix, Arizona), August 20, 1976, "Breaking Out of the Mold," with Gus Walker's review of *Hopes, Wishes and Dreams.*

The Daily Herald (Chicago, Illinois), August 27, 1976, "Playback: Members of Moody Blues Now Performing in Solo," by Tom Von Malder.

Stereo Review, September 1976, review of *The Promise.*

Beaver County Times (Pennsylvania), September 22, 1976, "Ray Thomas' Hopes, Wishes, Dreams, Fails," by Sandy Poiarkoff.

Circus, October 26, 1976, "Moody Blues Back with Solo Albums."

Stereo Review, December 1976, review of *Hopes, Wishes and Dreams.*

Beat Instrumental, January 1977, "Justin Hayward: In Search of the Lost Songwriter," by Tom Stock.

Record Mirror, January 29, 1977, Robin Smith's review of *Natural Avenue.*

Melody Maker, January 29, 1977, "Blue Jays Dead – Justin Time!" by Ray Coleman, and "Lodge Finds a Natural Avenue," by Harry Doherty.

Sounds, February 1977, Chas De Whalley's review of *Songwriter.*

Record Mirror, February 12, 1977, "The Singer and a Room," with Robin Smith's review of *Songwriter.*

Rock Star, February 19, 1977, review of "Lonely Room."

Billboard, February 26, 1977, review of *Songwriter.*

Melody Maker, February 26, 1977, Richard Green's review of *Songwriter.*

International Musician and Recording World, March 1977, with review of *Songwriter.*

Record Mirror, March 5, 1977, "John 'Clean Living' Lodge" and "Justin 'It's a Living' Hayward."

The Seattle Times, March 12, 1977, "Hayward's Album Ends Jinx," by Patrick MacDonald.

Record Mirror, March 26, 1977, review of "Children of Rock 'n' Roll" single.

Beaver County Times (Pennsylvania), March 23, 1977, "English Rock Alive & Well," with Bob Uhrinak's review of *Songwriter*.

Scottsdale Community College Free Press (Arizona) March 30, 1977, Patti Bruno's review of *Songwriter*.

Billboard, April 2, 1977, review of *Natural Avenue*.

Scottsdale Community College Free Press (Arizona), 1977, Patti Bruno's review of *Natural Avenue*.

The Pittsburgh Press (Pennsylvania), April 10, 1977, "Moody Blues Solo Listless," with Pete Bishop's review of *Songwriter*.

Circus, April 14, 1977, "Moody Blues Go Solo Again."

People, April 18, 1977, mini-review of *Songwriter*.

Rolling Stone, May 5, 1977, Alan Niester's review of *Songwriter*.

Record Mirror, May 7, 1977, Robin Smith's review of *Paradise Ballroom*.

Valley News (Van Nuys, California), May 13, 1977, Richard S. Ginell's review of *Songwriter*.

The Tennessean (Nashville, Tennessee), May 15, 1977, "John Lodge: 'I'm Still A Moody' – But Solo," by Lisa Hemby.

Ram (Australia), May 20, 1977, Simon Richardson's reviews of *Natural Avenue* and *Songwriter*.

Sounds, May 21, 1977, Phil Sutcliffe's review of *Paradise Ballroom*.

Denver Post (Colorado), May 22, 1977, "Hayward 'Changes Pace,' But for Lodge It's Reaffirmation," by Jared Johnson.

The Los Angeles Times, May 27, 1977, Robert Hilburn's review of *Songwriter*.

Billboard, May 28, 1971, review of *Caught Live + 5*.

Denver Post (Colorado), May 29, 1977, "Mood-ish Blues Drive Still Going Strong as Stars Do Their Own Thing," by Jared Johnson.

The Los Angeles Times (California), May 29, 1977, Robert Hilburn's review of *Natural Avenue*.

The Ottawa Journal (Ontario, Canada), June 3, 1977, "Moody Blues Must," with Ian Haysom's review of *Caught Live + 5*.

New Musical Express, June 11, 1977, Chris Salewicz reviews of *Paradise Ballroom* and *Caught Live + 5*.

Rolling Stone, June 16, 1977, Charley Walter's review of *Natural Avenue*.

The Los Angeles Times, June 17, 1977, Steve Rosen's review of *Caught Live + 5*.

Billboard, June 18, 1977, review of *Paradise Ballroom*.

The Pittsburgh Press (Pennsylvania), June 19, 1977, Pete Bishop's review of *Caught Live + 5*.

Variety, June 22, 1977, "Moody About Biz End of Disks."

Circus, July 7, 1977, Michael Bloom's review of *Songwriter*.

The Courier-News (Bridgewater, New Jersey), July 9, 1977, "Ever Apart They're Still Moody Blues," with Karen Herman Steffaro's review of *Natural Avenue*.

Muncie Evening Press (Indiana), July 30, 1977, "Moody Blues Reforming; New Album in the Making," by Sue Byrom.

Crawdaddy, August 1977, Moody Blues: Why They Sang the Blues," by Susan Ahrens.

Circus, August 18, 1977, "Solo Career Zooms for Ex-Moody Blue," by Liz Derringer.

Rock, September 1977, "Justin Hayward: Not Very Moody and Anything But Blue," by Jon Tiven.

Circus, October 27, 1977, Michel Bloom's reviews of *Caught Live + 5*, *Natural Avenue* and *Paradise Ballroom*.

Back Stage, April 21, 1978, "Moody Blues Reunite for New Album."

Union Recorder (Australia), May 1978, "On the Threshold of a Return," by Mark Robinson.

Billboard, May 6, 1978, "London Preps Moody Blues LP Push," by Adam White.

Billboard, June 3, 1978, "Moody Blues LP Wrapped in Security."

The Tennessean (Nashville), May 21, 1878, "Ask Showcase."

Union Recorder (Sydney, Australia), June 1978, Mark Robinson's review of *Octave*.

Music Week, June 3, 1978, "US premiere for Moody LP."

Muncie Evening Press (Indiana), June 10, 1978, United Features syndicated column by Sue Byron, estimating as high as 60 million might listen to premiere of *Octave* on 500 radio stations across America on this date.

Music Week, June 17, 1978, "Sir Edward: In a Rare Mood."

Melody Maker, June 17, 1978, "Back in the Moodies," with review of *Octave*.

New Musical Express, June 17, 1978, "Hairdressers and Brummie Businessmen Quit Day Jobs to Form Mystical Alliance (& Make Bucks)," by Bob Edmands.

Fort Lauderdale News (Florida), June 18, 1978, advance order stats for *Octave*, by Aaron Gold.

The Los Angeles Times, June 20, 1978, "Moody Blues Back in the Ring," with Robert Hilburn's review of *Octave*.

Semper Fi, June 21, 1978, Gus Strachan's review of *Octave*.

The Philadelphia Inquirer (Pennsylvania), June 23, 1978, "Alums," with Jack Lloyd's review of *Octave*.

Philadelphia Daily News (Pennsylvania), June 23, 1978, Rich Aregood's review of *Octave*.

Music Week, June 24, 1978, "Tony Clarke: The 'Invisible' Moody Blue."

Billboard, June 24, 1978, "Spotlight" album, *Octave*.

Cashbox, June 24, 1978, review of *Octave*.

Chicago Tribune, June 25, 1978, Lynn Van Matre's review of *Octave*.

Press and Sun-Bulletin (Binghamton, New York), June 28, 1978, Chris Carson's review of *Octave*.

Beaver County Times (Pennsylvania), June 28, 1978, Sandy Poiarkoff's review of *Octave*.

The Seattle Times, June 30, 1978, Patrick MacDonald's review of *Octave*.

Gallery magazine, Summer 1978, review of *Octave*.

Billboard, July 1, 1978, "Moody's *Octave* Given Big Push."

The Morning Call (Allentown, Pennsylvania), July 1, 1978, Paul Willistein Jr.'s review of *Octave*.

Muncie Evening Press (Indiana), July 1, 1978, Ron Hawkins's review of *Octave*.

The Morning News (Wilmington, Delaware), July 2, 1978, Gary Mullinax's review of *Octave*.

Hartford Courant (Connecticut), July 2, 1978, Henry McNulty's review of *Octave*.

The Pittsburgh Press (Pennsylvania), July 2, 1978, Pete Bishop's review of *Octave*.

Rolling Stone, July 13, 1978, "The Moody Blues' Days of Future," by Mikal Gilmore.

The Ottawa Journal (Ontario, Canada), July 14, 1978, Chris Cobb's review of *Octave*.

The Citizen (Ottawa, Canada), July 15, 1978, "Revolutions," with Bill Provick's review of *Octave*.

Melody Maker, July 15, 1978, "Why the Moodies Re-formed," by Ray Coleman.

Billboard, July 22, 1978, review of "Steppin' in a Slide Zone" single.

The Town Talk (Alexandria, Louisiana), July 22, 1978, Associated Press wire story: "Moody Blues Regroup," by James Simon.

The San Francisco Examiner & Chronicle, July 23, 1978, "The Moodiest of the Moody Blues Is Justin Hayward," by Bart Mills.

Sounds, July 29, 1978, "After the Goldrush," by Donna McAllister.

The Sun (London, England), August 5, 1978, interview with Justin and Marie Hayward.

People, August 7, 1978, "*People* Picks & Pans," with review of *Octave*.

Circus magazine, August 31, 1978, "Days of Future Passed?" by Mark Mehler.

Crawdaddy, September 1978, "Breathe Deep the Gathering Gloom," with Benson Worthington Laing's review of *Octave*.

Rolling Stone, September 7, 1978, Stephen Holden's review of *Octave*.

Asbury Park Press (New Jersey), September 29, 1979, "Moody Blues to Tour."

Melody Maker, September 30, 1978, "Moody Blues: Yes to the Moodies," by Chris Welch, plus "Moraz Replaces Mike Pinder in Moodies."

The Town Talk, October 3, 1978, "Off the Record," with review of *Octave*.

Billboard, October 7, 1978, "Moraz Will Tour with Moody Blues."

Billboard, October 21, 1978, "London Efforts Get Behind Moody Blues."

The Minneapolis Star (Minnesota), November 3, 1978, "Disciples Get Moodies to Tour," by Jon Bream.

St. Paul Pioneer Press, November 4, 1978, "Mood Is Quiet at Blues Concert."

St. Paul Pioneer Press, November 5, 1978, "Moody Blues Still Magical," by James M. Tarbox.

The Des Moines Register (Iowa), November 5, 1978, "11,000 Cheer Moody Blues at Ames Show," by Jonathan Engel.

St. Paul Pioneer Press, November 5, 1978, "Moody Blues Still Magical," by James M. Tarbox.

The Minneapolis Star, November 6, 1978, "Moraz Adds Energy, More Rock to Mood of Moodies," by Jon Bream.

Star Tribune (Minneapolis, Minnesota), November 6, 1978, "Moody Blues Powerful, but Lack

Polish," by Michael Anthony.

The Cincinnati Enquirer (Ohio), November 7, 1978, "Moody Blues on Second Honeymoon," by Cliff Radel.

The Cincinnati Enquirer (Ohio), November 8, 1978, "Even Moodies Get the Blues," by Cliff Radel.

Detroit Free Press, November 9, 1978, "Moody Blues Begin Long Road Back," by Linda Barber.

Chicago Tribune, November 13, 1978, "Moody Blues Keep Up the Good, Melodic Work," by Lynn Van Matre.

Chicago Sun-Times, November 13, 1978, "Moody Blues: In Concert, They're Mush," by Rick Kogan.

Atlantic Journal (Georgia), November 15, 1978, "Reunited Moodies Return to Fans," by Russ DeVault.

Washington [D.C.] Star, November 17, 1978, "Moody Blues Shows Signs of a Letdown," by Elaine Dickinson.

Washington Post, November 17, 1978, "Moody Blues," concert review by Jennefer Hirshberg.

The Michigan Daily, November 17, 1978, "Reunited Moody Blues Thriving," by John Dearing.

Billboard, November 17, 1978, "The Moody Blues: Madison Square Garden, New York," by Phil Gelormine.

Asbury Park Press (New Jersey), November 19, 1978, "Moody Blues Return in National Tour," with Pete Settles's review of *Octave*.

Philadelphia Daily News (Pennsylvania), November 22, 1978, "Encore for Moody Blues," by Jonathan Takiff.

Daily Press (Newport News, Virginia), November 22, 1978, United Press wire story: "Icy Highways Slow Rush-Hour Traffic."

New Haven Register (Connecticut), November 22, 1978, "Mellow Sound Worth the Wait," by Randall Beach.

The Philadelphia Inquirer (Pennsylvania), November 25, 1978, "Moody Blues' Sound: A Classic Wears Thin," by Jack Lloyd.

The New York Times, November 29, 1978, "Moody Blues Off Record," by Robert Palmer.

Star-Phoenix (Saskatoon, Saskatchewan, Canada), November 29, 1978, Canadian Press wire story: "Moody Blues Reunited with New Album, Tour."

Daily Press (Newport News, Virginia), November 30, 1978, "Moody Blues Serves Up Sloppy Show," by Mike Diana.

The Gazette (Montreal, Quebec, Canada), November 30, 1978, "Dreary Moodies Tread Old Waters in Nostalgic Wave," by Juan Rodriquez.

The Akron Beacon Journal (Ohio), December 2, 1978, "Moody Blues: Band Produces Tidal Wave of Sound," by Mark Faris.

Scene, December 1978, "The Moody Blues: The Coliseum, December 1," review by Bill Camarata.

Cleveland Press, December 2, 1978, "Moodies Remain at Head of Class," by Bruno Bornino.

The Morning Record (Meriden, Connecticut), December 2, 1978, "Blues Not in the Mood," by Ted Drozdowski.

Kansas City Star, December 5, 1978, "Moody Blues Rally Back, with Spheeris," by Nancy Bill.

Daily Press (Newport News, Virginia), December 6, 1978, "Review of Concert Draws Criticism."

The St. Louis Times (Missouri), December 6, 1978, "Blues For All Ages," by Kim Plummer.

Dallas Morning News, December 9, 1978, "Moody Blues Gather Steam in Thrilling Concert," by Pete Oppel.

Houston Post (Texas), December 9, 1978, "The Moody Blues," concert review by John Atkinson.

Dallas Morning News, December 10, 1978, "Moody Blues: Moraz May Move in as New Member," by Pete Oppel.

The Los Angeles Times, December 10, 1978, "Moody Blues: A New Sound," by Dennis Hunt.

The Los Angeles Times, December 13, 1978, "The Moody Blues: Updates Its Art," by Terry Atkinson.

Billboard, December 23, 1978, "Moody Blues: Forum, Inglewood, Calif." By Ed Harrison.

The Ithaca Journal (New York), December 29, 1978, Associated Press wire story: "Moody Blues Are Together Again After Failing Attempts to Go Solo," by Yardena Arar.

Hit Parader, March 1979, "Moody Blues: Time Warp Cosmology," by J.C. Costa.

North County Catholic, April 4, 1979, "Think Smart – Think Music: The Key to a Brand New World."

Melody Maker, April 21, 1979, review of Hayward's "Marie" single.

St. Petersburg Times, (Florida), May 7, 1979, "Moody Blues' Concert Quality Astonishing at Lakeland Civic Center," by Bob Ross.

The Orlando Sentinel (Florida), May 8, 1979, "Moody Blues: Their Music Stands by Itself," by Susan Marshall, and follow-up story, also by Marshall, in May 11th edition..

The Times (Shreveport, Louisiana), May 9, 1979, "Moody Blues Out of Balance," by John Andrew Prime, and letters regarding concert, from May 12th edition.

Omaha World Herald (Nebraska), May 12, 1979, "Moody Blues' Sound Still Basically Intact," by Steve Millburg.

The Waco Citizen (Texas), May 15, 1979, "Moody Blues 'Legendary.'"

Clarion-Ledger (Jackson, Mississippi), May 15, 1979, "Teen Inc. Staffer Enjoyed Moody Blues."

Dallas Morning News (Texas), May 16, 1979, "Moody Blues Concert: Close to Rock Bottom," by Pete Oppel.

Scottsdale Daily Progress (Arizona), May 18, 1979, "The Moody Blues Back Together Again," by Gary Houy.

Arizona Daily Star (Tucson), May 19, 1979, "Moody Blues, Crowd Take Trip Into Past," by Jose Galvez.

The Times (Shreveport, Louisiana), May 23, 1979, "Ticket Giveaway Blues," by John Andrew Prime.

The Seguin Gazette-Enterprise (Texas), May 24, 1979, "Moody Blues Flow at SEC," by Gary Parsons.

Oregonian (Portland, Oregon), May 25, 1979, "Moody Blues Present Nostalgia in Show," by John Wendeborn.

Melody Maker, May 26, 1979, "The Moody Blues: It's a Wonderful Life," by Chris Welch.

The Seattle Times (Washington), May 28, 1979, "Moody Blues Relive Past in 'Recital,'" by Patrick MacDonald, and letter from reader, protesting review, from June 3rd edition.

Suntracks, June 13, 1979, "The Moody Blues Survive the Activity Center," by Gene C. Siegel.

The Guardian (London, England), August 4, 1979, "Treasures from the Archives," by Edward Greenfield.

Clarion-Ledger (Jackson, Mississippi), August 7, 1979, Teen, Inc. wire story: "Moody Blues Is Still On Top."

The Baltimore Sun, August 12, 1979, "Slumping Sales Hit Record Business," by Eric Siegel.

Billboard, September 29, 1979, "Moodies Album In K-Tel $6M Drive."

Glasgow Herald, October 27, 1979, "Moody Blues Come Home to "Sell Out Tour," by Andrew Collier.

The Guardian (London, England), October 31, 1979, "When Genius Turns to Folly It Is Time for Someone Younger to Pick Up the Pieces," by Hamish McRae, and "Decca-Polygram Agree Deal," by James Erlichman.

Groove magazine, November 1979, "Will They Play Forever?" by Jon Marlowe.

The Burlington Free Press (Vermont), January 30, 1980, Associated Press wire story: "Decca Records Chairman Dies."

Melody Maker, February 9, 1980, "Death of an Old-School Capitalist," by Michael Watts.

Billboard, February 9, 1980, "Sir Edward's Death Marks an Era's End," by Mike Hennessey.

Variety, May 28, 1980, "Moody Blues to P/M for U.S. Rights; New Disks, Reissues Due."

Musicians Only, June 29, 1980, interview with Adrian Day.

Liverpool Echo, July 2, 1980, "Moody Blue Who Likes Going Solo," by Peter Trollope.

New Music News, Summer 1980, Nick Kemp's review of *Night Flight*.

Melody Maker, July 5, 1980, Ray Coleman's review of *Night Flight*.

Arizona Republic, July 6, 1980, with Gus Walker's review of *Night Flight*.

News-Press (Fort Myers, Florida), August 3, 1980, "Soundscale," with Ken Paulson's review of *Night Flight*.

The Morning Call (Allentown, Pennsylvania), August 9, 1980, Rich Harry's review of *Night Flight*.

The Pittsburgh Press (Pennsylvania), August 17, 1980, with Pete Bishop's review of *Night Flight*.

The Gazette (Montreal, Canada), August 28, 1980, with John Griffin's review of *Night Flight*.

Ram (Australia), Fall 1980, Bill Birch's review of *Night Flight*.

Beaver County Times (Pennsylvania), September 10, 1980, "Moody Blues Hayward Not a Workaholic on New Album," by Justin Hayward.

Melody Maker, October 14, 1980, Singles: Pure Pap for NOW! People," with review of John Lodge's "Street Café."

The Aquarian, November 12, 1980, "Justin Hayward Strikes New Notes on *Night Flight*," by Bruce Eber.

Melody Maker, May 23, 1980, Ray Coleman's review of *Long Distance Voyager*.

Variety, May 27, 1981, "International Music Notes: London," Pinder denied injunction to stop Moody Blues from using group's name on *Long Distant Voyager*.

Variety, June 3, 1981, "Record Reviews," with "Gemini Dream."

Pittsburgh Post-Gazette (Pennsylvania), June 5, 1981, Gary Graff's review of *LDV*.

Billboard, June 6, 1981, "Top Album Picks," with *Long Distance Voyager* as "Spotlight" pick, plus "Gemini Dream" as "Top Single Pick," and "Rock Albums & Top Tracks" chart.

Chicago Tribune, June 7, 1981, "Rush Spaces Out."

Arizona Republic, June 7, 1981, "Moody Blues' album Rehashes Old Sounds."

Hartford Courant, June 7, 1981, Henry McNulty's review of *Long Distance Voyager*.

Savannah News-Press (Richmond Hill, Georgia), June 7, 1981, review of *Long Distance Voyager*.

The Philadelphia Inquirer (Pennsylvania), June 7, 1981, review of *Long Distance Voyager*.

Daily Express (England), June 11, 1981, "And the Moody Blues Played On," by Anne Nightingale.

Fort Lauderdale News (Florida), June 12, 1981, review of *Long Distance Voyager*.

Muncie Evening Press (Indiana), June 13, 1981, syndicated column: Rick Shefchik's review of *Long Distance Voyager*.

Washington Post, June 14, 1981, "The Moody Blues Blues," by Eve Zibart.

The Daily Times (Salisbury, Maryland), June 14, 1981, "For the Record" with Rebecca Travis's review of *Long Distance Voyager*.

Variety, June 17, 1981, review of *Long Distance Voyager*.

American-Statesman (Austin, Texas), June 19, 1981, "Moody Blues Music, Demeanor Funeral," by Scott Bowles.

Melody Maker, June 20, 1981, "Moody Blues: Royal Albert Hall, London," with review by Ray Coleman.

Chicago Sun-Times, June 21, 1981, "The Moody Blues: Rock's Romantics On a Roundtrip Ticket," by Chuck Pratt.

The Los Angeles Times, June 21, 1981, "Voyaging Into Commercial Pop," by Dennis Hunt.

The Los Angeles Times, June 21, 1981, "Pop Album Briefs," with Steve Pond's review of *LDV*.

Daily Record (Morristown, New Jersey), June 21, 1981, Jim Bohen's review of *Long Distant Voyager*.

The Pittsburgh Press (Pennsylvania), June 21, 1981, "Voyager A Real Trip for Moodies' Fans," by Pete Bishop.

Arizona Daily Star (Tucson, Arizona), June 22, 1981, "Moodies Take Audience for a Stately, Cosmic Ride," by Jill Schensul.

Arizona Republic, June 21, 1981, "Moodies' Concert, LP Recapture Old Form," by Andrew Means.

San Francisco Chronicle, June 26, 1981, "The Moody Blues: Still Churning Out Their Patented Crud," by Joel Selvin.

The Los Angeles Times, June 29, 1981, "Something Old, New, Moody Blues," by Robert Hilburn.

Denver Post (Colorado), July 2, 1981, "Moraz on Keyboard Sabotages Moody Blues Red Rocks Concert," by G. Brown.

Rocky Mountain News (Denver, Colorado), July 3, 1981, "Oh, Like Wow – Moody Blues Return," by Paul Pershing.

Billboard, July 4, 1981, Ed Harrison's review of *Long Distance Voyager*.

Akron Beacon Journal, July 8, 1981, "The Moody Blues Captivate Blossom," by Mark Faris.

Cleveland Plain Dealer (Ohio), July 9, 1981, "Moody Blues Waxes Nostalgic," by Anastasia Pantsios.

The Age (Melbourne, Victoria, Australia), July 9, 1981, "Amazing, Colossal Wall-to-Wall Rock," by Mike Daily.

Detroit Free Press (Michigan), July 9, 1981, "Moody Blues Washes in on Wave of Romanticism," by Maryanne George.

Detroit Free Press (Michigan), July 11, 1981, "Moodys Play to Their Fans," by Maryanne George.

Good Times, July 14, 1981, "Lost in Space," by Bill McIlyaine.

New York Post, July 15, 1981, "Moody Blues Still Knights to Their Fans," by Ira Mayer.

Scene, July 16, 1981, "Livewire," with concert review of Moody Blues' Blossom concert, June 7.

New York Daily News, July 17, 1981, "Musicwatch," by Ernest Leogrande.

Chicago Sun-Times, July 20, 1981, "Moody Blues: A Turgid Musical Mush of Time and Confusion," by Don McLeese.

Chicago Tribune, July 20, 1981, "'Old' Moody Blues Fit the 'New' Mood of Rock," by Lynn Van Matre.

Melody Maker, July 25, 1981, "review" of "The Voice."

Sun-Herald (Biloxi, Mississippi), July 26, 1981, "On the Record," with Madeleine d'Haete's review of *Long Distance Voyager*.

Detroit Free Press, July 26, 1981, "Moody Blues Is Big Fish In Heavy Metal Sea," by Bruce Britt.

Good Times magazine, July 28, 1981, "The Moody Blues: Madison Square Garden, July 14," by Bill Milkowski.

Cream, August 1981, Jim Farber's review of *Long Distance Voyager*.

The Star Press (Muncie, Indiana), August 2, 1981, "*Long Distance Voyager*: The Moody Blues Return to Prominence with Latest Album," by Kim Teverbaugh.

Variety, August 5, 1981, review of "The Voice."

Gannett Today, August 11, 1981, Gannett News Service syndicated story: "Moody Blues Sink to Muddy Blahs," by Cliff Radel.

The Morning News (Wilmington, Delaware), August 23, 1981, Gary Mullinax's review of *LDV*.

WRNW 107 FM Concert & Club Guide, August 30, 1981, Alan Chapin's review of *Voyager*.

People, August 31, 1981, "The Moody Blues, Still Atmospheric After 17 Years, Have an Out-of-This-World Hit Again," by Salley Rayl.

Circus, August 31, 1981, "Longplayers," with John Swenson's review of *Long Distance Voyager*.

International Musician, September 1981, "Patrick Moraz: Still Playing After All these Years," by Tom Stock.

Us, September 1, 1981, "Moody," by Mark Morrison.

Rolling Stone, September 3, 1981, "The Moody Blues: Cosmic Voyage to Number One," by David Fricke.

Daily Press (Newport News, Virginia), September 18, 1981, "Cursed Moody Blues Return," by Mike Diana.

Circus, September 30, 1981, "Moody Blues Rock Again," by Richard Hogan.

Relix, October 1981, "It's Alive: Moody Blues – San Diego Sports Arena, June 22," by Thomas K. Arnold.

Stereo Review, October 1981, "M.P.'s" review of *Long Distance Voyager*.

The Seattle Times, October 19, 1981, "Moodies Create Studio Sound in Coliseum," by Patrick MacDonald.

The Minneapolis Star (Minnesota) October 21, 1981, "Moodies' Comeback Strong on Nostalgia," by Jon Bream.

The Des Moines Register (Iowa), October 23, 1981, "Blues Show Their Colors at the Hilton," by Jerry Perkins.

The Indianapolis Star (Indiana), October 29, 1981, "Moody Blues Disappoint At Arena," by Jill Warren.

Sounds, October 31, 1981, "John Lodge Talks It Out."

Song Hits, November 1981, "The Moody Blues: Pop Star of the Month."

Keyboard, November 1981, "Patrick Moraz."

The Seattle Times, November 1, 1981, "Letters."

The Buffalo News (New York), November 1, 1981, "Moody Blues Concert Has Upbeat Flavor," by Dale Anderson.

Pittsburgh Press, November 2, 1981, "Moody Blues Offer Rock at Its Best After 8-Year Absence," by Pete Bishop.

Pittsburgh Post-Gazette, November 2, 1981, "Moody Blues Play 'Safe' Rock," by Bill Stieg.

The Boston Globe, November 4, 1981, "Moody Blues: Grandiose Pop," by Jim Sullivan.

Billboard, November 7, 1981, review of "Talking Out of Turn."

The Courier-News (Bridgewater, New Jersey), November 7, 1981, "Moody Blues Concert," by Steve Libowitz.

The Orlando Sentinel (Florida), November 8, 1981, "Moody Blues in concert Cast Timeless Spell," by Gene Krukemyer.

Variety, November 11, 1981, "Concert Reviews: Moody Blues (Byrne Arena, N.J.," by "Ken."

Rolling Stone, November 11, 1981, "Parke Puterbaugh's review of *Long Distance Voyager*.

The Circle (Marist College), November 12, 1981, "Living Legends," by Michael Oliva.

Billboard, November 21, 1981, "Rock Albums & Tape Tracks," with "Meanwhile" a popular radio entry.

The Philadelphia Inquirer, November 22, 1981, "Moody Blues Return," by Edgar Koshatka.

Hartford Courant (Connecticut), November 23, 1981, "Ageing Moody Blues Band Grips Civic Center Fans," by Henry McNulty.

Hamilton Spectator (Ontario, Canada), November 24, 1981, "Moody Blues Retain Lush, Dreamy Style," by Greg McMillan.

The Blade (Toledo, Ohio), November 25, 1981, "Moody Blues Take Voyage to Toledo," by Randy Samborn.

Tallahassee Democrat (Florida), December 6, 1981, "High-Tech Affair Came Unplugged," by Christopher Farrell.

Tallahassee Democrat (Florida), December 13, 1981, "Concert-Goers Liked the Moody Blues."

Billboard, September 3, 1983, review of *The Present*.

Music Week, September 3, 1983, "The Moody Blues," by Chris Welch.

Evening Advertiser, September 16, 1983, "Time to Give Up Justin," by Barry Leighton.

The Los Angeles Times, September 25, 1983, "Moody Snooze," by Steve Pond.

The Boston Globe, October 1983, "Moody Blues: 'Now We're Like Family,'" by Steve Morse.

The Morning Call (Allentown, Pennsylvania), October 8, 1983, review of *The Present*.

The Michigan Daily, October 12, 1983, Jeff Segal's review of *The Present*.

San Jose Mercury News, October 16, 1983, Andrew Slater's review of *The Present*.

Hartford Courant (Connecticut), October 18, 1983, "Little Right and Lots Wrong As Moody Blues Struggle, Fail," by Frank Rizzo.

The Buffalo News, October 20, 1983, "Moody Blues Satisfy Everyone," by John Curran.

Echoes-Sentinel (Warren Township, New Jersey), October 20, 1983, Charles T. Zavalick's review of *The Present*.

Kerrang! magazine (England), October 20, 1983, "Blues for You," by Malcolm Dome.

The Age (Melbourne, Victoria, Australia), October 20, 1983, Mike Daly's review of *The Present*.

Philadelphia Daily News (Pennsylvania), October 21, 1983, review of *The Present*.

Logansport Pharos-Tribune (Indiana), October 23, 1983, Bill Missett's review of *The Present*.

The Record (Bergen County, New Jersey), October 24, 1983, "Moody Blues Long-Running Hit," by Barbara Jaeger.

New York Post, October 24, 1983, "Moody Blues Could Play It Just A Little Bit Less Cool," by Brian Chin.

USA Today, October 24, 1983, "Moody Blues Stay Tuned to Cosmic Rock," by Lloyd Sachs.

The New York Times, October 26, 1983, "Moody Blues Performs in Arena in Jersey," by Stephen Holden.

Rolling Stone, October 27, 1983, Errol Somay's review of *The Present*.

Journal Gazette (Mattoon, Illinois), October 27, 1983, Copley News Service wire story: "Moody Blues Banks on Melody," by Robin Wells.

Pittsburgh Post-Gazette (Pennsylvania), October 27, 1983, "Moody Blues Have Little New to Say," by John Spitzer.

The Pittsburgh Press (Pennsylvania), October 27, 1983, "Shaky Moody Blues, Sturdy Texas Blues Mix It Up at Arena," by Pete Bishop.

Daily Record (Morristown, New Jersey), October 28, 1983, Jim Bohen's review of *The Present*.

Santa Cruz Sentinel (California), October 28, 1983, Peter Field's review of *The Present*.

The Cincinnati Enquirer (Ohio), October 29, 1983, "It's 1983 – Collars Are Frayed, Magic Missing for Moody Blues," by Cliff Radel.

Detroit Free Press (Michigan), October 31, 1983, "Opening Band Outplays the Moody Blues," by Gary Graff.

The Daily Michigan, November 1, 1983, "The Moody Blues Travel in Time," by Mike Cramer.

Minneapolis Star and Tribune (Minnesota), November 2, 1983, "Enthusiastic Moodies Treat Enduring Fans," by Joe Bream.

Hartford Courant (Connecticut), November 3, 1983, "In Blue Mood Over Review."

Pittsburgh Post-Gazette (Pennsylvania), November 4, 1983, Ron Weikind's review of *The Present*.

Arizona Republic, November 6, 1983, "Moody Blues: Band's Work Withstands Test of Time," by Andrew Means.

Dallas Times Herald (Texas), November 7, 1983, "The Moody Blues Don't Belong in the '80s."

Austin American-Statesman (Texas), November 8, 1983, "Moody Blues Put on Consistent, Talented Show," by Ken Giles.

Detroit Free Press (Michigan), November 17, 1983, "Moody Success."

The Vancouver Province (Canada), November 18, 1983, "Moody Mellow," by Fiona McQuarrie.

The Calgary Sunday Sun (Canada), November 27, 1983, "Saddledome's A Star," by Mitch Potter.

Arizona Republic, November 31, 1983, "Moody Blues Resists Changes, Keeps Styling on Steady Course," by Andrew Means.

Rock Magazine, December 1983, Michael Leyland's review of *The Present*.

The Los Angeles Times, December 5, 1983, "Nothing New From the Moody Blues," with Duncan Strauss's review of *The Present*.

Daily Variety, December 6, 1983, "Concert Review: Moody Blues; Stevie Ray Vaughan," by "Kirk."

The Hollywood Reporter, December 8, 1983, "Concert Review: Moody Blues," by Mike Reynolds.

Stereo Review, January 1984, review of *The Present*.

Good Times, January 1, 1984, "Moody Blues Never Reaching the End," by Barry Millman.

Faces, February 1984, Rich Sutton's review of *The Present*.

Higher & Higher, #2, Summer 1984, "Justin Hayward: A Personal Sojourn," by Rosary Grande, and "The 4 Before: The Pre-Moodies Songs," by Mark Murley, and "Sneak Preview: The Jeff Wayne Interview."

Higher & Higher, #3, Autumn 1984, "A Canadian Interview with Patrick Moraz," by John Beaudoin.

Kerrang!, November 29, 1984, "The Story of the Moody Blues," by Malcolm Dome, plus review of *Voices in the Sky* compilation LP.

Higher & Higher, #5, Summer/Fall 1985, Mark S. Murley's review of *Moving Mountains*; "Ray Thomas: The Music's the Thing, Part I," by Mark Murley; and "Tony Clarke: The Master Producer Speaks," by Randy A. Salas.

Tracks, November 1985, "Mountain Man," by Justin Hayward.

Radio & Records, March 28, 1986, "Moodies Sign with Polygram."

New Musical Express, April 19, 1986, review of "Your Wildest Dreams."

Cashbox, April 26, 1986, review of *The Other Side of Life*.

Hartford Courant (Connecticut), April 27, 1986, Matt Damsker's review of *Other Side of Life*.

Harrisburg Patriot-News (Pennsylvania), 1986, review of *The Other Side of Life*.

Billboard, May 3, 1986, review of *The Other Side of Life*.

The Pittsburgh Press, May 5, 1986, Pete Bishop's review of *The Other Side of Life*.

New Braunfels Herald-Zeitung (Texas), May 15, 1986, "Moodies Stay Ahead of Pack," with Tom Labinski's review of *The Other Side of Life*.

Winnipeg Free Press, May 16, 1986, Glen Gore-Smith's review of *The Other Side of Life*.

The Los Angeles Times, May 18, 1986, Steve Hochman's review of *The Other Side of Life*.

The Akron Beacon Journal (Ohio), May 25, 1986, Knight-Ridder Newspapers wire story: "A Newfound Spirit of Unity," by Rick Shefchik.

Saskatoon Star (Canada), May 29, 1986, review of *The Other Side of Life*.

Higher & Higher, #6, Spring/Summer 1986, "Ray Thomas: The Music's the Thing, Part II," by Mark S. Murley; Randy A. Salas's review of *The Other Side of Life*.

Good Times, June 1986, Jim Jones's review of *The Other Side of Life*.

Niagara News (New York), "Moody Blues Show Lots of Punch, Knock Out Two Decades of

Hits," by Jeff Jones.

The Orlando Sentinel (Florida), June 1, 1986, Bill Henderson's review of *The Other Side of Life*.

People, June 9, 1986, David Hiltbrand's review of *The Other Side of Life*.

The Anniston Star, June 21, 1986, Mike Stedham's review of *The Other Side of Life*.

Journal-Gazette, June 21, 1986, "Twenty-Year Rockers Rarely Have the Blues," by Troy Cozad.

Chicago Tribune (Illinois), June 29, 1986, "Rocker Curnin Gets a Fix on the World with His Lyrics Even While Fans Dance," by Jae-Ha Kim.

Stereo Review, July 1986, M.P.'s review of *The Other Side of Life*.

Kansas City Star, July 1, 1986, "Moody Blues Push Message into '80s," by Brian McTavish.

Chicago Tribune, July 3, 1986, United Press wire story: "Graying Moody Blues Still a Rockin' Roll," by Bill Lohmann.

Billboard, July 5, 1986, "Talent in Action: Moody Blues, Chastain Park, Atlanta," by Russell Shaw.

Honolulu Star-Advertiser, July 5, 1986, Wayne Harada's review of *The Other Side of Life*.

Detroit Free Press (Michigan), July 6, 1986, "Moody Blues Stay in Rock Race," by Gary Graff.

Chicago Sun-Times (Illinois), July 7, 1986, "The Moody Blues Mix Past, Present and the Future," by Dave Hoekstra.

Detroit Free Press, July 8, 1986, "Live Concert Falls Short of the Dream," by Gary Graft.

Akron Beacon Journal (Ohio), July 9, 1986, "Impressive Blossom Show Proves Moody Blues Still Know the Score," by Mark Faris.

The Vindicator (Youngstown, Ohio), July 9, 1986, "Moody Blues, Fixx Turn Up the Heat in Blossom concert," by John P. Gatta.

Cleveland Plain Dealer (Ohio), July 10, 1986, "Old Favorites Playing It Cozy," by Anastasia Pantsios.

Hartford Courant (Connecticut), July 11, 1986, "Moody Blues Still Rolling with New Set of Listeners," by Frank Rizzo.

Philadelphia Daily News (Pennsylvania), July 11, 1986, "Live! This Week," by Jonathan Takiff.

Evening Express (Portland, Maine), July 12, 1986, "Moody Blues Bring Happiness," by Stephen Bartlett.

Hartford Courant (Connecticut), July 13, 1986, "Moody Blues Evokes Nostalgia; Does Best with Cosmic Concept,'" by Frank Rizzo, and "Summer Sounds," with Rizzo's review of "Your Wildest Dreams."

Valley News Dispatch (Tarentum, Pennsylvania), July 15, 1986, "Moody Blues Attracts Old Fans," by Rex Rutkoski.

Asbury Park Press (New Jersey), July 15, 1986, "Moody Blues Enthrall Fans," by Lee Cohen.

The Boston Herald, July 15, 1986, "Moody blues: Mega Fame, Micro emotion," by Craig Tomashoff.

The Boston Globe (Massachusetts), July 15, 1986, "Moodies Make Memories in Rain," by Steve Morse.

New York Register, July 15, 1986, "The Blues Come Back," by Mary Gay Johnson.

Democrat and Chronicle (Rochester, New York), July 16, 1986, "Moody Blues Put on Irresistible Show," by James Trowbridge.

Rolling Stone, July 17, 1986, Anthony DeCurtis's review of *The Other Side of Life*.

Scene, July 17, 1986, "The Moody Blues, The Fixx, Blossom, July 8," by Bill Camarata.

USA Today, July 18, 1986, "Back in the Mood for the Moody Blues," by John Milward.

Times Union (Albany, New York), July 18, 1986, "Thriving on Change," by Sean Daly.

The Pittsburgh Press, July 20, 1986, "Moody Blues: Rockin' 22 Years," by Pete Bishop.

The Saratogian (Saratoga Springs, New York), July 20, 1986, "Veteran Cosmic Rockers Prove They're Far From Extinct," by Kay Blough.

Press and Sun-Bulletin (Binghamton, New York), July 22, 1986, "Moody Blues Serve Nostalgia Treat," Eric Schafer.

Washington Post, July 24, 1986, "The Moody Blues," by Mike Joyce.

Milwaukee Sentinel, July 25, 1986, "Moody Blues Please Nostalgic Fans," by Tim Roets.

The Morning Call (Allentown, Pennsylvania), July 26, 1986, Len Righi's review of "Your Wildest Dreams."

Post-Dispatch (St. Louis, Missouri), July 26, 1986, "The Moody Blues Are Making a Comeback," by Louise King.

Buzz, August 1986, J.J. Ryan's review of *The Other Side of Life*.

Cashbox, August 9, 1986, review of "The Other Side of Life" single.

Days of Future Passed: The Story of the Moody Blues, August 11, 1986, including interview with John Lodge.

The Los Angeles Times, August 17, 1986, "Hayward Sings the Blues' Praises," by Dennis Hunt.

Seattle Post-Intelligencer, August 22, 1986, "Never Too Old to Rock 'N' Roll," by Roberta Penn.

San Francisco Chronicle, August 24, 1986, "Moody Blues Picks Up Where It Left Off," by Tom Lahham.

Tribune (Oakland, California), August 28, 1986, "Ever-Cosmic Moodies Fill Up Pavilion, But Forget Fine Points for Gun, Games," by Larry Kelp.

San Francisco Chronicle, August 28, 1986, "Moody Blues: The '60s Revived," by Michael Snyder.

Pasadena Star-News (California), August 30, 1986, "Moody Blues Light," by Rom Crow.

The Los Angeles Times, August 30, 1986, "Moody Blues Pose No Cosmic Questions," by Paul Grein.

The Island Ear (Long Island, New York), September 2, 1986, "The Moody Blues/The Fixx," by John Blenn.

The San Diego Union (California), September 2, 1986, "Moody Blues Attract Young Fans and Old," by Divina Infusino."

Variety, September 3, 1986, "Moody Blues (Universal Amphi, L.A.)," by "Sax."

The Tribune (San Diego, California), September 3, 1986, "Unbridled Egos, Volume Bring Down the Moodies," Robert J. Hawkins, and follow-up letter from reader, R. Scott Todd.

Akron Beacon Journal (Ohio), September 7, 1986, Associated Press wire story: "Granddads Never Sounded So Good," by Steven Wine.

Goldmine, September 12, 1986, Joseph Tortelli's review of *The Other Side of Life*.

Billboard, September 13, 1986, "Moody Blues, ELP Enjoy Renewed Success," by Steve Gett.

Evening Express, September 19, 1986, "Moody Blues Soars, But Fixx Really Clicks," by Dan R. Goddard.

Performance, September 19, 1986, "The Moody Blues – Success Beyond Their Wildest Dreams," by Theodora Goebel.

The Miami Herald, September 26, 1986, "Fans Still in Mood for Moodies," by Linda R. Thornton.

The Miami News (Florida), September 26, 1986, "The Blues Aren't Moody Any More," by Deborah Walker.

Savannah Morning News, September 27, 1986, "Years Have Been Kind to Moody Blues," by Frank Jossi.

Tampa Tribune (Florida), September 28, 1986, "Moody Blues Dazzled Crowd," by Bob Andelman.

South Florida Sun Sentinel, September 28, 1986, "Moody Blues: 'White Satin' to 'Wildest Dreams,'" by Scott Benarde.

St. Petersburg Times (Florida), September 29, 1986, "Moody Blues Energize for a Night," by Eric Snider.

The Miami Herald, September 30, 1986, "Moodies Mix New Tunes, Classics," by Linda R. Thornton.

Tower Records Pulse!, October 1986, "The Making of the Moody Blues' 'Your Wildest Dreams' Video."

The Palm Beach Post (Florida), October 1, 1986, "Moody Blues Strike Responsive Note with Fans," by Holly Gleason.

New York Post, October 8, 1986, "Moody Blues Freshness is All," by Dan Aquilante.

Newsday, October 8, 1986, "Rock Lullabyes for Moody Times," by Stephen Williams.

The Morning Call (Lehigh Valley, Pennsylvania), October 12, 1986, "Moody Blues Give Lackadaisical Concert," by Geoff Gerhman.

The Record (Bergen County, New Jersey), October 20, 1986, "The Moody Blues Renewed," by Barbara Jaeger.

The Salt Lake Tribune (Utah), October 21, 1986, "Moody Blues as Vibrant as Ever," by Jerry Spangker.

Higher & Higher, #7 & 8, Fall/Winter 1986, "Moody News"; "The Filming of 'Running Out of Love'," by Sharon M. Brown; "Gerry Levene & the Avengers: Brum Beat Revisited," by

Andy Whitlow; and "The Story of *Higher & Higher*."

The Arizona Republic, November 10, 1986, "Cosmic Rockers," by Andrew Means.

Reno Gazette-Journal (Nevada), November 12, 1986, "Moody Blues Betray Their Gray at Lawlor," by Eric McClary.

The Sacramento Bee (California), November 14, 1986, "Moody's Sound Still Smooth as Satin," by Cathy Cassinos.

The Sacramento Union (California), November 14, 1986, "Not Moody, or Blue – Just Good," by Steve Connell.

Denver Post (Colorado), November 17, 1986, "Moody Blues Take Fans on Journey to Past," by G. Brown.

Wisconsin State Journal, November 24, 1986, "Moody Blues, Next Time Turn Down the Volume," by Tony Ralenkotter.

The Courier-Journal (Louisville, Kentucky), November 24, 1986, "Music Reviews: The Moody Blues," by Scott Robinson.

Daily Express (England), November 27, 1986, "Moody Mania," by Louise Court.

Goldmine, December 5, 1986, Bruce Eder's review of *Moving Mountains*.

Newspaper clipping (unknown English publication), December 8, 1986, "Moodies Magic Back in Brum," by Paul Cole.

Modern Drummer, March 1987, "Graeme Edge," by Robyn Flans.

Variety, April 22, 1987, "Mason, Hayward Ink with Voyager."

Record Collector, May 1987, interview with Lonnie Donegan.

Higher & Higher, #9, Spring/Summer 1987, "The Graeme Edge Interview," and "Tony Visconti: The Dynamic Producer Reveals How Sampling Helped Him Clean Up on the Moody Blues."

Higher & Higher, #10, Fall/Winter 1987, "A Conversation with Martin Wyatt," by June Price.

Billboard, June 11, 1988, review of *Sur la Mer*.

New York Post Weekend, June 24, 1988, review of *Sur la Mer*.

The Orlando Sentinel (Florida), June 26, 1988, Bill Henderson's review of *Sur la mer*.

Hartford Courant (Connecticut), July 7, 1988, Frank Rizzo's review of *Sur la mer*.

Billboard, July 8, 1988, "Moodys Are True Blue," by Jim Bessman.

The Morning Call (Allentown, Pennsylvania), July 9, 1988, Harry Fisher's review of *Sur la mer*.

Scene, July 14, 1988, Doug Pinwinski review of *Sur la Mer*.

The Cincinnati Enquirer (Ohio), July 27, 1988, "Nights at the Gardens," by Cliff Radel.

Democrat and Chronicle (Rochester, New York), July 29, 1988, "10,000 Fans Get Memorable Show by Moody Blues at Finger Lakes," by Bruce Pilato.

Washington Post, July 29, 1988, Mark Jenkins's review of *Sur la Mer*.

Daily Record (Morristown, New Jersey), July 31, 1988, Jim Bohen's review of *Sur la Mer*.

The Daily Times (Salisbury, Maryland), August 1, 1988, "Moody Blues Concert Turns Back Clock," by Chris Estes.

Boston Globe (Massachusetts), August 4, 1988, "Sugar and Spice from Moody Blues," by Brett Milano.

Washington Post (Washington, D.C.), August 8, 1988, "The Moody Blues at Wolf Trap," by Alona Wartofsky.

The Daily Times (Salisbury, Maryland), August 4, 1988, "Moody Blues Were In Search of a Lost Plane," by Chris Estes.

Pittsburgh Post-Gazette (Pennsylvania), August 5, 1988, "Moody Blues Back, Explore Old Horizons," by Mark Madden.

The Pittsburgh Press (Pennsylvania), August 5, 1988, "Old, New Turns Don't Mix Well for Nostalgic-Ridden Moody Blues," by Peter E. King.

The Patriot-News (Harrisburg, Pennsylvania), "Moody Blues' Sound Problems Drown Lyrics, Dull Instruments," by Sandy Cullen.

Newsday (Long Island, New York), August 7, 1988, "Moody Blues," by Wayne Robins.

The Los Angeles Times, August 7, 1988, Guy Aoki's review of *Sur la mer*.

The Saratogian (Saratoga, New York), August 9, 1988, "Moody Blues Spend Dreamy Night at SPAC," by Holly Snyder.

Telemoustique (France), August 9, 1988, review of *Sur la Mer*.

The Times Union (Albany, New York), August 9, 1988, "Moody Blues Captivate SPAC Fans,

Old and New," by Michael Eck.

Scene, August 11, 1988, "The Moody Blues: Veteran Cosmic Rockers," by Mark Holan.

Toronto Star (Canada), August 12, 1988, "Magnificent Moody Blues Give Fans a Summer Tonic," by Dennis Morgan.

The Akron Beacon Journal (Ohio), August 13, 1988, "Moody Blues Still a Great Blending with Blossom Heat," by Mark Faris.

The Plain Dealer (Cleveland, Ohio), August 14, 1988, "Band Is Rocking After 20 Years," by Jane Scott.

The Wisconsin Journal, August 15, 1988, "Updated Moody Blues Keep Pop in Sharp Focus," by Dave Luhrssen.

The Kansas City Star, August 17, 1988, "Moody Blues Rock, a Faithful Replay at Sandstone," by Brian McTavish.

The Plain Dealer (Cleveland, Ohio), August 17, 1988, "Moodies Keep the Beat Strong," by Jane Scott.

The San Diego Union (California), August 19, 1988, "Virtuoso Saved Fading Blues: Keyboardist Creates Right Mood," by George Varga.

Las Vegas Review-Journal (Nevada), August 30, 1988, "Moody Blues Capitalize on Classic Past," Mike Weatherford.

The Speed of Sound, September 1988, "Moody Blues / Glass Tiger, Blossom Music Ctr, August 12," by K.L. Hagelberg.

The Los Angeles Times, August 28, 1988, "Moody Blues Delivers Too Much of a Good Thing," by Duncan Strauss, and reader's reply.

Daily Variety, August 30, 1988, "Concert Review: The Moody Blues; Glass Tiger (Greek Theatre: 6197 capacity; $20.50 Top)," by "Sax."

The Denver Post (Colorado), September 2, 1988, "Veteran Moody Blues Forges On," by G. Brown.

Rocky Mountain News (Denver, Colorado), September 2, 1988, "Album Leaves Member of Moody Blues Group Blue," by Justin Mitchell.

The Oshkosh Northwestern (Wisconsin), September 25, 1988: Associated Press wire story: "Rock Band Hangs Together Despite Discord," Bill Beechum.

Deseret News (Utah), "Magnetic, Middle-Aged Moodies Perform in Grand Style," by Brent Israelsen.

American-Statesman (Austin, Texas), September 6, 1988, "Moody Blues Fails to Grab Fest-Goers," by Michael MacCambridge.

St. Louis Post-Dispatch (Missouri), September 9, 1988, "Audience Energizes Moody Blues," by Louise King.

The Baltimore Sun (Maryland), September 9, 1988, J.D. Considine's review of *Sur la Mer*.

Albuquerque Journal (New Mexico), September 23, 1988, Christian Science Monitor wire story: "Moody Blues's Style Finds Younger Fans," by Shiv Cariappa.

People, September 26, 1988, review of *Sur la Mer*.

Creem, October 1988, "The Moody Blues Get Rhythm," by Hank Bordowitz.

Billboard, October 15, 1988, "Video Track," concerning making of "No More Lies" video.

The Columbus Dispatch (Ohio), October 21, 1988, "Popularity Timeless for Songs, Sounds of the Moody Blues," by T.C. Brown.

Billboard, October 22, 1988, review of "No More Lies" single.

New York Daily News, October 31, 1968, "Moodies: Music You Can Trust," by Matthew Auerbach.

Daily Press (Newport Beach, Virginia), November 2, 1988, "Moody Blues' Vision Dims with Age," Joseph Pryweller.

The Courier-Journal (Louisville, Kentucky), November 3, 1988, "Music Review: The Moody Blues," by Scott Robinson.

The Atlanta Journal and Constitution (Georgia), November 3, 1988, "Moody Blues Respond to the Curiosity Among Youth About the Vintage 1960s," by Russ DeVault.

Raleigh News & Observer, November 3, 1988, "Moody Blues Pulling off Balancing Act," by Michael Hetzer.

Pensacola News Journal (Florida), November 5, 1988, "Moody Drummer Beats on to Thrills of Young and Old," by Mike Suchcicki.

The Orlando Sentinel (Florida), November 6, 1988, Moody Blues," by Thom Duffy.

Pensacola News Journal (Florida), November 7, 1988, "Moody Blues' Granola Rock Rewinds Clock," by Troy Moon.

Showtime, November 11, 1988, "Moodies Only Get Better with Age," by Deborah Wilker.

Central Atlantic Musician, December 1988, "A Conversation On the Music Biz with John Lodge of the Moody Blues."

Music Makers, December 1988, "Questions of Balance," by Kevin Berger.

Audio, December 1988, Michael Tearson's review of *Sur la mer*.

Wilmington Morning Star (North Carolina), December 23, 1988, *New York Times* Regional Newspapers: "Blues Singing Through Generations," by Randy A. Salas.

Higher & Higher #11 & 12, Spring/Winter 1988, "John Lodge: Traveling the Natural Avenue," by Janet Tomey, and "John Lodge: The Story in His Eyes," by Kerry Fitzgerald.

Kaleidoscope, January/February 1989, "Moody Review," by Theodora Goelbel.

The Press (Atlantic City, New Jersey), March 3, 1989, "Nightclubs in White Satin," by David J. Spatz.

The Press (Atlantic City, New Jersey), March 7, 1989, "Moody Blues' TropWorld Success Spotlight Casino Versatility," by David J. Spatz.

Whoot! Weekly (Atlantic City, New Jersey), March 9, 1989, "Moody Blues Create Excitement with TropWorld Visit," by Bob Everland.

Reno Gazette-Journal (Nevada), March 9, 1989, Garnett News Service wire story: "Moody Blues Deposit Art-Rock in Platinum Accounts," by Joe DeChick.

Courier Post (Atlantic City, New Jersey), July 27, 1989, "Moody Blues Offer Fans Satin Nights Show," by Chuck Darrow.

Star-Ledger (Newark, New Jersey), July 28, 1989, "Casino Concerts New Deal for Moody Blues," by Charles Einstein.

Whoot! Weekly (Atlantic City, New Jersey), August 3, 1989, "New Generation of Fans for Moody Blues," by Bob Everland.

Daily Mail (London, England), November 21, 1989, "White Satin Has Lost Its Old Sheen," by Sophia Watson.

Higher & Higher #13, Winter 1989, Randy Salas's review of *Classic Blue*.

Billboard, December 9, 1989, "Moodys On Threshold Again," by Melinda Newman.

Billboard, December 23, 1989, "Media In the '90s: Focus on Baby Boomers," by Steve Berger.

Q, April 1990, "Moody Blues: Step This Way...," by Tom Hibbert.

Higher & Higher, #14, Spring 1990, "The Moody Blues Story" transcript of Unistar radio special; "Solo Works Now on CD"; "Moodies to Fans and Vice Versa: Lovely to See You Again," by Randy A. Salas.

The Bulletin (Bend, Oregon), May 6, 1990, Associated Press wire story: "Lennon Tribute Draws Fans."

Back Stage, May 16, 1990, "Broadways Video Stevenson Edits Moody Blues Music Video."

Nova Lepidoptera (The Barclay James Harvest Magazine), June 1990, Claire Powell's review of *Classic Blue*.

Richmond Times (Virginia), July 27, 1990, "Time Only Improves Moody Blues' Music," by Renee Pace.

The Courier-News (Bridgewater, New Jersey), August 1, 1990, *The Baltimore Evening Sun* syndicated story: "Moody Blues Goes on Tour to Keep Its Classic Sound Alive," by Nestor Aparicio.

Hartford Courant (Connecticut), August 4, 1990, "Beach Boys, Moody Blues Reprise Vitality of Past for Compounce Crowd," by Tony Angarano.

Pittsburgh Post-Gazette (Pennsylvania), August 9, 1990, "Moodies Tame, Beach Boys Worthy," by Dmitri Ragano.

St. Louis Dispatch (Missouri), August 18, 1990, "Moody Blues Brings Perennial Favorites to Fox," by Louise King.

The Los Angeles Times, August 29, 1990, "Moodies Engaging, With a Little Help," by Jean Rosenbluth.

Higher & Higher, #15, Winter 1990, "The Justin Hayward Interview," by June Price.

Billboard, January 19, 1991, review of *Legend of the Band* Home Video.

Goldmine, March 22, 1991, Bruce Eder's review of *Legend of a Band* Home Video.

Keyboard, May 1991, interview with Patrick Moraz, by Robert L. Doerschuk.

Amusement Business, May 20, 1991, "Alberto-Culver Signs On for Moody Blues Tour," by Patricia Bates.

Billboard, July 6, 1991, review of *Keys of the Kingdom*.

Chicago Tribune (Illinois), July 11, 1991, Patrick Kampert's review of *Keys of the Kingdom*.

Billboard, July 13, 1991, review of "Say It With Love."

Honolulu Star-Bulletin (Hawaii), July 15, 1991, Don Weller's review of *Keys of the Kingdom*.

Scene, July 18, 1991, Curt Goetz review of *Keys of the Kingdom*.

The Morning Call (Allentown, Pennsylvania), Paul Willistein's review of *Keys of the Kingdom*.

The Globe and Mail (Canada), July 29, 1991, Alan Niester's review of *Keys of the Kingdom*.

Orange Coast (Orange County, California), August 1991, "The Moody Blues' Timeless Journey," by Keith Tuber.

Scene, August 1, 1991, *"The Moody Blues: Long Distance Voyagers,"* by Mark Holan.

Ann Arbor News (Michigan), August 4, 1991, "The Moody Blues Keep on Moving," by Kevin Ransom.

Chicago Tribune (Illinois), August 5, 1991, "Their Days of Future Passed," by Dennis Polkow.

The Plain Dealer (Cleveland, Ohio), August 6, 1991, "Rocker Edge Scorns Soft Musical Edges," by Jane Scott.

The Milwaukee State Journal (Wisconsin), August 6, 1991, "Audience Likes Moody Blues Best When It Stays True to Its Colors," by Dave Luhrssen.

The Akron Beacon Journal (Ohio), August 7, 1991, "Moody Blues Seem Preprogrammed," by Joanne Draus Klein, plus rebuttals from reader Bruce M. Davie and James S. Tomicik.

Clarion-Ledger (Jackson, Mississippi), review of *Keys of the Kingdom* from "Wire Service Reports."

Milwaukee Sentinel (Wisconsin), August 8, 1991, "Moody Blues Look Back in Grand Style," by Dave Tianen.

Boston Globe (Massachusetts), August 9, 1991, "Singing the Moody Blues," by Steve Morse.

St. Louis Post-Dispatch (Missouri), August 9, 1091, *Rolling Stone*'s David Wild review of *Keys of the Kingdom*.

Daily Press (Newport News, Virginia), August 9, 1991, Dallas Morning News' review of *Keys of the Kingdom*.

Dayton Daily News (Ohio), August 9, 1991, "Nights in White Lightin'," by Dave Larson.

The Globe-Times (Bethlehem, Pennsylvania), August 10, 1991, "Moody Blues Still Best Cosmic Rockers," by Dana B. Grubb.

Chicago Tribune (Illinois), August 11, 1991, "Moody Blues Make Pretentiousness Pleasingly Palatable," by Mark Caro.

Chicago Sun-Times (Illinois), August 12, 1991, "Rock: Moody Blues Mix Old with New," by Jae-Ha Kim.

Idaho Press-Tribune, August 13, 1991, Associated Press wire story: "The Moody Blues: The Days of the Future Have Yet to Pass," by Mary Campbell.

The Buffalo News (New York), August 15, 1991, "English Rockers Are Enchanting as Ever," by Robbie Ann McPherson.

Scene, August 15, 1991, "Moody Blues / Neverland, Blossom, August 6," by Kymberli Hagelberg.

The Globe (Mansfield, Ohio), August 16, 1991, "Moody Blues Rock Like They Haven't in Years," by Steve Morse.

The Toronto Star (Ontario, Canada), August 19, 1991, "Good Ship Moody See-worthy," by Lenny Stoute.

Green Bay Press-Gazette (Wisconsin), August 20, 1991, William R. Macklin's review of *Keys of the Kingdom*.

Richmond-Times Dispatch (Virginia), August 21, 1991, "Moody Blues Keep up with Times," by Esther Benenson.

Washington Post (Columbia, Maryland), August 22, 1991, "Night of the Moody Blues," by Eric Brace.

Jam Entertainment News, August 23, 1991, "Justin Hayward: The Jam Interview," by June Price.

The Orlando Sentinel (Florida), August 23, 1991, "Moody Blues Still Upbeat About Their Music," by Jim Abbott.

The Orlando Sentinel (Florida), August 25, 1991, "Moody Blues Justifies Its Longevity," by Parry Gettelman.

The Daily Tar Heel (Chapel Hill, North Carolina), August 29, 1991, "Moody Blues Show Solid But Lacks Spontaneity," by Grant Halverson.

Denver Post (Colorado), August 30, 1991, "Moody Blues Spans Eras at Red Rocks," by G. Brown.

St. Louis Post-Dispatch (Missouri), August 31, 1991, "Kansas Is Lively Flip Side to Moody Blues," by Louise King.

Higher & Higher #16, Summer/Fall 1991, "A Conversation with Alan Tarney," interviewed by Randy Salas; Mark Murley's review of *Keys of the Kingdom*; Char Kemps's review of "Say It with Love" video.

Hi Fi News & Record Review, September 1991, Pete Clark's review of *Keys of the Kingdom*.

Vox (London, England), Nick Douglas's review of *Keys of the Kingdom*.

The Phoenix Gazette (Arizona), September 6, 1991, "Blues Cooking on 17th Album," by Dean Rhodes.

The Los Angeles Times (California), September 9, 1991, "Moody Blues Play Their Favorite Hits," by Mike Boehm.

Hollywood Reporter, September 12, 1991, "Moody Blues Sued by Ex-keyboardist," by Jeffrey Jolson-Colburn.

The Anniston Star (Alabama), Mike Stedham's review of *Keys to the Kingdom*.

The Orlando Sentinel (Florida), "Life After the Moody Blues Upbeat," by Jim Abbott.

Performance, October 11, 1991, "Keys of the Moody Blues Kingdom," by Debi Moen.

Cashbox, October 12, 1991, Talent Review: Moody Blues," by Jim Waligura and Mark Albert.

The Miami Herald (Florida), December 13, 1991, "Bare-bones Moody Blues Try to Recapture Their Roots," by Mario Tarradell.

The Daily Oklahoman, March 25, 1992, "Music Older, Wiser, Moody Blues Singer Says," by Bernice McShane.

Higher & Higher, Vol. 17, Winter/Spring 1992, "Pure Bliss: The Paul Bliss Interview," by Mark Murley; "Prince Charming of the Keys: A Conversation with Bias Boshell," by Jill Finan.

The Rocket-Courier (Wyalusing, Pennsylvania), May 7, 1992, "Bands Pair Up to Generate Summer Concert Interest," by D.C. Koviack.

The Sun (London, England), May 22, 1992, "Blues Sue for Dues."

The Dallas Morning Star (Texas), May 31, 1992, "Matched Set," by Tom Maurstad.

Scene, June 18, 1992, "Chicago, Moody Blues, Blossom, June 14," by Bruce Hackett.

The Morning Call (Allentown, Pennsylvania), June 21, 1992, "Moody Blues-Chicago Tour a Question of Balance," by D.L. Courville.

Easton Express-Times (Pennsylvania), June 28, 1992, "Moody Blues Leave Fans Wanting More at Allentown Show," by Theresa Anderson.

The Anniston Sun (Alabama), July 23, 1992, "Moodies Trust Own Judgment," by Norman Welch.

Press and Sun-Bulletin (Binghamton, New York), July 24, 1992, "A Change in Moody," by Gene Grey.

Recovery Network newsletter, September 1992, interview with Justin Hayward by Colleen Joy.

Gazette Telegraph (Colorado Springs, Colorado), September 12, 1992, "Orchestra Enhances Blues' Performance," by Todd Caudle.

Rocky Mountain News (Denver, Colorado), September 12, 1992, "Moody Blues Have Mellowed Well," by Justin Mitchell.

Kalamazoo Gazette (New York), October 4, 1992, "Groups Build on Basics," by Alexia Hayden.

Kalamazoo Gazette (New York), October 8, 1992, "Old Friends Entertain Old Friends," by Alexia Hayden.

Billboard, March 6, 1993, "PolyGram to Push Moody Blues Via PBS," by Greg Reibman.

Albuquerque Journal (New Mexico), March 19, 1993, "The Youth Express": Chris Young's review of *The Moody Blues in Concert at Red Rocks* on PBS, and rebuttal from Vikki Otero.

Billboard, April 7, 1993, "Video Previews: *Live at Red Rocks with the Colorado Symphony Orchestra*."

The Morning Call (Allentown, Pennsylvania), April 10, 1993, Paul Willistein's review of *A Night at Red Rocks with the Colorado Symphony Orchestra*.

The Indianapolis Star (Indiana), April 23, 1993, "Moody Blues "Live" Presents Hit Parade."

The Tennessean (Nashville, Tennessee), April 27, 1993, "Symphony Gets Moody Blues," by Brian Mansfield.

Honolulu Star-Bulletin (Hawaii), "April 30, 1993, "Don Weiler's review of *A Night at Red Rocks with the Colorado Symphony Orchestra.*

Higher & Higher, #18 & 19, Winter/Spring 1993, "The Moodies at Red Rocks: The Audience Response"; "Red Rocks: An Appreciation," by Blanch Horst; "Hayward on Red Rocks," by Alan Stock; "Larry Baird – In the Footsteps of Knight," by Randy Salas; "Rock 'n' Roll Thunder: A Talk with Gordon Marshall," by Jill Finan; "Part I: The Songwriter Evolves," by Russell Brown and Jill Finan; "Laura Vitez: Documenting the Magic of Red Rocks," by Mark Murley.

Rock Collector Disc Magazine, May 1993, review of *A Night at Red Rocks with the Colorado Symphony Orchestra.*

Fort Worth Star-Telegram (Texas), June 5, 1993, "Moody Blues: Veteran Rockers Keep Audience on the Threshold of a Dream," by Jeff Guinn.

Dallas Morning News (Texas), June 5, 1993, concert review.

Houston Chronicle (Texas), June 7, 1993, "Loyal Are as Laid-Back as Moodies," by Charles Ward.

The Miami Herald (Florida), June 9, 1993, Mario Tarradell's concert review: Sunrise Musical Theatre, Sunrise/Fort Lauderdale, Florida.

The Charlotte Observer (North Carolina), Knight-Ridder Newspapers wire story, "Moody Blues: In Harmony with Symphonies," by John Bordsen.

The Orlando Sentinel (Florida), June 11, 1993, "Moody Blues Find New Outlet with Orchestra," by Jim Abbott.

Tampa Tribune (Florida), June 12, 1993, "Orchestra Helps Moody Blues' Fans Tune in to Old Radio Standbys," by Philip Booth.

Orlando Sentinel (Florida), June 14, 1993, "Moody Blues, Live with Orchestra: Classic – Actually, Classical – Rock," by Parry Gettelman.

New York Post, June 18, 1993, review of Radio City Music Hall concert by Dan Aquilante.

Indianapolis Star (Indiana), June 30, 1993, "Moodys, ISO Slow Getting It Together," by Marc D. Allen.

Guitar World, July 1993, "The Moody Dude," by Andy Aledort.

Rag, July 1993, "The Moody Blues," by Jim Varsallone.

Pulse!, July 1993, Barry Gutman's review of *A Night at Red Rocks with the Colorado Symphony Orchestra.*

The Waukesha Journal (Wisconsin), July 1, 1993, "Moody Blues Still Has that Magic," by Tom Strini.

Scene, July 1, 1993, "The Moody Reviews: Blossom, June 26," review by Keith Kofron.

Washington Post (Washington, D.C.), July 2, 1993, Mike Joyce's review of *A Night at Red Rocks with the Colorado Symphony Orchestra.*

The Daily Gazette (New York, N.Y.), July 3, 1993, "Moody Blues Bring Pop Nostalgia to SPAC," by Michael Hochanadel.

Hartford Courant (Connecticut), July 5, 1993, "Moody Blues Mellow a Warm Evening," by Nichole M. Malec.

Washington Post (Washington D.C.), July 8, 1993, "Moody Blues & the NSO," review by Mark Carrington.

News Record (North Hills, Pennsylvania), July 8, 1993, "Orchestra Gives Backup to Moodys," by Rex Rutkowski.

Pittsburgh Post-Gazette (Pennsylvania), July 11, 1993, Tom Waseleski's review of *A Night at Red Rocks with the Colorado Symphony Orchestra*, and Ed Masley's concert review, "Orchestra Puts Moody Blues in the Mood."

Democrat and Chronicle (Rochester, New York), July 13, 1993, "Moody Blues and the RPO Hit Sweet Note," by Jeff Spevak.

The Sun Chronicle (Massachusetts), July 14, 1993, concert review.

Fairfax Times (Virginia), July 14, 1993, "Moody Blues and National Symphony Orchestra Find Lost Chord," by Angela Dawson.

Asbury Park Press (New Jersey), July 15, 1993, "Moody Blues Played Timeless Music," by

Albert H. Cohen.

The Buffalo News (New York), July 16, 1993, "Circles of Moods – Moody Blues Were Just That: Moody," by Michele Marcucci.

The Burlington Free Press (Vermont), July 17, 1993, "Moody Blues Get Better with Age," by Paul Kaza.

The Boston Globe (Massachusetts), June 19, 1993, "Moodies Orchestrate Unforgettable Evening," by Steve Morse.

The Patriot Ledger (Quincy, Massachusetts), July 19, 1993, "Orchestra Helps Moody Blues Do Its Magic at Great Woods," by Mick Skidmore.

Toronto Star (Ontario, Canada), July 21, 1993, "Too Bad It Was A One-Nighter," by Peter Howell.

The Courier-Journal (Louisville, Kentucky), July 24, 1993, concert review by Allen Howie.

The Dispatch (Moline, Illinois), July 25, 1993 "Moody Blues Touch Emotions," by Eileen Ford.

St. Louis Post-Dispatch (Missouri), July 25, 1993, "Crossover Style: '60s Group Starts a Trend," by Paul A. Harris.

St. Louis Post-Dispatch (Missouri), July 27, 1993, "Moody Blues: A Memorable Night," by Louise King.

Pollstar, July 26, 1993, "Moody Blues Play Meet the Beatles."

The Spokane-Review (Washington), September 15, 1993, concert review by Lonna Baldwin.

Visalia Times-Delta (California), September 16, 1993, "Moody Blues Turn Back Clock for Fans," by Warren Cederborg.

The San Diego Union-Tribune (California), September 18, 1994, "Music As Uneven As Regressing Hairline of Moody Blues," by Paul Hodgins, and reader responses.

Denver Post (Colorado), September 19, 1993, "Score One for Local Arranger at Rocks," by G. Brown.

Where It's Hot! (Las Vegas, Nevada), September 21, 1993, "The Moody Blues: They Ain't Heavy; They're Las Vegas," by Cia Romano McNear.

The Orange County Register (California), September 21, 1993, "Moodies Muster Majesty," by Steve Eddy.

Denver Post (Colorado), September 22, 1993, "Moody Blues, CSO Recapture Magic, by Butch Hause.

Las Vegas Sun (Nevada), September 24, 1993, "The Moody Blues Orchestrating a Long-Running Career," by Rick Velotta.

Wisconsin State Journal, October 11, 1993, "Moody Blues Create Pleasant Memories," by John Kovalic.

Variety, January 18, 1994, "Ex-Member Sues Over Moody Blues Booty," by Adam Sandler.

Battle Creek Enquirer (Michigan), March 3, 1994, "Fantastic Drama," by Mark Schwerin.

Kalamazoo Gazette (New York), March 3, 1994, "Lavish Moody Blues Recaptures the '60s," by Diana Dickerson.

Lansing State Journal (Michigan), March 7, 1994, "Moody Blues Still Strong," by Robin Welch.

Fargo Forum (North Dakota), March 9, 1994, "Moody Blues Weave Their Magic at the Fargodome," by Catherine Zalser.

Keyboard, May 1994, "Mike Pinder: The Many Moods of a Mellotron Master," by Ernie Rideout.

Higher & Higher, #20, Winter/Spring 1994, "Moody News"; "Michael Pinder: Reaching for the Beautiful Landscape," interview by Mark Murley; Mark Murley's review of *Off the Shelf;* "Behind the Scenes of the Moody Blues Concert Tour: An Orchestra Prepares," by Randy Salas; "The Sound Behind the Moodies," by Wendie Old; "Moody in St. Louie," by Doris Manda; "Fans Praise Tour"; "Once in a Blue Mood," a review by Blanche Horst.

Higher & Higher, #21 & 22, Summer 1994, "A Wilde Year," by Shelia Johnson, and "The Whispers & All Things Bright – The Early Pro Bands," by Mark Murley, and "Lesley Drewett: Remembering Justin," by Lesley Drewett, and "The Recovery Network Interview, by Colleen Joy; "Mike Pinder Update," by Theresa Murley.

St. Cloud Times, June 3, 1994, Gannett News Service wire story: "Reunion Summer Nets Another '70s Band in Trapeze."

Medina County Gazette, June 3, 1994, "Moodies Can Still Orchestrate Success," by Bill Murphy.

Milwaukee Sentinel, June 6, 1994, "Moody Blues Still Have Artistic Touch," by Dave Tianem.

The Denver Post (Colorado), September 9, 1994, "Moody Blues' Edge Will Listen to Sound from CSO This Time," by G. Brown.

New Times, September 22, 1994, "Moodies Enhancer," by Serene Dominic.

Higher & Higher, Vol. 23, Fall 1994, "*Time Traveller*: The Story Behind the New Moodies Boxed Set," by Randy A. Salas; "*Time Traveller*: Review/Commentary," by Randy A. Salas.

The Orange County Register (California), October 16, 1994, "*Time Traveler* Is a Worthwhile Set for All Moody Blues Fans," by Steve Eddy, and "His Moodies Days Are in the Past, and That's Fine," by Steve Eddy.

Goldmine, Vol. 20, No. 22, October 28, 1994, "The Moody Blues: Veteran Cosmic Rockers," by Bruce Eder.

Goldmine, November 11, 1994, "Trapeze: Flying High (Once Again) With the Greatest of Ease," by Lisa L. Barker.

Daily Mail (London, England), November 19, 1994, "I Loved Being the 'Prettiest Man' in Pop Music," by Justin Hayward.

Billboard, November 26, 1994, "Blues Are Gold."

Deseret News (Utah), December 16, 1994, Ray Boren's review of *Time Traveller*.

The Sacramento Bee (California), January 1, 1995, "Mellowing Out," by J. Freedom Du Lac.

The Tennessean (Nashville, Tenn.), Jeff Pearlman's review of *Among the Stars*.

The Indianapolis Star (Indiana), February 3, 1995, "Record Reviews," *Among the Stars*.

The Sun Herald (Biloxi, Mississippi), March 9, 1995, "Without the Blues," by Jeff Piorkowski.

Phoenix Gazette (Arizona), March 3, 1995, "Moody Man Back on the Album Track," by Andrew Means.

Tempe Daily News Tribune (Arizona), March 31, 1995, "Not Moody or Blue, Pinder Comes Back," by Betty Webb.

Express-Times (Allentown, Pennsylvania), May 5, 1995, "Ex-Moody Blue Taking a Step Back into the Light," by Deborah L. Courville.

Daily Herald (Chicago, Illinois), May 19, 1995, "In Search of the Lost Moody Blue," by Dan Kening.

Scene, May 25, 1995, "Following His Own Bliss," by Mark Holan.

Higher & Higher, #25, Spring 1995, "The Tony Visconti Interview," by Randy A. Salas.

Higher & Higher, #26/27, Summer 1995, "The Making of *To Our Children's Children's Children*," by Mark Murley; "The Art of *TOCCC*," by Mark Murley; "Derek Varnals: Engineering the Classic Moodies Sound," by Mark Murley; "Mike Pinder Update, including preview of *Conscious Living*, by Patty Anne McAdams.

The Performing Songwriter, July/August 1995, "The Long Distance Voyage of Moody Blues' Justin Hayward," by Bill DeMain.

Guitar Player, September 1995, "Moody Blues: Still Searching for the Lost Chord," by Chuck Crisafulli.

Higher & Higher, #28, Fall 1995, "Mike Pinder Update," with Theresa Murley's preview of *A Planet with One Mind*; "The Graeme Edge Band Project," by Mark Murley, "Graeme's Songs and Poems with The Moody Blues," by Mark Murley.

Seconds, October 1995, "The Moody Blues," by George Peters.

Goldmine, October 5, 1995, Bruce Eder's review of *Among the Stars*.

Reno Gazette-Journal (Nevada), October 26, 1995, AP wire story: "Golf, Rock 'n' Roll and Complications," by Mike Clark.

Higher & Higher, #29, Winter 1995, "The Tony Clarke Interview," by Mark Murley.

Holiday, March 1996, review of *A Planet with One Mind*.

Dane County Kids, March 1996, review of *A Planet with One Mind*.

King Apple Parents' Paper, March 1996, review of *A Planet with One Mind*.

Goldmine, March 1, 1996, "Airplane, Moody Blues Big Winners in Goldmine's Hall of Fame Ballot."

Genesee Valley Parent, April 1996, review of *A Planet with One Mind*.

The Albany Herald (New York), April 10, 1996, Associated Press wire story: "Band Sends Leary Get-Well Message."

Publisher's Weekly, April 15, 1996, review of *A Planet with One Mind*.

Star Tribune Entertainment (Minneapolis, Minnesota), April 21, 1996, Sharon Parker's review of *A Planet with One Mind*.

Higher & Higher, #31, Summer 1996, "The Making of *Long Distance Voyager*", "Hayward Solo Album Delayed," by Mark Murley; "New MB Album Underway"; "Timothy Leary: Dead at 75."

American Library Association, June 1, 1996, Lolly Gepson's review of *A Planet with One Mind*.

Tribune-Review (Pittsburgh, Pennsylvania), June 6, 1996, "Leary Death a Moody Flashback," by George Varga.

Tampa Tribune (Florida), June 8, 1996, "Moodies Delight Crowd with Mixed Bag of Old and New," by Charles Stovall.

Hartford Courant (Connecticut), June 12, 1996, "Future, Past Merge in Fully Orchestral Moody Blues Tour," by Roger Catlin.

Asbury Park Press (New Jersey), June 14, 1996, "A Touch of the Blues," by Kelly-Jane Cotter.

The Indianapolis Star (Indiana), June 16, 1996, "Moody Blues Revives 'Legend of a Mind,'" by Marc Allen.

The Beacon Journal (Ohio), June 20, 1996, "Still Moody, Still Blues," by Kevin C. Johnson.

St. Cloud Times (Minnesota), June 17, 1996, "Timothy Leary Lives, Moody Blues Now Sing," by Melanie Gilbert.

Tracks, Fall 1996, "Justin Hayward," by Lisa Ludwick.

Higher & Higher, #32, Fall 1996, "The Making of *The View From the Hill*," by Mark Murley; "Hayward Shows He's King of the Hill, with Randy A. Salas's review of *The View From the Hill*; "His Views on *The Hill*: Hayward on the New Album," interview by Lisa Ludwick; "A 20th Anniversary Stroll Down ... *Natural Avenue*," by Mark Murley; "Sur la Mer: A Visit to Mulinetti Studio," by Gian Antonio Cavanno.

The Dallas Morning News (Texas), November 1996, "Bits of Wisdom and Peace," by Laurie Wilson.

Bass Frontiers, November 1996, "John Lodge of the Moody Blues," by George A. Coelho.

Sound Check, November 1996, "Hayward's *View From the Hill*: Seamless Artistry, Innovative Arrangements," by Deborah Courville.

The Record Collector, November 1996, "Justin Hayward Interview," by John Reed.

Songwriter's Monthly, November 1996, "Justin Hayward, Part One: *The View From the Hill*."

Higher & Higher, #33, Winter 1996, "The Making of Question of Balance," by Mark Murley; "The Art of *A Question of Balance*," by Mark Murley.

The Los Angeles Times, December 2, 1996, "Riding a Seesaw Between the Moody Blues and a Solo Career," by Buddy Seigal.

The Los Angeles Times, December 5, 1996, "Hayward's Solo Mode: Still Moody," by Mike Boehm

The Union (Grass Valley, California), December 7, 1996, "Speaking with a New Voice," by Paul Harrar.

Second #37, 1996, "Capt. Robert 'Hoot' Gibson, U.S.N.," interviewed by George Petros.

The Los Angeles Times, January 1997, "Rocker's Current Gig Has No Tunes, Just Tales for Tots," by Bill Locey.

Hot Tickets, March 6, 1997, "Justin Hayward of the Moody Blues On..."

Good Housekeeping, April 1997, "And I Love You."

Albuquerque Journal (New Mexico), May 23, 1997, "The Moody Blues," by David Steinberg.

Goldmine, May 23, 1997, "Justin Hayward of the Moody Blues," by Geof O'Keefe.

Daily Mail (London, England), May 24, 1997, "Justin Hayward."

Higher & Higher, #35, Summer 1997, "A Conversation with 'Classic 7' Engineer Adrian Martins," by Mark Murley.

Seattle Post-Intelligencer (Washington), June 6, 1997, "Hindsight Alters Moody Blues' View of Leary Tribute," by Gene Stout.

Argus-Leader (Sioux Falls, South Dakota), June 12, 1997, "Blues in the Mood for Change," by Bob Keys.

Higher & Higher, #36, Fall 1997, "The *Higher & Higher* Denny Laine Interview, Part 1," by Mark Murley.

Highlands, November 1997, "Justin Hayward Interview, 5th November, Nice," by Didier Gonzalez.

Higher & Higher, #37, Winter 1997, "Denny Lane Interview, Part 2," by Mark Murley.

Highlands, October 1998, "Interview: Justin Hayward," from September 5, 1998, by Marie-Josée Jimenez and Didier Gonzalez.

Wildest Westerns Magazine, 1998, "Unsung Hero: Jay Silverheels Remembered," by John Lodge.

Higher & Higher, #39 & 40, Winter 1998/Spring 1999, "The Making of *The Present*," by Mark Murley, and "John Lodge on TP," interviewed by Mark Murley, and "Pip on TP"; "MB Album Still on for '99"; "Mike Pinder Update," by Theresa Murley; "Viva Los Moodies!," by Mark Murley.

Record Collector, May 1999, "The Voice of Rock!," by Tim Jones.

Moody Blues Fan Club Newsletter, Summer 1999.

Star-Banner (Ocala, Florida), August 13, 1999, NYT Regional Newspapers: "Moody Blues' Future Is Not Past," By Steve Webb.

Tallahassee Democrat (Florida), August 13, 1999, "*Strange Times* for the Moody Blues," by Kati Schardi.

Asheville Citizen-Times (North Carolina), August 15, 1999, "*Strange Times* with the Moody Blues," by Alan Sculley.

The Des Moines Register (Iowa), August 22, 1999, Kyle Munson's review of *Strange Days*.

St Louis Post-Dispatch (Missouri), August 26, 1999, "Moody Blues Gets Back on Track," by Kevin C. Johnson.

Goldmine, August 27, 1999, "The Moody Blues Back on Track with First New Album Since 1991," by Bruce Eder.

The Patriot Ledger (Quincy, Massachusetts), August 28, 1999, "Moody Blues Capture Band's Spirit in These *Strange Times*."

St. Louis Post-Dispatch (Missouri), August 30, 1999, "Moody Blues Deliver New and Old in Strong Show," by Joe Williams.

Higher & Higher, #41, Summer 1999, "Strange Tour Begins," review by Mark Murley; "The Making of *Strange Times*," by Mark Murley; Theresa Murley's review of *Strange Times*.

Milwaukee Journal (Wisconsin), September 1999, "Moody Blues Riding High on New Album, New Tour," by Dave Tianen.

Times-Dispatch (Richmond, Virginia), September 1999, "Moody Blues Not Resting on Laurels," by Melissa Ruggieri.

Washington Post, September 3, 1999, "Spotlight: Moody Blues On the Upswing."

The Record (Berger County, New Jersey), September 3, 1999, "More Moody than Ever."

Pittsburg Post-Gazette (Pennsylvania), September 4, 1999, "Moody Blues Cling Comfortably, Uninspiringly to Past," by John Young, plus reader's response from September 10th.

The Washington Times, September 8, 1999, "*Strange Times* for Moody Blues."

Higher & Higher, # 42, Fall 1999, "The Fans of *Strange Times*" with letters from readers; "The Graeme Edge Interview," by Dana Grubb; "Covering *Strange Times*," by Theresa Murley; "*Strange Times* on the Air," by Jane Fieberts; "The Moody Blues on A Composite Interview."

Hartford Courant (Connecticut), October 7, 1999, Steven Goode's review of *Strange Times*.

The Cincinnati Enquirer (Ohio), November 5, 1999, "Moody Blues Should Stick with Oldies," by Chris Varias, plus reader responses.

Highlands' Moody Blues Special Edition, December 12, 1999, "Justin Hayward: Interview, Part 3," by Marie-Josée Jimenez and Didier Gonzalez.

20th Century Guitar Magazine, April 2000, "Moody Blues: Still Walking on Air," by Robert Silverstein.

Outré Magazine, August 2000, "Interview with Justin Hayward."

Charisma, September 2000, "John Lodge: Bass Force Behind the Moody Blues."

Pollstar, 2000-2001 Edition, "Exclusive Interview: Peter Jackson, Idaho Center."

The Cincinnati Enquirer (Ohio), March 9, 2001, "Amazing Caves Scales New Heights of IMAX Excitement," by Margaret A. McGurk.

The Indianapolis Star (Indiana), March 23, 2001, "*Caves* Movie Inspires Awe," by Robert K. Elder.

The Star Press (Muncie, Indiana), May 5, 2001, *The Orlando Sentinel* syndicated story: "Veteran

Rock Band Is Touring Less and Enjoying It More," by Jim Abbott.

Higher & Higher, #44, Fall 2001, "Journey into Amazing Music," by Mark Murley.

The Desert Sun (Palm Springs, California), November 9, 2002, Knight-Ridder Newspapers wire-story: "The Moody Blues Are Still Searching for the Lost Chord," by Rod Harmon.

Highland's Moody Blues Special Edition, 2002, with Didier Gonzalez's interview with Justin Hayward from March 12, 1997.

The Record Collector, February 2003, "The Voice of the Moody Blues Reflects in His Colourful Career."

News-Press (Fort Myers, Florida), October 24, 2003, "British Rockers Kick Off Fall Tour Here," by Mark Marymont.

The Daily Times (Salisbury, Maryland), November 14, 2003, "A Moody Blues Holiday," by Bill De Young.

Sun Journal (Lewiston, Maine) November 21, 2003, "Moody Blues: Groundbreaking Band Coming to Maine on Tour to Promote its First Holiday Album," by Steve Sherlock.

The News Journal (Wilmington, Delaware), November 30, 2003, Gary Mullinax's review of *December*.

The Des Moines Register (Iowa), December 5, 2003, Kyle Munson's and Kevin Cox's review of *December*.

Argus-Leader (Sioux Falls, South Dakota), December 5, 2003, Joel Brown's review of *December*.

Pittsburgh Post-Gazette (Pennsylvania), December 5, 2003, Scott Mervis's review of *December*, and rebuttal from reader.

Music Connection, December 8, 2003, "A Moody Blues Christmas," by Dan Kimpel.

Philadelphia Daily News (Pennsylvania), December 10, 2003, Jonathan Takiff's review of *December*.

Journal and Courier (Lafayette, Indiana), December, 11, 2003, *Washington Post* syndicated Richard Harrington's review of *December*.

The Morning Call (Allentown, Pennsylvania), December 13, 2003, wire-service review of *December*.

Arizona Republic (Phoenix), December 13, 2003, Larry Rodgers's review of *December*.

Arizona Daily Star (Tucson), December 19, 2003, Ann Brown's review of *December*.

Music Connection, December 8, 2003, "A Moody Blues Christmas," by Dan Kimpel.

Higher & Higher, #46/47, Spring-Summer, 2004, "The Making of a Dream," by Mark Murley; "Hayward on *Threshold*," interviewed by Mark Murley; "Pinder on *Threshold*," interviewed by Mark Murley; "On *December*"; "A Brief Q&A with December Cover Artist Lucio De Giuseppe"; "December Provides a Winter of Fans' Content," by Jane Fieberts.

Library Journal, November 15, 2004, John Skrtic's review of *The Moody Blues: The Lost Performance, Live in Paris '70*.

Classic Rock, December 2004, "Justin Hayward," interviewed by Hugh Fielder.

Goldmine, December 5, 2008, "The Moody Blues Live," by Conrad L. Stinnett.

Sound On Sound, July 2009, "The Moody Blues 'Nights In White Satin,'" by Richard Buskin.

Jazz & Blues, August 2009, Bill Wahl's review of *The Moody Blues Threshold of a Dream: Live at the Isle of Wight Festival 1970*.

Goldmine, October 9, 2009, "Moody Blues and the Mellotron, Isle of Wight."

Record Collector, May/June 2012, "The Moody Blues," by Harvey Kubernik.

Goldmine, June 12, 2012, "Revisit the Moody Blues' Landmark Album, *Days of Future Passed*" and "Moody Blues Bassist John Lodge Looks Back on *Days of Future Passed*," by Lee Zimmerman.

PROG, March 2013, "The Moody Blues"; March 2013, Paul Sexton's review of *Spirits of the Western Sky*.

Goldmine, April 2013, "Moody Bluegrass," by Mike Greenblatt.

Rock Society, May/June 2013, "The Moody Blues: A Question of Balance."

PROG, June 2013, "Q&A: Justin Hayward," by Malcolm Dome.

The Guardian (England), January 14, 2014, "Jeff Wayne and David Essex: How We Made *The War of the Worlds*," by Andrew Pulver.

Classic Rock Magazine, May 28, 2014, "Revolution in the Head," by Rob Hughes.

Tape Op, September/October 2014, "Indigo Ranch: Richard Kaplan and Mike Pinder on Operating Malibu's Legendary Studio in the 70s & 80s," by Larry Crane.

Uncut, November 21, 2014, "The Making of The Moody Blues' 'Nights In White Satin.'"

PROG magazine, April 15, 2015, "King of Blue," by Paul Sexton.

Sonic Shocks, June 2015, "John Lodge," by Cristina Massei.

The Morning Call (Allentown, Pennsylvania), August 23, 2015, "He's Just a Singer in a Rock 'n' Roll Band," by John J. Moser.

Magnificent Moody Blues 50th Anniversary CD Set, 2015, pamphlet by Mark Powell.

Shindig magazine, 2015, Bye Bye Bird," by William James.

Cashbox Music Reviews, October 19, 2016, David Bowling's review of *All the Way*.

Cashbox Music Reviews, October 26, 2016, David Bowling's review of *Live In Concert at the Capital Theatre*.

North Coast Voice Magazine, November 9, 2016, Pete Roche's review of *All the Way*.

Goldmine, February 2017, "Justin's Moods," by Lee Zimmerman.

Rockcellar magazine, April 13, 2017, "Justin Hayward's 'Stage Door' – Conversation with the Moody Blues Legend," by Ken Sharp.

Goldmine, July 2017, "Moody Melodies," by Lee Zimmerman.

Quotes & specific references:

Allison, Guy | GA-AI17. Author interview, 2017.

Anger, Harry | HA-BB86. *Billboard*, September 13, 1986, "Moody Blues, ELP Enjoy Renewed Success," by Steve Gett.

Baccigaluppi, John | JB-TO14. *Tape Op*, September/October 2014, "Indigo Ranch: Richard Kaplan and Mike Pinder on Operating Malibu's Legendary Studio in the 70s & 80s," by Larry Crane.

Baird, Larry | LB-H&H93. *Higher & Higher, #18 & 19*, Winter/Spring 1993, "Larry Baird – In the Footsteps of Knight," by Randy Salas.

Baird, Larry | LB-H&H94. *Higher & Higher, #20*, Winter/Spring 1994, "Moody News"; "Michael Pinder: Reaching for the Beautiful Landscape," interview by Mark Murley; "Behind the Scenes of the Moody Blues Concert Tour: An Orchestra Prepares," by Randy Salas.

Baird, Larry | LB-DP93. *Denver Post* (Colorado), September 19, 1993, "Score One for Local Arranger at Rocks," by G. Brown.

Baker, Dave | DB-H&H96. *Higher & Higher, #32*, Fall 1996, "A 20th Anniversary Stroll Down … *Natural Avenue*," by Mark Murley.

Banks, Bessie | BB-SC04. Soundclick.com, "Larry and Jaibi," by Andy Croasdell for Dave Godin, with quote from Bessie Banks from November 2004.

Bassington, Mike | MB-CA07. *Classic Artists: Moody Blues*, April 24, 2007 (Image Entertainment).

Bevan, Bev | BB-BP64. *Birmingham Planet*, January 30, 1964, "A New Look for the Diplomats."

Bevan, Bev | BB-CA07. *Classic Artists: The Moody Blues*, April 24, 2007 (Image Entertainment).

Bliss, Paul | PB-H&H92. *Higher & Higher*, Vol. 17, Winter/Spring 1992, "Pure Bliss: The Paul Bliss Interview," by Mark Murley.

Boshell, Bias   BB-H&H92. *Higher & Higher*, Vol. 17, Winter/Spring 1992, "Prince Charming of the Keys: A Conversation with Bias Boshell," by Jill Finan.

Chapman, Marshall   MC-GLRAR04. *Goodbye, Little Rock and Roller*, by Marshall Chapman (Macmillan, 2004)

Clark, Tony   TC-NME71. *New Musical Express*, November 20, 1971, Paul McCartney Is Like a Man Who Has Dodged the Death Sentence," by Richard Green.

Clarke, Tony   TC-TCP69. *Threshold Concert Program*, December 5, 1969, "An Anatomy of Threshold."

Clarke, Tony   TC-RS70. *Rolling Stone*, April 3, 1970, "The Moody Blues, Chumps No More," by Charles Alverson.

Clarke, Tony   TC-MM70. *Melody Maker* , May 16, 1970, "Tony – the Sixth Moody," by Richard Williams.

Clarke, Tony   TC-MM70a. *Melody Maker*, October 10, 1970, "Giving Birth to Quads," by Tony Clarke.

Clarke, Tony   TC-HP71. *Hit Parader*, April 1971, "A Producer's View: Moody Blues," by Nick Logan.

Clarke, Tony   TC-RS72. *Rolling Stone*, December 21, 1972, "In Search of the Moody Blues," by James Horwitz.

Clarke, Tony   TC-NME73. *New Musical Express*, May 5, 1973, "The Tape Wizard of the Moodies," by Tony Tyler.

Clarke, Tony   TC-PBP74. *The Palm Beach Post* (West Palm Beach, Florida), December 16, 1974, "Moody Blues Alive and Well," by Thom Smith.

Clarke, Tony   TC-MW78. *Music Week*, June 24, 1978, "Tony Clarke: The 'Invisible' Moody Blue."

Clarke, Tony   TC-H&H85. *Higher & Higher*, #5, Summer/Fall 1985, "Tony Clarke: The Master Producer Speaks," by Randy A. Salas.

Clarke, Tony   TC-H&H94a. *Higher & Higher*, #26/27, Summer 1995, "The Making of *To Our Children's Children's Children*," by Mark Murley.

Clarke, Tony   TC-H&H95. *Higher & Higher*, #29, Winter 1995, "The Tony Clarke Interview," by Mark Murley.

Clarke, Tony   TC-H&H96. *Higher & Higher*, #33, Winter 1996, "The Making of Question of Balance," by Mark Murley.

Clarke, Tony   TC-H&H96a. *Higher & Higher*, #33, Winter 1996, "The Art of *A Question of Balance*," by Mark Murley.

Clarke, Tony   TC-H&H96. *Higher & Higher*, #32, Fall 1996, "A 20th Anniversary Stroll Down … *Natural Avenue*," by Mark Murley.

Clarke, Tony   TC-H&H04. *Higher & Higher*, Spring-Summer, 2004, "The Making of a Dream," by Mark Murley.

Clarke, Tony   TC-CA.TMB06. *Classic Artists: The Moody Blues*, 2009, Empire Media Holdings SL, Impact Film Sales Ltd..

Coppock, Bruce   BC-SLPD93. *St. Louis Post-Dispatch* (Missouri), July 25, 1993, "Crossover Style: '60s Group Starts a Trend," Paul A. Harris.

Crowley, Cliff   CC-CE88. *The Cincinnati Enquirer* (Ohio), July 27, 1988, "Nights at the Gardens," by Cliff Radel.

Curnin, Cy   CC-CT86. *Chicago Tribune* (Illinois), June 29, 1986, "Rocker Curnin Gets a Fix on the World with His Lyrics Even While Fans Dance," by Jae-Ha Kim.

Curtis, Dick   DC-SPI02. *Seattle Post-Intelligencer*, November 20, 2002, "Pat O'Day

Curtis, Dick	Pens His Page in Rock History," by Charles R. Cross. DC-BW11. BlatherWatch.com. October 2011, with excepts from *Me, Myself & I: We're On the Road Again*, unpublished book by Dick Curtis, with various postings by Michael Hood on October 11 and 26, 2011, and October 1, 2 and 9, 2015.
Day, Adrian	AD-MO80. *Musicians Only*, June 29, 1980, interview with Adrian Day
Diefendorf, Jennie	JD-TT93. *The Tennessean* (Nashville, Tennessee), April 27, 1993, "Symphony Gets Moody Blues," by Brian Mansfield.
Donegan, Lonnie	DL-RC87. *Record Collector*, May 1987, interview with Lonnie Donegan.
Drewett, Leslie	LD-H&H94. *Higher & Higher, #21 & 22*, Summer 1994, "Lesley Drewett: Remembering Justin," by Lesley Drewett.
Edge, Graeme	GE-BP64. *The Birmingham Planet*, June 11, 1964, "The Moody Blues Five," by Mary McGrane.
Edge, Graeme	GE-DW65. *Disc Weekly*, January 23, 1965, "'Brum Is Still Home!' Say the Chart-Topping Moody Blues," by Ted Scott.
Edge, Graeme	GE-NME65b. *New Musical Express*, February 12, 1965, "Top Ten by the Moody Blues."
Edge, Graeme	GE-R65. *Rave*, March 1, 1965, "The m'm'moody blues boys," by Lyn Carnell.
Edge, Graeme	GE-RM65. *Record Mirror*, April 10, 1965, "'How the Beatles Helped Us,' Say the Moody Blues," by Richard Green.
Edge, Graeme	GE-R65a. *Rave*, May 1, 1965, "Getting the Blues in Paris," by Maureen O'Grady.
Edge, Graeme	GE-PW65. *Pop Weekly*, September 11, 1965, cover story: "The Moody Blues on a Summer Day," by Gray Perell.
Edge, Graeme	GE-RM68. *Disc and Music Echo*, January 13, 1968, "Moodies Dislike Charts," by Derek Boltwood.
Edge, Graeme	GE-NME68. *New Musical Express*, February 3, 1968, "Moody Blues Deserve Much Greater Success," by Keith Altham.
Edge, Graeme	GE-RM68. *Record Mirror*, August 3, 1968, Derek Boltwood's review of *In Search of the Lost Chord*.
Edge, Graeme	GE-NME68a. *New Musical Express*, August 31, 1968, "Moody Blues Full of Surprises," by Richard Green.
Edge, Graeme	GE-R68. *Rave* magazine, September 1, 1968, "The Day the Moody Blues Should Have Been Called The Broody Moos!"
Edge, Graeme	GE-CP68. *Courier-Press* (Camden, New Jersey), November 16, 1968, interview with Graeme Edge, by Hoag Levins.
Edge, Graeme	GE-OC68. *Open City*, December 7, 1968, "Moody Blues," by Ramblin' Jim Martin.
Edge, Graeme	GE-HT69. *Hit Parader*, May 1969, "The Moody Blues Visit America."
Edge, Graeme	GE-MM69. *Melody Maker*, May 3, 1969, "Sex, Love and Pop."
Edge, Graeme	GE-MM69a. *Melody Maker*, May 10, 1969, ""Sex, Love and Pop" (Part 2), by Jean Elliott.
Edge, Graeme	GE-NME69. *New Musical Express*, September 20, 1969, "Moodies Write for You."
Edge, Graeme	GE-HPY70. *Hit Parader Yearbook*, Winter 1970, "The Moody Blues Speak Out."
Edge, Graeme	GE-MEP70. *Muncie Evening Press* (Indiana), February 14, 1970, UPI syndicated wire story: "Is Message of Rock Music Only for Young?" by John J. Meehan.
Edge, Graeme	GE-BS70. *The Baltimore Sun*, May 4, 1970, "The Moody Blues –

	Name No Reflection on Style," by Bob Lardine.
Edge, Graeme	GE-MM70. *Melody Maker*, May 9, 1970, "Moodies Aim for the Head and Heart," by Royston Eldridge.
Edge, Graeme	GE-NME70. *Disc and Music Echo*, August 15, 1970, "Graeme – the Drummer with a Head Full of Words."
Edge, Graeme	GE-NME70. *New Musical Express*, September 13, 1970, "Moodies Act as Music Guides," by Richard Green.
Edge, Graeme	GE-RM70. *Record Mirror*, October 10, 1970, "Why Do People Get Moody About the Moodies?" by Keith Altham.
Edge, Graeme	GE-NME71. *New Musical Express*, January 9, 1971, "The Day We Had to Con Our Label," by Graeme Edge, as told to Pamela Holman.
Edge, Graeme	GE-C71. *Circus*, April 1971, "The Moody Blues Flow Methodically Onward," by David Erlich.
Edge, Graeme	GE-MM71. *Melody Maker*, September 4, 1971, "Blunt Edge," by Roy Hollingworth.
Edge, Graeme	GE-RS71. *Rolling Stone*, September 16, 1971, "The Moody Blues" "What's Trite?" by Andrew Bailey.
Edge, Graeme	GE-TMN71. *The Morning News* (Wilmington, Delaware), September 25, 1971, "Teen Times" syndicated article, "Moody Blues Produce 'Total Concept Albums,'" by Jared Johnson.
Edge, Graeme	GE-S71. *Sounds*, September 25, 1971, "Percussion: Graeme's Got a Shocker, " by Penny Valentine.
Edge, Graeme	GE-J71. *Jackie*, September 25, 1971, "Pete Meets the Moody Blues."
Edge, Graeme	GE-S72. *Sounds*, September 30, 1972, "Graeme Edge Talking to Penny Valentine."
Edge, Graeme	GE-RS72. *Rolling Stone*, December 21, 1972, "In Search of the Moody Blues," by James Horwitz.
Edge, Graeme	GE-RS73. *Sounds*, February 3, 1973, "Days of Future Passed," by Penny Valentine.
Edge, Graeme	GE-NME73. *New Musical Express*, October 20, 1973, "Moody Blues: Saints or Sinners?," by Keith Altham.
Edge, Graeme	GE-T73. *Tambourine* magazine, November 26, 1973, "Moody Blues: Universal Experiences – Universal Sounds," by Daniel Goldberg.
Edge, Graeme	GE-S74. *Sounds*, July 20, 1974, "Edging His Bets," by Bill Henderson.
Edge, Graeme	GE-MS74. *Music Scene*, September 1974, "The Mixed Up Mood of the Moodies," by Richard Green.
Edge, Graeme	GE-PNJ74. *Pensacola News Journal* (Florida), September 24, 1974, Gannett-*Rolling Stone* wire story: "Moodys Pass Million Mark, Find Monster Needs Rest," by Andrew Bailey.
Edge, Graeme	GE-APP74. *Asbury Park Press* (New Jersey), September 26, 1974, "Moody Blues Taking Rest," by Andrew Bailey.
Edge, Graeme	GE-ZW74. *Zoo World*, October 10, 1974, "The Moody Blues."
Edge, Graeme	GE-NYT74. *The New York Times*, November 24, 1974, "A Requiem for the Moody Blues and the Days of Future Passed," by Barbara Rowes.
Edge, Graeme	GE-MM75. *Melody Maker*, September 6, 1975, "Edge of a Dream," by Chris Charlesworth.
Edge, Graeme	GE-MW75. *Music Week*, September 6, 1975, "Taking the Edge Off Exile, " by Terri Anderson.
Edge, Graeme	GE-MEP75. *Muncie Evening Press* (New Jersey), November 15, 1975, "Pop Scene Service" interview with Graeme Edge by Kim Garfield.
Edge, Graeme	GE-C75. *Circus*, November 25, 1975, "Moodies Planning to Record Again."
Edge, Graeme	GE-LR76. London Records press release, 1976.
Edge, Graeme	GE-NME78. "Hairdressers and Brummie Businessmen Quit Day Jobs to Form Mystical Alliance (& Make Bucks)," by Bob Edmands.
Edge, Graeme	GE-MM78. *Melody Maker*, September 30, 1978, "Moraz Replaces

	Mike Pinder in Moodies."
Edge, Graeme	GE-MM79. *Melody Maker*, May 26, 1979, "The Moody Blues: It's a Wonderful Life," by Chris Welch.
Edge, Graeme	GE-US81. *Us*, September 1, 1981, "Moody," by Mark Morrison.
Edge, Graeme	GE-MW83. *Music Week*, September 3, 1983, "The Moody Blues," by Chris Welch.
Edge, Graeme	GE-H&H86. *Higher & Higher*, #7 & 8, Fall/Winter 1986, "Gerry Levene & the Avengers: Brum Beat Revisited," by Andy Whitlow.
Edge, Graeme	GE-SPI. *Seattle Post-Intelligencer*, August 22, 1986, "Never Too Old to Rock 'N' Roll," by Roberta Penn.
Edge, Graeme	GE-MD87. *Modern Drummer*, March 1987, "Graeme Edge," by Robyn Flans.
Edge, Graeme	GE-H&H87. *Higher & Higher*, #9, Spring/Summer 1987, "The Graeme Edge Interview."
Edge, Graeme	GE-S88. *Scene*, August 11, 1988, "The Moody Blues: Veteran Cosmic Rockers," by Mark Holan.
Edge, Graeme	GE-DP88. *The Denver Post* (Colorado) September 2, 1988, "Veteran Moody Blues Forges On," by G. Brown.
Edge, Graeme	GE-PNJ88. *Pensacola News Journal* (Florida), November 5, 1988, "Moody Drummer Beats on to Thrills of Young and Old," by Mike Suchcicki.
Edge, Graeme	GE-ITS89. *In the Studio*, 1989, interview with Graeme Edge.
Edge, Graeme	GE-AAN91. *Ann Arbor News* (Michigan), August 4, 1991, "The Moody Blues Keep on Moving," by Kevin Ransom.
Edge, Graeme	GE-CT91. *Chicago Tribune* (Illinois), August 5, 1991, "Their Days of Future Passed," by Dennis Polkow.
Edge, Graeme	GE-PD91. *The Plain Dealer* (Cleveland, Ohio), August 6, 1991, "Rocker Edge Scorns Soft Musical Edges," by Jane Scott.
Edge, Graeme	GE-BG91. *Boston Globe* (Massachusetts), August 9, 1991, "Singing the Moody Blues," by Steve Morse.
Edge, Graeme	GE-DDN91. *Dayton Daily News* (Ohio), August 9, 1991, "Nights in White Lightin'," by Dave Larson.
Edge, Graeme	GE-PG91. *The Phoenix Gazette* (Arizona), September 6, 1991, "Blues Cooking on 17th Album," by Dean Rhodes.
Edge, Graeme	GE-DP94. *The Denver Post* (Colorado), September 9, 1994, "Moody Blues' Edge Will Listen to Sound from CSO This Time," by G. Brown.
Edge, Graeme	GE-H&H95a. *Higher & Higher, #26/27*, Summer 1995, "The Art of *TOCCC*," by Mark Murley.
Edge, Graeme	GE-H&H95. *Higher & Higher*, #28, Fall 1995, ""Graeme's Songs and Poems with The Moody Blues," by Mark Murley.
Edge, Graeme	GE-H&H96. *Higher & Higher, #33*, Winter 1996, "The Making of Question of Balance," by Mark Murley.
Edge, Graeme	GE-APP96. *Asbury Park Press* (New Jersey), June 14, 1996, "A Touch of the Blues," by Kelly-Jane Cotter.
Edge, Graeme	GE-AJ97. *Albuquerque Journal* (New Mexico), May 23, 1997, "The Moody Blues," by David Steinberg.
Edge, Graeme	GE-DOFP97. *Days of Future Passed*, issued 1997, sleeve notes and interviews by John Reed.
Edge, Graeme	GE-SB99. *Star-Banner* (Ocala, Florida), August 13, 1999, NYT Regional Newspapers: "Moody Blues' Future Is Not Past," By Steve Webb.
Edge, Graeme	GE-H&H99. *Milwaukee Journal* (Wisconsin), September 1999, "Moody Blues Riding High on New Album, New Tour," by Dave Tianen.
Edge, Graeme	GE-TD99. *Times-Dispatch* (Richmond, Virginia), September 1999, "Moody Blues Not Resting on Laurels," by Melissa Ruggieri.

Edge, Graeme	GE-H&H99. *Higher & Higher, # 42*, Fall 1999, "The Graeme Edge Interview," by Dana Grubb.
Edge, Graeme	GE-DS02. *The Desert Sun* (Palm Springs, California), November 9, 2002, Knight-Ridder Newspapers wire story: "The Moody Blues Are Still Searching for the Lost Chord," by Rod Harmon.
Edge, Graeme	GE-SJ03. *Sun Journal* (Lewiston, Maine) November 21, 2003, "Moody Blues: Groundbreaking Band Coming to Maine on Tour to Promote its First Holiday Album," by Steve Sherlock.
Edge, Graeme	GE-CB:TMB06. TC-CA.TMB06. *Classic Artists: The Moody Blues*, 2009, Empire Media Holdings SL, Impact Film Sales Ltd.
Edge, Graeme	GE-CA07. BB-CA07. *Classic Artists: The Moody Blues*, April 24, 2007 (Image Entertainment).
Edge, Graeme	GE-DT08. dailytribune.com, March 7, 2008, "Moody Blues Touch Down in Reno for Two shows," by Ryan Hoffman.
Edge, Graeme	GE-EGBDFCD08. *Every Good Boy Deserves Favour*, issued 2008, remastered edition, with booklet by Mark Powell.
Edge, Graeme	GE-SS08. RT-QOB08. *A Question of Balance,* issued 2008, Remastered edition, with booklet by Mark Powell.
Edge, Graeme	GE-GM12. *Goldmine*, June 12, 2012, "Revisit the Moody Blues' Landmark Album, *Days of Future Passed*."
Edge, Graeme	GE-UC12. *Uncut*, November 21, 2014, "The Making of The Moody Blues' 'Nights In White Satin.'"
Edge, Graeme	GE-PROG13. *PROG*, March 2013, "The Moody Blues."
Edge, Graeme	GE-GM14. GlideMagazine.com, February 10, 2014, "Graeme Edge of the Moody Blues (Interview)," by Leslie Michele Derroughin.
Edge, Graeme	GE-TT14. TechnologyTell.com. March 18, 2014. "Breathe Deep, The Moody Blues Cruise: Graeme Edge Gets Moody," by Howard Whitman, 2014.
Edge, Graeme	GE-TWN15. "More from *The Beat*'s interview with Graeme Edge of The Moody Blues," posted April 8, 2015.
Edge, Graeme	GE-MMCD15. *Magnificent Moody Blues* 50th Anniversary CD Set, 2015, pamphlet by Mark Powell.
Fiala, Danny	DF-NME72. *New Musical Express*, November 4, 1972, "Doug Jones on the Road with the Moody Blues," by Doug Jones.
Freeman, Alan	AF-MS67. marmalade-skies,co.uk, 1967 page.
Galley, Mel	MG-GM94. *Goldmine*, November 11, 1994, "Trapeze: Flying High (Once Again) With the Greatest of Ease," by Lisa L. Barker.
Gibson, "Hoot"	HG-SNDS96. *Second #37*, 1996, "Capt. Robert 'Hoot' Gibson, U.S.N.," interviewed by George Petros.
Goodman, Norman	NG-H&H96. *Higher & Higher, #31*, Summer 1996, "The Making of *Long Distance Voyager*."
Graves, Peter	PG-R93. *Rag*, July 1993, "The Moody Blues," by Jim Varsallone.
Greenland, Mike	MG-H&H94. *Higher & Higher, #21 & 22*, Summer 1994, "The Whispers & All Things Bright – The Early Pro Bands," by Mark Murley.
Gurvitz, Adrian	AG-S74. *Sounds*, July 20, 1974, "Edging His Bets," by Bill Henderson.
Hayward, Justin	JH-TB65/66. *Newspaper clipping*, likely the *Daily Mirror* (London,

England), mid-to-late December 1965. (Courtesy Tony Brown.)

Hayward, Justin	JH-TP67. *Top Pops*, November 25, 1967, "Gordon Coxhill Meets the Moody Blues," by Gordon Coxhill.
Hayward, Justin	JH-RM68. GE-RM68. *Disc and Music Echo*, January 13, 1968, "Moodies Dislike Charts," by Derek Boltwood.
Hayward, Justin	JH-CM68. *Croydon Midweek* (England), March 19, 1968, "Making Money Is A Gas, But It's Secondary," by Sandra Grant. (Courtesy Tony Brown.)
Hayward, Justin	JH-DME68. *Disc and Music Echo*, August 24, 1968, "Moodies Haven't Got the Blues Any More."
Hayward, Justin	JH-NME68. *New Musical Express*, August 31, 1968, "Moody Blues Full of Surprises," by Richard Green.
Hayward, Justin	JH-HP69. *Hit Parader*, May 1969, "The Moody Blues Visit America."
Hayward, Justin	JH-MM69. *Record Mirror*, May 10, 1969, "Getting Better All the Time," by Derek Boltwood.
Hayward, Justin	JH-NME69. *New Musical Express*, May 17, 1969, "Surprisingly, Moodies Miss Screams," by Richard Green.
Hayward, Justin	JH-NME69a. *New Musical Express*, September 20, 1969, "Moodies Write for You."
Hayward, Justin	JH-MM69. *Melody Maker*, November 1969, "New Blood on Moody's Label," by Richard Williams.
Hayward, Justin	JH-MM70. *Melody Maker*, January 3, 1970, interview with Justin Hayward, by Royston Eldridge.
Hayward, Justin	JH-F70, *Fabulous 208*, February 14, 1970, "Justin The Moody Blue," by Georgina Mells.
Hayward, Justin	JH-NME70. *New Musical Express*, February 21, 1970, "Doing a Moody: Justin Hayward," by Richard Green.
Hayward, Justin	JH-DME70. *Disc and Music Echo*, May 9, 1970, "How Justin Beat the Yokel Image," by Penny Valentine.
Hayward, Justin	JH-DME70a. *Disc and Music Echo*, May 30, 1970, "The Business of Being Moody," by David Hughes.
Hayward, Justin	JH-RM70. *Record Mirror*, October 10, 1970, "Why Do People Get Moody About the Moodies?" by Keith Altham.
Hayward, Justin	JH-HP71. *Hit Parader*, June 1971, "Moody Blues … From the Beginning," by Nancy Erlich.
Hayward, Justin	JH-NME72. *New Musical Express*, November 4, 1972, "Doug Jones on the Road with the Moody Blues," by Doug Jones.
Hayward, Justin	JH-CGD72. *Casa Grande Dispatch* (Arizona), November 8, 1972, AP Wire story: "Tension Is Absent in Moody Blues," by Mary Campbell.
Hayward, Justin	JH-S73. *Sounds*, August 18, 1973, "The Moody Machine Returns," by Ray Hammond.
Hayward, Justin	JH-RM73. *Record Mirror*, September 1, 1973, "Justin and Four Brum Teds," by Rick Sanders.
Hayward, Justin	JH-T73. *Tambourine* magazine, November 26, 1973, "Moody Blues: Universal Experiences – Universal Sounds," by Daniel Goldberg.
Hayward, Justin	JH-MHF74. *Modern Hi-Fi & Stereo Guide*, March/April 1974, "What's Happening with the Moody Blues?" by Robert V. Weinstein.
Hayward, Justin	JH-MOBJ75. *The Making of Blue Jays*, 1975, Threshold Records.
Hayward, Justin	JH-NME75. *New Musical Express*, March 22, 1975, "The Importance of Being Ernest," by Tony Stewart.
Hayward, Justin	JH-SJ75. *The Salina Journal* (Kansas), May 5, 1975, "Moody Blues Not Breaking Up: Blue Jays Just a Side Project," by Kim Garfield.
Hayward, Justin	JH-MM75. *Melody Maker*, May 24, 1975, "We're the Biggest Underground Band."
Hayward, Justin	JH-BI75. JL-BI75, *Beat Instrumental*, June 1975, "Blue Jays: Moodies Going Solo!" by Chris Simmons.
Hayward, Justin	JH-CR75. *Circus*, August 1975, "Moody Blues – How Hayward

	& Lodge's BLUEJAYS Keep the Astral Band Aloft," by Peter Crescenti.
Hayward, Justin	JH-RM75. *Record Mirror*, October 11, 1975, "The Blue Jays Say: 'We've Always Been Years Ahead or Years Behind," by Peter Harvey.
Hayward, Justin	JH-ZZ76. *Zigzag*, January 1976, "The Moody Blues," by Andy Childs.
Hayward, Justin	JH-BI76. *Beat Instrumental*, January 1977, "Justin Hayward: In Search of the Lost Songwriter," by Tom Stock.
Hayward, Justin	JH-MM76. *Melody Maker*, January 29, 1977, "Blue Jays Dead – Justin Time!" by Ray Coleman.
Hayward, Justin	JH-RM76. *Record Mirror*, March 5, 1977, "Justin 'It's a Living' Hayward."
Hayward, Justin	JH-DP77. *Denver Post* (Colorado), May 22, 1977, "Hayward 'Changes Pace,' But for Lodge It's Reaffirmation," by Jared Johnson.
Hayward, Justin	JH-DP77a. *Denver Post* (Colorado), May 29, 1977, "Mood-ish Blues Drive Still Going Strong as Stars Do Their Own Thing," by Jared Johnson.
Hayward, Justin	JH-C77. *Crawdaddy*, August 1977, Moody Blues: Why They Sang the Blues," by Susan Ahrens.
Hayward, Justin	JH-R77. *Rock*, September 1977, "Justin Hayward: Not Very Moody and Anything But Blue," by Jon Tiven.
Hayward, Justin	JH-TS78. *The Sun* (London, England), August 5, 1978, interview with Justin and Marie Hayward.
Hayward, Justin	JH-MM78. *Melody Maker*, July 15, 1978, "Why the Moodies Re-formed," by Ray Coleman.
Hayward, Justin	JH-TT78. *The Town Talk* (Alexandria, Louisiana), July 22, 1978, Associated Press write story: "Moody Blues Regroup," by James Simon.
Hayward, Justin	JH-SFE&C78. *The San Francisco Examiner & Chronicle*, July 23, 1978, "The Moodiest of the Moody Blues Is Justin Hayward," by Bart Mills.
Hayward, Justin	JH-S78. *Sounds*, July 29, 1978, "After the Goldrush," by Donna McAllister.
Hayward, Justin	JH-MS78. *The Minneapolis Star* (Minnesota), November 3, 1978, "Disciples Get Moodies to Tour," by Jon Bream.
Hayward, Justin	JH-CE78. *The Cincinnati Enquirer* (Ohio), November 7, 1978, "Moody Blues on Second Honeymoon," by Cliff Radel.
Hayward, Justin	JH-DFP78. *Detroit Free Press*, November 9, 1978, "Moody Blues Begin Long Road Back," by Linda Barber.
Hayward, Justin	JH-SP78. *Star-Phoenix* (Saskatoon, Saskatchewan, Canada), November 29, 1978, Canadian Press wire story: "Moody Blues Reunited with New Album, Tour."
Hayward, Justin	JH-IJ78. *The Ithaca Journal* (New York), December 29, 1978, Associated Press wire story: "Moody Blues Are Together Again After Failing Attempts to Go Solo," by Yardena Arar.
Hayward, Justin	JH-SDP79. *Scottsdale Daily Progress* (Arizona), May 18, 1979, "The Moody Blues Back Together Again," by Gary Houy.
Hayward, Justin	JH-MM79. *Melody Maker*, May 26, 1979, "The Moody Blues: It's a Wonderful Life," by Chris Welch.
Hayward, Justin	JH-G79. *Groove* magazine, November 1979, "Will They Play Forever?" by Jon Marlowe.
Hayward, Justin	JH-LE80. *Liverpool Echo*, July 2, 1980, "Moody Blue Who Likes Going Solo," by Peter Trollope.
Hayward, Justin	JH-TA80. *The Aquarian*, November 12, 1980, "Justin Hayward Strikes New Notes on Night Flight," by Bruce Eber.
Hayward, Justin	JH-OTR81. *Off the Record*, Westwood One, December 1981, interview with Justin Hayward.
Hayward, Justin	JH-BBC81. BBC radio, 1981, Anne Nightingale's interview with Justin

	Hayward.
Hayward, Justin	JH-LAT81. *The Los Angeles Times*, June 21, 1981, "Voyaging Into Commercial Pop," by Dennis Hunt.
Hayward, Justin	JH-US81. *Us*, September 1, 1981, "Moody," by Mark Morrison.
Hayward, Justin	JH-MW83. *Music Week*, September 3, 1983, "The Moody Blues," by Chris Welch.
Hayward, Justin	JH-BG83. *The Boston Globe*, October 1983, "Moody Blues: 'Now We're Like Family,'" by Steve Morse.
Hayward, Justin	JH-USAT83. *USA Today*, October 24, 1983, "Moody Blues Stay Tuned to Cosmic Rock," by Lloyd Sachs.
Hayward, Justin	JH-H&H84. *Higher & Higher, #2*, Summer 1984, "Justin Hayward: A Personal Sojourn," by Rosary Grande.
Hayward, Justin	JH-KR84. *Kerrang!*, November 29, 1984, "The Story of the Moody Blues," by Malcolm Dome.
Hayward, Justin	JH-T85. *Tracks*, November 1985, "Mountain Man," by Justin Hayward.
Hayward, Justin	JH-OTR86. *Off the Record*, Westwood One, May 10, 1986, interview with Justin Hayward & John Lodge; host Joe Benson.
Hayward, Justin	JH-JG86. *Journal-Gazette*, June 21, 1986, "Twenty-Year Rockers Rarely Have the Blues," by Troy Cozad.
Hayward, Justin	JH-CT86. *Chicago Tribune*, July 3, 1986, "Graying Moody Blues Still a Rockin' Roll," by Bill Lohmann.
Hayward, Justin	JH-DFP86. *Detroit Free Press* (Michigan), July 6, 1986, "Moody Blues Stay in Rock Race," by Gary Graff.
Hayward, Justin	JH-USAT86. *USA Today*, July 18, 1986, "Back in the Mood for the Moody Blues," by John Milward.
Hayward, Justin	JH-TU86. *Times Union* (Albany, New York), July 18, 1986, "Thriving on Change," by Sean Daly.
Hayward, Justin	JH-PD86. *Post-Dispatch* (St. Louis, Missouri), July 26, 1986, "The Moody Blues Are Making a Comeback," by Louise King.
Hayward, Justin	JH-LAT86. *The Los Angeles Times*, August 17, 1986, "Hayward Sings the Blues' Praises," by Dennis Hunt.
Hayward, Justin	JH-SFC86. *San Francisco Chronicle*, August 24, 1986, "Moody Blues Picks Up Where It Left Off," by Tom Lahham.
Hayward, Justin	JH-P86. *Performance*, September 19, 1986, "The Moody Blues – Success Beyond Their Wildest Dreams," by Theodora Goebel.
Hayward, Justin	JH-WNEW87. *WNEW*, 1987, interview with Justin Hayward.
Hayward, Justin	JH-BB88. *Billboard*, July 8, 1988, "Moodys Are True Blue," by Jim Bessman.
Hayward, Justin	JH-RL88. *Rockline*, August 1, 1988, interview with Justin Hayward.
Hayward, Justin	JH-ND88. *Newsday* (Long Island, New York), August 7, 1988, "Moody Blues," by Wayne Robins.
Hayward, Justin	JH-AJ88. *Albuquerque Journal* (New Mexico), September 23, 1988, Christian Science Monitor wire story: "Moody Blues's Style Finds Younger Fans," by Shiv Cariappa.
Hayward, Justin	JH-C88. *Creem*, October 1988, "The Moody Blues Get Rhythm," by Hank Bordowitz.
Hayward, Justin	JH-CD88. *The Columbus Dispatch* (Ohio), October 21, 1988, "Popularity Timeless for Songs, Sounds of the Moody Blues," by T.C. Brown.
Hayward, Justin	JH-AJC88. *The Atlanta Journal and Constitution* (Georgia), November 3, 1988, "Moody Blues Respond to the Curiosity Among Youth About the Vintage 1960s," by Russ DeVault.
Hayward, Justin	JH-OS88. *The Orlando Sentinel* (Florida), November 6, 1988, "Moody Blues," by Thom Duffy.
Hayward, Justin	JH-MM88. *Music Makers*, December 1988, "Questions of Balance," by Kevin Berger.

Hayward, Justin	JH-WMS88. *Wilmington Morning Star* (North Carolina), December 23, 1988, *New York Times* Regional Newspapers: "Blues Singing Through Generations," by Randy A. Salas.
Hayward, Justin	JH-H&H90. *Higher & Higher*, #15, Winter 1990, "The Justin Hayward Interview," by June Price.
Hayward, Justin	JH-MBS90. *The Moody Blues Story*, Unistar, February 17, 1990, hosted by Ray Sciaky, with Hayward and Lodge.
Hayward, Justin	JH-Q90. *Q*, April 1990, "Moody Blues: Step This Way…," by Tom Hibbert.
Hayward, Justin	JH-OC91. *Orange Coast* (Orange County, California), August 1991, "The Moody Blues' Timeless Journey," by Keith Tuber.
Hayward, Justin	JH-CT91. *Chicago Tribune* (Illinois), August 5, 1991, "Their Days of Future Passed," by Dennis Polkow.
Hayward, Justin	JH-IPT91. *Idaho Press-Tribune*, August 13, 1991, Associated Press wire story: "The Moody Blues: The Days of the Future Have Yet to Pass," by Mary Campbell.
Hayward, Justin	JH-JEN91. *Jam Entertainment News*, August 23, 1991, "Justin Hayward: The Jam Interview," by June Price.
Hayward, Justin	JH-ABJ91. *The Orlando Sentinel* (Florida), August 23, 1991, "Moody Blues Still Upbeat About Their Music," by Jim Abbott.
Hayward, Justin	JH-DP91. *Denver Post* (Colorado), "Moody Blues Spans Eras at Red Rocks," by G. Brown.
Hayward, Justin	JH-ET91. *Entertainment Tonight*, July 2, 1991, interview with Justin Hayward and John Lodge.
Hayward, Justin	JH-PFM91. *Performance*, October 11, 1991, "Keys of the Moody Blues Kingdom," by Debi Moen.
Hayward, Justin	JH-MH91. *The Miami Herald* (Florida), December 13, 1991, "Bare-bones Moody Blues Try to Recapture Their Roots," by Mario Tarradell.
Hayward, Justin	JH-DO92. *The Daily Oklahoman*, March 25, 1992, "Music Older, Wiser, Moody Blues Singer Says," by Bernice McShane.
Hayward, Justin	JH-MC92. *The Morning Call* (Allentown, Pennsylvania), June 21, 1992, "Moody Blues-Chicago Tour a Question of Balance," by D.L. Courville.
Hayward, Justin	JH-AS92. *The Anniston Sun* (Alabama), July 23, 1992, "Moodies Trust Own Judgment," by Norman Welch.
Hayward, Justin	JH-PASB92. *Press and Sun-Bulletin* (Binghamton, New York), July 24, 1992, "A Change in Moody," by Gene Grey.
Hayward, Justin	JH-RN92. *Recovery Network* newsletter, September 1992, interview with Justin Hayward by Colleen Joy.
Hayward, Justin	JH-H&H93. *Higher & Higher*, #18 & 19, Winter/Spring 1993, "Hayward on Red Rocks," by Alan Stock.
Hayward, Justin	JH-OS93. *The Orlando Sentinel* (Florida), June 11, 1993, "Moody Blues Find New Outlet with Orchestra," by Jim Abbott.
Hayward, Justin	JH-LVS93. *Las Vegas Sun* (Nevada), September 24, 1993, "The Moody Blues Orchestrating a Long-Running Career," by Rick Velotta.
Hayward, Justin	JH-H&H94. *Higher & Higher*, #21 & 22, Summer 1994, "A Wilde Year," by Shelia Johnson.
Hayward, Justin	JH-H&H94a. *Higher & Higher*, #21 & 22, Summer 1994, "The Recovery Network Interview, by Colleen Joy.
Hayward, Justin	JH-GM94. *Goldmine, Vol. 20, No. 22*, October 28, 1994, "The Moody Blues: Veteran Cosmic Rockers," by Bruce Eder.
Hayward, Justin	JH-DM94. *Daily Mail* (London, England), November 19, 1994, "I Loved Being the 'Prettiest Man' in Pop Music," by Justin Hayward.
Hayward, Justin	JH-GW93. *Guitar World*, July 1993, "The Moody Dude," by Andy Aledort.
Hayward, Justin	JH-PS95. *The Performing Songwriter*, July/August 1995, "The Long

	Distance Voyage of Moody Blues' Justin Hayward," by Bill DeMain.
Hayward, Justin	JH-GP95. *Guitar Player*, September 1995, "Moody Blues: Still Searching for the Lost Chord," by Chuck Crisafulli.
Hayward, Justin	JH-SNDS95. *Seconds*, October 1995, "The Moody Blues," by George Peters.
Hayward, Justin	JH-H&H96. *Higher & Higher, #31*, Summer 1996, "The Making of *Long Distance Voyager*," "Hayward Solo Album Delayed," by Mark Murley.
Hayward, Justin	JH-TR96. *Tribune-Review* (Pittsburgh, Pennsylvania), June 6, 1996, "Leary Death a Moody Flashback," by George Varga.
Hayward, Justin	JH-HC96. *Hartford Courant* (Connecticut), June 12, 1996, "Future, Past Merge in Fully Orchestral Moody Blues Tour," by Roger Catlin.
Hayward, Justin	JH-IS96. *The Indianapolis Star* (Indiana), June 16, 1996, "Moody Blues Revives 'Legend of a Mind,'" by Marc Allen.
Hayward, Justin	JH-TRKS96. *Tracks*, Fall 1996, "Justin Hayward," by Lisa Ludwick.
Hayward, Justin	JH-H&H96. *Higher & Higher, #32*, Fall 1996, "His Views on *The Hill*: Hayward on the New Album," interview by Lisa Ludwick.
Hayward, Justin	JH-SC96. *Sound Check*, November 1996, "Hayward's *View From the Hill*: Seamless Artistry, Innovative Arrangements, by Deborah Courville.
Hayward, Justin	JH-RC96. *The Record Collector*, November 1996, "Justin Hayward Interview," by John Reed.
Hayward, Justin	JH-SM96. *Songwriter's Monthly*, November 1996, "Justin Hayward, Part One: *The View From the Hill*."
Hayward, Justin	JH-LAT96. *The Los Angeles Times*, December 2, 1996, "Riding a Seesaw Between the Moody Blues and a Solo Career," by Buddy Seigal.
Hayward, Justin	JH-WPCH97. WPCH (Atlanta), 1997, Hayward interviewed by Steve Gross, early 1997.
Hayward, Justin	JH-HT97. *Hot Tickets*, March 6, 1997, "Justin Hayward of the Moody Blues On..."
Hayward, Justin	JH-GM97. *Goldmine*, May 23, 1997, "Justin Hayward of the Moody Blues," by Geof O'Keefe.
Hayward, Justin	JH-GH97. *Good Housekeeping,* April 1997, "And I Love You."
Hayward, Justin	JH-DM97. *Daily Mail* (London, England), May 24, 1997, "Justin Hayward."
Hayward, Justin	JH-SPI97. *Seattle Post-Intelligencer* (Washington), June 6, 1997, "Hindsight Alters Moody Blues' View of Leary Tribute," by Gene Stout.
Hayward, Justin	JH-HL97. *Highlands*, November 1997, "Justin Hayward Interview, 5th November, Nice," by Didier Gonzalez.
Hayward, Justin	JH-HL98. *Highland*, October 1998, "Interview: Justin Hayward," from September 5, 1998, by Marie-Josée Jimenez and Didier Gonzalez.
Hayward, Justin	JH-H&H98. *Higher & Higher, #39 & 40*, Winter 1998/Spring 1999, "The Making of *The Present*," by Mark Murley.
Hayward, Justin	JH-RL99. *Rockline*, August 4, 1999, with Bob Coburn, interviewing Hayward and Lodge.
Hayward, Justin	JH-ACT99. *Asheville Citizen-Times* (North Carolina), August 15, 1999, "*Strange Times* with the Moody Blues," by Alan Sculley.
Hayward, Justin	JH-GM99. *Goldmine*, August 27, 1999, "The Moody Blues Back on Track with First New Album Since 1991," by Bruce Eder.
Hayward, Justin	JH-PL99. *The Patriot Ledger* (Quincy, Massachusetts), August 28, 1999, "Moody Blues Capture Band's Spirit in These *Strange Times*."
Hayward, Justin	JH-WP99. *Washington Post*, September 3, 1999, "Spotlight: Moody Blues On the Upswing."

Hayward, Justin	JH-TR99. *The Record* (Berger County, New Jersey), September 3, 1999, "More Moody than Ever."
Hayward, Justin	JH-WT99. *The Washington Times*, September 8, 1999, "*Strange Times for Moody Blues.*"
Hayward, Justin	JH-RD99. RockDaily.com, September 24, 1999, "Moody Blues Profiled on Rock Daily.com, interviewed by Steve Reynolds.
Hayward, Justin	JH-GTYR99. "Go to Your Room" website, classicrockdaily.com, September 26, 1999 posting of interview with Justin Hayward.
Hayward, Justin	JH-HL99. *Highlands' Moody Blues Special Edition*, December 17, 1999, "Justin Hayward: Interview, Part 3," by Marie-Josée Jimenez and Didier Gonzalez.
Hayward, Justin	JH-NWE00. Interviewed by Robert Silverstein for mwe3.com in Winter, 2000.
Hayward, Justin	JH-10CG00, *20th Century Guitar Magazine*, April 2000, "Moody Blues: Still Walking on Air," by Robert Silverstein.
Hayward, Justin	JH-OM00. *Outré Magazine*, August 2000, "Interview with Justin Hayward."
Hayward, Justin	JH-H&H01. *Higher & Higher, #44*, Fall 2001, "Journey into Amazing Music," by Mark Murley.
Hayward, Justin	JH-HL02. *Highland's Moody Blues Special Edition*, 2002, with Didier Gonzalez's interview with Justin Hayward from March 12, 1997.
Hayward, Justin	JH-RC03. *The Record Collector*, February 2003, "The Voice of the Moody Blues Reflects in His Colourful Career."
Hayward, Justin	JH-MC03. *Music Connection*, December 8, 2003, "A Moody Blues Christmas," by Dan Kimpel.
Hayward, Justin	JH-H&H04. *Higher & Higher*, Spring-Summer, 2004, "The Making of a Dream," by Mark Murley; "Hayward on Threshold," interviewed by Mark Murley.
Hayward, Justin	JH-CR04. *Classic Rock*, December 2004, "Justin Hayward," interviewed by Hugh Fielder.
Hayward, Justin	JH-SWCD04. *Songwriter*, issued in 2004, remastered edition, with booklet by Mark Powell.
Hayward, Justin	JH-CA:TMB06. *Classic Artists: The Moody Blues*, 2009, Empire Media Holdings SL, Impact Film Sales Ltd..
Hayward, Justin	JH-CA07. BB-CA07. *Classic Artists: The Moody Blues*, April 24, 2007 (Image Entertainment).
Hayward, Justin	JH-GM08. *Goldmine*, December 5, 2008, "The Moody Blues Live," by Conrad L. Stinnett.
Hayward, Justin	JH-EGBDFCD08. *Every Good Boy Deserves Favour*, issued 2008, remastered edition, with booklet by Mark Powell.
Hayward, Justin	JH-QOBCD08. *A Question of Balance,* issued 2008, remastered edition, with booklet by Mark Powell.
Hayward, Justin	JH-SSCD08. *Seventh Sojourn*, issued 2008, remastered edition, with booklet by Mark Powell.
Hayward, Justin	JH-RC12. *Record Collector*, May/June 2012, "The Moody Blues," by Harvey Kubernik.
Hayward, Justin	JH-GM12. *Goldmine*, June 12, 2012, "Revisit the Moody Blues' Landmark Album, *Days of Future Passed.*"
Hayward, Justin	JH-TB13. www.TheBlog.com, February 9, 2013, "A Conversation with Justin Hayward," by Mike Ragogna.
Hayward, Justin	JH-SS13. Sammy Sultan interview with Justin Hayward, February 9, 2013, YouTube (Hotseat Entertainment).
Hayward, Justin	JH-PROG13. *PROG*, March 2013, "The Moody Blues."
Hayward, Justin	JH-SF13. Justin Hayward interviewed for songfacts, posted March 19,

	2013.
Hayward, Justin	JH-GM13. *Goldmine*, April 2013, "Moody Bluegrass," by Mike Greenblatt.
Hayward, Justin	JH-RS13. *Rock Society*, May/June 2013, "The Moody Blues: A Question of Balance."
Hayward, Justin	JH-PROG13a. *PROG*, June 2013, "Q&A: Justin Hayward," by Malcolm Dome.
Hayward, Justin	JH-GC13. www.grammy.com, December 11, 2013, "Nights in White Satin," interview with Justin Hayward, as told to John Sutton-Smith.
Hayward, Justin	JH-TB13. "A Conversation with Justin Hayward," by Mike Ragogna.
Hayward, Justin	JH-ERE13. Eaglerockent.com, 2013, "Justin Hayward – *Spirits of Western Skies*," by Jeb Wright.
Hayward, Justin	JH-ZOL14. "Exclusive Interview: Justin Hayward of the Moody Blues Talks Cruise Tour, Roger Daltrey, and Isle of Wight Festival."
Hayward, Justin	JH-UC14. *Uncut*, November 21, 2014, "The Making of The Moody Blues' 'Nights In White Satin.'"
Hayward, Justin	JH-MC15. *The Morning Call* (Allentown, Pennsylvania), August 23, 2015, "He's Just a Singer in a Rock 'n' Roll Band," by John J. Moser.
Hayward, Justin	JH-SWU16. Songwriteruniverse.com, January 4, 2016, "Legendary Artist Justin Hayward of the Moody Blues Talks about His Classic Song 'Nights in White Satin,' and His Other Hits," by Dale Kawashima.
Hayward, Justin	JH-MBT16. www.themoodybluestoday.com, September 19, 2016, "Wyatt Wendale interviews Justin Hayward for Planet Radio," posted on TheMoodyBluesToday.com.
Hayward, Justin	JH-FGPO16. "The Moody Blues' Justin Hayward Goes *All the Way*," by Gary Graff.
Hayward, Justin	JH-OFO16. otten.freeshell.org/moodyblues, updated 2016.
Hayward, Justin	JH-GM17. *Goldmine*, February 2017, "Justin's Moods," by Lee Zimmerman.
Hayward, Justin	JH-RC17. *Rockcellar* magazine, April 13, 2017, "Justin Hayward's 'Stage Door' – Conversation with the Moody Blues Legend," by Ken Sharp.
Hayward, Justin	JH-CB. www.classicbands.com, no date posted, "Gary James' Interview with Justin Hayward of The Moody Blues."
Hayward, Marie	MH-GH97. *Good Housekeeping,* April 1997, "And I Love You."
Hayward, Marie	MH-DM97. *Daily Mail* (London, England), May 24, 1997, "Justin Hayward."
Hoff, Gerry	GH-HP71. *Hit Parader*, June 1971, "Moody Blues … From the Beginning," by Nancy Erlich.
Hughes, Glenn	GH-SVT94. *St. Cloud Times*, June 3, 1994, Gannett News Service wire story: "Reunion Summer Nets Another '70s Band in Trapeze."
Hughes, Glenn	GH-GM94. *Goldmine*, November 11, 1994, "Trapeze: Flying High (Once Again) With the Greatest of Ease," by Lisa L. Barker.
Hughes, Glenn	GH-RC99. *Record Collector*, May 1999, "The Voice of Rock!," by Tim Jones.
Hulett, Tom	TH-P86. *Performance*, September 19, 1986, "The Moody Blues – Success Beyond Their Wildest Dreams," by Theodora Goebel.
Jackman, Greg	GJ-H&H96. *Higher & Higher*, *#31*, Summer 1996, "The Making of *Long Distance Voyager*."
Jackman, Greg	GJ-H&H98. *Higher & Higher*, *#39 & 40*, Winter 1998/Spring 1999,

"The Making of *The Present*," by Mark Murley.

Jackson, Peter	PJ-C72. *Circus*, December 1972, "Inside the Moody Blues' American Miracle," by Ward Beaverman.
Jackson, Peter	PJ-PS00. *Pollstar*, 2000-20001 Edition, "Exclusive Interview: Peter Jackson, Idaho Center."
James, Nicky	NJ-CA07. BB-CA07. *Classic Artists: The Moody Blues*, April 24, 2007 (Image Entertainment).
Kaplan, Richard	RK-TO14. *Tape Op*, September/October 2014, "Indigo Ranch: Richard Kaplan and Mike Pinder on Operating Malibu's Legendary Studio in the 70s & 80s," by Larry Crane.
King, Jonathan	JK-MM80. *Melody Maker*, February 9, 1980, "Death of an Old-School Capitalist," by Michael Watts.
Kudrna, Gary	GK-H&H94. *Higher & Higher, #20*, Winter/Spring 1994, "The Sound Behind the Moodies," by Wendie Old.
Laine, Denny	DL-BP64. *The Birmingham Planet*, June 11, 1964, "The Moody Blues Five," by Mary McGrane.
Laine, Denny	DL-NME65a. *New Musical Express*, January 15, 1965, "Moody Blues Are Really Quite Happy," by Ian Dove.
Laine, Denny	DL-DM65. *Daily Mirror*, January 19, 1965, "It's Go Now with the Moody Blues – They're Tops," by Patrick Doncaster.
Laine, Denny	DL-BEM65. *Birmingham Evening Mail*, January 19, 1965, "Moody Group Anything But Blue Today."
Laine, Denny	DL-RM65. *Record Mirror*, January 23, 1965, "Anyone Can Make the Top Ten," by Christine Osbourne.
Laine, Denny	DL-DW65. *Disc Weekly*, January 23, 1965, "Brum Is Still Home!' Say the Chart-Topping Moody Blues," by Ted Scott.
Laine, Denny	DL-NME65b. *New Musical Express*, February 12, 1965, "Top Ten by The Moody Blues."
Laine, Denny	DL-R65. *Rave*, March 1, 1965, "The m'm'moody blues boys," by Lyn Carnell.
Laine, Denny	DL-RM65. *Record Mirror*, April 10, 1965, "'How the Beatles Helped Us,' Say the Moody Blues," by Richard Green.
Laine, Denny	DL-R65a. *Rave*, May 1, 1965, "Getting the Blues in Paris," by Maureen O'Grady.
Laine, Denny	DL-RM65a. *Record Mirror*, June 19, 1965, "Story Behind That Scream," by Richard Green.
Laine, Denny	DL-RM65b. *Record Mirror*, October 30, 1965, "Moodies Lose Out to Brian Epstein!"
Laine, Denny	DL-SS73. *Senior Scholastic*, September 27, 1973, "On the Road with Paul McCartney," by Ed Sparn.
Laine, Denny	DL-GM94. *Goldmine, Vol. 20, No. 22*, October 28, 1994, "The Moody Blues: Veteran Cosmic Rockers," by Bruce Eder.
Laine, Denny	DL-H&H97. *Higher & Higher #36*, Fall 1997, "The *Higher & Higher* Denny Laine Interview, Part 1," by Mark Murley.
Laine, Denny	DL-H&H97a. *Higher & Higher #37*, Fall 1997, "The *Higher & Higher* Denny Laine Interview, Part 2," by Mark Murley.
Laine, Denny	DL-WS01. From www.wingspan.ru, January 2001, "An Interview with Denny Laine."
Laine, Denny	DL-BOTR03. *Band on the Run: A History of Paul McCartney and*

	Wings, by Garry McGee (Taylor Trade Publishing, 2003).
Laine, Denny	DL-CA07. BB-CA07. *Classic Artists: The Moody Blues*, April 24, 2007 (Image Entertainment).
Laine Denny	DL-RM09. From review-mag.com, 2009, "Moody Blues, Paul McCartney and Japanese Tears: The Denny Laine Interview."
Laine, Denny	DL-G10. From www.gibson.com, July 1, 2010, "The Gibson Interview – Denny Laine (Part One)," by Michael Wright.
Laine, Denny	DL-BB13. From www.brumbeat.net/dlaine, March 2013, "Denny Laine, Birmingham," article by John R. Woodhouse, with contributions from Nick Warburton.
Laine, Denny	DL-MMCD15. *Magnificent Moody Blues* 50th Anniversary CD Set, 2015, pamphlet by Mark Powell.
Laine, Denny	DL-HT17. Heraldtribune.com, March 29, 2017, "Denny Laine Talks Wings, Moody Blues Before Blue Rooster Show," by Jimmy Geurts.
Laine, Denny	DL-MNT. MiamaNewTimes.com, March 30, 2017, "Denny Laine Talks Moody Blues, Wings, and Never Retiring," by Celia Almeida.
Laine, Denny	DL-TH17. Tallahassee.com, September 21, 2017, interview with Denny Laine by Mark Hinson.
Laine, Denny	DL-HC17. From Hit-Channel.com, 2017, "Interview: Denny Laine (solo, Wings, Moody Blues)."
Lambert, Dennis	DL-H&H96. *Higher & Higher, #32*, Fall 1996, "The Making of *The View From the Hill*," by Mark Murley.
Leach, David	DL-BB86. *Billboard*, September 13, 1986, "Moody Blues, ELP Enjoy Renewed Success," by Steve Gett.
Levenson, Bill	BL-H&H94. *Higher & Higher, Vol. 23*, Fall 1994, "*Time Traveller*: The Story Behind the New Moodies Boxed Set," by Randy A. Salas.
Lewis, Jim	JL-BB86. *Billboard*, September 13, 1986, "Moody Blues, ELP Enjoy Renewed Success," by Steve Gett.
Lodge, John	JL-NME69. *New Musical Express*, September 20, 1969, "Moodies Write for You."
Lodge, John	JL-NME70. *New Musical Express*, January 17, 1970, "Moodies Success Secret Is Teamwork," by Richard Green.
Lodge, John	JL-NME70a. *New Musical Express*, February 28, 1970, "Doing A Moodie: John Lodge," by Richard Green.
Lodge, John	JL-RW70. *Record Mirror*, May 23, 1970, "The Moody Blues: When Is a Single Not a Single?" by Keith Altham.
Lodge, John	JL-C70. *Circus*, August 1970, "The Moody Blues: Gentle, Smooth and Nice."
Lodge, John	JL-NME70a. *New Musical Express*, September 13, 1970, "Moodies Act as Music Guides," by Richard Green.
Lodge, John	JL-NME71. *New Musical Express*, July 31, 1971, "Moodies Musical Advance," by Richard Green.
Lodge, John	JL-RS71. *Rolling Stone*, September 16, 1971, "The Moody Blues" "What's Trite?" by Andrew Bailey.
Lodge, John	JL-KP71. *Kingston Post*, November 11, 1971, "Moody Blues Are Noted for Simple Honesty, with Judy Hugg's review of *EGBDF*.
Lodge, John	JL-RM72. *Record Mirror*, April 22, 1972, "The Moody Blues," by Hal Speck.
Lodge, John	JL-S72. *Sounds*, June 3, 1972, "Moodies: Isn't Life Strange?" by Penny Valentine.
Lodge, John	JL-MS72. *Music Scene*, November 1972, "A Family of Moodies," by

Tony Norman.

Lodge, John	JL-RS72. *Rolling Stone*, December 21, 1972, "In Search of the Moody Blues," by James Horwitz.
Lodge, John	JL-DME73. *Disc and Music Echo*, August 25, 1973, "Coming Up the Hard Way: A Moody's View on the Struggle for Survival."
Lodge, John	JL-PV73. *The Popular Voice*, September 30, 1973, "Moody Blues, Happy Family."
Lodge, John	JL-MOBJ75. *The Making of Blue Jays*, 1975, Threshold Records.
Lodge, John	JL-SJ75. *The Salina Journal* (Kansas), May 5, 1975, "Moody Blues Not Breaking Up: Blue Jays Just a Side Project," by Kim Garfield.
Lodge, John	JL-MM75. JH-MM75. *Melody Maker*, May 24, 1975, "We're the Biggest Underground Band."
Lodge, John	JL-BI75, *Beat Instrumental*, June 1975, "Blue Jays: Moodies Going Solo!" by Chris Simmons.
Lodge, John	JL-CR75. *Circus*, August 1975, "Moody Blues – How Hayward & Lodge's BLUEJAYS Keep the Astral Band Aloft," by Peter Crescenti.
Lodge, John	JL-MM75. *Record Mirror*, November 22, 1975, "Blue, But Not Moody," by Peter Harvey.
Lodge, John	JL-ZZ76. *Zigzag*, January 1976, "The Moody Blues," by Andy Childs.
Lodge, John	JL-MM76. *Melody Maker*, January 29, 1977, "Lodge Finds a Natural Avenue," by Harry Doherty.
Lodge, John	JL-RM76. *Record Mirror*, March 5, 1977, "John 'Clean Living' Lodge."
Lodge, John	JL-DP77. *Denver Post* (Colorado), May 22, 1977, "Hayward 'Changes Pace,' But for Lodge It's Reaffirmation," by Jared Johnson.
Lodge, John	JL-DP77a. *Denver Post* (Colorado), May 29, 1977, "Mood-ish Blues Drive Still Going Strong as Stars Do Their Own Thing," by Jared Johnson.
Lodge, John	JL-V77. *Variety*, June 22, 1977, "Moody About Biz End of Disks."
Lodge, John	JL-C77. *Crawdaddy*, August 1977, Moody Blues: Why They Sang the Blues," by Susan Ahrens.
Lodge, John	JL-C78. *Circus* magazine, August 31, 1978, "Days of Future Passed?" by Mark Mehler.
Lodge, John	JL-PDN78. *Philadelphia Daily News* (Pennsylvania), November 22, 1978, "Encore for Moody Blues," by Jonathan Takiff.
Lodge, John	JL-OWH79. *Omaha World Herald* (Nebraska), May 12, 1979, "Moody Blues' Sound Still Basically Intact," by Steve Millburg.
Lodge, John	JL-DFP81. *Detroit Free Press* (Michigan), July 9, 1981, "Moody Blues Washes in on Wave of Romanticism," by Maryanne George.
Lodge, John	JL-C81. *Circus*, September 30, 1981, "Moody Blues Rock Again," by Richard Hogan.
Lodge, John	JL-S81. *Sounds*, October 31, 1981, "John Lodge Talks It Out."
Lodge, John	JL-TS83. *The Source*, November 1983, NBC, interview with John Lodge.
Lodge, John	JL-MW83. *Music Week*, September 3, 1983, "The Moody Blues," by Chris Welch.
Lodge, John	JL-K83. *Kerrang!* magazine (England), October 20, 1983, "Blues for You," by Malcolm Dome.
Lodge, John	JL-VP83. *The Vancouver Province* (Canada), November 18, 1983, "Moody Mellow," by Fiona McQuarrie.
Lodge, John	JL-GT84. *Good Times*, January 1, 1984, "Moody Blues Never Reaching the End," by Barry Millman.
Lodge, John	JL-OTR86. *Off the Record*, Westwood One, May 10, 1986, interview with Justin Hayward & John Lodge; host Joe Benson.
Lodge, John	JL-RL86. *Rockline*, June 30, 1986, interview with John Lodge.
Lodge, John	JL-OTR86. *Off the Record*, Westwood One, July 6, 1986, interview

	with John Lodge.
Lodge, John	JL-PDN86. *Philadelphia Daily News* (Pennsylvania), July 11, 1986, "Live! This Week," by Jonathan Takiff.
Lodge, John	JL-VND86. *Valley New Dispatch* (Tarentum, Pennsylvania), July 15, 1986, "Moody Blues Attracts Old Fans," by Rex Rutkoski.
Lodge, John	JL-USAT86. *USA Today*, July 18, 1986, "Back in the Mood for the Moody Blues," by John Milward.
Lodge, John	JL-SOMM86. John Lodge interview from "*Days of Future Passed*: The Story of the Moody Blues," August 11, 1986.
Lodge, John	JL-P86. *Performance*, September 19, 1986, "The Moody Blues – Success Beyond Their Wildest Dreams," by Theodora Goebel.
Lodge, John	JL-PC86. *Newspaper clipping* (unknown English publication), December 8, 1986, "Moodies Magic Back in Brum," by Paul Cole.
Lodge, John	JL-H&H88. *Higher & Higher #11 & 12*, Spring/Winter 1988, "John Lodge: Traveling the Natural Avenue," by Janet Tomey.
Lodge, John	JL-H&H88a. *Higher & Higher #11 & 12*, Spring/Winter 1988, "John Lodge: "John Lodge: The Story in His Eyes," by Kerry Fitzgerald.
Lodge, John	JL-BB88. *Billboard*, July 8, 1988, "Moodys Are True Blue," by Jim Bessman.
Lodge, John	JL-CE88. *The Cincinnati Enquirer* (Ohio), July 27, 1988, "Nights at the Gardens," by Cliff Radel.
Lodge, John	JL-C88. *Creem*, October 1988, "The Moody Blues Get Rhythm," by Hank Bordowitz.
Lodge, John	JL-CAM88. *Central Atlantic Musician*, December 1988, "A Conversation On the Music Biz with John Lodge of the Moody Blues."
Lodge, John	JL-TP89. *The Press* (Atlantic City, New Jersey), March 3, 1989, "Nightclubs in White Satin," by David J. Spatz.
Lodge, John	JL-TP89. *The Press* (Atlantic City, New Jersey), March 7, 1989, "Moody Blues' TropWorld Success Spotlight Casino Versatility," by David J. Spatz.
Lodge, John	JL-B89. *Billboard*, December 9, 1989, "Moodys On Threshold Again," by Melinda Newman.
Lodge, John	JL-MBS90. *The Moody Blues Story*, Unistar, February 17, 1990, hosted by Ray Sciaky, with Hayward and Lodge.
Lodge, John	JL-Q90. *Q*, April 1990, "Moody Blues: Step This Way…," by Tom Hibbert.
Lodge, John	JL-OC91. *Orange Coast* (Orange County, California), August 1991, "The Moody Blues' Timeless Journey," by Keith Tuber.
Lodge, John	JL-IPT91. *Idaho Press-Tribune*, August 13, 1991, Associated Press wire story: "The Moody Blues: The Days of the Future Have Yet to Pass," by Mary Campbell.
Lodge, John	JL-KG92. *Kalamazoo Gazette* (New York), October 4, 1992, "Groups Build on Basics," by Alexia Hayden, from same newspaper and writer, on October 8, 1992, "Old Friends Entertain Old Friends."
Lodge, John	JL-SP93. *Strauss' Place*, KTAR, Phoenix, Arizona, September 27, 1993, interview with John Lodge.
Lodge, John	JL-SLPD93. *St. Louis Post-Dispatch* (Missouri), July 25, 1993, "Crossover Style: '60s Group Starts a Trend," Paul A. Harris.
Lodge, John	JL-BCE94. *Battle Creek Enquirer* (Michigan), March 3, 1994, "Fantastic Drama," by Mark Schwerin.
Lodge, John	GP95. *Guitar Player*, September 1995, "Moody Blues: Still Searching for the Lost Chord," by Chuck Crisafulli.
Lodge, John	JL-SNDS95. *Seconds*, October 1995, "The Moody Blues," by George Peters.
Lodge, John	JL-RGJ95. *Reno Gazette-Journal* (Nevada), October 26, 1995, AP Wire story: "Golf, Rock 'n' Roll and Complications," by Mike Clark.
Lodge, John	JL-H&H96. *Higher & Higher, #31*, Summer 1996, "The Making of

	Long Distance Voyager."
Lodge, John	JL-H&H96. *Higher & Higher, #33*, Winter 1996, "The Making of Question of Balance," by Mark Murley.
Lodge, John	JL-H&H96. *Higher & Higher, #31*, Summer 1996, "New MB Album Underway."
Lodge, John	JL-BJ96. *The Beacon Journal* (Ohio), June 20, 1996, "Still Moody, Still Blues," by Kevin C. Johnson.
Lodge, John	JL-SCT96. *St. Cloud Times* (Minnesota), June 17, 1996, "Timothy Leary Lives, Moody Blues Now Sing," by Melanie Gilbert.
Lodge, John	JL-H&H96. *Higher & Higher, #32*, Fall 1996, "A 20th Anniversary Stroll Down ... *Natural Avenue*," by Mark Murley.
Lodge, John	JL-BF96. *Bass Frontiers*, November 1996, "John Lodge of the Moody Blues," by George A. Coelho.
Lodge, John	JL-AL97. *Argus-Leader* (Sioux Falls, South Dakota), June 12, 1997, "Blues in the Mood for Change," by Bob Keys.
Lodge, John	JL-DOFP97. *Days of Future Passed*, issued 1997, sleeve notes and interviews by John Reed.
Lodge, John	JL-H&H98. *Higher & Higher, #39 & 40*, Winter 1998/Spring 1999, "The Making of the Present," by Mark Murley; "John Lodge on TP," interviewed by Mark Murley.
Lodge, John	JL-WWM98. *Wildest Westerns Magazine*, 1998, "Unsung Hero: Jay Silverheels Remembered," by John Lodge.
Lodge, John	JL-H&H98/99. *Higher & Higher, #39 & 40*, Winder/Spring 1998/99, "MB Album Still on for '99."
Lodge, John	JL-RL99. *Rockline*, August 4, 1999, with Bob Coburn, interviewing Hayward and Lodge.
Lodge, John	JL-TD99. *Tallahassee Democrat* (Florida), August 13, 1999, "*Strange Times* for the Moody Blues," by Kati Schardi.
Lodge, John	JL-SLPD99. *St Louis Post-Dispatch* (Missouri), August 26, 1999, "Moody Blues Gets Back on Track," by Kevin C. Johnson.
Lodge, John	JL-GM99. *Goldmine*, August 27, 1999, "The Moody Blues Back on Track with First New Album Since 1991," by Bruce Eder.
Lodge, John	JL-10CG00, *20th Century Guitar Magazine*, April 2000, "Moody Blues: Still Walking on Air," by Robert Silverstein.
Lodge, John	JL-CH00. *Charisma*, September 2000, "John Lodge: Bass Force Behind the Moody Blues."
Lodge, John	JL-NWE00. Interviewed by Robert Silverstein for mwe3.com in Winter, 2000.
Lodge, John	JL-CA.TMB06. *Classic Artists: The Moody Blues*, 2009, Empire Media Holdings SL, Impact Film Sales Ltd..
Lodge, John	JL-CA07. *Moody Blues: Classic Artists*, April 24, 2007 (Image Entertainment).
Lodge, John	JL-ISOTLC08. *In Search of the Lost Chord*, 2008, remastered edition, with booklet by Mark Powell.
Lodge, John	JL-QOB08. *A Question of Balance,* issued 2008, remastered edition, with booklet by Mark Powell.
Lodge, John	JL-GM12. *Goldmine*, June 12, 2012, "Moody Blues Bassist John Lodge Looks Back on Days of Future Passed," by Lee Zimmerman.
Lodge, John	JL-PROG13. *PROG*, March 2013, "The Moody Blues."
Lodge, John	JL-RS13. *Rock Society*, May/June 2013, "The Moody Blues: A Question of Balance."
Lodge, John	JL-UC14. *Uncut*, November 21, 2014, "The Making of The Moody Blues' 'Nights In White Satin.'"
Lodge, John	JL-PROG15. *PROG* magazine, April 15, 2015, "King of Blue," by Paul Sexton.

Lodge, John	JL-SS15. *Sonic Shocks*, June 2015, "John Lodge," by Cristina Massei.
Madonia, Danilo	DM-H&H99. *Higher & Higher, #41*, Summer 1999 (out in September), "The Making of *Strange Times*," by Mark Murley.
Marshall, Gordon	GM-H&H93. *Higher & Higher, #18 & 19*, Winter/Spring 1993, "Rock 'n' Roll Thunder: A Talk with Gordon Marshall," by Jill Finan.
Martins, Adrian	AM-H&H97. *Higher & Higher, #35*, Summer 1997, "A Conversation with 'Classic 7' Engineer Adrian Martins," by Mark Murley.
Mattiussi, Jeanne	JM-BB93. *Billboard*, March 6, 1993, "PolyGram to Push Moody Blues Via PBS," by Greg Reibman.
McCartney, Paul	PM-NME71. *New Musical Express*, November 20, 1971, Paul McCartney Is Like a Man Who Has Dodged the Death Sentence," by Richard Green.
McCartney, Paul	PM-MM72. *Melody Maker*, December 2, 1972, "Mary Had a Little Lamb … Those Lyrics Are a Heavy Trip."
McCartney, Paul	PM-LAT73. *The Los Angeles Times*, August 31, 1973, "Paul Reliving the Beatles' Struggle with Wings Group," by Barbara Charone.
McCartney, Paul	PM-MM73. *Melody Maker*, December 1, 1973, "Paul McCartney," by Chris Welch.
McCartney, Paul	PM-BOTR03. *Band on the Run: A History of Paul McCartney and Wings*, by Garry McGee (Taylor Trade Publishing, 2003).
McCartney, Paul	PM-NCN. Nottingham *Campus News*, no date posted, found at Exchange.Nottingham.ac.uk.
McCormick, Derek	DM-SM67. *Sunday Mirror*, October 22, 1967, "Gear Change: Moodies Return with Millionaire Backer and Thirties Wardrobe," by Jack Bentley. (Article courtesy Tony Brown).
McCormick, Derek	DM-TJ67. *The Journal* (Newcastle, England), early November, 1967, "Making a Sound Investment." (Article courtesy Tony Brown).
McCormick, Derek	DM-HP70. *Hit Parader*, October 1970, "More Moody Blues News."
McCullough, Henry	HM-BOTR03. *Band on the Run: A History of Paul McCartney and Wings*, by Garry McGee (Taylor Trade Publishing, 2003).
Miller, Dave	DM-H&H94. *Higher & Higher, #21 & 22*, Summer 1994, "The Whispers & All Things Bright – The Early Pro Bands," by Mark Murley.
Mitchell, Gordon	GM-MBA12. Interviewed by Suzanne Rothberg, posted on website MoodyBluesAttitude on July 18, 2012.
Moraz, Patrick	PM-MM78. *Melody Maker*, September 30, 1978, "Moody Blues: Yes to the Moodies," by Chris Welch.
Moraz, Patrick	PM-MS78. *The Minneapolis Star*, November 6, 1978, "Moraz Adds Energy, More Rock to Mood of Moodies," by Jon Bream.
Moraz, Patrick	PM-LIT00. Let It Rock, demme.net, December 2000, interview with Patrick Moraz.
Moraz, Patrick	PM-DMN78. *Dallas Morning News*, December 10, 1978, "Moody Blues: Moraz May Move in as New Member," by Pete Oppel.
Moraz, Patrick	PM-IM81. *International Musician*, September 1981, "Patrick Moraz: Still Playing After All these Years," by Tom Stock.
Moraz, Patrick	PM-K81. *Keyboard*, November 1981, "Patrick Moraz."
Moraz, Patrick	PM-MW83. *Music Week*, September 3, 1983, "The Moody Blues," by

Chris Welch.

Moraz, Patrick	PM-H&H84. *Higher & Higher, #3*, Autumn 1984, A Canadian Interview with Patrick Moraz, by John Beaudoin.
Moraz, Patrick	PM-KCS86. *Kansas City Star*, July 1, 1986, "Moody Blues Push Message into '80s," by Brian McTavish.
Moraz, Patrick	PM-HC86. *Hartford Courant* (Connecticut), July 11, 1986, "Moody Blues Still Rolling with New Set of Listeners," by Frank Rizzo.
Moraz, Patrick	PM-PP86. *The Pittsburgh Press*, July 20, 1986, "Moody Blues: Rockin' 22 Years," by Pete Bishop.
Moraz, Patrick	PM-MH86. *The Miami Herald*, September 26, 1986, "Fans Still in Mood for Moodies," by Linda R. Thornton.
Moraz, Patrick	PM-MN86. *The Miami News* (Florida), "The Blues Aren't Moody Any More," by Deborah Walker.
Moraz, Patrick	PM-SDU88. *The San Diego Union* (California), August 19, 1988, "Virtuoso Saved Fading Blues: Keyboardist Creates Right Mood," by George Varga.
Moraz, Patrick	PM-RMN88. *Rocky Mountain News* (Denver, Colorado), September 2, 1988, "Album Leaves Member of Moody Blues Group Blue," by Justin Mitchell.
Moraz, Patrick	PM-ON88. *The Oshkosh Northwestern* (Wisconsin), September 25, 1988: Associated Press wire story: "Rock Band Hangs Together Despite Discord," Bill Beechum.
Moraz, Patrick	PM-K91. *Keyboard*, May 1991, interview with Patrick Moraz, by Robert L. Doerschuk.
Moraz, Patrick	PM-OS91. *The Orlando Sentinel* (Florida), "Life After the Moody Blues Upbeat," by Jim Abbott.
Murley, Mark	MM-H&H95a. *Higher & Higher, #26/27*, Summer 1995, "The Art of *TOCCC*," by Mark Murley.
Murray, Alex	AM-LP06. Correspondence, Alex Murray to Lucy Purdon, May 6, 2009.
Murray, Alex	AM-TB09. Correspondence, Alex Murray to Tony Brown, January 27, 2009.
Murray, Alex	AM-BB09. From brumbeat.net, 2009, "Alex Wharton – The Making of 'Go Now!'", by Bulls Head Bob.
Palmer, Phil	PP-H&H96. *Higher & Higher, #32*, Fall 1996, "The Making of *The View From the Hill*," by Mark Murley.
Parodi, Alberto	AP-H&H96. *Higher & Higher, #32*, Fall 1996, "Sur la Mer: A Visit to Mulinetti Studio," by Gian Antonio Cavanno.
Pinder, Mike	MP-NME65. *New Musical Express*, January 1, 1965, "Moody Blues Almost Gave Up!," by Ian Dove.
Pinder, Mike	MP-NME65a. *New Musical Express*, January 15, 1965, "Moody Blues Are Really Quite Happy," by Ian Dove.
Pinder, Mike	MP-RM65. *Record Mirror*, January 23, 1965, "Anyone Can Make the Top Ten," by Christine Osbourne.
Pinder, Mike	MP-DW65. *Disc Weekly*, January 23, 1965, "'Brum Is Still Home!' Say the Chart-Topping Moody Blues," by Ted Scott.
Pinder, Mike	MP-NME65b. *New Musical Express*, February 12, 1965, "Top Ten by the Moody Blues."
Pinder, Mike	MP-R65. *Rave*, March 1, 1965, "The m'm'moody blues boys," by Lyn Carnell.
Pinder, Mike	MP-RM65. *Record Mirror*, April 10, 1965, "'How the Beatles Helped Us,' Say the Moody Blues," by Richard Green.

Pinder, Mike	MP-R65a. *Rave*, May 1, 1965, "Getting the Blues in Paris," by Maureen O'Grady.
Pinder, Mike	MP-RM65a. *Record Mirror*, June 19, 1965, "Story Behind That Scream," by Richard Green.
Pinder, Mike	MP-RM65b. *Record Mirror*, October 30, 1965, "Moodies Lose Out to Brian Epstein!"
Pinder, Mike	MP-BI66. *Beat Instrumental*, approx. Summer 1966, "Profile: Mike Pinder," by Pete Goodman.
Pinder, Mike	MP-RM66. *Record Mirror*, October 8, 1966, "Single Truth," by Richard Green.
Pinder, Mike	MP-SM67. *Sunday Mirror*, October 22, 1967, "Gear Change: Moodies Return with Millionaire Backer and Thirties Wardrobe," by Jack Bentley (article courtesy Tony Brown).
Pinder, Mike	MP-PS67. *Pop Scene*, December 1967, "Moodies Meet a Millionaire!" by Dick Tatham.
Pinder, Mike	MP-DAME68. *Disc and Music Echo*, January 20, 1968, "Now the Moodies Ain't Got the Blues," by Mike Ledgerwood.
Pinder, Mike	MP-BI68. *Beat Instrumental*, March 1968, "Quality Paid off for The Moody Blues," by "P.G."
Pinder, Mike	MP-CM68. *Croydon Midweek* (England), March 19, 1968, "Making Money Is A Gas, But It's Secondary," by Sandra Grant. (Courtesy Tony Brown.)
Pinder, Mike	MP-VT68. *Valentine* magazine, March 22, 1968, "The Moodies Ride Again!" by Dick Tatham. (Courtesy Tony Brown.)
Pinder, Mike	MP-NME68. *New Musical Express*, September 28, 1968, "Moodies Sleeping Giants," by Keith Altham.
Pinder, Mike	MP-HP69. *Hit Parader*, May 1969, "The Moody Blues Visit America."
Pinder, Mike	MO-BB69. *Billboard*, September 13, 1969, "Mellotron Embellishes Moody Blues' Sound," by George Knemeyer.
Pinder, Mike	MP-RM69. *Record Mirror*, December 20, 1969, "Forget Pop! What About the More Aesthetic and Human Emotions?"
Pinder, Mike	MP-HPY70. *Hit Parader Yearbook*, Winter 1970, "The Moody Blues Speak Out."
Pinder, Mike	MP-MDE70. *Disc and Music Echo*, March 28, 1970, "Moody Mode of Travelling – On the Astral Plane," by David Hughes.
Pinder, Mike	MP-R70. *Rave* magazine, April 1, 1970, "Moody Blues Sound Effects," by Keith Altham.
Pinder, Mike	MP-RS70. *Rolling Stone*, April 3, 1970, "The Moody Blues, Chumps No More," by Charles Alverson.
Pinder, Mike	MP-C71. *Circus*, April 1971, "The Moody Blues Flow Methodically Onward," by David Erlich.
Pinder, Mike	MP-NP71. *News-Press* (Fort Myers, Florida), November 7, 1971, NEA wire story: "The Moody Blues Forever," by Dick Kleiner.
Pinder, Mike	MP-S71. *Sounds*, November 8, 1971, "The *Sounds* Talk-In: Mike Pinder," interviewed by Penny Valentine.
Pinder, Mike	MP-MM72. *Melody Maker*, March 18, 1972, Moody Views," by Andrew Means.
Pinder, Mike	MP-NME76. *New Musical Express*, April 17, 1976, Michael Pinder interview by Steve Turner.
Pinder, Mike	MP-H&H94. *Higher & Higher, #20*, Winter/Spring 1994, "Michael Pinder: Reaching for the Beautiful Landscape," interview by Mark Murley.
Pinder, Mike	MP-KB94. *Keyboard*, May 1994, "Mike Pinder: The Many Moods of a Mellotron Master," by Ernie Rideout.
Pinder, Mike	MP-OCR94. *The Orange County Register* (California), October 16, 1994, "His Moodies Days Are in the Past, and That's Fine," by Steve Eddy.

Pinder, Mike	MP-GM94. *Goldmine, Vol. 20, No. 22*, October 28, 1994, "The Moody Blues: Veteran Cosmic Rockers," by Bruce Eder.
Pinder, Mike	MP-SB95. *The Sacramento Bee* (California), January 1, 1995, "Mellowing Out," by J. Freedom Du Lac.
Pinder, Mike	MP-SH95. *The Sun Herald* (Biloxi, Mississippi), March 9, 1995, "Without the Blues," by Jeff Piorkowski.
Pinder, Mike	MP-PG95. *Phoenix Gazette* (Arizona), March 3, 1995, "Moody Man Back on the Album Track," by Andrew Means.
Pinder, Mike	MP-TDNT95. *Tempe Daily News Tribune* (Arizona), March 31, 1995, "Not Moody or Blue, Pinder Comes Back," by Betty Webb.
Pinder, Mike	MP-DH95. *Daily Herald* (Chicago, Illinois), May 19, 1995, "In Search of the Lost Moody Blue," by Dan Kening.
Pinder, Mike	MP-S95. *Scene*, May 25, 1995, "Following His Own Bliss," by Mark Holan.
Pinder, Mike	MP-H&H95. *Higher & Higher, #26/27*, Summer 1995, "The Making of *To Our Children's Children's Children*," by Mark Murley.
Pinder, Mike	MP-H&H95a. GE-H&H95a. *Higher & Higher, #26/27*, Summer 1995, "The Art of *TOCCC*," by Mark Murley.
Pinder, Mike	MP-CB95. Interviewed by Gary James, circa 1995, then posted on classicbands.com.
Pinder, Mike	MP-H&H96. *Higher & Higher, #33*, Winter 1996, "The Making of Question of Balance," by Mark Murley.
Pinder, Mike	MP-H&H96, *Higher & Higher, #31*, Summer 1996, "Timothy Leary: Dead at 75."
Pinder, Mike	MP-DMN96. *The Dallas Morning News* (Texas), November 1996, "Bits of Wisdom and Peace," by Laurie Wilson.
Pinder, Mike	MP-TU96. *The Union* (Grass Valley, California), December 7, 1996, "Speaking with a New Voice," by Paul Harrar.
Pinder, Mike	MP-LAT97. *The Los Angeles Times*, January 1997, "Rocker's Current Gig Has No Tunes, Just Tales for Tots," by Bill Locey.
Pinder, Mike	MP-H&H98/99. *Higher & Higher, #39 & 40*, Winter 1998/Spring 1999, "Mike Pinder Update," by Theresa Murley.
Pinder, Mike	MP-H&H04. *Higher & Higher*, Spring-Summer, 2004, "Pinder on *Threshold*," interviewed by Mark Murley.
Pinder, Mike	MP-CA:TMB06. TC-CA.TMB06. *Classic Artists: The Moody Blues*, 2009, Empire Media Holdings SL, Impact Film Sales Ltd..
Pinder, Mike	MP-CA07. *Moody Blues: Classic Artists*, April 24, 2007 (Image Entertainment).
Pinder, Mike	MP-GM09. *Goldmine*, October 9, 2009, "Moody Blues and the Mellotron, Isle of Wight."
Pinder, Mike	MP-SAV14. *Soundandvision.com*, February 12, 2014, "Former Magnificent Moody Blues Mellotron Maven Mike Pinder," by Mike Mettler.
Pinder, Mike	MP-CRM14. *Classic Rock Magazine*, May 28, 2014, "Revolution in the Head," by Rob Hughes.
Pinder, Mike	MP-TO14. *Tape Op*, September/October 2014, "Indigo Ranch: Richard Kaplan and Mike Pinder on Operating Malibu's Legendary Studio in the 70s & 80s," by Larry Crane.
Pinder, Mike	MP-UC14. *Uncut*, November 21, 2014, "The Making of The Moody Blues' 'Nights In White Satin.'"
Pinder, Mike	MP-CB15. ClassicBands.com, "Interview with Mike Pinder," August 26, 2015.
Pinder, Mike	MP-MMCD15. *Magnificent Moody Blues* 50th Anniversary CD Set, 2015, pamphlet by Mark Powell.
Pinder, Mike	MP-BCB17. From bestclassicbands.com, 2017, "Moody Blues Members Recall Days *Passed*," by Bill Kopp.

Pinder, Mike	MP-AI17. Author interview, 2017.
Rowley, Terry	TR-DME70. JH-DME70a. *Disc and Music Echo*, May 30, 1970, "The Business of Being Moody," by David Hughes.
Scher, John	JS-BB93. *Billboard*, March 6, 1993, "PolyGram to Push Moody Blues Via PBS," by Greg Reibman.
Stanley, Paul	PS-AB91. *Amusement Business*, May 20, 1991, "Alberto-Culver Signs On for Moody Blues Tour," by Patricia Bates.
Tarney, Alan	AT-H&H91. *Higher & Higher #16*, Summer/Fall 1991, "A Conversation with Alan Tarney," interviewed by Randy Salas.
Tayler, Stephen	ST-H&H96. *Higher & Higher, #32*, Fall 1996, "The Making of *The View From the Hill*," by Mark Murley.
Tayler, Stephen	ST-H&H99. H&H99. *Higher & Higher, #41*, Summer 1999 (out in September), "The Making of *Strange Times*," by Mark Murley.
Thomas, Ray	RT-NME65a. *New Musical Express*, January 15, 1965, "Moody Blues Are Really Quite Happy," by Ian Dove.
Thomas, Ray	RT-RM65. *Record Mirror*, January 23, 1965, "Anyone Can Make the Top Ten," by Christine Osbourne.
Thomas, Ray	RT-NME65b. *New Musical Express*, February 12, 1965, "Top Ten by The Moody Blues."
Thomas, Ray	RT-R65a. *Rave*, May 1, 1965, "Getting the Blues in Paris," by Maureen O'Grady.
Thomas, Ray	RT-PW65. *Pop Weekly*, September 11, 1965, cover story: "The Moody Blues on a Summer Day," by Gray Perell.
Thomas, Ray	RT-RM66. *Record Mirror*, October 8, 1966, "Single Truth," by Richard Green.
Thomas, Ray	RT-NME68. *New Musical Express*, September 28, 1968, "Moodies Sleeping Giants," by Keith Altham.
Thomas, Ray	RT-NME69. *New Musical Express*, May 3, 1969, "Moody Ray Talks About *Threshold*."
Thomas, Ray	RT-BB69. *Billboard*, September 13, 1969, "Mellotron Embellishes Moody Blues' Sound," by George Knemeyer.
Thomas, Ray	RT-NME69a. *New Musical Express*, September 20, 1969, "Moodies Write for You."
Thomas, Ray	RT-NME69b. *New Musical Express*, November 8, 1969, "Ray Thomas, New Moody Blues," by Richard Green.
Thomas, Ray	RT-TCP69. *Threshold Concert Program*, December 5, 1969, "An Anatomy of Threshold."
Thomas, Ray	NME70. *New Musical Express*, February 14, 1970, "Doing a Moody: Ray Thomas," by Richard Green.
Thomas, Ray	RT-MN70. *Music Now!*, May 9, 1970, "The Moody Blues Have Grown Up," by Tony Norman.
Thomas, Ray	RT-NME70a. *New Musical Express*, May 16, 1970, "A Hit Single? We're Just Getting Our Kicks, Says Moody Ray Thomas," by Richard Green.
Thomas, Ray	RT-DME70. *Disc and Music Echo*, May 30, 1970, "The Business of Being Moody," by David Hughes.
Thomas, Ray	RT-RM70. *Record Mirror*, October 10, 1970, "Why Do People Get Moody About the Moodies?" by Keith Altham.
Thomas, Ray	RT-HP71. *Hit Parader*, January 1971, "The Electronic Moodies: Mellotron and Moog."
Thomas, Ray	RT-RM71. *Record Mirror*, January 16, 1971, "The Moody Blues: Now

	I Know How McCartney Felt," by Keith Altham.
Thomas, Ray	RT-DME71. *Disc and Music Echo*, August 21, 1971, "Lord of the Manor," by David Hughes.
Thomas, Ray	RT-NP71. *News-Press* (Fort Myers, Florida), November 7, 1971, NEA Wire story: "The Moody Blues Forever," by Dick Kleiner.
Thomas, Ray	RT-S72. *Sounds*, April 15, 1972, "And the Rock Gods Came From On High," by Penny Valentine.
Thomas, Ray	RT-RM72. *Record Mirror*, April 22, 1972, "The Moody Blues," by Hal Speck.
Thomas, Ray	RT-NME72. *New Musical Express*, June 3, 1972, "Moody Music: The Place of Electronics," by Tony Stewart.
Thomas, Ray	RT-NME72. *New Musical Express*, October 6, 1972, "Moody Music."
Thomas, Ray	RT-NME72. *New Musical Express*, November 4, 1972, "Doug Jones on the Road with the Moody Blues," by Doug Jones.
Thomas, Ray	RT-RS72. *Rolling Stone*, December 21, 1972, "In Search of the Moody Blues," by James Horwitz.
Thomas, Ray	RT-PM73. *Pottstown Mercury*, October 30, 1973, *Chicago Daily News* Service wire story: "Moody Blues Keep Searching for Creativity," by Al Rudis.
Thomas, Ray	RT-PBP74. *The Palm Beach Post* (West Palm Beach, Florida), September 29, 1974, "The Moody Blues: The Monster Takes a Rest," by Andrew Bailey.
Thomas, Ray	RT-MSA74. *Music Scene Annual*, 1974, "Under The Moodies Influence," by Richard Green.
Thomas, Ray	RT-BI75. *Beat Instrumental*, March 1975, "Ray Thomas."
Thomas, Ray	RT-MM75. *Melody Maker*, July 12, 1975, "In the Moody," by Chris Charlesworth.
Thomas, Ray	RT-NME75. *New Musical Express*, August 2, 1975, "Mighty Acorn," by Tony Stewart.
Thomas, Ray	RT-PTP75. *PTP*, August 7, 1975, "Ray Thomas: 'What Else Can I Do?'"
Thomas, Ray	RT-DS75. *The Desert Sun*, August 28, 1975, NEA wire story: "Rock Millionaire Club's Elite," by Steven Ford.
Thomas, Ray	RT-RD75. *Reporter Dispatch*, September 17, 1975, "Ray Thomas Emerges from Blues," by Jack McDonough.
Thomas, Ray	RT-ID75. *New ... From The Moody Blues, Ray Thomas Discusses the Preparation and Production of His First Solo LP, From Mighty Oaks* (International Distribution vinyl album Threshold THSX-102, 1975).
Thomas, Ray	RT-MD78. *The Michigan Daily*, November 17, 1978, "Reunited Moody Blues Thriving," by John Dearing.
Thomas, Ray	RT-MM79. *Melody Maker*, May 26, 1979, "The Moody Blues: It's a Wonderful Life," by Chris Welch.
Thomas, Ray	RT-RS81. *Rolling Stone*, September 3, 1981, "The Moody Blues: Cosmic Voyage to Number One," by David Fricke.
Thomas, Ray	RT-MW83. *Music Week*, September 3, 1983, "The Moody Blues," by Chris Welch.
Thomas, Ray	RT-H&H85. *Higher & Higher, #5*, Summer/Fall 1985, "Ray Thomas: The Music's the Thing, Part 1," by Mark S. Murley.
Thomas, Ray	RT-H&H86. *Higher & Higher, #6*, Spring/Summer 1986, "Ray Thomas: The Music's the Thing, Part II," by Mark S. Murley.
Thomas, Ray	RT-GM94. *Goldmine, Vol. 20, No. 22*, October 28, 1994, "The Moody Blues: Veteran Cosmic Rockers," by Bruce Eder.
Thomas, Ray	RT-RFT95. As told to interview Pete Fame on the TV show *Rock Family Tree*, "The Birmingham Beat" segment, July 1, 1995.
Thomas, Ray	RT-DAFP97. *Days of Future Passed*, issued 1997, sleeve notes and interviews by John Reed.
Thomas, Ray	RT-OFCN99. *Moody Blues Fan Club Newsletter*, Summer 1999.

Thomas, Ray	RT-EGBDFCD08. *Every Good Boy Deserves Favour*, issued 2008, remastered edition, with booklet by Mark Powell.
Thomas, Ray	RT-QOB08. *A Question of Balance,* issued 2008, remastered edition, with booklet by Mark Powell.
Thomas, Ray	RT-SS08. *Seventh Sojourn*, issued 2008, remastered edition, with booklet by Mark Powell.
Thomas, Ray	RT-FMOCD11. *From Mighty Oaks*, issued 2011, liner notes by Ray Thomas.
Thomas, Ray	RT-PROG13. *PROG*, March 2013, "The Moody Blues."
Thomas, Ray	RT-CRM14. *Classic Rock Magazine*, May 28, 2014, "Revolution in the Head," by Rob Hughes.
Thomas, Ray	RT-UC14. *Uncut*, November 21, 2014, "The Making of The Moody Blues' 'Nights In White Satin.'"
Thomas, Ray	RT-DM15. discussionsmagazine.com, January 15, 2015, "True Story: The Magnificent Moodies Turns 50 – An Exclusive Interview with The Moody Blues Ray Thomas," by Stephen SPAZ Schnee.
Thomas, Ray	RT-RS15. raysasho.com, January 30, 2015, interview with Ray Thomas, by Rau Sasho.
Thomas, Ray	RT -MMCD15. *Magnificent Moody Blues* 50th Anniversary CD Set, 2015, pamphlet by Mark Powell.
Thomas, Ray	RT0SD15. *Shindig* magazine, 2015, Bye Bye Bird," by William James.
Thomas, Ray	RT-AC15. Annecarlini.com, Russell A. Trunk's interview with Ray Thomas.
Thomas, Ray	RT-OFO16. otten.freeshell.org/moodyblues, updated 2016.
Thomas, Ray	RT-BCB17. From bestclassicbands.com, 2017, "Moody Blues Members Recall Days *Passed*," by Bill Kopp.
Thomas, Ray	RT-AI17. Author interview, 2017.
Thompson, Jerry	JT-BS79. *The Baltimore Sun*, August 12, 1979, "Slumping Sales Hit Record Business," by Eric Siegel.
Travers, Phil	PT-H&H95a. *Higher & Higher, #26/27*, Summer 1995, "The Art of *TOCCC*," by Mark Murley.
Travers, Phil	PT0H&H96a. *Higher & Higher, #33*, Winter 1996, "The Art of *A Question of Balance*," by Mark Murley.
Travers, Phil	PT-TR08. "The Moody Blues' *In Search of the Lost Chord*, with Artwork by Philip Travers," by Mark Boudreau.
Travers, Phil	PT-TT15. From Tapatalk.com, May 7, 2015, "The Moody Blues – In Search of the Lost Chord," by Malcolm Dome.
Trempe, Monique	MT-H&H96. *Higher & Higher, #32*, Fall 1996, "The Making of *The View From the Hill*," by Mark Murley.
Varnals, Derek	DV-H&H95. *Higher & Higher, #26/27*, Summer 1995, "The Making of *To Our Children's Children's Children*," by Mark Murley.
Varnals, Derek	DV-H&H95b. *Higher & Higher, #26/27*, Summer 1995, "Derek Varnals: Engineering the Classic Moodies Sound," by Mark Murley.
Varnals, Derek	DV-H&H96. Higher & Higher #32, Fall 1996, "A 20th Anniversary Stroll Down … *Natural Avenue*," by Mark Murley.
Varnals, Derek	DV-H&H96. *Higher & Higher, #33*, Winter 1996, "The Making of Question of Balance," by Mark Murley.
Varnals, Derek	DV-H&H04. *Higher & Higher, #46/47*, Spring-Summer, 2004, "The Making of a Dream," by Mark Murley.
Varnals, Derek	DV-SOS09. *Sound On Sound*, July 2009, "The Moody Blues 'Nights In White Satin,'" by Richard Buskin.

Varnals, Derek   DV-UC14. *Uncut*, November 21, 2014, "The Making of The Moody Blues' 'Nights In White Satin.'"

Visconti, Tony   TV-H&H87. *Higher & Higher, #9*, Spring/Summer 1987, "The Graeme Edge Interview"; "Tony Visconti: The Dynamic Producer Reveals How Sampling Helped Him Clean Up on the Moody Blues."

Visconti, Tony   TV-H&H95. *Higher & Higher, #25*, Spring 1995, "The Tony Visconti Interview," by Randy A. Salas.

Vitez, Laura   LV-H&H93. *Higher & Higher, #18 & 19*, Winter/Spring 1993, "Laura Vitez: Documenting the Magic of Red Rocks," by Mark Murley.

Warwick, Clint   CW-RM65. *Record Mirror*, January 23, 1965, "Anyone Can Make the Top Ten," by Christine Osbourne.

Warwick, Clint   CW-DW65. *Disc Weekly*, January 23, 1965, "'Brum Is Still Home!' Say the Chart-Topping Moody Blues," by Ted Scott.

Warwick, Clint   CW-NME65b. *New Musical Express*, February 12, 1965, "Top Ten by the Moody Blues."

Warwick, Clint   CW-RM65a. *Record Mirror*, April 10, 1965, "'How the Beatles Helped Us,' Say the Moody Blues," by Richard Green.

Warwick, Clint   CW-RS02. Retrosellers.com, 2002 interview with Clint Warwick.

Wayne, Jeff   JW-H&H84. *Higher & Higher*, #2, Summer 1984, "Sneak Preview: The Jeff Wayne Interview."

Wayne, Jeff   JW-DOG09. DenOfGeek.com, June 11, 9009, "Interview with Jeff Wayne," by Michael Hague.

Wayne, Jeff   JW-TG14. *The Guardian* (England), January 14, 2014, "Jeff Wayne and David Essex: How We Made *The War of the Worlds*," by Andrew Pulver.

Williams, Pip   PW-MW83. *Music Week*, September 3, 1983, "The Moody Blues," by Chris Welch.

Williams, Pip   PW-H&H96. *Higher & Higher, #31*, Summer 1996, "The Making of *Long Distance Voyager.*"

Williams, Pip   PW-H&H98. *Higher & Higher, #39 & 40*, Winter 1998/Spring 1999, "The Making of *The Present*," by Mark Murley.

Williams, Pip   PW-H&H98b. *Higher & Higher, #39 & 40*, Winter 1998/Spring 1999, "John Lodge on TP," interviewed by Mark Murley, and "Pip on TP."

Woods, Steve   SW-H&H01. *Higher & Higher, #44*, Fall 2001, "Journey into Amazing Music," by Mark Murley.

Wyatt, Martin   MW-H&H87. *Higher & Higher, #10*, Fall/Winter 1987, "A Conversation With Martin Wyatt, by June Price.

Wyatt, Martin   MW-H&H94. *Higher & Higher, #2*, Summer 1984, "The 4 Before: The Pre-Moodies Songs," by Mark Murley.

Yates, Brian   BY-SM65. *Sunday Mercury* (Birmingham, England), October 1965, "John Bill – from Germany," by Mark Gardner.

You may also enjoy these other books published by
Jacobs Brown Press

These Are the Voyages: Star Trek the Original Series [TOS]
by Marc Cushman
Season One, ISBN 978-0-9892381-0-6
Season Two, ISBN 978-0-9892381-4-4
Season Three, ISBN 978-0-9892381-7-5

Irwin Allen's Lost in Space,
The Authorized Biography of a Classic Sci-Fi Series
by Marc Cushman
Volume One, ISBN 978-0-692-75018-6
Volume Two, ISBN 978-0-692-74756-8
Volume Three, ISBN 978-0-692-81426-0

The Show Runner – An Insider's Guide to Successful TV Production
by Cy Chermak
ISBN 978-0-9988663-1-4

Previously on X-Men – The Making of An Animated Series
By Eric Lewald
ISBN 978-0-9988663-2-1

Jacobs Brown Media Group, LLC
Jacobs Brown Press

"Where truth is better than fiction"

www.jacobsbrownmediagroup.com

Made in the USA
Las Vegas, NV
02 May 2023